Criminal Law

AND

Procedure

SIXTH EDITION

John M. Scheb, J.D., LL.M.

JUDGE, FLORIDA COURT OF APPEAL, SECOND DISTRICT (RET.)

John M. Scheb II, Ph.D.

PROFESSOR OF POLITICAL SCIENCE

UNIVERSITY OF TENNESSEE

WADSWORTH
CENGAGE Learning™

Australia • Brazil • Japan • Korea • Mexico • Singapore • Spain • United Kingdom • United States

WADSWORTH
CENGAGE Learning

Criminal Law and Procedure, Sixth Edition
John M. Scheb, John M. Scheb II

Senior Acquisitions Editor, Criminal Justice:
Carolyn Henderson Meier

Assistant Editor: Meaghan Banks

Editorial Assistant: Beth McMurray

Marketing Manager: Terra Schultz

Marketing Assistant: Emily Elrod

Marketing Communications Manager: Tami Strang

Project Manager, Editorial Production:
Jennie Redwitz

Creative Director: Rob Hugel

Art Director: Vernon Boes

Print Buyer: Linda Hsu

Permissions Editor: Bob Kauser

Production Service: Mary Keith Trawick,
Newgen–Austin

Text Designer: John Edeen

Copy Editor: Tess Roach

Illustrator: Newgen–Austin

Cover Designer: Yvo Reizebos Design

Compositor: Newgen

Image Credits:
Case-in-Point box icon: Steve Hamblin/Alamy
Supreme Court Perspectives box icon:
Photograph by Franz Jantzen, Collection of the
Supreme Court of the United States
Scales (cover): © Jodie Coston Stock/Alamy
Guard and prisoners (cover): William Fritsch/
Brand X Pictures Collection/PictureQuest

For product information and technology assistance, contact us at **Cengage Learning Customer Sales Support, 1-800-354-9706.**

For permission to use material from this text or product, submit all requests online at **cengage.com/permissions.**

Further permissions questions can be emailed to **permissionrequest@cengage.com.**

Library of Congress Control Number: 2007920855

ISBN-13: 978-0-495-09548-4
ISBN-10: 0-495-09548-6

Wadsworth
10 Davis Drive
Belmont, CA 94002-3098
USA

Cengage Learning is a leading provider of customized learning solutions with office locations around the globe, including Singapore, the United Kingdom, Australia, Mexico, Brazil, and Japan. Locate your local office at **international.cengage.com/region**

Cengage Learning products are represented in Canada by Nelson Education, Ltd.

For your course and learning solutions, visit **academic.cengage.com**

Purchase any of our products at your local college store or at our preferred online store **www.ichapters.com**

Printed in Canada
2 3 4 5 6 7 11 10 09 08

This edition of *Criminal Law and Procedure* is dedicated to
Ryan Patrick Scheb, John M. Scheb III, Mary Catherine Scheb, and Amy Elizabeth Scheb

About the Authors

John M. Scheb was born in Orlando, Florida, in 1926. He entered the practice of law in 1950. He served as associate municipal judge in Sarasota, Florida, from 1957 to 1959. From 1959 to 1970, he served as City Attorney for the city of Sarasota. In 1974, he was appointed to the Florida District Court of Appeal, second district, a position he held until his retirement in 1992. On retirement from the Florida Court of Appeal, Judge Scheb became an adjunct professor and later a distinguished professorial lecturer at the Stetson University College of Law. In 2006, he was named a distinguished professorial lecturer emeritus. Judge Scheb holds the B.A. from Florida Southern College, the J.D. from the University of Florida, and the LL.M. from the University of Virginia.

John M. Scheb II was born in Sarasota, Florida, in 1955. He attended the University of Florida from 1974 to 1982, receiving the B.A., M.A., and Ph.D. in political science. He is now Professor of Political Science and Chair of Legal Studies at the University of Tennessee, where he teaches courses in criminal law, constitutional law, civil rights and liberties, administrative law, and law in society. Professor Scheb has authored numerous articles in professional journals and is coauthor, with Otis H. Stephens Jr., of *American Constitutional Law,* Fourth Edition (2007).

Brief Contents

PART THREE
Law Enforcement and Criminal Procedure 385

Contents

CHAPTER 6

Offenses against Persons   107

CHAPTER 7

Property Crimes   160

PART THREE

Law Enforcement and Criminal Procedure   385

CHAPTER 15

Search and Seizure   386

CHAPTER 16

Arrest, Interrogation, and Identification Procedures   430

CHAPTER 17

The Pretrial Process   460

CHAPTER 18

The Criminal Trial   494

Preface

We are pleased to present to students in criminology, criminal justice, pre-law, political science, and paralegal studies the sixth edition of a concise yet comprehensive introduction to substantive and procedural criminal law. We believe this text is also an appropriate reference for the criminal justice professional who seeks a better understanding of the functioning of the criminal justice system in the United States. Of course, laws vary substantially across jurisdictions, and this text is not intended to be a substitute for independent legal research or competent legal advice.

An Overview of the Text

Criminal law is among the most dynamic fields of American law. In presenting the subject, we have divided the text into three basic components. Part One furnishes an overview of the criminal law and the criminal justice system. Chapter 1 explains the origin and sources of the criminal law and introduces the reader to basic concepts such as the legal definition of a crime, the statutory and judicial development of criminal law, the distinction between substantive and procedural criminal law, constitutional limitations on the definitions of crimes, and the stages of the criminal process. In Chapter 2, we follow up with surveys of the roles of key agencies involved in the enactment and enforcement of the criminal law as well as the adjudication of criminal cases.

Substantive Criminal Law

Part Two surveys the substantive criminal law from its common-law sources to its modern statutory development. In Chapter 3, we have attempted to give the reader an insight into the relevance of the U.S. Constitution and the state constitutions to the enactment and enforcement of criminal prohibitions. Chapter 4 discusses elements of crimes and parties to crimes. Chapter 5 examines the inchoate offenses: attempt, solicitation, and conspiracy. In Chapters 6 and 7, respectively, we survey crimes against persons and property crimes. Some textbooks on criminal law designed for undergraduate students stop at this point; our book goes on to examine offenses against public morality (Chapter 8), alcohol and drug offenses (Chapter 9), white-collar and organized crime (Chapter 10), offenses against public health and the environment (Chapter 11), offenses against public order, safety, and national security (Chapter 12), and offenses against justice and public administration (Chapter 13). Finally, our examination of the substantive criminal law concludes with a discussion on criminal responsibility and an easy-to-follow classification of criminal defenses, including some innovative defenses (Chapter 14).

Law Enforcement and Criminal Procedure

Part Three of the text examines law enforcement and criminal procedure. To better acquaint the reader with procedural aspects we include separate chapters on search and seizure (Chapter 15) and arrest, interrogation, and identification (Chapter 16). We then take the reader through the pretrial process (Chapter 17), the criminal trial (Chapter 18), and sentencing and punishment (Chapter 19). Part Three concludes with an outline of the appeals process and postconviction relief (Chapter 20). Throughout Part Three, we have included examples showing procedures being regulated by federal and state statutes, court rules, or judicial decisions.

What's New in the Sixth Edition?

We are grateful for the reception that instructors and students have accorded the previous editions of *Criminal Law and Procedure*. In this sixth edition, we have captured significant recent developments in the law, especially the implications of our nation's ongoing war on terrorism for domestic law enforcement and criminal justice. Throughout the book, we have reported on recent statutes and appellate court decisions impacting the criminal justice system. We have also added several new tables and figures to facilitate student understanding. And to bring life to the book, we have expanded the number of Case-in-Point boxes and have included such notable cases as the Enron prosecution, the Martha Stewart case, the O. J. Simpson trial, the historic Alger Hiss perjury trial, and the infamous Long Island Railroad Massacre case from the early 1990s.

Developments in the Substantive Law

With respect to crimes against persons, we have updated the discussion of stalking to include cyberstalking, and have updated our treatment of hate crimes, physician-assisted suicide, and rape trauma syndrome. In the field of economic crime, we have made more current the discussions of identity theft, computer crime, and intellectual property offenses. In terms of crimes against morality, we have updated the discussion of polygamy, expanded the treatment of child pornography, and addressed the growing phenomenon of Internet gambling. In the area of drug offenses, we have expanded our treatment of the methamphetamine crisis and the medical marijuana issue.

With regard to offenses against public order, we have addressed panhandling and homeless persons sleeping on public property, problems that are generating considerable controversy around the country. With respect to motor vehicle violations, we have expanded the discussion of offenses related to seat belts and cell phones. In the national security field, we have expanded our discussion of terrorism, including detention of terrorists, electronic surveillance, and military commissions. We have also discussed the 2006 amendments to the USA PATRIOT Act and the continuing controversy over this legislation, as well as customs and immigration issues.

Developments in the Procedural Law

In the area of search and seizure, we have updated and expanded the treatment of consent searches, anticipatory search warrants, and the "knock and announce" rule, all of which have been addressed recently by the Supreme Court. We updated the discussion of the USA PATRIOT Act with regard to procedural law, again focusing on the 2006 reauthorization. In the chapter on arrest and interrogation, we added a new subsection addressing arrests of persons with disabilities. We also added discussion of the police use of stun guns and updated the material on roadblocks and checkpoints.

With respect to the pretrial process, we updated the discussion of the federal Speedy Trial Act and discussed the problem of self-representation by persons of questionable competency. In the chapter dealing with the criminal trial, we have updated the subject of anonymous juries, provided detailed analysis of a case illustrating the use of circumstantial evidence, discussed new constitutional restrictions on the use of testimonial hearsay evidence, and have expanded the discussion of jurors asking questions at trial. In the area of sentencing and punishment, we have updated our discussion of the federal sentencing guidelines in light of recent Supreme Court decisions. We have also reorganized the material on capital punishment and added some discussion of the recent debate over lethal injection. With regard to the appeals process, we have reorganized the discussion of federal habeas corpus review of state criminal cases and have expanded our coverage of DNA evidence as a basis for federal and state postconviction relief.

Pedagogical Features

Many pedagogical features are included to help students understand and retain the book's content:

- Each chapter contains an outline delineating the major topics covered in the chapter.
- Beginning with Chapter 3, each chapter includes **Case-in-Point** boxes. These concise summaries of cases illustrate key concepts and have proven to be popular with students.
- Throughout the book, **Supreme Court Perspective** boxes provide brief excerpts from important Supreme Court decisions pertaining to specific issues of criminal law and procedure.
- A number of **Sidebars** furnish relevant information without disrupting the flow of the text.
- **Key terms** are identified in boldface type throughout each chapter and listed at the end of the chapter with page references.
- Chapters end with a set of **discussion questions** and (beginning with Chapter 3) one or more **hypothetical problems** to test understanding and stimulate classroom discussion, along with an option to pursue a **web-based research activity.**
- At the end of the book, a **comprehensive glossary** provides definitions of all key terms.
- For students and instructors who wish to venture into the realm of **legal research,** we have greatly expanded our comprehensive feature on this topic.

Appendix A, "Access to the Law through Legal Research," now includes up-to-date guidance on researching law through the Internet and computerized services.

Ancillaries

A number of supplements are provided by Thomson Wadsworth to help instructors use *Criminal Law and Procedure*, Sixth Edition, in their courses and to help students prepare for exams. These are available to qualified adopters. Please consult your local sales representative for details.

For the Instructor

EXAMVIEW® (WINDOWS/MACINTOSH)

Create, deliver, and customize tests and study guides (both print and online) in minutes with this easy-to-use assessment and tutorial system, which comes with all the book's test bank questions electronically preloaded. ExamView offers both a Quick Test Wizard and an Online Test Wizard that guide you step by step through the process of creating tests, while the unique WYSIWYG capability allows you to see the test you are creating onscreen exactly as it will print or display online. You can build tests of up to 250 questions using up to 12 question types. Using ExamView's complete word processing capabilities, you can enter an unlimited number of new questions or edit existing questions.

INSTRUCTOR'S MANUAL

Prepared by the core text authors, this valuable resource includes learning objectives, detailed chapter outlines, thorough coverage of key terms and concepts (including references to relevant cases), and class discussion "hypotheticals" for each chapter. In addition, the *Instructor Manual*'s robust test bank contains approximately 25 multiple-choice, 10 true-false, 10 fill-in-the-blank, and 10 essay questions for each chapter, along with a full answer key.

INSTANT ACCESS WEBTUTOR™ TOOLBOX FOR BLACKBOARD® AND WEBCT®

Available for standalone online purchase, the Instant Access Version of WebTutor ToolBox for either Blackboard or WebCT provides access from within a professor's course management system to all the content of this text's rich Book Companion Website. ToolBox is ready to use as soon as you log on, and offers a wide array of web quizzes, activities, exercises, and links. Robust communication tools—such as a course calendar, an asynchronous discussion tool, a real-time chat utility, a whiteboard, and an integrated e-mail system—make it easy to stay connected to the course.

THE WADSWORTH CRIMINAL JUSTICE VIDEO LIBRARY

So many exciting new videos—so many great ways to enrich your lectures and spark discussion of the material in this text! A list of our unique and expansive video programs follows. Or contact your Cengage Learning representative at **academic.cengage.com** for a complete, up-to-the-minute list of all of Wadsworth's video offerings—many of which are also available in DVD format—as well as clip lists and running times. The library includes these selections and many others:

- *ABC® Videos:* Featuring short, high-interest clips from current news events. Specially developed for courses including Introduction to Criminal Justice, Criminology, Corrections, Terrorism, and White-Collar Crime, these videos are perfect for use as discussion starters or lecture launchers to spark student interest. The brief video clips provide students with a new lens through which to view the past and present, one that will greatly enhance their knowledge and understanding of significant events and open up to them new dimensions in learning. Clips are drawn from such programs as *World News Tonight, Good Morning America, This Week, PrimeTime Live, 20/20,* and *Nightline,* as well as numerous ABC News specials and material from the Associated Press Television News and British Movietone News collections.

- *The Wadsworth Custom Videos for Criminal Justice:* Produced by Wadsworth and Films for the Humanities, these videos include short (5- to 10-minute) segments that encourage classroom discussion. Topics include white-collar crime, domestic violence, forensics, suicide and the police officer, the court process, the history of corrections, prison society, and juvenile justice.

- *Court TV Videos:* One-hour videos presenting seminal and high-profile cases, such as the interrogations of Michael Crowe and serial killer Ted Bundy, as well as crucial and current issues such as cyber crime, double jeopardy, and the management of the prison on Riker's Island.

- *A&E American Justice:* Forty videos to choose from, on topics such as deadly force, women on death row, juvenile justice, strange defenses, and Alcatraz.

- *Films for the Humanities:* Nearly 200 videos to choose from on a variety of topics such as elder abuse, supermax prisons, the making of an FBI agent, domestic violence, and more.

- *Oral History Project:* Developed in association with the American Society of Criminology, the Academy of Criminal Justice Society, and the National Institute of Justice, these videos will help you introduce your students to the scholars who have developed the criminal justice discipline. Compiled over the last several years, each video features a set of Guest Lecturers—scholars whose thinking has helped to build the foundation of present ideas in the discipline.

THE WADSWORTH CRIMINAL JUSTICE RESOURCE CENTER

academic.cengage.com/criminaljustice Designed with the instructor in mind, this website features information about Cengage Learning's technology and teaching solutions, as well as several features created specifically for today's criminal justice student. Supreme Court updates, timelines, and hot-topic polling can all be used to supplement in-class assignments and discussions. You'll also find a wealth of links to careers and news in criminal justice, book-specific sites, and much more.

For the Student

COMPANION WEBSITE

academic.cengage.com/criminaljustice/scheb One of the important features of our previous editions has been the inclusion of edited judicial decisions illustrating legal concepts affecting the criminal justice system. To allow for expanded coverage of important topics, we have moved these edited cases to the companion website. To facilitate use of this new resource, marginal references in each chapter indicate that a particular case discussed in the text is available on the website.

KEY CASES, COMMENTS, AND QUESTIONS ON SUBSTANTIVE CRIMINAL LAW

Written by Henry F. Fradella (The College of New Jersey), this book examines cases through comments, analyses, and discussion questions to help students grasp challenging material and test their knowledge. For more information, including the table of contents and pricing, contact your Cengage Learning representative.

LEGAL SPELL CHECK

Legal Spell Check contains 867 English and 564 Spanish legal terms. Delivered on CD-ROM, it is easily installed for use with Microsoft® Word. Legal terms are integrated into the existing spell checker on Word, so that users can quickly identify misspelled terms by using the standard spell check function. Legal Spell Check can be packaged with this text for a substantial discount.

CAREERS IN CRIMINAL JUSTICE WEBSITE

academic.cengage.com/criminaljustice/careers This unique website helps students investigate the criminal justice career choices that are right for them with the help of several important tools. Included are: Career Profiles, video testimonials from a variety of practicing professionals in the field, as well as information on many criminal justice careers, including job descriptions, requirements, training, salary and benefits, and the application process; Interest Assessment, a self-assessment tool to help students decide which careers suit their personalities and interests; Career Planner, résumé-writing tips and worksheets, interviewing techniques, and successful job search strategies; and Links for Reference—direct links to federal, state, and local agencies where students can get contact information and learn more about current job opportunities.

WADSWORTH'S GUIDE TO CAREERS IN CRIMINAL JUSTICE, THIRD EDITION

This handy guide, compiled by Caridad Sanchez-Leguelinel of John Jay College of Criminal Justice, gives students information on a wide variety of career paths, and includes requirements, salaries, training, contact information for key agencies, and employment outlooks.

WRITING AND COMMUNICATING FOR CRIMINAL JUSTICE

This book contains articles on writing skills, along with basic grammar review and a survey of verbal communication on the job, that will give students an introduction to academic, professional, and research writing in criminal justice. The voices of professionals who have used these techniques on the job will help students see the relevance of these skills to their future careers.

Acknowledgments

We gratefully acknowledge the contribution of the following reviewers, whose feedback was instrumental in shaping the revisions made to this newest edition: Andria

College; and Jeff Kleeger, Florida Gulf Coast University. Their names, and the names of the reviewers of all previous editions, are listed on page xxv as a tribute to their help—we thank them all for their excellent guidance.

We wish to acknowledge the assistance of Sally G. Waters, Esq., Head Reference Librarian & Adjunct Professor at Stetson College of Law in Gulfport, Florida. Professor Waters made a comprehensive review of our appendix on legal research and added up-to-date information on the methodology of computerized legal research and use of the Internet.

We also wish to thank the team at Wadsworth Publishing—in particular, Carolyn Henderson-Meier and Rebecca Johnson, for their excellent assistance throughout this project. We must also acknowledge the many e-mails we have received over the years from students and instructors who have used previous editions of our book. Their questions, comments, and suggestions have been extremely useful.

Finally, we thank our wives, Mary Burns Scheb and Sherilyn Claytor Scheb, for their patience and support, without which the project could not have been completed.

We have endeavored to make the sixth edition of *Criminal Law and Procedure* the most complete and interesting textbook in the field. We always welcome comments and suggestions from our readers. Of course, we assume responsibility for any errors contained herein.

John M. Scheb
judgescheb@comcast.net

John M. Scheb II
scheb@utk.edu

Reviewers of *Criminal Law and Procedure*

Simeon Acoba, Jr., Hawai'i State Judiciary

Jerry Armor, Calhoun Community College

Sherry Biddinger-Gregg, Indiana State University

Randal Boepple, Trinidad State Junior College

Donald Bradel, Bemidji State University

Jack Call, Radfort University

Elaine Cohen, Broward Community College

Andria Cooper, Fort Hays State University

Kevin Daugherty, Albuquerque TVI Community College

Paul Falzone, California State University–Sacramento

Jack Gregory, Rappahannock Community College

Jennifer Wells Hammack, Georgia College & State University

Thomas Jones, Sul Ross State University

Raymond Kessler

Jeff Kleeger, Florida Gulf Coast University

Bruce W. Lee

Bruce MacMurray, Anderson University

Richard Martin, Washburn University

Barbara May, Montgomery County Community College

Robert Peetz, Midland College

William Pizic, North Carolina Wesleyan College

Bob Plesha, Lakewood Community College

Elizabeth Raulerson, Indian River Community College

Lore Rutz-Burri, Southern Oregon University

Russ Slight, Iowa Lakes Community College

Joseph R. Steenbergen, Lindenwood University

R. Taskin

Stuart White, San Bernardino Valley College

Charles Wymer, Southwest Virginia Community College

Chet Zerlin, Miami-Dade Community College

PART ONE

Legal Foundations
of Criminal Justice

CHAPTER 1

Fundamentals of Criminal Law and Procedure

Introduction

A fundamental problem facing every society is how to achieve social control—protecting people's lives and property and establishing socially desirable levels of order, harmony, safety, and decency. Societies have developed several informal means of achieving this control, including family structures, social norms, and religious precepts. In contrast, law is a formal means of social control. Law can be defined as a body of rules prescribed and enforced by government for the regulation and protection of society. Criminal law is that branch of the law prohibiting certain forms of conduct and imposing penalties on those who engage in prohibited behavior.

All modern societies have developed systems for administering criminal justice. What distinguishes democratic societies from authoritarian ones is a commitment to the **rule of law.** In democratic societies such as ours, a person cannot be convicted of a crime unless he or she has committed a specific offense against a law that provides for a penalty. This principle is expressed in the maxim ***nullen crimen, nulla poena, sine lege,*** a Latin phrase meaning, "there is no crime, there is no punishment, without law." In the United States, formal law governs every aspect of criminal justice, from the enactment of criminal prohibitions to the imposition of punishment upon those who violate these prohibitions.

Our criminal law prescribes both substantive and procedural rules governing the everyday operation of the criminal justice system. **Substantive criminal law** prohibits certain forms of conduct by defining crimes and establishing the parameters of penalties. **Procedural criminal law** regulates the enforcement of the substantive law, the determination of guilt, and the punishment of those found guilty of crimes. For example, although substantive law makes the possession of heroin a crime, the procedural law regulates the police search and seizure that produce the incriminating evidence. The substantive law makes premeditated murder a crime; the procedural law determines the procedures to be observed at trial and, if a conviction ensues, at sentencing.

Figure 1.1 provides an overview of the system of criminal law and procedure that exists in this country. The figure suggests three fundamental principles at work:

- **Constitutional supremacy.** In keeping with the ideal of the rule of law, the entire system of criminal law and procedure is subordinate to the principles and provisions of the U.S. Constitution. The Constitution sets forth the powers of government, the limits of those powers, and the rights of individuals. The Constitution thus limits government's power to make and enforce criminal sanctions in several important ways. These limitations are enforced by **judicial review,** which is the power of courts of law to invalidate substantive laws and procedures that are determined to be contrary to the Constitution.

- **Federalism.** There is a fundamental division of authority between the national government in Washington, D.C., and the fifty state governments. Although both levels of government have authority and responsibility in the realm of criminal justice, most of the day-to-day peacekeeping function is exercised by the states and their political subdivisions (primarily counties and cities). Each of the states has its own machinery of government as well as its own constitution that empowers and limits that government. Each state constitution imposes limits on the criminal justice system within that state. Of course, the provisions of the state constitutions, as well as the statutes adopted by the state legislatures, are subordinate to the provisions of the U.S. Constitution and the laws adopted by Congress.

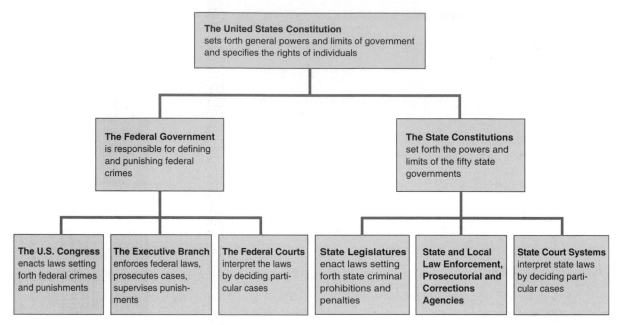

FIGURE 1.1 Overview of the American System of Criminal Law and Procedure

- **Separation of powers.** The national government and each of the fifty state governments are constructed on the principle that legislative, executive, and judicial powers must be separated into independent branches of government. Thus, the federal government and the states have their own legislative branches, their own executive branches, and their own systems of courts. The legislative branch is responsible for enacting laws that specify crimes and punishments. The executive branch is responsible for enforcing those prohibitions and for carrying out the punishments imposed by the judicial branch, but it is the judicial branch that interprets the laws and ensures that persons charged with crimes receive fair treatment by the criminal justice system.

What Is a Crime?

Every crime involves a wrongful act (*actus reus*) specifically prohibited by the criminal law. For example, in the crime of battery, the *actus reus* is the striking or offensive touching of another person. Even the failure to take action can be considered a wrongful act if the law imposes a duty to take action in a certain situation. For example, a person who fails to file a federal income tax return may be guilty of a federal offense.

In most cases, the law requires that the wrongful act be accompanied by criminal intent (*mens rea*). Criminal intent does not refer to a person's motive or reason for acting but merely to having formed a mental purpose to act. To convict a person of a crime, it is not necessary to know why a person committed the crime. It is only necessary to show that the individual intentionally committed a prohibited act. An unintentional act is usually not a crime, although, as we will discover, there are exceptions to this principle. Moreover, in certain instances, one may be held criminally responsible irrespective of intent. Crimes of this latter nature are classified as **strict liability offenses.**

A good example of a strict liability offense is selling liquor to a minor. (Strict liability offenses and general elements of crimes are discussed in Chapter 4.)

Felonies and Misdemeanors

Criminal law distinguishes between serious crimes, known as **felonies,** and less serious offenses, called **misdemeanors.** Generally speaking, felonies are offenses for which the offender can be imprisoned for more than one year; misdemeanors carry jail terms of less than one year. Common examples of felonies include murder, rape, robbery, burglary, aggravated assault, aggravated battery, and grand theft. Typical misdemeanors include petit theft, simple assault and battery, disorderly conduct, prostitution, and driving under the influence of alcohol.

Societal Interests Served by the Criminal Law

We can distinguish among types of crimes by the underlying societal interests that give rise to criminal prohibitions. Obviously, government has a duty to protect the lives and property of citizens—this is the essence of the social contract on which democratic government is based. But society also has an interest in protecting the public peace, order, and safety. Traditionally, the preservation of public morality has been regarded as an important function of the criminal law, although recently this notion has come under attack. Increasingly, the protection of the public health and the preservation of the natural environment are being recognized as societal interests that should be furthered by the criminal law. Finally, society has an interest in efficient and honest public administration and, in particular, the administration of justice.

Table 1.1 lists the societal interests served by the criminal law and shows some particular crimes that relate to each interest. The table also indicates the chapters in

Table 1.1	**An Overview of Types of Crimes and the Societal Interests Involved**	
Societal Interest Served	**Examples of Crimes**	**Discussed in Chapter(s)**
Protection of Persons against Violence	Assault and Battery, Rape and Sexual Battery, Murder, Manslaughter, Spousal and Child Abuse, Kidnapping, Stalking	Chapter 6, Offenses against Persons
Protection of Private Property	Vandalism, Theft, Burglary, Arson, Robbery, Extortion, Forgery, Larceny, Fraud, Embezzlement	Chapter 7, Property Crimes
Maintenance of Standards of Decency	Prostitution, Obscenity, Incest, Bigamy, Indecent Exposure, Lewd and Lascivious Conduct, Illegal Gambling, Animal Cruelty, Alcohol and Drug Offenses	Chapter 8, Offenses against Public Morality (see also Chapter 9, Alcohol and Drug Offenses)
Public Health and the Natural Environment	Fishing and Hunting Violations, Smoking Violations, Illegal Toxic Waste Disposal, Illegal Air Pollution	Chapter 11, Offenses against Public Health and the Environment
Public Peace, Order, and Safety	Disorderly Conduct, Incitement to Riot, Motor Vehicle Offenses, Vagrancy, Weapons Violations, Alcohol and Drug Offenses	Chapter 12, Offenses against Public Order, Safety, and National Security (see also Chapter 9, Alcohol and Drug Offenses)
National Security	Treason, Espionage, Sabotage, Sedition, Terrorism	Chapter 12, Offenses against Public Order, Safety, and National Security
Honest and Efficient Administration of Justice	Resisting Arrest, Bribery, Perjury, Obstruction of Justice, Contempt, Escape	Chapter 13, Offenses against Justice and Public Administration

this book that deal with the different types of crimes. Note that some of the crimes relate to more than one societal interest.

Crime: An Injury Against Society

As suggested by the previous discussion of the societal interests served by the criminal law, our legal system regards crimes not merely as wrongs against particular victims but as offenses against the entire society. Indeed, there does not have to be an individual victim for there to be a crime. For example, it is a crime to possess cocaine, even though it is unlikely that a particular individual will claim to have been victimized by another person's use of the drug. This is a crime because society, through its governing institutions, has made a collective judgment that cocaine use is inimical to the public welfare. Similarly, certain consensual sexual acts (for example, incest) remain crimes in some jurisdictions because communities continue to regard such actions as contrary to public morality. Of course, as society evolves and its standards change, behaviors that were once defined as crimes (for example, blasphemy) are no longer subject to criminal sanction. Over time, the particular prohibitions of the criminal law more or less reflect an evolving social consensus about both what is right and wrong and what is public and private. When a particular criminal prohibition is no longer supported by societal consensus (for example, adultery), it is apt to be unenforced or be stricken from the laws.

Because crime is an injury against society, the government, as society's legal representative, brings charges against persons accused of committing crimes. In the United States, we have a federal system—that is, a division of power and responsibility between the national and state governments. Both the national government and the states enact their own criminal laws. Thus, both the national government and the state governments may prosecute persons accused of crimes. The national government initiates a prosecution when a federal (national) law has been violated; a state brings charges against someone who is believed to have violated one of its laws.

Criminal Responsibility

The criminal law, indeed our entire legal system, rests on the idea that individuals are responsible for their actions and must be accountable for them. This is the essential justification and rationale for imposing punishments on persons convicted of crimes. On the other hand, society recognizes that certain individuals (for example, young children) lack the capacity to appreciate the wrongfulness of their conduct. Similarly, factors beyond individuals' control can lead them to commit criminal acts. In such instances the law exempts individuals from responsibility. Moreover, there are situations in which acts that would otherwise be crimes might be justified. The best example of this is committing a homicide in self-defense. Individuals can invoke a host of defenses beyond a simple denial of guilt. Indeed, a substantial body of law is devoted to the topic of criminal responsibility and defenses. We examine this topic in some detail in Chapter 14.

The Role of the Crime Victim

Because the government prosecutes criminals on behalf of society, the **victim** of a crime is not a party to the criminal prosecution. By filing a complaint with a law enforcement agency, a victim initiates the process that leads to prosecution, but once the prosecution begins, the victim's participation is primarily that of being a witness.

Quite often, victims feel lost in the shuffle of the criminal process. They sometimes feel that the system is insensitive or even hostile to their interests in seeing justice done. Some states are now taking steps to address victims' concerns. Despite some measures being proposed and others that have been adopted, crime victims remain secondary players in the criminal justice system. The principal parties in a criminal case are the prosecution (that is, the government) and the defendant (that is, the accused person). In some situations, however, the victim might have another remedy: a civil suit to recover damages for losses or injuries suffered.

Criminal Law Distinguished from Civil Law

The criminal law is not the only body of law that regulates the conduct of persons. The civil law provides remedies for essentially private wrongs, offenses in which the state has a less direct interest. Most civil wrongs are classified as **breaches of contract** or **torts.** A breach of contract occurs when a party to a contract violates the terms of the agreement. A tort, on the other hand, is a wrongful act that does not violate any enforceable agreement but nevertheless violates a legal right of the injured party. Common examples of torts include wrongful death, intentional or negligent infliction of personal injury, wrongful destruction of property, trespass, and defamation of character. A crime normally entails intentional conduct; thus, a driver whose car accidentally hits and kills another person would not necessarily be guilty of a crime, depending on the circumstances (see discussions of manslaughter and vehicular homicide in Chapter 6). If the accident resulted from the driver's negligence, the driver would have committed the tort of wrongful death and would be subject to a civil suit for damages.

The criminal law and the civil law often overlap. Conduct that constitutes a crime can also involve a tort. For example, suppose Randy Wrecker intentionally damages a house belonging to Harvey Homeowner. Wrecker's act might well result in both criminal and civil actions being brought against him. Wrecker may be prosecuted by the state for the crime of willful destruction of property and may also be sued by Homeowner for the tort of wrongful destruction of property. The state would be seeking to

CASE-IN-POINT

The O. J. Simpson Case

In what many in the media called the "trial of the century," former football and movie star O. J. Simpson was accused of murdering his ex-wife, Nicole Brown Simpson, and her companion, Ron Goldman. The trial began on January 24, 1995. On October 3, 1995, the jury delivered a stunning verdict, declaring Simpson not guilty of murder. A year later the families of the decedents initiated a civil suit against Simpson, alleging the tort of wrongful death. On February 4, 1997, a different jury found Simpson liable for the wrongful death of Nicole Brown Simpson and Ron Goldman and awarded the plaintiffs

$8.5 million in damages. The Simpson case illustrates dramatically how a defendant can be accused of a crime and a tort based on the same alleged act. Many observers have wondered how the two cases could have come out so differently. One answer is that they were independent legal actions resulting in separate trials before entirely different juries. Moreover, the standards of proof were different. In the criminal trial, the jury had to find Simpson guilty of murder beyond a reasonable doubt. In the civil case, the standard of proof was less demanding: the jury had only to find Simpson liable by a preponderance of the evidence.

punish Wrecker for his antisocial conduct, whereas Homeowner would be seeking compensation for the damage to his property. The criminal case would be designated *State v. Wrecker* (or *People v. Wrecker,* or even *Commonwealth v. Wrecker,* depending on the state); the civil suit would be styled *Homeowner v. Wrecker.*

Origins and Sources of the Criminal Law

Many antisocial acts classified as crimes have their origin in the norms of primitive societies. Humanity has universally condemned certain types of behavior since ancient times. Acts such as murder, rape, robbery, and arson are considered ***mala in se,*** or inherent wrongs. Other acts that the modern criminal law regards as offenses are merely ***mala prohibita;*** they are offenses only because they are so defined by the law. Many so-called victimless crimes, such as gambling or possession of marijuana, are generally not regarded as offensive to universal principles of morality. Rather, they are wrong simply because the law declares them wrong. In the case of *mala prohibita* offenses, society has made a collective judgment that certain conduct, although not contrary to universal moral principles, is nevertheless incompatible with the public good.

Development of Law in the Western World

The general consensus is that law developed in Western civilization as leaders began formalizing and enforcing customs that had evolved among their peoples. Eventually, informal norms and customs came to be formalized as codes of law. The Code of Hammurabi regulated conduct in ancient Babylonia some two thousand years before Christ. In the seventh century B.C., Draco developed a very strict code of laws for the Athenian city-states. Even today, one hears strict rules or penalties characterized as being "Draconian." These laws influenced the Romans in their development of the Twelve Tables in the fifth century B.C. And, of course, long before the time of Jesus, the Hebrews had developed elaborate substantive and procedural laws.

In the sixth century A.D., the Emperor Justinian presided over a codification of the Roman law that would prove to be very influential in the evolution of law on the European continent. The Napoleonic Code, promulgated under Napoleon Bonaparte in 1804 as a codification of all the civil and criminal laws of France, was based largely on the Code of Justinian. The Napoleonic Code became a model for a uniform system of law for Western European nations. This is why the legal systems of Western Europe are often said to be "Roman law" systems. Roman law systems are based on the primacy of statutes enacted by the legislature. These statutes are integrated into a comprehensive code designed to be applied by the courts with a minimum of judicial interpretation.

Development of the English Common Law

American criminal law is derived largely from the **English common law,** which dates from the eleventh century. Before the Norman Conquest of 1066, English law was a patchwork of laws and customs applied by local courts. The new Norman kings appointed royal judges to settle disputes based on the customs of the people. By 1300, the decisions of the royal judges were being recorded to serve as precedents to guide judges in future similar cases. Eventually a common body of law emerged throughout the entire kingdom, hence the term "common law." As the centuries passed, coherent principles of law and definitions of crimes emerged from the judges' decisions. Thus, in contrast with Roman law systems, which are based on legal codes, the common law developed primarily through judicial decisions. The common-law doctrine of following precedent, known as *stare decisis,* remains an important component of both the English and American legal systems today.

By 1600, the common-law judges had defined as felonies the crimes of murder, manslaughter, mayhem, robbery, burglary, arson, larceny, rape, suicide, and sodomy. They had also begun to define a number of lesser offenses as misdemeanors. In contrast with the criminal law that was developing on the continent, England developed trial by jury and trained barristers to argue cases on an adversarial basis. A barrister is a lawyer permitted to cross the "bar" in the courtroom that separates the bench from the spectators. Thus, in England, a barrister is a trial lawyer. Although we do not use the term "barrister" in the United States, we do refer to licensed attorneys as having been "admitted to the bar."

As representative government developed in England, the dominance of the common-law courts diminished. Parliament came to play a significant role in the formation of the criminal law by adopting **statutes** that revised and supplemented the common law. The adversarial system of justice continued, however, and the basic English felonies remain today defined essentially as they were by the common-law judges centuries ago.

Development of the American Criminal Law

Our criminal laws are basically derived from the common law as it existed when America proclaimed its independence from England in 1776. After independence, the new American states adopted the English common law to the extent that it did not conflict with the new state and federal constitutions. However, the federal government did not adopt the common law of crimes. From the outset, statutes passed by Congress defined federal crimes. Of the fifty states, Louisiana is the only one whose legal system is not based essentially on the common law. Rather, it is based primarily on the Napoleonic Code.

The new American judges and lawyers were greatly aided by Blackstone's *Commentaries on the Laws of England,* published in 1769, in which Sir William Blackstone, a professor at Oxford, codified the principles of the common law. Blackstone's seminal effort was a noble undertaking, but it demystified English law. Consequently, Blackstone's encyclopedic treatment of the law was less than popular among English barristers, who by this time had developed a close fraternity and took great pride in offering their services to "discover the law." In America, however, **Blackstone's *Commentaries*** became something of a "legal bible."

State and Local Authority to Enact Criminal Prohibitions

At the time of the American Revolution, the English common law constituted the criminal law of the new United States. As new states entered the Union, their legislatures usually enacted "reception statutes," adopting the common law to the extent that it did not conflict with the federal or their respective state constitutions. Eventually, most common-law definitions of crimes were superseded by legislatively defined offenses in the form of statutes adopted by the state legislatures. Today, the state legislatures are the principal actors in defining crimes and punishments. Persons who violate state criminal statutes are prosecuted in the state courts (see Chapter 2).

For the most part, modern state statutes retain the *mala in se* offenses defined by the common law, but many of the old common-law crime definitions have been modified to account for social and economic changes. For example, the offense of rape originated under English common law, but the offense is defined much differently under modern state statutes. Today, under most state laws, the offender and victim may be of either sex, and the offense encompasses anal and oral as well as vaginal penetrations by a sex organ or by another object. Indeed, the broader modern offense of sexual battery embraces all types of nonconsensual sexual impositions (see Chapter 6).

As we shall see in subsequent chapters, modern criminal statutes often go far beyond the common law in prohibiting offenses that are *mala prohibita.* Drug and alcohol offenses, environmental crimes, offenses against public health, and traffic violations fall into this category (see Chapters 9, 11, and 12).

When authorized by state constitutions or acts of state legislatures, cities and counties may adopt **ordinances** that define certain criminal violations. Local ordinances typically deal with traffic offenses, animal control, land use, building codes, licensing of businesses, and so forth. Usually these offenses are prosecuted in courts of limited jurisdiction, such as municipal or county courts (see Chapter 2).

Federal Authority to Define Crimes

As we have seen, the common law of crimes was more or less adopted by the various state legislatures. The U.S. Congress never adopted the common law, as there was no need for it to do so. The national government's responsibility in the criminal justice area has always been more limited than that of the states. Unlike the state legislatures, Congress does not possess **police power,** which is the broad authority to enact prohibitions to protect public order, safety, decency, welfare, etc. Yet Congress does possess authority to enact criminal statutes that relate to Congress's particular legislative powers and responsibilities. Thus, there are federal criminal laws that relate to military service, immigration and naturalization, use of the mail, civil rights, and so forth. In particular, Congress has used its broad power to regulate interstate commerce to criminalize a wide range of offenses, including carjacking, loan sharking, kidnapping, illicit drug dealing, wire fraud, and a variety of environmental crimes (see Chapters 3 and 11). Of course, persons who commit federal crimes are subject to prosecution in the federal courts (see Chapter 2).

The Model Penal Code

The American Law Institute (ALI) is an organization of distinguished judges, lawyers, and academics that have a strong professional interest in drafting model codes of laws. In 1962, after a decade of work that produced several tentative drafts, the ALI published its Proposed Official Draft of the **Model Penal Code** (MPC). The MPC consists of general provisions concerning criminal liability, definitions of specific crimes, defenses, and sentences. The MPC is not law; rather, it is designed as a model code of criminal law for all states. It has had a significant impact on legislative drafting of criminal statutes, particularly during the 1970s, when the majority of the states accomplished substantial reforms in their criminal codes. In addition, the MPC has been influential in judicial interpretation of criminal statutes and doctrines, thereby making a contribution to the continuing development of the decisional law. In this text, we illustrate many principles of law by selected statutes from federal and state jurisdictions; however, in some instances where the MPC is particularly influential, the reader will find references to specific provisions of the MPC.

United States v. Morrison, 529 U.S. 598, 120 S.Ct. 1740, 146 L.Ed.2d 658 (2000)

In this case, which arose from an alleged rape by football players at Virginia Tech University, the Supreme Court declared unconstitutional a federal statute that provided a federal civil remedy to victims of "gender-motivated violence." The Court found that the law exceeded Congress's authority to enact legislation regulating interstate commerce. The Court's decision in Morrison reinforced the traditional notion that Congressional authority to enact criminal law is much more limited than that of the states.

CHIEF JUSTICE [WILLIAM] REHNQUIST delivered the opinion of the Court, saying in part:

Under our written Constitution ... the limitation of congressional authority is not solely a matter of legislative grace.... We accordingly reject the argument that Congress may regulate noneconomic, violent criminal conduct based solely on that conduct's aggregate effect on interstate commerce. The Constitution requires a distinction between what is truly national and what is truly local.... In recognizing this fact we preserve one of the few principles that has been consistent since the [Commerce] Clause was adopted. The regulation and punishment of intrastate violence that is not directed at the instrumentalities, channels, or goods involved in interstate commerce has always been the province of the States.... Indeed, we can think of no better example of the police power, which the Founders denied the National Government and reposed in the States, than the suppression of violent crime and vindication of its victims.

Sources of Procedural Law

The procedural criminal law is promulgated by legislative bodies, through enactment of statutes, and by the courts, through judicial decisions and the development of rules of court procedure. The U.S. Supreme Court prescribes rules of procedure for the federal courts. Generally, the highest court of each state, usually called the state supreme court, is empowered to promulgate rules of procedure for all the courts of that state.

In addition to the common law, statutes, regulations, and ordinances, the federal and state constitutions contribute to the body of substantive and procedural law. For example, the U.S. Constitution defines the crime of treason, U.S. Const. Art. III, Sec. 3. The Constitution has much to say about criminal procedure, most notably as it relates to search and seizure, U.S. Const. Amend. IV; the protection against compulsory self-incrimination, U.S. Const. Amend. V; the right to counsel, U.S. Const. Amend. VI; and the right to trial by an impartial jury, U.S. Const. Amend. VI. Of course, the courts are primarily responsible for "fleshing out" the general principles of criminal procedure contained in the federal and state constitutions by deciding specific cases presented to them. Also, by adopting statutes, the Congress and the state legislatures provide more detailed rules in this area.

The Role of Courts in Developing the Criminal Law

Although substantive law and procedural criminal law are often modified by federal and state statutes, courts play an equally important role in the development of law. Trial courts exist primarily to make factual determinations, apply settled law to established facts, and impose sanctions. In reviewing the decisions of trial courts, appellate courts must interpret the federal and state constitutions and statutes. The federal and state constitutions are replete with majestic phrases such as "equal protection of the laws" and "privileges and immunities" that require interpretation. That is, courts must define exactly what these grand phrases mean within the context of particular legal disputes. Likewise, federal and state statutes often use vague language like "affecting commerce" or "reasonable likelihood." Courts must assign meaning to these and a multitude of other terms. Although most states have abolished all, or nearly all, common-law crimes and replaced them with statutorily defined offenses, the common law remains a valuable source of statutory interpretation. This is because legislatures frequently use terms known to the common law without defining such terms. For example, in proscribing burglary, the legislature might use the term "curtilage" without defining it. In such an instance, a court would look to the common law, which defined the term to mean "an enclosed space surrounding a dwelling."

In rendering interpretations of the law, appellate courts generally follow precedent, in keeping with the common-law doctrine of *stare decisis*. In our rapidly changing society, however, courts often encounter situations to which precedent arguably does not or should not apply. In such situations, courts will sometimes deviate from or even overturn precedent. Moreover, there are situations in which there is no applicable precedent. When this occurs, the appellate courts will have the opportunity to make new law. Thus, appellate courts perform an important **lawmaking function** as well as an **error correction function.** Therefore, any serious student of criminal law must follow developments in the **decisional law**—that is, law as developed by courts in deciding cases.

Constitutional Limitations

The prohibitions of the criminal and civil law are subject to limitations contained in the federal and state constitutions. For example, the U.S. Constitution (Art. I, Sec. 9 and 10) prohibits Congress and the state legislatures from enacting *ex post facto* laws. In essence, an act cannot be made a crime retroactively. To be criminal, an act must be illegal at the time it was committed (see Chapter 3 for more discussion).

The Bill of Rights

Many of the most important constitutional provisions relative to criminal justice are found in the **Bill of Rights** (the first ten amendments to the Constitution adopted by Congress in 1789 and ratified by the states in 1791). For example, the First Amendment to the U.S. Constitution prohibits government from using the civil or criminal law to abridge freedom of speech. In addition to limitations on the enactment of criminal laws, the Bill of Rights has much to say about the enforcement of these laws. These provisions, which constitute much of the basis of criminal procedure, include the Fourth Amendment prohibition of unreasonable searches and seizures, the Fifth Amendment injunction against compulsory self-incrimination, and the Sixth Amendment right to trial by jury. Finally, the Eighth Amendment prohibition of "cruel and unusual punishments" protects citizens against criminal penalties that are barbaric or excessive.

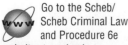 Go to the Scheb/ Scheb Criminal Law and Procedure 6e website at academic .cengage.com/criminaljustice/ scheb for an edited version of *Duncan v. Louisiana.*

Virtually all the provisions of the Bill of Rights have been held to apply with equal force to the states and to the national government. *Duncan v. Louisiana*, 391 U.S. 145, 88 S.Ct. 1444, 20 L.Ed.2d 491 (1968).

Thus, the Bill of Rights limits the adoption of criminal laws, whether by Congress, the state legislatures, or the myriad city and county legislative bodies. The Bill of Rights also limits the actions of police, prosecutors, judges, and corrections officers at the local, state, and national levels.

Due Process of Law

By far the broadest, and probably the most important, constitutional principle relating to criminal procedure is found in the due process clauses of the Fifth and Fourteenth Amendments to the Constitution. The same principle can be found in similar provisions of every state constitution. Reflecting a legacy that can be traced to the Magna Charta (1215), such provisions forbid the government from taking a person's life, liberty, or property, whether as punishment for a crime or any other reason, without **due process of law.** Due process refers to those procedural safeguards necessary to ensure the fundamental fairness of a legal proceeding. Most fundamentally, due process requires **fair notice** and a **fair hearing.** That is, persons accused of crimes must have ample opportunity to learn of the charges and evidence being brought against them as well as the opportunity to contest those charges and that evidence in open court.

One of the most basic tenets of due process in criminal cases is the **presumption of innocence.** Unless the defendant pleads guilty, the prosecution must establish the defendant's guilt by evidence produced in court. In a **criminal trial,** the standard of proof is "beyond a reasonable doubt." The **reasonable doubt standard** differs markedly from the preponderance of evidence standard that applies to civil cases. In a civil trial, the judge or jury must find only that the weight of the evidence favors the plaintiff or the defendant. In a criminal case, the fact finder must achieve the "moral certainty" that arises from eliminating "reasonable doubt" as to the defendant's guilt. Of course, it is difficult to define with precision the term "reasonable." Ultimately, this is a judgment call left to the individual judge or juror.

The Criminal Process

Certain basic procedural steps are common to all criminal prosecutions, although specific procedures vary greatly among jurisdictions. In every jurisdiction law enforcement agencies make arrests, interrogate persons in custody, and conduct searches and seizures. All of these functions are regulated by the law. In every jurisdiction there are procedures through which persons accused of crimes are formally notified of the charges against them and given an opportunity to answer these charges in court. The criminal trial is the crown jewel of criminal procedure, an elaborate, highly formal process for determining guilt or innocence. All court procedures, from the initial appearance of an accused before a magistrate to the decision of an appellate court upholding a criminal conviction, are governed by an elaborate framework of laws, rules, and judicial decisions. (Figure 1.2 illustrates the major components of the criminal process and indicates the chapter in which each is discussed.)

As cases move through the criminal justice system from arrest through adjudication and, in many instances, toward the imposition of punishment, there is considerable attrition. Of any one hundred felony arrests, perhaps as few as twenty-five will result in convictions. This "sieve effect" occurs for many reasons, including insufficient evidence, police misconduct, procedural errors, and the transfer of young offenders to juvenile courts.

14

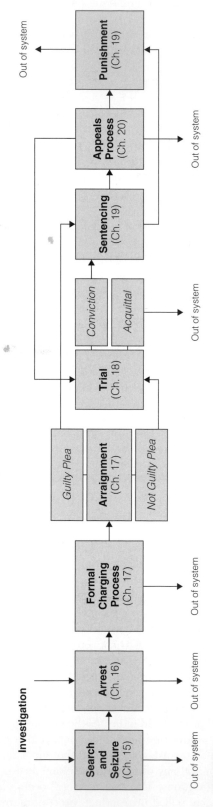

FIGURE 1.2 The Criminal Process

Plea Bargaining—The Reality of Criminal Justice

The criminal trial is the most dramatic aspect of the American system of justice. It is a highly formal process, governed by **rules of procedure** and **rules of evidence.** But the reality is that only a fraction of criminal cases results in trials. Some cases are dropped by the prosecutor for lack of evidence or due to obvious police misconduct. Others are dismissed by judges at preliminary hearings, usually for similar reasons. In those cases that are not dismissed, defendants usually enter pleas of guilty, almost always in exchange for concessions from the prosecution. To avoid trial, which is characterized by both delay and uncertainty, the prosecutor may attempt to persuade the defendant to plead guilty, either by reducing the number or severity of charges or by promising not to seek the maximum penalty allowed by law.

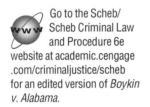 Go to the Scheb/ Scheb Criminal Law and Procedure 6e website at academic.cengage .com/criminaljustice/scheb for an edited version of *Boykin v. Alabama.*

The U.S. Supreme Court has upheld the practice of **plea bargaining** against claims that it violates the due process clauses of the Fifth and Fourteenth Amendments. *Brady v. United States,* 397 U.S. 742, 90 S.Ct. 1463, 25 L.Ed.2d 747 (1970); *North Carolina v. Alford,* 400 U.S. 25, 91 S.Ct. 160, 27 L.Ed.2d 162 (1970). However, because there is always a danger of coerced guilty pleas, especially when defendants are ignorant of the law, it is the judge's responsibility to ascertain whether the defendant's guilty plea is voluntarily and knowingly entered and that there is some factual basis for the offense charged. *Boykin v. Alabama,* 395 U.S. 238, 89 S.Ct. 1709, 23 L.Ed.2d 274 (1969).

Criminal Sanctions

Courts have at their disposal a variety of sanctions to impose on persons convicted of crimes. During the colonial period of American history, and indeed well into the nineteenth century, the death penalty was often inflicted for a variety of felonies, including rape, arson, and horse theft. Today, the death penalty is reserved for only the most aggravated forms of murder and is infrequently carried out. Incarceration is the conventional mode of punishment prescribed for persons convicted of felonies, while monetary fines are by far the most common punishment for those convicted of misdemeanors. For first-time offenders, especially those convicted of nonviolent crimes, probation is a common alternative to incarceration, although probation usually entails a number of restrictions on the offender's freedom.

As society becomes more cognizant of the rights of crime victims, courts are increasingly likely to require that persons convicted of crimes pay sums of money to their victims by way of restitution. Requiring offenders to make restitution and perform community service are common conditions of release on probation. Community service is often imposed as a condition as part of a **pretrial diversion program** in which first-time nonviolent offenders are offered the opportunity to avoid prosecution by completing a program of counseling or service. Increasingly, courts are requiring drug offenders to undergo treatment programs as conditions of probation.

■ CONCLUSION

The American system of criminal justice is deeply rooted in the common law, but the specifics of criminal law and procedure have evolved substantially from their medieval English origins. Today, American criminal law is largely codified in statutes adopted by Congress and the state legislatures, as interpreted by the courts in specific cases.

One of the more tragic aspects of the crime problem is that many Americans are losing faith in the ability of their government to protect them from criminals. Indeed, in some areas of the country, victims are unlikely even to report crimes to the police. Some victims are unwilling to endure the ordeal of being a witness. Others simply believe that the perpetrator will not be apprehended or, if so, will not be punished.

Our state and federal governments are severely constrained both by legalities and practicalities in their efforts to fight crime. Not only is the specter of "a cop on every corner" distasteful to most Americans, but it is impossible to achieve given the fiscal constraints on government.

Currently, the nation's prison system is filled beyond capacity, but the public is demanding that more convicted criminals be incarcerated and for longer periods of time. Yet the public appears unwilling to provide the revenues needed to build the additional prisons necessary to house these inmates.

Finally, society must confront the problem of the constitutional limitations on crime definition and law enforcement. Judges do have considerable discretion in interpreting the state and federal constitutions. Yet, if these documents are to be viable protections of our cherished liberties, we must accept that they place significant constraints on our efforts to control crime. For instance, to what degree is the public willing to allow the constitutional protection against unreasonable searches and seizures to be eroded? To what degree are we willing to sacrifice our constitutionally protected privacy and liberty to aid the ferreting out of crime? Today the question is amplified by the threat of terrorism and the belief of many that government needs greater powers of search and seizure to address the terrorist threat. These are the fundamental questions of criminal law and procedure in a society that prides itself on preserving the rights of the individual.

■ KEY TERMS

rule of law, 3

nullen crimen, nulla poena, sine lege, 3

substantive criminal law, 3

procedural criminal law, 3

judicial review, 3

actus reus, 4

mens rea, 4

strict liability offenses, 4

felonies, 5

misdemeanors, 5

victim, 6

breaches of contract, 7

torts, 7

mala in se, 8

mala prohibita, 8

English common law, 8

stare decisis, 9

statutes, 9

Blackstone's *Commentaries*, 9

ordinances, 10

police power, 10

Model Penal Code, 10

lawmaking function, 12

error correction function, 12

decisional law, 12

Bill of Rights, 12

due process of law, 13

fair notice, 13

fair hearing, 13

presumption of innocence, 13

criminal trial, 13

reasonable doubt standard, 13

rules of procedure, 15

rules of evidence, 15

plea bargaining, 15

pretrial diversion program, 15

■ WEB-BASED RESEARCH ACTIVITY

Go to http://www.findlaw.com/casecode/supreme.html. Use this page to locate the Supreme Court's decision in *Gonzales v. Raich* (2005). Read the decision. Identify the key issue and the Court's holding. What is the rationale for the Court's decision? What counterarguments are made by the dissenting opinion?

■ QUESTIONS FOR THOUGHT AND DISCUSSION

1. Should morality, in and of itself, be considered a sufficient basis for defining particular conduct as criminal?

2. What are the chief distinctions between the civil and criminal law? Why do the criminal and civil law sometimes overlap?

3. To what extent is the English common law significant in contemporary American criminal law?

4. What is the essential difference between substantive criminal law and procedural criminal law? Can you give examples of each?

5. What means of punishment for criminal offenses exist in your state? Is capital punishment available for persons convicted of first-degree murder? Which punishments, if any, do you think are most effective in controlling crime?

CHAPTER **2**

Organization of the Criminal Justice System

**CHAPTER
OUTLINE**

Introduction

In every modern country, criminal justice is a complex process involving a plethora of agencies and officials. In the United States, criminal justice is particularly complex, largely because of federalism, the constitutional division of authority between the national and state governments. Under this scheme of federalism, the national government operates one criminal justice system to enforce federal criminal laws, and each state has a justice system to apply its own criminal laws. As a result of this structural complexity, it is difficult to provide a coherent overview of criminal justice in America. The two systems are to some extent different in both substantive and procedural law.

Despite the differences that exist between federal and state criminal justice systems, there are certain similarities. All fifty-one criminal justice systems in the United States involve legislative bodies, law enforcement agencies, prosecutors, defense attorneys, courts of law, and corrections agencies (see Table 2.1). All follow certain general procedures beginning with arrest and, in some cases, ending in punishment. Finally, all systems are subject to the limitations of the U.S. Constitution, as interpreted by the courts. In this chapter we present an overview of the roles played by the institutions that make up the criminal justice system in the United States.

Legislatures

The governmental institution with primary responsibility for enacting laws is the **legislature.** Because the United States is organized on the principle of federalism, there arc fifty-one legislatures in this country—the **U.S. Congress** and the fifty state legislatures. Each of these bodies has the power to enact statutes that apply within its respective jurisdiction. The U.S. Congress adopts statutes that apply throughout the United States and its territories, whereas the Illinois General Assembly, for example, adopts laws that apply only within the state of Illinois. For the most part, federal and state statutes complement one another. When there is a conflict, the federal statute prevails.

Legislative Powers of Congress

Congress's legislative authority may be divided into two broad categories: **enumerated powers** and **implied powers.** Enumerated powers are those that are mentioned specifically in Article I, Section 8 of the Constitution, such as the power to tax and the power to borrow money on the credit of the United States. Among the constitutionally enumerated powers of Congress, there are only two direct references to criminal justice. Congress is explicitly authorized to "provide for the Punishment of counterfeiting the Securities and current Coin of the United States" and to "define and punish Piracies and Felonies committed on the high Seas, and Offenses against the Law of Nations." Of course, Congress's power to define federal crimes is much more extensive than these two clauses suggest.

The enumerated power to "regulate commerce among the states" has provided Congress with a vast reservoir of legislative power. Many of the criminal statutes enacted by Congress in recent decades have been justified on the basis of the Commerce Clause of Article I, Section 8 (see Chapter 3).

Table 2.1	Criminal Justice Agencies and Their Functions
Type of Agency	**Functions**
Legislative Bodies	Enacting Criminal Prohibitions
Law Enforcement Agencies	Enforcing Criminal Prohibitions
	Maintaining Public Order and Security
	Conducting Investigations and Gathering Evidence
	Performing Searches and Seizures
	Making Arrests of Persons Suspected of Crimes
	Interrogating Suspects
Prosecutorial Agencies	Enforcing Criminal Prohibitions
	Conducting Investigations
	Conducting Investigations and Gathering Evidence
	Initiating Criminal Prosecutions
	Representing the Government in Court
Public Defender Offices	Representing Indigent Persons Accused of Crimes
Grand Juries	Reviewing Evidence Obtained by Prosecutors
	Indicting Persons Accused of Crimes
	Granting Immunity to Witnesses
Courts of Law	Issuing Search Warrants
	Issuing Arrest Warrants
	Conducting Summary Trials in Minor Cases
	Conducting Initial Appearances
	Conducting Preliminary Hearings
	Conducting Arraignments
	Holding Hearings on Pretrial Motions
	Conducting Trials
	Sentencing Persons Convicted of Crimes
	Hearing Appeals from Lower Court Rulings
Corrections Agencies	Incarceration of Persons Convicted of Crimes
	Supervision of Persons on Probation or Parole
	Carrying Out Executions of Persons Sentenced to Death

Congress's implied powers are those that are deemed to be "necessary and proper for carrying into Execution the foregoing Powers, and all other Powers vested … in the Government of the United States, or in any Department or Officer thereof." As long as Congress's policy goal is permissible, any legislative means that are "plainly adapted" to that goal are likewise permissible. *McCulloch v. Maryland*, 17 U.S. (4 Wheat.) 316, 4 L.Ed. 579 (1819). Under the doctrine of implied powers, scarcely any area exists over which Congress is absolutely barred from legislating, because most social and economic problems have a conceivable relationship to the broad powers and objectives contained in the Constitution.

As the nation expanded and evolved, Congress became more active in passing social and economic legislation. In the twentieth century, and especially the last several decades, Congress established a host of federal crimes. There is now an elaborate body of criminal law. Of course, Congress may not enact laws that violate constitutional limitations such as those found in the Bill of Rights (see Chapter 3).

PUBLICATION OF FEDERAL STATUTES

Federal statutes are published in *United States Statutes at Large,* an annual publication dating from 1789 in which federal statutes are arranged in order of their adoption. Statutes are not arranged by subject matter, nor is there any indication of how they affect existing laws. Because the body of federal statutes is quite voluminous and because new statutes often repeal or amend their predecessors, it is essential that new statutes be merged into legal codes that systematically arrange the statutes by subject. To find federal law as it currently stands, arranged by subject matter, one must consult the latest edition of the *Official Code of the Laws of the United States,* generally known as the **U.S. Code.** The U.S. Code is broken down into fifty subjects, called "titles." Title 18, "Crimes and Criminal Procedure," contains many of the federal crimes established by Congress.

The most popular compilation of the federal law, used by lawyers, judges, and criminal justice professionals, is the **United States Code Annotated (U.S.C.A.).** Published by West Group, the U.S.C.A. contains the entire current U.S. Code, but each section of statutory law in U.S.C.A. is followed by a series of annotations consisting of court decisions interpreting the particular statute, along with historical notes, cross-references, and other editorial features (for more discussion, see Appendix A).

State Legislatures

Under the U.S. Constitution, each state must have a democratically elected legislature because that is the most fundamental element of a "republican form of government." State legislatures for the most part resemble the U.S. Congress. Each is composed of representatives chosen by the citizens of their respective states. All of them are bicameral (i.e., two-house) institutions, with the exception of Nebraska, which has a unicameral legislature. In adopting statutes, they all follow the same basic procedures. When state legislatures adopt statutes, they are published in volumes known as **session laws.** Then statutes are integrated into state codes. Lawyers make frequent use of annotated versions of state codes. These are available at law school libraries, and often at local law libraries, to those who wish to see how state statutes have been interpreted and applied by the state courts.

As we noted in Chapter 1, after the American Revolution, states adopted the English common law as their own state law. (Congress, on the other hand, never did.) Eventually, however, state legislatures codified much of the common law by enacting statutes, which in turn have been developed into comprehensive state codes. Periodically, states revise portions of their codes to make sure they remain relevant to a constantly changing society. For example, in 1989 the Tennessee General Assembly undertook a modernization of its criminal code. Old offenses that were no longer being enforced were repealed, other offenses were redefined, and sentencing laws were completely overhauled.

STATUTORY INTERPRETATION

Statutes are necessarily written in general language, so legislation often requires judicial interpretation. Because legislative bodies have enacted vast numbers of laws defining offenses that are *mala prohibita,* such interpretation assumes an importance largely unknown to the English common law. Courts have responded by developing certain techniques to apply when a statute appears unclear as related to a specific factual scenario. These techniques are generally referred to as **rules of statutory interpretation** and over the years have given rise to references to legislative history and various maxims that courts apply in attempting to determine the legislature's intention in enacting a statute.

Courts recognize that it is the legislative bodies and not the courts that exercise the power to define crimes and penalties. It follows that the most frequent maxim applied by courts in determining legislative intention is the **plain meaning rule.** As the U.S. Supreme Court observed early in the twentieth century, "Where the language [of a statutory law] is plain and admits of no more than one meaning the duty of interpretation does not arise...." *Caminetti v. United States,* 242 U.S. 470, 37 S.Ct. 192, 61 L.Ed. 442 (1917). The Court's dictum seems self-evident, yet even learned judges often disagree as to whether the language of a given statute is plain. This gives rise to certain **canons of construction** applied by courts to determine the **legislative intent** behind a statutory definition of a crime.

A primary canon of construction is that criminal statutes must be strictly construed. The rule originated at common law, when death was the penalty for committing a felony, but the rule has remained. However, it is now based on the rationale that every criminal statute should be sufficiently precise to give fair warning of its meaning. Today we see the rule applied most frequently in a constitutional context when courts determine a criminal statute to be **void for vagueness.** We address this aspect in more detail in the following chapter. Another canon of construction provides for an **implied exception** to a statute. For example, courts have ruled that there is an implied exception to a law imposing speed limits on the highway in instances where police or other emergency vehicles violate the literal text of the law. Would a court apply a statute that makes it an offense for any person to sleep in a bus terminal and thereby find a ticketed passenger guilty who fell asleep while waiting for a bus that was overdue? The implied exception doctrine seems to simply reflect a commonsense approach in determining the meaning of a statute.

Often a statute uses a term that has a definite meaning at common law. In general, courts interpret such terms according to their common-law meanings. Recall that in Chapter 1 we observed that in defining the crime of burglary a legislature might use the term "curtilage" without defining it. In such an instance, we noted that a court would ordinarily look to the common law, which defined the term to mean "an enclosed space surrounding a dwelling."

But this rule does not always apply when dealing with modern statutes, particularly at the federal level, where there is generally considerable legislative history in the form of committee reports and floor debates recorded in the *Congressional Record* that can aid in determining the true intent of a statute. Thus, in *Perrin v. United States,* 444 U.S. 37, 100 S.Ct. 311, 62 L.Ed.2d 199 (1979), the Supreme Court determined that the word "bribery" in a federal statute was not limited to its common-law definition because the legislative history revealed an intent to deal with bribery in organized crime beyond its common-law definition. In general, there is considerably less legislative history available at the state legislative level. However, at times courts seek to determine legislative intent based on available resources.

Law Enforcement Agencies

Law enforcement agencies are charged with enforcing the criminal law. They have the power to investigate suspected criminal activity, to arrest suspected criminals, and to detain arrested persons until their cases come before the appropriate courts of law. Society expects law enforcement agencies not only to arrest those suspected of crimes but also to take steps to prevent crimes from occurring.

Historical Development

Before the Norman Conquest in 1066, there were no organized police in England, but by the thirteenth century constables and justices of the peace came to symbolize enforcement of the rule of law in England. Large communities, somewhat similar to counties in America, were called "shires." The king would send a royal officer called a "reeve" to each shire to keep order and to exercise broad powers within the shire. The onset of the Industrial Revolution led to the development of large cities. Industrialists and merchants began to establish patrols to protect their goods and buildings. But the need for more effective policing became evident. In 1829 Sir Robert Peel, the British Home Secretary, organized a uniformed, but unarmed, police force for London. The name "Bobbies" is still applied to police officers in England in honor of Peel. In later years, Parliament required counties and boroughs to establish police departments modeled along the lines of the London force.

Colonial America basically followed the English system, with local constables and county sheriffs following the English concept of constables and shire reeves. These early law officers were often aided by local vigilante groups of citizens known as "posses." Once America became a nation, states and local communities began to follow the Peel model, and by the mid-1800s, Boston, New York, and Philadelphia had developed professional police departments. By the twentieth century, police were aided by technological developments, and by the 1930s, many departments were equipped with motorcycles and patrol cars. Detectives were soon added to the force, and police became equipped with modern communications equipment and were trained in ballistics and the scientific analysis of blood samples and handwriting.

Policing in Modern America

In the United States nearly 20,000 federal, state, and local agencies are involved in law enforcement and crime prevention. Collectively, these agencies employ nearly 800,000 **sworn officers.** Increasingly, law enforcement officers are trained professionals who must acquire a good working knowledge of the criminal law. At the local level, the typical police recruit now completes about 1,000 hours of training before being sworn in. Modern police forces are highly mobile and, except in the smallest communities, are equipped with computers, sophisticated communications technology, and scientific crime detection equipment.

POLICING AT THE NATIONAL LEVEL

At the national level, the **Federal Bureau of Investigation (FBI)** is the primary agency empowered to investigate violations of federal criminal laws. Located in the **Department of Justice,** the FBI is by far the most powerful of the federal law enforcement agencies, with broad powers to enforce the many criminal laws adopted by Congress. The FBI currently employs nearly 25,000 people, including more than 10,000 **special agents** spread out over fifty-six field offices in the United States and twenty-one foreign offices. With an annual budget exceeding two billion dollars, the FBI uses the most sophisticated methods in crime prevention and investigation. Its crime laboratory figures prominently in the investigation and prosecution of numerous state and federal crimes.

The **U.S. Marshals Service** is the oldest unit of federal law enforcement, dating back to 1790. The Marshals execute orders of federal courts and serve as custodians for the transfer of prisoners. U.S. Marshals played a prominent role in the crises in school integration during the civil rights struggles of the 1950s and early 1960s.

Nearly fifty other federal agencies have law enforcement authority in specific areas. Among them are the Bureau of Alcohol, Tobacco, and Firearms; the Internal Revenue Service; the Bureau of Indian Affairs; the Drug Enforcement Administration; the Bureau of Postal Inspection; the Tennessee Valley Authority; the National Park Service; the Forest Service; the U.S. Capitol Police; the U.S. Mint; the Secret Service; and the Bureau of Citizenship and Immigration Services within the new Department of Homeland Security.

STATE AND LOCAL POLICING

All states have law enforcement agencies that patrol the highways, investigate crimes, and furnish skilled technical support to local law enforcement agencies. Similarly, every state has a number of state agencies responsible for enforcing specific areas of the law, ranging from agricultural importation to food processing and from casino gambling to dispensing alcoholic beverages. Probably among the best known to all citizens are the state highway patrol and the fish and game warden. Generally, cases developed by state officers are processed through local law enforcement and prosecution agencies.

At the local level, we find both county and municipal law enforcement agencies. Nearly every county in America (more than three thousand of them) has a **sheriff.** In most states, sheriffs are elected to office and exercise broad powers as the chief law enforcement officers of their respective counties. They are usually dependent on funding provided by a local governing body, generally the county commission. In some areas, particularly the urban Northeast, many powers traditionally exercised by sheriffs have been assumed by state or metropolitan police forces. In the rest of the country, however, especially in the rural areas, sheriffs (and their deputies) are the principal law enforcement agents at the county level.

Nearly 15,000 cities and towns have their own **police departments.** Local police are charged with enforcing the criminal laws of their states, as well as of their municipalities. Although the county sheriff usually has jurisdiction within the municipalities of the county, he or she generally concentrates enforcement efforts on those areas outside municipal boundaries.

In addition to city and county law enforcement agencies, there are numerous special districts and authorities that have their own police forces. Most state universities have their own police departments, as do many airports and seaports.

Besides providing law enforcement in the strictest sense of the term, local law enforcement agencies initiate the criminal justice process and assist prosecutors in the preparation of cases. Sheriffs in many larger counties and many metropolitan police departments have developed SWAT (special weapons and tactics) teams to assist in the rescue of victims of catastrophes and persons taken hostage. They are also heavily involved in **order maintenance** or "keeping the peace," hence the term "peace officers." Often, keeping the peace involves more of a process of judgment and discretion rather than merely applying the criminal law.

Some of the newer and more innovative policing responsibilities include community relations departments that seek to foster better relations among groups of citizens, especially minorities and juveniles, and to assist social agencies in efforts to rehabilitate drug and alcohol abusers. Finally, the public looks to the police to prevent crime through their presence in the community and through education of the public on crime prevention measures. Under the rubric of **community policing,** police agencies are making an effort to become actively involved in their communities in order to earn the trust and confidence of the citizens they serve. Most police departments in cities of 50,000 people or more now have specialized community policing divisions.

Prosecutorial Agencies

Although law enforcement agencies are the "gatekeepers" of the criminal justice system, prosecutors are central to the administration of criminal justice. It is the **prosecutors** who determine whether to bring charges against suspected criminals. They have enormous discretion, not only in determining whether to prosecute but also in determining what charges to file. Moreover, prosecutors frequently set the tone for plea bargaining and have a powerful voice in determining the severity of sanctions imposed on persons convicted of crimes. Accordingly, prosecutors play a crucial role in the criminal justice system.

Historical Background

The early English common law considered many crimes to be private matters between individuals; however, the role of the public prosecutor evolved as early as the thirteenth century, when the King's counsel would pursue crimes considered to be offenses against the Crown and, in some instances, when injured victims declined to prosecute. Today in England, a public prosecutor prosecutes crimes that have great significance to the government, but the majority of offenses are handled by police agencies that hire barristers to prosecute charges. Unlike American prosecutors, the English barrister may represent the police in one case and in the next case represent the defendant.

The office of public prosecutor in England became the prototype for the office of attorney general in this country at the national and state levels. In colonial days, an attorney general's assistants handled local prosecutions. However, as states became independent, the practice ceased. The state attorneys general assumed the role of chief legal officers, and local governments began electing their own prosecuting attorneys.

Federal Prosecutors

In the United States, the chief prosecutor at the federal level is the **Attorney General,** who is the head of the Department of Justice. Below the Attorney General are several **U.S. Attorneys,** each responsible for prosecuting crimes within a particular federal district. The U.S. Attorneys, in turn, have a number of assistants who handle most of the day-to-day criminal cases brought by the federal government. The President, subject to the consent of the Senate, appoints the Attorney General and the U.S. Attorneys. Assistant U.S. Attorneys are federal civil service employees.

In addition to the regular federal prosecutors, Congress has provided for the appointment of **independent counsel** (special prosecutors) in cases involving alleged misconduct by high government officials. By far, the most infamous such case was "Watergate," which resulted in the convictions of several high-ranking officials and led to the resignation of President Richard Nixon in 1974. But there have been numerous cases where, under congressional direction, a special prosecutor has been appointed. The best-known recent example of this was Kenneth Starr's appointment to investigate the Whitewater scandal that involved close associates of President Bill Clinton and First Lady Hillary Rodham Clinton, an investigation that eventually culminated in President Clinton's impeachment and his subsequent acquittal by the U.S. Senate in February 1999.

State and Local Prosecutors

Each state likewise has its own attorney general, who acts as the state's chief legal officer, and a number of assistant attorneys general, plus a number of district or **state's attorneys** at the local level. Generally speaking, local prosecutors are elected for set terms of office and have the responsibility for the prosecution of crimes within the jurisdiction for which they are elected. In most states, local prosecutors act autonomously and possess broad discretionary powers. Many local prosecutors function on a part-time basis, but in the larger offices the emphasis is for the prosecutor and assistant prosecutors to serve on a full-time basis. Larger offices are establishing educational programs and developing specially trained assistants or units to handle specific categories of crime—for example, white collar and governmental corruption, narcotics offenses, and consumer fraud.

Cities and counties also have their own attorneys. These attorneys, generally appointed by the governing bodies they represent, sometimes prosecute violations of city and county ordinances, but increasingly their function is limited to representing their cities or counties in civil suits and giving legal advice to local councils and officials.

The Prosecutor's Broad Discretion

Federal and state prosecutors (whether known as district attorney, state attorney, or county prosecutor) play a vital role in the criminal justice system in the United States. As mentioned, a politically appointed U.S. Attorney supervises prosecutors at the federal level, whereas state and local prosecutors generally come into office by election in partisan contests. Thus, prosecutors become sensitive to the community norms while exercising the broad discretion that the law vests in prosecutorial decision making.

Prosecutors not only determine the level of offense to be charged; in exercise of their very broad discretion they exercise the power of ***nolle prosequi,*** usually called *nol pros,* which allows a prosecutor not to proceed in a given case irrespective of the factual basis for prosecution. Prosecutors sometimes *nol pros* cases to secure cooperation of a defendant in furthering other prosecution; in other instances, a prosecutor may allow a defendant to participate in some diversionary program of rehabilitation. In recent years, completion of a prescribed program in a drug court has often resulted in a case being *nol prossed* by a prosecutor. (See the discussion of drug courts in Chapter 9.)

Counsel for the Defense

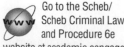

Go to the Scheb/ Scheb Criminal Law and Procedure 6e website at academic.cengage .com/criminaljustice/scheb for an edited version of *Mempa v. Rhay.*

In American criminal law, individuals accused of any crime, no matter how minor the offense, have the right to employ counsel for their defense. U.S. Const. Amend. VI. Indeed, the U.S. Supreme Court has held that a defendant has the right to be represented by an attorney at all criminal proceedings that may substantially affect the rights of the accused. *Mempa v. Rhay,* 389 U.S. 128, 88 S.Ct. 254, 19 L.Ed.2d 336 (1967).

In this country, many lawyers specialize in criminal defense work. Of course, defendants are free to employ an attorney of their choice at their own expense. Some well-known attorneys, such as Johnnie Cochran and Roy Black, are national celebrities who specialize in representing defendants in high-profile trials like the O. J. Simpson case. However, most criminal defendants are not wealthy, and few people accused of crimes can afford to hire such "dream teams" to represent them.

Many attorneys are highly skilled in handling criminal cases and are available for employment in federal and state criminal proceedings. In fact, it is not uncommon for attorneys who start their careers as prosecutors to eventually enter private practice in criminal matters. Today some state bar associations grant special recognition to lawyers who qualify by virtue of experience and examination as "certified criminal defense attorneys."

Representation of Indigent Defendants

Go to the Scheb/
Scheb Criminal Law
and Procedure 6e
website at academic.cengage
.com/criminaljustice/scheb for
edited versions of the *Gideon*
and *Argersinger* decisions.

Beginning in the 1960s, the U.S. Supreme Court greatly expanded the right to counsel by requiring states to provide attorneys to **indigent defendants.** *Gideon v. Wainwright,* 372 U.S. 335, 83 S.Ct. 792, 9 L.Ed.2d 799 (1963); *Argersinger v. Hamlin,* 407 U.S. 25, 92 S.Ct. 2006, 32 L.Ed.2d 530 (1972).

In some states, courts appoint attorneys from the private bar to represent indigent defendants. However, most states have chosen to handle the problem of indigent

**SUPREME COURT
PERSPECTIVE**

Gideon v. Wainwright, 372 U.S. 335; 83 S.Ct. 792; 9 L.Ed.2d. 799 (1963)

In this landmark case, the Supreme Court considers whether state courts must as a matter of course appoint counsel to represent indigent defendants accused of felonies. Clarence Earl Gideon was convicted of breaking and entering a poolroom with intent to commit a misdemeanor, a felony under Florida law. Unable to afford legal representation, Gideon requested that the trial judge appoint a lawyer to represent him. The judge refused, as Florida law at that time required judges to appoint counsel at public expense to represent indigent defendants only in capital cases. The Supreme Court held that this was a denial of the Sixth Amendment right to counsel as applied to the states under the Fourteenth Amendment. In his opinion for the Court, Justice Hugo Black reflected on the importance of defense counsel in criminal cases.

JUSTICE BLACK delivered the opinion of the Court, saying in part:

[I]n our adversary system of criminal justice, any person haled into court, who is too poor to hire a lawyer, cannot
be assured a fair trial unless counsel is provided for him. This seems to us to be an obvious truth. Governments, both state and federal, quite properly spend vast sums of money to establish machinery to try defendants accused of crime. Lawyers to prosecute are everywhere deemed essential to protect the public's interest in an orderly society. Similarly, there are few defendants charged with crime, few indeed, who fail to hire the best lawyers they can get to prepare and present their defenses. That government hires lawyers to prosecute and defendants who have the money hire lawyers to defend are the strongest indications of the widespread belief that lawyers in criminal courts are necessities, not luxuries. The right of one charged with crime to counsel may not be deemed fundamental and essential to fair trials in some countries, but it is in ours. From the very beginning, our state and national constitutions and laws have laid great emphasis on procedural and substantive safeguards designed to assure fair trials before impartial tribunals in which every defendant stands equal before the law. This noble ideal cannot be realized if the poor man charged with crime has to face his accusers without a lawyer to assist him.

defense by establishing the office of public defender. Like public prosecutors, **public defenders** are generally elected to set terms of office. Because of their constant contact with criminal cases, public defenders acquire considerable expertise in representing defendants. Moreover, because they are public officials who, like prosecutors, are provided budgets, public defenders are often able to hire investigators to aid their staff of assistant public defenders in their representation of indigent defendants. We discuss the right to appointed counsel and the right to self-representation in detail in Chapter 17.

The Role of Defense Attorneys

The role of the **defense attorney** is perhaps the most misunderstood in the criminal justice system. First and foremost, a defense attorney is charged with zealously representing his or her client and ensuring that the defendant's constitutional rights are fully protected. To anyone who has watched *Perry Mason* or a similar television program, the defense attorney's most visible role is that of vigorously cross-examining prosecution witnesses or passionately pleading for a client before a jury. The defense attorney's role is far greater than being a courtroom advocate. As a counselor, defense attorneys must evaluate the alternative courses of action that may be available to a defendant. They must attempt to gauge the strength of the prosecution's case, advise on the feasibility of entering a plea of guilty, and attempt to negotiate a fair and constructive sentence. In instances where a defendant elects to plead not guilty, defense attorneys challenge the police and prosecution. Many observers point out that these efforts by defense attorneys "keep the system honest" by causing police and prosecuting authorities to be scrupulous in their adherence to constitutional standards.

Perhaps the most frequently voiced reservation concerning defense attorneys relates to representation of a defendant who, from all facts available, is believed to be guilty. Defense attorneys are quick to point out that it is not their function to make a judgment of the defendant's guilt or innocence; there are other functionaries in the system charged with that responsibility. The answer does not easily satisfy critics. Nevertheless, in our system of adversarial justice the defense attorney is required to represent a defendant with fidelity, to protect the defendant's constitutional rights, to assert all defenses available under the law of the land, and to make sure before a defendant is found guilty that the prosecution has sustained its burden of proving the defendant guilty beyond a reasonable doubt. A defense attorney must make sufficient objections and other tactical moves to preserve any contention of error for review by a higher court. If the defendant is convicted, the duty continues to ensure imposition of a fair sentence, advise as to the right to appeal to a higher court, and, in some instances, seek postconviction relief if an appeal fails.

Juries

The **jury** is one of the great contributions of the English common law. By the twelfth century juries began to function in England, but not as we know juries today. Rather, these early juries comprised men who had knowledge of the disputes they were to decide, but eventually juries began to hear evidence and make their verdicts accordingly. By the eighteenth century, juries occupied a prominent role in the English common-law system and served as a buffer between the Crown and the citizenry. The colonists brought the concept to the New World. Today, juries composed of both men and women represent an important component of the American system of criminal justice.

There are two types of juries: the **grand jury** and the **petit (trial) jury.** The juries derive their names based on the number of persons who serve, the grand jury consisting of a larger number than the petit jury.

Grand Juries

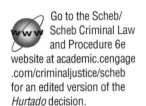

Go to the Scheb/ Scheb Criminal Law and Procedure 6e website at academic.cengage .com/criminaljustice/scheb for an edited version of the *Hurtado* decision.

Grand juries essentially serve to consider whether there is sufficient evidence to bring charges against a person; petit or trial juries sit to hear evidence at a trial and render a verdict accordingly. The Fifth Amendment to the U.S. Constitution stipulates that "[n]o person shall be held to answer for a capital, or otherwise infamous crime, unless on a presentment or indictment of a grand jury." The constitutional requirement binds all federal courts; however, the Supreme Court has held that states are not bound to abide by the grand jury requirement. *Hurtado v. California,* 110 U.S. 516, 4 S.Ct. 111, 28 L.Ed. 232 (1884).

Sixteen to twenty-three persons serve on a federal grand jury. The number varies according to each state but usually consists of between twelve and twenty-three citizens. Grand jurors serve for a limited time to hear evidence and to determine whether to hand down an indictment, sometimes referred to as a **true bill,** or to refuse to indict when the jury determines there is insufficient evidence of a crime by returning a **no bill.** Twelve must vote to return an indictment in federal court, and states usually require at least a majority of grand jurors to return an indictment. Courts have broad authority to call a grand jury into session, and grand juries are authorized to make wide-ranging inquiries and investigations into public matters. Grand juries may make accusations called *presentments* independently of a prosecutor.

Although the English common-law system gave birth to the grand jury, England abolished grand juries in the 1930s, having found that the return of **indictments** was almost automatic and that the use of grand juries tended to delay the criminal process. Today, critics argue that grand juries are so dominated by the prosecutors who appear before them that they cease to serve as an independent body to evaluate evidence. Indeed, many states have eliminated the requirement that a grand jury hand down indictments and have substituted a **prosecutor's information,** an accusatorial document charging a crime. Yet many reformers would retain the grand jury as an institution for investigation of corruption in government. We discuss grand juries in more detail in Chapter 17.

Trial Juries

Article III, Section 2 of the U.S. Constitution establishes the right to trial by jury in criminal cases. The Sixth Amendment guarantees "the right to a **speedy and public trial** by an impartial jury." The Seventh Amendment grants a right to a trial by jury in civil suits at common law. All state constitutions confer the right of trial by jury in criminal cases; however, the federal constitutional right to a jury trial applies to the states, thereby guaranteeing a defendant a right to a jury trial in a state criminal prosecution if such a right would exist in a federal prosecution. *Duncan v. Louisiana,* 391 U.S. 145, 88 S.Ct. 1444, 20 L.Ed.2d 491 (1968). However, as we note below, the right to trial by jury does not extend to juvenile delinquency proceedings.

A common-law trial jury consisted of twelve men. Today, twelve persons are required in federal juries; however, the number varies in states, although all states require twelve-person juries in capital cases. The Supreme Court has approved the use

Go to the Scheb/ Scheb Criminal Law and Procedure 6e website at academic .cengage.com/criminaljustice/ scheb for an edited version of *Williams v. Florida*.

of six-person juries in noncapital felony prosecutions. *Williams v. Florida,* 399 U.S. 78, 90 S.Ct. 1893, 26 L.Ed.2d 446 (1970).

Even though trial juries function in a relatively small number of criminal cases, their availability to serve has a considerable impact on the criminal justice system. In Chapter 18 we discuss in detail the various requirements concerning the right to trial by jury, the right to a public trial, the composition of trial juries, the selection of juries, and proposals for jury reforms.

The Courts

Courts of law are the centerpieces of the federal and state criminal justice systems. Courts of law are responsible for determining both the factual basis and the legal sufficiency of criminal charges and for ensuring that criminal defendants are provided due process of law. Essentially, the federal courts adjudicate criminal cases where defendants are charged with violating federal criminal laws; state courts adjudicate alleged violations of state laws.

Basically, there are two kinds of courts: trial and appellate courts. **Trial courts** conduct criminal trials and various pretrial and post-trial proceedings. **Appellate courts** hear appeals from the decisions of the trial courts. Trial courts are primarily concerned with ascertaining facts, determining guilt or innocence, and imposing punishments, whereas appellate courts are primarily concerned with matters of law. Appellate courts correct legal errors made by trial courts and develop law when new legal questions arise. In some instances appellate courts must determine whether there is legally sufficient evidence to uphold a conviction.

The first question facing a court in any criminal prosecution is that of **jurisdiction,** the legal authority to hear and decide the case. A court must have jurisdiction, over both the subject matter of a case and the parties to a case, before it may proceed to adjudicate that controversy. The jurisdiction of the federal courts is determined by both the language of Article III of the Constitution and the statutes enacted by Congress. The respective state constitutions and statutes determine the jurisdiction of the state courts.

The Federal Court System

Article III of the U.S. Constitution provides that "[t]he judicial Power of the United States shall be vested in one supreme Court, and in such inferior Courts as the Congress may from time to time ordain and establish." Under this authority Congress enacted the Judiciary Act of 1789, creating the federal court system. After passage of the Judiciary Act of 1801 the Supreme Court justices were required to "ride circuit," a practice that had its roots in English legal history. The circuit courts then consisted of district court judges who heard appeals alongside "circuit riding" Supreme Court justices. In 1891 Congress created separate appellate courts, and since then Supreme Court justices have remained as reviewing justices.

U.S. District Courts handle prosecutions for violations of federal statutes. In addition, federal courts sometimes review convictions from state courts when defendants raise issues arising under the U.S. Constitution. Appeals are heard by U.S. Courts of Appeals, and, of course, the Supreme Court is at the apex of the judicial system.

U.S. DISTRICT COURTS

The principal trial court in the federal system is the U.S. District Court. There are district courts in ninety-four federal judicial districts around the country. A criminal trial in the district court is presided over by a judge appointed for life by the President with the consent of the Senate. Federal magistrate judges, who are appointed by federal district judges, often handle pretrial proceedings in the district courts and trials of misdemeanors.

In the twelve-month period ending March 31, 2004, there were 70,746 criminal cases filed in U.S. District Courts (see Administrative Office of the United States Courts, Federal Judicial Caseload Statistics, March 31, 2004, Table D).

Since Congress created the district courts by the Judiciary Act of 1789, it has created specialized courts to handle specific kinds of cases (for example, the U.S. Court of International Trade and the U.S. Claims Court).

THE U.S. COURTS OF APPEALS

The **intermediate appellate courts** in the federal system are the **U.S. Courts of Appeals** (also known as circuit courts). Twelve geographical circuits (and one "federal circuit") cover the United States and its possessions. Figure 2.1 indicates the geographical distribution of the circuit courts. The circuit courts hear both criminal and civil appeals from the district courts and from quasi-judicial tribunals in the independent regulatory agencies. In the twelve-month period ending March 31, 2004, 45,769 appeals were commenced in the federal circuit courts. Of these, 12,056 were criminal cases. (Administrative Office of the United States Courts, Federal Judicial Caseload Statistics, March 31, 2004, Table B-7).

Generally, decisions of the courts of appeals are rendered by panels of three judges who vote to affirm, reverse, or modify the lower-court decisions under review. There is a procedure by which the circuit courts provide *en banc* **hearings,** where all judges assigned to the court (or a substantial number of them) participate in a decision. Like their counterparts in the district courts, federal appeals court judges are appointed to life terms by the President with the consent of the Senate.

Sidebar **Jurisdiction over Crimes Committed by Native Americans on Reservations**

Article I, Section 8 of the U.S. Constitution mentions Indian tribes as being subject to Congressional legislation. Congress has provided that federal courts have jurisdiction over specified offenses committed by Native Americans on Indian reservations. 18 U.S.C.A. 1153. At the same time, Congress has permitted certain states to exercise jurisdiction over such offenses. 18 U.S.C.A. 1162. Furthermore, offenses committed by one Native American against another on a reservation are generally subject to the jurisdiction of tribal courts, unless the crime charged has been expressly made subject to federal jurisdiction. *Keeble v. United States*, 412 U.S. 205, 93 S.Ct. 1993, 36 L.Ed.2d 844 (1973).

Courts of the state where a Native American reservation is located have jurisdiction over crimes on the reservation when the offense is perpetrated by a non-Indian against a non-Indian, but non-Indian defendants charged with committing a crime on a reservation are subject to federal jurisdiction if the victim is a member of the tribe. *United States v. Antelope*, 430 U.S. 641, 97 S.Ct. 1395, 51 L.Ed.2d 701 (1977).

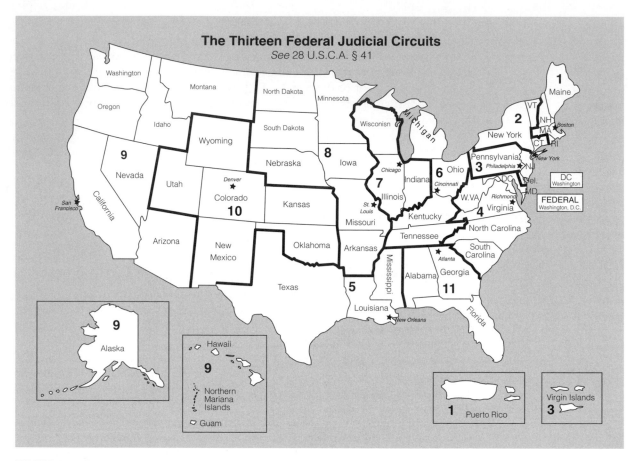

FIGURE 2.1 The Federal Judicial Circuits. Source: *Federal Reporter,* 2nd Series (West Publishing Company).

THE U.S. SUPREME COURT

The highest appellate court in the federal judicial system is the **U.S. Supreme Court.** The Supreme Court has jurisdiction to review, either on appeal or by **writ of certiorari** (discretionary review), all the decisions of the lower federal courts and many decisions of the highest state courts. The Supreme Court comprises nine justices who, like district and circuit judges, are appointed for life by the President with the consent of the Senate. These nine individuals have the final word in determining what the U.S. Constitution requires, permits, and prohibits in the areas of law enforcement, prosecution, adjudication, and punishment. The Supreme Court also promulgates rules of procedure for the lower federal courts to follow in both criminal and civil cases.

As of May 1, 2007, John Roberts was the chief justice of the Supreme Court, and the associate justices were John Paul Stevens, Antonin Scalia, Anthony Kennedy, David Souter, Clarence Thomas, Ruth Bader Ginsburg, Stephen Breyer, and Samuel Alito. During the 2004 term (which ended in June 2005), the Court received roughly 7,500 petitions for certiorari and granted review in only 87 (just over 1 percent) of these cases. During its 2004 term, the Court issued seventy-four signed opinions. (Chief Justice's *2005 Year-End Report on the Federal Judiciary,* January 1, 2006).

Supreme Court opinions are officially reported in the *United States Reports* (abbreviated U.S.) and in private publications, *Supreme Court Reporter* (abbreviated S.Ct.) and *Lawyers Edition, 2d* (abbreviated L.Ed.2d). Immediate access to a recently issued opinion may be found at www.findlaw.com.

MILITARY TRIBUNALS

Crimes committed by persons in military service are ordinarily prosecuted in proceedings before **courts-martial.** Article 1, Section 8 of the U.S. Constitution grants Congress the authority to regulate the armed forces. Under this authority, Congress has enacted the **Uniform Code of Military Justice (UCMJ),** 10 U.S.C.A. 801–940. The UCMJ gives courts-martial jurisdiction to try all offenses under the code committed by military personnel. Notwithstanding this grant of authority, the U.S. Supreme Court held in 1969 that military jurisdiction was limited to offenses that were service connected. *O'Callahan v. Parker,* 395 U.S. 258, 89 S.Ct. 1683, 23 L.Ed.2d 291 (1969). The *O'Callahan* decision greatly narrowed military jurisdiction over offenses committed by servicepersons. In 1987 the Court overruled *O'Callahan* and said that military jurisdiction depends solely on whether an accused is a military member. *Solorio v. United States,* 483 U.S. 435, 107 S.Ct. 2924, 97 L.Ed.2d 364 (1987). Thus, courts-martial may now try all offenses committed by servicepersons in violation of the UCMJ.

 Go to the Scheb/ Scheb Criminal Law and Procedure 6e website at academic.cengage .com/criminaljustice/scheb for an edited version of *Solorio v. U.S.*

Commanders of various military units convene court-martial proceedings and appoint those who sit similar to a civilian jury. These commanders are called the convening authorities and are assisted by military lawyers designated as staff judge advocates. Military trial procedures and rules of evidence are similar to the rules applied in federal district courts.

There are three classes of court-martial: summary, special, and general. The summary court-martial is composed of one military officer with jurisdiction to impose minor punishments over enlisted personnel. It is somewhat analogous to trial by a civilian magistrate, whereas special and general court-martial proceedings are formal military tribunals more analogous to civilian criminal courts of record.

A special court-martial must be composed of three or more members with or without a military judge, or a military judge alone, if requested by the accused. It can impose more serious punishments on both officers and enlisted personnel. A general court-martial tries the most serious offenses and must consist of five or more members and a military judge (or a military judge alone, if requested by the accused). A general court-martial may try any offense made punishable by the UCMJ and may impose any punishment authorized by law against officers and enlisted personnel, including death for a capital offense. Trial by a military judge alone is not permitted in capital cases.

A military judge presides at special and general courts-martial. A trial counsel serves as prosecutor, and a defendant is furnished legal counsel by the government unless the accused chooses to employ private defense counsel. The extent of punishment that may be imposed varies according to the offense and the authority of the type of court-martial convened.

Decisions of courts-martial are reviewed by military courts of review in each branch of the armed forces. In specified instances, appeals are heard by the U.S. **Court of Appeals for the Armed Forces.** This court is staffed by civilian judges who are appointed to fifteen-year terms by the President with the consent of the Senate.

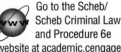 Go to the Scheb/ Scheb Criminal Law and Procedure 6e website at academic.cengage .com/criminaljustice/scheb for edited versions of *Ex parte Milligan* and *Ex parte Quirin.*

Only under conditions of martial law do military tribunals have the authority to try American citizens. *Ex parte Milligan,* 71 U.S. (4 Wall.) 2, 18 L.Ed. 281 (1866). Historically, the Supreme Court has permitted "enemy aliens" captured during wartime to be tried by military tribunals. See *Ex parte Quirin,* 317 U.S. 1, 63 S.Ct. 2, 87 L.Ed. 7 (1942). Under an executive order issued by President George W. Bush on November 13, 2001, the military established special tribunals to try foreign nationals accused of terrorism against the United States. Several accused terrorists detained at the U.S. Naval Base at Guantanamo Bay, Cuba, were brought to trial, but the proceedings were interrupted by a dramatic decision from the nation's highest court. In *Hamdan v. Rumsfeld,* ___ U.S. ___, 126 S.Ct. 2749, 165 L.Ed.2d 723 (2006), the U.S. Supreme

Court ruled that the military tribunals were neither authorized by federal law nor required by military necessity. Moreover, the Court held that they ran afoul of the Geneva Conventions governing the treatment of prisoners of war. Immediately after the *Hamdan* decision, some members of Congress indicated their willingness to support legislation to provide the authorization found lacking by the Court.

State Court Systems

Each state has its own independent judicial system. These courts handle more than 90 percent of criminal prosecutions in the United States. State judicial systems are characterized by variations in structure, jurisdiction, and procedure but have certain commonalities. Every state has one or more levels of trial courts and at least one appellate court. Most states have **courts of general jurisdiction,** which conduct trials in felony and major misdemeanor cases, and **courts of limited jurisdiction,** which handle pretrial matters and conduct trials in minor misdemeanor cases. Most states also have some form of intermediate appellate courts that relieve the **state supreme court** (known as the Court of Appeals in New York and Maryland) from hearing routine appeals. Many states also have separate **juvenile courts,** which operate in ways that differ significantly from the criminal courts for adults.

Some states, like North Carolina, have adopted tidy, streamlined court systems (see Figure 2.2). Other states' court systems are extremely complex, as is the case in

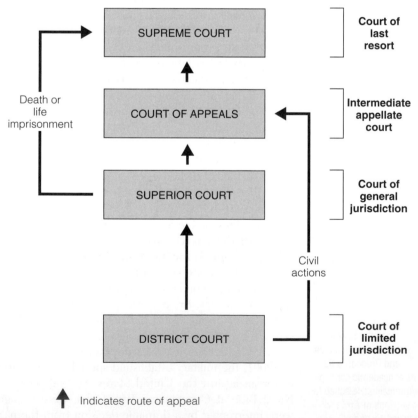

FIGURE 2.2 The North Carolina Court System. Source: U.S. Department of Justice/National Center for State Courts.

Texas (see Figure 2.3). In structural complexity, most states' systems fall somewhere between the two extremes.

Contrasting Judicial Functions and Environments

As we noted in Chapter 1, trial courts primarily make factual determinations, often assisted by juries; apply settled law to established facts; and impose sanctions. Appellate courts, on the other hand, interpret the federal and state constitutions and statutes,

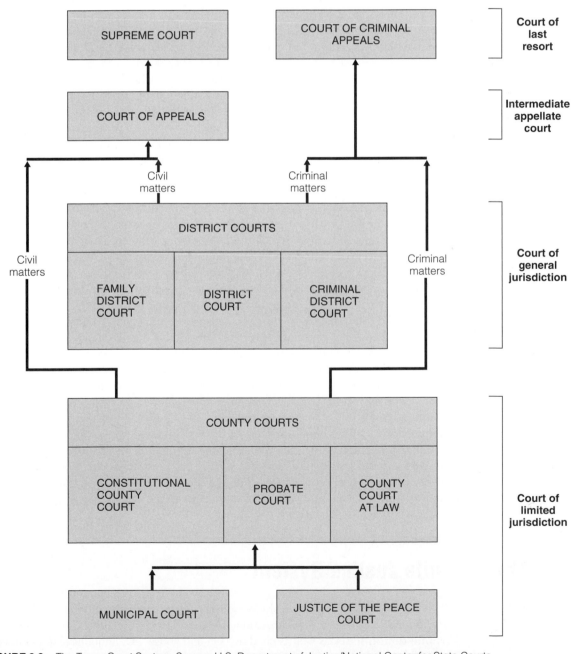

FIGURE 2.3 The Texas Court System. Source: U.S. Department of Justice/National Center for State Courts.

correct errors in law made by trial courts, and develop the law by "filling in the gaps" that often become apparent in the application of statutory laws.

The difference in the roles of trial and appellate courts is also evident in the environment where trial and appellate judges perform their functions. A trial court usually sits in a county courthouse or other county judicial building. Trial judges preside over courtrooms where there is considerable daily activity with juries being impaneled, witnesses providing testimony, and attorneys making objections and pleas for their clients. At other times the judges are busy hearing arguments in their chambers. In short, the trial scene is one of high visibility and is often attended by the comings and goings of numerous spectators and, where a high-profile case is being tried, by print and television media. In short, the trial court setting is a venue of daily interaction between court personnel and the citizens of the community.

In contrast, appellate courts are often described as "invisible courts" because their public proceedings are generally limited to hearing legal arguments by attorneys on prescribed oral argument days. Few clients and even fewer spectators are generally in attendance. Media representatives usually attend only when some high-profile appeal is being argued. Many of the documents arrive by mail to a staff of clerks. Proceedings are resolved primarily by review of records from the lower court or administrative agency, by study of the law briefs submitted by counsel, and by discussion among the panel of judges assigned a particular case, often supplemented by independent research conducted by judges and their staff attorneys.

Unlike the busy atmosphere that normally characterizes a trial court, an appellate court often sits in the state capitol building or in its own facility, usually with a complete law library. The décor in the buildings that house appellate courts is usually quite formal, often with portraits of former judges regarded as oracles of the law. When a panel of judges sits to hear oral arguments, they normally emerge from behind a velvet curtain on a precise schedule and to the cry of the court's marshal. When not hearing oral arguments, appellate judges usually occupy a suite of offices with their secretaries and law clerks. It is in these individual chambers that appellate judges study and write their opinions on cases assigned to them.

The U.S. Supreme Court occupies a majestic building in Washington, D.C., with spacious office suites and impressive corridors and library facilities. With enhanced attributes similar to those mentioned for appellate courts, the elegance and dignity of the facilities comport with the significant role of the Court as final arbiter in the nation's judicial system. Unlike the sparse attendance at most state and intermediate federal appellate courts, parties interested in the decisions that will result from arguments, a coterie of media persons, and many spectators will fill the courtroom to hear arguments that often significantly affect the economic, social, and political life of the nation. Photography is not allowed, and the arguments and dialogue between the counsel and the justices are observed silently and respectfully by those who attend. There is sometimes a contrasting scene outside the Supreme Court building, where demonstrators sometimes gather to give visibility to the causes they represent.

The Juvenile Justice System

The juvenile justice system includes specialized courts, law enforcement agencies, social services agencies, and corrections facilities designed to address problems of **juvenile delinquency** as well as child neglect and abuse. "Delinquency" refers to conduct that would be criminal if committed by an adult. In addition to being charged with delinquency, young people may be subjected to the jurisdiction of a juvenile court for engaging in conduct that is prohibited only for minors. Such behaviors, which include truancy (chronic absence from school) and incorrigibility, are often called **status offenses,** because they are peculiar to the status of children.

Historical Basis

The common law treated all persons above the age of fourteen as adults for purposes of criminal responsibility (see Chapter 14). Because the American legal system was based on English common law, American courts followed the common-law rules for the treatment of juveniles. Young teenagers were treated essentially as adults for the purposes of criminal justice. During the colonial period of American history, it was not uncommon for teenagers to be hanged, flogged, or placed in the public pillory as punishment for their crimes. Later, as state penitentiaries were established, it was not unusual for 20 percent of prison populations to be juveniles.

In the late nineteenth century, public outcry against treating juveniles like adults led to the establishment of a separate juvenile justice system in the United States. Reformers were convinced that the existing system of criminal justice was inappropriate for young offenders who were more in need of reform than punishment. Reformers proposed specialized courts to deal with young offenders not as hardened criminals, but as misguided youth in need of special care. This special treatment was justified legally by the concept of **parens patriae,** the power of the state to act to protect the interests of those who cannot protect themselves.

The first state to act in this area was Illinois in 1899. By the 1920s, many states had followed suit, and by 1945, juvenile court legislation had been enacted by Congress and all state legislatures. The newly created juvenile courts were usually separate from the regular tribunals; often, the judges or referees presiding over these courts did not have formal legal training. The proceedings were generally nonadversarial, and there was little in the way of procedural regularity or even the opportunity for the juvenile offender to confront his or her accusers. In fact, juvenile delinquency proceedings were conceived as civil, as opposed to criminal, proceedings. Dispositions of cases were usually nonpunitive in character; therefore, accused juvenile offenders were not afforded most of the rights of criminal defendants.

Because the juvenile justice system emphasized rehabilitation (rather than retribution, incapacitation, or deterrence), juveniles who were found delinquent were often placed in reformatories for indeterminate periods, sometimes until they reached the age of majority. Juvenile courts often suffered from a lack of trained staff and inadequate facilities, and by the 1960s, a system that was conceived by reformers was itself under attack by a new generation of reformers.

The Constitutional Reform of Juvenile Justice

Go to the Scheb/
Scheb Criminal Law
and Procedure 6e
website at academic.cengage
.com/criminaljustice/scheb for
an edited version of the *Gault*
decision.

The abuses that came to be associated with juvenile courts were addressed by the Supreme Court in the landmark case of *In re Gault,* 387 U.S. 1, 87 S.Ct. 1428, 18 L.Ed.2d 527 (1967). In *Gault,* the Court essentially required that juvenile courts adhere to standards of due process, applying most of the basic procedural safeguards enjoyed by adults accused of crimes. Moreover, *Gault* held that juvenile courts must respect the right to counsel, the freedom from compulsory self-incrimination, and the right to confront (cross-examine) hostile witnesses. Writing for a nearly unanimous bench, Justice Abe Fortas observed that "under our Constitution, the condition of being a boy does not justify a kangaroo court." 387 U.S. at 28, 87 S.Ct. at 1444, 18 L.Ed.2d at 546.

Four years later in *McKeiver v. Pennsylvania,* 403 U.S. 528, 91 S.Ct. 1976, 29 L.Ed.2d 647 (1971), the Court refused to extend the right to trial by jury to juvenile proceedings. In *Schall v. Martin,* 467 U.S. 253, 104 S.Ct. 2403, 81 L.Ed.2d 207 (1984), the Court upheld a pretrial detention program for juveniles that might well have been found violative of due process had it applied to adults. Writing for the Court, Justice William Rehnquist stressed that "the Constitution does not mandate elimination of all differences in the treatment of juveniles." 467 U.S. at 263, 104 S.Ct. at 2409, 81 L.Ed.2d at 216.

In the wake of *Gault,* a number of states revised their juvenile codes to reflect the requirements of those decisions and to increase the qualifications of persons serving as juvenile judges and to transform juvenile courts into courts of record. Today it is common for the juvenile court to simply be a division of a court of general jurisdiction, such as a circuit or a superior court. Nevertheless, juvenile courts retain their distinctive character. For example, juvenile court proceedings are not subject to the constitutional "public trial" requirement. The Federal Juvenile Delinquency Act, 18 U.S.C.A. 5031–5042, gives the court discretion on the issue of whether to close proceedings involving a child and whether to grant public access to the records of the proceedings. State laws vary, often allowing the presiding judge to exercise discretion in these matters.

There are significant differences in the adjudication of juvenile cases and adult criminal proceedings as well as the punishments imposed. We discuss some of the aspects of adjudication of juveniles in Chapter 18 and the distinctions between the punishments of juveniles and of adults in Chapter 19.

The Corrections System

The **corrections system** is designed to fulfill the criminal justice system's objective of providing punishment and rehabilitation of offenders. As with the court system, corrections facilities are operated at the federal and state levels. The system includes prisons and jails as well as a variety of programs that include probation, parole, and supervised community service.

Historical Background

Punishments inflicted under the English common law were quite severe—the death penalty was prescribed for most felonies, and those convicted of misdemeanors were generally subjected to such corporal punishment as flogging in the public square. The new American colonies generally followed common-law practice; by the time of the American Revolution, the death penalty was in wide use for a variety of felonies, and corporal punishment, primarily flogging, was widely used for a variety of crimes.

The American Bill of Rights (the first ten amendments to the Constitution, ratified in 1791) prohibited the imposition of "cruel and unusual punishments" (Eighth Amendment). The framers sought to prevent the use of torture, which had been common in Europe as late as the eighteenth century; however, they did not intend to outlaw the death penalty or abolish all forms of corporal punishment.

During the nineteenth century, reformers introduced the concept of the **penitentiary**—literally, "a place to do penance." The idea was that criminals could be reformed through isolation, Bible study, and hard labor. This gave rise to the notion of rehabilitation, the idea that the criminal justice system could reform criminals and reintegrate them into society. Many of the educational, occupational training, and psychological programs found in modern prisons are based on this theory.

Contemporary Developments in Criminal Punishment

By the twentieth century, incarceration largely replaced corporal punishment as the states, as well as the federal government, constructed prisons to house persons convicted of felonies. Even cities and counties constructed jails for the confinement of persons convicted of misdemeanors. The death penalty, an intensely controversial penalty, remains in effect today in more than half the states, although its use is now limited to the most aggravated cases of murder. Today, the focus of criminal punishment is on the goal of incapacitation to prevent commission of further crimes.

There are procedural as well as substantive issues in the area of sentencing and punishment. Sharp disagreements exist regarding the roles that legislatures, judges, and corrections officials should play in determining punishments. Specifically, criminal punishment is limited by the Eighth Amendment prohibition of cruel and unusual punishments, the due process clauses of the Fifth and Fourteenth Amendments, and similar provisions in all fifty state constitutions. Today the criminal law provides for a variety of criminal punishments, including monetary **fines,** incarceration, probation, community service, and, of course, the death penalty.

As with courts, there is a federal corrections system and fifty separate state corrections systems. Each of these systems is responsible for supervising those persons sentenced to prison by courts of law. Originally, prisons were conceived as places for criminals to reflect on their misdeeds and repent, hence the term "penitentiary." In the twentieth century, the emphasis shifted to rehabilitation through psychological and sociopsychological methods. Unfortunately, these efforts were less than successful. Ironically, prisons appear to "criminalize" individuals more than to rehabilitate them. Inmates are exposed to an insular society with norms of conduct antithetical to those of civil society. As essentially totalitarian institutions, prisons do not encourage individuals to behave responsibly; furthermore, prisons provide an excellent venue for the spreading of criminal techniques. It is probably unrealistic to expect rehabilitation programs to succeed in such an environment. Today, prisons are generally regarded as little more than a way to punish and isolate those persons deemed unfit to live in civil society.

The Burgeoning Prison Population

At the end of June 2005, there were nearly 2.2 million inmates in the United States. About 1.4 million prisoners were incarcerated in the federal and state prison systems; roughly 700,000 were held in local jails. The rest were held in juvenile facilities, territorial prisons, military prisons, detention facilities operated by federal immigration authorities, and jails located on the Indian reservations (U.S. Department of Justice, Office of Justice Programs, Bureau of Justice Statistics Bulletin, "Prison and Jail Inmates at Midyear 2005," May 2006, NCJ 213133).

During the 1990s, state and federal prison populations grew at an average rate of nearly 6 percent per year. Between June 30, 1998, and June 30, 1999, the federal prison population rose by nearly 10 percent, the largest twelve-month gain ever (U.S. Department of Justice, Office of Justice Programs, Bureau of Justice Statistics Bulletin, "Prison and Jail Inmates at Midyear 1999," April 2000, NCJ 181643). The dramatic increases in state and federal prison populations during the 1990s were not attributable to rising crime rates. In fact, both violent crime and property crime declined sharply in the 1990s. Rather, burgeoning prison populations resulted from the adoption of more punitive sentencing policies in the 1980s and 1990s. These policy changes included the elimination or curtailment of parole and the adoption of **"truth in sentencing" laws, "three strikes" laws,** and **mandatory minimum sentences** (see Chapter 19). As a result of these changes in policy, the nationwide incarceration rate nearly doubled, from approximately 300 to 600 inmates per 100,000 residents between 1985 and 1995 (U.S. Department of Justice, Office of Justice Programs, Bureau of Justice Statistics Bulletin, "Prison and Jail Inmates, 1995," August 1996, NCJ–161132).

During the first half of the current decade, the number of prisoners continued to grow, but the rate of increase slowed somewhat. Between June 2004 and June 2005, state prison populations grew by just over 1 percent; however, the federal prison population increased by 4 percent. In June 2005, state prisons were operating pretty much at capacity, but federal prisons were operating at 40 percent above capacity. At midyear 2005, 1 in every 136 U.S. residents was in prison or jail (U.S. Department of Justice, Office of Justice Programs, Bureau of Justice Statistics Bulletin, "Prison and Jail Inmates at Midyear 2005," May 2006, NCJ 213133). This is by far the highest incarceration rate among the democratic countries of the world.

The Future Outlook

The public continues to demand harsh sentences for convicted felons, but legislators (and taxpayers) are often unwilling to pay the price of constructing more prisons. Moreover, local residents often object to prisons being built in their "backyards." Even those states that have been aggressive in prison construction have found that demand for cell space continues to exceed supply. In many instances, federal courts have ordered prison officials to reduce overcrowding to comply with the U.S. Constitution's prohibition against "cruel and unusual punishments."

In many state prisons, cells originally designed for one or two inmates now house three or four prisoners. Increasingly, state prison systems must rely on local jails to house inmates, a situation that presents its own set of problems relating both to security and to conditions of confinement. Aside from the threat of federal judicial intervention, overcrowded prisons are more likely to produce inmate violence and even riots.

In addition to prisons, corrections systems include agencies that supervise probation, parole, community service, and other forms of alternative sentences. With burgeoning prison populations, these alternatives to incarceration are assuming more importance and consuming more resources, especially at the state level.

■ CONCLUSION

The American system of criminal justice is extremely complicated. The primary reason for this complexity is the principle of federalism, which refers to the division of political and legal authority in this country between one national government and fifty state governments. The U.S. Congress on behalf of the national government and each state legislature on behalf of its respective state enact their own criminal laws. The national government and all fifty state governments have their own law enforcement agencies, prosecutors, courts, and prison systems. No two systems are exactly alike. Indeed, there is tremendous variation from one jurisdiction to the next, both in the substantive criminal law and in the practices and procedures used by the various components of the criminal process. Yet, despite their substantive and procedural differences, all jurisdictions share two basic goals: to protect society from crime and, at the same time, to protect the rights of the individuals suspected of having committed offenses. Much of the conflict and inefficiency inherent in our criminal justice system stems from the need to balance these two competing objectives.

■ KEY TERMS

■ WEB-BASED RESEARCH ACTIVITY

Go to the Web. Locate the United States Code (hint: Try the "Legal Information Institute"). Locate Title 18, "Crimes and Criminal Procedure." Locate Chapter 115, "Treason, Sedition, and Subversive Activities." In addition to "treason" and "sedition," what specific offenses does this chapter proscribe? Locate section 2384, which proscribes the offense of "seditious conspiracy." What is the definition of the offense? What punishment does the law provide for this crime?

■ QUESTIONS FOR THOUGHT AND DISCUSSION

1. How does the concept of federalism complicate the administration of criminal justice in the United States?
2. Describe the functions of federal and state law enforcement agencies.

3. Compare and contrast the functions of trial and appellate courts. How are they similar? How are they different?

4. What function does a grand jury serve? Does replacement of the indictment function of grand juries at the state level with prosecutors authorized to charge crimes by filing a sworn information impair the rights of citizens charged with crimes?

5. Is there a justification for the broad discretion vested in a prosecutor?

6. To what extent does the U.S. Constitution protect the right to trial by jury in a criminal case?

7. What are the arguments for and against allowing trial judges broad discretion in criminal sentencing?

8. What factors do you think a prosecutor should take into consideration in determining whether to prosecute an individual the police have arrested for possession of illegal drugs?

9. What chief characteristics distinguish the military justice system under the Uniform Code of Military Justice from civilian criminal prosecutions?

10. What factors should a judge consider in determining whether to sentence a convicted felon to prison?

PART TWO

The Substantive Criminal Law

CHAPTER 3

Constitutional Limitations on the Prohibition of Criminal Conduct

CHAPTER OUTLINE

Introduction

In most democratic countries, legislative bodies are supreme in enacting statutes defining crimes and providing penalties. The only overarching authority is the will of the people manifested through the ballot box. Being very familiar with the English monarchy and its parliamentary system, the framers of the U.S. Constitution understood that unbridled power to make and enforce criminal prohibitions constitutes a serious threat to liberty. Thus, they framed a Constitution that delimits the power of Congress and state legislatures to enact criminal statutes. Although federal and state legislative bodies have authority to enact statutes defining crimes and setting penalties, various provisions of the U.S. Constitution and state constitutions limit that power.

Our goal in this chapter is to provide an overview of the various constitutional provisions that limit legislative authority in defining conduct as criminal and prescribing penalties for violations or offenses. We discuss the effect of judicial interpretations of criminal statutes and the power of courts to declare void laws that violate the constitutional principles.

The Importance of Judicial Review

Constitutional limits on the enactment and enforcement of criminal statutes do not depend for their vitality only on the voluntary compliance of legislators, prosecutors, and police officers. Under the doctrine of judicial review, courts are empowered to declare null and void laws that violate constitutional principles. In a landmark decision in 1803, the Supreme Court first asserted the power to invalidate legislation that is in conflict with the Constitution. *Marbury v. Madison,* 5 U.S. (1 Cranch) 137, 2 L.Ed. 60 (1803). Speaking for the Court in *Marbury,* Chief Justice John Marshall said, "It is emphatically the province and duty of the judicial department to say what the law is." 5 U.S. (1 Cranch) at 177, 2 L.Ed. at 175. Although the power of judicial review is generally associated with the Supreme Court, all courts of record, whether state or federal, can exercise the power to strike down unconstitutional legislation. It is doubtful whether constitutional limitations on governmental power would be meaningful in the absence of judicial review.

Throughout this textbook, we will be discussing constitutional limitations on the criminal justice system. Many of these principles are procedural in nature, imposing restrictions and obligations on law enforcement, prosecution, adjudication, and sentencing. (These procedural limitations are discussed in Part III of the textbook.) In this chapter we are concerned only with those constitutional provisions that place limits on the substantive criminal law, both in the types of laws that legislatures are barred from enacting and the situations in which police and prosecutors are barred from enforcing existing statutes.

Unconstitutional Per Se and Unconstitutional as Applied

In addressing constitutional assaults on criminal statutes, courts are sometimes asked to declare that a statute is unconstitutional under any circumstances, whereas in other instances a court might simply be asked to rule that the statute cannot constitutionally apply to certain conduct. A statute may be declared **unconstitutional per se** in that it inherently trenches on some constitutionally protected liberty or exceeds the constitutional powers of government. For example, a law that would restrict citizens' freedom to profess their religious beliefs would be inherently unconstitutional. Alternatively, a law that is facially valid, such as an ordinance prohibiting disorderly conduct, may be declared **unconstitutional as applied** if it is enforced in a way that impermissibly restricts or punishes the exercise of constitutional rights.

The Power to Enact Criminal Laws

Because our nation is committed to the rule of law, "there is no crime, there is no punishment, without law." As we saw in Chapter 1, no one can be guilty of a crime in the absence of a law that prohibits a particular type of wrongful conduct. As Chapter 2 pointed out, it is the role of legislatures to enact statutes that define crimes and provide for punishments.

Police Powers of State Legislatures

The police power of government is the authority to enact legislation to protect the public health, safety, order, welfare, and morality. Under our system of federalism, the police power of government is vested primarily in the state legislatures. State legislatures have comprehensive power to adopt statutes regulating the activities of individuals and corporations as long as these statutes do not violate limitations contained in the state and federal constitutions. State legislatures, in turn, may delegate some of this power to local governments, which enact ordinances defining criminal offenses within their jurisdictions.

The Federal Lawmaking Power

Unlike the state legislatures, the U.S. Congress does not possess plenary legislative authority (except over the District of Columbia and federal territories). As James Madison observed in 1788,

> The powers delegated by the proposed Constitution to the federal government are few and defined. Those which are to remain in the State governments are numerous and indefinite. *The Federalist* No. 45, pp. 292–293 (C. Rossiter ed., 1961).

Article I, Section 8 of the U.S. Constitution enumerates Congress's legislative powers. Several of these enumerated powers allow Congress to enact criminal laws in certain areas. These include the power to establish rules governing immigration and naturalization, to "define and punish piracies and felonies committed on the high seas," and to "provide for the punishment of counterfeiting the securities and current coin of the United States."

Congress also possesses a reservoir of implied powers, which are justified by the Necessary and Proper Clause of Article I, Section 8. The doctrine of implied powers was established by the Supreme Court in *McCulloch v. Maryland,* 17 U.S. (4 Wheat.) 316, 4 L.Ed. 579 (1819). Writing for the Court, Chief Justice Marshall articulated the doctrine as follows:

> Let the end be legitimate, let it be within the scope of the Constitution, and all means which are plainly adapted to that end, which are not prohibited, but consist with the letter and spirit of the Constitution, are constitutional. 17 U.S. (4 Wheat.) at 421, 4 L.Ed. at 605.

The doctrine of implied powers expands the legislative capabilities of Congress but by no means confers on Congress the plenary legislative authority possessed by state legislatures. To qualify as a valid expression of implied powers, federal legislation must be "plainly adapted" to the goal of furthering one or more of Congress's enumerated powers.

THE COMMERCE CLAUSE

In terms of the criminal law, by far the most significant of Congress's enumerated powers is the power to regulate **interstate commerce.** For example, Congress is not empowered to prohibit prostitution per se, but Congress may make it a crime to transport persons across state lines for "immoral purposes" by drawing on its broad power to regulate interstate commerce. *Hoke v. United States,* 227 U.S. 308, 33 S.Ct. 281, 57 L.Ed. 523 (1913). Congress has relied on the Commerce Clause to enact a wide variety of criminal laws, including prohibitions against the following:

- interstate transportation of kidnapped persons (see 18 U.S.C.A. § 1201)
- interstate transportation of stolen automobiles (see 18 U.S.C.A. § 2312)
- manufacture, sale, distribution, and possession of controlled substances (see 21 U.S.C.A. § 801 *et seq.*)
- carjacking (see 18 U.S.C.A. § 2119)
- fraudulent schemes that use interstate television, radio, or wire communications (see 18 U.S.C.A. § 1343)
- conspiracies to restrain trade (see 15 U.S.C.A. § 1 *et seq.*)
- loan sharking (see 18 U.S.C.A. § 891 *et seq.*)
- "computer crimes" (see 18 U.S.C.A. § 1030)
- racketeering and organized crime (see 18 U.S.C.A. §§ 1961–1963)
- various "environmental crimes" (see Chapter 11)

Go to the Scheb/ Scheb Criminal Law and Procedure 6e website at academic .cengage.com/criminaljustice/ scheb for an edited version of *U.S. v. Lopez.*

In the modern era, Congress has stretched the concept of interstate commerce to justify broader authority to enact criminal statutes. For the most part, the courts have been willing to accommodate this expansion of federal legislative power. See, for example, *Perez v. United States,* 402 U.S. 146, 91 S.Ct. 1357, 28 L.Ed.2d 686 (1971). However, in recent years the Supreme Court has circumscribed this authority somewhat. In *United States v. Lopez,* 514 U.S. 549, 115 S.Ct. 1624, 131 L.Ed.2d 626 (1995), the Court struck down the Gun-Free School Zones Act of 1990, which made it a federal crime for any person to knowingly possess a firearm while close to a school. Writing for the Court, Chief Justice William Rehnquist observed that the challenged statute

> has nothing to do with "commerce" or any sort of economic enterprise, however broadly one might define those terms. [The law] is not an essential part of a larger regulation of economic activity, in which the regulatory scheme could be undercut unless the intrastate activity were regulated. It cannot, therefore, be sustained under our cases upholding regulations of activities that arise out of or are connected with a commercial transaction, which viewed in the aggregate, substantially affects interstate commerce. 514 U.S. at 560, 115 S.Ct. at 1631, 131 L.Ed.2d at 639.

The Court's *Lopez* decision was reinforced by its decision in *United States v. Morrison,* 529 U.S. 598, 120 S.Ct. 1740, 146 L.Ed.2d 658 (2000), where the Court struck down a provision of the Violence Against Women Act of 1994 that provided a federal civil remedy to victims of gender-motivated violence. (An excerpt from the Supreme Court's *Morrison* decision is found in the "Supreme Court Perspective" feature in Chapter 1.)

Together, *Lopez* and *Morrison* called into question a number of the criminal statutes enacted by Congress under the Commerce Clause. One of these was the federal Controlled Substances Act, 21 U.S.C.A. § 801, *et seq.*, which defines federal drug crimes (see Chapter 9). In 1996 the U.S. Court of Appeals for the Second Circuit rejected a *Lopez*-based challenge to 21 U.S.C.A. § 841, which makes it a crime "for any person knowingly or intentionally to manufacture, distribute, or dispense, or possess with intent to manufacture, distribute, or dispense, a controlled substance." The statute criminalizes the mere possession of even small quantities of controlled substances and does not require proof that a particular defendant's conduct affected interstate commerce. The circuit court distinguished 21 U.S.C.A. § 841 from the statute struck down in *Lopez,* observing that

> the *Lopez* Court did not purport to overrule those cases that have upheld application of the Commerce Clause power to wholly intrastate activities, and we find no basis for extending the *Lopez* holding to the case before us. The Controlled Substances Act concerns an obviously economic activity. In addition, Congress has made specific findings that local narcotics activity has a substantial effect on interstate commerce. In contrast, the conduct that was criminalized in *Lopez* did not obviously concern economic activity, as the Court recognized. *United States v. Genao,* 79 F.3d 1333, 1337 (2nd Cir. 1996).

 Go to the Scheb/ Scheb Criminal Law and Procedure 6e website at academic .cengage.com/criminaljustice/ scheb for an edited version of *U.S. v. Genao.*

A more interesting problem was presented in *Gonzales v. Raich,* 545 U.S. 1, 125 S.Ct. 2195, 162 L.Ed.2d 1 (2005). The case involved two women who used marijuana for medical reasons based on the recommendation of their doctor as authorized by California's Compassionate Use Act of 1996. Under the federal Controlled Substances Act (CSA), the possession or use of marijuana is a crime and there is no exception for medicinal use (see *United States v. Oakland Cannabis Buyers' Cooperative,* 532 U.S. 483, 121 S.Ct. 1711, 149 L.Ed.2d 722 (2001). When agents of the federal Drug Enforcement Administration learned that one of the women was cultivating marijuana in her home, they obtained a search warrant and seized and destroyed the plants. Subsequently, the women brought suit in federal court, claiming that Congress had no authority under the Commerce Clause to prohibit the possession and use of marijuana that is not intended for interstate distribution. Although the District Court rejected the claim, the U.S. Court of Appeals for the Ninth Circuit reversed on the basis of *Lopez* and *Morrison.* The Supreme Court reversed the Ninth Circuit, however, holding that Congress may criminalize the possession and medicinal use of marijuana. Writing for the Court in *Gonzales v. Raich,* Justice John Paul Stevens stressed the commercial aspects of the marijuana prohibition:

 Go to the Scheb/ Scheb Criminal Law and Procedure 6e website at academic .cengage.com/criminaljustice/ scheb for an edited version of *U.S. v. Oakland Cannabis Buyers Cooperative.*

Go to the Scheb/ Scheb Criminal Law and Procedure 6e website at academic .cengage.com/criminaljustice/ scheb for an edited version of *Gonzales v. Raich.*

> One need not have a degree in economics to understand why a nationwide exemption for the vast quantity of marijuana (or other drugs) locally cultivated for personal use (which presumably would include use by friends, neighbors, and family members) may have a substantial impact on the interstate market for this extraordinarily popular substance. The congressional judgment that an exemption for such a significant segment of the total market would undermine the orderly enforcement of the entire regulatory scheme is entitled to a strong presumption of validity. 545 U.S. at 28, 125 S.Ct. at 2212, 162 L.Ed.2d at 26.

In a dissenting opinion joined by Chief Justice Rehnquist and Associate Justice Clarence Thomas, Justice Sandra Day O'Connor suggested that the Court had backtracked from the commitment to principles of federalism expressed in decisions like *Lopez* and *Morrison. Gonzales v. Raich* suggests that despite the decisions in *Lopez* and *Morrison,* Congress retains broad authority under the Commerce Clause to deal with social problems of national scope.

Delimiting the Crime of Treason

Treason involves betrayal of one's country, either by making war against it or giving aid and comfort to its enemies. At common law, treason was the most heinous crime a subject could commit. It was in a category by itself, considered far worse than any felony. Because all felonies were punishable by death, the common law provided a special punishment for the crime of treason:

> 1. That the offender be drawn to the gallows, and not be carried or walk.... 2. That he be hanged by the neck, and cut down alive. 3. That his entrails be taken out and burned, while he is yet alive. 4. That his head be cut off. 5. That his body be divided into four parts. 6. That his head and quarters be at the king's disposal. These refinements in cruelty ... were, in former times, literally and studiously executed; and indicate at once a savage and ferocious spirit, and a degrading subserviency to royal resentments, real or supposed. 3 J. Story, *Commentaries on the Constitution* § 1293.

English kings had used the crime of treason to punish and deter political opposition. For example, in 1683 one Algernon Sidney was executed for treason based primarily on published writings deemed to be subversive of the Crown. Being aware of these abuses of the criminal law, the framers of the U.S. Constitution sought to prohibit the federal government from using the offense of treason to punish political dissenters. Thus, they specifically defined treason against the United States in Article III, Section 3, paragraph 1, saying it "shall consist only in levying War against them, or in adhering to their Enemies, giving them Aid and Comfort." To make it more difficult for the government to prosecute people for treason, the same paragraph included the following injunction: "No Person shall be convicted of Treason unless on the Testimony of two Witnesses to the same overt Act, or on Confession in open Court." Thus no one may be convicted of treason against the United States based solely on circumstantial evidence.

Levying War Against the United States

As the constitutional language indicates, there are two types of treason—"levying war against" the United States and giving "aid and comfort" to its enemies. In *Ex Parte Bollman*, 8 U.S. (4 Cranch) 75 (U.S. Dist. Col. 1807), Chief Justice Marshall observed:

> As there is no crime which can more excite and agitate the passions of men than treason, no charge demands more from the tribunal before which it is made, a deliberate and temperate inquiry. Whether this inquiry be directed to the fact or to the law, none can be more solemn, none more important to the citizen or to the government; none can more affect the safety of both.... It is therefore more safe as well as more consonant to the principles of our constitution, that the crime of treason should not be extended by construction to doubtful cases; and that crimes not clearly within the constitutional definition, should receive such punishment as the legislature in its wisdom may provide. *Ex parte Bollman*, 8 U.S. (4 Cranch) at 125, 127.

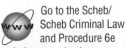 Go to the Scheb/ Scheb Criminal Law and Procedure 6e website at academic .cengage.com/criminaljustice/ scheb for an edited version of Chief Justice John Marshall's opinion in *U.S. v. Burr*.

Presiding over the trial of Aaron Burr in 1807, Chief Justice Marshall produced a lengthy opinion on the law of treason and its application to the Burr case. Marshall read the entire opinion aloud as a means of instructing the jury. The opinion made it clear that in Marshall's view, Burr could not be convicted of treason based on evidence that could lawfully be considered by the court. Consequently, in the most infamous treason trial in American history, the jury returned a verdict of not guilty. *United States v. Burr,* 25 F. Cas. 55 (Circuit Court of the District of Virginia, August 31, 1807).

The upshot of *Ex Parte Bollman* and the acquittal of Aaron Burr was to make it extremely difficult to convict a person of treason by virtue of levying war against the United States.

Giving Aid and Comfort to the Enemies of the United States

In *Cramer v. United States,* 325 U.S. 1, 65 S.Ct. 918, 89 L.Ed. 1441 (1945), the Supreme Court reversed the treason conviction of Anthony Cramer, a German immigrant accused of giving aid and comfort to two Nazi saboteurs who infiltrated the United States in 1942. Writing for the Court, Justice Robert Jackson pointed out that to be guilty of this form of treason, a defendant must both adhere to the enemy and provide them aid and comfort:

> A citizen intellectually or emotionally may favor the enemy and harbor sympathies or convictions disloyal to this country's policy or interest, but so long as he commits no act of aid and comfort to the enemy, there is no treason. On the other hand, a citizen may take actions, which do aid and comfort the enemy—making a speech critical of the government or opposing its measures, profiteering, striking in defense plants or essential work, and the hundred other things which impair our cohesion and diminish our strength—but if there is no adherence to the enemy in this, if there is no intent to betray, there is no treason. 325 U.S. at 29, 65 S.Ct. at 932, 89 L.Ed. at 1458.

Two years later, the Court upheld the conviction of a man who sheltered one of the Nazi saboteurs. *Haupt v. United States,* 330 U.S. 631, 67 S.Ct. 874, 91 L.Ed. 1145 (1947). Writing for the Court, Justice Jackson observed that "[t]he law of treason makes and properly makes conviction difficult but not impossible." 330 U.S. at 644, 67 S.Ct. at 880, 91 L.Ed. at 1155.

Bills of Attainder and *Ex Post Facto* Laws

Two historic abuses of the English Parliament that the framers of the Constitution sought to correct were bills of attainder and *ex post facto* laws. Article I, Section 9 of the Constitution prohibits Congress from adopting bills of attainder and *ex post facto* laws. Article I, Section 10 extends these same prohibitions to the state legislatures.

Bills of Attainder

A **bill of attainder** is a legislative act inflicting punishment on an individual or on a group of easily identifiable individuals. Laws of this character are antithetical to the basic principle that a person accused of wrongdoing is entitled to a fair trial in a court of law. Writing for the Supreme Court in *United States v. Lovett,* 328 U.S. 303, 66 S.Ct. 1073, 90 L.Ed. 1252 (1946), Justice Hugo Black reflected on the constitutional prohibition against bills of attainder:

> When our Constitution and Bill of Rights were written, our ancestors had ample reason to know that legislative trials and punishments were too dangerous to liberty to exist in the nation of free men they envisioned. And so they proscribed bills of attainder. 328 U.S. at 318, 66 S.Ct. at 1080, 90 L.Ed. at 1261.

In *United States v. Brown*, 381 U.S. 437, 85 S.Ct. 1707, 14 L.Ed.2d 484 (1965), the Supreme Court struck down a law barring Communist Party members from holding positions as officers of labor unions. The Court found the prohibition to constitute a bill of attainder in that it punished easily identifiable members of a class by imposing upon them the sanction of a mandatory forfeiture of a position to which they would otherwise be entitled. Subsequently, in *Nixon v. Administrator of General Services*, 433 U.S. 425, 97 S.Ct. 2777, 53 L.Ed.2d 867 (1977), the Supreme Court said that in reviewing a law challenged as a bill of attainder, a court must consider (1) whether the statute falls within the historic meaning of legislative punishment; (2) whether the statute, viewed in terms of the type and severity of the burdens imposed, reasonably can be said to further nonpunitive legislative purposes; and (3) whether the legislative record evinces a legislative intent to punish. A statute that fails any of the prongs of the test may be declared unconstitutional.

 Go to the Scheb/Scheb Criminal Law and Procedure 6e website at academic.cengage.com/criminaljustice/scheb for an edited version of *U.S. v. Brown*.

Ex Post Facto Laws

Sir William Blackstone, the great commentator on the English common law, wrote that an **ex post facto law** exists "when after an action (indifferent in itself) is committed, the legislator then for the first time declares it to have been a crime, and inflicts a punishment upon the person who has committed it." 1 W. Blackstone, *Commentaries* 46. Because the essence of the *ex post facto* law is retroactivity, it is flatly inconsistent with the **principle of legality,** which holds that individuals are entitled to know in advance if particular contemplated conduct is illegal. The framers of the U.S. Constitution viewed *ex post facto* laws as one of the "favorite and most formidable instruments of tyranny." *The Federalist* No. 84, p. 512 (C. Rossiter ed. 1961) (A. Hamilton). In his *Commentaries on the Constitution of the United States,* Justice Joseph Story expressed strong support for the prohibition of *ex post facto* laws:

> If the laws in being do not punish an offender, let him go unpunished; let the legislature, admonished of the defect of the laws, provide against the commission of future crimes of the same sort. The escape of one delinquent can never produce so much harm to the community, as may arise from the infraction of a rule, upon which the purity of public justice, and the existence of civil liberty, essentially depend.
> 3 J. Story, *Commentaries on the Constitution* § 1338, at 211, n. 2.

Although the phrase *"ex post facto* law" literally includes any law passed "after the fact," the Supreme Court has long recognized that the constitutional prohibition applies only to criminal statutes. Writing for the Supreme Court in *Calder v. Bull*, 3 U.S. (3 Dall.) 386, 1 L.Ed. 648 (1798), Justice Samuel Chase identified four types of laws that fall within the prohibition of the *ex post facto* laws:

> 1st. Every law that makes an action done before the passing of the law, and which was innocent when done, criminal, and punishes such action. 2d. Every law that aggravates a crime, or makes it greater than it was when committed. 3d. Every law that changes the punishment, and inflicts a greater punishment, than the law annexed to the crime when committed. 4th. Every law that alters the legal rules of evidence and receives less or different testimony than the law required at the time of the commission of the offense in order to convict the offender. 3 U.S. (3 Dall.) at 390, 1 L.Ed. at 651.

Although modern statutes are seldom invalidated as *ex post facto* laws, the courts continue to recognize Justice Chase's formulation. For example, in *Miller v. Florida*, 482 U.S. 423, 107 S.Ct. 2446, 96 L.Ed.2d 351 (1987), the Supreme Court held that Florida's sentencing guidelines, as revised by the state legislature in 1984, violated the *Ex Post Facto* clause of the federal Constitution insofar as their application caused an increase in punishment to persons whose crimes occurred before the effective date of the 1984 act.

A more interesting example is provided by *Carmell v. Texas,* 529 U.S. 513, 120 S.Ct. 1620, 146 L.Ed.2d 577 (2000). In 1997 Scott Leslie Carmell was convicted in a Texas court of sexual assault, aggravated sexual assault, and indecency with a child. Evidence showed that between 1991 and 1995, Carmell committed various sex acts with his stepdaughter, starting when she was only twelve years old. Carmell was sentenced to life in prison on two convictions for aggravated sexual assault and twenty years in prison on thirteen other counts. The U.S. Supreme Court reversed four of Carmell's convictions by a vote of 5–4. These convictions were for sexual assaults that were alleged to have occurred in 1991 and 1992, when Texas law provided that a defendant could not be convicted merely on the testimony of the victim unless she was under fourteen. At the time of the alleged assaults in question, the victim was fourteen or fifteen. The law was later amended to extend the "child victim exception" to victims under eighteen years old. Carmell was convicted under the amended law, which the Supreme Court held to be an unconstitutional *ex post facto* law as defined by *Calder v. Bull*, 3 U.S. (3 Dall.) 386, 1 L.Ed. 648 (1798).

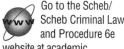

Go to the Scheb/ Scheb Criminal Law and Procedure 6e website at academic .cengage.com/criminaljustice/ scheb for an edited version of *Carmell v. Texas.*

Similarly, in *Stogner v. California,* 539 U.S. 607, 123 S.Ct. 2446, 156 L.Ed.2d 544 (2003), the Supreme Court broadened the prohibition against *ex post facto* laws. In 1994, California enacted a law lifting the statute of limitations in child molestation cases where the victim remembers the abuse after the statute of limitations runs out. In 2001, 72-year old Marion Stogner was charged with molesting his daughters nearly fifty years earlier. Before the enactment of the new law, the state's statute of limitations would have barred Stogner's prosecution, as it prohibited prosecution more than three years after the crime had occurred. In a 5–4 decision, the Supreme Court held that California's new law lifting the statute of limitations could not be constitutionally applied to allow prosecution of cases in which prosecution would have been foreclosed by the statute of limitations prior to the enactment of the new law.

Go to the Scheb/ Scheb Criminal Law and Procedure 6e website at academic .cengage.com/criminaljustice/ scheb for an edited version of *Stogner v. California.*

The Bill of Rights

Although the original Constitution contained few express limitations on legislative power, the Bill of Rights added several important constraints on Congress. Ratified in 1791, the Bill of Rights consists of the first ten amendments to the Constitution. For criminal law, the most significant of these are the **First Amendment** freedoms of expression, religion, and assembly; the Second Amendment protection of "the right to keep and bear arms"; the Fifth Amendment Due Process Clause; the Eighth Amendment Cruel and Unusual Punishments Clause; and the Ninth Amendment guarantee of "rights retained by the people."

The First Amendment begins with the injunction that *"Congress* shall make no law ..." [emphasis added]. Unlike certain provisions in the original, unamended Constitution, the Bill of Rights makes no mention of limitations on the state and local governments. Throughout much of the nineteenth century, the Bill of Rights was viewed as imposing limitations only on Congress, having no effect on state legislatures or local governing bodies. The Supreme Court officially adopted this view in *Barron v. Baltimore,* 32 U.S. (7 Pet.) 243, 8 L.Ed. 672 (1833). Under this interpretation of the Bill of Rights, citizens had to look to their state constitutions and state courts for protection against state and local actions that infringed on their rights and liberties.

Application of the Bill of Rights to State and Local Laws

The ratification of the **Fourteenth Amendment** in 1868 provided a justification for extending the scope of the Bill of Rights to apply against the states. Section 1 of the Fourteenth Amendment enjoins the states from depriving "any person of life, liberty, or property, without due process of law." It also prohibits states from adopting laws that "abridge the privileges and immunities of citizens of the United States."

 Go to the Scheb/ Scheb Criminal Law and Procedure 6e website at academic .cengage.com/criminaljustice/ scheb for an edited version of *Palko v. Connecticut.*

In a series of decisions, the Supreme Court has held that the **Due Process Clause** of the Fourteenth Amendment makes enforceable against the states those provisions of the Bill of Rights that are "implicit in the concept of ordered liberty." *Palko v. Connecticut,* 302 U.S. 319, 58 S.Ct. 149, 82 L.Ed. 288 (1937). This doctrine of incorporation has been employed by the Court to enforce the procedural guarantees of the Bill of Rights in state criminal prosecutions. For example, in *Wolf v. Colorado,* 338 U.S. 25, 69 S.Ct. 1359, 93 L.Ed. 1782 (1949), the Court said that the Fourth Amendment protection against unreasonable searches and seizures is applicable to state and local, as well as federal, law enforcement authorities. Similarly, in *Duncan v. Louisiana,* 391 U.S. 145, 88 S.Ct. 1444, 20 L.Ed.2d 491 (1968), the Court held that the Fourteenth Amendment requires states to observe the jury trial requirement of the Sixth Amendment.

In addition to incorporating the procedural protections of the Bill of Rights into the Fourteenth Amendment, the Court has extended the substantive limitations of the Bill of Rights to the states. In 1925 the Supreme Court recognized that the First Amendment protections of free speech and free press apply to state as well as federal laws. *Gitlow v. New York,* 268 U.S. 652, 45 S.Ct. 625, 69 L.Ed. 1138 (1925). Likewise, in 1934 the Court said that the First Amendment guarantee of free exercise of religion is enforceable against state and local governments. *Hamilton v. Regents of the University of California,* 293 U.S. 245, 55 S.Ct. 197, 79 L.Ed. 343 (1934).

The Supreme Court has incorporated virtually all the provisions of the Bill of Rights into the Fourteenth Amendment, making them applicable to state and local governments. The federal Constitution, and in particular the Bill of Rights, now stands as a barrier to unreasonable or oppressive criminal laws, whether they are enacted by Congress, a state legislature, or a local governing body.

The First Amendment Freedom of Expression

Perhaps the most treasured of our liberties, and the rights most essential to maintaining a democratic polity, are the First Amendment freedoms of speech and press. Often, freedom of speech and freedom of the press are referred to jointly as freedom of expression. Although the concept of free expression is fundamental to our democratic society, the Supreme Court has said that the First Amendment has "never been thought to give absolute protection to every individual to speak whenever or wherever he pleases, or to use any form of address in any circumstances that he chooses." *Cohen v. California,* 403 U.S. 15, 19, 91 S.Ct. 1780, 1785, 29 L.Ed.2d 284, 290 (1971). The task of the courts, of course, is to strike a reasonable balance between the right of expression and the legitimate interests of society in maintaining security, order, peace, safety, and decency. In what has become a classic phrase, Justice Oliver Wendell Holmes Jr. observed that the "most stringent protection of free speech would not protect a man in falsely shouting fire in a theater, and causing a panic." *Schenck v. United States,* 249 U.S. 47, 51, 39 S.Ct. 247, 249, 63 L.Ed. 470,

473 (1919). Moreover, the Supreme Court has said that certain types of speech are so inherently lacking in value as not to merit any First Amendment protection:

> There are certain well-defined and narrowly limited classes of speech, the prevention and punishment of which have never been thought to raise any constitutional problem. These include the lewd and obscene, the profane, the libelous, and the insulting or "fighting" words—those which by their very utterance inflict injury or tend to incite an immediate breach of the peace. It has been well observed that such utterances are no essential part of any exposition of ideas, and are of such slight social value as a step to truth that any benefit that may be derived from them is clearly outweighed by the social interest in order and morality. *Chaplinsky v. New Hampshire,* 315 U.S. 568, 571, 62 S.Ct. 766, 769, 86 L.Ed. 1031, 1035 (1942).

Advocacy of Unlawful Conduct

One of the most basic problems posed by the First Amendment is whether speech advocating unlawful conduct might itself be made unlawful. The Supreme Court first encountered this problem in *Schenck v. United States,* supra, where an official of the Socialist Party appealed a conviction under the Espionage Act of 1917, 40 Stat. at L. 217, 219. Charles T. Schenck had been convicted of participating in a conspiracy to cause insubordination in the military services and to obstruct military recruitment at a time when the United States was at war. The "conspiracy" consisted of activities surrounding the mailing of a leaflet to draftees urging them to resist induction into the military. The Supreme Court upheld Schenck's conviction, saying that

Go to the Scheb/ Scheb Criminal Law and Procedure 6e website at academic .cengage.com/criminaljustice/ scheb for an edited version of *Schenck v. U.S.*

> the question in every case is whether the words used are used in such circumstances and are of such a nature as to create clear and present danger that they will bring about the substantive evils that Congress has a right to prevent.… When a nation is at war many things that might be said in time of peace are such a hindrance to its effort that their utterance will not be endured so long as men fight, and that no court could regard them as protected by any constitutional right. 249 U.S. at 52, 39 S.Ct. at 249, 63 L.Ed. at 473.

The Supreme Court first invoked the **clear and present danger doctrine** to reverse a criminal conviction in a case involving a Georgia man who had been prosecuted under a state law prohibiting "any attempt, by persuasion or otherwise" to incite insurrection. *Herndon v. Lowry,* 301 U.S. 242, 57 S.Ct. 732, 81 L.Ed. 1066 (1937). Since then, the doctrine has been used by state and federal courts to reverse numerous convictions where persons have been prosecuted for merely advocating illegal acts.

The modern Supreme Court has refined the clear and present danger doctrine so that public advocacy may be prohibited only in situations when there is **imminent lawless action.** *Brandenburg v. Ohio,* 395 U.S. 444, 89 S.Ct. 1827, 23 L.Ed.2d 430 (1969). Today, it is questionable whether the courts would uphold a conviction in circumstances similar to those in the *Schenck* case. The courts might find that mailing a leaflet or standing on a street corner urging resistance to the draft—activities that were fairly common during the Vietnam War—are not fraught with imminent lawless action and therefore do not constitute a clear and present danger.

Go to the Scheb/ Scheb Criminal Law and Procedure 6e website at academic .cengage.com/criminaljustice/ scheb for an edited version of *Brandenburg v. Ohio.*

Symbolic Speech and Expressive Conduct

Freedom of expression is a broad concept embracing speech, publication, performances, and demonstrations. Even wearing symbols is considered to be constitutionally protected **symbolic speech.** *Tinker v. Des Moines Independent Community School District,* 393 U.S. 503, 89 S.Ct. 733, 21 L.Ed.2d 731 (1969). The Supreme Court has recognized a wide variety of conduct as possessing "sufficient communicative elements to bring the First Amendment to play." *Texas v. Johnson,* 491 U.S. 397, 404, 109 S.Ct. 2533, 2539, 105 L.Ed.2d 342, 353 (1989). The Court has accorded First Amendment protection to, among other things, "sit-ins" to protest racial segregation, *Brown v. Louisiana,* 383 U.S. 131, 86 S.Ct. 719, 15 L.Ed.2d 637 (1966); civilians wearing American military uniforms to protest the Vietnam War, *Schacht v. United States,* 398 U.S. 58, 90 S.Ct. 1555, 26 L.Ed.2d 44 (1970); and "picketing" over a variety of issues, *Amalgamated Food Employees Union v. Logan Valley Plaza, Inc.,* 391 U.S. 308, 88 S.Ct. 1601, 20 L.Ed.2d 603 (1968).

FLAG BURNING

Without question, the most controversial applications of the concept of expressive conduct have been the Supreme Court's decisions holding that the public burning of the American flag is protected by the First Amendment. In *Texas v. Johnson,* supra, the Court invalidated a Texas statute banning flag desecration. Gregory Johnson had been arrested after he publicly burned an American flag outside the Republican National Convention in Dallas in 1984. The Supreme Court's decision to reverse Johnson's conviction and strike down the Texas law resulted in a firestorm of public criticism of the Court as well as the enactment of a new federal statute. The Flag Protection Act of 1989, amending 18 U.S.C.A. § 700, imposed criminal penalties on anyone who knowingly "mutilates, defaces, physically defiles, burns, maintains upon the floor or ground, or tramples upon" the American flag. In *United States v. Eichman,* 496 U.S. 310, 110 S.Ct. 2404, 110 L.Ed.2d 287 (1990), the Supreme Court invalidated this federal statute as well, saying that "punishing desecration of the flag dilutes the very freedom that makes this emblem so revered, and worth revering." 496 U.S. at 319, 110 S.Ct. at 2410, 110 L.Ed.2d at 296. On several occasions, Congress has attempted to pass a constitutional amendment to overturn the Supreme Court's flag burning decisions, but in every instance the measure has failed to receive the necessary two-thirds vote in the Senate.

Go to the Scheb/ Scheb Criminal Law and Procedure 6e website at academic .cengage.com/criminaljustice/ scheb for an edited version of *Texas v. Johnson.*

Free Expression Versus Maintenance of the Public Order

One type of expression that sometimes transgresses the criminal law is public speech that threatens the public peace and order. Numerous state and local laws prohibit incitement to riot and disturbing the peace. The Supreme Court has said, "[w]hen clear and present danger of riot, disorder, interference with traffic upon the public streets, or other immediate threat to public safety, peace, or order appears, the power of the State to prevent and punish is obvious." *Cantwell v. Connecticut,* 310 U.S. 296, 308, 60 S.Ct. 900, 905, 84 L.Ed. 1213, 1220 (1940). Moreover, the Court has held that so-called **fighting words** are unprotected by the Constitution. *Chaplinsky v. New Hampshire,* supra. Fighting words are "those personally abusive epithets which, when addressed to the ordinary citizen, are, as a matter of common knowledge, inherently likely to provoke violent reaction." *Cohen v. California,* 403 U.S. at 20, 91 S.Ct. at 1785, 29 L.Ed.2d at 291.

Although government must have the authority to maintain order, it may not under the guise of preserving public peace unduly suppress free communication of views. Again, the problem for courts is to strike a reasonable balance between legitimate competing interests in the context of the particular facts in the case at hand.

Hate Speech

In recent years, legislatures and courts have become concerned with the problem of **hate speech.** Hate speech refers to any instance of hateful expression, whether verbal, written, or symbolic, that is based on racial, ethnic, or religious prejudice or some other similar animus. Because it constitutes expression, hate speech is generally protected by the Constitution unless it falls within one of the recognized exceptions to the First Amendment. Would a public cross burning by the Ku Klux Klan in a black neighborhood qualify as fighting words, or would it be considered expressive conduct protected by the First Amendment? What about the display of swastikas by Nazis parading through the streets of a predominantly Jewish city? Would police be justified in these instances to make arrests for incitement to riot? These questions became more real than hypothetical during the 1980s, when the country witnessed a resurgence of racist organizations, and cities and states countered with laws proscribing hate speech. One such law, the St. Paul, Minnesota, Bias-Motivated Crime Ordinance, provided:

> Whoever places on public or private property a symbol, object, appellation, characterization or graffiti, including, but not limited to, a burning cross or Nazi swastika, which one knows or has reasonable grounds to know arouses anger, alarm or resentment in others on the basis of race, color, creed, religion or gender commits disorderly conduct and shall be guilty of a misdemeanor. St. Paul, Minn. Legis. Code 292.02 (1990).

In *R.A.V. v. City of St. Paul,* 505 U.S. 377, 112 S.Ct. 2538, 120 L.Ed.2d 305 (1992), the Supreme Court declared this ordinance unconstitutional in the context of a criminal prosecution of a white teenager who burned a cross on the front lawn of a black family's home. Lest the public be tempted to conclude that the Supreme Court condoned racially motivated cross burnings, the Court stated the following:

> Let there be no mistake about our belief that burning a cross in someone's front yard is reprehensible. But St. Paul has sufficient means at its disposal to prevent such behavior without adding the First Amendment to the fire. 505 U.S. at 396, 112 S.Ct. at 2550, 120 L.Ed.2d at 326.

Go to the Scheb/ Scheb Criminal Law and Procedure 6e website at academic .cengage.com/criminaljustice/ scheb for an edited version of *Virginia v. Black.*

Notwithstanding its earlier decision in *R.A.V. v. City of St. Paul,* the Supreme Court in 2003 upheld a Virginia law banning cross burning with "an intent to intimidate a person or group of persons." Va. Code Ann. § 18.2-423 (1996). Writing for the Court, Justice O'Connor concluded that the "First Amendment permits Virginia to outlaw cross burnings done with the intent to intimidate because burning a cross is a particularly virulent form of intimidation." *Virginia v. Black,* 535 U.S. 343, 363, 123 S.Ct. 1536, 1549, 155 L.Ed.2d 535, 554 (2003).

Obscenity

Traditionally, state and local governments have proscribed speech, pictures, films, and performances regarded as obscene, generally classifying these as misdemeanor offenses. Despite challenges to the constitutionality of such obscenity laws, the Supreme Court has held that **obscenity** is beyond the pale of the First Amendment and thus subject to criminal prosecution. *Roth v. United States,* 354 U.S. 476, 77 S.Ct. 1304, 1 L.Ed.2d 1498 (1957).

The problem for the legislatures, police, prosecutors, and courts is to determine what is obscene and therefore unprotected by the First Amendment. The Supreme Court has held that for expression to be obscene, it must (1) appeal to a prurient interest in sex; (2) depict sexual conduct in a patently offensive way; and (3) lack serious literary, artistic, political, or scientific value. *Miller v. California,* 413 U.S. 15, 93 S.Ct. 2607, 37 L.Ed.2d 419 (1973). Despite this test, the concept of obscenity remains somewhat vague. Nevertheless, the Supreme Court has made it clear that obscenity refers only to "hard-core" pornography. *Jenkins v. Georgia,* 418 U.S. 153, 94 S.Ct. 2750, 41 L.Ed.2d 642 (1974). Today, with the easy availability of pornography on the

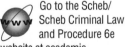

CASE-IN-POINT

Obscenity

Billy Jenkins managed a movie theater in Albany, Georgia, in which the film *Carnal Knowledge* was being shown. The film, which starred Jack Nicholson, Candice Bergen, Art Garfunkel, and Ann-Margret, appeared on many critics' "Ten Best" lists for 1971. The film contained scenes in which sexual conduct, including "'ultimate sexual acts," was understood to be taking place, but the camera did not focus on the bodies of the actors at such times. On January 13, 1972, local law enforcement officers entered the theater, pursuant to

a warrant, and seized the film. Jenkins was later convicted of distributing obscene material and was fined $750 and sentenced to twelve months' probation. By a divided vote, the Georgia Supreme Court affirmed the conviction. On appeal, the U.S. Supreme Court reversed Jenkins's conviction, holding that *Carnal Knowledge* was not hard-core pornography and was thus protected under the First Amendment standards delineated in *Miller v. California.*

Jenkins v. Georgia, 418 U.S. 153, 94 S.Ct. 2750, 41 L.Ed.2d 642 (1974).

Go to the Scheb/ Scheb Criminal Law and Procedure 6e website at academic .cengage.com/criminaljustice/ scheb for an edited version of *Miller v. California.*

Internet, police and prosecutors have shifted their focus away from the enforcement of traditional obscenity laws and toward enforcement of more recent statutes criminalizing child pornography. (The "intractable obscenity problem," as it has been called, is examined more fully in Chapter 8.)

Nude Dancing

Every state has a prohibition against indecent exposure. Generally, these statutes are applied in situations where individuals expose themselves in public or in private to unwilling viewers. But what if the exposure takes place by mutual consent, such as in a nightclub that features nude dancing? The Supreme Court has recognized that this form of entertainment is entitled to First Amendment protection under certain circumstances but has also expressed a willingness to uphold reasonable regulations, especially involving establishments that serve alcoholic beverages. *Doran v. Salem Inn,* 422 U.S. 922, 95 S.Ct. 2561, 45 L.Ed.2d 648 (1975). In *Barnes v. Glen Theatre, Inc.,* 501 U.S. 560, 111 S.Ct. 2456, 115 L.Ed.2d 504 (1991), the Court upheld an Indiana statute requiring that night club dancers wear "pasties" and "G-strings" when they dance. In an opinion expressing the view of three justices, Chief Justice Rehnquist observed that "Indiana's requirement that the dancers wear at least pasties and a G-string is modest, and the bare minimum necessary to achieve the state's purpose...." 501 U.S. at 571, 111 S.Ct. at 2463, 115 L.Ed.2d at 515.

Go to the Scheb/ Scheb Criminal Law and Procedure 6e website at academic .cengage.com/criminaljustice/ scheb for an edited version of *Barnes v. Glen Theatre.*

After the Supreme Court's decision in *Barnes v. Glen Theatre,* the city of Erie, Pennsylvania, adopted an ordinance making it an offense for anyone to "knowingly or intentionally appear in public in a state of nudity." To comply with the ordinance, erotic dancers were required to wear pasties and G-strings. The owners of Kandyland, a club that featured all-nude erotic dancers, filed suit in a state court to challenge the constitutionality of the new ordinance. The Court of Common Pleas declared the ordinance unconstitutional under the First Amendment, and the Pennsylvania Supreme Court agreed, concluding that the unstated purpose of the ordinance was the suppression of expression. On certiorari, the U.S. Supreme Court reversed and upheld the ordinance. Writing for a plurality of justices, Justice O'Connor concluded that the requirement that dancers wear pasties and G-strings was "a minimal restriction" that left dancers "ample capacity" to convey their erotic messages. *City of Erie et al. v. Pap's A. M.*, 529 U.S. 277, 120 S.Ct. 1382, 146 L.Ed.2d 265 (2000).

Profanity

Although in *Chaplinsky v. New Hampshire,* supra, the Supreme Court specifically enumerated profanity as being among those categories of speech so lacking in value as not to merit First Amendment protection, this view no longer prevails. In *Cohen v. California,* supra, the Supreme Court invalidated the "offensive conduct" conviction of a man who entered a courthouse wearing a jacket emblazoned with the slogan "Fuck the Draft." Writing for the Court, Justice John Marshall Harlan opined that

> while the particular four-letter-word being litigated here is perhaps more distasteful than others of its genre, it is nevertheless often true that one man's vulgarity is another's lyric. Indeed, we think it is largely because government officials cannot make principled distinctions in this area that the Constitution leaves matters of taste and style so largely to the individual. 403 U.S. at 25, 91 S.Ct. at 1788, 29 L.Ed.2d at 294.

Despite the Supreme Court's decision in *Cohen v. California,* most states and many cities retain laws proscribing profanity. These laws are seldom enforced and rarely challenged in court. One notable exception is the case of the "cussing canoeist" that made national news in 1998. When Timothy Boomer fell from his canoe into Michigan's Rifle River, he unleashed a tirade of profanities in a very loud voice. He was convicted of violating a nineteenth-century state law that prohibited the utterance of profanity in the presence of children. Boomer was fined $75 and ordered to perform four days of community service. With the assistance of the American Civil Liberties Union, Boomer appealed his conviction to the Michigan Court of Appeals, which reversed the conviction and struck down the statute on which it was based. Writing for the court, Judge William B. Murphy observed that the law, "as drafted, reaches constitutionally protected speech, and it operates to inhibit the exercise of First Amendment rights." *People v. Boomer,* 655 N.W.2d 255, 259 (Mich. App. 2002).

Freedom of Assembly

The First Amendment specifically protects the "right of the people peaceably to assemble." Yet, as we have seen, one of the most important purposes of the criminal law is to maintain public peace and order. Sometimes these values conflict, as in the civil rights struggle of the 1960s, when public demonstrations became an important part of a powerful political movement. See, for example, *Cox v. Louisiana,* 379 U.S. 559, 85 S.Ct. 476, 13 L.Ed.2d 487 (1965); *Adderley v. Florida,* 385 U.S. 39, 87 S.Ct. 242, 17 L.Ed.2d 149 (1966); *Walker v. City of Birmingham,* 388 U.S. 307, 87 S.Ct. 1824, 18 L.Ed.2d 1210 (1967).

In one of the most memorable cases from the civil rights era, the Supreme Court reversed the breach-of-the-peace convictions of 187 students who participated in a peaceful demonstration on the grounds of the South Carolina statehouse. *Edwards v. South Carolina,* 372 U.S. 229; 83 S.Ct. 680; 9 L.Ed.2d. 697 (1963). The Court characterized the students' conduct not as a breach of the peace but as "an exercise of … basic constitutional rights in their most pristine and classic form."

Governments may not ban assemblies in the **public forum** as long as they are peaceful and do not impede the operations of government or the activities of other

Go to the Scheb/ Scheb Criminal Law and Procedure 6e website at academic .cengage.com/criminaljustice/ scheb for an edited version of *Cohen v. California.*

Go to the Scheb/ Scheb Criminal Law and Procedure 6e website at academic .cengage.com/criminaljustice/ scheb for an edited version of *Edwards v. South Carolina.*

citizens. Yet, to promote the interests of safety, order, and peace, governments may impose reasonable **time, place, and manner regulations** on public assemblies. The character of a given place and the pattern of its normal activities determine the type of time, place, and manner regulations that the courts consider reasonable. *Grayned v. City of Rockford,* 408 U.S. 104, 92 S.Ct. 2294, 33 L.Ed.2d 222 (1972). For example, a restriction against the use of sound amplifiers near a courthouse or library might well be judged reasonable, whereas a ban on "picketing" on the steps of the same buildings would not. In imposing time, place, and manner regulations, governments must be careful not to deprive demonstrations or protests of their essential content by imposing excessive or unnecessarily burdensome regulations. *United States v. Grace,* 461 U.S. 171, 103 S.Ct. 1702, 75 L.Ed.2d 736 (1983).

Free Exercise of Religion

The value of **freedom of religion** is so deeply rooted in American culture that rarely have legislatures sought to impinge directly on that right. Yet from time to time lawmakers have sought to prevent certain unpopular religious groups from proselytizing. The Supreme Court has been quick to invalidate such efforts. In one leading case, the Court struck down a state statute that made it a misdemeanor for any person to solicit door to door for religious or philanthropic reasons without prior approval from local officials, who were authorized to make determinations as to whether solicitors represented *bona fide* religions. The law was successfully challenged by a member of the Jehovah's Witnesses sect who was prosecuted for engaging in door-to-door proselytizing without a permit. *Cantwell v. Connecticut,* supra.

Unusual Religious Practices

Much more problematic are government attempts to enforce criminal statutes designed to protect the public health, safety, and welfare against religious practices deemed inimical to these interests. Does the right to freely exercise one's religion permit a person to violate an otherwise valid criminal statute? In 1878 the Supreme Court answered this question in the negative by upholding the prosecution of a polygamist. *Reynolds v. United States,* 98 U.S. (8 Otto) 145, 25 L.Ed. 244 (1878). More recently, however, the Supreme Court granted to members of the Old Order Amish sect an exemption to the Wisconsin compulsory education law. The Court found that the law significantly interfered with the Amish way of life and thus violated their right to freely exercise their religion. *Wisconsin v. Yoder,* 406 U.S. 205, 92 S.Ct. 1526, 32 L.Ed.2d 15 (1972).

Several state courts have decided cases arising from unusual forms of worship. The Tennessee Supreme Court upheld the validity of a statute making it a crime to handle poisonous snakes in religious ceremonies against the claim that the law violated the right to free exercise of religion guaranteed by the state constitution. *Harden v. State,* 216 S.W.2d 708 (Tenn. 1949).

In a decision that cuts the other way, the California Supreme Court reversed the convictions of several members of the Native American Church for possession of peyote, which contains an illegal hallucinogen. *People v. Woody,* 394 P.2d 813 (Cal. 1964). In the court's view, the sacramental use of peyote was central to the worship by members of the Native American Church and thus protected by the First Amendment. In 1990, however, the U.S. Supreme Court held that the sacramental use of

Go to the Scheb/ Scheb Criminal Law and Procedure 6e website at academic .cengage.com/criminaljustice/ scheb for an edited version of *Wisconsin v. Yoder.*

peyote by members of the Native American Church was not protected by the Free Exercise Clause of the First Amendment. *Employment Division v. Smith,* 494 U.S. 872, 110 S.Ct. 1595, 108 L.Ed.2d 876 (1990). This decision by the nation's highest court means that state courts that have granted such protection might want to reconsider their positions. In our federal system, however, state courts are free to provide greater levels of protection to individual rights under the terms of their state constitutions than those provided by the federal constitution.

The principle that underlies *Employment Division v. Smith* is that the Free Exercise Clause does not provide the basis for an exemption to a generally applicable criminal statute. A law aimed specifically at the practices of one religious group is another matter, as the Supreme Court made clear in striking down a Hialeah, Florida, ordinance prohibiting animal sacrifices. After receiving a number of complaints about the practice of animal sacrifice associated with the Santeria religion, the city of Hialeah adopted an ordinance making it an offense to "unnecessarily kill, torment, torture, or mutilate an animal in a public or private ritual or ceremony not for the primary purpose of food consumption." Practitioners of Santeria sued to challenge the constitutionality of the ordinance. In a unanimous decision, the Supreme Court declared the ordinance unconstitutional. Writing for the Court, Justice Anthony Kennedy observed that "the laws in question were enacted by officials who did not understand, failed to perceive, or chose to ignore the fact that their official actions violated the Nation's essential commitment to religious freedom." *Church of the Lukumi Babalu Aye, Inc. v. City of Hialeah,* 508 U.S. 520, 524, 113 S.Ct. 2217, 2222, 124 L.Ed.2d 472, 477 (1993).

 Go to the Scheb/ Scheb Criminal Law and Procedure 6e website at academic .cengage.com/criminaljustice/ scheb for an edited version of the *Lukumi Babalu Aye* decision.

Refusal of Medical Treatment

One of the more troubling and tragic situations in which the Free Exercise Clause potentially conflicts with the criminal law involves the refusal of medical treatment. Certain religious groups, such as the Christian Scientists, believe that physical healing is to be achieved through spiritual power. Thus, when faced with an illness or injury, they are likely to refuse medical treatment. Other groups—for example, the Jehovah's Witnesses—believe that blood transfusions are specifically enjoined by scripture.

The courts have recognized the right of a competent adult to refuse medical treatment on religious grounds, even if the refusal results in death. See, for example, *In re Estate of Brooks,* 205 N.E.2d 435 (Ill. 1965); *In re Milton,* 505 N.E.2d 255 (Ohio 1987). It is another matter entirely when parents refuse to allow medical treatment for their children. The Supreme Court has recognized that

> parents may be free to become martyrs themselves. But it does not follow that they are free in identical circumstances to make martyrs of their children before they have reached the age of full legal discretion when they can make that choice for themselves. *Prince v. Massachusetts,* 321 U.S. 158, 170, 64 S.Ct. 438, 444, 88 L.Ed. 645, 654 (1944).

Accordingly, courts seldom allow freedom of religion as a defense to a criminal charge stemming from a situation in which parents refused to seek or allow medical treatment for their children. In one recent case, a member of the Christian Scientist faith was prosecuted for involuntary manslaughter after failing to seek medical treatment of her daughter's meningitis, which turned out to be fatal. The California Supreme Court rejected the defendant's free exercise of religion defense, saying that "parents have no right to free exercise of religion at the price of a child's life." *Walker v. Superior Court,* 763 P.2d 852 (Cal. 1988).

CASE-IN-POINT

The Right to Keep and Bear Arms

Article I, Section 2-a of the New Hampshire Constitution provides: "All persons have the right to keep and bear arms in defense of themselves, their families, their property and the state." At the same time, a New Hampshire statute proscribes possession of firearms by convicted felons. RSA 159:3. Scott Smith, who was convicted in the Rockingham Superior Court of being a felon in possession of a firearm, challenged the constitutionality of the statute. The New Hampshire Supreme Court affirmed the conviction and sustained the validity of the statute, saying, "the State constitutional right to keep and bear arms is not absolute and may be subject to restriction and regulation.... The governmental interest served by the statute, protection of human life and property, is patently significant."

State v. Smith, 571 A.2d 279, 281 (N.H. 1990).

The Right to Keep and Bear Arms

There are numerous criminal prohibitions—at the federal, state, and local levels—against the sale, possession, and use of certain types of firearms. "Gun control" laws are seen by many as antithetical to the **right to keep and bear arms.** The Second Amendment to the U.S. Constitution provides: "A well regulated Militia, being necessary to the security of a free state, the right of the people to keep and bear arms, shall not be infringed."

In *United States v. Miller,* 307 U.S. 174, 59 S.Ct. 816, 83 L.Ed. 1206 (1939), the Supreme Court upheld a federal law criminalizing the interstate shipment of sawed-off shotguns, saying that "the right to keep and bear arms" had to be interpreted in relation to the "well regulated militia." The Court concluded that possession of sawed-off shotguns had no reasonable relationship to serving in the militia. In reaffirming *Miller,* the Court said that "the Second Amendment guarantees no right to keep and bear a firearm that does not have some reasonable relationship to the preservation or efficiency of a well regulated militia." *Lewis v. United States,* 445 U.S. 55, 65 n.8, 100 S.Ct. 915, 921 n.8, 63 L.Ed.2d 198, 209 n.8 (1980). Like the federal constitution, many state constitutions contain language dealing with the right to keep and bear arms. Yet state courts tend to give wide latitude to state and local gun control laws. Conservatives and libertarians tend to criticize the courts for failing, in their view, to adequately protect the constitutional right to keep and bear arms. Members of the law enforcement community, however, are typically more supportive of legislative efforts to control the dissemination and use of firearms.

Go to the Scheb/Scheb Criminal Law and Procedure 6e website at academic.cengage.com/criminaljustice/scheb for an edited version of *U.S. v. Miller.*

The Doctrines of Vagueness and Overbreadth

The Fifth Amendment to the U.S. Constitution provides that "no person ... shall be deprived of life, liberty or property without due process of law." The two fundamental aspects of due process are fair notice and fair hearing. The principle of fair notice implies that a person has a right to know whether particular contemplated conduct is illegal.

Indeed, the Supreme Court has emphatically stated that "[n]o one may be required at peril of life, liberty or property to speculate as to the meaning of penal statutes." *Lanzetta v. New Jersey*, 306 U.S. 451, 453, 59 S.Ct. 618, 619, 83 L.Ed. 888, 890 (1939).

A criminal law that is excessively vague in its proscriptions offends this principle and is thus invalid under the Due Process Clause of the Fifth or Fourteenth Amendments (depending on whether it is a federal or state statute). However, we must realize that the **vagueness doctrine** is "designed more to limit the discretion of police and prosecutors than to ensure that statutes are intelligible to persons pondering criminal activity." *United States v. White*, 882 F.2d 250, 252 (7th Cir. 1989). Accordingly, the Supreme Court has held that the requisite specificity of criminal statutes may be achieved through judicial interpretation. *Rose v. Locke*, 423 U.S. 48, 96 S.Ct. 243, 46 L.Ed.2d 185 (1975). As interpreted by the Seventh Circuit Court of Appeals in *United States v. White*, "provided that conduct is of a sort widely known among the lay public to be criminal…, a person is not entitled to clear notice that the conduct violates a particular criminal statute." *United States v. White*, supra at 252.

In a landmark decision, the Supreme Court struck down a Jacksonville, Florida, ordinance that prohibited various forms of vagrancy, including loitering and "prowling by auto." *Papachristou v. City of Jacksonville*, 405 U.S. 156, 92 S.Ct. 839, 31 L.Ed.2d 110 (1972). Writing for the Court in *Papachristou*, Justice William O. Douglas objected to the "unfettered discretion" the ordinance placed in the hands of the police, allowing for "arbitrary and discriminatory enforcement of the law." (For further discussion of the vagueness doctrine as it relates to the crimes of vagrancy and loitering, see Chapter 12).

Closely related to the concept of vagueness, the **doctrine of overbreadth** was developed exclusively in the context of the First Amendment and concerns a criminal law that is written so broadly that it potentially infringes First Amendment freedoms. The evil of overbreadth of a law is that it may permit police to make arrests for

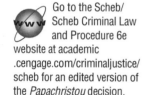

Go to the Scheb/ Scheb Criminal Law and Procedure 6e website at academic .cengage.com/criminaljustice/ scheb for an edited version of the *Papachristou* decision.

SUPREME COURT PERSPECTIVE

Kolender V. Lawson, 461 U.S. 352, 103 S.Ct. 1855, 75 L.Ed.2d 903 (1983)

In this case, the Supreme Court struck down a California statute requiring persons loitering on the streets to provide "credible and reliable" identification to police when requested to do so. The Court held the statute void for vagueness. In her opinion for the Court, Justice Sandra Day O'Connor discusses the vagueness doctrine.

JUSTICE O'CONNOR delivered the opinion of the Court.
As generally stated, the void-for-vagueness doctrine requires that a penal statute define the criminal offense with sufficient definiteness that ordinary people can understand what conduct is prohibited and in a manner that does not encourage arbitrary and discriminatory

enforcement.… Although the doctrine focuses both on actual notice to citizens and arbitrary enforcement, we have recognized recently that the more important aspect of the vagueness doctrine "is not actual notice, but the other principal element of the doctrine—the requirement that a legislature establish minimal guidelines to govern law enforcement." … Where the legislature fails to provide such minimal guidelines, a criminal statute may permit "a standardless sweep [that] allows policemen, prosecutors, and juries to pursue their personal predilections." …

The concern of our citizens with curbing criminal activity is certainly a matter requiring the attention of all branches of government. As weighty as this concern is, however, it cannot justify legislation that would otherwise fail to meet constitutional standards for definiteness and clarity.

constitutionally protected conduct, such as political speech, as well as for unprotected activity, such as inciting people to violence through the use of fighting words.

Coates v. City of Cincinnati, 402 U.S. 611, 91 S.Ct. 1686, 29 L.Ed.2d 214 (1971), illustrates both the vagueness doctrine and the doctrine of overbreadth. In *Coates* the Supreme Court struck down a Cincinnati ordinance that made it unlawful for "three or more persons to assemble … on any sidewalks and there conduct themselves in a manner annoying to persons passing by." The Court found the ordinance to be excessively vague in that "men of common intelligence must necessarily guess at its meaning." The Court also found that the ordinance was so broad that it criminalized speech and assembly protected by the First Amendment.

Ordinarily a person can contest only a law that has been directed against him or her. However, the doctrine of overbreadth enables a person to contest a law imposing restrictions on First Amendment freedoms even when that person has not been charged with violating the law. This doctrine was designed to bring to the courts' attention laws that have a "chilling effect" on the exercise of First Amendment rights.

In the 1980s, the Supreme Court appeared to be retreating somewhat from the overbreadth doctrine. In *New York v. Ferber,* 458 U.S. 747, 102 S.Ct. 3348, 73 L.Ed.2d 1113 (1982), for example, the Court rejected an overbreadth challenge to a child pornography statute that criminalized child pornography well beyond the legal test of obscenity delineated in *Miller v. California,* supra. Although expressing concern that the statute might possibly be applied to punish constitutionally protected artistic expression, the Court concluded that the law was not "substantially overbroad" and that impermissible applications of the statute should be addressed on a case-by-case basis. According to the *Ferber* Court, a statute should not be invalidated for overbreadth if its legitimate reach "dwarfs its arguably impermissible applications." 458 U.S. at 773, 102 S.Ct. at 3363, 73 L.Ed.2d at 1133.

The overbreadth doctrine was given new life by the Supreme Court in 1997, when the Court struck down provisions of the Communications Decency Act (CDA) of 1996, 47 U.S.C.A. §§ 223(a), 223(d) (Supp. 1997). Under the CDA, Congress had attempted to ban "indecent" as well as "obscene" speech from the Internet. Criminal penalties were provided for persons who transmitted such messages in a fashion that they could be received by children. The Court found that the law swept within its ambit constitutionally protected speech as well as obscenity. *Reno v. American Civil Liberties Union,* 521 U.S. 844, 117 S.Ct. 2329, 138 L.Ed.2d 874 (1997).

Go to the Scheb/ Scheb Criminal Law and Procedure 6e website at academic .cengage.com/criminaljustice/ scheb for an edited version of the *Coates* decision.

Go to the Scheb/ Scheb Criminal Law and Procedure 6e website at academic .cengage.com/criminaljustice/ scheb for an edited version of *New York v. Ferber.*

Go to the Scheb/ Scheb Criminal Law and Procedure 6e website at academic .cengage.com/criminaljustice/ scheb for an edited version of *Reno v. ACLU.*

Freedom from Compulsory Self-Incrimination

The Fifth Amendment to the U.S. Constitution provides that no person "shall be compelled in any criminal case to be a witness against himself." We normally think of the prohibition against compulsory self-incrimination in terms of a defendant's right not to testify in a criminal trial (see Chapter 18) or a suspect's right to remain silent in the face of police interrogation (see Chapter 16). But the courts have held that this clause also limits the degree to which legislatures can write statutes that require parties to report information to the government that can place them in jeopardy of criminal prosecution. Consider the following Supreme Court decisions from the late 1960s:

- In *Marchetti v. United States,* 390 U.S. 39, 88 S.Ct. 697, 19 L.Ed.2d 889 (1968), the defendant was convicted for conspiring to evade payment of an occupational tax relating to illegal wagers as required by 26 U.S.C.A. § 4411. The Supreme Court ruled that the requirements relative to registration and

CASE-IN-POINT

A Constitutional Challenge to Reporting Requirements of the Federal Gun Control Act

Virgilio Patricio Flores was convicted under the Federal Gun Control Act, 18 U.S.C.A. § 922(e), for failing to provide written notice to a carrier before shipping firearms. On appeal, citing the Supreme Court decisions in *Marchetti, Haynes,* and *Leary,* Flores argued that the reporting requirement violated his Fifth Amendment privilege against self-incrimination. The Ninth Circuit Court of Appeals rejected his arguments. The court noted that the cited decisions are distinguishable because in each the Supreme Court invalidated a notice requirement in an area of activity permeated with criminal statutes or directed at a group of persons inherently suspect of criminal activities. The court found that in those cases, compliance with the reporting requirements produced an immediate or real and appreciable hazard of self-incrimination. In contrast, the Court determined that the Gun Control Act is a general regulatory statute not directed at catching illegal firearm exporters but rather at helping the states regulate firearm distribution for the safety of their citizens by shutting off the flow of weapons across their borders. A divided Court affirmed Flores's conviction; however, dissenting judges argued that the Gun Control Act has penal aspects that go beyond mere regulation and is a law designed to facilitate the discovery of criminal activity.

United States v. Flores, 753 F.2d. 1499 (9th Cir. 1985).

payment of the tax would have had the "direct and unmistakable consequence of incriminating" the defendant and were thus unconstitutional under the Self-Incrimination Clause.

- In *Haynes v. United States,* 390 U.S. 85, 88 S.Ct. 722, 19 L.Ed.2d 923 (1968), the Court held that the privilege against self-incrimination provided a defense to prosecution either for failure to register a firearm under 26 U.S.C.A. § 5841 or for possession of an unregistered firearm under 26 U.S.C.A. § 5851.

- In *Leary v. United States,* 395 U.S. 6, 89 S.Ct. 1532, 23 L.Ed.2d 57 (1969), the Court held that the privilege against self-incrimination is a complete defense to a prosecution under 26 U.S.C.A. § 4744(a), the provision of the Marihuana Tax Act of 1937 that required payment of a tax when a person purchased marijuana (which was illegal under state laws at the time the statute was passed).

Go to the Scheb/Scheb Criminal Law and Procedure 6e website at academic.cengage.com/criminaljustice/scheb for an edited version of *Leary v. U.S.*

The Supreme Court's decisions in this area indicate that a statutory reporting requirement violates the freedom from compulsory self-incrimination if it (1) applies to an area of activity that is "permeated with criminal statutes," (2) is directed at a "highly selective" group of persons that is "inherently suspect of criminal activities," and (3) poses a "substantial hazard" or "direct likelihood" of self-incrimination.

The Prohibition against Cruel and Unusual Punishments

The Eighth Amendment prohibits the imposition of **cruel and unusual punishments.** This principle applies both to the procedures by which criminal sentences are imposed, *Furman v. Georgia,* 408 U.S. 238, 92 S.Ct. 2726, 33 L.Ed.2d 346 (1972), and to the

Go to the Scheb/ Scheb Criminal Law and Procedure 6e website at academic .cengage.com/criminaljustice/ scheb for an edited version of *Coker v. Georgia.*

substantive laws that define punishments. For example, in *Coker v. Georgia,* 433 U.S. 584, 97 S.Ct. 2861, 53 L.Ed.2d 982 (1977), the Supreme Court invalidated a provision of a state death penalty law that allowed capital punishment in cases of rape. Writing for the plurality, Justice Byron White concluded that "the death penalty, which is 'unique in its severity and its irrevocability,' is an excessive penalty for the rapist who, as such, does not take human life." 433 U.S. at 598, 97 S.Ct. at 2869, 53 L.Ed.2d at 993.

Generally, however, in Eighth Amendment cases the Supreme Court does not rule on the validity of a statute but rather confines its inquiry to the constitutionality of a particular sentence. For example, in *Ewing v. California,* 538 U.S 11, 123 S.Ct. 1179, 155 L.Ed.2d 116 (2003), the Court upheld a sentence imposed under California's "three strikes and you're out" law. The defendant, who had been previously convicted of four felonies and was out on parole, was convicted of grand larceny and was sentenced to twenty-five years to life in prison. Writing for the Court, Justice O'Connor observed the following: "Ewing's sentence is a long one. But it reflects a rational legislative judgment, entitled to deference, that offenders who have committed serious or violent felonies and who continue to commit felonies must be incapacitated." 538 U.S. at 30, 123 S.Ct. 1179 at 1190, 155 L.Ed.2d at 123. In dissent, Justice Stephen Breyer pointed out that "Ewing's sentence is, at a minimum, two to three times the length of sentences that other jurisdictions would impose in similar circumstances." 538 U.S at 52, 123 S.Ct. at 1202, 155 L.Ed.2d at 137.

Go to the Scheb/ Scheb Criminal Law and Procedure 6e website at academic .cengage.com/criminaljustice/ scheb for an edited version of *Robinson v. California.*

On occasion, the Eighth Amendment has even been employed to limit the definition of crimes. In *Robinson v. California,* 370 U.S. 660, 82 S.Ct. 1417, 8 L.Ed.2d 758 (1962), the Supreme Court, relying on the Cruel and Unusual Punishments Clause, struck down a state law that made it a crime for a person to be "addicted to the use of narcotics." The Court found it unacceptable that an individual could be punished merely for a "status" without regard to any specific criminal conduct. In effect, the Court "constitutionalized" the traditional requirement that a crime involve a specific *actus reus.*

The Constitutional Right of Privacy

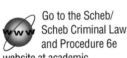

Go to the Scheb/ Scheb Criminal Law and Procedure 6e website at academic .cengage.com/criminaljustice/ scheb for an edited version of the *Griswold* decision.

Although there is no mention of "privacy" in the text of the Constitution, the Supreme Court has held that a sphere of intimate personal conduct is immune from legislative interference. In its first explicit recognition of this **constitutional right of privacy,** *Griswold v. Connecticut,* 381 U.S. 479, 85 S.Ct. 1678, 14 L.Ed.2d 510 (1965), the Court relied in part on the Ninth Amendment, which provides that "[t]he enumeration in the Constitution, of certain rights, shall not be construed to deny or disparage others retained by the people."

Go to the Scheb/ Scheb Criminal Law and Procedure 6e website at academic .cengage.com/criminaljustice/ scheb for an edited version of *Eisenstadt v. Baird.*

In the *Griswold* case, the Supreme Court invalidated a state law proscribing the use of birth control devices as applied to married couples. In *Eisenstadt v. Baird,* 405 U.S. 438, 92 S.Ct. 1029, 31 L.Ed.2d 349 (1972), the Court extended the principle to protect single individuals from a similar anti-contraception statute. Writing for the Court in *Eisenstadt,* Justice William J. Brennan stated that the right of privacy is "the right of the individual, married or single, to be free from unwarranted governmental intrusion into matters so fundamentally affecting a person as the decision whether or not to beget a child." 405 U.S. at 453, 92 S.Ct. at 1038, 31 L.Ed.2d at 362.

Abortion

The Supreme Court's *Griswold* and *Eisenstadt* decisions paved the way for its landmark abortion decision in *Roe v. Wade,* 410 U.S. 113, 93 S.Ct. 705, 35 L.Ed.2d 147 (1973). In *Roe,* the Court held that the right of privacy was broad enough to include a woman's decision to terminate her pregnancy. This 7–2 decision invalidated the Texas anti-abortion statute and rendered unenforceable similar laws in most states. The essential holding in *Roe v. Wade* has been reaffirmed by the Supreme Court on several occasions, most recently in 2000 when it struck down a Nebraska law banning a procedure commonly described as "partial-birth abortion." *Stenberg v. Carhart,* 530 U.S. 914, 120 S.Ct. 2597, 147 L.Ed.2d 743 (2000). Congress responded by enacting the federal Partial-Birth Abortion Ban Act, and the Court held the new act is not facially unconstitutional and does not impose an undue burden on a woman's right to an abortion. *Gonzales v. Carhart,* 127 S.Ct. 1610 (U.S., Apr 18, 2007) (05-380, 05-1382).

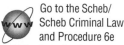 Go to the Scheb/ Scheb Criminal Law and Procedure 6e website at academic .cengage.com/criminaljustice/ scheb for an edited version of *Roe v. Wade.*

The continuing "pro-life" and "pro-choice" demonstrations around the country attest to the extremely controversial nature of legal abortion. (The abortion issue is discussed more thoroughly in Chapter 6.) Few questions today have greater philosophical, religious, ethical, medical, and political saliency than the issue of abortion. Seemingly irreconcilable views on the subject of abortion exist, and the issue continues to spawn legislative and judicial attention. The continuing clashes between demonstrators resulting in injuries and even death have caused some states to respond by restricting the proximity of demonstrators to clinics. In *Madsen v. Women's Health Center,* 512 U.S. 753, 114 S.Ct. 2516, 129 L.Ed.2d 593 (1994), the U.S. Supreme Court attempted to balance the constitutional rights of those seeking access to abortion clinics against the First Amendment rights of the protesters. In a 6–3 decision, the Court upheld the basic provisions of a state court injunction intended to keep disruptive protesters from blocking access to the clinics.

On May 26, 1994, President Clinton signed the Freedom of Access to Clinic Entrances (FACE) Act, 18 U.S.C.A. § 248. This federal law was prompted by the 1993 killing of an abortion doctor outside a Pensacola, Florida, clinic as well as by numerous episodes around the country in which persons working at or seeking access to abortion clinics had been harassed and threatened by anti-abortion activists. The new act provides civil and criminal remedies against whoever

> by force or threat of force or by physical obstruction, intentionally injures, intimidates or interferes with or attempts to injure, intimidate or interfere with any person because that person is or has been, or in order to intimidate such person or any other person or any class of persons from, obtaining or providing reproductive health services. 18 U.S.C.A. § 248(a)(1).

The Fourth Circuit held the FACE Act does not violate the First Amendment's free speech or free exercise of religion clauses and is neither overbroad nor vague. *American Life League, Inc. v. Reno,* 47 F.3d 642 (4th Cir. 1995).

Privacy and Sexual Conduct

Prior to the 1960s it was generally assumed that government had the authority to enforce traditional sexual mores through the criminal law. Even though laws against adultery, fornication, and sodomy were seldom enforced and had in fact been abolished in many states, few questioned the right of state and local governments to enact and enforce such prohibitions. Beginning in the 1960s, commentators began to question this assumption. The constitutional right of privacy recognized in *Griswold v. Connecticut*

The Virginia Supreme Court Strikes Down the State's Fornication Law

As recently as 2005, Virginia Code § 18.2-344 provided, "Any person, not being married, who voluntarily shall have sexual intercourse with any other person, shall be guilty of fornication, punishable as a Class 4 misdemeanor." Although the law had not been enforced against consenting adults for more than a century, the constitutionality of the statute was raised in a civil suit brought by a woman who accused a man of infecting her with a sexually transmitted disease. The defendant in the suit argued that the plaintiff could not recover damages inasmuch as she voluntarily participated in an unlawful act, to wit, the consensual sexual intercourse with him that resulted in her infection. The plaintiff then challenged the constitutionality of the fornication law, but the trial court upheld the statute as a rational means of protecting the public health. On appeal, the Virginia Supreme Court invalidated the prohibition as applied to consenting adults. Invoking the U.S. Supreme Court's decision in *Lawrence v. Texas* (2003), the state high court observed: "Because Code § 18.2-344, like the Texas statute at issue in *Lawrence,* is an attempt by the state to control the liberty interest which is exercised in making these personal decisions, it violates the Due Process Clause of the Fourteenth Amendment."

Martin v. Ziherl, 607 S.E.2d 367, 370 (Va. 2005).

(1965), *Roe v. Wade* (1973), and similar decisions came to be viewed by many commentators as a shield against governmental interference with private, consensual sexual conduct between adults. Beginning in the 1970s, activists in the gay rights movement sought to use the right of privacy to attack laws criminalizing homosexual conduct.

In 1986 the Supreme Court declined to extend the right of privacy to protect homosexual conduct between consenting adults. In *Bowers v. Hardwick,* 478 U.S. 186, 106 S.Ct. 2841, 92 L.Ed.2d 140 (1986), the Court upheld a Georgia sodomy law as applied to homosexual conduct. After the decision in *Bowers v. Hardwick,* however, a number of state courts invalidated sodomy laws on state constitutional grounds. See, for example, *Powell v. State,* 510 S.E.2d 18 (Ga. 1998); *Campbell v. Sundquist,* 926 S.W.2d 250 (Tenn. App. 1996).

In 2003, the Supreme Court revisited and overturned its decision in *Bowers v. Hardwick. Lawrence v. Texas,* 539 U.S. 558, 123 S.Ct. 2472, 156 L.Ed.2d 508 (2003). Writing for the Court, Justice Kennedy asserted that a Texas law criminalizing private, consensual homosexual conduct intruded upon personal liberty and autonomy without a sufficient justification. Dissenting, Justice Antonin Scalia argued that the Court had undercut the foundations of other long-standing criminal prohibitions such as those against incest, bestiality, and bigamy. Whether Justice Scalia was correct as a matter of legal reasoning, it was clear that by 2003 public attitudes about homosexuality had changed to the point that most Americans did not believe that the state should concern itself with such conduct. On the other hand, society continues to condemn bigamy, incest, and bestiality, and it is unlikely that courts will interpret constitutional principles so as to prevent government from expressing this condemnation through the criminal law.

Go to the Scheb/ Scheb Criminal Law and Procedure 6e website at academic .cengage.com/criminaljustice/ scheb for an edited version of *Lawrence v. Texas.*

The Right to Die

Since the mid-1970s, the right of privacy has been successfully asserted in state courts as a basis for refusing medical treatment. It is now settled law that a competent adult with a terminal illness has the **right to refuse medical treatment** that would unnaturally prolong his or her life. See, for example, *Satz v. Perlmutter,* 379

CASE-IN-POINT

The Landmark Karen Quinlan Case

Karen Quinlan was a healthy young woman who became permanently comatose after she ingested large quantities of drugs and alcohol. In this condition, she was unable to maintain normal breathing without a ventilator. After it became clear that Karen Quinlan would not regain consciousness, her parents asked her physicians to remove the respirator. The physicians refused, no doubt concerned about possible criminal prosecution or civil liability. The Quinlans went to court and obtained an order allowing removal of the life-support machine. According to the New Jersey Supreme Court, the right of privacy was "broad enough to encompass [Karen Quinlan's] decision to decline medical treatment under certain circumstances, in much the same way as it is broad enough to encompass a woman's decision to terminate pregnancy...." Of course, Karen Quinlan, lying comatose in the hospital, was unable to communicate her intentions to exercise this aspect of the right of privacy. According to the Court's opinion, the "only practical way to prevent destruction of [Karen Quinlan's] right is to permit the guardian and family ... to render their best judgment as to whether she would exercise [the right to decline treatment] in these circumstances." After Karen Quinlan was taken off the breathing machine, she lived for nine years in a coma, taking food and water through a nasogastric tube. Her parents never asked that this feeding be discontinued.

In re Quinlan, 355 A.2d 647 (N.J. 1976).

So.2d 359 (Fla. 1980). Under certain circumstances courts have allowed the family of a comatose individual the direct removal of extraordinary means of life support. See, for example, *In re Quinlan,* 355 A.2d 647 (N.J. 1976). This manifestation of rights of privacy and personal autonomy came to be known as the **right to die.**

The right to die, if extended beyond the right of a terminally ill person to refuse artificial means of life support, runs headlong into criminal prohibitions against suicide and, potentially, homicide (see Chapter 6). As yet, courts have been unwilling to extend the right of privacy this far. For example, in *Gilbert v. State,* 487 So.2d 1185 (Fla. App. 1986), a Florida appeals court rejected Roswell Gilbert's "euthanasia" defense to the charge that he committed premeditated murder against his wife, who suffered from osteoporosis and Alzheimer's disease. More recently, the U.S. Supreme Court upheld state laws criminalizing doctor-assisted suicide. *Washington v. Glucksberg,* 521 U.S. 702, 117 S.Ct. 2258, 138 L.Ed.2d 772 (1997). Writing for the Court, Chief Justice Rehnquist observed:

> Throughout the Nation, Americans are engaged in an earnest and profound debate about the morality, legality, and practicality of physician assisted suicide. Our holding permits this debate to continue, as it should in a democratic society. 521 U.S. at 735, 117 S.Ct. at 2275, 138 L.Ed.2d at 797.

Go to the Scheb/ Scheb Criminal Law and Procedure 6e website at academic .cengage.com/criminaljustice/ scheb for an edited version of *Washington v. Glucksberg.*

Equal Protection of the Laws

The Fourteenth Amendment of the U.S. Constitution forbids states from denying persons **equal protection of the laws.** The Due Process Clause of the Fifth Amendment has been interpreted to impose a similar prohibition on the federal government. *Bolling v. Sharpe,* 347 U.S. 497, 74 S.Ct. 693, 98 L.Ed. 884 (1954). Most state

Go to the Scheb/
Scheb Criminal Law
and Procedure 6e
website at academic
.cengage.com/criminaljustice/
scheb for an edited version of
Loving v. Virginia.

constitutions contain similar requirements. On occasion, the concept of equal protection has been used to challenge the validity of criminal statutes. For example, in *Loving v. Virginia,* 388 U.S. 1, 87 S.Ct. 1817, 18 L.Ed.2d 1010 (1967), the Supreme Court relied on the Equal Protection Clause of the Fourteenth Amendment in striking down a state statute that criminalized interracial marriage. The effect of *Loving* was that any law that criminalized conduct solely on the basis of the race of the parties was rendered null and void.

In *Eisenstadt v. Baird,* supra, the Court invoked the Equal Protection Clause in striking a Massachusetts law that criminalized the use of birth control devices by single persons but not by married couples. And in *Craig v. Boren,* 429 U.S. 190, 97 S.Ct. 451, 50 L.Ed.2d 397 (1976), the Court invalidated an Oklahoma law that forbade the sale of beer containing 3.2 percent alcohol to females under the age of eighteen and males under the age of twenty-one. The Court concluded that the state lacked a sufficient justification for discriminating between the sexes regarding the legal availability of the contested beverage.

In recent years, women have challenged the constitutionality of laws that permit men but not women to go topless in public. For the most part these challenges have failed. For example, in *State v. Vogt,* 775 A.2d 551 (N.J. App. 2001), a New Jersey appellate court upheld an ordinance that prohibited "indecent or unnecessary exposure" of the human body in public. The law was challenged by Arlene Vogt, who was arrested for going topless on a public beach. Vogt argued that application of the law to topless women but not men "creates an invidious discrimination on the basis of gender in violation of both the federal and state constitutional guarantees of equal protection." 775 A.2d at 557. The appellate court rejected her challenge, observing: "Restrictions on exposure of the female breast are supported by the important governmental interest in safeguarding the public's moral sensibilities, and this ordinance is substantially related to that interest." 775 A.2d at 557. As the public's "moral sensibilities" change, it is likely that such restrictions will continue to be challenged.

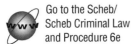

Go to the Scheb/
Scheb Criminal Law
and Procedure 6e
website at academic
.cengage.com/criminaljustice/
scheb for an edited version of
State v. Vogt.

Standards of Judicial Review

At a minimum, a criminal law prohibition that touches on a constitutionally protected interest must be "rationally related to furthering a legitimate government interest." *Massachusetts Board of Retirement v. Murgia,* 427 U.S. 307, 96 S.Ct. 2562, 49 L.Ed.2d 520 (1976). For example, a state law that makes it a crime for a person to perform surgery without a license is obviously a rational means of advancing the state's legitimate interests in public health and safety. Thus, even though the law deprives laypersons of their right to make contracts freely and discriminates against those unable to obtain a license, there is little doubt it would withstand judicial review under the **rational basis test.**

Criminal laws that infringe **fundamental rights** such as the First Amendment freedoms of speech and press are judged by a more stringent standard of review. Such laws are subject to **strict judicial scrutiny,** which means, in effect, that they are presumed to be unconstitutional. To survive judicial review, government must show that the challenged law furthers a **compelling government interest** and is narrowly tailored to that purpose. *Shapiro v. Thompson,* 394 U.S. 618, 89 S.Ct. 1322, 22 L.Ed.2d 600 (1969). This is a heavy burden for the government to carry. Consequently, most laws subjected to strict judicial scrutiny are declared unconstitutional. However, the application of strict scrutiny is not necessarily equivalent to a declaration of unconstitutionality. For example, in *New York v. Ferber,* supra, the Supreme Court upheld a child pornography law that impinged on the First Amendment freedom of expression because, in the view of the Court, the law served a compelling interest in protecting children from the abuse typically associated with the pornography industry.

The Importance of State Constitutions

Under our federal system of government, the highest court of each state possesses the authority to interpret with finality its state constitution and statutes. A decision by a state court is not subject to review by the U.S. Supreme Court, except insofar as the state law on which it is based is being challenged as a violation of the federal constitution or statutes. Because every state constitution contains language protecting individual rights and liberties, many state court decisions implicate both state and federal constitutional provisions. Under the relevant language of their constitutions and statutes, state courts are free to recognize greater (but not lesser) protections of individual rights than are provided by the U.S. Constitution as interpreted by the federal courts. As a result of the increased conservatism of the federal judiciary, and in particular the Supreme Court, over the last two decades, there has been a resurgence of interest in state constitutional law as it relates to civil rights and liberties.

In *Michigan v. Long,* 463 U.S. 1032, 1040, 103 S.Ct. 3469, 3476, 77 L.Ed.2d 1201, 1214 (1983), the U.S. Supreme Court said that "when a state court decision fairly appears to rest primarily on federal law, or to be interwoven with the federal law, and when the adequacy and independence of any possible state law ground is not clear from the face of the opinion, we will accept as the most reasonable explanation that the state court decided the case the way it did because it believed that federal law required it to do so." However, the Court also indicated that "if the state court decision indicates clearly and expressly that it is alternatively based on *bona fide* separate, adequate, and independent grounds, we, of course, will not undertake to review the decision." 463 U.S. at 1041, 103 S.Ct. at 3476, 77 L.Ed.2d at 1214 (1983).

Michigan v. Long effectively invited the state courts to consider the parallel provisions of their state constitutions independently. Some state courts have accepted the invitation. For example, in *In re T.W.,* 551 So.2d 1186 (Fla. 1989), the Florida Supreme Court struck down as a violation of the right of privacy a statute that required parental consent in cases where minors sought abortions. The constitutionality of a similar law had been upheld on federal grounds by the U.S. Supreme Court in *Planned Parenthood v. Ashcroft,* 462 U.S. 476, 103 S.Ct. 2517, 76 L.Ed.2d 733 (1983). In *T.W.,* the Florida Supreme Court made it clear that it was basing its decision on an amendment to the Florida Constitution that (unlike the federal constitution) explicitly protects the right of privacy. Similarly, in *State v. Kam,* 748 P.2d 372 (Hawaii 1988), the Hawaii Supreme Court adopted an interpretation of its state constitution that affords considerably broader protection to pornography than that provided by the U.S. Constitution. These decisions, and many others like them, mean that a person interested in constitutional limitations on the prohibition of criminal conduct must not ignore the provisions of state constitutions that parallel the U.S. Constitution.

■ CONCLUSION

Enacting laws defining crimes and specifying punishments is a legislative function carried out by Congress and by state legislatures. The power to exercise that function is subject to the limitations in various provisions of the U.S. Constitution and state constitutions. Criminal laws must be rationally related to a legitimate public interest and must be specific to avoid being declared void for vagueness. Moreover, laws that restrict such fundamental rights as First Amendment freedoms are subject to strict judicial scrutiny. As you read later chapters, you will find that these constitutional restraints are especially evident in the definition of offenses against public morality, discussed in Chapter 8, where the constitutional right of privacy has assumed increasing importance, and in the definition of offenses against public order, discussed in Chapter 12, where courts are scrupulous in upholding the freedoms of expression and assembly. Courts address not only definitions of crimes but also the application of those definitions to specific conduct. These serious constraints on the definition of criminal conduct and the enforcement of the criminal law are sustained through the well-established power of judicial review. This protects the constitutional rights of the individual and ensures that the rule of law will prevail in the nation.

■ KEY TERMS

unconstitutional per se, 45
unconstitutional as applied, 46
interstate commerce, 47
treason, 49
bill of attainder, 50
ex post facto law, 51
principle of legality, 51
First Amendment, 52
Fourteenth Amendment, 53
Due Process Clause, 53
clear and present danger doctrine, 54
imminent lawless action, 54
freedom of expression, 54
symbolic speech, 54
fighting words, 55
hate speech, 55

obscenity, 56
public forum, 58
time, place, and manner regulations, 59
freedom of religion, 59
right to keep and bear arms, 61
vagueness doctrine, 62
doctrine of overbreadth, 62
cruel and unusual punishments, 64
constitutional right of privacy, 65
right to refuse medical treatment, 67
right to die, 68
equal protection of the laws, 68
rational basis test, 69
fundamental rights, 69
strict judicial scrutiny, 69
compelling government interest, 69

■ WEB-BASED RESEARCH ACTIVITY

 Log on to http://supreme.lp.findlaw.com/supreme_court. Examine the pending cases on the Supreme Court's docket. Do any of these cases involve constitutional limitations on criminal law? How would you predict that the Court will rule in these cases?

■ QUESTIONS FOR THOUGHT AND DISCUSSION

1. Can you think of an example of an *ex post facto* law?
2. Is it possible for the criminal law to define the crime of obscenity precisely enough to avoid the "vice of vagueness" or the problem of overbreadth?

3. Can a municipality enforce an ordinance totally banning religious organizations from canvassing neighborhoods in search of new members? What about an ordinance that prohibits such canvassing between the hours of 8 P.M. and 8 A.M.?

4. Should the constitutional right of privacy invalidate criminal statutes that require a minor to obtain parental consent to obtain an abortion?

5. Would the constitutional right of privacy provide a defense to a charge of possession of obscene materials where videotapes were viewed only by the defendant in the privacy of his or her home?

6. Could a father who, without judicial approval, unplugs the respirator sustaining the breathing of his comatose, terminally ill child be prosecuted for murder?

7. Would a law making it an offense for a person to carry prescription medicine in other than the original, labeled container meet the test of being rationally related to a legitimate government interest?

8. How does the doctrine of judicial review affect the power of a state legislature to define criminal conduct? Would the constitutional limitations on legislative power be as stringent without the power of courts to declare laws unconstitutional?

9. Give an example of a law that would be constitutional per se, and point out how such a law may be unconstitutional in its application to a specific conduct.

10. Give an example of a law defining a crime that, although held to be constitutional by the U.S. Supreme Court, has been declared unconstitutional by some state courts. Why can such a result occur in our federal system?

■ **PROBLEMS FOR DISCUSSION AND SOLUTION**

1. Amelia Eyeland has been arrested for trespass, disorderly conduct, and resisting arrest. The charges stem from an incident in which Amelia and other members of the Green Warriors staged a raucous protest in a privately owned shopping mall during regular business hours. The protest was aimed at the decision of the mall's owners to expand the parking lot into a wetlands area known to be a habitat for a number of animals. Amelia's attorney is considering a defense based on the First Amendment freedoms of speech and assembly. What chance does the attorney have at being successful with this defense?

2. John Masters, a licensed psychotherapist, has been charged with violating a new state statute making it a crime for "any licensed psychologist, psychiatrist, or psychotherapist to have sexual intercourse with a patient during the existence of the professional relationship." Masters is challenging the constitutionality of the statute on two principal grounds: (a) that it intrudes on his right of privacy and (b) that it violates the Equal Protection Clause of the Fourteenth Amendment in that it fails to apply the same prohibition to other health care professionals. Do you think Masters is likely to prevail in his challenge to the statute? If you were a judge faced with these constitutional questions, how would you be inclined to rule? What additional information would you need to render your decision?

Elements of Crimes and Parties to Crimes

Introduction

The essential elements of a crime are a physical act, often referred to as the *actus reus* (wrongful act), and the intent or state of mind, frequently called the *mens rea* (guilty mind). To establish that a defendant is guilty of a crime, the prosecution must prove the defendant committed some legally proscribed act or failed to act when the law required certain action. The prosecution must also prove that such act or failure to act occurred with a concurrent criminal intent. It would be contrary to our common-law heritage to punish someone who accidentally or unwittingly committed a wrongful act without any intent to commit a crime, but there are some exceptions to this common-law principle. Likewise, a person cannot be punished for a mere intention, however wrongful that intention may be.

Certain offenses, primarily regulatory and public-welfare–type offenses, are classified as strict liability crimes and are exceptions to the common-law concept of requiring proof of a defendant's criminal intent. They came into prominence in America during the Industrial Revolution, and today they form a significant part of the substantive criminal law, particularly in the so-called "public welfare offenses" such as food and drug laws and traffic offenses.

In addition to the basic requirement of establishing a physical act and intent, in some instances the prosecution must establish that certain circumstances existed at the time the act was committed. For example, in some sexual battery offenses the prosecution must establish that the defendant's acts occurred without the victim's consent. Moreover, in other situations the prosecution must establish that a defendant's acts caused specific results. For instance, in homicide cases the prosecution must prove a causal relationship between the defendant's act and the victim's death.

The English common law classified crimes as felonies and misdemeanors. Felonies were very serious crimes; misdemeanors were lesser offenses. Early English common law imposed the death penalty on felons but developed categories of offenders to lessen the punishment meted out to those who assisted in the commission of felonies. At common law, parties to crimes were classified as **principals** in the first and second degree, **accessories before the fact,** and **accessories after the fact;** crimes were classified as felonies and misdemeanors. An awareness of the history of these terms leads to a better understanding of their function in contemporary American criminal law and the procedure of federal and state court systems. In this chapter we first explain the elements of a crime; then we discuss parties to crimes.

The *Actus Reus* (The Act Requirement)

The term *actus reus* means "the act of a criminal." But simply committing a wrongful act does not mean that one has committed a crime. To fulfill the requirements of the criminal law, the actor must willfully commit a proscribed physical act or intentionally fail to act where the law requires a person to act. The rationale for the *actus reus* requirement is to prevent a person from being guilty of an offense based on thoughts or intent alone. Common-law crimes required commission of an act or omission and not merely an evil state of a person's mind. Of course, in the United States, a law that made it a criminal offense simply to entertain an evil thought would be patently unconstitutional.

What Is an Act?

Probably the most complete definition of an "act" as contemplated by the criminal law is found in the Model Penal Code (MPC), which we introduced in Chapter 1. In section 1.13(2) the MPC defines "act" as a "bodily movement whether voluntary or involuntary"; however, section 2.01(1) states that "a person is not guilty of an offense unless his liability is based on conduct that includes a voluntary act or the omission to perform an act of which he is capable." Indeed, courts have generally held that some outward manifestation of voluntary conduct must occur to constitute the physical act necessary in criminal law. The rationale for the requirement of a voluntary act is simple: Only those persons whose acts result from free choice should be criminally punished. Most acts are voluntary. For example, when you raise your hand, it is considered a voluntary act, but when your hand moves as a result of a muscle spasm, it is not a voluntary act. Likewise, movements committed by a person who is unconscious, or acts by someone having an epileptic seizure or sleepwalking, are not regarded as voluntary acts. On the other hand, a driver who takes sleeping pills before beginning to operate an automobile and then falls asleep at the wheel would generally be held criminally responsible for a traffic accident because the driver voluntarily committed the act of taking the pills. Consider the following examples:

- John enters Tom's house or strikes Tom. John has quite obviously committed an "act."
- John picks up a pistol and fires it in the direction of Tom. John, by pulling the trigger of the gun, has committed an "act."
- John hands Tom a glass of liquid to be given to Bob. Unknown to Tom, John added poison to the glass of liquid before handing it to Tom. Tom gives the liquid to Bob, who drinks it and dies. Here John has acted through Tom, an innocent agent; thus, John has committed the "act."
- While riding as a passenger on a bus, John suffers an unexpected attack of epilepsy. As a consequence, John violently kicks his leg, inflicting an injury on Tom, a fellow passenger. John would not be criminally responsible for the injury to Tom.

When Does Failure to Act Constitute an Act?

The requirement for an act is usually fulfilled by an affirmative act. But even a person's failure to act—that is, an **act of omission**—can satisfy the requirements of a physical act in the criminal law. To be guilty of a crime for failure to act, there must have been a legal duty to act in the first place. Such a duty can arise in one of three ways: (1) by relationship of the actor to the victim, for example, parent–child or husband–wife; (2) by a statutory duty; or (3) by contract between the actor and the victim. Consider these examples:

- Mark, an expert swimmer, is lying on the beach and sees a young girl, unrelated to him, struggling to stay afloat and crying for help. Mark disregards her cries, and she drowns. Is Mark criminally liable? The answer is no, for although we might agree that Mark had a strong moral obligation to attempt to save the child, there was no legal obligation to do so. If, on the other hand, Mark were the child's parent or guardian, or a lifeguard on duty, then Mark's failure to act would most likely qualify as a criminal act.
- Jennifer receives an annual income of $50,000 from the operation of her business. She fails to file a federal income tax return as required by the laws of the

The *Actus Reus* Requirement

Law officers found two whiskey stills and all the paraphernalia for making liquor on the defendant's land. Seeing no activity, they drove away. As they did, they met a car driven by the defendant heading toward the property. The car contained a quantity of sugar and other indicators of the illegal activity the officers suspected. The defendant committed no act of making liquor in the presence of the officers, but on the basis of what they observed, they arrested the defendant, and he was convicted of making liquor unlawfully.

On appeal, the South Carolina Supreme Court reversed the conviction, observing that "the evidence overwhelmingly tends to show an intention to manufacture liquor.... But intent alone, not coupled with some overt act ... is not cognizable by the court. [T]he act must always amount to more than mere preparation, and move directly toward the commission of the crime." Citing respectable textbook authority, the court explained that the law does not concern itself with mere guilty intention unconnected with any overt act.

State v. Quick, 19 S.E.2d 101 (S.C. 1942).

United States. Is Jennifer's omission a criminal act? Clearly it is, for she has violated a statutory obligation, the breach of which is punishable by law.

- Dr. Gore, a surgeon, undertakes to perform an operation on a patient for a fee. Before completing the operation, Dr. Gore decides to cease his efforts. As a result of such inattention, the patient dies. Would Dr. Gore's failure to complete what he undertook professionally qualify as an act within the meaning of the criminal law? Yes, because Dr. Gore had a contractual relationship with his patient.

In some instances, failure to perform an **administrative-type act** required by law might not be a crime. In *Lambert v. California*, 355 U.S. 225, 78 S.Ct. 240, 2 L.Ed.2d 228 (1957), the U.S. Supreme Court reviewed a case where the defendant, a convicted felon, was charged with failing to register with authorities as required by a Los Angeles city ordinance. The Court held that as applied to one who has no actual knowledge of a duty to register and where no showing is made of the probability of such knowledge, the ordinance violates the Due Process Clause of the Fourteenth Amendment to the U.S. Constitution. In contrasting the ordinance requiring felon registration with various public welfare offenses it had upheld, the Court noted that public welfare offenses punish failure to act only in "circumstances that should alert the doer to the consequences of his deed." *Lambert v. California*, 355 U.S. at 228, 78 S.Ct. at 243, 2 L.Ed.2d at 231. However, *Lambert's* reach has been limited. In *Texaco, Inc. v. Short*, 454 U.S. 516, 537-38 n. 33, 102 S.Ct. 781, 70 L.Ed.2d 738 (1982), the Supreme Court noted that its application has been so circumscribed that it gives "some credence to Justice Frankfurter's colorful prediction in dissent [in *Lambert*] that the case would stand as 'an isolated deviation from the strong current of precedents—a derelict on the waters of the law'" (quoting *Lambert*, 355 U.S. at 232, 78 S.Ct. 240 [Frankfurter, J., dissenting]).

Possession as a Criminal Act

In certain crimes, **possession** alone is considered to be the wrongful act. For example, in the offense of carrying a concealed weapon, the possession of the weapon concealed from ordinary observation is the wrongful act. Likewise, possession of contraband such as illegal drugs or untaxed liquors constitutes the wrongful act element of certain offenses. Possession is not usually defined in criminal statutes; however, courts generally define possession as the power to control something. The law recognizes two classes of possession: actual and constructive. **Actual possession** exists when a person has something under his or her direct physical control. An example of actual possession would be when an item is on your person, within your reach, or located in a place where you alone have access. **Constructive possession,** on the other hand, is a more difficult concept because it is based on a legal fiction. A person who has the power and intention to control something either directly or through another person is said to be in constructive possession. The exact meaning of these terms is usually determined by the context of the situation. The difficulty is exacerbated when two or more persons are in joint possession of the premises or vehicle where an object is found. Consider the following examples:

- Sarah and Tiffany rent and jointly share an apartment. A police search yields contraband drugs found on the coffee table in the living room used by both Sarah and Tiffany. Can both be charged with possession of the contraband? They probably can: Possession by both Sarah and Tiffany can be inferred because the drugs are in plain view and located in a place to which both have access.

- Under the same circumstances of a shared apartment, drugs are found in a privately owned, closed container in a dresser drawer where only Sarah keeps clothing and valuables. Because Tiffany has no access to this area, the law does not infer that Tiffany has constructive possession of the contents in the drawer. Of course, there might be circumstances under which the prosecution could prove that Tiffany actually had rights to the drugs, knowledge of their whereabouts, and access to them. Then the prosecution could establish that Tiffany was in constructive possession of the contraband.

Status as a Criminal Act

"**Status**" refers to a person's state of being, and ordinarily the state cannot criminalize a person's status. For example, a person's race or gender represents a status. But is addiction to narcotics a status that cannot be criminalized? In *Robinson v. California,* 370 U.S. 660, 82 S.Ct. 1417, 8 L.Ed.2d 758 (1962), the U.S. Supreme Court declared unconstitutional a California statute that made it an offense for a person "to be addicted to the use of narcotics." The Court observed that

> we deal with a statute which makes the "status" of narcotic addiction a criminal offense, for which the offender may be prosecuted "at any time before he reforms." … We hold that a state law which imprisons a person thus afflicted as a criminal, even though he has never touched any narcotic drug within the State or been guilty of any irregular behavior there, inflicts a cruel and unusual punishment in violation of the Fourteenth Amendment. 370 U.S. at 666-667, 82 S.Ct. at 1420, 8 L.Ed.2d at 762-763.

Go to the Scheb/ Scheb Criminal Law and Procedure 6e website at academic .cengage.com/criminaljustice/ scheb for an edited version of *Robinson v. California.*

The issue of when a criminal statute proscribes status, as opposed to conduct, can be very close. This is illustrated by the Supreme Court's decision in *Powell v. Texas,* 392 U.S. 514, 88 S.Ct. 2145, 20 L.Ed.2d 1254 (1968). Powell was a chronic alcoholic who was convicted of public intoxication. Four justices held that Powell had been punished for being in a public place on a particular occasion while intoxicated rather than for his status as a chronic alcoholic. A fifth justice concurred in affirming Powell's conviction. But the four dissenting justices thought the case was indistinguishable from *Robinson v. California,* supra. In their view, both cases involved defendants who were prosecuted for being in a condition that they had no capacity to alter or avoid.

Go to the Scheb/ Scheb Criminal Law and Procedure 6e website at academic .cengage.com/criminaljustice/ scheb for an edited version of *Powell v. Texas.*

The *Mens Rea* (The Criminal Intent Requirement)

The common law developed the doctrine that there should be no crime without a *mens rea,* or "guilty mind." This element is customarily referred to as the criminal intent. To constitute a crime, there must be a concurrence of the *actus reus* with a person's criminal intent. Strict liability offenses, discussed later, are an exception to this principle.

Criminal intent must be distinguished from **motive.** To obtain a conviction, a prosecutor must establish the defendant's criminal intent but not necessarily the defendant's motive for committing a crime. A person's motive often equates with an impulse, an incentive, or a reason for certain behavior, and proof of one's motive can assist in establishing criminal intent. To illustrate, if the prosecution relies on circumstantial evidence to establish the defendant's guilt in a homicide case, the fact that the defendant had vowed "to get even" with the victim might be a relevant factor in the proof. Yet the failure to establish a defendant's motive is not fatal to proving guilt. On the other hand, good motives do not exonerate a person from a crime. Thus, one who steals food simply to give it to a poor, hungry family might have a noble motive. Nevertheless, such a person would be guilty of a crime because of his or her act and intent.

The basic reason that the law requires proof of a criminal intent as well as an act or omission is to distinguish those acts or omissions that occur accidentally from those committed by a person with a "guilty mind." As the California Supreme Court observed in *In re Hayes,* 442 P.2d 366, 369 (Cal. 1968), "an essential element of every orthodox crime is a wrongful or blameworthy mental state of some kind."

Concurrence of Act and Intent

To constitute a crime, there must be a concurrence of the *mens rea* and the *actus reus.* Very early the Massachusetts Supreme Court articulated this traditional common-law standard when it observed: "An evil intention and an unlawful action must concur in order to constitute a crime." *Commonwealth v. Mixer,* 93 N.E. 249 (Mass. 1824). In 1872, California stipulated in Section 20 of the California Penal Code that "the defendant's wrongful intent and his physical act must concur in the sense that the act must be motivated by the intent." See *People v. Green,* 609 P.2d 468, 500 (Cal. App. 1980). Concurrence of the act and intent usually, but not always, occurs simultaneously. For example, suppose an owner accidentally starts a fire in his or her building without any intention to defraud. The owner then takes no steps to extinguish the fire or notify the fire department. The owner's omission to act concurs with the owner's intent to defraud the insurer of the premises. See *Commonwealth v. Cali,* 141 N.E.510 (Mass. 1923). On the other hand, suppose Andrew forms an intent to kill his enemy, Bryan, but after completely abandoning the idea, Andrew later inadvertently kills Bryan in a traffic accident. There would be no concurrence of the original intent with the subsequent act.

General and Specific Intent

At common law, crimes were classified as requiring either general intent or specific intent. *United States v. Bailey,* 444 U.S. 394, 100 S.Ct. 624, 62 L.Ed.2d 575 (1980). American courts followed that tradition. **General intent** is the intent to do an act but not necessarily to cause the results that occur from that act.

Where a crime requires only proof of a general intent, the fact finder (that is, the judge or jury) may infer the defendant's intent from the defendant's acts and the circumstances surrounding those acts. Thus, the prosecution does not have to prove that the defendant had any specific intent to cause a particular result when the act was committed: "General intent exists when from the circumstances the prohibited result may reasonably be expected to follow from the offender's voluntary act, irrespective of a subjective desire to have accomplished such result." *Myers v. State,* 422 N.E.2d 745, 750 (Ind. App. 1981).

Historically, many trial judges would instruct a jury that "the law presumes that a person intends the ordinary consequences of his voluntary acts." In 1979, in *Sandstrom v. Montana,* 442 U.S. 510, 99 S.Ct. 2450, 61 L.Ed.2d 39, the Supreme Court ruled that it is unconstitutional for a judge to so instruct the jury. The Court held that such a presumption conflicts with the presumption of innocence of the accused and violates the Due Process Clause of the Fourteenth Amendment, which requires that the state prove every element of a criminal offense beyond a reasonable doubt.

Criminal statutes that prohibit particular voluntary acts are generally classified as **general-intent statutes.** General intent means the intent to do that which the law prohibits; an individual need not have intended the precise harm or precise result which eventuated." *State v. Poss,* 298 N.W.2d 80, 83 (S.D. 1980). Statutory words such as "willfully" or "intentionally" generally indicate that the offender must have only intended to do the act and not to accomplish any particular result. Thus, a statute making it the crime of arson to "willfully and unlawfully" set fire to a building is generally viewed as defining a general-intent crime. *Linehan v. State,* 476 So.2d 1262 (Fla. 1985). On the other hand, **specific intent** refers to an actor's mental purpose to accomplish a particular result beyond the act itself. Again, in the context of the crime of arson, suppose the statute read that it was an offense for any person "to willfully and with the intent to injure or defraud an insurance company set fire to any building." In this instance the prosecution would be required to prove that the defendant had the specific intent to injure or defraud an insurance company when the proscribed act was perpetrated. Specific intent is the intent to accomplish the precise act that the law prohibits. *State v. Poss,* 298 N.W.2d 80, 83 (S.D.1980). Again, a statute defining murder that includes the language "premeditated killing of a human being" requires the prosecution to prove the defendant's specific intent. Courts have consistently said that a **specific-intent statute** designates "a special mental element which is required above and beyond any mental state required with respect to the *actus reus* of the crime." See, for example, *State v. Bridgeforth,* 750 P.2d 3, 5 (Ariz. 1988).

Assume that State X charged a defendant with burglary of a dwelling under a specific-intent statute that defines the offense as "the unauthorized entry of a dwelling by a person with the intent to commit theft therein." Three basic elements must be established to convict the defendant. First, the state must prove the defendant made an unauthorized entry. Second, it must prove that the entry was made into a dwelling. Finally, it must establish that the defendant made such unauthorized entry with the intent to commit a theft. Intent, of course, is a state of mind, but it can be (and almost always is) inferred from the defendant's actions and surrounding circumstances. Therefore, if some of the dwelling owner's property had been moved and other items left in disarray, the inference would be that the defendant who made the unauthorized entry intended to commit theft from the dwelling. And this would be true whether the defendant did in fact commit a theft within the dwelling.

The Michigan Supreme Court summed up the difference between specific and general intent in 2000 when it observed that its decisions have held that "the distinction between specific intent and general intent crimes is that the former involve a particular criminal intent beyond the act done, while the latter involve merely the intent to do the physical act." *People v. Nowack,* 614 N.W.2d 78, 84 (Mich. 2000).

In a situation where the defendant might not have had a specific intent to cause a particular result but there was a substantial likelihood of the result occurring, and the act was done with conscious disregard or indifference for the consequences, some courts have developed the concept of **constructive intent** as a substitute for the defendant's specific intent.

The Model Penal Code Approach to Intent

Over the years, the common-law classifications of general and specific intent have become subject to many variations in court decisions in the various jurisdictions. In the chapters of this text that discuss substantive offenses, the reader will find a variety of terms that legislatures and courts have used to describe the *mens rea* requirements of various crimes. Such terms include *unlawfully, feloniously, willfully, maliciously, wrongfully, deliberately, recklessly, negligently, with premeditated intent, with culpable negligence, with gross negligence,* and numerous others.

The wide variety of terms used to describe the mental element of crimes and the dichotomy between general and specific intent have led to considerable difficulty in determining intent requirements in statutory crimes. In 1980 the Supreme Court recognized the common-law classification of crimes as requiring either "general intent" or "specific intent." Nevertheless, the Court pointed out that this distinction has been a continuing source of confusion. The Court suggested the merits of the Model Penal Code classification (referring to the 1962 tentative draft of the MPC) that replaces the term "intent" with a hierarchy of culpable states in a descending order as purpose, knowledge, recklessness, and negligence. *United States v. Bailey,* 444 U.S. 394, 100 S.Ct. 624, 62 L.Ed.2d 575 (1980). However, courts must deal with the intent requirement that legislative bodies include when defining statutory crimes. Thus, in its decision in *Holloway v. United States,* 526 U.S. 1, 119 S.Ct. 966, 143 L.Ed.2d 1 (1999), the Court referred to a federal statute in 18 U.S.C.A. § 2119, which defined carjacking as "tak[ing] a motor vehicle … from … another by force and violence or by intimidation … with the intent to cause death or serious bodily harm," as a law including a specific-intent element (see Supreme Court Perspective below).

Today, almost all crimes are statutory, and in 1985 the American Law Institute published the official draft of the MPC, with some revisions of the earlier tentative draft published in 1962. The MPC rejects the common-law terms for intent. Instead, it simplifies the terms describing culpability and proposes four states of mind: purposely, knowingly, recklessly, and negligently. M.P.C. § 2.02(2). Section 2.02(4) states that the prescribed culpability requirement applies to all material elements of an offense. (The term "purposely" seems to roughly correspond to the common-law specific-intent requirement while other MPC categories seem to fall within the general-intent category.)

Several legislative revisions of state criminal codes have followed the MPC in setting standards of culpability. For example, in 1977 Alabama adopted section 13A-2-2 of its Criminal Code to provide as follows:

The following definitions apply to this Criminal Code:

1. Intentionally. A person acts intentionally with respect to a result or to conduct described by a statute defining an offense, when his purpose is to cause that result or to engage in that conduct.

2. Knowingly. A person acts knowingly with respect to conduct or to a circumstance described by a statute defining an offense when he is aware that his conduct is of that nature or that the circumstance exists.

Holloway v. United States, 526 U.S. 1, 119 S.Ct. 966, 143 L.Ed.2d 1 (1999)

In this case the Supreme Court examines the question of the intent required to establish a violation of the federal carjacking statute. The petitioner was charged with three counts of carjacking in violation of 18 U.S.C. § 2119. In each of the crimes, the petitioner and an armed accomplice approached the driver, produced a gun, and threatened to shoot unless the driver turned over the car keys. At trial, the accomplice testified that the plan was to steal the cars without harming the victims but that he would have used his gun if any of the drivers had given him "a hard time." The trial judge instructed the jury that the intent requisite under section 2119 may be "conditional" and that this element of the offense is met as long as the defendant intended to cause death or serious bodily harm if the victims refused to surrender their automobiles. The conviction was upheld by the Court of Appeals, which rejected the petitioner's view that the trial judge misconceived the *mens rea* requirement under section 2119.

JUSTICE JOHN PAUL STEVENS delivered the opinion of the Court.

The specific issue in this case is what sort of evil motive Congress intended to describe when it used the words "with the intent to cause death or serious bodily harm" in the 1994 amendment to the carjacking statute. More precisely, the question is whether a person who points a gun at a driver, having decided to pull the trigger if the driver does not comply with a demand for the car keys, possesses the intent, at that moment, to seriously harm the driver. In our view, the answer to that question does not depend on whether the driver immediately hands over the keys or what the offender decides to do after he gains control over the car. At the relevant moment, the offender plainly does have the forbidden intent.

The opinions that have addressed this issue accurately point out that a carjacker's intent to harm his victim may be either "conditional" or "unconditional." The statutory phrase at issue theoretically might describe (1) the former, (2) the latter, or (3) both species of intent. Petitioner argues that the "plain text" of the statute "unequivocally" describes only the latter: that the defendant must possess a specific and unconditional intent to kill or harm in order to complete the proscribed offense. To that

end, he insists that Congress would have had to insert the words "if necessary" into the disputed text in order to include the conditional species of intent within the scope of the statute.... Because Congress did not include those words, petitioner contends that we must assume that Congress meant to provide a federal penalty for only those carjackings in which the offender actually attempted to harm or kill the driver (or at least intended to do so whether or not the driver resisted).

We believe, however, that a commonsense reading of the carjacking statute counsels that Congress intended to criminalize a broader scope of conduct than attempts to assault or kill in the course of automobile robberies....

This interpretation of the statute's specific intent element does not, as petitioner suggests, render superfluous the statute's "by force and violence or by intimidation" element. While an empty threat, or intimidating bluff, would be sufficient to satisfy the latter element, such conduct, standing on its own, is not enough to satisfy § 2119's specific intent element. In a carjacking case in which the driver surrendered or otherwise lost control over his car without the defendant attempting to inflict, or actually inflicting, serious bodily harm, Congress' inclusion of the intent element requires the Government to prove beyond a reasonable doubt that the defendant would have at least attempted to seriously harm or kill the driver if that action had been necessary to complete the taking of the car.

In short, we disagree with petitioner's reading of the text of the Act and think it unreasonable to assume that Congress intended to enact such a truncated version of an important criminal statute. The intent requirement of § 2119 is satisfied when the Government proves that at the moment the defendant demanded or took control over the driver's automobile the defendant possessed the intent to seriously harm or kill the driver if necessary to steal the car (or, alternatively, if unnecessary to steal the car). Accordingly, we affirm the judgment of the Court of Appeals.

JUSTICE ANTONIN SCALIA, dissenting.

This seems to me not a difficult case. The issue before us is not whether the "intent" element of some common-law crime developed by the courts themselves—or even the "intent" element of a statute that replicates the common-law definition—includes, or should include, conditional

(continued)

Holloway v. United States (continued)

intent. Rather, it is whether the English term "intent" used in a statute defining a brand new crime bears a meaning that contradicts normal usage. Since it is quite impossible to say that longstanding, agreed-upon legal usage has converted this word into a term of art, the answer has to be no. And it would be no even if the question were doubtful. I think it particularly inadvisable to introduce the new possibility of "conditional-intent" prosecutions into a modern federal criminal-law system characterized by plea bargaining, where they will predictably be used for in terrorem effect. I respectfully dissent.

JUSTICE CLARENCE THOMAS, dissenting.

I cannot accept the majority's interpretation of the term "intent" in 18 U.S.C. § 2119 to include the concept of conditional intent. The central difficulty in this case is that the text is silent as to the meaning of "intent"—the carjacking statute does not define that word, and Title 18 of the United States Code, unlike some state codes, lacks a general section defining intent to include conditional intent.... As the majority notes, there is some authority to support its view that the specific intent to commit an act may be conditional. In my view, that authority does not demonstrate that such a usage was part of a well-established historical tradition. Absent a more settled tradition, it cannot be presumed that Congress was familiar with this usage when it enacted the statute. For these reasons, I agree with Justice Scalia the statute cannot be read to include the concept of conditional intent and, therefore, respectfully dissent.

3. Recklessly. A person acts recklessly with respect to a result or to a circumstance described by a statute defining an offense when he is aware of and consciously disregards a substantial and unjustifiable risk that the result will occur or that the circumstance exists. The risk must be of such nature and degree that disregard thereof constitutes a gross deviation from the standard of conduct that a reasonable person would observe in the situation. A person who creates a risk but is unaware thereof solely by reason of voluntary intoxication, as defined in subdivision (e)(2) of Section 13A-3-2, acts recklessly with respect thereto.

4. Criminal negligence. A person acts with criminal negligence with respect to a result or to a circumstance which is defined by statute as an offense when he fails to perceive a substantial and unjustifiable risk that the result will occur or that the circumstance exists. The risk must be of such nature and degree that the failure to perceive it constitutes a gross deviation from the standard of care that a reasonable person would observe in the situation. A court or jury may consider statutes or ordinances regulating the defendant's conduct as bearing upon the question of criminal negligence.

Commentary following section 13A-2-2 points out that this section "is derived principally from Michigan Revised Criminal Code § 305, which followed New York Penal Law § 15.05, which in turn is based on the Model Penal Code § 2.02." Some other states have essentially adopted the MPC proposals, but, like Alabama, several have opted to use the term "intentionally" instead of the MPC term "purposely." This difference appears to be only one of terminology.

Section 13A-6-3 of Alabama's Criminal Code now begins defining "manslaughter" by stating, in part, that "[a] person commits the crime of manslaughter if (1) He recklessly causes the death of another person ... ," whereas a state that has not adopted the MPC classifications might define manslaughter in terms of "an unlawful killing of a person by culpable negligence" or "a killing of a human being without malice aforethought."

In addition to understanding traditional concepts of general and specific intent, a student should become acquainted with previously quoted sections of the MPC that define "act" and relate to levels of culpability. While these are among the most widely relied-on provisions of the MPC, in later chapters dealing with substantive crimes we

The *Mens Rea* Requirement

The defendant was convicted under a statute that made it an offense to fondle or caress the body of a child less than sixteen years "with the intent to gratify the sexual desires or appetites of the offending person or … to frighten or excite such child." On appeal, the Indiana Supreme Court noted that the strongest evidence in favor of the prosecution was that both the defendant's daughters admitted that during playfulness the father touched and came in contact with the breasts of one of his daughters. However, there was no evidence that this was done with the intent to gratify the sexual desires of the defendant or to frighten the child.

In reversing the defendant's conviction, the court observed that "[a] crime has two components—an evil intent coupled with an overt act. The act alone does not constitute the crime unless it is done with a specific intent declared unlawful by the statute in this state.… There must also be proved beyond a reasonable doubt, the specific intent at the time of touching to gratify sexual desires or to frighten the child as stated in the statute."

Markiton v. State, 139 N.E.2d 440 (Ind. 1957).

refer to instances where the MPC has been influential in the revision of criminal statutes.

In 1978 Arizona adopted the four culpable mental states of intention, knowledge, recklessness, and criminal negligence, as defined in A.R.S. § 13-105; M.P.C. § 2.02(2). These replaced all previous mental states used in Arizona's criminal laws. See *State v. Robles*, 623 P.2d 1245, 1246 (Ariz. App.1981).

The Doctrine of Transferred Intent

The **doctrine of transferred intent** transfers an actor's original intent against an intended victim to an unintended victim who suffers the consequences. An English court invoked the doctrine in 1576 in the classic case *Regina v. Saunders & Archer*, 75 Eng. Rep. 706, where Saunders gave his wife a poisoned apple. After tasting it but suffering no consequences, the wife gave the apple to her daughter, who died from the poison. The court found that Saunders caused his daughter's death despite the fact he intended no harm to her. American courts apply the doctrine primarily in assaultive and homicide cases, often referred to as the "missed aim" cases, but it can apply to other crimes such as, for example, arson. Because the doctrine supplies an intent to commit a crime against a person where no such intent existed, it is often referred to as a "legal fiction." It is designed to avoid an otherwise unjust result by obviating the need for the prosecution to establish that it was predictable an accused's actions would have caused harm to an unintended victim. Instead of following the doctrine of transferred intent, the MPC deals with such a situation on the basis of causation. M.P.C. Sec. 2.02(2)(a).

In *State v. Gardner*, 203 A.2d 77 (Del. 1964), the Delaware Supreme Court ruled that where a defendant whose express malice aforethought was directed toward an intended victim but not in fact toward the actual victim who was killed, a defendant can nevertheless be convicted of first-degree murder. The court noted that courts in the great majority of other states consider the defendant guilty of the same crime as if the defendant had accomplished the original purpose. As more recently explained by the North Carolina Supreme Court,

[U]nder the doctrine of transferred intent, it is immaterial whether the defendant intended injury to the person actually harmed; if he in fact acted with the required or elemental intent toward someone, that intent suffices as the intent element of the crime charged as a matter of substantive law. *State v. Locklear,* 415 S.E.2d 726, 730 (N.C. 1992).

Most transferred intent cases involve homicides. As the doctrine developed, some courts expressed disagreement as to whether a defendant's specific intent to kill an individual is transferred to an unintended victim. But even if the actor's *specific intent* is not transferred, the killing of an unintended victim can be prosecuted as a homicidal crime or other offense not requiring proof of the defendant's specific intent. Because the doctrine is designed to punish an offender who "misses aim" and kills or injures an unintended victim, jurisdictions have split on whether it also applies when the accused kills or injures both the intended and the unintended victims. Some courts reason that it is unnecessary to apply the doctrine in such cases. But in *Poe v. State,* 671 A.2d 501 (Md. 1996), Maryland's highest court held that the doctrine of transferred intent applied where the defendant, intending to kill a woman, fired a shot that wounded the woman who was targeted, passed through her, and killed a child standing nearby.

The Importance of Determining the Intent Required

There are two reasons why it is essential to determine whether a particular offense is a general-intent or a specific-intent crime or, in some recent statutory revisions, whether it meets the MPC culpability requirements. First, the intent requirement in a criminal statute determines the extent of proof that must be offered by the prosecution. Second, as we will explain in later chapters, in certain crimes the intent required to be proven determines whether particular defenses are available to the defendant.

Strict Liability Offenses

As we previously noted, common-law crimes consist of a criminal act or omission known as the *actus reus* and the mental element known as the *mens rea.* However, legislative bodies have the power to dispense with the necessity for the mental element and authorize punishment of particular acts without regard to the actor's intent (see Figure 4.1). Such crimes are known as strict liability offenses.

As we pointed out in Chapter 1, **mala in se offenses** are inherent wrongs, whereas **mala prohibita offenses** are considered wrongs because they are so defined by the law. In such common-law felonies as murder, rape, robbery, and larceny, the proscribed conduct is considered *mala in se,* and the intent is deemed inherent in the offense. This holds true today even if the statute proscribing such conduct fails to specify intent as an element of the offense.

Many of the *mala prohibita* crimes are defined as strict liability offenses. For the most part, these include "regulatory" or "public welfare" types of offenses, which often are tailored to address public safety, environmental, and public health concerns. We see some of the earliest examples of strict liability in cases involving the sale of liquor and adulterated milk. Examples of strict liability laws today include mostly traffic regulations, food and drug laws, and laws prohibiting the sale of liquor and cigarettes to minors. Strict liability offenses now constitute a substantial part of the criminal law.

The fact that a statute is silent on the matter of criminal intent does not necessarily mean that it defines a strict liability offense. If the prohibited conduct falls

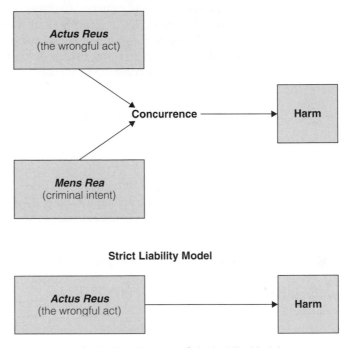

FIGURE 4.1   Elements of a Crime: Traditional and Strict Liability Models

Go to the Scheb/
Scheb Criminal Law
and Procedure 6e
website at academic
.cengage.com/criminaljustice/
scheb for an edited version of
Morrisette v. U.S.

within a traditional common-law crime category, courts will likely interpret such statutes to contain a *mens rea* requirement. For example, in *Morissette v. United States,* 342 U.S. 246, 72 S.Ct. 240, 96 L.Ed. 288 (1952), the defendant had been convicted of violating federal law by taking some old bomb casings from a government bombing range. At trial, the district court refused to instruct the jury on the issue of intent, in effect holding that the government was required to prove only the defendant's act, not his intent, because the statute required proof of only the prohibited act. The Supreme Court reversed Morissette's conviction. The Court held that the crime for which he was prosecuted was a variant of the common-law offense of larceny and that failure to include the intent requirement in the statute did not eliminate the element of intent.

In *United States v. United States Gypsum Co.,* 438 U.S. 422, 98 S.Ct. 2864, 57 L.Ed.2d 854 (1978), the Supreme Court was called on to decide whether a criminal violation of the Sherman Act required proof of criminal intent or whether intent may be presumed conclusively from the anticompetitive effect of the defendants' actions. Despite the fact that the Sherman Act does not use the words "willfully" or "knowingly," the Court held that intent is an essential element of a criminal antitrust offense and must be established not only by proof of anticompetitive effects but by proof that the defendants had knowledge that the proscribed effects were probable.

Critics of strict liability offenses argue that they run counter to the standards of criminal culpability. Others argue that it is desirable to classify these offenses as regulatory or administrative, thereby removing the "criminal" stigma. Still others counter that to remove the criminal aspect from these offenses would remove their deterrent factor. One thing seems certain: In a rapidly urbanizing, technological society with increased awareness of the necessity to protect the public health, safety, and environment, strict liability offenses will become even more prominent.

In the chapters that follow, note that as penalties for statutory offenses become heavier, courts are more reluctant to dispense with proof of intent. This is true in environmental crimes (see Chapter 11) and in some serious motor vehicle violations. For example, many state courts have addressed the issue of whether proof of a criminal intent is necessary to convict someone of the statutory crime of driving with a revoked or suspended license. In *Jeffcoat v. State,* 639 P.2d 308 (Alaska App. 1982), the Alaska Court of Appeals held that even though the statute is silent, the element of *mens rea* must be read into it by implication. In *State v. Keihn,* 542 N.E.2d 963 (Ind. 1989), the Indiana Supreme Court agreed that in a prosecution for driving with a suspended license, the State was required to prove the defendant's knowledge of the suspension. However, in 1998 the Connecticut Supreme Court disagreed with the Indiana Supreme Court's decision in *State v. Keihn* and held that actual knowledge of a license suspension is not an essential element of the crime of operating a motor vehicle with a suspended license as long as there was proof of a bulk certified mailing of the suspension notice. *State v. Swain,* 718 A.2d 1 (Conn. 1998).

The Causation Requirement

When an offense is defined in a manner that a specific result must occur, the concept of **causation** becomes important. This is most commonly associated with homicide offenses. For example, the various degrees of homicide require that to be guilty of murder or manslaughter, the accused's conduct must have resulted in the death of a human being. Sometimes lawyers refer to legal causation as **proximate cause,** defined as "a cause that in a natural, continuous sequence, unbroken by any intervening causes, produces the consequences that occur." Proximate cause is satisfied if the result that occurs was foreseeable. Sometimes the "but for" test is employed here, meaning that "but for" the accused's actions, the harm would not have occurred. This can be illustrated by an instance where, but for the accused's firing a pistol, the victim would not have been killed. But suppose the victim was only slightly injured by the accused's having fired a pistol and was later taken to a hospital, where through the negligence of health care providers the victim died. If the victim's death occurred from such an intervening cause, it would likely result in the perpetrator's being charged with a lesser offense such as assault with a dangerous weapon.

Although causation is important in many crimes to link the elements of the accused's act and intent, in Chapter 5 we will study the incomplete offenses of attempt, solicitation, and conspiracy, which are classified as inchoate (incomplete) offenses. These offenses, among others that we will later study, do not require that certain specified results occur.

Parties to a Crime

Historically, the common law classified parties to crimes as either principals or accessories. Principals were persons whose conduct involved direct participation in a crime; accessories were **accomplices** or those who gave aid and comfort to principals. The common law classified crimes other than treason as felonies and misdemeanors. Felonies were very serious; in fact, at times, a person found guilty of a felony could be deprived of all worldly possessions and suffer either death or lengthy imprisonment. Because of the serious nature of felonious conduct and because all persons involved might not be equally guilty, the common law developed several technical distinctions among the various participants.

Common-Law Distinctions Among Participants in Crime

To comprehend present criminal law regarding participants in a crime, a basic knowledge of the common-law scheme is essential. At common law, a person directly involved in committing a felony was classified as a principal; a person whose conduct did not involve direct participation was classified as an accessory. Principals were further classified by the degree of their participation. A person who directly or through the acts of an innocent agent actually committed the crime was a principal in the first degree. A principal in the second degree was a person not directly involved but actually or constructively present at the commission of the crime who aided and abetted the perpetrator. To be constructively present, one had to be sufficiently close to render assistance to the perpetrator. For example, suppose a man led a woman's escort away from her so that another man could sexually attack the woman. The man who led the escort away would probably be constructively present and would be classified as a principal in the second degree because he was **aiding and abetting** a crime. Aiding and abetting another in the commission of a crime means assenting to an act or lending countenance or approval, either by active participation in it or by encouraging it in some other manner.

An accessory at common law was classified as either an accessory before or after the fact. An accessory before the fact was one who procured or counseled another to commit a felony but who was not actually or constructively present at the commission of the offense. An accessory after the fact was one who, with knowledge of the other's guilt, rendered assistance to a felon in an effort to hinder the felon's arrest or punishment.

Because misdemeanors were far less serious than felonies, the common law found it unnecessary to distinguish between participants in misdemeanor offenses. As with treason, all participants in misdemeanors were regarded as principals.

Accessories to felonies were not regarded as being as culpable as the principals, so they were punished less severely at common law. Moreover, under the common law there were some procedural distinctions applicable to principals and accessories; for example, a party had to be charged as a principal or as an accessory. The principal had to be tried first, and if the principal were found not guilty, the accessory could not be tried for the offense.

The Modern American Approach

The American approach has been to abolish both the substantive and procedural distinctions between principals and accessories before the fact. Federal law stipulates that "[w]hoever commits an offense against the United States or aids, abets, counsels, commands, induces, or procures its commission, is punishable as a principal...." 18 U.S.C.A. § 2(a). The federal statute reflects the law of most of the states insofar as it abolishes the distinction between principals and accessories before the fact. As early as 1872, California enacted a statute defining principals as "all persons concerned in the commission of a crime, whether it be felony or misdemeanor, and whether they directly commit the act constituting the offense, or aid and abet in its commission, or, not being present, have advised and encouraged its commission." West's Ann. Cal. Penal Code § 31. As explained by the Supreme Court of Appeals of West Virginia in *State v. Fortner*, 387 S.E.2d 812, 822 (W.Va. 1989),

Being an accessory before the fact or a principal in the second degree is not, of itself, a separate crime, but is a basis for finding liability for the underlying crime.... In essence, evidence of such complicity simply establishes an alternative theory of criminal liability, i.e., another way of committing the underlying substantive offense.

The common-law distinction between principals and accessories before the fact has been largely abolished, but the concept of accessory after the fact as a separate offense has been retained by many jurisdictions. Modern statutes view an accessory after the fact as less culpable than someone who plans, assists, or commits a crime. Thus, statutes generally define being an accessory after the fact as a separate offense and provide for a less severe punishment. See, for example, West's Ann. Cal. Penal Code § 33. In most states, a lawful conviction as an accessory after the fact requires proof that a person knew that the person he or she aided or assisted had committed a felony. The gist of being an accessory after the fact lies essentially in obstructing justice, and a person is guilty who knows that an offense has been committed and receives, relieves, comforts, or assists the offender to hinder his or her apprehension, trial, or punishment. *United States v. Brown*, 33 F.3d 1002 (8th Cir. 1994). However, federal law does not distinguish whether the person assisted has committed a felony or a misdemeanor. 18 U.S.C.A. § 3.

The common law rule that a woman who gave comfort and aid to her husband was exempt from being an accessory after the fact no longer prevails, yet some state statutes exempt spouses and other classes of relatives from penalty for being accessories after the fact. For example, Florida law has long prevented the prosecution as an accessory after the fact of any person standing in the relation of husband or wife, parent or grandparent, child or grandchild, or brother or sister, either by blood or marriage. West's Fla. Stat. Ann. § 777.03(1)(a). In 1999 the legislature amended the statute to add that, regardless of relation to the offender, a person who maintains or assists a principal or accessory before the fact knowing the offender has committed child abuse or a related offense is subject to prosecution as an accessory after the fact unless the court finds that such person is a victim of domestic violence. West's Fla. Stat. Ann. § 777.03(1)(b).

Defendant with Intent to Commit Felony Convicted as an Accomplice Irrespective of Active Participation in Killing a Victim

Defendant Vernell Dixon appealed his conviction of capital felony murder that occurred during the course of an aggravated robbery. He argued that his conviction should not stand because the evidence showed that he did not take an active part in the killing of the victim.

In rejecting Dixon's argument the Arkansas Supreme Court observed: "A defendant must only have the requisite intent for the underlying felony. Substantial evidence established defendant as an accomplice to the underlying aggravated robbery, and it was committed under circumstances manifesting extreme indifference to the value of human life. Under the capital

murder statute, Ark. Code Ann. § 5-10-101(a)(1) (Repl.1993), it is not necessary that the State show that the defendant took an active part in the killing so long as he assisted in the commission of the underlying crime.... A defendant must only have the requisite intent for the underlying felony.... The proof showed that [the defendant] was an accomplice and had the requisite intent for the aggravated robbery, supplied the .25 caliber pistol used in the robbery, and was present when the victim was killed in the course of the robbery. Such proof is sufficient to sustain the conviction for capital felony murder."

Dixon v. State, 891 S.W.2d 59 (Ark. 1995).

■ CONCLUSION

The concepts discussed in this chapter, though technical, are basic to an understanding of the criminal law in the United States. At this stage, concepts like *actus reus* and the *mens rea* may seem abstract, but they will become more concrete in later chapters as we relate them to specific offenses.

Common-law crimes were considered *mala in se,* or wrongs in themselves, and required proof of a general or specific intent. The classification of intent as being general or specific remains viable; however, in some criminal code revisions today, these traditional categories of intent are being replaced by categories of culpability recommended by the MPC. In contrast, many modern statutory offenses are classified as *mala prohibita*—that is, they are offenses simply because a legislative body has classified them as wrongs, and they are considered strict liability crimes. Yet even where a statute describes a strict liability crime, courts will imply an intent requirement if the crime is basically of common-law origin or imposes a heavy punishment.

The elements of crimes discussed in this chapter will be relevant throughout the text. In contrast, except for the offense of being an accessory after the fact, the common-law designation of parties to crimes is largely of historical importance. This is because modern criminal law generally treats parties who are complicit to crimes as principals, whether perpetrators or accomplices. Society has found this approach necessary, and this principle has become firmly ingrained in modern criminal law.

■ KEY TERMS

principals, 74	general-intent statutes, 79
accessories before the fact, 74	specific intent, 79
accessories after the fact, 74	specific-intent statute, 79
act of omission, 75	constructive intent, 80
administrative-type act, 76	doctrine of transferred intent, 80
possession, 76	*mala in se* offenses, 80
actual possession, 77	*mala prohibita* offenses, 82
constructive possession, 77	causation, 82
status, 77	proximate cause, 83
motive, 78	accomplices, 84
general intent, 78	aiding and abetting, 84

■ WEB-BASED RESEARCH ACTIVITY

 Go to the web. Locate your state's criminal statutes (or another state's if yours are not available online). Determine whether your state uses Model Penal Code terminology ("purposely," "knowingly," "recklessly," and "negligently") in defining criminal intent. Download examples of crime definitions using the MPC terminology.

■ QUESTIONS FOR THOUGHT AND DISCUSSION

1. Distinguish between the concepts of motive and intent in the criminal law. Can you cite an instance where, despite good motives, a person would be guilty of a crime?

2. What justifies the criminal law making mere possession of contraband articles illegal? Do you think this rationale extends to criminalizing the mere possession of

such innocent items as a screwdriver, a pair of pliers, or an ice pick that could be used to commit burglary?

3. Given the fact that the common-law requirement of intent is not an element of strict liability crimes, what rationale supports legislative enactment of such offenses?

4. Should the criminal law punish a person whose mere carelessness, as opposed to willfulness, causes harm to another?

5. Is there a justification for the criminal law not punishing a person for failing to act when there is a clear moral duty to act?

6. Has the moral integrity of the criminal law been jeopardized by the increasing number of offenses for which a person can be convicted without proof of any criminal intent?

7. Why has the common-law doctrine distinguishing between principals and accessories before the fact diminished in importance in contemporary criminal law?

8. Contrast an offense that requires proof of causation with one that does not.

9. Is it fair to assess the same degree of fault and impose the same punishment on an accomplice as on a perpetrator? What rationale supports your conclusion?

10. Is there a valid reason to exempt close family relatives from punishment as accessories after the fact to felonious conduct?

■ PROBLEMS FOR DISCUSSION AND SOLUTION

1. Sol Toolmaker visited his long-time friend, I. N. Mate, a prisoner in a state institution. Mate had previously told Toolmaker how much he wanted to escape from the prison. So on this occasion, Toolmaker brought Mate two small saws. Mate hid the saws in a place where he thought the prison guards would not find them, but the guards promptly discovered and confiscated the saws. The warden turned this evidence over to the prison's legal counsel with a request that charges be prepared against Mate for attempting to escape from prison. Assuming Mate intended to escape from prison, did his conduct constitute a criminal act?

2. Alice Alpha had a long-standing grievance against Benjamin Beta and had threatened to kill him. When Alpha saw Beta standing on a street corner amidst a crowd of people, Alpha pulled a gun and fired a shot. The bullet grazed Beta's arm, injuring him slightly. But it struck and killed Gerry Gamma, who was unknown to Alpha. Considering the concepts discussed in this chapter, what crime or crimes has Alpha committed?

CHAPTER 5

Inchoate Offenses

CHAPTER OUTLINE

Introduction
Attempt
Solicitation
Conspiracy

Introduction

The word "inchoate" means "underdeveloped" or "unripened." Thus, an **inchoate offense** is one involving activity or steps directed toward the completion of a crime. There are three such offenses: attempt, solicitation, and conspiracy. These are not crimes in themselves; rather there must be an attempt to commit a crime—for example, attempted murder—the solicitation of someone to commit a crime, or a conspiracy to commit an offense—for example, to sell contraband. Although preparatory to the commission of other offenses, they are separate and distinct crimes. During the 1800s each was recognized as a misdemeanor at English common law, too late to become a part of the common law under the reception statutes adopted by most new American states. Most American jurisdictions now define these offenses by statute, frequently classifying them as felonies.

The development of the law in this area has been primarily through the courts. Courts have often found difficulty in determining when mere preparatory activity has reached the stage of criminal conduct. Yet, by recognizing an actor's design toward commission of an offense, the law permits police to apprehend dangerous persons who have not yet accomplished their criminal objectives, thereby affording them an opportunity to terminate such conduct at an early stage.

Attempt

Attempt is the most frequently charged of the inchoate crimes. Attempt, of course, means an effort to accomplish a particular purpose. As the Tennessee Supreme Court has explained, "An attempt, by nature, is a failure to accomplish what one intended to do." *State v. Kimbrough,* 924 S.W.2d 888 (Tenn. 1996). State penal codes often specifically provide for attempts to commit the most serious crimes, such as murder. The remaining offenses are then covered by a general attempt statute. A typical statute that covers all attempts provides that "[w]hoever attempts to commit an offense prohibited by law and in such attempt does any act toward the commission of such an offense, but fails in the perpetration or is intercepted or prevented in the execution of the same, commits the offense of criminal attempt." West's Fla. Stat. Ann. § 777.04(1). The "act" requirement contemplates an **overt act** that constitutes a **substantial step** toward the commission of an offense. Although the quoted statute makes no distinction between felony or misdemeanor offenses, statutes in some states limit the crime of attempt to attempts to commit felonies or certain specified crimes.

No specific federal statute proscribes or defines attempts generally; rather, various statutes focus on attempts to commit specific offenses. For example, Title 18 U.S.C.A. § 1113 proscribes attempts to commit murder or manslaughter. In general, federal courts have recognized the requisite elements of attempt as (1) an intent to engage in criminal conduct and (2) the performance of an act that constitutes a substantial step toward the completion of the substantive offense. See *United States v. Manley,* 632 F.2d 978 (2d Cir. 1980). This follows the Model Penal Code Section 5.01 view that the requisite elements of attempt are intent to engage in criminal conduct and the performance of acts, which constitute a "substantial step" toward the commission of the substantive offense. *United States v. Jackson,* 560 F.2d 112 (2d Cir. 1977).

The Act Requirement

As we have noted, the "act" element in the crime of attempt requires an act that constitutes a substantial step toward the commission of an offense; that is, it must be conduct beyond mere preparation. The Model Penal Code distinguishes **preparatory conduct** from an attempt. It allows conviction for the crime of attempt, where the actor engages in "an act or omission constituting a substantial step in a course of conduct planned to culminate in the commission of the crime." M.P.C. § 501 (1)(c). Federal courts apply this test. In *United States v. Mandujano*, 499 F.2d 370, 376 (5th Cir. 1974), the court observed, "A substantial step must be conduct strongly corroborative of the firmness of the defendant's criminal intent." Where multiple intentions underlie an act, one act may establish several different criminal attempts. For example, in *State v. Walker*, 804 P.2d 1164 (Or. 1991), the court held that the defendant's conduct established an attempt to commit kidnapping, rape, and sodomy.

Many state statutes also include the term "substantial step" in defining the act requirement. Where they do not, courts usually imply that the act must constitute a substantial step toward the commission of a substantive offense. In either instance, it becomes necessary to distinguish between mere preparatory acts of planning or arranging means to commit a crime and those acts that constitute a direct movement toward the commission of an offense. Appellate courts have taken various approaches as to how close that act must be to accomplishment of the intended crime. This issue frequently turns on the specific factual situation involved. An early, and demanding, test held that an actor must have engaged in the "last proximate act necessary to accomplish the intended crime," but most courts have now rejected that test and apply a more realistic test that the actor's conduct must be "within dangerous proximity to success." An Illinois decision is illustrative. Two men armed with guns were found hiding behind a service station. One had a black nylon stocking in his pocket. The Illinois Supreme Court affirmed their convictions for attempted armed robbery because it found their act of "lying in wait … reconnoitering the place contemplated for the commission of the crime [while in] possession of materials to be employed in the commission of the crime." The court found their conduct sufficient to constitute a substantial step toward the commission of armed robbery. *People v. Terrell*, 459 N.E.2d 1337 (Ill. 1984).

New York courts have summed it up in a practical manner, opining simply that an accused's conduct must be "very near" to the completion of the intended crime. *People v. Mahboubian*, 543 N.E.2d 34 (N.Y. 1989).

CASE-IN-POINT

What Constitutes an Overt Act beyond the Preparation Stage?

A defendant was found guilty of attempting to escape from prison. He appealed, contending the state failed to prove beyond a reasonable doubt that he had committed an overt act as required by law. He characterized his actions as preparatory steps indicative only of an intention to attempt an escape. The Supreme Judicial Court of Maine recognized that the State must prove more than mere preparation; it must prove "a positive action … directed towards the execution of the crime." Yet the court rejected his contention and affirmed his conviction, stating: "[T]here was undisputed evidence that a dummy was found in defendant's cell; that defendant was in an unauthorized area attempting to conceal his presence; and that a rope ladder was found in a paper bag close to where he was concealed. [Defendant] had gone far beyond the preparation stage."

State v. Charbonneau, 374 A.2d 321, 322 (Me. 1977).

The Requisite Criminal Intent

To find a defendant guilty of the crime of attempt, most courts require the prosecution to prove that the defendant had a specific intent to commit the intended offense, frequently referred to as the **target crime.** See, for example, *Thacker v. Commonwealth,* 114 S.E. 504 (Va. 1922); *State v. Earp,* 571 A.2d 1227 (Md. 1990). The rationale for this view is that it is logically impossible to attempt an unintended result. But the specific intent requirement raises an issue on which courts disagree: Can a person intend to commit a crime by unintentionally causing a result? Because specific intent is not an element of certain offenses, for example, manslaughter, some courts hold that a defendant cannot be convicted of an attempt to commit such a crime. See, for example, *State v. Zupetz,* 322 N.W.2d 730 (Minn. 1982). Other courts hold that if the prosecution is not required to show a defendant's specific intent to successfully prosecute the completed crime, it is not required to establish specific intent to successfully prosecute an attempt to commit such a crime. In *Gentry v. State,* 437 So.2d 1097 (Fla.1983), the Florida Supreme Court held: "If the state is not required to show specific intent to successfully prosecute the completed crime, it will not be required to show specific intent to successfully prosecute an attempt to commit that crime." In any event, courts require at least the level of intent that must be established in proof of the target crime.

Attempts in Relation to Substantive Crimes

When a criminal attempt completes a substantive crime, the attempt usually merges into the target offense. The actor is then guilty of the substantive crime, rather than merely an attempt to commit it. Thus, a person who is successful in an attempt to commit murder is guilty of murder. However, there can be no attempt to commit certain crimes because some substantive offenses by definition embrace an attempt. To illustrate, consider the statutory crime of uttering a forged instrument. Statutes usually define the crime as including an attempt to pass a forged instrument to someone to obtain something of value. Therefore, one who makes such an attempt would be guilty of uttering a forged instrument, not merely an attempt to do so. In effect, the attempt is subsumed by the very definition of the substantive crime. Needless to say, it would be redundant to charge someone with attempting to attempt to commit a given crime.

Defenses to the Crime of Attempt

The Model Penal Code proposes that an accused who "purposely engages in conduct that would constitute the crime if the attendant circumstances were as he believed them to be" is guilty of an attempt. M.P.C. § 5.01(1)(a). Although many state statutes track this Model Penal Code language, it raises the issue of whether the law should pursue a conviction for an attempt to commit a crime that is impossible to commit.

The rule developed in most jurisdictions is that **legal impossibility** is a defense to the crime of attempt but that **factual impossibility** is not. The distinction can be very close. For example, attempted rape requires a human victim. Therefore, a man who assaults a mannequin dressed as a woman would not be guilty of attempted rape because it would be legally impossible to commit that offense. Yet this example must be distinguished from the classic illustration in *State v. Mitchell,* 71 S.W. 175 (Mo. 1902). There, a man was held responsible for attempted murder when he shot into the room in which his target usually slept but who, fortuitously, was sleeping elsewhere in the house at the time of the shooting. Although the bullet struck the target's customary pillow, attainment of the criminal objective was factually impossible. Likewise, a person who picks another's pocket intending to steal money may be found guilty of attempted theft even if the victim's pocket is empty. In these instances courts have said that although it was factually impossible to commit the crime, it was legally possible to do so.

New York law now provides that it is no defense to a prosecution that the crime charged to have been attempted was either factually or legally impossible to commit if it could have been committed had the circumstances been what the defendant believed them to be. McKinney's N.Y. Penal Law § 110.10; *People v. Davis,* 526 N.E.2d 20 (N.Y. 1988). The trend is toward finding an attempt to commit a crime in instances where the actor's intent has been frustrated merely because of some factor unknown at the time. Thus, if the accused believed a victim was alive when the accused shot at the victim, it follows that such an attempt to kill a dead person would constitute an attempt under New York law. *People v. Dlugash,* 363 N.E.2d 1155 (N.Y. 1977).

Some jurisdictions have laws providing that it is a defense to the crime of attempt if the defendant abandons an attempt to commit an offense or otherwise prevents its consummation. See, for example, Vernon's Tex. Ann. Penal Code § 15.04(a). Where recognized as a defense, abandonment must be wholly voluntary. It cannot be the result of any outside cause such as the appearance of the police on the scene. See, for example, *People v. Walker,* 191 P.2d 10 (Cal. 1948).

Solicitation

By the 1800s, the English common law specified that a person who counseled, incited, or solicited another to commit either a felony or a misdemeanor involving breach of the peace committed the offense of **solicitation.** A person who solicited another to commit a crime was guilty of solicitation even if the crime counseled, incited, or solicited was not committed. The offense of solicitation is now defined by statute in most American jurisdictions. Numerous federal statutes define solicitation as a crime in various contexts. See, for example, Title 18 U.S.C.A. § 373 proscribing solicitation to commit a crime of violence.

Conviction under federal law requires the solicitation to be of a federal offense. *United States v. Korab,* 893 F.2d 212 (9th Cir. 1989). In explaining why its penal code makes solicitation an offense, a California appellate court offered two reasons: first, to protect individuals from being exposed to inducement to commit or join in the commission of crime, and second, to prevent solicitation from resulting in the commission of the crime solicited. *People v. Cook,* 199 Cal. Rptr. 269 (Cal. App. 1984).

The Act Requirement

The request, command, or enticement constitutes the *actus reus* required for solicitation. The statutory definition of solicitation in Illinois is typical: "A person commits solicitation when, with intent that an offense be committed, other than first-degree murder, he commands, encourages, or requests another to commit the offense." 720 I.L.C.S. 5/8-1.1, Il. Stat. Ch. 720 § 5/8-1.1. (A separate statute defines solicitation for first-degree murder.) The gist of the offense is the solicitation itself, so the offender may be found guilty irrespective of whether the solicited crime is ever committed.

Commission of the crime of solicitation does not require direct solicitation of another; it may be perpetrated through an intermediary. Thus, if Abel solicits Barnes to solicit Cummings to commit a crime, Abel would be liable even though he did not directly contact Cummings because Abel's solicitation of Barnes itself involves the commission of the offense.

Is an Uncommunicated Solicitation an Offense?

The Model Penal Code states, "It is immaterial … that the actor fails to communicate with the person he solicits to commit a crime if his conduct was designed to effect such communication." M.P.C. § 5.02(2). Nevertheless, courts have been reluctant to uphold a conviction of solicitation where there has been no communication of the solicitation to the intended solicitee. For example, in *State v. Cotton,* 790 P.2d 1050 (N.M. App. 1990), the New Mexico Court of Appeals explained that the language of its criminal code describes the offense of criminal solicitation in a manner that differs in several material respects from the Model Penal Code by specifically omitting that portion of the Model Penal Code subsection that declares an uncommunicated solicitation to commit a crime may constitute the offense of criminal solicitation. Thus the court concluded that the legislative intent was to require some form of actual communication from the defendant to either an intermediary or the intended solicitee. In *People v. Saephanh,* 94 Cal.Rptr.2d 910 (Cal. App. 2000), a corrections officer intercepted the defendant's letter of solicitation to commit murder. In a case of first impression, a California appellate court held that solicitation of murder requires receipt of solicitation by the intended recipient. The court, however, held that the defendant could be convicted of attempted solicitation of murder.

The Requisite Criminal Intent

The statutory language making solicitation a crime might not seem to require the prosecution to establish the defendant's specific intent. However, most courts hold that to commit solicitation, the solicitor must have specifically intended to induce or entice the

CASE-IN-POINT

When Is the Crime of Solicitation Committed?

Defendant Roger Gardner, an alleged contract killer, subcontracted the killing of Alvin Blum to a man named Tim McDonald for a fee of $10,000. Gardner met with McDonald and gave him some expense money, a gun, and ammunition. In talking with McDonald, Gardner said that he (Gardner) would first kill a man named Hollander, and if this did not create the desired result, then McDonald would be directed to kill Blum. Gardner's attempts were foiled when he was arrested and charged with solicitation to murder. It turned out that McDonald was a police informant whose assistance led to Gardner's arrest.

On appeal, Gardner argued that he did not commit the crime of solicitation because he did not actually direct McDonald to proceed with the murder of Blum or pay him all of the money he had promised. In affirming Gardner's conviction, the Maryland Court of Appeals said "the crime of solicitation was committed when he asked McDonald to commit the murder." The Court explained that "[n]either a final direction to proceed nor fulfillment of conditions precedent (paying of the money) was required." In holding that the crime of solicitation was committed, the Court observed that "[t]he gist of the offense is incitement."

Gardner v. State, 408 A.2d 1317, 1322 (Md. 1979).

person solicited to commit the target offense. See, for example, *Kimbrough v. State,* 544 So.2d 177 (Ala. Crim. App. 1989). If the particular jurisdiction does not require proof of the defendant's specific intent, the prosecution must at least establish that the actor who solicits someone to commit a crime had the requisite intent for the crime solicited.

Solicitation Distinguished from Other Inchoate Crimes

The offenses of solicitation and attempt are different crimes, analytically distinct in their elements. Although each is an inchoate offense, solicitation is complete when the request or enticement to complete the intended offense is made, and it is immaterial if the solicitee agrees, if the offense is carried out, or if no steps are taken toward consummation of the offense. In contrast, mere solicitation is generally not sufficient to constitute an attempt because attempt requires proof of an overt act to commit the intended criminal act. This principle was succinctly explained by the Idaho Supreme Court: "The solicitation of another, assuming neither the solicitor nor solicitee proximately acts toward the crime's commission, cannot be held for an attempt." *State v. Otto,* 629 P.2d 646, 650 (Idaho 1981).

Is solicitation more serious than attempt? The Tennessee Supreme Court has suggested that it is not, stating, "There is not the same degree of heinousness in solicitation as in attempts, nor is solicitation as likely to result in a completed crime, there not being the same dangerous proximity to success as found in attempts." *Gervin v. State,* 371 S.W.2d 449, 451 (Tenn. 1963). The Connecticut Supreme Court has taken the contrary point of view, observing, "The solicitation to another to [commit] a crime is as a rule far more dangerous to society than the attempt to commit the same crime. For the solicitation has behind it an evil purpose, coupled with the pressure of a stronger intellect upon the weak and criminally inclined." *State v. Schleifer,* 121 A. 805, 809 (Conn. 1923).

If the crime solicited is committed or attempted by the solicitee, then the offense of solicitation ordinarily merges into the target crime. For example, if Andrew solicits Bob to murder Carl and Bob then murders or attempts to murder Carl, then Andrew would become an accessory before the fact to murder or attempted murder. As discussed in Chapter 4, this complicity would make Andrew a principal to the crime of murder or attempted murder. If, however, Bob refuses Andrew's solicitation, Andrew would still be guilty of solicitation.

Solicitation is distinguished from conspiracy because although solicitation requires an enticement, conspiracy, as we explain later, requires an agreement. Sometimes a solicitation results in a conspiracy, and some courts have regarded the offense of solicitation as "an offer to enter into a conspiracy." See, for example, *Commonwealth v. Carey,* 439 A.2d 151, 155 (Pa. Super. 1981).

Defenses to the Crime of Solicitation

Generally, the fact that the solicitor countermands the solicitation is not a defense to the crime of solicitation. Nor is it a defense that it was impossible for the person solicited to commit the crime. The Model Penal Code provides that a complete and voluntary renunciation of the accused's criminal purpose is a defense to a charge of solicitation. M.P.C. § 5.02(3). Some states have adopted this position. Kentucky law agrees; however, Section 506.060 of the Kentucky Statutes stipulates:

A renunciation is not "voluntary and complete" … when it is motivated in whole or in part by: (a) A belief that circumstances exist which pose a particular threat of

apprehension or detection of the accused or another participant in the criminal enterprise or which render more difficult the accomplishment of the criminal purpose;
or (b) A decision to postpone the criminal conduct until another time or to transfer
the criminal effort to another victim or another but similar object.

Conspiracy

Under English common law, **conspiracy** consisted of an agreement by two or more
persons to accomplish a criminal act or to use unlawful means to accomplish a noncriminal objective. The gist of the offense was the unlawful agreement between the
parties, and no overt act was required.

The common law regarded a husband and wife as one person for most purposes;
therefore, a husband and wife could not be guilty of conspiring with each other. In
recent years courts have recognized the separate identities of spouses, and there is
no valid reason to continue the common-law approach. See, for example, *People v.
Pierce*, 395 P.2d 893 (Cal. 1964). Thus, a husband and wife who conspire only between themselves ordinarily cannot claim immunity from prosecution for conspiracy
on the basis of their marital status.

Today the offense of conspiracy is defined by statute in all jurisdictions. Most
state laws define the elements of the offense along the lines of the common law.
Thus, the agreement becomes the *acts reus* of the offense. Typically, as the Florida
law states, "A person who agrees, conspires, combines, or confederates with another
person or persons to commit any offense commits the offense of criminal conspiracy." West's Fla. Stat. Ann. § 777.04(3). Thus, under Florida law, both an agreement
and an intention to commit an offense are necessary elements to support a conviction for conspiracy. *Webster v. State*, 646 So.2d 752 (Fla. App. 1994).

Several states, however, require proof of an overt act to convict someone for
conspiracy. Where an overt act is required, courts simply require that the act be one
taken in furtherance of the conspiracy without the qualifications required of an act
required in an attempt to commit a crime. For example, Texas law provides that "[a]
person commits criminal conspiracy if, with intent that a felony be committed, (1) he
agrees with one or more persons that they or one or more of them engage in conduct
that would constitute the offense, and (2) he or one or more of them performs an
overt act in pursuance of the agreement." Vernon's Tex. Penal Code Ann. § 15.02(a).
Note that the Texas statute also requires an intent that a felony be committed,
whereas in many states it is necessary only to prove an intent to commit a criminal
offense.

Federal law (with some exceptions) requires proof of an overt act in a conspiracy
to commit an offense or to defraud the United States. 18 U.S.C.A. § 371. In *United
States v. Jobe*, 101 F.3d 1046, 1063 (5th Cir. 1996), the court stated, "In order to establish a conspiracy under 18 U.S.C.A. § 371, the government must prove beyond a
reasonable doubt the existence of an agreement between two or more people to violate a law of the United States and that any one of the conspirators committed an
overt act in furtherance of that agreement."

Because of the variations encountered in statutory language, in reviewing any
statute defining conspiracy it is necessary to determine at the outset (1) the type of
the offense or unlawful activity the statute proscribes and (2) whether it requires
proof of an overt act in furtherance of the parties' agreement.

CASE-IN-POINT

The Enron Conspiracy Case

In one of the most dramatic white-collar crime cases ever prosecuted in the United States, Enron founder Kenneth Lay and former chief executive Jeffrey Skilling were convicted in federal court in May of 2006 of conspiracy to commit securities fraud and wire fraud. The government charged that Lay and Skilling entered into a conspiracy to defraud investors and employees by giving them false information about the giant energy company's financial health. Enron's dramatic collapse in 2001 left more than five thousand employees jobless and cost investors billions of dollars. In her closing argument to the jury, prosecutor Kathryn Ruemmler insisted that Lay and Skilling committed their crimes "through accounting tricks, fiction, hocus-pocus, trickery, misleading statements, half-truths, omissions and outright lies...." Prosecution witnesses included eight former Enron employees who had pleaded guilty to other charges stemming from the scandal or entered into immunity agreements with the government. The jury deliberated for six days before returning guilty verdicts against Lay and Skilling. In July 2006, before sentences were imposed, Lay died of a heart attack. In October 2006, Skilling was sentenced to twenty-four years and four months in prison.

Justification for the Offense of Conspiracy

Why is conspiracy considered an offense distinct from the substantive offense the conspirators agree to commit? The late U.S. Supreme Court Justice Felix Frankfurter articulated one of the most cogent responses to this question. In *Callanan v. United States,* 364 U.S. 587, 593–594, 81 S.Ct. 321, 325, 5 L.Ed.2d 312, 317 (1961), Frankfurter observed:

Go to the Scheb/ Scheb Criminal Law and Procedure 6e website at academic .cengage.com/criminaljustice/ scheb for an edited version of *Callanan v. U.S.*

> Concerted action both increases the likelihood that the criminal object will be successfully attained and decreases the probability that the individuals involved will depart from their path of criminality. Group association for criminal purposes often, if not normally, makes possible the attainment of ends more complex than those which one criminal could accomplish.... Combination in crime makes more likely the commission of crimes unrelated to the original purpose for which the group was formed. In sum, the danger that a conspiracy generates is not confined to the substantive offense that is the immediate aim of the enterprise.

The Range of Conspiracies in Society

The range of conspiracies cuts across socioeconomic classes in society. Traditionally, state prosecutions for conspiracy have been directed at criminal offenses such as homicide, arson, perjury, kidnapping, and various offenses against property. In recent years an increasing number of both state and federal conspiracy prosecutions have been related to illicit drug trafficking. In addition to the numerous narcotics violations, federal prosecutions include a variety of conspiracies not found under state laws. Among these are customs violations, counterfeiting of currency, copyright violations, mail fraud, lotteries, and violations of antitrust laws and laws governing interstate commerce and other areas of federal regulation. Recently, several federal prosecutions have involved conspiracies to deprive persons of their civil rights secured by the Constitution or laws of the United States. See 18 U.S.C.A. § 241. Lower federal courts have held that this section, which prohibits conspiracy against rights of citizens, does not require proof of an overt act. See, for example, *United States v. Morado*, 454 F.2d 167 (5th Cir. 1972).

The Act Element in Conspiracy

In general, the *actus reus* of the crime of conspiracy is the unlawful agreement. But the agreement need not be formal or written. A simple understanding is sufficient. Where an overt act is required, such act need not be a substantial movement toward the target offense. For example, in California, where the law requires an overt act, the courts have said that an overt act tending to effect a conspiracy may merely be a part of preliminary arrangements for the commission of the ultimate crime. *People v. Buono*, 12 Cal. Rptr. 604 (Cal. App. 1961). In *Bannon v. United States*, 156 U.S. 464, 15 S.Ct. 467, 39 L.Ed. 494 (1895), the U.S. Supreme Court held that an act committed by any one of the conspirators applies to all present members of the conspiracy. In fact, a single act such as a telephone conversation arranging a meeting has been held to be sufficient proof of an overt act. *United States v. Civella*, 648 F.2d 1167 (8th Cir. 1981).

In *State v. Dent*, 869 P.2d 392 (Wash. 1994), the Supreme Court of Washington articulated the difference between the *actus reus* requirement in the crimes of attempt and conspiracy. The court observed that the two crimes differ in the nature of the conduct sought to be prohibited and in the significance of the "substantial step" requirement (known as the "overt act" requirement in some jurisdictions) in each context. "A substantial step," the court noted, "is required in the context of attempt to prevent the imposition of punishment based on intent alone." But the court explained that the purpose of the substantial step or overt act requirement is different in the context of conspiracy: "The purpose of the 'substantial step' requirement is, therefore, to manifest that the conspiracy is at work, and is neither a project still resting solely in the minds of the conspirators nor a fully completed operation no longer in existence." 869 P.2d at 397.

Contrary to some popular views, the participants in a conspiracy need not even know or see one another as long as they otherwise participate in common deeds. The essence of the offense is the mutual agreement of the parties to the conspiracy, not the acts done to accomplish its objective. Moreover, the agreement need not be explicit. In fact, it seldom is. In most instances, the agreement is implied from the acts of the parties and the circumstances surrounding their activities. Furthermore, all the conspirators do not have to join the conspiracy at the same time.

The Requisite Criminal Intent

Statutes frequently fail to encompass the intent requirement in the offense of conspiracy. This difficulty is compounded by failure of the courts to clearly define the intent required for a conviction. In general, the prosecution must prove that a defendant intended to further the unlawful object of the conspiracy, and such intent must exist in the minds of at least two of the parties to the alleged conspiracy. *People v. Cohn*, 193 N.E. 150 (Ill. 1934). Many courts refer to the crime as requiring a specific intent. See, for example, *People v. Marsh*, 376 P.2d 300 (Cal. 1962). As previously noted relative to attempts, such intent may be inferable from the conduct of the parties and the surrounding circumstances. Although many federal court decisions have not required proof of a specific intent, the U.S. Supreme Court has said that in federal prosecutions there must be proof of at least the criminal intent necessary for the requirements of the substantive offense. *United States v. Feola*, 420 U.S. 671, 95 S.Ct. 1255, 43 L.Ed.2d 541 (1975).

Salinas v. United States, 522 U.S. 52, 118 S.Ct. 469, 139 L.Ed.2d 352 (1997)

In this case, the Supreme Court upholds a conviction for conspiracy to violate the federal racketeering laws (see discussion of the "RICO" statute in Chapter 10). Writing for a unanimous Court, Justice Anthony Kennedy discusses the characteristics of the offense of conspiracy.

JUSTICE KENNEDY delivered the opinion of the Court.

A conspiracy may exist even if a conspirator does not agree to commit or facilitate each and every part of the substantive offense.... The partners in the criminal plan must agree to pursue the same criminal objective and may divide up the work, yet each is responsible for the acts of each other.... If conspirators have a plan which calls for some conspirators to perpetrate the crime and others to provide support, the supporters are as guilty as the perpetrators. As Justice Holmes observed: "[P]lainly a person may conspire for the commission of a crime by a third person." ... A person, moreover, may be liable for conspiracy even though he was incapable of committing the substantive offense."

Conspiracy Distinguished from Aiding and Abetting and Attempt

As we noted in Chapter 4, aiding and abetting someone in the commission of a crime makes a person either a principal or an accessory before the fact. Conspiracy is a separate offense and must be distinguished from aiding and abetting. Conspiracy involves proof of an agreement between two or more persons, an element often present, but not essential, in proving that a defendant aided and abetted a crime. On the other hand, aiding and abetting requires some actual participation. Conspiracy differs from the crime of attempt in that it focuses on intent, whereas attempt places more emphasis on the defendant's actions.

The *Pinkerton* Rule

In *Pinkerton v. United States,* 328 U.S. 640, 66 S.Ct. 1180, 90 L.Ed. 1489 (1946), Pinkerton was charged with conspiring with his brother for tax evasion, including some offenses allegedly committed by his brother during times that Pinkerton was incarcerated. The trial court instructed the jury that it could find Pinkerton guilty if it found he was a party to a conspiracy and that the offenses were in furtherance of the conspiracy. Pinkerton was convicted, and on review the U.S. Supreme Court upheld his conviction, stating that a member of a conspiracy is liable for all offenses committed in furtherance of the conspiracy. The Court did indicate that a different result may occur if the offenses were not reasonably foreseeable as a natural consequence of the unlawful agreement of the conspirators. This has come to be known as the ***Pinkerton* Rule.** It is based on the theory that conspirators are agents of one another, and just as principals are bound by the acts of their agents within the scope of the agency relationship, so too conspirators are bound by the acts of their co-conspirators. See *United States v. Troop,* 890 F.2d 1393 (7th Cir. 1989).

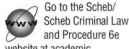

Go to the Scheb/ Scheb Criminal Law and Procedure 6e website at academic .cengage.com/criminaljustice/ scheb for an edited version of *Pinkerton v. U.S.*

    The *Pinkerton* doctrine has broad implications, and not all courts have accepted it. For example, in *People v. McGee,* 399 N.E.2d 1177 (N.Y. 1979), the court rejected the *Pinkerton* doctrine and observed that "[i]t is not offensive to permit a conviction of conspiracy to stand on the overt act committed by another, for the act merely provides corroboration of the existence of the agreement and indicates that the agreement has reached a point where it poses a sufficient threat to society to impose sanctions…. But it is repugnant to our system of jurisprudence, where guilt is generally personal to the defendant … to impose punishment, not for the socially harmful agreement to which the defendant is a party, but for substantive offenses in which he did not participate."

Some Unique Aspects of the Offense of Conspiracy

Because the courts view each conspirator as an agent of the others, it follows that each will be held responsible for the acts of the others within the context of their common design. *Commonwealth v. Thomas,* 189 A.2d 255 (Pa. 1963). This principle permits an exception to the rule of evidence that ordinarily excludes hearsay statements from being used in a trial over the defendant's objection. Thus, statements made "in furtherance of" the conspiracy may be admitted into evidence. These include statements to inform other conspirators of the activities or status of the conspiracy and those identifying other conspirators. Federal courts have upheld the use of statements to establish the source or purchaser of controlled substances. Before receiving this type of evidence, a court must receive independent evidence that a conspiracy exists. In some instances, courts receive the hearsay evidence subject to its being tied into the offense by independent evidence of the conspiracy. Court procedures in this area are very technical because the court must determine the scope of the conspiracy and the inception of the conspirator's participation.

The Supreme Court of Hawaii properly characterized the judicial approach to conspiracy:

> In the eyes of the law conspirators are one man, they breathe one breath, they speak one voice, they wield one arm, and the law says that the acts, words, and declarations of each, while in the pursuit of the common design, are the words and declarations of all. *Territory v. Goto,* 27 Hawaii 65 (1923).

Courts have held that once formed, a conspiracy continues to exist until consummated, abandoned, or otherwise terminated by some affirmative act. *Cline v. State,* 319 S.W.2d 227 (Tenn. 1958). Consequently, upon joining a conspiracy and not withdrawing, a conspirator is not insulated from the actions of his or her co-conspirators.

These unique aspects are significant. They assist the prosecution in proof of cases that might be otherwise unprovable. Perhaps the law has established these exceptions in recognition of the difficulties of prosecuting persons involved in conspiracies, which are generally formed in secret.

Conspiracy is among the most commonly charged federal offenses. A law review article explains why this is the case:

> Conspiracy, the prosecutor's "darling," is one of the most commonly charged federal crimes. The offense of conspiracy is construed broadly by courts and is therefore applied by prosecutors to a variety of situations…. A conspiracy charge gives the prosecution certain unique advantages and … one who must defend against such a charge bears a particularly heavy burden. Raphael Prober and Jill Randall, *Federal Criminal Conspiracy,* 39 Am. Crim. L. Rev. 571 (Spring 2002).

Conspiracy Does Not Merge into the Target Crime

Conspiracy is regarded as a separate and distinct crime; therefore, it does not merge into the target offense. See *People v. Carter,* 330 N.W.2d 314 (Mich. 1982). A pragmatic consideration is that by not merging conspiracy into the target offense, the law can more effectively deal with organized crime, criminal street gangs, and other dangerous collective efforts to commit crimes.

The Wharton's Rule Exception

Wharton's Rule, named after Francis Wharton, a well-known commentator on criminal law, provides an exception to the principle that conspiracy does not merge into the target crime. Wharton's Rule holds: "An agreement by two persons to commit a particular crime cannot be prosecuted as a conspiracy when the crime is of such a nature as to necessarily require the participation of two persons for its commission." 1 R. Anderson, Wharton's Criminal Law and Procedures 89, p. 191 (1957). Thus, Wharton's Rule holds that two people cannot conspire to commit a crime such as adultery, incest, or bigamy because these offenses require only two participants.

The rationale behind Wharton's Rule is that, unlike the usual conspiracy (often viewed as a wheel with many spokes or as a chain of circumstances), the offenses named do not endanger the public generally. Wharton's Rule has been applied in many state and federal courts, but it has its limitations. In holding Wharton's Rule inapplicable to various federal gambling offenses under the Organized Crime Control Act of 1970, the Supreme Court pointed out that the rule itself is simply an aid to the determination of legislative intent and must defer to a discernible legislative judgment. *Iannelli v. United States*, 420 U.S. 770, 786, 95 S.Ct. 1284, 1294, 43 L.Ed.2d 616, 628 (1975).

Go to the Scheb/
Scheb Criminal Law
and Procedure 6e
website at academic
.cengage.com/criminaljustice/
scheb for an edited version of
Iannelli v. U.S.

Criticism of the Conspiracy Laws

There has been an increased tendency in recent years to prosecute defendants for conspiracies as well as target crimes. The offense of conspiracy is a potent weapon for prosecutors, particularly as they try to cope with the problem of organized crime.

CASE-IN-POINT

Conspiracy to Deliver Controlled Substances

Cook, an undercover police officer, agreed to purchase fifty doses of LSD from Erickson at a park in Snohomish, Washington. Erickson asked Smith for a ride to go there, ostensibly to meet Hensler (who owed Smith $600). When Smith and Erickson arrived in Smith's vehicle, Cook approached the car and asked Erickson if he had the LSD. When Erickson produced a bag of LSD, Cook asked Smith if he had tried it. Smith replied that "he was going to college … and couldn't afford to get messed up, but that his wife had taken some of it, and … 'it really [messed] her up.'" At that point Cook agreed to purchase the LSD, handed the money to Erickson, and arrested both Smith and Erickson. Smith was found guilty of conspiracy to deliver LSD.

On appeal, Smith argued that there was no proof beyond a reasonable doubt (1) that he agreed to engage in delivery of LSD and (2) that he intended that it be delivered. The appellate court rejected both contentions and affirmed Smith's conviction. The court first pointed out that "a formal agreement is not necessary to the formation of a conspiracy." Then the court observed that although Smith's primary purpose in giving Erickson a ride to the park was to meet Hensler, his secondary purpose was to assist in delivering LSD. In finding the evidence sufficient to show that Smith intended to assist Erickson, the court opined that "there was evidence not only of knowledge of Erickson's unlawful purpose, but an agreement to assist with the plan by providing the necessary transportation.… Here there were two overt acts: first, that Smith drove Erickson to Snohomish knowing, according to Cook, Erickson's purpose for the trip; and second, that Smith provided encouragement for the sale by assuring the officer of the potency of the drug."

State v. Smith, 828 P.2d 654, 656, 657 (Wash. App. 1992).

Because the intent requirement and the form of agreement required are somewhat imprecise, a conspiracy is easier to prove than specific substantive crimes. On this basis, some critics argue that prosecutors, judges, and juries are given too much latitude in finding a defendant guilty.

Critics also argue that prosecution for conspiracy can chill a person's exercise of First Amendment freedom of speech, especially in matters involving political dissent. Courts, however, have ruled that conduct is not protected by the First Amendment merely because it involves the use of language. This became an issue in the 1968 prosecution of the late Dr. Benjamin M. Spock, the renowned pediatrician and author. Dr. Spock and three alleged co-conspirators were convicted of violating the Universal Military Training and Service Act, § 12(a) as amended, 50 U.S.C.A. App. § 462(a), for conspiring to urge men to evade the military draft. The U.S. Court of Appeals found that the evidence at Spock's trial was insufficient and set aside his conviction. *United States v. Spock*, 416 F.2d 165 (1st Cir. 1969). Nevertheless, the court explained that the First Amendment did not, per se, require acquittal on the charge of conspiracy to counsel men to resist the draft.

Defenses to the Charge of Conspiracy

In some states, statutes specifically provide for a defense of withdrawal from and renunciation of a conspiracy. As an illustration, Missouri law specifies that "[n]o one shall be convicted of conspiracy if, after conspiring to commit the offense, he prevented the accomplishment of the objectives of the conspiracy under circumstances manifesting a renunciation of his criminal purpose." Vernon's Mo. Ann. Stat. § 564.016(5)(1). In the absence of statutory authority, courts have been reluctant to approve a person's withdrawal as a defense. One difficulty in approving withdrawal as a defense is that even though a conspirator withdraws, the criminal objective of the conspiracy may proceed. Therefore, it seems reasonable to require that a person who would rely on such defense not only renounce any criminal purpose but also take the necessary steps to thwart the objective of the conspiracy. To accomplish this result, the conspirator would probably have to notify law enforcement authorities of the pertinent details of the conspiracy. In any event, if an accused is allowed to offer such a defense, the defendant has the burden of establishing his or her withdrawal from the conspiracy.

Entrapment, a defense to be examined in Chapter 14, may under some circumstances be a defense to conspiracy. For example, in *Stripling v. State*, 349 So.2d 187 (Fla. App. 1977), the court found reversible error in the trial judge's having instructed the jury that the defense of entrapment was not available to a defendant if the officer acted in good faith and merely furnished an opportunity for commission of a crime by one who already had the intent to commit the crime. As the appellate court said, "A defendant could deny being a party to a conspiracy and yet raise the issue that any overt acts done by him or her were done because of entrapment; that rationale being that inconsistencies in defenses in criminal cases are allowable so long as the proof of one does not necessarily disprove the other." *Id.* at 191.

■ CONCLUSION

By criminalizing attempt, solicitation, and conspiracy, the law endeavors to prevent the occurrence of criminal acts that pose prospective harm to persons. These inchoate offenses often pose substantial problems for law enforcement agencies, courts, and legislative bodies.

Police and courts experience difficulty determining the stage at which an act tends toward commission of a crime such that it qualifies as criminal attempt. Moreover, there are difficulties in distinguishing between what is legally impossible and what is factually impossible.

Solicitation poses a major problem because the solicitor often exerts power by manipulating the solicitee to commit a crime. There remains controversy whether legislatures should make it a criminal offense to solicit another person to commit a misdemeanor.

In conspiracy, group action can accomplish criminal purposes not otherwise likely from individual efforts. The offense of conspiracy affords prosecutors considerable leeway in proving offenses sometimes remote from a conspirator's intention. Yet, as will become apparent in later chapters, the offense of conspiracy has become a vital tool in coping with racketeering, drug trafficking, and white-collar crime. It is also an essential weapon in the ongoing war on terrorism.

Despite the problems associated with inchoate offenses, there is strong public support for criminalizing conduct directed toward future injuries to society. Most American jurisdictions have statutes making it an offense to attempt to commit a crime; some are directed at attempts to commit specific crimes. Not all jurisdictions make solicitation a crime, and those that do sometimes limit solicitation to certain classes of felonies. Conspiracy has been made a crime by statute in all jurisdictions. Criminalizing such incomplete and preparatory conduct permits timely intervention of law enforcement agencies to restrain dangerous persons and prevent intended crimes.

■ KEY TERMS

inchoate offense, 92	legal impossibility, 94
attempt, 92	factual impossibility, 94
overt act, 92	solicitation, 95
substantial step, 92	conspiracy, 98
preparatory conduct, 93	*Pinkerton* Rule, 101
target crime, 94	Wharton's Rule, 103

■ WEB-BASED RESEARCH ACTIVITY

Go to the Web. Locate your state's statutes on line. Does your state have a generic statute defining attempt, solicitation, and conspiracy? If not, find a state that does have such a statute. Download the statutory definitions of the three inchoate offenses. How do they compare with the definitions offered in this text?

■ QUESTIONS FOR THOUGHT AND DISCUSSION

1. What justifies criminalizing attempt, solicitation, and conspiracy?

2. How does the criminal law distinguish between mere preparatory conduct and the overt act required for a criminal attempt? Can you think of a situation in which preparatory conduct might have the appearance of prospective criminal conduct but would not constitute a criminal attempt?

3. Should it be a defense to a charge of attempt that the accused voluntarily abandoned the attempt?

4. Describe a scenario where an attempt to commit a crime is subsumed by the definition of the crime.

5. What is the rationale for making solicitation a crime even where a solicitor's requests are completely unheeded?

6. Which do you think poses a more serious threat to society: an attempt or a solicitation to commit murder? Why?

7. Should statutes defining conspiracy require proof of an overt act in furtherance of the conspirators' agreement? Why or why not?

8. Given the First Amendment protections of freedom of expression and association, can members of a revolutionary political organization be prosecuted for conspiring to overthrow the government of the United States?

9. Name some instances where the offense of conspiracy provides a means to protect the public from dangers incident to group activities.

10. What distinguishes the offense of conspiracy from the crime of aiding and abetting, discussed in Chapter 4?

■ PROBLEMS FOR DISCUSSION AND SOLUTION

1. Leo Lothario was having an affair with Lucy Slarom, a woman separated from her husband, Joe. One night while Lothario and Lucy were playing tennis in her backyard, Joe appeared on the scene. Lothario demanded that Joe leave, but he declined and sat in one of the yard chairs. Lothario went to the garage, picked up a rifle, pointed it at Joe, and from a distance of approximately seventy-five feet, fired a shot in the direction of Joe. The bullet missed Joe by about eighteen inches. Lothario explained to the police that he was simply trying to scare Lucy's estranged husband so he would not bother her. On the strength of these facts, do you think there is a basis to charge Lothario with attempted murder?

2. John and Jane were running a student loan "scam." They were convicted of soliciting several students to make false applications in exchange for a "cut" of the loan proceeds and also for aiding and abetting those same students in making false applications for loans. On appeal, they argue that the solicitation charges merged into their convictions for aiding and abetting the making of the false applications. The state responds that John and Jane were guilty of both crimes because the solicitation offenses were completed before John and Jane assisted the students in making the false applications. How should the appellate court rule on this appeal? Why?

3. A state statute makes it a criminal offense for "three or more persons to conduct, direct, or own a gambling business." Several defendants were convicted of "conspiring to violate the statute." In addition, each was convicted of the substantive offense of gambling. On appeal, each defendant argues that the conspiracy offense merged into the substantive offense of gambling because the offense of gambling required participation of a number of persons. The state counters that the harm attendant upon commission of the offense of gambling is not limited to the parties to the conspiracy. Moreover, it points out that those prosecuted for the conspiracy would not necessarily be identical to those who are prosecuted for the substantive offense of gambling. How do you think an appellate court should rule in this instance? Why?

CHAPTER **6**

Offenses against Persons

Introduction

Every civilized society attempts to protect its members from injury or death at the hands of wrongdoers. As the English common law developed, the judges created criminal offenses to protect individuals from conduct that society deemed wrongful and injurious. The American colonists inherited the offenses defined by the English common law, and as colonies became states, legislatures enacted statutes adopting these common-law offenses. Since then, many social changes have occurred in America, and federal and state statutes have redefined many of these offenses and have created new ones. In this chapter, we examine the common-law crimes against persons and discuss their statutory development in the United States. We also explore some representative statutes defining present-day offenses against persons.

The Common-Law Background

By the time of the English colonization in America, the common law had identified four basic groups of offenses against persons. These consisted of (1) the assaultive crimes—that is, assault, battery, and mayhem; (2) the homicidal crimes of murder, manslaughter, and suicide; (3) sex-related offenses of rape, sodomy, and abortion; and (4) offenses known as false imprisonment and kidnapping. Murder, manslaughter, suicide, rape, and sodomy were common-law felonies; the other offenses named were classified as misdemeanors.

The American Development

Early substantive criminal law in America was essentially a continuation of the English common law of crimes. By the 1800s, however, America's quest for representative government and its penchant for definiteness and certainty, combined with the standards of written constitutions, resulted in legislative definitions of crimes. Defining offenses against persons became primarily a state rather than a federal legislative function, and the new states basically followed the common-law themes with variations deemed necessary in the new social, economic, and political environment.

As the United States became urbanized, more densely populated, and increasingly mobile, the areas of conduct initially defined as criminal offenses against persons required revision and, in many instances, enlargement. Under modern statutes, assault and battery have been classified according to their seriousness, the character of the victim, and the environment in which these crimes are committed, and legislatures have created new crimes against persons such as stalking and, more recently, "cyberstalking." Murder has been classified based on the degree of the offender's culpability, and a new offense of vehicular homicide has been created to cope with the dangers inherent in vehicular traffic. At early common law, suicide was punished by causing the forfeiture of the decedent's goods and chattels to the king. Suicide statutes are now designed primarily to punish those who assist others in committing suicide. Conduct that constituted the offense of mayhem at common law is now often prosecuted under various forms of assaultive crimes.

In recent years contemporary moral standards have caused the offense of rape to be expanded into a more comprehensive, gender-neutral offense of sexual battery, with new emphasis on the victim's age and vulnerability.

Abortion, a common-law misdemeanor, is now regarded as a woman's constitutional right. *Roe v. Wade*, 410 U.S. 113, 93 S.Ct. 705, 35 L.Ed.2d 147 (1973). And laws prohibiting consensual sodomy between adults, a felony at common law, have been found unconstitutional by the U.S. Supreme Court. *Lawrence v. Texas,* 539 U.S. 558, 123 S.Ct. 2472, 156 L.Ed.2d 508 (2003).

Laws prohibiting doctor-assisted suicide have become controversial, and statutes now address such conduct as child and spousal abuse and abuse of the elderly. The offense of false imprisonment is essentially the same as at common law, but the crime of kidnapping, which today focuses on child abduction, serves a much different role in American society than it did under the English common law.

As noted in Chapter 4, common-law crimes required proof of a criminal intent. In contrast, many statutory crimes—for example, the sale of intoxicants to minors and consensual sexual relations between an adult and a minor—now fall in the category of strict liability offenses. In contemporary society there is a new emphasis on enforcement of civil rights laws that originated in the post-Civil War environment and have been supplemented by modern enactments. Finally, in an effort to curb intimidation, many states now proscribe certain conduct as "hate crimes."

Assaultive Offenses

Assault and **battery,** though commonly referred to together, were separate misdemeanor offenses at common law. An assault was basically an attempted battery consisting of an offer to do bodily harm to another by using force and violence; a battery was a completed or consummated assault. Although an actual touching was not required, words alone did not constitute an assault. The common law made no distinction between classes or degrees of assault and battery but dealt more severely with aggravated cases.

Modern Statutory Development

Today all jurisdictions make assault an offense, and most make battery a crime as well. Assault is defined by statute, as is battery, and sometimes the term "assault and battery" is used to indicate one offense. Simple assaults and batteries generally remain misdemeanors, whereas those perpetrated against public officers (for example, fire and police personnel) are frequently classified as felonies. Legislatures commonly classify as felonies more egregious assaultive conduct such as **aggravated assault, aggravated battery,** and assault with intent to commit other serious crimes.

The California Penal Code defines an assault as "an unlawful attempt, coupled with a present ability, to commit a violent injury on the person of another." West's Ann. Cal. Penal Code § 240. It imposes increased penalties for an assault committed on a person engaged in performing the duties of a peace officer, firefighter, lifeguard, process server, paramedic, physician, or nurse. West's Ann. Cal. Penal Code § 241(b). Like most states, California makes it a felony to commit an assault with a deadly weapon or with force likely to produce great bodily injury. West's Ann. Cal. Penal Code § 245. Many states classify this latter offense as aggravated assault. For example, under Florida law, a person who commits an assault with a deadly weapon without intent to kill or an assault with intent to commit a felony is guilty of aggravated assault, a felony offense. West's Fla. Stat. Ann. § 784.021.

The California Penal Code defines as battery "any willful and unlawful use of force or violence upon the person of another." West's Ann. Cal. Penal Code § 242. The code

CASE-IN-POINT

Assault with a Deadly Weapon

Rasor, a police officer, stopped a vehicle and attempted to arrest the driver, Jackson, for driving while intoxicated. As he did, a fight broke out between the officer and Jackson. At that point the defendant, Lloyd Gary, a passenger in Jackson's car, approached the two combatants, removed the officer's pistol, and pointed it at Rasor and Jackson. Gary was convicted of assault with a deadly

weapon. On appeal, he argued that the trial judge erred in not directing the jury to return a verdict of not guilty because the evidence showed no attempt to commit a physical injury. The Arizona Supreme Court rejected Gary's argument, saying that "[t]he pointing of a gun may constitute 'an assault' … and it is not necessary to show in addition that there was an intent to do physical harm to the victim."

State v. Gary, 543 P.2d 782, 783 (Ariz. 1975).

also specifies increased punishment for batteries committed against specific classes of officers, West's Ann. Cal. Penal Code § 243.6, or those committed on school property, park property, or hospital grounds, West's Ann. Cal. Penal Code § 243.2. Consistent with its handling of aggravated assaults, Florida law classifies a battery resulting in great bodily harm, permanent disability, or permanent disfigurement or one committed with a deadly weapon as an aggravated battery, an even more serious felony than aggravated assault. West's Fla. Stat. Ann. § 784.045.

Although most assault and battery prosecutions occur under state laws, the federal government also has a role in this area. Federal statutes proscribe assault within the maritime and territorial jurisdiction of the United States. 18 U.S.C.A. § 113. Interestingly, federal courts have held that the statute covers the entire range of assaults, *United States v. Eades,* 615 F.2d 617 (4th Cir. 1976), and that the word "assault" includes acts that would constitute batteries under most state laws. *United States v. Chaussee,* 536 F.2d 637 (7th Cir. 1976). Additional federal statutes proscribe assaults on federal officers, including members of the uniformed services engaged in the performance of official duties, 18 U.S.C.A. § 111, and assaults of foreign diplomatic and other official personnel, 18 U.S.C.A. § 112.

Common Illustrations of Simple and Aggravated Assault and Battery

Statutory definitions vary, but under most statutes a simple assault would include a threat to strike someone with the fist or a small stone or simply a missed punch. Firing a shot in the direction of a person or threatening someone with a weapon would probably qualify as aggravated assaults. A battery, on the other hand, involves some physical contact with the victim. Common illustrations of simple battery include hitting or pushing someone, a male hugging and kissing a female—or even an offensive touching—if against her will, using excessive force in breaking up a fight, intentionally tripping another individual, or using excessive force (by a parent or teacher) in disciplining a child. The acts referred to above as constituting aggravated assault, if completed, would most likely be prosecuted as aggravated batteries. When courts must determine whether an assault or battery is "aggravated," two questions commonly arise. First, what constitutes a "deadly weapon," and second, whether the defendant's conduct results in "great bodily harm." For example, the South Carolina Supreme Court recently observed, "Circumstances of aggravation include the use of a deadly weapon, the intent to commit a felony, infliction of serious bodily injury, great disparity in the ages or physical conditions of the parties, a difference in gender, the purposeful infliction of shame and disgrace, taking indecent liberties or familiarities with a female, and resistance to lawful authority." *State v. White,* 605 S.E.2d 540 (S.C. 2004).

Courts have no difficulty in finding that a gun, a knife, a club, or an axe is a deadly weapon. Other objects such as a pocketknife, hammer, rock, or walking cane, while not dangerous instruments per se, may under certain circumstances cause death or serious bodily injury.

What constitutes great or serious bodily injury is a factual determination not subject to a precise definition; however, the Indiana Supreme Court has stated that the term "great bodily harm" means "great as distinguished from slight, trivial, minor or moderate harm, and as such does not include mere bruises as are likely to be inflicted in a simple assault and battery." *Froedge v. State,* 233 N.E.2d 631, 636 (Ind. 1968). In making factual determinations of whether an injury constitutes a "serious" or "great" bodily injury, courts consider the type of injury the victim has suffered, as well as the instrument by which the injury was inflicted, and any disability that the victim will suffer. In many instances courts make the determination of whether the use of one's body can be a "deadly weapon" by focusing on the manner in which such body parts are used in committing an assault or battery. For example, in *Jefferson v. State,* 974 S.W.2d 887 (Tex. App. 1998), the court upheld a defendant's conviction for aggravated assault where the defendant struck the victim in the face four times with his fist and the victim suffered a broken nose, lacerations, and bleeding. In *State v. Bolarinho,* 850 A.2d 907, 910 (R.I. 2004), the Rhode Island Supreme Court noted that it is the object's capability and manner of use that is determinative of whether an object qualifies as a dangerous weapon. The court held that a person's foot can qualify as a dangerous weapon, particularly when employed with karate-like precision. Many other courts have considered hands and fists to be deadly weapons for purposes of assault with a deadly weapon, given the manner in which they were used and the relative size and condition of the parties involved. See, for example, West's N.C.G.S.A. § 14-33; *State v. Yarrell,* 616 S.E.2d 258 (N.C. App. 2005).

In *State v. Flemming,* 19 S.W.3d 195, 197 (Tenn. 2000), the Tennessee Supreme Court took a contrary view and held that feet and fists are not deadly weapons under Tennessee Code Annotated section 39-11-106(a)(5). The court commented, "Were we to interpret the statute to be written broadly enough to include one's fists and feet within the statutory definition of 'deadly weapon,' it would lead to an absurd result—the merger of simple and aggravated offenses—which would contradict the expressed intent of the General Assembly."

The Burden of the Prosecution

Go to the Scheb/ Scheb Criminal Law and Procedure 6e website at academic .cengage.com/criminal justice/scheb to *find State v. Towers* (1973), a decision in which the Maine Supreme Court upholds a conviction for aggravated assault and battery.

The proof required to establish assaultive offenses depends on the statutory language of the offense. To convict a defendant of simple assault or battery, the prosecution generally needs only to prove the act and the defendant's general, not specific, intent. In aggravated assault and aggravated battery prosecutions, courts have arrived at different interpretations of the intent requirement, but proof of the defendant's general intent is usually sufficient. In contrast, if a defendant is prosecuted for committing an assault or battery "with the intent to do great bodily harm" or "with the intent to commit a specific felony, for example, murder," courts generally require the prosecution to prove the defendant's specific intent to accomplish those results.

Defenses to Charges of Assault and Battery

Many forms of conduct involving intentional use of physical force do not constitute batteries. In many instances, there is an express or implied consent of the person against whom the physical force is exerted. Reasonableness is the test applied in sports contests and friendly physical encounters. Everyday examples include such contact sports as football, in which the participants obviously consent to forceful bodily contact. The physician who performs surgery with consent of the patient provides another example of physical contact that, if properly applied, does not constitute a battery. Reasonableness is also the test applied to interpersonal relationships. Thus, although a person might imply consent to a friendly kiss or caress, seldom could a person imply consent to an act of violence, even when done under the guise of affection.

Statutory law regulates the degree of force that can be used by teachers, police officers, and correction officials, and an excessive use of force may constitute a battery. Likewise, parents and guardians and those standing *in loco parentis* have a right to impose reasonable punishment when disciplining a child but must consider the child's age, health, size, and all other relevant circumstances. Parents who inflict injury on a child or who impose excessive punishment may be guilty of committing a simple or even an aggravated battery. They may also be subject to prosecution under modern statutes proscribing child abuse.

A person charged with battery can defend the action by showing that the touching or hitting was unintentional, that the physical force used was reasonable, or that the action was taken in self-defense. Self-defense is subject to qualifications, as we explain in Chapter 14. Defenses applicable to the offense of battery generally apply as well to a charge of assault. The theory is that a person who fails to make physical contact with another can defend on the same basis of reasonableness or self-defense as a person who successfully commits a battery.

Mayhem

At common law, **mayhem** consisted of willfully and maliciously injuring another so as to render the victim less able in fighting. Mayhem became a statutory crime in most states, with some statutes extending the common-law definition to include injuries that disfigure a person. In most instances it is a general-intent offense; however, some statutes require proof of the actor's specific intent to maim or disfigure the victim. Mayhem statutes are less common today because many of the acts formerly prosecuted under these laws are now prosecuted under such statutory crimes as aggravated battery and attempted murder.

Hazing

Hazing consists of intentional or reckless physical or mental harassment, abuse, or humiliation. It frequently occurs in the process of initiation into clubs, fraternities, sororities, athletic teams, and other groups. Hazing sometimes merely consists of foolish pranks, but too often it has resulted in serious injuries to the initiate. In recent years state legislatures in the great majority of states have enacted statutes making hazing in all schools and colleges either a misdemeanor or felony, depending on the degree of injury to the initiate. The objective of anti-hazing statutes is to prevent or severely curtail the practice of hazing. Currently many national fraternities and sororities have adopted prohibitions or restrictions on the hazing activities of local chapters. Likewise, many colleges and universities have explicit prohibitions on hazing.

See, for example, *Buttny v. Smiley,* 281 F.Supp. 280 (D.Colo. 1968) (upholding anti-hazing rule at University of Colorado). Hazing is also prohibited in the armed forces academies. See 10 U.S.C.A. §§ 4352, 6964, 6965, 9352. Moreover, anti-hazing statutes do not restrict prosecutions, and egregious conduct can be prosecuted under other statutes as a felony, for example, aggravated battery.

The Maryland legislature has enacted a rather typical anti-hazing statute. MD Code, Criminal Law, § 3-607 provides:

(a) A person may not recklessly or intentionally do an act or create a situation that subjects a student to the risk of serious bodily injury for the purpose of an initiation into a student organization of a school, college, or university.

(b) A person who violates this section is guilty of a misdemeanor and on conviction is subject to imprisonment not exceeding 6 months or a fine not exceeding $500 or both.

(c) The implied or express consent of a student to hazing is not a defense under this section.

In rejecting an attack on the constitutionality of the statute, the Maryland Court of Special Appeals held that the state has a compelling interest in preventing violent or dangerous initiation activities on campuses and found that the law is not vague nor does it violate freedoms of association and assembly guaranteed by the First Amendment. The court further observed that the statute "does not reach students' rights to participate in fraternities, sororities, or other organizations, does not reach such conduct as yelling at or insulting pledges, and does not reach such conduct as requiring pledges to don matching tee shirts, memorize silly songs, or run errands for and serve meals to regular members...." *McKenzie v. State,* 748 A.2d 67, 72 (Md. App. 2000).

Stalking

By the late 1980s, persons who were being continually followed, threatened, or harassed by others were beginning to file complaints with law enforcement officers. Most complainants were women targeted by former suitors or celebrities who were being constantly followed by obsessive fans. Police began to refer to this type of behavior as **stalking,** but they were hampered in taking action to protect victims until after harm occurred to them. Police and prosecutors who felt that the traditional protections of the criminal law were not always sufficient to protect victims from stalking urged legislators to adopt statutes to help them combat the problem.

In California an obsessed fan shot and killed actress Rebecca Schaeffer after stalking her for two years. In 1990 this led the California legislature to enact the first law making stalking a crime. By 1994 all states and the District of Columbia had enacted laws defining stalking and making it either a misdemeanor or a felony. These laws generally stipulate that a person who willfully, maliciously, and repeatedly follows or harasses another and makes a credible threat against that person is guilty of stalking. Some stalking statutes require proof of a stalker's specific intent, while in others proof of a general intent suffices.

In 1996 Congress enacted a law to protect persons against stalking when the perpetrator has crossed state lines to commit the crime. The federal statute was amended as part of the Violence against Women Act (VAWA) of 2000 and makes it a crime to stalk someone across state or tribal lines where the stalker has the intent to kill, injure, harass, or intimidate a victim. 18 U.S.C.A. § 2261A(1).

In what is often considered to be one of the toughest laws on stalking, the Illinois Criminal Code makes stalking another person a felony and provides that a person guilty of aggravated stalking is guilty of an even more serious felony. As amended, Illinois law now provides:

(a) A person commits stalking when he or she, knowingly and without lawful justification, on at least two separate occasions follows another person or places the person under surveillance or any combination thereof and:

(1) at any time transmits a threat of immediate or future bodily harm, sexual assault, confinement or restraint and the threat is directed towards that person or a family member of that person; or

(2) places that person in reasonable apprehension of immediate or future bodily harm, sexual assault, confinement or restraint; or

(3) places that person in reasonable apprehension that a family member will receive immediate or future bodily harm, sexual assault, confinement, or restraint.

(a-5) A person commits stalking when he or she has previously been convicted of stalking another person and knowingly and without lawful justification on one occasion:

(1) follows that same person or places that same person under surveillance; and

(2) transmits a threat of immediate or future bodily harm, sexual assault, confinement or restraint; and

(3) the threat is directed towards that person or a family member of that person.

Subsection (d) of the statute states that a defendant "places a person under surveillance" by remaining present outside the person's school, place of employment, vehicle, other place occupied by the person, or residence other than the residence of the defendant. Subsection (e) stipulates that the words "follows another person" mean "(i) to move in relative proximity to a person as that person moves from place to place or (ii) to remain in relative proximity to a person who is stationary or whose movements are confined to a small area." However, subsection (e) points out that to follow another person does not include following within the residence of the defendant. Subsection (g) defines "transmit a threat" as giving a "verbal or written threat or a threat implied by a pattern of conduct or a combination of verbal or written statements or conduct." Finally, subsection (h) broadly defines "family member." ILL. ST. 720 ILCS 5/12-7.3.

In Illinois a person commits aggravated stalking when he or she, in conjunction with committing the offense of stalking, also does any of the following:

(1) causes bodily harm to the victim;

(2) confines or restrains the victim; or

(3) violates a temporary restraining order, an order of protection, or an injunction prohibiting the behavior described in subsection (b)(1) of Section 214 of the Illinois Domestic Violence Act of 1986. Ill. ST. 720 ILCS 5/12-7.4(a).

Defendants charged with stalking offenses often challenge stalking statutes on the grounds that they are unconstitutionally overbroad and vague. During the 1990s a number of defendants attacked stalking laws on grounds of violating the First Amendment to the U.S. Constitution. In *People v. Bailey*, 657 N.E.2d 953 (Ill. 1995), the Illinois Supreme Court upheld its stalking laws against challenges that the statutes are unconstitutionally vague and overbroad and that they intrude on the right to freedom of speech. As pointed out in *People v. Baer*, 973 P.2d 1225 (Colo. 1999), the majority of courts have upheld the constitutionality of stalking laws in various states. Nevertheless, in some instances defendants have prevailed in such attacks. For example, in *Commonwealth v. Kwiatkowski*, 637 N.E.2d 854 (Mass 1994), the Massachusetts Supreme Judicial Court held that state's stalking statute to be unconstitutional because the uncertain meaning of "repeated patterns of conduct" or "repeated series of acts" rendered the statute vague, thereby failing to give a person of ordinary intelligence fair notice of what conduct is forbidden. Where appellate courts have found infirmities in statutory language, state legislatures usually have made necessary changes in wording to avoid such further challenges. For example, litigation over what constitutes a "credible threat" caused some state legislatures to eliminate that term from their stalking statutes.

In reversing a lower appellate court holding that an attempt to stalk did not constitute a crime, the Supreme Court of Georgia concluded that attempted stalking is an offense because such conduct constitutes an attempt to follow, place under surveillance, or contact another person. *State v. Rooks*, 468 S.E.2d 354 (Ga. 1996). There is a paucity of judicial opinions on the issue, possibly because prosecutors have seldom filed charges of attempts to stalk as opposed to actual stalking; however, some legal scholars contend there can be no attempt to commit stalking. (See the discussion of inchoate offenses in Chapter 5.)

Cyberstalking

Following the increased use of computers, many women have complained of being victims of relentless e-mail messages. The problem is exacerbated by the availability of personal data on the Internet. Often **cyberstalking** involves some prankster or disappointed suitor placing a female's name online with suggestive data directed to third parties. This is sometimes referred to as "stalking by proxy." The anonymity of the Internet makes it extremely difficult for law enforcement agencies to track down cyberstalkers.

Title 18 U.S.C.A. § 2261A(2) makes it a federal crime to stalk someone across state, tribal, or international lines using regular mail, e-mail, or the Internet with the intent to kill or injure the victim, or to place the victim, a family member, or a spouse or intimate partner of the victim in fear of death or serious bodily injury.

Illinois has now specifically criminalized cyberstalking. Illinois Statutes, Ch. 720, Sec. 5/12-7.5 provides:

(a) A person commits cyberstalking when he or she, knowingly and without lawful justification on at least 2 separate occasions, harasses another person through use of electronic communication and:

(1) at any time transmits a threat of immediate or future bodily harm, sexual assault, confinement, or restraint and the threat is directed toward that person or a family member of that person, or

(2) places that person or a family member of that person in reasonable apprehension of immediate or future bodily harm, sexual assault, confinement, or restraint.

Several other states have amended their statutory definitions of stalking to include cyberstalking or to define "contacts" to include the use of electronic communications. For example, in 2000 Georgia enacted a law defining "contact" in its stalking law to include any communication by telephone, mail, broadcast, computer, computer network, or any other electronic devices. O.C.G.A. § 16-5-90. Similarly, in 2004 the Florida legislature amended Fla. Stat. § 784.048, which includes cyberstalking, to define cyberstalking as "to engage in a course of conduct to communicate, or to cause to be communicated, words, images, or language by or through the use of electronic mail or electronic communication, directed at a specific person, causing substantial emotional distress to that person and serving no legitimate purpose."

Homicide

The word *homicide* means the taking of the life of one human being by another. The English common law recognized both criminal and noncriminal homicides. Criminal homicide embraced the crimes of murder and manslaughter; noncriminal homicide included those killings of humans deemed either justifiable or excusable. The killing of a human being was the common factor in all classes of homicide; however, the perpetrator's state of mind was significant in determining whether an offense had been committed and, if so, the category of that offense.

At common law, murder was the unlawful killing of one person by another with **malice aforethought.** The required malice could be either express or implied. There were no degrees of murder. **Manslaughter** was the unlawful killing of one human being by another when no malice was involved. There were two categories: voluntary and involuntary. Voluntary manslaughter consisted of an intentional, unlawful killing that occurred in the **heat of passion** as a result of some adequate provocation. Involuntary manslaughter was the unintentional killing of another by the accused's gross or wanton negligence. Simply stated, the difference between the two was that the former was intentional whereas the latter was unintentional.

At common law, homicide was justifiable if performed by the command or permission of the law; it could be excusable if it occurred through accident or when committed for necessary self-protection.

Modern Statutory Classifications of Homicide

With some variations, the basic scheme of common-law homicide has been carried over into the statutory law of American jurisdictions. However, most states classify murder as either first or second degree. First-degree murder is usually defined as requiring either malice aforethought or premeditation. Second-degree murder commonly requires proof that the accused was guilty of imminently dangerous or outrageous conduct, albeit not malicious in the common-law sense of malice aforethought.

All states make manslaughter a crime, although some statutes have abolished the distinction between **voluntary manslaughter** and **involuntary manslaughter.** Moreover, modern statutes extend the offense of manslaughter to embrace a person's responsibility for death resulting from an omission to act in instances where the law imposes a duty to act.

Modern criminal codes generally provide that it is **justifiable homicide** for one to take another's life by authority of the law (for example, an executioner performing a duty). It is usually considered **excusable homicide** if death results from the inadvertent taking of another's life when the actor is not guilty of criminal negligence (for example, death occurring from an unavoidable traffic accident).

The overwhelming majority of homicide prosecutions are brought under state laws. However, federal statutes provide jurisdiction over the killing of certain officers and employees of the United States engaged in performance of their official duties, 18 U.S.C.A. § 1114, as well as certain foreign officials, 18 U.S.C.A. § 1116. Federal statutes classify criminal homicide as murder in the first degree, felony murder, and manslaughter (voluntary and involuntary). 18 U.S.C.A. § 1111–1112.

First-Degree Murder

The California Penal Code illustrates a modern statutory approach to homicide. It defines murder as the "unlawful killing of a human being, or a fetus, with malice aforethought" but stipulates that the death of a fetus is not murder when an abortion is performed by a physician when the mother's life is endangered or with the mother's consent. West's Ann. Cal. Penal Code § 187. The malice required by the code may be either express or implied. When a deliberate intention is manifested to take a person's life unlawfully, the malice is considered express; it may be implied when no considerable **provocation** appears or under other circumstances indicating malice. West's Ann. Cal. Penal Code § 188. In defining degrees of murder, the California code states that

> all murder which is perpetrated by means of a destructive device or explosive, knowing use of ammunition designed primarily to penetrate metal or armor, poison, lying in wait, torture, or by any other kind of willful, deliberate, and premeditated killing, or which is committed in the perpetration of, or attempt to perpetrate, arson, rape, carjacking, robbery, burglary, mayhem, kidnapping … is murder of the first degree; and all other kinds of murder are of the second degree. West's Ann. Cal. Penal Code § 189.

The penalties in California and other jurisdictions for **first-degree murder** are the most severe, with decreasing penalties provided for second-degree murder and manslaughter.

First-degree murder is the highest classification of homicide. It contemplates a true "intent to kill" and, as noted, usually requires proof of either malice aforethought or **premeditation.** Thus, to obtain a conviction, the prosecution must establish the defendant's specific intent to take another's life.

The California Supreme Court has said that "when a defendant with a wanton disregard for human life, does an act that involves a high degree of probability that it will result in death, he acts with malice aforethought." Moreover, the court has opined that "willful, deliberate, and premeditated" as used in the statute indicates its intent to require as an essential element of first-degree murder substantially more reflection "than the mere amount of thought necessary to form the intention to kill." *People v. Cruz,* 605 P.2d 830, 834 (Cal. 1980). The Pennsylvania Supreme Court has defined malice aforethought more elaborately, saying it is "not only a particular ill will, but a hardness of heart, cruelty, recklessness of consequences, and a mind regardless of social duty." *Commonwealth v. Buzard,* 76 A.2d 394, 396 (Pa. 1950). Such malice may be expressed or may be implied from the circumstances under which a homicidal act is performed; yet that court has noted that a single punch to a victim's face was insufficient to support a finding of malice. *Commonwealth v. Thomas,* 594 A.2d 300 (Pa. 1991).

Many jurisdictions define first-degree murder based on the "premeditated intent" of the offender. For example, Florida classifies a homicide as a first-degree murder if the unlawful killing of a human being is "perpetrated from a premeditated design to effect the death of the person killed or any human being." West's Fla. Stat. Ann. § 782.04. Initially, one might be inclined to think of a premeditated act as requiring a lengthy period of deliberation. Indeed, dictionaries commonly define "premeditation" as a conscious and deliberate preplanning over a period of time. However, judicial decisions defining premeditation emphasize that although it requires thought beforehand, no particular length of time is required. The length of time necessary to deliberate, or to form a specific intent to kill, need only be time enough to form the required intent

First-Degree Murder: Evidence of Premeditation

Defendant Phillip Lee Young suggested to his two companions that they rob and kill John Cooke in order to obtain money to buy liquor. After the three men used a ruse to gain entry to Cooke's house, Young stabbed Cooke twice in the chest, and one of the companions stabbed the victim several times in the back. Cooke died as a result of the injuries. A jury found Young guilty of first-degree murder, and he appealed. After explaining that first-degree murder is the unlawful killing of a person with malice and with premeditation and deliberation, the North Carolina Supreme Court rejected Young's contention that the evidence was insufficient to support a conviction.

State v. Young, 325 S.E.2d 181 (N.C. 1985).

Go to the Scheb/ Scheb Criminal Law and Procedure 6e website at academic .cengage.com/criminaljustice/ scheb to find *State v. Corder* (1991), a decision of the South Dakota Supreme Court that illustrates the factors that courts consider in determining whether evidence is sufficient to establish a defendant's premeditated design to effect the death of the victim.

before the killing. It matters not how short that time may be, as long as the process of premeditation occurs at any point before the killing. See, for example, *State v. Corn*, 278 S.E.2d 221 (N.C. 1981). On the issue of premeditation, courts consider defendants' acts and comments before and after killing, use of grossly excessive force or infliction of lethal blows after the deceased has been felled, and history of altercations or ill will between the parties.

The prosecution usually attempts to establish either malice aforethought or premeditation by introducing a variety of evidentiary facts and circumstances bearing on the defendant's motive and state of mind. These include the defendant's previous relationship with the victim including threats, quarrels, and expressions of ill will as well as conversations of the defendant at the time of and before and after the act of killing. Prosecutors also point to the nature of the wound inflicted, prior attacks on the victim, the defendant's actions before and after the crime, and the circumstances of the killing itself, including the weapon used and the nature and location of wounds inflicted.

Felony Murder

The common law developed a doctrine that where an accused was engaged in the commission of a felony and a homicide occurred, the felonious act was regarded as a substitute for the proof of malice aforethought required to find the defendant guilty of murder. Thus, it became **felony murder** when an accused unintentionally killed a human being while committing, or attempting to commit, such common-law felonies as burglary, arson, rape, or robbery. The theory was that if a killing resulted, even though unintentional or accidental, the required malice was carried over from the original felony. Consequently, the felon would be found guilty of murder.

The felony murder doctrine has been incorporated into most criminal codes in the United States. See *People v. Aaron*, 299 N.W.2d 304 (Mich. 1980). With the proliferation of crimes classified as felonies, legislatures have generally limited the applicability of felony murder to felonies involving violence or posing great threat to life or limb (for example, rape, robbery, kidnapping, arson, and burglary). See, for example, West's Ann. Cal. Penal Code § 189, quoted above. Some state legislatures have sought to equate certain felonious drug offenses with violent felonies. Some statutes provide for degrees of felony murder depending on the seriousness of the felony attempted or perpetrated by the accused, whether the killing occurred by a person other than the person perpetrating or attempting to perpetrate the felony, and whether the accused was present at the scene when the killing occurred. See, for example, West's Fla. Stat. Ann. § 782.04. Felony murder statutes have produced much litigation in the criminal courts. Some of the pertinent questions raised include the following:

- Can a felon who perpetrates an offense be guilty of felony murder where the victim of the intended offense kills a co-felon?
- Should a felon committing a crime such as robbery be guilty of felony murder if a police officer mistakenly kills the felon's intended victim?
- Can a felon be guilty of felony murder when a co-felon accidentally kills a bystander or a police officer?

Most courts have held that the doctrine of felony murder does not extend to a killing stemming from the commission of the felony if it is directly attributable to the act of someone other than the defendant or those actively participating with the defendant in the unlawful enterprise. Nevertheless, courts have arrived at different solutions to these and other problems arising under felony murder laws.

Perhaps questions such as these led the Michigan Supreme Court in 1980 to abrogate the felony murder doctrine. After commenting on how its prior decisions had already significantly restricted the doctrine, the court concluded that the rule that substitutes the intent to commit the underlying felony for the malice element of murder had to be abolished. Its abrogation of the doctrine does not make irrelevant the fact that a death occurred in the course of a felony. Rather, the court noted that a jury could properly infer malice from evidence that a defendant intentionally set in motion a force likely to cause death or great bodily harm. However, Michigan juries are no longer instructed to find malice if they are satisfied from all the evidence that it does not exist. *People v. Aaron,* supra.

A cogent argument can be made that the felony murder rule violates the basic requirement of moral culpability in the criminal law. Moreover, critics point out that under the early common law, conviction of a felony was punishable by death. Consequently, they note, when a death occurred in the commission of a felony and the accused was guilty of felony murder, no additional consequences resulted. With the exception of certain federal offenses recently classified as capital crimes, no felony except murder committed under aggravating circumstances is punishable by death. Nevertheless, the felony murder doctrine is well established in most jurisdictions. With legislatures perceiving the need to take a "hard line" on crime, it is doubtful that many states will be motivated to repeal felony murder statutes. Therefore, courts have become increasingly conscious of the need to strictly interpret such statutes. Observing that it is the commission of a specified felony that supplants the requirement of premeditation for first-degree murder, the Florida Supreme Court declared that for the felon to be guilty of felony murder there must be some causal connection between the homicide and the underlying felony. *Bryant v. State,* 412 So.2d 347 (Fla. 1982). The State must prove that there was no break in the chain of circumstances beginning with the felony and ending with the murder. *Santiago v. State,* 874 So.2d 617 (Fla. App. 2004).

Second-Degree Murder

In many jurisdictions, **second-degree murder** is a residual classification applied to unlawful homicides not evidenced by malice aforethought or premeditation, not occurring in conjunction with other felonies, and not falling within the statutory definition of manslaughter. More commonly, second-degree murder is defined as an unlawful killing of a human being by a person having a **depraved mind or heart.** For example, in South Dakota second-degree murder is defined as follows:

> Homicide is murder in the second degree when perpetrated by any act imminently dangerous to others and evincing a depraved mind, regardless of human life, although without any premeditated design to effect the death of any particular individual. S.D. St. § 22-16-7.

The South Dakota Supreme Court has held that the statutory language "although without any premeditated design" distinguishes premeditated murder from second-degree murder. *State v. Satter,* 543 N.W.2d 249 (S.D. 1996). Two years later that court held that a trial court properly defined the phrase "evincing a depraved mind" as conduct demonstrating an indifference to the life of others, that is, not only disregard for the safety of another but also a lack of regard for the life of another. *State v. Hart,* 584 N.W.2d 863 (S.D. 1998).

Shooting a firearm into a crowd or into an occupied house or automobile is a classic example of a depraved-heart-or-mind murder. But courts have also found such conduct as a parent who spanked and shook a young child so hard as to cause death, a driver running a police roadblock at a high rate of speed, a golfer swinging a golf club with great force against a victim, and a person tossing heavy stones from a building onto a busy street below to be conduct evidencing a depraved heart or depraved mind.

In practice, convictions for second-degree murder often reflect a **jury pardon.** A classic example is when the state prosecutes a defendant for first-degree murder and the jury determines that the circumstances surrounding the killing do not show malice aforethought or premeditation or simply do not justify the penalty, often death. In such an instance a jury sometimes returns a verdict for the lesser offense of second-degree

Second-Degree Murder: Evidence of Depraved Indifference

The state charged a fifteen-and-a-half-year-old boy with murder in the second degree under section 125.25(2) of the McKinney's N.Y. Penal Law, which provides as follows: "A person is guilty of murder in the second degree when: … (2) Under circumstances evincing a depraved indifference to human life, he recklessly engages in conduct which creates a grave risk of death to another person, and thereby causes the death of another person." The evidence at trial revealed the defendant loaded a mix of "live" and "dummy" shells at random into the magazine of a 12-gauge shotgun and then pumped a shell into the firing chamber, not knowing whether it was a dummy or live round. He next raised the gun to his shoulder and, pointing it directly at the victim, exclaimed, "Let's play Polish roulette," and asked, "Who is first?" Then the defendant pulled the trigger, discharging a live round into the thirteen-year-old victim's chest, resulting in the eventual death of the victim.

On appeal, the defendant challenged the sufficiency of the evidence to support his conviction. In its review the court first distinguished the crime of second-degree murder by depraved indifference from manslaughter by saying that it must be shown that the actor's reckless conduct is imminently dangerous and presents a grave risk of death, whereas in manslaughter the conduct need only present the lesser "substantial risk" of death. Then pointing out that the defendant had an intense interest in and a detailed knowledge of weapons and analogizing the incident to a macabre game of chance, the New York Court of Appeals held the evidence was legally sufficient to support the defendant's conviction of second-degree murder.

People v. Roe, 542 N.E.2d 610 (N.Y. 1989).

murder, always a noncapital felony. One might generalize that second-degree murder convictions often occur when a jury is convinced the defendant acted recklessly or even outrageously but with no intent to take the victim's life.

Manslaughter

As we have noted, there were two classes of manslaughter at common law: voluntary and involuntary. California, like many states, preserves that distinction and defines manslaughter as the "unlawful killing of a human being without malice." California law enumerates three categories: voluntary, involuntary, and vehicular. Voluntary manslaughter refers to instances where death of the victim occurs in a sudden quarrel or in the heat of passion. Involuntary manslaughter occurs where a death results from the commission of a lawful act that might produce death in an unlawful manner, or without due caution and circumspection. The third category, vehicular homicide, involves death resulting from the perpetrator's driving a vehicle while in the commission of an unlawful act not amounting to a felony and not with gross negligence, or driving a vehicle in the commission of a lawful act that might produce death in an unlawful manner, and with gross negligence. West's Ann. Cal. Penal Code § 192.

Many other states define manslaughter without categorizing it as voluntary or involuntary. Still other state legislatures have defined manslaughter by degrees. For example, New York law provides that a person who recklessly causes the death of another person, commits an unlawful abortion on a female that causes her death, or intentionally causes or aids another to commit suicide commits manslaughter in the second degree. McKinney's N.Y. Penal Law § 125.15. However, a person who inflicts certain intentional serious injuries that cause the death of another under circumstances that do not constitute murder may be guilty of the more serious offense of manslaughter in the first degree if he or she (1) acts under the influence of extreme emotional disturbance or (2) commits an unlawful abortional act that causes the death of a female pregnant for more than twenty-four weeks unless it is an abortional act deemed justifiable by statutory exceptions. McKinney's N.Y. Penal Law § 125.20. Irrespective of whether a statute classifies manslaughter as voluntary, involuntary, or by degree, certain situations generally fall within the definition of the offense. Common examples include a death resulting from mutual combat or killing someone by use of excessive force while defending oneself or a family member or acting in defense of property.

The intent the prosecution must establish to obtain a conviction of manslaughter may depend on the nature of the charge and whether the particular statute defines voluntary or involuntary manslaughter. To establish voluntary manslaughter, the prosecution may have to establish the defendant's specific intent. On the other hand, in a prosecution for involuntary manslaughter, the prosecution need only establish the defendant's general intent, and that may be inferred from the defendant's act and surrounding circumstances.

Often a charge of involuntary manslaughter is based on allegations of criminal negligence. A highly publicized example of this arose from a tragic accident occurring in the film industry. In 1982, a movie crew shooting a scene for the movie *The Twilight Zone* used a helicopter that crashed on the set, decapitating an actor and a child and crushing another child. The state prosecuted the director and four of his associates for involuntary manslaughter, claiming they were guilty of criminal negligence. The defendants argued that the tragic deaths resulted from an unforeseeable accident. In May 1987, after a dramatic five-month trial, a jury found them all not guilty.

Provocation is frequently a factor in manslaughter trials. Provocation that would cause a reasonable person to lose control may be sufficient to convert an otherwise

Manslaughter by Culpable Negligence

William Burge and Juanita Calloway became involved in an argument over the fact that Calloway was apparently sleeping with one of her sons. When Calloway displayed a knife, Burge pulled a gun that he carried to kill snakes that lurked in the walls of his house. Burge pointed the gun at Calloway and cocked it. Burge then pushed Calloway in an attempt to get her into his car. When he did, Calloway's hand hit the gun and it went off, severely wounding Calloway. While driving her to the hospital,

Burge ran out of gas and called an ambulance. Calloway died en route to the hospital. Despite his plea of self-defense, a jury found Burge guilty of manslaughter by culpable negligence. In affirming the conviction, the Mississippi Supreme Court rejected the defendant's contentions of self-defense and excusable and justifiable homicide. The court observed that the jury could reasonably have determined that although the victim was holding a knife, the defendant was not in danger of great personal injury.

Burge v. State, 472 So.2d 392 (Miss. 1985).

intentional killing of another to manslaughter. Mere words, however gross or insulting, are not sufficient to constitute provocation. Rather, to reduce a homicide from murder to manslaughter, it must generally be shown that there was sufficient provocation to excite in the defendant's mind such anger, rage, or terror as would obscure an ordinary person's reasoning and render the person incapable of cool reflection. A classic example is discovering one's spouse in an act of adultery with significant sexual contact taking place. The Maryland Special Court of Special Appeals has observed that

> if one spouse discovers another in an unexpected act of adultery, a killing of spouse or paramour in hot-blooded fury may lower the blameworthiness from the murder level to the manslaughter level. The blood, however, must indeed be hot and, generally speaking, only the hot-blooded killer can attest to that. By an objective standard, moreover, the time frame must be close enough so that an average and reasonable man would not have had an adequate 'cooling period' for the first fury to abate. *Bartram v. State,* 364 A.2d 1119, 1153 (Md. App. 1976).

The Indiana Supreme Court has noted that

> all that is required to reduce a homicide from murder to voluntary manslaughter is sufficient provocation to excite in the mind of the defendant such emotions as either anger, rage, sudden resentment, or terror as may be sufficient to obscure the reason of an ordinary man, and to prevent deliberation and premeditation, to exclude malice, and to render the defendant incapable of cool reflection. *Hardin v. State,* 404 N.E.2d 1354, 1357 (Ind. 1980).

Modern statutes often provide that negligent performance of a legal duty or the doing of a lawful act in an unlawful manner constitutes manslaughter. In addition to the more common instances, courts have upheld manslaughter convictions under such statutes for death occurring because of criminal negligence of medical practitioners or because of parental failure to provide medical attention or adequate nourishment for their children. See, for example, *People v. Ogg,* 182 N.W.2d 570 (Mich. App. 1970) (the mother of a young child who left the home while her child was locked in a bedroom and the child was killed in a fire of undetermined origin was guilty of manslaughter). The California Supreme Court held that a parent of a seriously ill child who makes only provision for prayer may be guilty of such criminal negligence that the parent can be found guilty of involuntary manslaughter or child endangerment. *Walker v. Superior Court,* 763 P.2d 852 (Cal. 1988). Other courts

Distinction Between Second-Degree Murder and Manslaughter

William Manuel challenged his conviction, after jury trial, for second-degree murder. The evidence revealed that while walking along a street on a dark night, he carelessly fired his pistol toward a garbage area, not aiming at anyone. Unfortunately, the shot killed a youngster noiselessly playing nearby.

The appellate court pointed out that section 782.04(2) of the Florida statutes defines second-degree murder as "the unlawful killing of a human being, when perpetrated by any act imminently dangerous to another and evincing a depraved mind regardless of human life, although without any premeditated design to effect the death of any particular individual...." In contrast, section 782.07 defines manslaughter as "the killing of a human being by the ... culpable negligence of another, without lawful justification...."

The court found no evidence that Manuel observed the victim or had any notice (actual or constructive) of his possible presence. Rather than evincing a depraved mind, the court found that Manuel's conduct exhibited culpable negligence by consciously doing an act with utter disregard for the safety to some other person, although without an intent to injure any person. "Thus," the court explained, "the noiseless playing of the victim, the inky blackness of the night and the lack of demonstrated ill will on the part of [Manuel] point more toward culpable negligence than the evincing of a depraved mind regardless of human life." Accordingly, the court reduced the defendant's conviction to manslaughter.

Manuel v. State, 344 So.2d 1317 (Fla. App. 1977).

Go to the Scheb/Scheb Criminal Law and Procedure 6e website at academic.cengage.com/criminaljustice/scheb to find *Manuel v. State* (1977), where a Florida appellate court distinguishes second-degree murder from man-slaughter.

have rejected the First Amendment right to free exercise of religion as a defense in such situations.

In a high-profile case, in October 1997, a Massachusetts jury found Louise Woodward, a young British *au pair* serving an American family, guilty of second-degree murder in the death of an eight-month-old child under her care. The child died a few days after receiving a severe head trauma while in Woodward's care. There was no evidence the defendant had ever abused or injured the child prior to the fatal injury. Fearing a compromise verdict, Woodward's counsel requested that the court not instruct the jury on the offense of manslaughter. After the jury returned a verdict of murder, the trial judge found the defendant's actions "were characterized by confusion, inexperience, frustration, immaturity and some anger, but not malice (in the legal sense) supporting a conviction for second degree murder" and reduced the defendant's conviction to manslaughter. The prosecution challenged the trial judge's action; however, the Massachusetts Supreme Judicial Court concluded that the trial judge did not abuse his discretion. *Commonwealth v. Woodward,* 694 N.E.2d 1277 (Mass. 1998).

Vehicular Homicide

The carnage on American highways has prompted many states to enact statutes making **vehicular homicide** a specific felony rather than opting to rely on prosecutors charging a defendant with manslaughter for causing a traffic death. Such statutes were originally directed at motor vehicles but now frequently include boats and airplanes.

In Kansas the legislature has provided that vehicular homicide is a class A misdemeanor and defines the offense as follows:

Vehicular homicide is the unintentional killing of a human being committed by the operation of an automobile, airplane, motor boat or other motor vehicle in a manner

Vehicular Homicide: Criminal Liability for Second Accident

On the evening of February 14, 1987, Gary Dawson was a passenger in a car driven by Richard Peaslee Jr. on a snow-packed, icy road in Maine. As a result of Peaslee's intentional "fishtailing," the car went out of control and overturned, throwing Dawson onto the road. Dawson, unable to move, lay on the road, where he was run over by another vehicle several minutes later. Dawson died before help arrived on the scene. A jury found Peaslee guilty of vehicular manslaughter, and he appealed. In affirming Peaslee's conviction, the Maine Supreme Court rejected his contention that he was not criminally responsible for the second accident. "The separate accidents were not independent of each other," said the court, "because Dawson would not have been lying immobile on the road in the path of the other car were it not for Peaslee's conduct." Moreover, the court concluded that "[w]hether Dawson was killed by the first or second impact makes no difference."

State v. Peaslee, 571 A.2d 825 (Me. 1990).

which creates an unreasonable risk of injury to the person or property of another and which constitutes a material deviation from the standard of care which a reasonable person would observe under the same circumstances. K.S.A. § 21-3405.

Many states have opted to classify vehicular homicide as a felony. See, for example, West's Fla. Stat. Ann. § 782.071. ("Vehicular homicide" is the killing of a human being, or the killing of a viable fetus by any injury to the mother, caused by the operation of a motor vehicle by another in a reckless manner likely to cause the death of, or great bodily harm to, another.) The Florida Supreme Court has said that in enacting its vehicular homicide statute, the legislature created a separate offense with a lesser standard of proof than is required for conviction under the state's manslaughter statute. Thus, the statute enables the prosecution to secure a conviction where the state is unable to meet the level of proof otherwise required in establishing manslaughter. Therefore, the court said the state could charge a defendant with manslaughter for operating a motor vehicle in a culpably negligent manner that causes the death of a human being or could proceed under vehicular homicide, a lesser included offense. *State v. Young*, 371 So.2d 1029 (Fla. 1979).

Justifiable and Excusable Homicide

As in most jurisdictions, California classifies nonculpable homicide as excusable or justifiable. It is excusable "when committed by accident or misfortune or in doing any other lawful act by lawful means, with usual and ordinary caution, and without any unlawful intent." It may also be excusable "when committed in the heat of passion, or on sudden and sufficient provocation, or on sudden combat where no undue advantage is taken nor any dangerous weapon is used and the killing is not done in a cruel or unusual manner." West's Ann. Cal. Penal Code § 195. Examples of excusable homicide include killing someone when resisting attempts to murder or to inflict great bodily injury upon a person; when in defense of a person's home under certain circumstances; or in some instances of self-defense where there is a reasonable ground to apprehend imminent danger of great bodily harm to a person's self, spouse, parent, or child. See West's Ann. Cal. Penal Code § 196; *People v. Collins*, 11 Cal. Rptr. 504 (Cal. App. 1961).

Under California law, homicide is justifiable when committed by public officers and those acting by their command in their aid and assistance,

1. In obedience to any judgment of a competent Court; or,

2. When necessarily committed in overcoming actual resistance to the execution of some legal process, or in the discharge of any other legal duty; or,

3. When necessarily committed in retaking felons who have been rescued or have escaped, or when necessarily committed in arresting persons charged with felony, and who are fleeing from justice or resisting such arrest. West's Ann. Cal. Penal Code § 196; *People v. Young,* 29 Cal. Rptr. 595 (Cal. App. 1963).

Removal of Life-Support Systems

Another area of contemporary concern has resulted from technological advances in medicine that has enabled physicians to use sophisticated life-support systems to prolong life for indefinite periods. In a landmark case involving Karen Quinlan, the New Jersey Supreme Court in 1976 reviewed the request of Karen's parents to remove the life-support systems sustaining the life of their daughter, who lay in a comatose state with no reasonable medical probability of regaining a sapient existence. The court ruled that withdrawal of such life-support systems, under the circumstances, would not constitute a criminal homicide. *In re Quinlan,* 355 A.2d 647 (N.J. 1976).

A significant body of decisional law has now developed on the issue of when life-sustaining measures should be initiated and when they may be removed. Generally, a competent adult who is terminally ill may decide to forgo such extraordinary measures or may order such measures discontinued. *McKay v. Bergstedt,* 801 P.2d 617 (Nev. 1990). Moreover, the Florida Supreme Court has held that terminally ill incompetent

CASE-IN-POINT

The Terri Schiavo Case

Problems can result in acrimonious litigation when a patient has no living will or other written instructions on the issue of removal of life support and close family members disagree. This was dramatized in litigation involving the late Terri Schiavo. In 1990, Schiavo, age 26, suffered cardiac arrest and remained in a coma for several weeks. She was then diagnosed as being in a persistent vegetative state. In 1998, Michael, her husband and guardian, petitioned a Florida court to remove her feeding tube. She had no living will. Over the strong objections of her parents, the court found the evidence revealed that Schiavo did not wish to be kept alive and ordered her feeding tube removed. The court's decision engendered numerous unsuccessful appeals in state courts. The Florida legislature became involved in the controversy, and even the U.S. Congress passed a law granting federal court jurisdiction over this particular case, an action that raised critical constitutional issues. The U.S. Supreme Court denied review of court decisions, denying the parents relief. Even Florida governor Jeb Bush then unsuccessfully attempted to prohibit removal of the feeding tube. Finally, Schiavo's feeding tube was removed for the third time. While the media kept the public constantly advised of the progress of the legal proceedings, Schiavo died on March 31, 2005, at the age of 41.

The Schiavo case did not develop any new legal principles or procedures. It did, however, focus national attention on the need for individuals to execute legal directives clearly defining the extent of extraordinary medical procedures to be taken in the event a person is in a persistent vegetative state.

persons have the same right to refuse extraordinary measures as competent persons and that family members or guardians may exercise such rights on their behalf. *John F. Kennedy Memorial Hosp., Inc. v. Bludworth,* 452 So.2d 921 (Fla. 1984).

Judicial opinions vary as to when, under what circumstances, and by whom discontinuance of medical treatments may be ordered for minors and incompetents. Statutes in several states now address many of the problems in this area, yet there is no statutory or judicial consensus on the procedures to effect discontinuance. However, courts have been cautious not to allow criminal prosecutions where life-sustaining medical procedures have been discontinued in good faith based on competent medical advice and consent of a competent patient and the patient's family. See, for example, *Barber v. Superior Court,* 195 Cal. Rptr. 484 (Cal. App. 1983).

Prosecutorial Burdens in Homicide Cases

To obtain a conviction in a homicide case, the prosecution bears several burdens peculiar to homicide cases. The victim of the crime must have been alive, the defendant's actions must be the cause of the victim's death, and, in some jurisdictions, death of the victim must occur within a stated period of time. Although these might appear to be matters easily proven, sometimes they pose problems for prosecutors.

THE REQUIREMENT THAT THE VICTIM WAS ALIVE BEFORE THE HOMICIDAL ACT

By definition, a criminal homicide consists of someone taking another person's life. It follows that before the accused can be found guilty of a homicidal crime, the prosecution must establish that the victim was alive before the accused's criminal act. In most instances this is not too difficult, but consider, for example, the killing of a fetus. Under common law a child was not considered born until the umbilical cord had been severed and the child's circulation became independent of its mother's.

In the highly publicized case of *Keeler v. Superior Court,* 470 P.2d 617 (Cal. 1970), the California Supreme Court held that in enacting its homicide statute, the legislature intended it to have the settled common-law meaning that to be the subject of homicide, a fetus must be "born alive." Consequently, the court overturned a murder conviction where the defendant stomped on a pregnant woman's abdomen, thereby causing the death of her fetus. As a result, California amended section 187(a) of its penal code that defines murder to include the present language, *"the unlawful killing of a human being, or a fetus, with malice aforethought"* [emphasis added].

Lower courts began holding that viability of a fetus was essential for an accused to be guilty of murder of a fetus; however, the California Supreme Court has now held that "[V]iability is not an element of fetal homicide under section 187, subdivision (a)," but the state must demonstrate "that the fetus has progressed beyond the embryonic stage of seven to eight weeks." *People v. Taylor,* 86 P.3d 881 (Cal. 2004).

From the standpoint of California state law, when a defendant commits murder of a pregnant woman, the prosecution can also charge the defendant with murder of an unborn child where the fetal development has gone beyond the embryonic stage. Nevertheless, in states where legislatures have not enacted fetal homicide statutes, courts tend to follow the common law and have not extended the protection to the unborn.

THE *CORPUS DELICTI* REQUIREMENT

In addition to establishing that a human being was alive before a killing took place, the prosecution must always establish the **corpus delicti,** or body of the crime. The *corpus delicti* consists of the fact that a human being is dead and that the death was caused by the criminal act or agency of another person. In most jurisdictions the *corpus delicti* rule requires independent evidence beyond a defendant's confession. Some argue that this requirement is simply a technicality that impedes the search for truth. They argue that modern constitutional protections of confessions render the rule unnecessary. Others contend that by requiring some independent evidence to link a defendant to the crime charged ensures that no one is convicted based on a mistake or a coerced or fabricated confession. This rule is firmly implanted in American law, although several states have modified the rule in the last few decades. To prove the *corpus delicti,* the prosecution must show by either direct or circumstantial evidence, independent of the accused's statements, that the victim died as a result of a criminal act. Usually, the victim's body is available for medical examination, and a physician can testify about the cause of death. If the deceased's body is not recovered and the victim's death cannot be determined to have resulted from a criminal act, a conviction cannot be lawfully obtained. Consider the case of *Ex parte Flodstrom,* 277 P.2d 101 (Cal. 1954). There, it could not be determined if a baby died from the mother's alleged homicidal act or whether death occurred as a result of natural causes. Consequently, because there was no evidence available to establish the *corpus delicti,* the appellate court discharged the accused mother from custody on the ground that she was being held to answer charges of murder without probable cause.

To hold a defendant responsible for the death of a victim, the prosecution must also establish that the defendant's act was the **proximate cause** of the victim's death. This means that the victim's death must have been the natural and probable consequence of the defendant's unlawful conduct. Where A shoots or physically beats B, A pushes B out of a window or overboard from a boat, or A administers poison to B, medical evidence can usually establish the cause of the victim's death. However, killings can be accomplished in hundreds of ways. For example, death can be precipitated by fright, shock, or other means not involving physical contact with the victim. The accused's acts or omissions need not be the immediate cause of the victim's death as long as the death results naturally from the accused's conduct.

Some situations present perplexing issues for medical experts and courts. For example, a defendant fired a shot into the water about six feet from a boat occupied by two boys. When a second shot struck nearer to the boat than the first, one of the boys leaped out of the boat into the water. The boat capsized with the remaining boy in it. Both boys drowned. The defendant argued that he could not be guilty of causing the death of the boy who drowned when the boat overturned. The Tennessee Supreme Court rejected his contention and upheld the defendant's conviction for involuntary manslaughter, concluding that it was his shots, not the act of the boy who caused the boat to capsize, that caused the decedent's death. *Letner v. State,* 299 S.W. 1049 (Tenn. 1927).

In another instance, a wife who had been severely beaten by her husband in the past was impelled by fear of another beating at his hands to jump from a moving automobile. She died from injuries sustained. Her husband was charged with her murder and was found guilty of the lesser offense of manslaughter. On appeal, the Florida Supreme Court upheld the conviction. *Whaley v. State,* 26 So.2d 656 (Fla. 1946).

In a recent prosecution for several counts of attempted murder, the evidence revealed that the defendant was aware that he had tested positive for human immunodeficiency virus (HIV). The defendant's probation officer had even informed him that if he passed HIV to another person, "he would be killing someone." Nevertheless, he repeatedly and intentionally engaged in sexual activity with multiple partners and refused to take "safe sex" precautions. The defendant was convicted and appealed. He argued that he meant only to satisfy himself sexually and such was insufficient to prove intent to cause death. The Oregon Court of Appeals rejected his appeal and held that the defendant did not act impulsively merely to satisfy his sexual desire; rather, he acted deliberately to cause his victims serious bodily injury and death. *State v. Hinkhouse,* 912 P.2d 921 (Or. App. 1996).

Prosecutions of HIV-positive defendants under statutes proscribing attempted murder pose difficult problems for prosecutors. For example, proof of the element of intent is problematic, and proof of causation can pose great difficulty when the victim has had sexual relations with multiple partners. In *Smallwood v. State,* 680 A.2d 512 (Md. 1996), an HIV-positive defendant who pleaded guilty to attempted first-degree rape and robbery was then convicted of assault with intent to murder and attempted murder. On appeal, the Maryland Court of Appeals reversed the defendant's convictions for assault with intent to murder and attempted murder. The court held that evidence that the defendant knew he was HIV positive when he raped three women was insufficient to prove that he had an intent to kill.

Some states allow the prosecution of persons who are HIV positive under reckless endangerment statutes, thus eliminating proof of intent and causation. A number of states have adopted statutes that proscribe a person who has been diagnosed with HIV from engaging in sexual activity with another person without first informing a sexual partner of the HIV diagnosis.

WHEN DEATH OCCURS

Just as it is necessary to determine that a homicide victim was alive before the injury that caused death, it is also necessary to establish that death has, in fact, occurred. In most instances, the classic definition will suffice: Death occurs when the heart stops beating and respiration ends. However, technological advances have rendered this definition obsolete as the sole means of determining when death occurs. Many state legislatures have now adopted a definition of **brain death** that specifies that irreversible cessation of total brain functions constitutes death. For example, North Carolina law states:

> Brain death, defined as irreversible cessation of total brain function, may be used as a sole basis for the determination that a person has died, particularly when brain death occurs in the presence of artificially maintained respiratory and circulatory functions. This specific recognition of brain death as a criterion of death of the person shall not preclude the use of other medically recognized criteria for determining whether and when a person has died. N.C.G.S.A. § 90-323.

All states and the District of Columbia, either by statute or judicial decision, now recognize brain death as a criterion of death.

THE "ONE YEAR AND A DAY" RULE

Another obstacle to the prosecution of homicide cases can be the **one year and a day rule.** Although the rule originated during the early development of the English common law, in 1894 the U.S. Supreme Court acknowledged its applicability to criminal prosecutions in this country, stating:

> In cases of murder the rule at common law undoubtedly was that no person should be adjudged "by any act whatever to kill another who does not die by it within a year and a day thereafter...." And such is the rule in this country in prosecutions for murder, except in jurisdictions where it may be otherwise prescribed by statute. *Louisville, Evansville, & St. Louis R.R. Co. v. Clarke,* 152 U.S. 230, 239, 14 S.Ct. 579, 581, 38 L.Ed. 422, 424 (1894).

This inflexible rule continued because of uncertainties of medical science in establishing the cause of a victim's death after a lengthy period had elapsed. But in an age of advancing medical technology, the "one year and a day" rule has little relevance.

Either by statute or judicial decision the vast majority of states have abolished the rule; a few have modified it. California amended its statute in 1996 to stipulate that "[i]f death occurs beyond the time of three years and a day, there shall be a rebuttal presumption that the killing was not criminal." West's Ann. Cal. Penal Code § 194. Tennessee is one of the latest states to abolish the rule by judicial decision. In *State v. Rogers*, 992 S.W.2d 393 (Tenn. 1999), the Tennessee Supreme Court concluded that the reasons that prompted common-law courts to recognize the rule no longer exist, observing, "Modern pathologists are able to determine the cause of death with much greater accuracy than was possible in earlier times." *Id.* at 400. The U.S. Supreme Court upheld the Tennessee Supreme Court's retroactive abolition of the one year and a day rule. Justice Sandra Day O'Connor, writing for the majority of the Court, pointed out that the rule was an outdated relic of the common law and that modern medicine no longer necessitated the rule. Further, her opinion held that judicial abrogation of the year and a day rule was not unexpected, and thus Rogers had fair warning the rule may be abolished and there was no violation of the *Ex Post Facto* provision of the Constitution. *Rogers v. Tennessee,* 532 U.S. 451, 121 S.Ct. 1693, 149 L.Ed.2d 697 (2001).

Defenses to Homicidal Crimes

Defendants charged with murder or manslaughter frequently plead either self-defense or insanity. These defenses are discussed in detail in Chapter 14. Where an accused defends against a charge of murder, the heat of passion defense discussed earlier may be available in some instances, as would be the defense of reasonable care or accidental killing in others.

Suicide

The early English common law defined the offense of **suicide** as the intentional taking of a person's life by self-destruction. Suicide was not only regarded as being contrary to nature; it was regarded as an offense against the biblical commandment "Thou shalt not kill." Suicide was a species of felony punishable by forfeiture of the decedent's goods and chattels because it deprived the king of one of his subjects.

In the United States, the thrust of the criminal law has been to make it an offense to cause or aid another person to commit suicide, with many states making **assisted suicide** a crime. New York law provides that a person who "intentionally causes or aids another person to commit suicide" is guilty of manslaughter in the second degree. McKinney's N.Y. Penal Law § 125.15. In Texas, a person who, with intent to promote or assist in the commission of suicide, aids or attempts to aid another to commit suicide is guilty of a misdemeanor. If the actor's conduct causes a suicide or an attempted suicide that results in serious bodily injury, the offense becomes a felony. Vernon's Tex. Penal Code Ann. § 22.08. Until recently, the validity of laws of this character went unchallenged. As we explain in the following sections, this is no longer the case.

On November 8, 1994, Oregon voters adopted a Death with Dignity Act that allows terminally ill adult patients to obtain a physician's prescription for a lethal dose of medication. Two doctors must determine that the patient has less than six months to live and is mentally competent. The patient must request a lethal dose of medicine both orally and in writing and must wait at least fifteen days to obtain it. Although a federal district court originally enjoined the enforcement of the act, the U.S. Court of Appeals vacated the injunction. *Lee v. State of Oregon,* 107 F.3d 1382 (9th Cir. 1997). The U.S. Supreme Court declined to review the case. 522 U.S. 927, 118 S.Ct. 328, 139 L.Ed.2d 254 (1997).

On November 6, 2001, U.S. Attorney General John Ashcroft advised the Drug Enforcement Administration that assisting suicide was not a "legitimate medical purpose" and that the use of controlled substances to do so would violate the Controlled Substances Act (CSA). He pointed out that prescribing controlled substances for assisting suicide would make a physician's license subject to suspension or revocation. The State of Oregon filed suit, arguing that the Attorney General's actions exceeded his authority under the CSA. A federal court issued a permanent injunction against enforcement of the Attorney General's Directive on the ground that the Directive exceeded authority delegated to the Attorney General by the CSA. *Oregon v. Ashcroft,* 192 F.Supp.2d 1077 (D.Or. 2002). The Ninth Circuit Court of Appeals agreed. The U.S. Supreme Court granted review and held that the CSA did not authorize the Attorney General to prohibit doctors from prescribing regulated drugs for use in physician-assisted suicide, as authorized by the Oregon Death with Dignity Act. *Gonzales v. Oregon,* 546 U.S 243, 126 S.Ct. 904, 163 L.Ed.2d 748 (2006).

The Michigan Experience

Over the past several years, a series of judicial decisions have held that physicians may withhold or withdraw medical treatment at a patient's request. But the courts recognized a sharp distinction between such activity and administering drugs to assist a person to take his or her own life. Michigan, and several other states, had no laws against assisted suicide. This was dramatized on June 4, 1990, when a fifty-four-year-old woman suffering from Alzheimer's disease took her life by pressing a button that injected a lethal substance into her system through use of a suicide machine developed by Dr. Jack Kevorkian, a retired Michigan pathologist. Murder charges filed against the doctor were dismissed on the grounds that Michigan had no law against assisted suicide and that the prosecutors failed to show that the doctor tripped the device used to effect the death. After additional instances of assisted suicide of terminally ill patients, the Michigan legislature enacted a bill banning assisted suicide effective on April 1, 1993.

In succeeding years, the media reported numerous instances of alleged participation by Kevorkian in assisting terminally ill persons to commit suicide. After several unsuccessful attempts to prosecute Kevorkian, in 1999 a Michigan jury found him guilty of second-degree murder in the death of a man suffering from Lou Gehrig's disease. The court sentenced him to serve ten to twenty-five years in prison. The Michigan Court of Appeals affirmed his conviction and sentence. *People v. Kevorkian,* 639 N.W.2d 291 (Mich. App. 2001). The Supreme Court of Michigan denied his request for a further appeal, *People v. Kevorkian,* 642 N.W.2d 681 (Mich. 2002), and the U.S. Supreme Court denied his petition for a writ of certiorari. *Kevorkian v. Michigan,* 537 U.S. 881, 123 S.Ct. 90, 154 L.Ed.2d 137 (2002).

During the 1990s, state laws that prohibit assisted suicide were challenged on constitutional grounds in instances where terminally ill patients seek to end their lives with the aid of a physician. Soon the state of Washington became the venue for a direct challenge to a state statute prohibiting assisted suicide, a challenge that would eventually lead to a seminal decision by the U.S. Supreme Court.

The Washington Experience

To prevent assisted suicide in the state of Washington, the legislature enacted a law providing that "[a] person is guilty of promoting a suicide attempt when he knowingly causes or aids another person to attempt suicide." Wash. Rev. Code § 9A.36.060(1) (1994). "Promoting a suicide attempt" is a felony, punishable by up to five years' imprisonment and up to a $10,000 fine. § 9A.36.060(2). However, Washington's Natural

Death Act, enacted in 1979, states that the "withholding or withdrawal of life sustaining treatment" at a patient's direction "shall not, for any purpose, constitute a suicide." Wash. Rev. Code § 70.122.070(1).

In 1994 the U.S. District Court for the Western District of Washington ruled that Washington's statute banning assisted suicide was unconstitutional. *Compassion in Dying v. Washington,* 850 F. Supp. 1454, 1459 (W.D. Wash. 1994). A panel of the Court of Appeals for the Ninth Circuit reversed, emphasizing that "[i]n the two hundred and five years of our existence no constitutional right to aid in killing oneself has ever been asserted and upheld by a court of final jurisdiction." *Compassion in Dying v. Washington,* 49 F.3d 586, 591 (1995). Following the reversal by the three-judge appellate panel, the Ninth Circuit reheard the case *en banc,* reversed the panel's decision, and affirmed the District Court. *Compassion in Dying v. Washington,* 79 F.3d 790, 798 (1996). In its *en banc* decision the Ninth Circuit concluded that "the Constitution encompasses a due process liberty interest in controlling the time and manner of one's death—that there is, in short, a constitutionally recognized 'right to die.'" 79 F.3d at 816. After "[w]eighing and then balancing" this interest against Washington's various interests, the court held that the state's assisted suicide ban was unconstitutional "as applied to terminally ill competent adults who wish to hasten their deaths with medication prescribed by their physicians." 79 F.3d 836, 837.

The U.S. Supreme Court granted certiorari and on June 26, 1997, in *Washington v. Glucksberg,* 521 U.S. 702, 117 S.Ct. 2258, 138 L.Ed.2d 772 (1997), reversed the Ninth Circuit's decision. Writing for a unanimous Court, Chief Justice William Rehnquist discussed the historical and cultural background of laws prohibiting assisted suicide. He pointed out that in almost every state it is a crime to assist in a suicide and that the statutes banning assisted suicide are long-standing expressions of the states' commitment to the protection and preservation of all human life.

Go to the Scheb/ Scheb Criminal Law and Procedure 6e website at academic .cengage.com/criminaljustice/ scheb for an edited version of *Washington v. Glucksberg.*

The Court's opinion analyzed the interests that come into play in determining whether a statute banning assisted suicide passes constitutional muster. In doing so, the Court rejected any parallel between a person's right to terminate medical treatment and the "right" to have assistance in committing suicide. As the Court opined,

> We need not weigh exactly the relative strengths of these various interests. They are unquestionably important and legitimate, and Washington's ban on assisted suicide is at least reasonably related to their promotion and protection. We therefore hold that [the challenged statute] does not violate the Fourteenth Amendment, either on its face or "as applied to competent, terminally ill adults who wish to hasten their deaths by obtaining medication prescribed by their doctors." 521 U.S. at 735, 117 S.Ct. at 2275, 138 L.Ed.2d at 797.

Expressing deference to the lawmaking role of the states, the Court noted:

> Throughout the Nation, Americans are engaged in an earnest and profound debate about the morality, legality, and practicality of physician assisted suicide. Our holding permits this debate to continue, as it should in a democratic society. 521 U.S. at 735, 117 S.Ct. at 2275, 138 L.Ed.2d at 797.

Competing Values in Suicide Laws

Laws against assisted suicide bring into play significant policy issues and require legislatures to carefully balance competing claims of individual liberty, ethics, and the interest of society. Some proponents of allowing assisted suicide argue that it simply enables a person who has a rational capacity to make a choice. Those who reject this view argue that the state has an interest in the preservation of life and that some individuals may elect to die needlessly as a result of misdiagnosis. Moreover, opponents

Assisted Suicide

In 1997 Charles E. Hall, a mentally competent but terminally ill patient, and his physician, Cecil McIver, M.D., sought to have a Florida court declare that section 782.08, Florida Statutes, which prohibits assisted suicide, violated the Privacy Clause of the Florida Constitution and the Due Process and Equal Protection Clauses of the Fourteenth Amendment to the U.S. Constitution. They sought an injunction against the state attorney from prosecuting the physician for giving deliberate assistance to Hall in committing suicide. Basing its conclusion on Florida's privacy provision and the federal Equal Protection Clause, the trial court held that the Florida law could not be constitutionally enforced against Hall and McIver. The Florida Supreme Court granted an expedited review. By the time it rendered its decision on July 17, 1997, the U.S. Supreme Court had ruled that state laws prohibiting assisted suicide pass muster under the federal constitution. On the basis of that decision, the Florida Supreme Court summarily disposed of the contention that the Florida law violated the U.S. Constitution. The court then proceeded to find that neither was the explicit privacy provision in the Florida constitution offended by the state's 129-year-old statute prohibiting assisted suicide. In concluding its opinion, the court opted to leave "social policy" to the state legislature when it observed that "[w]e do not hold that a carefully crafted statute authorizing assisted suicide would be unconstitutional."

Krischer v. McIver, 697 So.2d 97 (Fla. 1997).

of legalizing assisted suicide argue that allowing it leads to an indifference to the value of life. As a result of the Supreme Court's 1997 decision in *Washington v. Glucksberg, supra,* the states may enforce statutory bans on assisted suicide with more assurance, yet as the terminally ill population continues to increase, the debate is destined to continue. The Supreme Court's decision places that debate in the state legislatures and the state judicial tribunals.

Public opinion would seem to support the legalization of doctor-assisted suicide, at least in some instances. In a series of national surveys conducted between 1996 and 2005, the Gallup Organization asked, "When a person has a disease that cannot be cured and is living in severe pain, do you think doctors should or should not be allowed by law to assist the patient to commit suicide if the patient requests it?" In 1996, 52 percent of respondents said yes; in 2005, 58 percent answered in the affirmative. The Gallup Organization, Inc., The Gallup Poll, December 29, 2005.

Less than one month after the Supreme Court's decision in *Washington v. Glucksberg,* the Florida Supreme Court ruled that the state statute prohibiting assisted suicide did not offend the state constitution. *Krischer v. McIver,* 697 So.2d 97 (Fla. 1997). (See the Case-in-Point on assisted suicide.) In 2001 the Alaska Supreme Court held that the state constitution's guarantees of privacy and liberty do not afford terminally ill patients the right to a physician's assistance in committing suicide. *Sampson v. State,* 31 P.3d 88 (Alaska 2001).

Rape and Sexual Battery

There are early biblical accounts of the offense of rape; however, the law of rape, as it exists today, has its roots in the early English common law. It was a felony for a male to have unlawful **carnal knowledge** (that is, sexual intercourse) of a female by force and against her will. This is usually referred to as **common-law rape** or **forcible rape.** In later stages of the English law, it became a statutory offense for a man to have carnal knowledge of a female child less than ten years of age with or without the child's consent. This latter offense came to be known as **statutory rape.**

The common-law offenses required penetration, however slight, of the female's sexual organ by the male sexual organ; no emission of seed was required. At common law, there was a conclusive presumption that a male under age fourteen could not commit the crime of rape.

Common-law rape contemplated unlawful intercourse; therefore, a husband could not be guilty of raping his wife. Although this **marital exception** is of somewhat dubious judicial origin, it is generally credited to the writings of Sir Matthew Hale, who served as Lord Chief Justice in England from 1671 to 1676. Of course, in egregious cases the husband could be charged with assault or battery of his wife. Furthermore, a husband or even another woman could be charged as an aider or abettor if he or she assisted or procured another man to rape his wife.

More than two centuries after Hale's demise, in March 1991, England's Court of Appeal dismissed an appeal by a man who was convicted of an attempted rape of his estranged wife. In delivering the opinion of the five-judge court, the Lord Chief Justice observed that a rapist remains a rapist irrespective of his relationship with his victim. Further, the court observed that the centuries-old legal doctrine that a husband could not be guilty of raping his wife no longer represented the law, considering the position of a wife in contemporary society.

The American Approach

The new American states followed the common-law scheme in statutorily defining rape; however, two principal changes soon occurred. First, many states explicitly rejected the common-law presumption that males under age fourteen could not commit the offense. Second, legislatures in most states made consensual intercourse with a young female an offense (statutory rape) if the female was younger than sixteen or eighteen, rather than ten. Some, however, added the qualification that the female must have been "of previous chaste character."

American courts disagreed on the intent required for a defendant to be guilty of rape. Some held that no intent other than that evidenced by the act of intercourse was needed. See, for example, *Walden v. State,* 156 S.W.2d 385 (Tenn. 1941). An earlier Oklahoma judicial opinion required proof of the defendant's specific intent. *Thomas v. State,* 95 P.2d 658 (Okl. Cr. 1939). But in 1977, the requirement of specific intent was expressly overruled. *Boyd v. State,* 572 P.2d 276 (Okl. Cr. 1977).

Courts in American jurisdictions struggled with the requirements of **force** and **consent** in the law of forcible rape. Some judges instructed juries that "for the defendant to be found guilty of rape, you must find that the woman resisted to her utmost." Later cases recognized that it was not necessary for a female victim to resist to the utmost; rather, the degree of resistance came to be regarded as a relative matter dependent on all the circumstances surrounding the incident. Yet courts continued to recognize that resistance generally had to be more than a mere negative verbal response by a female.

All courts recognized that to constitute common-law rape, sexual intercourse had to be without the female's consent. However, there could be no valid consent by a woman who was asleep, unconscious, or mentally incapable. Likewise, consent obtained by fraud or impersonation or through pretext was invalid. Thus, if a man impersonated a woman's husband and caused her to submit to sexual intercourse, he would be guilty of rape. Likewise, a physician who had intercourse with female patients who were not conscious of the nature of the doctor's acts because of the treatments being administered was properly found guilty of rape. *People v. Minkowski*, 23 Cal. Rptr. 92 (Cal. App. 1962).

Statutory Rape Laws

In America, state legislatures enacted laws to protect young women from acts of sexual intercourse. These statutory rape laws usually stipulate that carnal knowledge (sexual intercourse) with a female under age sixteen, seventeen, or eighteen is a crime. In contrast with common-law rape, the elements of force and consent are irrelevant in statutory rape laws. In effect, underage females are deemed unable to validly consent to sexual relations. A few states have allowed a male to defend against a charge of statutory rape on the basis that he was mistaken about the female's age, but most hold a male defendant strictly liable even if he made a reasonable inquiry in good faith to determine the victim's age. (The concept of a strict liability offense is explained in Chapter 4.)

A California law making statutory rape a crime was challenged on the basis of gender discrimination because only males could be prosecuted for the offense. The U.S. Supreme Court rejected the challenge. *Michael M. v. Superior Court*, 450 U.S. 464, 101 S.Ct. 1200, 67 L.Ed.2d 437 (1981).

Statutory rape laws are now gender-neutral in most states, and some impose penalties only if there is at least a two to five-year disparity between the ages of the perpetrator and the underage party. Obviously, it would be inconceivable to prosecute every minor who has a consensual sexual relationship. The original objective of statutory rape laws was to protect the chastity of young females; however, those who support these laws now emphasize both the psychological effects and the threat of disease that accompany sexual encounters involving minors. They also point out that it is adult males who impregnate most teenage mothers and that, when vigorously enforced, statutory rape laws that focus on sexual relationships involving age discrepancies of several years are one solution to the problem of teenage pregnancy. Some states have graded voluntary sexual battery offenses by considering the age of a perpetrator who engages in sex with a minor. For example, in 1996 the Florida legislature made it a second-degree felony for a person age twenty-four or older to engage in sex with a person age sixteen or seventeen. West's Fla. Stat. Ann. § 794.05.

There is universal agreement that very young children should be protected from sexual predators, but there is considerable opposition to statutory rape laws. Opponents argue that these laws are out of touch with present-day sexual mores. Some see statutory rape laws as depriving women in their late teens of exercising a personal choice; others point out that these laws are largely unobserved and lend themselves to selective enforcement along the lines of race and social class. Despite the conflict in views, it appears that for the foreseeable future statutory rape laws, now often termed "voluntary sexual assault or battery" laws, will remain on the American legal scene.

Reform in the American Law of Rape

During the late 1970s and the 1980s, protests led to several statutory and judicial reforms in the law of rape. Initially, many such protests were by women's groups who complained of traumatic encounters between female victims and police, prosecutors, defense attorneys, and courts. Women's advocacy groups contended that in all too many instances, a female rape victim was degraded and made to feel ashamed for the assault she suffered. As societal awareness increased, significant changes in the law occurred. Before examining a modern criminal code proscribing sexual offenses, we will examine the more significant legislative and judicial reforms in this area.

LEGISLATIVE REFORMS

Legislative reforms have focused on making rape a **gender-neutral offense,** dividing the offense into categories, and adopting rape shield laws. Denominating rape as sexual battery and making it a gender-neutral offense became a basic reform. No longer was the offense limited to the common-law concept of vaginal rape of a female. The offender and victim may be of either sex, and newer statutes embrace all types of sexual impositions, including anal, oral, or vaginal penetrations by a sex organ or by another object, excepting acts performed for *bona fide* medical purposes. In many states, either statutes or judicial decisions now provide that a husband may be charged with rape of his wife.

The trend of the newer statutes has been to divide the offense of sexual battery into various classifications. Punishment varies according to the type of sexual conduct or contact, the character and extent of force used, and the age and vulnerability of the victim. Those who commit sexual batteries against the helpless and those who take advantage of their position of familial or supervisory authority can be singled out for special punishment. The proper classification of offenses has led to convictions when merited by the evidence and has achieved more just results in punishing offenders.

One of the most significant legal reforms concerning rape has been the enactment of **rape shield laws.** In a prosecution for rape (or sexual battery), these laws preclude presentation of evidence of a victim's prior sexual activity with anyone other than the defendant. In 1999 the West Virginia Supreme Court summarized the objective of rape shield statutes when it observed:

> Like rape shield statutes in other jurisdictions, this State's rape shield statute was enacted to protect the victims of sexual assault from humiliating and embarrassing public fishing expeditions into their sexual conduct; to overcome victims' reluctance to report incidents of sexual assault; and to protect victims from psychological or emotional abuse in court as the price of their cooperation in prosecuting sex offenders. *State v. Guthrie,* 518 S.E.2d 83, 96 (W.Va. 1999).

Even where the defendant seeks to introduce evidence of prior relations with a victim, statutes commonly require such evidence to be first presented to the court *in camera* (in the judge's private chambers) for the court to determine whether the evidence of the defendant's prior relationship with the victim is relevant to the victim's consent. For example, New Jersey law provides:

> In prosecutions for the crime of rape, assault with intent to commit rape, and breaking and entering with intent to commit rape, evidence of the complaining witness' previous sexual conduct shall not be admitted nor reference made to it in the presence of the jury except as provided in this act. N.J.S.A. 2A:84A-32.1.

The New Jersey statute goes on to state that before permitting evidence of a complaining witness's sexual history, the court must first conduct a hearing *in camera* to determine whether such evidence is relevant and whether its probative value is not outweighed by the prejudice or confusion it will create or by its unwarranted invasion of the complaining witness's privacy.

Rape shield laws are based on the theory that a victim's prior sexual activity is not probative of whether the victim has been violated in the instance for which the defendant stands accused. Thus, in *State v. Madsen,* 772 S.W.2d 656 (Mo. 1989), the Missouri Supreme Court held that neither evidence of a victim having a "live-in" boyfriend or having two illegitimate children was relevant in a prosecution for rape.

But can a female victim offer testimony of a prior rape to explain her conduct in failing to resist an attacker? In *Raines v. State*, 382 S.E.2d 738 (Ga. App. 1989), the appellate court found this to be appropriate.

In interpreting the applicability of rape shield laws to some unusual factual situations, courts have faced some difficult judgments. In a Massachusetts decision, the court ruled that a defendant charged with rape should have been allowed to question the complainant as to whether she had sexual intercourse with anyone else on the night of the attack. The court concluded that such evidence would not constitute an attack on the complainant's credibility. Rather, the court held that such evidence tended to support the defendant's theory that someone else had attacked the complainant and that she had wrongly accused him. *Commonwealth v. Fitzgerald*, 590 N.E.2d 1151 (Mass. 1992).

A Virginia appellate court ruled that evidence that a victim did not report the alleged rape until a month after the incident, when she learned that she had contracted gonorrhea, was admissible to show ill will of the complainant. The court found that such evidence did not relate to the sexual conduct of the victim and was therefore not barred by the Virginia rape shield statute. *Evans v. Commonwealth*, 415 S.E.2d 851 (Va. App. 1992).

JUDICIAL REFORMS

Go to the Scheb/ Scheb Criminal Law and Procedure 6e website at academic .cengage.com/criminaljustice/ scheb to find *State v. Studham* (1977), where the Utah Supreme Court explains how force can be psychological as well as physical in the context of sexual assault.

Significant judicial reforms have also occurred in the law of rape. For example, for many years courts have not insisted that a woman must "resist to the utmost" to establish that her sexual privacy has been violated. This is consistent with the advice of law enforcement officers, who frequently caution women that violent resistance to a rapist's attack can result in the victim's serious injury or death. In considering whether a victim's resistance has been overcome, courts consider such factors as the extent of the offender's force, the physical capacity of the victim to resist, and the psychological and emotional stress of a victim whose sensibilities are outraged by fear of violation of her bodily integrity.

Courts have also come to realize that there is no unique reason to single out the testimony of a sexual battery victim and instruct juries that it deserves more scrutiny than the testimony of other crime victims. The low conviction rate for rape defendants belies the need for special scrutiny for the uncorroborated testimony of a rape victim. In fact, data compiled several years ago by the Federal Bureau of Investigation revealed that of the FBI's four violent crimes (murder, forcible rape, robbery, and aggravated assault), rape had the highest rate of acquittal or dismissal. See *People v. Rincon-Pineda*, 538 P.2d 247, 257 (Cal. 1975).

CASE-IN-POINT

Does Asking an Attacker to Wear a Condom Constitute Consent to Sex?

In May 1993, in Travis County, Texas, Joel Valdez, a twenty-eight-year-old defendant who was charged with rape, claimed that the female with whom he admittedly had sexual intercourse had asked him to wear a condom. Valdez testified that he complied with the woman's request and that accordingly they were simply "making love." But the twenty-six-year-old complainant explained that she pleaded with her attacker to wear a condom only to protect herself from acquired immunodeficiency syndrome (AIDS). The jury in Austin, Texas, found Valdez guilty of rape, implicitly finding that asking the attacker to wear a condom does not constitute consent to sexual intercourse.

A Contemporary Statutory Treatment of Sexual Offenses

Michigan has modern, comprehensive laws that classify criminal sexual conduct by various degrees, depending on whether it involves sexual penetration or sexual contact with another person as well as other factors. It defines **sexual penetration** as sexual intercourse, cunnilingus, fellatio, anal intercourse, or any other intrusion, however slight, of any part of a person's body or of any object into the genital or anal openings of another person's body, but emission of seed is not required. Sexual contact is defined as including the intentional touching of the victim's intimate parts or the intentional touching of the clothing covering the immediate area of the victim's intimate parts, if that intentional touching can reasonably be construed as being for the purpose of sexual arousal or gratification. Mich. Comp. Laws Ann. § 750.520a(k)(l).

Section 720.520(b) deals with first-degree criminal sexual conduct and provides:

1. A person is guilty of criminal sexual conduct in the first degree if he or she engages in sexual penetration with another person and if any of the following circumstances exists:

(a) That other person is under 13 years of age.

(b) That other person is at least 13 but less than 16 years of age and any of the following:

(i) The actor is a member of the same household as the victim.

(ii) The actor is related to the victim by blood or affinity to the fourth degree.

(iii) The actor is in a position of authority over the victim and used this authority to coerce the victim to submit.

(iv) The actor is a teacher, substitute teacher, or administrator of the public or nonpublic school in which that other person is enrolled.

(c) Sexual penetration occurs under circumstances involving the commission of any other felony.

(d) The actor is aided or abetted by 1 or more other persons and either of the following circumstances exists:

(i) The actor knows or has reason to know that the victim is mentally incapable, mentally incapacitated, or physically helpless.

(ii) The actor uses force or coercion to accomplish the sexual penetration. Force or coercion includes but is not limited to any of the circumstances listed in subdivision (f)(i) to (v).

(e) The actor is armed with a weapon or any article used or fashioned in a manner to lead the victim to reasonably believe it to be a weapon.

(f) The actor causes personal injury to the victim and force or coercion is used to accomplish sexual penetration. Force or coercion includes but is not limited to any of the following circumstances:

(i) When the actor overcomes the victim through the actual application of physical force or physical violence.

(ii) When the actor coerces the victim to submit by threatening to use force or violence on the victim, and the victim believes that the actor has the present ability to execute these threats.

(iii) When the actor coerces the victim to submit by threatening to retaliate in the future against the victim, or any other person, and the victim believes that the actor has the ability to execute this threat. As used in this subdivision, "to retaliate" includes threats of physical punishment, kidnapping, or extortion.

(iv) When the actor engages in the medical treatment or examination of the victim in a manner or for purposes which are medically recognized as unethical or unacceptable.

(v) When the actor, through concealment or by the element of surprise, is able to overcome the victim.

(g) The actor causes personal injury to the victim, and the actor knows or has reason to know that the victim is mentally incapable, mentally incapacitated, or physically helpless.

(h) The other person is mentally incapable, mentally disabled, mentally incapacitated, or physically helpless, and any of the following:

(i) The actor is related to the victim by blood or affinity to the fourth degree.

(ii) The actor is in a position of authority over the victim and uses this authority to coerce the victim to submit.

2. Criminal sexual conduct in the first degree is a felony of the first degree.... Mich. Comp. Laws Ann. § 520(b).

Second-degree criminal sexual conduct follows substantially along the lines of the preceding section, but instead of penetration it makes sexual contact with a victim unlawful. Violation is a second-degree felony. Mich. Comp. Laws Ann. § 750.520(c).

Third-degree criminal sexual conduct includes two of the same elements as a first-degree offense (that is, penetration and use of force or coercion) but does not include the element that the defendant was aided or abetted in the act by one or more persons. Violation is a third-degree felony. Mich. Comp. Laws Ann. § 750.520(d).

Fourth-degree criminal sexual conduct involves **sexual contact** with another person involving force or coercion; an actor who knows or has reason to know that the victim is mentally incapable, mentally incapacitated, or physically helpless; or a victim who is under jurisdiction of the department of corrections and an actor who is associated with that department. It is a serious misdemeanor. Mich. Comp. Laws Ann. § 750(e).

Note that the Michigan law makes no distinction as to the sex of the actor or victim—in other words, it is gender-neutral. It broadly defines sexual penetration and sexual contact and divides the offense of criminal sexual conduct into degrees considering the conduct of the actor and the vulnerability of the victim. Thus, it is a comprehensive sexual battery statute that embodies many of the reforms discussed earlier.

Demise of the Marital Exception

As noted, Lord Hale, the seventeenth-century English jurist, wrote that a husband could not be guilty of the rape of his wife. To support this rationale, the common-law courts offered three reasons. First, the wife is a chattel belonging to her husband; second, a husband and wife are "one," and obviously a husband cannot rape himself; and finally, by marriage the wife irrevocably consents to intercourse with her husband on a continuing basis. Until the late 1970s, American courts almost universally accepted Hale's Rule, although not the rationale that Lord Hale proffered.

The 1980s witnessed the erosion of **Hale's Rule.** Today courts generally disavow the unity concept of marriage. In 1981 the New Jersey Supreme Court held that the state's rape statute that used the language "any person who has carnal knowledge of a woman forcibly against her will" did not except from its operation a husband who was living apart from his wife. *State v. Smith,* 426 A.2d 38 (N.J. 1981).

The marital exception has been abrogated in a number of ways. Pending adoption of gender-neutral sexual battery statutes, some courts addressed challenges to traditional rape statutes on constitutional grounds. For example, in *People v. Liberta,*

474 N.E.2d 567 (N.Y. 1984), New York's highest court termed the notion of a wife's implied consent to intercourse as "irrational and absurd" and emphasized that a married woman should have the same right to bodily autonomy as a single woman. It dismissed any idea of the wife being property of the husband because the state recognizes that wives and husbands are separate legal entities. In rejecting any distinction between marital and nonmarital rape, appellate courts in other states began to rely on constitutional arguments similar to those expounded by the New York court. See, for example, *Shunn v. State*, 742 P.2d 775 (Wyo. 1987). By the mid 1990s about half the states had abolished the marital exception completely; the majority of the remaining states had abolished the exception where the spouses are living apart from each other.

Many state legislatures have now enacted statutes either redefining "rape" or defining "sexual battery" as gender-neutral offenses. For example, in 1990 Louisiana made rape a gender-neutral offense by redefining it as "the act of anal or vaginal sexual intercourse with a male or female person committed without the person's lawful consent." West's L.S.A.-R.S. 14:41. In other instances, states have enacted statutes specifically excluding marriage as a defense to rape or sexual battery. Several states now criminalize forced sexual relations between spouses or cohabiters. For example, Connecticut law follows this approach and defines "sexual intercourse" very broadly:

> No spouse or cohabiter shall compel the other spouse or cohabiter to engage in sexual intercourse by the use of force against such other spouse or cohabiter, or by the threat of the use of force against such other spouse or cohabiter which reasonably causes such other spouse or cohabiter to fear physical injury. C.G.S.A. § 53a-70b.

Some argue that prosecution of a husband for rape might make reconciliation of marital differences impossible. Furthermore, they contend that proof of guilt will be difficult to obtain because of the usual lack of corroborating evidence of the incident. Nevertheless, legislatures and courts have come to realize that marriage in contemporary society is regarded as a partnership and should not be deemed a license to enjoy sex on demand by a forcible encounter with one's spouse.

Prosecutorial Burdens

As in all criminal cases, the prosecution must prove the *corpus delicti*—that is, the fact that the crime has been committed. Proof that an act of sexual intercourse (or other sexual imposition, depending on the statutory definition of the offense) has taken place with the victim is usually sufficient in a sexual battery case. In addition, in a statutory rape case, proof must be offered of the age of the victim (usually the female) and, in some instances, the age of the offender (usually the male). In sexual battery prosecutions, proof of the defendant's general intent is usually sufficient, absent a statute requiring proof of the defendant's specific intent.

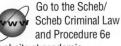 Go to the Scheb/Scheb Criminal Law and Procedure 6e website at academic .cengage.com/criminaljustice/ scheb to find *State v. Rothenberg* (1985), where the Connecticut Supreme Court examines the sufficiency of evidence to support a conviction for sexual assault.

One common problem in sexual battery prosecutions is the lack of independent eyewitness testimony. Consequently, it frequently becomes the victim's word against the defendant's word. Thus, police and prosecutors place paramount importance on a "fresh complaint" by a victim. Preservation of semen, photographs of bruises, torn clothing, and even pubic hairs become valuable evidence to corroborate a victim's testimony. Seldom is the credibility of a complaining witness as vital as in sexual battery prosecutions. To appear in court and testify concerning a sexual assault is a traumatic experience for a victim of sexual assault. This is particularly true for young children. To assist youngsters, many courts permit them to illustrate their testimony through the use of anatomically detailed dolls.

Sufficiency of Evidence to Support a Conviction for Sexual Assault

Rothenberg met the complainant in a bar. After dancing with her, Rothenberg asked the complainant to accompany him to a party at a friend's condominium. The complainant agreed and drove to the condominium in her own car. When she arrived at the condo, there appeared to be no one there except Rothenberg. The complainant and Rothenberg sat on a couch in the living room where they kissed and exchanged back massages. The complainant then told Rothenberg that she wanted to leave, but he refused to let her go. She ran to the front door and attempted to open it, but Rothenberg closed the door and prevented her from leaving. The com-plainant then locked herself in the bathroom where she remained for thirty minutes. Rothenberg promised to let the complainant leave if she would come out of the bathroom. When she came out, Rothenberg forced her onto the couch. At that point the complainant submitted to sexual intercourse. In sustaining Rothenberg's conviction for sexual assault, the Connecticut Supreme Court noted that "the complainant's unambiguous request to leave the condominium disabused the defendant of any misinterpretation of her wishes" and that "the defendant's conduct thereafter was knowingly coercive."

State v. Rothenberg, 487 A.2d 545 (Conn. 1985).

Rape Trauma Syndrome

In 1974, to describe a recurring pattern of physical and emotional symptoms experienced by rape victims, psychiatrists coined the term **rape trauma syndrome,** which refers to a set of psychological manifestations (for example, fear, depression, and a sense of guilt) of victims usually following a sexual assault. Since then, prosecutors have sought to introduce expert testimony at rape trials to establish that a victim's symptoms are consistent with those of the syndrome. This type of evidence has particular relevance to prosecutions where the defendant claims consent of the victim as a defense. On review of convictions, appellate courts have disagreed on whether such evidence is admissible. The Kansas Supreme Court was the nation's first appellate court to address the question of the admissibility of expert testimony concerning rape trauma syndrome. The court allowed the introduction of psychiatric testimony that a rape victim suffered from rape trauma syndrome, noting that such expert evidence is relevant where the defendant claims consent. *State v. Marks,* 647 P.2d 1292 (Kan. 1982). Other state supreme courts have reached a similar conclusion. *State v. Liddell,* 685 P.2d 918 (Mont. 1984); *State v. Huey,* 699 P.2d 1290 (Ariz. 1985). An Ohio appellate court held that such expert psychiatric testimony is admissible but only where its value outweighs its prejudicial impact. The court noted that expert opinions of this type assist laypersons in interpreting reactions of a victim, especially in child rape cases. *State v. Whitman,* 475 N.E.2d 486 (Ohio App. 1984).

There is respectable judicial authority to the contrary. In 1982 the Minnesota Supreme Court ruled that the diagnosis of rape trauma syndrome is not a fact-finding tool but rather a therapeutic tool and that admission of expert testimony on the subject at a rape trial is erroneous. *State v. Saldana,* 324 N.W.2d 227 (Minn. 1982). Several other appellate courts have held that expert testimony concerning the syndrome is not admissible to prove that a rape in fact occurred. For example, in *People v. Pullins,* 378 N.W.2d 502 (Mich. App. 1985), the court held evidence of rape trauma syndrome inadmissible to establish that a rape occurred. This came the year after the Missouri Supreme Court, in *State v. Taylor,* 663 S.W.2d 235 (Mo. 1984), concluded that such testimony was beyond the proper basis of expert opinion.

In 1990 New York's highest court concluded that the scientific community has now generally accepted that rape is a highly traumatic event that triggers the onset of certain identifiable symptoms. The court agreed that expert testimony of the rape trauma syndrome may be admitted to aid the jury's understanding of the victim's behavior after the assault. Nevertheless, the court observed that identifiable symptoms in rape victims do not indicate whether an incident did or did not occur; thus, trial judges cannot allow such testimony to be introduced for this purpose. *People v. Taylor,* 552 N.E.2d 131 (N.Y. 1990). In 1995 the Kansas Supreme Court, noting that it was the first high court to allow introduction of qualified expert psychiatric testimony regarding the existence of rape trauma syndrome, ruled that a social worker was not qualified to testify on the subject. *State v. Willis,* 888 P.2d 839 (Kan. 1995).

Appellate courts still disagree on the admissibility of evidence of the rape trauma syndrome. Much of the controversy focuses on the purpose of the evidence and the qualifications of experts. Yet the trend is to allow such evidence. As the New Mexico Court of Appeals recently pointed out, an expert's testimony on victimization and impact of trauma on victims is relevant in a trial for sex offenses. *State v. Maestas,* 112 P.3d 1134 (N.M. App. 2005).

Can a defendant charged with rape introduce expert testimony concerning the rape trauma syndrome to establish that a rape did not occur? In *Henson v. State,* 535 N.E.2d 1189 (Ind. 1989), the defense presented a witness who testified to seeing the victim dancing and drinking at a bar on the evening after the alleged rape. The defense then sought to introduce expert testimony on the subject, but the trial judge would not allow it. The state supreme court ruled that the testimony must be permitted because it would be unfair to allow the prosecution to present expert testimony on rape trauma syndrome but deny a defendant the same opportunity.

Some commentators contend that to allow a defendant to inquire about the victim's lack of rape trauma syndrome can thwart the purpose of rape shield laws.

SUPREME COURT PERSPECTIVE

Coker v. Georgia, 433 U.S. 584, 97 S.Ct. 2861, 53 L.Ed.2d 982 (1977)

In this case, the Supreme Court invalidated a Georgia statute allowing the death penalty for defendants convicted of rape. In his opinion announcing the judgment of the Court, Justice Byron White commented on the crime of rape.

JUSTICE WHITE announced the judgment of the Court and filed an opinion in which JUSTICE STEWART, JUSTICE BLACKMUN, and JUSTICE STEVENS joined.
[Rape] is highly reprehensible, both in a moral sense and in its almost total contempt for the personal integrity and autonomy of the female victim and for the latter's privilege of choosing those with whom intimate relationships are to be established. Short of homicide, it is the "ultimate violation of self." It is also a violent crime because it nor-

mally involves force, or the threat of force or intimidation, to overcome the will and the capacity of the victim to resist. Rape is very often accompanied by physical injury to the female and can also inflict mental and psychological damage. Because it undermines the community's sense of security, there is public injury as well.

Rape is without doubt deserving of serious punishment; but in terms of moral depravity and of the injury to the person and to the public, it does not compare with murder, which does involve the unjustified taking of human life. Although it may be accompanied by another crime, rape by definition does not include the death of or even the serious injury to another person. The murderer kills; the rapist, if no more than that, does not. Life is over for the victim of the murderer; for the rape victim, life may not be nearly so happy as it was, but it is not over and normally is not beyond repair.

Sex Offender Registration Laws

On June 20, 1997, a Trenton, New Jersey, court sentenced Jesse Timmendequas to death for the rape and murder of seven-year-old Megan Kanka in 1994. The case attracted national attention after it was revealed that Timmendequas had a record of committing sex offenses against children. Public outrage led the New Jersey legislature to enact a law requiring convicted sex offenders who are released from prison, move into the state, or simply change their addresses to register with local law enforcement agencies. Registration must include the individual's address, description, and other personal data along with a complete criminal history. These agencies in turn must make this information available to the public. The New Jersey statute became widely known as **Megan's Law** in memory of Megan Kanka. Failure to comply with the registration requirement is itself a criminal offense. After fifteen years with no violations, an offender may request a court to terminate sex offender status. See, generally, N.J.S.A. 2C: 7-1 *et seq.*

Similar laws have been enacted in most states, and most of these laws have survived constitutional attack (see the following Case-in-Point). In 1996 Congress enacted a federal version of Megan's Law. 42 U.S.C.A. § 14071. The federal statute sets forth guidelines for state programs and encourages states to adopt such programs by threatening them with the loss of federal funds. All states and the District of Columbia have adopted variations of Megan's Law.

It remains to be seen how effective the various versions of Megan's Law will be in protecting children from sexual predators. There is also concern that these laws may be too inclusive in that persons convicted in the past of minor sexual offenses are subjected to undeserved community scorn. Megan's Law and similar laws are also subject to the criticism that they impose penalties based on status rather than on wrongful acts. However, the public has demanded that the justice system do more to protect people from sexual predators, and such individuals often remain a serious threat to the community even after they have paid their debt to society.

State registration laws modeled after Megan's Law have survived constitutional attacks based on double jeopardy, vagueness, equal protection, the right to privacy, and cruel and unusual punishment, constitutional doctrines such as discussed in Chapter 3. The Case-in-Point below illustrates an unsuccessful challenge to Tennessee's version of Megan's Law on the basis of the Double Jeopardy Clause in the U.S. Constitution.

CASE-IN-POINT

Constitutionality of Sex Offender Registration Laws

In 1990 Arthur Cutshall pled guilty to aggravated sexual battery of a five-year-old child and was sentenced to prison. When he learned that his name and address would be forever placed on the state's sex offender registry upon his release from prison, he brought suit in federal district court to challenge the constitutionality of Tennessee's version of Megan's Law. See Tenn. Code § 40-39-106. Among other things, Cutshall argued that the law constituted double jeopardy. A federal district judge rejected the challenge, as did the U.S. Court of Appeals for the Sixth Circuit. In upholding the statute, the Sixth Circuit observed that "the focus of the act is not on circumscribing the conduct of the offender, but on the protection of the public...." The U.S. Supreme Court denied certiorari, leaving the Sixth Circuit's decision intact.

Cutshall v. Sundquist, 193 F.3d 466 (6th Cir. 1999).

In March 2003 the U.S. Supreme Court upheld Alaska's version of Megan's Law against an attack based on the constitutional prohibition against *ex post facto* laws. *Smith v. Doe,* 538 U.S. 84, 123 S.Ct. 1140, 155 L.Ed.2d 164 (2003). The majority found that although the act was retroactive, it was nonpunitive in nature; therefore, the *Ex Post Facto* Clause did not apply. In dissent, Justice Ruth Bader Ginsburg (joined by Justice Stephen Breyer) asserted that the legislative intent behind the act was ambiguous but that its effect was punitive. In her view, the act was an unconstitutional *ex post facto* law. Justice John Paul Stevens also dissented, noting the severe stigma that sex offender registration places on the convicted sex offender. In Stevens's view, it was "clear beyond peradventure that these unique consequences of conviction of a sex offense are punitive." 538 U.S. at 112, 123 S.Ct. at 1157, 155 L.Ed.2d at 189.

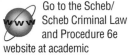
Go to the Scheb/ Scheb Criminal Law and Procedure 6e website at academic .cengage.com/criminaljustice/ scheb for an edited version of *Smith v. Doe.*

Defenses to Charges of Sexual Battery

Beyond a general denial of the charges, the most common defense asserted in a rape case is that the victim consented. For consent to be a defense, it must be voluntarily given before the sexual act. As we pointed out previously, the defense of consent is not available where the victim is unconscious, asleep, or mentally deficient.

The defense of consent would not be valid in a case of voluntary sexual battery (that is, statutory rape) because persons under a certain age are legally incapable of consent. Moreover, it is usually not a defense to a charge of voluntary sexual battery that the defendant believed the victim was older than the prohibited age. In the majority of states this is true despite the victim's appearance or if the victim misrepresented his or her age. The Model Penal Code, however, allows a defense when the victim is over the age of ten years, but it requires the actor "to prove by a preponderance of the evidence that he reasonably believed the child to be above the critical age." M.P.C. § 213.61. Legislatures in about one-third of the states have enacted statutes allowing a mistake-of-age defense, often with variations such as the age of the victim and in instances when a mistake is based on declarations of age by the victim.

Impotency (that is, the inability to engage in sexual intercourse) can be asserted as a defense to a charge of rape. The majority of cases where the defense of impotency is asserted involve charges against young males and men of an advanced age. However, this defense is seldom successful. Modern laws have so broadened the definition of sexual battery as to render impotency irrelevant in many sexual impositions.

Finally, if the statute under which the defendant is prosecuted requires proof of a specific intent, the defendant may be able to show an inability to form such intent due to voluntary intoxication (see Chapter 14).

Sodomy

Sodomy refers to oral or anal sex between humans and sexual intercourse between humans and animals (the latter is often termed bestiality). In his landmark commentaries on the English common law, Sir William Blackstone defined sodomy as "the infamous crime against nature" and asserted that it was an offense of "deeper malignity" than rape. Sodomy can be consensual or nonconsensual. Nonconsensual sodomy is considered a crime against a person and is often charged along with rape in states with older, narrower statutory definitions of rape. (Of course, in jurisdictions with more modern rape statutes, any nonconsensual sexual penetration is considered rape.) Consensual sodomy, on the other hand, has been viewed as an offense against public morality. Prior to 2003, many states had abolished the offense either through legislative or judicial action. In June 2003 the U.S. Supreme Court found a Texas law that proscribed private, consensual sodomy between same-sex partners to be unconstitutional.

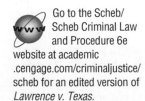
Go to the Scheb/ Scheb Criminal Law and Procedure 6e website at academic .cengage.com/criminaljustice/ scheb for an edited version of *Lawrence v. Texas.*

Lawrence v. Texas, 539 U.S. 558, 123 S.Ct. 2472, 156 L.Ed.2d 508 (2003). The Supreme Court's decision sounded the death knell for state laws prohibiting consensual sodomy.

Abortion

Abortion has been legally defined as the willful bringing about of the miscarriage of a pregnant woman. It was a common-law misdemeanor for a woman who was "quick" with child to have an abortion. The stage of "quickening" referred to the point during a woman's pregnancy when the fetus stirred in the womb.

Most American jurisdictions adopted statutes proscribing abortion, and many made abortion criminal throughout pregnancy. However, there was a tendency to provide that abortion was justified if physicians found it essential to save the mother's life. More liberal statutes allowed abortions to be performed when one or two physicians advised that it was necessary to preserve the life or health of the mother. By 1970, a few states had even repealed criminal penalties for abortions where they were performed under medical supervision in the very early stages of a woman's pregnancy.

The 1960s and 1970s, a period of liberalized views on sexual practices, witnessed a clamor for liberalization of abortion laws. But before significant reforms occurred in most states, the U.S. Supreme Court entertained a challenge to the constitutionality of a Texas law that permitted abortion only on medical advice that it was necessary to save the mother's life. In a landmark 7–2 decision in 1973, the Court in *Roe v. Wade,* supra, held that a fetus was not a "person" within the meaning of the Fourteenth Amendment to the U.S. Constitution. Therefore, the fetus was not entitled to the constitutional protection of the law granted persons. The Court then extended its views on privacy by holding that a woman's personal right of privacy was involved in the decision whether to abort a fetus. The Court's decision had the effect of invalidating most state laws proscribing or regulating abortions. A decision whether to abort during the first trimester of a pregnancy, the Court said, was a matter between the woman and her physician without state regulation. After the first trimester, procedures for abortion could be regulated when "necessarily related to maternal health." In the final trimester, when the fetus has become "viable," the state may prohibit abortion except "when it is necessary, in appropriate medical judgment, to preserve the life or health of the mother."

The controversial issue of abortion has philosophical, religious, ethical, medical, and political dimensions. As part of the national debate, Congress in the early 1980s considered but rejected a constitutional amendment to restrict abortions. A more conservative Supreme Court has modified *Roe* to allow states greater leeway in regulating abortions in such areas as waiting periods and required counseling. In the wake of one of these decisions, *Planned Parenthood v. Casey,* 505 U.S. 833, 112 S.Ct. 2791, 120 L.Ed.2d 674 (1992), supporters of abortion rights clamored for Congress to adopt a statute that would codify the holding in *Roe v. Wade.* That has yet to happen.

 Go to the Scheb/ Scheb Criminal Law and Procedure 6e website at academic .cengage.com/criminaljustice/ scheb for an edited version of *Roe v. Wade.*

Go to the Scheb/ Scheb Criminal Law and Procedure 6e website at academic .cengage.com/criminaljustice/ scheb for an edited version of *Planned Parenthood v. Casey.*

The Conflict over Partial Birth Abortion

In 1997 Congress passed a bill making it a crime for a physician to perform an infrequently used procedure commonly known as **partial birth abortion.** President Clinton vetoed the bill, preventing it from becoming law. However, several states have enacted similar laws, several of which have been declared unconstitutional.

On June 28, 2000, the U.S. Supreme Court struck down a Nebraska statute banning partial birth abortion. *Stenberg v. Carhart*, 530 U.S. 914, 120 S.Ct. 2597, 147 L.Ed.2d 743 (2000). The statute defined partial birth abortion as "an abortion procedure in which the person performing the abortion partially delivers vaginally a living unborn child before killing the unborn child and completing the delivery." Neb. Rev. Stat. Ann. § 28-326(9) (Supp. 1999). The Supreme Court, dividing 5–4, invalidated the law because it lacked an exception for the preservation of the health of the mother and imposed an undue burden on a woman's right to choose abortion.

Writing for the Court, Justice Breyer recognized that millions of Americans believe that abortion is akin to causing the death of an innocent child while millions of others fear that a law that forbids abortion would condemn many American women to lives that lack dignity and would lead to illegal abortions with the attendant risk of death and suffering. He observed that under the Nebraska law,

> some present prosecutors and future Attorneys General may choose to pursue physicians who use … the most commonly used method for performing previability second trimester abortions. All those who perform abortion procedures using that method must fear prosecution, conviction, and imprisonment. The result is an undue burden upon a woman's right to make an abortion decision. 530 U.S. at 934, 120 S.Ct. at 2617, 147 L.Ed.2d at 745.

Dissenting, Justice Anthony Kennedy observed the following:

> The decision nullifies a law expressing the will of the people of Nebraska that medical procedures must be governed by moral principles having their foundation in the intrinsic value of human life, including life of the unborn. Through their law the people of Nebraska were forthright in confronting an issue of immense moral consequence. The State chose to forbid a procedure many decent and civilized people find so abhorrent as to be among the most serious of crimes against human life, while the State still protected the woman's autonomous right of choice.… The Court closes its eyes to these profound concerns. 530 U.S. at 952, 120 S.Ct. at 2635, 147 L.Ed.2d at 795.

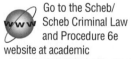 Go to the Scheb/ Scheb Criminal Law and Procedure 6e website at academic .cengage.com/criminaljustice/ scheb for an edited version of *Stenberg v. Carhart* and *Gonzales v. Carhart.*

In April 2007, the Supreme Court upheld a federal statute banning partial birth abortion, but did so without overturning *Stenberg v. Carhart.* In another controversial 5–4 decision, the Court found that the Partial-Birth Abortion Ban Act of 2003, 18 U.S.C.A. § 1531, was "more specific concerning the instances to which it applies and in this respect more precise in its coverage." *Gonzales v. Carhart,* 2007 WL 1135596 (April 18, 2007).

Abusive Offenses

Laws proscribing abuse of one person by another are modern concepts. Many of these laws have been proposed by social agencies that bear the responsibility of coping with problems of members of society who require protection from abusive behavior. Increasingly, legislatures and, even more recently, Congress have responded by enacting laws designed to protect children, spouses and other intimate partners, and, in some instances, the elderly.

Child Abuse

Since the 1980s, complaints of **child abuse** have increased dramatically. Many cases involve commission of assault, battery (or aggravated categories thereof), or some category of sexual assault or sexual battery and are prosecuted under one or more of such statutes. Nevertheless, with the rise of neglect, abuse, and violence against children, many states have enacted specific child abuse laws to cover a broader range of abusive behavior. These laws often refer to **endangering the welfare of a child,** and they hold a parent or guardian responsible for abuse of a child regardless of the source of the mistreatment. These concerns appear to be reflected in McKinney's N.Y. Penal Law § 260.10. That law makes endangering the welfare of a child a misdemeanor and provides that a person is guilty of endangering the welfare of a child when

> 1. He knowingly acts in a manner likely to be injurious to the physical, mental or moral welfare of a child less than seventeen years old or directs or authorizes such child to engage in an occupation involving a substantial risk of danger to his life or health; or

> 2. Being a parent, guardian or other person legally charged with the care or custody of a child less than eighteen years old, he fails or refuses to exercise reasonable diligence in the control of such child to prevent him from becoming an "abused child," a "neglected child," a "juvenile delinquent," or a "person in need of supervision," as those terms are defined in articles ten, three and seven of the family court act.

Because of the age and vulnerability of minors, statutes proscribing child abuse are strict liability crimes in many states. Since 2000 several states have enacted statutes making it a misdemeanor to allow young children to remain unattended in a vehicle. For example, a defendant's actions in leaving a three-week-old child locked in a van on a hot summer day posed substantial risk of harm to the child and thus was a violation of an Ohio child endangerment statute that provided that "[n]o person, who is the parent … or person *in loco parentis* of a child under eighteen years of age … shall create a substantial risk to the health or safety of the child, by violating a duty of care, protection, or support. *State v. Morton,* 741 N.E.2d 202 (Ohio App. 2000).

The prosecution of parents for leaving a child unattended in a vehicle has engendered some debate. Some argue that parents should not be punished criminally for their lack of judgment. But the more prevalent view is that punishing parents for such lapses of judgment forces parents to face the consequences of their actions. Moreover, such statutes raise public awareness as to the danger of leaving children alone in vehicles. In other instances a parent has been charged with endangering a child's welfare by transporting a child in an auto while the parent was driving under the influence of intoxicating beverages.

Statutes now commonly require medical professionals and social workers to report instances of suspected child abuse to the enforcement authorities. When such cases of child abuse reach the courts, they often involve legal issues as to whether parents, social workers, and others who discuss these matters with an abused child are to be permitted to testify in court concerning communications with the child. Moreover, expert testimony of physicians, psychologists, and social workers is often relied on to explain a child's sometimes-curious behavior that might be a result of certain types of abuse.

The widespread drug problem has led to prosecutions of women for child abuse when expectant mothers ingested cocaine or other controlled substances and demonstrable adverse medical effects were present in their children at birth. Courts have generally declined to hold that such action constitutes child abuse, often based on their interpretation of statutes proscribing child endangerment or delivery of controlled substances. For example, Kentucky Revised Statute § 508.110 criminalizes abuse of "another person of whom [the offender] has actual custody" which "places him in a situation that may cause … serious physical injury" to a person twelve years of age or less or who is physically helpless or mentally helpless.

In a leading decision on the subject, the Kentucky Supreme Court held the statute does not apply to a mother whose baby suffered injuries as the result of the mother's ingestion of drugs during her pregnancy. *Commonwealth v. Welch,* 864 S.W.2d 280 (Ky. 1993). In reaching its decision, the court cited *Johnson v. State,* 602 So.2d 1288 (Fla. 1992). There, the Florida Supreme Court held that cocaine passing through a baby's umbilical cord after birth but before the cord was cut did not violate a Florida law making it a crime for an adult to deliver a controlled substance to a minor.

In *Reinesto v. Superior Court,* 894 P.2d 733 (Ariz. App. 1995), the state prosecuted a mother for having knowingly caused injury to her unborn child under circumstances likely to produce death or serious physical injury in violation of A.R.S. § 13-3623.B. The statute makes it a felony for "any person" who "[u]nder circumstances likely to produce death or serious physical injury ... causes a child ... to suffer physical injury...." The statute defines a child as "an individual who is under eighteen years of age" and physical injury as "the impairment of physical condition ... or any physical condition which imperils health or welfare." A.R.S. § 13-3623.A. The defendant challenged the right of the state to bring charges against her. The appellate court granted her petition and held:

> The plain language of section 13-3623 indicates that the legislature intended to proscribe conduct by any person that causes physical harm to a child. Applying the ordinary meaning of these words leads us to conclude that the statute refers to conduct that directly endangers a child, not to activity that affects a fetus and thereby ultimately harms the resulting child. *Id.* at 735–736.

Because it concluded that Arizona's child abuse statute does not reach the defendant's conduct, the court declined to reach that constitutional issue of whether the statute violated her right of privacy.

Many court decisions hold that maternal conduct before the birth of the child does not give rise to criminal prosecution under state child abuse/endangerment or drug distribution statutes. However, in *Whitner v. State,* 492 S.E.2d 777 (S.C. 1997), the South Carolina Supreme Court held that a mother of a newborn infant could be criminally prosecuted on the statutory theory of child abuse or endangerment for injuries to her child resulting from prenatal substance abuse.

Spousal Abuse

In recent years, legislatures and courts have given increased attention to **spousal abuse.** Many of these abuses constitute criminal violations of one or more traditional statutes previously discussed. Nevertheless, laws have been enacted in many states to provide for issuance of court injunctions to protect spouses from domestic violence and provide for the arrest of those who violate these orders. In many instances, courts issue protective orders of this character during litigation. In *Cole v. Cole,* 556 N.Y.S.2d 217 (Fam. Ct. 1990), a wife petitioned the court to have her husband held in contempt for violating such an order. A question arose about the effectiveness of such an order when the wife voluntarily seeks reconciliation with her husband. The court explained that a victim of domestic violence who has procured such an order is entitled to the court's protection from violence throughout the duration of the order, even if the victim is desirous of pursuing a goal of voluntary reconciliation with the offending spouse.

Prosecutions for spousal abuses are sometimes hindered by the difficulty of showing which instances of domestic violence have occurred in which legal jurisdiction. Recognizing this, Congress included in the Violent Crime Control and Law Enforcement Act of 1994 (commonly referred to as "the federal Crime Bill") an offense of "interstate domestic violence." Section 40221 of the act inserts a new chapter titled "Domestic Violence" after Chapter 110 in 18 U.S.C.A. Title 18 U.S.C.A. § 2261 now provides:

> (a) Offenses.—
>
> > (1) Travel or conduct of offender.—A person who travels in interstate or foreign commerce or enters or leaves Indian country or within the special maritime and territorial jurisdiction of the United States with the intent to kill, injure, harass, or intimidate a spouse, intimate partner, or dating partner, and who, in the course of or as a result of such travel, commits or attempts to commit a crime of violence against that spouse or intimate partner, shall be punished as provided in subsection (b).
> >
> > (2) Causing travel of victim.—A person who causes a spouse, intimate partner, or dating partner to travel in interstate or foreign commerce or to enter or leave Indian country by force, coercion, duress, or fraud, and who, in the course of, as a result of, or to facilitate such conduct or travel, commits or attempts to commit a crime of violence against that spouse or intimate partner, shall be punished as provided in subsection (b).

Shortly after the new act took effect, Christopher Bailey was charged with violating it for assaulting his spouse and driving her around West Virginia and Kentucky until he finally carried her into an emergency room. A jury found Bailey guilty of kidnapping and interstate domestic violence under the new federal act. The U.S. Court of Appeals for the Fourth Circuit affirmed his convictions for violating 18 U.S.C.A. § 1201(a)(1), kidnapping, and 18 U.S.C.A. § 2261(a)(2), the new act. The court rejected Bailey's constitutional argument that the new federal statute was beyond the power of Congress to enact. *United States v. Bailey,* 112 F.3d 758 (4th Cir. 1997). The court in *United States v. Lankford,* 196 F.3d 563 (5th Cir. 1999), held that the enactment of the Violence Against Women Act, 18 U.S.C.A. § 2261(a)(1), did not exceed the scope of Congress's authority under the Commerce Clause, U.S. Const. Art. 1, § 8.

Abuse of the Elderly

Abuse of the elderly is often handled through regulatory agencies. Frequently, this has involved resorting to civil court processes, but in recent years some state legislatures have created criminal offenses to punish caregivers who abuse, neglect, or exploit elderly persons. Generally these statutes define caregivers broadly to include adults who are close relatives and persons appointed by agencies or otherwise employed to assist the elderly and disabled. New York and Illinois have been leaders in enacting legislation that provides criminal sanctions for endangering the welfare of a vulnerable elderly person.

McKinney's N.Y. Penal Law, Chapter 260, makes it a felony for a caregiver to endanger the welfare of a vulnerable elderly person. A "caregiver" is defined as one who assumes responsibility for the care of a vulnerable elderly person pursuant to a court order or who receives monetary or other valuable consideration for providing care for a vulnerable elderly person. A "vulnerable elderly person" is one sixty years of age or older who is suffering from a disease or infirmity associated with advanced age and manifested by demonstrable physical, mental, or emotional dysfunction to the extent that the person is incapable of adequately providing for his or her own health or personal care. It is endangering in the second degree (and a felony) for a caregiver for a vulnerable elderly person to recklessly cause physical injury to such person or subject the person to sexual contact without that person's consent. § 260.32. It is endangering in the first degree (and a felony) for a caregiver to intentionally cause injury to a vulnerable elderly person. § 260.34.

Under Illinois law, the caregiver of an elderly or disabled person commits a felony if he or she knowingly:

(1) performs acts which cause the elderly or disabled person's life to be endangered, health to be injured, or pre-existing physical or mental condition to deteriorate; or

(2) fails to perform acts which he knows or reasonably should know are necessary to maintain or preserve the life or health of the elderly or disabled person and such failure causes the elderly or disabled person's life to be endangered, health to be injured or pre-existing physical or mental condition to deteriorate; or

(3) abandons the elderly or disabled person. 720 ILCS 5/12-21 (West 1994).

In *People v. Simester,* 678 N.E.2d 710 (Ill. App. 1997), Janice and Dale Simester, husband and wife, were convicted of two counts of criminal neglect of an elderly person and sentenced to 30 months' probation and 1,000 hours of community service. The victim, Stanley Pierzga, the wife's seventy-four-year-old uncle, had lived with the couple for several years. At trial the evidence revealed that when paramedics responded to a call to the home they found Mr. Pierzga lying on the floor in a coma in a fetal position. An emergency room physician found him covered with dried urine and crusted feces. Medical evidence further revealed the victim had no nutritional intake for at least one week, that his rigid fetal position took at least two weeks to develop, and that his deep coma had to have existed for several days before his hospitalization.

On appeal the defendants argued that the statute (quoted above) presumptively imposes medical and psychiatric knowledge on a layperson for diagnosing and correctly treating the pre-existing ailments of the elderly or disabled and that by making it an offense to fail to give adequate care to the victim on the basis that one "should reasonably know" the proper care, the statute "impermissibly adopts a civil negligence standard and enforces it as a criminal felony." The appellate court rejected their contentions and in affirming their convictions observed that both defendants should have reasonably known of the victim's condition long before the paramedics were summoned.

False Imprisonment and Kidnapping

In recognition of the need to protect an individual's freedom of movement, the common law developed two misdemeanor offenses: **false imprisonment** and **kidnapping.** False imprisonment consisted of confining someone against the person's will, whereas kidnapping involved forcibly abducting and taking a person to another country.

The Statutory Offense of False Imprisonment

Not all states have adopted statutes making false imprisonment an offense. Those that have generally classify it as a misdemeanor and define it much as did the common law, which defined the offense as the unlawful detention of a person.

Typically, the Texas statute states that "[a] person commits an offense if he intentionally and knowingly restrains another person." Vernon's Tex. Penal Code Ann. § 20.02(a). Texas law declares the offense to be a misdemeanor but provides that it becomes a felony if the offender recklessly exposes the victim to a substantial risk of serious bodily injury. Vernon's Tex. Penal Code Ann. § 20.02(c). Usually, a prosecution

Go to the Scheb/ Scheb Criminal Law and Procedure 6e website at academic .cengage.com/criminaljustice/ scheb to find *State v. Snider* (1991), where the Iowa Court of Appeals considers whether there is sufficient evidence to support the defendant's conviction for false imprisonment.

for false imprisonment requires only proof of a defendant's general intent, although this depends on the language of the particular statute.

Four hypothetical situations illustrate the crime of false imprisonment:

• A police officer takes a person into custody under an unlawful arrest.

• A prison warden fails to release a prisoner who has served his or her term.

• A storekeeper detains a customer when the storekeeper has a hunch the customer has shoplifted but has no reasonable basis for such suspicion.

• An overzealous male refuses to allow his female companion to leave his apartment without yielding to his sexual demands.

In recent years, false imprisonment has not been a commonly charged offense. Three reasons chiefly account for this: (1) serious charges involving restraint of a person frequently reveal elements constituting the statutory offense of kidnapping; (2) persons claiming to have been falsely imprisoned often seek to recover damages in a civil suit rather than press criminal charges; and (3) on close investigation, many restraints undoubtedly are determined to have been imposed based on authority, or at least a reasonable belief that there was authority to have restrained the complaining party.

Modern Statutory Treatment of Kidnapping

Unlike false imprisonment, the crime of kidnapping is a serious felony universally proscribed by state and federal jurisdictions. It plays a far greater role in our society than it did at common law, where to constitute kidnapping the victim had to be taken to another country.

Under modern legislation the elements of the crime necessarily depend on the precise wording of the statute in a particular jurisdiction, but in general, to constitute kidnapping there must be an unlawful taking and forcible carrying away (sometimes called **asportation**) of a victim without that person's consent. Intimidation and coercion can substitute for the required force, and even where consent has been given, a person who has the capacity to consent must have voluntarily given it. Therefore, young children and incompetent persons cannot legally consent to an act of asportation.

Most states classify kidnapping as **simple kidnapping** and **kidnapping for ransom.** Others classify the offense by degrees. In New York, kidnapping in the second degree is a felony that merely involves the abduction of another person. McKinney's N.Y. Penal Law § 135.20. Kidnapping in the first degree is a more serious felony, and the statute proscribing it states:

A person is guilty of kidnapping in the first degree when he abducts another person and when:

1. His intent is to compel a third person to pay or deliver money or property as ransom, or to engage in other particular conduct, or to refrain from engaging in particular conduct; or

2. He restrains the person abducted for a period of more than twelve hours with intent to:

    (a) Inflict physical injury upon him or violate or abuse him sexually; or

    (b) Accomplish or advance the commission of a felony; or

    (c) Terrorize him or a third person; or

    (d) Interfere with the performance of a governmental or political function; or

3. The person abducted dies during the abduction or before he is able to return or to be returned to safety. McKinney's N.Y. Penal Law § 135.25.

The Requirement of Asportation in Kidnapping

The asportation or movement of the victim distinguishes the crime of kidnapping from the offense of false imprisonment. One of the more commonly litigated issues in kidnapping prosecutions concerns the extent of movement of the victim required to meet this element of the crime. In *People v. Martinez*, 973 P.2d 512 (Cal. 1999), the California Supreme Court noted that there are two requirements under the asportation standard. First, the movement of the victim must not be merely incidental to the commission of the underlying crime, and second, it must increase the risk of harm to the victim over and above that necessarily present in the underlying crime itself. See West's Ann. Cal. Penal Code § 209(b)(2).

In recent years, courts have tended to limit the scope of kidnapping statutes by deciding that the required movement of a victim must be something more than that inherent in or incidental to the commission of another felony. The proliferation of court decisions on this subject might be the result of prosecutors' tendencies to levy multiple charges against a criminal defendant for conduct arising from a single criminal episode.

When is the offender's movement of a victim in conjunction with an independent offense such as assault, rape, or robbery sufficient to constitute an independent offense of kidnapping? If the movement is merely incidental to a crime and does not involve an additional significant risk to the victim, courts generally will not sustain a conviction for kidnapping in addition to the other offense. Appellate court decisions are instructive. The New Hampshire Supreme Court has held that a defendant was properly convicted for kidnapping as an accomplice of a defendant who forced a woman into a car and drove her to an apartment where the principal defendant assaulted her. *State v. Goodwin*, 395 A.2d 1234 (N.H. 1978). In the same vein, two years later, the North Carolina Supreme Court sustained a kidnapping conviction where a handyman forced a woman off the street and into her home for purposes of sexually assaulting her. *State v. Adams*, 264 S.E.2d 46 (N.C. 1980).

Two 1983 appellate court decisions addressed the extent of movement required to meet the asportation element of kidnapping. The Florida Supreme Court held that the statutory requirement of "confining, abducting, or imprisoning another person … with intent to commit or facilitate commission of any felony" does not include movement or confinement that is inconsequential or inherent in the nature of the felony. *Faison v. State*, 426 So.2d 963 (Fla. 1983). In applying this rationale, a California appellate court held that moving a robber's victim across a room or from one room to another was an insufficient movement to meet the requirement for kidnapping. *People v. John*, 197 Cal. Rptr. 340 (Cal. App. 1983).

Federal Kidnapping Laws

Perhaps the most notorious kidnapping to have occurred in the United States was the abduction of the infant son of Charles A. Lindbergh, the "Lone Eagle" who, in 1927, made the first nonstop solo flight across the Atlantic Ocean. The Lindbergh baby was abducted from the family home in New Jersey in 1932. Bruno Richard Hauptmann was convicted of the crime after a spectacular trial and was executed in 1936. The Lindbergh kidnapping led to a demand for federal laws to enable the FBI to become involved in apprehending kidnappers. This, in turn, led to sweeping changes in state and federal laws on kidnapping. The Federal Kidnapping Act, commonly called the Lindbergh Law, provides that:

> Whoever unlawfully seizes, confines, inveigles, decoys, kidnaps, abducts, or carries away and holds for ransom or reward or otherwise any person, except in the case of a minor by a parent thereof … shall be punished by imprisonment. 18 U.S.C.A. § 1201(a).

Subsection (b) of the statute raises a presumption that if the kidnapped victim is not returned within twenty-four hours after the taking, then the defendant did, in fact, take the victim across state lines. This presumption effectively allows the federal government to act promptly to bring federal agents into the investigation of an alleged kidnapping.

A recent federal statute makes **hostage taking** an offense. 18 U.S.C.A. § 1203. Other federal statutes make it a crime to knowingly receive, possess, or dispose of any money or property that has been delivered as ransom for a victim of a kidnapping, 18 U.S.C.A. § 1202, or for a bank robber to avoid apprehension by forcing someone to accompany him, 18 U.S.C.A. § 2113(e).

Defenses to Charges of False Imprisonment and Kidnapping

It is not false imprisonment for a person to detain another under authority of the law. Thus, an officer, or even a private citizen, who makes a lawful arrest or a jailer who detains a prisoner lawfully committed to custody is not guilty of an offense. Likewise, a parent who reasonably disciplines a child or a teacher who reasonably restrains a pupil would not be guilty of false imprisonment.

Consent can also be a defense to false imprisonment or kidnapping. Of course, the consent must not have been induced by threat, coercion, or misrepresentation and must have been given by a person competent to give consent. A person who relies on consent as a defense has the burden of establishing the validity of such consent.

CASE-IN-POINT

Rape and Kidnapping: Required Resistance in the Face of Threats

Late one night after leaving work, a woman responded to a request by two men to assist them in getting their car off the road. When she began to leave, both men grabbed her, ordered her into the back seat of the car, and threatened to kill her unless she cooperated. The men told her that they had escaped from prison and were holding her as a hostage. They then drove their victim to a tent, disrobed her, and forced her to submit to sexual acts with each of them. When they drove her back to her car the next morning, they told her that they would kill her if she reported the incident to the police.

The defendants were convicted of rape, kidnapping, and several other offenses. On appeal, they argued that the victim had cooperated in their endeavors; hence, they were not guilty of either rape or kidnapping. The Indiana Supreme Court rejected their contentions and explained that the resistance necessary to protect against sexual attack is dependent on all circumstances. Further, the court noted that a victim need not physically resist after being confronted with threats and being in fear of injury.

Ballard v. State, 385 N.E.2d 1126 (Ind. 1979).

Finally, as we have noted, a defendant may challenge whether there was sufficient movement of the victim to constitute the asportation element of kidnapping.

Child Snatching

In recent years, marital disputes have given rise to many serious problems concerning the custody of children of divorced or separated parents. It has been estimated that in excess of 300,000 children are abducted by family members each year. The term **child snatching** is now commonly applied to situations in which one parent deliberately retains or conceals a child from the other parent. The problem has resulted partly from the ability of one parent to seize a child from the custodial parent, travel to another state, and petition the court in the latter state for custody of the child.

In 1995 the Supreme Judicial Court of Maine affirmed the conviction of a father who took his children from their home where their mother had equal legal custody rights. The evidence revealed the defendant's purpose was to keep the children away from their mother and to hold them in a place where they were not likely to be found. The court found this evidence sufficient to support the conviction of the father for violating a statute defining criminal restraint to include taking a child "from the custody of his other parent." *State v. Butt*, 656 A.2d 1225 (Me. 1995).

Most states have made child snatching a felony, thereby subjecting violators to extradition for prosecution in the state where the offense occurs. In addition, child snatching is now being curbed by several approaches:

- In many states, trial judges include a provision in a divorce judgment requiring court approval to remove a child from the state where the divorce is granted. Violation may subject the offending party to being held in contempt of court or, in some states, to be prosecuted for a felony.

- The **Uniform Child Custody Jurisdiction Act (UCCJA),** proposed in 1968 and now in force in all fifty states, generally continues jurisdiction for custody in the home or resident state of the child. Cooperation between the courts in the different states is becoming increasingly effective in preventing "judge shopping."

- In 1980 Congress enacted the **Parental Kidnapping Prevention Act (PKPA),** 28 U.S.C.A. § 1738A. The federal act is designed to prevent jurisdictional conflicts over child custody, and it takes precedence over any state law, including the UCCJA. Its primary goal is to reduce any incentive for parental child snatching.

- Federal and state governments, as well as religious and civic organizations and the media, have initiated programs for identifying children and for collecting and disseminating information on missing children.

Prosecuting international parental kidnapping presents additional problems, most notably the difficulties encountered in dealing with a foreign legal system.

Civil Rights Offenses

A category of offenses unknown to the common law involves injuries to the **civil rights** of individuals. After the Civil War, Congress adopted a series of laws designed to protect the civil rights of the newly freed former slaves. Today, these statutes as amended can be used to initiate federal prosecutions against individuals who conspire or use their official positions to deprive persons of rights guaranteed by the U.S. Constitution or the laws of the United States. The relevant provisions are as follows:

18 U.S.C.A. § 241. Conspiracy against rights

If two or more persons conspire to injure, oppress, threaten, or intimidate any inhabitant of any State, Territory, Commonwealth, Possession, or District in the free exercise or enjoyment of any right or privilege secured to him by the Constitution or laws of the United States, or because of his having so exercised the same; or

If two or more persons go in disguise on the highway, or on the premises of another, with intent to prevent or hinder his free exercise or enjoyment of any right or privilege so secured—

They shall be fined under this title or imprisoned not more than ten years, or both; and if death results from the acts committed in violation of this section or if such acts include kidnapping or an attempt to kidnap, aggravated sexual abuse or an attempt to commit aggravated sexual abuse, or an attempt to kill, they shall be fined under this title or imprisoned for any term of years or for life, or both, or may be sentenced to death.

18 U.S.C.A. § 242. Deprivation of rights under color of law

Whoever, under color of any law, statute, ordinance, regulation, or custom, willfully subjects any person in any State, Territory, or District to the deprivation of any rights, privileges, or immunities secured or protected by the Constitution or laws of the United States, or to different punishments, pains, or penalties, on account of such person being an alien, or by reason of his color, or race, than are prescribed for the punishment of citizens, shall be fined under this title or imprisoned not more than one year, or both; and if bodily injury results from the acts committed in violation of this section or if such acts include the use, attempted use, or threatened use of a dangerous weapon, explosives, or fire, shall be fined under this title or imprisoned not more than ten years, or both; and if death results from the acts committed in violation of this section or if such acts include kidnapping or an attempt to kidnap, aggravated sexual abuse, or an attempt to commit aggravated sexual abuse, or an attempt to kill, shall be fined under this title, or imprisoned for any term of years or for life, or both, or may be sentenced to death.

These statutes are used most frequently to prosecute in federal court individuals who engage in criminal acts that are racially motivated. Thus, although a conspiracy to commit arson may be prosecuted as such under state law, if it is racially motivated, it may also constitute a federal civil rights violation under 18 U.S.C.A. § 241. Instances of police brutality are sometimes prosecuted under 18 U.S.C.A. § 242. Increasingly, section 242 is being used to prosecute state officials who engage in other types of egregious conduct. To be guilty of willfully depriving a person of constitutional rights under this section, the defendant's actions must be done under color of law; where use of force is involved, the force used must be unreasonable and unnecessary. *United States v. Stokes,* 506 F.2d 771 (5th Cir. 1975). As a result of judicial interpretation, federal civil rights laws now protect individuals from a wide range of injurious conduct by public officials or other persons acting under the authority of the government.

Among the most common types of civil rights offenses is the excessive use of force by police. In a highly publicized case in March 1991, four Los Angeles police officers were charged with the beating of Rodney King, an African American motorist who was stopped by the police after a high-speed automobile chase. After the officers were acquitted in a state court trial, highly destructive riots erupted in South Central Los Angeles. Federal authorities then prosecuted the officers under 18 U.S.C.A. § 242 for violating King's civil rights, in particular, his Fourth Amendment right to be free from an unreasonable seizure. In April 1993, two of the officers, Stacey Koon and

CASE-IN-POINT

Criminal Prosecution under Federal Civil Rights Laws

In 1992, David Lanier, a Tennessee state judge, was charged with violating the constitutional rights of five women by sexually assaulting them in his chambers. In a somewhat novel theory of the scope of 18 U.S.C.A. § 242, the federal indictment alleged that the judge, acting willfully and under color of state law, had deprived his victims of their federal constitutional right to be free from sexual assault. The jury returned verdicts of guilty on seven counts, and the defendant was sentenced to twenty-five years in federal prison. The U.S. Court of Appeals for the 6th Circuit reversed the conviction, but the U.S. Supreme Court reversed the circuit court's ruling. After the Supreme Court's decision, Judge Lanier was apprehended in Mexico, where he had fled to avoid imprisonment. He is currently serving his sentence in federal prison.

United States v. Lanier, 520 U.S. 259, 117 S.Ct. 1219, 137 L.Ed.2d 432 (1997).

Go to the Scheb/ Scheb Criminal Law and Procedure 6e website at academic .cengage.com/criminaljustice/ scheb for an edited version of *U.S. v. Lanier.*

Laurence Powell, were convicted and sentenced to prison; the two other officers were found not guilty. Their convictions were upheld by the U.S. Court of Appeals, *United States v. Koon*, 34 F.3d 1416 (9th Cir. 1994). (Later review by the Supreme Court was limited to issues regarding sentencing. *Koon v. United States*, 518 U.S. 81, 116 S.Ct. 2035, 135 L.Ed.2d 392 [1996]).

Hate Crimes

Hate crimes are offenses motivated by bias against a person's race, religion, nationality, gender, disability, or sexual orientation. Hate crimes can be offenses against property—for example, an instance of synagogue vandalism that is motivated by anti-Semitism. But most hate crimes are violent crimes against persons. In recent years there have been a number of highly publicized homicides where the only apparent motive was animus based on the victim's race, religion, gender, or sexual orientation. One of the most grisly such crimes was the racially motivated murder of James Byrd Jr. in Jasper, Texas, in 1998. Byrd, an African American, was chained by his ankles to the back of a pickup truck and dragged for three miles. He died when he was decapitated when his body struck a culvert. A Texas court sentenced two of the three white males convicted of Byrd's murder to death; the third was sentenced to life in prison.

Concerned about an apparent rise in hate crimes, Congress in 1990 enacted the Hate Crime Statistics Act, 28 U.S.C.A. § 534, which requires the U.S. Justice Department to acquire data on such offenses. In 2004 the Justice Department recorded 9,035 hate crimes nationwide. These included crimes against persons and property motivated by race, ethnicity, religion, sexual orientation, and disability. U.S. Department of Justice, Federal Bureau of Investigation, *Hate Crime Statistics, 2004*, FBI Uniform Crime Reports (Washington, D.C.: U.S. Department of Justice, 2005), p. 10.

Federal law currently limits federal prosecution of hate crimes to civil rights offenses, 18 U.S.C.A. § 245, which criminalizes interference with "federally protected activities" such as voting. Advocates of a stronger federal role in this area have called on Congress to enact the Hate Crimes Prevention Act, which was introduced in Congress in 1999. The proposed legislation would criminalize willful acts of violence involving guns, explosives, or fire directed at individuals because of their actual or perceived race, color, nationality, religion, gender, disability, or sexual orientation. On June 20, 2000, the Senate voted to pass this legislation, but the bill failed to pass the House of Representatives. Since then, civil rights activists have been urging Congress to reconsider the legislation.

Some opponents of the Hate Crimes Prevention Act base their objections on what they perceive to be a federal usurpation of state and local law enforcement responsibilities. Others question the very concept of the hate crime. Not everyone agrees that a crime should be punished more severely because the perpetrator was motivated by racial hatred rather than greed, lust, or any other motive. Others argue that existing criminal sanctions are adequate to punish hate crimes. On the other hand, criminalizing hate crimes clearly communicates society's strong aversion to bigotry.

Hate crimes are mostly subject to state legislation. There are two categories of state hate crime laws: substantive and penalty enhancement statutes. Many states with such laws protect against biases not included in the proposed Hate Crimes Prevention Act, thus addressing additional local preferences. Most states now have laws permitting courts to enhance criminal penalties when defendants are convicted of hate crimes.

In 2001 the New Jersey Legislature revised its laws to effectively target both goals. New Jersey Statutes section 16-1 now provides: "A person is guilty of the crime of bias intimidation if he commits, attempts to commit, conspires with another to commit, or threatens the immediate commission of an offense specified (in certain chapter of New Jersey statutes) (1) with a purpose to intimidate an individual or group of individuals because of race, color, religion, gender, handicap, sexual orientation, or ethnicity...." The law goes on to provide for a grading of the offense and specifies that "the court shall impose separate sentences upon a conviction for bias intimidation and a conviction of any underlying offense."

Go to the Scheb/ Scheb Criminal Law and Procedure 6e website at academic .cengage.com/criminaljustice/ scheb for an edited version of *Apprendi v. New Jersey.*

The Supreme Court has upheld hate crime laws of the penalty enhancement variety—see *Wisconsin v. Mitchell,* 508 U.S. 476, 113 S.Ct. 2194, 124 L.Ed.2d 436 (1993)—but it has also said that the factual question of whether a crime was motivated by animus against a particular group is an element of the crime that must be proved beyond a reasonable doubt. In a jury trial, this question must be submitted to the jury. *Apprendi v. New Jersey,* 530 U.S. 466, 120 S.Ct. 2348, 147 L.Ed.2d 435 (2000). For further discussion of the penalty enhancement approach to hate crimes, see Chapter 19, "Sentencing and Punishment."

■ CONCLUSION

Crimes against persons usually result in either death or injury to the victim. Surviving victims of violent personal crimes often suffer emotional and psychological damage, as well as physical injury. In addition, offenses resulting in death or injury frequently have long-lasting social and economic effects on the victim. Consider the economic plight of a family where a penniless assailant disables a working family member or the strains imposed on a marital union in which the young bride has been sexually assaulted or kidnapped and ravished.

Over the centuries the assaultive, homicidal, sexual, and detention crimes have been a stable base for prosecuting persons whose antisocial conduct offended the basic norms of civilized people. Yet laws must change to cope with the needs of a dynamic society. In addition to such well-known offenses involving persons, in this chapter we have attempted to broaden the scope of the usual coverage of crimes against persons by explaining the impact of newer offenses such as stalking; abuse of children, spouses, and the elderly; and child snatching, as well as federal laws concerning violations of civil rights, that have become integral parts of the criminal justice system.

■ KEY TERMS

assault, 109
battery, 109
aggravated assault, 109
aggravated battery, 109
mayhem, 112
hazing, 112
stalking, 113
cyberstalking, 115
homicide, 116
malice aforethought, 116
manslaughter, 116
heat of passion, 116
voluntary manslaughter, 116
involuntary manslaughter, 116
justifiable homicide, 116
excusable homicide, 116
provocation, 117
first-degree murder, 117
premeditation, 117
felony murder, 118
second-degree murder, 119
depraved mind or heart, 120
jury pardon, 120
vehicular homicide, 123
corpus delicti, 126
proximate cause, 127
brain death, 128
one year and a day rule, 128
suicide, 129
assisted suicide, 129
carnal knowledge, 132
common-law rape, 133
forcible rape, 133

statutory rape, 133
marital exception, 133
force, 133
consent, 133
gender-neutral offense, 135
rape shield laws, 135
sexual penetration, 137
sexual contact, 138
Hale's Rule, 138
rape trauma syndrome, 140
Megan's Law, 142
impotency, 143
sodomy, 143
abortion, 144
partial birth abortion, 144
child abuse, 145
endangering the welfare of a child, 146
spousal abuse, 147
abuse of the elderly, 148
false imprisonment, 149
kidnapping, 149
asportation, 150
simple kidnapping, 150
kidnapping for ransom, 150
hostage taking, 152
child snatching, 153
Uniform Child Custody Jurisdiction Act
  (UCCJA), 153
Parental Kidnapping Prevention Act
  (PKPA), 153
civil rights, 153
hate crimes, 155

■ WEB-BASED RESEARCH ACTIVITY

Go to the Web. Locate your state's criminal statutes online. Find the statute defining homicidal crimes. How does your state define the various gradations of homicide? Locate the online statutes for a nearby state. How does that state's homicide statute differ from your own state's laws in this area? Does your state have a broad gender-neutral statute that defines sexual battery? Does the law in your state provide for a defense to the offense of statutory rape based on the actor's good-faith mistake of fact as to the victim's age?

■ QUESTIONS FOR THOUGHT AND DISCUSSION

1. What elements, in addition to those required for assault or battery, must the prosecution prove to convict a defendant of aggravated assault or battery?
2. Is it legitimate for a jury to find a defendant guilty of manslaughter in a case where there is evidence of premeditation simply because members of the

jury feel that the defendant was somewhat justified in taking the life of the victim?

3. How can the prosecution establish the *corpus delicti* in a murder case when the body of the victim cannot be found?

4. Compare the U.S. Supreme Court's 1997 opinion holding that there is no constitutional right to have assistance in committing suicide with the constitutional right of privacy discussed in Chapter 3. Can these views be logically reconciled?

5. Why has the common-law doctrine of felony murder become controversial among courts and legal scholars in recent years?

6. Is a state law making it a crime to kill a viable fetus constitutional, notwithstanding the Supreme Court's decision in *Roe v. Wade*?

7. A male who is aware that he has been diagnosed with acquired immunodeficiency syndrome (AIDS) engages in sexual intercourse with a female. He does not inform the female that he has AIDS. As a result, the female contracts AIDS and dies from the disease two years later. Under the laws of your state, could the male be convicted of a homicidal act?

8. What interests does the law seek to protect in proscribing (a) forcible rape and (b) statutory rape?

9. Which statutory and judicial reforms of the 1970s and 1980s in the law of rape were the most significant from a female victim's standpoint? Are there other biases against female victims of sexual assault that should be addressed?

10. Does Hale's Rule, which creates a marital exception in the law of rape, apply in your state?

11. What role do the Uniform Child Custody Jurisdiction Act (UCCJA) and the Parental Kidnapping Prevention Act (PKPA) play in controlling child snatching?

12. Do the federal statutes making it unlawful to deprive persons of their civil rights under color of law have a significant deterrent effect on misconduct of law enforcement personnel? Or do these statutes hamper effective police action?

13. Explain the necessity for the prosecution to prove asportation in order to establish the offense of kidnapping.

14. Why have most state courts rejected prosecution of a mother whose child suffers adverse medical effects from the mother's ingestion of cocaine during her pregnancy?

15. Assume you are a staff member of a state criminal justice agency. The director asks you to compose a draft of a statute to prohibit endangerment to children. What key points would you include in your draft?

■ PROBLEMS FOR DISCUSSION AND SOLUTION

1. Shortly before midnight, a man is driving through a residential area in an attempt to get his wife, who is in labor, to the hospital. The posted speed limit is 30 mph, but the anxious husband is driving 50 mph. In a dark area, the car strikes and kills a ten-year-old boy who is playing in the middle of the street. Can the driver be convicted of (a) manslaughter or (b) vehicular homicide?

2. A store manager observes Lucy Grabit stuffing a pair of nylon hose into her purse before going through the checkout counter in a supermarket. The manager

detains her and promptly directs his employee to call the police. Is the store manager guilty of false imprisonment? Why or why not?

3. Several college freshmen enter the dean's private office and remain there for several hours. They refuse to let the dean leave until he yields to their demands to allow unrestricted visitation in all dormitories. Under contemporary criminal statutes, what offense, if any, have the students committed? Explain.

4. An intoxicated driver recklessly drove his vehicle into a car being driven by a woman who was seven months pregnant. As a result of the accident, the woman's baby was born prematurely, suffered from extensive brain damage, and died two days later. The state law defines a person as an individual "who has been born and is alive." Nevertheless, the state prosecuted the intoxicated driver, and a jury found him guilty of manslaughter. Do you think an appellate court should uphold the defendant's conviction? Why or why not?

5. The defendant was convicted of battery under a statute that provides that "a person commits a battery who either intentionally or knowingly, and without legal justification, makes physical contact of an insulting or provoking nature with an individual." The evidence disclosed that one morning the male defendant picked up a female friend whom he had invited to have breakfast with him. En route to the restaurant he unbuttoned her blouse and placed his hand on her breast; after she removed his hand and asked him to stop, he again placed his hand on her breast. On appeal, the defendant argues that his conviction should be reversed because his acts were not insulting, there was no struggle, and the female did not testify that she was traumatized or disturbed by his acts. Moreover, he points out that the evidence disclosed that after the incident the female complainant accompanied him to a restaurant where they had breakfast together. Should the appellate court reverse this conviction on the ground that the evidence is insufficient? Why or why not?

6. The defendant and her husband have two sons, ages five and three. Without notifying her husband, she left the family home with both children while no court proceedings were pending concerning either their marriage or custody of their children. Two weeks later, and without the wife's knowledge, the husband obtained a court order granting him custody of the two children. An arrest warrant was eventually issued for the wife. She was arrested in another state and brought back to her home state, where she now faces prosecution under a statute that provides, "Whoever, being a relative of a child … without lawful authority, holds or intends to hold such a child permanently or for a protracted period, or takes or entices a child from his lawful custodian … shall be guilty of a felony." The wife's attorney stipulates that the facts are correct as stated but contends the wife cannot be convicted of parental kidnapping under the quoted statute. What result do you think should occur? Why?

7. A nineteen-year-old woman returns home from an evening at the beach. She tells her mother that she has been raped and sodomized by an attacker she does not know. Some hours later, the woman identifies her attacker to her mother, and they notify the police. At trial, the prosecution seeks to admit expert testimony on rape trauma syndrome to explain the victim's reticence in promptly identifying her attacker. The defense objects. Should the court allow expert testimony on this subject to explain the reactions of the female victim in the hours following her attack and to explain why she may initially have been unwilling to report the defendant who attacked her? Why or why not?

CHAPTER **7**

Property Crimes

Introduction

Private property is a basic value of American society and a fundamental tenet of American law. In early America, property interests beyond raw land were often meager, consisting primarily of possessions necessary for survival. Dwellings for most people were modest. At that time, enforcement of the law largely depended on "self-help." As the nation developed, property interests became a vital part of the American economy, and professional law enforcement became the rule rather than the exception. The law recognized the need to deter people from infringing on the property interests of others and to punish transgressors. In today's affluent society and with the rapid technological advances of the past few decades, crimes against property have assumed even greater significance. In this chapter we examine the background of basic common-law property and habitation offenses and provide a sampling of the present-day statutory crimes in this area.

The Common-Law Background

When the common law emerged, England was an agrarian country with relatively little commercial activity. Possession of private property was an important concept, but beyond the right to occupy a dwelling, the property interests of most people consisted largely of what the law refers to as **tangible property** (that is, such things as animals, cooking implements, and tools). Today, in contrast to tangible property (such as automobiles, household goods, and books), a majority of households own some intangible property, such as bank accounts, stocks, bonds, and notes. Thus, in contrast to the early common-law period, intangible assets are now of great economic importance.

The common-law offenses involving property reflect the environment in which they matured. It was a very serious offense for someone to permanently deprive another of the possession of personal property, whether through stealth or through force, violence, or intimidation. However, it was of far less consequence to cheat someone by the use of false tokens or false weights and measures. When it came to such breaches of ethics as misrepresentations and violations of trust, the common law generally left victims to their civil remedies. This view gave rise to such early maxims as *caveat emptor,* meaning, "let the buyer beware." Because commercial transactions were not a major concern, forgery remained a misdemeanor. Likewise, extortion and malicious mischief were also misdemeanors because the conduct involved in these offenses did not qualify for the severe punishment meted out for felonies. Finally, offenses concerning the rights of landholders were dealt with largely through the civil law.

The Common-Law Theft Offenses

By 1776 the English common law recognized two offenses dealing with theft: larceny and false pretenses. Theft offenses of embezzlement and receiving stolen property were later created by statutes passed by the English Parliament.

Larceny

The basic common-law offense against infringement of another's personal property was **larceny,** the crime from which all other theft offenses developed. Larceny was a felony that consisted of (1) the wrongful taking and carrying away of (2) the personal property of another (3) with the intent to permanently deprive the other person of the property. The taking was called the "caption," the carrying away was called the "asportation," and the personal property had to have a "corporeal" (that is, a physical) existence. The wrongful act of taking was described as a "trespass," and the intent to permanently deprive the victim of the property was known as the *animus furundi.* Although many of these terms are not in common use today, the reader will find that courts frequently use them in judicial opinions when interpreting modern-day theft statutes.

To constitute common-law larceny, the taking had to be a deprivation of the owner's or possessor's interest in personal property. Real estate and the property attached to it were not subject to larceny; neither were trees nor crops wrongfully severed from the land. But if the owner of property had already severed crops and a thief carried them away, it was larceny because the thief was carrying away personal property rather than merely infringing on the owner's real property.

These distinctions are difficult to appreciate today, but they were significant in the development of the common law, where wrongs concerning a person's land gave rise to civil, as opposed to criminal, remedies. Also, at common law, anyone wrongfully deprived of possession of personal property was entitled to recover damages based on the tort (civil wrong) of conversion. Thus, there was overlap between the crime of larceny and the tort of conversion.

As the common law developed, personal property consisted largely of tools, household items, and domestic animals. Items such as promissory notes were not subject to larceny because they represented intangible legal rights; however, coins and bills were because they had a physical existence.

A taking by a person who had a lawful right to possession was not larceny. As we will discuss later, this led Parliament to enact the crime of embezzlement. Because the property had to be taken from another, a co-owner or partner did not commit larceny by taking jointly owned property. Nor did a spouse commit larceny by taking the other spouse's property because at common law, spouses were considered one.

To find an accused guilty of larceny, it was necessary to prove that the taker carried the property away. This element was usually satisfied by even a slight removal of the property. It was also essential to prove the taker's intent to permanently deprive the owner or possessor of the property. A person could not be convicted for just borrowing or using property under a reasonable belief of a right of possession. Consequently, a person who temporarily took another's horse would not be guilty of larceny because there was no intent to permanently deprive the owner of the horse. Furthermore, had someone taken a horse that reasonably appeared to be the taker's own, the taker would likely have been acting under a *bona fide* mistake of fact and hence would not have been guilty of larceny. (See Chapter 14 for a discussion of the mistake-of-fact defense.) Yet a person who secured possession of goods through trickery could be found guilty of larceny if there was proof that the trickster intended to permanently deprive the owner of the goods.

False Pretenses, Embezzlement, and Receiving Stolen Property

Many technical and often subtle distinctions developed in the common-law crime of larceny. Perhaps one reason for this was the reluctance of courts to find a thief guilty of larceny because the penalty at early common law was death. As commerce became more significant in England, the crime of larceny was not adequate either to deal with those who obtained financial advantage through false pretenses or to deter or punish servants who fraudulently appropriated property that rightfully came into their possession. Consequently, by the late 1700s, the English Parliament created two supplemental misdemeanor offenses: false pretenses and embezzlement. The offense of **false pretenses** came into being in 1757, before the American Revolution. The offense thereby became a part of the common law of those states that adopted it with the statutory modifications made by Parliament before the American Revolution. **Embezzlement,** on the other hand, did not become a statutory crime until an enactment by Parliament in 1799. Although as early as 1691 a receiver of stolen goods could be prosecuted as an accessory after the fact to larceny, in 1827 Parliament enacted a statute making receiving stolen property a misdemeanor. Thus embezzlement and receiving stolen property became English laws too late to become part of the common law adopted by the new American states. By subsequent enactments, the English Parliament broadened the scope of embezzlement.

The offense of false pretenses was committed by a person who obtained someone else's property by (1) the accused obtaining wares or merchandise of another (2) by false pretenses and (3) with the intent to cheat or defraud the other person. Parliament's enactment of the offense of false pretenses during the Industrial Revolution represented an important development in the English criminal law. Because false pretenses became an offense just before the American Revolution, few English court decisions interpreting these offenses became a part of the common law adopted by the new American states. Yet the English law in this area influenced both American legislation and judicial decisions.

In contrast with larceny, embezzlement occurred where an accused who had lawful possession of another's property (for example, a servant or employee) wrongfully appropriated the property. A series of enactments by the English Parliament brought not only servants but also brokers, bankers, lawyers, and trustees within the scope of embezzlement. Thus, an embezzlement occurred when someone occupying a position

CASE-IN-POINT

Receiving Stolen Property: Sufficient Evidence to Convict

Defendant Lynn Belt was convicted of receiving stolen property in violation of Utah Code Ann. 76–6–408(1) (Supp. 1989), which makes it a crime for a person to receive property of another "knowing that it has been stolen or believing that it probably has been stolen … with a purpose to deprive the owner thereof." Belt appealed, contending the evidence was legally insufficient to support his conviction. The evidence revealed that the defendant purchased videocassette recorders from Sgt. Illsley of the Metro Major Felony Unit during an undercover operation involving the purchase and sale of stolen property. Defendant met Illsley at an empty parking lot, where Illsley offered the new recorders to the defendant at a very low price, explaining that the store name and serial numbers had been cut off. Defendant replied, "I don't want to hear about the serial number or store names—just do our business." Illsley testified that at one point the defendant said, "I wish you wouldn't cut the serial numbers off. That makes it look hot." The Court of Appeals of Utah held that the evidence was sufficient for the jury to have found that the defendant believed the goods he purchased were stolen and affirmed Belt's conviction.

State v. Belt, 780 P.2d 1271 (Utah App. 1989).

of trust converted another's property to his or her own use, whereas larceny required proof of a wrongful taking and carrying away of the personal property of another. Nevertheless, to convict a defendant of embezzlement, it was necessary to prove that the accused intended to defraud the victim. **Receiving stolen property** consisted of receiving possession and control of another's personal property knowing it was stolen and with the intent to permanently deprive the owner of possession of such property.

The Modern Approach to Theft Offenses

A review of the various technical distinctions that developed in the common-law offenses of larceny, receiving stolen property, and false pretenses and the early statutory offenses of embezzlement and receiving stolen property makes it obvious that significant reforms were needed. A redefinition of these basic property offenses was required to cope with the various aspects of theft in American society. Modern theft ranges from the theft of vehicles, shoplifting, and looting to such sophisticated forms of larceny as credit card fraud, identity theft, and theft of intellectual property (see Figure 7.1). Indeed, theft is a nationwide problem that must be dealt with by both state and federal authorities.

Federal Approaches

Congress has enacted a series of statutes comprehensively proscribing theft and embezzlement. The first, 18 U.S.C.A. § 641, provides:

> Whoever embezzles, steals, purloins, or knowingly converts to his use or the use of another, or without authority, sells, conveys or disposes of any record, voucher, money, or thing of value of the United States or any department or agency thereof, or any property made or being made under contract for the United States or any department or agency thereof; or
>
> Whoever receives, conceals, or retains the same with intent to convert it to his use or gain, knowing it to have been embezzled, stolen, purloined or converted; …
>
> Shall be fined….

The purpose of 18 U.S.C.A. § 641 is to place in one part of the criminal code crimes so kindred as to belong in one category. The Supreme Court has said that despite the

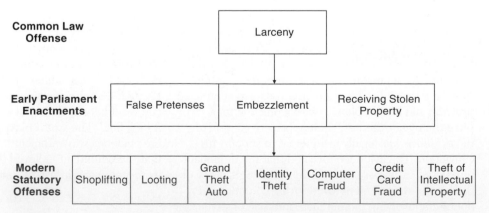

FIGURE 7.1 Evolution of Theft Offenses

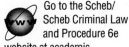 Go to the Scheb/
Scheb Criminal Law
and Procedure 6e
website at academic
.cengage.com/criminaljustice/
scheb for an edited version of
Morissette v. U.S.

failure of Congress to expressly include the common-law intent requirement for larceny, section 641 should not be construed to eliminate that intent requirement. The statute has been held to apply not only to larceny and embezzlement but also to all instances in which a person may obtain wrongful advantage from another's property. *Morissette v. United States,* 342 U.S. 246, 72 S.Ct. 240, 96 L.Ed. 288 (1952).

Another federal statute, 18 U.S.C.A. § 659, provides penalties for embezzling or unlawfully taking the contents of any vehicle moving in interstate or foreign commerce or from any passenger therein. Federal appellate courts have characterized the intent requirement under this statute as the intent to appropriate or convert the property of the owner. Furthermore, the federal appellate courts have said that a simultaneous intent to return the property or make restitution does not make the offense any less embezzlement. See, for example, *United States v. Waronek,* 582 F.2d 1158 (7th Cir. 1978).

A variety of other federal statutes define embezzlement and theft by public officers or employees of the United States and custodians of federal funds, bank examiners, and bank officers and employees. See 18 U.S.C.A. §§ 641–665. During the 1990s Congress added statutes creating offenses involving theft concerning programs involving federal funds, theft of livestock and artwork, and theft or embezzlement in connection with health care. 18 U.S.C.A. §§ 666–669.

State Approaches

All states have enacted statutes expanding the common-law concept of larceny to include all types of tangible and intangible property. Historically, the states maintained numerous statutes basically adopting the concepts of common-law larceny and false pretenses and the later English statutes proscribing embezzlement and receiving stolen property. As new problems developed, legislative bodies attempted to fill the gaps by creating new offenses. This resulted in the legislative creation of numerous statutory offenses proscribing various forms of stealing and dishonest dealings. Often, these statutes were confusing and in many instances contradictory.

In recent years, many states have replaced their various statutes with a consolidated theft statute that proscribes stealing in very broad terms. These new statutes make it unlawful for a person to commit any of the common-law theft offenses mentioned as well as other crimes, and penalties are based on the amount and character of the property stolen.

Florida, for example, passed the Florida Anti-Fencing Act in 1977. Despite its narrow title, the act defines theft as including all the common-law theft offenses, several former statutory offenses, possession of property with altered or removed identifying features, and dealing in stolen property (that is, fencing). As do other modern theft statutes, the statute defines theft by degrees based on the seriousness of the offender's conduct. West's Fla. Stat. Ann. § 812.012–037. Section 812.014(1) provides:

A person commits theft if he or she knowingly obtains or uses, or endeavors to obtain or to use, the property of another with intent to, either temporarily or permanently: (a) Deprive the other person of a right to the property or a benefit from the property. (b) Appropriate the property to his or her own use or to the use of any person not entitled to the use of the property.

Under the comprehensive Florida theft statute, the phrase "obtains or uses" replaces the old common-law requirement of "taking and carrying away." This statute defines "obtains or uses" as

any manner of (a) taking or exercising control over property; (b) making any unauthorized use, disposition, or transfer of property; (c) obtaining property by fraud, willful misrepresentation of a future act, or false promise; or (d) by conduct previously known as stealing, larceny, purloining, abstracting, embezzlement, misapplication, misappropriation, conversion, or obtaining money or property by false pretenses, fraud, or deception; or (e) other conduct similar in nature. § 812.012(1)(2).

"Property" is broadly defined to include "(a) Real property, including things growing on, affixed to, and found in land; (b) Tangible or intangible personal property, including rights, privileges, interests, and claims; and (c) Services." § 812.012(4).

"Property of another" means "property in which a person has an interest upon which another person is not privileged to infringe without consent, whether or not the other person has an interest in the property." § 812.012(5).

"Services" means "anything of value resulting from a person's physical or mental labor or skill, or from the use, possession, or presence of property, and includes: (a) Repairs or improvements to property. (b) Professional services. (c) Private, public, or government communication, transportation, power, water, or sanitation services. (d) Lodging accommodations. (e) Admissions to places of exhibition or entertainment." § 812.012(6).

The value and type of property stolen categorize the seriousness of the offense. **Grand theft** in the first degree is the most serious felony. It involves stealing property valued at $100,000 or more, or an offender who commits any grand theft and in the course of committing the offense uses a motor vehicle as an instrumentality, other than merely as a getaway vehicle, to assist in committing the offense and thereby damages the real property of another or causes damage to the real or personal property of another in excess of $1,000. § 812.014(2)(a)(b).

Grand theft in the second degree, a somewhat less serious felony, involves theft of property valued at $20,000 or more but less than $100,000. § 812.014(2)(b). It is grand theft in the third degree and a lesser felony if the property stolen is valued at $300 or more but less than $20,000 or if the property stolen is a will, codicil, or other testamentary instrument; firearm; motor vehicle; livestock; fire extinguisher; 2,000 or more pieces of citrus fruit; a stop sign; property taken from an identified construction site; or anhydrous ammonia. § 812.014(2)(c). If the property stolen is valued at $100 or more but less than $300 and is taken from a dwelling or from the unenclosed curtilage of a dwelling, the offense is also classified as a third-degree felony. § 812.014(2)(d). Otherwise, except for the specified articles, theft of property having a value under $300 is petit theft, a misdemeanor. § 812.014 (2)(e).

CASE-IN-POINT

Larceny Committed through a Phony Night-Deposit Box

A Massachusetts jury convicted Brian Donovan and Robert Grant of larceny. Evidence introduced at trial showed that they had constructed a phony night-deposit box and attached it to the wall of a bank building. The box was constructed of heavy-gauge steel just like a real depository. Seven depositors lost an estimated $37,000 by making deposits to the phony box. Although the phony box was never recovered, a witness testified that he overheard the defendants in a bar talking about the phony deposit box as "a helluva'n idea." Another witness stated that Grant had admitted to her that he had robbed a bank using a phony deposit box. On appeal, the Massachusetts Supreme Court rejected the defendants' contentions that certain testimony had been improperly admitted into evidence and that the evidence produced at trial was legally insufficient to prove the crime of larceny.

Commonwealth v. Donovan, 478 N.E.2d 727 (Mass. 1985).

Go to the Scheb/
Scheb Criminal Law
and Procedure 6e
website at academic
.cengage.com/criminaljustice/
scheb to find *State v. Richard*
(1984), where the Nebraska
Supreme Court reverses a larceny conviction in a case
where the defendant was convicted of shoplifting a pound
of bacon from a
supermarket.

Finally, a person previously convicted of theft who commits **petit theft** is guilty of a more serious misdemeanor, § 812.014(3)(b), though one who has been convicted of theft two or more times commits a felony of the third degree, § 812.014(3)(c). Special penalties include suspension of a driver's license for a person who drives away from a filling station without paying for gasoline. § 812.014(5). Penalties are also upgraded where the victim of theft is over age 65. § 812.0145.

Theft remains a specific-intent crime, but like many newer theft statutes, the Florida statute simply refers to the **intent to deprive.** The Florida Supreme Court has said this simply means the "intent to steal" and not necessarily the intent to permanently deprive the owner of the property. *State v. Dunmann,* 427 So.2d 166 (Fla. 1983). Because the statutory definition of theft includes an endeavor to commit theft, the crime is fully proved when an attempt, along with the requisite intent, is established. *State v. Sykes,* 434 So.2d 325 (Fla. 1983) (see Chapter 5).

Computer Crime: New Offenses to Cope with High-Tech Crime

Once computers became common in society, criminals began to employ them to commit a variety of offenses. Indeed, the pervasiveness of computers poses some unique challenges to law enforcement agencies and prosecutors. Most computer crimes violate laws defining theft, fraud, or embezzlement at the state level and, often, mail fraud at the federal level. Nevertheless, since 1978 nearly every state has enacted laws specifically defining computer crimes. These laws define *access, computer program, software, database, hacking, financial instrument,* and other terms used in modern computer parlance and address such activities as computer manipulation, theft of intellectual property, telecommunications crimes, and software piracy. They also create such offenses as **theft of computer services, computer fraud,** and **computer trespass.** The Virginia legislature has addressed each of these offenses by enacting the Virginia Computer Crimes Act.

Section 18.2–152.3 provides:

Any person who uses a computer or computer network without authority and with the intent to:

1. Obtain property or services by false pretenses;

2. Embezzle or commit larceny; or

3. Convert the property of another shall be guilty of the crime of computer fraud.

Depending on the value of property or services actually obtained, the offense is either a felony or a serious misdemeanor.

Section 18.2–152.4 provides:

A. It shall be unlawful for any person, with malicious intent, to:

1. Temporarily or permanently remove, halt, or otherwise disable any computer data, computer programs or computer software from a computer or computer network;

2. Cause a computer to malfunction, regardless of how long the malfunction persists;

3. Alter, disable, or erase any computer data, computer programs or computer software;

4. Effect the creation or alteration of a financial instrument or of an electronic transfer of funds;

5. Use a computer or computer network to cause physical injury to the property of another; or

6. Use a computer or computer network to make or cause to be made an unauthorized copy, in any form, including, but not limited to, any printed or electronic form of computer data, computer programs or computer software residing in, communicated by, or produced by a computer or computer network.

Depending on the damages caused, the offense is either a felony or a serious misdemeanor.

A Unique Prosecutorial Burden in Theft Offenses

Except where statutorily specified articles are stolen, theft offenses are usually classified as grand theft or petit theft. Statutes commonly grade the felony and misdemeanor offenses based on ranges of market value of goods stolen. Therefore, the prosecution must establish the market value of goods or services stolen. The determining factor is generally the market value at the time and in the locality of the theft. *State v. Kimbel*, 620 P.2d 515 (Utah 1980). This may be shown by proof of the original market cost, the manner in which the property stolen has been used, and its general condition and quality. *Negron v. State*, 306 So.2d 104 (Fla. 1974). Judges customarily instruct juries that if the value of the property cannot be ascertained, they must find the value to be less than that required for grand theft. But consider the theft of a credit card. Usually, holders of these cards have set credit limits available to them on proper signature. Therefore, a credit card has no market value in lawful channels for a third person. In *Miller v. People*, 566 P.2d 1059 (Colo. 1977), the Colorado Supreme Court held that

CASE-IN-POINT

Unauthorized Access to a Voice Mailbox

Andrea M. Gerulis was convicted in a bench trial of two counts of unlawful use of a computer and two counts of violating a statute that criminalized intentionally obtaining various electronic services "available only for compensation" by deception, unauthorized connection, etc. Gerulis was ordered to make restitution. The evidence revealed that Gerulis had deposited and retrieved information from voice mailboxes (VMBs) of a hospital and a telephone message company without authority from either to do so. By altering passwords, she thereby prevented authorized users from using their VMBs. Gerulis appealed, contending the evidence was insufficient to sustain her convictions.

The appellate court found that VMBs are "computers" within the meaning of the statute, and Gerulis's disruption of normal use of the VMBs

violated the statute. The court then addressed Gerulis's convictions for theft of services. The court observed that the prosecution had charged Gerulis under a statute that makes it an offense if a person "intentionally obtains services for himself or for another which he knows are available only for compensation." Because the evidence revealed that the VMBs that Gerulis accessed were provided by the hospital and message company without charge for their employees, the court found that Gerulis's mere intent to obtain free services did not violate that statute. Accordingly, the court affirmed Gerulis's convictions for unlawful use of a computer, reversed her convictions for theft of services, and remanded the case to the trial court to modify the restitution order imposed as Gerulis's sentence.

Commonwealth v. Gerulis, 616 A.2d 686 (Pa. Super. 1992).

the amount that could be purchased on the stolen card in the "illegitimate" market could be considered in determining whether a defendant was guilty of felony theft. In *Owolabi v. Commonwealth*, 428 S.E.2d 14 (Va. App. 1993), a Virginia appellate court disagreed. Where there was no evidence of the value of the credit cards stolen, only of the lines of credit they represented, the evidence did not support a finding that the card had a value greater than $200. Thus, the court held the defendant could be convicted only of petit larceny, not grand larceny.

Proof of value is very important in a theft case because it can often mean the difference between the defendant's being convicted of a misdemeanor or a felony, or even of a felony of various degrees. For this reason, courts often receive expert testimony on this issue.

Identity Theft

The theft or misappropriation of personal identifying information and documents, commonly referred to as **identity theft,** has become a theft offense of major proportions in the United States. In April 2006 the *Bureau of Justice Statistics Bulletin* reported that in 2004, 3.6 million households, representing three percent of the households in the United States, discovered that at least one member of the household had been the victim of identity theft during the previous six months.

A person's identity is closely tied to personal and numerical identification of bank accounts; credit cards; Social Security, Medicare, telephone, insurance, and utility accounts; and many other identifying documents. Thieves obtain information about a person through many means. These include such obvious means as theft of wallets and purses, mail, and computer data and gathering information from home and car burglaries. They also obtain information from such less obvious means as "shoulder surfing" when someone is paying by check or credit card and "dumpster diving" into trash to obtain discarded identifying documents such as unused pre-approved credit card applications. Information obtained from e-mail and other computer transactions, including responses to requests for passwords and other information, is increasingly becoming a source of identifying information. Armed with such information, a thief can then assume the victim's identity, change the victim's address, open new accounts, buy a car, borrow money, and otherwise injure the victim's assets, credit standing, and reputation. Most victims of identity theft are unaware of how a thief obtained their personal information. Often the victim is unaware of the fraud until substantial damage has been inflicted. Victims often incur large expenses and expend considerable time in opening new accounts and repairing their credit ratings.

Federal Legislation

To address the growing problem of identity theft, Congress enacted the Identity Theft and Assumption Deterrence Act of 1998 (ITADA), which amends 18 U.S.C.A. § 1028 by adding subsection (a)(7), making it a felony to "knowingly transfer or use, without lawful authority, a means of identification of another person with the intent to commit, or to aid or abet, any unlawful activity that constitutes a violation of Federal law, or that constitutes a felony under any applicable State or local law." Conduct involving identity theft or fraud may in some instances also be a violation of 18 U.S.C.A. § 1341 (credit card fraud); 18 U.S.C.A. 1030 (computer fraud); 18 U.S.C.A. 1341 (mail fraud);

18 U.S.C.A. 1343 (wire, radio and television fraud); and 18 U.S.C.A. § 1344 (financial institution fraud).

The Federal Trade Commission maintains a Web site (www.consumer.gov/idtheft) that furnishes considerable information about identity theft. It explains how the crime occurs, what steps can be taken to prevent it, and what measures should be taken when people discover that they have been victimized by identity theft. The site also features a comprehensive survey of federal and state legislation criminalizing identity theft.

State Legislation

By 2003 most states had enacted specific statutes criminalizing identify theft and fraud, but even without specific statutes such activity could be prosecuted under statutes proscribing theft and fraud. Section 943.210(2) of the Wisconsin Statutes, as recently amended, provides that:

> (2) Whoever, for any of the following purposes, intentionally uses or, attempts to use, or possess with intent to use any personal identifying information or personal identification document of an individual, including a deceased individual, without the authorization or consent of the individual and by representing that he or she is the individual, that he or she is acting with the authorization or consent of the individual, or that the information or document belongs to him or her is guilty of a Class H felony:
>
>> (a) To obtain credit, money, goods, services, employment, or any other thing of value or benefit.
>>
>> (b) To avoid civil or criminal process or penalty.
>>
>> (c) To harm the reputation, property, person, or estate of the individual.

In *State v. Ramirez,* 633 N.W.2d 656 (Wis. App. 2001), the court upheld the conviction of a defendant found guilty under Wis. Stat. § 943.201(2) for misappropriating the personal identifying information of another. The defendant had used someone else's Social Security number without authorization to obtain employment.

In 2005 the Washington Court of Appeals rejected a defendant's contention that the state's choice of prosecuting him for the felony of identity theft rather than the misdemeanor offenses of use of a false name or a false identity denied him his constitutional right to equal protection of the law. The court rejected his contention because the misdemeanor offense did not require assuming the identity of an actual person. *State v. Presba,* 26 P.3d 1280 (Wash. App. 2005).

Intellectual Property Offenses

The term **intellectual property** refers to products of the human intellect such as patents, copyrights, trademarks, and trade secrets. In the information age, intellectual property is as important as real estate or tangible personal property. The U.S. Constitution, Article 1, Section 8, cl. 8, grants Congress the power to secure for a limited time to authors and inventors the exclusive rights to their writings and discoveries. Congress has legislated pursuant to such authority and has granted federal courts exclusive jurisdiction over civil and criminal actions based on federal statutes. See 28 U.S.C.A. §§ 1338, 1355. While most disputes involving intellectual property are civil matters, there are several important criminal prohibitions in this area, most notably patent infringement, copyright infringement, trademark counterfeiting, and theft of trade secrets.

Patent Infringement

A **patent** is a federal government grant of the right to exclude others from producing or using a discovery or invention. Patents are issued by the U.S. Patent and Trademark Office for inventions and discoveries that are novel, useful, and not something of an obvious nature. See 35 U.S.C.A. §§ 101–103. Patents are issued for a period of 20 years. 35 U.S.C.A. § 154.

Patent infringements are generally remedied through civil litigation. Indeed, there are few instances of criminal penalties being imposed. The Patent Act, however, establishes criminal liability of $500 per infringement for falsely affixing or marking in connection with sales or advertising of any imitation of the name of the patentee, the patent number, or using the words "patent," "patentee," "patent applied for," or "patent pending" to falsely convey the status of a patent. To prove any of the above violations, the prosecution must show the deceitful intent of the defendant. 35 U.S.C.A. § 292. Title 18 U.S.C.A. § 497 makes it an offense for "Whoever passes, utters, or publishes, or attempts to pass, utter, or publish as genuine, any such letters patent, knowing the same to be forged, counterfeited or falsely altered." The statute calls for a fine or imprisonment.

Copyright Infringement

A **copyright** is a form of legal protection that is provided to the authors of original works. Congress has enacted statutes to expand the protection of literary work to include musical, artistic, and architectural works as well as videos, computer software, and databases. Copyrights are registered in the Copyright Office in the Library of Congress, and a copyright for a work created after January 1, 1978, is given statutory protection for the life of the author plus 70 years after the author's death. 17 U.S.C.A. § 302(a). Section 506 of the Copyright Act provides for the criminal prosecution of certain types of infringement.

Section 506(a) of the Copyright Act, 17 U.S.C.A. § 506(a), provides that anyone "who infringes a copyright willfully either (1) for purposes of commercial advantage or private financial gain, or (2) by the reproduction or distribution, including by electronic means of 1 or more copies or phonorecords … shall be punished as provided in 18 U.S.C.A. § 2319." (The term "willfully" distinguishes the crime from infringement in civil litigation.) Under this latter statute the determination of whether such violation is a felony or misdemeanor depends on the quantity and value of items distributed in a specified period of time. Penalties are also provided for fraudulent removal of copyright notices and for false representations in copyright applications. 17 U.S.C.A. § 506(d) & (e).

Knowingly trafficking in counterfeit labels affixed or designed to be affixed to a phonorecord or copy of a computer program, motion pictures, or other audiovisual works is **bootlegging,** an offense punishable by fine or imprisonment under 18 U.S.C.A. § 2318.

Section 506(b) of the Copyright Act provides for the "forfeiture and destruction … of all infringing copies or phonorecords and all implements, devices, or equipment used in the manufacture of such infringing copies or phonorecords." 17 U.S.C.A. § 506(b).

It is a misdemeanor to fraudulently place a copyright notice on an article, to distribute such an article, to fraudulently remove the copyright notice from a validly copyrighted article, or to knowingly make false representations in an application for

Criminal Copyright Infringement

In August of 1999, Jeffrey G. Levy, a twenty-two-year-old senior at the University of Oregon, pleaded guilty to criminal copyright infringement. According to a statement issued by the U.S. Attorney's Office in Oregon, Levy admitted that he illegally posted computer software, music files, and digitally recorded movies on the Internet, which allowed anyone accessing his site to download and copy these products. Officials at the University of Oregon brought the matter to the attention of the FBI after noting an unusually large volume of bandwidth traffic being generated from Levy's Web site, which was hosted on the University's file server. The FBI's investigation confirmed that thousands of computer programs, movies, and musical recordings had been made available for downloading from Levy's site. Although Levy faced a possible $250,000 fine and three years in prison, his negotiated guilty plea led to a sentence of two years' probation. As a condition of probation, Levy was ordered not to access the Internet from his home computer.

Source: United States Attorney's Office, District of Oregon, "Defendant Sentenced for First Criminal Copyright Conviction Under the 'No Electronic Theft' (NET) Act for Unlawful Distribution of Software on the Internet," November 23, 1999.

copyright. 17 U.S.C.A. § 506(c), (d), & (e). Some states have also enacted laws making bootlegging of copyrighted materials an offense.

Title 18 U.S.C.A. § 2319 provides that it is a felony to reproduce or distribute ten or more copies or phonorecords, of one or more copyrighted works, having a retail value of more than $2,500 in any 180-day period. The reproduction or distribution of fewer copies or phonorecords, or of goods having a value below $2,500, is a misdemeanor.

INTERNET-BASED COPYRIGHT INFRINGEMENT

In 1997, Congress enacted the No Electronic Theft (NET) Act, 111 STAT. 2678, Public Law 105–147, specifically to address Internet-based copyright infringement. Prior to this legislation, copyright infringement could be prosecuted only where the defendant derived a financial benefit from the infringement. The proliferation of file sharing via the Internet prompted Congress to change the law. The NET Act amended 17 U.S.C.A. § 506 and 18 U.S.C.A. § 2319 to make it unlawful to reproduce or distribute copyrighted works even where a defendant lacks a commercial or financial motive. One who reproduces or distributes ten or more copyrighted works that have a total value of more than $2,500 can be charged with a felony punishable by up to three years in prison and a fine of up to $250,000. A defendant who reproduces or distributes one or more copies of copyrighted works with a value of more than $1,000 can be charged with a misdemeanor punishable by up to one year in prison and a fine of up to $100,000.

Trademark Counterfeiting

A **trademark** is a distinctive word, phrase or graphic symbol used to distinguish a product. To be protected by federal law, trademarks used in interstate or foreign commerce may be registered with the U.S. Patent and Trademark Office. Once registered, a trademark has nationwide protection. See 15 U.S.C.A. §§ 1051–1127. Trademark disputes are generally resolved in civil courts, but federal law does provide criminal penalties for **trademark counterfeiting.** The Trademark Counterfeiting Act of 1984 provides that:

> Whoever intentionally traffics or attempts to traffic in goods or services and knowingly uses a counterfeit mark on or in connection with such goods or services shall, if an individual, be fined not more than $2,000,000 or imprisoned not more than 10 years, or both, and, if a person other than an individual, be fined not more than $5,000,000. 18 U.S.C.A. § 2320.

The statute defines "counterfeit mark" to mean "a spurious mark … that is identical with, or substantially indistinguishable from, a mark registered in the United States Patent and Trademark Office … and the use of which is likely to cause confusion, to cause mistake, or to deceive…." 18 U.S.C.A. § 2320(e). When a genuine trademark is affixed to a counterfeit product, it becomes a "spurious mark" within the meaning of the statutory prohibition against trafficking in counterfeit goods. To establish a violation of the statute, the government must prove that the mark is counterfeit and that the defendant knew the mark was counterfeit. Section 2320 requires the government to establish, beyond a reasonable doubt, four elements: (1) that the defendant trafficked or attempted to traffic in goods or services; (2) that such trafficking, or the attempt to traffic, was intentional; (3) that the defendant used a "counterfeit mark" on or in connection with such goods or services; and (4) that the defendant "knew" that the counterfeit mark was so used. *United States v. Sultan,* 115 F.3d 321, 325 (5th Cir. 1997).

Theft of Trade Secrets

A **trade secret** is generally a formula, pattern, physical device, idea, process, compilation of information, or other information that provides a business with a competitive advantage. Trade secrets include "all forms and types of financial, business, scientific, technical, economic, or engineering information … whether tangible or intangible, and whether or how stored, compiled, or memorialized physically, electronically, graphically, photographically, or in writing." 18 U.S.C.A. § 1839(3). Controversies concerning the use and misuse of trade secrets are frequently handled in civil courts where state statutes and the common law provide remedies. However, in 1996, Congress enacted the Economic Espionage Act of 1996 (EEA), creating the first national criminal penalty for theft of trade secrets. The EEA prohibits foreign governments from stealing trade secrets (18 U.S.C.A. § 1831) and criminalizes domestic trade secret theft (18 U.S.C.A. § 1832). Title 18 U.S.C.A. § 1832, provides that:

> (a) Whoever, with intent to convert a trade secret, that is related to or included in a product that is produced for or placed in interstate or foreign commerce, to the economic benefit of anyone other than the owner thereof, and intending or knowing that the offense will, injure any owner of that trade secret, knowingly—
>
> (1) steals, or without authorization appropriates, takes, carries away, or conceals, or by fraud, artifice, or deception obtains such information;
>
> (2) without authorization copies, duplicates, sketches, draws, photographs, downloads, uploads, alters, destroys, photocopies, replicates, transmits, delivers, sends, mails, communicates, or conveys such information;
>
> (3) receives, buys, or possesses such information, knowing the same to have been stolen or appropriated, obtained, or converted without authorization;
>
> (4) attempts to commit any offense described in paragraphs (1) through (3); or
>
> (5) conspires with one or more other persons to commit any offense described in paragraphs (1) through (3), and one or more of such persons do any act to effect

Violation of the Economic Espionage Act

CASE-IN-POINT

Dr. Victor Lee was employed by Avery Dennison Inc. to conduct scientific research on adhesives. In 1989, while making a presentation in Taiwan, Lee was introduced to Pin-Yen Yang, the head of Four Pillars Enterprise Company, Ltd., a competing firm. According to the indictment, Yang and Lee agreed that Lee would receive $25,000 to serve as a secret consultant to Four Pillars. Some time later Lee provided Yang with confidential materials belonging to Avery Dennison, including informa-

tion regarding a new adhesive product. After learning of Lee's activities, the FBI confronted him and persuaded him to participate in a "sting" operation in which the FBI videotaped a meeting between Lee and Yang at which Lee provided Yang with confidential Avery Dennison materials. After a jury trial, Yang was convicted of attempt and conspiracy to commit theft of a trade secret. The U.S. Court of Appeals for the Sixth Circuit upheld the conviction.

United States v. Yang, 281 F.3d 534 (6th Cir. 2002).

---

the object of the conspiracy, shall, except as provided in subsection (b), be fined under this title or imprisoned not more than 10 years, or both.

(b) Any organization that commits any offense described in subsection (a) shall be fined not more than $5,000,000. 18 U.S.C.A. § 1832.

Title 18 U.S.C.A. § 1834 provides for forfeiture to the United States of any profits and proceeds derived from violation of section 1832.

In July 2006 the media reported that three people had been arrested for allegedly violating the EEA. An employee of the Coca-Cola Company and two others were charged with stealing the confidential files and a sample of a new drink product and offering to sell these items to Coca-Cola's main rival, PepsiCo. Reportedly, the plot was foiled when Coca-Cola learned of the crime and reported it to the FBI. On February 2, 2007, a federal jury in Atlanta convicted Joya Williams, a former executive assistant at Coca-Cola, of conspiracy to steal trade secrets.

Robbery

At common law, **robbery** was a felony that consisted of (1) a taking of another's personal property of value (2) from the other person's possession or presence (3) by force or placing the person in fear and (4) with the intent to permanently deprive the other person of that property. In reality, robbery was an aggravated form of larceny where the taking was accomplished by force or threats of force with the same specific-intent requirement as in common-law larceny. The intent to steal (*animus furundi*), for example, was the same as in larceny and the taking of property had to be from the victim's actual or constructive possession. To constitute robbery, the violence or intimidation had to overcome the victim's resistance and precede or accompany the actual taking of property. Property in the victim's dwelling or vicinity was regarded as being in the victim's possession. To illustrate a significant difference between larceny and robbery, a person who spirited a person's wallet from his pocket would be guilty of larceny, but if the victim resisted and the thief took the wallet by force or violence, the offense constituted robbery.

Statutory Approaches to Robbery

In some respects, robbery is an offense against the person because it usually involves an assault or battery. See, for example, *State v. Shoemake*, 618 P.2d 1201 (Kan. 1980). Yet it also involves a taking of property and is generally classified as an offense against property.

FEDERAL LAWS

A federal statute makes it an offense to take, or attempt to take, by force and violence or intimidation from the person or presence of another any property or money belonging to or in the care of a bank, credit union, or savings and loan association. 18 U.S.C.A. § 2113(a). In addition, 18 U.S.C.A. § 1951 (Hobbs Act) defines the obstruction of interstate commerce in the context of robbery.

Federal jurisdiction is established where the bank is a federally chartered institution or where its deposits are federally insured. *United States v. Harris*, 530 F.2d 576 (4th Cir. 1976). The statutory offense varies from the common-law crime of robbery in that the government need only establish the defendant's general intent. *United States v. Klare*, 545 F.2d 93 (9th Cir. 1976).

STATE LAWS

Robbery is an offense in every state. Many states have enacted statutes simply defining it as did the common law, a practice sometimes referred to as codifying the common law. Other states classify robbery according to degree, with the seriousness of the offense usually based on whether the assailant is armed, the degree of force used, and, in some instances, on the vulnerability of the victim. The value of the property taken does not usually affect the degree of the crime of robbery, as it does that of theft.

CASE-IN-POINT

Robbery

On the morning of July 26, 1984, Lamont Julius McLaughlin and a companion, both wearing masks, entered a bank in Baltimore. McLaughlin brandished a handgun and told those in the bank to put up their hands and not to move. While McLaughlin held the gun, his companion leaped over the counter and stuffed several thousand dollars into a brown paper bag. Police officers were waiting outside and promptly arrested the pair. It was then determined that McLaughlin's gun was not loaded.

McLaughlin was found guilty in federal court of bank robbery "by the use of a dangerous weapon." 18 U.S.C.A. § 2113(d). On appeal, McLaughlin argued that his unloaded gun did not qualify as a "dangerous weapon" under the federal bank robbery statute. The U.S. Supreme Court rejected the argument and upheld McLaughlin's conviction. Justice Stevens opined:

"Three reasons, each independently sufficient, support the conclusion that an unloaded gun is a 'dangerous weapon.' First, a gun is an article that is typically and characteristically dangerous; the use for which it is manufactured and sold is a dangerous one, and the law reasonably may presume that such an article is always dangerous even though it may not be armed at a particular time or place. In addition, the display of a gun instills fear in the average citizen; as a consequence, it creates an immediate danger that a violent response will ensue. Finally, a gun can cause harm when used as a bludgeon."

McLaughlin v. United States, 476 U.S. 16, 106 S.Ct. 1677, 90 L.Ed.2d 15 (1986).

The Colorado Criminal Code provides a good illustration of classification of robbery offenses: "A person who knowingly takes anything of value from the person or presence of another by the use of force, threats, or intimidation commits robbery." West's Colo. Rev. Stat. Ann. § 18–4–301(1). Property is taken from the "presence of another" under Colorado law when it is so within the victim's reach, inspection, or observation that he or she would be able to retain control over the property but for the force, threats, or intimidation directed by the perpetrator. *People v. Bartowsheski*, 661 P.2d 235 (Colo. 1983). This is "simple robbery," in contrast with the statutory offense of **aggravated robbery.** The Colorado statute further provides:

(1) A person who commits robbery is guilty of aggravated robbery if during the act of robbery or immediate flight therefrom:

(a) He is armed with a deadly weapon with intent, if resisted, to kill, maim, or wound the person robbed or any other person; or

(b) He knowingly wounds or strikes the person robbed or any other person with a deadly weapon or by the use of force, threats, or intimidation with a deadly weapon knowingly puts the person robbed or any other person in reasonable fear of death or bodily injury; or

(c) He has present a confederate, aiding or abetting the perpetration of the robbery, armed with a deadly weapon, with the intent, either on the part of the defendant or confederate, if resistance is offered, to kill, maim, or wound the person robbed or any other person, or by the use of force, threats, or intimidation puts the person robbed or any other person in reasonable fear of death or bodily injury; or

(d) He possesses any article used or fashioned in a manner to lead any person who is present reasonably to believe it to be a deadly weapon or represents verbally or otherwise that he is then and there so armed. West's Colo. Rev. Stat. Ann. § 18–4–302.

Go to the Scheb/ Scheb Criminal Law and Procedure 6e website at academic .cengage.com/criminaljustice/ scheb to find *Jones v. Commonwealth* (1992), where a Virginia appellate court considers the sufficiency of the evidence to support a robbery conviction.

The Colorado Supreme Court has said that the gist of the crime of robbery under the Colorado statutes is "the putting in fear and taking of property of another by force or intimidation." *People v. Small*, 493 P.2d 15 (Colo. 1972). Aggravated robbery is distinguished from simple robbery by the fact that an accomplice or confederate is armed with a dangerous weapon with intent, if resisted, to maim, wound, or kill. The Colorado Supreme Court has observed that simple and aggravated robbery are but two degrees of the same offense. *Atwood v. People,* 489 P.2d 1305 (Colo. 1971).

The Temporal Relationship of Force to the Taking

Is it essential in the crime of robbery that the element of violence or intimidation occur before or at the same time as the taking of the victim's property? State appellate courts are divided on this issue, often based on the specific statutory language. Note that the Colorado statute in addressing aggravated robbery includes the language "if during the act of robbery or immediate flight therefrom." The Colorado Supreme Court has said that force used in robbery need not occur simultaneously with the taking. *People v. Bartowsheski,* supra. Other courts have agreed. In *Hermann v. State,* 123 So.2d 846 (Miss. 1960), a defendant, after stealthily obtaining gasoline, made a getaway from a filling station by pointing a deadly weapon at the attendant. The attendant stuck his hand through the window of the vehicle but was pushed away by the offender. The Mississippi Supreme Court held that this act of pushing the victim away constituted the force element of robbery. Again, in *People v. Kennedy,* 294 N.E.2d 788 (Ill. App. 1973), the court held that while the taking may be without force, the offense is robbery if the departure with the property is accomplished by the use of force. Likewise, a Utah appellate court noted that if force or fear is used at any time prior to or concurrent with the victim actually losing the ability to control his chattel (personal property), then a robbery has occurred. *State in Interest of D.B.,* 925 P.2d 178 (Utah App. 1996).

In 1986 the Florida Supreme Court held that defendants who used force while fleeing a retail store after committing theft in the store could not be convicted of robbery. The court followed the traditional common-law view that the use of force must occur before or at the same time as the taking of property. *Royal v. State,* 490 So.2d 44 (Fla. 1986). The state legislature promptly amended the statutory definition of robbery to add "an act shall be deemed 'in the course of committing the robbery' if it occurs in an attempt to commit robbery or in flight after the attempt or commission." West's Fla. Stat. Ann. § 812.13(3)(a). The statute also added that "an act shall be deemed 'in the course of taking' if it occurs either prior to, contemporaneous with, or subsequent to the taking of the property and if it and the act of taking constitute a continuous series of acts and events." § 812.13(3)(b). See *Perry v. State,* 801 So.2d 78 (Fla. 2001) (recognizing the change under the revised statute).

Carjacking

Depending on the circumstances, a person who forcibly takes another's vehicle is subject to prosecution under various state statutes. Recognizing the serious national threat that forcible auto theft poses to persons and their motor vehicles, and after a nationwide spree of **carjacking,** in 1992 Congress enacted the Anti-Car Theft Act of 1992. 18 U.S.C.A. § 2119. As originally enacted, the statute made it a crime for anyone who "takes a motor vehicle that has been transported, shipped, or received in interstate or foreign commerce from the person or presence of another by force and violence or by intimidation, or attempts to do so." The Ninth Circuit interpreted the 1992 statute as creating a general-intent offense. *United States v. Martinez,* 49 F.3d 1398 (9th Cir. 1995).

In 1994 Congress amended section 2119 to provide:

> Whoever, *with the intent to cause death or serious bodily harm* [emphasis added] takes a motor vehicle that has been transported, shipped, or received in interstate or foreign commerce from the person or presence of another by force and violence or by intimidation or attempts to so shall
>
> (1) be fined under this title or imprisoned not more than 15 years, or both,
>
> (2) if serious bodily injury (as defined in section 1365 of this title, including any conduct that, if the conduct occurred in the special maritime and territorial jurisdiction of the United States, would violate section 2241 or 2242 of this title) results, be fined under this title or imprisoned not more than 25 years, or both, and
>
> (3) if death results, be fined under this title or imprisoned for any number of years up to life, or both, or sentenced to death.

Thus the statute describes three offenses with different statutory elements: (1) a carjacking (or attempted carjacking), § 2119(1); (2) a carjacking (or attempted carjacking) resulting in a serious bodily injury, § 2119(2); and (3) a carjacking (or attempted carjacking) resulting in a death, § 2119(3).

In 1999, the Supreme Court reconciled the views of lower federal courts and held that section 2119 merely requires proof of an unconditional intent to seriously harm or kill the driver if necessary or a conditional intent to kill or seriously harm the driver if necessary to steal the car. *Holloway aka Ali v. United States,* 526 U.S. 1, 119 S.Ct. 966, 143 L.Ed.2d 1 (1999).

Go to the Scheb/ Scheb Criminal Law and Procedure 6e website at academic .cengage.com/criminaljustice/ scheb for an edited version of *Holloway aka Ali v. U.S.*

In recent years the Supreme Court has indicated that there are limits to congressional authority to create new federal crimes under the auspices of the Commerce Clause of the U.S. Constitution. See *United States v. Lopez,* 514 U.S. 549, 115 S.Ct. 1624, 131 L.Ed.2d 626 (1995). Some critics have suggested that the Court might also invalidate the federal carjacking statute, but this seems unlikely inasmuch as the automobile is a major article of interstate commerce and a primary vehicle of interstate transportation. In fact, lower federal courts have upheld the constitutionality of the act as a valid expression of Congressional power under the Commerce Clause. See, for example, *United States v. Coleman,* 78 F.3d 154 (11th Cir. 1996).

Forgery and Uttering a Forged Instrument

Blackstone defined common-law **forgery** as "the fraudulent making or alteration of a writing to the prejudice of another man's right." The early cases reveal that such writings as wills, receipts, and physicians' certificates were subject to forgery. To convict a defendant of forgery under common law, it was essential to establish the accused's intent to defraud. **Uttering a forged instrument** was also a common-law offense, but one separate and distinct from forgery. "Utter," a term of art synonymous with "publish," distinguishes the actual forgery from the act of passing a forged instrument to someone. As an indication of the lesser importance of commercial matters in early English society, the common law classified both forgery and uttering a forged instrument as misdemeanors.

Statutory Expansion of Forgery Offenses

Unlike the common law, federal and state statutes generally classify forgery as a felony. Reflecting the importance of written and printed documentation in our modern economy, statutes in all American jurisdictions have extended the crime of forgery to almost every type of public or private legal instrument.

FEDERAL STATUTES

Under federal law, "[w]hoever, with intent to defraud, falsely makes, forges, counterfeits, or alters any obligation or other security of the United States" commits the crime of forgery. 18 U.S.C.A. § 471. Federal courts have stated that the manifest purpose of these laws is to protect all currency and obligations of the United States, *United States v. LeMon,* 622 F.2d 1022 (10th Cir. 1980), and that the prosecution must prove not only the passing but also the defendant's "intent to pass the bad money," *United States v. Lorenzo,* 570 F.2d 294, 299 (9th Cir. 1978).

Title 18, Section 472 provides that "Whoever, with intent to defraud, passes, utters, publishes, or sells, or attempts to pass, utter, publish, or sell, or with like intent brings into the United States or keeps in possession or conceals any falsely made, forged, counterfeited, or altered obligation or other security of the United States, shall be fined under this title or imprisoned...." In *United States v. Drumright,* 534 F.2d 1383 (10th Cir. 1976), a defendant seeking a reversal of his conviction under section 472 argued that the federal reserve bill he uttered was not of an appearance calculated to deceive an unsuspecting person of ordinary observation. The court disagreed, however, pointing out that the bill was "a falsely made and altered obligation of the United States because it was composed of parts of three genuine bills which had been fastened together with transparent tape. When folded with the right half of the obverse side showing, it has the appearance of a good $50 bill.... Although the workmanship on the bill was crude, it was of such character that under favorable circumstances it could be uttered and accepted as genuine." *Id.* at 1385. The court concluded that these circumstances presented in the peculiar facts were sufficient to establish a violation of the statute.

Several other federal statutes relate to forgery and the **counterfeiting** of federal securities, postage stamps, postage meters, money orders, public records, judges' signatures, and court documents. See 18 U.S.C.A. §§ 472–509. Many prosecutions are brought under 18 U.S.C.A. § 495, which provides that:

> Whoever falsely makes, alters, forges, or counterfeits any deed, power of attorney, order, certificate, receipt, contract, or other writing, for the purpose of obtaining or receiving, or of enabling any other person, either directly or indirectly, to obtain or receive from the United States or any officers or agents thereof, any sum of money; or
>
> Whoever utters or publishes as true any such false, forged, altered, or counterfeited writing, with intent to defraud the United States, knowing the same to be false, altered, forged, or counterfeited; or
>
> Whoever transmits to, or presents at any office or officer of the United States, any such writing in support of, or in relation to, any account or claim, with intent to defraud the United States, knowing the same to be false, altered, forged, or counterfeited—
>
> Shall be fined under this title or imprisoned....

To convict someone under this statute, the government must establish the defendant's specific fraudulent intent. *United States v. Sullivan,* 406 F.2d 180 (2d Cir. 1969).

STATE STATUTES

Most states have substantially adopted the common-law definition of forgery but have expanded the number of instruments that can be forged to include a lengthy list of public and private documents. For example, the Arizona Criminal Code makes forgery a felony and provides the following:

> A. A person commits forgery if, with intent to defraud, the person:
>
> 1. Falsely makes, completes or alters a written instrument; or
>
> 2. Knowingly possesses a forged instrument; or
>
> 3. Offers or presents, whether accepted or not, a forged instrument or one which contains false information. Ariz. Rev. Stat. § 13–2002.

Under this section, the offenses of forgery and uttering have been coupled under the term "forgery," but the distinction as separate offenses must still be observed because the elements of the offenses are not the same and the proof required can differ. *State v. Reyes,* 458 P.2d 960 (Ariz. 1969). Thus, under Arizona law the crime of forgery has three elements: (1) signing the name of another person, (2) intending to defraud, and (3) knowing that there is no authority to sign. *State v. Nettz,* 560 P.2d 814 (Ariz. App. 1977). On the other hand, uttering is the passing or publishing of a false, altered, or counterfeited paper or document. *State v. Reyes,* supra. Proof of the intent to defraud is essential to obtain a conviction of forgery, *State v. Maxwell,* 445 P.2d 837 (Ariz. 1968), but such intent may be inferred from circumstances in which the false instrument is executed or issued, *State v. Gomez,* 553 P.2d 1233 (Ariz. App. 1976). Note that based on the wording of the Arizona statute proscribing forgery, a conviction for "attempt to pass" is a conviction of forgery, not of an attempt. *Ponds v. State,* 438 P.2d 423 (Ariz. App. 1968) (see Chapter 5).

Go to the Scheb/ Scheb Criminal Law and Procedure 6e website at academic .cengage.com/criminaljustice/ scheb to find *State v. Gomez.*

Forgery

The state prosecuted defendant Donald E. Hicks for forgery. At trial, the evidence revealed that on August 4, 1984, Hicks went to see Edmond Brown to make a payment on a debt. Hicks told Brown he could pay him $100 on his debt if Brown could cash a two-party check for him. Hicks presented Brown with a check for $349 made out to Hicks on the account of Gott, Young, and Bogle, P.A., a Wichita law firm. The check was signed "Gott Young." The defendant told Brown that the check was a partial payment of a settlement of a claim stemming from an automobile accident. Hicks assured Brown that the check was good and endorsed it over to him. Brown accepted the check and returned $249 to Hicks. When the check was returned by the bank, Brown contacted the law firm. He was told that there was no one by the name of Gott Young at the firm and that the firm had never represented Hicks. He further learned that some twenty-five checks from the firm's petty cash account were missing. Hicks was found guilty by a jury, and his conviction was affirmed on appeal.

State v. Hicks, 714 P.2d 105 (Kan. App. 1986).

Common Examples of Forgery and Uttering a Forged Instrument

Among the more common examples of forgery today are the following:

- Signing another's name to an application for a driver's license
- Printing bogus tickets to a concert or sports event
- Signing another's name to a check on his or her bank account without authority
- Altering the amount of a check or note
- Signing another's name without authority to a certificate transferring shares of stock
- Signing a deed transferring someone's real estate without authorization
- Making an unauthorized change in the legal description of property being conveyed under a deed
- Altering the grades or credits on a college transcript.

Uttering a forged instrument commonly occurs when a person knowingly delivers a forged check to someone in exchange for cash or merchandise, knowingly sells bogus tickets for an event, or submits a deed with forged signatures for official recording.

Falsification of computerized records such as college credits and financial records poses new challenges to laws proscribing forgery. The increasing use of computers gives rise to the need for new applications of statutes proscribing forgery and uttering a forged instrument.

Worthless Checks

As commercial banking developed, the passing of "bad checks" became a serious problem. A person who writes a worthless check on his or her bank account does not commit a forgery. In early cases, some courts referred to issuance of checks without funds in the bank as use of a "false token." These cases were prosecuted under statutes making it unlawful to use false pretenses to obtain property.

States have now enacted a variety of statutes making it unlawful to issue checks with insufficient funds to cover payment. Earlier statutes often provided that to be guilty of false pretenses for issuing a worthless check, a person had to fraudulently obtain goods. This proved to be an impracticable method to control issuance of checks by depositors who misgauged their checking account balances. The widespread use of commercial and personal banking led legislatures to enact **worthless check statutes** to cope with the problem. These statutes usually classify such an offense as a misdemeanor, and legislatures have increasingly opted to allow offenders to make restitution of losses caused by worthless checks. State laws often allow a recipient of a bad check to assess a fee against one who issues or transfers a bad check. Many retail stores have signs posted notifying customers of such fees.

A Texas law that makes issuance of bad checks a misdemeanor stipulates the following:

> A person commits an offense if he issues or passes a check or similar sight order for the payment of money knowing that the issuer does not have sufficient funds in or on deposit with the bank or other drawee for the payment in full of the check or order as well as all other checks or orders outstanding at the time of issuance. Vernon's Tex. Penal Code Ann. § 32.41(a).

The Texas Penal Code presumes the issuer knows that there are insufficient funds if he or she had no account with the bank or other drawee when the check was issued, or if payment is refused by the bank on presentation within thirty days after issue and the person who wrote the check failed to pay the holder in full within ten days after receiving notice of such refusal. Vernon's Tex. Penal Code Ann. § 32.41(b)(1–2). A person charged with an offense under section 32.41 is permitted to make restitution under certain conditions. Vernon's Tex. Penal Code Ann. § 32.41(e).

Ohio R.C. § 2913.11(B) makes it an offense to "issue or transfer or cause to be issued or transferred a check or other negotiable instrument, knowing that it will be dishonored." The statute further provides that one who issues or transfers such a negotiable instrument is presumed to know that it will be dishonored if either the drawer had no account with the drawee bank or the negotiable instrument was properly refused payment for insufficient funds upon presentment within thirty days and the liability of any person liable on the instrument was not discharged by payment or satisfaction within ten days after receiving notice of dishonor. See Ohio R.C. § 2913.11(C)(1–2). If a bad check is for less than $500, the offense is a misdemeanor; beyond that amount it becomes a felony, the degree of which is dependent on the amount of the check, with a check for $100,000 or more becoming a felony of the third degree. See Ohio R.C. 2913.11 (F). Ohio courts have held that where the payee of a check knows that the check is not collectible at the time it is tendered, there is no criminal violation of passing a bad check. *State v. Edwards* 751 N.E.2d 510 (Ohio App. 2001).

Access Device Fraud

Debit cards and credit cards, automated teller machine (ATM) cards, account numbers, personal identification numbers (PINs), and other means are now commonly available to named persons who assume the obligation of their use. Because of their widespread use, state legislatures have realized the necessity to enact comprehensive statutes proscribing the fraudulent use of devices to secure cash, goods, and services through means beyond the traditional credit card.

In 1998 Pennsylvania rewrote its statute titled "Credit Card Fraud" to proscribe a variety of means of gaining fraudulent access to money, goods, and services. As amended, the revised section of Purdon's Pennsylvania Consolidated Statutes Annotated now provides:

Section 4106. Access device fraud

(a) Offense defined.—A person commits an offense if he:

(1) uses an access device to obtain or in an attempt to obtain property or services with knowledge that:

(i) the access device is counterfeit, altered or incomplete;

(ii) the access device was issued to another person who has not authorized its use;

(iii) the access device has been revoked or canceled; or

(iv) for any other reason his use of the access device is unauthorized by the issuer or the device holder; or

(2) publishes, makes, sells, gives, or otherwise transfers to another, or offers or advertises, or aids and abets any other person to use an access device knowing that the access device is counterfeit, altered or incomplete, belongs to another person who has not authorized its use, has been revoked or canceled or for any reason is unauthorized by the issuer or the device holder; or

(3) possesses an access device knowing that it is counterfeit, altered, incomplete or belongs to another person who has not authorized its possession.

(a.1) Presumptions.—For the purpose of this section as well as in any prosecution for theft committed by the means specified in this section:

(1) An actor is presumed to know an access device is counterfeit, altered or incomplete if he has in his possession or under his control two or more counterfeit, altered or incomplete access devices.

(2) Knowledge of revocation or cancellation shall be presumed to have been received by an access device holder seven days after it has been mailed to him at the address set forth on the access device application or at a new address if a change of address has been provided to the issuer.

(b) Defenses.—It is a defense to a prosecution under subsection (a)(1)(iv) if the actor proves by a preponderance of the evidence that he had the intent and ability to meet all obligations to the issuer arising out of his use of the access device.

Subsection (c) of the Pennsylvania statute stipulates that if the value involved is $500 or more, the offense constitutes a felony; if less than $500, the offense constitutes a misdemeanor. The degree of felony or misdemeanor depends on the value involved.

Subsection (d) includes the following definitions:

- "Access device." Any card, including, but not limited to, a credit card, debit card and automated teller machine card, plate, code, account number, personal identification number or other means of account access that can be used alone or in conjunction with another access device to obtain money, goods, services or anything else of value or that can be used to transfer funds.

- "Altered access device." A validly issued access device which after issue is changed in any way.

- "Counterfeit access device." An access device not issued by an issuer in the ordinary course of business.

- "Device holder." The person or organization named on the access device to whom or for whose benefit the access device is issued by an issuer.

Because of the widespread use of access devices, many states have adopted statutes prohibiting **access device fraud.** Offenses proscribed by the above statute could likely be prosecuted under modern comprehensive theft or forgery statutes; however, given such statutes, an issue has arisen as to whether the existence of a statute proscribing credit card use (more recently included in statutes proscribing access device fraud) precludes prosecution under a theft or forgery proscribing more severe penalties. Several courts have held that such specific statutes did not preclude prosecution under a statute based on theft or forgery. See, for example, *People v. James* 497 P.2d 1256 (Colo. 1972); *Garcia v. State,* 669 S.W.2d 169 (Tex. App. 1984).

In *Commonwealth v. Sargent,* 823 A.2d 174 (Pa. Super. 2003), a Pennsylvania appellate court rejected a defendant's argument that, because he obtained property valued at $450 through fraudulent use of a credit card, he could not be convicted under a statute making forgery a felony. He argued that because of the existence of section 4106, his offense would be a misdemeanor as he obtained property valued at only $450. The court held that the defendant's action of signing the victim's name to credit card receipts was a felony of the third degree because the receipts constituted documents within the meaning of a statute providing that forgery is a felony of the third degree. The court concluded, "We find meritless Appellant's argument that the Legislature did not intend the fraudulent signing of credit card receipts to constitute a felony of the third degree under the facts in this case since the Legislature specifically provided for the unauthorized use of credit cards in 18 Pa. C.S.A. § 4106." *Id.* at 177.

Many states have adopted statutes similar to the Pennsylvania law. Courts have generally held that the existence of a statute specifically addressing access devices does not preclude the state from prosecution of an access device offense as forgery, where the facts warrant it, under a forgery statute proscribing more severe penalties. See, for example, *Garcia v. State,* 669 S.W.2d 169 (Tex. App. 1984); *People v. James,* 497 P.2d 1256 (Colo. 1972).

Habitation Offenses

Two felonies developed at common law reflect the value of privacy and the need to protect the security of a person's dwelling. The offenses of **burglary** and **arson** gave credence to the old English saying "A man's home is his castle." These offenses were created to protect not only the dwelling house but also the buildings within the **curtilage,** an enclosed area around the dwelling that typically included the cookhouse and other outbuildings. In England the enclosure had to be formed by a stone fence or wall; however, this custom has not been established in the United States. *State v. Bugg,* 72 P. 236 (Kan. 1903). Rather, American courts tend to define curtilage as the ground surrounding a dwelling that is used for domestic purposes or for the convenience of the family.

Both burglary and arson became felonies in the United States. Modern statutes have greatly broadened the scope of the common-law crimes of burglary and arson and extended the protection of the criminal law far beyond the traditional concept of offenses against habitation. Nevertheless, to understand their historic development, it is helpful to classify them as offenses against habitation.

Evidence Sufficient to Establish Burglary

On the morning of October 18, 1981, Philadelphia police were called to Cramer's Kiddy Shop. Entering the store, they heard footsteps on the roof. They went up to the second floor, where they discovered a two-foot hole in a wall with access to the roof. One of the officers went through the hole and found himself covered with plaster dust. He then observed two males climbing down an exterior wall. One of them was apprehended. His hands were dirty, and his clothes were covered with plaster dust. In the alley behind the store, police located several items of children's clothing that had been taken from the store, along with a crowbar. Patrick Carpenter, who was apprehended, was found guilty of burglary and other offenses. On appeal, Carpenter argued that the evidence was insufficient to warrant a conviction for burglary. The appellate court rejected the contention and upheld Carpenter's conviction.

Commonwealth v. Carpenter, 479 A.2d 603 (Pa. Super. 1984).

Burglary at Common Law

According to Blackstone, common-law burglary consisted of (1) breaking and entering of (2) a dwelling of another (3) during the nighttime (4) with intent to commit a felony therein. The "breaking" at common law could be either "actual" or "constructive." An actual breaking could be merely technical, such as pushing open a door or opening a window. An entry gained through fraud or deception was considered a "constructive" breaking. Even the slightest entry was deemed sufficient; for instance, a hand, a foot, or even a finger within the dwelling was regarded as a sufficient entry. Proof of the defendant's intent to commit a felony was essential: A breaking and entering did not constitute burglary at common law unless the perpetrator had a specific intent to commit a felony (for example, murder, rape, or larceny); however, it was not necessary to prove that any felony was committed. "Dwelling" was defined as the house or place of habitation used by the occupier or member of the family "as a place to sleep in." Finally, to constitute burglary at common law, it was essential that the offense be committed at nighttime, generally defined as the period between sunset and sunrise.

Statutory Revisions of Burglary

Many states have enacted statutes proscribing **breaking and entering,** thereby placing a new label on the common-law crime of burglary. At a minimum, these statutes expand the offense of burglary beyond dwelling houses and eliminate the requirement that the offense take place in the nighttime. Most states retain the common-law requirement that the accused break and enter with intent to commit a felony, and others include the language "or theft." Even where the offense is still labeled burglary, legislatures have made significant changes in the common-law definition. In addition to eliminating the nighttime requirement, they have broadened the offense to include buildings and structures of all types. Today, most criminal codes include vehicles, aircraft, and vessels either in the definition of burglary or by a separate statute. Finally, modern statutes frequently provide that a person who enters a structure with consent but who remains therein with intent to commit a felony may be found guilty of burglary notwithstanding an original lawful entry. An example of this would be someone intentionally remaining in a department store intending to

What Constitutes "Entry" Within the Meaning of a Burglary Statute?

On February 4, 1998, a man later identified as the defendant was seen removing a screen from a bathroom window of the Floreas' house and unsuccessfully attempting to open the window itself. Then, after unsuccessfully attempting to open the front door of the house, the defendant banged on the wall and drove away. Shortly thereafter he was arrested and charged with burglary under California law, which provides that the crime of burglary is committed when a person "enters any ... building," including a "house," "with intent to commit ... larceny or any felony." A jury found the defendant guilty of burglary in the first degree because it involved an inhabited dwelling house. The trial court sentenced him to four years in prison. In 2001, a California appellate court reversed his conviction on the ground that penetration into the area behind a window screen did not constitute an entry as required by the burglary statute.

The California Supreme Court granted review, and in reversing the court of appeals' decision, opined, "We recognize that penetration into the area behind a window screen without penetration of the window itself usually will effect only a minimal entry of a building in terms of distance. But it has long been settled that "[a]ny kind of entry, complete or partial, ... will suffice." *Id.* at 927. A dissenting judge argued that the defendant committed attempted burglary because he tried, but failed, to enter the house.

People v. Valencia, 46 P.3d 920 (Cal. 2002).

commit an offense therein after the store closes for the day. Michigan law illustrates a modern statutory approach and specifies the following:

> A person who breaks and enters with intent to commit any felony, or any larceny therein, a tent, hotel, office, store, shop, warehouse, barn, granary, factory or other building, structure, boat or ship, or railroad car shall be guilty of a felony. Mich. Comp. Laws Ann. § 750.110.

The Michigan statute states that if the dwelling is occupied, the offender shall be punished more severely. Mich. Comp. Laws Ann. § 750.110(a)(2). Another Michigan statute makes it a felony for a person to enter even if the person does not break into any of the structures or vehicles enumerated in the breaking and entering statute. Mich. Comp. Laws Ann. § 750.111.

Courts tend to liberally construe the terms "breaking" and "entering" commonly found in burglary statutes. In *State v. Jaynes,* 464 S.E.2d 448, 466 (N.C. 1995), the North Carolina Supreme Court said that for purposes of burglary, "any force, however slight, employed to effect entrance through any usual or unusual place of ingress, whether open, partly open, or closed ... by any use of force, however slight, ... will suffice as the 'breaking' required for burglary." A New York appellate court has said that a defendant "enters" a building within the meaning of that state's burglary statute when a defendant's person or any part of a defendant's body intrudes. *People v. Jackson*, 638 N.Y.S.2d 140 (1996).

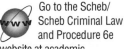 Go to the Scheb/ Scheb Criminal Law and Procedure 6e website at academic .cengage.com/criminaljustice/ scheb to find *State v. Feldt* (1989), where the Montana Supreme Court considers an appeal by a convenience store employee who was convicted of burglary.

Possession of Burglar's Tools

Michigan, like most states, makes **possession of burglar's tools** a felony if the possessor has the intent to use the tools for burglarious purposes. Michigan law provides:

> Any person who shall knowingly have in his possession any nitroglycerine, or other explosive, thermite, engine, machine, tool or implement, device, chemical or

substance, adapted and designed for cutting or burning through, forcing or breaking open any building, room, vault, safe or other depository, in order to steal therefrom any money or other property, knowing the same to be adapted and designed for the purpose aforesaid, with intent to use or employ the same for the purpose aforesaid, shall be guilty of a felony. Mich. Comp. Laws Ann. § 750.116.

Many years ago, the Michigan Supreme Court emphasized that to obtain a conviction, the state must prove the accused knowingly had possession of burglar's tools, knew the tools could be used for a criminal purpose, and intended to use them for such purpose. *People v. Jefferson,* 126 N.W. 829 (Mich. 1910).

Arson at Common Law

Like burglary, arson was a felony at common law designed to protect the security of the dwelling place. The crime consisted of (1) the willful and malicious burning (2) of a dwelling (3) of another. There was no requirement that the dwelling be destroyed or even that it be damaged to a significant degree. In fact, a mere charring was sufficient, but scorching or smoke damage did not constitute arson at common law. The common law defined the term "dwelling" the same as in burglary. Consequently, the burning of buildings within the curtilage constituted arson. The common law regarded arson as a general-intent crime, with the required malice being presumed from an intentional burning of someone's dwelling. However, setting fire to one's own home was not arson at common law. Yet some early English cases indicate that under circumstances where burning one's own house posed a danger to others, "houseburning" was a misdemeanor offense.

Statutory Revision of Arson

Modern statutes have extended the offense of arson to include the intentional burning of buildings, structures, and vehicles of all types. Frequently, this even includes a person's own property. Several states have enacted statutes that provide that the use of explosives to damage a structure constitutes arson. As in burglary, the modern offense of arson is designed to protect many forms of property. Therefore, arson can no longer be considered strictly a habitation offense. By categorizing arson, legislatures can make appropriate distinctions and provide penalties accordingly.

Michigan law embraces four categories of arson. Mich. Comp. Laws Ann. § 750.72 provides:

> Any person who wilfully or maliciously burns any dwelling house, either occupied or unoccupied, or the contents thereof, whether owned by himself or another, or any building within the curtilage of such dwelling house, or the contents thereof, shall be guilty of a felony.

In *People v. Williams,* 318 N.W.2d 671 (Mich. App. 1982), the court held that to establish the *corpus delicti* (see Chapter 6) of arson of a dwelling house, the state must show not only a burning of the house but also that it resulted from an intentional criminal act. The court explained that where only a burning is shown, a presumption arises that it was accidentally caused.

Section 750.73 makes it a lesser felony for anyone to willfully or maliciously burn any building or other real property or contents thereof, while section 750.74 makes it a misdemeanor or felony to willfully and maliciously burn personal property, the level of offense being determined by the value of the property involved. For a fire to be "willfully" set by the accused requires that the defendant commit such act stubbornly

Proving the Crime of Arson

Early on the morning of September 23, 1981, a fire destroyed a log cabin belonging to Henry Xavier Kennedy. Investigators determined the fire was incendiary in origin. A hot plate with its switch in the "on" position was found in the most heavily burned area of the cabin. Investigators also determined that kerosene poured around the area of the hot plate had accelerated the fire.

Five days before the fire, Kennedy had renewed a $40,000 insurance policy on the cabin. Evidence

was also presented that Kennedy's building business was slow. Kennedy introduced evidence of an alibi from midnight until 4:00 A.M. Although the fire was reported at 3:42 A.M., investigators testified that the incendiary device could have been set before midnight.

Kennedy was convicted of arson, and his conviction was upheld on appeal.

Kennedy v. State, 323 S.E.2d 169 (Ga. App. 1984).

and for an unlawful purpose. Mere proof of carelessness or accident is not sufficient to establish guilt. *People v. McCarty,* 6 N.W.2d 919 (Mich. 1942).

In contrast with Michigan, many state statutes broaden the scope of the offense by referring to "damage caused by fire" rather than "burning." And in contrast with the common law, under many modern statutes proof of damage by smoke or scorching is sufficient to constitute arson. See, for example, *State v. McVeigh,* 516 P.2d 918 (Kan. 1973).

BURNING PROPERTY WITH THE INTENT TO DEFRAUD AN INSURANCE COMPANY

Most jurisdictions have enacted statutes making it a crime to burn any property with the intent to defraud an insurance company, usually requiring the prosecution to prove the defendant's specific intent to defraud. In this respect, Mich. Comp. Laws Ann. § 750.75 stipulates the following:

> Any person who shall wilfully burn any building or personal property which shall be at the time insured against loss or damage by fire with intent to injure and defraud the insurer, whether such person be the owner of the property or not, shall be guilty of a felony.

Malicious Mischief

A mere trespass to land or personal property was not a crime at common law unless it was committed forcibly or maliciously. However, it was a common-law misdemeanor called **malicious mischief** for a person to damage another's real or personal property. Modern statutes usually define the offense much as did the common law, often referring to the offense as **vandalism** and imposing penalties based on the extent of damage inflicted on the victim's property. For example, section 594(a) of the California Penal Code states the following:

> Every person who maliciously commits any of the following acts with respect to any real or personal property not his or her own, in cases other than those specified by state law, is guilty of vandalism:
>
> (1) Defaces with graffiti or other inscribed material.
>
> (2) Damages.
>
> (3) Destroys.

The California statute sets the penalty based on the amount of defacement, damage, or destruction. Damage to state-owned furniture or equipment located in a prison would be punishable as malicious mischief, a misdemeanor.

 Go to the Scheb/ Scheb Criminal Law and Procedure 6e website at academic .cengage.com/criminaljustice/ scheb to find *State v. Tonnisen,* where the Appellate Division of the New Jersey Superior Court rejects an appeal by a defendant who was found guilty of malicious mischief.

Section 806.13(1)(a), Florida Statutes, provides that "A person commits the offense of criminal mischief if he willfully and maliciously injures or damages by any means any real or personal property belonging to another, including, but not limited to, the placement of graffiti thereon or other acts of vandalism thereto." Florida appellate courts have held that to be found guilty of the offense, the actor must possess the specific intent to damage the property of another. *In Interest of J.G.,* 655 So.2d 1284 (Fla. App. 1995). The offense is a misdemeanor with the value of property determining the punishment. If, however, the defendant has had one or more previous convictions, the offense is reclassified as a felony of the third degree.

Extortion

In describing common-law **extortion,** Blackstone said it was "the taking by color of an office of money or other thing of value, that is not due, before it is due, or more than is due." Under most modern statutes, extortion has been extended beyond acts by public officers. As the California law provides,

> Extortion is the obtaining of property from another, with his consent, or the obtaining of an official act of a public officer, induced by a wrongful use of force or fear, or under color of official right. West's Ann. Cal. Penal Code § 518.

It further stipulates the following:

> Fear, such as will constitute extortion, may be induced by a threat, either:
>
> 1. to do an unlawful injury to the person or property of the individual threatened or of a third person; or,
>
> 2. to accuse the individual threatened, or any relative of his, or member of his family, of any crime; or,
>
> 3. to expose, or to impute to him or them any deformity, disgrace or crime, or,
>
> 4. to expose any secret affecting him or them. West's Ann. Cal. Penal Code § 519.

There are both similarities and distinctions between the offenses of extortion and robbery. As explained by a California appellate court:

> The crime of extortion is related to and sometimes difficult to distinguish from the crime of robbery.... Both crimes have their roots in the common law crime of larceny. Both crimes share the element of an acquisition by means of force or fear. One distinction between the robbery and extortion frequently noted by courts and commentators is that in robbery property is taken from another by force or fear "against

his will" while in extortion property is taken from another by force or fear "with his consent." The two crimes, however, have other distinctions. Robbery requires a "felonious taking" which means a specific intent to permanently deprive the victim of the property.... Robbery also requires the property be taken from the victim's "person or immediate presence." ... Extortion does not require proof of either of these elements.... Extortion does, however, require the specific intent of inducing the victim to consent to part with his or her property. *People v. Torres,* 39 Cal. Rptr. 2d 103, 110–111 (Cal. App. 1995).

Extortion under Federal Law

In many instances, the statutory offense of extortion has become synonymous with the common understanding of **blackmail.** In fact, 18 U.S.C.A. § 873—a federal statute that provides that "Whoever, under a threat of informing, or as a consideration for not informing, against any violation of any law of the United States, demands, or receives any money or other valuable thing, shall be fined ..."—is often referred to as the "blackmail statute." Another federal statute, 18 U.S.C.A. § 876, makes it a crime to mail through the Postal Service a demand for ransom or a threat to injure a person's property or reputation. The only specific intent required to support a conviction under section 876 is that the defendant knowingly deposited a threatening letter in the mail, not that he or she intended to carry out the threat. *United States v. Chatman,* 584 F.2d 1358 (4th Cir. 1978).

Defenses to Property Crimes

At common law, the offenses of larceny and robbery were specific-intent crimes. This intent requirement has been carried over in statutes proscribing theft, either comprehensively or in various descriptive crimes, but the intent requirement in modern robbery statutes varies. Therefore, in a prosecution for theft, a defendant may raise the defense of mistake of fact (but this does not necessarily follow when defending a charge of robbery—see Chapter 14). This means that a defendant who took items of property from another person in the good-faith belief that they belonged to the taker may have a defense. A classic example: Sherry leaves a coat on a coat rack, and later Mary does also. The jackets are similar, and Sherry mistakenly walks away with Mary's jacket. The problem becomes more acute if Mary has left a wallet in her jacket with hundreds of dollars of currency in it. These mistakes justify requiring the prosecution to prove a defendant's specific intent in theft offenses. Have you ever opened the door of a car like yours in a shopping center parking lot, thinking the car was your own?

In some theft prosecutions, mistake of law has been held to be a defense. This is limited to situations where there are exceedingly technical questions concerning ownership rights (see Chapter 14).

In a prosecution for forgery, an accused can defend by proving that he or she was authorized to sign another's name. Under certain circumstances, a person accused of forgery can also assert the defense of "mistake of fact" (see Chapter 14).

In some instances, a person charged with burglary can also assert mistake of fact as a defense. For example, an intoxicated person who enters a "row-house" identical to his or her own may have a defense. And, of course, the requirement that the prosecution prove "an intent to commit a felony" would make it difficult to prove that a person who took refuge from a storm on the porch of an unoccupied dwelling did so with intent to commit a felony therein (see Chapter 14). Arson, on the other hand, is usually a general-intent crime. This imposes a limitation on defenses beyond consent, where a person intentionally commits the proscribed acts. Because statutes proscribing the commission of arson with the intent to defraud an insurer usually require proof of the defendant's specific intent to defraud, the lack of such intent can be shown in defense.

■ CONCLUSION

Most statutory property crimes parallel the basic common-law scheme but have been broadened to meet the demands of our changing society. Although the common-law crimes against property and habitation provide a good starting point for legislating against offenses involving property, there is a need for continuing statutory revision to consolidate the laws proscribing certain property offenses that have proliferated over the years.

Statutes that proscribe various forms of theft and forgery need to be updated, particularly because of computer crimes and identity theft, which increasingly create serious problems in both the public and private sectors. Definitions must be reviewed to ensure adequate protection against those who willfully take computer data or access computer systems without authority and to cope with the increasing problem of identity theft.

Although issues regarding intellectual property rights are largely resolved through civil proceedings, modern forms of communication may give rise to criminal sanctions for patent, copyright, trademark, and trade names violations.

Consumers are no longer willing to acquiesce in outmoded doctrines such as *caveat emptor.* Thus, laws concerning representations made in commercial transactions assume a role of importance in today's society. Consumer fraud, intentional false advertising, credit card fraud, and a variety of other scams need to be specifically proscribed or included in omnibus definitions of theft and forgery statutes and more recently in statutes specifically addressing computer fraud and access device fraud.

The laws proscribing burglary and arson must protect more than homes. These offenses pose serious threats to lives and property, regardless of whether they are committed in a residential or business property, whether the structure involved is private or public, and whether it is a vehicle, vessel, building, or other structure. These offenses have moved from being crimes against habitation to being crimes against property. Modern statutes tend to make these offenses crimes against persons as well. With the almost universal dependence on insurance to protect against casualty losses, the need for a close look at statutes proscribing insurance fraud is also essential.

■ KEY TERMS

tangible property, 161
larceny, 162
false pretenses, 163
embezzlement, 163
receiving stolen property, 164
grand theft, 166
petit theft, 167
intent to deprive, 167
theft of computer services, 167

computer fraud, 167
computer trespass, 167
identity theft, 169
intellectual property, 170
patent, 171
copyright, 171
bootlegging, 171
trademark, 172
trademark counterfeiting, 173

■ WEB-BASED RESEARCH ACTIVITY

 Go to the Web. Locate the decisions of your state's highest appellate court. Find a recent decision in which the court discussed the definition of one of the crimes covered in this chapter. If you cannot locate such a decision from your state's highest court, try another state.

■ QUESTIONS FOR THOUGHT AND DISCUSSION

1. What advantages do you see for a state that adopts a comprehensive theft statute?
2. What measures can be taken to protect oneself against identity theft?
3. Is it a crime to share digital music files with a friend if there is no commercial purpose or monetary gain in doing so?
4. How does the crime of burglary as it is typically defined under modern statutes differ from the definition of this offense under English common law?
5. Is it more important for theft offenses to be classified as specific-intent crimes than robbery? Why?
6. What provisions would you include in a model statute making arson a crime? Would you provide for separate degrees of the offense?
7. Should the offense of forgery be divided into degrees based on the importance of the forged documents? If so, what criteria would you propose for the various degrees of the crime?
8. Give some examples of actions that would probably fall within the conduct proscribed by (a) extortion and (b) vandalism or malicious mischief statutes.
9. What offense would a person who destroyed or damaged data in someone's computer have committed? If a person electronically accessed another's computer without permission, would this constitute a criminal offense?
10. Name some important similarities and distinctions between the offenses of robbery and extortion.
11. What is the rationale for courts to require that to obtain a conviction for possession of burglary tools the state must prove the accused knowingly had possession of burglar's tools, knew the tools could be used for a criminal purpose, and intended to use them for such purpose?
12. Assume you are working as a staff assistant to a legislator who desires to introduce a bill to assist merchants who are experiencing losses from "bad checks." What types of provisions and penalties would you recommend?

■ PROBLEMS FOR DISCUSSION AND SOLUTION

1. A. H. Hacker is a skilled computer operator at a business office. Through stealthful operation of his computer, he successfully obtains a list of names and addresses of a competitor's customers without the knowledge or consent of the competitor. For what offense would Hacker most likely be prosecuted in your state?

2. Laura Lightfingers steals a package of filet mignon priced at $19.99 from the meat counter in a supermarket. As she leaves the store, she is approached by a security guard. Lightfingers kicks and injures the security guard in her attempt to leave with the meat she has stolen. In your state, would Lightfingers be charged with petit theft, grand theft, or robbery? Why?

3. Sally Spendthrift has an established bank account at a local bank. She gives a check to a merchant for the purchase of a new stereo. Her bank returns the check to the merchant because Spendthrift's account has insufficient funds to cover payment. Do you think Spendthrift should face criminal charges or simply be required to compensate the bank and anyone who suffered a loss?

CHAPTER 8

Offenses against Public Morality

Introduction

Traditionally, one of the functions of the law has been to express and reinforce the prevailing morality of the society. In this chapter we discuss a number of crimes traditionally classified as offenses against public morality. These offenses include various forms of sexual misconduct as well as several forms of **public indecency.** Some of the offenses discussed in this chapter, notably gambling, prostitution, and obscenity, are often classified as **vice crimes.** All of these offenses have evolved substantially in recent decades, reflecting tremendous changes in society.

Offenses involving alcohol and drugs, although they can be viewed as crimes against morality, can also be seen as offenses against public order and safety. Given the importance of these offenses in contemporary society, we have chosen to place them in a separate chapter (Chapter 9).

The Common-Law Background

The common-law crimes developed largely because of society's demands for security of persons and property, the need to maintain public order, and the judges' perceptions of society's concepts of morality. Many ideas of morality were based on the Bible and church doctrine; others were simply the product of the shared experiences of the people. These concepts became the foundation for the criminal laws in this country in the pre-Revolutionary days, when early settlers tended to equate sin with crime. Later, as legislative bodies defined crimes, the statutes more closely reflected the moral standards of the new American society. Eventually, the equation of crime with sin gave way to a more secular approach to crime.

Religious Influences

It has been said that religion is the greatest single moral force in our society. Conflicts sometimes surface because this pluralistic nation has a constitutional prohibition against the establishment of religion and a guarantee of the free exercise thereof. Therefore, questions arise concerning whether a law with a religious origin can be enforced without offending these basic constitutional guarantees. The short answer is that most criminal laws that proscribe behavior forbidden by the Bible have also been found to serve a recognized secular purpose. Obviously, certain moral principles must be enforced for the protection of society. No one suggests that murder is a crime simply because of the biblical injunction "Thou shall not kill." All civilized societies throughout history have prohibited murder. Historically, some of our ancestors imposed severe criminal sanctions for blasphemy or taking the Lord's name in vain. For example, under the Articles, Laws, and Orders, Divine, Politic, and Martial for the Colony in Virginia (1610–1611), the offense of blasphemy was punishable by death.

In a number of American colonies, the law prescribed punishments for failing to attend worship services and even for entertaining heretical opinions. Today, it would be unthinkable for any jurisdiction in the United States to attempt to enact such prohibitions. Yet the Judeo-Christian moral tradition continues to exercise powerful influence on our criminal law.

Is Morality a Legitimate Basis for Legislation?

An essential characteristic of a sovereign state is its police power, the power to legislate in pursuit of public health, safety, welfare, and morality. More than a century ago the U.S. Supreme Court assumed that regulation of morality was among the purposes of government: "Whatever differences of opinion may exist as to the extent and boundaries of the police power, and however difficult it may be to render a satisfactory definition of it, there seems to be no doubt that it does extend to … the preservation of good order and the public morals." *Boston Beer Co. v. Massachusetts,* 97 U.S. (7 Otto) 25, 33, 24 L.Ed. 989 (1878).

Today this assumption is often questioned by those who believe that morality, like religion, is a personal matter. Persons of a libertarian persuasion generally believe that the state should be neutral in matters of morality, much as it is with respect to religion. Others, stressing the practical aspect of the problem, cite the aphorism "you can't legislate morality." However, critics must realize that the moral basis of the law extends far beyond prohibitions of sexual conduct. Many proscriptions of the criminal law, from animal cruelty to insider stock trading, are based on collective societal judgments about what is right and what is wrong. Writing for the U.S. Supreme Court in *Bowers v. Hardwick,* 478 U.S. 186, 106 S.Ct. 2841, 92 L.Ed.2d 140 (1986), Justice Byron White observed that "the law … is constantly based on notions of morality, and if all laws representing essentially moral choices are to be invalidated … , the courts will be very busy indeed." 478 U.S. at 196, 106 S.Ct. at 2846, 92 L.Ed.2d at 149.

Police Power and the Social Consensus

It has long been assumed that legislative bodies have the authority to criminalize conduct they determine to be contrary to the health, safety, and morals of the people, as long as such prohibitions do not infringe on rights protected by the state and federal constitutions. The problem is primarily one of legislative perception of the standards that society requires and is willing to accept. Historically, enforcement of the criminal law has largely depended on community acceptance of certain conduct being forbidden by law. But public opinion about law changes. A societal consensus resulted in a constitutional amendment in 1919 prohibiting the sale of intoxicating liquors. It proved unworkable, and after a strong consensus developed against Prohibition, the amendment was repealed in 1933. See U.S. Const. Amendments XVIII and XXI.

Today, there are varying attitudes about whether certain forms of conduct should be illegal. For example, public opinion is divided on the need for laws making it a crime to engage in certain forms of gambling. Consequently, the criminal prohibitions against gambling vary considerably throughout the United States. Since the sexual revolution of the 1960s, the consensus supporting laws prohibiting sexual activities between consenting adults has eroded. This decline in consensus has led many legislatures to revise their criminal codes to remove prohibitions against certain sexual conduct. In other states, the courts have invalidated prohibitions in this area.

Constitutional Limitations

In the United States, legislative bodies have broad authority to define conduct as criminal and to set the punishment to be meted out to violators. Of course, the U.S. Constitution and the constitutions of every state impose limitations on government efforts to criminalize certain forms of conduct (see Chapter 3). For example, in *Griswold v. Connecticut,* 381 U.S. 479, 85 S.Ct. 1678, 14 L.Ed.2d 510 (1965), the U.S. Supreme

CASE-IN-POINT

Marital Privacy and Reproductive Freedom

Estelle Griswold, the director of Planned Parenthood in Connecticut, was convicted and fined $100 for aiding and abetting persons in using contraceptive devices, an offense under Connecticut law. Before the U.S. Supreme Court, Griswold's attorneys argued that the Connecticut statute infringed a right of privacy implicit in the Bill of Rights, as embodied in the concept of personal liberty protected by the Fourteenth Amendment. Moreover, they maintained that the Connecticut statute lacked a reasonable relationship to a legitimate legislative purpose. The State of Connecticut responded by emphasizing its broad police powers, arguing that the birth control law was a rational means of promoting the welfare of Connecticut's people. Interestingly, however, Connecticut's brief failed to state the particular legislative purpose behind the birth control law. Rather, the brief was designed chiefly to convince the justices that they should not second-guess the wisdom or desirability of social legislation.

On June 7, 1965, the Supreme Court announced its 7–2 decision striking down the Connecticut birth control law. Writing for the Court, Justice William O. Douglas asserted that "specific guarantees in the Bill of Rights have penumbras, formed by emanations from those guarantees that help give them life and substance." Douglas reasoned that the explicit language of the Bill of Rights, specifically the First, Third, Fourth, Fifth, and Ninth Amendments, when considered along with their "emanations" and "penumbras" as defined by previous decisions of the Court, add up to a general, independent right of privacy. In Douglas's view, this general right was infringed by the State of Connecticut when it outlawed birth control. In the sharpest language of the majority opinion, Douglas wrote, "Would we allow the police to search the sacred precincts of marital bedrooms for telltale signs of the use of contraceptives? The very idea is repulsive to the notions of privacy surrounding the marriage relationship."

Griswold v. Connecticut, 381 U.S. 479, 85 S.Ct. 1678, 14 L.Ed.2d 510 (1965).

Go to the Scheb/ Scheb Criminal Law and Procedure 6e website at academic .cengage.com/criminaljustice/ scheb for edited versions of *Griswold v. Connecticut* and *Roe v. Wade.*

Court struck down a state law that made it a crime for all persons, even married couples, to use birth control devices (see Case-in-Point above). The Court said that the law violated the **right of privacy** that inheres in the Bill of Rights and is imposed on the states via the Fourteenth Amendment. In *Eisenstadt v. Baird,* 405 U.S. 438, 92 S.Ct. 1029, 31 L.Ed.2d 349 (1972), the Court extended the *Griswold* decision to protect single individuals from a similar anti-contraception statute. The Court's decisions in *Griswold* and *Eisenstadt,* as well as its landmark decision in *Roe v. Wade* (the 1973 decision striking down Texas's abortion law), are often viewed as establishing a fundamental constitutional principle that competent adults have the right to make their own decisions in matters of sex and reproduction. This principle runs counter to the traditional common-law notion that the criminal law may be used to prohibit private conduct that violates society's moral code.

Criminal Prohibitions of Consensual Sexual Conduct

Debate concerning offenses against public morality usually focuses primarily on the statutory prohibitions against fornication, adultery, seduction, sodomy, prostitution, and, to a lesser degree, incest. Many people today believe that such behavior is, or at least ought to be, private in character and thus beyond the reach of the criminal law. In contrast, many still subscribe to the classical conservative view that such prohibitions are necessary to maintain a proper moral climate.

Fornication, Adultery, and Seduction

Fornication is sexual intercourse between unmarried persons. **Adultery** is generally defined as sexual intercourse between a male and female, at least one of whom is married to someone else. Fornication and adultery were regarded as offenses against morality and were punishable in the ecclesiastical courts in England. Neither was considered a common-law crime unless committed openly. In such instances the act was prosecuted as a public nuisance. Historically, the rationale for criminalizing these acts was threefold: (1) to avoid disharmony in family relationships, (2) to prevent illegitimate births, and (3) to prevent the spread of sexually transmitted diseases.

Because of changing societal attitudes, these offenses are rarely prosecuted today. Indeed, many states have eliminated these offenses altogether. Adultery and fornication might be widespread, but they generally occur under the most private of circumstances. Consequently, complaints about these sexual encounters are seldom reported to the authorities. In instances where sexual conduct is the subject of a complaint by a participant, it may fall under the classification of sexual battery (see Chapter 6). As we noted in Chapter 3, in 2005 the Virginia Supreme Court struck down that state's prohibition of fornication as a violation of the liberty guaranteed by the Fourteenth Amendment. *Martin v. Ziherl*, 607 S.E.2d 367 (Va. 2005). The constitutionality of the statute was raised in an unusual civil suit. As the court noted in its opinion, the prohibition had not been enforced criminally against consenting adults in more than a hundred years.

Seduction was not a crime at common law; hence, it exists only by statute. The essence of the offense is that a male obtains sexual intercourse with a virtuous female on the unfulfilled promise of marriage. Historically, prosecution for seduction served the role of persuading a recalcitrant suitor to marry the woman he seduced. Most states have repealed their seduction statutes, and where such laws remain on the books, prosecution is rare.

Incest

Incest is sexual intercourse within or outside the bonds of marriage between persons related within certain prohibited degrees. *Haller v. State*, 232 S.W.2d 829 (Ark. 1950). Incest was not a crime at common law but was punishable by the ecclesiastical courts.

There are strong religious and moral taboos against incest. Furthermore, it has been almost universally believed that incest not only disrupts family relationships but also leads to genetically defective offspring. For these reasons, all states prohibit marriage or sexual relations between certain close relatives. Once the prosecution establishes the defendant's knowledge of the prohibited relationship, proof of the act of sexual intercourse is sufficient to show violation of the statute.

Statutes that prohibit intermarriage or sexual relations between persons within certain degrees of kinship usually refer to relationship by consanguinity (that is, blood relationships). Typically, Florida law provides as follows:

> Whoever knowingly marries or has sexual intercourse with a person to whom he is related by lineal consanguinity, or a brother, sister, uncle, aunt, nephew, or niece, commits incest, which constitutes a felony of the third degree. West's Fla. Stat. Ann. § 826.04.

Statutes do not usually distinguish between relationships of half-blood and full-blood. But, historically some went further than the Florida statute and classified as incestuous close relationships between persons related by affinity (that is, marriage) as well as relationships by the bloodline. For example, effective July 1, 2006, South Dakota repealed S.D. Codified Laws § 22–22–19.1, which formerly proscribed affinity as a basis of incest. SL 2005, ch. 120, § 22.

Bigamy

Like most sexual offenses, **bigamy** was originally a canonical offense punishable by the ecclesiastical courts in England; later it became a common-law offense. All American jurisdictions prohibit bigamy (that is, marriage between two persons when one is already legally married to another). Usually these statutes require the prosecution to prove that the defendant had knowledge of the prior marital status of the person whom he or she married. Since everyone is presumed to know the consequences of his or her acts, no further intent need be shown.

During the 1800s arguments were advanced that polygamy—the practice of one person being married to several spouses at the same time—was a religious practice protected by the First Amendment. The U.S. Supreme Court soundly rejected these contentions when it held that a religious belief cannot be made a justification for commission of an overt act made criminal by the state. *Reynolds v. United States,* 98 U.S. (8 Otto) 145, 25 L.Ed. 244 (1878). The *Reynolds* case involved a Mormon polygamist who challenged the constitutionality of the federal statute prohibiting polygamy in federal territories. Subsequently the Church of Jesus Christ of Latter-Day Saints disavowed the practice of polygamy, but the practice continues to this day in some "fundamentalist" Mormon communities in the western United States. Prosecutions are rare (see Case-in-Point below).

Go to the Scheb/ Scheb Criminal Law and Procedure 6e website at academic .cengage.com/criminaljustice/ scheb for an edited version of *Reynolds v. U.S.*

Sodomy: The Demise of a Historic Offense

The word "sodomy" is derived from the biblical account of Sodom, the city that was destroyed because of its vices. **Sodomy** consists of committing acts that were once commonly referred to as "crimes against nature." Sodomy was originally an ecclesiastical offense but became a felony in the later stages of the common law. In his *Commentaries on the Laws of England,* Blackstone described sodomy as an offense "the very mention of which is a disgrace to human nature" and "a crime not fit to be named." In general, the offense includes oral or anal sex between humans and sexual intercourse between humans and animals (the latter is often termed bestiality). Until 1961 all states had statutes outlawing sodomy; however, during the 1970s and 1980s

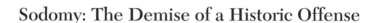

Criminal Prosecution of a Polygamist

CASE-IN-POINT

In what was described in the press as the country's first major polygamy case in nearly five decades, Thomas Arthur Green was found guilty on four counts of bigamy and one count of child rape in May of 2001. Green, a fundamentalist Mormon polygamist, had five wives and thirty children.

Green was sentenced to five years in prison. In reviewing the case in 2004, the Utah Supreme Court rejected Green's argument that the state bigamy statute violated the federal constitutional right to free exercise of religion. It also held that the bigamy statute was not unconstitutionally vague as applied.

State v. Green, 99 P.3d 820 (Utah 2004).

many of these statutes were either repealed or invalidated by courts. The few that remained on the books were not actively enforced.

In the mid-1980s, a federal appeals court in Georgia struck down that state's sodomy law on the ground that it violated the constitutional right of privacy, but in 1986, in a 5–4 decision, the U.S. Supreme Court overturned the ruling and upheld the law. *Bowers v. Hardwick,* 478 U.S. 186, 106 S.Ct. 2841, 92 L.Ed.2d 140 (1986). Writing for the Court, Justice White concluded that the Constitution did not confer "a fundamental right to homosexuals to engage in acts of consensual sodomy." 478 U.S. at 192, 106 S.Ct. at 2844, 92 L.Ed.2d at 146. The Court's decision left open the question of whether sodomy laws would be enforceable against acts of heterosexual sodomy, whether within or without the bounds of marriage. As we noted in Chapter 3, a state constitution may afford more protection to its citizens than does the federal constitution. Thus, on the ground the law infringed on the right of privacy under the state constitution, the Georgia Supreme Court struck down the same sodomy law the U.S. Supreme Court had upheld in *Bowers v. Hardwick. Powell v. State,* 510 S.E.2d 18, 26 (Ga. 1998).

By the beginning of the twenty-first century, only a few states had laws making sodomy an offense. In Texas two men were convicted of having anal sex with a member of the same sex in violation of Tex. Penal Code Ann. § 21.06(a), which makes it an offense "to engage in deviate sexual intercourse with another individual of the same sex." A Texas appellate court, in a divided opinion, rejected the defendants' federal constitutional arguments under both the Equal Protection and Due Process Clauses of the Fourteenth Amendment and affirmed the defendants' convictions. *Lawrence v. State,* 41 S.W.3d 349 (Tex. App. 2001). When the Supreme Court granted certiorari to review the decision upholding the Texas statute, the stage was set for the continuing campaign to obtain a reversal of the 1986 decision in *Bowers v. Hardwick.*

In *Lawrence v. Texas,* 539 U.S. 558, 123 S.Ct. 2472, 156 L.Ed.2d 508 (2003), Justice Anthony Kennedy, writing for the Court in a 6–3 decision, opined that the Texas statute "furthers no legitimate state interest which can justify its intrusion into the personal and private life of the individual." 539 U.S. at 578, 123 S.Ct. at 2484, 156 L.Ed.2d at 526.

The Court expressly overruled its decision in *Bowers v. Hardwick* on the ground that the Due Process Clause of the Fourteenth Amendment prohibits states from making private consensual sexual conduct of adults a crime. After referencing the English experience and decisions of the European Court of Human Rights, Justice Kennedy pointed out that the deficiencies in *Bowers* had become apparent in the years following its announcement. Observing that the twenty-five states with laws prohibiting the conduct referred to in *Bowers* were now reduced to thirteen, of which four enforce their laws only against homosexual conduct, Kennedy stated, "In those States, including Texas, that still proscribe sodomy (whether for same-sex or heterosexual conduct), there is a pattern of nonenforcement with respect to consenting adults acting in private." 539 U.S. at 573, 123 S.Ct. at 2481, 156 L.Ed.2d at 522.

In concurring in the Court's judgment, Justice Sandra Day O'Connor wrote separately to note that while she agreed the Texas law was unconstitutional, she would have invalidated it on the ground that it violated the Equal Protection Clause because it was directed only against homosexual and not heterosexual conduct.

The Court was careful to note that its decision does not involve minors, persons who might be injured or coerced or who are situated in relationships where consent might not easily be refused, public conduct, or prostitution. Finally, the Court emphasized that its decision does not bear on the issue of whether the government must give formal recognition to any relationship that homosexual persons seek to enter.

Chief Justice William Rehnquist and Justice Clarence Thomas joined with Justice Antonin Scalia in dissenting. Scalia argued, "What Texas has chosen to do is well within the range of traditional democratic action, and its hand should not be stayed through the invention of a brand-new 'constitutional right' by a Court that is impatient of democratic change." 539 U.S. at 603, 123 S.Ct. at 2497, 156 L.Ed.2d at 542.

Finally, in a separate dissent, Justice Thomas observed, "I join Justice Scalia's dissenting opinion. I write separately to note that the law before the Court today 'is … uncommonly silly.… If I were a member of the Texas Legislature, I would vote to repeal it. Punishing someone for expressing his sexual preference through noncommercial consensual conduct with another adult does not appear to be a worthy way to expend valuable law enforcement resources. Notwithstanding this, I recognize that as a member of this Court I am not empowered to help petitioners and others similarly situated." 539 U.S. at 605, 123 S.Ct. at 2498, 156 L.Ed.2d at 543.

Go to the Scheb/ Scheb Criminal Law and Procedure 6e website at academic .cengage.com/criminaljustice/ scheb for edited versions of *Bowers v. Hardwick, Powell v. State,* and *Lawrence v. Texas.*

Prostitution

Although **prostitution** was not a crime at common law, statutes proscribing prostitution have been part of the laws directed against public immorality since the early history of the United States. Lawmakers have officially deplored the existence of prostitution, and law enforcement authorities have long linked the activity with vice, narcotics offenses, and the exploitation of women.

A prostitute is a person who indulges in indiscriminate sexual activity for hire. Today, prostitution is illegal in all states except Nevada, where it exists by local option in some counties, although it is strictly regulated by law. See Nev. Rev. Stat., Chapter 201, Crimes Against Public Decency and Good Morals. Despite the limited legalization in Nevada, arrests for prostitution are still quite numerous in that state, as shown in Table 8.1. This is largely explained by the fact that prostitution is rampant in Las Vegas, where it remains illegal.

Historically, statutes prohibiting prostitution have been directed at females who have sexual intercourse with males for compensation, but in recent years, as prostitution by males has increased, enforcement has come to be directed at males as well.

Historically, laws prohibiting prostitution were directed almost exclusively at the prostitute. However, newer statutes provide for conviction of customers as well as prostitutes. Indeed, if the statutes are not so construed, they might be vulnerable to constitutional attack as a denial of equal protection under the law.

In addition to making prostitution an offense, most states make it an offense to solicit for a prostitute or to live off the earnings of a person engaged in prostitution. Statutes also commonly declare brothels and houses of prostitution as public nuisances.

Texas statutes provide that a person who offers or agrees to engage or engages in sexual conduct for a fee, or who solicits another in a public place to engage in such conduct, commits the misdemeanor offense of prostitution. Vernon's Tex. Penal Code Ann. § 43.02. Texas also makes promotion of prostitution a misdemeanor offense. § 43.03. One who owns or manages a prostitution enterprise that uses two or more prostitutes commits a felony. § 43.04. Finally, Texas law makes it a serious felony for a person to knowingly cause another by force, threat, or fraud or to cause by any means a person younger than seventeen years to commit prostitution. § 43.05.

Go to the Scheb/ Scheb Criminal Law and Procedure 6e website at academic .cengage.com/criminaljustice/ scheb to find *Austin v. State* (1990), in which the Texas Court of Criminal Appeals determines whether there is sufficient evidence to support a conviction for prostitution.

Prostitution has been dealt with primarily at the state and local levels, but the federal government has also shown an interest in coping with the problem. The Mann Act, 18 U.S.C.A. § 2421 *et seq.,* prohibits interstate transportation of an individual for purposes of prostitution or with the intent to compel an individual to become a prostitute or to engage in any other immoral practice. The Supreme Court has held that the act applies to transporting persons for immoral purposes even if

Table 8.1	Prostitution Arrests in the United States by State, 2005		
California	13,911	Connecticut	493
Texas	5,999	Oklahoma	456
Florida	5,715	Louisiana	447
Illinois	4,931	Utah	344
Nevada	4,633	Hawaii	341
Pennsylvania	2,552	Arkansas	301
New Jersey	2,342	New Mexico	300
Minnesota	2,133	Iowa	215
Tennessee	2,025	West Virginia	163
Maryland	1,861	Nebraska	148
Indiana	1,809	Delaware	140
Michigan	1,776	Alabama	124
New York	1,743	Alaska	123
Georgia	1,681	Wisconsin	121
Arizona	1,611	Rhode Island	110
Washington	1,567	New Hampshire	74
North Carolina	1,370	Mississippi	63
Ohio	1,282	Maine	18
Missouri	1,271	Kansas	8
Colorado	869	Idaho	3
South Carolina	742	South Dakota	3
Virginia	737	Wyoming	3
Massachusetts	672	Montana	2
Oregon	635	North Dakota	1
Kentucky	509	Vermont	1

Source: U.S. Department of Justice, Federal Bureau of Investigation, *Uniform Crime Reports 2005.*

commercial vice is not involved. *Cleveland v. United States,* 329 U.S. 14, 67 S.Ct. 13, 91 L.Ed. 12 (1946).

Criticism of Laws Regulating Consensual Sexual Conduct

Considerable criticism is leveled at laws that proscribe sexual conduct between consenting adults. Those who advocate the repeal of statutes making fornication, adultery, and seduction crimes argue that sexual conduct between consenting adults is essentially a matter of private moral concern. They believe such behavior should be left to the discretion of the participants. Furthermore, they contend that the resources needed to fight serious crime should not be wasted in attempts to apprehend violators of sexual mores. Moreover, they argue that because laws against these activities are largely unenforced, they lend themselves to charges of arbitrary enforcement against persons whose lifestyles are socially unacceptable. Finally, many critics contend that the very fact that these laws are not enforced breeds disrespect and encourages violation of laws that society regards as essential.

There is considerably less support for repealing laws forbidding incest. Some who do advocate the repeal of these laws advance the same arguments as for decriminalizing fornication, adultery, and seduction. In addition, many who see incest as a genuine concern urge that government should approach the problem through counseling and by furnishing psychiatric assistance to transgressors rather than by making incest a penal offense.

Those who oppose the prostitution laws now extant in the United States point to the fact that the so-called oldest profession has survived many centuries of condemnation yet exists as a cultural institution. Thus, they argue, it fulfills a socially desirable function because it furnishes an outlet for certain sexual impulses and tends to lessen the incidence of forcible sexual attacks on women. In addition to the need to conserve scarce resources to fight serious crime and the futility of trying to eradicate an ingrained institution, reformers contend that legalization of prostitution would lead to needed regulation. This, they point out, could provide for medical inspections to diminish the spread of sexually transmitted diseases. Finally, many critics of the present laws concerning prostitution contend that legalization would allow the police to take this activity from the grips of organized crime and control more effectively many of the vices that now accompany prostitution.

Bigamy and polygamy are still practiced in some areas. Given that such marriages are considered null and void, some argue that criminalizing such conduct is unnecessary. However, there is no great movement to abolish such laws, and any such effort would probably be to little avail.

The Prognosis for Reform

The repeal of laws prohibiting fornication is not a priority item for legislators. When criminal codes are revised, however, such laws often disappear. In our monogamous society, laws proscribing adultery will most likely remain as a public statement on morality, but they will be largely unenforced. Seduction has been mostly relegated to civil suits for breach of promise to marry, but even this type of action has been outlawed in many jurisdictions. In view of the Supreme Court's decision in *Lawrence v. Texas*, supra, it appears that laws prohibiting private noncommercial consensual sodomy between adults are no longer enforceable.

The practice of incest among those related by consanguinity is widely condemned in Western civilization, and laws forbidding it will undoubtedly remain. However, one area for limited reform is statutes that forbid marriage among certain persons related by affinity. For example, changing the incest statutes that prohibit such practices as a brother marrying his deceased brother's wife would be inoffensive to most and welcomed by many. In some cultures, such a practice is regarded as an obligation.

Monogamy is an ingrained institution in contemporary American culture, and it seems safe to predict that scattered efforts to revise laws prohibiting bigamy will continue to be ignored by legislators.

The prognosis on prostitution is a difficult one. One certainty is that increasingly, buyers as well as sellers of sexual services will be prosecuted. Despite the cries for reform, any decriminalization of prostitution will most likely be in selected locations only and will confine activities to prescribed areas. The inherent privacy of the scene of offenses makes it very difficult to apprehend prostitutes and their customers. Therefore, enforcement should focus on those who are the procurers of prostitutes and solicitors for their services and not merely on those who render their services.

Indecent Exposure

At common law, it was a misdemeanor for persons to intentionally expose their "private parts" in a public place. Today, statutes and local ordinances in most jurisdictions make it a misdemeanor to expose one's private parts to the view of another under offensive circumstances. However, such laws have been generally interpreted not to prohibit public exposure of the buttocks. See, for example, *Duvallon v. District of Columbia,* 515 A.2d 724 (D.C. App. 1986). Frequently state statutes and local ordinances specify that the prohibited exposure must be in public or visible to the public. Questions are often raised as to what constitutes being "in public" or "visible to the public."

Some statutes proscribing indecent exposure do not include the requirement that the exposure must be open to the public. For example, in *People v. Neal,* 702 N.W.2d 696 (Mich. App. 2005), the defendant exposed his erect penis to a minor victim while they were in his home and not in a public place. The court held that the Michigan statute providing that "[a]ny person who shall knowingly make any open or indecent exposure of his or her person or of the person of another is guilty of a misdemeanor ..." does not require that the offending act take place in public.

Several state courts have upheld laws criminalizing **indecent exposure** against a variety of constitutional challenges. See, for example, *Keller v. State,* 738 P.2d 186 (Okl. Crim. App. 1987); *State v. Ludwig,* 468 So.2d 1151 (La. 1985).

Frequently, the offense of indecent exposure is termed **lewd and lascivious conduct.** Because a person can expose himself or herself either accidentally or of necessity, laws generally provide that indecent exposure must be done willfully and in an offensive manner. See, for example, *People v. Randall,* 711 P.2d 689 (Colo. 1985).

 Go to the Scheb/ Scheb Criminal Law and Procedure 6e website at academic .cengage.com/criminaljustice/ scheb to find *State v. Fly* (1998), a North Carolina Supreme Court decision involving the offense of indecent exposure.

Often, statutes require that offensive exposure must be in the *presence* of another person. Interpreting the term "presence" has become problematical. In 1992, the Florida Supreme Court ruled that presence "encompasses sensory awareness as well as physical proximity." Consequently, the court reversed the conviction of a man who admitted to masturbating in the presence of his thirteen-month-old child. In the court's view, the child did not have "sensory awareness" of the act in question. *State v. Werner,* 609 So.2d 585 (Fla. 1992). The Supreme Court of Kansas took a contrasting view. In *State v. Bryan,* 130 P.3d 85 (Kan. 2006), the court held that there is no awareness requirement associated with the offense of publicly exposing a sex organ in the presence of a person.

CASE-IN-POINT

Indecent Exposure

A man exposing himself in a second-story apartment in New Orleans was seen from below by persons in the apartment parking lot. He was prosecuted for indecent exposure under a statute that had been interpreted as criminalizing indecent exposure if it was viewable from any location open to the public. In upholding his conviction, the Louisiana Supreme Court noted that the parking lot from which the victims observed the man exposing himself was not enclosed, nor was it posted as private property, and was open to any visitors to the apartment complex.

State v. Clark, 372 So.2d 1218 (La. 1979).

Nude Dancing in Places of Public Accommodation

Is nude dancing for entertainment in a bar or theater a form of indecent exposure? Or is it a form of expression protected by the First Amendment? In *Barnes v. Glen Theatre, Inc.,* 501 U.S. 560, 111 S.Ct. 2456, 115 L.Ed.2d 504 (1991), the U.S. Supreme Court upheld an Indiana law that prohibited totally nude dancing. Writing for a plurality of justices, Chief Justice Rehnquist observed that "the governmental interest served by the text of the prohibition is societal disapproval of nudity in public places and among strangers." 501 U.S. at 572, 111 S.Ct. at 2463, 115 L.Ed.2d at 515. In Rehnquist's view, "Indiana's requirement that the dancers wear at least pasties and a G-string is modest, and the bare minimum necessary to achieve the state's purpose." 501 U.S. at 572, 111 S.Ct. at 2463, 115 L.Ed.2d at 515.

In 2000 the Supreme Court reaffirmed its decision in *Barnes v. Glen Theatre.* The Court upheld an Erie, Pennsylvania, ordinance that was interpreted to require dancers in clubs to wear pasties and G-strings. *City of Erie v. Pap's A.M.,* 529 U.S. 277, 120 S.Ct. 1382, 146 L.Ed.2d 265 (2000). Writing for a plurality, Justice O'Connor concluded that "Erie's asserted interest in combating the negative secondary effects associated with adult entertainment establishments … is unrelated to the suppression of the erotic message conveyed by nude dancing." 529 U.S. at 296, 120 S.Ct. at 1394, 146 L.Ed.2d at 282.

 Go to the Scheb/ Scheb Criminal Law and Procedure 6e website at academic .cengage.com/criminaljustice/ scheb for an edited version of *Barnes v. Glen Theatre.*

Nudity and Seminudity on Public Beaches

Historically, public nudity has been taboo in Western societies. Yet only a few states have imposed outright bans. Many states maintain that public nudity on beaches and other recreational areas violates laws proscribing lewd and lascivious conduct or indecent exposure. For example, in Florida, where public beaches are popular attractions, signs are commonly posted notifying beachgoers that nude sunbathing is a violation of Florida Statutes section 877.03. Actually, that law prohibits "such acts as are of a nature to corrupt the public morals, or outrage the sense of public decency, or affect the peace and quiet of persons who may witness them." In 1976 the Florida Supreme Court held that the legislative intent of the statute prohibits adult females from openly exposing their breasts on public beaches. *Moffett v. State,* 340 So.2d 1155 (Fla. 1976). Arrests under this provision are not common. In fact, Miami Beach and other Florida cities that attract large numbers of tourists have set aside specified areas where topless or nude sunbathing is permitted. In 2001 a Florida appellate court held that a state statute and a county ordinance that prohibited exposure of the female breast in circumstances where the exposure of the male breast would not be prohibited did not violate the equal protection guarantee of the state constitution because the classification served an important governmental objective. *Frandsen v. County of Brevard,* 800 So.2d 757 (Fla. App. 2001). The Florida Supreme Court denied review. 828 So.2d 386.

Voyeurism

Voyeurism refers to obtaining sexual gratification from seeing another person's sexual organs or sexual activities. Historically voyeurism has been addressed under "Peeping Tom" statutes and ordinances based on a trespass theory. Modern photography and the availability to publish photos on the Internet have caused some states

"Up-skirt" Video Voyeurism

Tony O. Morris was convicted of "interference with privacy" under Minnesota Statutes § 609.746 (2000). The evidence showed that Morris carried a bag containing a concealed video camera into a J.C. Penney department store and surreptitiously positioned the lens underneath a sales clerk's skirt so as to photograph her underwear. Morris was sentenced to 90 days in jail and fined $1,000. On appeal, the conviction was affirmed. The appellate court concluded that "[b]ecause appellant surreptitiously positioned a video camera lens underneath [the victim's] skirt, a place where [the victim] had a reasonable expectation of privacy, so as to photograph the clothing covering the immediate area of the intimate parts of her body, with the intent to intrude upon or interfere with her privacy, he was lawfully found guilty of interference with privacy...."

State v. Morris, 644 N.W.2d 114 (Minn. App. 2002).

to revisit such prohibitions in order to protect the privacy of persons, not only in their homes but also in public where a person would ordinarily expect a reasonable degree of privacy.

Although most state statutes defining voyeurism prohibit nonconsensual viewing only in "private" places, Florida Statutes now take a modern approach to prohibiting voyeurism. Section 810.14 provides, "A person commits the offense of voyeurism when he or she, with lewd, lascivious, or indecent intent, secretly observes, photographs, films, videotapes, or records another person when such other person is located in a dwelling, structure, or conveyance and such location provides a reasonable expectation of privacy." Another recently enacted statute makes it unlawful for any merchant to directly observe or make use of video cameras or other visual surveillance devices to observe or record customers in the merchant's dressing room, fitting room, changing room, or restroom when such room provides a reasonable expectation of privacy. Fla. Stat. § 877.26.

Obscenity and Pornography

At common law, vulgar and obscene language and indecent public exhibitions were considered public nuisances, punishable as misdemeanors. Historically, federal and state governments in the United States passed laws banning various forms of obscenity. By the late 1800s, Congress had made it an offense to mail any "obscene, lewd or lascivious paper or writing" and provided that the word "obscene" should be given fully as broad a significance as it had at common law. *Knowles v. United States,* 170 F. 409 (8th Cir. 1909). The states also passed laws making the sale or distribution of obscene materials a crime. Typically, section 6567 of the Connecticut General Statutes (1949 Revision) provided that "[b]uying, selling, giving or showing any obscene, indecent or impure book, paper or picture is a crime." Likewise, most municipalities adopted ordinances proscribing various forms of obscenity.

Historically, statutes and ordinances making obscenity an offense seldom defined it. Thus, they were vulnerable to contentions that they were vague and did not provide an ascertainable standard of guilt. As questions arose, the courts tended to define obscenity as sexual or erotic speech or conduct. The word "obscene" came to mean something offensive to the senses—that is, repulsive, disgusting, foul, or filthy.

The Emerging Constitutional Standards

As mass communications developed, laws banning obscene speech, materials, and performances became subject to scrutiny under the First Amendment. The Supreme Court's first direct encounter with regulating obscenity came in *Roth v. United States,* 354 U.S. 476, 77 S.Ct. 1304, 1 L.Ed.2d 1498 (1957). Roth was found guilty of sending erotic materials through the mail, and his conviction was affirmed on appeal. The Supreme Court granted review and announced that the dispositive issue was "whether obscenity is utterance within the area of protected speech and press." The Court held that obscenity was not constitutionally protected; rather, the Court viewed it as "utterly without redeeming social importance." After observing that "sex and obscenity are not synonymous," Justice William J. Brennan, writing for the Court, said the test for determining obscenity was "whether to the average person applying contemporary community standards, the dominant theme of the material taken as a whole, appeals to the prurient interest." 354 U.S. at 489, 77 S.Ct. at 1311, 1 L.Ed.2d at 1509 (1957).

By the late 1950s, there was a flood of erotic materials on the market. Whether particular materials were obscene had become an increasingly important issue. *Roth* effectively made the definition of obscenity a matter of federal constitutional law. It also evidenced the Court's concern for First Amendment freedoms and for protecting the free flow of expression from local interpretations of what constituted obscenity. Because of the problems in determining whether materials were obscene under the *Roth* standards, law enforcement officers experienced great difficulty in enforcing obscenity laws.

From 1957 to 1973, the Supreme Court granted review of several lower court decisions determining that particular books, plays, and movies were obscene, often explicating due process guidelines to be followed by lower courts in determining what constitutes obscenity. During this period the Court found the French film *The Lovers* not to be obscene and implied that national standards would govern in determining whether materials were obscene. There Justice Potter Stewart, in expressing the view that obscenity is limited to **hard-core pornography,** made his oft-quoted remark on obscenity: "I know it when I see it." *Jacobellis v. Ohio,* 378 U.S. 184, 197, 84 S.Ct. 1676, 1683, 12 L.Ed.2d 793 (1964) (Stewart, J. concurring).

As the 1970s approached, observers speculated that the Supreme Court was taking a more liberal approach. In *Stanley v. Georgia,* 394 U.S. 557, 89 S.Ct. 1243, 22 L.Ed.2d 542 (1969), the Court reviewed a defendant's conviction for violating a statute making the knowing possession of obscene materials a crime. In *Stanley,* the police had seized materials (which the Court assumed to be obscene) from the defendant's home. In reversing the defendant's conviction, the Court held that "the State may no more prohibit mere possession of obscene matter on the ground that it may lead to antisocial conduct than it may prohibit possession of chemistry books on the ground that they may lead to the manufacture of homemade spirits." 394 U.S. at 567, 89 S.Ct. at 1249, 22 L.Ed.2d at 551. Some read *Stanley* as an indication the Court was relaxing its standards on regulating obscenity. They were mistaken.

The Intractable Obscenity Problem

When the Supreme Court decided the seminal case of *Miller v. California,* 413 U.S. 15, 93 S.Ct. 2607, 37 L.Ed.2d 419 (1973), it referred to "the intractable obscenity problem." 413 U.S. at 16, 93 S.Ct. at 2610, 37 L.Ed.2d at 426. In *Miller,* the defendant had mailed unsolicited material containing explicit sexual drawings in violation of a California law. A jury found him guilty, and an appellate court upheld the judgment without opinion. At the outset, Chief Justice Warren Burger reiterated that obscene materials were unprotected by the Constitution. Then the Court suggested that local juries could base their judgments on local and not national standards. Most significantly, the Court redefined the standards for determining obscenity, saying that the

> basic guidelines for the trier of fact must be: (1) whether "the average person, applying contemporary community standards" would find that the work, taken as a whole, appeals to the **prurient interest;** (b) whether the work depicts or describes, in a **patently offensive** way, sexual conduct specifically defined by the applicable state law; and (c) whether the work, taken as a whole, lacks serious literary, artistic, political, or scientific value. 413 U.S. at 24, 93 S.Ct. 2614, 37 L.Ed.2d at 431.

Go to the Scheb/ Scheb Criminal Law and Procedure 6e website at academic .cengage.com/criminaljustice/ scheb for an edited version of *Miller v. California.*

Finally, the Court expressly rejected any requirement that the challenged materials be found to be "utterly without redeeming social importance." 413 U.S. at 24, 93 S.Ct. at 2614, 37 L.Ed.2d at 431. The Court gave examples of "patently offensive" by saying it meant "representations or descriptions of ultimate sexual acts, normal or perverted, actual or simulated … , representations or descriptions of masturbation, excretory functions, and lewd exhibition of genitals." 413 U.S. at 25, 93 S.Ct. at 2615, 37 L.Ed.2d at 431. The Court made it clear that no one would be subject to prosecution unless the materials alleged to be obscene described patently offensive, "hardcore" sexual conduct.

In a companion case, *Paris Adult Theatre I v. Slaton,* 413 U.S. 49, 93 S.Ct. 2628, 37 L.Ed.2d 446 (1973), the Court observed that the states have a right to "maintain a decent society" and may challenge obscene material even if it is shown only to consenting adults.

These decisions indicated an increasing concern over the issue of obscenity and allowed local juries to make judgments based on more explicit standards. These decisions also tended to eliminate the practice of using expert witnesses to testify on such issues as contemporary community standards and whether materials were "utterly without redeeming social value."

Significant Post-*Miller* Developments

Go to the Scheb/ Scheb Criminal Law and Procedure 6e website at academic .cengage.com/criminaljustice/ scheb for an edited version of *Jenkins v. Georgia.*

Miller may have clarified the tests for obscenity, but it did not satisfy those who sought to ban pornographic materials. For example, *Carnal Knowledge,* a very successful movie in the early 1970s, was held not obscene under the *Miller* test. There were scenes in which "ultimate sexual acts" were understood to be taking place; however, the camera did not focus on the bodies of the actors, nor was there any exhibition of genitals during such scenes. The Court said that the film was not a "portrayal of hard core sexual conduct for its own sake, and for the ensuing commercial gain" and did not depict sexual conduct in a patently offensive way. *Jenkins v. Georgia,* 418 U.S. 153, 161, 94 S.Ct. 2750, 2755, 41 L.Ed.2d 642, 650 (1974).

In *Pope v. Illinois,* 481 U.S. 497, 107 S.Ct. 1918, 95 L.Ed.2d 439 (1987), the Supreme Court said that the application of "contemporary community standards" is appropriate in evaluating the first two prongs of the *Miller* test for obscenity—that is, the work's appeal to the prurient interest and its patent offensiveness. However, the Court concluded that the third prong concerning the work's value cannot be tested by "community standards." The Court said the third prong must be determined on an objective basis, with the proper inquiry being not whether an ordinary member of any given community would find serious literary, artistic, political, or scientific value in allegedly

Obscenity

In the first federal appeals court decision applying the *Miller v. California* obscenity test to a musical composition, the Eleventh Circuit Court of Appeals ruled that the recording *As Nasty as They Wanna Be* by 2 Live Crew was not obscene. The Eleventh Circuit ruled that even assuming the work was "patently offensive" and appealed to a "prurient interest," the trial judge erred in concluding, simply on the basis of his own listening to a tape recording, that the work lacked "serious artistic value."

Luke Records, Inc. v. Navarro, 960 F.2d 134 (11th Cir. 1992).

obscene material but whether a reasonable person would find such value in the material taken as a whole. 481 U.S. at 500, 107 S.Ct. at 1921, 95 L.Ed.2d at 445.

Noting that the First Amendment protection extends to rap music and is not weakened because the music takes on an unpopular or even dangerous viewpoint, in 2000 a federal district court in Louisiana found that "gangster rap" did not lack serious artistic value so as to constitute obscene speech devoid of First Amendment protection. *Torries v. Hebert,* 111 F. Supp.2d 806 (W.D. La. 2000).

State and Local Regulation of Obscenity

States, of course, may interpret their own constitutions to allow greater freedom of expression than is allowed under the current federal constitutional interpretations. In that vein, in 1987 the Oregon Supreme Court held that "any person can write, print, read, say, show or sell anything to a consenting adult even though that expression may be generally or universally condemned as 'obscene.'" *State v. Henry,* 732 P.2d 9, 18 (Or. 1987).

Some states classify violations of their obscenity statutes by degree. For example, in New York a person is guilty of obscenity in the third degree when, knowing its content and character, he or she

1. Promotes, or possesses with intent to promote, any obscene material; or

2. Produces, presents or directs an obscene performance or participates in a portion thereof which is obscene or which contributes to its obscenity. McKinney's N.Y. Penal Law § 235.05.

A person is guilty of obscenity in the second degree "when he commits the crime of obscenity in the third degree … and has been previously convicted of obscenity in the third degree." § 235.06. A person is guilty of obscenity in the first degree "when, knowing its content and character, he wholesale promotes or possesses with intent to wholesale promote, any obscene material." § 235.07. New York law makes third-degree obscenity a misdemeanor, whereas second-degree or first-degree obscenity is a felony.

States generally set higher penalties for exposing juveniles to pictures or shows where obscenity or even pornography is involved, and some state laws have been updated to proscribe disseminating indecent material to minors through computers. For example, McKinney's N.Y. Penal Law § 235.22 provides:

A person is guilty of disseminating indecent material to minors in the first degree when:

1. knowing the character and content of the communication which, in whole or in part, depicts actual or simulated nudity, sexual conduct or sado-masochistic abuse,

and which is harmful to minors, he intentionally uses any computer communication system allowing the input, output, examination or transfer, of computer data or computer programs from one computer to another, to initiate or engage in such communication with a person who is a minor; and

2. by means of such communication he importunes, invites or induces a minor to engage in sexual intercourse, deviate sexual intercourse, or sexual contact with him, or to engage in a sexual performance, obscene sexual performance, or sexual conduct for his benefit.

Under the statute, disseminating indecent material to minors in the first degree is a class D felony. In *People v. Foley,* 731 N.E.2d 123 (N.Y. 2000), the New York Court of Appeals, the state's highest court, upheld the constitutionality of section 235.22 against challenges that it is vague and that, by its content-based restrictions, violates the First Amendment. The court ruled that by criminalizing computerized dissemination of indecent material to sexually exploit children, the law was a carefully tailored means of serving a compelling State interest. Accordingly the court found the statute was not an unconstitutional content-based restriction on speech. The court distinguished its decision from the U.S. Supreme Court's decision's in *Reno v. American Civil Liberties Union,* 521 U.S. 844, 117 S.Ct. 2329, 138 L.Ed.2d 874 (1997). In *Reno,* the Court struck down the Communications Decency Act (47 U.S.C.A. § 223), which prohibited the knowing transmission of "obscene or indecent" comments to any person under the age of 18. (We discuss the *Reno* decision in a later topic in this chapter.)

Defenses to Charges of Obscenity

New York law provides a defense for those charged with obscenity if they can establish that the allegedly obscene material was disseminated to or performed for an audience of persons having scientific, educational, governmental, or other similar justification for possessing or viewing the material. McKinney's N.Y. Penal Law § 235.15. Moreover, it is a defense for disseminating indecent material to minors if the defendant had reasonable cause to believe that the minor involved was seventeen years old or older and exhibited official documentation to the defendant to establish that fact. McKinney's N.Y. Penal Law § 235.23. This latter provision was undoubtedly inserted to protect theater personnel from conviction on a strict liability basis.

Problems of Enforcement

Police and prosecutors often experience difficulty in determining what is to be considered obscene based on "contemporary community standards." Juries in most instances now determine the issue of obscenity simply by reviewing the material. As a result, it is not unusual for a given work to be determined obscene by a jury in one locality and not obscene by another jury in a different locality. For example, the rock musical stage production *Hair* was found not to be obscene by a federal court in Georgia. *Southeastern Promotions, Ltd. v. Atlanta,* 334 F. Supp. 634 (N.D. Ga. 1971). The following year, it was found to be obscene by another federal court in Tennessee, but this decision was reversed by the Supreme Court. *Southeastern Promotions, Inc. v. Conrad,* 341 F. Supp. 465 (E.D. Tenn. 1972), aff'd., 486 F.2d 894 (6th Cir. 1973), rev'd., 420 U.S. 546, 95 S.Ct. 1239, 43 L.Ed.2d 448 (1975).

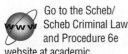 Go to the Scheb/ Scheb Criminal Law and Procedure 6e website at academic .cengage.com/criminaljustice/ scheb to find *Radey v. State* (1989), where an Ohio appellate court reverses an obscenity conviction.

Legal problems incident to searches and seizures of allegedly obscene materials can be very technical. Because books, movies, and even live performances are presumptively protected by the First Amendment, the Supreme Court has held that police must obtain a search warrant before conducting searches and seizures of such materials. *Roaden v. Kentucky,* 413 U.S. 496, 93 S.Ct. 2796, 37 L.Ed.2d 757 (1973).

However, the Court has explained that the Fourth Amendment does not prohibit undercover police officers from purchasing allegedly obscene materials because such a purchase would not constitute a "seizure." *Maryland v. Macon,* 472 U.S. 463, 105 S.Ct. 2778, 86 L.Ed.2d 370 (1985).

Pornography on the Internet

Amid growing public concerns about the prevalence of sexually explicit material on the Internet, and especially the relatively easy access of children to such material, Congress enacted the Communications Decency Act of 1996 (CDA). The CDA contained two provisions aimed at pornography on the Internet. The "indecent transmission" provision, codified at 47 U.S.C.A. § 223(a) (Supp. 2000), prohibited the knowing transmission of obscene or indecent messages to any recipient under eighteen years of age. The "patently offensive display" provision, codified at 47 U.S.C.A. § 223(d) (Supp. 1997), prohibited the knowing sending or displaying of patently offensive messages in a manner that is available to a person under eighteen years of age and was amended in 2003 by striking out "patently offensive as measured by contemporary community standards, sexual or excretory activities or organs" and inserting "is obscene or child pornography." Immediately after the CDA was signed into law by President Clinton, twenty plaintiffs, including the American Civil Liberties Union, brought suit challenging its constitutionality. In *Reno v. American Civil Liberties Union,* 521 U.S. 844, 117 S.Ct. 2329, 138 L.Ed.2d 874 (1997), the Supreme Court struck down the CDA on First Amendment grounds. Focusing on the statute's proscription of "indecent" transmissions, the Court concluded that the CDA presented a real threat of censoring expression entitled to First Amendment protection. Thus, the Court held that the statute was unconstitutionally overbroad. However, the Court left open the possibility that a more carefully drafted statute might pass constitutional muster. A statute limited to the prohibition of "obscene," as distinct from merely "indecent," material might survive constitutional scrutiny.

 Go to the Scheb/ Scheb Criminal Law and Procedure 6e website at academic .cengage.com/criminaljustice/ scheb for an edited version of *Reno v. ACLU.*

In an attempt to overcome some of the constitutional defects of the CDA, in 1998 Congress passed the Child Online Protection Act (COPA). 47 U.S.C.A. § 231. COPA states:

> Whoever knowingly and with knowledge of the character of the material, in interstate or foreign commerce by means of the World Wide Web, makes any communication for commercial purposes that is available to any minor and that includes any material that is harmful to minors shall be fined not more than $50,000, imprisoned not more than 6 months, or both.

Subsection (6) of COPA relies on "community standards" to determine whether materials are harmful to minors. Lower federal courts enjoined enforcement of COPA on the ground that it improperly relied on community standards to identify what material is harmful to minors and was unconstitutionally overbroad in violation of the First Amendment. The Supreme Court then held COPA's reliance on community standards did not by itself render the statute substantially overbroad for First Amendment purposes; however, it remanded the case to the Third Circuit Court of Appeals to determine whether COPA suffers from substantial overbreadth for other reasons. *Ashcroft v. American Civil Liberties Union,* 535 U.S. 564, 122 S.Ct. 1700, 152 L.Ed.2d 771 (2002). On March 6, 2003, the Third Circuit found the plaintiffs established a substantial likelihood of prevailing on their claim that COPA is unconstitutionally overbroad and continued a preliminary injunction against enforcement of the act. 322 F.3d 240 (3rd Cir. 2003). The Supreme Court granted review and held the District Court did not abuse its discretion when it entered the preliminary injunction. However, the Court remanded the case to enable the District Court to consider whether recent technological developments in the Internet and recent Congressional enactments might enable the government to meet its constitutional burden of showing that COPA is the least restrictive alternative available to accomplish Congress's goal. *Ashcroft v. American Civil Liberties Union,* 542 U.S. 656, 124 S.Ct. 2783, 159 L.Ed.2d 690 (2004). As of April 2007 the constitutionality of COPA remained undetermined.

Child Pornography

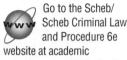
Go to the Scheb/ Scheb Criminal Law and Procedure 6e website at academic .cengage.com/criminaljustice/ scheb for an edited version of the *Ferber* decision.

In *New York v. Ferber,* 458 U.S. 747, 102 S.Ct. 3348, 73 L.Ed.2d 1113 (1982), the Supreme Court unanimously held that **child pornography,** like obscenity, is unprotected by the First Amendment to the Constitution. The Court upheld a New York law prohibiting persons from distributing materials that depict children engaging in lewd sex. The Court found such laws valid even if the material does not appeal to the prurient interest of the average person and is not portrayed in a patently offensive manner. The Court found a compelling state interest in protecting the well-being of children and perceived no value in permitting performances and photo reproductions of children engaged in lewd sexual conduct.

Most states have also criminalized the possession of child pornography. For example, Ohio law makes it a crime to "possess or view any material or performance that shows a minor who is not the person's child or ward in a state of nudity." Ohio Rev. Code Ann. 2907.323(A)(3) (Supp. 1989). In 1990, the Supreme Court upheld this prohibition against a constitutional challenge that the statute was overbroad. *Osborne v. Ohio,* 495 U.S. 103, 110 S.Ct. 1691, 109 L.Ed.2d 98 (1990). Together, the *Ferber* and *Osborne* decisions suggested that the Supreme Court would not be sympathetic to any First Amendment claim that would protect from criminal prosecution those who produce, distribute, or consume child pornography.

Having determined that virtual child pornography is as destructive as pornography using real children and in an effort to keep up with developing technology, Congress enacted the Child Pornography Prevention Act of 1996 (CPPA). 18 U.S.C.A. § 2252A. The Act prohibited any type of virtual or simulated child pornography, even if real children were not involved. In *Ashcroft v. Free Speech Coalition,* 535 U.S. 234, 122 S.Ct. 1389, 152 L.Ed.2d 403 (2002), the Supreme Court surprised some observers in striking down the prohibition of virtual child pornography. The Court noted that in upholding the ban on child pornography *Ferber* focused on how the depictions of child pornography were made, not on what was communicated, and held that *virtual* child pornography is distinguishable from *real* child pornography, which, under *New York v. Ferber,* supra, may be banned without regard to whether it depicts works of value. The Court found that the ban on virtual child pornography in the CPPA abridges the freedom to engage in a substantial amount of lawful speech, and thus is overbroad and therefore unconstitutional under the First Amendment. Three justices dissented from this ruling.

Profanity

Historically, many states and cities maintained criminal prohibitions against public **profanity.** In many instances these prohibitions have been incorporated into broader prohibitions of offensive or disorderly conduct (see Chapter 12). In recent decades, the courts have often invalidated such laws for vagueness (see Chapter 3). In other instances, courts have upheld their validity but ruled that such laws can be applied only where the defendant's language consisted of "fighting words" or the defendant's conduct threatened a breach of the peace (see Chapter 12).

New York v. Ferber, 458 U.S. 747, 102 S.Ct. 3348, 73 L.Ed.2d 1113 (1982)

At issue before the Court was the constitutionality of a New York law that made it a crime to knowingly promote sexual performances by children under the age of 16 by distributing material which depicts such performances. Ferber, who was convicted of violating the statute, claimed that the law violated the First Amendment.

JUSTICE WHITE delivered the opinion of the Court.

First. It is evident beyond the need for elaboration that a state's interest in "safeguarding the physical and psychological well being of a minor" is "compelling." ... "A democratic society rests, for its continuance, upon the healthy well-rounded growth of young people into full maturity as citizens." ...

The prevention of sexual exploitation and abuse of children constitutes a government objective of surpassing importance....

Second. The distribution of photographs and films depicting sexual activity by juveniles is intrinsically related to the sexual abuse of children in at least two ways. First, the materials produced are a permanent record of the children's participation and the harm to the child is exacerbated by their circulation. Second, the distribution network for child pornography must be closed if the production of material which requires the sexual exploitation of children is to be effectively controlled. Indeed, there is no serious contention that the legislature was unjustified in believing that it is difficult, if not impossible, to halt the exploitation of children by pursuing only those who produce the photographs and movies. While the production of pornographic materials is a low-profile, clandestine industry, the need to market the resulting products requires a visible apparatus of distribution. The most expeditious if not the only practical method of law enforcement may be to dry up the market for this material by imposing severe criminal penalties on

persons selling, advertising, or otherwise promoting the product....

Third. The advertising and selling of child pornography provides an economic motive for and is thus an integral part of the production of such materials, an activity illegal throughout the nation. "It rarely has been suggested that the constitutional freedom for speech and press extends its immunity to speech or writing used as an integral part of conduct in violation of a valid criminal statute." ...

Fourth. The value of permitting live performances and photographic reproductions of children engaged in lewd sexual conduct is exceedingly modest, if not de minimis. We consider it unlikely that visual depictions of children performing sexual acts or lewdly exhibiting their genitals would often constitute an important and necessary part of a literary performance or scientific or educational work.... Nor is there any question here of censoring a particular literary theme or portrayal of sexual activity. The First Amendment interest is limited to that of rendering the portrayal somewhat more "realistic" by utilizing or photographing children.

Fifth. Recognizing and classifying child pornography as a category of material outside the protection of the First Amendment is not incompatible with our earlier decisions. "The question whether speech is, or is not protected by the First Amendment often depends on the content of the speech." ... Thus, it is not rare that a content-based classification of speech has been accepted because it may be appropriately generalized that within the confines of the given classification, the evil to be restricted so overwhelmingly outweighs the expressive interests, if any, at stake, that no process of case-by-case adjudication is required. When a definable class of material, such as that covered by [the challenged statute], bears so heavily and pervasively on the welfare of children engaged in its production, we think the balance of competing interests is clearly struck and that it is permissible to consider these materials as without the protection of the First Amendment....

In *Cohen v. California,* 403 U.S. 15, 19, 91 S.Ct. 1780, 1785, 29 L.Ed.2d 284, 290 (1971), the Supreme Court invalidated the "offensive conduct" conviction of a man who entered a courthouse wearing a jacket emblazoned with the slogan "Fuck the Draft." Writing for the Court, Justice John M. Harlan noted that "while the particular four-letter-word being litigated here is perhaps more distasteful than others of

CASE-IN-POINT

The Case of the Cussing Canoeist

When Timothy Boomer, age twenty-five, fell out of his canoe and into the Rifle River in Michigan, he let loose a three-minute tirade of profanity. Two sheriff's deputies patrolling the river heard Boomer and ticketed him. Boomer was charged with violating an 1897 Michigan statute that provides, "Any person who shall use any indecent, immoral, obscene, vulgar or insulting language in the presence or hearing of any woman or child shall be guilty of a misdemeanor." M.C.L. § 750.337

Standing before the Arenac County Circuit Court, Boomer said, "[I]f my words offended anyone, I'm sorry. I've said from the beginning that I did not know that there were children in the area and I would not have said what I said if I had known there were

children around." A jury found Boomer guilty, and the court sentenced him to four days' community service and imposed a $75 fine.

On appeal the Michigan Court of Appeals reversed Boomer's conviction, noting, "Allowing a prosecution where one utters 'insulting' language could possibly subject a vast percentage of the populace to a misdemeanor conviction. M.C.L. § 750.337 fails to provide fair notice of what conduct is prohibited, and it encourages arbitrary and discriminatory enforcement…. Here, it would be difficult to conceive of a statute that would be more vague than M.C.L. § 750.337. There is no restrictive language whatsoever contained in the statute that would limit or guide a prosecution for indecent, immoral, obscene, vulgar, or insulting language."

People v. Boomer, 655 N.W.2d 255 (Mich. App. 2002).

Go to the Scheb/ Scheb Criminal Law and Procedure 6e website at academic .cengage.com/criminaljustice/ scheb for an edited version of *Cohen v. California.*

its genre, it is nevertheless often true that one man's vulgarity is another's lyric." 403 U.S. at 25, 91 S.Ct. at 1788, 29 L.Ed.2d at 294.

Despite the Supreme Court's decision in *Cohen v. California,* a number of jurisdictions retain laws proscribing profanity. For example, consider the following ordinance enacted by the city of Rockville, Maryland:

Sec. 13-53. Profanity; violation of section declared misdemeanor.

(a) A person may not profanely curse and swear or use obscene language upon or near any street, sidewalk or highway within the hearing of persons passing by, upon or along such street, sidewalk or highway.

(b) A person may not act in a disorderly manner by profanely cursing, swearing or using obscene language.

(c) Any person who violates this section is guilty of a misdemeanor. Laws of Rockville, Ch. 12, § 12-1.00.

Such laws are seldom enforced and even more rarely challenged in court. A notable exception occurred in 1999 in the widely publicized case of the "cussing canoeist" (see the Case-in-Point above).

Gambling

Traditionally, to gamble has meant to risk money on an event, chance, or contingency in the hope of realizing a gain. See *State v. Stripling,* 21 So. 409 (Ala. 1897). The common law did not regard gambling as an offense. However, many of the new American states, either by constitution or statute, made all or certain forms of **gambling** illegal. Today, federal laws and a variety of state statutes and local ordinances prohibit gambling. Laws regulating gambling come under the police power of the state, and the U.S. Supreme Court has recognized that there is no constitutional right to gamble. *Lewis v. United States*, 348 U.S. 419, 75 S.Ct. 415, 99 L.Ed. 475 (1955).

Bingo, craps, baccarat, poker, raffles, bookmaking, and slot machines are just a few common forms of gambling. Gambling also includes betting on sports events and card games. Many forms of gambling are legal; therefore, when considering gambling, we must separate the legal from the illegal. For example, those who pay something of value to take a chance to win a prize in a **lottery** are gambling. In many jurisdictions, this is a criminal offense. Yet in several states, lotteries are not only legal, they are an important source of public revenue. In effect, it is unregulated gambling that is illegal. A common form of unregulated gambling is "numbers." To play, you place a bet on a number with the hope that it will correspond to a preselected number. The **numbers racket** is widespread and, along with prostitution, is a major source of income for organized crime.

What Constitutes Gambling?

To constitute gambling, gaming activity must generally include three elements: **consideration, prize, and chance.** Retail stores conduct a variety of promotional schemes; local carnivals and fairs offer opportunities to play a variety of games for prizes. When are they gambling, and when are they games of skill? And if games of skill, are they exempt from laws prohibiting gambling? Some statutes regulating gambling provide the answer. In other instances, courts may be called on to determine whether a particular activity offends a statutory prohibition against gambling.

Most statutes prohibiting gambling are interpreted to exclude athletics or other contests in which participants pit their physical or mental skills against one another for a prize. Courts tend to be practical in their interpretations. For example, an Ohio appellate court found that a pinball machine that allowed the outcome of its operation to be determined largely by the skill of the user was not "a game of chance," and the

CASE-IN-POINT

What Constitutes an Illegal Gaming Machine?

The Michigan Liquor Control Commission imposed a $250 fine on the Sanford Eagles Club for having a "video poker" machine on its premises. The machine had five windows, and when a quarter was deposited, a playing card appeared in each window. Essentially, the contestant played a game of five-card draw against the machine. A "winner" could gain credits entitling the player to free replays based on a random "reshuffling" of the cards. After administrative and judicial hearings, the court of appeals held that the machine was not an illegal gaming device because there was no monetary payoff. The Michigan Supreme Court reversed. The court based its decision on a provision of the statute addressing gambling devices that exempted mechanical amusement devices that reward a player with replays as long as the device is not allowed to accumulate more than fourteen replays at one time. Because the video poker machine at issue in this case permitted the player to accumulate more than fourteen replays, it did not fall within the statutory exemption.

Automatic Music and Vending Corp. v. Liquor Control Comm., 396 N.W.2d 204 (Mich. 1986).

pinball operators were not in violation of the Ohio gambling statute. *Progress Vending, Inc. v. Department of Liquor Control,* 394 N.E.2d 324 (Ohio App. 1978).

Statutory Regulation of Gambling

A federal statute called the Travel Act, 18 U.S.C.A. § 1952, prohibits interstate travel in aid of gambling. The act is not aimed at local criminal activity; rather, its purpose is to attack crime that has a definite interstate aspect. *United States v. O'Dell,* 671 F.2d 191 (6th Cir. 1982).

Many states broadly proscribe gambling much the same as Florida law, which provides:

> Whoever plays or engages in any game at cards, keno, roulette, faro or other game of chance, at any place, by any device whatever, for money or other thing of value, shall be guilty of a misdemeanor of the second degree. West's Fla. Stat. Ann. § 849.08.

Typically, Florida law creates certain exemptions. Nonprofit organizations are permitted to conduct bingo games under strict regulations, section 849.0931, and charitable and nonprofit organizations are allowed to conduct certain drawings by chance, section 849.0935. Subject to specific restrictions, certain retail merchandising promotions with prizes awarded to persons selected by lot are permitted. Section 849.092. Another exception allows penny-ante card games with participants age eighteen or older provided that the games are conducted in a dwelling in which the winnings of any player in a single round or game do not exceed $10 in value. Section 849.085.

Where gambling is prohibited, states customarily make it unlawful to possess gambling devices and provide for their confiscation. See, for example, West's Fla. Stat. Ann. §§ 849.231, 849.232.

Prosecutorial Problems and Defenses

The problems encountered in enforcing prostitution and sexual laws are also obstacles to enforcing gambling statutes. Because of the consensual nature of gambling, apprehension of violators largely depends on the use of informants by police. Procedures for obtaining search and arrest warrants are technical and require close adherence to Fourth Amendment standards. The prosecution, of course, must prove all elements of the offense. In most instances, this requires proof of a consideration, a prize, and a chance; however, some statutes have eliminated the consideration requirement. If the statute prohibiting gambling makes intent an element of the offense, the prosecution must prove the defendant's intent; otherwise, it is sufficient merely to prove the act of gambling.

Texas law makes it an offense to bet on results of games, contests, political nominations, or elections or to play games with cards and dice. See Vernon's Tex. Penal Code Ann. § 47.02(a). The state legislature has taken a pragmatic approach by providing that it is a defense to prosecution under that section of the statute if

> (1) the actor engaged in gambling in a private place; (2) no person received any economic benefit other than personal winnings; and (3) except for the advantage of skill or luck, the risks of losing and the chances of winning were the same for all participants. Vernon's Tex. Penal Code Ann. § 47.02(b).

Section 47.02(c) provides that it is a defense to prosecution if the actor reasonably believed that the gambling conduct was permitted under bingo or a charitable raffle or occurred under a lottery approved by a parks and wilderness agency for determination of hunting privileges.

In some instances a defendant charged with gambling might succeed in establishing entrapment, a defense discussed in Chapter 14.

The Paradox of Gambling Laws

Go to the Scheb/ Scheb Criminal Law and Procedure 6e website at academic .cengage.com/criminaljustice/ scheb to find *U.S. v. Pinelli*, a federal appeals court decision dealing with gambling offenses.

The law on gambling seems paradoxical. Some laws authorize nonprofit organizations to conduct certain forms of gambling that are otherwise forbidden. In some states, people can legally bet at dog tracks and horse tracks yet may still be prosecuted for betting in their own homes on the World Series or the Kentucky Derby. Many reformers contend that present laws are ineffective to suppress gambling. Instead, they claim these laws actually lend support to the activities of organized crime.

Certain forms of legalized gambling, particularly state lotteries and state-franchised dog and horse tracks, have become increasingly acceptable. Yet unregulated forms of gambling will most likely continue to be prohibited in most instances. In any event, if inroads are to be made in controlling unregulated gambling, enforcement efforts must be directed primarily toward gambling activity that is under the control of organized crime syndicates.

Today, gambling via the Internet is widespread and very easily accessible. Because these Web sites tend to be hosted on servers located in foreign countries, prosecution of those who operate the sites is not possible. And, without the cooperation of those parties, it is very difficult to obtain the identities of persons in this country who use the sites. Thus, prosecutions for Internet-based gambling are extremely rare.

Animal Cruelty

Today there are a number of interest groups advocating the cause of "animal rights." Yet animals do not have rights as such under American law. Nevertheless they can be and in some instances are protected by law. As we will see in Chapter 11, there are laws today that protect certain animal species and their habitats. Such laws can be justified on the basis of the need to conserve wildlife and maintain a healthy natural environment. But every state today has laws protecting animals from unnecessary harm. For example, the Tennessee Code provides:

(a) A person commits an offense who intentionally or knowingly:

(1) Tortures, maims or grossly overworks an animal;

(2) Fails unreasonably to provide necessary food, water, care or shelter for an animal in the person's custody;

(3) Abandons unreasonably an animal in the person's custody;

(4) Transports or confines an animal in a cruel manner; or

(5) Inflicts burns, cuts, lacerations, or other injuries or pain, by any method, including blistering compounds, to the legs or hooves of horses in order to make them sore for any purpose including, but not limited to, competition in horse shows and similar events.

(b) It is a defense to prosecution under this section that the person was engaged in accepted veterinary practices, medical treatment by the owner or with the owner's consent, or bona fide experimentation for scientific research. T.C.A. § 39–14–202.

Violation of these cruelty to animals laws is a misdemeanor; however, a second or subsequent conviction for cruelty to animals is a felony.

Tennessee law also proscribes cockfighting, dog fighting, and other forms of animal fighting, T.C.A. § 39–14–203, as well as the intentional killing of animals belonging to other persons, except where necessary to protect oneself, T.C.A. § 39–14–205. There is also a statute governing offenses involving farm animals and animal research facilities. T.C.A. § 39–14–803. Tennessee law classifies all of these offenses as crimes against property, but these offenses can be committed against stray animals over which no one claims ownership. These offenses do not serve the goal of conservation of wildlife because they are most commonly committed against household pets, which are hardly endangered species. Clearly, these behaviors are prohibited because the great majority of Tennesseans, like people throughout the country, are repulsed by the wanton or unnecessary infliction of suffering on animals. As such, they are properly viewed as offenses against public morality. It is important to recognize that the notion of public morality embraces much more than puritanical strictures against vice. Rather, it encompasses the "evolving standards of decency that mark the progress of a maturing society." *Trop v. Dulles,* 356 U.S. 86, 101, 78 S.Ct. 590, 598, 2 L.Ed.2d 630, 642 (1958).

■ CONCLUSION

In addition to defining crimes against persons and property and establishing rules necessary to preserve public order, the law proscribes certain forms of conduct simply because they offend societal morality. Chief among these prohibitions are the laws prohibiting certain forms of sexual activity, public indecency, obscenity, profanity, and gambling. Offenses involving the use of alcohol and drugs, although sometimes categorized as offenses against public morality, can also be seen as threats to public order, safety, and peace. Thus, we have dealt with them in a separate chapter.

The prohibition of consensual sexual acts and of vices like pornography and gambling has its roots in Judeo-Christian morality. As our society has become more religiously diverse and our legal system more secularized, people have come to question whether the criminal law ought to be a vehicle for enforcing moral standards that originated from religious traditions. However, the courts have not rejected morality as a proper basis for the criminal law, even if that morality is rooted in a particular religious tradition. Clearly, the fact that a form of conduct was or is proscribed by one or more religious traditions is not a sufficient basis for criminalizing that activity. But if an act violates societal consensus, even if that consensus derives from religious traditions, it may be legitimately prohibited by the criminal law. As societal consensus changes—as it surely has with respect to sexual activities, pornography, and gambling—the prohibitions of the criminal law must, and do, change as well. Thus, the offenses against public morality constitute a particularly dynamic area of the criminal law.

■ KEY TERMS

public indecency, 194
vice crimes, 194
right of privacy, 196
fornication, 197
adultery, 197
seduction, 197
incest, 197
bigamy, 198
sodomy, 198
prostitution, 200
indecent exposure, 203

lewd and lascivious conduct, 203
voyeurism, 204
hard-core pornography, 206
prurient interest, 207
patently offensive, 207
child pornography, 211
profanity, 211
gambling, 214
lottery, 214
numbers racket, 214
consideration, prize, and chance, 214

■ WEB-BASED RESEARCH ACTIVITY

 Go to the Web. Locate your state's criminal statutes online. What forms of gambling are legal in your state? Using other resources available on the Internet, determine whether there are efforts underway in your state legislature to change the gambling laws in your state.

■ QUESTIONS FOR THOUGHT AND DISCUSSION

1. Assume you are a legislative assistant for a member of the state house of representatives. Your representative intends to introduce a bill to prohibit up-skirt videography in public shopping areas. She asks you to prepare a memo of suggested language for the bill. What suggestions would you offer to be included in the text of the bill?

2. Should it be a defense to a charge of bigamy that both persons in the alleged bigamous union are adherents to a religious faith that sanctions polygamy?

3. Do you think proponents of same-sex marriage can use the Supreme Court's decision in *Lawrence v. Texas* as a basis for constitutional assaults on state laws that prohibit such unions?

4. Would prostitution be more injurious or less injurious to the public health, welfare, and morality if it were legalized and regulated?

5. Is "mooning," a common adolescent prank, a form of indecent exposure in your state?

6. How are laws proscribing obscenity susceptible to the overbreadth and vagueness challenges discussed in Chapter 3?

7. Given the fact that there are millions of Internet users throughout the United States, is it appropriate for courts to apply the "contemporary community standards" test in making determinations concerning obscenity on the Internet?

8. Do you think Congress can devise a law that will pass constitutional muster to protect children from Internet pornography? What suggestions do you have in this area?

9. What, if any, constitutional objections could be raised against a city ordinance making it a criminal offense "to use profane language in a public place"?

10. What forms of gambling are legal and illegal in your state? Are there any particular games that fall into a gray area between permitted and prohibited activity? Is church bingo legal in your state?

■ PROBLEMS FOR DISCUSSION AND SOLUTION

1. Tanya Thong has been convicted of indecent exposure stemming from an incident in which she appeared topless on a public beach. On appeal, Thong argues that the indecent exposure statute amounts to unconstitutional sex discrimination because it prohibits women, but not men, from baring their breasts in public. Does Thong have a valid argument?

2. Gerald N. runs a video game arcade. One of his most popular games is called Video Blackjack. Essentially, the game is a computerized form of blackjack in which the contestant plays against the computer. The cost of playing the game is fifty cents. The contestant who wins the game is issued a token that can be used to play any other game in the arcade. Suppose your state gambling statute prohibits all "games involving valuable consideration, chance, and a possible prize." If you were the prosecutor, would you be concerned about the legality of this game?

CHAPTER 9

Alcohol and Drug Offenses

CHAPTER OUTLINE

Introduction

In this chapter we examine several offenses involving the misuse of alcohol and drugs. Because the English common law had little to say about the abuse of alcohol and nothing to say about illicit drugs, these offenses are based on relatively recent statutory enactments. These prohibitions reflect the modern awareness of the adverse social consequences of drug and alcohol abuse. Drug and alcohol offenses can be, and often are, classified as crimes against public morality. Others would argue that these offenses are really crimes against public health. Certainly, public intoxication is an offense against public order, and driving under the influence of alcohol or drugs is an offense against the public safety. Certain drug offenses, such as the production of methamphetamine in makeshift laboratories, can even be viewed as environmental crimes. Because alcohol and drug offenses are sufficiently distinctive in character and frequent in their occurrence, we place them in a category unto themselves.

Prohibition and Regulation of Alcoholic Beverages

Alcohol is the oldest and most widely abused drug known to mankind. There is evidence of alcohol consumption in Mesopotamia four thousand years before Christ. Nearly two thousand years B.C., the Code of Hammurabi regulated commercial establishments where alcoholic beverages were consumed. In Judeo-Christian culture, consumption of alcoholic beverages was tolerated, even encouraged, and wine took on a ceremonial importance in Judaism and a sacramental importance in Christianity. However, Judeo-Christian culture frowned upon drunkenness. Islam, which dates from the seventh century A.D., has from its inception prohibited the consumption of alcohol.

In England, the common law had little to say about alcohol, except that drunkenness was not regarded as a defense to a criminal prosecution (see Chapter 14). However, in 1603 an English court took the view that not only was intoxication no defense, it was a wrong in itself in the sense that it aggravated a crime committed. *Beverly's Case*, 4 Co. Rep. 125 (1603).

In colonial America, alcohol use was very widespread, the favorite libations being beer, ale, and rum. In 1619 the colony of Virginia passed the first law in America against public drunkenness. In 1697 New York adopted the first law requiring that drinking establishments be closed on Sundays. The sale of alcohol was prohibited altogether by the State of Georgia in 1735, but this early experiment in "prohibition" proved unsuccessful and was repealed after only seven years. The rise of evangelical Protestantism in the early nineteenth century led to the Temperance Movement, which condemned the use of alcohol, and by the mid-1800s, thirteen states had enacted laws prohibiting the sale of alcohol. The Civil War dealt a setback to the Prohibition Movement, but the movement was revitalized in the early twentieth century as women became politically active and acquired the right to vote.

"Prohibition"

In response to growing, but far from unanimous, public sentiment, Congress proposed the Eighteenth Amendment to the U.S. Constitution, which was ratified by the states in 1919. This amendment, widely referred to as "Prohibition," made unlawful the "manufacture, sale, or transportation of intoxicating liquors" within the United States. Prohibition actually began with the passage of the National Prohibition Act of 1920, 41 Stat. 305, better known as the Volstead Act. Section 3 of the Act provided:

> No person shall on or after the date when the Eighteenth Amendment to the Constitution of the United States goes into effect, manufacture, sell, barter, transport, import, export, deliver, furnish or possess any intoxicating liquor except as authorized in this act, and all the provisions of this act shall be liberally construed to the end that the use of intoxicating liquor as a beverage may be prevented.

Prohibition was widely violated and contributed greatly to the development of organized crime syndicates in this country. Rates of murder and other violent crimes rose dramatically during Prohibition and then declined steadily after Prohibition was repealed. Many commentators believe that Prohibition also weakened public respect for the law, the courts, and law enforcement agencies. Jury nullification, a phenomenon we discuss in Chapter 18, was common during Prohibition, as citizens were reluctant to convict people for doing something (albeit illegal) they did on a regular basis. By the beginning of the 1930s, public opinion demanded that Prohibition be repealed.

Ultimately, Prohibition was repealed by the Twenty-First Amendment, ratified in 1933. Under the Twenty-First Amendment, however, state and local governments retain the authority to ban or regulate the manufacture, sale, and use of alcohol within their borders. As the U.S. Supreme Court recognized in *California Retail Liquor Dealers Assn. v. Midcal Aluminum, Inc.*, 445 U.S. 97, 110, 100 S.Ct. 937, 946, 63 L.Ed.2d 233, 246 (1980), the "Twenty-First Amendment grants the States virtually complete control over whether to permit importation or sale of liquor and how to structure the liquor distribution system." Indeed, even though the sale of alcohol is widespread today, there are still a number of so-called "dry counties" throughout the United States, mainly in the South and Midwest, where the sale of all or some alcoholic beverages is prohibited. Although no state has chosen to ban the sale of alcohol altogether, all states regulate the sale and use of alcoholic beverages and retain a number of alcohol-related offenses.

Offenses Related to the Consumption of Alcohol by Minors

All states prohibit minors from purchasing, possessing, and consuming alcoholic beverages and also make it an offense for an adult to sell, serve, or otherwise provide alcohol to a minor. Such offenses are misdemeanors, but the recent trend is to punish these offenses severely. For example, Texas law makes furnishing alcohol to a minor a class A misdemeanor punishable by up to one year in jail and a fine of up to $4,000. Texas Alcoholic Beverages Code § 106.03(c). However, it is not a strict liability offense; an adult who furnishes alcohol to a minor is not guilty of a crime if the minor uses a plausible but false identification card to represent himself or herself as an adult. Texas Alcoholic Beverages Code §106.03(b).

Although states are free to set their own drinking ages, Congress has used its considerable fiscal power to induce states to raise the drinking age to twenty-one. Under a 1984 act, the Secretary of Transportation is required to withhold a percentage of a state's otherwise allocable federal highway funds if the state does not establish a minimum age of twenty-one for "the purchase or public possession" of alcoholic beverages. 23 U.S.C.A. § 158. The act has effectively established twenty-one as the minimum age for drinking. In *South Dakota v. Dole*, 483 U.S. 203, 107 S.Ct. 2793, 97 L.Ed.2d 171 (1987), the Supreme Court upheld this measure as a valid exercise of congressional spending power.

Go to the Scheb/ Scheb Criminal Law and Procedure 6e website at academic .cengage.com/criminaljustice/ scheb for an edited version of *South Dakota v. Dole*.

Public Intoxication

Laws and ordinances making **public drunkenness** an offense have long been enforced by all jurisdictions, with most states and municipalities simply providing that whoever shall become intoxicated from the voluntary use of intoxicating liquors shall be punished. The offense merely involves a person being found in a public place in a state of intoxication. This offense is usually classified as a minor misdemeanor. A common police practice has been to take offenders into custody and release them once they have "sobered up," a practice sometimes described as a "revolving door." In a great many cases, people who are repeatedly arrested for public intoxication suffer from alcoholism and are in need of treatment. For such individuals, the application of a criminal sanction is not likely to curb their unlawful behavior.

There is a growing awareness that alcoholism is a disease, and many have argued that the criminal law is an inappropriate mechanism to deal with it. In addition, some reformers have contended that criminalizing the public presence of an intoxicated person is contrary to the Eighth Amendment's prohibition of cruel and unusual punishments. However, the Supreme Court has declined to accept such a view. Instead, in *Powell v. Texas,* 392 U.S. 514, 88 S.Ct. 2145, 20 L.Ed.2d 1254 (1968), the Court upheld a public intoxication law. In effect, the Court ruled that the defendant, Powell, was not being punished for his status as an alcoholic but rather for his presence in a public place in an inebriated condition.

Go to the Scheb/ Scheb Criminal Law and Procedure 6e website at academic .cengage.com/criminaljustice/ scheb for an edited version of *Powell v. Texas.*

In recent years, some states have enacted statutes directing police officers to take persons found intoxicated in public places to treatment facilities rather than to incarcerate them. Consistent with this approach, many statutes now criminalize only **disorderly intoxication.** This newer offense involves the offender's being intoxicated in a public place or on a public conveyance and endangering the safety of others, not merely being in a state of intoxication in public. See, for example, Tex. Penal Code § 49.02. In 1992 a Texas appellate court ruled that a police officer had sufficient probable cause for a warrantless arrest for public intoxication. The officer believed that the defendant could have fled from the scene, posing a danger to himself and others. Witnesses testified that the defendant ran into a parked car while intoxicated. *Segura v. State,* 826 S.W.2d 178 (Tex. App. 1992).

Driving under the Influence

The carnage on the American highways attests to the urgent need for states to take stern measures to keep drunk drivers off the road, and all states have enacted laws attempting to accomplish this goal. Perhaps these measures contributed to the decline from over 1.5 million arrests for driving while under the influence of intoxicants in 1985 to approximately 871,000 in 2000, a decrease of 41 percent (U.S. Department of Justice, Bureau of Justice Statistics, *Sourcebook of Criminal Justice Statistics 2001,* p. 358).

The "classical" offense in this area is **driving while intoxicated (DWI)** or, more accurately, operating a motor vehicle while intoxicated. In the 1950s the laws in many states stipulated that a level of 0.15 percent or more alcohol in the bloodstream evidenced intoxication. In the 1960s and 1970s, many jurisdictions expanded the offense to prohibit **driving under the influence (DUI)** of intoxicating liquors or drugs. DWI and DUI laws sometimes allowed a defendant to avoid conviction because of the ambiguity of his or her subjective behavior. In response to this problem, most states have modified their statutes to prohibit **driving with an unlawful blood-alcohol level (DUBAL).** For many years most states defined "an unlawful blood-alcohol level" as 0.10 percent or more alcohol in the bloodstream. Today, as a result of federal fiscal incentives, all fifty states have lowered the prohibited blood-alcohol level to 0.08 percent. Moreover, most states now impose harsher penalties on DUBAL offenders whose blood-alcohol levels are especially high, typically defined as 0.15 to 0.20 percent.

Most states now require mandatory minimum jail terms (usually 24 or 48 hours) for first-time DWI, DUI, or DUBAL offenders. Jail terms increase with subsequent offenses. Other penalties include monetary fines, suspension or revocation of driving privileges, and alcohol education or treatment programs. In several states, repeat offenders may have their vehicles confiscated. A number of states allow judges to require repeat offenders to install devices that measure the driver's blood-alcohol level before the vehicle can be started.

Zero Tolerance for Juveniles

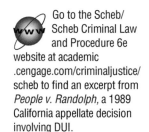

Go to the Scheb/ Scheb Criminal Law and Procedure 6e website at academic .cengage.com/criminaljustice/ scheb to find an excerpt from *People v. Randolph,* a 1989 California appellate decision involving DUI.

In 1996 Kentucky enacted a **zero tolerance law,** also known as the juvenile DUI law, which makes it an offense for a person under age twenty-one to drive with a blood-alcohol content of 0.02 percent or higher. In *Commonwealth v. Howard,* 969 S.W.2d 700 (Ky. 1998), the Kentucky Supreme Court upheld the law as being rationally related to a legitimate legislative purpose of reducing teenage traffic fatalities and protecting all members of the public. Therefore, the court held that it does not violate the equal protection rights of those who are prosecuted. By 2003, all fifty states had followed Kentucky's lead in establishing a lower permissible blood-alcohol level for juveniles (in most states, 0.02 percent).

Prosecution of DWI, DUI, and DUBAL Charges

To obtain a conviction for DWI, DUI, or DUBAL, the prosecution must first establish that the defendant charged with driving while intoxicated or driving under the influence was operating the vehicle. This may be accomplished by either eyewitness testimony or circumstantial evidence. In *State v. Harrison,* 846 P.2d 1082 (N.M. App. 1992), the court reviewed a DUI conviction where the defendant's only contention was that the prosecution failed to prove he was driving a vehicle. Evidence at the defendant's trial revealed that he was found asleep behind the steering wheel of his car parked on the roadway with the key in the ignition, the motor running, and the transmission in drive. The court determined that this evidence established that the defendant was in actual physical control of the vehicle and therefore was sufficient to prove that the defendant was driving the automobile.

Next, the prosecution must establish the intoxication. Statutes, it should be noted, often refer to intoxication occurring as a result of alcohol or from ingestion of **contraband** substances. Intoxication is often a difficult state to articulate. Therefore, in addition to frequently offering evidence of a defendant's blood and urine alcohol content, law enforcement officers who observed the defendant are permitted to testify as to the defendant's appearance, speech, or conduct and whether the officer detected the odor of an alcoholic beverage on the defendant's person. These factors are relevant evidence of the defendant's mental and physical impairment.

In *Berkemer v. McCarty,* 468 U.S. 420, 104 S.Ct. 3138, 82 L.Ed.2d 317 (1984), the U.S. Supreme Court held that an officer's roadside questioning and administration of a **field sobriety test** to an individual stopped for irregular driving was not a "custodial interrogation" that required giving the suspect the *Miranda* warnings. However, the Court cautioned that the *Miranda* warnings apply once the suspect is under arrest. (For more discussion of field sobriety tests, see Chapter 16.)

Evidence indicates that field sobriety tests can be somewhat unreliable, and courts are beginning to scrutinize cases that rely solely on field sobriety tests without supporting chemical testing of the blood, urine, or breath of the suspect. Still, most courts permit persons to be convicted of DUI without chemical tests, especially when multiple sobriety tests have been performed by more than one officer.

Increasingly, police videotape suspects' performance on field sobriety tests and make audiotape recordings of suspects' speech. Many police agencies today have mobile blood-alcohol testing units ("Batmobiles") equipped with **breathalyzer** testing machines, videotape equipment, and voice recorders. These vans, available at the call of the arresting officer, give the police the opportunity to promptly collect evidence at or near the scene of the arrest.

One of the most sophisticated methods of alcohol detection is measuring the grams of alcohol in a volume of breath by use of a spectrophotometer, which measures the absorption of infrared light by a sample of a gas. The sampled gas is human breath, and the absorption of infrared light by a sample of the gas is affected by the concentration of alcohol in the gas. A formula can be used to determine the concentration of alcohol. An instrument called the Intoxilyzer 5000 is increasingly used to perform this calculation electronically and provide a printout of the results.

Although generally regarded as superior to field sobriety tests from an evidentiary standpoint, chemical tests are not devoid of problems. We mention some of these problems in the following topic. Ideally, to obtain a conviction, a prosecutor would like to have evidence that the defendant was driving abnormally, smelled of alcohol, exhibited slurred speech, failed a battery of field sobriety tests administered by several officers, and registered an impermissibly high blood-alcohol level on one or more chemical tests performed by a trained technician. Of course, in the real world of law enforcement, such thorough evidence is seldom obtained.

DEFENSE OF DWI, DUI, AND DUBAL CHARGES

Historically, counsel who represent a defendant charged with DWI, DUI, or DUBAL have challenged the methodology of an officer's administration of field sobriety tests, particularly where the defendant suffers from any physical impairment or has been taking medication that might make it difficult to perform these tests. Today defense counsel must have a basic knowledge of scientific evidence and be prepared to also challenge the reliability and validity of chemical testing equipment and the operator's level of competence. Counsel often challenge the results of breath tests made by such machines as the Intoxilyzer 5000, referred to above. They present expert testimony challenging the chemicals that breath machines measure and offer evidence of a defendant's illnesses and the medications a defendant was taking at the time of the tests.

States have administrative rules that specify the procedure to be followed in administering a breath test. Defense counsel often seeks to suppress the results of Intoxilyzer tests on grounds that the prosecution has not established a proper predicate for their admissibility. For example, in *Davis v. State,* 712 So.2d 1115 (Ala. Crim. App. 1997), the defense objected to the introduction of the results of the Intoxilyzer tests on the ground that it was not properly calibrated at the time the blood-alcohol test was performed. The trial court denied the motion. On appeal, the Alabama Criminal Appeals Court agreed with the defense. The court held there was no evidence the equipment used to perform the tests had been inspected as required by rules of the Alabama Department of Forensics.

State administrative rules usually require an observation period before administering a breath test to ensure that no substance enters the defendant's mouth that might affect the validity of the test results. For example, an Illinois administrative rule governing alcohol breath tests stipulated that the test was valid only if the driver did not regurgitate within an observation period of 20 minutes before the test. In *People v. Bonutti*, 817 N.E.2d 489 (2004), defense counsel had objected to the introduction of the tests, asserting what has become known as the "acid reflux defense." The Illinois Supreme Court reversed the lower court's ruling and suppressed the results of the breath alcohol test because the evidence revealed the defendant suffered an acid reflux episode while waiting to take the breath test.

Implied Consent Statutes

Go to the Scheb/ Scheb Criminal Law and Procedure 6e website at academic .cengage.com/criminaljustice/ scheb for an edited version of *Mackey v. Montrym*.

To facilitate chemical testing in DWI, DUI, and DUBAL cases, California and most other jurisdictions have enacted **implied consent statutes.** Under these laws, a person who drives a motor vehicle is deemed to have given consent to a urine test for drugs and to blood, breath, or urine testing to determine blood-alcohol content. The testing is made incident to a lawful arrest of a driver. See, for example, West's Ann. Cal. Vehicle Code § 23157. In most instances, refusal to submit to the tests required by an implied consent law will result in an administrative suspension of licensing privileges. The Supreme Court has upheld the validity of the Massachusetts implied consent law providing for suspension of the driver's license of a person who refuses to take a breathalyzer test. *Mackey v. Montrym*, 443 U.S. 1, 99 S.Ct. 2612, 61 L.Ed.2d 321 (1979).

Origins of the Prohibition of Drugs

Though not as widespread as alcohol, drugs like marijuana and opium have been used by people in various parts of the world for thousands of years. The indigenous peoples of South America knew of the stimulating properties of coca leaves, although cocaine was not invented until the nineteenth century. In that century, cocaine and opium derivatives were widely used by Americans with no legal prohibitions or regulations. Opium derivatives were routinely used to treat diarrhea, sleeplessness, and anxiety. In 1875, the City of San Francisco prohibited the smoking of opium, a common practice among Chinese immigrants. But the city did not criminalize other means of ingesting opium that were popular among white citizens, such as the liquid preparation laudanum. As the twentieth century dawned, Americans were becoming more aware of the addictive nature of narcotics, and people began to call for governmental restrictions on such products.

The Harrison Act

The Harrison Act of 1914, 38 Stat. 785, was the first attempt by the federal government to regulate the sale and use of opium and cocaine. Ostensibly a revenue measure, the act was styled "An Act To provide for the registration of, with collectors of internal revenue, and to impose a special tax on all persons who produce, import, manufacture, compound, deal in, dispense, sell, distribute, or give away opium or coca leaves, their salts, derivatives, or preparations, and for other purposes." However, the act levied criminal penalties on those who distributed cocaine or opium and failed to register and pay the requisite taxes. Although the act allowed doctors to prescribe cocaine and opiates for legitimate medical reasons, it criminalized their prescription merely to satisfy the cravings of addicts. The Supreme Court upheld the Harrison Act against the challenge that it was not a valid revenue measure and usurped the police powers of the states. *United States v. Doremus,* 249 U.S. 86, 39 S.Ct. 214, 63 L.Ed. 493 (1919). In the wake of the Harrison Act, state legislatures enacted statutes criminalizing the sale and possession of opiates and cocaine. By the 1930s, these prohibitions were nearly universal among the states. During this period, rates of cocaine and opium use declined, but the country also saw the emergence of an underground drug economy that persists to this day.

Prohibition of Marijuana

Marijuana or hemp, which has been used in parts of the world for thousands of years, was widely cultivated in the United States in the nineteenth century. Used primarily as a source of fiber for making rope, marijuana was also used as medicine, both for people and animals. Smoking marijuana for "recreational" purposes was not widespread in the United States until the early twentieth century, when an influx of immigrants from Mexico brought the practice to this country. During Prohibition, many people turned to marijuana as a cheap and legal alternative to alcohol. After Prohibition was repealed in 1933, federal and state authorities turned their attention to marijuana.

Harry Anslinger, who headed the Federal Bureau of Narcotics, led a successful crusade to criminalize marijuana. By 1937, forty-six of the forty-eight states had banned the cultivation, sale, possession, and use of the cannabis plant. Marijuana use declined dramatically during the 1940s and 1950s, at least partly due to the new criminal prohibitions, but rose again in the 1960s.

The Marihuana Tax Act of 1937 was the federal government's first attempt to control marijuana. Not a direct prohibition, the act criminalized the failure to pay a tax on the transfer of cannabis. Of course, compliance with the law exposed a person to criminal prosecution under state laws, which is why the U.S. Supreme Court declared the statute unconstitutional in 1969. Writing for the Court in a case involving Dr. Timothy Leary, an icon of the counterculture of the 1960s, Justice John M. Harlan observed that "the Marihuana Tax Act compelled petitioner to expose himself to a 'real and appreciable' risk of self-incrimination." *Leary v. United States,* 395 U.S. 6, 16, 89 S.Ct. 1532, 1537, 23 L.Ed.2d 57, 70 (1969).

 Go to the Scheb/ Scheb Criminal Law and Procedure 6e website at academic .cengage.com/criminaljustice/ scheb for an edited version of *Leary v. U.S.*

Modern Drug Laws

In the 1960s, the United States saw a resurgence of illicit drug use. Whereas illegal drug use had previously been concentrated in big cities, among ethnic minorities, and among the lower socioeconomic strata, in the 1960s drug use proliferated within the middle-class white population, especially young people. During the 1960s marijuana use increased dramatically and new hallucinogenic drugs like LSD came on the scene. The use of such drugs was encouraged by a "counterculture" movement that eschewed middle-class conventions and encouraged young people to experiment with alternative lifestyles.

Responding to concern over the rise in drug use, Congress enacted the Comprehensive Drug Abuse Prevention and Control Act of 1970. 21 U.S.C.A. § 801 *et seq.* The act, commonly referred to as the **Controlled Substances Act,** establishes the criteria for classification of substances and lists controlled substances according to their potential for abuse. Offenses involving the manufacture, sale, distribution, and possession with intent to distribute are defined and the penalties are prescribed in

21 U.S.C.A. § 841. Penalties for simple possession of controlled substances are prescribed in 21 U.S.C.A. § 844. Provision is made in 21 U.S.C.A. § 823 for registered practitioners to dispense narcotics for approved purposes.

Modern State Drug Laws

In 1972 the Uniform Controlled Substances Act was drafted by the Commission on Uniform Laws, whose purpose was to achieve uniformity among state and federal laws. There are three versions of the Uniform Controlled Substances Act: 1970, 1990, and 1994. Provisions within each version are similar. All fifty states and the Virgin Islands have adopted one of the three versions. Like the federal statute, the uniform act classifies controlled substances according to their potential for abuse (see Table 9.1). For example, opiates are included in Schedule I because they are unsafe for use even under medical treatment, whereas Schedule II includes drugs that have a high potential for abuse but may be medically acceptable under certain conditions. The remaining schedules include controlled substances that have lesser potential for abuse and dependency. The range of controlled substances includes such well-known drugs as cocaine, amphetamines, tranquilizers, and barbiturates.

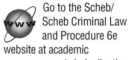 Go to the Scheb/ Scheb Criminal Law and Procedure 6e website at academic .cengage.com/criminaljustice/ scheb for an edited version of *Robinson v. California*.

All states make the manufacture, sale, and possession of **controlled substances** illegal. Offenses involving drugs that have a high potential for abuse (for example, heroin and cocaine) are usually very serious felonies. Although it is constitutionally permissible to enact such laws, the U.S. Supreme Court has ruled that states may not criminalize the mere status of being addicted to such drugs. *Robinson v. California*, 370 U.S. 660, 82 S.Ct. 1417, 8 L.Ed.2d 758 (1962).

Table 9.1	Schedule of Controlled Substances under Tennessee Law	
Schedule I	High potential for abuse; no accepted medical use in treatment or lacks accepted safety for use in treatment under medical supervision.	This includes certain opiates (e.g., heroin); hallucinogens (e.g., LSD); depressants (e.g., methaqualone); and stimulants (e.g., MDMA).
Schedule II	High potential for abuse; has currently accepted medical use in treatment, or currently accepted medical use with severe restrictions; abuse of the substance may lead to severe psychic or physical dependence.	Examples: Cocaine, morphine, amphetamines, amobarbital.
Schedule III	Potential for abuse less than the substances listed in Schedules I and II; has currently accepted medical use in treatment; and may lead to moderate or low physical dependence or high psychological dependence.	Examples: Anabolic steroids.
Schedule IV	Low potential for abuse relative to substances in Schedule III; has currently accepted medical use in treatment; and may lead to limited physical dependence or psychological dependence relative to the substances in Schedule III.	Example: Phenobarbital.
Schedule V	Low potential for abuse relative to the controlled substances listed in Schedule IV; has currently accepted medical use in treatment in the United States; and has limited physical dependence or psychological dependence liability relative to the controlled substances listed in Schedule IV.	Example: A medicine containing not more than two hundred (200) milligrams of codeine per one hundred (100) grams.
Schedule VI	Tetrahydrocannabinols.	Marijuana; hashish; synthetic equivalents.
Schedule VII	Butyl nitrite and any isomer thereof.	

Source: Tennessee Drug Control Act of 1989, T.C.A. § 39–17–401 *et seq.*

The following California statute is fairly typical of state drug laws:

(a) Except as otherwise provided in this division, every person who transports, imports into this state, sells, furnishes, administers, or gives away, or offers to transport, import into this state, sell, furnish, administer, or give away … any controlled substance … shall be punished by imprisonment in the state prison for three, four, or five years. West's Ann. Cal. Codes, Health and Safety Code, § 11352(a) (1989).

Offenses involving the mere possession of less harmful substances are often classified as lesser-degree felonies or, where a very small quantity of marijuana is involved, are frequently classified as misdemeanors. In Nebraska, for example, possession of more than one ounce but less than one pound of marijuana is a misdemeanor, see Rev. Stat. Neb. § 28–416 (11); however, possession of more than one pound is a felony. Rev. Stat. Neb. § 28–416 (12). During the 1970s several states decriminalized their anti-marijuana laws by removing the threat of a jail sentence for possession offenses. In Nebraska, possession of less than one ounce of marijuana is considered an "infraction" for which a first-time offender may be fined no more than one hundred dollars and made to attend a drug education course. Rev. Stat. Neb. § 28–416 (13)(a).

The Marijuana Controversy

Marijuana violations lead to nearly half of all drug arrests in the United States. Of the 1,586,902 drug arrests in the United States during 2001, 5.2 percent were for marijuana sales or manufacturing and 40.4 percent were for marijuana possession. Federal Bureau of Investigation, *Crime in the United States 2001,* October 2002. In 2001, the National Household Survey on Drug Abuse estimated that 37 percent of Americans aged twelve and over had tried marijuana at least once and that approximately 5 percent are frequent users of the drug.

Despite aggressive law enforcement, marijuana remains widely available and exemplifies the difficulty of enforcing a law that has less-than-universal public support. Nevertheless, courts have generally declined to reassess legislative judgments in this area, and statutes making it a criminal offense to possess marijuana have withstood numerous constitutional challenges. For example, in *State v. Smith,* 610 P.2d 869 (Wash. 1980), the Supreme Court of Washington held that criminal penalties for possession of marijuana did not violate the constitutional prohibition against cruel and unusual punishments. More recently, in *State v. Harland,* 556 So.2d 256 (La. App. 1990), a Louisiana appellate court rejected the contention that such penalties violated a state constitutional provision protecting the right of privacy.

Perhaps the most notable court ruling dealing with marijuana use is an Alaska Supreme Court decision in 1975. In *Ravin v. State,* 537 P.2d 494 (Alaska 1975), the court held that the explicit right to privacy contained in the Alaska state constitution protects the possession and personal use of marijuana by an adult in the home. In interpreting the right to privacy under the Alaska Constitution, the court took note of the individualistic nature of Alaska's political culture. The court concluded that, given the relatively innocuous nature of marijuana, the state had an insufficient basis for criminalizing its use in the home. The court recognized that the distribution of marijuana could still be criminalized.

Responding to the *Ravin* decision, the Alaska legislature in 1982 decriminalized the possession by an adult of up to four ounces of marijuana for personal use. However, in 1990 Alaska voters approved a ballot initiative that stated:

Under Alaska law it is currently legal for adults over 18 years old to possess under four ounces of marijuana in a home or other private place. The penalty for adults over 18 years old for possessing less than one ounce in public is a fine of up to $100. This

Go to the Scheb/ Scheb Criminal Law and Procedure 6e website at academic .cengage.com/criminaljustice/ scheb for an edited version of *Ravin v. State.*

initiative would change Alaska's laws by making all such possession of marijuana criminal, with possible penalties of up to 90 days in jail and/or up to a $1000 fine.

In *Noy v. State*, 83 P.3d 545 (Alaska App. 2003), the Alaska Court of Appeals struck down the statute adopted by voter initiative in 1990. The court noted that the voters are bound, as is the legislature, to respect the provisions of the state constitution as interpreted by the state's highest court. The court determined that the legislature had acted properly in its 1982 enactment decriminalizing possession of up to four ounces of marijuana for personal use. Unless and until the Alaska Supreme Court says otherwise, or the people of Alaska amend their state constitution, Alaskans have a constitutional right to possess up to four ounces of cannabis in one's home for personal use. As noted in *State v. Crocker*, 97 P.3d 93, 95 (Alaska App. 2004), "Not all marijuana possession is a crime in Alaska. Under *Ravin* and *Noy*, an adult may possess any amount of marijuana less than four ounces in their home, if their possession is for personal use."

Go to the Scheb/ Scheb Criminal Law and Procedure 6e website at academic .cengage.com/criminaljustice/ scheb for an edited version of *Noy v. State*.

MARIJUANA FOR MEDICINAL USE

As we noted earlier in the chapter, marijuana was sometimes used in the nineteenth century for medicinal purposes. Today, there is a growing demand that marijuana be made legal for medical use, especially for the relief of nausea experienced by persons undergoing chemotherapy for cancer or acquired immunodeficiency syndrome (AIDS). In 1991 a Florida appellate court permitted a husband and wife suffering from AIDS to assert a medical necessity defense (see Chapter 14) in a marijuana possession case. *Jenks v. State*, 582 So.2d 676 (Fla. App. 1991). That decision and similar decisions in other states helped give rise to a national movement to legalize marijuana for medicinal use.

Since 1996, medical marijuana ballot initiatives have received a majority of votes in Alaska, Arizona, California, Colorado, the District of Columbia, Nevada, Oregon, and Washington state. Opponents of medical marijuana initiatives claim that they are a cleverly disguised first step toward drug legalization rather than a genuine effort to alleviate suffering due to cancer or AIDS.

Go to the Scheb/ Scheb Criminal Law and Procedure 6e website at academic .cengage.com/criminaljustice/ scheb for an edited version of the *Oakland Cannabis Buyers' Cooperative* decision.

The federal authorities have thus far taken the position that marijuana has no legitimate medical use. In *United States v. Oakland Cannabis Buyers' Cooperative*, 532 U.S. 483, 121 S.Ct. 1711, 149 L.Ed.2d 722 (2001), the Court refused to recognize a "medical necessity exception" to the Controlled Substances Act. As yet, Congress has not amended the act to create a medical necessity exception.

The legalization of marijuana for medical use creates a conflict between state and federal law. As we noted in Chapter 3, in *Gonzales v. Raich*, 545 U.S. 1, 125 S.Ct. 2195, 162 L.Ed.2d 1 (2005), the Supreme Court held that Congress does have the power under the Commerce Clause to prohibit the mere possession of small quantities of marijuana, even if it is solely for personal medicinal use authorized by state law. Thus, a person using marijuana with a doctor's prescription pursuant to a state "compassionate use" statute is still subject to arrest and prosecution by federal authorities, although it is safe to say that the enforcement of the marijuana prohibition against such individuals is not a high priority for federal prosecutors or law enforcement agencies.

The Crystal Meth Crisis

In the 1980s, cocaine (especially "crack") emerged as the leading drug problem in this country. Today, law enforcement agencies are confronting a new epidemic—that of homemade methamphetamines. Also known as "crystal meth" or "crank," this powerful stimulant can be easily made by amateur chemists with products readily available in the marketplace. However, the making of the drug is itself extremely dangerous, as it involves highly volatile, explosive, and noxious chemicals. The process also produces highly toxic by-products that, when disposed of, present a serious threat to the natural environment. Meth labs tend to be located in rural areas where they can operate without detection. Often the authorities become aware of them only after a fire, explosion or serious environmental contamination has occurred. In a statement before a subcommittee of the U.S. House of Representatives Appropriations Committee on April 6, 2006, Drug Enforcement Administration Administrator Karen P. Tandy claimed that in fiscal year 2005, the DEA "spent an estimated $176 million to combat methamphetamine, including $18.8 million to administer 8,897 clandestine laboratory cleanups."

Prosecutors have begun to take a new and dramatic approach to the meth lab problem. They have begun to charge operators of labs with environmental crimes (see Chapter 11) as well as drug crimes. A Watauga County, North Carolina, prosecutor made national news in 2003 when he announced that he would charge meth lab operators with violating a recent statute aimed at the use of chemical weapons by terrorists. The law, adopted after the terrorist attacks of September 11, 2001, defines as a chemical weapon of mass destruction "any substance that is designed or has the capability to cause death or serious injury and … is or contains toxic or poisonous chemicals or their immediate precursors." Critics argued out that the legislature did not intend for the statute to be used in the war on drugs. The prosecutor, Jerry Wilson, defended his novel approach saying, "Not only is the drug methamphetamine in itself a threat to both society and those using it, but the toxic compounds and deadly gases created as side products are also real threats. I feel that, as a prosecutor, I have to address this. Something has to be done to protect society."

THE COMBAT METHAMPHETAMINE EPIDEMIC ACT

In 2005, Congress passed an important measure to address the crystal meth crisis. In addition to increasing penalties for smuggling and selling methamphetamine, the Combat Methamphetamine Epidemic Act of 2005, now codified at 21 U.S.C.A. § 865, is designed to make it more difficult to acquire the precursor chemicals used to make meth. The new law limits purchases of ephedrine, pseudoephedrine, and phenylpropanolamine, which are commonly found in over-the-counter cold and sinus products as well as appetite suppressants. The law requires stores to keep products containing these ingredients behind the counter or in locked display cases. Vendors are prohibited from selling more than 3.6 grams per day or 9 grams per month of these chemicals to any customer, regardless of the number of transactions. Of course, those who are intent on acquiring large quantities of these products can go from store to store. That is why vendors are required to keep a log book in which they record the names and addresses of purchasers, who must show valid identification in order to purchase the regulated products. These log books must be made available on demand to state and federal authorities investigating meth production.

Prohibition of Drug Paraphernalia

Possession of **drug paraphernalia** is also commonly a criminal offense under many state laws and local ordinances. For example, Missouri law provides:

1. It is unlawful for any person to deliver, possess with intent to deliver, or manufacture, with intent to deliver, drug paraphernalia, knowing, or under circumstances where one reasonably should know, that it will be used to plant, propagate, cultivate, grow, harvest, manufacture, compound, convert, produce, process, prepare, test,

analyze, pack, repack, store, contain, conceal, inject, ingest, inhale, or otherwise introduce into the human body a controlled substance or an imitation controlled substance in violation of sections 195.005 to 195.425.

2. Possession of more than twenty-four grams of any methamphetamine precursor drug or combination of methamphetamine precursor drugs shall be prima facie evidence of intent to violate this section. This subsection shall not apply to any practitioner or to any product possessed in the course of a legitimate business.

3. A person who violates this section is guilty of a class D felony. V.A.M.S. 195.235.

Under federal law, it is a crime to import, export, sell, offer for sale, or use the mails to transport any drug paraphernalia. 21 U.S.C.A. § 863(a). Violation of this prohibition is punishable by a fine and imprisonment up to three years. 21 U.S.C.A. § 863(b). Federal law defines drug paraphernalia to include "any equipment, product, or material of any kind which is primarily intended or designed for use in manufacturing, compounding, converting, concealing, producing, processing, preparing, injecting, ingesting, inhaling, or otherwise introducing into the human body a controlled substance, possession of which is unlawful under this subchapter." 21 U.S.C.A. § 863(d). Under federal law, drug paraphernalia is subject to confiscation. 21 U.S.C.A. § 863(c). In *United States v. Janus Industries*, 48 F.3d 1548 (10th Cir. 1995), a federal appeals court upheld the federal prohibitions and penalties associated with drug paraphernalia.

Problems of Drug Enforcement and Prosecution

Federal and state laws on controlled substances mirror one another in many respects. Federal enforcement is usually directed against major interstate or international drug traffickers; states usually concentrate on those who possess or distribute controlled substances. Many drug-trafficking violations of federal law involve prosecution for conspiracy. Unlike many state laws, the federal law on conspiracy to violate the Controlled Substances Act does not require proof of an overt act. 21 U.S.C.A. § 846; *United States v. Pulido,* 69 F.3d 192 (7th Cir. 1995); *United States v. Wilson,* 657 F.2d 755 (5th Cir. 1981).

Because those involved in narcotics transactions are usually willing participants, enforcement often depends on the use of confidential informants by police. Obtaining search warrants and making arrests based on probable cause often present difficult Fourth Amendment problems (see Chapter 15).

The level of intent that the prosecution must establish in contraband cases can vary according to the particular statutory offense (see Chapter 4). However, courts have generally held that statutes making possession, distribution, or trafficking of contraband unlawful require the prosecution to prove only the defendant's general intent. See, for example, *State v. Williams,* 352 So.2d 1295 (La. 1977) (Intent established by mere proof of voluntary distribution); *State v. Bender,* 579 P.2d 796 (N.M. 1978).

Actual and Constructive Possession

In drug possession cases, a critical problem is proving that the defendant was in possession of a controlled substance. The prosecution may prove either actual or constructive possession of contraband to satisfy the possession requirement. Proof of actual possession is established by evidence that the contraband was found on the accused's person or that the accused was in exclusive possession of the premises or vehicle where the contraband was discovered. Where the accused is not in actual possession, however, or where the accused and another person jointly occupy a dwelling or automobile where contraband is discovered, the prosecution must attempt to prove what the law calls constructive possession.

A person has constructive possession of contraband if he or she has ownership, dominion, or control over the contraband itself or over the premises in which it is concealed. *United States v. Schubel,* 912 F.2d 952 (8th Cir. 1990). The prosecution usually attempts to establish constructive possession by evidence of incriminating statements and circumstances from which the defendant's ability to control the contraband may be inferred. This can pose a formidable difficulty.

In *State v. Somerville,* 572 A.2d 944 (Conn. 1990), the defendant appealed his conviction for possession of cocaine with intent to sell sixty-nine vials of crack cocaine. He argued that no evidence was presented at his trial to establish that he possessed the drugs in question. He pointed to the fact that no drugs and no large sums of money were found on his person. The evidence revealed that the police found the sixty-nine vials of cocaine underneath a garbage can at the defendant's neighbor's house. Witnesses had seen the defendant selling crack cocaine in small vials before his arrest. They testified that he had been stooping near the garbage can under which the police found the vials of cocaine. The Connecticut Supreme Court rejected the defendant's contention and found the evidence sufficient to establish that the defendant had dominion and control over the cocaine and had knowledge of the character of the contraband and its presence.

 Go to the Scheb/ Scheb Criminal Law and Procedure 6e website at academic .cengage.com/criminaljustice/ scheb to find *Embry v. State* (1990), where the Arkansas Supreme Court considers the sufficiency of the evidence to support the convictions of two individuals for possession of illegal drugs with intent to deliver.

PROOF OF INTENT TO SELL OR DISTRIBUTE DRUGS

Intent to distribute controlled substances may be proved by either direct or circumstantial evidence. It may be inferred from the presence of equipment to weigh and measure narcotics and paraphernalia used to aid in their distribution. Large sums of

Constructive Possession of Drugs

CASE-IN-POINT

After Minneapolis police obtained a tip that crack cocaine was being sold out of cars parked in front of a certain duplex, an officer observed a blue Cadillac parked in front of the building. A female later identified as the defendant, Nina Knox, made several trips between the car and the duplex. At one point she drove the car from the scene but returned shortly and sat in the car for a period of time as a number of men approached the car and walked away after brief encounters. The officer, who was experienced in dealing with drug offenses, believed the activities he witnessed to be drug transactions, although he was unable to observe money and drugs being exchanged. Knox was arrested, and a search of the car produced 14.3 grams of crack cocaine and $2,200 in cash. A search of Knox's purse produced a large amount of money and food stamps. Knox was convicted in federal court of possession with intent to distribute a controlled substance.

On appeal, Knox argued that the evidence failed to establish that she was in physical control of the cocaine and was intending to sell it. The U.S. Court of Appeals rejected Knox's contention, concluding that the evidence supported a finding that Knox had exercised "dominion over the premises in which the contraband [was] concealed" since she was observed driving the car, sitting in the car, and entering it on several occasions. The court further concluded that intent to distribute could be inferred from the fact that sizable amounts of cash and cocaine were found at the scene. Knox's conviction was affirmed.

United States v. Knox, 888 F.2d 585 (8th Cir. 1989).

cash and narcotics are common indicia of circumstantial evidence of intent to distribute illegal drugs. See, for example, *United States v. Brett,* 872 F.2d 1365 (Mo. 8th Cir. 1989).

Defenses in Drug Cases

Defendants on trial for drug offenses sometimes assert that they were entrapped by the police, a defense discussed in Chapter 14. More frequently, defense counsel attempt to suppress the contraband seized by police on the ground that it was obtained in violation of the Fourth Amendment prohibition against unreasonable searches and seizures. In some instances, a defendant presents an expert witness to contest the type of contraband introduced in evidence, and frequently defendants challenge the chain of custody of the contraband from the time it was seized until the time it was introduced into evidence. Because the gravity of the offense is often based on the amount of contraband seized, defendants sometimes challenge the weight of the contraband being introduced into evidence. Possession with intent to deliver drugs within a certain proximity of a school is a more serious offense that can carry severe penalties. Defendants charged with this offense often challenge the measurement of the distance between the school and the place where the offense allegedly occurred.

In a number of cases, courts have rejected such defenses as economic coercion and duress, but, as we noted above, in some instances courts have accepted the defense of "medical necessity" in possession of marijuana cases.

The "War on Drugs"

President Richard Nixon first "declared war" on illegal drugs in 1973. President Ronald Reagan "redeclared" the war in 1982, as did the first President Bush in 1988. Since 1973 the war on drugs has been waged on numerous fronts, from elementary schools to Colombian coca farms, and has employed a number of controversial weapons and tactics. Federal and state drug laws have been made more stringent, budgets for drug enforcement activities have been increased dramatically, teachers, police officers and other public employees have been subjected to random drug testing, and constitutional restrictions on searches and seizures have been relaxed. Millions of dollars have been spent on public information campaigns on the dangers of drug abuse. To supporters of the drug war, it is a war for national survival, nearly as important as the current war on terrorism. Its detractors see it as a war on people or, alternatively, a war on the Constitution.

The Drug Enforcement Administration

In 1973, President Nixon issued an executive order creating the Drug Enforcement Administration (DEA) within the Department of Justice to concentrate federal drug enforcement responsibilities within one agency of government. Since then, the DEA has been involved in all facets of the drug war, including joint operations with state and local law enforcement agencies as well as agencies in other countries. The DEA has even worked in tandem with the Coast Guard in an effort to interdict smuggling operations into the United States. The DEA has employed a number of controversial tactics, including **drug courier profiling,** in which a set of behavioral characteristics believed to typify drug smugglers is employed to identify, monitor and sometimes detain suspected drug couriers. Such tactics have generated considerable litigation—with disparate results. See, for example, *Reid v. Georgia,* 448 U.S. 438, 100 S.Ct. 2752, 65 L.Ed.2d 890 (1980); *United States v. Sokolow,* 490 U.S. 1, 109 S.Ct. 1581, 104 L.Ed.2d 1 (1989). (This issue is given considerable attention in Chapter 16.)

The DEA employs more than 9,000 people, including more than 4,500 special agents. Its annual budget exceeds $1.8 billion. Yet according to a Performance and Management Assessment released by the White House in February 2003, the DEA "is unable to demonstrate its progress in reducing the availability of illegal drugs in the U.S." The report cited a lack of cooperation with other law enforcement agencies, misplaced priorities, and a lack of internal evaluation and accountability mechanisms, all of which may be valid criticisms. The reality may well be that the problem that DEA is tasked with solving is beyond the capabilities of any government agency.

Mandatory Minimum Sentences

In 1969, amidst public outcry over drugs and street crime, the New York legislature enacted the first of the so-called Rockefeller Drug Laws, which required mandatory prison terms for persons convicted of serious drug crimes. In 1973, the legislature strengthened these laws by establishing more severe penalties and by restricting plea bargaining in drug cases. By and large, these laws remain in effect today. As an example of the harshness of the laws, a person convicted of selling two ounces or possessing four ounces of cocaine or heroin is required to serve at least fifteen years in prison before being eligible for parole. While their effect on deterring illegal drug use is debatable, the Rockefeller Drug Laws have certainly had the effect of dramatically increasing the size of the prison population in New York. In 1998 the prison population in New York State stood at roughly 70,000 inmates, nearly three times as many prisoners as in 1979. By 1998, non-violent drug offenders accounted for 30 percent of the state prison population. See Spiros A.Tsimbinos, *Is It Time to Change the Rockefeller Drug Laws?,* 13 St. John's J. Legal Comment 613–34, Spring 1999.

In the late 1970s and 1980s, other states and the federal government followed New York's example. Beginning in 1986, Congress required mandatory minimum prison terms for drug felonies. For example, a person charged with possession with the intent to distribute more than five kilograms of cocaine is subject to a mandatory minimum sentence of ten years in prison. See 21 U.S.C.A. § 841(b)(1)(A). Consequently, the federal prison population has swelled with drug offenders who theretofore received probation. In 1991, 58 percent of federal prisoners were convicted of drug offenses; by 1997 the proportion had risen to 63 percent. (U.S. Department of Justice, Bureau of Justice Statistics, *Sourcebook of Criminal Justice Statistics, 2001,* p. 499). In 2000 there were 112,329 federal offenders sentenced to prison. Of these, 63,898 or 55.5 percent were sentenced for drug offenses. (*Sourcebook of Criminal Justice Statistics, 2001,* p. 512). As a result of mandatory sentencing under federal law, a significantly higher percentage of federal drug defendants are sentenced to prison than are state drug defendants.

Drug Testing of Public Employees and Public School Students

As a means of reducing drug use among public employees, numerous local, state, and federal government agencies in the 1980s adopted **drug-testing requirements** for their employees. In 1989 the U.S. Supreme Court sustained a Customs Service policy requiring drug tests for persons seeking positions as customs inspectors. *Treasury Employees Union v. Von Raab,* 489 U.S. 656, 109 S.Ct. 1384, 103 L.Ed.2d 685 (1989). As yet, the Supreme Court has not addressed the issue of general, random drug testing of public employees. However, it has invalidated a policy under which all political candidates were required to submit to drug testing as a condition of qualifying for the ballot. *Chandler v. Miller,* 520 U.S. 305, 117 S.Ct. 1295, 137 L.Ed.2d 513 (1997). Several state courts have addressed the question of random drug testing of public employees, and at least one state appellate court has found such a policy to be unconstitutional. *City of Palm Bay v. Bauman,* 475 So.2d 1322 (Fla. App. 1985).

 Go to the Scheb/ Scheb Criminal Law and Procedure 6e website at academic .cengage.com/criminaljustice/ scheb for an edited version of the *Von Raab* decision.

In many school districts around the country, teachers and students are subjected to drug testing. Teachers are required to submit to drug testing as a condition of employment, and this requirement has generally been upheld by the courts. See, for example, *Knox County Education Association v. Knox County Board of Education,* 158 F.3d 361 (6th Cir. 1998). With respect to students, most policies require drug testing as a condition of participation in sports or other extracurricular activities. One such policy established by the city of Tecumseh, Oklahoma, was upheld by the U.S. Supreme Court in 2002. See *Board of Education v. Earls,* 536 U.S. 822, 122 S.Ct. 2559, 153 L.Ed.2d 735 (2002). Writing for the Court, Justice Clarence Thomas concluded, "Given the nationwide epidemic of drug use, and the evidence of increased drug use in Tecumseh schools, it was entirely reasonable for the School District to enact this particular drug testing policy." 536 U.S. at 836, 122 S.Ct. at 2568, 153 L.Ed.2d at 748. (See Chapter 15 for additional material on the issue of drug testing.)

Asset Forfeiture

In passing the Comprehensive Drug Abuse Prevention and Control Act of 1970, Pub.L. No. 91-513, 84 Stat. 1276, Congress for the first time provided for forfeiture of property used in connection with federal drug crimes. Since then Congress has legislated frequently in this area, so that today there is a fairly complex body of federal forfeiture law. It should be noted that asset forfeiture is not limited to drug offenses but applies to a number of federal crimes, including counterfeiting, mail and wire fraud, forgery, money laundering, and carjacking. However, it is in the area of drug enforcement that forfeitures are most common. Today federal law authorizes forfeiture of illegal drugs themselves, drug paraphernalia, money and other assets furnished or intended to be furnished in drug exchanges, proceeds from illegal drug transactions, real estate used or intended to be used in illegal drug transactions, as well as aircraft, vessels, and vehicles used to transport or otherwise facilitate illegal drug transactions. Most states have enacted similar laws. See, for example, Oklahoma's Uniform Controlled Dangerous Substances Act, 63 Okl. St. Ann. § 2–503.

CRIMINAL FORFEITURES

Federal asset forfeitures can be criminal or civil. In a **criminal forfeiture,** a person convicted of a federal drug offense is ordered to forfeit property involved in that offense. However, in order for that to occur, the property sought by the government must be specifically identified in the indictment so that the owner has the opportunity to contest the forfeiture. Furthermore, the standard of proof with respect to the forfeiture is lower than that required to convict the defendant. As in any criminal prosecution, the government must prove the defendant's guilt beyond a reasonable doubt. But the standard of proof with respect to the associated forfeiture of property is merely "by a preponderance of the evidence." The two principal statutes governing criminal forfeiture in federal drug cases are 18 U.S.C.A. § 982 and 21 U.S.C.A. § 853.

CIVIL FORFEITURES

In contrast to a criminal forfeiture, a **civil forfeiture** (see 18 U.S.C.A. § 983) does not require a criminal conviction, or even prosecution of the owner, because the legal action is brought against the property itself in what is known as an *in rem* action. Thus a civil forfeiture case is likely to be styled something like *United States v. 2003 Porsche 911 Carrera Cabriolet.* Property may be seized as long as agents have probable cause to believe it is subject to forfeiture. A subsequent civil proceeding determines whether the property is to be forfeited or returned to the owner. Civil forfeiture thus rests on the legal fiction that the property itself is in violation of the law and can be the target of legal action. Of course, the real target of the action is the property owner, who may or may not be simultaneously defending against a criminal prosecution. The Supreme Court has essentially ratified this approach, holding that civil forfeitures are neither punishment nor criminal for purposes of the Double Jeopardy Clause. *United States v. Ursery*, 518 U.S. 267, 116 S.Ct. 2135, 135 L.Ed.2d 549 (1996).

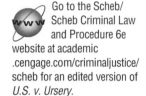

Go to the Scheb/
Scheb Criminal Law
and Procedure 6e
website at academic
.cengage.com/criminaljustice/
scheb for an edited version of
U.S. v. Ursery.

CRITICISM AND REFORM

In the 1980s, the federal government became much more aggressive in the use of civil forfeitures as part of the war on drugs. The Comprehensive Crime Control Act of 1984, Pub. L. 98-473, 98 Stat. 1976, directed that proceeds of forfeitures be disbursed to law enforcement agencies that made seizures, thus creating a powerful incentive for the seizure of assets in connection with drug arrests. As a result, civil forfeitures increased dramatically. Critics charged that the practice was being abused and called on Congress and the courts to limit the government's power in this area.

The Supreme Court limited civil forfeitures in several important decisions handed down in 1993. In *United States v. A Parcel of Land,* 507 U.S. 111, 113 S.Ct. 1126, 122 L.Ed.2d 469 (1993), the Court ruled that although proceeds traceable to an unlawful drug transaction are subject to forfeiture, an owner's lack of knowledge that her home had been purchased with proceeds of illegal drug transactions constitutes a defense to a forfeiture proceeding under federal law. In *United States v. Good Real Property,* 510 U.S. 43, 114 S.Ct. 492, 126 L.Ed.2d 490 (1993), the Court held that due process requires government to provide property owners adequate notice and a meaningful opportunity to be heard before seizing real estate that is subject to civil forfeiture. And in *Austin v. United States,* 509 U.S. 602, 113 S.Ct. 2801, 125 L.Ed.2d 488 (1993), the Court ruled that civil *in rem* forfeitures, although not technically criminal proceedings, are subject to the Excessive Fines Clause of the Eighth Amendment. However, the Court declined to establish any test for determining when a forfeiture is constitutionally excessive.

Go to the Scheb/
Scheb Criminal Law
and Procedure 6e
website at academic
.cengage.com/criminaljustice/
scheb for an edited version of
Austin v. U.S.

Responding to continuing criticism of civil forfeitures, Congress enacted the Civil Asset Forfeiture Reform Act (CAFRA) of 2000, Pub. L. No. 106-185, 114 Stat. 202. Previously, the property owner carried the burden of proving by a preponderance of the evidence that the property seized by the government is not subject to forfeiture. CAFRA reversed the burden of proof so that it now rests on government. 18 U.S.C.A. § 983(c). It also established a uniform "innocent owner defense" applicable to all federal forfeiture statutes. To prevail in this defense, owners must prove either that they did not know of the unlawful activity associated with their property or that they did all they could reasonably be expected to do to prevent or halt it. 18 U.S.C.A. § 983(d). The new law also provides counsel to indigent property owners who have standing to challenge forfeitures. 18 U.S.C.A. § 983(b)(2). While CAFRA represents a serious attempt to reform civil forfeitures, it does not severely retard the government's ability to use this powerful weapon in the war on drugs.

United States v. Ursery, 518 U.S. 267, 116 S.Ct. 2135, 135 L.Ed.2d 549 (1996)

In this excerpt from the Court's majority opinion, Chief Justice William Rehnquist discusses the nature of *in rem* forfeiture proceedings, concluding that they are not limited by the constitutional prohibition against double jeopardy.

CHIEF JUSTICE REHNQUIST delivered the opinion of the Court, saying in part:

In sum, "[b]y creating such distinctly civil procedures for forfeitures …, Congress has indicate[d] clearly that it intended a civil, not a criminal sanction." … [W]e find that there is little evidence, much less the "clearest proof" that we require, suggesting that forfeiture proceedings … are so punitive in form and effect as to render them criminal despite Congress' intent to the contrary.…

Most significant is that [forfeitures], while perhaps having certain punitive aspects, serve important nonpunitive goals.… Requiring the forfeiture of property used to commit federal narcotics violations encourages property owners to take care in managing their property and ensures that they will not permit that property to be used for illegal purposes.… In many circumstances, the forfeiture may abate a nuisance.…

To the extent that [the forfeiture law] applies to "proceeds" of illegal drug activity, it serves the additional nonpunitive goal of ensuring that persons do not profit from their illegal acts.

Other considerations that we have found relevant to the question whether a proceeding is criminal also tend to support a conclusion that [the challenged forfeitures] are civil proceedings.… First, in light of our decisions … and the long tradition of federal statutes providing for a forfeiture proceeding following a criminal prosecution, it is absolutely clear that in rem civil forfeiture has not historically been regarded as punishment, as we have understood that term under the Double Jeopardy Clause. Second, there is no requirement in the statutes that we currently review that the Government demonstrate scienter in order to establish that the property is subject to forfeiture; indeed, the property may be subject to forfeiture even if no party files a claim to it and the Government never shows any connection between the property and a particular person.… [W]e do not think that such a

provision, without more indication of an intent to punish, is relevant to the question whether a statute is punitive under the Double Jeopardy Clause. Third, though both statutes may fairly be said to serve the purpose of deterrence, we long have held that this purpose may serve civil as well as criminal goals.… Finally, though both statutes are tied to criminal activity,… this fact is insufficient to render the statutes punitive.… It is well settled that "Congress may impose both a criminal and a civil sanction in respect to the same act or omission." … By itself, the fact that a forfeiture statute has some connection to a criminal violation is far from the "clearest proof" necessary to show that a proceeding is criminal.…

JUSTICE [JOHN PAUL] STEVENS, concurring in the judgment in part and dissenting in part, observed:

In recent years, both Congress and the state legislatures have armed their law enforcement authorities with new powers to forfeit property that vastly exceed their traditional tools. In response, this Court has reaffirmed the fundamental proposition that all forfeitures must be accomplished within the constraints set by the Constitution.… This Term the Court has begun dismantling the protections it so recently erected.… [T]oday, for the first time it upholds the forfeiture of a person's home. On the way to its surprising conclusion that the owner is not punished by the loss of his residence, the Court repeatedly professes its adherence to tradition and time-honored practice.…

There is simply no rational basis for characterizing the seizure of this respondent's home as anything other than punishment for his crime. The house was neither proceeds nor contraband and its value had no relation to the Government's authority to seize it. Under the controlling statute an essential predicate for the forfeiture was proof that respondent had used the property in connection with the commission of a crime. The forfeiture of this property was unquestionably "a penalty that had absolutely no correlation to any damages sustained by society or to the cost of enforcing the law." … Fidelity to both reason and precedent dictates the conclusion that this forfeiture was "punishment" for purposes of the Double Jeopardy Clause.

The Office of National Drug Control Policy

In 1988, Congress enacted the Anti-Drug Abuse Act, which established the Office of National Drug Control Policy (ONDCP) within the Executive Office of the President to coordinate federal and state drug control policies. The ONDCP spends considerable time, effort, and money on public relations and advertising in an attempt to persuade people not to use illicit drugs and to defeat efforts by various interest groups to ease existing drug laws. The director of the ONDCP is known colloquially as the "drug czar." To emphasize the importance of the war on drugs, President Reagan made the drug czar a member of his Cabinet, and subsequent presidents have followed suit. As the official responsible for coordinating federal drug policy, the drug czar deals with every federal agency involved in the war on drugs, including the FBI, the Customs Service, the DEA, the Department of Transportation, the Department of Health and Human Services, the State Department, and even the Department of Defense. But the role is more than one of coordinator. The drug czar helps set the tone for national policy on illicit drug use, including the use of criminal prohibitions. By rhetoric and directive, the drug czar is in a position to greatly influence whether the war on drugs continues along its present course.

Assessing the War on Drugs

Some commentators, believing that the national "war on drugs" has failed, have argued for the legalization of such drugs as marijuana, cocaine, and heroin. These commentators would prefer to see the use of these drugs legalized, although highly regulated, with increased efforts directed toward educational and treatment programs. Advocates of legalization contend that criminal prohibition of drug use has led to a vast underground economy and that the war on drugs has debased the rule of law by ineffective attempts to alter personal conduct. They argue that imprisonment of nonviolent drug offenders is excessive, unjust, and ruinous to lives that might otherwise be productive. They also object to what they perceive to be the curtailment of individual rights that has accompanied the drug war. Although the number of Americans who are sympathetic to such arguments may be increasing, there remains substantial public support for maintaining criminal prohibitions in this area. Although the attitude toward legalization appears to be more favorable toward marijuana than other drugs, in 2000 only 32 percent of Americans thought its use should be made legal (U.S. Department of Justice, Bureau of Justice Statistics, *Sourcebook of Criminal Justice Statistics, 2001*, pp. 158–159).

Despite widespread criticism, the war on drugs continues. According to the Uniform Crime Reports compiled by the FBI, local, state and federal authorities made nearly 1.6 million arrests for drug violations in 2000. And during the 2002 fiscal year, the federal government spent more than $19 billion in the war on drugs—with even greater spending earmarked for fiscal year 2003.

Libertarians argue that drug use should be strictly a moral question, where each person is free to decide his or her own limits. Yet drug abuse affects more than just the individual user. Drug abuse creates many dramatic economic, social, and health problems in our society. Illegal trafficking in drugs has led to many violent crimes as well as to instances of official corruption. Moreover, many violent crimes are committed by people under the influence of illicit drugs. The correlation between drug abuse and crime is demonstrated by the fact that in twenty-three of the largest cities in the United States, between 50 and 77 percent of male arrestees test positive for drugs. (See National Institute of Justice, *Drug Use Forecasting: 1999 Annual Report on Adult and Juvenile Arrestees*.) Most Americans want their government to continue to fight the war on drugs, although citizens and officials are often frustrated with the rate of progress.

Drug Courts: A New Approach

By the late 1980s, judges began to recognize that traditional court processes were neither deterring substance abusers nor addressing the medical, social, and economic problems associated with drug abuse. In an effort to use the court's authority to divert certain offenders to closely monitored programs, courts began to develop the concept of a **drug court.** Rather than sending nonviolent defendants to jail, a drug court—in collaboration with prosecutors, defense counsel, and other professionals—would monitor their progress through status hearings and prescribe sanctions and rewards.

Proliferation of Drug Courts

The first drug court was implemented in 1989 in Miami, Florida. Between 1989 and 1994, forty-two drug court programs were established. The Violent Crime Control and Law Enforcement Act of 1994 (**Violent Crime Act**) authorizing federal grants for drug court programs that include court-supervised drug treatment, accelerated the development of drug courts. The ONDCP has reported that as of April 2006, there were 1,557 drug courts operating in the United States, and 394 more were in the planning phases. Currently, 50 states plus the District of Columbia, Northern Mariana Islands, Puerto Rico, Guam, two federal districts, and 136 tribal programs have drug courts that are in operation or are being planned.

Methodology of Drug Court Programs

The methodology of processing defendants who might be eligible for participation in a drug court program varies from standard post-arrest processes. After an individual who has not committed a violent crime is arrested for possession of a controlled substance, a background check is made. If the arrestee meets the drug court eligibility requirements and the prosecuting attorney agrees, the defendant may opt to be diverted to a drug court program. Prosecution is deferred as long as the participant progresses. Once in the program, the participant must obtain a sponsor, attend certain meetings and counseling sessions, give frequent urine samples, and attend required court status hearings. The participant signs a "contract" to complete the program within a specified period, usually twelve months. The treatment phases consist of detoxification, counseling sessions, and often assistance in job training or employment. In some programs a participant who agrees is given acupuncture treatments to aid in detoxification and to make the participant more receptive to counseling sessions.

The status hearings before the drug court are central to the program. They are held in open court with all participants present. The judge may begin with a short orientation emphasizing the need for sobriety and gainful employment. The judge then reviews each participant's progress file and commends those whose urine samples are "clean" and who are in complete compliance with their contract. Participants applaud those with outstanding records of performance. The judge encourages those who have minor deviations in their performance and admonishes those who have relapsed. Often the court prescribes additional counseling, treatment, community service, or a short stay in jail for those who have seriously relapsed in their efforts.

Most programs countenance some relapse; however, positive urine tests, additional arrests, or failure to attend status hearings or treatment sessions may cause a participant to be terminated and prosecution resumed. Successful completion of a drug court program usually results in the charges against the participant being dropped or the plea of guilty being stricken from the record.

Evaluation of Drug Courts

Although the preceding topics provide a general outline of drug court programs, many variations exist. Some focus on women or juveniles; others handle both male and female adults. Some provide support services such as health and housing assistance and job placement; others do not. Some operate with a professional staff; in other instances, the assigned judge might have minimal professional assistance. These factors, along with the relative newness of the programs and the problem of comparing a given group of drug court participants with a control group of those whose offenses are handled in the traditional manner, make it difficult to evaluate the success of the drug court program. Nevertheless, the relapse rate of the participants and the frequency of new arrests are criteria that can be used to assess the program's effectiveness. And, though still a new and innovative institution, drug courts appear to hold considerable promise to deter repetitive criminal behavior of drug abusers. They also hold a promise to relieve courts and other functionaries in the criminal justice system of the burden of repetitive arrests and overloaded trial and sentencing dockets of criminal cases where drugs play an important role.

■ CONCLUSION

The American public is committed to continue strict enforcement of laws proscribing drunk driving. Fortunately, this is an area where positive results are being achieved. Increased education of the consequences of driving while intoxicated is having a positive effect. And better-educated law enforcement officers utilizing sophisticated on-the-scene methods are leading to increased enforcement. Nevertheless, these instances of undesirable behavior will remain criminal offenses and will continue to provide major problems for police, prosecutors, courts, and prison officials.

The control of the use of illegal drugs has been less promising. The widespread abuse of drugs is a serious social problem with many undesirable consequences. Society has responded to this problem largely through the criminal justice system. However, there are those who believe that criminalizing drug possession is undesirable public policy. At this time, the public appears to be strongly committed to maintaining the criminal sanctions against the manufacture, sale, and possession of drugs. The public continues to place emphasis primarily on criminal enforcement against drug dealers while being receptive to increasing education designed to control demand. Moreover, a few jurisdictions are minimizing penalties for the possession of small amounts of marijuana. Many are stepping up efforts to deter drug abuse by nonviolent offenders through treatments administered by drug courts, which continue to proliferate. Efforts to control the supply of illegal drugs has proved extremely difficult, so increasingly efforts are attempting to control the demand by educating the public of the consequences of drug abuse and by rehabilitating minor offenders.

■ KEY TERMS

public drunkenness, 222
disorderly intoxication, 222
driving while intoxicated (DWI), 222
driving under the influence (DUI), 222

driving with an unlawful blood-alcohol level (DUBAL), 223
zero tolerance law, 223
contraband, 223

■ WEB-BASED RESEARCH ACTIVITY

 Go to the Web. Locate your state's criminal statutes. Determine whether possession of small amounts of marijuana is a felony, a misdemeanor, or a noncriminal infraction in your state.

■ QUESTIONS FOR THOUGHT AND DISCUSSION

1. Should chronic alcoholism be a defense to intoxication offenses such as public drunkenness or driving under the influence?

2. Is requiring a person suspected of driving while intoxicated to submit to a blood-alcohol test a violation of the Fifth Amendment prohibition against compulsory self-incrimination?

3. Is it sensible to maintain the criminal prohibitions against illicit drugs, or should these substances be legalized, carefully regulated, and their abuse dealt with through other means?

4. What are the typical difficulties facing prosecutors in drug possession cases?

5. Why, according to *Robinson v. California*, may a person not be held criminally liable for being addicted to illicit narcotics? Is this decision distinguishable from *Powell v. Texas*?

6. Is the drug court method of dealing with nonviolent drug offenders superior to the traditional methods of imposing a fine or jail term or placing the defendant on probation? Should drug courts limit eligibility to participate to first-time offenders?

7. How does the prosecution establish that a defendant is in constructive possession of illicit drugs?

8. To what extent have the federal courts approved drug testing of students in public institutions?

9. To what extent has the U.S. Supreme Court placed restrictions on forfeiture of real estate involved in drug trafficking operations?

10. Name some items that would ordinarily be subject to confiscation under a statute proscribing possession of drug paraphernalia.

■ PROBLEMS FOR DISCUSSION AND SOLUTION

1. Late one night, a deputy sheriff found Ronald Rico in his car parked on the side of a road in a rural area of the county. Rico was at the wheel, the headlights were on, and the radio was playing at a loud volume. The motor was not running. No one else was in the vehicle. A field sobriety test and a later chemical test indicated that Rico had a 0.14 blood alcohol concentration level. Under these circumstances, should Rico be prosecuted for driving under the influence of alcohol? What defenses would a lawyer representing Rico likely raise?

2. During the late afternoon, police were called to quell a disturbance at a motel where the management had reported some disorderly conduct and apparent drug use. Outside the motel, the police observed Henry Egad standing by a tree. About eighteen inches from Egad's feet, the police discovered a matchbox on the ground. Their examination revealed that the matchbox contained a substance that later proved to be PCP, an illegal drug. Police placed Egad under arrest and charged him with possession of a controlled substance. Based on these facts alone, do you think the prosecutor can establish that Egad was in possession of the PCP?

CHAPTER **10**

White-Collar and Organized Crime

**CHAPTER
OUTLINE**

Introduction

Criminologists often classify offenses committed by persons in the upper socioeconomic strata of society as white-collar crimes. This approach focuses on the status of perpetrators. From this perspective, all offenses committed by persons in the upper socioeconomic strata of society would be classified as white-collar crimes. In this chapter, however, we take a legalistic approach and focus on the nature of the offenses. In this sense, **white-collar crimes** are economic offenses characterized by deceit, concealment, and violation of trust. Thus, bribery, forgery, extortion, embezzlement, and obtaining property by false pretenses, which we discuss in Chapter 7, "Property Crimes," can properly be considered white-collar crimes. Beyond these classic crimes, there are a number of modern economic offenses that are uniquely classified as white-collar crimes. In this chapter we discuss these offenses, which include antitrust violations, bid rigging, price fixing, money laundering, insider trading, securities fraud, wire and mail fraud, false claims, and bankruptcy and tax fraud. Essentially, these offenses involve the use of deceit and concealment (as opposed to force or violence) to obtain economic benefits or advantages.

Today, the nearly universal reach of computers and the Internet provides abundant opportunities for the commission of crimes. Some of these crimes, such as "hacking" (unauthorized surreptitious access to computer files, usually from a remote computer) and "phishing" (using fraudulent e-mails and Web sites to obtain access to credit cards or bank accounts) are clearly economic in nature and thus fall within our definition of white-collar crime. Other computer-related crimes, such as trafficking in child pornography or operating illegal gambling sites on the Internet, are crimes against public decency and morality and are addressed in Chapter 8. Others, such as "cyberstalking," are crimes against persons and are discussed in Chapter 6. The use of computers and the Internet to promote or facilitate terrorism are crimes against national security and are addressed in Chapter 12.

Organized crime involves offenses committed by persons or groups who conduct their business through illegal enterprises. Organized crime figures often attempt to gain political influence through graft and corruption, and they frequently resort to threats and acts of violence in the commission of white-collar offenses. Organized crime gained its greatest foothold during the Prohibition era, when the Eighteenth Amendment to the U.S. Constitution prohibiting the sale and distribution of alcoholic beverages was in effect. By the time Prohibition was repealed in 1933, organized crime had become involved in many phases of our economy, often pursuing its interests through such illegal activities as **loan sharking,** gambling, prostitution, and drug trafficking. Protection rackets and other forms of **racketeering** have become the methodology of organized crime as it has infiltrated many legitimate business operations.

White-collar crime is responsible for the loss of billions of dollars annually to government, businesses, and citizens nationwide. The FBI, the investigative division of the U.S. Department of Justice, has special units that handle investigations in economic crimes, financial institution fraud, government fraud, and public corruption. In addition, the Internal Revenue Service, Secret Service, U.S. Customs, Environmental Protection Agency, and Securities and Exchange Commission are active in the enforcement of federal white-collar crime legislation. In recent years most states have become more active in establishing enforcement agencies to address state legislation that proscribes white-collar crimes.

The U.S. Department of Justice also has an Organized Crime and Racketeering Section (OCRS), which coordinates the department's program to combat organized crime. OCRS coordinates with other investigative agencies such as the FBI and the Drug Enforcement Administration and works with the Attorney General's Organized Crime Council. OCRS also reviews all proposed federal prosecutions under the Racketeer Influenced and Corrupt Organizations (RICO) statute and provides advice to prosecutors.

Although white-collar crime and organized crime often overlap, in this chapter we first address white-collar crime, followed by organized crime.

Legal Principles Governing White-Collar Crimes

The principles discussed in relation to the elements of crimes and parties generally also apply to white-collar offenses. Requirements under both state and federal laws for an *actus reus, mens rea,* their concurrence and causation of harm, as well as the definition of principals and accessories, are explained in Chapter 4. In prosecuting white-collar crimes in federal court, the government is usually required to prove that the accused committed the prohibited act "knowingly and willfully." Frequently, federal prosecutors charge white-collar defendants with conspiracy, either under 18 U.S.C.A. § 371 or under one of the conspiracy provisions pertaining to substantive offenses. As pointed out in Chapter 5, the prosecution enjoys certain procedural advantages in using conspiracy as a basis for criminal charges.

Most white-collar crimes prosecuted as federal violations are based on statutes enacted by Congress under the authority of Article I, Section 8, of the U.S. Constitution, which grants Congress power over postal, bankruptcy, and taxing matters and authority to regulate interstate and foreign commerce. Of course, state legislatures have broad authority to proscribe such offenses as contrary to the public welfare.

While the most notable prosecutions of white-collar crimes involve large-scale corporate frauds, white-collar offenses more frequently entail telephone, mail, and e-mail solicitations by those who commit frauds and swindles as they furnish their victims "opportunities" to buy unregistered securities, obtain undeserved diplomas, participate in phony contests, and the like. Also common are "scams" involving fraudulent home improvement schemes, bogus land sales, and spurious investments.

Many statutes defining offenses that have become known as white-collar crimes also provide civil remedies designed to compensate those who have suffered pecuniary losses as a result of a defendant's activities. These laws provide an example of the overlap between the civil and criminal law discussed in Chapter 1. In instances where a civil proceeding and a criminal proceeding are conducted at the same time, courts often stay the civil proceeding pending resolution of the criminal action.

Prosecution of Corporate Defendants

Under common law, a corporation was not held criminally responsible for its acts. This was because a corporation is an artificial being that cannot form the mental element necessary for imposition of criminal liability and cannot be imprisoned. Nevertheless, its members could be held responsible. As strict liability offenses not requiring proof of a *mens rea* developed, corporations were held criminally responsible. Eventually, courts began to interpret the words "person" and "whoever" in criminal statutes to include corporations. Where statutes prescribed punishment other than death or incarceration, courts began to impose criminal liability based on acts of the corporation's agents and to punish corporations by imposing fines. In some jurisdictions, however, a corporation cannot be held criminally liable for crimes against persons unless the offense is based on the corporation's negligence rather than on a crime based on specific intent. The rationale for this is that the corporation cannot form the necessary *mens rea.*

Acts by Corporate Agents

Today, prosecutions of white-collar crime are frequently directed against **corporate defendants,** and corporations are held criminally liable for the acts of their agents committed within the **scope of an agent's authority.** In 1909 the U.S. Supreme Court first held that a corporation could be held criminally liable based on acts of its agents attributed to the corporation. *N.Y. Cent. & Hudson River R.R. Co. v. United States,* 212 U.S. 481, 29 S.Ct. 304, 53 L.Ed. 613 (1909). Today, corporations are held criminally liable for the unlawful acts of its agents, provided that such conduct is within the scope of the agent's authority, actual or apparent. *United States v. Bi-Co Pavers, Inc.,* 741 F.2d 730 (5th Cir. 1984). An agent's knowledge is imputed to the corporation where the agent is acting within the scope of his or her authority and where the knowledge relates to matters within the scope of that authority. See *In re Hellenic, Inc.,* 252 F.3d 391, 395 (5th Cir. 2001). State and federal courts tend to broadly define what constitutes scope of authority, generally holding that the agent's acts must be intended to benefit the corporation in some way.

A few states have adopted section 2.07 of the Model Penal Code or some version of it. Section 2.07(1) provides that a corporation may be convicted of an offense under the following guidelines:

(a) the offense is a violation defined by a statute in which a legislative purpose to impose liability on corporations plainly appears and the conduct is performed by an agent of the corporation acting in behalf of the corporation within the scope of his office or employment, except that if the law defining the offense designates the agents for whose conduct the corporation is accountable or the circumstances under which it is accountable, such provisions shall apply; or

(b) the offense consists of an omission to discharge a specific duty of affirmative performance imposed on corporations by law; or

(c) the commission of the offense was authorized, requested, commanded, performed or recklessly tolerated by the board of directors or by a high managerial agent acting in behalf of the corporation within the scope of his office or employment.

In other jurisdictions, courts simply seek to determine whether the corporate agent or employee was acting within the scope of his or her authority. If so, the courts impute that action to the corporation. Although a corporation may be prosecuted for crimes, that does not exonerate individuals committing an unlawful act. In fact, in prosecutions for white-collar crimes committed by or on behalf of a corporation, it is not uncommon for corporate executives to be individually punished, generally by the imposition of large fines.

Common Federal White-Collar Crimes

In addition to those categories of offenses mentioned earlier and those discussed in other chapters, among the more common federal white-collar crimes are those committed in the following areas.

Antitrust Violations

The **Sherman Antitrust Act,** 15 U.S.C.A. § 1 *et seq.,* makes it a crime to enter any contract or engage in any combination or conspiracy in restraint of trade or to monopolize or attempt to monopolize trade. The act is designed to protect and preserve a system of free and open competition. Its scope is broad and reaches individuals and entities in profit and nonprofit activities as well as local governments and educational institutions. The act includes civil remedies as well as criminal sanctions.

To prove a criminal violation of the act, the government must establish that (1) two or more entities formed a combination or conspiracy; (2) the combination or conspiracy produces, or potentially produces, an unreasonable restraint of trade or commerce; (3) the restrained trade or commerce is interstate in nature; and (4) the defendant's general intent is to violate the law.

Principles outlined in Chapter 5 concerning conspiracies come into play in prosecutions for **antitrust violations.** The antitrust statutes are unclear whether intent must be proven to convict a defendant. In *United States v. U.S. Gypsum Co.,* 438 U.S. 422, 98 S.Ct. 2864, 57 L.Ed.2d 854 (1978), a case involving alleged price fixing, the Supreme Court rejected any idea that criminal violations of the act were intended to be strict liability crimes. Rather, the Court observed that intent is an indispensable element of a criminal antitrust case as in any other criminal offense.

The essence of a Sherman Antitrust Act violation is a combination and conspiracy in restraint of trade. For example, in 1998 the Tenth Circuit Court of Appeals held that the NCAA's rules restricting earnings of a class of coaches to an annual salary of $16,000 was an unreasonable restraint of trade as having an anticompetitive effect. *Law v. National Collegiate Athletic Ass'n.,* 134 F.3d 1010 (10th Cir. 1998).

Among the more common violations are **price fixing** and **bid rigging.** Bid rigging involves interference with competitive bidding for the award of a contract. Illustrative convictions are the following:

- Parties made an agreement not to bid competitively at a bankruptcy auction and to hold a later auction and then split the profits. *United States v. Seville Industrial Machinery Corp.,* 696 F. Supp. 986 (D.N.J. 1988).

- An agent for a public contractor agreed to rig bids with another on a county construction project. *United States v. Bi-Co Pavers, Inc.,* 741 F.2d 730 (5th Cir. 1984).

- Parties entered into a conspiracy to submit collusive noncompetitive bids on a project. *United States v. Mobile Materials, Inc.,* 881 F.2d 866 (10th Cir. 1989).

The U.S. Justice Department alone is authorized to enforce the criminal sanctions of the act. Criminal violations are felonies. Corporations may be fined as much as $100,000,000, while individuals may be fined as much as $1,000,000, sentenced to a maximum of ten years' imprisonment, or both.

Corporate defendants often seek to avoid liability for violations committed by their agents. But courts have generally held that as long as an agent acts within the scope of employment or apparent authority, the corporation may be held legally responsible.

Most state legislatures have enacted statutes under which intrastate violations of securities laws are prosecuted. The text of state statutes and their judicial interpretations often parallel the federal views.

Computer Crimes

The **Computer Fraud and Abuse Act,** 18 U.S.C.A. § 1030, proscribes crimes involving "protected computers," which are those used in interstate commerce or communications, including computers connected to the Internet. As amended in 1996, 18 U.S.C.A.

§ 1030(a)(5)(A) makes it a crime to "knowingly cause the transmission of a program, information, code, or command" in interstate commerce with intent to cause damage to a computer exclusively used by a financial institution or the U.S. government. In addition, the act prohibits "knowingly and with intent to defraud, trafficking in passwords to permit unauthorized access to a government computer, or to affect interstate or foreign commerce." 18 U.S.C.A. § 1030(a)(6)(A)(B). Subsection 1030(a)(7) makes it illegal to transmit in interstate or foreign commerce any threat to cause damage to a protected computer with intent to extort something of value.

It is also a federal crime to "knowingly with intent to defraud" produce, use, or traffic in counterfeit **access devices.** 18 U.S.C.A. § 1029(a). Access devices include cards, plates, codes, electronic serial numbers, mobile identification numbers, personal identification numbers, telecommunications services, equipment, instrument identifiers, or other means that can be used to obtain goods or services. 18 U.S.C.A. § 1029(e). To obtain a conviction for using or trafficking in unauthorized access devices, the government must prove that a defendant acted knowingly and with intent to defraud, but proof of such intent may be established with circumstantial evidence. *United States v. Ismoila,* 100 F.3d 380 (5th Cir. 1996).

THE USA PATRIOT ACT

After the tragic attacks of September 11, 2001, Congress hastily passed important legislation officially known as the Uniting and Strengthening America by Providing Appropriate Tools Required to Intercept and Obstruct Terrorism Act of 2001. Better known by its acronym, the **USA PATRIOT Act** was signed into law by President George W. Bush on October 25, 2001. This 342-page legislation was designed to deter and punish terrorist acts in the United States and around the world and to enhance the federal government's law enforcement investigatory tools. On March 9, 2006, President Bush signed legislation essentially renewing the USA PATRIOT Act. Section 814 of the act makes a number of changes in federal statutes designed to strengthen the Computer Fraud and Abuse Act, 18 U.S.C.A. § 1030.

Section 814 of the PATRIOT Act amends the definition of "protected computer" to include computers outside of the United States that affect "interstate or foreign commerce or communication of the United States." 18 U.S.C.A. § 1030(e)(2)(B). Section 814 of the act raises the maximum penalty for violations for damaging a protected computer to ten years for first-time offenders and twenty years for repeat offenders. 18 U.S.C.A. § 1030(c)(4). Under previous law, first-time offenders who violate section 1030(a)(5) by damaging a protected computer could be punished by no more than five years' imprisonment, while repeat offenders could receive up to ten years.

Section 814 of the act created 18 U.S.C.A. 1030(c)(2)(C) and (e)(8) to clarify that a hacker need only intend to damage a protected computer or the information on it, not to cause a specific dollar amount of loss or other special harm.

Most states have enacted computer crimes statutes, some of which we discussed in Chapter 7. Often these statutes expand the traditional definitions of "property" to include computer technologies and make it a criminal offense to alter, delete, or destroy computer programs or files; to access computer programs or files without consent; or to contaminate computers with viruses. Other state statutes prohibit accessing or using computer systems without the consent of the owner or rightful possessor.

INTERNATIONAL EFFORTS TO COMBAT CYBERCRIME

Because of its global reach, Internet crime poses an especially difficult challenge to law enforcement agencies. In 2006, the United States joined more than forty other countries by ratifying the Convention on Cybercrime, a treaty designed to harmonize national laws and strengthen international cooperation in this area. In addition to its provisions dealing with sexual exploitation of children, terrorism, and "hate crimes," the treaty addresses several problems in the area of international white-collar crime, including computer-related fraud, "hacking," the dissemination of computer viruses, and electronic attacks on financial institutions.

False Statements and Bankruptcy Fraud

The federal **False Statements Act** (18 U.S.C.A. § 1001) prohibits knowingly and willfully making a false statement that is material to a matter within the jurisdiction of any department or agency of the United States. "Congress intentionally drafted § 1001 in an expansive fashion in order that it be accorded the broadest possible interpretation regarding the situations in which it would come into play." *Moser v. United States,* 18 F.3d 469, 473 (7th Cir. 1994).

When proceeding under the False Statements Act, the government must prove that the accused knowingly and willfully submitted to a government agency or department a statement that was false and material. The issue of materiality is one for the court to consider. *United States v. Rodgers,* 466 U.S. 475, 104 S.Ct. 1942, 80 L.Ed.2d 492 (1984). (A false statement in any matter within the jurisdiction of any department or agency of the United States encompasses criminal investigations conducted by the FBI and Secret Service.)

Federal statutes criminalize **bankruptcy fraud,** which is defined as the knowing and fraudulent concealment of assets, avoiding distribution of nonexempt assets, taking false oaths, and related conduct in connection with bankruptcy proceedings. 18 U.S.C.A. § 152. To convict, the government must prove the defendant acted willfully; however, one who acts with willful blindness can be found to have acted with the requisite criminal intent. Although the statute does not expressly state a materiality requirement, 18 U.S.C.A. § 152 has been construed "to require that [a] false oath be given in relation to some material matter." *United States v. O'Donnell,* 539 F.2d 1233, 1237 (9th Cir. 1976).

The False Claims Act

Medicare and Medicaid provide health care benefits to millions of Americans. Medicare is designed to provide medical care primarily to older citizens, whereas Medicaid is a program that furnishes health care services to the needy. Historically, criminal violations of the federal statutes providing these benefits, as well as other false claims to federal entitlements, have been prosecuted under the **False Claims Act,** 18 U.S.C.A. § 287, and the False Statements Act. To prove Medicare or Medicaid fraud under the False Claims Act, the government must prove that (1) the defendant presented a claim seeking reimbursement from the government for medical services or goods, (2) the claim was false or fraudulent, and (3) the accused knew of the claim's falsity. See *United States v. Upton,* 91 F.3d 677 (5th Cir. 1996), where the court, after reciting these elements of proof, affirmed the defendants' convictions under 18 U.S.C.A. for filing a false claim with the U.S. Air Force for reimbursement of unpaid bond premiums.

Go to the Scheb/ Scheb Criminal Law and Procedure 6e website at academic .cengage.com/criminaljustice/ scheb for an edited version of *U.S. v. Upton.*

THE HEALTH INSURANCE PORTABILITY AND ACCOUNTABILITY ACT

In 1996 Congress enacted the Health Insurance Portability and Accountability Act of 1996, Public Law 104–191. Section 244 of the act, codified at 18 U.S.C.A. § 1035, establishes a new false statement offense that prohibits making material false or fraudulent statements or entries in connection with delivery of or payment for health

CASE-IN-POINT

Criminal Prosecution Under the False Claims Act

Evidence at trial disclosed that the defendant had submitted false claims to Pennsylvania Blue Shield and the Travelers Insurance Company but not to any federal agency or official. These insurance companies processed and paid the claims and were reimbursed by the federal government for their payments and costs of processing the claims. The defendant was convicted and appealed. A question arose whether the insurance carriers could be considered "agencies" of the United States for purposes of criminal prosecution. The court doubted that the insurance carriers were agencies of the United States; however, it cited another federal statute, 18 U.S.C.A. § 2(b), which provides that "[w]hoever willfully causes an act to be done which if directly performed by him or another would be an offense against the United States, is punishable as a principal." Finding the proof established that the defendant "caused" the private carriers to submit false claims to the government, the court affirmed the defendant's conviction.

United States v. Catena, 500 F.2d 1319 (3d Cir. 1974).

care benefits. This new section covers statements and concealments made to private insurers that could not be prosecuted under the False Statements Act. The new act also includes several other criminal provisions. Section 242 makes it an offense for any person to knowingly and willfully execute or attempt to execute a scheme or artifice to defraud any health care benefit program or to fraudulently obtain money or property of such programs in connection with the delivery of or payment for health care benefits, items, or services. 18 U.S.C.A § 1347. Section 243 proscribes knowingly and willfully embezzling assets of a health care benefit program. 18 U.S.C.A. § 669. Section 245 creates a new crime that prohibits willfully obstructing, misleading, or delaying communication of information or records to a criminal investigator relating to a violation of a federal health care offense. 18 U.S.C.A. § 1518.

CASE-IN-POINT

Criminal Prosecution Under the Health Insurance Portability and Accountability Act

Three defendants participated in staged automobile accidents and fabricated personal injury claims to take advantage of the operation of the New York No-Fault Act. They contended that they were not subject to prosecution under 18 U.S.C.A. § 1347 because they were not health professionals. The court rejected their contention and held that "[W]hether that person is a medical professional, a patient, or otherwise—who purposefully endeavors to defraud a health care benefit program may be found guilty of health care fraud, if his or her conduct otherwise conforms to the elements of the offense. The broad language of section 1347 shows that Congress intended for this statute to include within its scope a wide range of conduct so that all forms of health care fraud would be proscribed, regardless of the kind of specific schemes unscrupulous persons may concoct."

United States v. Lucien, 347 F.3d 45, 51 (2d Cir. 2003).

The Federal Mail Fraud and Wire Fraud Statutes

The Federal Mail Fraud Statute, 18 U.S.C.A. § 1341, makes it a crime to use the mail to defraud. **Mail fraud** consists of (1) a scheme devised or intended to defraud or to obtain money or property by fraudulent means and (2) the use of or causing to use the mails in furtherance of the fraudulent scheme. Courts have held that to obtain a conviction, the government must prove the existence of a scheme committed by the defendant with a specific intent to defraud the government through use of the U.S. mail or some other interstate commercial carrier. The government is not required to prove that the scheme to defraud was successful. It is sufficient for the government to prove that a scheme existed in which use of the mails was reasonably foreseeable and that an actual mailing occurred in furtherance of the scheme. *United States v. Dick*, 744 F.2d 546, 550 (7th Cir. 1984).

A companion statute, the Federal Wire Fraud Statute, 18 U.S.C.A. § 1343, parallels the mail fraud statute and makes fraudulent schemes that use interstate television, radio, or wire communications a crime. Although the U.S. Constitution grants Congress jurisdiction over the postal service, Congress enacted the **wire fraud** statute under its authority to regulate interstate commerce. U.S. Const., Art. I, § 8. Therefore, a violation of this statute exists only if the communication crosses state lines.

Shortly after the tragedy of September 11, 2001, Americans were again shocked by allegations of fraud affecting the rights of employees and shareholders of once highly regarded corporations. One of the most highly publicized was that involving the Enron Corporation, an energy company that had become one of the largest corporations in America. In July 2004 a federal jury convicted a former Enron financial executive and four former investment brokers of conspiracy and fraud. On May 25, 2006, a federal jury convicted former Enron chief executive Jeffrey Skilling and founder Kenneth Lay of conspiracy to commit securities and wire fraud. Lay died before sentencing. Because his demise occurred before the sentencing and appeal process was completed, the U.S. District Judge in Houston, Texas, on October 17, 2006, vacated the proceedings against Lay. See *United States v. Moehlenkamp*, 557 F.2d 126, 127–28 (7th Cir. 1977) (Defendant's death pending appeal from final judgment of conviction deprives the defendant of the right to an appellate decision and requires vacating of a conviction). At a sentencing hearing on October 23, 2006, the court sentenced Skilling to serve twenty-four years and four months in confinement.

CASE-IN-POINT

Mail Fraud

Wayne T. Schmuck, a used-car distributor, purchased used cars, rolled back their odometers, and then sold the automobiles to Wisconsin retail dealers for prices artificially inflated because of the low-mileage readings. The dealers, in turn, mailed the title applications to the state transportation department. Finding that the mailings by the dealers were essential to the defendant distributor's fraudulent acts, the Supreme Court upheld Schmuck's conviction under 18 U.S.C.A. § 1341, observing that the mailings were "part of the execution of the scheme as conceived by the perpetrator at the time."

Schmuck v. United States, 489 U.S. 705, 109 S.Ct. 1443, 103 L.Ed.2d (1989).

Money Laundering and Currency Reporting Violations

Money laundering is the crime of disguising illegal income to make it appear legitimate and is prohibited by the Money Laundering Control Act of 1986, 18 U.S.C.A. §§ 1956, 1957. Section 1956 (a)(1) provides as follows:

> Whoever, knowing that the property involved in a financial transaction represents the proceeds of some form of unlawful activity, conducts, or attempts to conduct such a financial transaction which in fact involves the proceeds of specified unlawful activity

> (A)(i) with the intent to promote the carrying on of specified unlawful activity; or (ii) with intent to engage in conduct constituting a violation of section 7201 or 7206 of the Internal Revenue Code of 1986; or

> (B) knowing that the transaction is designed in whole or in part (i) to conceal or disguise the nature, the location, the source, the ownership, or the control of the proceeds of specified unlawful activity; or (ii) to avoid a transaction reporting requirement under State or Federal law, shall be sentenced to a fine of not more than $500,000 or twice the value of the property involved in the transaction, whichever is greater, or imprisonment for not more than twenty years, or both.

Thus, crimes under section 1956 fall into three categories: (1) acts committed with intent to promote unlawful activity; (2) those committed with knowledge that a transaction is to conceal ownership, control, or source of funds; and (3) those designed to avoid certain currency reporting laws.

Section 1957 makes it a crime to engage in or attempt to engage in a transaction involving criminally derived property. To convict a defendant of money laundering, the government must show that (1) the defendant took part in a financial transaction and knew that the property in the transaction involved proceeds of illegal activity; (2) that the property involved was in fact proceeds of illegal activity; and (3) that the defendant knew that the transaction was designed in whole or part to conceal or disguise the nature, source, location, ownership, or control of illegal proceeds. The government bears a heavy burden to establish that a defendant is guilty of money laundering. It must show the accused has "actual knowledge" or is guilty of "willful blindness" to the criminal acts; simply showing that a defendant "should have known" is insufficient to establish guilt.

Often, federal appellate courts have had to determine whether certain acts constitute a financial transaction within the meaning of the statute. In *United States v. Jackson*, 935 F.2d 832 (7th Cir. 1991), the defendant appealed his conviction on three counts of money laundering in violation of section 1956(a) and other violations. The evidence revealed the defendant had deposited funds derived from both legitimate and illegal activities in a local savings and loan institution and had written checks on the account. After first pointing out that writing a check on an account in a financial institution is a "transaction" within the money laundering statute, the court of appeals rejected the defendant's argument that the prosecution failed to establish that the financial transactions involved the proceeds of unlawful activity within the meaning of the statute because the checks involved were written on an account that contained both legitimate funds and drug profits. The court held it was sufficient for the government to show that the transaction in question involved the proceeds of one of the types of criminal conduct specified. Federal courts have also held that the term "financial transaction" includes making a deposit into an account. See *United States v. Reynolds*, 64 F.3d 292 (7th Cir. 1995). But the Fifth Circuit has held that transportation of drug proceeds by car does not constitute a financial transaction within the meaning of section 1956. *United States v. Puig-Infante*, 19 F.3d 929 (5th Cir. 1994).

ILLEGALLY STRUCTURING CASH TRANSACTIONS TO AVOID REPORTING REQUIREMENTS

Federal statutes require financial institutions to file currency transaction reports with the Secretary of the Treasury for cash transactions in excess of $10,000. 31 U.S.C.A. § 5313. A related provision, 31 U.S.C.A. § 5324, prohibits a person from causing or attempting to cause a financial institution from making the required reports or from **structuring** or assisting in structuring a transaction with one or more institutions to evade the requirement and provides penalties for persons who willfully conduct a transaction to evade this structuring requirement.

On October 20, 1988, Waldemar Ratzlaf ran up a debt of over $100,000 playing blackjack at a casino in Reno, Nevada. The casino gave him one week to pay. On the due date, Ratzlaf returned to the casino with cash totaling $100,000 in hand. When Ratzlaf offered to pay $100,000 on his gambling debt, the casino informed him that payment by a check in that amount would trigger the currency reporting requirements under federal law. Ratzlaf then proceeded to obtain a series of $10,000 cashier's checks from various banks to pay his debt. The government charged him with "structuring transactions" in violation of 31 U.S.C.A. § 5322 and § 5324. Section 5324 provides that it is illegal to "structure" financial transactions "for the purpose of evading" a financial institution's reporting requirements. Section 5322(a) established that "a person willfully violating" the anti-structuring provision (section 5324) is subject to criminal penalties. A jury found him guilty.

On review, the U.S. Supreme Court, in a 5–4 decision, interpreted "willfully" in 31 U.S.C.A. § 5322 to require the government to prove that a defendant acted with knowledge that his conduct was unlawful and reversed his conviction. *Ratzlaf v. United States,* 510 U.S. 135, 114 S.Ct. 655, 126 L.Ed.2d 615 (1994). The Court based its holding upon a strict reading of the statutory language of the two sections. Section 5324 provides that it is illegal to "structure" financial transactions "for the purpose of evading" a financial institution's reporting requirements. Section 5322(a) establishes that a person "willfully violating" the anti-structuring provision (section 5324) is subject to criminal penalties.

After *Ratzlaf,* Congress amended section 5324 to no longer include the requirement that the defendant acted "willfully." See 31 U.S.C.A. § 5324. Apparently the only mental state now required is a purpose to evade the reporting requirement. See *United States v. Vazquez,* 53 F.3d 1216, 1218 n. 2 (11th Cir. 1995).

Securities Fraud

A variety of federal and state statutes criminalize conduct involving misrepresentations, omissions, **insider trading,** and other aspects of fraud in securities dealing. The most significant federal acts are the Securities Act of 1933, 15 U.S.C.A. § 77a *et seq.,* and the **Securities and Exchange Act** of 1934, 15 U.S.C.A. § 78a *et seq.* Again, these statutes provide for civil remedies as well as criminal sanctions. The Securities and Exchange Commission (SEC) refers most criminal prosecutions to the Department of Justice. Convictions can result in fines in millions of dollars and imprisonment.

Not all misrepresentations or omissions involving securities give rise to criminal violations. Rather, the government must prove the accused's *willful* intent to commit a substantive fraud in connection with the purchase or sale of a security or in the offering or sale of a security involving interstate commerce or through use of the mails. Courts uniformly hold that to sustain a conviction, the omission or misrepresentation must be material and be made in reckless disregard for the truth or falsity of the information provided. See, for example, *United States v. Farris,* 614 F.2d 634 (9th Cir.

1979). The specific intent that must be proven to sustain a criminal prosecution can be found in a defendant's deliberate and intentional acts or reckless disregard for the facts. *United States v. Boyer*, 694 F.2d 58 (3d Cir. 1982).

Churning and Insider Trading

In recent years, many financial executives and securities brokers have been prosecuted under the Securities and Exchange Act for fraudulent conduct known as churning and insider trading. **Churning** is a term applied to transactions made in a customer's account without regard to the customer's investment objectives; they are made simply to generate commissions for the broker. When determining whether a broker is guilty of churning, courts often focus on whether the trading by a broker was disproportionate to the size of the customer's account. Insider trading usually occurs when a person who operates "inside" a corporation has access to material, nonpublic information and uses that information to trade securities without first disclosing that information to the public.

Securities and Exchange Commission rule 10(b) proscribes (1) using any "deceptive device" (2) "in connection with the purchase or sale of any security," in contravention of rules promulgated by the SEC. Insider trading qualifies as a "deceptive device" because the insider occupies a position of trust and confidence with regard to the corporation's shareholders. This position of trust requires the insider to abstain from trading based on information he or she has acquired by virtue of the insider status. *Chiarella v. United States*, 445 U.S. 222, 100 S.Ct. 1108, 63 L.Ed.2d 348 (1980). (See Case-in-Point.)

The late 1980s witnessed sensational cases involving insider trading by prominent Wall Street financiers. Since then, the SEC has secured indictments under rule 10(b) against numerous prominent individuals and corporations for securities violations.

IS ANYONE WHO PROFITS FROM INSIDE INFORMATION AN INSIDER?

During 1975–76, Vincent Chiarella worked as a "markup man" for a company that printed announcements of corporate takeover bids. From the copy submitted for printing, he discerned information that enabled him to purchase stock in companies

CASE-IN-POINT

Domestic Diva Investigated for Insider Trading

In one of the most highly publicized insider trading cases in history, "domestic diva" Martha Stewart was investigated by the Securities and Exchange Commission in 2002 for selling 4,000 shares of stock in a company called ImClone after allegedly receiving insider information that the company's new cancer drug was going to be rejected by the Food and Drug Administration (FDA). The day after Stewart sold her stock, the FDA announced its rejection of the cancer drug and ImClone stock declined 16 percent. Although the SEC charged Stewart with insider trading via a civil complaint, she was charged criminally with conspiracy, obstruction of justice, making false statements to investigators, and securities fraud. Although Stewart was acquitted of securities fraud, a federal jury found her guilty of the other offenses. On July 16, 2004, a federal district judge sentenced Stewart to five months in prison followed by two years of supervised release (including five months' house arrest and electronic monitoring). On January 6, 2006, a federal appeals court upheld Stewart's conviction.

United States v. Stewart, 433 F.3d 273 (2d Cir. 2006).

targeted for takeover before this information was disclosed to the general public. Chiarella made a profit in excess of $30,000 from the purchase, and later sale, of stock in the targeted companies. He was convicted in the U.S. District Court for violating section 10(b) of the Securities Exchange Act of 1934. 15 U.S.C.A. §§ 78b, 78j(b). In 1978 the U.S. Court of Appeals for the Second Circuit affirmed his conviction.

On review, the Supreme Court recognized that a corporate insider must not trade in shares of a corporation without having first disclosed all material insider information. But the Court ruled that the obligation to disclose is based on having the "duty to disclose arising from a relationship of trust and confidence between parties to a transaction." Thus, the Court held that the trial court erred when, in effect, it instructed the jury that Chiarella owed a duty to everyone, to all sellers—indeed, to the market as a whole. Accordingly, the Court reversed his conviction. *Chiarella v. United States*, 445 U.S. 222, 100 S.Ct. 1108, 63 L.Ed.2d 348 (1980).

The Hobbs Act

Congress enacted the Anti-Racketeering Act of 1934 in an effort to control racketeering activities. However, the act did not specifically mention racketeering, and as a result of certain judicial interpretations, in 1946 Congress enacted the **Hobbs Act.** 18 U.S.C.A. § 1951. Subsection (a) provides:

> Whoever in any way or degree obstructs, delays, or affects commerce or the movement of any article or commodity in commerce, by robbery or extortion or attempts or conspires so to do, or commits or threatens physical violence to any person or property in furtherance of a plan or purpose to do anything in violation of this section shall be fined under this title or imprisoned not more than twenty years, or both.

Note that the act includes the inchoate offenses of attempt and conspiracy. Other subsections define "robbery," "extortion," and "commerce." The Hobbs Act was enacted under the power of Congress to regulate interstate commerce; however, the courts have held that it is sufficient if the government simply proves that an act has an effect on interstate commerce. Courts allow this to be established by proof of an actual impact, however small, or, in the absence of actual impact, by proof of a probable or potential impact.

Originally, most prosecutions under the Hobbs Act were based on extortion by public officials using force, violence, or fear. Now prosecutors frequently rely on the act as a basis to prosecute state and local officials based on extortion "under color of official rights."

In *Evans v. United States*, 504 U.S. 255, 112 S.Ct. 1881, 119 L.Ed.2d 57 (1992), Evans, a commissioner in DeKalb County, Georgia, was approached by an undercover FBI agent who posed as a real estate developer seeking assistance in a rezoning petition. The agent gave Evans a $1,000 check payable to a campaign fund and $7,000 in cash. Evans reported the $1,000 campaign contribution but failed to report the cash payment of $7,000 on either his campaign disclosure form or his income tax return. In upholding his conviction for extortion under the Hobbs Act, the U.S. Supreme Court stated that "[w]e hold today the Government need only show that a public official has obtained a payment to which he was not entitled, knowing that the payment was made in return for official acts." 504 U.S. at 268, 112 S.Ct. at 1889, 119 L.Ed.2d at 72.

 Go to the Scheb/ Scheb Criminal Law and Procedure 6e website at academic .cengage.com/criminaljustice/ scheb for an edited version of *Evans v. U.S.*

Tax Fraud

Prosecutions for white-collar crime often include charges of violating federal tax statutes. Although the government can employ a wide variety of federal criminal statutes to prosecute those who commit **tax fraud,** most prosecutions are based on the

Internal Revenue Code, 26 U.S.C.A. § 7201 *et seq.* Some of the more common violations include deliberately underreporting or omitting income and overstating the amount of deductions. Whether violations are felonies or misdemeanors, to obtain a conviction the government must prove the defendant's willfulness to commit the proscribed act. *United States v. Bishop,* 412 U.S. 346, 93 S.Ct. 2008, 36 L.Ed.2d 941 (1973). To establish "willfulness," the government must prove the defendant's "intentional violation of a known legal duty." *United States v. Pomponio,* 429 U.S. 10, 97 S.Ct. 22, 50 L.Ed.2d 12 (1976). In reaffirming this standard of proof, the Supreme Court observed in *Cheek v. United States,* 498 U.S. 192, 111 S.Ct. 604, 112 L.Ed.2d 617 (1991), that the term "willfully" as used in federal criminal tax statutes serves to "carve out an exception to the traditional rule [that ignorance of the law or mistake of law is no defense to prosecution]."498 U.S. at 200, 111 S.Ct. at 609, 112 L.Ed.2d at 628.

Many prosecutions for tax evasion occur under section 7201, which makes it a felony to willfully attempt to evade or to evade federal taxes. A successful prosecution requires that the government prove willfulness, the existence of a tax deficiency, and an affirmative act of evasion or attempted evasion of the tax. *Sansone v. United States,* 380 U.S. 343, 85 S.Ct. 1004, 13 L.Ed.2d 882 (1965).

Section 7202 also makes it a crime to willfully fail to collect, account truthfully for, or pay over taxes. Although most employers do not fail to collect taxes, a more common violation is the employer's failure to pay over those taxes to the Internal Revenue Service (IRS).

Section 7203 makes it a misdemeanor to willfully fail to pay an estimated tax, file a tax return, keep records, or supply information required by law. To successfully prosecute an accused, the government must establish that the accused had knowledge of a duty to file a return and willfully failed to file.

Section 7206 makes it a felony to commit fraud or make false statements in conjunction with tax obligations. To convict a person of "tax perjury," under section 7206(1) the government must prove the defendant acted willfully and (1) filed a return containing a written declaration (2) made under penalty of perjury, (3) did not believe that the return was true and correct as to every material matter, (4) and exercised willfulness with the specific intent to violate the law. The defendant's willfulness may be inferred from the existence of unreported or misreported tax information. In *United States v. Tarwater,* 308 F.3d 494 (6th Cir. 2002), the court pointed out that this is a perjury statute that criminalizes lying on any document filed with the IRS and that "the government need only prove that a defendant willfully made and subscribed a return, that the return contained a written declaration that it was made under penalties of perjury, and that the defendant did not believe the return to be true and correct as to every material matter." *Id.* at 504.

Section 7206(2) makes it a felony to willfully aid and assist another in a material falsity. To convict, the government must prove (1) an act of aiding and assisting in the preparation of a return or other document, (2) material falsity, and (3) willfulness. Tax preparers are sometimes prosecuted under this provision of the statute.

Additional sections of 26 U.S.C.A. criminalize the furnishing of false and fraudulent statements to the IRS, interfering with the administration of the tax laws, and delivering a fraudulent tax return.

Criminal Prosecution of Tax Violations

In April 2006, the U.S. Department of Justice (DOJ) announced that during 2005, the department's Tax Division authorized prosecutions against 1,256 defendants for tax crimes, an increase of more than 43 percent over the 877 defendants authorized for prosecution in 2001 (see "Justice Department and IRS Highlight Tax Enforcement Efforts," U.S.

Department of Justice, April 11, 2006, online at www.usdoj.gov/tax/txdv06212.htm). According to the DOJ's press release, the Tax Division's criminal enforcement priorities include investigating and prosecuting schemes that involve the following:

- Using trusts or other entities to conceal control over income and assets;
- Shifting assets and income to hidden offshore accounts;
- Claiming fictitious deductions;
- Using frivolous justifications for not filing truthful tax returns;
- Failing to withhold, report, and pay payroll and income taxes;
- Failing to report income; and
- Failing to file tax returns.

Organized Crime

During the Prohibition era, organized gangs trafficked in liquor and became involved in prostitution and other vices. After the repeal of the Eighteenth Amendment in 1933, these **crime syndicates** expanded into loan sharking, gambling, narcotics, and extortion. As they did, they infiltrated legitimate businesses and conducted widespread illegal operations through their own complex and secretive structures.

As we have pointed out in other chapters, the common-law development of crimes and the legislative acts defining crimes focused on particular acts of wrongdoing and on inchoate activities. This approach did not cover the ongoing criminal activity by organized groups. To that extent, the traditional definitions of crime left a void in the criminal justice system.

In 1961 Congress enacted three statutes to combat the growing problem of organized crime. These acts gave the FBI jurisdiction over gambling violations and interstate and foreign travel or transportation in aid of racketeering, 18 U.S.C.A. 1952; interstate transportation of wagering paraphernalia, 18 U.S.C.A. 1953; prohibition of illegal gambling, 8 U.S.C.A. § 1955; and laundering of monetary instruments, 18 U.S.C.A. § 1956. In 1968 Congress passed the Omnibus Crime Control and Safe Streets Act. This act provided for the conduct of court-authorized electronic surveillance. 18 U.S.C.A. §§ 2510–2521.

The Organized Crime Control Act of 1970

Notwithstanding the FBI's increased attention to organized crime, the problem continued to grow. Congress found that organized crime had weakened the stability of the nation's economy through infiltration of legitimate businesses and labor unions and threatened to subvert and corrupt our democratic processes. Under its power to regulate foreign and interstate commerce, Congress enacted the **Organized Crime Control Act of 1970.** Title IX of the act, titled **Racketeer Influenced and Corrupt Organizations (RICO),** prohibits the infiltration of legitimate organizations by racketeers where foreign or interstate commerce is affected. 18 U.S.C.A. §§ 1961–1963. In addition to increased criminal penalties, the RICO statute provided for forfeiture of property used in criminal enterprises and permitted the government to bring civil actions against such enterprises. (See the discussion of civil forfeiture in Chapter 9).

RICO created new crimes and a new approach to criminal prosecution. First, it makes it a crime for any person "who has received any income derived, directly or indirectly, from a pattern of racketeering activity or through collection of an unlawful debt … to use or invest [in] any enterprise which is engaged in interstate or foreign commerce." 18 U.S.C.A. § 1962(a). Second, RICO makes it unlawful for any such person to participate, directly or indirectly, in the conduct of the enterprise's affairs through a "pattern of racketeering." 18 U.S.C.A. § 1962(b). Third, it is a crime for any person "employed by or associated with any enterprise engaged in, or the activities of which affect, interstate or foreign commerce, to conduct or participate, directly or indirectly, in the conduct of such enterprise's affairs through a pattern of racketeering activity or collection of unlawful debt." 18 U.S.C.A. § 1962(c). This latter subsection has become the most frequently used provision by prosecutors. Finally, the act prohibits conspiracies to violate any of these proscriptions. 18 U.S.C.A. § 1962(d).

THE EXPANSIVE SCOPE OF RICO

RICO broadly defines racketeering activity to include a variety of federal offenses as well as nine state crimes that are characteristically felonies. 18 U.S.C.A. § 1961(1). Establishing a **pattern of racketeering** activity requires proof of at least two of these acts of racketeering having occurred within a period of ten years, excluding any period of imprisonment. 18 U.S.C.A. § 1961(5). Courts frequently refer to these acts as **predicate acts,** and any combination of two or more can constitute a pattern of racketeering. To obtain a conviction under RICO, the government must establish the defendant's involvement in a "pattern of racketeering or collection of an unlawful debt." There is no requirement that a state conviction be obtained before the state offense can be used as a predicate act of the racketeering activity charged. *United States v. Malatesta,* 583 F.2d 748 (5th Cir. 1978). RICO provides for a maximum of twenty years' imprisonment, a heavier penalty than many of the predicate offenses on which a RICO conviction can be based.

RICO does not criminalize a person for being a racketeer—it criminalizes that person's conduct of an enterprise through a pattern of racketeering. Therefore, a jury that finds a defendant has committed the required predicate acts must still find that these acts were committed in connection with a pattern of racketeering or collection of an unlawful debt.

WHAT CONSTITUTES AN ENTERPRISE?

In RICO, Congress has defined **enterprise** broadly to include "any individual, partnership, corporation, association, or other legal entity, and any union or group of individuals associated in fact although not a legal entity." 18 U.S.C.A. § 1961(4). The Supreme Court has said that the term encompasses both legitimate and illegitimate entities and groups. *United States v. Turkette,* 452 U.S. 576, 101 S.Ct. 2524, 69 L.Ed.2d 246 (1981). Lower federal courts have held the term includes both private and public entities such as corporations, banks, and decedents' estates, as well as state agencies, police departments, traffic courts, and prostitution rings.

EXTENSION OF RICO BEYOND ITS ORIGINAL SCOPE

RICO was conceived as a weapon for prosecution of organized crime, but it has become the basis of prosecution against white-collar criminals as well. Prosecutors have long experienced difficulty in securing convictions of organized crime leaders for violating specific criminal statutes. In part, this occurs because the evidence of a specific statutory violation might be unconvincing to a judge or jury. The reaction of a judge or jury is likely to be different when the prosecution parades before the court evidence of a series of violations that reveal a pattern of criminal behavior.

RICO has been justified because the harm that organized crime inflicts on society is far greater than the harm inflicted by those who commit statutory crimes. It can be an effective tool to help prosecutors fight against crime syndicates. Yet membership in

Defendant's Conspiracy Conviction Upheld Despite Acquittal of Substantive RICO Charge

The federal government charged Mario Salinas, a deputy sheriff of Hidalgo County, Texas, with one count of violating the RICO Act, 18 U.S.C.A. § 1962 (c), one count of conspiracy to violate RICO, section 1962(d), and other offenses. The government alleged that Deputy Salinas accepted two watches and a truck in exchange for permitting women to make "contact visits" to a federal prisoner housed in the county jail. A jury acquitted Salinas of the substantive RICO count but convicted him on the conspiracy charge. The U.S. Court of Appeals for the Fifth Circuit affirmed, and the Supreme Court granted review.

Salinas contended he could not be convicted of conspiracy under the RICO statute because he was found not guilty of the substantive RICO offense. In rejecting his contention, Justice Anthony Kennedy, writing for the Court, noted that the RICO conspiracy statute provides, "It shall be unlawful for any person to conspire to violate any of the provisions of subsection (a), (b), or (c) of this section." 18 U.S.C.A. § 1962(d). Kennedy stated, "There is no requirement of some overt act or specific act in the statute before us, unlike the general conspiracy provision applicable to federal crimes, which requires that at least one of the conspirators have committed an 'act to effect the object of the conspiracy.'" 18 U.S.C.A. § 371. "The RICO conspiracy provision, then, is even more comprehensive than the general conspiracy offense in § 371."

Salinas v. United States, 522 U.S. 52, 118 S.Ct. 469, 139 L.Ed.2d 352 (1997).

organized crime is not a necessary element for a conviction under RICO. Unlike criminal statutes that historically have been narrowly construed, Congress provided that RICO is to be liberally interpreted to effect its remedial purposes. The liberal construction of the enterprise requirement and the fact that the pattern requirement of racketeering activity is cast in numerical terms have engendered some criticism. Critics contend that RICO is a "catch-all" statute that gives prosecutors too much discretion to expand the range of indictable offenses. Examples of RICO prosecutions include the following:

- Several members of the Outlaws Motorcycle Club were prosecuted for a RICO violation based on narcotics and prostitution offenses. *United States v. Watchmaker,* 761 F.2d 1459 (11th Cir. 1985).

- Vogt, a U.S. Customs Services Officer, accepted payment for information that was used to facilitate a drug smuggling operation. The bribe money was invested in foreign bank accounts, thus constituting a money laundering enterprise. *United States v. Vogt,* 910 F.2d 1184 (4th Cir. 1990).

- A gambler and a police officer were convicted for their involvement in a police protection racket. *United States v. Sanders,* 962 F.2d 660 (7th Cir. 1992).

- Gang members were convicted of racketeering offenses for extorting protection money from local Chinese businesses, committing robberies, and kidnapping and murdering rival gang members, potential witnesses, and business owners who refused to pay protection money. *United States v. Wong,* 40 F.3d 1347 (2d Cir. 1994).

- An attorney was convicted of violating RICO based on participating in a scheme involving bribery of judges where evidence revealed that the defendant had agreed to seek to corruptly use the court system by bribing judges to appoint

RICO, Predicate Offenses, and Double Jeopardy

Sixty members of the Nicodemo Scarfo crime family allegedly controlled Mafia operations in parts of Pennsylvania and New Jersey. The government alleged that over the course of eleven years the family's activities included a number of felony offenses. All the defendants were found guilty of conspiring to participate and participating in an enterprise through a pattern of racketeering in violation of 18 U.S.C.A. § 1962.

On appeal, Scarfo contended that the use of his former convictions as predicate offenses on which to base the RICO prosecution violated his constitutional right not to be placed in jeopardy twice for the same offense. In rejecting Scarfo's claims, the U.S. Court of Appeals pointed out the following: (1) As to state convictions used as predicate offenses, there could be no double jeopardy because different sovereigns were involved; and (2) as to federal convictions used as predicate offenses, the court in previous cases has ruled that a RICO offense "is not, in a literal sense, the 'same' offense as one of the predicate offenses" because a RICO violation requires proof of a "pattern of racketeering" and is intended to deter continuous criminal conduct whereas the predicate offenses are intended to deter discrete criminal acts. Accordingly, the court rejected Scarfo's contentions.

United States v. Pungitore, 910 F.2d 1084 (3d Cir. 1990).

Go to the Scheb/ Scheb Criminal Law and Procedure 6e website at academic .cengage.com/criminaljustice/ scheb to find *U.S. v. Gambino* (1977), a federal appeals court decision that provides an interesting example of a RICO prosecution.

attorneys as special assistant public defenders. *United States v. Massey*, 89 F.3d 1433 (11th Cir. 1996).

RICO has been extended beyond its original purpose to target such nonorganized criminals as white-collar criminals and corrupt government officials. Thus, through RICO a prosecutor can circumvent statutes of limitation and seek to inflict multiple punishments for the same offenses.

Most states have adopted RICO-type statutes. Some closely parallel the federal act, whereas others have varying provisions concerning prohibited acts, sanctions, forfeitures of property, and the procedures involved.

Despite criticism, RICO is firmly established as a weapon in the arsenal of federal and, in many instances, state prosecutors. It has proved to be a useful tool in the war against racketeering and corruption, both private and public, whether organized or not.

CONSTITUTIONAL ASSAULTS ON RICO

Since its enactment in 1970, RICO has withstood a number of constitutional assaults. In *United States v. Martino*, 648 F.2d 367 (5th Cir.1981), the Fifth Circuit found that RICO does not violate the *ex post facto* prohibition of the U.S. Constitution, nor does it violate the Ninth and Tenth Amendments by intruding on state sovereignty. Prior to that the Ninth Circuit rejected a contention that the RICO term "pattern of racketeering" is vague and ambiguous, concluding that any ambiguity was cured by the definitions of "pattern" and "racketeering activity" in section 1961. *United States v. Campanale*, 518 F.2d 352, 364 (9th Cir. 1975). Perhaps a more serious challenge to RICO has been the allegation that it violates the Double Jeopardy Clause of the Constitution. But because a RICO violation involves a separate criminal proceeding; courts have generally denied such contention. For example, the Fifth Circuit has held that the Double Jeopardy Clause does not prohibit the government from prosecuting a defendant for a RICO charge where the defendant has been previously prosecuted for a substantive offense used as one of the predicate crimes. *United States v. Smith*, 574 F.2d 308 (5th Cir. 1978).

Go to the Scheb/ Scheb Criminal Law and Procedure 6e website at academic .cengage.com/criminaljustice/ scheb for an edited version of *Scheidler v. NOW* (2003).

National Organization for Women v. Scheidler, 510 U.S. 249, 114 S.Ct. 798, 127 L.Ed.2d 99 (1994)
Scheidler v. National Organization for Women, 537 U.S. 393, 123 S.Ct. 1057, 154 L.Ed.2d 991 (2003)
Scheidler v. National Organization for Women, 547 U.S. 9, 126 S.Ct. 1264, 164 L.Ed.2d 10 (2006)

The National Organization for Women (NOW) and some abortion clinics brought a class action suit against some organizers of an antiabortion protest network, alleging the organizers violated the RICO Act by engaging in a nationwide conspiracy to shut down abortion clinics through a pattern of racketeering activity that included acts of extortion in violation of the Hobbs Act (18 U.S.C.A. § 1951). After lower federal courts dismissed their claims, the U.S. Supreme Court granted review to resolve a conflict between lower federal courts as to whether the term "enterprise" was limited to entities that involved an economic motive. After examining the term as used in RICO, the Court concluded that an "enterprise" was not required to have an economic motive. The Court sent the case back for further proceedings. A jury found the activities by Scheidler et al. included a pattern of racketeering activity that consisted of violations or attempts or conspiracy to violate the Hobbs Act, state extortion law, and the Travel Act. The jury awarded damages, and the District Court entered a permanent nationwide injunction prohibiting Scheidler et al. from obstructing access to the clinics, trespassing on clinic property, damaging clinic property, or using violence or threats of violence against the clinics, their employees, or their patients. Scheidler et al. appealed to the U.S. Seventh Circuit Court of Appeals. The Seventh Circuit, affirming in relevant part, held the women's right to seek medical services from the clinics, the clinic doctors' rights to perform their jobs, and the clinics' rights to conduct their business constituted "property" that Scheidler et al. obtained in violation of the Hobbs Act. The court also upheld the issuance of the nationwide injunction. Once again, the U.S. Supreme Court granted review. In an 8–1 decision, the Supreme Court held that Petitioners [Scheidler et al.] did not commit extortion within the meaning of the Hobbs Act because they did not "obtain" property from Respondents [NOW et al.].

Writing for the Court, Chief Justice William Rehnquist stated,
"We hold that Petitioners did not commit extortion because they did not 'obtain' property from respondents as required by the Hobbs Act. We further hold that our determination with respect to extortion under the Hobbs Act renders insufficient the other bases or predicate acts of racketeering supporting the jury's conclusion that petitioners violated RICO."

The Court recognized that the petitioners interfered with, disrupted, and in some instances completely deprived respondents of their ability to exercise their property rights. But because all of the predicate acts supporting the jury's finding of a RICO violation could not stand, the Court vacated the judgment that the petitioners violated RICO. Justice John Paul Stevens dissented, noting his disagreement with what he termed the Court's narrow interpretation of "obtaining property."

On remand, the Court of Appeals did not order the District Court to terminate the cases or to vacate its injunction. Instead, the Court of Appeals considered the respondents' argument that the jury's RICO verdict rested not only upon many instances of extortion-related conduct but also upon four instances (or threats) of physical violence unrelated to extortion. The Court of Appeals decided that the parties had not presented this theory to this Court and, as a result, the U.S. Supreme Court had not considered whether these four acts alone might be sufficient, as predicate acts under RICO, to support the nationwide injunction. The Court of Appeals remanded the cases to the District Court to make that determination.

Again, the Supreme Court granted review. In an 8–0 decision (Justice Samuel Alito not participating), the Court explained that the Hobbs Act says that an individual commits a federal crime if he or she "obstructs, delays, or affects commerce" by (1) "robbery," (2) "extortion," or (3) "commit[ting] or threaten[ing]

(continued)

National Organization for Women v. Scheidler
Scheidler v. National Organization for Women (continued)

physical violence to any person or property in further-ance of a plan or purpose to do anything in violation of this section" (emphasis added). Section 1951(a). The Court held that threatening or committing physical violence unre-lated to robbery or extortion which obstructs, delays, or af-fects commerce falls outside the scope of the Hobbs Act.

Writing for the Court, Justice Stephen Breyer observed:
"Respondents' [NOW et al.] Hobbs Act interpretation … would federalize much ordinary criminal behavior, rang-ing from simple assault to murder, behavior that typically is the subject of state, not federal, prosecution…. We con-clude that Congress did not intend to create a freestand-

ing physical violence offense in the Hobbs Act. It did in-tend to forbid acts or threats of physical violence in furtherance of a plan or purpose to engage in what the statute refers to as robbery or extortion (and related at-tempts or conspiracies). The judgment of the Court of Appeals is reversed, and the cases are remanded for entry of judgment for petitioners."

Although the Scheidler litigation involved civil RICO actions, the Supreme Court's decisions drew heavily from criminal precedents and appears to ef-fectively preclude the use of RICO as a basis to prose-cute unruly anti-abortion demonstrators on the theory that the demonstrators are guilty of the predicate crime under state and federal extortion acts.

Defenses in White-Collar and Organized Crime Cases

Many of the defenses available to defendants charged with white-collar and orga-nized crime offenses are similar to those available to defendants generally. The most common defense to prosecutions involving fraud is that the defendant had a good faith belief that allegedly "fraudulent" representations were, in fact, true. In a prose-cution under a statute that requires the government to prove the defendant acted willfully, an effective defense is one that negates the defendant's willfulness. In tax prosecutions a defendant who in good faith relied on the advice of a professional tax preparer can assert such reliance as a defense provided the taxpayer disclosed all rel-evant information to the tax preparer.

In prosecutions under RICO, the defenses of entrapment, double jeopardy, and selective prosecution appear more frequently than in other situations (see Chapter 14). In organized crime prosecutions, the defense often attacks the validity of the underly-ing predicate offenses. Moreover, the complexities involved in many federal statutes aimed at organized crime raise more issues of statutory construction and legislative in-tent than do the more traditionally defined crimes.

■ CONCLUSION

Unlike transactional criminal offenses, white-collar crime and organized crime are not easily defined, and the conduct involved is often elusive. We lack the accurate data and statistical information that is available on the traditional defined offenses; hence, the extent of white-collar offenses and organized crime is not readily quantifiable. Some conduct criminalized today as white-collar crimes might have passed as simply unethi-cal business practices in our earlier history. Other behavior, although long recognized as offensive, did not fit into the molds developed at common law and has become stat-utorily forbidden only in recent years. In today's society, so dependent on electronic transactions, the computer criminal might become as significant a danger to our well-being as is the street criminal who robs, burglarizes, and steals.

Organized crime is a phenomenon of our modern social and economic institutions. Through a variety of coercive and illegal tactics, it has infiltrated legitimate business operations. White-collar and underworld figures cater to people's desire for goods and services that cannot be legally supplied but that can be made available to them at minimal risks to the providers. On the positive side, there is an increased awareness of organized crime operations and an increased emphasis, particularly at the federal level, on investigation and prosecution. RICO and other measures have provided the legal system with effective tools to prosecute criminal enterprise activity and those who engage in racketeering. If the public demands increased efforts in this area, we should see considerable progress in ferreting out and punishing those who threaten the safety and economic well-being of society.

■ KEY TERMS

white-collar crimes, 244
organized crime, 244
loan sharking, 244
racketeering, 244
corporate defendants, 246
scope of an agent's authority, 246
Sherman Antitrust Act, 247
antitrust violations, 247
price fixing, 247
bid rigging, 247
Computer Fraud and Abuse Act, 247
access devices, 248
USA PATRIOT Act, 248
False Statements Act, 249
bankruptcy fraud, 249
False Claims Act, 249
mail fraud, 251

wire fraud, 251
money laundering, 252
structuring, 253
insider trading, 253
Securities and Exchange Act, 253
churning, 254
Hobbs Act, 255
tax fraud, 255
crime syndicates, 257
Organized Crime Control Act of
    1970, 257
Racketeer Influenced and Corrupt
    Organizations (RICO), 257
pattern of racketeering, 258
predicate acts, 258
enterprise, 258

■ WEB-BASED RESEARCH ACTIVITY

Go to the Web. Locate your state's criminal statutes online. Determine whether your state has its own laws against racketeering or other forms of organized crime. Use your state government's Internet resources to determine whether your state attorney general's office has an active criminal enforcement effort underway in the area of organized crime or in some other area of white-collar crime.

■ QUESTIONS FOR THOUGHT AND DISCUSSION

1. Is it appropriate to define "white-collar offenses" by focusing on the offender's social and economic status?

2. What is the federal constitutional authority for enacting (a) antitrust and wire fraud laws? (b) postal offenses? (c) securities laws? (d) bankruptcy laws?

3. Why do federal criminal statutes figure so prominently in the context of white-collar offenses?

4. Under what circumstances can a corporation be held legally responsible for a white-collar offense committed by one of its agents or employees?

5. Why does the rationale for federal antitrust and securities laws require the availability of both civil and criminal sanctions?

6. What criminal offenses described in Chapters 5 through 9 can be committed by using a computer?

7. Describe a factual scenario that could occur in the operation of a municipal or county government in your state that could likely result in a person's being prosecuted under the Hobbs Act.

8. What led Congress to the realization that the traditional common-law transactional approach to crime was inadequate to deal with organized crime?

9. What is required to establish a "pattern of racketeering activity" under RICO?

10. How does RICO define "enterprise," and what is its significance in prosecution of RICO offenses?

■ PROBLEMS FOR DISCUSSION AND SOLUTION

1. An elderly widow whose income was derived primarily from Social Security and a small pension owned $100,000 in government bonds that she inherited from her late husband. Other than her home and a modest checking account, her bonds constituted her estate. On advice of A. Brokero, a licensed securities broker, she converted the bonds into cash and deposited the proceeds with Brokero to manage. She explained her financial situation and investment objectives. She and Brokero agreed that her funds should be invested in conservative, income-producing investments. Instead, Brokero, who had trading authorization from the widow, bought and sold numerous issues of aggressive stocks for the account, and at the end of two years the account had dwindled to $28,500. During the two-year period, Brokero had earned thousands of dollars in commissions for buying and selling the investments. What, if any, criminal violation is suggested by this scenario?

2. At a state peace officers' convention, two police officers from Sedateville, a small rural community, developed a friendship with two officers from Trendville, a metropolitan city. Gambling, except for a state lottery, was prohibited in the state. As their friendship developed, they enjoyed "a friendly game of poker" with modest betting. They all agreed that "after all, gambling is really not all bad" and probably should not be prohibited. As the rural officers began to lament their modest salaries, the Trendville officers introduced them to some "prominent businessmen." They all agreed that "it would hurt no one" to allow these businessmen to conduct some private gambling operations in Sedateville. But, of course, the operation would require some protection by the local police. With cooperation of the officers, the businessmen opened a bar where gambling was conducted in a back room. The new operation also accommodated male patrons seeking prostitutes by transporting the men to Trendville for a weekend "sports event." Through the cooperation of the officers, the new operation was "overlooked" by the Sedateville police. In turn, the officers from Trendville and Sedateville enjoyed some of the profits from the gambling and prostitution activities. The four officers' gains eventually exceeded their salaries as police officers, and as they later said, "No one was hurt in this operation—people were just allowed to have a good time." Under what circumstances would this scenario present a basis for a RICO prosecution?

CHAPTER 11

Offenses against Public Health and the Environment

CHAPTER OUTLINE

Introduction

In the wake of the Industrial Revolution, society recognized the need for government to protect the **public health.** In the latter decades of the twentieth century, society became aware of the need for governmental action to protect the natural environment as well. Obviously, these two societal interests are closely related, as public health is greatly dependent on a healthy natural environment. Increasingly, governments at all levels (i.e., federal, state and local) are making use of criminal sanctions as means of protecting the public health and the environment.

In addition to offenses involving the adulteration or misbranding of foods, medicines, and cosmetics and the unlawful exposure of others to germs or toxins, this chapter examines **environmental crime,** which includes, among other things, the unlawful pollution of the air and water; unlawful transportation, handling, or storage of hazardous materials; and unlawful destruction of protected animal and plant species or their habitats.

Beyond protecting natural resources and public health, the criminal law seeks to promote aesthetic values. Laws forbidding **littering** or dumping of refuse along the roadside are based on aesthetic considerations as well as environmental and public health concerns. **Antismoking laws,** which we discuss later in this chapter, are motivated by aesthetic as well as public health concerns. **Noise ordinances** also seek to protect the aesthetic quality of the living environment that people share.

Sources of Law Defining Crimes against the Public Health and the Environment

As we have seen throughout the foregoing chapters, common-law crimes were originally recognized by courts and later revised and expanded by legislatures. But crimes against public health and the environment do not have their origin in the English common law. Rather, these offenses originated directly from Congress and state legislatures in response to the needs of a changing society. Offenses relating to public health originated in the late nineteenth and early twentieth centuries as a result of the widespread distribution of food, drugs, and cosmetics and the need to control communicable diseases. By the early 1900s, municipalities perceived the need for zoning to control nuisances and to regulate land use. Since the middle of the twentieth century, pollution of the ground, water, and air has been recognized as a major threat to the health and welfare of the people and, indeed, to the ecological balance of the Earth.

Enforcing regulations in these fields is accomplished largely through regulatory agencies and measures imposing civil liability. Nevertheless, legislatures have found it necessary to impose criminal sanctions to effectively enforce standards and to deter violators. Although not faced with the severe environmental problems of our age, the common law did regard wildlife, game, and fish as resources to be preserved by government. In the United States, the state and federal governments have for many years imposed criminal sanctions against **poaching** to protect these resources for the benefit of the public.

In contrast with the typical common-law crimes, many offenses against the public health and environment consist of an offender's neglect to comply with required standards or failure to take action required by law. These offenses are *mala prohibita,* and statutes criminalizing conduct in these areas generally contemplate a lower level of intent, frequently imposing a standard of **strict liability.** For example, in *State v. Budd Co.*, 425 N.E.2d 935 (Ohio App. 1980), the defendant was convicted under a state law that made it a criminal offense to dispose of garbage or other pollutants in any ditch, pond, stream, or other watercourse. On appeal, the court rejected the appellant's argument that it was necessary for the state to prove his criminal intent. The court observed that the law did not require proof of intent and that "the destruction of wildlife through pollution, will occur whenever the waterways are intentionally or accidentally polluted." 425 N.E.2d at 938.

Public Health Legislation

The authority of government to enact laws to protect the public health is a basic component of the police power of the state. Statutes delegating to public health agencies the power to declare quarantines, and later to require inoculations to control communicable diseases, were among the earliest applications of this police power. At the turn of the century, the U.S. Supreme Court reviewed a defendant's sentence to pay a fine for refusing to be vaccinated for smallpox as required by a Cambridge, Massachusetts, ordinance. The defendant argued that a compulsory vaccination law invaded his liberty secured by the Constitution. Rejecting this contention, the Court observed that "persons and property are subjected to all kinds of restraints and burdens in order to secure the general comfort, health, and prosperity of the state." *Jacobson v. Massachusetts*, 197 U.S. 11, 26, 25 S.Ct. 358, 361, 49 L.Ed. 643, 650 (1905). Today all states require vaccinations of public school students; however, some states provide exemptions where parents show that vaccinations are contrary to their religious beliefs.

Today, numerous federal, state, and local laws address health concerns, providing criminal penalties for serious violations. Modern statutes address a variety of contemporary problems. California, like other states, has a comprehensive collection of laws concerning prevention and control of communicable disease and sexually transmitted disease. Section 120600 of the California Health and Safety Code stipulates the following:

> Any person who refuses to give any information to make any report, to comply with any proper control measure or examination, or to perform any other duty or act required by this chapter, or who violates any provision of this chapter or any rule or regulation of the state board issued pursuant to this chapter, or who exposes any person to or infects any person with any venereal disease; or any person infected with a venereal disease in an infectious state who knows of the condition and who marries or has sexual intercourse, is guilty of a misdemeanor.

In *Reynolds v. McNichols*, 488 F.2d 1378 (10th Cir. 1973), a federal appeals court upheld a Denver, Colorado, "hold and treat" ordinance authorizing detention and treatment, if necessary, of a woman arrested for prostitution who was reasonably suspected of having a venereal disease. Indeed, many states now have statutes imposing criminal penalties on health care professionals who fail to report communicable diseases. See, for example, West's Colo. Stat. Ann. §§ 25-4-402–407. A California appellate court has held that under the "special needs" doctrine, the state, without individualized suspicion, may require that a person convicted of prostitution be tested for AIDS. *Love v. Superior Court*, 276 Cal. Rptr. 660 (Cal. App. 1990). In *Fosman v. State*, 664 So.2d 1163 (Fla. App. 1995), the court held that a court order requiring a defendant charged with sexual battery to submit to an HIV test did not constitute an unreasonable search and seizure. Florida has also enacted laws criminalizing intentional sexual transmission of HIV without a partner's consent and making it a felony for a person who knows that he or she is HIV-positive to donate blood or organs. West's Fla. Stat. Ann. §§ 381.0041(11), 384.24. In Nevada, a licensed prostitute who practices with knowledge of a positive HIV test result is guilty of a felony. Nev. Rev. Stat. § 201.358. Most public health laws that impose criminal penalties do not include any intent requirement. In those instances the government need only prove the defendant violated the statute. Offenses of this type are known as strict liability offenses, a concept we introduced in Chapter 4.

The Federal Pure Food, Drug, and Cosmetic Act

In 1848 Congress first enacted legislation to prevent the importation of adulterated drugs and medicines. Today, numerous federal acts relate to foods and drugs, but the basic **Pure Food, Drug, and Cosmetic Act (FDCA)** dates back to 1906. It was comprehensively amended in 1938 and subsequently amended many times. 21 U.S.C.A. §§ 301–392. The present law prohibits traffic in food, drugs, and cosmetics being prepared or handled under unsanitary circumstances or under conditions that render them injurious to health. Included in its broad sweep are prohibitions against misbranding and adulteration of food, drugs, and cosmetics, as well as requirements for truthful labeling.

The U.S. Supreme Court has declared that the purpose of the FDCA is "to safeguard the consumer by applying the act to articles from the moment of their introduction into interstate commerce all the way to the moment of their delivery to the ultimate consumer." *United States v. Sullivan,* 332 U.S. 689, 696, 68 S.Ct. 331, 336, 92 L.Ed. 297, 303 (1948).

Violations of the FDCA are punishable by criminal penalties, civil fines, and injunctive relief, and, in some instances, by seizure of the articles found to be adulterated or misbranded.

Specifically, the FDCA prohibits

(a) The introduction or delivery for introduction into interstate commerce of any food, drug, device, or cosmetic that is adulterated or misbranded.

(b) The adulteration or misbranding of any food, drug, device, or cosmetic in interstate commerce.

(c) The receipt in interstate commerce of any food, drug, device, or cosmetic that is adulterated or misbranded, and the delivery or proffered delivery thereof for pay or otherwise. 21 U.S.C.A. § 331.

The FDCA defines adulterated food, 21 U.S.C.A. § 342; sets out standards for considering whether drugs and devices are adulterated, 21 U.S.C.A. § 351; and sets out criteria for adulterated cosmetics, 21 U.S.C.A. § 361. In general an item is considered adulterated if its ingredients are poisonous, filthy, putrid, or otherwise unsanitary or if it has come into contact with unsanitary substances.

Misbranding includes false or misleading labels, packaging, and containers. Specifically, 21 U.S.C.A. § 343 defines misbranded foods; 21 U.S.C.A. § 352 classifies misbranded drugs and devices; and 21 U.S.C.A. § 362 defines misbranded cosmetics.

In 1952, the Eighth Circuit declared that "It is not necessary that [food] actually become contaminated.... [T]he statute is designed to prevent adulterations 'in their incipiency' by condemning unsanitary conditions which may result in contamination." *Berger v. United States,* 200 F.2d 818, 821 (8th Cir. 1952). Numerous federal court decisions have interpreted what constitutes adulteration and misbranding under the FDCA. Illustrative decisions include:

- *United States v. Kohlback,* 38 F.3d 832 (6th Cir. 1994), where the court found that orange juice had been adulterated by adding beet sugar, other additives, and preservatives in order to extend the product's shelf life.
- *United States v. Bhutani,* 175 F.3d 572 (7th Cir. 1999), where the court noted the jury had found that a manufacturer adulterated a liver drug by "spiking" it with sodium hydroxide and repacking it with falsified expiration dates.
- *United States v. Haas,* 171 F.3d 259 (5th Cir. 1999), where the court upheld a conviction for aiding and abetting the illegal delivery of misbranded drugs into interstate commerce by sale of non–FDA-approved drugs.

In addition to provisions prohibiting adulteration and misbranding. the FDCA proscribes:

> The alteration, mutilation, destruction, obliteration, or removal of the whole or any part of the labeling of, or the doing of any other act with respect to, a food, drug, device, or cosmetic, if such act is done while such article is held for sale (whether or not the first sale) after shipment in interstate commerce and results in such article being adulterated or misbranded. 21 U.S.C.A. § 331(k).

The Supreme Court has held that section 331(k) defines two distinct offenses with respect to products held for sale after interstate shipment: (1) acts relating to misbranding and (2) acts relating to adulteration of the product. *United States v. Wiesenfeld Warehouse Co.,* 376 U.S. 86, 84 S.Ct. 559, 11 L.Ed.2d 536 (1964).

Strict Liability Offenses

As with most public health laws, violations of federal food and drug statutes fall in the category of **regulatory offenses,** which traditionally courts have regarded as strict liability crimes. In *United States v. Dotterweich,* 320 U.S. 277, 64 S.Ct. 134, 88 L.Ed. 48 (1943), the U.S. Supreme Court established a standard of strict liability for violations of the FDCA by holding that proof of the defendant's intent to commit a violation was not required to obtain a misdemeanor conviction. In felony prosecutions, however, the government must prove the defendant's intent. Moreover, in prosecution under certain sections of the FDCA, lower federal courts have held that to obtain a felony conviction, the government must establish the defendant's specific intent. See, for example, *United States v. Mitcheltree,* 940 F.2d 1329 (10th Cir. 1991), where the defendant was prosecuted for violating 21 U.S.C.A. §§ 331(a) and 333(a)(2) for introducing a misbranded drug into interstate commerce with the intent to mislead or defraud.

Many legal scholars criticize the imposition of strict liability in regulatory offenses, such as food, drug, and health laws. They contend that it brands as criminals people who are without moral fault. Arguing against making the violation of such laws punishable by incarceration, critics suggest decriminalization, with liability predicated on a **negligence standard** rather than on strict liability, or punishment by only a monetary fine. These criticisms notwithstanding, Congress has determined that the interest of society requires a high standard of care and has been unwilling to eliminate either the strict liability standard or incarceration. The courts follow *United States v. Park,* 421 U.S. 658, 670, 95 S.Ct. 1903, 1910, 44 L.Ed.2d 489, 500 (1975), in which the U.S. Supreme Court held that a corporate agent who bears a responsible relationship to the operation of the enterprise, and has power to take measures necessary to ensure compliance, can be found guilty of violating such regulatory statutes.

United States v. Wiesenfeld Warehouse Co., 376 U.S. 86, 84 S.Ct. 559, 11 L.Ed.2d 536 (1964)

In this case the Supreme Court discusses the standard of criminal liability under Section 301 (k) of the Federal Pure Food, Drug, and Cosmetic Act.

JUSTICE POTTER STEWART delivered the opinion of the Court:

Section 301 (k) of the Federal Food, Drug, and Cosmetic Act prohibits the "alteration, mutilation, destruction, obliteration, or removal of the whole or any part of the labeling of, or the doing of any other act with respect to, a food, drug, device, or cosmetic, if such act is done while such article is held for sale ... after shipment in interstate commerce and results in such article being adulterated or misbranded.... The question presented by this appeal is whether a criminal information which alleges the holding of food by a public storage warehouseman (after interstate shipment and before ultimate sale) under unsanitary conditions in a building accessible to rodents, birds and insects, where it may have become contaminated with filth, charges an offense under 301 (k)....

The language of 301 (k) unambiguously defines two distinct offenses with respect to food held for sale after interstate shipment. As originally enacted in 1938, the subsection prohibited "[t]he alteration, mutilation, destruction, obliteration, or removal" of the label, or "the doing of any other act" with respect to the product which "results in such article being misbranded." The section was amended in 1948 to prohibit additionally "the doing of any other act" with respect to the product which "results in such article being adulterated." The acts specifically enumerated in the original enactment relate to the offense of misbranding through labeling or the lack thereof. The separate offense of adulteration, on the other hand, is concerned solely with deterioration or contamination of the commodity itself. For the most part, acts resulting in misbranding and acts resulting in adulteration are wholly distinct. Consequently, since the enumerated label-defacing offenses bear no textual or logical

relation to the scope of the general language condemning acts of product adulteration, application of the rule of ejusdem generis to limit the words "the doing of any other act" resulting in product adulteration in 301 (k) to acts of the same general character as those specifically enumerated with respect to misbranding is wholly inappropriate....

Section 301 (k), as amended, prohibits "any ... act" which results in adulteration of the product. And food is adulterated if it "has been prepared, packed, or held under unsanitary conditions whereby it may have become contaminated with filth." This language defines with particularity an explicit standard of conduct. Section 301 (k), read together with the definition of food adulteration contained in 402 (a) (4), therefore, gives ample warning that the "holding" or storing of food under unsanitary conditions whereby it may have become contaminated is prohibited.

It is settled law in the area of food and drug regulation that a guilty intent is not always a prerequisite to the imposition of criminal sanctions. Food and drug legislation, concerned as it is with protecting the lives and health of human beings, under circumstances in which they might be unable to protect themselves, often "dispenses with the conventional requirement for criminal conduct—awareness of some wrongdoing. In the interest of the larger good it puts the burden of acting at hazard upon a person otherwise innocent but standing in responsible relation to a public danger....

It is argued, nevertheless, that the Government in this case is seeking to impose criminal sanctions upon one "who is, by the very nature of his business powerless" to protect against this kind of contamination, however high the standard of care exercised. Whatever the truth of this claim, it involves factual proof to be raised defensively at a trial on the merits. We are here concerned only with the construction of the statute as it relates to the sufficiency of the information, and not with the scope and reach of the statute as applied to such facts as may be developed by evidence adduced at a trial.

Criminal Liability of Responsible Corporate Officers

Food, drugs, and cosmetics are usually produced and distributed by corporate enterprises. To effectively enforce regulatory laws imposing criminal sanctions in these areas, government agencies must be able to affix responsibility on individuals in supervisory positions as well as on corporate entities. The Supreme Court first recognized the concept of a **responsible corporate officer** in *United States v. Dotterweich,* 320 U.S. 277, 64 S.Ct. 134, 88 L.Ed. 48 (1943). There, a pharmacy company and Dotterweich, its president and general manager, were charged with shipping misbranded and adulterated drugs in violation of the FDCA. The jury declined to find the company guilty but did find Dotterweich guilty. A federal appellate court reversed his conviction. The U.S. Supreme Court granted review, upheld Dotterweich's conviction, and held that a "responsible corporate officer" could be held accountable for corporate violations of the FDCA. The Court reasoned that Dotterweich was in a responsible position to prevent any public danger.

Until 1975 there were conflicting federal court decisions about whether a corporate officer who failed to take measures to prevent violations of the food and drug laws from occurring could be held criminally liable. Recognizing this conflict, the Supreme Court again addressed the standard of liability of corporate officers under the FDCA in *United States v. Park,* 421 U.S. 658, 95 S.Ct. 1903, 44 L.Ed.2d 489 (1975). There, a national retail food chain and its president and chief executive officer were charged with causing food shipped in interstate commerce to be held in a building accessible to rodents and exposed to contamination. The food chain pled guilty, but its president contested the charges against him. He argued that although he retained authority over corporate affairs, he delegated "normal operating duties," including sanitation, to lower-level personnel. In rejecting his contention as a basis of nonliability, the Court explained that the prosecution established a *prima facie* case of the guilt of the accused when it established that the defendant had, by reason of his position in the corporation, responsibility and authority either to prevent in the first instance or promptly to correct the violation complained of and that he failed to do so. The Court left open a means for a defendant to establish that he or she was powerless to prevent or correct a violation but noted that "If such a claim is made, the defendant has the burden of coming forward with evidence, but this does not alter the Government's ultimate burden of proving ... the defendant's guilt, including his power, in light of the duty imposed by the Act, to prevent or correct the prohibited condition." *United States v. Park,* 421 U.S. at 673, 95 S.Ct. at 1912, 44 L.Ed.2d at 502. The Court agreed with the government that Park was subject to strict criminal liability because he failed to use his authority in operating the company to prevent the storage of food in an area where it could be contaminated by rodents.

Defenses under the FDCA

Defendants charged with violations of the FDCA have challenged warrantless inspections, but in most cases this has not proved to be successful because the courts have ruled that the Fourth Amendment allows considerable latitude in inspection of commercial establishments (see Chapter 15). A corporate officer charged with a violation of the act may assert the defense of objective impossibility. In *United States v. Gel Spice Co., Inc.,* 773 F.2d 427 (2d Cir. 1985), the court noted that to establish the impossibility defense, the corporate officer must introduce evidence that he or she exercised extraordinary care but was nevertheless powerless to prevent or correct violations of the act. The defense is very difficult to establish and fails in most situations. In cases where the government prosecutes for misbranding of articles, the defense will sometimes rely on experts to establish the validity of the defendant's branding.

CASE-IN-POINT

Responsibility Follows Authority

Dean Starr, secretary-treasurer of Cheney Brothers Food Corporation, was convicted of violating the Federal Pure Food, Drug, and Cosmetic Act, 21 U.S.C.A. §§ 301–391, for allowing contamination of food stored in a company warehouse over which he had operational responsibility. After an inspector from the Food and Drug Administration (FDA) pointed out the problem, the janitor for the warehouse was instructed to make corrections, but no action was taken. A month later,

a second inspection by the FDA disclosed that the problem had not been corrected. On appeal, Starr contended that he was not responsible because the janitor in charge had failed to comply with instructions to clean up the warehouse. The court rejected his argument, noting that Starr was aware of the problem after the first inspection and had ample time to remedy the situation. In affirming his conviction, the court also observed that supervisory officers have a duty to anticipate the shortcomings of their delegates.

Planning and Zoning Laws

Although sometimes used interchangeably, the terms "zoning" and "planning" are not synonymous. Zoning is primarily concerned with the use and regulation of buildings and structures, whereas planning is a broader term embracing the systematic and orderly development of a community. *State ex rel. Kearns v. Ohio Power Co.*, 127 N.E.2d 394, 399 (Ohio 1955).

In *Village of Euclid, Ohio v. Ambler Realty Co.*, 272 U.S. 365, 47 S.Ct. 114, 71 L.Ed. 303 (1926), the Supreme Court first upheld the concept of **zoning,** which allows local governments to divide areas of the community and to designate the permitted and prohibited land uses in the respective districts. This is often referred to as Euclidean zoning. Today land-use zoning has become widespread and sophisticated. For example, newer concepts such as the "planned unit development" (PUD) may permit a mixture of land uses on the same tract of land. See, for example, *Rouse-Fairwood Development Ltd. Partnership v. Supervisor of Assessments for Prince George's County*, 773 A.2d 535 (Md. App. 2001). Comprehensive planning has evolved into complex land-use management and guides the development of a community, and that planning is implemented to a large degree by local zoning ordinances (their enactment usually preceded by studies and recommendations of professional consultants). Building codes are generally encompassed within the overall local zoning requirements. Local citizens are enlisted to sit on planning and zoning boards that make recommendations to the governing body. Any comprehensive zoning ordinance must provide for a board of adjustment to act in a quasi-judicial capacity. The board must have the power to grant variances where strict enforcement of an ordinance would cause an undue hardship to property owners. It may also be empowered to approve special exceptions based on criteria specified in a zoning ordinance.

As with other regulatory measures, enforcement of local zoning codes is accomplished administratively in most instances. Failing this, local governments often resort to civil court actions, commonly seeking injunctive relief against violators. Most zoning ordinances classify violations as misdemeanors and provide for a fine and a jail term on conviction. Zoning ordinances, like most health regulations, generally do not include an intent requirement. Prosecution of violators is usually undertaken only as a last resort. But once a state or local government commences prosecution of a defendant for violating a zoning ordinance, it must meet all burdens placed on the prosecution in criminal proceedings. *People v. St. Agatha Home for Children,* 389 N.E.2d 1098 (N.Y. 1979).

Numerous federal statutes and agencies play a part in regulating and enforcing the laws affecting our environment. Among the older agencies are the Army Corps of Engineers, the Coast Guard, and the Departments of the Interior, Commerce, Transportation, and Justice. A newer agency, the **Environmental Protection Agency** (EPA), acts under the authority of major congressional enactments and has significant responsibilities in numerous areas, including hazardous wastes, toxic substances, and air and water pollution. State environmental agencies became active in the 1970s, and planning and coordinating councils now function at state, regional, and local levels. They play an important part in environmental regulation by establishing pollution controls, water management programs, and wastewater and solid-waste disposal programs.

The Scope of Federal and State Environmental Statutes

Environmental regulation at the federal and state levels has become a vast undertaking. Those enacted by federal and state governments are enforced by regulatory agencies, by civil suits, and by criminal prosecutions. At the federal level, the EPA, which came into being in 1970, coordinates national efforts to reduce environmental risks and enforce federal laws protecting health and the environment. During the 1970s government agencies relied almost exclusively on civil penalties as an enforcement tool. The concept changed in the 1980s and 1990s when criminal enforcement of environmental laws became prominent, particularly in instances of egregious waste disposal, water pollution, and air pollution.

The trend toward prosecution of violators, particularly at the federal level, is shown by the increase in prosecutions. According to the Transactional Records Access Clearinghouse (TRAC) at Syracuse University, the EPA referred 139 cases to the U.S. Department of Justice (DOJ) for criminal prosecution during the 1992 fiscal year. During fiscal year 2001, the EPA referred 328 criminal cases to the DOJ. The high-water mark in EPA criminal referrals was fiscal year 1998, when 486 criminal cases were referred to the DOJ.

Most states now have environmental agencies that coordinate with the EPA in the enforcement of national environmental laws as well as in supervising the enforcement of state environmental laws. The California Environmental Protection Agency is a good example. In 1991 the governor, by executive order, established the agency as a cabinet level position in order to restore, protect, and enhance the environment and to ensure public health, environmental quality, and economic vitality.

Some environmental crimes (usually punishable as misdemeanors) require only proof that the defendant committed a proscribed act or failed to comply with a required standard. In prosecutions of these strict liability offenses, the government may establish the defendant's guilt in a manner similar to prosecuting many crimes against the public health. Other statutes (usually those that impose felony punishment) require the government to establish the defendant's negligent conduct or a willful or knowing violation, and many court decisions in environmental prosecutions turn on whether the evidence is sufficient to meet the required statutory standard.

Major Federal Environmental Legislation Providing Criminal Sanctions

Congress enacted its first major environmental law, the **Rivers and Harbors Act,** in 1899. 33 U.S.C.A. §§ 401–467. This act makes it a misdemeanor to discharge refuse into the navigable waters of the United States. Notwithstanding the act's provisions for criminal enforcement, the federal government traditionally has sought enforcement through the civil courts. In recent years, the following acts of Congress have provided significant means to enforce criminal violations of environmental laws and regulations.

- **Clean Air Act** of 1970, 42 U.S.C.A. §§ 7401–7642.
- Federal Water Pollution Control Act of 1972 (**Clean Water Act),** 33 U.S.C.A. §§ 1251–1376.
- **Resource Conservation and Recovery Act** of 1976 (RCRA), 42 U.S.C.A. §§ 6901–6992.
- **Toxic Substances Control Act** of 1976 (TSCA), 15 U.S.C.A. §§ 2601–2692.
- **Comprehensive Environmental Response, Compensation and Liability Act** of 1980 (CERCLA), 42 U.S.C.A. §§ 9601–9675.

The Clean Air Act

The Clean Air Act sets federal standards designed to enhance the quality of the air by deterring air polluters. In 1977 Congress passed a series of amendments establishing stricter standards for air quality. As amended, the act provides criminal sanctions for the violation of any provisions for which civil penalties apply and for any person who knowingly makes any false representation in a document filed under the act.

The Clean Air Act recognizes that the prevention and control of air pollution at its source is the primary responsibility of states and local governments. It provides that enforcement may be delegated to the states pursuant to the State Implementation Plan (SIP), 42 U.S.C.A. § 7410, but the states are not required to enact minimum criminal provisions to receive EPA approval of their implementation plans. Nevertheless, states are increasingly toughening criminal penalties in this area. State penalties for violations of air pollution laws vary. For example, violation of Oklahoma's Clean Air Act entails a fine of $25,000 or up to one year in jail per day for misdemeanor violations and a fine of $250,000 or up to ten years' imprisonment for violations classified as felonies. 27A Okl. Stats. Ann. § 2–5–116. Rhode Island law provides for substantial fines and imprisonment for violations of air pollution laws and regulations, yet it stipulates:

> No person shall be convicted or found liable in any criminal prosecution … brought by or in behalf of the state, the director or the public to enjoin, suppress, prohibit, or punish air pollution unless he or she knowingly violated a rule or regulation or order of the director, issued under the authority conferred upon him or her by [Ch. 23]. R.I. Stat. § 23-23-11.

There have been fewer criminal prosecutions for violation of air pollution laws compared with prosecutions for violations of hazardous waste and water pollution laws. Two reasons have been advanced: first, the cost of criminal enforcement in this area is apparently great; second, the problems of enforcement are made exceedingly difficult for states because air pollution is a less stationary category of pollution.

The *Exxon Valdez* Spill Prosecution and Subsequent Civil Suit

In March 1989, the supertanker *Exxon Valdez* ran aground and ruptured, spilling more than 240,000 barrels of oil into Alaska's Prince William Sound and wreaking havoc on the natural environment. Subsequently, the federal government brought criminal charges against the Exxon Shipping Co. and its parent, Exxon Corporation, under the Clean Water Act, the Migratory Bird Act, the Ports and Waterway Safety Act, and the Dangerous Cargo Act. In October 1991, one week before the case was scheduled to go to trial, Exxon accepted a plea bargain under which it agreed to plead guilty and pay $25 million in federal fines and another $100 million in restitution, split between the federal and state governments. The $125 million fine was the largest environmental criminal fine in U.S. history.

In 1994, a federal district court in Anchorage, Alaska, ordered Exxon to pay roughly $287 million in compensatory damages to commercial salmon and herring fishermen, plus $5 billion in punitive damages. However, the Ninth Circuit Court of Appeals remanded the case to the district court to reconsider the punitive damages. *In re Exxon Valdez,* 270 F.3d 1215 (9th Cir. 2001). On remand, the district court concluded the $5 billion in punitive damages was still fair, but in compliance with the Ninth Circuit mandate, it reduced the award to $4 billion. *In re Exxon Valdez,* 236 F. Supp.2d 1043 (2002). After further litigation, on December 22, 2006, the Ninth Circuit Court of Appeals ordered the district court to reduce the punitive damage award against Exxon to $2.5 billion.

In re Exxon Valdez, 472 F.3d 600 (9th Cir. 2006).

The Clean Water Act

The Federal Water Pollution Control Act of 1972 (Clean Water Act, or CWA), 33 U.S.C.A. §§ 1251–1376, is designed to control water pollution and regulate industrial and other discharges into navigable waters. The CWA prohibits the discharge of pollutants from any **point source** into the navigable waters of the United States unless such discharge complies with a permit issued by the EPA pursuant to the National Pollutant Discharge Elimination System (NPDES) or by an EPA-authorized state agency. See 33 U.S.C.A. §§ 1311(a) and 1342. Although the CWA is enforced primarily through civil means, criminal sanctions have been imposed for willful or negligent violations of certain provisions concerning permits and the making of false statements. Amendments in 1987 substituted the term "knowingly" for the earlier intent requirement of "willfully" and imposed more stringent penalties for negligent violations and even more severe penalties for knowing violations of the act's criminal provisions. 33 U.S.C.A. § 1319(c)(2).

Courts have construed the term "knowingly" to find that a defendant's acts violate the CWA if those acts are proscribed, even if the defendant was not aware of the proscription. Thus, courts have held the government need only prove the defendant performed acts intentionally; it is not required to prove the defendant knew those acts violated the CWA. *United States v. Hopkins,* 53 F.3d 533 (2d Cir. 1995).

Courts tend to construe the penal provisions of the CWA broadly and generally hold supervisory personnel vested with authority to a high standard of compliance. The trend in the federal courts is to hold responsible corporate officers criminally liable in environmental offenses despite their lack of "consciousness of wrongdoing."

In *United States v. Hanousek,* 176 F.3d 1116 (9th Cir. 1999), Edward Hanousek Jr., a roadmaster for a railroad company, was convicted under a *respondeat superior* (supervisory responsibility) theory for the negligent discharge of oil into navigable waters, a violation of 33 U.S.C.A. § 1319(c)(1). The accident occurred due to a backhoe's punc-ture of a high-pressure oil line and resulted in the release of up to 5,000 gallons of oil directly into the Skagway River. Although Hanousek held a supervisory position of re-sponsibility for construction and maintenance of the railroad track, he was home at the time of the accident. On appeal, he argued that the trial judge had violated his right to due process of law by failing to instruct the jury that the government had to prove that he acted with *criminal* and not ordinary negligence. The U.S. Court of Appeals for the Ninth Circuit rejected his argument, observing, "The criminal provisions of the CWA constitute public welfare legislation.… Public welfare legislation is designed to protect the public from potentially harmful or injurious items … and may render criminal 'a type of conduct that a reasonable person should know is subject to stringent public reg-ulation and may seriously threaten the community's health or safety.'" The court then noted that "a public welfare statute may subject a person to criminal liability for ordi-nary negligence without offending due process." *Id.* at 1121–1122. The Ninth Circuit's decision sends a message to those who occupy supervisory roles that a supervisor can be held criminally liable for ordinary negligence in failing to take precautions to prevent another person from committing a violation of the CWA.

A majority of the states have programs approved by the EPA. Although states vary somewhat in their approaches, many provide penalties similar to those in the federal act for either willful or negligent violations of water pollution provisions.

The Government's Requirement of Proof of Violation of the Clean Water Act

In *United States v. Wilson*, 133 F.3d 251, 264 (4th Cir. 1997), the court stated:

> To establish a felony violation of the Clean Water Act, we hold [the government] must prove:
>
> 1) that the defendant knew that he was discharging a substance, eliminating a prose-cution for accidental discharges;
>
> 2) that the defendant correctly identified the substance he was discharging, not mistaking it for a different, unprohibited substance;
>
> 3) that the defendant knew the method or instrumentality used to discharge the pollutants;
>
> 4) that the defendant knew the physical characteristics of the property into which the pollutant was discharged that identify it as a wetland, such as the presence of water and water-loving vegetation;
>
> 5) that the defendant was aware of the facts establishing the required link between the wetland and waters of the United States; and
>
> 6) that the defendant knew he did not have a permit.

The Point Source Problem

As noted, the CWA prohibits the discharge of pollutants from any point source into the navigable waters of the United States unless such discharge complies with a per-mit issued by the EPA. The CWA states:

> The term "point source" means any discernible, confined and discrete conveyance, including but not limited to any pipe, ditch, channel, tunnel, conduit, well, discrete fissure, container, rolling stock, concentrated animal feeding operation, or vessel or other floating craft, from which pollutants are or may be discharged. This term does

Criminal Prosecution Under the Clean Water Act

David W. Boldt was the chemical engineering manager for Astro Circuit Corporation, a Massachusetts company that manufactured circuit boards using an electroplating process. Boldt's duties included supervising the company's pretreatment process, a part of the pollution control system. He was charged with six counts of violating the Clean Water Act. He was convicted on two counts: one for knowingly aiding and abetting the discharge of pollutants into a municipal sewer in 1987, when the copper level in Astro's effluent greatly exceeded the federal standards, and another for ordering a subordinate in 1988 to dump 3,100 gallons of partially treated industrial wastewater containing excessive metals into the municipal sewer. At trial, Boldt asserted the defense of impossibility to the first incident, arguing he was only a mid-level manager who was not responsible for the discharge. Boldt acknowledged responsibility for the

second discharge but pleaded the defense of necessity, arguing it was necessary to authorize the discharge to avoid a worse harm.

In upholding both convictions, the appellate court observed that the evidence showed that pollution control was part of Boldt's area of responsibility and that, regarding the 1987 violation, he was aware of the practice of bypassing the pollution control system and had condoned it on the occasion at issue. Regarding the 1988 incident, the court found the evidence undisputed that Boldt directly ordered his subordinate to dump the copper wastewater, a conclusion bolstered by his subordinate's testimony that Boldt attempted to cover up the incident. Finally, the appellate court observed that the record of the trial disclosed that the president of Astro testified that Boldt was authorized to shut down the plant.

United States v. Boldt, 929 F.2d 35 (1st Cir. 1991).

---

not include agricultural stormwater discharges and return flows from irrigated agriculture. 33 U.S.C.A. 1362 (14)

Courts generally have interpreted "point source" broadly. For example, in *Froebel v. Meyer,* 217 F.3d 928, 938 (7th Cir. 2000), the court noted that several circuit courts have even considered that a dam can act as point sources if an artificial mechanism introduces pollutants. In *Avoyelles Sportsmen's League, Inc. v. Marsh,* 715 F.2d 897 (5th Cir. 1983), the U.S. Court of Appeals for the Fifth Circuit held that bulldozers and backhoes are point sources within the meaning of the CWA.

The issue of whether a human being can be a point source came into sharp focus in 1988 after schoolchildren on a field trip discovered glass vials of blood in the Hudson River. The vials were traced to Plaza Health Laboratories, Inc. (Plaza Health), a blood testing laboratory in Brooklyn, New York. In 1989 a federal grand jury handed down a four-count indictment against Plaza Health and its co-owner and vice president, Geronimo Villegas, for violating the CWA. At Villegas's trial the evidence revealed that Villegas had thrown the vials into water with his hands. The court instructed the jury that under the CWA, the act of physically throwing the pollutants into the water constituted a discharge from a point source. The jury found Villegas guilty on all four counts. On appeal by Villegas, the U.S. Court of Appeals for the Second Circuit found that the language and legislative history of the CWA and the case law interpreting the term "point source" supported a conclusion that "the statute was never designed to address the random, individual polluter like Villegas." Rather, the court noted the term "point source" in the CWA was defined to include a "pipe, ditch, channel, tunnel, conduit, well, [and] discrete fissure" and to "evoke images of physical structures and instrumentalities that systematically act as a means of conveying pollutants from an industrial source to navigable waterways." Thus, applying the rule of lenity (a rule often applied

Go to the Scheb/ Scheb Criminal Law and Procedure 6e website at academic .cengage.com/criminaljustice/ scheb for an edited version of *U.S. v. Plaza Health Laboratories.*

in criminal prosecutions), the court found the CWA did not clearly proscribe Villegas's conduct and therefore did not give him fair warning that he was violating the law. *United States v. Plaza Health Laboratories, Inc.*, 3 F.3d 643, 646 (2d Cir. 1993). A dissenting judge pointed out "the discharge was directly into the water, and came from an identifiable point," *Id.* at 653, and concluded that Villegas had fair warning that his actions were illegal and proscribed by the CWA. At the time this book was written, Congress had not acted to indicate that the intent of the CWA is that a discharge of pollutants into the water by an individual is illegal, although many observers had expected that it would do so.

The Resource Conservation and Recovery Act

Enactment of the Resource Conservation Recovery Act (RCRA) in 1976 was a significant step in environmental control. It establishes detailed provisions for the regulation of hazardous wastes. Its objective is to encourage the states—through grants, technical assistance, and advice—to establish standards and provide for civil and criminal enforcement of state regulations. The EPA sets minimum standards requiring the states to enact criminal penalties against any person who knowingly stores or transports any hazardous waste to an unpermitted facility, who treats such waste without a permit, or who makes false representations to secure a permit. All states have enacted criminal statutes pursuant to the criteria specified in the RCRA.

The RCRA proscribes a comprehensive list of illegal actions and imposes criminal penalties on any person who

1. knowingly transports or causes to be transported any hazardous waste to an unpermitted facility, 42 U.S.C.A. § 6928(d)(1);

2. knowingly treats, stores, or disposes of any hazardous waste without a permit, in knowing violation of any material condition or requirement of the interim status, 42 U.S.C.A. § 6928(d)(2)(A)-(C); or one who

3. knowingly omits material information or makes any false statement or representation in any record or document required to be maintained under the regulations or submitted to the [EPA] or any state which is authorized to run RCRA programs. 42 U.S.C.A. § 6928(d)(3).

The RCRA contains criminal penalties of up to five years' imprisonment and $50,000 per day fines, or both. In addition, section 6928(e), often referred to as the "knowing endangerment" provision, makes it a criminal offense to knowingly place another person in imminent danger of death or serious bodily injury in conjunction with the transportation, storage, or disposal of hazardous wastes. This provision carries fines of up to $250,000 and up to fifteen years' imprisonment, or both.

The RCRA has become an important tool for enforcement, and prosecutors frequently rely on it when prosecuting persons who illegally dispose of hazardous wastes. In *United States v. Johnson & Towers, Inc.*, 741 F.2d 662, 664 (3d Cir. 1984), the court held that the term "person" in RCRA section 6928(d) includes employees as well as owners and operators but that employees can be subject to criminal prosecution only if they knew or should have known that there had been no compliance with the permit requirement of section 6925. Proof of the knowledge element required may be inferred for those individuals holding responsible corporate positions.

In *United States v. Hayes International Corp.*, 786 F.2d 1499 (11th Cir. 1986), the court affirmed a conviction under section 6928(d)(1) for unlawfully transporting hazardous waste materials to an unpermitted facility and ruled that neither a lack of knowledge that paint waste was a hazardous material nor ignorance of the permit requirement was

Prosecution of a "Responsible Corporate Officer" under the Clean Water Act

During 1996, Avion Environmental employees discharged untreated wastewater directly into the Richmond, Virginia, sewer system in violation of Avion's discharge permit. Based on these activities, the government charged James Hong, as a responsible corporate officer of Avion, with thirteen counts of negligently violating pretreatment requirements under the CWA, 33 U.S.C.A. § 1319(c)(1)(A) (West Supp. 2000). Hong, the sole shareholder of Avion Environmental, was convicted. Although he played a substantial role in the corporation's operations, Hong was not identified as an officer or as having direct oversight responsibility for operations from which the releases occurred. On appeal, Hong contended the government failed to prove he was a formally designated officer of Avion Environmental. Alternatively, he argued that there was no proof that he had sufficient control over the operations of Avion to be liable for violations of the CWA. The U.S. Fourth Circuit Court of Appeals rejected his arguments. The court held that the government was not required to prove that Hong was formally designated an officer of Avion. Rather, the court stated, "[T]he pertinent question is whether the defendant bore such a relationship to the corporation that it is appropriate to hold him criminally liable for failing to prevent the charged violations of the CWA." Holding that he did not prevent the violations, the court affirmed his convictions.

United States v. Hong, 242 F.3d 528, 531 (4th Cir. 2001).

a defense. Conviction for the treatment, storage, or disposal of hazardous waste without an RCRA permit has been more problematic. In *United States v. Hoflin,* 880 F.2d 1033 (9th Cir. 1989), the court held that the government is not required to prove the defendant's knowledge of the lack of a permit to secure a conviction in either transport or storage cases; nevertheless, a person who does not know that the waste material he or she is disposing of is hazardous cannot be guilty of violating section 6928(d)(2)(a).

One of the most serious cases brought under the RCRA involved section 6928(e) (the knowing endangerment provision), which makes it a criminal violation to knowingly place employees "in imminent danger of death or serious bodily injury." *United States v. Protex Industries, Inc.,* 874 F.2d 740 (10th Cir. 1989), involved a company that operated a drum-recycling facility and, in connection with its business, purchased drums that previously contained toxic chemicals. The evidence revealed that the company's safety provisions were inadequate to protect its employees and, as a result, certain company employees suffered from solvent poisoning and exhibited serious maladies. The court upheld a conviction of Protex for placing employees in an industrial environment without sufficient protection against exposure to toxic chemicals.

The Government's Requirement of Proof of RCRA Offenses

Actions that violate the RCRA are often quite evident, yet proof of an offending person's intent is often the key to successful prosecution under the RCRA. To successfully prosecute a defendant charged with illegally transporting hazardous materials to a facility that lacks a permit, the government must prove that the substance being transported fit within the parameters of the definition of "hazardous waste," not that the defendant had knowledge that the material was hazardous and waste. *United States v. Kelly,* 167 F.3d 1176 (7th Cir. 1999). A corporate officer who does not "directly"

Criminal Prosecution under the RCRA: No Requirement that Defendant Knew Waste Would Be Harmful if Improperly Disposed

James Ralph Sellers was convicted of knowingly and willfully disposing of methylethylketone (M.E.K.), a hazardous waste, without obtaining a permit, a violation of 42 U.S.C.A. § 6928(d)(2)(A) (RCRA). At his jury trial the evidence revealed that residents discovered sixteen fifty-five-gallon drums of hazardous paint waste on the embankment of a creek that flows into the Leaf River. These drums contained paint waste and M.E.K., a paint solvent. The evidence further revealed that Sellers did not have a permit for disposing of hazardous waste, nor did he take the waste to a licensed disposal area.

The trial court instructed the jury that the government must prove (1) that the defendant knowingly disposed of, or commanded and caused others to dispose of, wastes as charged in the indictment;

(2) the defendant knew what the wastes were; (3) the wastes were listed or identified or characterized by the EPA as a hazardous waste pursuant to the RCRA, and (4) the defendant had not obtained a permit from either the EPA or the State of Mississippi authorizing the disposal under the RCRA.

On appeal, Sellers argued that the jury charge should have required the government to prove that Sellers knew that the paint waste could be hazardous or harmful to persons or the environment. The U.S Court of Appeals rejected Sellers's contention and held that in a prosecution for knowingly and willfully disposing of methylethylketone (M.E.K.), a hazardous waste, without obtaining a permit, there was no requirement that defendant knew that waste would be harmful if improperly disposed of.

United States v. Sellers, 926 F.2d 410 (5th Cir. 1991).

cause the violations may still be culpable. *United States v. Hansen*, 262 F.3d 1217, 1243 (11th Cir. 2001).

It is not necessary that the government prove that the defendant knew a chemical waste had been defined as a "hazardous waste" by the EPA. *United States v. Goldsmith,* 978 F.2d 643, 646 (11th Cir. 1992). The government need only prove that a defendant had knowledge of "the general hazardous character" of the chemical. *United States v. Dee*, 912 F.2d 741, 745 (4th Cir. 1990).

The Toxic Substances Control Act

The Toxic Substances Control Act (TSCA) of 1976 authorizes the EPA to require testing and to prohibit the manufacture, distribution, or use of certain chemical substances that present an unreasonable risk of injury to health or the environment and to regulate their disposal. Section 14 of TSCA prohibits the commercial use of substances that the user knew or had reason to know were manufactured, processed, or distributed in violation of any provision of TSCA. 15 U.S.C.A. § 2614(2). Although the act depends primarily on civil penalties, a person who knowingly or willfully fails to maintain records or submit reports as required violates the criminal provisions of the act. 15 U.S.C.A. §§ 2614, 2615(b). There have been relatively few criminal prosecutions under TSCA; however, in 1982 a court upheld the conviction of Robert Earl Ward Jr., the chairman of the board of Ward Transformer Company, on eight counts of the unlawful disposal of toxic substances (PCB-containing oils from used transformers) and the willful aiding and abetting of the unlawful disposal of toxic substances. The evidence at trial revealed that although the defendant himself did not dispose of the toxic substances, the company's employees performed the task while he was kept advised of the progress. *United States v. Ward*, 676 F.2d 94 (4th Cir. 1982). In 1995 the U.S. Court of Appeals for the First Circuit found sufficient evidence to uphold a conviction of a defendant who allowed others to take PCB-laden transformers, knowing they would dump them unlawfully. *United States v. Catucci,* 55 F.3d 15 (1st Cir. 1995).

The Comprehensive Environmental Response, Compensation, and Liability Act

In 1980 Congress enacted the Comprehensive Environmental Response, Compensation, and Liability Act (CERCLA), commonly known as the Superfund Law. Its purpose is to finance cleanup and provide for civil suits by citizens. As revised in 1986, the act requires notice to federal and state agencies of any "release" of a "reportable quantity" of a listed hazardous substance. "Release" is broadly defined, and "reportable quantity" is related to each of the several hundred "hazardous substances." CERCLA also allows the EPA to promulgate regulations for the collection and disposal of solid wastes. The act imposes criminal sanctions against those who fail to report as required or who destroy or falsify records. 42 U.S.C.A. § 9603(d)(2).

Standard of Liability of Corporate Officers

Many violations in the public health area are caused by corporate entities; therefore, courts often focus on whether an accused, by reason of his or her position in the corporate enterprise, had sufficient responsibility and authority to either prevent or correct the violation charged. Courts hold responsible corporate officers liable in environmental crimes just as in prosecutions under the FDCA. In fact, Congress has adopted the "responsible corporate officer" doctrine in the Clean Air Act, 42 U.S.C.A. § 7413(c)(6), and the Clean Water Act, 33 U.S.C.A. § 1319(c)(3)(6). And the doctrine has been upheld in CERCLA cases by federal appeals courts. For example, in *United States v. Carr,* 880 F.2d 1550 (2d Cir. 1989), the court rejected a maintenance supervisor's argument that he could not be guilty because he was a relatively low-level employee. The court explained that CERCLA imposes criminal responsibility on a person "even of relatively low rank" who acts in a supervisory capacity and is "in a position to detect, prevent, and abate a release of hazardous substances." 880 F.2d at 1554. Thus, a responsible corporate officer not only cannot avoid criminal liability by delegating tasks to others but also must remedy any violations that occur. At the state level, corporate executives have been charged with criminally negligent homicide and manslaughter where employees' deaths have resulted from the improper use of hazardous substances. See, for example, *State ex rel. Cornellier v. Black,* 425 N.W.2d 21 (Wis. App. 1988).

Lack of Uniformity in Environmental Laws

Disparate environmental standards, enforcement policies, and sanctions in the areas of water and air pollution and disposal of hazardous wastes can lead to "shopping" by industrial companies to secure locations that will enable them to be more competitive by not having to comply with stringent environmental standards. Significant differences exist among the fifty states in the standards of proof required and in the sanctions imposed for criminal violations of hazardous waste, water pollution, and air pollution laws.

Compare the differences between the statutory language in the Kentucky and Vermont offenses set out in Tables 11.1 and 11.2. What level of proof should be required for establishing a defendant's guilt under the "knowingly" standard of the

Table 11.1	Kentucky Environmental Laws Imposing Criminal Penalties Concerning Hazardous Wastes, Water Pollution, and Air Pollution	
	Unlawful Acts	**Penalties**
HAZARDOUS WASTES	Knowingly engaging in the generation, treatment, storage, transportation, or disposal of hazardous wastes in violation of this chapter, or contrary to a permit, order, or administrative regulation issued or promulgated under the chapter; or knowingly making a false statement, representation, or certification in an application for, or in form pertaining to, a permit, or in a notice or report required by the terms and conditions of an issued permit. Ky. Rev. Stat. Ann. § 224.99–010(6).	Imprisonment between one and five years or a fine up to $25,000 per day of violation, or both. § 224.99–010(6).
WATER POLLUTION	Knowingly violating any of the following: § 224.70–110 (water pollution) § 224.73–120 (monitoring and reporting) § 224.40–100 (waste disposal) § 224.40–305 (unpermitted waste disposal facilities) Or violating any determination, permit, administrative regulation, or order of the Cabinet promulgated pursuant to those sections which have become final; or knowingly providing false information in any document filed or required to be maintained under this chapter; or knowingly rendering inaccurate any monitoring device or method required to be maintained. § 224.99–010(4).	Imprisonment between one and five years or a fine up to $25,000 per day of violation, or both. § 224.99–010(4).
AIR POLLUTION	Knowingly violating § 224.20–110 (air pollution), or any determination, permit, administrative regulation, or order of the Cabinet promulgated pursuant to those sections which have become final; or knowingly providing false information in any document filed or required to be maintained under this chapter; or knowingly rendering inaccurate any monitoring device or method required to be maintained. § 224.99–010(4).	Imprisonment between one and five years or a fine up to $25,000 per day of violation, or both. § 224.99–010(4).

Source: Kentucky Revised Statutes Annotated.

Kentucky laws? Would a different standard of proof be required under Vermont's laws concerning hazardous wastes and air pollution?

Unfortunately, fines imposed on violators of environmental laws are too often regarded as "costs of doing business" because in reality these costs can be passed on to the ultimate consumer. The threat of imprisonment, on the other hand, is one cost that cannot be passed on to consumers; therefore, it is a powerful deterrent to those who would pollute the environment. As states more aggressively prosecute environmental crimes, more uniformity of criminal sanctions will undoubtedly develop, much as it has for the more common criminal offenses.

Defenses to Environmental Crimes

Defendants' attacks on most environmental statutes as being vague and ambiguous have largely failed. Defenses asserting that a criminal prosecution constitutes double jeopardy (see Chapter 14) because the government has previously exacted a civil fine against the defendant have also been unsuccessful. Nevertheless, courts must provide an opportunity for assertion of defenses. In *United States v. Pa. Industrial Chemical Corp.*, 411 U.S. 655, 93 S.Ct. 1804, 36 L.Ed.2d 567 (1973), a manufacturing corporation was convicted under the Rivers and Harbors Act of discharging refuse into navigable waters without a permit. The Court reversed a conviction where the trial court failed to allow the defendant to present evidence at trial that he had been misled

Table 11.2	Vermont Environmental Laws Imposing Criminal Penalties Concerning Hazardous Wastes, Water Pollution, and Air Pollution	
HAZARDOUS WASTES	Violating any provision of the waste management chapter (transportation, storage, disposal, or treatment of hazardous waste; permit and manifest requirements), rules promulgated therein, or terms or conditions of any order of certification. Vt. Stat. Ann., Title 10, § 6612(a).	Imprisonment up to six months or a fine up to $25,000 per day of violation, or both. Title 10, § 6612(a).
	Violating any provision of the waste management chapter by the knowing or reckless (1) transport, treatment, storage or disposal of any hazardous waste; (2) transport, treatment, storage or disposal of more than one cubic yard of solid waste or more than 275 pounds of solid waste; or release of any hazardous material. Title 10, § 6612(d).	Imprisonment up to five years; or a fine not to exceed $250,000 or both. Title 10, § 6612(d).
WATER POLLUTION	Violating any provision of the water pollution control subchapter, or failing, neglecting, or refusing to obey or comply with any order or the terms of any permit issued under this subchapter. Title 10, § 1275(a).	Imprisonment up to six months or a fine up to $25,000 per day of violation, or both. Title 10, § 1275(a).
	Knowingly making any false statement, representation, or certification in any document filed or required to be maintained under the water pollution control subchapter, or by any permit, rule, regulation, or order issued thereunder; or falsifying, tampering with, or knowingly rendering inaccurate any monitoring device or method required to be maintained under this subchapter, or by any permit, rule, regulation, or order issued thereunder. Title 10, § 1275(b).	Imprisonment up to six months or a fine up to $10,000 or both. Title 10, § 1275(b).
AIR POLLUTION	Violating a provision of the air pollution control chapter (discharge of air contaminants without a permit or in violation of pollution standards) except § 563 and § 567 (relating to motor vehicles and confidential records), or any rule issued thereunder. Title 10, § 568(a).	Imprisonment up to five years, a fine up to $100,000 per violation, or both. Title 10, § 568(a).
	Knowingly making any false statement, representation or certification in any application, record, report, plan or falsifying, tampering with, or knowingly rendering inaccurate any monitoring devices required to be maintained under chapter or by permit, rule, regulation, or order issued under chapter. Title 10, § 568(b).	Imprisonment up to one year, a fine up to $50,000 per violation, or both. Title 10, § 568(b).

Source: Vermont Statutes Annotated.

deliberately by the government about required permits and thus deprived of presenting a defense.

Environmental cases can be very technical. Frequently they involve challenging the government's test results that form the basis of the charges. Some prosecutions under the CWA where defendants have eventually prevailed provide illustrations of defenses under environmental statutes. For example, in *United States v. Borowski*, 977 F.2d 27 (1st Cir. 1992), the First Circuit reversed a conviction where company officers had directed employees to pour toxic chemicals into a drain that led to a public treatment plant. And while observing that the defendants' conduct was reprehensible, the court held that it did not violate the CWA because prosecution for knowing endangerment under the CWA cannot be premised upon danger that occurs before a pollutant reaches publicly owned sewer or treatment works. As noted earlier in this chapter, in *United States v. Plaza Health Labs*, in a prosecution under the CWA, defense counsel succeeded in establishing a restrictive application of what constitutes a discharge from a point source.

In *Village of Oconomowoc Lake v. Dayton Hudson Corp.*, 24 F.3d 962 (7th Cir. 1994), the Seventh Circuit held that a six-acre artificial retention pond that discharged only to ground water did not constitute "waters of the United States," a predicate for conviction under the CWA's proscription on discharges of pollutants into navigable waters. In *Solid Waste Agency of Northern Cook County v. United States Army Corps of Engineers*, 531 U.S. 159, 121 S.Ct. 675, 148 L.Ed.2d 576 (2001), the U.S. Supreme Court held that isolated ponds, some used only seasonally as a habitat by migratory birds, did not fall within the CWA's definition of "navigable waters" merely because these waters served as a habitat for migratory birds. The Court's decision has caused speculation as to the viability of the so-called Migratory Bird Rule.

Noise Pollution

Congress enacted the **Quiet Communities Act** of 1978, 42 U.S.C.A. §§ 4901–4918, to protect the environment against noise pollution, which has become perceived as a growing danger to the health and welfare of the population. Section 4909 details prohibited acts, and section 4910 provides criminal penalties for those who knowingly or willfully import, manufacture, or distribute products that fail to comply with noise standards specified in the statute. However, the act recognizes that the primary responsibility for protecting communities against noise pollution lies with state and local governments.

Historically, local governments have adopted ordinances that prohibit excessive noise. In the twentieth century, ordinances have reflected concern about amplified sound equipment. Noise control ordinances often prohibit the use of loud audio equipment in an apartment building where residents live in close quarters and are directed at loud late-night parties that disturb neighbors or against persons whose car stereos are played so loudly as to be an annoyance or even a safety hazard.

Most persons charged with violations of noise ordinances do not choose to contest the charges. Instead, they pay a small fine or agree to abate the violation. Those who do choose to contest the charge often attack the constitutionality of the ordinance. As we pointed out in Chapter 3, the vagueness doctrine requires that a statute that defines a criminal offense must be definite so that ordinary persons can understand what conduct is prohibited. Local ordinances that vaguely prohibit unnecessary noise are subject to constitutional challenge. In 1991 the Supreme Court of Mississippi held that Gulfport's noise control ordinance, by prohibiting "unnecessary or unusual noises ... which either annoys, injures or endangers the comfort, repose, health or safety of others ... fails to provide clear notice and sufficiently definite warning of the conduct that is prohibited." As a result, the court said that persons of "common intelligence must necessarily guess at its meaning and differ as to its application." *Nichols v. City of Gulfport*, 589 So.2d 1280, 1282 (Miss. 1991). Likewise the Supreme Court of Georgia invalidated a county ordinance that prohibited "any ... unnecessary or unusual sound or noise which ... annoys ... others." The court held that the ordinance failed to provide the requisite clear notice and sufficiently definite warning of the conduct that is prohibited. *Thelen v. State*, 526 S.E.2d 60, 62 (Ga. 2000).

The City of Sarasota, Florida adopted an ordinance that amended its zoning code by prohibiting all amplified sound in non-enclosed structures in an area zoned

"Commercial Business-Newtown" during specified times of day. Daley, who owned a restaurant that provided both live and recorded musical entertainment for its customers, challenged the ordinance's validity. A Florida appellate court invalidated the ordinance. *Daley v. City of Sarasota,* 752 So.2d 124 (Fla. App. 2000). The court recognized that music, as a form of expression and communication, is protected under the First Amendment and observed,

> The goal of regulating unreasonable sound is unquestionably a matter within the city's province. However, that goal, no matter how laudable, cannot be achieved by the overbroad regulation of activities protected by the First Amendment. As currently written, the city's ordinance can be used to suppress First Amendment rights far more severely than can be justified by the city's interest in regulating unreasonable sound. 752 So.2d at 126.

Narrowly drafted noise control ordinances fare better before judicial tribunals. In *City of Janesville v. Garthwaite,* 266 N.W.2d 418 (Wis. 1978), the city charged the defendant with violation of an ordinance that states, "No person shall make unnecessary and annoying noise with a motor vehicle by squealing tires, excessive acceleration of engine or by emitting unnecessary and loud muffler noises." The Supreme Court of Wisconsin held the ordinance was a valid exercise of the city's police power to manage and control its streets.

In 2001 the Ohio Court of Appeals upheld the village of Kelleys Island antinoise ordinance, which provides:

> No person shall generate or permit to be generated noise or loud sound which is likely to cause inconvenience or annoyance to persons of ordinary sensibilities by means of a live performance, radio, phonograph, television, tape player, compact disc player, loudspeaker or any other sound amplifying device which is plainly audible at a distance of 150 feet or more from the source of the noise or loud sound.

The owner of a bar that featured karaoke or live bands on an outdoor patio was cited for violation of the ordinance. The owner contended the ordinance was vague and therefore unconstitutional under the First Amendment to the U.S. Constitution. The court, however, found the ordinance was sufficiently definite to allow a person to determine what conduct violated the ordinance and prevent arbitrary enforcement. Addressing concerns as to the ordinance's constitutionality, the court explained that the "noise or loud sound" is made definite by adding that it must be "plainly audible" or "clearly heard" by a person using his or her "normal hearing faculties." Also, the noise or sound must be inconvenient or annoying to persons of "ordinary sensibilities." "Time and distance limitations also aid in providing fair warning of the nature of the unlawful conduct." The distance requirement puts "an objective quantifiable number into the ordinance, thus narrowing the scope of its operations." Thus, it held the ordinance was a valid exercise of police power and not unconstitutionally vague. *Kelleys Island v. Joyce,* 765 N.E.2d 387, 393 (Ohio App. 2001).

Antismoking Legislation

As society has become more aware of the ill effects of smoking and, in particular, the hazards of "secondhand smoke," governments have restricted smoking in public buildings and places of public accommodation and transportation. Perhaps the best-known example is the Federal Aviation Administration regulation prohibiting all smoking on domestic passenger airline flights. The last few years has witnessed enactment of no-smoking laws by states; by 2003 most states had laws restricting smoking in public places, and several have laws restricting smoking in private workplaces. In some instances state laws have preempted the subject, and local communities have been prevented from enacting conflicting ordinances. In other instances local communities have acted where the states have not. Often antismoking laws carry minor civil penalties, and local ordinances frequently impose penalties analogous to parking fines.

The Florida Initiative

In November 2002, Florida voters, by a margin in excess of 70 percent, adopted a state constitutional amendment that required the state legislature to enact a comprehensive ban on smoking in restaurants and other public places. The state legislature promptly enacted laws that generally prohibit smoking in workplaces and restaurants, with exceptions that allow smoking in "stand alone" bars that serve incidental snacks, on outdoor patios at restaurants, at membership associations, in designated smoking rooms at public lodging establishments, and at designated smoking areas at airports. The new laws make violations noncriminal and impose civil fines for violators. West's Fla. Stat. Ann., Ch. 386.

New York's Comprehensive Smoking Ban

In 2003 the New York legislature enacted a comprehensive antismoking law. Effective July 24, 2003, McKinney's Public Health Law § 1399-o provides that smoking shall not be permitted and no person shall smoke in places of employment, indoor areas of bars and restaurants, subways, and numerous other enclosed areas. Smoking is permitted in private automobiles and homes, unless the home is used to provide day care. This far-ranging and controversial statute is enforced through administrative fines, not criminal penalties. The statute is praised by public health authorities and antismoking groups and severely criticized by "smokers' rights" organizations. Many smokers resent laws that they see as infringements on their freedom and often assert that their decision to smoke is no one else's business. But because smoking negatively affects others who are in close proximity, there is little question that government has a legitimate basis upon which to restrict smoking in public places. How far government chooses to go in this area is a political issue, not a constitutional one.

 As noted, the clear trend is to prohibit or restrict smoking in public places. Thus, the great majority of the other states have enacted laws prohibiting or restricting smoking in a variety of areas—for example, public transportation vehicles, hospitals, medical offices, public offices and meeting rooms, schools, child care centers, libraries, motion picture theaters, stage performance theaters, restaurants, waiting and meeting rooms owned or operated by the executive and judicial branches of the state and local governments, and specified areas of sports arenas.

Wildlife Protection Laws

Since the early common law, fish and game have been viewed as animals *ferae naturae*, meaning that the state as sovereign owns them in trust for the people. *Bayside Fish Flour Co. v. Gentry*, 297 U.S. 422, 56 S.Ct. 513, 80 L.Ed. 772 (1936). As trustee, the state has the duty to preserve and protect wildlife by regulating fishing in public and private streams and by controlling the taking of game. *Shively v. Bowlby*, 152 U.S. 1, 14 S.Ct. 548, 38 L.Ed. 331 (1894). Federal courts have said that under the public trust doctrine, the U.S. and state governments have the right and the duty to protect and preserve the public's interest in natural wildlife resources. See, for example, *Toomer v. Witsell*, 334 U.S. 385, 68 S.Ct. 1156, 92 L.Ed. 1460 (1948). Owners of private property retain a qualified interest, so those seeking to take fish or game from the confines of private property must secure the owner's permission.

The Migratory Bird Act

Although it is generally within the jurisdiction of the states to regulate wildlife, fish, and game, the federal government has jurisdiction to enact statutes to carry out treaties for migratory birds. The jealous regard that the states have over wildlife within their borders led Missouri to challenge the constitutionality of the **Migratory Bird Conservation Act,** 16 U.S.C.A. §§ 703–712, a statute Congress enacted to enforce the provisions of the Migratory Bird Treaty entered into by the United States in 1916. Missouri claimed the federal statute infringed rights reserved to the states by the Tenth Amendment to the U.S. Constitution. The Supreme Court rejected that challenge, thereby settling the issue of federal control. The Court held that Article II, Section 2 of the Constitution grants the president the power to make treaties, and Article I, Section 8 gives Congress the power to enact legislation to enforce those treaties. *Missouri v. Holland*, 252 U.S. 416, 40 S.Ct. 382, 64 L.Ed. 641 (1920). Of course, the federal government retains jurisdiction to protect all wildlife, game, and fish within national game preserves. *Hunt v. United States*, 278 U.S. 96, 49 S.Ct. 38, 73 L.Ed. 200 (1928).

Enforcement of the Migratory Bird Act (MBA) remains a viable part of the federal environmental enforcement program. In *Humane Society v. Glickman*, 217 F.3d 882 (D.C. Cir. 2000), the U.S. Court of Appeals for the D.C. Circuit held that federal agencies are subject to the provisions of the MBA. Its broad proscription makes it "unlawful … to pursue, hunt, take, capture, kill, attempt to take, capture, or kill, possess, offer for sale, sell, offer to barter, barter, offer to purchase, purchase, deliver for shipment, ship, export, import, cause to be shipped, exported, or imported, deliver for transportation, transport or cause to be transported, carry or cause to be carried, or receive for shipment, transportation, carriage, or export birds protected under the treaty." 16 U.S.C.A. §§ 703–712. A violation of a regulation issued under the MBA is a misdemeanor, but a person guilty of knowingly taking a migratory bird with intent to sell or offer for sale or barter is guilty of a felony and subject to up to two years' imprisonment and a substantial fine. 16 U.S.C.A. § 707.

In 1986 Congress inserted the word "knowingly" into the section of the act providing criminal sanctions, thus requiring the prosecution to prove the defendant's *mens rea* as well as *actus reus* to establish a violation (see Chapter 4). Although section 707 requires the government to prove a knowing act, it does not require it to establish that a defendant's act is willful. Thus, in *United States v. Pitrone*, 115 F.3d 1 (1st Cir. 1997), in upholding the defendant's conviction for unlawfully selling a Harlequin duck, the appellate court rejected the defendant's contention that the government was required to prove his specific intent in order to establish that he knowingly violated the law. In effect, the government must show that the defendant's actions were intentional but need not show that the defendant knew they were illegal.

In an appeal from conviction for possessing more migratory game birds than the daily bag limit imposed under 16 U.S.C.A. § 703, another defendant argued that his hunting dog had simply picked up birds from other hunters. Thus, he contended he had no intent to violate the law. But the U.S. Court of Appeals for the Fifth Circuit rejected his argument, holding that a misdemeanor violation of the MBA for possessing more migratory game birds than the daily limit allowed is a strict liability offense. *United States v. Morgan,* 283 F.3d 322 (5th Cir. 2002).

The Endangered Species Act

Modern efforts of the federal government to preserve the environment through protection of wildlife is illustrated by the Federal **Endangered Species Act** of 1973 (ESA), 16 U.S.C.A. §§ 1531–1544. This act is designed to conserve ecosystems by preserving wildlife, fish, and plants. And although enforcement is largely through civil penalties, criminal liability is imposed against any person who knowingly violates regulations issued under the act. 16 U.S.C.A. § 1540(b). The ESA prohibits several specific acts regarding endangered species, and the Secretary of the Interior is further authorized to prohibit any of those acts with regard to threatened species.

The powerful role the ESA plays in the preservation of endangered species was dramatized in 1978 when the U.S. Supreme Court upheld a permanent injunction against construction of the Tellico Dam and Reservoir, a nearly complete $100 million water project in Tennessee. According to the plaintiffs in the case, the project would have eradicated or destroyed the remaining habitat of the only known population of an endangered species of fish, the snail darter. In upholding an injunction against the continuance of the project, the Court held that "the plain intent of Congress in enacting this statute was to halt and reverse the trend toward species extinction, whatever the cost." 437 U.S. 153, 184, 98 S.Ct. 2279, 2297, 57 L.Ed.2d 117 (1978). Subsequently, Congress enacted legislation restarting the project and the Tellico Dam was completed in 1979.

Under the ESA, criminal liability is imposed for the knowing violation of one of the specific prohibitions listed in the act, a regulation issued to implement those prohibitions, or a permit or certificate issued pursuant to the act. Violators may be fined up to $50,000 or imprisoned for up to a year, or both. ESA also authorizes fines of up to $25,000 or imprisonment for up to six months, or both, for violations of any other regulation promulgated under the act.

In *United States v. Billie,* 667 F. Supp. 1485 (S.D. Fla. 1987), the defendant was charged with killing a Florida panther, an endangered species. He argued that the prosecution had to prove his specific intent—that is, that he knew the animal he shot was a Florida panther, as opposed to a species of panther not on the list of "endangered species." The U.S. District Court rejected his argument and held that the government "need prove only that the defendant acted with general intent when he shot the animal in question." 667 F. Supp. at 1493. The court discussed the fact that the defendant was charged with violating a regulatory statute enacted to conserve and protect endangered species and that its purposes would be eviscerated if the government had to prove that a hunter who killed an animal recognized the particular subspecies as being protected under the act. 667 F. Supp. at 1492–1493. The following year a defendant was convicted for illegally taking a grizzly bear. The court held that the government had to establish that the defendant knowingly took the bear without a permit, but the government was not required to prove the defendant knew he was shooting at a grizzly bear. *United States v. St. Onge,* 676 F. Supp. 1044 (D. Mont. 1988).

Despite the existence of criminal penalties for the violation of environmental laws, often the most effective means of enforcement is to secure an injunction against actual or threatened violations. This is illustrated by an action against Volusia County, Florida, filed under the citizen-suit provision of the ESA, 16 U.S.C.A. § 1540(g)(1)(A), discussed in the 1998 decision from the Fifth Circuit Court of Appeals in *Turtles v. Volusia County,* illustrated in the Case-in-Point.

CASE-IN-POINT

A Federal Appellate Court Grants Protection to Nesting Sea Turtles

In 1978 the U.S. Fish and Wildlife Service listed the loggerhead sea turtle as a threatened species and the green sea turtle as an endangered species. In the spring, the female sea turtles come ashore on the beaches in Volusia County, Florida, and deposit their eggs in the sand and return to the ocean. Nesting females avoid bright lights. Months later, the hatchlings break out of their shells at night and instinctively crawl toward the brightest light on the horizon, which on an undeveloped beach is the moon's reflection off the surf. But on a developed beach, the brightest light can be artificial and can lead to disorientation of the turtles. Citizens acting on behalf of the endangered turtles sought an injunction against the county's refusal to ban beach driving and beachfront artificial light sources that adversely impact sea turtles during sea turtle nesting season, arguing that the county had violated the

"take" prohibition of 16 U.S.C.A. § 1538(a)(1)(B). The county responded that it had implied permission to "take" federally protected sea turtles through artificial beachfront lighting because it had a federal permit conditioned on its implementation of detailed lighting-related mitigatory measures. The district court enjoined the county from permitting beach driving during the nesting season but denied relief as to the beachfront lighting. The turtles appealed.

In a case of first impression, the U.S. Court of Appeals for the Eleventh Circuit held that the ESA's incidental take permit exception to its "take prohibition" did not apply to an activity performed as a purely mitigatory measure upon which the permit is conditioned and thus did not authorize the county to take protected sea turtles through measures associated with artificial beachfront lighting.

Turtles v. Volusia County, 148 F.3d 1231 (11th Cir. 1998).

State Regulation of Wildlife

State legislatures may make it a strict liability offense to take or possess fish and game in violation of regulations. *Cummings v. Commonwealth,* 255 S.W.2d 997 (Ky. 1953). Most states have done so, usually imposing strict liability for taking quantities of game or fish in excess of permitted allowances and for hunting and fishing during closed seasons. But it can be quite difficult to determine whether a given law that imposes a criminal penalty for violating a fishing or game regulation is a strict liability statute. If a wildlife penal statute includes language incorporating a *mens rea* requirement, it is clear that the prosecution must prove the defendant's intent. Although it is difficult to generalize, if a wildlife penal law does not explicitly require intent by including such words as "willfully" or "knowingly," only proof of the *actus reus* of the offense is required. The courts have tended to make an exception to imposing strict liability where the offense is of a more serious criminal character (for example, smuggling and chemical trafficking) or where the offense is designated as a felony or otherwise carries a severe punishment.

In *State v. Rice,* 626 P.2d 104 (Alaska 1981), the court considered a game regulation that lacked any requirement for criminal intent. As we have noted, this type of regulation is generally treated as a strict liability offense, much like a traffic law. The Alaska Supreme Court took a different approach, saying, "strict liability is an exception to the rule that requires criminal intent" and that criminal statutes will be "strictly construed to require some degree of *mens rea* absent a clear legislative intent to the contrary." *Id.* at 108.

Statutes also commonly make it a strict liability offense to use improper types of fishing nets, to hunt with artificial lights, and to shoot over baited fields. In addition, statutes provide for forfeiture of illegal equipment used to hunt or fish in violation of laws. See, for example, *State v. Billiot,* 229 So.2d 72 (La. 1969), where the Louisiana Supreme Court upheld the forfeiture of seines and other devices used in trawling for shrimp during a closed season.

Irrespective of whether a penal statute imposes strict liability or requires proof of intent, the prosecution is not required to establish that a person accused of fishing in a closed season actually caught fish, *State v. Parker,* 167 A. 854, 855 (Me. 1933), nor is it a defense that a hunter has failed to kill any game, *Key v. State,* 384 S.W.2d 22 (Tenn. 1964).

What Constitutes Possession?

Recall that in Chapter 9 we discussed the difference between actual and constructive possession and the elements of joint possession, concepts that often come into play in regard to possession of illegal drugs and drug paraphernalia. These same concepts become important in wildlife laws where proof of violation of game and fish laws can be based on constructive possession and even constructive joint possession as well as actual possession of game and fish.

The concept of constructive possession of wildlife is illustrated by the Vermont Supreme Court's decision in *State v. Letourneau,* 503 At.2d 553 (Vt. 1985). There, the defendants appealed their convictions for illegal possession of moose where a game warden had searched their premises and found packages of moose meat in the defendants' freezers. The trial judge had instructed the jury that if a person deposited unlawful property in a place of concealment on his own premises or otherwise, he nevertheless had possession of the property even though he might have been absent from the place he was using for its concealment. The court rejected the defendants' contention that the instruction was improper and held the instruction was consistent with statutory and case law.

In *Ford v. State,* 344 S.E.2d 514 (Ga. App. 1986), a Georgia appellate court reviewed a conviction for possession of a wild turkey with the knowledge that it had been taken in violation of Ga. Code Ann. § 27-1-31. The court reversed the defendant's conviction because there was no evidence that the defendant knew or reasonably should have known that the turkey was taken in violation of the law. Nevertheless, the court took the occasion to explain the law of constructive possession of the turkey. The court observed that the jury could have inferred the defendant's joint constructive possession of a turkey where the defendant waited for a companion who shot a wild turkey. The court found the defendant knew her companion was to hunt for turkey on the morning in question; she waited for him during the hunt and cooked and ate the game he killed.

Defenses Rejected

Defendants have attacked certain wildlife regulations as being vague and ambiguous, but in most cases such challenges have failed. In other cases defendants have challenged warrantless searches, a subject we discuss in detail in Chapter 15. Historically, a "subsistence" defense—that is, a contention that game or fish was taken as a means of subsistence—may have been allowed, but this defense generally fails today. See *State v. Eluska,* 742 P.2d 514 (Alaska 1986). In *State v. Gibbs,* 797 P.2d 928 (Mont. 1990), a defendant charged with illegal possession of a bobcat pelt claimed he had killed the bobcat in defense of his son, whom the animal had attacked. (We discuss defense of another person in Chapter 14). He based his defense on Mont. Code Ann. § 87-3-112, which provided there was no criminal liability for the taking of wildlife that was molesting or threatening to kill a person. The trial court refused to submit the issue of defense of another person to the jury, noting the statute that the defendant relied upon required notification to the Department of Fish, Wildlife, and Parks within seventy-two hours and that the defendant failed to comply with the statutory reporting requirement. The Montana Supreme Court upheld the trial court's action in refusing to submit the defense to the jury and affirmed the defendant's conviction.

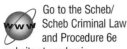

Go to the Scheb/ Scheb Criminal Law and Procedure 6e website at academic .cengage.com/criminaljustice/ scheb for an edited version of *State v. Billie*.

In *State v. Billie,* 497 So.2d 889 (Fla. App. 1986), a Florida appellate court held that the State of Florida had jurisdiction to charge a member of the Seminole tribe with unlawfully killing a panther pursuant to Florida Statutes § 372.671. The court rejected claims that the ESA preempted state law, finding that the state law in this area was more protective than the federal ESA.

■ CONCLUSION

The authority of federal and state governments to enact laws to protect the public health is a basic component of their police power. Imposing strict criminal liability on responsible corporate officers has proven to be successful in deterring violations of laws protecting the purity and safety of food and drugs. Moreover, the concept of strict liability is firm relative to traditional public health statutes.

Formerly, governmental agencies relied almost exclusively on civil penalties to punish violators of environmental laws, but the regulatory climate is changing. The coming years will continue to witness an increased reliance by federal and state authorities on criminal sanctions, often with greatly increased penalties. As this trend continues, legislatures (or, in their absence, courts of law) will most likely include a *mens rea* requirement in regulatory statutes that subject violators of environmental laws to severe punishment.

Strict liability is also applied to transgressors of wildlife regulations, although— whenever a violation rises to the level of a felony or involves a substantial penalty— courts are inclined to require proof of the defendant's intent before upholding a conviction that visits serious consequences on the offender.

Noise pollution and smoking in public places are increasingly viewed by society as detrimental. Statutes and ordinances that regulate noise must be sufficiently precise to avoid constitutional infirmity. Increased concern about the deleterious effects of second-hand smoke have caused the public to demand restrictions on smoking in public buildings, restaurants, bars, and workplaces. It is reasonable to expect that criminal sanctions—which, after all, mirror societal norms—will be increasingly applied to these problems.

■ KEY TERMS

public health, 266
environmental crime, 266
littering, 266
antismoking laws, 266
noise ordinances, 266
poaching, 266
strict liability, 267
Pure Food, Drug, and Cosmetic Act (FDCA), 268
regulatory offenses, 269
negligence standard, 269
responsible corporate officer, 271
zoning, 272
Environmental Protection Agency, 273

Rivers and Harbors Act, 274
Clean Air Act, 274
Clean Water Act, 274
Resource Conservation and Recovery Act, 274
Toxic Substances Control Act, 274
Comprehensive Environmental Response, Compensation and Liability Act, 274
point source, 275
Quiet Communities Act, 284
Migratory Bird Conservation Act, 287
Endangered Species Act, 288

■ WEB-BASED RESEARCH ACTIVITY

 Go to the Web. Locate your state's statutes. Search your state's environmental laws. Determine which, if any, prohibitions involve criminal sanctions. What, if any, additional criminal sanctions would you support if you were elected to your state legislature?

■ QUESTIONS FOR THOUGHT AND DISCUSSION

1. Are criminal sanctions essential to the effective enforcement of food, drug, and cosmetic laws?

2. Should the term "responsible corporate officer" be explicitly defined by statute, or should courts make this determination on a case-by-case basis?

3. Does your community impose criminal penalties for violations of zoning regulations? If so, are violations treated as strict liability offenses? Why is it often more effective for a local governmental body to seek injunctive relief against zoning violators?

4. Should efforts be made to formulate a model state code of environmental regulations?

5. Should environmental crimes that carry major penalties be strict liability offenses, or should prosecutors be required to prove that a defendant knowingly or willfully committed an offense?

6. Do you think hunting and fishing violations should be decriminalized and treated as civil infractions in the way that many states treat less serious traffic offenses?

7. Can you describe some instances where it is advisable to seek injunctive relief rather than imposing criminal penalties for violations of environmental laws?

8. Where smoking is prohibited by law in workplaces, restaurants, and bars, should violations be treated as civil or criminal infractions? What, if any, exceptions should be provided in such laws?

■ PROBLEMS FOR DISCUSSION AND SOLUTION

1. Two boys died of asphyxiation after playing in a dumpster in which a toxic solvent was disposed of improperly. The solvent was placed in the dumpster by workers at a nearby industrial plant. Under which, if any, federal statute can the plant manager be prosecuted?

2. Hoss Tile is arrested after police are called to the scene of a private social club where Tile is a member. The police are called because Tile refuses to extinguish his cigarette in the dining room and is becoming belligerent. He is charged with a misdemeanor under a new ordinance that prohibits smoking in "restaurants and other places of public accommodation other than those in which alcoholic beverages are sold for consumption on the premises." The club in which he was arrested does not sell or serve alcohol. How might Tile defend himself in this case?

CHAPTER 12

Offenses against Public Order, Safety, and National Security

Introduction

Government has a fundamental obligation to protect the public order and safety. The criminal law is one means by which government performs this function—by criminalizing acts that threaten society's interests in order and safety. Government is also obligated to protect the security of the nation itself. It does this primarily through its military capabilities and intelligence agencies, but the criminal law also plays a role in the protection of national security. Since September 11, 2001, protection of the homeland against acts of terrorism has become a high priority for the criminal law.

As with most basic criminal offenses, the crimes against public order and safety are rooted in the English common law. The common law recognized the right of the people to assemble peaceably for lawful purposes. Nevertheless, maintaining public order was given a high priority. To maintain order, the common law developed three misdemeanors: **unlawful assembly, rout,** and **riot.** If three or more persons met together with the intention of cooperating to disturb the public peace by doing an unlawful act, their gathering was considered an unlawful assembly. If they took steps to achieve their purpose, it was a rout, and if they actually executed their plans, they committed a riot.

Modern statutes have modified these common-law crimes somewhat. Today, the category of offenses known as **breaches of the peace** includes unlawful assembly, riot, **inciting a riot,** and **disorderly conduct,** as well as violations of noise ordinances. While these offenses are very important in carrying out the day-to-day peacekeeping function of the police, they do raise constitutional problems in certain instances. The First Amendment guarantees the rights of free expression and assembly. Of course, the exercise of these freedoms sometimes poses a threat to public order and safety. The line between what the Constitution protects and what the criminal law legitimately forbids can sometimes be difficult to perceive (see Chapter 3).

To discourage idleness, the common law also developed the offense of **vagrancy,** which was the crime of "going about without visible means of support." Historically, this offense allowed the police tremendous discretion in dealing with suspicious persons. Accordingly, it has been the subject of considerable controversy. Today, the offense of vagrancy has been largely supplanted by the modern offense of **loitering,** although it too is subject to criticism. Numerous vagrancy and loitering laws have been attacked as being excessively vague and therefore in violation of the constitutional requirement that criminal laws provide fair notice as to what specific conduct is prohibited.

Offenses against public order and safety also include **motor vehicle violations** and **weapons offenses,** which, while unknown to the common law, exist by virtue of modern legislation aimed at protecting the public safety. While there is little constitutional debate over traffic safety laws, weapons offenses are sometimes challenged under the Second Amendment to the Constitution, which protects the right to keep and bear arms. Today, there is a strident political debate taking place in this country on both the desirability and constitutionality of **gun control laws.**

In the wake of the horrific terrorist attacks of September 11, 2001, offenses against national security have taken on renewed importance. Many offenses that were far less prominent before 9-11, such as sabotage, espionage, and sedition, are receiving renewed attention. So too are immigration offenses, not only due to the threat of terrorists entering the country illegally but also because in the last two decades the country has experienced an enormous wave of unlawful immigrants, primarily coming across the Mexican border.

The USA PATRIOT Act, enacted shortly after 9-11 and essentially reauthorized in 2006, has updated many federal criminal laws by relating new technologies to new terrorist threats. In interpreting the application of these laws, the courts will bear the responsibility of balancing the need to effectively combat terrorism with the need to preserve the freedom and due process of law guaranteed by the U.S. Constitution.

Breaches of the Peace

In the United States, the responsibility for maintaining public order and peace rests primarily with state and local governments, although the federal government has a significant role as well. A variety of state statutes and local ordinances prohibit unlawful assemblies, riots, and disorderly conduct. Control of unlawful assemblies and riots is aimed at group behavior, whereas laws proscribing disorderly conduct are aimed at both group and individual behavior. By enforcing laws prohibiting disorderly conduct, state and local governments attempt to prevent such undesirable conduct as violent and tumultuous behavior, excessive noise, offensive language and gestures, actions impeding movement of persons on public sidewalks and roads, and disturbances of lawfully conducted meetings.

On the other hand, the First Amendment to the U.S. Constitution guarantees citizens the rights of free speech and free assembly in the public forum. Courts must carefully weigh the community's interests in maintaining order and peace against these fundamental freedoms. The exercise of freedom of speech and assembly in the public forum may be restricted only where necessary to achieve a compelling public interest. *United States v. Grace,* 461 U.S. 171, 103 S.Ct. 1702, 75 L.Ed.2d 736 (1983).

Unlawful Assembly and Riot

Most states have enacted statutes proscribing unlawful assemblies and riots. For example, the Indiana Code defines unlawful assembly as "an assembly of five or more persons whose common object is to commit an unlawful act, or to commit a lawful act by unlawful means." West's Ann. Ind. Code § 35–45–1–1. It further defines tumultuous conduct as "conduct that results in, or is likely to result in, serious bodily injury to a person or substantial damage to property." West's Ann. Ind. Code § 35–45–1–1. Under the Indiana Code, a person who is a "member of an unlawful assembly who recklessly, knowingly, or intentionally engages in tumultuous conduct commits rioting." Under Indiana law, the offense is punishable as a misdemeanor unless committed while armed with a deadly weapon, in which case it becomes a felony. West's Ann. Ind. Code § 35–45–1–2.

THE FEDERAL ANTI-RIOT ACT

Historically, federal statutes have made it a crime to riot. However, the controversy over the Vietnam War, racial unrest, poverty, and a host of other social ills during the 1960s became catalysts for riotous behavior beyond proportions previously experienced. To better cope with riots, Congress enacted the **Federal Anti-Riot Act** of 1968. The

Evidence Sustaining a Conviction for Inciting a Riot

A jury convicted Powell of inciting a riot. He appealed, challenging the sufficiency of the evidence. The jury heard evidence that after fourteen-year-old Anderson rejected Powell's request to have sex with him, Powell threatened to have his eighteen-year-old girlfriend, Johnson, beat her. Powell then informed Johnson that Anderson had been talking about her and suggested that Johnson go up the street to meet Anderson. As Anderson and her friends Lattimore and Faust walked down the street, Johnson cursed them, and at Powell's direction, Johnson jumped on Lattimore's back and began pulling her hair and punching her. When Lattimore's sister attempted to break up the fight, Powell insisted on keeping the fight going and shoved away everyone who tried to stop it. Before Faust returned with Lattimore's mother and uncle, who ended the fight, between twenty-five and sixty onlookers had gathered.

In affirming Powell's conviction, the Georgia Court of Appeals noted that the essential elements of inciting a riot are (1) engaging in conduct which urges, counsels, or advises others to riot; (2) with intent to riot; and (3) at a time and place and under circumstances which produce a clear and present danger of a riot. OCGA § 16–11–31(a). The court observed that Powell encouraged Johnson to confront Anderson and that after Johnson attacked Lattimore, Powell directed Johnson's moves and yelled, "You ought to be beating this bitch" and "Don't stop the fight, the bitch got too much mouth." Further, Powell shoved and bullied several people in the gathering crowd in order to prevent any interference with the fight.

Powell v. State, 462 S.E.2d 447 (Ga. App. 1995).

act applies to persons who travel in or use any facility of interstate and foreign commerce. It proscribes interstate travel and use of the mail, telegraph, telephone, radio, or television with intent to incite, encourage, participate in, or carry on a riot; or to aid or abet any person in inciting or participating in a riot or committing any act of violence in furtherance of a riot. 18 U.S.C.A. § 2101(a). The act comprehensively defines riot by stating that

> the term "riot" means a public disturbance involving (1) an act or acts of violence by one or more persons part of an assemblage of three or more persons, which act or acts shall constitute a clear and present danger of, or shall result in, damage or injury to the property of any other person or to the person of any other individual or (2) a threat or threats of the commission of an act or acts of violence by one or more persons part of an assemblage of three or more persons having, individually or collectively, the ability of immediate execution of such threat or threats, where the performance of the threatened act or acts of violence would constitute a clear and present danger of, or would result in, damage or injury to the property of any other person or to the person of any other individual. 18 U.S.C.A. § 2102(a).

It defines "to incite a riot" by explaining that

> the term "to incite a riot," or "to organize, promote, encourage, participate in, or carry on a riot," includes, but is not limited to, urging or instigating other persons to riot, but shall not be deemed to mean the mere oral or written (1) advocacy of ideas or (2) expression of belief, not involving advocacy of any act or acts of violence or assertion of the rightness of, or the right to commit, any such act or acts. 18 U.S.C.A. § 2102(b).

In 1972 the U.S. Court of Appeals for the Seventh Circuit held that the Anti-Riot Act is not unconstitutionally vague or overbroad in relation to the First Amendment. *United States v. Dellinger,* 472 F.2d 340 (7th Cir. 1972).

Disorderly Conduct

Closely related to statutes prohibiting unlawful assembly and riot are laws making disorderly conduct an offense. The Indiana Code concisely, yet comprehensively, proscribes disorderly conduct by providing that

> [a] person who recklessly, knowingly or intentionally: (1) engages in fighting or in tumultuous conduct; (2) makes unreasonable noise and continues to do so after being asked to stop; (3) disrupts a lawful assembly of persons; commits disorderly conduct.... West's Ann. Ind. Code § 35–45–1–3.

Statutes and ordinances similar to those in Indiana are found in virtually every state. There is no constitutional problem when such laws are applied to conduct that is violent or threatens to produce imminent lawless action. *Brandenburg v. Ohio,* 395 U.S. 444, 89 S.Ct. 1827, 23 L.Ed.2d 430 (1969). Nor is there any constitutional barrier against applying such statutes to the utterance of fighting words. *Chaplinsky v. New Hampshire,* 315 U.S. 568, 571, 62 S.Ct. 766, 769, 86 L.Ed. 1031, 1035 (1942). However, the Constitution "does not permit a State to make criminal the peaceful expression of unpopular views." *Edwards v. South Carolina,* 372 U.S. 229, 237, 83 S.Ct. 680, 684, 9 L.Ed.2d 697, 703 (1963). (For more discussion of these First Amendment concepts, see Chapter 3.)

In *Edwards v. South Carolina,* supra, the Supreme Court reviewed a set of convictions that stemmed from a civil rights protest. On the morning of March 2, 1961, a large group of black students congregated on the lawn of the statehouse in Columbia, South Carolina, to protest the state's segregation laws. Speeches were made; songs were sung. The students responded by clapping and stamping their feet. A large crowd of onlookers gathered nearby. Nobody among the crowd caused or threatened any trouble, and there was no obstruction of pedestrian or vehicular traffic. A contingent of thirty or more police officers was present to meet any foreseeable possibility of disorder. After refusing to obey a police order to disperse, many of the students were arrested and found guilty of breach of the peace. In reversing their convictions, the U.S. Supreme Court said the following:

> These petitioners were convicted of an offense as to be, in the words of the South Carolina Supreme Court, "not susceptible of exact definition." And they were convicted upon evidence which showed no more than that the opinions which they were peaceably expressing were sufficiently opposed to the views of the majority of the community to attract a crowd and necessitate police protection.... The Fourteenth Amendment does not permit a State to make criminal the peaceful expression of unpopular views. 372 U.S. at 237, 83 S.Ct. at 684, 9 L.Ed.2d at 703.

It is instructive to compare *Edwards v. South Carolina* with *Adderley v. Florida,* 385 U.S. 39, 87 S.Ct. 242, 17 L.Ed.2d 149 (1966). Here the Supreme Court affirmed the convictions of African American student protesters who blocked a driveway to the local jail. Emphasizing the use of the driveway for vehicles providing service to the jail, the Supreme Court observed, "The State, no less than a private owner of property, has power to preserve the property under its control for the use to which it is lawfully dedicated." 385 U.S. at 47, 87 S.Ct. at 247, 17 L.Ed.2d at 156.

In *People v. Barron,* 808 N.E.2d 1051 (Ill. App. 2004) the defendant was convicted of disorderly conduct for violating an Illinois statute proscribing specific categories of conduct. 720 ILCS 5/26-1(a)(3) provided:

> A person commits disorderly conduct when he knowingly ... [t]ransmits or causes to be transmitted in any manner to another a false alarm to the effect that a bomb or other explosive of any nature ... is concealed in such place that its explosion or

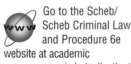 Go to the Scheb/ Scheb Criminal Law and Procedure 6e website at academic .cengage.com/criminaljustice/ scheb for an edited version of *Brandenburg v. Ohio.*

 Go to the Scheb/ Scheb Criminal Law and Procedure 6e website at academic .cengage.com/criminaljustice/ scheb for an edited version of *Edwards v. South Carolina.*

Go to the Scheb/ Scheb Criminal Law and Procedure 6e website at academic .cengage.com/criminaljustice/ scheb for an edited version of *Adderley v. Florida.*

United States v. Grace, 461 U.S. 171, 103 S.Ct. 1702, 75 L.Ed.2d 736 (1983)

Mary Grace stood on the sidewalk in front of the Supreme Court building in Washington, D.C., and held up a sign displaying the text of the First Amendment. A police officer approached Grace and informed her she would be arrested if she did not move across the street. Grace complied with the officer's request but later filed suit to challenge the constitutionality of 40 U.S.C.A. § 13k, which made it unlawful to "parade, stand, or move in processions or assemblages in the Supreme Court Building or grounds," or "display therein any flag, banner, or device designed or adapted to bring into public notice any party." The federal district court dismissed the suit, but Grace appealed and the case eventually reached the Supreme Court. The High Court declared the statute unconstitutional insofar as it restricted expression on the sidewalk in front of the Supreme Court building. In his opinion for the Court, Justice Byron White discusses the concept of "public forum" and the government's justification for prohibiting demonstrations in front of the Court.

JUSTICE WHITE delivered the opinion of the Court, saying in part:

It is ... true that "public places" historically associated with the free exercise of expressive activities, such as streets, sidewalks, and parks, are considered, without more, to be "public forums." ... In such places, the government's ability to permissibly restrict expressive conduct is very limited: the government may enforce reasonable time, place, and manner regulations as long as the restrictions "are content-neutral, are narrowly tai-lored to serve a significant government interest, and leave open ample alternative channels of communication." ... Additional restrictions such as an absolute prohibition on a particular type of expression will be upheld only if narrowly drawn to accomplish a compelling governmental interest....

Publicly owned or operated property does not become a "public forum" simply because members of the public are permitted to come and go at will.... There is little doubt that in some circumstances the government may ban the entry on to public property that is not a "public forum" of all persons except those who have legitimate business on the premises. The government, "no less than a private owner of property, has the power to preserve the property under its control for the use to which it is lawfully dedicated." ...

But ... we are unconvinced that the prohibitions of § 13k ... sufficiently serve that purpose to sustain its validity insofar as the public sidewalks on the perimeter of the grounds are concerned. Those sidewalks are used by the public like other public sidewalks. There is nothing to indicate to the public that these sidewalks are part of the Supreme Court grounds or are in any way different from other public sidewalks in the city. We seriously doubt that the public would draw a different inference from a lone picketer carrying a sign on the sidewalks around the building than it would from a similar picket on the sidewalks across the street.

We thus perceive insufficient justification for [the] prohibition of carrying signs, banners, or devices on the public sidewalks surrounding the building. We hold that under the First Amendment the section is unconstitutional as applied to those sidewalks.

release would endanger human life, knowing at the time of such transmission that there is no reasonable ground for believing that such bomb ... is concealed in such place.

The evidence at the defendant's trial disclosed that although the defendant was not actually in possession of a concealed explosive device, he informed two airline ticket agents that he had a bomb in his shoe. He claimed the ticket agents knew he was joking; however, one of the agents called the police, who used bomb searching dogs and arrested the defendant. On appeal, the defendant argued that section 26–1(a)(3) requires that, once transmitted, the alarm must cause actual fear in the mind of the listener. In a case of first impression, the court rejected his arguments and held that the crime of disorderly conduct is complete upon the transmission of a false alarm to another person, regardless of the effect the false alarm has upon the individual who receives it. The court affirmed the defendant's conviction.

In *Colten v. Kentucky,* 407 U.S. 104, 92 S.Ct. 1953, 32 L.Ed.2d 584 (1972), the Supreme Court upheld a conviction for disorderly conduct arising from a confrontation between a police officer and a student protester. After conducting a political demonstration, several students got into their cars and formed an entourage. A police officer stopped one of the vehicles after noting that its license plate had expired. The other cars in the group also pulled over. One of the students approached the officer to find out what was wrong. After explaining the situation, the officer asked the student to leave. The student refused to do so and was arrested for violating section 437.016(1)(f) of the Kentucky Revised Statutes, which provided that a person was guilty of disorderly conduct "if, with intent to cause public inconvenience, annoyance or alarm, or recklessly creating a risk thereof," he "congregates with other persons in a public place and refuses to comply with a lawful order of the police to disperse." A conviction for disorderly conduct was upheld by the Kentucky Court of Appeals. *Colten v. Commonwealth,* 467 S.W.2d 374 (Ky. 1971). In upholding the conviction, the U.S. Supreme Court said this:

> As the Kentucky statute was construed by the state court, … a crime is committed only where there is no *bona fide* intention to exercise a constitutional right—in which event, by definition, the statute infringes no protected speech or conduct—or where the interest so clearly outweighs the collective interest sought to be asserted that the latter must be deemed to be insubstantial.… Individuals may not be convicted under the Kentucky statute merely for expressing unpopular or annoying ideas. The statute comes into operation only when the individual's interest in expression, judged in the light of all relevant factors, is "minuscule" compared to a particular public interest in preventing that expression or conduct at that time and place. 407 U.S. at 111, 92 S.Ct. at 1958, 32 L.Ed.2d at 590.

Go to the Scheb/Scheb Criminal Law and Procedure 6e website at academic.cengage.com/criminaljustice/scheb for an edited version of *Hess v. Indiana.*

In a similar case, *Hess v. Indiana,* 414 U.S. 105, 94 S.Ct. 326, 38 L.Ed.2d 303 (1973), the Supreme Court reversed a conviction of a student protestor who had been arrested after the sheriff heard him shout, "We'll take the fucking street later." The Supreme Court found that the defendant's language did not amount to fighting words or represent imminent lawless action.

In *Cavazos v. State,* 455 N.E.2d 618 (Ind. App. 1983), an Indiana appellate court found that a defendant calling a police officer an "asshole" and continuing to debate with him about the arrest of her brother was insufficient to support her conviction for disorderly conduct. The court reasoned that the defendant's words to the police officer did not constitute fighting words or fall within any of the other unprotected classes of speech.

In 1999 a Georgia appellate court reversed a defendant's conviction for disorderly conduct. The court held that although the defendant's statement to a female medic that she had "nice tits" was crude and socially unacceptable, such words were not such as to incite a breach of the peace. *Lundgren v. State,* 518 S.E.2d 908 (Ga. App. 1999). But vulgar language, when combined with physical action, may constitute disorderly conduct. In 1999 the Supreme Judicial Court of Maine affirmed a defendant's conviction for disorderly conduct where, in addition to the use of foul and vulgar language, the defendant, an emergency room patient, "head butted" a physician. *State v. McKenzie,* 605 A.2d 72 (Me. 1999).

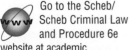

Go to the Scheb/Scheb Criminal Law and Procedure 6e website at academic.cengage.com/criminaljustice/scheb to find *Commonwealth v. Young* (1988), where a Pennsylvania appellate court upholds a conviction for disorderly conduct.

Excessive Noise

Local governments often use disorderly conduct ordinances to control **excessive noise.** To sustain a conviction based on unreasonable noise, the prosecution must show that the speech at issue infringed on the peace and tranquility enjoyed by others.

Allegations of Disorderly Conduct and Inciting to Riot

Reggie Upshaw was charged with disorderly conduct and inciting to riot. He moved to dismiss the charges, contending the complaint failed to allege facts from which it could be inferred that he intended to cause a riot or disturbance or to present a clear and present danger of creating unrest. The court found the complaint was supported by sworn allegations that shortly after the September 11, 2001, terrorist attacks on the World Trade Center, the defendant and several accomplices confronted a gathering street crowd in the vicinity of Times Square in New York City. They allegedly boasted that they supported the attacks and were disappointed the carnage had not been greater, yelling in the faces of the crowd, "We've got something for your asses." The complaint further alleged that the defendant and his accomplices refused to disperse after police officers asked them to do so. In ruling against the motion to dismiss, the court concluded that the defendant's remarks went beyond speech protected by the First Amendment and constituted a real threat of violence.

People v. Upshaw, 741 N.Y.S.2d 664 (N.Y. City Crim. Ct. 2002).

Hooks v. State, 660 N.E.2d 1076 (Ind. App. 1996). For example, the noise produced by a late-night party with a live band might be actionable under a breach of the peace ordinance, but only if the party is in fact disturbing the peace of the neighborhood. Courts are inclined to uphold the application of ordinances that proscribe making excessive noise in areas such as hospitals and nursing homes. Police officers responding to complaints about excessive noise usually first request that the offending party "turn it down." If this fails, the offender may be charged with a breach of the peace.

Vagrancy, Loitering, Curfews, and Panhandling

Elites in feudal England placed great emphasis on able-bodied serfs performing labor and not straying from their assigned tasks. This was motivated by both the need for laborers and the desire to prevent idle persons from becoming public charges. With the breakup of feudal estates, England found it necessary to prevent workers from moving from one area to another in search of improved working conditions. Thus, to regulate the economics of the populace, the common law developed the misdemeanor offense of vagrancy. The offense comprised three elements: (1) being without visible means of support, (2) being without employment, and (3) being able to work but refusing to do so. *Fenster v. Leary,* 229 N.E.2d 426 (N.Y. 1967). In sixteenth-century England, persons who loitered idly for three days were subject to punishment under the Enslavement Acts.

Eventually the emphasis shifted from merely punishing idleness toward the prevention of crime, as England enacted statutes defining vagrancy. The objective then became to protect the people and their property from persons considered potential criminals or simply regarded as undesirables. Thus, by the time the American colonists settled in their new environment, the concept of punishing vagrants had become firmly implanted, and the colonists found it to be a desirable way to prevent idleness and to outlaw conduct offensive to their social mores.

The American Approach to Vagrancy

During the 1800s, virtually all American states and most cities enacted statutes and ordinances punishing a wide variety of conduct as vagrancy. Statutory language was intentionally rather vague, presumably to allow police broad discretion to arrest persons they deemed undesirable to the community. Vagrancy laws not only proscribed such acts as disorderly conduct, begging, and loitering; they also criminalized the condition of being poor, idle, of bad reputation, or simply "wandering around without any lawful purpose." By 1865, Alabama's vagrancy statute included "runaway" and "stubborn servants." By making a person's status an offense, these laws ran counter to the historical concept that a crime consisted of the commission of an unlawful act or the failure to perform a required act. Frequently, vagrancy laws were directed against persons without the means to contest their validity or to challenge the application of such laws to them. Moreover, the U.S. Supreme Court had sanctioned them in 1837 by saying that

> [w]e think it [is] as competent and as necessary for a state to provide precautionary measures against the moral pestilence of paupers, vagabonds, and possibly convicts; as it is to guard against … physical pestilence…. *City of New York v. Miln,* 36 U.S. (11 Pet.) 102, 142, 9 L.Ed. 648, 664 (1837).

In the first half of the 1900s, arrests and convictions for vagrancy were common, as were appellate court decisions upholding convictions in a variety of circumstances. For example, in Minnesota a defendant's conviction was affirmed for wandering about the streets with no place of abode and without giving a good account of himself. *State v. Woods,* 163 N.W. 518 (Minn. 1917). In Virginia, an appellate court held that a defendant's conduct in consorting with gamblers and idlers constituted the offense of vagrancy. *Morgan v. Commonwealth,* 191 S.E. 791 (Va. 1937). Even a defendant's conduct as part of "a group of 4 or 5 suspicious men" at a saloon was, under the particular circumstances, held to be vagrancy. *State v. Carroll,* 30 A.2d 54 (N.J. 1943).

The wide range of vaguely proscribed conduct in vagrancy laws made them susceptible to arbitrary enforcement by law enforcement agencies. In their efforts to prevent crime and control "undesirables," these laws became somewhat of a catchall of the criminal justice system. Police commonly used them as a basis to arrest a suspect, who was then held pending investigation, or as a method of getting the suspect to confess. Vagrancy laws also furnished a convenient basis for police to justify a search incident to arrest as an exception to the warrant requirement of the Fourth Amendment.

By the 1950s, the vagrancy laws were enforced primarily against loafers, alcoholics, derelicts, and tramps when they left the environs of "skid row" and ventured into the more "respectable" neighborhoods, where residents found their presence offensive. The constitutionality of the vagrancy laws was frequently challenged on grounds that they were vague, violated due process of law requirements, and exceeded the police power of the states. But such challenges were rejected by state and federal courts, which generally upheld the right of the legislature to define what constitutes being a vagrant. During the 1960s, however, a number of statutes defining a vagrant as a person "without visible means of support," who "wanders around the streets at late hours," or who "fails to give account of himself" were declared unconstitutional.

The Death Knell of Vagrancy Laws

In 1972 the U.S. Supreme Court issued an opinion that had a profound effect on the enforcement of vagrancy laws in the United States. *Papachristou v. City of Jacksonville,* 405 U.S. 156, 92 S.Ct. 839, 31 L.Ed.2d 110 (1972).

In Jacksonville, Florida, eight defendants were convicted under a municipal ordinance that broadly defined vagrancy and levied criminal penalties on violators of as many as ninety days in jail, a $500 fine, or both. The ordinance included language common to many of the statutes and ordinances extant at the time:

> Rogues and vagabonds, or dissolute persons who go about begging, common gamblers, persons who use juggling or unlawful games or plays, common drunkards, common night walkers, thieves, pilferers or pickpockets, traders in stolen property, lewd, wanton and lascivious persons, keepers of gambling places, common railers and brawlers, persons wandering or strolling around from place to place without any lawful purpose or object, habitual loafers, disorderly persons, persons neglecting all lawful business and habitually spending their time by frequenting houses of ill fame, gaming houses, or places where alcoholic beverages are sold or served, persons able to work but habitually living upon the earnings of their wives or minor children shall be deemed vagrants.... Quoted in *Papachristou,* 405 U.S. at 158–159, n. 1, 92 S.Ct. at 841, 31 L.Ed.2d at 112.

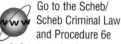 Go to the Scheb/ Scheb Criminal Law and Procedure 6e website at academic .cengage.com/criminaljustice/ scheb for an edited version of the *Papachristou* decision.

Speaking for a unanimous Supreme Court, Justice William O. Douglas said that the Jacksonville ordinance was void for vagueness, both in the sense that it "fails to give a person of ordinary intelligence fair notice that his contemplated conduct is forbidden by the statute and because it encourages arbitrary and erratic arrests and convictions." 405 U.S. at 162, 92 S.Ct. at 843, 31 L.Ed.2d at 115.

Despite the Supreme Court's ruling in *Papachristou,* the effects of the vagrancy ordinances lingered on. In 1968 a Nevada police officer arrested Lloyd Powell under a Henderson, Nevada, vagrancy ordinance. In a search incident to the arrest, the officer discovered a .38-caliber revolver with six spent cartridges in the cylinder. Laboratory analysis determined that the weapon was used in a recent murder. Powell was convicted of second-degree murder, and although a federal court later declared the vagrancy ordinance unconstitutional, the use of the evidence against Powell, and his conviction for murder, were ultimately sustained. *Stone v. Powell,* 428 U.S. 465, 96 S.Ct. 3037, 49 L.Ed.2d 1067 (1976).

State legislatures and local governments continued to enact ordinances in an attempt to control conduct they deemed objectionable; however, courts have invalidated such laws when they criminalize a person's status (for example, homelessness or intoxication) as opposed to proscribing a person's actions, frequently on the ground that such laws are vague and lead to arbitrary enforcement. One state supreme court took the view that a vagrancy statute that made it an offense to be a habitual drunkard violated the constitutional prohibition against cruel and unusual punishment for punishing a person's status. *State v. Pugh,* 369 So.2d 1308 (La. 1979).

Loitering

After the Supreme Court's decision in *Papachristou,* a new generation of laws making loitering a crime came on the scene. These new laws are narrower and often focus on preventing such crimes as prostitution and drug dealing. Courts scrutinize these ordinances carefully because they often prohibit or restrict constitutionally protected activities. Some have met the same fate as the traditional vagrancy ordinances.

One such ordinance enacted by Akron, Ohio, made it an offense to loiter "for the purpose of engaging in drug-related activity." The ordinance then listed eleven factors that may be considered in determining whether such purpose is manifested. The Ohio Supreme Court found the ordinance to be unconstitutionally vague under both the federal and state constitutions because it did not give persons of ordinary intelligence a reasonable opportunity to know what conduct was prohibited. Moreover, the court held that the enumerated factors to be considered—for example, looking like a drug user, being in an area known for unlawful drug use, and so on—could well be innocent and constitutionally protected conduct. Finally, the court pointed out that the ordinance was flawed because it delegated matters to enforcement authorities without providing necessary objective standards. *Akron v. Rowland*, 618 N.E.2d 138 (Ohio 1993).

In 1992 the Nevada Supreme Court held that the Nevada statute and Las Vegas Municipal Code provision criminalizing "loitering" on private property when the person has "no lawful business with owners or occupant thereof" lacked guidelines to avoid arbitrary and discriminatory enforcement and were unconstitutionally vague under the due process clauses of the federal and state constitutions. *State v. Richard*, 836 P.2d 622 (Nev. 1992).

Any ordinance that proscribes loitering without clearly defining the activities prohibited and without providing objective guidelines for enforcement is vulnerable to constitutional objections; however, courts have upheld loitering ordinances with a more narrow scope. For example, in 1989 the Oregon Supreme Court rejected a defendant's argument that the phrase "loiter in a manner and under circumstances manifesting the purpose of soliciting prostitution" did not meet the required constitutional standard of certainty. *City of Portland v. Levi*, 779 P.2d 192 (1989).

Police often use loitering ordinances and statutes to remove suspected drug dealers from the streets. At least one appellate court has approved this approach. See *Griffin v. State*, 479 S.E.2d 21 (Ga. App. 1996), where the court held that the sale of drugs on the streets violated a state loitering statute.

CHICAGO'S GANG LOITERING ORDINANCE

In a major decision of the 1996–1997 term, the U.S. Supreme Court held unconstitutional the "Gang Congregation Ordinance" enacted by the Chicago City Council in 1992. The ordinance made it a criminal offense for gang members to loiter with one another in any public place "with no apparent purpose." It required police to order a group of people who were standing around with no apparent purpose to move along if an officer believed that at least one of them belonged to a street gang. Those who disregarded an order to disperse were subject to arrest. Some 45,000 people were arrested in the three years the ordinance was enforced before the Illinois Supreme Court struck down the ordinance as violating due process of law by giving the police too much discretion and impermissibly restricting personal liberty. *City of Chicago v. Morales*, 687 N.E.2d 53 (Ill. 1997).

Go to the Scheb/ Scheb Criminal Law and Procedure 6e website at academic .cengage.com/criminaljustice/ scheb for an edited version of the Supreme Court's decision in *Chicago v. Morales*.

On review, the Supreme Court agreed with the Illinois Supreme Court. Writing for a divided Court, Justice John Paul Stevens criticized the ordinance for telling people to move on without inquiring about their purpose for standing around. He wrote that the ordinance "affords too much discretion to the police and too little notice to citizens who wish to use the public streets." *City of Chicago v. Morales*, 527 U.S. 41, 119 S.Ct. 1849, 144 L.Ed.2d 67 (1999).

To withstand constitutional attack, it appears that any ordinance proscribing loitering must, at a minimum, focus on a person's conduct and not a person's status or association, give fair notice as to what is proscribed, and afford a person an opportunity to explain his or her presence before being ordered to disperse.

HOMELESS PERSONS SLEEPING ON PUBLIC PROPERTY—THE FLORIDA EXPERIENCE

In recent years Florida municipalities have attempted to control the problem of homeless persons sleeping on public property in attempts to remove such persons from the streets and parks. They faced a background of courts' invalidating ordinances. In

State v. Penley, 276 So.2d 180 (Fla. App. 1973), the court invalidated a city ordinance that provided, "No person shall sleep upon or in any street, park, wharf or other public place." The appellate court determined the ordinance was unconstitutional in that it might result in arbitrary and erratic arrests and convictions.

A decade later, in *City of Pompano Beach v. Capalbo,* 455 So.2d 468 (Fla. App. 1984), another Florida appellate court reviewed a municipal ordinance that provided, "It shall be unlawful for any person to lodge or sleep in, on, or about any automobile, truck, camping or recreational vehicle or similar vehicle in any public street, public way, right of way, parking lot or other public property, within the limits of the city." The court found the ordinance void for vagueness "because it leaves in the unbridled discretion of the police officer whether or not to arrest one asleep in a motor vehicle on a public street or way or in a parking lot. A wide range of persons may violate [the ordinance] from the tired child asleep in his car-seat while a parent drives or while the car is parked, to the alternate long-distance driver asleep in the bunk of a moving or parked tractor-trailer, to the tired or inebriated driver who has … chosen to go to sleep in his parked car rather than take his life or others' lives in his hands.," 455 So.2d at 470.

Against this background, section 43.52 of the City of Orlando's Code prohibited "camping" on public property, which was defined to include, among other things, "sleeping out-of-doors." After James Joel, a homeless person, was arrested for violating the ordinance, he filed suit against the city, contending the ordinance violated his rights under the Fifth, Eighth, and Fourteenth Amendments to the U.S. Constitution. He contended the ordinance (1) encouraged discriminatory, oppressive, and arbitrary enforcement, (2) was unconstitutionally vague, (3) bore no rational relationship to a legitimate governmental purpose, (4) violated his right to travel, and (5) violated his right to be free from cruel and unusual punishment. He sought a declaratory judgment, injunctive relief, and monetary damages under 42 U.S.C.A. § 1983. The federal district court ruled in favor of the city, and Joel appealed. On appeal, the U.S. Court of Appeals affirmed, noting the ordinance was rationally related to the city's interest in promoting aesthetics, sanitation, public health, and safety and did not violate equal protection rights of the homeless, notwithstanding that it may have had disproportionate impact on homeless persons. *Joel v. City of Orlando,* 232 F.3d 1353 (11th Cir. (2000).

Curfews

In an attempt to combat juvenile crime and protect children by keeping them off the streets at night, most large cities and many counties have enacted **curfew ordinances.** While restrictions vary considerably, most curfew laws define juveniles as unmarried persons under age eighteen and prohibit them from being on public streets or in other public places from midnight to 6:00 A.M. unless accompanied by a parent or guardian or another adult approved by the juvenile's parent or guardian. Many curfew ordinances provide that parents and guardians violate the ordinance if they knowingly allow their child to commit a violation. Curfew laws often provide exceptions concerning work, school and civic events, travel, and emergencies.

Considerable litigation has ensued concerning the validity of curfews. Those who seek to sustain them argue that a juvenile curfew is a valid exercise of the government's police power. They liken the curfew regulations to requirements that minors are required to attend school, are prohibited from purchasing alcoholic beverages, and are subject to restrictions on operation of motor vehicles. Challengers contend that curfew regulations are vague and violate First Amendment rights of association, abridge Fourth Amendment rights to be free from unreasonable detention, deny juveniles the equal protection of the law, and interfere with parental rights.

In *City of Wadsworth v. Owens,* 536 N.E.2d 67 (Ohio 1987), a city ordinance prohibited anyone under age eighteen from being on the streets, sidewalks, or other public places during certain nighttime hours unless accompanied by a parent or some other responsible adult having the parent's permission. The court found the ordinance unconstitutionally overbroad, pointing out that it contained no exceptions, thereby restricting a minor's church, school, and work activities. Courts in New Jersey, Ohio, Hawaii, and the state of Washington have also found curfew ordinances unconstitutional. On the other hand, in *Panora v. Simmons,* 445 N.W.2d 363 (Iowa 1989), the Iowa Supreme Court upheld an ordinance making it unlawful for any minor to be or remain upon any street or in any public place between 10:00 P.M. and 5:00 A.M. The ordinance provided exceptions for a minor accompanied by a parent or other adult custodian and for a minor traveling between home and places of employment, and to church, civic, or school functions.

More recent curfew ordinances that have been upheld have included an expanded number of exceptions. For example, in May 1997, Pinellas Park, Florida, adopted a curfew ordinance along the lines described above. In addition to permitting a juvenile to be accompanied by a parent or an adult authorized by a custodial parent, the ordinance includes numerous exceptions such as when a juvenile is exercising First Amendment rights to attend religious, political, and governmental meetings or events sponsored by civic and governmental groups, during or going to and from lawful employment and school-sponsored or theme-park events, when on the sidewalk at home or at a neighbor's home with the neighbor's permission, or when involved in interstate travel. The trial court, applying a strict scrutiny test (see Chapter 3), invalidated the ordinance on the basis that it violates a juvenile's parents' fundamental right to raise their children without governmental intrusion. On appeal, the court applied a "heightened scrutiny" test and reversed the trial court's ruling, noting that the ordinance includes adequate exceptions to limit the scope of the curfew. *State v. T.M.,* 761 So.2d 1140 (Fla. App. 2000). On review, the Florida Supreme Court ruled that the appellate court had erred in applying the "heightened scrutiny" test and remanded the case to the appellate court to apply a "strict standard" in reviewing the ordinance. *T.M. v. State,* 784 So.2d 442 (Fla. 2001). On remand, the district court of appeal held that the city's juvenile curfew ordinance was unconstitutional under the "strict scrutiny test." 832 So.2d 118 (Fla. App. 2002).

Courts in Texas, Virginia, and Washington, D.C., have also upheld curfew ordinances. Those who oppose curfews recognize the authority of parents to impose the restrictions, but they claim the government should not intrude into the parental sphere. They also point to studies showing no correlation between arrests for curfew violations (which are quite common) and the incidence of juvenile crime. The American Civil Liberties Union (ACLU) has been very active in attacking curfew laws in the courts. In a September 1999 press release, ACLU of New Jersey Legal Director Lenora Lapidus observed that "police already have the ability to arrest juvenile criminals; the curfew adds nothing more than the discretion to arrest the innocent as well." In her view, "The proper response to juvenile crime is to arrest the criminals, not to place thousands of law-abiding young people under house arrest."

Despite the controversial nature of juvenile curfews, law enforcement officials and local governing bodies overwhelmingly support these measures. They are likely to remain on the scene as long as juvenile crime continues to plague our nation's cities, although to be upheld the ordinances must recognize reasonable exceptions.

EMERGENCY CURFEWS

Although most curfews involve restrictions on juveniles, the law recognizes that governments can also impose curfews to cope with emergencies. Curfews restrict a person's right of movement, but the Supreme Court has stated that the constitutional right to travel may be legitimately curtailed when a community has been ravaged by flood, fire, or disease and its safety and welfare are threatened. *Zemel v. Rusk,* 381 U.S. 1, 85 S.Ct. 1271, 14 L.Ed.2d 179 (1965).

State laws usually grant local governments the authority to impose limited curfews during emergencies where floods, fires, riots, looting, and other situations threaten the safety and welfare of a community. West's Ann. Cal. Gov. Code § 8634 is illustrative. It provides:

> During a local emergency the governing body of a political subdivision, or officials designated thereby, may promulgate orders and regulations necessary to provide for the protection of life and property, including orders or regulations imposing a curfew within designated boundaries where necessary to preserve the public order and safety. Such orders and regulations and amendments and rescissions thereof shall be in writing and shall be given widespread publicity and notice.

Courts generally uphold the exercise of emergency powers by local governing bodies or their authorized representatives to declare a curfew where life and property are threatened as long as the curfew regulations are reasonable. To be reasonable, curfew regulations must not be directed at any one class of persons, must not unduly restrict the right of expression, and must allow necessary exemptions.

In April 1992, widespread rioting, looting, and arson occurred in Los Angeles County following the jury verdict acquitting police officers in the Rodney King beating. Long Beach, California, imposed curfew regulations that prohibited anyone from being on the public streets and in public places between 7:00 P.M. and 6:00 A.M. so long as the emergency existed. The regulations were not directed at any particular class or group, regulated conduct and not the content of speech, exempted law enforcement officers and firefighters, and permitted arrest of only those who refused, after notice, to obey the curfew. A California appellate court upheld the curfew regulations. *In re Juan C.,* 33 Cal.Rptr.2d 919 (Cal. App. 1994).

Panhandling

Before the Supreme Court's 1972 seminal decision in *Papachristou v. City of Jacksonville,* supra, vagrancy ordinances commonly included a prohibition on begging on public streets and sidewalks. Once catchall vagrancy ordinances were invalidated, cities began to look for new ways to prohibit begging, often called **panhandling.** Some local ordinances proscribe all begging on public ways; others prohibit "aggressive begging." Prohibitions against begging subordinate a beggar's right of expression on the public ways to a pedestrian's right to be left alone. The issue becomes whether the activity of begging is conduct that can be proscribed under local "police power" or whether such activity constitutes expression protected by the First Amendment. In some instances courts have analyzed the problem based on the "time, place, and manner" doctrine that guides the regulation of expressive conduct in the public forum (see the discussion in Chapter 3). The U.S. Supreme Court has held that government can regulate, but not prohibit, solicitation of funds for charities on public ways. *Village of Schaumburg v. Citizens for a Better Environment,* 444 U.S. 620, 100 S.Ct. 826, 63 L.Ed.2d 73 (1980). But the Court has not yet spoken directly on the issue of begging on public streets and sidewalks. Decisions from lower federal and state courts make it difficult to generalize as to whether such ordinances pass constitutional muster. Federal courts have held that any ordinance that restricts begging must be narrowly drawn to avoid conflict with the First Amendment.

In 1990 the U.S. Court of Appeals for the Second Circuit upheld a prohibition against begging and panhandling in the New York City subway system. The court observed that begging and panhandling in the city subway system was not expression protected by the First Amendment and that the regulations furthered the government's interest in preventing disruption and startling of passengers. *Young v. New York City Transit Authority,* 903 F.2d 146 (2d Cir. 1990). The U.S. Supreme Court denied certiorari. 498 U.S. 984, 111 S.Ct. 516, 112 L.Ed.2d 528 (1990). Seven years later in *Loper v. New York City Police Dept.,* 999 F.2d 699, 705 (2d Cir. 1993), the same federal appellate court declared unconstitutional a New York statute that provided, "A person is guilty of loitering when he loiters, remains or wanders about in a public place for the purpose of begging...." The court distinguished its 1990 decision in *Young v. New York City Transit Authority,* supra, saying, "[W]e observed that the prohibition on panhandling in the subway did not foreclose begging throughout all of New York City." *Young,* 903 F.2d at 160. The court found the regulation was neither content neutral nor justifiable as a proper time, place, or manner restriction on protected speech. Finally, the court found no compelling state interest served by excluding those who beg in a peaceful manner from communicating their messages of indigency with their fellow citizens.

State courts have commonly struck down local ordinances that prohibit begging on the public streets. For example, in *Ledford v. State,* 652 So.2d 1254 (Fla. App. 1995), a Florida appellate court struck down a St. Petersburg Beach ordinance that provided,

> It shall be unlawful for any person to beg for money in the City while about or upon any public way, and it shall be unlawful for any persons to be in or upon any public way in the City for the purpose of begging money for themselves or any other person.

In holding the ordinance unconstitutional, the court stated:

> [B]egging is communication entitled to some degree of First Amendment protection.... [S]ince the ordinance restricts speech on the "public ways," a traditional public forum, the regulation is subject to intense scrutiny. Such regulations survive only if: (1) they are narrowly drawn to achieve a compelling governmental interest; (2) the regulations are reasonable; and (3) the viewpoint is neutral. *Id.,* at 1256.

In subjecting the ordinance to strict scrutiny, the court pointed out that it was vague and neither defined the terms "beg" or "begging" nor distinguished between "aggressive" and "passive" begging.

In recent years federal appellate courts have approved ordinances that restrict "aggressive panhandling." An Indianapolis ordinance restricting panhandling is illustrative. The ordinance prohibited solicitation of cash on any day after sunset or before sunrise. It also prohibited solicitation at a bus stop, near a public transportation vehicle or facility, at a parked or stopped vehicle, at a sidewalk cafe, or in an area within twenty feet in any direction from an automatic teller machine or entrance to a bank. It also made it unlawful to engage in an act of panhandling in an aggressive manner, which entails blocking the path of a person being solicited or the entrance to any building or vehicle; following behind, ahead, or alongside a person who walks away from the panhandler after being solicited; or using profane or abusive language, either during the solicitation or following a refusal to make a donation. In 2000 the U.S. Court of Appeals for the Seventh Circuit held that the ordinance was narrowly tailored to promote the city's legitimate interest in safety and convenience of its citizens on public streets and that it allowed feasible alternatives to reach both daytime and nighttime downtown crowds. In upholding the ordinance the court pointed out, "Under the ordinance, panhandlers may ply their craft vocally or in any manner they deem fit (except for those involving conduct defined as aggressive) during all the daylight hours on all of the city's public streets." *Gresham v. Peterson,* 225 F.3d 899, 907 (7th Cir. 2000).

Motor Vehicle Violations

Go to the Scheb/ Scheb Criminal Law and Procedure 6e website at academic .cengage.com/criminaljustice/ scheb to find *State v. Young* (1988), where an Ohio appellate court reviews a man's conviction for failure to yield to oncoming traffic.

States, and many municipalities, have adopted laws defining a wide range of motor vehicle violations. These are generally strict liability offenses; therefore, there is generally no requirement to prove criminal intent to find a defendant guilty of a traffic violation (see Chapter 4). Among other offenses, these laws proscribe speeding; failing to yield the right-of-way; failing to observe traffic officers, signs, and signals; and driving without required equipment. By the 1980s, many states adopted a number of "model" laws, providing legal uniformity to the **rules of the road.** Such uniformity is highly desirable given the mobility of today's populace and the volume of traffic on the nation's highways. People driving along the nation's highways, often passing through several states on a single trip, would be ill served by variance in state traffic laws.

When a driver is stopped for a traffic violation, police may observe conduct or evidence that gives rise to probable cause to conduct a search or make an arrest. Frequently drugs, alcohol, and weapons are discovered by police officers stopping automobiles for routine traffic violations. (We discuss these aspects further in Chapters 15 and 16.)

Decriminalization of Traffic Offenses

Historically, traffic offenders were treated like persons committing other misdemeanors: they were arrested and required to post bond to avoid confinement pending the adjudication of their cases. Since the 1960s, most states and municipalities have decriminalized minor traffic offenses, which means that these offenses are now considered **civil infractions** rather than misdemeanors. For example, consider the following excerpt from the Maine Revised Statutes, Title 29–A:

§ **103. Traffic infraction**

1. Traffic infraction. A traffic infraction is not a crime. The penalty for a traffic infraction may not be deemed for any purpose a penal or criminal punishment.

2. Jury trial. There is no right to trial by jury for a traffic infraction.

3. Exclusive penalty. The exclusive penalty for a traffic infraction is a fine of not less than $25 nor more than $500, unless specifically authorized, or suspension of a license, or both.

In Maine and most other states, traffic violators are now commonly issued citations or "tickets" instead of being subject to arrest. Offenders may avoid a court appearance by simply paying a fine according to a predetermined schedule of fines. Of course, offenders may elect to contest the charge by appearing in the appropriate court, often a municipal court or **traffic court.** In addition to fines, most states assess "points" against a driver for traffic violations, and an accumulation of points can lead to suspension or revocation of a driver's license.

The **decriminalization of routine traffic offenses** has proved to be an expeditious and efficient means of maintaining discipline and order on the public thoroughfares. Under most traffic codes, however, the more serious motor vehicle offenses—such as driving while intoxicated, eluding a police officer, and reckless driving—are still defined as misdemeanors, and offenders are subject to arrest.

Seat Belts and Cell Phones

During the 1980s and the 1990s many state legislatures enacted **mandatory seat belt laws** and **mandatory child restraint laws.** Such laws usually provide for a violator to pay a small fine and have generally been accepted by the driving public and upheld by the courts. But it came as a surprise to many observers when the Supreme Court in 2001 upheld a custodial arrest for the violation of a seat belt law. A police officer in Lago Vista, Texas, arrested Gail Atwater for driving without wearing a seat belt as required by Texas law. The law provided for punishment by payment of a fine, and police officers had discretion to issue citations to violators. Instead of simply issuing a citation, the officer arrested and detained Atwater at jail. The Court held the warrantless custodial arrest did not violate Atwater's Fourth Amendment rights. *Atwater v. City of Lago Vista,* 532 U.S. 318, 121 S.Ct. 1536, 149 L.Ed.2d 549 (2001). Dissenting, Justice Sandra Day O'Connor contended the majority "cloaks the pointless indignity that Gail Atwater suffered with the mantle of reasonableness." 532 U.S. at 373, 121 S.Ct. at 1567, 149 L.Ed.2d at 589 (2001).

By 2000 state legislatures began to express concern that using a cell phone had become a mental and visual distraction from driving. In 2001 New York enacted the first prohibitory law. McKinney's Vehicle and Traffic Law § 1225-c provides:

> 2. (a) Except as otherwise provided in this section, no person shall operate a motor vehicle upon a public highway while using a mobile telephone to engage in a call while such vehicle is in motion.
>
> (b) An operator of a motor vehicle who holds a mobile telephone to, or in the immediate proximity of his or her ear while such vehicle is in motion is presumed to be engaging in a call within the meaning of this section. The presumption established by this subdivision is rebuttable by evidence tending to show that the operator was not engaged in a call.

The new law makes exceptions for use of mobile phones in emergency communications; by fire, police, and other persons in the performance of official duties; and for use of a hands-free mobile phone. A violation of the statute is treated as a traffic infraction and is punishable by a fine not to exceed $100. In an initial assault on the statute, a New York Justice Court upheld its constitutionality. *People v. Neville,* 737 N.Y.S.2d 251 (N.Y. Just. Ct. 2002). But the law has been held not to apply to a parking lot in a public shopping center because such property does not qualify as a "public highway" under the above-quoted statute. *People v. Moore,* 765 N.Y.S.2d 218 (N.Y. Just. Ct. 2003).

On May 11, 2007, Governor Christine Gregoire of the state of Washington signed the nation's first statute to ban "DWT"—driving while texting with a cell phone, BlackBerry, or similar device. The new law subjects violators to a $100 fine.

Weapons Offenses

Firearms are commonly used in the perpetration of serious crimes. Although the incidence has receded somewhat in recent years, more than 300,000 murders, robberies, and assaults in the United States were known to have been committed with firearms in 2005 alone (see Figure 12.1). For this reason, governing bodies have enacted laws restricting access to and limiting use of firearms. The Second Amendment to the U.S. Constitution provides that "a well regulated Militia, being necessary to the security of a free state, the right of the people to keep and bear Arms, shall not be infringed." Nevertheless, there are numerous state and federal statutory prohibitions against the manufacture, sale, possession, and use of firearms and other weapons. For example, federal law prohibits the sale, possession, and use of machine guns and other automatic weapons.

Go to the Scheb/ Scheb Criminal Law and Procedure 6e website at academic .cengage.com/criminaljustice/ scheb for an edited version of *U.S. v. Miller.*

The Supreme Court has said that federal gun control laws do not violate the Second Amendment because the amendment protects the keeping and bearing of arms only in the context of a **well-regulated militia.** See *United States v. Miller*, 307 U.S. 174, 59 S.Ct. 816, 83 L.Ed. 1206 (1939); *Lewis v. United States*, 445 U.S. 55, 100 S.Ct. 915, 63 L.Ed.2d 198 (1980).

Under Iowa law, any unauthorized person who knowingly possesses an offensive weapon commits a class D felony, I.C.A. § 724.3; however, the statute makes exceptions for peace officers and certain other instances. In *State v. Winders*, 366 N.W.2d 193 (Iowa App. 1985), the court held that the term "knowingly" in section 724.3 merely requires that the defendant had knowledge that he or she possessed a weapon within the general meaning of such term, rather than knowledge that he or she possessed an "offensive weapon" as statutorily defined. "To hold otherwise," the court said, "would only serve to undermine the very purpose of the provision in regulating possession of weapons in the interest of public safety." 366 N.W.2d at 196.

The Iowa law stipulates that offensive weapons include machine guns, short-barreled rifles and shotguns, bombs, grenades, mines, poison gases, ballistic knives, bullets, and projectiles containing any explosive mixtures or chemical compounds. Section 724.1. A person who goes armed with a dangerous weapon concealed on or about the person, or who, within the limits of any city, goes armed with a pistol or revolver, or any loaded firearm of any kind, whether concealed or not, or who knowingly carries or transports in a vehicle a pistol or revolver, commits an aggravated misdemeanor. Section 724.4 (Exceptions include peace officers whose duties require carrying weapons and members of the armed forces whose members are required to carry weapons). "A 'dangerous weapon' is any instrument or device designed primarily for use in inflicting death or injury upon a human being or animal, and which is capable of inflicting death upon a human being when used in the manner for which it was designed." *State v. Mitchell*, 371 N.W.2d 432 (Iowa App. 1985).

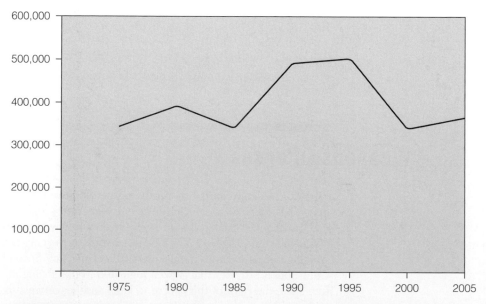

FIGURE 12.1 Number of Murders, Robberies, and Assaults Committed with Firearms, 1975–2005. Source: U.S. Department of Justice, Federal Bureau of Investigation, *Uniform Crime Reports 2005.*

Concealed Weapons

States commonly enact statutes making it unlawful to carry a **concealed weapon.** Most define a concealed weapon as one being carried on or about a person in such a manner as to conceal it from the ordinary sight of another person. It follows that a defendant was properly convicted of carrying a concealed weapon in her purse when it was disclosed by a metal detector at a courthouse. *Schaaf v. Commonwealth*, 258 S.E.2d 574 (Va. 1979). But more often, litigation involves less than absolute concealment. For example, a Georgia appellate court ruled that even though the handle of a pistol tucked in a defendant's pants was visible to some extent through a slit in his shirt, the weapon was concealed. *Marshall v. State*, 200 S.E.2d 902 (Ga. App. 1973). Similarly, in *People v. Charron*, 220 N.W.2d 216 (Mich. App. 1974), a Michigan appellate court held that a knife slightly protruding from a defendant's rear pocket was a concealed weapon.

Many concealed-weapons statutes also make it an offense to carry a concealed weapon in a vehicle, and in numerous cases courts have been asked to rule on the application of these laws. For example, a defendant reached into his automobile and withdrew a revolver from a shelf behind the driver's seat. In affirming the defendant's conviction, the Wisconsin Supreme Court said that "[i]f the weapon is hidden from ordinary observation, it is concealed." The court noted that "absolute invisibility to other persons" was not "indispensable to concealment." The question was this: "Was [the weapon] carried so as not to be discernible by ordinary observation?" *Mularkey v. State*, 230 N.W. 76, 77 (Wis. 1930). More recently, an Illinois appellate court observed that "[i]t is well settled … that a weapon is 'concealed' … even though there is some notice of its presence to an alert police officer who can see part of the gun when he approaches the vehicle." *People v. Williams*, 350 N.E.2d 81, 83 (Ill. App. 1976).

Federal Gun Control Laws

The **Federal Gun Control Act** of 1968, 18 U.S.C.A. § 921 *et seq.*, established a fairly comprehensive regime governing the distribution of firearms. The statute prohibits firearms dealers from transferring handguns to persons who are under twenty-one, nonresidents of the dealer's state, or those who are otherwise prohibited by state or local laws from purchasing or possessing firearms. 18 U.S.C.A. § 922(b). The law also forbids possession of a firearm by, and transfer of a firearm to, persons in several categories, including convicted felons, users of controlled substances, persons adjudicated as incompetent or committed to mental institutions, persons dishonorably discharged from the military, persons who are illegally in the United States, persons who have renounced their citizenship, and fugitives from justice. 18 U.S.C.A. §§ 922(d) and (g).

In the early 1990s, Congress enacted three important gun control statutes. The **Gun-Free School Zones Act** of 1990, 18 U.S.C.A. § 922, made it unlawful for any individual knowingly to possess a firearm in a school zone, regardless of whether the school is in session. The 1993 **Brady Bill,** also codified at 18 U.S.C.A. § 922, requires a five-working-day waiting period for the purchase of a handgun. And the 1994 Crime Bill banned the manufacture, transfer, or possession of firearms classified as "assault weapons." 18 U.S.C.A. § 922(v)(1).

In 1995 the U.S. Supreme Court struck down the Gun-Free School Zones Act of 1990 and reversed a student's conviction for carrying a handgun to school. The Court found that the law, in its full reach, was beyond the power of Congress to regulate interstate commerce. *United States v. Lopez*, 514 U.S. 549, 115 S.Ct. 1624, 131 L.Ed.2d 626 (1995).

 Go to the Scheb/ Scheb Criminal Law and Procedure 6e website at academic .cengage.com/criminaljustice/ scheb for an edited version of *U.S. v. Lopez.*

CASE-IN-POINT

Unlawful Possession of a Firearm

South Carolina law provides that it is unlawful for any person to carry a pistol about his or her person, regardless of whether the pistol is concealed. S.C. Code § 16–23–20. The statute provides twelve exceptions to the prohibition. Barry Clarke was convicted of violating the statute after he was stopped for a traffic violation and the police officer noticed a gun in a holster next to the driver's seat. On appeal, Clarke argued that the burden of proof should have been on the prosecution to show that he did not qualify to carry the weapon under any of the twelve exceptions to the prohibition. The South Carolina Supreme Court disagreed, saying that "[t]he general rule, when dealing with statutory crimes to which there are exceptions, is that the defendant 'has the burden of excusing or justifying his act; and hence the burden may be on him to bring himself within an exception in the statute or to prove the issuance of a license or permit.'"

State v. Clarke, 396 S.E.2d 827 (S.C. 1990).

Go to the Scheb/ Scheb Criminal Law and Procedure 6e website at academic .cengage.com/criminaljustice/ scheb for edited versions of the Supreme Court's *Lopez* and *Printz* decisions.

In 1997 the Court dealt another blow to federal gun control efforts when it invalidated a section of the Brady Bill requiring local law enforcement officers to conduct background checks of prospective gun purchasers. *Printz v. United States,* 521 U.S. 898, 117 S.Ct. 2365, 138 L.Ed.2d 914 (1997). Despite the Supreme Court's decisions in *Lopez* and *Printz,* the extensive regime of federal gun control legislation remains essentially intact.

After several catastrophic incidents involving firearms, state legislatures began to focus on gun safety legislation. Many states have enacted laws that require background checks of gun buyers at gun shows. Most states require registration or permits to purchase firearms and prohibit sales to persons convicted of serious felonies.

New Jersey has been very active in enacting gun safety laws. Licensing of retail dealers and their employees is strictly regulated. No handgun shall be delivered to any person unless such person possesses and exhibits a valid permit to purchase a firearm and at least seven days have elapsed since the date of application for the permit. Applications must be submitted to designated officials. The purchaser of a firearm must be personally known to the seller or present evidence of his or her identity. N.J. Stat. 2C:58-2. Trigger locks are required on handguns. N.J. Stat. 2C:58-2. Sawed-off shotguns and silencers are prohibited. N.J. Stat. 2C:39-3. Laws strictly regulate the possession and use of handguns. Any person who knowingly has in his possession any handgun, including any antique handgun, without first having obtained a permit to carry the same as provided in N.J. Stat. 2C:58-4 is guilty of a crime of the third degree. N.J. Stat. 2C:39-5.

Offenses against National Security

The preamble to the U.S. Constitution appropriately refers to the role of the federal government "to promote the common defense." The federal government performs this function by relying on the immense military capabilities of the United States and also upon various agencies devoted to the gathering of foreign intelligence. But it also relies on the criminal justice system to deter and punish violations of the national security. While there are a number of specific offenses in this category, the principal crimes against national security are treason, **espionage, sabotage** and **sedition.**

Treason

As we discussed in Chapter 3, Article III, Section 3 of the U.S. Constitution provides that treason against the United States "shall consist only in levying War against them, or in adhering to their Enemies, giving them Aid and Comfort." Following this constitutional language, the current federal statute on treason provides:

> Whoever owing allegiance to the United States, levies war against them or adheres to their enemies, giving them aid and comfort within the United States or elsewhere, is guilty of treason and shall suffer death, or shall be imprisoned not less than five years and fined under this title but not less than $10,000; and shall be incapable of holding any office under the United States.... 18 U.S.C.A. § 2381.

No one has been convicted of treason since the Second World War. Many people incorrectly believe that Julius and Ethel Rosenberg, who provided the Soviet Union with top-secret information about the construction of the atomic bomb, were convicted of treason. Prosecutors considered charging the Rosenbergs with treason but concluded that they could not obtain a conviction due to the constitutional two-witness requirement. Instead, they elected to charge the Rosenbergs with espionage. The defendants were convicted in 1951 and sentenced to death.

More recently, some believed that John Walker Lindh, the so-called American Taliban, was guilty of treason based on his involvement with the Taliban regime in Afghanistan and Osama bin Laden's al-Qaeda terrorist organization. Lindh, an American citizen, was captured by American forces after a battle in Afghanistan in December 2001. As in the Rosenberg case, federal prosecutors elected not to charge Lindh with treason. Rather, he agreed to plead guilty to two lesser offenses and was sentenced to twenty years in prison.

Espionage

Known in the popular parlance as "spying," espionage consists of turning over state secrets to a foreign government. First criminalized by the Espionage Act of 1917, 40 Stat. 217, espionage is now covered by a number of federal statutes. 18 U.S.C.A. § 793 criminalizes gathering or transmitting defense information "with intent or reason to believe that the information is to be used to the injury of the United States, or to the advantage of any foreign nation." 18 U.S.C.A. § 794(b) prohibits collection or transmission of information about American military activities during time of war "with intent that the same shall be communicated to the enemy."

In recent years there have been a number of high-profile espionage cases in the United States. In 1986, Jonathan Pollard, a former U.S. Navy intelligence analyst, was sentenced to life imprisonment after he was convicted of selling classified information to Israel. Pollard admitted that he provided Israel with American intelligence about weapons programs in Syria, Iraq, Pakistan, and Libya. In 1994, former CIA analyst Aldrich Ames was sentenced to life in prison after he was convicted of selling classified information to the Soviet Union. The investigation revealed that Ames had received $2.7 million from Moscow for exposing covert American operations and betraying fellow CIA agents. In 2001, former FBI agent Robert Hanssen pleaded guilty to fifteen counts of espionage and conspiracy to commit espionage and was sentenced to life in prison. The government's investigation revealed that Hanssen received nearly $1.5 million from Russia in exchange for classified information.

The Intelligence Identities Protection Act of 1982, 50 U.S.C.A. § 421, *et seq.,* prohibits disclosure of the identities of undercover intelligence officers, agents, informants, and their "sources." The public became acutely aware of this law in the fall of 2003 when the FBI began an investigation of the Bush administration after it was alleged that senior administration officials had intentionally exposed an undercover CIA operative as an act of political retaliation. The operative was married to a former ambassador who had accused the Bush administration of selectively using intelligence to exaggerate the threat from Iraq in order to justify making war against Saddam Hussein's regime. A *Washington Post/BBC* News survey reported on October 2, 2003, found that more than eight in ten Americans viewed the allegation as "serious" and more than seven in ten thought it likely that a White House official was behind the leak. Ultimately, after a two-year investigation, it was determined that the leak came from an official in the State Department and not the White House.

Sabotage

Sabotage is the intentional destruction of a country's military infrastructure by an enemy agent or a civilian with the objective of hindering that country's war efforts or reducing its military capabilities. Several federal statutes criminalize particular forms of sabotage, but the broadest of these statutes is found at 18 U.S.C.A. § 2155. It provides:

> (a) Whoever, with intent to injure, interfere with, or obstruct the national defense of the United States, willfully injures, destroys, contaminates or infects, or attempts to so injure, destroy, contaminate or infect any national-defense material, national-defense premises, or national-defense utilities, shall be fined under this title or imprisoned not more than 20 years, or both, and, if death results to any person, shall be imprisoned for any term of years or for life.

18 U.S.C.A. § 2153 prohibits sabotage during time of war or national emergency and carries a thirty-year maximum prison term. Most states have similar laws, many of them enacted during World War II.

Sedition

Sedition is the incitement of insurrection or revolution. At common law there was no offense of sedition per se, but English law did proscribe seditious libel, seditious meetings, and seditious conspiracies. In 1798, the U.S. Congress enacted the infamous Sedition Act, which prohibited "false, scandalous and malicious" utterances and publications against the federal government or any of its officials. Thomas Jefferson and his followers assailed the act as a violation of the First Amendment to the U.S. Constitution, and after Jefferson was elected president and his party won both houses of Congress in 1801, the Sedition Act was promptly repealed.

In 1918, during the First World War, Congress enacted a new Sedition Act aimed primarily at communists, socialists, anarchists, and other radicals. More than two thousand persons were prosecuted under this prohibition. In *Abrams v. United States,* 250 U.S. 616, 40 S.Ct. 17, 63 L.Ed. 1173 (1919), the Supreme Court upheld the conviction of five Russian immigrants who published leaflets criticizing America's role in World War I and attacking the capitalist system. In dissent, Justice Oliver Wendell Holmes questioned the need for governmental suppression of dissent, saying "the best test of truth is the power of the thought to get itself accepted in the competition of the market …" 250 U.S. at 630, 40 S.Ct. at 22, 63 L.Ed. at 1180.

In 1940, Congress adopted the Smith Act, 54 Stat. 670, 671. The act has been amended several times. In its present form, codified at 18 U.S.C.A. § 2385, the act makes it a crime if a person

> knowingly or willfully advocates, abets, advises, or teaches the duty, necessity, desirability, or propriety of overthrowing or destroying the government of the United States or the government of any State, Territory, District or Possession thereof, or the government of any political subdivision therein, by force or violence, or by the assassination of any officer of any such government.

In *Dennis v. United States,* 341 U.S. 494, 71 S.Ct. 857, 95 L.Ed. 1137 (1951), the Supreme Court upheld the convictions under the Smith Act of eleven officials of the Communist Party, rejecting their First Amendment challenge to the statute. But in *Yates v. United States,* 354 U.S. 298, 77 S.Ct. 1064, 1 L.Ed.2d 1356 (1957), the Court set aside the convictions of another set of Communist Party officials. In so doing, the Court distinguished between "advocacy of abstract doctrine and advocacy directed at promoting unlawful action" and held that the Smith Act prohibited only the latter. In 1969, in *Brandenburg v. Ohio,* 395 U.S. 444, 89 S.Ct. 1827, 23 L.Ed.2d 430, the Court went so far as to hold that mere advocacy could never be criminalized in the absence of "imminent lawless action." Although the *Brandenburg* case did not arise under the Smith Act, but rather under a state law prohibiting "criminal syndicalism," most commentators have concluded that the "imminent lawless action" doctrine applies equally to federal prosecutions under the Smith Act. Today, however, such prosecutions are rare.

Terrorism and Weapons of Mass Destruction

Before the 1980s there were some sporadic acts of **terrorism** by radical political protesters and by persons involved in protests during the fight for racial equality. The 1980s and 1990s witnessed the continuing attacks by Theodore Kaczynski, the so-called Unabomber who sent packages with bombs in his protest against modern technology. Antiabortion extremists committed sporadic acts of terrorism at abortion clinics. During the 1980s and 1990s terrorists attacked several American military bases overseas. Militant Islamists were convicted of damaging the World Trade Center in 1993. Timothy McVeigh and Terry Nichols, who bore extreme hatred for the government, were convicted of the massive bombing of a federal government building in Oklahoma City in 1995. And everyone is familiar with the tragic loss of thousands of lives when hijackers crashed aircraft into the World Trade Center and the Pentagon on September 11, 2001.

Antiterrorism Legislation

The Omnibus Diplomatic Security and Antiterrorism Act of 1986, Pub. L. 99-399, now codified as 18 U.S.C.A. § 2332, makes it a federal offense for a terrorist overseas to kill, attempt to kill, conspire to kill, or engage in physical violence with the intent to cause serious bodily injury to an American citizen. The **Antiterrorism and Effective Death Penalty Act** of 1996, Pub. L. 104-132, 110 Stat. 1214, enacted after the Oklahoma City bombing of 1995, expanded federal jurisdiction with respect to investigation and prosecution of international terrorism. It also made it a crime for persons in the United States or subject to U.S. jurisdiction to provide material support to groups designated as terrorist organizations by the U.S. Department of State. 18 U.S.C.A. § 2339B.

Since terrorists attacked the United States on 9-11, the president and the Congress have responded in new ways in attempts to maintain the security of the country. These include the creation of the federal Department of Homeland Security; stricter safety measures in mass transportation systems; increased protective measures to safeguard borders, ports, utility systems, and government buildings; and training programs for police, fire, and medical personnel to cope with the potential use of weapons of mass destruction. From a legislative standpoint, enactment of the USA PATRIOT Act has become an important part of the criminal justice system.

THE USA PATRIOT ACT

As we explained in Chapter 10, Congress enacted the USA PATRIOT Act shortly after the terrorist attacks of 9-11. Title VIII of the USA PATRIOT Act strengthens numerous federal criminal laws against terrorism. (In Chapter 15 we explain the ramifications of the act in respect to search and seizure.) Section 801 creates a detailed new offense for willfully attacking mass transportation facilities. Section 802 defines domestic terrorism as "activities that occur primarily within U.S. jurisdiction, that involve criminal acts dangerous to human life that appear to be intended to intimidate or coerce a civilian population, to influence government policy by intimidation or coercion, or to affect government conduct by mass destruction, assassination, or kidnapping." Section 803 prohibits knowingly harboring persons who have committed or who are about to commit an act of terrorism.

The act establishes federal jurisdiction over crimes committed at U.S. facilities abroad, (§ 804) and, by amending 18 U.S.C.A. § 2339A, applies prohibitions against providing material support for terrorism offenses outside of the United States (§ 805). It also subjects to civil forfeiture all assets, foreign or domestic, of individuals and terrorist organizations that plan or perpetrate domestic or international terrorism against the United States (§ 806).

Section 809 extends the statute of limitations for certain offenses and provides that there shall be no statute of limitations for certain terrorism offenses if the commission of such an offense resulted in, or created a foreseeable risk of, death or serious bodily injury to another person. Section 810 provides for alternative maximum penalties for specified terrorism crimes, while section 811 provides the same penalties for attempts and conspiracies as for terrorist acts and provides for post-release supervision for terrorists whose offenses resulted in foreseeable risk of death or serious bodily injury. Certain acts of terrorism are deemed to be racketeering activity (§ 813), and penalties regarding fraud and related activity in connection with specified cyberterrorism offenses are included (§ 814). Finally, section 817 creates a new offense of possession of biological weapons when not justified for research, etc.

On March 9, 2006, President Bush signed legislation making permanent all but two provisions of the USA PATRIOT Act. In signing the USA PATRIOT Improvement and Reauthorization Act of 2005, President Bush stated:

> The law allows our intelligence and law enforcement officials to continue to share information. It allows them to continue to use tools against terrorists that they use against drug dealers and other criminals. It will improve our nation's security while we safeguard the civil liberties of our people. The legislation strengthens the Justice Department so it can better detect and disrupt terrorist threats. And the bill gives law enforcement new tools to combat threats to our citizens from international terrorists to local drug dealers.

Although recognizing the need to protect the security of the United States, critics argue that certain sections of the act unduly restrict personal liberties, thereby offending basic constitutional protections. For example, they cite language in section 802 defining terrorism to include "activities … that appear … to influence government policy by intimidation or coercion" as having the potential to chill political dissent. Among the sharpest critics of the PATRIOT Act is the American Civil Liberties Union, which has challenged several of the act's provisions in court. In 2007, the litigation was still ongoing.

Weapons of Mass Destruction

While terrorism using conventional explosives can produce massive destruction and widespread panic, as we saw in New York City on 9-11, the prospect of terrorists using chemical, biological, or nuclear weapons is almost too horrible to contemplate. In recent years Congress has enacted a number of statutes that provide criminal jurisdiction over the use of **weapons of mass destruction** (WMDs). For example, 18 U.S.C.A. § 175(a) provides:

> Whoever knowingly develops, produces, stockpiles, transfers, acquires, retains, or possesses any biological agent, toxin, or delivery system for use as a weapon, or knowingly assists a foreign state or any organization to do so, or attempts, threatens, or conspires to do the same, shall be fined under this title or imprisoned for life or any term of years, or both. There is extraterritorial Federal jurisdiction over an offense under this section committed by or against a national of the United States.

Additional provisions found in Title 18 of the U.S. Code impose similar prohibitions with respect to toxic chemicals, § 229, nuclear materials, § 831, and other weapons of mass destruction, § 2332a.

Detention and Trial of Accused Terrorists Captured Abroad

On November 13, 2001, just weeks after the terrible attacks on 9-11, President George W. Bush issued an executive order authorizing the use of military tribunals to try foreign nationals apprehended in the war on terrorism. In early 2002, the military began to incarcerate "enemy aliens" at the American Naval Base at Guantanamo Bay, Cuba. Detainees were held in solitary confinement in small cells and were not permitted to have any contact with the outside world. No judicial or administrative process was established to determine whether detainees were in fact terrorists or enemies of the United States. The government essentially asserted the authority to detain these inmates indefinitely without trial or recourse to the courts. But in *Rasul v. Bush*, 542 U.S. 466, 124 S.Ct. 2686, 159 L.Ed.2d 548 (2004), the Supreme Court held that federal courts had jurisdiction over habeas corpus petitions brought on behalf of the Guantanamo detainees. However, the Court withheld comment on the legality of the government's actions or the constitutionality of President Bush's November 2001 executive order.

Following *Rasul v. Bush*, the Pentagon created special three-member military panels to review the question of whether the Guantanamo detainees had been properly classified as enemy combatants. Although a number of detainees were released pursuant to these reviews, critics argued that the belated review procedures fell short of the due process of law required by the Constitution. In January 2006, the government resumed military trials of two Guantanamo detainees who had been formally accused of terrorism based on their activities within the al-Qaeda organization.

In *Hamdan v. Rumsfeld,* 548 U.S. ___, 126 S.Ct. 2749, 165 L.Ed.2d 723 (2006), the Supreme Court held that the Bush administration's plan to try Guantanamo Bay detainees before military commissions was unauthorized by statute and violated international law. The overarching rationale of the Court's decision is summed up by Justice Stevens's assertion: "Even assuming that Hamdan is a dangerous individual who would cause great harm or death to innocent civilians given the opportunity, the executive nevertheless must comply with the prevailing rule of law in undertaking to try him and subject him to criminal punishment." 548 U.S. at ___, 126 S.Ct. 2749 at 2757, ___ L.Ed.2d at ___. The majority indicated that Congress could, through appropriate legislation, provide for the use of military tribunals to try Guantanamo Bay detainees.

Congress began work on such legislation during the summer of 2006, and in October President Bush signed the Military Commissions Act (MCA). Denounced by civil liberties groups but defended as essential to the war on terrorism by the White House, the Act not only authorizes the use of military commissions for the trial of the Guantanamo detainees, it permits statements obtained from coercive interrogation methods (as distinct from "torture") to be used at trial. It also removes the habeas corpus jurisdiction of the federal courts over "unlawful enemy combatants." On the other hand, the statute requires that military commissions respect the presumption of innocence and afford defendants the right to representation by counsel.

Immigration Offenses

Article I, Section 8 of the U.S. Constitution vests in Congress the power "[t]o establish an uniform Rule of Naturalization...." The courts have interpreted this language as providing Congress plenary power over immigration. In exercising this power, Congress has created several **immigration offenses.** 8 U.S.C.A. § 1325 prohibits improper entry by aliens, while 8 U.S.C.A. § 1326 makes it an offense for an alien who has been removed from the United States to reenter the country. Specific immigration offenses include entering or attempting "to enter the United States at any time or place other than as designated by immigration officers," 8 U.S.C.A. § 1325(a)(1); eluding "examination or inspection by immigration officers," 8 U.S.C.A. § 1325(a)(2); attempting to enter or obtaining entry to the United States "by a willfully false or misleading representation or the willful concealment of a material fact," 8 U.S.C.A. § 1325(a)(3); knowingly entering into a marriage "for the purpose of evading any provision of the immigration laws," 8 U.S.C.A. § 1325(c); and knowingly establishing "a commercial enterprise for the purpose of evading any provision of the immigration laws," 8 U.S.C.A. § 1325(d).

Lax enforcement of immigration laws in the face of massive illegal immigration across the nation's southern border has led to a divisive political battle over "immigration reform." On one hand, there is broad public support for tightening security at the borders and more vigorously enforcing existing laws. The need for greater border control is particularly acute in an age of international terrorism. On the other hand, it is unrealistic to deport or prosecute the millions of immigrants who have come to this country illegally, most simply looking to improve their lives through hard work at low wages, performing jobs than many Americans are unwilling to do.

In 2006 the president and Congress began to seriously address the problem of illegal immigration. The president sent National Guard troops to augment the U.S. Border Patrol's operations on the southern border, and additional funds were provided to increase measures to protect the border. The U.S. Senate and the U.S.

House of Representatives crafted very different approaches to the problems of border protection and the resolution of the status of illegal immigrants. But by 2007 major political differences continued to thwart Congressional action to achieve a unified approach to resolve the numerous issues surrounding immigration and border control.

■ CONCLUSION

Offenses against public order, safety, and security present a picture of the dynamic development of the law in a constitutional democracy. The need to maintain order and protect the public safety are high-priority items for any organized society. Yet the U.S. Constitution mandates that government maintain a delicate balance between these interests and the rights of citizens. Of particular relevance to offenses against public order are the protections of the First Amendment. Today, our society faces a new threat, that of terrorism, which adds more pressure to limit individual rights and freedoms and grant more power to law enforcement agencies. Americans today are engaged in a great debate about where the balance should be struck between freedom on one hand and order, safety, and security on the other.

■ KEY TERMS

unlawful assembly, 294
rout, 294
riot, 294
breaches of the peace, 294
inciting a riot, 294
disorderly conduct, 294
vagrancy, 294
loitering, 294
motor vehicle violations, 294
weapons offenses, 294
gun control laws, 294
Federal Anti-Riot Act, 295
excessive noise, 299
curfew ordinances, 304
panhandling, 306
rules of the road, 308
civil infractions, 308
traffic court, 308

decriminalization of routine traffic offenses, 308
mandatory seat belt laws, 308
mandatory child restraint laws, 308
well-regulated militia, 310
concealed weapon, 311
Federal Gun Control Act, 311
Gun-Free School Zones Act, 311
Brady Bill, 311
espionage, 313
sabotage, 313
sedition, 313
terrorism, 315
Antiterrorism and Effective Death Penalty Act, 315
weapons of mass destruction, 317
immigration offenses, 318

■ WEB-BASED RESEARCH ACTIVITY

Go to the Web. Locate your state's criminal statutes. Examine your state's gun control laws. In your judgment, are these laws too permissive or too restrictive? Are any of these statutes susceptible to challenge under your state constitution? If you were elected to serve in the state legislature, what changes would you propose to your state's weapons laws?

■ QUESTIONS FOR THOUGHT AND DISCUSSION

1. Why has it been necessary for American courts to interpret laws proscribing breach of peace and vagrancy more strictly than did the English common-law courts?

2. How does the Federal Anti-Riot Act seek to prevent the definition of "to incite a riot" from being applied in such a way that it violates First Amendment guarantees of freedom of expression?

3. Is an ordinance that defines "disturbing the peace" simply as "tumultuous or offensive conduct" sufficiently precise to meet the constitutional standard of giving a person of ordinary intelligence fair notice of what conduct is forbidden?

4. How did the Jacksonville, Florida, vagrancy ordinance invalidated by the Supreme Court in the *Papachristou* case offend the Constitution of the United States? Have the reforms in vagrancy laws at the state and local levels sufficiently removed the threat of criminalizing a person's status? Are they now written with the precision necessary to protect citizens from arbitrary enforcement of the law?

5. Based on the ruling of the Supreme Court in *City of Chicago v. Morales,* what protections of the individual do you think must be included in an ordinance proscribing loitering?

6. Assume you are working as a staff assistant to a state legislator who intends to introduce a law making it an offense to solicit funds by "panhandling" on streets and in parks. You are asked to prepare a memorandum of provisions to be considered in order to avoid the proposed act's being declared unconstitutional. What would you recommend?

7. Have traffic offenses been decriminalized in your state? To what extent? What procedures are available to contest a traffic ticket?

8. Why have the courts refused to interpret the Second Amendment's protection of the "right to keep and bear arms" to prohibit gun control legislation? On what bases other than the Second Amendment can one make constitutional attacks on federal gun control laws?

9. To what extent does the First Amendment protect the right of citizens to advocate on behalf of groups that have been labeled as terrorist organizations by the federal government?

10. Under what circumstances does the law permit the government to prosecute a person who publicly advocates the violent overthrow of the U.S. government? What constitutional considerations come into play?

11. Evaluate the criticism leveled against the USA PATRIOT Act that the sections quoted in the text unconstitutionally deprive individuals of their civil liberties by such vague terms as "acts intended to influence government policy by intimidation or coercion."

12. Are acts of terrorism perpetrated against the United States by foreign nationals more appropriately viewed as crimes or acts of war? Is the criminal justice system the appropriate means of dealing with foreign terrorists?

13. What should be done about the millions of foreign nationals who have entered the United States illegally? Should they be prosecuted for immigration offenses, deported to their countries of origin, or granted some sort of amnesty whereby they can remain in this country and work legally?

■ **PROBLEMS FOR DISCUSSION AND SOLUTION**

1. Consider the following hypothetical case: Members of the American Nazi Party announced a demonstration to be held in Pleasant Ridge, a predominantly Jewish suburb of Metropolis. The Pleasant Ridge City Council quickly adopted an

ordinance requiring groups planning demonstrations to obtain a permit from the police department. Under the ordinance, to hold a demonstration without a permit was a misdemeanor, punishable by a $1,000 fine and 60 days in jail. The Nazis applied for a permit and were denied on the grounds that their presence in Pleasant Ridge constituted a "clear and present danger to the public order." The Nazis held their demonstration anyway. Approximately one hundred demonstrators congregated on the city square. Many were dressed in Nazi uniforms, others carried banners emblazoned with swastikas, and others held signs on which were printed anti-Semitic slogans. Pleasant Ridge police arrived at the scene and asked the demonstrators to disperse. When they refused, police arrested some demonstrators; others ran to avoid arrest. The leader of the Nazi group, Asa Houle, was convicted of a number of offenses, including violation of the new ordinance. On appeal, Houle is challenging the constitutionality of the ordinance. What do you think the court's ruling should be? Explain your reasoning.

2. The city of Dystopia experienced difficulties with groups of rowdy individuals congregating on downtown sidewalks and harassing passersby. When the local police were unable to control the situation by enforcing the disorderly conduct statute, the city council enacted the following ordinance:

Sec. 1. It shall be unlawful for three or more persons to assemble on any public sidewalk or walkway within the city while conducting themselves in a manner that is annoying or bothersome to surrounding persons.

Sec. 2. Anyone found guilty of violating this ordinance shall be punished as provided in the city charter.

After the ordinance went into effect, three college students congregated on a public sidewalk and made loud, obnoxious remarks to passersby. The police arrested the students and charged them under the ordinance. The students admit that they were rowdy but argue that the ordinance unduly restricts their First Amendment rights. What constitutional arguments could they, or their counsel, present to a court in an effort to reverse their convictions? Do you think they would prevail?

CHAPTER **13**

Offenses against Justice and Public Administration

CHAPTER OUTLINE

Introduction

The English common-law judges found it necessary to create a number of offenses to maintain the integrity of the law and the administration of justice. Principally, these offenses were bribery, perjury and subornation of perjury, resisting arrest, obstruction of justice, compounding a crime, and escape. At common law, these offenses were misdemeanors. In addition, the common law developed the concept of criminal contempt to enable judges to maintain the dignity and authority of the courts and the respect due judicial officers. All of these common-law crimes remain an important part of contemporary criminal law in the United States, although they have been expanded and augmented by a variety of modern statutes. The offenses against public administration and the administration of justice in particular serve as a means to punish those who breach the public trust and whose actions corrupt the orderly processes of government and the justice system.

Bribery

The concept of **bribery** dates back to biblical times when it was regarded as sinful to attempt to influence the judge with a gift because the judge represented the divine. Thus, when the common law developed the crime of bribery, it sought to penalize only persons whose actions were designed to improperly influence those identified with the administration of justice. Later, it was considered bribery for anyone to give or receive anything of value or any valuable service or promise with the intent to influence any public officer in the discharge of a legal duty. Bribery is generally a felony under modern law.

The Modern Statutory Offense of Bribery

Today, a variety of federal statutes proscribe bribery of specific public officers and witnesses as well as of jurors and government employees and functionaries. The most prominent among these is 18 U.S.C.A. § 201. To convict an accused of violating section 201(b)(1), the government is required to prove that something of value was requested, offered, or given to a federal public official with a corrupt intent to influence some official act. Other subsections of the statute make it a crime to offer a bribe to a witness or for a witness to solicit or accept a bribe.

State statutes generally define bribery in broad terms and frequently address specific situations as well. The trend has been to enlarge the common-law approach by extending the offense to new categories of persons and conduct and by making the punishment more severe. The broad statutory definition of bribery is illustrated by a Florida law that makes bribery a felony and provides

> "Bribery" means corruptly to give, offer, or promise to any public servant, or, if a public servant, corruptly to request, solicit, accept, or agree to accept for himself or herself or another, any pecuniary or other benefit with an intent or purpose to influence the performance of any act or omission which the person believes to be, or the public servant represents as being, within the official discretion of a public servant, in violation of a public duty, or in performance of a public duty. West's Fla. Stat. Ann. § 838.015(1).

Section 838.015(2) makes explicit that the person sought to be bribed need not have authority to accomplish the act sought or represented.

Courts generally construe such terms as "public servant" and "benefit" broadly to accomplish the intended legislative purpose of statutes defining bribery.

Arizona law adds the term "party officer" to its statute proscribing bribery. It defines that term as "a person who holds any position or office in a political party, whether by election, appointment or otherwise." Ariz. Rev. Stat. § 13–2601.

Section 13–2602 of the Revised Arizona Statutes provides

A. A person commits bribery of a public servant or party officer if with corrupt intent:

1. Such person offers, confers or agrees to confer any benefit upon a public servant or party officer with the intent to influence the public servant's or party officer's vote, opinion, judgment, exercise of discretion or other action in his official capacity as a public servant or party officer; or

2. While a public servant or party officer, such person solicits, accepts or agrees to accept any benefit upon an agreement or understanding that his vote, opinion, judgment, exercise of discretion or other action as a public servant or party officer may thereby be influenced.

B. It is no defense to a prosecution under this section that a person sought to be influenced was not qualified to act in the desired way because such person had not yet assumed office, lacked jurisdiction or for any other reason.

C. Bribery of a public servant or party officer is a class 4 felony.

Although the Florida statute is explicit on the subject, irrespective of statutes, courts generally hold that where the act intended to be influenced is connected with a person's public duty, it is immaterial whether the person bribed has, or has not, the authority to do a specific act. See, for example, *State v. Hendricks,* 186 P.2d 943 (Ariz. 1947).

The Range of Bribery Offenses

Acts sought to be accomplished by bribes cover a wide range of conduct, and as we pointed out in Chapter 10, the offense of bribery is frequently present in white-collar and organized crime situations. Common examples of bribery include obtaining the release or acquittal of an arrestee, securing an award of a government contract, and even obtaining a favorable vote by a legislator on a pending bill. The Arizona statute just quoted expands the traditional concept of "public servant" by recognizing the potential for bribery within the ranks of political parties. Although we commonly think of money being offered or requested as a bribe, a variety of other things are offered, sought, or exchanged. These not only include cash or its equivalent but also such tangible and intangible benefits as price advantages, use of vehicles, vacation homes, and even sexual favors. Bribes often occur in subtle or disguised ways. For example, a sale of property for less than its true value would likely be considered bribery if the seller's real purpose was to benefit the purchaser to influence his or her official governmental action.

The Burden of the Prosecution

The gist of the crime of bribery is the unlawful offer or agreement to do something under color of office. Ordinarily, the prosecution must prove not only the offer or agreement or the request or acceptance of a benefit but also that the defendant had a false or corrupt intent. One difficulty encountered in prosecuting a bribery charge

Bribery: What Constitutes a Thing of Value?

McDonald, a male trial court judge in Alabama, was prosecuted for solicitation of sexual favors in exchange for affording a female favorable treatment in pending court cases. He was convicted of bribery under a state statute that provided that it was bribery for any public official to accept "any gift, gratuity, or other thing of value." On appeal, McDonald argued that "sexual intercourse, or the promise of sexual intercourse, or the promise of other sexual favors or relationship" did not meet the test of being a "thing of value" under the bribery statute. The Alabama Court of Criminal Appeals rejected the defendant's contention, saying, "The word 'thing' does not necessarily mean a substance.... [I]t includes an act, or action."

McDonald v. State, 329 So.2d 583 (Ala. Crim. App. 1975).

is establishing the corrupt intent element. For example, it can be extremely difficult to prove that a person received employment or was granted a contract as a result of a bribe. The difficulty is compounded because, not infrequently, bribes are disguised as gifts or even as political or charitable contributions.

Offenses Extending the Concept of Bribery

Many states have enacted statutes to extend the offense of bribery to encompass conduct of persons other than public officials and employees. The two principal areas of extension have been commerce and sports.

COMMERCIAL BRIBERY

Section 224.8 of the Model Penal Code outlines an offense known as **commercial bribery.** Some states have classified certain corrupt business practices, for example, fraudulent acts of purchasing agents, as commercial bribery. The New Jersey law making commercial bribery a crime includes many of the provisions outlined in the Model Penal Code. As amended in 1986, the statute provides

A. A person commits a crime if he solicits, accepts or agrees to accept any benefit as consideration for knowingly violating or agreeing to violate a duty of fidelity to which he is subject as:

(1) An agent, partner or employee of another;

(2) A trustee, guardian, or other fiduciary;

(3) A lawyer, physician, accountant, appraiser, or other professional adviser or informant;

(4) An officer, director, manager or other participant in the direction of the affairs of an incorporated or unincorporated association;

(5) A labor official, including any duly appointed representative of a labor organization or any duly appointed trustee or representative of an employee welfare trust fund; or

(6) An arbitrator or other purportedly disinterested adjudicator or referee.

B. A person who holds himself out to the public as being engaged in the business of making disinterested selection, appraisal, or criticism of commodities, real properties or services commits a crime if he solicits, accepts or agrees to accept any benefit to influence his selection, appraisal or criticism.

C. A person commits a crime if he confers, or offers or agrees to confer, any benefit the acceptance of which would be criminal under this section. N.J. Stat. Ann. § 2C:21–10.

Under the New Jersey statute, the benefit offered, conferred, agreed to be conferred, solicited, accepted, or agreed to determines the degree of the crime and the penalty.

SPORTS BRIBERY

Because of the increased role of both professional and amateur sports in society, most states now have made **sports bribery** a crime. Sports bribery statutes generally make it an offense for a person to offer anything of value to a participant or official in an amateur or professional athletic contest to vary his or her performance. Likewise, it is a crime for a participant or official in a sports event to accept a bribe under such circumstances. See, for example, Iowa Code Ann. § 722.3; *State v. Di Paglia,* 71 N.W.2d 601 (Iowa 1955).

 Go to the Scheb/ Scheb Criminal Law and Procedure 6e website at academic .cengage.com/criminaljustice/ scheb to find *State v. Gustafson* (1986), in which a Minnesota appellate court addresses the offenses of bribery and conspiracy to commit perjury.

Defenses to the Crime of Bribery

Of course, the fact that an offer to bribe is not legally enforceable is no defense. The only recognized defense to a charge of bribery, other than denial, is entrapment. See *State v. Harrington,* 332 So.2d 764 (La. 1976). We discuss the defense of entrapment in Chapter 14.

CASE-IN-POINT

A State Supreme Court Upholds a Conviction for Sports Bribery

Following a bench trial, Angelo Trosclair III, was convicted of two counts of bribery of sports participants on February 14, 1981, in violation of La.R.S. 14:118.1. That statute defines bribery of a jockey as "the giving or offering to give, directly or indirectly, anything of apparent present or prospective value to any jockey with the intent to influence him to lose or cause to be lost, or corruptly to affect or influence the result of a horse race or to limit his mount or beast's margin of victory in any race." On appeal Trosclair contended the evidence was legally insufficient to support a finding that he was guilty beyond a reasonable doubt.

In rejecting his contention, the Louisiana Supreme Court noted, "The state presented two witnesses who testified that they had been offered, and

had actually received, significant sums of money in exchange for their promises not to finish first, second or third in the fourth race at the Fairgrounds on February 14, 1981. The testimony of the two jockeys, Hale and Durousseau, undoubtedly provided an adequate basis for a finding of guilt beyond a reasonable doubt by a rational trier of fact." Despite the defendant's claim that the credibility of these two witnesses was destroyed, the court further noted, "[I]t is not our function to assess credibility or reweigh the evidence. Our review for minimal constitutional sufficiency of evidence is a limited one which ends upon our finding that the rational trier-reasonable doubt standard has been satisfied." The court affirmed the defendant's convictions.

State v. Trosclair, 443 So.2d 1098 (La. 1983).

Perjury

Like bribery, the crime of **perjury** has its roots in biblical times. The Mosaic Code included an admonition against the bearing of false witness. At common law, perjury came to consist of willfully giving under oath in a judicial proceeding false testimony material to the issue. Because of the narrow scope of the offense, it was eventually supplemented by the common-law offense of false swearing, a crime committed when an oath was taken in other than a judicial proceeding.

Elements of the Offense of Perjury

These common-law offenses have been codified by federal law, 18 U.S.C.A. § 1621, which provides

> Whoever (1) having taken an oath before a competent tribunal, officer, or person, in any case in which a law of the United States authorizes an oath to be administered, that he will testify, declare, depose, or certify truly, or that any written testimony, declaration, deposition, or certificate by him subscribed, is true, willfully and contrary to such oath states or subscribes any material matter which he does not believe to be true; or (2) in any declaration, certificate, verification, or statement under penalty of perjury as permitted under section 1746 of title 28, United States Code, willfully subscribes as true any material matter which he does not believe to be true; is guilty of perjury....

The reference to 28 U.S.C.A. § 1746 covers certifications subscribed under a rule, regulation, or order pursuant to any law where the subscriber signs a document in substantially the following form: "I declare (or certify, verify, or state) under penalty of perjury under the laws of the United States of America that the foregoing is true and correct." Probably the most common example of this is the declaration a taxpayer signs when filing a U.S. Income Tax Return. 26 U.S.C.A. § 6065.

All states have laws making perjury a criminal offense. For example, the California perjury statute provides that a person who has taken an oath to tell the truth and who "willfully and contrary to the oath, states as true any material matter which he or she knows to be false" is guilty of perjury. West's Ann. Cal. Penal Code § 118. Although section 118 relates to oaths in administrative and judicial proceedings, section 118a makes it perjury for a person to give a false affidavit to be used in those proceedings. Section 118 is applicable whether the statement, testimony, declaration, deposition, or certification is made or subscribed within or without the State of California. As in other jurisdictions, additional California statutes make it unlawful for anyone to give a false statement under oath in various applications, certificates, and reports. Courts have ruled that a grant of immunity (discussed in Chapter 14) will not protect a witness from prosecution for perjury if the witness testifies falsely. The courts reason that although a witness may be compelled to testify, nevertheless the witness is not compelled to testify falsely. See, for example, *DeMan v. State*, 677 P.2d 903 (Alaska App. 1984).

The Burden of the Prosecution

To convict a defendant of perjury, the prosecution must establish that the defendant took an oath to tell the truth and knowingly made a false statement of fact. Statutes usually permit anyone with scruples against taking an oath to affirm that a statement is true. In either event, a person cannot be lawfully convicted of perjury unless there is proof that he or she was administered the oath by or made an affirmation before someone with legal authority. *Whitaker v. Commonwealth,* 367 S.W.2d 831 (Ky. 1963). Furthermore, the defendant's statement must have been material. This means that the testimony given by the defendant must have been capable of influencing the tribunal on the issues before it. *United States v. Jackson,* 640 F.2d 614 (8th Cir. 1981).

Historically, courts in many jurisdictions held that the question of whether a witness's statement was material was a matter to be decided by the judge. In the 1990s some courts reasoned that because materiality is an element of the crime of perjury, a jury must determine that such element has been proved beyond a reasonable doubt. See, for example, *State v. Anderson,* 603 A.2d 928 (N.J. 1992). Their view prevailed in 1995, for as pointed out in the following Supreme Court Perspective, the Constitution requires that in a perjury prosecution the materiality of the defendant's statements, like all other elements of a crime, is a jury question.

Some statutes that define perjury require the prosecution to prove that the defendant's statement was made with the "intent to deceive." See, for example, Vernon's Tex. Penal Code Ann. § 37.02(a). Irrespective of statutory requirements, most jurisdictions require the prosecution to prove that the defendant's false statement was made "willfully and corruptly" because at common law, perjury was a specific-intent crime. Requiring the prosecution to prove the defendant's specific intent generally eliminates the likelihood of a defendant's being convicted for simply having made a careless or offhanded statement.

Perjury is one of the most difficult crimes to prove. The inherent difficulty of convicting a defendant of this offense is exacerbated by the **two-witness rule** that prevails in most jurisdictions. Under this rule the prosecution must prove the falsity of a defendant's statements by two witnesses. For example, McKinney's N.Y. Penal Code § 210.50 provides

> In any prosecution for perjury, except a prosecution based upon inconsistent statements pursuant to section 210.20, or in any prosecution for making an apparently sworn false statement, or making a punishable false written statement, falsity of a statement may not be established by the uncorroborated testimony of a single witness.

Perjury by Contradictory Statements

Go to the Scheb/ Scheb Criminal Law and Procedure 6e website at academic .cengage.com/criminaljustice/ scheb to find *U.S. v. Scott* (1982), in which a federal appeals court discusses perjury by contradictory statements.

Early American cases followed the common-law principle that a defendant could not be convicted of **perjury by contradictory statements** unless the prosecution established which one of the statements was false. Modern statutes make it unnecessary for the prosecution to establish which of two contradictory statements is false. See, for example, McKinney's N.Y. Penal Law § 210.20 (Inability of the prosecution to establish specifically which of the two statements is the false one does not preclude a prosecution for perjury).

Subornation of Perjury

At common law, **subornation of perjury** consisted of instigating or procuring another person to commit perjury. Statutes now generally define subornation of perjury much as did the common law. To convict a defendant of the offense, the prosecution must first establish that the defendant induced another to testify falsely and that an

The Perjury Trial of the Twentieth Century

In one of the most famous perjury prosecutions in American history, Alger Hiss, a former law clerk to a Supreme Court Justice and an adviser to President Franklin D. Roosevelt, was convicted of two counts of perjury by a federal court on January 21, 1950.

On August 3, 1948, Whitaker Chambers, a magazine editor, acknowledged before a Congressional committee investigating subversive activities of governmental employees that he operated as a spy for the Soviet Union during 1934–1938. Chambers charged that during this time Alger Hiss, a highly respected official of the U.S. Department of State, had turned over U.S. government documents to him in his former role as a spy. Hiss appeared before the committee and categorically denied that he was, or ever had been, a communist or a communist sympathizer. He asserted that he did not know anyone by the name of Whittaker Chambers.

On December 15, 1948, Hiss testified under oath as a witness before a federal grand jury investigating charges of espionage activities by communists in the U.S. government. Hiss stated that he had never, nor had his wife in his presence, turned over any documents of the State Department to Chambers or to any other unauthorized person. He also testified before the same grand jury on the same day that he thought he could definitely say that he did not see Chambers after January 1, 1937. This grand jury indicted Hiss with having committed perjury when he testified that he did not turn over government documents to Chambers and when he denied knowing Chambers. (The statute of limitations had tolled, so the government could not charge Hiss with espionage.)

In a bizarre controversy that involved vast media coverage, the nation was kept spellbound during the late 1940s as the Chambers-Hiss spy controversy excited the American public and greatly affected the American political scene.

Hiss was tried by jury twice, the jury at the first trial having failed to agree upon a verdict. At the second trial, the government presented Chambers as Hiss's prime accuser along with a witness to corroborate Chambers's testimony that Hiss had formerly had ties with the Soviet Union. The government also presented evidence of certain government documents prepared for espionage purposes that were typed on a typewriter owned by Hiss. It was established that the documents came from Hiss's typewriter but not that Hiss had typed them. Hiss denied knowing Chambers, denied any involvement with the communists, and branded Chambers a liar. He presented excellent character witnesses and a well-known expert who categorized Chambers as a psychopathic personality given to repetitive lying.

Hiss was convicted on both counts of perjury and sentenced to five years in prison. His conviction was based on statements he had made on December 15, 1948, to the federal grand jury investigating espionage activities by communists in the U.S. government.

On appeal to the U.S. Court of Appeals for the Second Circuit, Hiss contended the evidence was legally insufficient under the law of perjury. The court acknowledged there must be either two witnesses who testify that the accused violated his oath or one witness to that and corroboration by other evidence the jury believes. The court affirmed, however, because in addition to Chambers's direct testimony, there was sufficient independent evidence of the documents of which Chambers produced copies and which were all available to the defendant at the Department of State. Further, the court found that the evidence established the documents were copied on a typewriter when in the defendant's possession. As to count 2, the court noted that both Chambers and his wife testified that the defendant met and saw Chambers after January 1, 1937. Notwithstanding the decisions of the courts, Hiss stoutly maintained his innocence until his death in 1996.

United States v. Hiss, 185 F.2d 822 (2nd Cir. 1951). Review denied, 340 U.S. 948, 71 S.Ct. 532 95 L.Ed. 683 (1951).

actual perjury has been committed. *State v. Devers*, 272 A.2d 794 (Md. 1971). Thus, the Tennessee Supreme Court upheld a subornation of perjury conviction of an attorney for counseling four men charged with illegally selling whiskey to commit perjury. The attorney was prosecuted, however, only after his four clients were convicted. *Grant v. State*, 374 S.W.2d 391 (Tenn. 1964).

Defenses to the Crime of Perjury

Truth, of course, is a complete defense to a charge of perjury; therefore, a defendant who while under oath gives an answer that is "literally accurate, technically responsive or legally truthful" cannot lawfully be convicted of perjury. *United States v. Wall*, 371 F.2d 398, 400 (6th Cir. 1967).

After making a false statement under oath, a witness sometimes recants and tells the truth. Federal law provides for a **recantation** defense to a prosecution for perjury where in the same continuous court or grand jury proceeding in which a declaration is made, the person making the declaration admits such declaration to be false "if the declaration has not substantially affected the proceeding, or it has not become manifest that such falsity has been or will be exposed." 18 U.S.C.A. § 1623(d).

In reviewing a state statute similar to the federal statute, in *Nelson v. State*, 500 So.2d 1308 (Ala. Cr. App. 1986), the court held that retraction of a false statement is a defense if the retraction occurs in the same proceeding and the statement is retracted before it becomes manifest that the fabrication is or will be exposed.

New York courts have held that recantation is a defense provided it occurs promptly, before the body conducting the inquiry (for example, a grand jury) has been

SUPREME COURT PERSPECTIVE

United States v. Gaudin, 515 U.S. 506, 115 S.Ct. 2310, 132 L.Ed.2d 444 (1995)

Michael E. Gaudin was charged with making false statements on Department of Housing and Urban Development (HUD) loan documents in violation of 18 U.S.C.A. § 1001. At trial, the judge instructed the jury that the prosecution had to prove that the alleged false statements were material to HUD's decision with regard to the loans. The question of materiality, the court ruled, was an issue to be determined by the court and not by the jury. Gaudin was convicted, but the Ninth Circuit Court of Appeals reversed. They held that the trial judge erred in withholding the question of materiality from the jury and that Gaudin's rights to due process and trial by jury were infringed. Reviewing the case on certiorari, the Supreme Court agreed. The following are excerpts from Justice Antonin Scalia's opinion for a unanimous Court:

The Fifth Amendment to the United States Constitution guarantees that no one will be deprived of *liberty without "due process of law"; and the Sixth, that "[i]n all criminal prosecutions, the accused shall enjoy the right to a speedy and public trial, by an impartial jury." We have held that these provisions require criminal convictions to rest upon a jury determination that the defendant is guilty of every element of the crime with which he is charged, beyond a reasonable doubt....*

[O]ne of the elements in the present case is materiality; respondent therefore had a right to have the jury decide materiality.... [W]e find nothing like a consistent historical tradition supporting the proposition that the element of materiality in perjury prosecutions is to be decided by the judge. Since that proposition is contrary to the uniform general understanding (and we think the only understanding consistent with principle) that the Fifth and Sixth Amendments require conviction by a jury of all elements of the crime, we must reject those cases that have embraced it.

CASE-IN-POINT

Perjury: The Truth Must Be Unequivocal

A police officer was convicted of committing perjury on the basis of his denial of having received money from certain persons while in performance of his police duties. On appeal, he argued that his answer, "No sir. Not for my duties," to the prosecutor's question whether he received any money from any persons while on official duty as a Chicago policeman was literally true and therefore formed no basis for his conviction. The U.S. Court of Appeals, Seventh Circuit, rejected his contention. The court explained his initial response, "No sir," was directly responsive and false, so that his nonresponsive attempted hedge that followed was not effective.

United States v. Nickels, 502 F.2d 1173 (7th Cir. 1974).

deceived or any prejudice has occurred and before the defendant's perjury has most likely become known to the authorities. *People v. Ezaugi,* 141 N.E.2d 580 (N.Y. 1957). The rationale for the recantation defense is that the object of judicial investigations and trials is to ascertain the truth. It follows, therefore, that the law should encourage a witness to correct a false statement without fear of perjury charges as long as the false statement has prejudiced no one.

Obstruction of Justice

At common law it was a crime to commit an act obstructing or tending to obstruct public justice. Any act that prevented, obstructed, impeded, or hindered the administration of justice was considered a common-law misdemeanor. This included a host of acts such as obstructing an officer, tampering with jurors or witnesses, preparing false evidence, and secreting or destroying evidence. As statutory law came into being, some offenses that had been prosecuted as **obstructions of justice,** for example, **escape** and rescue and later **resisting arrest,** were dealt with as distinct crimes.

Modern Statutory Developments

Federal statutes proscribe a lengthy list of actions that constitute obstruction of justice. Among the actions made unlawful are assault on a process server; theft or alteration of process; endeavoring to influence or impede grand or petit jurors; obstructing proceedings before departments, agencies, and committees; tampering with or retaliating against a witness, victim, or an informant; and obstructing court orders. 18 U.S.C.A. 1501–1518. Postal laws make it an offense to willfully and knowingly obstruct or retard the passage of the mail. 18 U.S.C.A. § 1701. Thus, in *United States v. Upshaw,* 895 F.2d 109 (3d Cir. 1990), a federal appeals court upheld a defendant's conviction for obstructing mail where a postal truck driver took home a package after he signed out from work.

All jurisdictions have statutes proscribing interference with officers in the performance of their duties. Some laws define obstruction to embrace many forms of conduct. Common examples include statutes making it unlawful to

• Give false information to an officer with the intent to interfere with the officer's lawful performance of duties.

- Knowingly give a false fire or emergency alarm.
- Impersonate an officer.
- Intimidate a victim or witness.
- Tamper with a juror.
- Destroy or tamper with public records or physical evidence to be offered in official proceedings.

Go to the Scheb/ Scheb Criminal Law and Procedure 6e website at academic .cengage.com/criminaljustice/ scheb for an edited version of *People v. Brake.*

Under Illinois law it is obstruction of justice, a felony, to knowingly destroy, alter, conceal, or disguise physical evidence, plant false evidence, or furnish false information with the intent to prevent the apprehension or to obstruct the prosecution or defense of any person, 720 ILCS 5/31-4(a). In 2003, an Illinois appellate court held that a defendant who swallowed a plastic bag containing drugs, of which an arresting officer was aware, was guilty of violating the statute by concealing or destroying evidence of the defendant's possessory offense. *People v. Brake,* 783 N.E.2d 1084 (Ill. App. 2003).

The Citizen's Duty to Assist Law Enforcement Officers

The common law imposed a duty on citizens to assist the sheriff and, on request, to keep the peace and apprehend wrongdoers. Modern statutes impose on citizens the duty to come to the assistance of law enforcement officers on request. Rather typical is the Ohio law that makes it a misdemeanor to fail to aid a law enforcement officer. Ohio Rev. Code Ann. § 2921.23(a) states

> No person shall negligently fail or refuse to aid a law enforcement officer, when called upon for assistance in preventing or halting the commission of an offense, or in apprehending or detaining an offender, when such aid can be given without a substantial risk of physical harm to the person giving it.

Many states also have comprehensive statutes making it an offense to prevent, hinder, or delay the discovery or apprehension of persons sought by law enforcement.

Resisting Arrest

All jurisdictions make resisting arrest a crime. The common law did not permit a person to resist a lawful arrest by an authorized officer of the law. It did, however, permit a person to use force to resist an unlawful arrest. *United States v. Heliczer,* 373 F.2d 241 (2d Cir. 1967). Until recently this rule of law was applied in most American jurisdictions, but the functioning of the rule in modern society brought about the need to change it. The legality of an arrest may frequently be a close call, and because officers will normally overcome resistance with necessary force, there is a great danger of escalating violence between the officer and the arrestee. Thus, in recent years many courts have reexamined this common-law doctrine and have held that there is no longer authority to use physical force to resist an arrest by a police officer or by one the arrestee knows or has good reason to believe is an authorized peace officer performing his or her duties, whether such arrest is legal or illegal. See *Miller v. State,* 462 P.2d 421 (Alaska 1969).

Legislatures, too, have reexamined the issue of using physical force in resisting arrest. In 1980, the New York legislature amended its penal law to provide

> A person may not use physical force to resist an arrest, whether authorized or unauthorized, which is being effected or attempted by a police officer or peace officer

when it would reasonably appear that the latter is a police officer or peace officer. McKinney's N.Y. Penal Law § 35.27.

Oregon law now provides, "A person commits the crime of resisting arrest if the person intentionally resists a person known by the person to be a peace officer in making an arrest." Or. Rev. Stat. § 162.315(1). In *State v. Wright,* 799 P.2d 642 (Or. 1990), the Oregon Supreme Court held that a person may not lawfully resist arrest, even if the arresting officer lacks the legal authority to make the arrest, provided that the officer was acting under color of official authority. In addition, the court observed that if a police officer uses excessive force in making an arrest, the arrestee may use only such physical force as is reasonably necessary to defend against such excessive force.

Go to the Scheb/ Scheb Criminal Law and Procedure 6e website at academic .cengage.com/criminaljustice/ scheb to find *State v. Blanton* (1979), which involves resisting arrest and other related offenses.

The modern statutory and judicial revisions to the common-law approach make sense. It is not too great a burden today for a person who believes that he or she has been unlawfully arrested to submit to the officer and seek legal remedies in court. The circumstances surrounding an arrest are completely different from those that prevailed at common law. An arrestee today must be promptly taken before a magistrate, and legal counsel is readily available. Moreover, today's detention facilities do not resemble the crude dungeons where arrestees were incarcerated for lengthy periods before trial under the early English common law. The abandonment of the common-law rule is another example of a rule of law ceasing to exist when the rationale for it has ceased to exist.

Compounding a Crime

At common law a person who accepted money or something else of value in exchange for agreeing not to prosecute a felony was guilty of compounding a felony. In the later history of the common law, it became a misdemeanor to compound a misdemeanor if the conduct constituted an offense against public justice and was dangerous to society. To conceal a felony was also a common-law offense known as **misprision of felony,** which was based on the common-law duty to inform authorities about any felony of which that person had knowledge. A person who saw someone commit a felony and used no means to prevent the felony or apprehend the felon committed the offense of misprision of felony.

The Modern Statutory Approach

The legal theory underlying making it an offense to **compound a crime** is that justice is debased when an offender bargains to escape the consequences of his or her crime. Most states have enacted statutes making it a crime to compound a felony, but some have expanded the common-law rule by making it a crime to compound any offense. To illustrate, New Hampshire law provides that a person is guilty of a misdemeanor who

1. Solicits, accepts, or agrees to accept any benefit as consideration for his refraining from initiating or aiding in a criminal prosecution; or

2. Confers, offers, or agrees to confer any benefit upon another as consideration for such person refraining from initiating or aiding in a criminal prosecution.

3. It is an affirmative defense that the value of the benefit did not exceed an amount which the actor believed to be due as restitution or indemnification for the loss caused, or to be caused by the offense. N.H. Rev. Stat. Ann. § 642:5.

Most states have not made misprision of felony a statutory crime, probably relying on enforcement of statutes making it an offense to become an accessory after the fact to an offense (see Chapter 4). The federal criminal code, however, specifically makes misprision of felony a crime, the gist of the offense being concealment and not merely the failure to report a felony. 18 U.S.C.A. § 4. The U.S. Court of Appeals for the Second Circuit has held that the elements of misprision of felony are that the defendant had full knowledge that the principal has committed and completed an alleged felony and that the defendant failed to notify authorities and took steps to conceal the crime. *United States v. Cefalu,* 85 F.3d 964 (2nd Cir. 1996).

A Common Scenario of Compounding a Crime

The offense of compounding a crime often appears where a crime victim whose goods have been stolen agrees with the thief to take back the goods in exchange for not prosecuting. Such an action would ordinarily constitute an offense by the victim. But the New Hampshire statute makes it an affirmative defense that the value of the benefit did not exceed that which the actor believed due as restitution for a loss. In some instances courts will approve dismissal of a prosecution based on an agreement for restitution to the victim, but persons should not reach such an agreement without prior court approval.

Escape

At common law a person who departed from lawful custody committed the crime of escape. Where the prisoner used force, the offense came to be known as prison break. Finally, a person who forcibly freed another from lawful custody was guilty of the offense of rescue.

Modern Statutory Approaches to Escape

Statutes proscribing escape are generally broad enough to embrace all three common-law offenses relating to escape. Often the punishment is more severe when force has been used. Federal statutes prohibit a person who has been lawfully arrested or confined from escaping or attempting to escape from custody, 18 U.S.C.A. § 751, or from rescuing or attempting to rescue a federal prisoner, 18 U.S.C.A. § 752.

Most state statutes define escape in rather simple terms. For example, Texas law provides that a person commits the offense of escape "if he escapes from custody when he is: (1) under arrest for, charged with, or convicted of an offense; or (2) in custody pursuant to a lawful order of court." Vernon's Tex. Penal Code Ann. § 38.06.

The Elements of the Offense of Escape

The gist of the offense of escape is the prisoner's unauthorized departure from lawful custody. Lawful custody is generally presumed once the prosecutor establishes that the escapee was confined to an institution specified by law. In other instances it may be essential for the prosecutor to establish proof of lawful custody; however, those who escape from a jail, juvenile detention home, penal institution, or reformatory are usually presumed to have been in lawful custody. Likewise, a person who fails to return to detention following a temporary release or furlough generally falls within the ambit of escape statutes.

Absent an explicit statutory requirement, courts differ on whether the prosecution must prove the defendant's specific intent to avoid lawful confinement. Of course, if a statute requires specific intent, the prosecution must establish this before a conviction can be lawfully obtained. The Supreme Court has held that under the federal statute, the government need only prove that the escapee knew that his or her actions would result in leaving confinement without permission. *United States v. Bailey,* 444 U.S. 394, 100 S.Ct. 624, 62 L.Ed.2d 575 (1980).

State appellate courts differ on whether the prosecution must prove that the escapee intended to leave or be absent from lawful custody. Recognizing that a slim majority of jurisdictions hold that intent is not an element of the crime, a Florida appellate court in 1975 held that the state must prove that a defendant intended to leave or be absent from lawful custody. Despite the lack of such a statutory requirement in Florida law, the court justified its position by raising some interesting "horribles" under which a defendant charged with escape could be improperly convicted if the state were not required to establish the escapee's specific intent to avoid lawful confinement. In one scenario the court hypothesized that a road gang member had fallen asleep under a tree and was left behind by a negligent guard. The prisoner awakened only to find that the guards and work detail had returned to the prison. Because of such possibilities the court opted for requiring the prosecution to establish the defendant's specific intent to escape. *Helton v. State,* 311 So.2d 381 (Fla. App. 1975).

Defenses to the Charge of Escape

Occasionally an innocent person is unlawfully confined. Nevertheless, if custody was lawful, the fact that a person was innocent is not generally recognized as a defense to a charge of escape. See *Woods v. Commonwealth,* 152 S.W.2d 997 (Ky. 1941). Of course, a person who escapes can always assert the defense of unlawful confinement or custody. *State v. Dickson,* 288 N.W.2d 48 (Neb. 1980).

CASE-IN-POINT

Was Defendant Released on Bail "In Custody" Within the Meaning of the Statute?

After Douglas Owen Davis pled guilty to several drug offenses, the trial court released him on bond pending a presentencing investigation. He was ordered to report to jail on August 1, 2003, prior to his sentencing date. When Davis failed to report as ordered, the trial court, in a bench trial, found him guilty of escape under Virginia Statute § 18.2-479(B), which provides that "[I]f any person lawfully confined in jail or lawfully in the custody of any court or officer thereof or of any law-enforcement officer on a charge or conviction of a felony escapes, otherwise than by force or violence or by setting fire to the jail, he shall be guilty of a Class 6 felony."

In reviewing the conviction, the state appellate court framed the issue as whether Davis was "the custody of [the] court" within the meaning of Code § 18.2-479(B) when he failed to report to jail after the trial court released him on bond. Noting the case presented an issue of first impression, the court observed, "Appellant in the instant case had been released from the trial court pending sentence and allowed to remain free on bond. At that point he was no longer in the physical custody or even presence of the court. Thus, the sufficient restraint to have physical control over him 'did not presently exist.'" Accordingly, the court ordered the trial court to dismiss the charges against Davis, commenting in a footnote, "We do not preclude by this holding the trial court's other remedies for failure to abide by its orders."

Davis v. Commonwealth, 608 S.E.2d 482 (Va. App. 2005).

During the 1970s there was considerable attenton to the conditions of prisons, particularly at the state level. This is illustrated by a landmark 1974 California decision. Defendant Marsha Lovercamp was attacked by other inmates demanding sex. Prison authorities failed to provide Lovercamp with adequate protection, and she escaped. She was found guilty of escape, but an appellate court awarded her a new trial because the trial judge had denied her the opportunity to submit evidence of her plight as a justification for her escape. In reversing Lovercamp's conviction, the appellate court enumerated guidelines for asserting the defense of duress or necessity in these situations. *People v. Lovercamp,* 118 Cal. Rptr. 110 (Cal. App. 1974). The court opined that a limited defense is available if the following conditions exist:

(1) The prisoner is faced with a specific threat of death, forcible sexual attack or substantial bodily injury in the immediate future;

(2) There is no time for a complaint to the authorities or there exists a history of futile complaints which make any result from such complaints illusory;

(3) There is no time or opportunity to resort to the courts;

(4) There is no evidence of force or violence used toward prison personnel or other "innocent" persons in the escape; and

(5) The prisoner immediately reports to the proper authorities when he has attained a position of safety from the immediate threat.

In 1991, the Kansas Court of Appeals observed that the great majority of courts now follow the principles outlined in *Lovercamp. State v. Pichon,* 811 P.2d 517 (Kan. App. 1991). See, for example, *People v. Unger,* 338 N.E.2d 442 (Ill. App. 1975), aff'd., 362 N.E.2d 319 (Ill. 1977); *State v. Alcantaro,* 407 So.2d 922 (Fla. App. 1981).

In 1980, the U.S. Supreme Court recognized the defense of necessity as being valid in the context of the crime of escape. To sustain the defense, the Court said a prisoner must demonstrate (1) that because of an imminent threat of harm, escape was the prisoner's only reasonable alternative; and (2) that the prisoner made a *bona fide* effort to surrender or return to custody as soon as the duress or necessity lost its coercive force. *United States v. Bailey,* supra.

Legislatures respond to public opinion, and improvement of prison conditions is not a high priority for most voters. Because courts tend to focus on issues where the legislative process affords no relief, they will undoubtedly continue to give attention to complaints concerning prison conditions. As they do, prisoners will most likely seek to extend the defense of necessity to justify an escape based on the inadequacy of prison conditions. Some have already argued that the denial of needed medical care should be recognized as a defense to escape. See, for example, *People v. Martin,* 298 N.W.2d 900 (Mich. App. 1980) (Allowing defendant to present to jury whether lack of medical attention could rise to the defense of necessity.) Courts, however, have generally refused to accept either lack of medical care or inhumane living conditions as a defense to escape.

Go to the Scheb/ Scheb Criminal Law and Procedure 6e website at academic .cengage.com/criminaljustice/ scheb to find *State v. Ring* (1978), in which the Maine Supreme Court addresses the offense of attempted escape.

Contempt

Early in the history of the common law, judges began to exercise the power to punish persons whose conduct interfered with the orderly functioning of the courts in the administration of justice. Federal and state courts exercise the power to hold an offender—sometimes called a **contemnor**—in either civil or criminal contempt.

In *Bessette v. W.B. Conkey Co.,* 194 U.S. 324, 327, 24 S.Ct. 665, 666, 48 L.Ed. 997, 1001 (1904), the U.S. Supreme Court observed,

> The power to punish for contempts is inherent in all courts; its existence is essential to the preservation of order in judicial proceedings, and to the enforcement of the judgments, orders, and writs of the courts, and, consequently to the due administration of justice. The moment the courts of the United States were called into existence and invested with jurisdiction over any subject, they became possessed of this power.

State courts have universally recognized that the power to punish for contempt is an inherent one that springs from the nature and constitution of a judicial tribunal. See, for example, *Martin v. Waters,* 259 S.E.2d 153 (Ga. App. 1979); *Little v. State,* 90 Ind. 338 (Ind. 1883).

Civil Contempt

Because it is not considered a crime, we will deal very briefly with the concept of **civil contempt.** Usually it is a sanction imposed to coerce a recalcitrant person to obey a court order. For example, a court may hold someone in civil contempt for failing to pay court-ordered support for dependents. Perhaps the best known example of a civil contempt citation occurred in 1999 when Chief Judge Susan Webber Wright of the Federal District Court in the Eastern District of Arkansas found former president William Jefferson Clinton in civil contempt in a sexual harassment suit filed by Paula Jones because "the President responded to plaintiff's questions by giving false, misleading and evasive answers that were designed to obstruct the judicial process." *Jones v. Clinton,* 36 F. Supp.2d 1118, 1127 (E.D. Ark. 1999). As a result the court ordered Clinton to pay approximately $90,000 to attorneys and others for expenses they incurred as a result of his actions. *Jones v. Clinton,* 57 F. Supp.2d 719 (E.D. Ark. 1999).

Criminal Contempt

A court imposes **criminal contempt** to punish an offender whose deliberate conduct is calculated to obstruct or embarrass the court or to degrade a judicial officer in the role of administering justice. Intent is always an element in criminal contempt proceedings. Legislative bodies can regulate the power to punish for contempt, and, in recent years the Supreme Court has referred to 18 U.S.C.A. § 401, where Congress has provided that

> A court of the United States shall have power to punish by fine or imprisonment, or both, at its discretion, such contempt of its authority, and none other, as—
>
> (1) Misbehavior of any person in its presence or so near thereto as to obstruct the administration of justice;
>
> (2) Misbehavior of any of its officers in their official transactions;
>
> (3) Disobedience or resistance to its lawful writ, process, order, rule, decree, or command.

Direct and Indirect Criminal Contempt

Criminal contempt is classified as either direct or indirect. **Direct contempt** is contemptuous behavior committed in the presence of the court or so close to the court as to interrupt or hinder the judicial proceedings. Disruptions of the examination of a witness or an assault on a judge or juror are examples of direct contempt. **Indirect contempt,** sometimes called constructive contempt, refers to acts that occur outside

Defense Counsel Cited for Criminal Contempt

In 1949, after a turbluent trial that lasted nine months, eleven officials of the Communist Party were found guilty of violating the Smith Act (now codified at 18 U.S.C.A. § 2385), which prohibits activities aimed at the violent overthrow of the U.S. government (see Chapter 12). When the trial was concluded, the defense counsel were cited for contempt for "their persistent obstructive colloquies, objections, arguments, and many groundless charges against the court...." *United States v. Sacher,* 182 F.2d 416, 423 (2nd Cir., 1950). On reviewing the case, the Supreme Court upheld the convictions for contempt. Speaking for the Court, Justice Robert Jackson rejected the argument that the lawyers were merely performing their duty by providing a vigorous defense of their clients.

"But that there may be no misunderstanding, we make clear that this Court, if its aid be needed, will unhesitatingly protect counsel in fearless, vigorous and effective performance of every duty pertaining to the office of the advocate on behalf of any person whatsoever. But it will not equate contempt with courage or insults with independence. It will also protect the processes of orderly trial, which is the supreme object of the lawyer's calling."

Sacher v. United States, 343 U.S. 1, 72 S.Ct. 451, 96 L.Ed. 717 (1952).

the court's presence that tend to degrade the court or hinder the proceedings of the court. Illustrations of indirect contempt are an attorney charged with responsibility of a case who is willfully absent from the courtroom or a juror discussing the facts of a case with a news reporter before the trial of a case has been completed.

One reason for classifying contempt as direct or indirect is to determine the processes that must be followed. Direct criminal contempt proceedings are usually handled summarily. The judge must inform the contemnor of the accusation and ask if he or she can show any cause to preclude the court from entering a judgment of contempt. The court then proceeds to enter its judgment accordingly. Courts justify the summary character of these proceedings because the contemptuous act has occurred in the presence of the judge.

The process is more formal in indirect contempt proceedings. The judge is required to issue a written order to the contemnor to show cause as to why he or she should not be held in contempt of court. The order must set forth the essential facts of the charge and allow the contemnor a reasonable time to prepare a defense. The judge tries all issues of law and fact, but the contemnor has the right to counsel, to the compulsory process to secure witnesses, and to refuse to testify.

U.S. Supreme Court decisions have established basic due process rights that must be accorded contemnors in these proceedings. Of course, if there are statutes or court rules in a particular jurisdiction that prescribe the method of processing criminal contempt, the judge must not deviate from those rules to the prejudice of the contemnor's rights. In any contempt proceeding, if the contemnor is to be sentenced to a term of imprisonment for more than six months, he or she is entitled to a jury trial. *Baldwin v. New York,* 399 U.S. 66, 90 S.Ct. 1886, 26 L.Ed.2d 437 (1970).

Is Criminal Contempt Really a Crime?

Until the 1960s there was considerable division of thinking on this subject. In 1968, the U.S. Supreme Court in *Bloom v. Illinois,* 391 U.S. 194, 88 S.Ct. 1477, 20 L.Ed.2d 522 (1968), held that criminal contempt is a crime in the ordinary sense and may be punished by fine, imprisonment, or both. A person charged with criminal contempt is presumed innocent and must be afforded the procedural and substantive benefits of due process of law. Consequently, a contemnor must be proven guilty beyond a reasonable doubt before being held in criminal contempt. In some states, criminal contempt has been made a statutory crime. See, for example, McKinney's N.Y. Penal Law § 215.50–51, which provides that contempt in the second degree includes such misbehavior before the court, a misdemeanor (§ 215.50); while contempt in the first degree is a felony and concerns refusal to be sworn before the grand jury or refusal to answer proper questions after having been sworn in.(§ 215.51).

LEGISLATIVE CONTEMPT

Legislative bodies also have the power to punish by contempt those persons whose deliberate acts impede legislative activities. Some states have enacted statutes to cover specific instances of criminal contempt in respect to legislative functions. New York, for example, makes criminal contempt of the legislature a misdemeanor. McKinney's N.Y. Penal Law § 215.60 provides

> A person is guilty of criminal contempt of the legislature when, having been duly subpoenaed to attend as a witness before either house of the legislature or before any committee thereof he:
>
> 1. Fails or refuses to attend without lawful excuse; or
>
> 2. Refuses to be sworn; or
>
> 3. Refuses to answer any material and proper questions; or

Sidebar

Rule 42. Criminal Contempt

(a) Disposition After Notice. Any person who commits criminal contempt may be punished for that contempt after prosecution on notice.

(1) *Notice.* The court must give the person notice in open court, in an order to show cause, or in an arrest order. The notice must:

(A) state the time and place of the trial;

(B) allow the defendant a reasonable time to prepare a defense; and

(C) state the essential facts constituting the charged criminal contempt and describe it as such.

(2) *Appointing a Prosecutor.* The court must request that the contempt be prosecuted by an attorney for the government, unless the interest of justice requires the appointment of another attorney. If the government declines the request, the court must appoint another attorney to prosecute the contempt.

(3) *Trial and Disposition.* A person being prosecuted for criminal contempt is entitled to a jury trial in any case in which federal law so provides and must be released or detained as Rule 46 provides. If the criminal contempt involves disrespect toward or criticism of a judge, that judge is disqualified from presiding at the contempt trial or hearing unless the defendant consents. Upon a finding or verdict of guilty, the court must impose the punishment.

(b) Summary Disposition. Notwithstanding any other provision of these rules, the court (other than a magistrate judge) may summarily punish a person who commits criminal contempt in its presence if the judge saw or heard the contemptuous conduct and so certifies; a magistrate judge may summarily punish a person as provided in 28 U.S.C. sec. 636(e). The contempt order must recite the facts, be signed by the judge, and be filed with the clerk.

Direct Criminal Contempt

Attorney Terrence M. Spears represented Gary Kaeding in an indirect criminal contempt proceeding. During the Kaeding proceeding, the judge stated that he would give Spears five days to file a motion for substitution of judge. Thereafter, the following exchange took place between the court and counsel for the parties:

THE COURT: Also I am going to *sua sponte* enter an order ordering Mr. Kaeding to be examined by a psychiatrist of the choice of the Court, because I do not know whether he is competent to stand trial.

MR. SPEARS: You cannot rule since there has been a Motion for Leave—

THE COURT: (Interrupting) I can; anybody can request a psychiatric examination. I am going to do that.

MR. SPEARS: I will be asking for one for you, Judge; have that on the record.

MR. SCHARF: [Prosecutor] Judge, I would ask he be found in contempt for that.

THE COURT: I am going to hold you in contempt, $500 fine.

MR. SPEARS: Praise God, praise the Lord Almighty God. May you—

MR. SCHARF: (Interrupting) I ask for jail.

MR. SPEARS: May you reap what you sow, Judge, by the good book.

THE COURT: You have 24 hours to pay the fine, or you are going to jail.

In affirming the trial court's finding that attorney Spears was in contempt, the appellate court noted, "Direct criminal contempt is contemptuous conduct occurring in the very presence of the judge, making all the elements of the offense matters within his own personal knowledge. Direct criminal contempt may be found and punished summarily without the usual procedural due process rights being followed. Criminal contempt is conduct which is calculated to embarrass, hinder, or obstruct a court in its administration of justice or derogate from its authority or dignity, thereby bringing the administration of law into disrepute.

"We find that Spears' comments were calculated to embarrass the court and to derogate from the court's authority and dignity. Accordingly, we hold that based on this conduct, the trial court's finding of direct criminal contempt was proper."

People v. Kaeding, 607 N.E.2d 580 (Ill. App. 1993).

4. Refuses, after reasonable notice, to produce books, papers, or documents in his possession or under his control which constitute material and proper evidence.

Criminal contempt of the legislature is a first-degree misdemeanor.

Courts have been zealous in assuring that legislative bodies afford contemnors due process of law before adjudging them to be in contempt. See, for example, *Watkins v. United States*, 354 U.S. 178, 77 S.Ct. 1173, 1 L.Ed.2d 1273 (1957), where the Supreme Court invalidated a conviction for contempt of Congress because a witness was not adequately advised as to the pertinency of a subcommittee's questions. In practice, the Congress and state legislative bodies frequently make citations for contempt and then turn the matter over to the courts to handle.

■ CONCLUSION

The fair and impartial administration of justice and the orderly processes of democratic government depend on the honesty and integrity of those who occupy positions of authority. Hence, the basic common-law offenses described in this chapter have endured over the centuries. The offense of bribery seeks to avoid corruption of those in positions of trust, whereas the crime of perjury seeks to maintain the integrity of the judicial system and agencies of government.

To safeguard the security and effectiveness of law enforcement personnel, all jurisdictions make it a crime to resist arrest, even if the arrest is later declared to be unlawful. Society must ensure confinement of those it has chosen to incarcerate, so it is essential to maintain the offense of escape. With increased awareness of inhumane prison conditions and the rights of prisoners, however, courts have recognized that under some circumstances necessity can be a defense to a charge of escape. The abandonment of the common-law principle that allowed a person to forcibly resist an unlawful arrest and the recognition of the necessity defense in the law of escape both demonstrate the dynamic nature of the criminal law in response to societal change.

Finally, to maintain the effectiveness and the dignity of the judicial and legislative processes, courts and legislatures must have the authority to hold persons in contempt, although that authority must be exercised with due regard for the constitutional rights of contemnors.

■ KEY TERMS

bribery, 323	escape, 331
commercial bribery, 325	resisting arrest, 331
sports bribery, 326	misprision of felony, 333
perjury, 327	compound a crime, 333
two-witness rule, 328	contemnor, 336
perjury by contradictory statements, 328	civil contempt, 337
subornation of perjury, 328	criminal contempt, 337
recantation, 330	direct contempt, 337
obstructions of justice, 331	indirect contempt, 337

■ WEB-BASED RESEARCH ACTIVITY

 Go to the Web. Locate the decisions of your state's highest appellate court. Search the court's recent decisions for references to any of the offenses discussed in this chapter. Find the most recent of these decisions and write a synopsis of the decision.

■ QUESTIONS FOR THOUGHT AND DISCUSSION

1. To what extent have contemporary legislative bodies expanded the scope of bribery to cover classes of persons beyond public officials?

2. How does the requirement that the prosecution prove a defendant's specific intent to deceive protect citizens from unwarranted prosecutions for perjury?

3. Contrast the common-law rule allowing a person to resist an unlawful arrest with the modern trend of requiring citizens to submit to unlawful arrests by police officers. Which approach makes more sense in today's society?

4. Is a state statute that makes it a criminal offense "to hinder or delay a law enforcement officer in the performance of his or her duties" likely to be held void for vagueness under the tests outlined in Chapter 3?

5. Would a person who accepts the return of stolen goods from a thief without agreeing to refrain from filing a criminal complaint be guilty of compounding a crime?

6. Name some acts that would likely be considered obstruction of justice under federal and state statutes.

7. Despite the wording of most statutes proscribing the offense of escape, courts increasingly require the prosecution to prove the defendant's specific intent to avoid lawful confinement. Are courts justified in imposing such a requirement on the statutory law?

8. Have courts aided society by allowing escapees from prison to defend their actions on the basis of intolerable prison conditions? Are such conditions likely to be remedied by the legislative process?

9. Should courts allow an escapee from prison to assert as a defense the prison's failure to provide essential medical treatement to the prisoner? If this is to be recognized as a basis for a defense of necessity, what stipulations would you recommend to protect the public?

10. Describe some specific acts that a trial judge could justifiably consider to be direct contempts of court.

11. Why does the law require more formal proceedings in cases of indirect contempt than in cases of direct criminal contempt?

■ PROBLEMS FOR DISCUSSION AND SOLUTION

1. The state charged Larcen Inmatio with escape from prison. The court appointed the public defender to represent him. You are assigned to investigate the case and report your findings to the public defender. Your investigation reveals that Inmatio was convicted of burglary of a dwelling and was serving the second year of a five-year sentence in the state prison. He complained to the warden that another inmate had sexually molested him and requested transfer to another prison or at least another cell block. After confirming that an inmate in Inmatio's cell block had molested him on one occasion, the warden told Inmatio that he would place him in another cell block. During the next three days the warden took no action. On the fourth day, while Inmatio and other prisoners were on a work detail picking up trash from the roadside outside the prison, Inmatio left without permission and caught a ride to a nearby city where he obtained a construction job. He had no contact with the prison until two weeks later when the local police apprehended him and returned him to prison. Based on your investigation, do you think the public defender can successfully establish the defense of necessity on behalf of Inmatio?

2. Early one evening Alden Dancio was sitting at a table in a tavern with his girlfriend and two other couples. They had been drinking beer and were talking and laughing. A local uniformed police officer, who was patrolling the area, stopped in to have a sandwich. Annoyed by the loud talking and laughing, the officer walked over to the table. There he saw Angela Mellow, a female he occasionally dated, sitting with her arm around Dancio. No one at the table was intoxicated. The officer demanded that Dancio produce some identification and, when he refused, the officer told him he was under arrest for disorderly conduct and ordered him to get in the patrol car. Dancio refused and, after an altercation between the two, the officer handcuffed Dancio and placed him in the patrol car. After reviewing the police file, the prosecutor acknowledged that Dancio should not have been arrested for disorderly conduct. He dismissed that charge. Nevertheless, the prosecutor decided to file an information against Dancio for resisting arrest. Is there a basis for charging Dancio with resisting arrest in the state where you live?

CHAPTER **14**

Criminal Responsibility and Defenses

CHAPTER OUTLINE

Introduction

As the English common law developed, the concept of **criminal responsibility** became a significant consideration. As it did, various defenses to criminal conduct emerged. Incapacity to commit a crime because of infancy, insanity, or, under some circumstances, intoxication came to be recognized as defenses. Self-defense, defense of others, and defense of habitation and other property were also recognized as defenses because of justification for a defendant's use of force in those instances. Moreover, the common law allowed a defendant to assert certain matters as an excuse or justification for having committed a criminal act. Mistake of fact that occurred honestly, necessity, duress, and—under limited circumstances—consent were recognized as defenses.

Essentially these defenses have been recognized in the various jurisdictions in the United States, although they have been modified over the years. The Fifth Amendment to the U.S. Constitution and corresponding provisions of the state constitutions furnish defendants two additional defenses: immunity and double jeopardy. Legislatures initiated the concept of a statute of limitations on the prosecution of most crimes. Through judicial development, entrapment has become a recognized defense where improper governmental conduct has induced an otherwise innocent person to commit a crime. In rare instances, defendants have successfully asserted the defense of selective prosecution—that is, being singled out for prosecution.

In previous chapters, we have mentioned some defenses applicable to specific substantive crimes. We revisit some of those defenses in this chapter, further examining the scope of common-law, constitutional, and statutory defenses to criminal charges.

Defenses in General

Defendants who plead not guilty to a criminal charge may not only rely on their general denial; they may also offer any defense (sometimes called a **negative defense**) not required to be specifically pled. A defendant merely has the burden of raising some evidence of a negative defense. This is sometimes referred to as the defendant's **burden of production of evidence;** in some instances, however, the prosecution's own evidence might raise the issue. Once such evidence is produced, the prosecution usually has the burden to overcome it. For example, Henry Homeowner is charged with the manslaughter of a person who forced entry into his home one night after Homeowner had gone to bed. Homeowner claims to have acted in self-defense by using deadly force to defend his home. If any evidence discloses that he acted in self-defense, then to establish that Homeowner is guilty of manslaughter, the prosecution must ordinarily prove that he did not act reasonably. But in some jurisdictions, depending on the specific defense, the defendant not only must be required to produce evidence but must also carry the burden of proving the defense by the greater weight of the evidence, usually referred to as the **preponderance of the evidence.**

A defense that must be specifically pled is classified as an **affirmative defense** —that is, one that does not simply negate an element of the crime but, rather, consists of new matters relied on as an excuse or justification for the defendant's otherwise illegal conduct. To illustrate, suppose Larry Boatman is charged with burglary of a vacant beach cottage. He pleads not guilty, raising the affirmative defense of necessity. He argues that although he entered the cottage with the intent to take food from within, it was an act of necessity because he and his starving companions were shipwrecked in a desolate area without other means of obtaining food or drinking water. Ordinarily, a defendant has the burden to prove the matters offered as an affirmative defense. Therefore, it is up to Boatman to prove by the preponderance of the evidence that he acted out of necessity. Courts sometimes vary in their views about whether a defense is a negative or affirmative one.

For purposes of analysis and study, we have divided defenses to crimes (beyond simply negative defenses) into five categories:

1. Those asserting lack of capacity (infancy, intoxication, insanity, automatism)
2. Those asserting excuse or justification (duress, necessity, consent, mistake of law or of fact)
3. Those justifying the use of force (self-defense, defense of others, defense of property and habitation, and using force to resist an arrest)
4. Those relying on constitutional or statutory rights (immunity, double jeopardy, statutes of limitation)
5. Those assailing governmental conduct (entrapment, selective prosecution)

It is difficult to generalize whether a specific defense is or is not an affirmative one. The defenses we categorized are generally classified as affirmative defenses, but this is not always true. The prosecution is always required to prove the defendant guilty beyond any reasonable doubt. Still, the law may constitutionally place the burden on a defendant to establish an affirmative defense as long as that defense is not one that simply negates an element of the crime the prosecution must prove to convict the defendant. *Patterson v. New York,* 432 U.S. 197, 97 S.Ct. 2319, 53 L.Ed.2d 281 (1977). Defenses authorized by statute are often styled as affirmative defenses, but merely labeling a defense an affirmative defense is not sufficient. Courts look to the substance to make certain that an affirmative defense is one that alleges lack of capacity to commit a crime or seeks to excuse or justify conduct that would otherwise lead to criminal responsibility, rather than one that simply negates an element of the crime.

Defenses Asserting Lack of Capacity to Commit a Crime

In proffering a defense asserting the lack of capacity to commit a crime, the defendant admits the *actus reus* alleged by the prosecution but denies criminal responsibility for that act on the ground that he or she lacked the mental capacity to form the requisite criminal intent. There are four principal defenses asserting the lack of capacity to commit a crime: infancy, intoxication, insanity, and automatism.

Infancy

The common law regarded a child under age seven as incapable of forming criminal intent. Thus, **infancy** gave rise to a conclusive presumption of incapacity for a child younger than seven. This presumption of incapacity was rebuttable regarding a child between seven and fourteen years old, with the prosecution having the burden to demonstrate that a child younger than fourteen was capable of comprehending the wrongdoing involved in commission of an offense. Children over age fourteen were treated as adults. *Commonwealth v. Cavalier,* 131 A. 229 (Pa. 1925).

The rationale for these common-law presumptions was that young children require protection from the harshness of the adversarial processes of the law. Some jurisdictions have abolished these presumptions because legislatures have provided that children under certain ages, usually sixteen to eighteen, are subject to the jurisdiction of the juvenile courts, where the procedures are tailored toward less mature offenders. In establishing juvenile courts, the legislatures frequently intend to eliminate the common-law presumption of incapacity of infants. See *People v. Miller,* 334 N.E.2d 421 (Ill. App. 1975), for the court's perception of legislative intent under Illinois law. Under federal law, a juvenile is a person who has not attained age eighteen at the time of the commission of an offense. 18 U.S.C.A. § 5031.

Starting with Illinois in 1899, all states developed juvenile court systems. These courts traditionally handled juvenile offenders separately from adults in nonadversarial proceedings. The theory was that the state acted as *parens patriae,* taking a clinical and rehabilitative, rather than an adversarial or punitive, approach to youthful offenders. Nevertheless, the system suffered from many deficiencies, such as inadequate staffing and substandard facilities, and the results were disappointing. Many youthful offenders were not rehabilitated, nor were they afforded even the most basic constitutional rights accorded adults in the criminal justice system. In the words of the U.S. Supreme Court, "[T]he child receives the worst of both worlds: that he gets neither the protections accorded to adults nor the solicitous care and regenerative treatment postulated for children." *Kent v. United States,* 383 U.S. 541, 556, 86 S.Ct. 1045, 1054, 16 L.Ed.2d 84, 94 (1966). Although juvenile courts remain as part of the judicial scene, statutes commonly provide that for certain offenses a juvenile may be tried as an adult.

Intoxication

Intoxication can result from ingestion of alcohol or drugs. The common law did not excuse from responsibility for criminal conduct a person who voluntarily became intoxicated. In an early English case, the court approved a death sentence for a homicide committed by an extremely intoxicated defendant. *Regina v. Fogossa,* 75 Eng. Rep. 1 (1550).

In evaluating whether intoxication is a defense, **voluntary intoxication** must first be distinguished from **involuntary intoxication.** In most jurisdictions, voluntary intoxication may be considered in determining whether a defendant can formulate the specific intent the prosecution must establish in such crimes as larceny, burglary, and premeditated murder. Most courts reject the defense of voluntary intoxication for general-intent crimes. See, for example, *United States v. Hanson,* 618 F.2d 1261 (8th Cir. 1980) (assault on a federal officer); *Commonwealth v. Bridge,* 435 A.2d 151 (Pa. 1981) (voluntary manslaughter); *State v. Keaten,* 390 A.2d 1043 (Me. 1978) (gross sexual misconduct). These decisions are grounded in the public policy of not excusing conduct by those who voluntarily impair their own judgment. Three decades ago the South Carolina Supreme Court judicially adopted a rule that voluntary intoxication, where it has not produced permanent insanity, is never an excuse for or a defense to a general intent or specific crime. *State v. Vaughn,* 232 S.E.2d 328, 330 (S.C. 1977). In contrast, in *Johnson v. State,* 584 N.E.2d 1092 (Ind. 1992), the Indiana Supreme Court held that a defendant can offer a defense of voluntary intoxication to any crime.

In 1996 the U.S. Supreme Court, in a 5–4 decision, upheld a Montana law that does not allow a jury to consider a defendant's voluntary intoxication in determining whether the defendant possessed the mental state necessary for the commission of a crime. *Montana v. Egelhoff,* 518 U.S. 37, 116 S.Ct. 2013, 135 L.Ed.2d 361 (1996). In

1999 the Florida Legislature enacted a statute that eliminates voluntary intoxication as a defense. The new law specifies that evidence of voluntary intoxication is not admissible to show a lack of specific intent or to show insanity at the time of the offense. However, the statute makes an exception for controlled substances taken pursuant to a doctor's prescription. West's Fla. Stat. Ann. § 775.051.

 Go to the Scheb/ Scheb Criminal Law and Procedure 6e website at academic .cengage.com/criminaljustice/ scheb to find *Lattimore v. State* (1988), where an Alabama appeals court addresses a defendant's contention that his voluntary intoxication should be accepted as a defense to a charge of murder.

Florida courts have held that the statute excluding the right to assert the defense does not violate a defendant's constitutional right to due process. *Barrett v. State,* 862 So.2d 44 (Fla. App. 2003); *Cuc v. State,* 834 So.2d 378 (Fla. App. 2003). The trend is for states to disallow the defense of voluntary intoxication on the theory that a defendant who voluntarily deprives himself or herself of the ability to distinguish between right and wrong is criminally responsible for acts committed. In *Law on the Rocks: The Intoxication Defenses Are Being Eighty-Sixed,* Meghan Paulk Ingle has noted that, in addition to Florida, legislatures in Arizona, Arkansas, Delaware, Georgia, Hawaii, Idaho, Indiana, Missouri, Montana, Ohio, Oklahoma, and Texas have now passed statutes barring the admission of voluntary intoxication evidence. 55 Vand. L. Rev. 607, 645 n. 49 (March 2002).

Involuntary intoxication rarely occurs, but when it does, it relieves the criminality of an act committed under its influence if, as a result of intoxication, the defendant no longer knows right from wrong. *State v. Mriglot,* 564 P.2d 784 (Wash. 1977). A person can become involuntarily intoxicated through the trickery or fraud of another person—see, for example, *Johnson v. Commonwealth,* 115 S.E. 673 (Va. 1923)—or through inadvertent ingestion of medicine. See *People v. Carlo,* 361 N.Y.S.2d 168 (N.Y. App. Div. 1974). The New Hampshire Supreme Court summarized the law in this area:

> Generally the defense of involuntary intoxication will only be considered when it is shown that the intoxication was the product of external pressures such as fraud, force, or coercion, or when intoxication resulted from a medical prescription. *State v. Plummer,* 374 A.2d 431, 435 (N.H. 1977).

Intoxication as a defense to criminal liability has been codified in some jurisdictions. Section 939.42 of the Wisconsin Statutes is rather typical:

> An intoxicated or a drugged condition of the actor is a defense only if such condition:
>
> (1) Is involuntarily produced and renders the actor incapable of distinguishing between right and wrong in regard to the alleged criminal act at the time the act is committed; or
>
> (2) Negatives the existence of a state of mind essential to the crime *except as provided in § 939.24(3).* Wis. Stat. Ann. § 939.42.

The Wisconsin legislature inserted the italicized exception in 1987 to stipulate that a voluntarily produced intoxicated or drugged condition is not a defense to liability for criminal recklessness.

Wisconsin courts have said that to establish the defense of involuntary intoxication, the accused must show the inability to tell right from wrong at the time of the offense. To establish voluntary intoxication, the defendant must show that the defendant's condition negated the existence of the state of mind necessary to commit the crime. *State v. Repp,* 342 N.W.2d 771 (Wis. App. 1983), aff'd. 362 N.W.2d 415 (Wis. 1985).

Insanity

All persons are presumed sane unless previously adjudicated insane. Even a person who has been adjudicated legally insane may still be found guilty of a criminal act if it was committed during a lucid interval. Insanity is a legal concept and is defined differently in various jurisdictions in the United States. A person who meets the requirements of the definition at the time of commission of an offense may plead **insanity** as a defense to criminal conduct.

Few cases have caused as great a concern about how the criminal justice system functions as did the verdict of **not guilty by reason of insanity** in John Hinckley's federal court trial for the 1981 shooting of President Ronald Reagan, his press secretary, and two law officers. The defense of insanity has never been popular with the public. It has sometimes been called "a rich person's defense" because defendants who invoke it frequently expend considerable financial resources to present psychiatric testimony. The Hinckley verdict motivated Congress and several state legislatures to review the status of insanity defenses.

HISTORICAL ROOTS OF THE INSANITY PLEA

The concept of mental responsibility has deep roots in Anglo American law—the common-law crimes included a *mens rea,* the mental element. Nevertheless, the common law was slow to develop any standard for a mental condition that would excuse a person from criminal responsibility. By the eighteenth century, some English courts applied what has sometimes been called a "wild beast" test. For example, one English judge opined that "a man ... totally deprived of his understanding and memory, ... and doth not know what he is doing, no more than an infant, than a brute, or a wild beast ... is never the object of punishment." *Rex v. Arnold,* 16 Howell's State Trials 695 (Eng. 1724).

THE *M'NAGHTEN* RULE

Little progress occurred in the development of the defense of insanity until 1843, when an event in England caused even greater consternation than the Hinckley verdict caused in the United States. Suffering from delusions that he was being persecuted by government officials, Daniel M'Naghten decided to kill Sir Robert Peel, the British Home Secretary. (Peel was the founder of the British Police System; hence, the term "bobbies" is still applied to British law officers.) From outside Peel's home, M'Naghten saw Peel's secretary, Edward Drummond, leave the house. Believing Drummond to be Peel, M'Naghten shot and killed him. At trial, M'Naghten's barristers argued that he was insane at the time of the shooting and therefore should be found not guilty. The jury agreed. Enraged by the verdict, Queen Victoria insisted that the law provide a yardstick for the defense of insanity. The House of Lords responded, and the test they developed is still referred to as the **M'Naghten rule.** It provides that insanity cannot be a defense to a crime unless "at the time of committing the act, the party accused as labouring under such a defect of reason, from disease of the mind, as not to know the nature and quality of the act he was doing; or, if he did know it, that he did not know what he was doing was wrong." *M'Naghten's Case,* 8 Eng. Rep. 718 (1843).

The *M'Naghten* rule became the test for insanity used in both federal and state courts in the United States. As psychology and psychiatry developed new theories of mental capacity, critics attacked the rule as being based solely on cognition (that is, a process of the intellect) and ignoring a person's emotions. In response, some courts accepted the **irresistible impulse** test that stressed volition (that is, self-control) as a supplement to the *M'Naghten* rule. See *Parsons v. State,* 2 So. 854 (Ala. 1887). This allowed a person who knew an act was wrong but who acted under an uncontrollable desire or the duress of mental disease to be excused from a criminal act.

THE *DURHAM* TEST

Another test for insanity evolved from *Durham v. United States,* where the U.S. Court of Appeals for the District of Columbia held that an accused is not criminally responsible if that person's unlawful act was "the product of mental disease or defect." 214 F.2d 862, 876 (D.C. Cir. 1954). Many psychiatrists applauded the **Durham test,** but it gained little judicial support outside of the District of Columbia. It was eventually discarded even there. *United States v. Brawner,* 471 F.2d 969 (D.C. Cir. 1972).

THE ALI STANDARD

In 1962 the American Law Institute (ALI), an association of distinguished lawyers and judges, proposed a new standard combining both cognitive and volitional capacities as a test for insanity. It is sometimes referred to as the **ALI Standard** or **substantial capacity test** and reads as follows:

> A person is not responsible for criminal conduct if at the time of such conduct, as a result of mental disease or defect, a person lacks substantial capacity either to appreciate the wrongfulness of his conduct or to conform his conduct to the requirements of the law.

Go to the Scheb/ Scheb Criminal Law and Procedure 6e website at academic .cengage.com/criminaljustice/ scheb for an edited version of *U.S. v. Freeman.*

The ALI Standard was adopted by most federal courts and has sometimes been referred to as the *Freeman* rule, stemming from an endorsement of the test by the U.S. Court of Appeals for the Second Circuit in *United States v. Freeman,* 357 F.2d 606 (2d Cir. 1966). State courts, however, remained divided in their approaches to the defense of insanity. Many opted to follow the new substantial capacity test; the remainder adhered to the basic *M'Naghten* **right from wrong test.**

The substantial capacity concept was applied as the test for insanity in the infamous John Hinckley case. Under the ALI criteria, a showing of substantial impairment of a person's mental faculties is enough to meet the test of insanity. In contrast, establishing insanity under a strict *M'Naghten* approach requires a showing of total incapacity, and evidence that does not tend to prove or disprove the defendant's ability to distinguish right from wrong is irrelevant.

THE CURRENT FEDERAL STANDARD

Dissatisfied with the ALI test, Congress decided to eliminate the volitional prong in the federal test for insanity and to revert substantially to the *M'Naghten* rule when it enacted the **Insanity Defense Reform Act of 1984.** This act provides that in federal courts:

> It is an affirmative defense to a prosecution under any federal statute that, at the time of the commission of the acts constituting the offense, the defendant, as a result of a severe mental disease or defect, was unable to appreciate the nature and quality or the wrongfulness of his acts. Mental disease or defect does not otherwise constitute a defense. 18 U.S.C.A. § 17(a).

In addition, the act stipulates that "[t]he defendant has the burden of proving the defense of insanity by clear and convincing evidence." 18 U.S.C.A. § 17(b). The **clear and convincing evidence standard** is higher than the usual civil evidentiary standard of preponderance of the evidence but somewhat lower than the standard of **beyond a reasonable doubt,** the evidentiary standard required for criminal convictions. Although there has been some controversy concerning the legitimacy of placing the burden of proof of insanity on the defendant, the U.S. Supreme Court has held that this type of "burden shifting" does not violate the defendant's right of due process of law under the U.S. Constitution. *Patterson v. New York,* supra. Moreover, federal appellate court decisions in 1986 affirmed the constitutionality of this burden shifting under the 1984 federal act. *United States v. Freeman,* 804 F.2d 1574 (11th Cir. 1986); *United States v. Amos,* 803 F.2d 419 (8th Cir. 1986).

On April 4, 1995, a federal jury found Francisco Martin Duran guilty of attempting to assassinate President Bill Clinton. Duran pleaded insanity. His counsel argued that Duran was a paranoid schizophrenic who was shooting at the White House as a symbol of a government he hated. Unlike the John Hinckley trial, the new federal standard for insanity applied in Duran's trial. The jury rejected Duran's plea of insanity and found him guilty of attempting to assassinate the president, as well as guilty of several other charges.

THE INSANITY DEFENSE REFORM ACT: THE EFFECT ON THE USE OF PSYCHIATRIC EVIDENCE

Under the Insanity Defense Reform Act, psychiatric evidence of impaired volitional control is inadmissible to support an insanity defense. After passage of the new law, a question arose as to whether Congress also intended to prohibit the use of psychiatric evidence to negate a defendant's specific intent to commit an offense. In 1990 the U.S. Court of Appeals for the Eleventh Circuit addressed the issue: "Both Congress and the courts have recognized the crucial distinction between evidence of psychological impairment that supports an 'affirmative defense,' and psychological evidence that negates an element of the offense charged." The court ruled that the language of the new federal act does not bar the use of psychiatric evidence to negate specific intent where that level of intent is an element of the offense charged by the government. *United States v. Cameron,* 907 F.2d 1051, 1063 (11th Cir. 1990).

CONTEMPORARY STATE DEVELOPMENTS

Although Congress has placed the burden on defendants who plead insanity in federal courts to prove their defense, state courts are divided on the issue. In some states, where insanity is classified as an affirmative defense, the defendant bears the burden of proof of insanity, usually by a preponderance of the evidence. See, for example, *State v. Baker,* 424 A.2d 171 (N.H. 1980).

Tennessee is now among the states that place the burden on the defendant to establish the affirmative defense of insanity by clear and convincing evidence. West's TCA § 39-11-501; *State v. Flake,* 114 S.W.3d 487 (Tenn. 2003). In many other states, because of the presumption of insanity, when a defendant pleads insanity and introduces some evidence of insanity, the presumption disappears and the prosecution must then establish the defendant's sanity usually by proof beyond a reasonable doubt, the standard required for establishing a defendant's guilt. See, for example, *State v. Milam,* 260 S.E.2d 295 (W.Va. 1979). Courts usually permit laypersons as well as expert witnesses to testify about a defendant's sanity.

Unlike a defendant who is simply found not guilty, a defendant who is found not guilty by reason of insanity is exposed to institutionalization and may, in some circumstances, be committed to a mental institution. *Jones v. United States,* 463 U.S. 354, 103 S.Ct. 3043, 77 L.Ed.2d 694 (1983). This is generally accomplished subsequent to the verdict by the trial judge, who determines whether the protection of the public requires that the defendant be confined.

On the premise that a person should not be found not guilty on the basis of insanity, some states have recently resorted to verdicts of **guilty but mentally ill** in cases where the defendant's insanity has been established. For example, in *People v. Sorna,* the court explained that this category of verdict deals with situations "where a defendant's mental illness does not deprive him of substantial capacity sufficient to satisfy the insanity test but does warrant treatment in addition to incarceration." 276 N.W.2d 892, 896 (Mich. App. 1979).

Kansas became the fourth state to abolish the defense of insanity when it enacted Kan. Stat. Ann. § 22–3220, effective January 1, 1996. Montana, Idaho, and Utah had previously abolished insanity as a defense. In *State v. Cowan,* 861 P.2d 884 (Mont. 1993), the Montana Supreme Court held that its state law abolishing insanity as a defense did not violate the federal constitution. The defendant, asserting a constitutional right to plead the defense, asked the U.S. Supreme Court to review his case. In March 1994, the Court refused to review the *Cowan* decision. *Cowan v. Montana,* 511 U.S. 1005, 114 S.Ct. 1371, 128 L.Ed.2d 48 (1994). Although the Court declined to definitively settle the issue, its action suggests that the federal constitution does not require that states allow a defendant to plead insanity.

In 1995 the Nevada Legislature enacted a law effectively abolishing insanity as a complete defense to a criminal offense. In *Finger v. State,* 27 P.3d 66 (Nev. 2001), the Nevada Supreme Court held the new statutory scheme to be unconstitutional under both the Nevada and U.S. Constitutions and ordered that the insanity defense as it previously existed be reinstated. The court noted that "legal insanity is a well-established and fundamental principle of the law of the United States," and "it is therefore protected by the Due Process Clauses of both the United States and Nevada Constitutions." 27 P.3d at 84. The State of Nevada sought review of the court's decision in the U.S. Supreme Court, but the Court denied its request without opinion. *Nevada v. Finger,* 534 U.S. 1127, 122 S.Ct. 1063, 151 L.Ed.2d 967 (2002).

It is sometimes difficult to classify the results that occur from a plea of insanity when a jury acquits the defendant. For example, in 1994 Lorena Bobbitt was charged with severing her husband's penis, a fact that was not in controversy. She relied on insanity as a defense but in a novel way. She testified about her husband's alleged cruel and abusive behavior toward her and characterized herself as a victim. A jury in Manassas, Virginia, acquitted her. Some observers have characterized her acquittal as a jury nullification rather than a finding of not guilty by reason of insanity.

In 1993, the Arizona legislature deleted a reference to the defendant's knowledge of the "nature and quality" of his act, a traditional component of the *M'Naghten* Rule, thereby deleting the cognitive capacity aspect from its statutory test for insanity. Eric Clark, a young man, was charged with first-degree murder for the June 21,

CASE-IN-POINT

Insanity Defense

Joy Ann Robey was charged with involuntary manslaughter and child abuse in connection with the death of her ten-month-old daughter, Christina. At trial, Robey admitted to beating the child severely and repeatedly over a two-month period but pleaded not guilty by reason of insanity. The trial court found that the defendant was temporarily insane each time she beat the child but that she returned to sanity thereafter. Accord-

ingly, the defendant could not be held criminally liable for the beatings but was responsible for her failure to seek medical care for her child. Robey was convicted of involuntary manslaughter and child abuse and sentenced to three concurrent ten-year terms in prison. Her conviction was upheld on appeal over her contention that the trial court erred in holding her criminally responsible after acknowledging that she was insane at the time of the beatings.

Robey v. State, 456 A.2d 953 (Md. App. 1983).

2000, killing of a Flagstaff, Arizona, police officer, Jeff Moritz. Clark, who was suffering from paranoid schizophrenia at the time he shot the officer, pleaded "guilty, but insane" and waived the right to a jury trial. At a bench trial, the judge found Clark did not establish that his schizophrenia distorted his perception of reality so severely that he did not know his actions were wrong. After the Arizona Court of Appeals affirmed his conviction, the U.S. Supreme Court granted review. Clark argued that the Arizona definition of insanity violates due process of law because it does not allow a defendant to be judged insane if he did not understand the "nature and quality of his act," as has historically been an essential part of the *M'Naghten* Rule. Thus, Clark contended that, by not allowing evidence of mental disease or defect, the Arizona law violated his right to due process under the Fourteenth Amendment to the U.S. Constitution. Moreover, Clark's counsel pointed out that at least thirty-eight states, the District of Columbia, and the federal government employ insanity standards under which those satisfying either part of the *M'Naghten* Rule qualify as legally insane.

In *Clark v. Arizona,* ___ U.S. ___, 126 S.Ct. 2709, 165 L.Ed.2d 842 (2006), in a 6–3 decision written by Justice David Souter, the Supreme Court found that Clark's appeal presented two questions: (1) whether due process prohibits Arizona's use of an insanity test stated solely in terms of the capacity to tell whether an act charged as a crime was right or wrong, and (2) whether the Arizona insanity statute violates due process in restricting the consideration of defense evidence of mental illness and incapacity to its bearing on a claim of insanity, thus eliminating its significance directly on the issue of the mental element of the crime charged. The Court concluded there was no violation of due process in either instance. In affirming the judgment of the Arizona Court of Appeals, Justice Souter pointed out that "Arizona's rule serves to preserve the State's chosen standard for recognizing insanity as a defense and to avoid confusion and misunderstanding on the part of jurors." ___ U.S. ___, 126 S.Ct. at 2737, 165 L.Ed.2d at ___.

Thus, the Court upheld Arizona's elimination of the cognitive capacity aspect not only from its statutory test for insanity but also in refusing to allow psychiatric testimony short of insanity to negate the *mens rea* element of the crime charged. In affirming the judgment of the Arizona Court of Appeals, Justice Souter pointed out that "Arizona's rule serves to preserve the State's chosen standard for recognizing insanity as a defense and to avoid confusion and misunderstanding on the part of jurors." ___ U.S. ___, 126 S.Ct. at 2737, 165 L.Ed.2d at ___. Justice Anthony Kennedy, joined by Justices John Paul Stevens and Ruth Bader Ginsburg, contended "the Court is incorrect in holding that Arizona may convict … Clark of first-degree murder for the intentional or knowing killing of a police officer when Clark was not permitted to introduce critical and reliable evidence showing he did not have that intent or knowledge." ___ U. S. ___, 126 S.Ct. at 2738, 165 L.Ed.2d at ___.

Automatism

Older cases treated defendants who claimed that their unlawful acts were committed because of an involuntary condition such as somnambulism (that is, sleepwalking) within the context of the insanity defense. Newer cases tend to classify such involuntary actions as **automatism** and view automatism similar to unconsciousness as a basis for an affirmative defense independent from insanity. The defense is usually limited to a situation where criminal conduct is beyond a person's knowledge and control. *Sellers v. State,* 809 P.2d 676 (Okla. Cr. App. 1991). In *Fulcher v. State,* 633 P.2d 142 (Wyo. 1981), the court explained that one reason for regarding automatism as a separate defense is that there are generally no follow-up consequences such as institutionalization, which usually occurs in an acquittal by reason of insanity. The defense of sleepwalking is infrequently pled. In November 1994, a defendant in Butler, Pennsylvania, contended that his sleep apnea disorder depleted his oxygen and caused him to shoot his wife. The prosecution countered by arguing the man shot his wife because she had planned to leave him. The jury rejected the defendant's claim and found him guilty of murder.

Defenses Asserting Excuse or Justification

A defendant who asserts an excuse admits the act charged by the prosecution but claims that under the circumstances his or her conduct should not result in punishment. A defendant who asserts a justification for conduct says, in effect, that it was justified under the circumstances. Five principal defenses are based on a defendant's asserting an excuse or justification: duress, necessity, consent, mistake of law, and mistake of fact. For convenience, we also discuss **alibi** under this topic although, rather than offering an excuse, a defendant who pleads alibi simply says that he or she was elsewhere when an offense was committed.

Duress

The common law recognized that duress can be a defense to criminal charges if the coercion exerted involved the use of threats of harm that were "present, imminent and pending" and "of such nature as to include well-grounded apprehensions of death or serious bodily harm if the act was not done." Nevertheless, no form of **duress,** even the threat of imminent death, was sufficient to excuse the intentional killing of an innocent human being. American courts have generally followed this approach, with both federal and state courts having made it clear that threats of future harm are not sufficient to constitute duress. See, for example, *United States v. Agard,* 605 F.2d 665 (2d Cir. 1979); *State v. Clay,* 264 N.W. 77 (Iowa 1935).

The defense of duress, sometimes referred to as coercion, compulsion, or duress, is recognized today by either statute or decisional law. Duress has been asserted most frequently by defendants who have committed robberies and thefts and by prisoners who have escaped from custody. Some courts look on duress as negating an element of the offense charged and classify it as a negative defense. See *People v. Graham,* 129 Cal. Rptr. 31 (Cal. App. 1976) (a defendant who raised a reasonable doubt as to whether he had acted in the exercise of free will did not have the burden of showing duress by a preponderance of evidence). However, most courts classify duress as an affirmative defense and require the defendant to prove the defense by the preponderance of the evidence.

The common-law presumption was that if a wife committed a felony other than murder or treason in her husband's presence, she did so under coercion of her husband. That presumption has little significance in modern America and has been abolished in some jurisdictions either by statute—see, for example, Wis. Stat. Ann. § 939.46(2)—or by judicial decision—see *People v. Statley,* 206 P.2d 76 (Cal. App. 1949).

In November 1992, a California appellate court announced a new development in the law of duress. The court held that evidence of **battered woman syndrome** (BWS) is admissible to support a woman's defense that she committed robbery offenses because she was afraid the man she lived with would kill her if she did not do as he demanded. *People v. Romero,* 13 Cal. Rptr. 2d 332 (Cal. App. 1992). The court compared the situation to California decisions allowing evidence of BWS when a

Rejecting Economic Duress as a Defense

The defendant was arrested on board a boat in the Gulf of Mexico just off the coast of Florida and was charged with trafficking in cannabis in excess of ten thousand pounds. He pled not guilty and asserted the defense of duress. At trial, the defendant and his wife testified that economic reasons forced him to participate in trafficking in cannabis by piloting the boat. The trial judge declined to instruct the jury on duress, and the defendant was convicted. On appeal, the court affirmed the conviction and said that such claim of economic coercion was insufficient to call for a jury instruction on duress.

Corujo v. State, 424 So.2d 43 (Fla. App. 1982), rev. denied, 434 So.2d 886 (Fla. 1983).

woman is accused of killing a man she lives with who batters her (see the later discussion of self-defense in this chapter).

Prisoners who escape custody frequently plead duress. As pointed out in Chapter 13, the requirement for establishing duress as a defense to escape requires the defendant to show that a *bona fide* effort was made to surrender or return to custody as soon as the claimed duress had ended or lost its coercive force. See *United States v. Bailey*, 444 U.S. 394, 100 S.Ct. 624, 62 L.Ed.2d 575 (1980).

There is a conflict among jurisdictions about whether a threat against persons other than the defendant is a sufficient basis for a defendant to invoke the defense of duress. Kan. Stat. Ann. § 21-3209 provides:

(1) A person is not guilty of a crime other than murder or voluntary manslaughter by reason of conduct which he performs under the compulsion or threat of the imminent infliction of death or great bodily harm, if he reasonably believes that death or great bodily harm will be inflicted upon him or upon his spouse, parent, child, brother or sister if he does not perform such conduct.

(2) The defense provided by this section is not available to one who willfully or wantonly places himself in a situation in which it is probable that he will be subjected to compulsion or threat.

Necessity

Whereas in duress the situation has its source in the actions of others, in the defense of **necessity,** forces beyond the actor's control are said to have required a person's choice of the lesser of two evils. Early common-law cases recognized that "a man may break the words of the law … through necessity." *Regina v. Fogossa*, supra. Contemporary American judicial authorities hold that if there is a reasonable legal alternative to violating the law, the defense of necessity fails.

Suppose several people are shipwrecked on a cold night. One person swims to shore, breaks into an unoccupied beach cottage, and takes food and blankets to assist the injured until help can be secured. Prosecution in such an event would be unlikely, but if prosecuted, the defendant would properly plead the defense of necessity.

Is the defense of necessity applicable to a person with a suspended license driving a motor vehicle? In South Carolina, a defendant admitted to the offense but justified his actions on the ground that he needed to get help for his pregnant wife, who was suffering. He had no telephone, and his neighbor who did was not at home. The defendant drove to the nearest phone booth to request a relative to take his wife to the hospital. As he left, the police stopped him for having a broken taillight. He was then arrested for driving with a suspended license. At his trial, the judge refused his request to instruct the jury on the defense of necessity. The jury found him guilty, and he appealed. In a 3–2 decision, the Supreme Court of South Carolina ruled that under the circumstances the defendant was entitled to plead the defense of necessity. *State v. Cole,* 403 S.E.2d 117 (S.C. 1991).

In 1991 a Florida court of appeal allowed a husband and wife who contracted AIDS to assert the defense of necessity to charges of possession and cultivation of marijuana. *Jenks v. State,* 582 So.2d 676 (Fla. App. 1991). Courts in a few other states have allowed the medical necessity defense. Although Maryland has not legalized the use of medical marijuana, it has enacted legislation that allows a person prosecuted for use or possession of marijuana to have the court consider as a mitigating factor any evidence of medical necessity. If a conviction results, the maximum penalty is a fine not exceeding $100. MD Crim. Law, § 5-601(c)(3).

In November 1996 California voters approved Proposition 215 (Compassionate Use Act of 1996) to make marijuana legally available as a medicine to patients or their caregivers on recommendation of a physician. (In Chapter 9, we mention other states that have adopted initiatives to allow marijuana to be used for medical purposes.) The Oakland Cannabis Buyers' Cooperative began to distribute marijuana to qualified patients for medical purposes. In 1998, the United States sued to enjoin the cooperative's operation, arguing its activities violated the Controlled Substances Act's prohibitions on distributing, manufacturing, and possessing with the intent to distribute or manufacture a controlled substance. The litigation culminated in 2001 with an 8–0 decision from the U.S. Supreme Court holding there is no implied medical necessity exception to the Controlled Substances Act's prohibitions. Justice Clarence Thomas, writing for the Court, observed, "For purposes of the Controlled Substances Act, marijuana has 'no currently accepted medical use' at all." *United States v. Oakland Cannabis Buyers' Co-op.,* 532 U.S. 483, 491, 121 S.Ct. 1711, 1718, 149 L.Ed.2d 722, 732 (2001). Many commentators predict that Congress will eventually make provision for medical uses of marijuana. In the meantime the Court's decision has tended to thwart the use of medical necessity as a defense by those charged with marijuana offenses.

A number of defendants have attempted to justify actions involving "civil disobedience" on the ground of necessity in instances where they have forcefully asserted their personal or political beliefs. One of the most dramatic of these incidents occurred in 1980 when a group of antinuclear activists entered a factory in Pennsylvania, damaged components of nuclear bombs, and poured human blood on the premises. An appellate court approved of the defendants' entering a defense of necessity; however, the Pennsylvania Supreme Court reversed the decision. *Commonwealth v. Berrigan,* 501 A.2d 226 (Pa. 1985). Other attempts to plead the necessity defense by antinuclear activists have also failed.

In most, but not all cases, the necessity defense has been unavailing to defendants espousing other social and political causes. In another instance, several defendants were charged with criminal trespass when they refused to leave an abortion clinic in Anchorage, Alaska. They claimed their actions were necessary to avert the imminent peril to human life that would result from abortions being performed. They were convicted, and on appeal they argued that the trial court erred in refusing to instruct the jury on their claim of necessity as a defense. In rejecting their contention, the Alaska Supreme Court outlined three requirements that must be met by a person who pleads the defense of necessity: (1) the act charged must have been done to prevent a significant evil, (2) there must have been no adequate alternative, and (3) the harm caused must not have been disproportionate to the harm avoided. *Cleveland v. Municipality of Anchorage,* 631 P.2d 1073, 1078 (Alaska 1981).

A Wisconsin statute codifies the defense of necessity by providing that

> [p]ressure of natural physical forces which causes the actor reasonably to believe that his or her act is the only means of preventing imminent public disaster, or imminent death or great bodily harm to the actor or another and which causes him or her so to act, is a defense to a prosecution for any crime based on that act, except that if the prosecution is for first-degree intentional homicide, the degree of the crime is reduced to second-degree intentional homicide. Wis. Stat. Ann. § 939.47.

Consent

Because in most instances a victim may not excuse a criminal act, American courts have said that consent is not a defense to a criminal prosecution. See, for example, *State v. West,* 57 S.W. 1071 (Mo. 1900). Yet there are exceptions to this general statement. For example, where lack of consent is an element of the offense, as in larceny, consent is a defense. This can also be true today in a prosecution for rape, but only where competent adults freely consent before having sexual relations. Thus consent would not be a defense to a charge of statutory rape (the strict liability offense of having sexual intercourse with a minor).

Consent is commonly given to physicians who perform surgery. In contact sports, such as football and boxing, consent is implied and may be a defense to reasonable instances of physical contact that would otherwise be regarded as batteries. Some state legislatures have enacted statutes defining when consent is a defense. For example, section 565.080 of the Missouri Statutes specifies that, for consent to be a defense, the physical injury consented to or threatened must result from conduct that is not intended to cause serious physical injury or that the conduct and harm are reasonably foreseeable occupational or athletic event hazards. Nevertheless section 565.080 does not apply to hazing or homicide cases, where consent is no defense.

Of course, a valid consent presupposes that it is voluntarily given by a person legally competent to do so and is not induced by force, duress, or deception. Moreover, a victim cannot ratify a criminal act by giving consent after the offense has been committed. *State v. Martinez,* 613 P.2d 974 (Mont. 1980).

Mistake of Law

One of the oft-quoted maxims of the law is that "ignorance of the law is no excuse." The safety and welfare of society demand that persons not be excused from commission of criminal acts on the basis of their claims that they did not know they committed crimes. Although this is the generally accepted view, in some instances a defendant's honest but mistaken view of the law may be accepted as a defense. One example is where such a mistake negates the specific-intent element of a crime. Thus, a **mistake of law** may be asserted as a defense in a larceny case where there is a technical question of who has legal title to an asset. *State v. Abbey,* 474 P.2d 62 (Ariz. App. 1970). Likewise, a defendant's good-faith but mistaken trust in the validity of a divorce has been held to be a defense to a charge of bigamy. *Long v. State,* 65 A.2d 489 (Del. 1949).

The Illinois Criminal Code lists four exceptions to the general rule that a person's ignorance of the law does not excuse unlawful conduct:

> A person's reasonable belief that certain conduct does not constitute a criminal offense is a defense if:

(1) The offense is defined by an administrative regulation which is not known to him and has not been published or otherwise made reasonably available to him, and he could not have acquired such knowledge by the exercise of due diligence pursuant to facts known to him; or

(2) He acts in reliance upon a statute which later is determined to be invalid; or

(3) He acts in reliance upon an order or opinion of an Illinois Appellate or Supreme Court, or a United States appellate court later overruled or reversed; or

(4) He acts in reliance upon an official interpretation of the statute, regulation or order defining the offense, made by a public officer or agency legally authorized to interpret such statute. 720 ILCS 5/4–8(b).

Citing the preceding statutory exceptions, the Illinois Supreme Court held that a taxpayer who contended that she reasonably believed that she would be subject only to civil penalties, not to criminal sanctions, for failure to file an occupational tax return did not present a mistake of law defense. *People v. Sevilla,* 547 N.E.2d 117 (Ill. 1989).

In *United States v. Moore,* 627 F.2d 830 (7th Cir. 1980), the court said that "the mistake of law defense is extremely limited and the mistake must be objectively reasonable." 627 F.2d at 833. Furthermore, a court will never recognize a dishonest pretense of ignorance of the law as a defense. *State v. Carroll,* 60 S.W. 1087 (Mo. 1901).

A defendant can always raise the unconstitutionality of a statute as a defense to a prosecution for its violation. But a person who violates a statute thinking it unconstitutional does so at his or her peril; courts have said that a person's belief that a statute is unconstitutional, even if based on advice of counsel, does not constitute a valid defense for violating the law. *State v. Thorstad,* 261 N.W.2d 899 (N.D. 1978).

Mistake of Fact

In contrast with the ancient common-law maxim that "ignorance of the law is no excuse," at common law, ignorance or **mistake of fact,** guarded by an honest purpose, afforded a defendant a sufficient excuse for a supposed criminal act. American courts have agreed but have generally said that a mistake of fact will not be recognized as a defense to a general-intent crime unless the mistake is a reasonable one for a person to make

CASE-IN-POINT

When a Penalty Is Imposed for Failure to Act, Reasonable Notice of a Local Ordinance May Be Required

A Los Angeles, California, ordinance made it unlawful for any "convicted persons" to remain in the city for more than five days without registering with the police, or if they lived outside of the city, to enter the city on five or more occasions during a thirty-day period without registering. Virginia Lambert, a convicted felon, was found guilty of failing to register, fined $250, and placed on probation for three years.

On appeal to the U.S. Supreme Court, Lambert's conviction was reversed. Writing for the Court

was Justice William O. Douglas: "Engrained in our concept of due process is the requirement of notice. Notice is sometimes essential so that the citizen has the chance to defend charges…. Notice is required in a myriad of situations where a penalty or forfeiture might be suffered from mere failure to act."

Lambert v. California, 355 U.S. 225, 78 S.Ct 240, 2 L.Ed.2d 228 (1957).

under the circumstances. However, even an unreasonable mistake may be asserted as a defense to a crime that requires a specific intent. The decisions in recent years have indicated that a mistake of fact may be a defense as long as it negates the existence of the mental state essential to the crime charged. See, for example, *State v. Fuentes*, 577 P.2d 452 (N.M. App. 1978). Some jurisdictions have codified the mistake-of-fact defense. In Indiana, for example, mistake of fact is an affirmative defense by statute:

> It is a defense that the person who engaged in the prohibited conduct was reasonably mistaken about a matter of fact if the mistake negates the culpability required for commission of the offense. West's Ind. Code Ann. § 35–41–3–7.

In strict liability offenses, the defense of mistake of fact is unavailing because these offenses are not based on intent (see Chapter 4). In pointing out that this view represents the weight of authority, the Montana Supreme Court held that ignorance or even a *bona fide* belief that a minor was of legal age did not constitute a defense to prosecution for selling intoxicating liquor to a minor unless expressly made so by the statute. *State v. Parr*, 283 P.2d 1086 (Mont. 1955). Likewise, because having consensual sexual relations with a minor is generally considered a strict liability offense, a mistake of fact as to a minor's age is generally not a defense to a charge of statutory rape. Even if a court finds that a statutory rape statute requires proof of a general criminal intent to convict, a defendant's reasonable mistake of fact concerning a female's age is generally not available as a defense. *State v. Stiffler*, 788 P.2d 220 (Idaho 1990). In 1964, however, the California Supreme Court departed from this almost universally accepted rule and held that an accused's good-faith, reasonable belief that a female had reached the age of consent would be a defense to statutory rape. *People v. Hernandez*, 393 P.2d 673 (Cal. 1964).

Other state courts have noted, but not followed, the view of the Supreme Court of California. In 1993 the Court of Appeals in Maryland held that a rape statute prohibiting sexual intercourse with underage persons defines a strict liability offense. The court explained that the statute does not require the prosecution to prove *mens rea* and makes no allowance for a mistake-of-fact defense. *Garnett v. State*, 632 A.2d 797 (Md. App. 1993). A dissenting judge acknowledged the rationale for protecting very young females but challenged such statutes that protect young, mature women: "But when age limits are raised to sixteen, eighteen, and twenty-one, when the young girl becomes a young woman, when adolescent boys as well as young men are attracted to her, the sexual act begins to lose its quality of abnormality and physical danger to the victim. Bona fide mistakes in the age of girls can be made by men and boys who are no more dangerous than others of their social, economic and educational level." *Id.* at 815.

In the past few years, in cases of statutory rape, some trial courts have heard arguments based on a minor's right to privacy. The contention is that because a minor female can consent to an abortion, she should be able to consent to sexual intercourse. Although this argument has generally fallen on deaf ears, some trial judges have questioned the need to continue to employ a strict liability standard in consensual sexual relationships where the female is a minor and appears to be an adult and represents herself as such.

 Go to the Scheb/ Scheb Criminal Law and Procedure 6e website at academic .cengage.com/criminaljustice/ scheb to find *State v. Freeman* (1990), where the Iowa Supreme Court considers the defense of mistake of fact in the context of a conviction for "delivering a simulated controlled substance."

Alibi

Alibi means "elsewhere," and the defense of alibi may be interposed by a defendant who claims to have been at a place other than where the crime allegedly occurred. A criminal defendant who relies on an alibi as a defense does not deny that a crime was committed. Rather, he or she denies the ability to have perpetrated such crime because of having been elsewhere at the time.

The Colorado Supreme Court has pointed out that most jurisdictions that have addressed the issue have concluded that an alibi is not an affirmative defense. *People v. Huckleberry,* 768 P.2d 1235 (Colo. 1989). A few, however, characterize the defense as an affirmative one requiring proof of alibi by the defendant. Generally, a defendant who asserts an affirmative defense essentially admits the conduct charged and seeks to excuse or justify it. One who claims an alibi does not so admit. Therefore, it seems logical not to classify alibi as an affirmative defense. As explained by the Missouri Supreme Court,

> The theory of alibi is that the fact of defendant's presence elsewhere is essentially inconsistent with his presence at the place where the alleged offense was committed and, therefore, defendant could not have personally participated. Although the defense is not an affirmative one, the fact of defendant's presence elsewhere is an affirmative fact logically operating to negative his presence at the time and place. *State v. Armstead,* 283 S.W.2d 577, 581 (Mo. 1955).

Statutes or court rules commonly require that to assert alibi as a defense, a defendant must notify the prosecution in advance of trial and furnish the names of witnesses the defendant intends to use to support the alibi. The Supreme Court has said that this requirement does not violate the defendant's right to due process of law. *Williams v. Florida,* 399 U.S. 78, 90 S.Ct. 1893, 26 L.Ed.2d 446 (1970). In 1973, however, the Court held that when the state requires such information, the prosecution must make similar disclosures to the defendant concerning refutation of the evidence that the defendant furnishes. *Wardius v. Oregon,* 412 U.S. 470, 93 S.Ct. 2208, 37 L.Ed.2d 82 (1973). Alibi-notice statutes and court rules now commonly require disclosure by both defense and the prosecution.

Defenses Justifying the Use of Force

When offering a defense justifying the use of force, a defendant admits to an offense but claims that his or her conduct was justified under the circumstances. The use of force may be a defense to a criminal charge that the defendant caused injury or death to another. Therefore, the defense of **justifiable use of force** applies to the assaultive and homicidal offenses.

As a starting point, the use of **deadly force** (that is, force likely to cause death or serious bodily injury) must be distinguished from the use of **nondeadly force.** In general, the use of deadly force in self-defense requires that the person using such force (1) be in a place where he or she has a right to be, (2) act without fault, and (3) act in reasonable fear or apprehension of death or great bodily harm. *Lilly v. State,* 506 N.E.2d 23 (Ind. 1987). In evaluating whether the use of deadly force is reasonable, courts consider numerous factors. Among these are the sizes, ages, and physical abilities of the parties; whether the attacker was armed; and the attacker's reputation for violence. Ordinarily, a person may use whatever nondeadly force appears reasonably necessary under the circumstances. *State v. Clay,* 256 S.E.2d 176 (N.C. 1979).

Self-Defense

Defendants frequently admit the commission of acts that constitute an assaultive or homicidal offense but claim to have acted in **self-defense.** Generally, when a defendant raises the issue of self-defense, the prosecution must prove beyond a reasonable doubt that the accused did not act in self-defense. *Wash v. State,* 456 N.E.2d 1009 (Ind. 1983). Variations exist in the law on the permitted degree of force that can be used in self-defense, but the test of reasonableness appears common to all views. In determining the lawfulness of force used in self-defense, courts first look to see if the force used by the aggressor was unlawful. If so, the defender must show there was a necessity to use force for self-protection and that the degree of force used by the defender was reasonable considering the parties and circumstances.

At common law, a person attacked had a duty "to retreat to the wall" before using deadly force in self-defense. *State v. Sipes*, 209 N.W. 458 (Iowa 1926). In *Scott v. State*, 34 So.2d 718 (Miss. 1948), the court explained that to justify the slaying of another in self-defense at common law, there must have been actual danger of loss of life or suffering of great bodily harm. But the court said that the American approach has been that the danger need not be actual but must be "reasonably apparent and imminent."

Most courts reject the common-law doctrine of requiring a person to retreat to the greatest extent possible before meeting force with force. Rather, they say that a person attacked or threatened may stand his or her ground and use any force reasonably necessary to prevent harm. Courts that take this view often state it in positive terms, as did the Oklahoma Court of Criminal Appeals when citing one of its 1912 precedents: "The law in Oklahoma is clear: There is no duty to retreat if one is threatened with bodily harm." *Neal v. State*, 597 P.2d 334, 337 (Okl. Crim. App. 1979).

A substantial minority of courts, however, have adopted the principle that a person who can safely retreat must do so before using deadly force. But courts that follow the **retreat rule** have generally adopted the principle that a person does not have to retreat in his or her own dwelling. *State v. Bennett*, 105 N.W. 324 (Iowa 1905).

The Wisconsin Statutes codify the general law on use of force in self-defense:

> A person is privileged to threaten or intentionally use force against another for the purpose of preventing or terminating what the actor reasonably believes to be an unlawful interference with his or her person by such other person. The actor may intentionally use only such force or threat thereof as he reasonably believes is necessary to prevent or terminate the interference. The actor may not intentionally use force which is intended or likely to cause death or great bodily harm unless the actor reasonably believes that such force is necessary to prevent imminent death or great bodily harm to himself or herself. Wis. Stat. Ann. § 939.48(1).

The use of deadly force presents the greatest issue in self-defense. As we noted earlier, deadly force may be used only where it reasonably appears necessary to use such force to prevent death or serious injury. In considering whether a defendant is justified in using deadly force, the law has traditionally applied an **objective test for the use of deadly force.** See, for example, *State v. Bess*, 247 A.2d 669 (N.J. 1968). Today, however, there is a conflict in the decisional law. Some courts apply a **subjective standard of reasonableness** to determine whether circumstances are sufficient to induce in the defendant an honest and reasonable belief that force must be used. See, for example, *State v. Wanrow*, 559 P.2d 548 (Wash. 1977). Although the objective test requires the jury to place itself in the shoes of a hypothetical "reasonable and prudent person," the subjective test permits a jury "to place itself in the defendant's own shoes."

 Go to the Scheb/ Scheb Criminal Law and Procedure 6e website at academic .cengage.com/criminaljustice/ scheb to find *People v. Greene* (1987), where an Illinois appellate court upholds a trial judge's rejection of the defendant's claim of self-defense to a charge of homicide.

Much of the impetus for courts' applying the subjective test to determine whether the use of deadly force is reasonable has resulted from cases where women charged with committing assaultive or homicidal offenses against men have defended their use of force. In *State v. Wanrow*, supra, a woman on crutches was convicted of second-degree murder and first-degree assault in her fatal shooting of a large, intoxicated man who refused to leave her home. In reversing her convictions, the Washington Supreme Court held that the trial judge erred by giving instructions to the jury that did not make it clear that Wanrow's actions were to be judged against her own subjective impressions and not those that the jury might determine to be objectively reasonable.

The Law of Self-Defense

Defendant Ernest Young was distributing religious literature on the street when he was approached by George Coleman, who began to harass and swear at him. Later, Coleman again accosted Young, this time at a table in a fast-food restaurant. Coleman began swearing at Young and grabbed his arm. Young pulled out a handgun and shot Coleman three times, killing him. Young was charged with and tried for murder. Notwithstanding his plea of self-defense, the jury returned a verdict of guilty of voluntary manslaughter. As the appellate court reviewing the conviction said, "The jury heard appellant's story and it determined that he acted in the heat of the moment rather than in self-defense. There is ample evidence to support its verdict." The defendant's conviction was affirmed.

Young v. State, 451 N.E.2d 91 (Ind. App. 1983).

THE BATTERED WOMAN SYNDROME

Beyond the subjective standard of self-defense, in recent years the concept of self-defense by women has been expanded where a woman claims to have been continually battered by a man. The "battered spouse syndrome" soon became the "battered woman syndrome" (BWS). It describes a pattern of psychological and behavioral symptoms of a woman living with a male in a battering relationship. Some jurisdictions now permit a female in that situation who is charged with assaulting or killing a man to show that even though she did not face immediate harm, her plea of self-defense should be recognized because her actions were her response to constant battering by the man with whom she lived.

Decisional law is in the developing stage on the admissibility of expert testimony concerning the battered woman syndrome, with the trend being to hold that when a woman kills her batterer and pleads self-defense, expert testimony about BWS is admissible to explain how her particular experiences as a battered woman affected her perceptions of danger and her honest belief in its imminence. *State v. Hill,* 339 S.E.2d 121 (S.C. 1986); *People v. Aris,* 264 Cal. Rptr. 167 (Cal. App. 1989). In *Commonwealth v. Rodriquez,* 633 N.E.2d 1039 (Mass. 1994), the Supreme Judicial Court of Massachusetts found the trial court erred in refusing to admit evidence of the battered woman syndrome where a defendant who stabbed her boyfriend during an argument claimed she did so in self-defense.

In some instances, legislatures have enacted statutes to provide for admission of such evidence. See, for example, section 563.033 of the Missouri Statutes Annotated, which provides: "Evidence that the actor was suffering from the battered spouse syndrome shall be admissible upon the issue of whether the actor lawfully acted in self-defense or defense of another."

Increasingly, courts are recognizing the role of the battered woman syndrome, not as an independent defense but as furnishing support for a woman's defense where a woman shows that she has been acting under coercion of a male. In *United States v. Brown,* 891 F. Supp. 1501, 1505 (D. Kan. 1995), the court explained that although a woman cannot rely on the syndrome as a complete defense,

> it is some evidence to be considered to support a defense, such as self-defense, duress, compulsion, and coercion. Because women who suffer from the battered woman syndrome do not act in a typical manner as compared with women who do not suffer from it, evidence of the syndrome is used to explain their behavior.

Evidence of the syndrome is presented through expert testimony to assist the jury's evaluation of the defendant's state of mind.

THE BATTERED CHILD SYNDROME

Following the same rationale, where there is evidence that a child has been abused continually over an extended period, there is a movement now to assert the **battered child syndrome** (BCS) in defense of a child accused of assaulting or killing a parent. Many prosecutors claim that the use of BCS is undermining the law of self-defense, yet there are experts who claim that a child's perceptions of the need to use force are shaped by his or her experience of constant abuse by a parent. These experts argue that when juries hear such evidence, they may be persuaded that a child acted in self-defense and not out of retribution.

In the state of Washington, a boy who killed his stepfather was convicted of second-degree murder and two counts of second-degree assault. At his trial, the court held that evidence of the battered child syndrome could not, as a matter of law, support a finding of self-defense because there was no "imminent threat" to the defendant. In a much-discussed opinion, the appellate court held that this ruling was in error: "Neither law nor logic suggest any reason to limit to women recognition of the impact a battering relationship may have on the victim's actions or perceptions.... [T]he rationale underlying the admissibility of testimony regarding the battered women syndrome is at least as compelling, if not more so, when applied to children." *State v. Janes*, 822 P.2d 1238, 1243 (Wash. App. 1992).

In 1993 California charged Erik and Lyle Menendez, ages eighteen and twenty-one, respectively, with the murder of their parents. Although the defendants admitted killing their parents, they claimed to have been victims of parental abuse. Their first two trials ended in mistrials because the jurors could not agree on a verdict. In March 1996, the Menendez brothers were convicted and sentenced to life in prison without the possibility of parole.

Defense of Others

At common law, a defender had the right to use reasonable force to prevent commission of a felony or to protect members of the household who were endangered, a principle that was codified in many jurisdictions. See, for example, *State v. Fair*, 211 A.2d 359 (N.J. 1965). The trend in American jurisdictions is to allow a person "to stand in the shoes of the victim" and to use such **reasonable force** as is necessary to defend anyone, irrespective of relationship, from harm. As the court noted in *State v. Grier*, "What one may do for himself, he may do for another." 609 S.W.2d 201, 203 (Mo. App. 1980). Today a number of states have statutes that permit a person to assert force on behalf of another. To illustrate, the Wisconsin statute provides as follows:

> A person is privileged to defend a third person from real or apparent unlawful interference by another under the same conditions and by the same means as those under and by which the person is privileged to defend himself or herself from real or apparent unlawful interference, provided that the person reasonably believes that the facts are such that the third person would be privileged to act in self-defense and that the person's intervention is necessary for the protection of the third person. Wis. Stat. Ann. § 939.48(4).

Like the quoted Wisconsin statute, statutes in many other states limit a person's right to defend another individual from harm to those persons who "reasonably believe" that force is necessary to protect another. Some courts take a more restrictive view and hold that an intervenor is justified in using force to defend another only if the party being defended would have been justified in using the same force in self-defense. Under either standard, however, the right to go to the **defense of others** does not authorize a person to resort to retaliatory force.

In *People v. Kurr,* 654 N.W.2d 651 (Mich. App. 2002), a Michigan appellate court held that the defense-of-others concept extends to the protection of a nonviable fetus from an assault against the mother. The court concluded that in enacting M.C.L.A. § 750.90a *et seq.* (Fetal Protection Act), which provides penalties for harming a fetus or embryo during an intentional assault against a pregnant woman, the legislature determined that fetuses are worthy of protection as living entities.

Defense of Habitation

The common law placed great emphasis on the security of a person's dwelling and permitted the use of deadly force against an intruder. *Russell v. State,* 122 So. 683 (Ala. 1929). This historical view was chronicled by the Illinois Supreme Court in *People v. Eatman:*

> As a matter of history the defense of habitation has been the most favored branch of self-defense from the earliest times. Lord Coke, in his Commentaries, says: "A man's home is his castle—for where shall a man be safe if it be not in his house?" 91 N.E.2d 387, 390 (Ill. 1950).

Referring to a person's **defense of habitation,** the *Eatman* court opined that "he may use all of the force apparently necessary to repel any invasion of his home."

CASE-IN-POINT

Defense of Habitation

Defendant Raines was charged with murder in connection with the death of Ricky Stinson. Stinson was the passenger in a car driven by James Neese. The evidence showed that Neese had threatened to kill Raines and that Neese had driven past Raines's trailer and fired some shots out the window of his car. Raines was not home at the time, but when he returned, his live-in companion, Sharon Quates, told him what had happened. A few minutes later they heard a car approaching and went outside. Quates identified the car as the same one from which the shots had been fired. As the car drove away, Raines fired five shots from a semiautomatic rifle. Quates testified that Raines said that "he'd just shoot the tire out and stop it and we'd go get the law and find out who it was." However, one of the bullets struck Ricky Stinson in the head, killing him. Despite his plea that he acted in self-defense and defense of his habitation, Raines was convicted of manslaughter.

The conviction was upheld on appeal, with the appellate court saying that "although Raines may well have been in fear of danger when the … car approached, such fear alone did not justify his firing at the car as it drove down the public road past his trailer." As the court further observed, "One assaulted in his house need not flee therefrom. But his house is his castle only for the purposes of defense. It cannot be turned into an arsenal for the purpose of offensive effort against the lives of others."

Raines v. State, 455 So.2d 967 (Ala. Crim. App. 1984).

91 N.E.2d at 390. This is sometimes referred to as the **castle doctrine.** Even though a householder may, under some circumstances, be justified in using deadly force, the householder would not be justified in taking a life to repel a mere trespass.

In *State v. McCombs,* 253 S.E.2d 906 (N.C. 1979), the North Carolina Supreme Court addressed the issue of using deadly force to protect one's home. The court said that the use of deadly force is generally justified to prevent a forcible entry into the habitation in circumstances such as threats or where the occupant reasonably apprehends death or great bodily harm to self or other occupants or reasonably believes the assailant intends to commit a felony. Although this decision states the law generally applied by the courts, some statutory and decisional variations exist.

Defense of Property

The right to defend your property is more limited than the right to defend your home or yourself. The common law allowed a person in lawful possession of property to use reasonable, but not deadly, force to protect it. *Russell v. State,* supra. Today, the use of force to protect a person's property is often defined by statute. Typically, Iowa law provides that "[a] person is justified in the use of reasonable force to prevent or terminate criminal interference with his or her possession or other right to property." Iowa Code Ann. § 704.4. The quoted statutory language generally represents contemporary decisional law even in the absence of a statute.

Some older court decisions hold that a person may oppose force with force, even to the extent of taking a life in defense of his or her person, family, or property against a person attempting to commit a violent felony such as murder, robbery, or rape. However, these decisions focus on preventing a dangerous felony rather than simply on protecting or recapturing property. The prevailing view of the courts is that, in the absence of the felonious use of force by an aggressor, a person must not inflict deadly harm simply for the protection or recapture of property. *State v. McCombs,* supra. This is because the law places higher value on preserving the life of the wrongdoer than on protecting someone's property.

One method of defending property has been through the use of a mechanical device commonly known as a "spring gun" that is set to go off when someone trips a wire or opens a door. In the earlier history of the country, these devices were used on farms, in unoccupied structures, and sometimes in a residence at night to wound or kill an intruder. Some early court decisions said that use of a spring gun that resulted in the death of an intruder into a person's home was justified in instances where a homeowner, if present, would have been authorized to use deadly force.

Today, if someone is killed or injured as a result of a spring gun or similar mechanical device, the party who set it (and anyone who caused it to be set) generally will be held criminally responsible for any resulting death or injury. This is true even if the intruder's conduct would ordinarily cause a party to believe that the intrusion threatened death or serious bodily injury, conditions that might justify the use of deadly force.

The Model Penal Code § 3.06(5) takes the position that a device for the protection of property may be used only if

(a) the device is not designed to cause or known to create a substantial risk of causing death or serious bodily harm; and

(b) the use of the particular device to protect the property from entry or trespass is reasonable under the circumstances, as the actor believes them to be; and

(c) the device is one customarily used for such a purpose or reasonable care is taken to make known to probable intruders the fact that it is used.

Even courts in jurisdictions that have not adopted the MPC view take a harsh view of the use of such mechanical devices, reasoning that to allow persons to use them can imperil the lives of innocent persons such as firefighters, police officers, and even children at play. Finally, some courts point to another reason: although a deadly mechanical device acts without mercy or discretion, there is always the possibility that a human being protecting property would avoid taking a human life or injuring someone. See *People v. Ceballos,* 526 P.2d 241 (Cal. 1974).

FLORIDA'S NEW "STAND YOUR GROUND" LAW—A TRENDSETTER ON SELF-DEFENSE

In April 2005, Governor Jeb Bush signed a new law enacted by the Florida Legislature expanding the right of self-defense for individuals. The law amends Florida Statutes section 776.013 effective October 1, 2005, and provides:

(1) A person is presumed to have held a reasonable fear of imminent peril of death or great bodily harm to himself or herself or another when using defensive force that is intended or likely to cause death or great bodily harm to another if:

(a) The person against whom the defensive force was used was in the process of unlawfully and forcefully entering, or had unlawfully and forcibly entered, a dwelling, residence, or occupied vehicle, or if that person had removed or was attempting to remove another against that person's will from the dwelling, residence, or occupied vehicle; and

(b) The person who uses defensive force knew or had reason to believe that an unlawful and forcible entry or unlawful and forcible act was occurring or had occurred.

(2) [Includes provisions to protect anyone who has a right to be in a residence, those under lawful guardianship, and law enforcement officers]

(3) A person who is not engaged in an unlawful activity and who is attacked in any other place where he or she has a right to be has no duty to retreat and has the right to stand his or her ground and meet force with force, including deadly force if he or she reasonably believes it is necessary to do so to prevent death or great bodily harm to himself or herself or another or to prevent the commission of a forcible felony.

(4) A person who unlawfully and by force enters or attempts to enter a person's dwelling, residence, or occupied vehicle is presumed to be doing so with the intent to commit an unlawful act involving force or violence.

The new law expands the "castle doctrine" discussed above and allows individuals to use deadly force in public places without the duty to retreat. It also forbids the arrest, detention, or prosecution of those covered by the law and prohibits civil suits against them. Since the enactment of the new law, the media has reported that several other states have enacted or are considering enacting similar laws designed to allow individuals to use deadly force to defend themselves in public places without the duty to retreat. Critics of the new law have dubbed it a "shoot first" law and predict that it may lead to pre-emptive shootings.

Defense to Being Arrested

At common law, a person had the right to use such force as reasonably necessary, short of killing, to resist an unlawful arrest. The common-law rule developed at a time when bail was largely unavailable, arraignments were delayed for months until a royal judge arrived, and conditions in English jails were deplorable. Most American courts followed the English view. See, for example, *State v. Small,* 169 N.W. 116 (Iowa 1918). In some states a person may still forcibly resist an unlawful arrest.

Tennessee v. Garner, 471 U.S. 1, 105 S.Ct. 1694, 85 L.Ed.2d 1 (1985)

In this case the Supreme Court holds that use of deadly force by police to prevent the escape of an unarmed felony suspect who does not pose a threat of serious harm is an unreasonable seizure under the Fourth Amendment. The case stems from an incident in which a Memphis police officer shot and killed an unarmed burglary suspect who was attempting to flee the scene of the crime.

JUSTICE BYRON WHITE delivered the opinion of the Court, saying in part:
The use of deadly force to prevent the escape of all felony suspects, whatever the circumstances, is constitutionally unreasonable. It is not better that all felony suspects die than that they escape. Where the suspect poses no immediate threat to the officer and no threat to others, the harm resulting from failing to apprehend him does not justify the use of deadly force to do so. It is no doubt unfortunate when a suspect who is in sight escapes, but the fact that the police arrive a little late or are a little slower afoot does not always justify killing the suspect. A police officer may not seize an unarmed, nondangerous suspect by shooting him dead.

JUSTICE SANDRA DAY O'CONNOR dissented, saying in part:
Although the circumstances of this case are unquestionably tragic and unfortunate, our constitutional holdings must be sensitive both to the history of the Fourth Amendment and to the general implications of the Court's reasoning. By disregarding the serious and dangerous nature of residential burglaries and the longstanding practice of many States, the Court effectively creates a Fourth Amendment right allowing a burglary suspect to flee unimpeded from a police officer who has probable cause to arrest, who has ordered the suspect to halt, and who has no means short of firing his weapon to prevent escape. I do not believe that the Fourth Amendment supports such a right, and I accordingly dissent.

As pointed out in Chapter 13, however, the rationale for the rule has substantially eroded. Increasingly, legislatures and courts recognize that resisting an arrest exposes both the officer and the arrestee to escalating violence. Moreover, defendants are now promptly arraigned, and counsel is generally available to debate the legality of an arrest in court. See *United States v. Ferrone,* 438 F.2d 381 (3d Cir. 1971). Today the majority of states, either by statute or judicial decision, provide that a person may not resist an arrest, even if it is illegal.

Use of Force by Police

Most states have statutes or police regulations that specify the degree of force that may be used to apprehend violators. Officers are usually permitted to use such force as is reasonably necessary to effect an arrest and are not required to retreat from an aggressor. In practice, deadly force is seldom used by modern police forces, yet many states have statutes that authorize the use of deadly force by police in apprehending felons.

The Supreme Court's decision in *Tennessee v. Garner,* 471 U.S. 1, 105 S.Ct. 1694, 85 L.Ed.2d 1 (1985), limits an officer's use of deadly force to situations where it is necessary to prevent the escape of a suspect who poses a significant threat of death or serious injury to the officer or others. A law enforcement officer who injures or kills a person or damages someone's property in the line of duty is sometimes charged with a criminal offense. As long as the officer acted reasonably and not in violation of the Fourth Amendment, a statute, or valid police regulations, the defense of having performed a public function is available to the officer.

Defenses Based on Constitutional and Statutory Authority

In earlier chapters we mentioned that, subject to certain exceptions, the First Amendment to the Constitution provides a defense for legitimate speech, press, assembly, and religious activities. We also discussed how the Due Process Clauses of the Fifth and Fourteenth Amendments permit one to defend against criminal charges based on statutes that are void for vagueness.

In this section we discuss two significant constitutional defenses asserted by defendants in criminal cases: immunity and double jeopardy. In addition, we mention here the defense provided by statutes of limitations, which are legislative enactments establishing time limits for prosecution of most offenses.

Constitutional Immunity

Everyone is familiar with the scenario of the witness who invokes the constitutional privilege against self-incrimination based on the Fifth Amendment to the Constitution, which provides that "no person ... shall be compelled in any criminal case to be a witness against himself." The privilege against self-incrimination is applicable to the states through the Fourteenth Amendment, *Malloy v. Hogan,* 378 U.S. 1, 84 S.Ct. 1489, 12 L.Ed.2d 653 (1964), although states have similar protections in their constitutions.

The privilege against self-incrimination guaranteed by the federal constitution is a personal one that applies only to natural persons and not corporations. *United States v. White,* 322 U.S. 694, 64 S.Ct. 1248, 88 L.Ed. 1542 (1944). A strict reading of the clause would limit the privilege to testimony given in a criminal trial. However, the Supreme Court has held that an individual may refuse "to answer official questions put to him in any ... proceeding, civil or criminal, formal or informal, where the answers might incriminate him in future criminal proceedings." *Lefkowitz v. Turley,* 414 U.S. 70, 77, 94 S.Ct. 316, 322, 38 L.Ed.2d 274, 281 (1973). A classic example is the privilege of suspects in police custody to invoke their *Miranda* rights. See *Miranda v. Arizona,* 384 U.S. 476, 86 S.Ct. 1602, 16 L.Ed.2d 694 (1966) (discussed in Chapter 16).

Frequently, when a witness invokes the Fifth Amendment and refuses to testify, the court is requested to compel the witness's testimony. This may be accomplished by conferring **immunity** on the witness, which is a grant of amnesty to protect the witness from prosecution through the use of compelled testimony. A witness compelled to give incriminating testimony thus receives **use immunity** (that is, the testimony given cannot be used against the witness). This form of immunity (sometimes referred to as "derivative immunity") is coextensive with the scope of the privilege against self-incrimination and meets the demands of the Constitution. *Kastigar v. United States,* 406 U.S. 441, 92 S.Ct. 1653, 32 L.Ed.2d 212 (1972).

In some states a witness who testifies under a grant of immunity is given **transactional immunity,** a broader protection than is required under the federal constitution. Transactional immunity protects a witness from prosecution for any activity mentioned in the witness's testimony. An example of requiring broader protection occurred in 1993 when the Alaska Supreme Court ruled that its state constitution requires that witnesses who are compelled to testify be given the more protective transactional immunity from prosecution, not just use immunity or derivative immunity as required by the federal constitution. *State v. Gonzalez,* 853 P.2d 526 (Alaska

1993). A defendant may assert the defense of immunity by a pretrial motion. Despite a grant of immunity, a witness may be prosecuted for making material false statements under oath. *United States v. Apfelbaum,* 445 U.S. 115, 100 S.Ct. 948, 63 L.Ed.2d 250 (1980) (see Chapter 13).

Other Forms of Immunity

Sometimes a prosecutor, with approval of the court, grants a witness **contractual immunity.** The purpose is to induce a suspect to testify against someone and thereby enable the prosecution to obtain a conviction not otherwise obtainable because of constitutional protection against self-incrimination. This type of immunity is rarely granted if other available evidence will lead to a conviction. The authority to grant immunity in federal courts is vested in the U.S. Attorney with approval of the Attorney General or certain authorized assistants. 18 U.S.C.A. § 6003(b). At the state level, such authority is generally vested in the chief prosecuting officer (that is, the district or state attorney).

Under international law, a person who has diplomatic status and serves as part of a diplomatic mission, as well as members of the diplomat's staff and household, is immune from arrest and prosecution, thus enjoying **diplomatic immunity.** The expectation, of course, is that American diplomats and their dependents and staff members will enjoy like immunity in foreign nations. Diplomatic immunity attaches to the sovereign state, not to the individual diplomat. In instances of egregious misconduct, a foreign state may be asked to waive the diplomat's immunity. In 1997, Republic of Georgia envoy Gueorgui Makharadze was involved in a traffic accident in Washington, D.C., while driving while intoxicated. The accident resulted in the death of one person and injuries to four others. At the request of the U.S. Government, Georgia withdrew Makharadze's diplomatic immunity. He pled guilty to involuntary manslaughter and aggravated assault and was sentenced to prison.

Double Jeopardy

The concept of forbidding retrial of a defendant who has been found not guilty developed from the common law. *Ex parte Lange,* 85 U.S. (18 Wall.) 163, 21 L.Ed. 872 (1873). The Fifth Amendment to the U.S. Constitution embodies this principle: "[N]or shall any person be subject for the same offence to be twice put in jeopardy of life or limb." The Double Jeopardy Clause was made applicable to the states through the Fourteenth Amendment in *Benton v. Maryland,* 395 U.S. 784, 89 S.Ct. 2056, 23 L.Ed.2d 707 (1969). Even before that, all states provided essentially the same protection through their constitutions, statutes, or judicial decisions recognizing common-law principles.

Justice Hugo Black expressed the rationale underlying the Double Jeopardy Clause:

> The underlying idea, one that is deeply ingrained in at least the Anglo-American system of jurisprudence, is that the State with all its resources and power should not be allowed to make repeated attempts to convict an individual for an alleged offense, thereby subjecting him to embarrassment, expense and ordeal and compelling him to live in a continuing state of anxiety and insecurity, as well as enhancing the possibility that even though innocent he may be found guilty. *Green v. United States,* 355 U.S. 184, 187–188, 78 S.Ct. 221, 223, 2 L.Ed.2d 199, 204 (1957).

The subject of **double jeopardy** is very complex, but certain principles seem clear. Jeopardy attaches once the jury is sworn in, *Crist v. Bretz,* 437 U.S. 28, 98 S.Ct. 2156, 57 L.Ed.2d 24 (1978), or when the first witness is sworn in to testify in a nonjury trial, *Serfass v. United States*, 420 U.S. 377, 95 S.Ct. 1055, 43 L.Ed.2d 265 (1975). The defense of double jeopardy may be asserted by pretrial motion.

The Double Jeopardy Clause forbids a second prosecution for the same offense after a defendant has been acquitted. *Ball v. United States*, 163 U.S. 662, 16 S.Ct. 1192, 41 L.Ed. 300 (1896). In recent years, this principle has been applied even after a conviction. *United States v. Wilson*, 420 U.S. 332, 95 S.Ct. 1013, 43 L.Ed.2d 232 (1975). But if a defendant appeals a conviction and prevails, it is not double jeopardy for the prosecution to retry the defendant unless the appellate court rules that there was insufficient evidence to sustain the defendant's conviction. *Burks v. United States*, 437 U.S. 1, 98 S.Ct. 2141, 57 L.Ed.2d 1 (1978). Note the distinction between a conviction reversed by a higher court on the basis of **insufficient evidence** and a defendant's conviction being vacated and a new trial ordered based on the **weight of the evidence.** In the latter case, a retrial of the defendant would not constitute double jeopardy. *Tibbs v. Florida*, 457 U.S. 31, 102 S.Ct. 2211, 72 L.Ed.2d 652 (1982). Nor is it double jeopardy to retry a defendant if the trial court, at the defendant's request, has declared a mistrial. *Oregon v. Kennedy*, 456 U.S. 667, 102 S.Ct. 2083, 72 L.Ed.2d 416 (1982). If, however, the government moves for a mistrial, the defendant objects, and the court grants the mistrial, the prosecution must establish a **manifest necessity** for the mistrial in order for a retrial to be permitted. An example of a manifest necessity might be a highly improper opening statement by the defendant's counsel. *Arizona v. Washington*, 434 U.S. 497, 98 S.Ct. 824, 54 L.Ed.2d 717 (1978).

Some offenses are crimes against both the federal and state governments. The policy, and in some instances state law, forbids a second prosecution once an offender has been prosecuted in a different jurisdiction. Nevertheless, because separate sovereigns are involved, under our federal system the Double Jeopardy Clause does not preclude a prosecution by both the federal and state governments. *Bartkus v. Illinois*, 359 U.S. 121, 79 S.Ct. 676, 3 L.Ed.2d 684 (1959). Yet this principle does not allow two courts within a state to try an accused for the same offense. Therefore, a person who has been prosecuted in a city or county court cannot be tried again in any court in the state for the same offense. *Waller v. Florida*, 397 U.S. 387, 90 S.Ct. 1184, 25 L.Ed.2d 435 (1970). In addition to protecting against a second prosecution for the same offense after conviction or acquittal, the Double Jeopardy Clause protects against multiple punishments for the same offense. *North Carolina v. Pearce*, 395 U.S. 711, 89 S.Ct. 2072, 23 L.Ed.2d 656 (1969). However, the Constitution does not define "same offense." In 1932 the Supreme Court said the following:

> The applicable rule is that, where the same act or transaction constitutes a violation of two distinct statutory provisions, the test to be applied to determine whether there are two offenses or only one is whether each provision requires proof of an additional fact which the other does not. *Blockburger v. United States*, 284 U.S. 299, 304, 52 S.Ct. 180, 182, 76 L.Ed. 306, 309 (1932).

The ***Blockburger* test** compares the elements of the crimes in question. It is a tool of interpretation and creates a presumption of legislative intent, but it is not designed to contravene such intent. Rather, the Supreme Court has said that the "legislative intent," if clear, determines the scope of what constitutes "same offenses." *Missouri v. Hunter*, 459 U.S. 359, 103 S.Ct. 673, 74 L.Ed.2d 535 (1983); *Albernaz v. United States*, 450 U.S. 333, 101 S.Ct. 1137, 67 L.Ed.2d 275 (1981). In 1980 the Supreme Court reviewed a case where the defendant was first convicted of failing to slow down to avoid an accident with his car. Later he was charged with manslaughter arising from the same incident. After reciting the "elements" test in *Blockburger*, the Court stated that

> if in the pending manslaughter prosecution Illinois relies on and proves a failure to slow to avoid an accident as the reckless act necessary to prove manslaughter, Vitale

[the defendant] would have a substantial claim of double jeopardy under the Fifth and Fourteenth Amendments of the U.S. Constitution. *Illinois v. Vitale,* 447 U.S. 410, 420, 100 S.Ct. 2260, 2267, 65 L.Ed.2d 228, 238 (1980).

The *Blockburger* test examines the elements, not the facts. Since the Supreme Court's decision in *Illinois v. Vitale,* supra, not all courts have regarded *Blockburger* as the exclusive method of determining whether successive prosecutions violate the principle of double jeopardy. Indeed, some courts look also to the evidence to be presented to prove those crimes. For example, the Connecticut Supreme Court, citing *Vitale,* held that the prosecution of a defendant for operating a vehicle under the influence of intoxicants after being acquitted for manslaughter with a motor vehicle while intoxicated was barred by principle of double jeopardy. Even though the offenses were not the same under the *Blockburger* test, the evidence offered to prove a violation of the offense charged in the first prosecution was to be the sole evidence offered to prove an element of the offense charged in the second prosecution. Thus, the court held the second prosecution barred by the principle of double jeopardy. *State v. Lonergan,* 566 A.2d 677 (Conn. 1989). Other courts continue to determine the issue of double jeopardy by applying the *Blockburger* test. See, for example, *Butler v. State,* 816 S.W.2d 124 (Tex. App. 1991).

In *Grady v. Corbin,* 495 U.S. 508, 110 S.Ct. 2084, 109 L.Ed.2d 548 (1990), the Supreme Court, by a 5–4 vote, continued to follow the approach in *Vitale.* The Court said that "if to establish an essential element of an offense charged in that prosecution, the government will prove conduct that constitutes an offense for which the defendant has already been prosecuted," a second prosecution may not be undertaken. 495 U.S. at 510, 110 S.Ct. at 2087, 109 L.Ed.2d at 557. This became known as the **same evidence test** and barred a second prosecution based on the same conduct by the defendant that was at issue in the first prosecution. In June 1993, however, in *United States v. Dixon,* 509 U.S. 688, 113 S.Ct. 2849, 125 L.Ed.2d 556 (1993), by a 5–4 margin, the Court overruled *Grady v. Corbin,* replacing the same evidence test for double jeopardy analysis by a return to the **same elements test** from *Blockburger,* which bars punishment for offenses that have the same elements, or when one offense includes or is included in another offense. In *Dixon,* the Court also ruled that a criminal contempt conviction represents a "jeopardy" that triggers the bar against a second prosecution for the same offense. After the Supreme Court's decision in *United States v. Dixon,* the Connecticut Supreme Court revisited its decision in *State v. Lonergan,* 566 A.2d 677 (Conn. 1989) and adopted the *Blockburger* "same elements" approach. *State v. Alvarez,* 778 A.2d 938 (Conn. 2001).

In 1994 the U.S. Supreme Court invalidated a Montana tax on the possession of illegal drugs, imposed on a party already convicted of possession of illegal drugs. The Court ruled that the added tax was punishment in violation of the Double Jeopardy Clause. *Dept. of Revenue of Montana v. Kurth Ranch,* 511 U.S. 767, 114 S.Ct. 1937, 128 L.Ed.2d 767 (1994). After a defendant won dismissal of DUI-related charges in Colorado on the basis that his driver's license had already been revoked because of the offense, defense attorneys began to assert a double jeopardy defense to DUI prosecutions. They argued that, on the basis of *Montana v. Kurth Ranch,* an administrative revocation of the accused's driver's license constituted "punishment" that barred a subsequent prosecution for DUI. In July 1996, the Colorado Supreme Court unanimously held that "imposition of criminal sanctions, subsequent to an administrative driver's license revocation proceeding does not constitute the imposition of multiple punishments and does not violate the Double Jeopardy Clause." *Deutschendorf v. People,* 920 P.2d 53, 61 (Colo. 1996). The court's opinion appears to be consistent with what other courts have said on this issue. In *United States v. Reyes,* 87 F.3d 676 (5th Cir. 1996), the government imposed a three-day unpaid suspension of a civilian air force

Double Jeopardy

In a high-profile case in 1992, four Los Angeles police officers were tried by jury in a California state court on charges arising out of the beating of Rodney King, an African American motorist stopped by the police for traffic infractions. The event was videotaped by an onlooker and televised nationally. The jury's verdict of not guilty was followed by considerable outrage and large-scale rioting in Los Angeles. Despite the acquittal on state charges, the federal government brought new charges against the officers for violating King's civil rights. Their pleas that the new federal charges were barred by the Double Jeopardy Clause of the Fifth Amendment were rejected by the U.S. District Court, and in April 1993 two of the four officers were convicted after a jury trial. 833 F. Supp. 769. On appeal, the Ninth Circuit said that "there is no evidence that the federal prosecution was a 'sham' or a 'cover' for the state prosecution."

United States v. Koon, 34 F.3d 1416 (9th Cir. 1994).

employee for operating a motor vehicle while intoxicated on an air force base. In that instance, the court held, the government was acting as an employer, not as a sovereign, and the suspension was not "punishment" under the Double Jeopardy Clause.

As we noted earlier, the dual sovereignty of the federal government and the states allow separate trials of a defendant for the same offense. In the past, this has not been a major problem because it has been governmental policy not to cause duplicate prosecutions. Some deviations from this policy have occurred in recent years, however.

Statutes of Limitation

A **statute of limitations** is a legislative enactment that places a time limit on the prosecution of a crime. Common law placed no time limits on prosecution. There is no federal constitutional basis to limit the time in which a prosecution can be initiated. Nonetheless, the federal government and almost all states have enacted laws that prescribe certain time limits for prosecution of most offenses, excluding murder. There are two primary public policy reasons for enacting statutes of limitations on the prosecution of crimes. First, it is generally accepted that a person should not be under threat of prosecution for too long a period. Second, after a prolonged period, proof is either unavailable or, if available, may not be credible.

Statutes of limitations seldom place time limits on prosecutions for murder and other very serious offenses. This was dramatized in 1994, when Byron de la Beckwith was convicted for the June 1963 murder of Medgar Evers. Evers was an official of the National Association for the Advancement of Colored People, and his death galvanized support for the enactment of civil rights laws in the 1960s. Two trials in 1964 ended in deadlocked juries. But after extended litigation and a lapse of more than thirty years since the victim's death, a Mississippi jury found Beckwith guilty of killing Evers. On December 22, 1997, the Mississippi Supreme Court affirmed Beckwith's conviction. *Beckwith v. State,* 707 So.2d 547 (Miss. 1997).

Under most statutes of limitations, the period for prosecution begins when a crime is committed rather than when it is discovered. The period ends when an arrest warrant is issued, an indictment is returned, or an information is filed. The period of limitations is interrupted while a perpetrator is a fugitive or conceals himself or herself from authorities. This cessation of the statute of limitations is often referred to as the **tolling** of the statutory period.

Federal statutes of limitations provide a five-year limitation on the prosecution of noncapital crimes. 18 U.S.C.A. § 3282 *et seq.* Although limitation periods vary among the states, the Ohio law appears representative:

Except as otherwise provided in this section, a prosecution shall be barred unless it is commenced within the following periods after an offense is committed:

(1) For a felony other than aggravated murder or murder, six years;

(2) For a misdemeanor other than a minor misdemeanor, two years;

(3) For a minor misdemeanor, six months.

Page's Ohio Rev. Code Ann. § 2901.13 (A).

There is a conflict among the various jurisdictions as to whether a statute of limitations in a criminal action is an affirmative defense. An affirmative defense that is not pled is ordinarily deemed waived, but some courts have said that such a waiver must be knowing and voluntary. In *State v. Pearson,* 858 S.W.2d (Tenn. 1993), the Tennessee Supreme Court treated the statute of limitations as waivable by a defendant when it is about to run out, indicating that a defendant may wish to waive the protection of the statute. The court cited an instance where a defendant needs to gain time for plea bargaining and another instance where a defendant who is charged with a more serious offense that is not time-barred might want to waive the statute of limitations on a lesser included offense. But, as the court pointed out, any waiver of the statute of limitations must be knowingly and voluntarily entered. Other courts follow the rule that the statute of limitations is jurisdictional and that if the state's information or indictment discloses that the prosecution is initiated beyond the period allowed by the applicable statute of limitations, the prosecution is barred.

Defenses Based on Improper Government Conduct

There are two defenses that are based on improper government conduct. The defense of entrapment aims to prevent the government from manufacturing crime. This defense is widely asserted in prosecution for narcotics violations, for these cases are frequently based on undercover police operations. The defense of selective prosecution is infrequently imposed and has achieved very limited success. Nevertheless, it is designed to prevent the government from singling out an individual for prosecution based on impermissible grounds.

Entrapment

Law enforcement officers may provide an opportunity for a predisposed person to commit a crime, but they are not permitted to "manufacture" crime by implanting criminal ideas into innocent minds. Therefore, a person who has been induced to commit an offense under these latter circumstances may plead the defense of **entrapment.** A defendant who claims to have committed an offense as a result of inducement by an undercover police officer or a confidential police informant often asserts the defense of entrapment. It is not available to a defendant who has been entrapped by a person not associated with the government or police. See *Henderson v. United States,* 237 F.2d 169 (5th Cir. 1956).

Entrapment was not a defense under the common law, and, strictly speaking, it is not based on the Constitution. Nevertheless, it has long been recognized in federal and state courts in the United States. In 1980 the Tennessee Supreme Court acknowledged that Tennessee was the only state in the Union that did not allow entrapment as a defense and proceeded to remedy the situation by declaring, "From this day forward entrapment is a defense to a Tennessee criminal prosecution." *State v. Jones,* 598 S.W.2d 209, 212 (Tenn. 1980). In 1989 the Tennessee legislature codified the law on entrapment and required a defendant who pleads entrapment to so advise the prosecution. Tenn. Code Ann. § 39-11-505.

In a landmark case arising during Prohibition days, the U.S. Supreme Court held that a federal officer had entrapped a defendant by using improper inducements to cause him to buy illegal liquor for the officer. The Court observed that the evidence revealed that the defendant, Sorrells, had not been predisposed to commit a crime but had been induced by the government agent to do so. The Court opined that entrapment occurs when criminal conduct involved is "the product of the creative activity of [law enforcement officers]." *Sorrells v. United States,* 287 U.S. 435, 451, 53 S.Ct. 210, 216, 77 L.Ed. 413, 422 (1932).

In *Sorrells,* the majority of the justices viewed entrapment as an issue of whether the defendant's criminal intent originated in the mind of the officer or whether the defendant was predisposed to commit the offense. This focus on the predisposition of the defendant has come to be known as the **subjective test of entrapment.** A minority of justices in *Sorrells* would have applied what is now known as the **objective test of entrapment.** Under this view, the court would simply determine whether the police methods were so improper that they likely induced or ensnared a person into committing a crime.

In the past, the majority of federal and state courts followed the subjective view. Thus, a person who pled entrapment was held to have admitted commission of the offense. See, for example, *United States v. Sedigh,* 658 F.2d 1010 (5th Cir. 1981); *State v. Amodei,* 563 P.2d 440 (Kan. 1977). A jury would then proceed to determine whether the defendant committed the crime because of a predisposition or was improperly induced to do so by the police.

The subjective approach to entrapment has the disadvantage of not providing the police with any bright lines for enforcement. Moreover, in proving predisposition, the prosecutor often brings in evidence of a defendant's past conduct that may be otherwise inadmissible. This can prejudice the jury with respect to arriving at a verdict on the principal offense charged.

In *United States v. Dion,* 762 F.2d 674 (8th Cir. 1985), modified, 476 U.S. 734 (1986), the U.S. Court of Appeals for the Eighth Circuit provided a detailed list of factors appropriate for distinguishing predisposed defendants from nonpredisposed defendants. They are:

(1) whether the defendant readily responded to the inducement offered;

(2) the circumstances surrounding the illegal conduct;

(3) "the state of mind of a defendant before government agents make any suggestion that he shall commit a crime";

(4) whether the defendant was engaged in an existing course of conduct similar to the crime for which he is charged;

(5) whether the defendant had already formed the "design" to commit the crime for which he is charged;

(6) the defendant's reputation;

(7) the conduct of the defendant during the negotiations with the undercover agent;

(8) whether the defendant has refused to commit similar acts on other occasions;

(9) the nature of the crime charged; and

(10) "[t]he degree of coercion present in the instigation law officers have contributed to the transaction" relative to the "defendant's criminal background."

Although the traditional view of courts has been that a defendant who asserts entrapment as a defense admits the offense charged, there have been conflicting decisions in the federal courts between this view and the more modern view, which holds that a defendant may assert entrapment without being required to concede commission of the crime or any element thereof. The U.S. Supreme Court resolved the issue in *Mathews v. United States,* 485 U.S. 58, 108 St. 883, 99 L.Ed.2d 54 (1988). The Court ruled that a defendant who pleads entrapment does not necessarily admit to the crime charged or any element thereof. The Court's decision affects only the federal courts; state courts vary in their approach as to whether a defendant who pleads entrapment admits the crime charged, their views sometimes being based on state laws providing for the defense of entrapment.

Where courts follow the objective view, the judge, not the jury, determines whether the police methods were so improper as to constitute entrapment. See, for example, *People v. D'Angelo,* 257 N.W.2d 655 (Mich. 1977). Some federal courts have simply said that where police conduct is outrageous, it becomes a question of law for the judge to determine whether governmental misconduct is so shocking as to be a violation of due process of law. See, for example, *United States v. Wylie,* 625 F.2d 1371 (9th Cir. 1980). In courts that strictly follow the objective view, the defendant's predisposition to commit an offense is irrelevant. The objective approach has the advantage of enabling the courts to scrutinize governmental action to ensure that outrageous methods are not employed in seeking to ferret out crime.

In 1993 the Wyoming Supreme Court declined to adopt the objective theory of entrapment. Nevertheless, it indicated that a defendant can rely on "outrageous government conduct" as a defense if the circumstances reveal police conduct that violates fundamental fairness and is shocking to the universal sense of justice mandated by the Due Process Clauses of the Fifth and Fourteenth Amendments. *Rivera v. State,* 846 P.2d 1 (Wyo. 1993).

Recent decisions indicate that the subjective and objective tests can coexist. Some state courts now first determine whether a defendant who pleads entrapment has been ensnared by outrageous police methods. If so, the judge dismisses the charges against the ensnared defendant. If not, the court then allows the defendant to attempt to establish the defense of entrapment by proving improper inducement. The prosecution usually counters with evidence showing the defendant's prior criminal activity and ready acquiescence in committing the crime charged. The court then instructs the jury to determine whether the defendant committed the crime because of his or her predisposition or through inducement by the police. At least two states have adopted this general approach. *Cruz v. State,* 465 So.2d 516 (Fla. 1985); *State v. Talbot,* 364 A.2d 9 (N.J. 1976).

Dissatisfied with the Florida Supreme Court's decision in *Cruz v. State,* which provided for the trial court to first determine whether a defendant who pleads entrapment has been ensnared by outrageous police methods, the Florida legislature enacted a new subjective-model entrapment statute. West's Fla. Stat. 777.201. After passage of the statute, the Supreme Court of Florida held that, in enacting section 777.201, the legislature effectively eliminated the objective test in *Cruz.* Nevertheless, the court observed that the legislature cannot prohibit the judiciary from objectively reviewing the issue of entrapment to the extent such a review involves the Due Process Clause of Article I, Section 9 of the Florida Constitution. *Munoz v. State,* 629 So.2d 90 (Fla. 1993).

Two principal reasons account for the increased assertion of the defense of entrapment in recent years. First, numerous violations of narcotics laws have been prosecuted

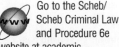

Go to the Scheb/ Scheb Criminal Law and Procedure 6e website at academic .cengage.com/criminaljustice/ scheb for an edited version of *Cruz v. State.*

A Promise of Sex—Entrapment as a Matter of Law

Law enforcement officers told a female that she might not be prosecuted for possession of cocaine if she would become a confidential informant. She agreed and met with the defendant, James Banks, a suspected drug dealer, on two nights. The meetings included "kissing and hugging," after which she told Banks that if he "could get her something [they] would get together for the weekend, fool around and party." The defendant obtained some cocaine for her, and as a result, he was arrested. The trial judge dismissed the charges because the uncontested facts established that the officers used a method with a substantial risk of persuading or inducing the defendant to commit a criminal offense.

The state appealed the dismissal. The appellate court affirmed: "When law enforcement agencies utilize confidential informants who use sex, or the express or implied promise thereof, to obtain contraband the defendant did not already possess, there is no way for the courts or anyone else to determine whether such inducement served only to uncover an existing propensity or created a new one. This violates the threshold objective test."

State v. Banks, 499 So.2d 894 (Fla. App. 1986).

on the basis of undercover police activity and evidence given by confidential police informants. Second, there has been increased attention to prosecuting corruption involving government officials.

One of the most highly publicized cases resulted from the 1980 Abscam operation, in which FBI agents posed as wealthy Arab businessmen and attempted to buy influence from members of Congress. Despite their claims of entrapment, several members of Congress were found guilty of offenses involving misuse of office. See, for example, *United States v. Jenrette*, 744 F.2d 817 (D.C. Cir. 1984).

In 1987 Keith Jacobson was indicted for violating the Child Protection Act of 1984, 18 U.S.C.A. § 2252(a)(2)(A), which criminalizes the knowing receipt through the mails of a "visual depiction [that] involves the use of a minor engaging in sexually explicit conduct." At trial, Jacobson contended the government entrapped him into committing the crime. A jury found him guilty, and his conviction was affirmed by the court of appeals. The U.S. Supreme Court granted review.

In evaluating the evidence at Jacobson's trial, the Supreme Court found that when it was still legal to do so, Jacobson ordered some magazines containing photos of nude boys. After Congress enacted the Child Protection Act, making this illegal, two government agencies learned that Jacobson had ordered the magazines. The agencies sent mail to Jacobson through fictitious organizations to explore his willingness to break the law. He was literally bombarded with solicitations, which included communications decrying censorship and questioning the legitimacy and constitutionality of the government's efforts to restrict availability of sexually explicit materials. He finally responded to an undercover solicitation to order child pornography and was arrested after a controlled delivery of the explicit sexual materials.

After pointing out that for twenty-six months government agents had made Jacobson the target of repeated mailings, the Court held that the prosecution failed to produce evidence that Jacobson was predisposed to break the law before the government directed its efforts toward him. Adding that government agents may not implant a criminal design in an innocent person's mind and then induce commission of a crime, the Court reversed his conviction, observing that Congress had not intended

Rejecting the Defense of Selective Prosecution

In 1982 David Alan Wayte was indicted for willfully failing to register under the Military Selective Service Act. Wayte sought dismissal of the indictment on the ground of selective prosecution. He contended that he and the others being prosecuted had been singled out of an estimated 674,000 nonregistrants because they had voiced opposition to the Selective Service requirements. The district court dismissed the indictment on the ground that the government had failed to rebut Wayte's *prima facie* showing of selective prosecution. The case was eventually heard by the U.S. Supreme Court. The Court held that the government's passive enforcement policy, under which it prosecuted only those nonregistrants who reported themselves or were reported by others, did not violate the First or Fifth Amendments to the Constitution.

Wayte v. United States, 470 U.S. 598, 105 S.Ct. 1524, 84 L.Ed.2d 547 (1985).

Go to the Scheb/ Scheb Criminal Law and Procedure 6e website at academic .cengage.com/criminaljustice/ scheb for an edited version of *Jacobson v. U.S.*

for government officials to instigate crime by luring persons otherwise innocent to commit offenses. *Jacobson v. United States,* 503 U.S. 540, 112 S.Ct. 1535, 118 L.Ed.2d 174 (1992).

In 1994 the U.S. Court of Appeals for the Seventh Circuit rendered an *en banc* decision holding that when a defendant pleads entrapment, the government must prove that the defendant was not only "willing" to commit the offense charged but also that he or she was "ready" to commit the offense in the absence of official encouragement. *United States v. Hollingsworth,* 27 F.3d 1196 (7th Cir. 1994).

Because the Supreme Court's decision in *Jacobson v. United States* is not grounded on constitutional principles, it affects only federal law enforcement activities. Nonetheless, it signals state enforcement authorities not to play on the weaknesses of innocent parties to beguile them into committing crimes.

Selective Prosecution

Selective enforcement of the criminal law is not itself a constitutional violation; therefore, without more, it does not constitute a defense. *Oyler v. Boles,* 368 U.S. 448, 82 S.Ct. 501, 7 L.Ed.2d 446 (1962). There are many cases rejecting the defense of **selective prosecution.** To prevail, a defendant must ordinarily demonstrate that other similarly situated persons have not been prosecuted for similar conduct and that the defendant's selection for prosecution was based on some impermissible ground such as race, religion, or exercise of the First Amendment rights of free speech. *United States v. Jennings,* 991 F.2d 725 (11th Cir.1993); *United States v. Arias,* 575 F.2d 253 (9th Cir. 1978).

In 1996 the Supreme Court reviewed a case where defendants indicted for federal narcotics violations filed a pretrial motion for the discovery of information that they contended would show that they were being selectively prosecuted because of their race. The Court held that the defendants failed to establish an entitlement to discovery based on their claim because they failed to produce any credible evidence that similarly situated defendants of other races could have been prosecuted but were not. *United States v. Armstrong,* 517 U.S. 456, 116 S.Ct. 1480, 134 L.Ed.2d 687 (1996).

In *United States v. Eagleboy,* 200 F.3d 1137 (8th Cir. 1999), the defendant, who was not a member of a federally recognized Indian tribe, was charged with possessing hawk parts in violation of the Migratory Bird Treaty Act (MBTA). Had the defendant been a member of a federally recognized Indian tribe, he would not have been charged with a violation of the MBTA. Pointing to this policy, the defendant moved to dismiss on the ground of selective prosecution. The U.S. Court of Appeals for the Eighth Circuit held that Eagleboy was not selectively prosecuted. The court said that the government's policy of not enforcing the act against recognized Indian tribes distinguished between persons on the basis of membership in a federally recognized Indian tribe, not on the basis of race.

Nontraditional Defenses

Although they are seldom successful, defendants sometimes employ **novel and innovative defenses.** We previously discussed the status of the battered women and battered children syndrome defenses, which, though not traditional, can no longer be considered novel. In this section, we discuss some of the more interesting novel defenses. These include unusual religious practices, the victim's negligence, premenstrual syndrome (PMS), compulsive gambling, post-traumatic stress syndrome (PTSS), the junk food defense, television intoxication, and pornographic intoxication. In instances where a novel defense leads to an acquittal, appellate courts do not have an opportunity to evaluate the legal basis of the defense. This is because the prosecution is not permitted to appeal an acquittal.

Unusual Religious Beliefs and Practices

The courts have long rejected contentions by defendants that they have been commanded by God or the scriptures to commit illegal acts. See *Hotema v. United States,* 186 U.S. 413, 22 S.Ct. 895, 46 L.Ed. 1225 (1902). Moreover, laws prohibiting religious rites that endanger the lives, health, or safety of the participants or others are customarily upheld by the courts. This is illustrated by the Kentucky Court of Appeals decision in *Lawson v. Commonwealth,* 164 S.W.2d 972 (Ky. 1942). There, despite the defendants' contentions that their constitutional guarantees of freedom of religion were violated, the court upheld the constitutionality of a statute making it a misdemeanor for anyone to handle snakes or reptiles in connection with any religious service.

Courts have traditionally upheld the right of parents to raise their children by their own religious beliefs, ruling that the state's interest must yield to the parents' religious beliefs that preclude medical treatment when the child's life is not immediately imperiled. See, for example, *In re Green,* 292 A.2d 387 (Pa. 1972). Nevertheless, the courts have held that where a child's life is imperiled, the parents have an affirmative duty to provide medical care that will protect the child's life. Thus, an appellate court upheld a conviction of parents for manslaughter when it found that a child's death was directly caused by the parents' failure to secure needed medical care. *Commonwealth v. Barnhart,* 497 A.2d 616 (Pa. Super. 1985). In about half of the states, child abuse and criminal neglect statutes permit parents to choose spiritual means or prayer as a response to illness without regard to a child's medical condition. In *State v. McKown,* 461 N.W.2d 720 (Minn. App. 1990), aff'd 475 N.W.2d 63 (1991), the court upheld the dismissal of manslaughter charges against a parent and stepparent who relied on spiritual means and failed to secure medical treatment for an eleven-year-old boy. The child died allegedly as a result of medical problems resulting from diabetes.

The need to furnish medical care to children poses a problem of balancing the parents' interests in bringing up their offspring in accordance with their religious beliefs against the interest of the state in the preservation of life. In January 1988, the press reported that the American Academy of Pediatrics urged the repeal of laws allowing parents to reject medical treatment for their children on religious grounds. The academy pointed out that about three-fourths of the states have laws that permit some rejection of medical care on religious or philosophical grounds. However, the academy noted that courts have frequently intervened to order certain treatments for minors.

Victim's Negligence

Federal and state courts hold that a victim's negligence, credulity, or wrongdoing is not a defense to a prosecution. *United States v. Kreimer,* 609 F.2d 126 (5th Cir. 1980); *State v. Lunz,* 273 N.W.2d 767 (Wis. 1979). Likewise, because a crime is an offense against society as well as against the victim, it follows that a victim's forgiveness or condoning does not relieve an actor of criminal responsibility.

Premenstrual Syndrome

Premenstrual syndrome (PMS) refers to certain physiological changes that occur in some women, usually in the days close to the onset of menstruation. This results from hormonal imbalance and can cause serious depression and irritability. In certain cases, medical treatment is required. Some argue that a woman so affected should be allowed to assert PMS as a defense to criminal conduct because some physicians say that PMS directly affects behavior. Nevertheless, PMS has not been accepted as a defense in the United States. In England, it has been recognized as a basis to mitigate punishment.

Compulsive Gambling

Evidence of compulsive gambling is generally not considered as a defense unless it rises to the level of insanity. For example, a defendant was convicted of entering a bank with intent to commit larceny and robbery. On appeal, he argued that the trial court erred in instructing the jury that "as a matter of law pathological gambling disorder is not a disease or defect within the meaning of the American Law Institute test for insanity." The U.S. Court of Appeals, while still applying the former ALI standard, rejected his contention. *United States v. Gould,* 741 F.2d 45 (4th Cir. 1984).

Post-Traumatic Stress Syndrome

Post-traumatic stress syndrome (PTSS) commonly refers to the unique stresses suffered during combat, often manifesting such symptoms as flashbacks, outbursts of anger, and blocked-out memories. After World War I, these conditions were usually referred to as "shell shock." Following World War II, the term "combat fatigue" was often used to describe such anxiety disorders. Present generations have heard these conditions described as "post-traumatic stress syndrome." Because of the bizarre type of warfare that service personnel endured in Vietnam, the unpopularity of the war, the availability of drugs, and the difficulties encountered in adjusting to civilian life, many veterans suffered severe psychological reactions. To a lesser extent, the stress of combat in Operation Desert Storm also caused delayed traumatic stress syndrome. Undoubtedly, the stress of combat operations in the present military operations in Afghanistan and Iraq can be expected to cause similar results.

Although not a legal defense in itself, in some instances PTSS may affect a defendant's understanding to the point of allowing a plea of insanity. More frequently, PTSS will be introduced as evidence bearing on a defendant's intent or offered at a sentencing hearing in an effort to mitigate punishment.

The "Junk Food" Defense

Dan White, a former city supervisor, shot and killed the mayor of San Francisco in 1978. Following this, he killed another supervisor, who was a leader of the local gay community. In defense to charges of first-degree murder, White's counsel sought to establish that his client was depressed by having gorged himself on junk food. White was convicted of manslaughter instead of murder, giving some credence to reports that the jury may have accepted White's defense. This was jury action, so it set no precedent to establish any such defense.

Television Intoxication

An adolescent boy was tried in Miami for the first-degree murder of an elderly woman. He attempted to establish insanity on the basis of psychiatric testimony concerning the effects of "involuntary subliminal television intoxication." The trial court rejected his claim. An appellate court, stating that the trial judge correctly limited the evidence to the requirements of the *M'Naghten* rule, found no difficulty in upholding the trial court's decision. *Zamora v. State*, 361 So.2d 776 (Fla. App. 1978).

Pornographic Intoxication

There is a lively academic debate over the effect of pornography on the psyche. Does it stimulate sexual violence? Some defendants have attempted to employ a "pornography intoxication defense," but with little success. For example, in *Schiro v. Clark*, 963 F.2d 962 (7th Cir. 1992), a federal appellate court held that acting under the influence of pornography could not be used to mitigate the defendant's death sentence for rape and murder.

XYY Chromosome Abnormality

Growing evidence indicates that a person's genes influence behavior, and there has been speculation in media reports that people accused of violent crimes might find a medical basis to assert a "my genes made me do it" defense. While this is not recognized as a specific defense, there is some medical evidence indicating that the presence of an extra Y chromosome may lead to physical and mental problems that cause an affected person to act aggressively. Some defendants have used evidence of this abnormality as a basis for the insanity defense.

Multiple Personality Defense

One who asserts a multiple personality argues that he or she did not commit the offense alleged; rather, another personality of which the defendant has no memory and no control committed the crime. In October 2000, the press reported that a woman named Mary in Kansas City, Missouri, who pled not guilty by reason of insanity to several offenses, contended that her multiple personalities were responsible for the deaths of her two young sons in 1999. Her lawyers and expert witnesses said she had severe psychosis and a personality named Sharon who controlled her actions. Notwithstanding her claim, the defendant was found guilty of murder and a series of child abuse charges.

Black Rage and Urban Survival Defenses

Based on claims that have developed over the years in response to perceptions of social needs are the black rage defense and the urban survival defense. These are usually offered with the hope that a defendant's punishment will be mitigated by the social conditions they expose.

In the black rage defense, some African American defendants charged with violent crime against a white person have sought to absolve or mitigate their conduct on the basis of years of oppression and racist hostility endured at the hands of white Americans. Proponents contend that as a result of racism, substandard education, inadequate employment opportunities, and substandard housing and medical care, African American defendants seek to justify retaliatory action against white citizens. Critics point out that if courts were to accept black rage as a legal defense, it could lead to an impossible task of assessing claims of discrimination by criminal defendants of a variety of ethnic, and even religious, backgrounds.

Similar to the black rage defense is the advocacy of an "urban survival syndrome" defense based upon a defendant's having lived under substandard environmental conditions in a deteriorated urban neighborhood plagued with drug dealers and acts of violence that often include threats of deadly force.

■ CONCLUSION

Despite the fact that the prosecution has met its burden of proving the elements of a crime, a defendant has the opportunity to not only dispute such proof but also to affirmatively assert defenses to the conduct charged. A defendant may assert the incapacity to commit a crime. The law does not hold an insane person responsible, but as we have pointed out, legislatures and courts continue to struggle with the definition of insanity and the disposition of persons found to be insane. Young children are not held responsible, but, here again, the law encounters problems in determining at what age a child should be held responsible for crime. The use of alcohol and drugs now plagues the courts, as evidenced by the various approaches now taken to defenses asserting voluntary intoxication.

A person's right to use reasonable force in self-defense and defense of habitation and property has always been regarded as basic in Anglo American jurisprudence, yet in modern society it becomes increasingly difficult to determine the extent of force that may be used in other situations. The use of force by police, by parents, and by guardians and teachers who serve *in loco parentis* often present difficult questions. To what extent should police be permitted to use force in making arrests? When does the legitimate use of disciplinary force cease and child abuse begin? And what about the battered woman who seeks to justify her use of force against a charge of homicide or assault on the man she lives with? Or the abused child who assaults his or her parent?

Mistake of fact and mistake of law are merely expository of the commonsense foundation of the criminal law. They are a part of the civilized application of law. So too are the defenses of necessity and duress. However, courts have not been receptive to claims of necessity based on sociopolitical claims. Nor have they been receptive to claims of duress on the ground of economic coercion.

The defenses of immunity and double jeopardy are based squarely on the Constitution. The statute of limitations defense emerged from our penchant for certainty and our distrust of prosecutions resting on stale testimony. Our inherent distaste for "frame-ups" and outrageous conduct by the police has caused entrapment to become a viable defense to admitted criminal conduct.

The concepts of criminal responsibility and of criminal defenses will continue to evolve in response to our increased knowledge of human behavior and society's balance of the rights of the individual against society's legitimate demand for protection. Some nontraditional defenses could become viable, given new social science and medical research. In some instances, a nontraditional defense may result in the defendant's acquittal, may lead to a conviction for a lesser offense, or may be a mitigating factor in sentencing.

■ KEY TERMS

criminal responsibility, 344
negative defense, 344
burden of production of evidence, 344
preponderance of the evidence, 344
affirmative defense, 344
infancy, 345
intoxication, 346
voluntary intoxication, 346
involuntary intoxication, 346
insanity, 348
not guilty by reason of insanity, 348
M'Naghten rule, 348
irresistible impulse, 348
Durham test, 349
ALI Standard, 349
substantial capacity test, 349
right from wrong test, 349
Insanity Defense Reform Act of 1984, 349
clear and convincing evidence standard, 349
beyond a reasonable doubt, 349
guilty but mentally ill, 350
automatism, 352
alibi, 353
duress, 353
battered woman syndrome, 353
necessity, 354
mistake of law, 356
mistake of fact, 357
justifiable use of force, 359
deadly force, 359

nondeadly force, 359
self-defense, 359
retreat rule, 360
objective test for the use of deadly force, 360
subjective standard of reasonableness, 360
battered child syndrome, 362
reasonable force, 362
defense of others, 363
defense of habitation, 363
castle doctrine, 364
immunity, 367
use immunity, 367
transactional immunity, 367
contractual immunity, 368
diplomatic immunity, 368
double jeopardy, 368
insufficient evidence, 369
weight of the evidence, 369
manifest necessity, 369
Blockburger test, 369
same evidence test, 370
same elements test, 370
statute of limitations, 371
tolling, 371
entrapment, 372
subjective test of entrapment, 373
objective test of entrapment, 373
selective prosecution, 376
novel and innovative defenses, 377

■ WEB-BASED RESEARCH ACTIVITY

Use the Internet to examine your state statute dealing with the insanity defense and any judicial decisions interpreting the statute. What is the test for determining insanity in your state? Who bears the burden of proof? What is the standard of proof? What are the rules governing the introduction of psychiatric testimony?

■ QUESTIONS FOR THOUGHT AND DISCUSSION

1. In general, courts permit intoxication evidence only to the extent that it negates the *mens rea* of a specific-intent crime. Should evidence of voluntary intoxication be allowed for both general-intent and specific-intent crimes? Several states

have recently enacted statutes making voluntary intoxication inadmissible as a defense to any crime. What position have the courts of your state taken on this issue?

2. What is the test for insanity in your state? Who has the burden of proof once the defendant introduces some evidence of insanity? Do you think the test in your state adequately protects (a) the public and (b) the defendant's rights?

3. Should the courts recognize battered woman syndrome as a defense to assaultive and homicidal crimes by a woman living with a man who continually batters her? What position does your state take on this issue?

4. Explain the difference between the objective and subjective approaches to the defense of entrapment. Which approach is more just? Why?

5. Should the law require a person to retreat when attacked in his or her own home? Should the law make a distinction between co-occupants? Explain the justification for your view.

6. A few states have recently enacted statutes removing any duty to retreat if a person is attacked in a vehicle where he or she has a right to be. Some allow a person attacked to presume the attacker intends to do bodily harm and allows the vehicle occupant to use any force necessary in defense, with no duty to retreat. Supporters often characterize them as "stand your ground" laws. Some opponents call them "shoot first" laws. Do you think such laws are justifiable?

7. Increasingly, states have enacted "anti-hazing" laws aimed particularly at the initiation procedures of certain fraternal organizations. Most make it a misdemeanor; a few make it a felony where serious injury results from hazing. Should these laws permit defendants accused of hazing to assert the victim's consent as a defense?

8. The Fifth Amendment to the U.S. Constitution requires the court to grant use immunity to a witness who is required to testify over a legitimately invoked right of self-incrimination. In some states, a witness who testifies under a grant of immunity is given transactional immunity, a broader protection than the federal constitution requires. Explain the difference between the two categories of immunity.

9. To what extent, if at all, do you think the courts should interfere with the right of a parent to opt for spiritual, as opposed to medical, healing for a child who suffers from a curable disease?

10. Can one make a credible argument that any one of the nontraditional defenses outlined in the chapter should be accepted as a defense to criminal conduct?

11. The majority of courts hold that ignorance or even a *bona fide* belief that a minor is of legal age does not constitute a defense to prosecution of such strict liability offenses as (a) voluntary sexual relations with a minor and (b) sale of intoxicating liquor to a minor. Do you think a state should adopt a statute that would excuse such offenses where the defendant made an inquiry as to a person's age and the person appeared to be of legal age?

12. The maxim "ignorance of the law is no excuse" is derived from an age when laws were much simpler than today's sophisticated legal codes. Assume you are working as a staff person for a state legislator who tells you she intends to introduce a bill to "clearly define when a person's 'mistake of the law' should be excused." She asks you to do some research and prepare a memorandum of points that such a bill should include to enable her to discuss her proposal with a legislative committee. What are some of the key points that you would recommend?

■ PROBLEMS FOR DISCUSSION AND SOLUTION

1. While taking his nightly walk, Charley Goodneighbor saw Joe Macho commit a battery on Charlene Loverly, a fourteen-year-old girl. Goodneighbor came to Loverly's defense and struck Macho so hard it fractured his skull. The police arrested both Macho and Goodneighbor. Goodneighbor explained to the police that he came to Loverly's aid to prevent her from being injured by Macho. What factors will the prosecutor probably consider in determining whether to file charges against Goodneighbor?

2. Nathan Ninja, who holds a black belt in karate, arrives at his home to find an intruder fleeing from the garage. Ninja pursues the intruder across the front yard and catches him in the street. An exchange of blows renders the intruder unconscious. A medical examination reveals substantial brain damage to the intruder as a result of the blows inflicted by Ninja. In a prosecution for aggravated battery, can Ninja successfully assert as a defense that his use of force was necessary to protect his habitation?

3. Sally Shopper drives a 1995 gray Honda Accord. She parks it in a shopping center lot while she shops. Two hours later, Shopper enters a car parked nearby that is almost identical to hers. As she drives away, the owner spots her and demands that a nearby police officer stop her. Just as the officer approaches her, Shopper realizes that she is in someone else's vehicle. Had she looked at the vehicle more carefully, she would have observed that it had a license tag from a different state and some unique bumper stickers. On complaint of the owner, the officer arrests Shopper and charges her with theft. What is Shopper likely to assert in her defense?

4. A destitute homeless man steals food from a convenience market. When prosecuted for theft, he pleads the defense of necessity. The prosecutor urges the trial judge to strike the defense on the ground that the defendant could have qualified for assistance from local welfare organizations. Should the defendant be allowed to present his defense to the jury? Do you think he has a credible defense? Why or why not?

5. A defendant was found guilty of having forcible sexual intercourse with a fifteen-year-old female of previous chaste character. He is charged, convicted, and sentenced for violating two statutes: (a) common-law rape involving force and lack of consent and (b) statutory rape involving intercourse with a minor of previous chaste character. On appeal, the defendant contends that his sentence violates the Double Jeopardy Clause of the Fifth Amendment. What arguments are his counsel likely to present to the appellate court? What should be the appellate court's decision?

6. The police suspect Mary Jane Hemphill of having sold marijuana at the Sibanac Bar. An undercover agent approaches her and asks her to go out with him. After a movie, the agent says that he would like to buy some marijuana for his close friend. At first, Hemphill makes no response. They make another date, and after a very pleasant evening together, the undercover agent pleads with Hemphill to help him find marijuana for his friend. She agrees, and the next day she delivers a quantity of the contraband to the agent, who gives her $200. As he concludes his purchase, the undercover agent arrests Hemphill and charges her with the sale of contraband. Hemphill's attorney pleads entrapment at her trial. Do you think her defense will be successful? Why or why not?

7. Boris Bottlemore has just finished celebrating his new job promotion by consuming ten double shots of bourbon in a bar near his home. He staggers from

the bar to his home, which is one of twenty identical row houses on his block. In his inebriated state, Bottlemore mistakes his neighbor's home for his own. Finding the door unlocked, he enters and promptly raids the refrigerator. He then collapses on a couch in the living room and passes out. The next morning, Patty Purebred is shocked to find a stranger sleeping in her living room and her refrigerator standing open, with food strewn across the kitchen floor. She telephones the police, who arrive and take Bottlemore into custody, charging him with burglary. What defense or defenses are available to Bottlemore? How would you assess his chances before a jury?

PART THREE

Law Enforcement and Criminal Procedure

CHAPTER **15**

Search and Seizure

**CHAPTER
OUTLINE**

Introduction

Search and seizure have always been essential tools of law enforcement. A **search** occurs when government agents look for evidence in a manner that intrudes into a person's legally protected zone of privacy. A **seizure** takes place when agents take possession or control of property or persons. Today, as America simultaneously prosecutes a "war on drugs" and a "war on terrorism," search and seizure are crucial issues for law enforcement agencies, courts, and citizens. Without the powers to conduct searches and seize evidence, law enforcement agencies would be unable to perform their historic missions, let alone combat drug trafficking, organized crime, and international terrorism. On the other hand, unrestricted powers of search and seizure are antithetical to the American traditions of individual liberty and limited government.

Because search and seizure often entail serious invasions of privacy, the power of law enforcement agencies to conduct searches and seizures is limited by the federal and state constitutions and by a number of federal and state statutes. Most important among these legal limitations is the Fourth Amendment to the U.S. Constitution, which provides:

> The right of the people to be secure in their persons, houses, papers and effects, against unreasonable searches and seizures, shall not be violated, and no Warrants shall issue but upon probable cause, supported by Oath or affirmation, and particularly describing the place to be searched and the persons or things to be seized.

As a general rule, the Fourth Amendment requires law enforcement officers to obtain a **warrant** before conducting searches and seizures. Although some warrantless searches and seizures are permissible, they all must conform to a standard of reasonableness. Law enforcement officers are not permitted to conduct searches and seizures arbitrarily or even based on their hunches about criminal activity. For a search to be reasonable under the Fourth Amendment, police generally must have **probable cause** to believe that a search will produce evidence of crime. In certain instances, police may conduct limited searches based on the lesser standard of **reasonable suspicion.** Subject to certain exceptions, evidence obtained through unreasonable searches and seizures is not admissible in criminal prosecutions.

Historical Background

Before the late seventeenth century, there was very little protection at common law against invasions of privacy by unreasonable searches and seizures. Although a system of warrants had long been in place to provide legal authority for arrests, searches, and seizures, executive as well as judicial authorities could issue warrants. Moreover, there was no requirement that a search warrant specify the location to be searched or the items to be seized. For hundreds of years, English subjects (and, later, American colonists) were subjected to the abuse of the **general warrant**—that is, a warrant authorizing searches of unspecified persons and places.

In the wake of the Glorious Revolution of 1688, English courts began to place more stringent and effective limitations on the Crown's power. The power of search and seizure was one area in which courts moved to limit royal authority.

By far the most significant English case in the area of search and seizure before the American Revolution was *Entick v. Carrington,* 95 Eng. Rep. 807 (1765). John Entick, who edited a newspaper highly critical of the government, was arrested on a charge of seditious libel. A warrant was issued calling for the seizure of all his books, letters, and papers. Entick successfully sued for trespass. On appeal, the judgment was upheld and the practice of general warrants declared illegal. The opinion in *Entick v. Carrington* proved to be very influential. The next year, Parliament declared the notorious general warrant invalid. Addressing the House of Commons, William Pitt declared that

> [t]he poorest man may, in his cottage, bid defiance to all the forces of the Crown. It may be frail; its roof may shake; the wind may blow through it; the storm may enter; but the King of England may not enter; all his force dares not cross the threshold of the ruined tenement.

Adoption of the Fourth Amendment

Although the common law provided some protection against general warrants, the framers of the Bill of Rights adopted a more explicit, and more thorough, proscription of unreasonable searches and seizures. To a great extent they were motivated by a distaste for the Writs of Assistance, which gave customs officials in the American colonies unlimited powers to search for smuggled goods. In a famous debate in 1761, James Otis called the Writs of Assistance "the worst instrument of arbitrary power, the most destructive of English liberty and the fundamental principles of law, that ever was found in an English law book." Quoted in *Boyd v. United States,* 116 U.S. 616, 625, 6 S.Ct. 524, 529, 29 L.Ed. 746, 749 (1886). The Fourth Amendment was adopted to ensure that officials of the U.S. government would never be able to exercise such unlimited powers of search and seizure.

Their distaste for general warrants led the framers of the Bill of Rights to write a particularity requirement into the Warrant Clause of the Fourth Amendment. The Supreme Court has recognized that "limiting the authorization to search to the specific areas and things for which there is probable cause to search … ensures that the

SUPREME COURT PERSPECTIVE

Weeks v. United States, 232 U.S. 383, 34 S.Ct. 341, 58 L.Ed. 652 (1914)

In this landmark decision, the U.S. Supreme Court held that evidence obtained by federal agents in violation of the Fourth Amendment is inadmissible in a federal criminal trial.

JUSTICE WILLIAM R. DAY delivered the opinion of the court, saying in part:
The effect of the 4th Amendment is to put the courts of the United States and Federal officials, in the exercise of their power and authority, under limitations and restraints as to the exercise of such power and authority, and to forever secure the people, their persons, houses, papers, and effects, against all unreasonable searches and seizures under the guise of law. This protection reaches all alike, whether accused of crime or not, and the duty of giving to it force and effect is obligatory upon all entrusted under our Federal system with the enforcement of the laws. The tendency of those who execute the criminal laws of the country to obtain conviction by means of unlawful seizures and enforced confessions, the latter often obtained after subjecting accused persons to unwarranted practices destructive of rights secured by the Federal Constitution, should find no sanction in the judgments of the courts, which are charged at all times with the support of the Constitution, and to which people of all conditions have a right to appeal for the maintenance of such fundamental rights.

search will be carefully tailored to its justifications, and will not take on the character of the wide-ranging exploratory searches the Framers intended to prohibit." *Maryland v. Garrison*, 480 U.S. 79, 84, 107 S.Ct. 1013, 1016, 94 L.Ed.2d 72, 80 (1987).

Extension of the Fourth Amendment to Apply to State and Local Action

The Fourth Amendment, like all the protections of the Bill of Rights, was originally conceived as a limitation on the powers of the newly created national government. Under the original conception of the Bill of Rights, citizens seeking legal protection against actions of state and local governments had to look to their state constitutions and state courts for relief. *Barron v. Baltimore*, 32 U.S. (7 Pet.) 243, 8 L.Ed. 672 (1833). However, the protection of the Fourth Amendment, along with most of the protections contained in the Bill of Rights, has been extended to defendants in state criminal prosecutions on the basis of the Fourteenth Amendment's limitations on state action. In 1949 the Supreme Court held that the freedom from unreasonable searches and seizures is "implicit in 'the concept of ordered liberty' and as such enforceable against the States through the Due Process Clause [of the Fourteenth Amendment]." *Wolf v. Colorado*, 338 U.S. 25, 27–28, 69 S.Ct. 1359, 1361, 93 L.Ed. 1782, 1785 (1949). The judicial extension of the Fourth Amendment and other protections of the Bill of Rights to limit the actions of the state and local governments are referred to as the **doctrine of incorporation.** Under this doctrine, provisions of the Bill of Rights deemed to be essential to a scheme of ordered liberty are incorporated into the Fourteenth Amendment's broad limitations on state and local authority. *Palko v. Connecticut*, 302 U.S. 319, 58 S.Ct. 149, 82 L.Ed. 288 (1937).

JUDICIAL FEDERALISM AND THE FOURTH AMENDMENT

As a result of *Wolf v. Colorado,* supra, the Fourth Amendment limits search and seizure activities by law enforcement agencies at all levels of government, whether federal, state, or local. The application of the Fourth Amendment to state prosecutions ensures a minimal national standard governing search and seizure. Under our system of federalism, state courts are free to provide higher levels of protection for individuals under applicable provisions of their state constitutions than are provided by the Fourth Amendment. But they cannot provide less protection to the individual without running afoul of the Fourteenth Amendment. Indeed, this is true of all constitutional protections. As long as state courts make clear that decisions that favor the rights of suspects, defendants, and prisoners rest on independent state constitutional grounds, those decisions are not subject to review by the federal courts. *Michigan v. Long*, 463 U.S. 1032, 103 S.Ct. 3469, 77 L.Ed.2d 1201 (1983).

State constitutional law in the search and seizure area has become extremely complex, as there are numerous issues on which certain state courts have refused to follow federal decisions restricting Fourth Amendment protections. We will mention a few examples on the pages that follow. In an attempt to reduce confusion and unnecessary complexity owing to different federal and state standards of search and seizure, Florida amended its constitution in 1982 to render its prohibition of unreasonable searches and seizures coextensive with that of the Fourth Amendment. West's Fla. Const. Art. 1, § 12 (as amended 1982). Interpreting this novel amendment, the Florida Supreme Court has held that, in effect, the Florida Constitution incorporates all decisions of the U.S. Supreme Court interpreting the Fourth Amendment, regardless of when they were rendered. *Bernie v. State*, 524 So.2d 988 (Fla. 1988).

When, Where, and to Whom the Fourth Amendment Applies

Because the Constitution limits government action, the Fourth Amendment protects a person's rights against the police and other government agents but not against searches and seizures conducted by private individuals. The Supreme Court has said that the Fourth Amendment "is wholly inapplicable to a search or seizure, even an unreasonable one, effected by a private individual not acting as an agent of the Government or with the participation or knowledge of any government official." *United States v. Jacobsen,* 466 U.S. 109, 113, 104 S.Ct. 1652, 1656, 80 L.Ed.2d 85, 94 (1984). In determining whether a private citizen has acted as an agent of the government, the court must consider (1) whether the government knew of and acquiesced in the activity and (2) whether the citizen was motivated on the basis of assisting the government. *United States v. Feffer,* 831 F.2d 734, 739 (7th Cir. 1987). Thus, a search by a privately employed security guard is ordinarily considered a search by a private citizen. Likewise, a search of a package by an employee of a common carrier is not considered a violation of the Fourth Amendment unless the search was instigated by government action. *United States v. Monroe,* 943 F.2d 884 (8th Cir. 1991).

Border Searches and Searches Outside the United States

Go to the Scheb/ Scheb Criminal Law and Procedure 6e website at academic .cengage.com/criminaljustice/ scheb for an edited version of *Rochin v. California.*

Travelers crossing the borders of the United States are routinely subjected to searches even when they are not the targets of suspicion. Suspicionless **border searches** are justified by the view that persons crossing the national border are not entitled to the protections of the Fourth Amendment. *United States v. Ramsey,* 431 U.S. 606, 97 S.Ct. 1972, 52 L.Ed.2d 617 (1977). This is not to say that agents conducting border searches are beyond the law. Regardless of the applicability of the Fourth Amendment, methods of search and seizure may not be so severe or extreme as to "shock the conscience." *Rochin v. California,* 342 U.S. 165, 72 S.Ct. 205, 96 L.Ed. 183 (1952).

The border search exception to the Fourth Amendment extends to searches conducted at established stations near the border or other functional equivalents of a border search. An example would be the search of a ship when it first docks after entering the territorial waters of the United States. *United States v. Prince,* 491 F.2d 655 (5th Cir. 1974). On the other hand, in *Almeida-Sanchez v. United States,* 413 U.S. 266, 93 S.Ct. 2535, 37 L.Ed.2d 596 (1973), the Supreme Court invalidated a search by a roving patrol some twenty-five miles within the border because agents lacked probable cause.

The Fourth Amendment does not apply to searches and seizures conducted by U.S. agents outside the territory of the United States. The purpose of the amendment is to restrict only those searches and seizures conducted domestically. *United States v. Verdugo-Urquidez,* 494 U.S. 259, 110 S.Ct. 1056, 108 L.Ed.2d 222 (1990).

The Home, Its Curtilage, and the Open Fields Doctrine

The English common law held that "a man's home is his castle," and it sought to protect persons in their homes by, among other things, creating the crime of burglary. The Fourth Amendment specifically mentions the right of the people to be secure in their houses. Of course, it also mentions their persons, papers, and effects. But it is fair to say that when a person is in his or her home, the protection afforded by the Fourth Amendment is at its maximum.

At common law, the concept of curtilage was developed to afford the area immediately surrounding a house the same protection under the law of burglary as afforded the house itself. The term "curtilage" refers to the enclosed space of ground surrounding a dwelling. The Supreme Court has held that the Fourth Amendment provides the same protection to the curtilage as to the house itself. On the other hand, the open fields surrounding the house and curtilage are not entitled to Fourth Amendment protection. *Hester v. United States,* 265 U.S. 57, 44 S.Ct. 445, 68 L.Ed. 898 (1924). Writing for the Supreme Court in *Hester,* Justice Oliver Wendell Holmes noted that

> the special protection accorded by the Fourth Amendment to the people in their "persons, houses, papers and effects," is not extended to the open fields. The distinction between the latter and the house is as old as the common law. 265 U.S. at 59, 44 S.Ct. at 446, 68 L.Ed. at 900.

The **open fields doctrine** was reaffirmed by the Supreme Court in *Oliver v. United States,* 466 U.S. 170, 104 S.Ct. 1735, 80 L.Ed.2d 214 (1984). In *Oliver,* narcotics officers entered the defendant's land by going around a locked gate and ignoring "No Trespassing" signs. When they observed a field of marijuana, they arrested the owner of the property for manufacturing contraband. The Court upheld the search because it concluded that the Fourth Amendment did not apply to the open fields around his home, despite his attempt to protect it by posting signs.

State courts are divided on whether to provide greater protection under their state constitutions. In *People v. Scott,* 593 N.E.2d 1328 (N.Y. 1992), New York's highest court ruled that where property owners fence or post "No Trespassing" signs on their private property or, by some other means, indicate that entry is not permitted, they have a reasonable expectation of privacy that must be respected. The New York decision illustrates that a state is free to provide greater protection under its state constitution than the U.S. Supreme Court determines is required under the federal constitution. A New Jersey appellate court was unwilling to grant greater protection than afforded by the federal constitution when it excused a warrantless entry onto private lands by conservation officers investigating a suspected violation of fish and game law. *State v. Gates,* 703 A.2d 696 (N.J. Super. 1997).

Go to the Scheb/ Scheb Criminal Law and Procedure 6e website at academic .cengage.com/criminaljustice/ scheb for an edited version of *Hester v. U.S.*

Applicability of the Fourth Amendment to Administrative Searches

Although the Fourth Amendment refers to "houses," its protections are extended to stores, offices, and places of business. *See v. City of Seattle,* 387 U.S. 541, 87 S.Ct. 1737, 18 L.Ed.2d 943 (1967). However, an exception is made for those areas of commercial properties that carry an implied invitation for the public to enter. *Maryland v. Macon,* 472 U.S. 463, 105 S.Ct. 2778, 86 L.Ed.2d 370 (1985). Moreover, various statutes provide for unannounced inspections of "pervasively regulated businesses," such as establishments that sell alcoholic beverages. In 1998 the Michigan Supreme Court considered a massage parlor to be a pervasively regulated business and on that basis upheld a warrantless search of the premises. *Gora v. City of Ferndale,* 576 N.W.2d 141 (Mich. 1998).

Local ordinances also allow routine inspections to enforce building codes and other regulations. The Supreme Court has recognized these **administrative searches** as exceptions to normal Fourth Amendment protections. *Colonnade Catering Corp. v. United States,* 397 U.S. 72, 90 S.Ct. 774, 25 L.Ed.2d 60 (1970). The Fourth Amendment applies, but the standard is one of "reasonableness" rather than the more stringent test required of searches conducted by the police. *Camara v. Municipal Court,* 387 U.S. 523, 87 S.Ct. 1727, 18 L.Ed.2d 930 (1967). To determine whether an administrative search meets the reasonableness requirement, courts balance the need to search against the invasion that such search entails. *United States v. Bulacan,* 156 F.3d 963 (9th Cir. 1998).

Searches of Abandoned Property

Because it mentions "effects," the Fourth Amendment applies to items of personal property as well as to real estate. However, it should be noted that the Fourth Amendment does not apply to property that has been abandoned. Therefore, police may search abandoned premises and seize **abandoned property** without the necessity of legally justifying their actions. *Abel v. United States,* 362 U.S. 217, 80 S.Ct. 683, 4 L.Ed.2d 668 (1960). The key question in such cases is whether the property was abandoned at the time of the search. In a 1960 decision, the Supreme Court observed that a "passenger who lets a package drop to the floor of the taxicab in which he is riding can hardly be said to have 'abandoned' it. An occupied taxicab is not to be compared to an open field … or a vacated hotel room." *Rios v. United States,* 364 U.S. 253, 262, n. 6, 80 S.Ct. 1431, 1437, 4 L.Ed.2d 1688, 1694 (1960). Similarly, in 1990 the Supreme Court held that "a citizen who attempts to protect his private property from inspection, after throwing it on a car to respond to a police officer's inquiry, clearly has not abandoned that property." *Smith v. Ohio,* 494 U.S. 541, 543–544, 110 S.Ct. 1288, 1290, 108 L.Ed.2d 464, 468 (1990).

Automobile Inventory Searches

Most law enforcement agencies that impound automobiles for parking violations or abandonment, or pursuant to the arrest of a motorist, routinely conduct an inventory of the contents and remove any valuables for safekeeping. When conducted according to standard police procedures, an **inventory search** is generally regarded as an administrative search not subject to ordinary Fourth Amendment requirements. Inventory searches are justified by the need for protection of the owner's property while the vehicle remains in police custody, protection of the police from claims of lost property, and protection of the police from potential dangers that might be lurking inside closed automobiles. Of course, if a routine inventory search yields evidence of

CASE-IN-POINT

Does the Fourth Amendment Apply to Garbage Placed by the Curb?

A police officer requested a trash collector to turn over bags of garbage collected from the Greenwood home in Laguna Beach, California. The officer searched the garbage bags and found evidence indicating illicit drug use. She used this evidence as a basis for obtaining a warrant to search the Greenwood home. During the search, the police discovered cocaine and hashish. As a result, the police charged the defendants with possession of illicit drugs. The trial court dismissed the charges on the ground that the warrantless trash search violated the Fourth Amendment, and the California appellate court affirmed. The U.S. Supreme Court granted review and reversed on the ground that the defendants, by placing their garbage outside the curtilage, had exposed their garbage to the public, and regardless of whether they may have had an expectation of privacy in their garbage, it was not an expectation that society is prepared to accept as being objectively reasonable.

California v. Greenwood, 486 U.S. 35, 108 S.Ct. 1625, 100 L.Ed.2d 30 (1988).

crime, it may be seized and admitted into evidence without violating the Fourth Amendment. *South Dakota v. Opperman,* 428 U.S. 364, 96 S.Ct. 3092, 49 L.Ed.2d 1000 (1976).

It should be recognized that police are not permitted to use an inventory search as a pretext for a criminal investigation. *Colorado v. Bertine,* 479 U.S. 367, 107 S.Ct. 738, 93 L.Ed.2d 739 (1987). Nevertheless, once the police have legitimately taken a vehicle into custody, they are not required to overlook contraband articles discovered during a valid inventory search, and such items may be used as evidence. Lower federal and state courts have emphasized that an inventory search must be in accordance with established inventory procedures. See, for example, *United States v. Velarde,* 903 F.2d 1163 (7th Cir. 1990). In 1998 the Arkansas Supreme Court held that the fact that the defendant lacked a valid driver's license constituted good cause to justify a police officer's impounding his vehicle and completing a warrantless inventory of its contents pursuant to the police department's standards. *Thompson v. State,* 966 S.W.2d 901 (Ark. 1998).

Searches Based on Consent

Constitutional rights may be waived, and Fourth Amendment rights are no exception. Voluntary cooperation with police officers often results in fruitful searches and seizures. The Supreme Court has refused to require law officers to inform suspects of their right to refuse to **consent to a search.** *Schneckloth v. Bustamonte,* 412 U.S. 218, 93 S.Ct. 2041, 36 L.Ed.2d 854 (1973). More recently, the Court held that police are not required to inform motorists who are stopped for other reasons that they are "free to go" before asking them to consent to a search of their automobile. *Ohio v. Robinette,* 519 U.S. 33, 117 S.Ct. 417, 136 L.Ed.2d 347 (1996).

THE VOLUNTARINESS REQUIREMENT

To be valid, consent must be truly voluntary. If a person actually assists the police in conducting a search, or consents after having been advised that consent is not required, courts have little difficulty in finding that consent was voluntary. Yet consent has to involve more than mere acquiescence to the authority of the police. Thus, in *Bumper v. North Carolina,* 391 U.S. 543, 88 S.Ct. 1788, 20 L.Ed.2d 797 (1968), the Court held that a claim of police authority based on a nonexistent warrant was so coercive as to invalidate the defendant's consent. Similarly, a Georgia appellate court invalidated an automobile search where the defendant and a companion were surprised by six heavily armed law officers, were searched at gunpoint, and were then asked to consent to a search of their automobile. *Love v. State,* 242 S.E.2d 278 (Ga. App. 1978).

When a person summons the police to the home to investigate a crime that has allegedly taken place there, there is an **implied consent** to a search of the premises related to the routine investigation of the offense. Of course, once police are lawfully on the premises, any evidence of crime that is in their plain view may be seized, even if the person who initially summoned the police may be ultimately prosecuted as a result of such evidence.

THIRD-PARTY CONSENT

A perennial problem in the area of consent searches is that of **third-party consent.** The problem is especially acute in situations where several persons share a single dwelling, as is common among college students. For example, may an apartment dweller consent to the search of his or her roommate's bedroom? The Supreme Court has said that the consent of a third party is valid only when there is mutual use of the property by persons generally having joint access or control. Thus, any of the co-occupants has the right to permit the inspection. The others have assumed the risk that one of their number might permit the common area to be searched. *United States v. Matlock,* 415 U.S. 164, 94 S.Ct. 988, 39 L.Ed.2d 242 (1974). *Matlock* stands for the principle that the validity of third-party consent is tested by the degree of dominion and control exercised by the third party over the searched premises and that a joint occupant may provide valid consent only if the other party is not present.

In *Illinois v. Rodriguez,* 497 U.S. 177, 110 S.Ct. 2793, 111 L.Ed.2d 148 (1990), the Supreme Court shifted the focus from the dominion and control of the third party to the police officer's subjective belief that the third party has the authority to grant consent to a search of the premises. Writing for the Court, Justice Antonin Scalia opined that a warrantless entry is valid when based on the consent of a third party whom the police reasonably believe to possess common authority over the premises, even if the third party does not in fact have such authority.

There are a number of well-established situations in which third-party consent is not valid. Tenancy arrangements are a good example. A landlord does not have the implied authority to consent to the search of a tenant's premises. *Chapman v. United States,* 365 U.S. 610, 81 S.Ct. 776, 5 L.Ed.2d 828 (1961). Likewise, a hotel manager or clerk does not have the right to consent to the search of a guest's room during the time the guest has a legal right to occupy the room. *Stoner v. California,* 376 U.S. 483, 84 S.Ct. 889, 11 L.Ed.2d 856 (1964).

Courts have taken different approaches to searches of college dormitory rooms, often depending on the regulations the student agrees to when occupying the dormitory room. A search routinely performed by college officials for reasons of health or safety that reveals incriminating evidence in plain view would probably not be in violation of the Fourth Amendment. On the other hand, a search of a dormitory room by police would ordinarily require a search warrant issued on the basis of probable cause. In *Commonwealth v. McCloskey,* 272 A.2d 271 (Pa. Super. 1970), the court held that absent **exigent circumstances,** police entry into a college dormitory room by means of a pass key possessed by the head resident was improper. Even though the university had reserved the right to check the room for damage and use of unauthorized appliances, the court found that in the absence of exigent circumstances the university did not have authority to consent to a governmental search of the student's room.

Some current problems in the area of third-party consent involve parental consent to searches of premises occupied by their adult children and spousal consent to searches of the other spouse's property, such as an automobile. But again, the Supreme Court has shifted the focus to the police officer's subjective belief regarding the authority of third parties. In general, state courts have followed the *Matlock* approach. The Louisiana Supreme Court did that in 1999 by holding that a warrantless search may be valid even if consent was given by one without authority if the facts available to officers at the time of entry justified the officers' reasonable, albeit erroneous, belief that the one consenting to the search had authority over the premises. *State v. Edwards,* 750 So.2d 893 (La. 1999). But not all state courts have been willing to follow *Matlock;* some provide more protection to their citizens. For example, Oregon courts have ruled that the state constitution requires that consent by a third party must be based on actual authority. See *State v. Will,* 885 P.2d 715 (Or. App. 1994).

WHAT HAPPENS WHEN SPOUSES DISAGREE AS TO WHETHER POLICE MAY SEARCH THEIR RESIDENCE?

In *Georgia v. Randolph,* ___ U.S. ___, 126 S.Ct. 1515, 164 L.Ed.2d 208 (2006), the Supreme Court granted review of a case in order to resolve a split of authority in lower federal courts in instances where one co-occupant gives the police consent to search shared premises, yet another co-occupant who is present refuses to permit the search. In 2006 the Court reviewed a case in which police entered a home based on a wife's consent even though her husband, who was present at the time, objected to the entry. The wife led police to cocaine belonging to her husband. In reversing the conviction on the ground that the police had made an unlawful search and seizure, the Court said that police may not search a home when one resident invites them in but another refuses to grant access. In a strongly worded dissenting opinion, Chief Justice John Roberts expressed concern about the impact of the decision on the ability of police to protect women from their abusive partners.

The Scope of Privacy Protected by the Fourth Amendment

 Go to the Scheb/ Scheb Criminal Law and Procedure 6e website at academic .cengage.com/criminaljustice/ scheb for an edited version of *Olmstead v. U.S.*

The term "seizure" refers to the taking into custody of physical evidence, property, or even a person. What constitutes a "search"? The answer is not so clear. Originally, the protection of the Fourth Amendment was limited to physical intrusions to one's person or property. *Olmstead v. United States,* 277 U.S. 438, 48 S.Ct. 564, 72 L.Ed. 944 (1928). Historically, courts looked at whether a trespass had taken place in deciding whether the Fourth Amendment was implicated. Thus, surveillance without physical contact with the suspect or the suspect's property was deemed to fall outside the protections of the Fourth Amendment. Accordingly, the Fourth Amendment was not deemed applicable to **wiretapping** or **electronic eavesdropping.**

In *Katz v. United States,* 389 U.S. 347, 88 S.Ct. 507, 19 L.Ed.2d 576 (1967), the Supreme Court overruled *Olmstead* and abandoned the trespass doctrine, saying "the Fourth Amendment protects people, not places." 389 U.S. at 361, 88 S.Ct. at 516, 19 L.Ed.2d at 582. The contemporary approach to determining the scope of protected privacy under the Fourth Amendment is nicely stated in Justice John M. Harlan's concurring opinion in *Katz:*

Go to the Scheb/ Scheb Criminal Law and Procedure 6e website at academic .cengage.com/criminaljustice/ scheb for an edited version of *Katz v. U.S.*

> My understanding of the rule as it has emerged from prior decisions is that there is a twofold requirement, first that a person have exhibited an actual (subjective) expectation of privacy and, second, that the expectation be one that society is prepared to recognize as "reasonable." 389 U.S. at 361, 88 S.Ct. at 516, 19 L.Ed.2d at 587.

Reasonable Expectations of Privacy

Potentially, the term "search" applies to any official invasion of a person's reasonable expectation of privacy as to one's person, house, papers, or effects. In *Katz,* the Court held that a suspected bookie who was using a public telephone allegedly in conduct of a gambling business enjoyed a **reasonable expectation of privacy** and that a police wiretap of the phone booth was a search within the meaning of the Fourth Amendment. This decision brought wiretapping and other forms of electronic eavesdropping within the limitations of the Fourth Amendment. Currently, any means of invading a person's reasonable expectation of privacy is considered a search for Fourth Amendment purposes. The critical question that courts must address in reviewing cases where police conduct surveillance or eavesdropping without probable cause or prior judicial authorization is whether such surveillance intruded on a person's reasonable expectation of privacy.

The issue of what constitutes a reasonable expectation of privacy has been litigated in hundreds of cases in federal and state courts. Police techniques such as canine sniffs are considered among the least intrusive means of government investigation. Thus, police were allowed to conduct a "sniff test" of a passenger's luggage at an airport without reasonable suspicion because it did not violate a person's reasonable expectation of privacy. *United States v. Place,* 462 U.S. 696, 106 S.Ct. 2637, 77 L.Ed.2d 110 (1983). However, the uniqueness of individual situations has resulted in disparate views, with police frequently complaining that judicial decisions fail to furnish any "bright line" rules. In a number of well-defined situations, however, courts have upheld minimally intrusive, suspicionless searches on the assumption that people's privacy expectations are reduced in such situations.

With increased concern over airplane hijacking and terrorism has come increased security at the nation's airports. Passengers attempting to board aircraft routinely pass through metal detectors; their carry-on baggage and checked luggage are routinely subjected to X-ray scans. Should these procedures suggest the presence of suspicious objects, physical searches are conducted to determine what the objects are. There is little question that such searches are reasonable given their minimal intrusiveness, the gravity of the safety interests involved, and the reduced privacy expectations associated with airline travel. Indeed, travelers are often notified through airport public address systems and signs that "all bags are subject to search." Such announcements place passengers on notice that ordinary Fourth Amendment protections do not apply.

Sobriety Checkpoints

In the last twenty-five years society has become incensed about drunk driving and the resulting carnage on the nation's highways. One method increasingly used by law enforcement to combat this problem is the use of **sobriety checkpoints,** in which all drivers passing a certain point are stopped briefly and observed for signs of intoxication.

CASE-IN-POINT

The Privacy Expectations of Bus Passengers

Steven D. Bond was traveling on a Greyhound bus from California to Little Rock, Arkansas. When the bus stopped at a border patrol checkpoint in Texas, an agent boarded the bus to check for undocumented aliens. During the course of the inspection, the agent squeezed the soft luggage in the overhead storage space above the seats. In squeezing a canvas bag belonging to Bond, the agent detected a "brick-like" object that aroused his suspicions. Upon the agent's request, Bond consented to a search of the bag, which produced a brick of methamphetamine wrapped in duct tape.

After his motion to suppress the contraband was denied, Bond was convicted of possession with intent to distribute methamphetamine and was sentenced to fifty-seven months in prison. The Court of Appeals upheld the denial of the suppression motion, holding that the agent's action in squeezing the canvas bag

was not a search within the meaning of the Fourth Amendment. On certiorari, the Supreme Court reversed, dividing 7–2. Writing for the Court, Chief Justice William Rehnquist opined, "When a bus passenger places a bag in an overhead bin, he expects that other passengers or bus employees may move it for one reason or another.... He does not expect that other passengers or bus employees will, as a matter of course, feel the bag in an exploratory manner. But this is exactly what the agent did here." In dissent, Justice Stephen Breyer, joined by Justice Antonin Scalia, observed that "the traveler who wants to place a bag in a shared overhead bin and yet safeguard its contents from public touch should plan to pack those contents in a suitcase with hard sides, irrespective of the Court's decision today."

Bond v. United States, 529 U.S. 334, 120 S.Ct. 1462, 146 L.Ed.2d 365 (2000).

To the extent that police officers at these checkpoints visually inspect the passenger compartments of stopped automobiles, these brief encounters involve searches, although in most instances these procedures entail only minor intrusion and inconvenience. Critics of sobriety checkpoints object to the fact that police temporarily detain and visually search cars without any particular suspicion. Yet the courts have generally approved such measures. See, for example, *Michigan Dept. of State Police v. Sitz,* 496 U.S. 444, 110 S.Ct. 2481, 110 L.Ed.2d 412 (1990). It is noteworthy, however, that in 2000, the U.S. Supreme Court disallowed a checkpoint that was established primarily for the purpose of detecting illegal drugs. *City of Indianapolis v. Edmond*, 531 U.S. 32, 121 S.Ct 447, 148 L.Ed.2d 333 (2000). (This topic is explored further in the next chapter.)

Go to the Scheb/ Scheb Criminal Law and Procedure 6e website at academic .cengage.com/criminaljustice/ scheb for an edited version of *Indianapolis v. Edmond.*

Jail and Prison Searches and Strip Searches

Obviously, anyone lawfully incarcerated in a prison or jail has no reasonable expectation of privacy. Jail and prison cells are routinely "swept" for weapons and other contraband, and inmates are routinely subjected to searches of their persons. The Supreme Court in *Bell v. Wolfish,* 441 U.S. 520, 99 S.Ct. 1861, 60 L.Ed.2d 447 (1979), upheld **strip searches** of prison inmates because of the demands for institutional security. But the Court did not give prison officials carte blanche. Rather, the Court held that the Fourth Amendment requires balancing the need for the particular search against the invasion of personal rights. Thus, courts must consider the justification and scope of the intrusion and the manner and place in which it is conducted.

Absent cause for suspicion, visitors to a prison may be subjected to reasonable searches—for example, a pat-down search or a metal detector sweep. However, before conducting a strip search of a visitor, prison authorities must have at least a reasonable suspicion that the visitor is bearing contraband. *Spear v. Sowders,* 71 F.3d 626 (6th Cir. 1995).

Courts have generally disapproved of blanket policies that allow strip searches of all persons who have been arrested, particularly where traffic violators are concerned. Some courts hold that strip searches are violative of Fourth Amendment rights unless there is probable cause to believe the arrestee is concealing weapons or contraband. See, for example, *Mary Beth G. v. Chicago,* 723 F.2d 1263 (7th Cir. 1983). Other courts have permitted such searches where there is a reasonable suspicion that the arrestee is concealing weapons or contraband. See, for example, *Weber v. Dell,* 804 F.2d 796 (2d Cir. 1986).

Strip searches can also have civil consequences. For example, in *Jones v. Edwards,* 770 F.2d 739 (8th Cir. 1985), Marlin E. Jones was arrested and taken into custody for failing to sign a summons and complaint on an animal leash law violation. He was subjected to a visual strip search of his anal and genital area. The court ruled that such a search, under these circumstances, subjected the police and jail personnel to liability for the violation of the arrestee's civil rights. The court emphasized that the police had no reason to suspect that Jones was harboring weapons or contraband on his person.

The Warrant Requirement

As pointed out, when searches are challenged as being unreasonable, courts must first determine if the Fourth Amendment is applicable. The Fourth Amendment does not apply to border searches or searches conducted outside the United States, nor does it apply to open fields or abandoned property. Indeed, the Fourth Amendment does not apply to any situation where a person lacks a reasonable expectation of privacy. Where it does apply, the Fourth Amendment expresses a decided preference for searches and seizures to be conducted pursuant to a warrant. The warrant requirement is designed to ensure that the impartial judgment of a judge or a magistrate is interposed between the citizen and the state. The right of privacy is "too precious to entrust to the discretion of those whose job is the detection of crime and the arrest of criminals." *McDonald v. United States*, 335 U.S. 451, 455–456, 69 S.Ct. 191, 195–96, 93 L.Ed. 153, 158 (1948).

The Probable Cause Requirement

With the exception of warrants permitting administrative searches, search warrants must be based on probable cause. Like many legal terms, "probable cause" is not susceptible to precise definition. Probable cause exists when prudent and cautious police officers have trustworthy information leading them to believe that evidence of crime might be obtained through a particular search. See *Brinegar v. United States*, 338 U.S. 160, 69 S.Ct. 1302, 93 L.Ed. 1879 (1949); *Carroll v. United States*, 267 U.S. 132, 45 S.Ct. 280, 69 L.Ed. 543 (1925).

The Supreme Court has said that courts should view the determination of probable cause as a "commonsense, practical question" that must be decided in light of the **totality of circumstances** in a given case. *Illinois v. Gates*, 462 U.S. 213, 230, 103 S.Ct. 2317, 2328, 76 L.Ed.2d 527, 543 (1983). This approach has been amplified by lower federal courts, which have observed that even though an innocent explanation might be consistent with the facts alleged in an affidavit seeking a search warrant, this does not negate probable cause. See, for example, *United States v. Fama*, 758 F.2d 834 (2d Cir. 1985).

Although state courts are free to impose a higher standard, most have followed this approach. For example, the Ohio Supreme Court ruled that an affidavit by a police agent saying that he observed a tall marijuana plant growing in an enclosed backyard furnished probable cause for a magistrate to conclude there was marijuana or related paraphernalia in the residence. *State v. George*, 544 N.E.2d 640 (Ohio 1989). Some state courts have declined to follow the *Gates* approach and have opted to provide their citizens more protection than allowed by the federal view. In some instances, these state views result from linguistic variations in state constitutional counterparts to the Fourth Amendment. For example, in *Commonwealth v. Upton*, 476 N.E.2d 548 (Mass. 1985), the court noted the Massachusetts Constitution provides more substantive protection to criminal defendants than does the Fourth Amendment in the determination of probable cause. Thus, the court held that an affidavit based on a telephone tip from an anonymous informer whose veracity was not shown did not establish probable cause for issuance of a warrant to search a mobile home.

Issuance of the Search Warrant

Under normal circumstances, a police officer with probable cause to believe that evidence of a crime is located in a specific place must submit under oath an application for a search warrant to the appropriate judge or magistrate. Rule 41 of the Federal Rules of Criminal Procedure allows a federal agent to obtain a search warrant from a federal magistrate or a judge of a state court of record within the district wherein the property or person sought is located. Whether by statute or judicial rules, states usually provide similar authorization.

In *Coolidge v. New Hampshire,* 403 U.S. 443, 91 S.Ct. 2022, 29 L.Ed.2d 564 (1971), the Supreme Court invalidated a warrant issued by the state attorney general. The Court said that a warrant must be issued by a neutral and detached magistrate and certainly not by an official responsible for criminal prosecutions. Similarly, in *United States v. United States District Court,* 407 U.S. 297, 92 S.Ct. 2125, 32 L.Ed.2d 752 (1972), the Court invalidated a statute that permitted electronic eavesdropping to be authorized solely by the U.S. Attorney General in cases involving national security. Writing for the Court, Justice Lewis Powell observed that "unreviewed executive discretion may yield too readily to pressures to obtain incriminating evidence and overlook potential invasions of privacy...." 407 U.S. at 317, 92 S.Ct. at 2136, 32 L.Ed.2d at 766.

Go to the Scheb/ Scheb Criminal Law and Procedure 6e website at academic .cengage.com/criminaljustice/ scheb for an edited version of *U.S. v. U.S. District Court.*

The Supporting Affidavit

An **affidavit** is a signed document attesting under oath to certain facts of which the **affiant** (the person submitting the affidavit) has knowledge (see Figure 15.1). Generally, an affidavit by a law enforcement officer requesting issuance of a search warrant is presented to a judge or magistrate. The manner in which the affidavit is recorded and transmitted may vary. For example, the Idaho Supreme Court, finding that electronically recorded testimony is no less reliable than a sworn, written statement, held that the word "affidavit" under the Idaho constitution was sufficiently broad to include a tape recording of oral testimony. *State v. Yoder,* 534 P.2d 771 (Idaho 1975).

Rule 41(d)(3)(A) of the Federal Rules of Criminal Procedure provides that a federal magistrate judge may issue a warrant based upon sworn oral testimony communicated by phone or other appropriate means, including facsimile transmission. Some states follow this approach—for example, California law permits police officers to complete affidavits using the telephone to expedite the issuance of a warrant. West's Ann. Cal. Pen. Code. § 1526(b).

The officer's affidavit in support of a search warrant must always contain a rather precise description of the place(s) or person(s) to be searched and the things to be seized. Moreover, the affidavit must attest to specific facts that establish probable cause to justify a search. An affidavit cannot establish probable cause for issuance of a search warrant if it is based merely on the affiant's suspicion or belief without stating the facts and circumstances that the belief is based on.

The information on which an affidavit is based must be sufficiently fresh to ensure that the items to be seized are probably located on the premises to be searched. The issue of when a search warrant becomes invalid because the information the affidavit is based on is stale has been litigated in many cases, with varying results. No set rule can be formulated. For example, a Delaware appellate court invalidated a search warrant where there was a delay of twenty-three days between the last alleged fact and the issuance of the warrant. In *State v. Pulgini,* 374 A.2d 822 (Del. 1977), the Delaware Supreme Court reversed the decision, noting the affidavit for the warrant recited facts indicating activity of a protracted and continuous nature during the period of delay. The court said that under such circumstances the passage of time becomes less significant. In *United States v. Rosenbarger,* 536 F.2d 715 (6th Cir. 1976), a twenty-one-day time lapse between observation of the receipt of stolen property and issuance of the warrant did not invalidate the warrant because the magistrate could determine there was a reasonable probability that the stolen goods were still in the defendant's home.

In *State v. Carlson,* 4 P.3d 1122 (Idaho App. 2000), an Idaho appellate court held that a warrant to search a defendant's residence was not based upon stale information even though there was a lapse of twenty-four days between the informant's initial observations and the issuance of the search warrant. The court considered the

ACODC NO. 29

Commonwealth of Massachusetts

Middlesex _____ , ss.

Concord District Court
Court

AFFIDAVIT IN SUPPORT OF APPLICATION FOR SEARCH WARRANT*

G.L. c. 276, ss. 1 to 7; St. 1964, c. 557 As Amended

I, __Sam Buckley_____ , being duly sworn, depose and say: __21__   __June__ , 19 __80__
   Name of applicant

1. I am ____Police Chief of Concord, Massachusetts_____
      (Describe position, assignment, office, etc.)

2. I have information based upon (describe sources, facts indicating reliability of source and nature of information; if based on personal knowledge and belief, so state) (If space is insufficient, attach affidavit or affidavits hereto)

   Based on information from a Federal Drug Enforcement Officer, the above has reason to belive at 123 Smith Street, one-story red brick house, with garage, 2 bedrooms, kitchen, living room, and bathroom, there is a small brown suitcase containing a controlled substance believed to be heroin.

*3. Based upon the foregoing reliable information - and upon my personal knowledge and belief - and ~~searched affidavits~~ - there is probable cause to believe that the property hereinafter described - has been stolen - or is being concealed, etc.
   and may be found in the possession of __Miss Francine Taggart_____
                                          Name or person or persons

   at premises ____123 Smith Street, Concord_____
              (Identify number, street, place, etc.)

4. The property for which I seek the issuance of a search warrant is the following (here describe the property as particularly as possible).

   One small brown suitcase taken from a station locker by Francine Taggart on June 19, 1980, containing heroin.

WHEREFORE, I respectfully request that the court issue a warrant and order of seizure, authorizing the search of (identify premises and the person or persons to be searched)

and directing that if such property or evidence or any part thereof be found that it be seized and brought before the court; together with such other and further relief that the court may deem proper.

Police Chief Sam Buckley
Signature of applicant

Then personally appeared the above named _Chief Buckley_____
and made oath that the foregoing affidavit by him subscribed is true.

Before me this __21__ day of _June_ , 19 __80__

J. P. Jones - Special Justice
Justice of Special Justice
Clerk or Assistant Clerk of the   Municipal
                                   District   Court.

* Strike inapplicable clauses

APPROVED BY THE CHIEF JUSTICE OF THE DISTRICT COURTS

FIGURE 15.1   Application for a Search Warrant

fact that the information was supplemented by a second report regarding observation of a marijuana plant three days prior to the issuance of the warrant and the implication that a marijuana operation continued in the interim period.

In *Hemler v. Superior Court,* 118 Cal. Rptr. 564 (Cal. App. 1975), the court acknowledged that the question of "stale" information depends upon the facts of each case. The court stated that an affidavit clearly furnished probable cause for the issuance of a search warrant either immediately or within a short time after observation of the sale of narcotics in an apartment. Nevertheless, the court held that the affidavit did not furnish probable cause for the issuance of a search warrant thirty-four days later.

Most appellate courts have not set specific time limits as to when information supporting the issuance of a search warrant becomes stale. However, in *House v. State,* 323 So.2d 659 (Fla. App. 1975), the court stated that if the observation of an alleged offense was no more than thirty days before the issuance of a warrant, a trial court's finding that probable cause existed would not be disturbed.

Tips from Police Informants

A magistrate's finding of probable cause may be based on hearsay evidence. See, for example, Fed. R. Crim. P. 41(c)(1), which permits police to obtain search warrants based on tips from anonymous or **confidential informants.** Confidential informants, or CIs, are often persons who have been involved with the police and are seeking favorable consideration in respect to their own offenses. Because their motivation may be suspect, their reliability is checked carefully. For many years the Supreme Court required magistrates to apply a rigorous two-pronged test to determine probable cause. See *Aguilar v. Texas,* 378 U.S. 108, 84 S.Ct. 1509, 12 L.Ed.2d 723 (1964); *Spinelli v. United States,* 393 U.S. 410, 89 S.Ct. 584, 21 L.Ed.2d 637 (1969). The *Aguilar–Spinelli* test required that the officer's affidavit satisfy two criteria: (1) it had to demonstrate that the informant was both credible and reliable, and (2) it had to reveal the informant's basis of knowledge.

 Go to the Scheb/Scheb Criminal Law and Procedure 6e website at academic.cengage.com/criminaljustice/scheb for an edited version of *Illinois v. Gates.*

The *Aguilar–Spinelli* test made it very difficult for police to use anonymous tips. In 1983 the Supreme Court relaxed the test and permitted magistrates to consider the totality of circumstances when evaluating applications based on hearsay evidence. *Illinois v. Gates,* supra. The following year, the Court held that the standard for determining probable cause announced in the *Gates* decision was to be given a broad interpretation by lower courts. *Massachusetts v. Upton,* 466 U.S. 727, 104 S.Ct. 2085, 80 L.Ed.2d 721 (1984).

Despite the Supreme Court's relaxed standard for determining probable cause based on tips from informants, several states have chosen to follow the stricter standards formerly imposed by the *Aguilar* and *Spinelli* decisions. This, of course, is the prerogative of the states. In a comprehensive opinion in *State v. Cordova,* 784 P.2d 30 (N.M. 1989), the New Mexico Supreme Court reviewed an affidavit for a search warrant that recited that Cordova had brought heroin into town and was selling it at the house in question. However, the affidavit was devoid of explanation about how the informant gathered this information. Further, although the affidavit stated that the informant had personal knowledge that "heroin users" had been at the residence in question, there was nothing to indicate the source of the informant's knowledge and no explanation of how the informant knew that the persons in question were heroin users. Because the affidavit did not establish that the informant was both credible and reliable, the court found it did not provide a substantial basis for believing the informant and for concluding that the informant gathered the information in a reliable manner. Further, the affidavit did not adequately state the informant's basis of knowledge that the defendant was selling heroin. In rejecting the state's appeal, the New Mexico Supreme Court declined to follow the *Gates* totality-of-circumstances rule and found the affidavit did not meet the requirements of the New Mexico Constitution and its rules of criminal procedure.

In 1985 the Connecticut Supreme Court criticized the totality-of-circumstances test as being "too amorphous" and an inadequate safeguard against unjustified police intrusions. Nevertheless, that court has recently held that if the information supplied by a CI fails the *Aguilar–Spinelli* test, probable cause may still be found if the affidavit sets forth other circumstances that bolster any deficiencies. *State v. Barton*, 594 A.2d 917 (Conn. 1991). Four years later, the Tennessee Supreme Court held that the two-pronged standard for probable cause inquiries incident to the issuance of a search warrant announced in the *Aguilar* and *Spinelli* cases, if not measured hypertechnically, is the standard to measure whether there is probable cause to issue a warrant. *State v. Jacumin*, 778 S.W.2d 430 (Tenn. 1989).

When a defendant demands to know the identity of the informant who provided the police with information on which they based their affidavit for a search warrant, courts face a delicate problem. There is a limited privilege to withhold the identity of the confidential informant. In determining whether to require disclosure, the court balances the interest of the public in preserving the anonymity of the informant against the defendant's need to have this information to prepare a defense, and where the questioned identity "is relevant and helpful to the defense of an accused, or is essential to a fair determination of a cause, the privilege must give way." *Roviaro v. United States*, 353 U.S. 53, 77 S.Ct. 623, 1 L.Ed.2d 639 (1957).

In *State v. Litzau*, 650 N.W.2d 177 (Minn. 2002), the Minnesota Supreme Court, citing *Roviaro*, pointed out that where an informant is merely a transmitter of information rather than an active participant in or a material witness to the crime, that disclosure is generally not required. But the court said, "Where an informant is an eyewitness to the crime, an *in camera* hearing is appropriate to determine whether there is a reasonable probability that the informer's testimony is necessary to a fair determination of guilt or innocence." *Id.* at 184. In considering a request for disclosure of the identity of an informant, the Minnesota court stated that the trial court considers (1) whether the informant is a material witness, (2) whether the informant's testimony will be material to the issue of guilt, (3) whether the state's evidence is suspect, and (4) whether the informant's testimony might disclose entrapment. *Id.* at 184.

Required Specificity of a Search Warrant

The Fourth Amendment mandates that "no warrants shall issue" except those "particularly describing the place to be searched and the persons or things to be seized." Thus, the scope of a search and seizure is bound by the terms of the warrant (see Figure 15.2). Consequently, a warrant that described property to be seized as "various long play phonographic albums, and miscellaneous vases and glassware" was held insufficient. Nevertheless, in 1999 the Maine Supreme Judicial Court upheld a search warrant that authorized the seizure of all computer-related equipment in the defendant's house. The police knew only that images of minors who were allegedly sexually exploited were taken by digital camera and downloaded on a computer. *State v. Lehman*, 736 A.2d 256 (Me. 1999).

Courts tend to be less strict when it comes to the description of contraband (such as heroin), because it is illegal per se, but stricter in cases involving First Amendment rights. For example, a federal appeals court invalidated a warrant authorizing the seizure of "a quantity of obscene materials, including books, pamphlets, magazines, newspapers, films and prints." *United States v. Guarino*, 729 F.2d 864, 865 (1st Cir.

```
ACODC NO. 30
```

Commonwealth of Massachusetts

Middlesex _____ , ss.   Concord District
                                                                Court

(Search Warrant)

TO THE SHERIFFS OF OUR SEVERAL COUNTIES, OR THEIR DEPUTIES, ANY STATE POLICE OFFICER, OR ANY CONSTABLE OR POLICE OFFICER OF ANY CITY OR TOWN, WITHIN OUR SAID COMMONWEALTH:

Proof by affidavit having been made this day before Special Justic J.Q. Jones
                                                    (Name of person issuing warrant)

by   Police Chief Sam Buckley
              (Name of person or persons signing affidavit)

*that there is probable cause for believing that certain property has been stolen, embezzled, or obtained by false pretenses — certain property is intended for use or has been used as the means of committing a crime — certain property has been concealed to prevent a crime from being discovered — certain property is unlawfully possessed or kept or concealed for an unlawful purpose.

WE THEREFORE COMMAND YOU in the daytime (or at any time of the day or night) to make an immediate search of   123 Smith Street, Concord
                                          (Identify premises)

(occupied by   Francine Taggart   ) and of the person of
                      (Name of occupant)

_____ , and of any person present who may
              (Name of person)

be found to have such property in his possession or under his control or to whom such property may have been delivered, for the following property:

_____

(Description of property)

One small brown suitcase believed to contain heroin.

and if you find any such property or any part therof to bring it and the persons in who possession it is found before the Concord District Court
                          (Name of Court)

at   Concord, Massachusetts
                  (Court location)

in said County and Commonwealth, as soon as it has been served and in any event not later than seven days of issuance thereof. (Officer to make return on reverse side)

Witness _J.D. Jones_ , Esquire, Justice, at _Concord_ ,

_____ aforesaid, this _21_ day of _June_

in the year of our Lord one thousand nine hundred and _80_

* Strike inapplicable clauses   Justice
                                       Clerk
                                       Assistant Clerk

G.L. c. 276, ss. 1 to 7; St. 1964, c. 557

APPROVED BY THE CHIEF JUSTICE OF THE DISTRICT COURTS

FIGURE 15.2   A Typical Search Warrant

1984). In *United States v. Hall*, 142 F.3d 988 (7th Cir. 1998), the court held that search warrants were written with sufficient particularity "because the items listed on the warrants were qualified by … such phrases as 'child pornography,' 'minors engaged in sexually explicit conduct,' and 'sexual conduct between adults … and minors.'" *Id.* at 996–997.

CASE-IN-POINT

Required Specificity of a Search Warrant

A police officer was executing a search warrant that specified a particular copyrighted software program, gave its serial number, and added "all other computer related software." The officer was unable to find a floppy disk containing the program but did locate the program on the hard drive of the defendant's computer. After making a diskette copy of the program, the officer seized the manuals for the program, the computer keyboard and terminal, and numerous related documents. In affirming the defendant's conviction for an offense involving intellectual property, the court held that these materials were properly seized even though not specifically listed in the warrant.

State v. Tanner, 534 So.2d 535 (La. App. 1988).

Anticipatory Search Warrants

The dramatic increase in drug trafficking over the last few decades has given rise to a countermeasure known as the **anticipatory search warrant.** Traditionally, police wait until a suspect receives contraband and then prepare an affidavit to obtain a search warrant. If the magistrate finds that probable cause exists at that time, a search warrant is issued. In the case of an anticipatory warrant, probable cause does not have to exist until the warrant is executed and the search conducted.

During the 1980s, several state appellate courts approved anticipatory search warrants. See, for example, *State v. Coker,* 746 S.W.2d 167 (Tenn. 1987). In one of these cases, *Bernie v. State,* supra, a freight delivery service notified police that a package that broke in transit revealed a suspicious substance that later proved to be cocaine. An anticipatory warrant was issued to search the residence to which the package was addressed. Police were on the scene when the freight company delivered the package. The warrant was served, the cocaine seized, and the defendant taken into custody. On appeal, the search was upheld by the state supreme court, which observed that neither the federal nor the state constitution prohibited issuance of a search warrant to be served at a future date in anticipation of the delivery of contraband.

The Alaska Supreme Court has cautioned that a magistrate issuing an anticipatory warrant should make its execution contingent on the occurrence of an event that evidences probable cause that the items to be seized are in the place to be searched rather than directing that the warrant be executed forthwith. *Johnson v. State,* 617 P.2d 1117 (Alaska 1980).

In January 2000, a Michigan appellate court first addressed the issue; following the trend of appellate courts, it concluded that an anticipatory search warrant does not violate the federal and state constitutional prohibitions against unreasonable searches and seizures. *People v. Kaslowski,* 608 N.W.2d 539 (Mich. App. 2000).

While there has been a split of authority, the majority of federal appellate courts have upheld the basic concept that contraband does not have to be currently located at the place described in a search warrant if there is probable cause to believe it will be there when the warrant is executed. In 1986 the Ninth Circuit Court of Appeals held that an anticipatory search warrant is permissible "where the contraband to be seized is on a sure course to its destination." *United States v. Hale,* 784 F.2d 1465, 1468 (9th Cir. 1986). Two years later, the U.S. Court of Appeals for the Fourth Circuit upheld an anticipatory search warrant permitting an inspector to search an apartment for child pornography where the issuing magistrate conditioned the validity of the warrant on the contraband being placed in the mail. Thus, when the mailing was accomplished, the contraband was on a certain course to its destination. *United States v. Dornhofer,* 859 F.2d 1195 (4th Cir. 1988).

In *United States v. Grubbs,* ___ U.S. ___, 126 S.Ct. 1494, 164 L.Ed.2d 195 (2006), the Supreme Court held that anticipatory search warrants do not contravene the Fourth Amendment. In an opinion by Justice Scalia, the Court said,

> Anticipatory warrants are … no different in principle from ordinary warrants. They require the magistrate to determine (1) that it is now probable that (2) contraband, evidence of a crime, or a fugitive will be on the described premises (3) when the warrant is executed. It should be noted, however, that where the anticipatory warrant places a condition (other than the mere passage of time) upon its execution, the first of these determinations goes not merely to what will probably be found if the condition is met…. Rather, the probability determination for a conditioned anticipatory warrant looks also to the likelihood that the condition will occur, and thus that a proper object of seizure will be on the described premises. In other words, for a conditioned anticipatory warrant to comply with the Fourth Amendment's requirement of probable cause, two prerequisites of probability must be satisfied. It must be true not only that if the triggering condition occurs "there is a fair probability that contraband or evidence of a crime will be found in a particular place," … but also that there is probable cause to believe the triggering condition will occur. The supporting affidavit must provide the magistrate with sufficient information to evaluate both aspects of the probable-cause determination. ___ U.S. at ___, 126 S.Ct. at 1500, 164 L.Ed.2d at ___.

Execution of a Search Warrant

Applicable federal and state laws and rules of criminal procedure govern the manner and time in which warrants are executed. Rule 41(e) of the Federal Rules of Criminal Procedure provides that the warrant

> shall command the officer to search, within a specified period of time not to exceed 10 days, the person or place named or the property or person specified. The warrant shall be served in the daytime, unless the issuing authority … authorizes its execution at times other than daytime.

Rule 41(a)(2)(B) defines "daytime" as the period between 6:00 A.M. and 10:00 P.M. according to local time. States have varying provisions governing the period of time within which a search warrant may be executed. Texas allows three days, excluding the date of issuance and the date of execution, Vernon's Ann. Texas C.C.P. Art. 18.07, whereas California allows ten, West's Ann. Cal. Penal Code § 1534. Likewise, state laws vary on the hours during which a search warrant may be executed. California law provides that upon a showing of good cause, the magistrate may, in his or her discretion, insert a direction in a search warrant that it may be served at any time of the day or night. In the absence of such a direction, the warrant shall be served only between the hours of 7 A.M. and 10 P.M. West's Ann. Cal. Penal Code § 1533. Some states, including Texas, do not impose restrictions on the hours when a warrant may be executed; others allow nighttime searches under special circumstances.

The Knock-and-Announce Rule

At the time the Constitution was adopted, there was a principle of the English common law that law enforcement officers should ordinarily announce their presence and authority before entering a residence to conduct a search or make an arrest pursuant to a warrant. Under federal law an officer is required to **knock and announce** on arrival at the place to be searched. 18 U.S.C.A. § 3109. That section stipulates:

> The officer may break open any outer or inner door or window of a house, or any part of a house, or anything therein, to execute a search warrant, if, after notice of his authority and purpose, he is refused admittance or when necessary to liberate himself or a person aiding him in the execution of the warrant.

Go to the Scheb/ Scheb Criminal Law and Procedure 6e website at academic .cengage.com/criminaljustice/ scheb for an edited version of *Wilson v. Arkansas.*

Most states have similar "knock-and-announce" requirements, but courts have created some exceptions to protect officers and to prevent the destruction of evidence. In *Wilson v. Arkansas,* 514 U.S. 927, 115 S.Ct. 1914, 131 L.Ed.2d 976 (1995), the U.S. Supreme Court elevated the knock-and-announce rule to constitutional status under the Fourth Amendment. However, the Court did recognize that exigent circumstances may render the knock-and-announce requirement unnecessary.

The purpose of the knock-and-announce requirement is to reduce the potential for violence and to protect the right of privacy of the occupants. Courts have generally ruled that there are no rigid limits as to the time that must elapse between the announcement and the officers' entry. A few seconds may even suffice. Moreover, courts frequently excuse compliance when to require it would endanger the lives of the officers or simply provide an occasion for occupants to dispose of evidence. The most common example of disposing of evidence after police have announced their presence is the flushing of contraband down a toilet. For example, in *State v. Stalbert,* 783 P.2d 1005 (Or. App. 1989), the court found no violation of the knock-and-announce rule where police officers arrived at the defendant's residence to execute a search warrant, yelled "Police officers, search warrant," and paused no more than two seconds between knocking and breaking through the door.

In *Wilson v. Arkansas,* supra, the Supreme Court noted that officers facing exigent circumstances such as the need to preserve evanescent evidence could dispense with the knock-and-announce requirement. But in *Richards v. Wisconsin,* 520 U.S. 385, 117 S.Ct. 1416, 137 L.Ed.2d 615 (1997), the Court ruled that states may not create a blanket "drug exception" to the requirement that police officers knock and announce prior to executing a search warrant. Writing for a unanimous bench, Justice John Paul Stevens observed that

> the fact that felony drug investigations may frequently present circumstances warranting a no knock entry cannot remove from the neutral scrutiny of a reviewing court the reasonableness of the police decision not to knock and announce in a particular case. Instead, in each case, it is the duty of a court confronted with the question to determine whether the facts and circumstances of the particular entry justified dispensing with the knock and announce requirement. 520 U.S. at 394, 117 S.Ct. at 1421, 137 L.Ed.2d at ___.

In *Hudson v. Michigan,* ___ U.S. ___, 126 S.Ct. 2159, 165 L.Ed.2d 56 (2006), the Supreme Court retreated from the position taken in *Wilson v. Arkansas,* holding that violations of the knock-and-announce requirement do not require the suppression of all evidence seized as the result of such violations. Speaking for a sharply divided Court, Justice Scalia concluded that when it comes to knock-and-announce violations, "[r]esort to the massive remedy of suppressing evidence of guilt is unjustified." ___ U.S. at ___, 126 S.Ct. at 2168, 165 L.Ed.2d at ___. Scalia also noted, "In addition to the grave adverse consequence that excluding relevant incriminating evidence always entails—the risk of releasing dangerous criminals—the imposing such a massive remedy would generate a constant flood of alleged failures to observe the rule...." ___ U.S. at ___, 126 S.Ct. at 2161, 165 L.Ed.2d at ___. Writing for four dissenters, Justice Breyer observed that the decision "destroys the strongest legal incentive to comply with the Constitution's knock-and-announce requirement." ___ U.S. at ___, 126 S.Ct. at 2171, 165 L.Ed.2d at ___.

Testing the Sufficiency of the Basis for Issuing a Search Warrant

In *Franks v. Delaware*, 438 U.S. 154, 98 S.Ct. 2674, 57 L.Ed.2d 667 (1978), the Supreme Court was faced with the issue of whether a defendant can challenge the affidavit for a search warrant in a pretrial proceeding. The Delaware Supreme Court had ruled that a defendant could not challenge the veracity of the statements made by the police to obtain their search warrant. The U.S. Supreme Court reversed and held that the Fourth Amendment requires an evidentiary hearing (called a ***Franks* hearing**) into the truthfulness of allegations in an affidavit in support of an application for a search warrant "where the defendant makes a substantial preliminary showing that a false statement knowingly and intentionally, or with reckless disregard for the truth, was included by the affiant in the warrant affidavit, and if the allegedly false statement is necessary to the finding of probable cause." 439 U.S. 154, 155–156, 98 S.Ct. 2674, 2676, 57 L.Ed.2d 667 (1978).

Return of Seized Property

Illegally seized property must be returned to the owner; however, the government may retain property lawfully seized as long as the government has a legitimate interest in its retention. Whether seized legally or illegally, contraband or property subject to forfeiture is not subject to being returned. See *United States v. Carter*, 859 F. Supp. 202 (E.D. Va. 1994). The return of other seized property is generally handled expeditiously based on a motion of the party seeking return. See, for example, Fed. R. Crim. P. 41(g).

Exceptions to the Warrant Requirement

Courts have recognized that an absolute warrant requirement would be impractical. Consequently, they have upheld the reasonableness of **warrantless searches** under so-called exigent circumstances. Yet, despite a number of exceptions, the warrant requirement remains a central feature of Fourth Amendment law. Whenever possible, police officers should obtain warrants because their failure to do so can jeopardize the fruits of a successful search. The following are well-defined exceptions to the warrant requirement. However, it is important to understand that all these exceptions assume that police officers have probable cause to believe that a given search is likely to produce evidence of crime.

Evidence in Plain View

The Supreme Court has said that evidence in plain view of a police officer is not subject to the warrant requirement. *Harris v. United States*, 390 U.S. 234, 88 S.Ct. 992, 19 L.Ed.2d 1067 (1968). Police officers are not required to close their eyes or wear blinders in the face of evidence of a crime. Police officers have long been permitted to seize evidence that comes to their attention inadvertently, provided that (1) the officer has a legal justification to be in a constitutionally protected area when the seizure occurs, (2) the evidence seized is in the plain view of the officer who comes across it, and (3) it is apparent that the object constitutes evidence of a crime. *Coolidge v. New*

Hampshire, supra. An officer may not seize anything and everything in plain view—the officer must have probable cause.

The "inadvertent discovery" requirement announced in *Coolidge v. New Hampshire* remained in effect for more than a decade. However, in *Horton v. California,* 496 U.S. 128, 110 S.Ct. 2301, 110 L.Ed.2d 112 (1990), the Supreme Court noted that the inadvertence requirement was not an essential part of the plurality opinion in *Coolidge v. New Hampshire.* As the Court observed in 1983, "There is no reason [the police officer] should be precluded from observing as an officer what would be entirely visible to him as a private citizen." *Texas v. Brown,* 460 U.S. 730, 740, 103 S.Ct. 1535, 1542, 75 L.Ed.2d 502 (1983). Notwithstanding, some state courts have continued to insist that the inadvertence requirement is a limitation on the plain view exception to the warrant requirement. See, for example, *State v. Davis,* 828 A.2d 293 (N.H. 2003).

The **plain-view doctrine** may apply both where the item seized is in plain view before the commencement of a search and where it comes into the plain view of an officer conducting an otherwise valid search or entry. For example, in *United States v. Pacelli,* 470 F.2d 67 (2d Cir. 1972), the court invoked the plain view doctrine to uphold the seizure of illegal chemicals found during a search based on a warrant to search for heroin. The search warrant gave police officers the right to enter and search the premises; other items of contraband found in plain view during the search were deemed properly seized.

In contrast with *Pacelli,* consider the case of *Arizona v. Hicks,* 480 U.S. 321, 107 S.Ct. 1149, 94 L.Ed.2d 347 (1987). There, police who had lawfully entered an apartment to search for weapons noticed stereo equipment that seemed out of place, given the squalid condition of the apartment. His suspicion aroused, an officer moved the stereo equipment to locate the serial numbers. A check of the numbers indicated that the equipment was stolen. The Supreme Court disallowed the "search" of the serial numbers because they were not in plain view when the police entered the apartment.

Emergency Searches

Police frequently must respond to emergencies involving reports of crime or injuries. In other instances, they accompany firefighters to the scene of a fire. Increasingly, law enforcement authorities are called to investigate bomb threats where explosive devices are possibly sequestered inside buildings. Although these are among the most dramatic emergencies, in many other situations police are called to conduct **emergency searches.** The law recognizes that police do not have the time to obtain search warrants in such instances. Of course, police must possess probable cause to make warrantless emergency searches of dwellings. While they are on premises in response to an emergency, police may seize evidence in plain view during the course of their legitimate emergency activities. *Michigan v. Tyler,* 436 U.S. 499, 98 S.Ct. 1942, 56 L.Ed.2d 486 (1978).

Even when investigating a crime scene, police are not permitted to search anything and everything found. In *Flippo v. West Virginia,* 528 U.S. 11, 120 S.Ct. 7, 145 L.Ed.2d 16 (1999), the police responded to a 9-1-1 call reporting that a man and his wife had been attacked in a cabin at a state park. When they arrived, the police found the woman fatally wounded. While investigating the crime scene, they discovered a briefcase. They opened it and an envelope within it and found photographs that tended to incriminate the husband. The prosecutor attempted to justify the seizure based on a "crime scene" exception to the warrant requirement. While recognizing that police may make warrantless searches for perpetrators and victims at a crime scene, the Supreme Court rejected the contention that there is a "crime scene exception" to the Warrant Clause of the Fourth Amendment. In remanding the case to the lower court, the Court allowed that the police might have secured the evidence by consent, under the plain view doctrine, or under the inventory exception to the warrant requirement but not on the basis of a claimed crime scene exception.

Police do not violate the Fourth Amendment if they stop a vehicle when they have adequate grounds to believe the driver is ill or falling asleep. *State v. Pinkham,* 565 A.2d 318 (Me. 1989). Likewise, police who make warrantless entries and searches when they reasonably believe that a person within is in need of immediate aid do not violate the protections against unreasonable search and seizure. Once inside, the police may justifiably seize evidence in plain view. See *Mincey v. Arizona,* 437 U.S. 385, 392, 98 S.Ct. 2408, 2413, 57 L.Ed.2d 290, 300 (1978). An officer's belief that an emergency exists must be reasonable, however. Chief Justice (then judge) Warren Burger in *Wayne v. United States,* 318 F.2d 205, 212 (D.C. Cir. 1963), opined that "the need to protect or preserve life or avoid serious injury is justification for what would be otherwise illegal absent an exigency or emergency." In *United States v. Al-Azzawy,* 784 F.2d 890 (9th Cir. 1985), the court upheld a warrantless search where a suspect was believed to be in possession of explosives and in such an agitated state as to create a risk of endangering the lives of others.

Preservation of Evidence

A frequently invoked justification for a warrantless search and seizure is the preservation of **evanescent evidence**—evidence that might be lost or destroyed. Where there is a reasonable belief that loss or destruction of evidence is imminent, a warrantless entry of premises may be justified, *United States v. Gonzalez,* 967 F.2d 1032 (4th Cir. 1992), but a mere possibility of such is insufficient, *United States v. Hayes,* 518 F.2d 675, 678 (6th Cir. 1975). The leading case in this area is *Schmerber v. California,* 384 U.S. 757, 86 S.Ct. 1826, 16 L.Ed.2d 908 (1966), where the Supreme Court upheld a warrantless blood-alcohol test of a person who appeared to be intoxicated. The Court characterized the forcible blood test as a "minor intrusion" and noted that the test was performed by qualified medical personnel. However, the most significant fact of the case was that the suspect's blood-alcohol level was rapidly diminishing, and the time required for police to obtain a search warrant could well have changed the results of the test.

In 1984 the Supreme Court narrowed the doctrine, saying that destruction of evidence does not constitute exigent circumstances if the underlying offense is relatively minor. *Welsh v. Wisconsin,* 466 U.S. 740, 104 S.Ct. 2091, 80 L.Ed.2d 732 (1984). Since then, lower courts have disagreed over what constitutes a "relatively minor" offense. In particular, drug offenses, many of which are felonies or misdemeanors depending on the quantity of contraband involved, have proven vexing to police and courts trying to apply the "relatively minor" standard. In 1993 the Idaho Supreme Court said that a minor offense is one that is nonviolent; thus, drug possession offenses, even if felonies, are "minor offenses." The court announced its decision in a case where police, acting with probable cause but without a warrant, entered a home and seized marijuana they believed was about to be destroyed. *State v. Curl,* 869 P.2d 224 (Idaho 1993). It remains to be seen whether other states will take the position adopted by the Idaho Supreme Court.

Search Incident to a Lawful Arrest

A **search incident to a lawful arrest** is an exception to the warrant requirement in order that the police may disarm an arrestee and preserve evidence. It has long been recognized that such a search is permissible. *Weeks v. United States,* 232 U.S. 383, 34 S.Ct. 341, 58 L.Ed. 652 (1914). For many years, this rule was interpreted quite broadly. For example, in *United States v. Rabinowitz,* 339 U.S. 56, 70 S.Ct. 430, 94 L.Ed. 653 (1950), the Supreme Court upheld a warrantless search of an entire home incident to a lawful arrest that occurred there. In 1969 the Supreme Court narrowed the permissible scope of searches incident to lawful arrests. *Chimel v. California,* 395 U.S. 752, 89 S.Ct. 2034, 23 L.Ed.2d 685 (1969). Under *Chimel,* police may search the body of an arrestee and the area within that person's immediate control. The area of immediate control is often defined as the area within the "grasp" or "lunge" of the arrestee. To conduct a more extensive search, police must generally obtain a search warrant.

Even if a formal arrest is not made until after a search, the search will be upheld as one incident to arrest if there was probable cause for the arrest before the search was begun. *Bailey v. United States,* 389 F.2d 305 (D.C. Cir. 1967). On the other hand, courts will not uphold a search where it is shown that the arrest was a mere pretext to conduct a warrantless search. See, for example, *United States v. Jones,* 452 F.2d 884 (8th Cir. 1971).

There are definite limitations on police conducting a search incident to arrest. Despite the existence of probable cause, absent extraordinary circumstances, the police have no right to search a dwelling when an arrest occurs outside it. As the Supreme Court observed in *Payton v. New York,* 445 U.S. 573, 591, 100 S.Ct. 1371, 1382, 63 L.Ed.2d 639, 653 (1980), "The Fourth Amendment has drawn a firm line at the entrance to the house. Absent exigent circumstances, that threshold may not reasonably be crossed without a warrant." Exigent circumstances would most likely include a situation where, after an arrest, the officers have a reasonable basis to suspect there may be others on the premises who pose a danger to the police or who may destroy evidence. See *Vale v. Louisiana,* 399 U.S. 30, 90 S.Ct. 1969, 26 L.Ed.2d 409 (1970). Thus, police who made an arrest outside a residence and had knowledge regarding cocaine trafficking taking place inside were not barred from entering the house to conduct a "protective sweep" for other persons who might pose a threat to their safety. *United States v. Hoyos,* 892 F.2d 1387 (9th Cir. 1989). Nevertheless, once a person is arrested and in custody, searching that person's car at another location is not a search incident to arrest. *Preston v. United States,* 376 U.S. 364, 84 S.Ct. 881, 11 L.Ed.2d 777 (1964).

Hot Pursuit

Officers in **hot pursuit** of a fleeing suspect already have probable cause to make an arrest. The Supreme Court has long recognized that police may pursue the suspect into a protected place, such as a home, without having to abandon their pursuit until a warrant can be obtained. *Warden v. Hayden,* 387 U.S. 294, 87 S.Ct. 1642, 18 L.Ed.2d 782 (1967). As the police enter a building and look for a suspect therein, they are by definition engaged in a search. If they find the suspect and make an arrest, they have in effect made a seizure. Once the suspect is in custody, police may engage in a warrantless search of the immediate area, which might produce evidence such as discarded weapons or contraband.

Automobile Stops and Roadside Searches of Motor Vehicles

Police may stop an automobile without a warrant and temporarily detain the driver as long as they have probable cause to believe that criminal activity is taking place or

Go to the Scheb/Scheb Criminal Law and Procedure 6e website at academic.cengage.com/criminaljustice/scheb for an edited version of *Chimel v. California.*

Go to the Scheb/ Scheb Criminal Law and Procedure 6e website at academic .cengage.com/criminaljustice/ scheb for an edited version of *Whren v. U.S.*

that traffic laws or automobile regulations are being violated. *Whren v. United States,* 517 U.S. 806, 116 S.Ct. 1769, 135 L.Ed.2d 89 (1996). Sometimes, police use a minor traffic or equipment violation as a pretext for stopping an automobile that they wish to investigate. When police make such stops, evidence of drug or alcohol use or some other criminal violation may become readily apparent, which allows police to make a warrantless arrest and a warrantless search incident to that arrest.

In *New York v. Belton,* 453 U.S. 454, 101 S.Ct. 2860, 69 L.Ed.2d 768 (1981), the Supreme Court held that a police officer who makes a valid arrest of an occupant of an automobile may search the passenger compartment of the car even in the absence of probable cause to believe there is evidence located there. This search incident to arrest is justified on the assumption that the arrestee could reach into the passenger compartment to destroy evidence or obtain a weapon. Of course, if a person is in handcuffs or otherwise under the control of the police, it would seem unlikely that he or she could exercise any control over the passenger compartment of the car. Thus, *Belton* has been criticized as moving beyond the rationale of *Chimel.* Most state courts have followed the *Belton* approach, but several have not. For example, in *People v. Belton,* 432 N.E.2d 745 (N.Y. 1982) (a different case involving a different Belton), the New York Court of Appeals declined to adopt the U.S. Supreme Court's decision in *Belton* (discussed above) as a matter of state constitutional law. Likewise, in *State v. Brown,* 588 N.E.2d 113 (Ohio 1992), the Ohio Supreme Court rejected *Belton,* which it characterized as allowing police "to search every nook and cranny of an automobile just because the driver is arrested for a traffic violation." 588 N.E.2d at 115. Of course, if a driver is taken into custody and there is no one else legally able to take control of the car, police may impound the vehicle and conduct an inventory search.

As interpreted by the state supreme court, Iowa law allowed an officer to conduct a full-blown search of an automobile and its driver when the officer stopped a motorist for speeding and issued a traffic citation. The officer searched the vehicle without consent or probable cause, and the search revealed a bag of marijuana and a "pot pipe." The search was upheld by the Iowa Supreme Court. *State v. Knowles,* 569 N.W.2d 601 (Iowa 1997). But the U.S. Supreme Court granted review and the following year held that a search under these circumstances (where a traffic citation was issued and no custodial arrest was involved) violates the Fourth Amendment. *Knowles v. Iowa,* 525 U.S. 113, 119 S.Ct. 484, 142 L.Ed.2d 492 (1998).

Go to the Scheb/ Scheb Criminal Law and Procedure 6e website at academic .cengage.com/criminaljustice/ scheb for an edited version of *Knowles v. Iowa.*

THE SCOPE OF WARRANTLESS ROADSIDE AUTOMOBILE SEARCHES

Quite often, automobile stops involve fairly extensive roadside searches and seizures. The Supreme Court has long recognized the validity of the so-called **automobile exception** to the warrant requirement, as long as police have probable cause to believe the vehicle contains contraband or evidence of crime, on the premise that the mobile character of a motor vehicle creates a practical necessity for an immediate search. *Carroll v. United States,* supra. The Court has held that once begun under exigent circumstances, a warrantless search of an automobile may continue after the vehicle has been taken to the police station. *Chambers v. Maroney,* 399 U.S. 42, 90 S.Ct. 1975, 26 L.Ed.2d 419 (1970).

Several state supreme courts have refused to go along with *Chambers v. Maroney.* For example, in August 1993, the Connecticut Supreme Court refused to adopt *Chambers v. Maroney* as a matter of state constitutional law. In *State v. Miller,* 630 A.2d 1315 (Conn. 1993), the court noted that any exigent circumstances that might justify a roadside automobile search disappear once the vehicle has been impounded. Writing for the court was Chief Justice Ellen A. Peters:

SUPREME COURT PERSPECTIVE

Delaware v. Prouse, 440 U.S. 648, 99 S.Ct. 1391, 59 L.Ed.2d 660 (1979)

In this case the Supreme Court held that singling out and stopping an automobile in order to check the driver's license and registration is unreasonable under the Fourth Amendment unless there is at least reasonable suspicion to believe that the driver is unlicensed, the vehicle is unregistered, or some other criminal activity is afoot. In the course of his opinion for the Court, Justice Byron White discusses the approach that courts should take in judging the reasonableness of particular police practices that are challenged under the Fourth Amendment.

JUSTICE WHITE delivered the Opinion of the Court, saying in part:

The essential purpose of the proscriptions in the Fourth Amendment is to impose a standard of "reasonableness" upon the exercise of discretion by government officials, including law enforcement agents, in order "to safeguard the privacy and security of individuals against arbitrary invasions." … Thus, the permissibility of a particular law enforcement practice is judged by balancing its intrusion on the individual's Fourth Amendment interests against its promotion of legitimate governmental interests. Implemented in this manner, the reasonableness standard usually requires, at a minimum, that the facts upon which an intrusion is based be capable of measurement against "an objective standard," whether this be probable cause or a less stringent test. In those situations in which the balance of interests precludes insistence upon "some quantum of individualized suspicion," other safeguards are generally relied upon to assure that the individual's reasonable expectation of privacy is not "subject to the discretion of the official in the field."

We tolerate the warrantless on-the-scene automobile search only because obtaining a warrant would be impracticable in light of the inherent mobility of automobiles and the latent exigency that that mobility creates. The balance between law enforcement interests and individuals' privacy interests thus tips in favor of law enforcement in the context of an on-the-scene automobile search. If the impracticability of obtaining a warrant no longer exists, however, our state constitutional preference for warrants regains its dominant place in that balance, and a warrant is required. 630 A.2d at 1325.

One perennial problem associated with warrantless automobile searches is how closed containers, such as suitcases, found inside automobiles should be treated. In 1982 the U.S. Supreme Court held that a police officer having probable cause to believe that evidence of a crime is concealed within an automobile may conduct a search as broad as one that could be authorized by a magistrate issuing a warrant. *United States v. Ross,* 456 U.S. 798, 102 S.Ct. 2157, 72 L.Ed.2d 572 (1982). This ruling effectively allowed police officers to search closed containers found during the course of an automobile search without first having to obtain a warrant. In *United States v. Johns,* 469 U.S. 478, 105 S.Ct. 881, 83 L.Ed.2d 890 (1985), the Court upheld the warrantless search of plastic containers seized during an automobile search even though the police had waited several days before opening the containers. The Court reasoned that since police legitimately seized the containers during the original search of the automobile, no reasonable expectation of privacy could be maintained once the containers came under police control. The search of the containers, which produced a substantial quantity of marijuana, was therefore not unreasonable simply because it was delayed.

In 1998 a highway patrol officer in Wyoming stopped a speeding car. While speaking to the driver, the officer noticed a syringe in the driver's pocket. The driver admitted using the syringe to inject drugs. Having probable cause to search the car,

Go to the Scheb/ Scheb Criminal Law and Procedure 6e website at academic .cengage.com/criminaljustice/ scheb for an edited version of *U.S. v. Ross.*

the officer then opened a passenger's purse on the back seat and found contraband. The Wyoming Supreme Court ruled that the search that yielded the contraband was not within the permissible scope of search of the vehicle and thus violated the Fourth Amendment. *Houghton v. State,* 956 P.2d 363 (1998). On review, the U.S. Supreme Court held that police officers who have probable cause to search a vehicle may search the belongings of passengers who are capable of concealing objects of the search. *Wyoming v. Houghton,* 526 U.S. 295, 119 S.Ct. 1297, 140 L.Ed.2d 408 (1999).

Exceptions to the Probable Cause Requirement

Warrantless searches are now well established in the law, and although reasonable people might disagree about specific cases, there is consensus that warrantless searches are often necessary and proper. The same cannot be said for the next category of searches—those based on something less than probable cause. In these special situations, courts permit limited searches based on the lesser standard of reasonable suspicion. Reasonable suspicion is the belief, based on articulable circumstances, that criminal activity might be afoot. The classic application of the reasonable suspicion standard is to the so-called "stop-and-frisk."

Stop-and-Frisk

The **stop-and-frisk** is a routine law enforcement technique whereby police officers stop, question, and sometimes search suspicious persons. In *Terry v. Ohio,* 392 U.S. 1, 88 S.Ct. 1868, 20 L.Ed.2d 889 (1968), the Supreme Court upheld the authority of police officers to detain and conduct a limited "pat-down" search of several men who were acting suspiciously. Given the limited intrusiveness of the pat-down and the compelling need to protect officers in the field, the Court allowed the warrantless search for weapons on a reasonable suspicion standard instead of imposing the traditional probable cause requirement. Subsequently, the Court stressed the narrow scope of the stop-and-frisk exception by saying that "nothing in *Terry* can be understood to allow … any search whatever for anything but weapons." *Ybarra v. Illinois,* 444 U.S. 85, 93–94, 100 S.Ct. 338, 343, 62 L.Ed.2d 238, 247 (1979).

 Go to the Scheb/ Scheb Criminal Law and Procedure 6e website at academic .cengage.com/criminaljustice/ scheb for an edited version of *Terry v. Ohio.*

In *Michigan v. Long,* 463 U.S. 1032, 103 S.Ct. 3469, 77 L.Ed.2d 1201 (1983), the Supreme Court held that seizure of contraband other than weapons during a lawfully conducted *Terry* search was justified under the plain view doctrine. Going a step further in *Minnesota v. Dickerson,* 508 U.S. 366, 113 S.Ct. 2130, 124 L.Ed.2d 334 (1993), the Court said that police may seize nonthreatening contraband detected through their sense of touch during a protective pat-down search as long as that search stays within the bounds of a *Terry* search. This extension of *Terry* is sometimes referred to as a "plain feel" exception to the warrant requirement of the Fourth Amendment. Nevertheless, in *Dickerson* the Court found the search and seizure of contraband invalid because the officer conducting the search determined that the item he seized was contraband only after searching beyond the scope authorized in *Terry*. (More attention is given to the so-called *Terry* stop in Chapter 16.)

IS A STOP-AND-FRISK PERMISSIBLE BASED ON AN ANONYMOUS TIP?

In *Alabama v. White,* 496 U.S. 325, 110 S.Ct. 2412, 110 L.Ed.2d 301 (1990), police received an anonymous tip that a certain female was carrying cocaine and that she would leave a certain apartment at a specified time, get into a car matching a

Go to the Scheb/
Scheb Criminal Law
and Procedure 6e
website at academic
.cengage.com/criminaljustice/
scheb for an edited version of
Florida v. J.L.

particular description, and drive to a particular motel. The police conducted surveillance of the woman, which verified elements of the tip. Only then did they move in to stop her car, detain her, and seize the cocaine. Characterizing the case as a "close" one, the Supreme Court upheld the police procedure but said that the tip alone would not have justified the stop-and-frisk. It was on that basis that the Court invalidated a seizure of a firearm in *Florida v. J.L.,* 529 U.S. 266, 120 S.Ct. 1375, 146 L.Ed.2d 254 (2000). In the latter case, the Court observed that "an anonymous tip lacking indicia of reliability … does not justify a stop and frisk whenever and however it alleges the illegal possession of a firearm." 529 U.S. at 274, 120 S.Ct. at 1380, 146 L.Ed.2d at 262.

Drug Courier Profiles

Go to the Scheb/
Scheb Criminal Law
and Procedure 6e
website at academic
.cengage.com/criminaljustice/
scheb for an edited versions
of *Reid v. Georgia* and *U.S.
v. Sokolow.*

In attempting to identify and to apprehend drug smugglers, law enforcement agencies have developed drug courier profiles. These profiles are sets of characteristics that typify drug couriers, such as paying for airline tickets in cash, appearing nervous, carrying certain types of luggage, and so forth. In *Reid v. Georgia,* 448 U.S. 438, 100 S.Ct. 2752, 65 L.Ed.2d 890 (1980), the Supreme Court suggested that fitting a drug courier profile was not in itself sufficient to constitute the reasonable suspicion necessary to allow police to detain an airline passenger. Therefore, the stopping of an airline passenger on that basis violated the Fourth Amendment. However, in *United States v. Sokolow,* 490 U.S. 1, 109 S.Ct. 1581, 104 L.Ed.2d 1 (1989), the Court upheld a similar investigatory detention in which a drug courier profile was employed. It is instructive to examine these decisions side by side to determine how and why the Court distinguished the two situations.

School Searches

In the First Amendment context, the Supreme Court has said that students in public schools do not "shed their constitutional rights … at the schoolhouse gate." *Tinker v. Des Moines Independent Community School District,* 393 U.S. 503, 506, 89 S.Ct. 733, 736, 21 L.Ed.2d 731, 737 (1969). Following this premise, the Court has held that the Fourth Amendment protects children in the public schools from unreasonable searches and seizures. However, the Court has said that such searches are to be judged by a reasonableness standard and are not subject to the requirement of probable cause. Moreover, the Court has said that the warrant requirement is particularly unsuited to the unique

CASE-IN-POINT

Detention and Search of a Suspected Drug Courier Based on "Reasonable Suspicion"

A suspected drug courier was held incommunicado in an airport security room for sixteen hours while officers obtained a court order permitting an X-ray and rectal examination. During the examination a plastic balloon containing cocaine was retrieved. Over the next several days, the defendant passed some eighty-eight cocaine-filled balloons. The Supreme Court upheld the protracted detention and search, despite the lack of probable cause. The Court said that in such circumstances the lesser standard of reasonable suspicion was sufficient.

United States v. Montoya de Hernandez, 473 U.S. 531, 105 S.Ct. 3304, 87 L.Ed.2d 381 (1985).

circumstances of the school environment. *New Jersey v. T.L.O.,* 469 U.S. 325, 105 S.Ct. 733, 83 L.Ed.2d 720 (1985). The pervasive problem of illicit drug use in the schools as well as the notorious incidents of school violence in recent years have added pressure to relax Fourth Amendment standards in the public school context. Although there are certainly exceptions, most search and seizure policies implemented by public schools have been upheld by the courts. These include "sweeps" for drugs and guns using such devices as drug sniffing dogs and metal detectors, as well as routine searches of backpacks, lockers, and even automobiles coming onto school grounds.

In *Commonwealth v. Cass,* 709 A.2d 350 (Pa. 1998), a leading case decided by the Pennsylvania Supreme Court, a public high school principal brought in police and drug sniffing dogs to detect drugs sequestered in student lockers. When a dog "alerted" to a particular locker, school officials would open it and search the contents. Eighteen lockers were searched, and one of them was found to contain a small amount of marijuana and some related paraphernalia. The student to whom that locker was assigned was suspended from school for ten days, required to attend drug counseling, and charged criminally with possession of marijuana and possession of drug paraphernalia. In rejecting a challenge to the constitutionality of the search that led to the discovery of the contraband, the Pennsylvania Supreme court observed:

> Common sense dictates that when a student is given permission to store his or her belongings in a locker designated for his or her personal and exclusive use, that student can reasonably expect a measure of privacy within that locker. Common sense further dictates that when the student's use of the locker is expressly conditioned upon the acknowledgment that the locker belongs to the school, that measure of privacy is necessarily limited. *Id.* at 359.

Drug Testing

Go to the Scheb/ Scheb Criminal Law and Procedure 6e website at academic .cengage.com/criminaljustice/ scheb for an edited version of *Treasury Employees v. Von Raab.*

Because of the paramount interest in ensuring the public safety, courts have upheld the constitutionality of regulations permitting supervisory personnel to order urinalysis testing of public safety officers based on reasonable suspicion of drug abuse. See, for example, *Turner v. Fraternal Order of Police,* 500 A.2d 1005 (D.C. App. 1985). In 1989 the U.S. Supreme Court upheld federal regulations requiring drug and alcohol testing of railroad employees involved in train accidents. *Skinner v. Railway Labor Executives' Association,* 489 U.S. 602, 109 S.Ct. 1402, 1411, 103 L.Ed.2d 639 (1989). The Court has also sustained a Customs Service policy requiring drug tests for persons seeking positions as customs inspectors. *Treasury Employees Union v. Von Raab,* 489 U.S. 656, 109 S.Ct. 1384, 103 L.Ed.2d 685 (1989). As yet, the Supreme Court has not addressed the issue of general, random drug testing of public employees. However, it has invalidated a policy under which all political candidates were required to submit to drug testing as a condition of qualifying for the ballot. *Chandler v. Miller,* 520 U.S. 305, 117 S.Ct. 1295, 137 L.Ed.2d 513 (1997).

In 1995 the U.S. Supreme Court stated that a public school district's student athlete drug policy, which authorized random urinalysis drug testing of students who participated in athletic programs, did not violate a student's right to be free from unreasonable searches. While mandatory drug testing is a search, Justice Scalia, writing for a 6–3 majority of the Court, pointed out that, given the decreased expectation of privacy of a public school student, the relative unobtrusiveness of the search, and the severity of the need, such a search was not unreasonable. *Vernonia School District v. Acton,* 515 U.S. 646, 115 S.Ct. 2386, 132 L.Ed.2d 564 (1995).

Several state courts have addressed the question of random drug testing of public employees, and at least one state appellate court has found such a policy to be unconstitutional. *City of Palm Bay v. Bauman,* 475 So.2d 1322 (Fla. App. 1985). Given the scope of the drug problem and the governmental resolve to do something about it, the issue of random drug testing is certain to be litigated for some time to come.

When administrative personnel turn over results of drug tests to law enforcement agencies for criminal prosecution, courts tend to exercise a higher level of scrutiny. The leading case in this regard is *Ferguson v. City of Charleston,* 532 U.S. 67, 121 S.Ct. 1281, 149 L.Ed.2d 205 (2001), in which the U.S. Supreme Court invalidated a policy under which a public hospital turned over to police urine samples of pregnant women who had tested positive for cocaine. The High Court noted that

> The fact that positive test results were turned over to the police does not merely provide a basis for distinguishing our prior cases applying the "special needs" balancing approach to the determination of drug use. It also provides an affirmative reason for enforcing the strictures of the Fourth Amendment. 532 U.S. at 84, 121 S.Ct. at 1292, 149 L.Ed.2d at 220.

Go to the Scheb/ Scheb Criminal Law and Procedure 6e website at academic .cengage.com/criminaljustice/ scheb for an edited version of *Ferguson v. Charleston.*

Electronic Surveillance

The drafters of the Fourth Amendment obviously did not contemplate present-day technology. Yet, in framing the Bill of Rights, they used simple, straightforward language that has endured through the centuries—language capable of being adapted to the needs of the people. Today's technology makes possible silent and invisible intrusions on the privacy of the individual, and the courts are responding to these new, innovative means of surveillance, always cognizant that the touchstone of the Fourth Amendment is its prohibition of "unreasonable" searches and seizures. Of course, the interpretation of what is "reasonable" is apt to be affected by pressing public needs. The attacks on American cities on September 11, 2001, and the subsequent "war on terrorism" have had an enormous impact in the area of electronic surveillance, both in terms of what law enforcement agencies are now doing and what legislation and judicial opinions authorize.

Expectations of Privacy with Respect to Electronic Surveillance

Generally speaking, the use of wiretaps, microphones, video recorders, and other devices that permit agencies to intercept the content of what would otherwise be private communications implicates the Fourth Amendment. *Katz v. United States,* supra. However, merely using technology to augment the senses does not necessarily trigger Fourth Amendment protections. For example, the Supreme Court has approved the use of searchlights, field glasses, aerial photography, and various other means of enhancing the police's powers of observation, even in the absence of a warrant or probable cause. *United States v. Lee,* 274 U.S. 559, 47 S.Ct. 746, 71 L.Ed. 1202 (1927); *Texas v. Brown,* 460 U.S. 730, 103 S.Ct. 1535, 75 L.Ed.2d 502 (1983). Lower federal courts have even approved miniaturized television camera surveillance. *United States v. Torres,* 751 F.2d 875 (7th Cir. 1984). The question is whether the police use methods that infringe on a person's reasonable expectations of privacy. If so, they need a warrant or some other form of judicial authorization before deploying these technologies.

CORDLESS AND CELLULAR TELEPHONES: A CASE STUDY IN PRIVACY EXPECTATIONS

Changes in technology often create new legal questions. An excellent example is the proliferation of cordless telephones in the 1980s. When one uses a cordless phone, one is essentially broadcasting a low-power radio signal to a nearby receiver (the base unit) that is connected to a phone line. But any nearby receiver tuned to the correct frequency can intercept a conversation being conducted on a cordless phone. Analog cellular telephones operate in much the same way, although their signals are more powerful so they can communicate with towers located within "cells." The new digital cell phones are more difficult to eavesdrop upon as their signals are encrypted. Realizing the potential for monitoring conversations on cordless telephones and analog cellular phones, police sometimes employ receivers or scanners mounted in vehicles to eavesdrop on conversations. In doing this without a warrant or even probable cause, are police in violation of the Fourth Amendment?

In *Tyler v. Berodt,* 877 F.2d 705 (8th Cir. 1989) and *United States v. Smith,* 978 F.2d 171, 177 (5th Cir. 1992), two federal courts ruled that users of cordless phones had no reasonable expectation of privacy; therefore, the interception of their calls was not a "search" within the meaning of the Fourth Amendment. However, in *State v. Mozo,* 655 So.2d 1115 (Fla. 1995), the Florida Supreme Court held that nonconsensual interception of cordless phone calls without prior judicial approval violates a state statute protecting the privacy of communications. That court declined to reach the constitutional issues in the case, preferring to base its decision on statutory grounds. In 1986 Congress enacted a statute to provide nationwide protection against eavesdropping on cellular phone conversations, and in 1994 the statute was amended to provide protection for cordless phones as well. Thus Congress provided through legislation protection to individual privacy that federal courts were unable or unwilling to provide via the Fourth Amendment.

The Supreme Court's Major Decisions in the Area of Electronic Surveillance

The U.S. Supreme Court has rendered only a few decisions affecting the legality of electronic surveillance by police, but these decisions have had a major impact on law enforcement practices. In *Smith v. Maryland,* 442 U.S. 735, 99 S.Ct. 2577, 61 L.Ed.2d 220 (1979), the Court determined that the employment of a **pen register** is not a search within the meaning of the Fourth Amendment. A pen register is a device that records the phone numbers that are dialed from a particular phone number. Writing for the Court, Justice Harry Blackmun observed that merely by using the phone, the defendant "voluntarily conveyed numerical information to the telephone company and 'exposed' that information to its equipment in the ordinary course of business." 442 U.S. at 744, 99 S.Ct. at 2582, 61 L.Ed.2d at 229. Blackmun concluded that in so doing, the defendant "assumed the risk that the company would reveal to police the numbers he dialed." *Ibid.* In a vigorous dissenting opinion, Justice Potter Stewart asserted, "It is simply not enough to say, after *Katz,* that there is no legitimate expectation of privacy in the numbers dialed because the caller assumes the risk that the telephone company will disclose them to the police." 442 U.S. at 747, 99 S.Ct. at 2583, 61 L.Ed.2d at 231. In another dissenting opinion, Justice Thurgood Marshall observed that "[p]rivacy in placing calls is of value not only to those engaged in criminal activity" and predicted that "[t]he prospect of unregulated governmental monitoring will undoubtedly prove

Go to the Scheb/ Scheb Criminal Law and Procedure 6e website at academic .cengage.com/criminaljustice/ scheb for an edited version of *Smith v. Maryland.*

disturbing even to those with nothing illicit to hide." 442 U.S. at 751, 99 S.Ct. at 2586, 61 L.Ed.2d at 234.

In *Dow Chemical Company v. United States,* 476 U.S. 227, 106 S.Ct. 1819, 90 L.Ed.2d 226 (1986), the Supreme Court held that high-altitude photography of a chemical plant was not a search within the meaning of the Fourth Amendment. The Court concluded that the means of surveillance was incapable of revealing intimate activities that would give rise to constitutional concerns. That same year, in *California v. Ciraolo,* 476 U.S. 207, 106 S.Ct. 1809, 90 L.Ed.2d 210 (1986), the Court upheld a conviction where police, acting on a tip, conducted a low-altitude flight and photographed marijuana plants growing in the defendant's backyard. The police then used the photos to obtain a warrant and seize the contraband. In upholding the search, the Court said, "[W]e readily conclude that [the defendant's] expectation that his garden was protected from [aerial] observation is unreasonable and is not an expectation that society is prepared to honor." 476 U.S. at 214, 106 S.Ct. at 1813, 90 L.Ed.2d at 217. Dissenting, Justice Powell suggested that the Court's decision was inconsistent with the broad interpretation of the Fourth Amendment suggested by the Court's seminal decision in *Katz v. United States:*

> Rapidly advancing technology now permits police to conduct surveillance in the home itself, an area where privacy interests are most cherished in our society, without any physical trespass. While the rule in *Katz* was designed to prevent silent and unseen invasions of Fourth Amendment privacy rights in a variety of settings, we have consistently afforded heightened protection to a person's right to be left alone in the privacy of his house. The Court fails to enforce that right or to give any weight to the longstanding presumption that warrantless intrusions into the home are unreasonable. 476 U.S. at 226, 106 S.Ct. at 1819, 90 L.Ed.2d at 225.

In the 1980s, police looking for marijuana being grown indoors under artificial light began to use infrared thermal imagers, which detect heat waves. These devices can provide a strong indication of whether marijuana is being grown inside a closed structure. Prior to 2001, most courts that considered this issue ruled that using thermal imaging devices was not a search within the meaning of the Fourth Amendment. See, for example, *United States v. Pinson,* 24 F.3d 1056 (8th Cir. 1994); *United States v. Ford,* 34 F.3d 992 (11th Cir. 1994); and *United States v. Penny-Feeney,* 773 F. Supp. 220 (D.C. Hawaii 1991). A notable exception was *State v. Young,* 867 P.2d 593 (Wash. 1994), where the Washington Supreme Court held that the use of a thermal imaging device was a search within the meaning of the Washington state constitution. In *Kyllo v. United States,* 533 U.S. 27, 121 S.Ct. 2038, 150 L.Ed.2d 94 (2001), the U.S. Supreme Court adopted the view taken by the Washington Supreme Court. Writing for the Court, Justice Scalia concluded that when "the Government uses a device that is not in general public use, to explore details of the home that would previously have been unknowable without physical intrusion, the surveillance is a 'search' and is presumptively unreasonable without a warrant." 533 U.S. at 40, 121 S.Ct. at 2046, 150 L.Ed.2d at 106.

Go to the Scheb/ Scheb Criminal Law and Procedure 6e website at academic .cengage.com/criminaljustice/ scheb for an edited version of *Kyllo v. U.S.*

Federal Legislation Governing Interception of Electronic Communications

As noted above, Congress has enacted legislation governing the interception of electronic communications. The cornerstone of this statutory edifice is Title III of the Omnibus Crime Control and Safe Streets Act of 1968, codified at 18 U.S.C.A. §§ 2510–20. The act prohibits interception of electronic communications without a court order unless one party to the conversation consents. Interception is defined as "aural or other acquisition of the contents of any wire, electronic or oral communication through the use of any electronic, mechanical, or other device." 18 U.S.C.A. § 2510(4). In 1986 Congress expanded the meaning of "wire communications" to include conversations through "switching stations." 18 U.S.C.A. § 2510(1). Therefore, the statute now covers cellular telephones.

WIRETAP ORDERS

Title III permits issuance of **wiretap orders** by federal and state courts on sworn applications authorized by the U.S. Attorney General, a specially designated assistant, or a state official at a similar level. The act expressly preempts state law. Therefore, to permit the use of electronic surveillance, a state must adopt legislation along the lines of the federal act, and many states have done so. See, for example, the New Jersey Wiretapping and Electronic Surveillance Control Act of 1968, N.J. Stat. Ann. § 2A: 156A–(1), *et seq.*

An application for a wiretap order must contain considerable detailed information along with an explanation of why less intrusive means of investigation will not suffice. 18 U.S.C.A. § 2518(1)(c). The statute requires that normal investigative procedures be employed first. But it does not require an officer to exhaust all possible investigative methods before applying for a wiretap order. Before a court may issue a wiretap order, it must find probable cause that the subject of the wiretap has committed or is committing one of a series of enumerated crimes for which wiretapping is authorized and that conventional modes of investigation will not suffice. 18 U.S.C.A. § 2518(3). Originally these offenses included narcotics, organized crime, and national security violations. In 1986 the act was amended to include numerous other serious crimes, including interstate transportation of stolen vehicles, bribery in sports contests, weapons of mass destruction threats, sex trafficking of children by force, fraud or coercion, mail fraud, and money laundering. 18 U.S.C.A. § 2516(1)(c).

Court orders permit surveillance for no longer than a thirty-day period. 18 U.S.C.A. § 2518(5). At the period's expiration, the recordings made of intercepted communications must be delivered to the judge who issued the order. They are then sealed under the judge's direction. 18 U.S.C.A. § 2518(8)(a).

THE ELECTRONIC COMMUNICATIONS PRIVACY ACT OF 1986

The Electronic Communications Privacy Act of 1986 (ECPA), 18 U.S.C.A. § 2701 *et seq.,* established federal standards for access to e-mail and other electronic communications and to "transactional records," including subscriber identifying information, call logs, phone bills, and so forth. The law established a high standard for access to the contents of electronic communications but allowed agencies to easily gain access to transactional records. One part of the act, 18 U.S.C.A. § 3121 *et seq.,* governs the use of pen registers and **trap and trace devices.** It requires judges to issue orders to allow the use of such devices when properly requested by prosecutors. There is no standard of proof that prosecutors have to meet in order to get such orders. The courts have generally taken the position that users of telephones have no reasonable expectations of privacy with regard to numbers associated with incoming or outgoing phone calls. Congress has chosen not to provide significant statutory protection in this area, much to the chagrin of civil libertarians.

Go to the Scheb/ Scheb Criminal Law and Procedure 6e website at academic .cengage.com/criminaljustice/ scheb to find *U.S. v. Fregoso* (1995), where the U.S. Court of Appeals for the Eighth Circuit discusses the federal statute pertaining to pen registers and trap and trace devices.

THE USA PATRIOT ACT

Many of the measures enacted into law by the USA PATRIOT Act (discussed in Chapters 10 and 12) are outside the scope of this chapter; however, Title II, "Enhanced Surveillance Procedures" includes provisions of particular relevance to our discussion of search and seizure. Title II enables law enforcement to access Internet communication and expands the authority for use of pen registers and trap and trace surveillance by including a number of salient features in respect to search and seizure. Listed below are several significant changes, most of which focus on expanding the government's power to conduct electronic surveillance:

- § 202. Computer fraud and abuse are added to the predicate crimes listed in 18 U.S.C.A. § 2516(1)(c) for seeking authorization for interception of wire, oral, or electronic communications.

- § 203. Rule 6(e)(3)(C), Federal Rules of Criminal Procedure and 18 U.S.C.A. § 2517 are amended to allow intelligence obtained in grand jury proceedings and from wiretaps to be shared with federal law enforcement and national security personnel for use in connection with their official duties.

- § 204. The act amends 18 U.S.C.A. § 2511(2)(f) in regard to interception and disclosure of electronic communications by inserting "wire, oral and electronic" in place of "wire and oral," thereby broadening the right of government to intercept electronic communications in foreign intelligence matters.

- § 206. The act also amends 18 U.S.C.A. § 1805(c)(2)(B) to authorize federal courts to issue "roving" surveillance orders in connection with foreign intelligence matters, enabling investigators to intercept e-mail and cell phone communications where suspects frequently change their account numbers.

- § 209. The act amends 18 U.S.C.A. § 2510 to authorize law enforcement officers to seize voice-mail messages pursuant to a search warrant instead of a wiretap order.

- § 210. The act amends 18 U.S.C.A. § 2703(c) to allow law enforcement officers to obtain by subpoena subscriber records of local and long distance telephone connection records, "records of session times and durations," and means of payment including credit card numbers from Internet Service Providers (ISPs).

- § 212. ISPs are allowed to reveal data concerning their customers without first notifying them if the ISP reasonably believes that "death or serious physical injury to any person" requires such disclosure without delay.

- § 214. The government only has to certify that the information that it obtains would be relevant to an "ongoing investigation" to secure a pen register or trap and trace order. Formerly, under 50 U.S.C.A. § 1842(c)(3), the government had to certify that it had reason to believe that surveillance was being conducted on a line or device that is or was used in "communications with" someone involved in international terrorism or intelligence activities that may violate U.S. criminal law, or a foreign power or its agent whose communication is believed to concern terrorism or intelligence activities that violate U.S. law.

- § 215. Among the very controversial provisions of the act is an amendment to the Foreign Intelligence Security Act (FISA), 50 U.S.C.A. § 1861 *et seq.*, which removes the limitations on the FBI's ability to obtain business records pursuant to an *ex parte* court order and grants the FBI the power in terrorism investigations to obtain records and other "tangible things" from entities that include libraries and Internet providers. The act forbids those served such orders from disclosing such fact to other than official sources (nondisclosure orders). (Section 215 became the focus of the first direct constitutional assault on the act in a suit filed by the American Civil Liberties Union and other organizations in July of 2003.) (See amendments to the act in the topic that follows on the 2006 Reauthorization Act.)

- § 216. Sections of the Electronic Communications Privacy Act (ECPA), 18 U.S.C.A. §§ 3121, 3123 (previously discussed), are amended to add the terms "routing" and "addressing" to the phrase "dialing and signaling information," thus expanding the federal government's authority to monitor Internet activities, as well as telephone conversations, by using systems similar to pen registers and trap and trace devices. This enables a U.S. Attorney, acting at the behest of the FBI, to obtain a court order allowing use of technology that records e-mail addresses and URLs of Web sites being accessed from a particular computer.

- § 216. The act also amends 18 U.S.C.A. § 3123(a) to provide that the court shall enter an *ex parte* order authorizing the installation and use of a pen register or trap and trace device anywhere within the United States if the court finds that the attorney for the Government has certified to the court that the information likely to be obtained by such installation and use is relevant to an ongoing criminal investigation. (Recall our previous discussion that a pen register or trap and trace device ordinarily reveals only such telephone transactions as numbers called from particular telephones.)

- § 219. The act also permits federal magistrate judges in any district in which terrorism-related activities may have occurred to issue search warrants for searches within or outside the district. This greatly facilitates the issuance of nationwide warrants for investigations involving terrorism.

As Americans come to rely more extensively on computers, e-mail, and the Internet, many see these new measures of exposing their Internet communications as a necessary evil in pursuit of a greater good, namely, the war on terrorism. Others find their constitutional rights being substantially diminished. While acknowledging that effective legislation is essential to protect the national security of the United States, they believe that greatly expanding the government's right to eavesdrop on e-mail and other Internet communications increases the potential for official mischief and diminishes individual liberty and privacy. Many Americans also see the right of law enforcement to share information revealed to a grand jury with intelligence-gathering agencies as unfairly impeding on the privacy of persons under investigation, many of whom are never indicted.

Although recognizing the imperatives of national security, many Americans would ask courts, legislatures, and their fellow citizens to heed the words of Justice Louis Brandeis written in a dissenting opinion more than seventy-five years ago:

> The makers of our Constitution undertook to secure conditions favorable to the pursuit of happiness. They recognized the significance of man's spiritual nature, of his feelings and of his intellect. They knew that only a part of the pain, pleasure and satisfactions of life are to be found in material things. They sought to protect Americans in their beliefs, their thoughts, their emotions and their sensations. They conferred, as against the government, the right to be let alone—the most comprehensive of rights and the right most valued by civilized men. To protect that right, every unjustifiable intrusion by the government upon the privacy of the individual, whatever the means employed, must be deemed a violation of the 4th Amendment.... *Olmstead v. United States,* 277 U.S. 438, 478, 48 S.Ct. 564, 572, 72 L.Ed. 944, 956 (1928).

THE 2006 REAUTHORIZATION ACT

Soon after the hasty adoption of the USA PATRIOT Act in October 2001, controversy erupted about the necessity and constitutionality of several provisions of the act. Congress engaged in serious arguments concerning the act in general, and especially in respect to particular provisions. Some of the most significant complaints were lodged by libraries (section 215) that could be directed to turn over records to the FBI and that those served with section 215 orders were prohibited from disclosing that fact to anyone. Finally, Congress enacted—and on March 9, 2006, President George W. Bush signed—the Reauthorizing Amendments Act of 2006.

The new legislation contains a number of technical revisions of the original USA PATRIOT Act. Many are designed to clarify that individuals who receive Foreign Intelligence Service Act (FISA) orders can challenge nondisclosure requirements. Specifically, recipients of a section 215 order (often libraries) are granted the right to petition a FISA judge to modify or quash the nondisclosure requirement of such an order. The new act removes the requirement that recipients of section 215 orders or National Security Letters (NSLs) provide the FBI with the name of the attorney they consulted. Finally, it clarifies that libraries, whose services include offering patrons access to the Internet, are not subject to NSLs unless they are functioning as electronic communication service providers.

The Exclusionary Rule

The **exclusionary rule** is a judicially created rule that prohibits the use of illegally obtained evidence in a criminal prosecution of the person whose rights were violated by the police in obtaining that evidence. In 1914 the U.S. Supreme Court first held that evidence obtained through an unlawful search and seizure could not be used to convict a person of a federal crime. *Weeks v. United States,* supra. The rationale for the rule is to deter illegal searches and seizures by police and thereby enforce the constitutional requirements. In 1949, in *Wolf v. Colorado,* supra, the Supreme Court refused to require the states to follow the exclusionary rule, saying that it was not an essential element of Fourth Amendment protection. But in *Mapp v. Ohio,* 367 U.S. 643, 81 S.Ct. 1684, 6 L.Ed.2d 1081 (1961), the Court held that there was no other effective means of enforcing the protections of the Fourth Amendment. The Court reasoned that if the Fourth Amendment was applicable to the states under the Fourteenth Amendment, then the exclusionary rule was also because it was the only effective means of enforcing the Fourth Amendment against overzealous police officers. The *Mapp* decision had an immediate impact. In New York City, for example, in the year preceding *Mapp,* police officers had not bothered to obtain a single search warrant. In the year following *Mapp,* they obtained more than eight hundred.

Go to the Scheb/ Scheb Criminal Law and Procedure 6e website at academic .cengage.com/criminaljustice/ scheb for an edited version of *Mapp v. Ohio.*

The Fruit of the Poisonous Tree Doctrine

The **fruit of the poisonous tree doctrine** holds that evidence derived from other evidence that is obtained through an illegal search or seizure is itself inadmissible. *Wong Sun v. United States,* 371 U.S. 471, 83 S.Ct. 407, 9 L.Ed.2d 441 (1963). The general rule is that where there has been an illegal seizure of property, such property cannot be introduced into evidence and no testimony may be given relative to any facts surrounding the seizure. However, the Fourth Amendment does not require evidence to be excluded, even if it was initially discovered during an illegal search of private property, if that evidence is later discovered during a valid search that is wholly independent of the initial illegal activity. *Murray v. United States,* 487 U.S. 533, 108 S.Ct. 2529, 101 L.Ed.2d 472 (1988). The Supreme Court has also held that evidence obtained through a search guided by information obtained from an inadmissible confession is inadmissible unless the search would inevitably have recovered

Go to the Scheb/ Scheb Criminal Law and Procedure 6e website at academic .cengage.com/criminaljustice/ scheb for an edited version of *Nix v. Williams.*

the evidence in the absence of the tainted information. *Nix v. Williams,* 467 U.S. 431, 444, 104 S.Ct. 2501, 2509, 81 L.Ed.2d 377 (1984).

The Erosion of the Exclusionary Rule

The exclusionary rule is justified by the need to deter police misconduct, but it exacts a high price to society in that "the criminal is to go free because the constable has blundered." As crime rates rose dramatically during the 1960s and 1970s, the exclusionary rule came under attack from critics who argued that the social cost of allowing guilty persons to avoid prosecution outweighed the benefit of deterring police from violating the Fourth Amendment. During the 1970s the Supreme Court used this sort of cost-benefit analysis in curtailing the scope of the exclusionary rule in a series of controversial decisions. In *United States v. Calandra,* 414 U.S. 338, 94 S.Ct. 613, 38 L.Ed.2d 561 (1974), the Court held that illegally obtained evidence could be used to obtain grand jury indictments. In *Michigan v. DeFillippo,* 443 U.S. 31, 99 S.Ct. 2627, 61 L.Ed.2d 343 (1979), the Court allowed the use of evidence obtained through a search incident to arrest pursuant to a law that was later ruled unconstitutional. But the most significant erosions of the rule came in the 1980s.

 Go to the Scheb/ Scheb Criminal Law and Procedure 6e website at academic .cengage.com/criminaljustice/ scheb for an edited version of *U.S. v. Calandra.*

The Good-Faith Exception

In the most significant exclusionary rule cases decided in the 1980s, the Supreme Court held that evidence obtained on the basis of a search warrant that is later held to be invalid may be admitted as evidence at trial if the police officer who conducted the search relied on the warrant in "good faith." *United States v. Leon,* 468 U.S. 897, 104 S.Ct. 3405, 82 L.Ed.2d 677 (1984); *Massachusetts v. Sheppard,* 468 U.S. 981, 104 S.Ct. 3424, 82 L.Ed.2d 737 (1984). In *Illinois v. Krull,* 480 U.S. 340, 107 S.Ct. 1160, 94 L.Ed.2d 364 (1987), the Court held that the **good-faith exception** to the exclusionary rule permits the introduction of evidence obtained by an officer in reliance upon a statute authorizing warrantless administrative searches where the statute is later determined to be unconstitutional. It must be noted that the good-faith exception to the exclusionary rule, as it has been developed thus far by the Supreme Court, applies only to cases where police officers rely on warrants that are later held to be invalid; it does not apply to warrantless searches.

In *United States v. Leon,* supra, the Supreme Court identified four situations involving police reliance on a warrant where the good-faith exception to the exclusionary rule does not apply:

 Go to the Scheb/ Scheb Criminal Law and Procedure 6e website at academic .cengage.com/criminaljustice/ scheb for an edited version of *U.S. v. Leon.*

1. If the magistrate was misled by an affidavit that the affiant knew was false or would have known was false except for reckless disregard for the truth;
2. If the magistrate wholly abandons his or her judicial role;
3. If the affidavit is so lacking in indicia of probable cause as to render belief in its existence unreasonable;
4. If the warrant is so facially deficient that the executing officer cannot reasonably presume its validity.

THE GOOD-FAITH EXCEPTION UNDER STATE CONSTITUTIONAL LAW

As previously noted, the Fourth Amendment sets a minimal national standard. Most states have adopted the good-faith exception. As pointed out, state courts are free to provide greater levels of protection under the search and seizure sections of state

The Good-Faith Exception Under State Constitutional Law

Acting on the basis of an informant's tip, police obtained a warrant to search a building owned by the defendant. Inside the building they discovered seventeen growing marijuana plants, as well as cultivating equipment. After a suppression hearing, the trial judge determined that the warrant upon which the search was based was defective in that it had not been adequately supported by probable cause. Nevertheless, the judge refused to suppress the evidence, citing the good-faith exception to the exclusionary rule created by the U.S. Supreme Court's decision in *United States v. Leon.* On appeal, the Pennsylvania Supreme Court interpreted its state constitution as affording more protection to a defendant against unreasonable searches and seizures than the federal constitution as interpreted in *Leon.* Thus, the court concluded that the Pennsylvania Constitution does not permit a *Leon-style* good-faith exception to the exclusionary rule.

Commonwealth v. Edmunds, 586 A.2d 887 (Pa. 1991).

constitutions. This latter approach was followed by the New Jersey Supreme Court in *State v. Novembrino,* 519 A.2d 820 (N.J. 1987), where it refused to follow the good-faith exception to the exclusionary rule as a matter of state law. The court observed that the exclusionary rule was firmly embedded in its own jurisprudence and that a good-faith exception would "ultimately reduce respect for and compliance with the probable cause standard." 519 A.2d 854.

Standing to Invoke the Exclusionary Rule

A person who seeks the benefits of the exclusionary rule must have **standing** to invoke the rule. The concept of standing limits the class of defendants who may challenge an allegedly illegal search and seizure. In *Jones v. United States,* 362 U.S. 257, 80 S.Ct. 725, 4 L.Ed.2d 697 (1960), the Supreme Court granted automatic standing to anyone who was legitimately on the premises searched. In *Rakas v. Illinois,* 439 U.S. 128, 99 S.Ct. 421, 58 L.Ed.2d 387 (1978), however, the Court restricted the *Jones* doctrine by refusing to allow passengers of an automobile to challenge the search of the vehicle in which they were riding.

In *United States v. Salvucci,* 448 U.S. 83, 100 S.Ct. 2547, 65 L.Ed.2d 619 (1980), the Court took the final step in overruling the automatic-standing rule of *Jones v. United States.* Salvucci was charged with possession of stolen mail. The evidence was recovered by police in a search of an apartment that belonged to the mother of Salvucci's accomplice. The federal district court granted Salvucci's motion to suppress the evidence, relying on the automatic-standing doctrine. The Supreme Court reversed, holding that Salvucci was not automatically entitled to challenge the search of another person's apartment. Justice William H. Rehnquist explained the Court's more conservative stance on the issue of standing:

> We are convinced that the automatic standing rule … has outlived its usefulness in this Court's Fourth Amendment jurisprudence. The doctrine now serves only to afford a windfall to defendants whose Fourth Amendment rights have not been violated. 448 U.S. at 95, 100 S.Ct. at 2554, 65 L.Ed.2d at 630.

The Court's current approach is to grant standing only to those persons who have a possessory or legitimate privacy interest in the place that was searched. Thus, a casual visitor to an apartment has no legitimate expectation of privacy in an apartment hallway that would grant standing to contest a search of those premises. *United States v. Burnett,* 890 F.2d 1233 (D.C. Cir. 1989). To successfully invoke the exclusionary rule now, a defendant must show that a legitimate expectation of privacy was violated.

In *United States v. Edwards,* 242 F.3d 928 (10th Cir. 2001), the court held the defendant lacked standing to challenge the search of a rented car because it was rented in another person's name and he was not an authorized driver of the vehicle, whereas in *United States v. Walker,* 237 F.3d 845 (7th Cir. 2001), the defendant had standing to challenge the search of a rental car because he was listed on the rental agreement as an authorized driver.

In 1983 the Pennsylvania Supreme Court determined that under its state constitution a defendant accused of a possessory crime who seeks to challenge a search and seizure must be accorded automatic standing notwithstanding the more restrictive view announced by the U.S. Supreme Court. *Commonwealth v. Sell,* 470 A.2d 457 (Pa. 1983). Of course, states may still grant automatic standing to challenge seized evidence. For example, "under Louisiana jurisprudence, any defendant against whom evidence is acquired as a result of an allegedly unreasonable search and seizure, whether or not it was obtained in violation of his rights, has standing to challenge the constitutionality of the search or seizure." *State v. Dakin,* 495 So.2d 344, 346 (La. 1986). Likewise, in *Commonwealth v. Amendola,* 550 N.E.2d 121, 126 (Mass. 1990), the court refused to abandon the automatic-standing rule: "When a defendant is charged with a crime in which possession of the seized evidence at the time of the contested search is an essential element of guilt, the defendant shall be deemed to have standing to contest the legality of the search and the seizure of that evidence." Courts in Michigan, New Hampshire, New Jersey, and Vermont have reached similar conclusions.

■ CONCLUSION

The constitutional protection against unreasonable searches and seizures is a fundamental right, yet determining the precise scope and meaning of the right is not easy. The constitutional law governing search and seizure is extremely complex. Moreover, it is highly dynamic, as courts decide countless cases in this area each year. Figure 15.3 provides an overview of search and seizure law—actually, a decision tree that highlights the important questions that courts must answer in determining whether a particular search or seizure was lawful.

The threshold question in evaluating a given search or seizure is whether the Fourth Amendment is applicable. Certain searches, including those conducted by private individuals where the government does not take part and searches of open fields or abandoned property, are beyond the pale of the Fourth Amendment. In a nutshell, the Fourth Amendment protects persons from unreasonable intrusions where they have a reasonable expectation of privacy. To guard against unreasonable intrusions of privacy, police are normally required to obtain a warrant before engaging in a search and seizure. Courts rigorously enforce the Fourth Amendment requirement that search warrants be issued only "upon probable cause, supported by Oath or affirmation" and are specific as to "the place to be searched and the persons or things to be seized." U.S. Const., Amend. 4. In addition to searches based on consent or those conducted incident to a lawful arrest, a number of exceptions to the warrant requirement are based on the doctrine of exigent circumstances. Hot pursuit, evanescent evidence, and certain emergencies qualify as exigent circumstances allowing warrantless searches.

Normally, police must have probable cause before conducting a search. Here, too, there are exceptions—the so-called stop-and-frisk situation, the airport search,

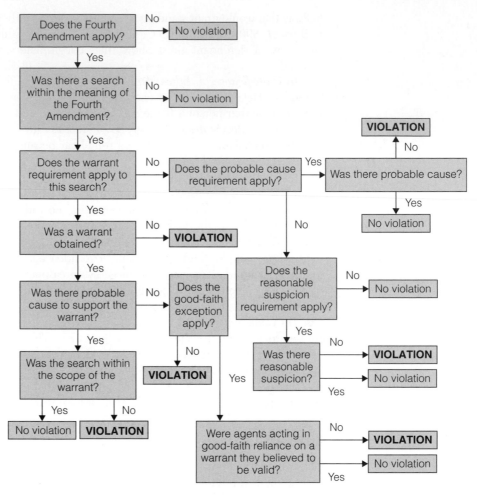

FIGURE 15.3 Fourth Amendment Decision Tree. The decision tree depicted here is based on general principles of federal law and may not correctly portray applicable laws in all states.

and the school search—where police may conduct searches on the basis of a less stringent standard of reasonableness.

One of the most controversial Fourth Amendment issues is how to deter law enforcement officials from conducting improper searches and seizures. The Supreme Court has fashioned a rule excluding illegally obtained evidence from criminal trials. Here again, there are exceptions to the rule, such as the limited good-faith exception announced in the *Leon* case and the issue of whether a defendant has standing to contest an illegal search or seizure.

Although technological advances have afforded law enforcement new means to ferret out crime, the use of helicopters and such high-tech devices as infrared sensors, supersensitive microphones, and miniature radio transmitters challenges the traditional right of privacy enjoyed by citizens in a free country. The current war on terrorism creates new demands for law enforcement agencies to conduct surveillance as well as considerable pressures on courts to allow such activities. Most Americans recognize the need to allow intelligence and law enforcement agencies additional authorities to combat terrorism. Thus, there is broad support for the USA PATRIOT Act despite its significant incursions into rights of privacy.

The Fourth Amendment has applicability beyond the seizure of evidence. Because the arrest of a suspect is considered a "seizure," the Fourth Amendment applies to arrests and various lesser police–citizen encounters, as well as to the use of force by police in making arrests. We examine these issues, along with police interrogation and identification procedures, in the next chapter.

■ KEY TERMS

search, 387

seizure, 387

warrant, 387

probable cause, 387

reasonable suspicion, 387

general warrant, 387

doctrine of incorporation, 389

border searches, 390

open fields doctrine, 391

administrative searches, 391

abandoned property, 392

inventory search, 392

consent to a search, 393

implied consent, 393

third-party consent, 393

exigent circumstances, 394

wiretapping, 395

electronic eavesdropping, 395

reasonable expectation of privacy, 395

sobriety checkpoints, 396

strip searches, 397

totality of circumstances, 398

affidavit, 399

affiant, 399

confidential informants, 401

anticipatory search warrant, 404

knock and announce, 406

Franks hearing, 407

warrantless searches, 407

plain-view doctrine, 408

emergency searches, 408

evanescent evidence, 409

search incident to a lawful arrest, 409

hot pursuit, 410

automobile exception, 411

stop-and-frisk, 413

pen register, 417

wiretap orders, 419

trap and trace devices, 419

exclusionary rule, 422

fruit of the poisonous tree doctrine, 422

good-faith exception, 423

standing, 424

■ WEB-BASED RESEARCH ACTIVITY

Go to http://www.findlaw.com/casecode/supreme.html. Locate the Supreme Court's decision in *United States v. Ramirez,* decided March 4, 1998. Read the decision. Write a brief summary of the decision in which you describe the key facts, the issue before the Supreme Court, the Court's holding, and the rationale for its decision. In your opinion, did the Court make the correct decision? Why or why not?

■ QUESTIONS FOR THOUGHT AND DISCUSSION

1. Today many security personnel are "private police," yet Fourth Amendment protection has been extended only to those searches conducted by government officials. What arguments can be made for and against expanding the prohibitions of the Fourth Amendment to include security personnel?

2. What rationale supports the "search incident to arrest" exception to the warrant requirement? What limitations do the courts impose on such searches?

3. Should one have a reasonable expectation of privacy from infrared detectors and other high-tech devices that enable law enforcement officers to "see" heat emanating from a person's home? Why or why not?

4. Does a person using a public restroom in a government office building have a reasonable expectation of privacy from television security surveillance?

5. In *New Jersey v. T.L.O.* (1985), the Supreme Court adopted a reasonableness standard for public school searches. Should this standard be applied to searches of students in public colleges and universities? What about private colleges? Does it make a difference if the search is conducted in a public setting or in the student's dormitory room?

6. What is the rationale for excluding from trial evidence obtained in violation of the Fourth Amendment? Is this a compelling justification for the exclusion of criminal evidence from the trial of a defendant accused of a serious felony such as aggravated battery?

7. What alternatives to the exclusionary rule might be adopted to enforce the protections of the Fourth Amendment? How effective are such alternatives likely to be?

8. The Supreme Court has created a "good-faith" exception to the exclusionary rule where police rely on a search warrant that is later held to be invalid because the magistrate erred in finding probable cause for a search. Should the good-faith exception be extended to cases where police acting in good faith conduct *warrantless* searches that are later held to be unlawful?

9. What is meant by the "fruit of the poisonous tree doctrine" in relation to searches and seizures?

10. What is the "standing" requirement in the law of search and seizure? What is its purpose?

11. In 2006 in *Hudson v. Michigan*, Justice Scalia, writing for a sharply divided Supreme Court, concluded that when it comes to knock-and-announce violations, "[r]esort to the massive remedy of suppressing evidence of guilt is unjustified." Writing for the four dissenters, Justice Breyer contended that the decision "destroys the strongest legal incentive to comply with the Constitution's knock-and-announce requirement." Evaluate these opposing views.

12. In *United States v. Salvucci* (1980), the U.S. Supreme Court concluded that "the automatic standing rule … has outlived its usefulness in this Court's Fourth Amendment jurisprudence." Yet, several state courts have held that under their state constitutions a defendant accused of a possessory crime who challenges a search and seizure must be accorded automatic standing. What are the merits of states, based on their own constitutions, affording defendants in this area more protection than required by the Supreme Court?

■ PROBLEMS FOR DISCUSSION AND SOLUTION

1. Police observed an automobile traveling at a high rate of speed and swerving on the road. They gave pursuit and stopped the vehicle after a five-minute chase. The driver, later identified as Jerome Johnson, emerged from the car and began to verbally abuse and threaten the officers. Johnson appeared intoxicated but refused to take any of the standard field sobriety tests. Under state law, refusal to perform a sobriety test results in the loss of a driver's license for a period of one year. The law does not authorize police to force suspects to perform any sobriety

tests against their will. Johnson was arrested and transported to a local hospital, where he was forcibly restrained and asked to submit to a blood-alcohol test. Johnson refused, saying "I'd rather lose my license than let you stick me with that needle." The test was administered over Johnson's objection, and the results indicated that Johnson's blood-alcohol level was substantially above the legal limit. Johnson was charged with driving under the influence of alcohol. Before trial, Johnson's attorney moved to suppress the results of the blood-alcohol test, arguing that it was taken without Johnson's consent, without probable cause, and in violation of the state's implied consent law. If you were the judge in this case, how would you be inclined to rule on the admissibility of this evidence? What additional information would you need to render your decision?

2. Acting without a search warrant, police arrive at a home after receiving an anonymous tip that a man has been making illegal explosives in his workshop. The officers find that the man is not at home. Can the man's wife consent to a warrantless search of her husband's workshop, or must police wait until the husband returns to obtain his consent?

3. The sheriff's department in a rural north Georgia county receives an anonymous letter stating that there is a "meth lab" being operated in a trailer home belonging to Danny Dawgmire and that children living in the trailer are being exposed to methamphetamine and other toxic chemicals. Without obtaining a warrant, deputies drive to the trailer home, where they detect strong chemical odors associated with the production of methamphetamines. The deputies knock and announce their presence, but no one answers. They then forcibly enter the trailer, where they discover large quantities of methamphetamines and associated equipment, paraphernalia, and supplies. No children are found in the trailer. The deputies call a hazardous materials disposal unit to the scene. Two hours later, as the meth lab is being cleaned up and evidence secured, Dawgmire arrives at the scene in his pick-up truck and is promptly arrested and charged with manufacture of and possession with intent to distribute a controlled substance. In a pretrial motion, Dawgmire's attorney moves to suppress the evidence on the ground that no warrant had been obtained to authorize the search. The attorney claims that Dawgmire, who is unmarried, lives in the trailer alone and that at no time had any children been inside the trailer. How would the state likely counter the motion? How would the judge likely rule on the motion to suppress?

CHAPTER 16

Arrest, Interrogation, and Identification Procedures

Introduction

In its most general sense, the term **arrest** refers to the deprivation of a person's liberty by someone with legal authority. In the contemporary criminal justice system, an arrest usually occurs when police take an individual into custody and charge that person with the commission of a crime. Generally, an arrest is made by a police officer, although there are some circumstances in which an arrest can be effected by a private individual.

As a form of "seizure," an arrest is governed by requirements of the Fourth Amendment. However, the formal arrest is not the only type of encounter between police and citizens that implicates the Fourth Amendment. A seizure, for Fourth Amendment purposes, occurs when a police officer, "by means of physical force or show of authority, has in some way restrained the liberty of a citizen." *Terry v. Ohio,* 392 U.S. 1, 19 n. 16, 88 S.Ct. 1868, 1879 n. 16, 20 L.Ed.2d 889, 905 n. 16 (1968). The traditional full-blown arrest clearly constitutes a seizure. So too does a police officer's fatal shooting of a fleeing suspect. *Tennessee v. Garner,* 471 U.S. 1, 105 S.Ct. 1694, 85 L.Ed.2d 1 (1985). Other instances may not be so clear, however. In 1988 the Supreme Court declined to formulate a "bright line" rule delineating what constitutes a seizure; rather, the Court asserted that the test requires an assessment of whether, in view of all the circumstances surrounding an incident, "a reasonable person would have believed that he was not free to leave." *Michigan v. Chesternut,* 486 U.S. 567, 108 S.Ct. 1975, 100 L.Ed.2d 565 (1988). The following year, the Court ruled that stopping a motorist at a police roadblock is a seizure for Fourth Amendment purposes. *Brower v. County of Inyo,* 489 U.S. 593, 109 S.Ct. 1378, 103 L.Ed.2d 628 (1989).

Encounters between citizens and police range from formal arrests to situations in which police approach an individual and ask questions. Police–citizen encounters can be placed in four categories:

1. Arrest
2. Investigatory detention (also referred to as stop-and-frisk, as discussed in Chapter 15)
3. The use of roadblocks and sobriety checkpoints
4. The **request for information or identification**

Each type of encounter is unique from the standpoint of the Fourth Amendment. Accordingly, we examine each of these separately in this chapter.

Interrogation refers to the questioning of a suspect by law enforcement officers to elicit a confession, an admission, or information that otherwise assists them in solving a crime. Typically, interrogation takes place behind closed doors in a law enforcement facility, although today a suspect being questioned is often accompanied by an attorney. Because interrogation of a suspect carries with it a risk of coercion, confessions obtained by police are subject to constitutional attack under the Self-Incrimination Clause of the Fifth Amendment.

Identification procedures are techniques employed by law enforcement agencies to identify suspects. These fall into two basic categories: scientific means to match physical evidence taken from a suspect with that found at a crime scene and procedures to determine whether victims or witnesses can identify perpetrators. Both types of identification procedure are extremely important in building cases against defendants, and both present unique legal problems.

Arrest

Because arrest is the most serious type of police–citizen encounter, it is subject to the most stringent constitutional requirements. Specifically, arrest is subject to the probable cause and warrant requirements of the Fourth Amendment, although there are exceptions to the latter. The Supreme Court has said that the legality of arrests by state and local officers is to be judged by the same constitutional standards applicable to federal agents. *Ker v. California*, 374 U.S. 23, 83 S.Ct. 1623, 10 L.Ed.2d 726 (1963).

The Probable Cause Requirement

For any arrest or significant deprivation of liberty to occur, police officers must have probable cause. Although not easy to define, probable cause in the context of arrest means the same thing as in the context of search and seizure (see Chapter 15). The Supreme Court has said that probable cause exists where "the facts and circumstances within [the officers'] knowledge and of which they had reasonably trustworthy information [are] sufficient in themselves to warrant a man of reasonable caution in the belief" that a particular crime had been or was being committed. *Carroll v. United States*, 267 U.S. 132, 162, 45 S.Ct. 280, 288, 69 L.Ed. 543, 555 (1925).

Police can establish probable cause without personally observing the commission of a crime as long as they have sufficient information to conclude that the suspect probably committed it. Officers often obtain their information from crime victims, eyewitnesses, official reports, and confidential or even anonymous informants.

The Warrant Requirement

An **arrest warrant** (see Figure 16.1) is routine in cases where an arrest is to be made based on an indictment by a grand jury. When a prosecutor files an accusatorial document known as an information, the court issues a **capias,** a document directing the arrest of the defendant. In such cases, suspects are often not aware that they are under

CASE-IN-POINT

The Need for Probable Cause to Make an Arrest

On March 26, 1971, the owner of a pizza parlor in Rochester, New York, was killed during an attempted armed robbery. Acting without a warrant, police took Irving Dunaway into custody and interrogated him in connection with the attempted robbery and murder. Dunaway was not told that he was under arrest, but he was interrogated, he confessed, and he was ultimately convicted. On appeal, Dunaway contended the police officers violated his rights under the Fourth and Fourteenth Amendments when, without probable cause, they

seized him and transported him to the police station for interrogation. The state argued that although the police did not have probable cause to make an arrest, the "station-house detention" and interrogation of the suspect could be allowed on the lesser standard of reasonable suspicion. The Supreme Court reversed the conviction, saying that probable cause was necessary to justify a station-house detention and interrogation, irrespective of whether it is termed an "arrest."

Dunaway v. New York, 442 U.S. 200, 99 S.Ct. 2248, 60 L.Ed.2d 824 (1979).

```
                        WARRANT OF ARREST
        County of _____. State of _____.

        To any peace officer of said state:

        Complaint on oath having this day been laid before me that the
        crime of _____ (designating it
        generally) has been committed and accusing
        _____ (naming defendant) thereof,
        you are therefore commanded forthwith to arrest the above named
        defendant and bring him/her before me at
        _____ (naming the place), or in case of
        my absence or inability to act, before the nearest or most accessible
        magistrate in this county. Dated at _____ (place)
        this _____ day of _____, 20 __.


                      _____
                  (signature and full official title of magistrate)
```

FIGURE 16.1   Typical Format of an Arrest Warrant

investigation, and police officers have ample time to obtain an arrest warrant without fear that suspects will flee. However, most arrests are not made pursuant to secret investigations but are made by police officers who observe a criminal act, respond to a complaint filed by a crime victim, or have probable cause to arrest after completing an investigation. In such cases it is often unnecessary for police to obtain an arrest warrant, but it is always essential that they have probable cause to make the arrest.

Warrantless Arrests

At common law, police had the right to make a **warrantless arrest** if they observed someone in the commission of a felony or had probable cause to believe that a person had committed or was committing a felony. To make a warrantless arrest for a misdemeanor, an officer had to observe someone in the commission of the act. Otherwise, to make an arrest, a warrant was required. Many states adopted common-law rules of arrest in statutes allowing police officers broad discretion to make warrantless arrests. As with warrantless searches and seizures, the Supreme Court has approved warrantless arrests (1) where crimes are committed in **plain view** of police officers or (2) where officers possess probable cause to make an arrest but exigent circumstances prohibit them from obtaining a warrant. Absent plain view or compelling exigencies, the need to obtain an arrest warrant is unclear. As a matter of policy, it makes sense for police officers to obtain arrest warrants when possible. However, given the time that it takes to obtain an arrest warrant and the fact that magistrates are not always available around the clock, it is not always feasible for police to obtain warrants before making arrests.

The Supreme Court has upheld the authority of police officers to make warrantless arrests in public, assuming they have probable cause to do so. *United States v. Watson*, 423 U.S. 411, 96 S.Ct. 820, 46 L.Ed.2d 598 (1976). More problematic are warrantless arrests involving the forcible entry of a dwelling. Here we encounter the classic Fourth

Amendment concern for the sanctity of the home. For example, in *Payton v. New York,* 445 U.S. 573, 100 S.Ct. 1371, 63 L.Ed.2d 639 (1980), the Supreme Court held that, absent exigent circumstances, a warrantless, nonconsensual entry into a suspect's home to make a routine felony arrest violates the Fourth Amendment. In a footnote, the Court pointed out that at that time, twenty-three states had laws permitting a warrantless entry into the home for the purpose of making an arrest, even in the absence of exigent circumstances. 445 U.S. at 598, n. 46, 100 S.Ct. at 1386, n. 46, 63 L.Ed.2d at 658, n. 46. Courts are generally inclined to uphold warrantless entries into homes for the purpose of making an arrest if the following conditions are met:

1. There is probable cause to arrest the suspect.
2. The police have good reason to believe the suspect is on the premises.
3. There is good reason to believe the suspect is armed and dangerous.
4. There is a strong probability that the suspect will escape or evidence will be destroyed if the suspect is not soon apprehended.
5. The entry can be effected peaceably.
6. The offense under investigation is a serious felony.

The Right of an Arrestee to a Prompt Appearance Before a Magistrate

Although the Supreme Court has recognized the practical necessity of permitting police to make warrantless arrests, it has stressed the need for immediate *ex post facto* judicial review of the detention of a suspect. Writing for the Supreme Court in *Gerstein v. Pugh,* 420 U.S. 103, 95 S.Ct. 854, 43 L.Ed.2d 54 (1975), Justice Potter Stewart observed that "once the suspect is in custody, … the reasons that justify dispensing with the magistrate's neutral judgment evaporate." 420 U.S. at 114, 95 S.Ct. at 863, 43 L.Ed.2d at 65. When a suspect is in custody pursuant to a warrantless arrest, "the detached judgment of a neutral magistrate is essential if the Fourth Amendment is to furnish meaningful protection from unfounded interference with liberty." 420 U.S. at 114, 95 S.Ct. at 863, 43 L.Ed.2d at 65. In *County of Riverside v. McLaughlin,* 500 U.S. 44, 111 S.Ct. 1661, 114 L.Ed.2d 49 (1991), the Supreme Court ruled that if an arrested person is brought before a magistrate within forty-eight hours, the requirements of the Fourth Amendment are satisfied.

Actually, any person who is arrested, regardless of whether the arrest was based on a warrant, must be brought promptly before a court of law. Although this is not a federal constitutional right in instances where arrests are made pursuant to warrants, all states now have rules that require the police to promptly bring an arrestee before a magistrate. Similarly, as Fed. R. Crim. P. 5(a) states,

> A person making an arrest within the United States must take the defendant without unnecessary delay before a magistrate judge, or before a state or local judicial officer as Rule 5(c) provides, unless a statute provides otherwise.

Use of Force by Police Making Arrests

Because suspects frequently resist attempts to take them into custody, police officers often must use force in making arrests. Sometimes, the use of force by police is challenged in civil suits seeking damages. Typically, in such cases, the courts have said that in making a lawful arrest, police officers may use such force as necessary to effect the arrest and prevent the escape of the suspect. See, for example, *Martyn v. Donlin,* 198 A.2d 700 (Conn. 1964). Generally, a police officer has less discretion to use force in apprehending suspected misdemeanants than suspected felons. See, for example, *City of Mason v. Banks,* 581 S.W.2d 621 (Tenn. 1979). Most states have statutes providing that police officers have the right to require bystanders to assist them in making arrests. See, for example, West's Ann. Cal. Penal Code § 839. Nearly every state has a law governing the use of force by police attempting to make arrests. The Illinois statute is typical:

> (a) A peace officer, or any person he has summoned or directed to assist him, need not retreat or desist from efforts to make a lawful arrest because of resistance or threatened resistance to the arrest. He is justified in the use of any force which he reasonably believes to be necessary to effect the arrest and of any force which he reasonably believes to be necessary to defend himself or another from bodily harm while making the arrest. However, he is justified in using force likely to cause death or great bodily harm only when he reasonably believes that such force is necessary to prevent death or great bodily harm to himself or other such person, or when he reasonably believes both that:
>
> > 1. Such force is necessary to prevent the arrest from being defeated by resistance or escape; and
> >
> > 2. The person to be arrested has committed or attempted a forcible felony which involves the infliction or threatened infliction of great bodily harm or is attempting to escape by use of a deadly weapon, or otherwise indicates that he will endanger human life or inflict great bodily harm unless arrested without delay.
>
> (b) A peace officer making an arrest pursuant to an invalid warrant is justified in the use of any force which he would be justified in using if the warrant were valid, unless he knows that the warrant is invalid. S.H.A. 720 ILCS 5/7–5(a).

Go to the Scheb/ Scheb Criminal Law and Procedure 6e website at academic .cengage.com/criminaljustice/ scheb for an edited version of *Tennessee v. Garner.*

In *Tennessee v. Garner,* supra, the Supreme Court struck down a state statute that permitted police to use deadly force against fleeing suspects even when there was no threat to the safety of the officer or the public. This ruling effectively narrowed the discretion of police officers in using force to make arrests and broadened the possibility for civil actions against police for using excessive force.

THE RODNEY KING EPISODE

Concern over police brutality took center stage in 1991, when the nation viewed on television a videotape of what appeared to be the unnecessarily brutal beating of motorist Rodney King by Los Angeles police officers. In response to public outrage, four police officers involved in the incident were prosecuted by state authorities for assault and battery and related crimes. On the motion of the defense, the trial was moved from Los Angeles to a suburban community. No one can forget the riot that ensued in Los Angeles in April 1992 after the jury returned its verdict of not guilty. In response to the widespread perception that a miscarriage of justice had occurred, the U.S. Justice Department launched its own investigation of the case. In the summer of 1992, a federal grand jury indicted the four officers for violating Rodney King's Fourth Amendment rights. In April 1993, a trial jury returned verdicts of guilty against two of the officers; the other two were acquitted. See *Koon v. United States,* 518 U.S. 81, 116 S.Ct. 2035, 135 L.Ed.2d 392 (1996). In 1997, Rodney King was awarded $3.8 million in a civil suit he brought against the City of Los Angeles.

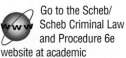

Go to the Scheb/ Scheb Criminal Law and Procedure 6e website at academic .cengage.com/criminaljustice/ scheb for an edited version of *Koon v. U.S.*

THE AMADOU DIALLO CASE

In February 1999, four New York City police officers looking for a serial rapist shot and killed Amadou Diallo, a recent immigrant from the African nation of Guinea. The officers cornered Diallo in the vestibule of his apartment building in the Bronx. It remains unclear as to whether the officers considered Diallo to be a suspect in the rapes. The officers later claimed that they had ordered Diallo to put his hands in the air and that he had not complied but instead turned around and reached into his pocket. The officers claimed that they believed that Diallo was armed and was going for a gun. Reacting immediately, the officers fired forty-one bullets, nine of which struck Diallo. It turned out that Diallo was unarmed. Some speculated that he might have been reaching into his pocket for his identification card. The shooting spawned a wave of protest and demands that the officers be held criminally responsible for Diallo's death. The State of New York charged the four police officers with second-degree murder and reckless endangerment. On the motion of the defense, the trial was moved upstate from the Bronx to Albany. In February 2000, after deliberating for roughly twenty hours, a jury composed of seven white males, one white female, and four African American females acquitted the police officers on all counts. The verdict prompted protests around the country and rekindled a debate over police treatment of minorities. Although the Diallo case was national news, there have been many such cases around the country. In many of these cases, what appears to be reckless or wanton use of force by the police appears more understandable when all of the evidence comes to light in court.

USE OF POLICE DOGS TO APPREHEND SUSPECTS

In addition to using trained dogs to sniff for drugs and other contraband, police often use dogs to assist them in apprehending uncooperative or fleeing suspects. Sometimes the use of a dog to take down a suspect results in serious injury to that person. Police dogs are trained to bite and hold a suspect on the arm. The bite of a German Shepherd has a force in the range of 1,200 to 1,600 pounds per square inch. If the bite lasts more than a few seconds, it can result in a severe wound, a fracture, or possibly even the severing of the arm. Of course, police are trained that once the dog has subdued the suspect, the dog is called off. The dogs tend to be very well trained and almost always obey immediately when given the command to release the suspect. In an interesting case decided by the U.S. Court of Appeals for the Ninth Circuit in August of 2003, a deputy sheriff sent a police dog into a wooded area to apprehend a suspect who had fled on foot into the woods. Before the deputy dispatched the dog, he yelled into the woods, "This is the Sheriff's Office. You have five seconds to make yourself known, or a police dog will be sent to find you." When the suspect did not respond after five seconds, the deputy sent the dog into the woods. About a minute later loud screaming could be heard from the woods. The deputy moved toward the sound and within about forty-five seconds located the police dog with a firm bite on the suspect's arm. The deputy called off the dog and arrested the suspect, whose badly injured arm required immediate surgery. The suspect eventually brought suit under 42 U.S.C.A. § 1983 against the deputy and the county, claiming that the use of the police dog constituted excessive force in violation of the Fourth Amendment. The federal district judge who tried the case entered judgment in favor of the defendants, holding that the use of the dog was not unreasonable under the circumstances. In a unanimous opinion, the Ninth Circuit agreed. The court noted that the suspect was being sought for a felony, that the deputy had reason to believe the suspect was armed with a knife and therefore posed a danger, and that because it was nighttime the deputy would have had great difficulty in locating the suspect promptly without the assistance of the dog. Given the totality of the circumstances, the court determined that the deputy's use of the police dog was reasonable. *Miller v. Clark County,* 340 F.3d 959 (9th Cir. 2003).

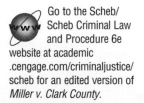

Go to the Scheb/ Scheb Criminal Law and Procedure 6e website at academic .cengage.com/criminaljustice/ scheb for an edited version of *Miller v. Clark County.*

USE OF TASERS TO SUBDUE PERSONS WHO RESIST ARREST

Taser is the trade name of a stun gun that shoots metal barbs attached to wires. The barbs stick into a person's skin or clothing, whereupon 50,000 volts of electricity are transmitted from the gun via the wires. Tasers are now in wide use among police departments and are certainly effective in incapacitating most suspects who resist arrest. Typically, persons subjected to Taser shocks experience tremendous pain for about five seconds, but in most cases there is no permanent injury. However, a number of persons subjected to Taser shocks have been hospitalized and, according a February 2003 report by Amnesty International, at least three persons died in the United States in 2002 as the result of being struck by Tasers. Generally, the courts have upheld the use of Tasers as an alternative to more injurious force. For example, in *Ewolski v. City of Brunswick,* 287 F.3d 492 (6th Cir. 2003), a federal appeals court held that use of a Taser to subdue a potentially homicidal individual did not constitute excessive force. Of course, courts will not permit police to use Tasers against resisting suspects when equally effective but less risky measures are readily available.

Arrest of Persons with Disabilities

There are special concerns stemming from police encounters with persons with disabilities. Persons who are deaf or mentally retarded may appear to be uncooperative. Persons experiencing epileptic seizures are likely to be perceived as "drunk and disorderly." Similarly, one experiencing the effects of hypoglycemia may appear to be intoxicated. A disabled motorist who reaches behind the seat when stopped by the police may simply be trying to retrieve a walking assistance device, but this might be perceived by police as an attempt to retrieve a weapon. Arresting and booking someone confined to a wheelchair poses obvious problems. According to the U.S. Department of Justice, the Americans with Disabilities Act requires public agencies "to make reasonable modifications in their policies, practices, and procedures that are necessary to ensure accessibility for individuals with disabilities, unless making such modifications would fundamentally alter the program or service involved." U.S. Department of Justice, Civil Rights Division, Disability Rights Section, "Commonly Asked Questions about the Americans with Disabilities Act and Law Enforcement," last revised April 4, 2006. The document recommends modifying the "regular practice of handcuffing arrestees behind their backs, and instead handcuff[ing] deaf individuals in front in order for the person to sign or write notes." The document also suggests that "[s]afe transport of other individuals who use manual or power wheelchairs might require departments to make minor modifications to existing cars or vans, or to use lift-equipped vans or buses."

Citizen's Arrest

At common law, a private individual could make a **citizen's arrest** without a warrant for a felony or breach of the peace committed in the presence of that individual. The common-law rule prevails in some states; in others, it has been revised by statute. A California law enacted in 1872 broadens the common law in that it permits a private person to make a warrantless arrest in any of three situations:

> A private person may arrest another:
>
> 1. For a public offense committed or attempted in his presence.
>
> 2. When the person arrested has committed a felony, although not in his presence.
>
> 3. When a felony has been in fact committed, and he has reasonable cause for believing the person arrested to have committed it. West's Ann. Cal. Penal Code § 837.

Arrests for Minor Traffic Offenses

In most states, a police officer is vested with discretion to make an arrest or issue a citation to a person who commits a minor traffic violation. Generally, police exercise their discretion by giving the motorist a "ticket," yet there is little judicial guidance for the proper action to be taken in such situations. That this area of broad police discretion is subject to abuse was recognized in *State v. Hehman,* 578 P.2d 527 (Wash. 1978), where the Washington Supreme Court ruled that arrests for minor traffic offenses are unjustified if the defendant signs a promise to appear in court as provided by statute. By contrast, an Illinois appellate court upheld the arrest and jailing of a motorist for lacking a front license plate and being unable to produce a driver's license. *People v. Pendleton,* 433 N.E.2d 1076 (Ill. App. 1982).

In *Atwater v. City of Lago Vista,* 532 U.S. 318, 121 S.Ct. 1536, 149 L.Ed.2d 549 (2001), the U.S. Supreme Court ruled that the Fourth Amendment does not forbid a warrantless arrest for a minor traffic offense, specifically a seat belt violation. Writing for the Court, Justice David Souter concluded that

> Atwater's arrest was surely "humiliating," … but it was no more "harmful to … privacy or … physical interests" than the normal custodial arrest. She was handcuffed, placed in a squad car, and taken to the local police station, where officers asked her to remove her shoes, jewelry, and glasses, and to empty her pockets. They then took her photograph and placed her in a cell, alone, for about an hour, after which she was taken before a magistrate, and released on $310 bond. The arrest and booking were inconvenient and embarrassing to Atwater, but not so extraordinary as to violate the Fourth Amendment. 532 U.S. at 354, 121 S.Ct. at 1558, 149 L.Ed.2d at 577.

Four justices dissented, characterizing Atwater's arrest for not wearing a seat belt as a "pointless indignity." Writing for the dissenters, Justice Sandra Day O'Connor opined:

> The majority takes comfort in the lack of evidence of "an epidemic of unnecessary minor-offense arrests." … But the relatively small number of published cases dealing with such arrests proves little and should provide little solace. Indeed, as the recent debate over racial profiling demonstrates all too clearly, a relatively minor traffic infraction may often serve as an excuse for stopping and harassing an individual. After today, the arsenal available to any officer extends to a full arrest and the searches permissible concomitant to that arrest. An officer's subjective motivations for making a traffic stop are not relevant considerations in determining the reasonableness of the stop.… But it is precisely because these motivations are beyond our purview that we must vigilantly ensure that officers' poststop actions—which are properly within our reach—comport with the Fourth Amendment's guarantee of reasonableness. 532 U.S. at 372, 121 S.Ct. at 1567, 149 L.Ed.2d at 587.

State courts can interpret their state constitutions to provide more protection than the federal constitution as interpreted in the *Atwater* decision. Perhaps a more feasible solution is for state legislatures to provide that misdemeanor offenses are subject to "ticketing" under a "cite and release" statute. A Tennessee law is illustrative in this regard. Tenn. Code Ann. § 40-7-118 (1997) provides that "[a] peace officer who has arrested a person for the commission of a misdemeanor committed in such peace officer's presence … shall issue a citation to such arrested person to appear in court in lieu of the continued custody and taking of the arrested person before a magistrate." In 1999 the legislature added, "No citation shall be issued under the provisions of this section if … [t]he person arrested cannot or will not offer satisfactory evidence of identification, including the providing of a field-administered fingerprint or thumbprint which a peace officer may require to be affixed to any citation.…" Tenn. Code Ann. § 40-7-118(c)(3) (Supp.1999). The state's "cite and release" statute creates a presumptive right to be cited and released for the commission of a misdemeanor. *State v. Walker,* 12 S.W.3d 460 (Tenn. 2000).

Search Incident to Arrest

Go to the Scheb/
Scheb Criminal Law
and Procedure 6e
website at academic
.cengage.com/criminaljustice/
scheb for an edited version of
Chimel v. California.

When making an arrest, police usually conduct a limited search. As we noted in Chapter 15, the Supreme Court has said that such a search incident to arrest must be limited to the body of an arrestee and the area within that person's immediate control. *Chimel v. California*, 395 U.S. 752, 89 S.Ct. 2034, 23 L.Ed.2d 685 (1969).

Normally, a search incident to arrest takes place after the arrest has been effected. In *Rawlings v. Kentucky*, 448 U.S. 98, 100 S.Ct. 2556, 65 L.Ed.2d 633 (1980), however, the Supreme Court upheld a search incident to arrest even though the search briefly preceded the arrest. The key point is that probable cause to make the arrest must precede the search; police may not use the search as a means to justify the arrest.

The Supreme Court has limited the ability of police to conduct an automobile search incident to arrest when issuing a traffic citation. See *Knowles v. Iowa*, 525 U.S. 113, 119 S.Ct. 484, 142 L.Ed.2d 492 (1998). In some instances, police may opt to make an arrest rather than issue a citation so that they can conduct a search of the automobile. See *Gustafson v. Florida*, 414 U.S. 260, 94 S.Ct. 488, 38 L.Ed.2d 456 (1973). If a driver is arrested and there is no one else who is authorized to take possession of the vehicle, police will impound the vehicle and thoroughly search its contents. This will often lead to the discovery of incriminating evidence that has been sequestered in the vehicle. There is no Fourth Amendment barrier to using such evidence in a criminal prosecution. *South Dakota v. Opperman*, 428 U.S. 364, 96 S.Ct. 3092, 49 L.Ed.2d 1000 (1976). (For more information on inventory searches of impounded automobiles, see Chapter 15.)

Investigatory Detention

Go to the Scheb/
Scheb Criminal Law
and Procedure 6e
website at academic
.cengage.com/criminaljustice/
scheb for an edited version of
Minnesota v. Dickerson.

The second major category of police–citizen encounters involves the so-called stop-and-frisk, discussed in Chapter 15. A more descriptive term for this type of encounter is **investigatory detention.** Police are permitted to detain persons temporarily for questioning as long as they have reasonable suspicion that criminal activity is afoot. If they have reasonable suspicion that the detained person is armed, police may perform a **pat-down search** of the suspect's outer clothing to locate weapons. *Terry v. Ohio*, supra. In conducting the "frisk," police may seize items that plainly feel like contraband. *Minnesota v. Dickerson*, 508 U.S. 366, 113 S.Ct. 2130, 124 L.Ed.2d 334 (1993).

What Constitutes Reasonable Suspicion?

After the U.S. Supreme Court's 1968 decision in *Terry v. Ohio*, supra, the concept of what constitutes "reasonable suspicion" became extremely important both in law enforcement and in criminal procedure in the courts. The concept does not lend itself to a precise definition; however, in *United States v. Cortez*, 449 U.S. 411, 101 S.Ct. 690, 66 L.Ed.2d 621 (1981), after defining it in a rather technical way, Chief Justice Warren E. Burger offered a practical explanation. He said that a trained officer develops a reasonable suspicion that a person is, or is about to be, engaged in criminal activity from the officer's objective observations and from inference and deductions.

Go to the Scheb/
Scheb Criminal Law
and Procedure 6e
website at academic
.cengage.com/criminaljustice/
scheb for an edited version of
U.S. v. Arvizu.

Thousands of federal and state judicial decisions have applied the standard of reasonable suspicion, often with degrees of variation. However, courts generally agree that the totality of the circumstances of any given scenario must be examined to determine whether a law officer had a reasonable suspicion as a basis for making an investigatory stop. In *United States v. Arvizu,* 534 U.S. 266, 122 S.Ct. 744, 151 L.Ed.2d 740 (2002), the Supreme Court said that courts are not to view in isolation the factors upon which police officers develop reasonable suspicion. Instead, courts should consider all of an officer's observations, giving appropriate weight to any inferences drawn by an officer based on his or her training or experience.

The Length of an Investigatory Detention

The Supreme Court has said that investigatory detentions must be brief (unless, that is, they confirm police suspicions of criminal conduct). *Dunaway v. New York,* 442 U.S. 200, 99 S.Ct. 2248, 60 L.Ed.2d 824 (1979). Nevertheless, the Supreme Court has been disinclined to place an arbitrary time limit on detention. Instead, the Court has considered the purpose of the stop and the reasonableness of the time required for the police to obtain any additional required information. This approach looks at the totality of the circumstances to determine whether there has been an infringement of the suspect's Fourth Amendment rights. In *Florida v. Royer,* 460 U.S. 491, 103 S.Ct. 1319, 75 L.Ed.2d 229 (1983), the Court held that a fifteen-minute detention of a suspect in a police room was unreasonable when the police detained the suspect while they brought his luggage to him. Yet a twenty-minute detention of a truck driver stopped on suspicion of transporting marijuana was found to be reasonable because the time was used by police in pursuing a second, related vehicle necessary to the investigation, and the suspect's actions contributed to the delay. *United States v. Sharpe,*

CASE-IN-POINT

Reasonable Suspicion to Justify a Stop-and-Frisk

On September 9, 1995, William Wardlow was standing in front of a building around noon in a high-crime area in Chicago known for narcotics trafficking. When he saw a caravan of four police cars pass by, he ran through an alley. Officers in one of the patrol cars pursued and eventually stopped him, patted him down in a protective search for weapons, and searched an opaque bag he was holding. They found him in possession of a handgun and arrested him. Wardlow sought to suppress the weapon on the ground that the officers had no reasonable suspicion to stop and frisk him. Therefore, he argued the seizure of the handgun was in violation of the Fourth Amendment. His motion was denied, and he was convicted. The Illinois Supreme Court reversed, holding the stop illegal. On

review, the U.S. Supreme Court, in a 5–4 decision, reversed the Illinois Supreme Court. The justices agreed that the "totality of the circumstances" governs in determining if there is reasonable suspicion for the stop, but they disagreed on the application of that test to the factual situation here. Writing for the majority, Chief Justice William Rehnquist found that the officers had a reasonable suspicion based on Wardlow's presence in a high-crime area coupled with his headlong, unprovoked flight from the police. Four justices, in an opinion written by Justice John Paul Stevens, disagreed with the majority's conclusion that the Chicago police were justified in stopping Wardlow.

Illinois v. Wardlow, 528 U.S. 119, 120 S.Ct. 673, 145 L.Ed.2d 570 (2000).

470 U.S. 675, 105 S.Ct. 1568, 84 L.Ed.2d 605 (1985). Consequently, although detention must be brief in stop-and-frisk situations, the time span must be evaluated in light of the totality of circumstances. In *State v. Merklein,* 388 So.2d 218 (Fla. App. 1980), a Florida appellate court said it was reasonable for officers to detain suspects for twenty to forty minutes pending arrival of another officer, witnesses, and the victim of a robbery. The key is whether the police are diligently investigating to confirm or dispel the suspicions that led to the stop. *State v. Werner,* 848 P.2d 11 (N.M. App. 1992).

When May Police Conduct a Frisk?

A valid **Terry-stop** (a synonym for investigatory detention) does not necessarily permit an officer to conduct a frisk. Rather, the need for protecting the police justifies a frisk. Therefore, an officer who undertakes to frisk a suspect must be able to point to specific facts and reasonable inferences to believe that the individual is armed. Initially, a frisk is limited to a pat-down search of an individual's outer garments. If during the pat-down search the officer feels an object that may be a weapon, the officer may seize it. If it turns out that the object is other than a weapon, it may still be seized if it is contraband. As we have noted, a stop-and-frisk may be based on reasonable suspicion, but absent probable cause, an officer is not justified in simply searching a suspect for contraband when a pat-down does not reveal any weapon-like objects. *Terry v. Ohio,* supra.

In *Ybarra v. Illinois,* 444 U.S. 85, 100 S.Ct. 338, 62 L.Ed.2d 238 (1979), the Supreme Court ruled that because police could not point to any specific facts to support their belief that the suspect was armed and dangerous, they had no grounds for frisking him. The Court has made it amply clear that a frisk must be based on an officer's reasonable suspicion that the suspect is armed rather than on a desire to locate incriminating evidence. *Sibron v. New York,* 392 U.S. 40, 88 S.Ct. 1889, 20 L.Ed.2d 917 (1968). Under the doctrine of plain view (discussed in Chapter 15), however, contraband that is discovered during a legitimate pat-down for weapons may be admissible in evidence. For example, if during the course of a lawful frisk a police officer feels what the officer suspects is a knife concealed in the suspect's pocket, the officer may retrieve the object. If the object turns out to be a metal smoking pipe wrapped inside a plastic bag containing crack cocaine, the crack would most likely be admissible as evidence of crime under the plain-view doctrine.

Investigatory Automobile Stops

Lower federal and state courts have routinely applied the stop-and-frisk doctrine to stops of vehicles as well as individuals. In many instances, this was stipulated in state statutes codifying the *Terry* standard; otherwise, it was based on the *Terry* rationale. Of course, as in the case of the individual on the street, police must have reasonable suspicion that criminal activity is afoot before they can stop a single motor vehicle. *Delaware v. Prouse,* 440 U.S. 648, 99 S.Ct. 1391, 59 L.Ed.2d 660 (1979).

Normal police practice is for the officer who makes an automobile stop to examine the suspect's driver's license, vehicle registration, and license plate. A rapid computer check can reveal whether there are any outstanding warrants on the driver, whether the license has been suspended or revoked, or whether the automobile has been reported stolen. During the stop the officer also visually scans the driver, any passengers, and any objects in plain view. Such visual scans sometimes provide probable cause to make an arrest or conduct a warrantless automobile search.

Even without probable cause, a police officer may perform a limited automobile search based on reasonable suspicion. In 1983 the Supreme Court held that when police stop an automobile based on reasonable suspicion, they may search the passenger compartment for weapons, assuming they have reason to believe—based on specific and articulable factors, together with rational inferences—that a suspect is dangerous. The search, of course, must be limited to those areas in which a weapon may be placed or hidden. *Michigan v. Long,* 463 U.S. 1032, 103 S.Ct. 3469, 77 L.Ed.2d 1201 (1983). In determining whether an officer possessed such a reasonable suspicion, courts look at many factors. Among these are the knowledge, expertise, and experience of the officer; the physical appearance of a person or vehicle as fitting the description of a person or vehicle wanted for a crime; the item and place where the suspect or vehicle is seen; and their nearness to the scene of a crime. In addition, the suspect's demeanor and any furtive gestures or attempts to flee are relevant considerations. See Chapter 15 for more discussion of automobile searches.

Automobile Stops Based on Anonymous Tips

An issue that often comes before appellate courts is whether reasonable suspicion can be developed on the basis of an anonymous tip. In *Alabama v. White,* 496 U.S. 325, 110 S.Ct. 2412, 110 L.Ed.2d 621 (1990), the U.S. Supreme Court reviewed a case where the police stopped a vehicle based on an anonymous phone tip. The Court held that an anonymous tip corroborated by independent police work was sufficient to establish a reasonable suspicion to make an investigatory stop of the vehicle described by the one who gave police the tip.

Since the Supreme Court's decision in *Alabama v. White,* state courts have been addressing cases where police have made an investigatory stop based on an anonymous tip. State courts have been disinclined to approve an investigatory stop where the anonymous tip lacks indicia of credibility and is not sufficiently verified by independent

CASE-IN-POINT

An Anonymous Tip as the Basis of Reasonable Suspicion

Police in Memphis, Tennessee received an anonymous telephone tip through a "drug hotline" that a number of African American men were dealing drugs at a particular street corner known to police as a "hot spot" for drug sales. When an officer and his partner approached the area, they saw a group of around eight African American males standing by the curb. When the officers approached the group, the men began to walk away. One of the men made a throwing motion toward the bushes. At this point the officers instructed the men to stop, take their hands out of their pockets, and place them on a nearby vehicle. A pat-down search of one of the men revealed a .40 caliber revolver tucked into his waistband. The man, who had been previously convicted of a felony, was subse-quently convicted in federal court of violating 18 U.S.C. § 922(g), which prohibits the possession of a firearm by a convicted felon. In reversing the defendant's conviction, the U.S. Court of Appeals for the Sixth Circuit held that the anonymous tip the police received failed to provide sufficient specific information in support of reasonable suspicion and that, in the absence of the tip, the defendant's behavior was insufficient to support reasonable suspicion. One judge dissented, arguing that the court's approach departed from that required by the Supreme Court's 2002 decision in *United States v. Arvizu,* supra, which instructs lower courts not to consider in isolation the factors that support determinations of reasonable suspicion.

United States v. Patterson, 340 F.3d 368 (6th Cir. 2003).

evidence. See, for example, *State v. Hjelmstad,* 535 N.W.2d 663 (Minn. App. 1995). In 2000 the Supreme Court of Pennsylvania held that an uncorroborated anonymous tip alleging a defendant was selling marijuana did not create a reasonable suspicion that would justify an investigatory stop of the defendant's car. *Commonwealth v. Goodwin,* 750 A.2d 795 (2000). Nevertheless, many state courts now agree that information supplied by an anonymous source can warrant an investigatory stop if verified by sufficient independent evidence of criminal activity. See, for example, *People v. George,* 914 P.2d 367 (Colo. 1996).

Pretextual Automobile Stops

Police have been known to use a minor or technical motor vehicle infraction as a pretext for stopping a vehicle and conducting an investigatory detention. In the past, most federal courts ruled that the police may not use minor traffic violations to justify **pretextual stops.** For example, in *United States v. Smith,* 799 F.2d 704 (11th Cir. 1986), the court said the appropriate analysis was whether a reasonable officer would have stopped the car absent an additional invalid purpose. Many state courts followed this approach.

Go to the Scheb/ Scheb Criminal Law and Procedure 6e website at academic .cengage.com/criminaljustice/ scheb for an edited version of *Whren v. U.S.*

In *Whren v. United States,* 517 U.S. 806, 116 S.Ct. 1769, 135 L.Ed.2d 89 (1996), the U.S. Supreme Court ruled that the motives of an officer in stopping a vehicle are irrelevant as long as there is an objective basis for the stop. Thus, the Court held there is no violation of the Fourth Amendment as long as there is probable cause to believe that even a minor violation has taken place. It remains to be seen whether the states, which may apply a stricter standard under their constitutions, will follow the federal standard.

Can Police Require Drivers and Passengers to Exit Their Vehicles?

During automobile stops, police routinely request that drivers exit their cars. Sometimes they also request that passengers exit. These practices are justified by the need to protect police officers from weapons that might be concealed inside the passenger compartment of a stopped vehicle. In upholding these practices, the U.S. Supreme Court noted that in 1994 eleven police officers were killed and more than five thousand officers assaulted during traffic stops. *Maryland v. Wilson,* 519 U.S. 408, 117 S.Ct. 882, 137 L.Ed.2d 41 (1997). Of course, when drivers and passengers are required to exit their automobiles, police often discover contraband or observe behavior indicative of intoxication. Such was the case in *Maryland v. Wilson,* where a passenger who had been ordered to exit a vehicle dropped a quantity of crack cocaine onto the ground. This evidence was used to secure a conviction for possession with intent to distribute; ultimately, the conviction was sustained by the Supreme Court.

Use of Drug Courier Profiles

In recent years, police have developed drug courier profiles based on typical characteristics and behaviors of drug smugglers. The profiles include such factors as paying cash for airline tickets, taking short trips to drug-source cities, not checking luggage, and appearing nervous. Police often use these profiles to identify and detain suspected drug couriers, a controversial practice that has resulted in disparate court decisions. As we pointed out in Chapter 15, the Supreme Court has held that fitting a drug courier profile is not by itself sufficient to constitute the reasonable suspicion necessary to allow police to detain an airline passenger. *Reid v. Georgia,* 448 U.S. 438, 100 S.Ct. 2752, 65 L.Ed.2d 890 (1980). The critical question is whether the behavior of the suspect is inherently suspicious. In 1989 the Supreme Court upheld an investigative stop of an air passenger for which a number of circumstances, including the use of the profile, furnished the police a reasonable suspicion of criminal activity. Although the Court found that any one of the several factors relied on by the police may have been consistent with innocent travel, it observed that the evaluation of the stop requires a consideration of the "totality of the circumstances." *United States v. Sokolow,* 490 U.S. 1, 109 S.Ct. 1581, 104 L.Ed.2d 1 (1989).

Go to the Scheb/ Scheb Criminal Law and Procedure 6e website at academic .cengage.com/criminaljustice/ scheb for an edited version of *Reid v. Georgia.*

Although the Supreme Court has upheld the use of profiles in locating suspicious persons, courts must remain on guard against abuse of the practice. In 1990 a Minnesota appellate court reversed a conviction in which the defendant, who was in an automobile, had been stopped not on the basis of a particular suspicion but because the driver's behavior loosely fit the police profile of a person looking for prostitutes. In rejecting the use of the profile, the court distinguished the case from *Sokolow,* supra, saying that "the observable facts taken together do not approach the composite bundle available to the DEA in *Sokolow.*" *City of St. Paul v. Uber,* 450 N.W.2d 623, 626 (Minn. App. 1990). The court concluded that "we cannot sustain what was, in effect, a random stop." 450 N.W.2d at 629.

Racial Profiling

Recent years have seen a continuing controversy over **racial profiling,** a term loosely applied to a variety of police practices that are alleged to be racially biased. The Department of Justice defines racial profiling as "any police-initiated action that relies on the race, ethnicity or national origin rather than the behavior of an individual or information that leads the police to a particular individual who has been identified as being, or having been, engaged in criminal activity." Deborah Ramirez, Jack McDevitt, and Amy Farrel, *A Resource Guide on Racial Profiling Data Collection Systems: Promising Practices and Lessons Learned,* Washington, D.C.: U.S. Department of Justice, 2000, p. 3.

Most of the debate over racial profiling has focused on motor vehicle stops. The sarcastic phrase "driving while black" has been used to denote what critics allege to be a widespread police practice of stopping African American motorists solely or primarily based on their race. A national survey conducted in 1999 found that 42 percent of African Americans believed they had been stopped by police because of their race and 77 percent of African Americans believed racial profiling was widespread. While only 6 percent of whites believed they had been stopped by police because of their race, 56 percent of whites believed racial profiling was widespread. *The Gallup Poll,* September 24–November 16, 1999.

In February 2001, President George W. Bush proclaimed, "Racial profiling is wrong, and we will end it in America." The movement to halt racial profiling has taken both legislative and judicial directions. Several state legislatures have passed laws to require data collection for police stops, while defendants who contend they were stopped on the basis of race have sought to dismiss charges arising out of police stops, arguing they were denied due process and equal protections of the laws. Others have sought and won relief through civil litigation under 42 U.S.C.A. § 1983. See, for example, *National Congress of Puerto Rican Rights v. City of New York,* 191 F.R.D. 52 (S.D.N.Y. 1999).

Roadblocks, Sobriety Checkpoints, and Drug Checkpoints

The third major category of police–citizen encounters includes **roadblocks** and sobriety checkpoints. Police often set up roadblocks for apprehending fleeing suspects, conducting field sobriety tests, or even for merely performing safety checks on automobiles. In addition to locating drunk drivers, roadblocks often lead to the discovery of illegal weapons, drugs, and other contraband. Because roadblocks do constitute a restraint on the liberty of the motorist, courts have held that they are susceptible to challenge under the Fourth Amendment. Therefore, police agencies must take care that roadblocks are established and operated according to guidelines that minimize the inconvenience to motorists and constrain the exercise of discretion by police officers.

In *Michigan Dept. of State Police v. Sitz*, 496 U.S. 444, 110 S.Ct. 2481, 110 L.Ed.2d 412 (1990), the Supreme Court recognized that a Fourth Amendment "seizure" occurs when a vehicle is stopped at a checkpoint but upheld the use of roadblocks for conducting field sobriety tests. In *Sitz*, the Michigan State Police operated a pilot roadblock program under guidelines drafted by an advisory committee. The guidelines set forth procedures governing checkpoint operations, site selection, and publicity. The sobriety checkpoints operated essentially as follows: Police set up roadblocks at predetermined points along state highways. All vehicles passing through the checkpoints were stopped, and drivers were briefly observed for signs of intoxication. The average length of the stop was less than thirty seconds, except where drivers appeared to be intoxicated. These drivers were instructed to pull their vehicles over to the side of the road for a license and registration check and, if indicated, a field sobriety test. Those who failed the test were placed under arrest. At one checkpoint, which was in operation for 75 minutes, 126 vehicles were stopped. Two drivers were given field sobriety tests, and one was arrested for driving under the influence of alcohol. One vehicle failed to stop at the roadblock but was apprehended and its driver arrested for driving under the influence.

Drug Checkpoints

After the Supreme Court's 1990 decision upholding sobriety checkpoints, some police departments began running drug checkpoints that would operate in much the same way but would often involve the use of drug-sniffing dogs. In 2000, the U.S. Supreme Court invalidated an Indianapolis police practice of establishing checkpoints primarily for the purpose of detecting illegal drugs. Writing for the Court, Justice O'Connor distinguished between sobriety checkpoints, which are geared toward elimination of an imminent public safety threat, and drug checkpoints designed primarily to snare traffickers in contraband. *City of Indianapolis v. Edmond*, 531 U.S. 32, 121 S.Ct 447, 148 L.Ed.2d 333 (2000).

 Go to the Scheb/ Scheb Criminal Law and Procedure 6e website at academic .cengage.com/criminaljustice/ scheb for an edited version of *City of Indianapolis v. Edmond.*

An interesting (and often productive) variation of the drug checkpoint procedure is for the police to place a sign on an interstate highway indicating "Notice: Drug Checkpoint Ahead." The sign is placed just before an exit, tempting drivers who wish to avoid the checkpoint to take the exit. Of course, there really is no drug checkpoint on the interstate highway. Rather, police are waiting at the bottom of the exit ramp to see who takes the exit. Typically, the exit chosen is one where there is little or no commercial activity and no connection to a major road. When a van with out-of-state plates takes the exit, is this inherently suspicious? Can police assume that the only reason the driver took the exit was to avoid the spurious drug checkpoint? Can police stop this vehicle, order the driver and passengers to exit the vehicle, and bring out a drug-sniffing canine? Federal courts have reached different conclusions on this issue. For example, in *United States v. Huguenin,* 154 F.3d 547 (6th Cir. 1998), the Sixth Circuit held that it was a pretextual seizure for police to selectively detain motorists without a traffic violation or reasonable suspicion of drug trafficking. But in *United States v. Brugal,* 209 F.3d 353 (4th Cir. 2000), the Fourth Circuit held that the totality of factors used by police in screening motorists eliminated a substantial portion of innocent travelers and that the conduct of the particular motorist involved gave officers reasonable suspicion to instruct him to pull his vehicle over.

After the Supreme Court's decision in the Indianapolis case, some law enforcement agencies expressed their intention to continue running drug checkpoints featuring the deceptive tactic described above. In their view, a drug checkpoint of this type is distinguishable from that which was invalidated in the Indianapolis case. It will be interesting to see if the Supreme Court examines this practice and whether it recognizes a distinction that can salvage the constitutionality of the deceptive drug checkpoint.

CASE-IN-POINT

The Use of Roadblocks

On August 8, 1992, Deputy Sheriff Robert Starnes stopped Sarah Hutton Downey at a highway roadblock on Hixson Pike in Hamilton County, Tennessee. The roadblock had been set up with no advance publicity by Lt. Ronnie Hill of the Tennessee Highway Patrol, who was assisted by members of the Chattanooga Police Department DUI task force, the Hamilton County DUI task force, and auxiliary sheriffs' officers. Hill did not obtain the approval of a superior officer regarding the establishment, time, or location of the roadblock. When Deputy Starnes checked Downey's driver's license, he smelled an odor of alcohol. After field sobriety testing, he arrested her for driving under the influence.

At trial, evidence revealed the defendant did nothing to arouse the deputy's suspicion as she approached the roadblock; rather, she was stopped for the same purpose and in the same manner as other motorists. The defendant moved to suppress the evidence on grounds there was no suspicion that a crime had been committed before the stop, and therefore her detention violated the section of the state constitution that parallels the Fourth Amendment to the U.S. Constitution. The trial court denied her motion.

The Court of Criminal Appeals ruled that use of the roadblock was not a per se violation of the state constitution, but in this case no General Order was in effect granting authority to set up highway roadblocks. Thus, the court ruled, the defendant's arrest constituted an unreasonable seizure. The Tennessee Supreme Court granted review to determine the constitutionality of highway roadblocks.

Referring to the U.S. Supreme Court's 1990 decision in *Michigan Dept. of State Police v. Sitz,* the court agreed that highway roadblocks established and operated in accordance with predetermined guidelines do not violate the Tennessee Constitution. But here, the court observed, "[T]he decision to set up a roadblock was made by an officer in the field … the site selected for the roadblock and the procedure to be used in operating the roadblock were matters left to the discretion of an officer in the field. No supervisory authority was sought or obtained, and no administrative decisions were made with regard to these critical factors." Because the roadblock was not conducted in accordance with proper, predetermined guidelines, the court found it constituted an unreasonable seizure under the Tennessee Constitution and affirmed the Court of Criminal Appeals.

State v. Downey, 945 S.W.2d 102 (Tenn. 1997).

The Latest Word from the U.S. Supreme Court on Checkpoints

In *Illinois v. Lidster,* 540 U.S. 419, 124 S.Ct. 885, 157 L.Ed.2d 843 (2004), the Supreme Court reversed a state supreme court decision striking down a police checkpoint based on *Indianapolis v. Edmond,* supra. Police in Lombard, Illinois, set up a checkpoint along a highway, stopping motorists to ask them if they knew anything about a recent hit-and-run accident. Approaching the checkpoint in his minivan, Lidster swerved and nearly hit a police officer. Detecting the odor of alcohol, police performed a field sobriety test, determined that Lidster was impaired, and placed him under arrest. Lidster challenged his DUI conviction on the ground that the government obtained evidence through use of a checkpoint stop that violated the Fourth Amendment. The Illinois appellate courts agreed that, based on *Indianapolis v. Edmond,* the automobile stop was unconstitutional. The U.S. Supreme Court reversed, making clear in an opinion by Justice Stephen Breyer that *Indianapolis v. Edmond* was not intended to prevent the police from using checkpoints to obtain the motoring public's assistance in locating the perpetrator of a crime involving a traffic accident.

Requests for Information or Identification

The lowest level of police–citizen encounter takes place when a police officer approaches an individual in public and asks questions or requests identification. Is there a legal duty to cooperate with the police in such instances? In a concurring opinion in *Terry v. Ohio,* supra, Justice Byron White observed:

> There is nothing in the Constitution which prevents a policeman from addressing questions to anyone on the streets. Absent special circumstances, the person approached may not be detained or frisked but may refuse to cooperate and go on his way. However, given the proper circumstances … , the person may be briefly detained against his will while pertinent questions are directed to him. Of course, the person stopped is not obliged to answer, answers may not be compelled, and refusal to answer furnishes no basis for an arrest, although it may alert the officer to the need for continued observation. 392 U.S. at 34, 88 S.Ct. at 1886, 20 L.Ed.2d at 913.

Historically, many states had laws making it a misdemeanor for persons to refuse to identify themselves when asked to do so by police. In *Brown v. Texas,* 443 U.S. 47, 99 S.Ct. 2637, 61 L.Ed.2d 357 (1979), the Supreme Court reviewed the constitutionality of this Texas statute: "A person commits an offense if he intentionally refuses to report or gives a false report of his name and residence address to a peace officer who has lawfully stopped him and requested the information." The Court held that the statute could not be constitutionally applied in the absence of reasonable suspicion that the individual who was asked for identification was engaged in or had engaged in criminal conduct.

In *Kolender v. Lawson,* 461 U.S. 352, 103 S.Ct. 1855, 75 L.Ed.2d 903 (1983), the Supreme Court reviewed a California statute that required persons who were loitering or wandering on the streets to provide a "credible and reliable" identification and to account for their presence when requested to do so by a police officer. The Court found that the statute was "unconstitutionally vague on its face because it encourages arbitrary enforcement by failing to describe with sufficient particularity what a suspect must do in order to satisfy the statute." 461 U.S. at 361, 103 S.Ct. at 1860, 75 L.Ed.2d at 911.

Validity of an Ordinance Requiring Self-Identification

Section 17–13 of the Arlington, Virginia, County Code provides that "[i]t shall be unlawful for any person at a public place … to refuse to identify himself by name and address at the request of a uniformed police officer … if the surrounding circumstances are such as to indicate to a reasonable man that the public safety requires such identification." The defendant was convicted of failing to identify himself at the request of a police officer and appealed. The Virginia Supreme Court held that the police validly stopped the defendant under a *Terry v. Ohio* standard and that the "stop and identify" provision in the county code did not violate the Fourth Amendment. The court distinguished the case from the statute the U.S. Supreme Court struck down in *Kolender,* saying that the California statute at issue there required an individual to provide a credible and reliable identification and required a person to account for his or her presence.

Jones v. Commonwealth of Virginia, 334 S.E.2d 536 (Va. 1985).

Interrogation and Confessions

Although the courts have long recognized the need for police interrogation of suspects, they have also recognized the potential for abuse inherent in the practice of incommunicado interrogation. At early common law, any confession was admissible even if extracted from the accused by torture. As the common law progressed, judges came to insist on proof that a confession was made voluntarily before it could be admitted in evidence.

In 1897 the Supreme Court held that to force a suspect to confess violates the Self-Incrimination Clause of the Fifth Amendment. *Bram v. United States,* 168 U.S. 532, 18 S.Ct. 183, 42 L.Ed. 568. In 1936 the Court held that a **coerced confession** deprived a defendant in a state criminal case of due process of law as guaranteed by the Fourteenth Amendment. *Brown v. Mississippi,* 297 U.S. 278, 56 S.Ct. 461, 80 L.Ed. 682 (1936). In 1964 the self-incrimination clause was made applicable to state criminal prosecutions. *Malloy v. Hogan,* 378 U.S. 1, 84 S.Ct. 1489, 12 L.Ed.2 653 (1964). As a result, federal and state police are held to the same standards in evaluating the voluntariness of confessions of guilt. In *Malloy,* the Court said that the Fifth Amendment prohibits the extraction of a confession by "exertion of any improper influence." 378 U.S. at 7, 84 S.Ct. at 1493, 12 L.Ed.2d at 659. A confession is voluntary when it is made with knowledge of its nature and consequences and without duress or inducement. *United States v. Carignan,* 342 U.S. 36, 72 S.Ct. 97, 96 L.Ed. 48 (1951).

In *Escobedo v. Illinois,* 378 U.S. 478, 84 S.Ct. 1758, 12 L.Ed.2d 977 (1964), the Supreme Court recognized the right of suspects to have counsel present during interrogation. Anticipating the criticism that the Court's decision would hamper law enforcement, Justice Arthur Goldberg observed the following: "If the exercise of constitutional rights will thwart the effectiveness of a system of law enforcement, then there is something very wrong with that system." However, the Court's work in this area was not finished. Two years later, in its landmark decision in *Miranda v. Arizona,* 384 U.S. 436, 86 S.Ct. 1602, 16 L.Ed.2d 694 (1966), the Supreme Court held that before interrogating suspects who are in custody, police must warn them of their

Go to the Scheb/ Scheb Criminal Law and Procedure 6e website at academic .cengage.com/criminaljustice/ scheb for an edited version of the *Miranda* decision.

Coerced Confessions

As an example of psychological coercion, a confession was ruled involuntary where a defendant was incarcerated and subjected to questioning over a four-day period. The defendant's relatives were denied permission to see him, and he was unable to communicate with anyone outside the jail. At one point during the interrogation, the defendant was forced to hold for twenty-five minutes a gory picture of the deceased lying in a pool of blood.

Davis v. State, 308 S.W.2d 880, 882 (Tex. Crim. App. 1957).

right to remain silent and their right to have counsel present during questioning. The typical form of the *Miranda* **warnings** used by law enforcement is as follows:

> You are under arrest. You have the right to remain silent. Anything you say can and will be used against you in a court of law. You are entitled to have an attorney present during questioning. If you cannot afford an attorney, one will be appointed to represent you.

Unless these warnings have been given, no statement made by the suspect may be used in evidence, subject to certain narrow exceptions.

The *Miranda* decision was severely criticized by law enforcement interests when it was handed down in 1966. But now it is accepted, even supported, by most law enforcement agencies and has been integrated into routine police procedure. It is also firmly established in the Supreme Court's jurisprudence, as evidenced by the Court's recent decision in *United States v. Dickerson* (2000) (see the Supreme Court Perspective following).

The Fruit of the Poisonous Tree Doctrine

The *Miranda* decision essentially established an exclusionary rule applicable to statements made by suspects during custodial interrogation. But the loss of a confession or statement may have consequences for other evidence gathered by the police. Under the fruit of the poisonous tree doctrine, evidence that is derived from inadmissible evidence is likewise inadmissible. *Wong Sun v. United States,* 371 U.S. 471, 83 S.Ct. 407, 9 L.Ed.2d 441 (1963). For example, if police learn of the location of a weapon used in the commission of a crime by interrogating a suspect who is in custody, that weapon is considered **derivative evidence.** If the police failed to provide the *Miranda* warnings, not only the suspect's responses to their questions but also the weapon discovered as the fruit of the interrogation are tainted. On the other hand, if the physical evidence was located on the basis of independently and lawfully obtained information, it may be admissible under the **independent source doctrine.** *Segurra v. United States,* 468 U.S. 796, 104 S.Ct. 3380, 82 L.Ed.2d 599 (1984). Thus, in our hypothetical case, if police learned of the location of the weapon from an informant, the weapon might well be admissible in court, even though the suspect's admissions are still inadmissible.

A variation on the independent source doctrine is what is termed the **inevitable discovery doctrine.** A grisly case that illustrates this doctrine is *Nix v. Williams,*

United States v. Dickerson, 530 U.S. 428, 120 S.Ct. 2326, 147 L.Ed.2d 405 (2000)

In 2000 the Supreme Court reaffirmed its landmark 1966 decision in *Miranda v. Arizona.* The following are brief excerpts from the majority opinion and a dissent authored by Justice Antonin Scalia.

CHIEF JUSTICE WILLIAM H. REHNQUIST delivered the opinion of the Court, saying in part:

In Miranda ... *we held that certain warnings must be given before a suspect's statement made during custodial interrogation could be admitted in evidence. In the wake of that decision, Congress enacted 18 U.S.C. § 3501, which in essence laid down a rule that the admissibility of such statements should turn only on whether or not they were voluntarily made....*

Petitioner Dickerson was indicted for bank robbery, conspiracy to commit bank robbery, and using a firearm in the course of committing a crime of violence.... Before trial, Dickerson moved to suppress a statement he had made at a Federal Bureau of Investigation field office, on the grounds that he had not received "Miranda warnings" before being interrogated. The District Court granted his motion to suppress, and the Government took an interlocutory appeal to the United States Court of Appeals for the Fourth Circuit. That court, by a divided vote, reversed ... [holding] that our decision in Miranda *was not a constitutional holding, and that therefore Congress could by statute have the final say on the question of admissibility.*

We do not think there is ... justification for overruling Miranda. Miranda *has become embedded in routine police practice to the point where the warnings have become part of our national culture.... While we have overruled our precedents when subsequent cases have undermined their doctrinal underpinnings, ... we do not believe that this has happened to the* Miranda *decision. If anything, our subsequent cases have reduced the impact of the* Miranda *rule on legitimate law enforcement while reaffirming the decision's core ruling that unwarned statements may not be used as evidence in the prosecution's case in chief.*

JUSTICE ANTONIN SCALIA, joined by JUSTICE CLARENCE THOMAS, dissented, concluding:

I am not convinced by petitioner's argument that Miranda *should be preserved because the decision occupies a special place in the "public's consciousness." As far as I am aware, the public is not under the illusion that we are infallible. I see little harm in admitting that we made a mistake in taking away from the people the ability to decide for themselves what protections (beyond those required by the Constitution) are reasonably affordable in the criminal investigatory process.*

www Go to the Scheb/ Scheb Criminal Law and Procedure 6e website at academic .cengage.com/criminaljustice/ scheb for an edited version of *Nix v. Williams.*

467 U.S. 431, 104 S.Ct. 2501, 81 L.Ed.2d 377 (1984). In this case, a jury in a murder defendant's retrial was not permitted to learn of the defendant's incriminating statements because the police had violated *Miranda.* He was convicted nevertheless, largely on evidence derived from the girl's corpse. The body was discovered when Williams, before meeting with his attorney, led police to the place where he had dumped it. On appeal, Williams argued that evidence of the body was improperly admitted at trial because its discovery was based on inadmissible statements and thus constituted the fruit of the poisonous tree. In reviewing the case, the U.S. Supreme Court held that the evidence of the body was properly admissible at trial because a search party operating in the area where the body was discovered would eventually have located the body, even without assistance from the defendant.

The Public Safety Exception to *Miranda*

Police generally provide the *Miranda* warnings immediately on arrest or as soon as is practicable to preserve as evidence any statements that the suspect might make, as well as any other evidence that might be derived from these statements. In some situations, however, the *Miranda* warnings are delayed because police are preoccupied with apprehending other individuals or taking actions to protect themselves or others on the scene. In *New York v. Quarles,* 467 U.S. 649, 104 S.Ct. 2626, 81 L.Ed.2d 550 (1984), the Supreme Court recognized a **public safety exception** to the *Miranda* exclusionary rule. Under *Quarles,* police may ask suspects questions designed to locate weapons that might be used to harm the police or other persons before providing the *Miranda* warnings. If this interaction produces incriminating statements or physical evidence, the evidence need not be suppressed.

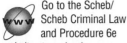 Go to the Scheb/ Scheb Criminal Law and Procedure 6e website at academic .cengage.com/criminaljustice/ scheb for an edited version of *N.Y. v. Quarles.*

What Constitutes an Interrogation?

Although interrogation normally occurs at the station house after arrest, it may occur anywhere. For the purpose of determining when the *Miranda* warnings must be given, the Supreme Court has defined interrogation as "express questioning or its functional equivalent," including "any words or actions on the part of the police that the police should know are reasonably likely to elicit an incriminating response from the suspect." *Rhode Island v. Innis,* 446 U.S. 291, 301, 100 S.Ct. 1682, 1693, 64 L.Ed.2d 297, 308 (1980). Before police may engage in such interaction, they must provide the *Miranda* warnings or risk the likelihood that useful **incriminating statements** will be suppressed as illegally obtained evidence.

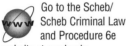 Go to the Scheb/ Scheb Criminal Law and Procedure 6e website at academic .cengage.com/criminaljustice/ scheb for an edited version of *Rhode Island v. Innis.*

Waiver of *Miranda* Rights

It is axiomatic that all constitutional rights may be waived. A suspect may elect to waive the right to remain silent or the right to have counsel present during questioning as long as he or she does so knowingly and voluntarily. Courts are apt to strictly scrutinize a **waiver of *Miranda* rights** to make sure it is not the product of some coercion or deception by police. In *United States v. Carra,* 604 F.2d 1271 (10th Cir. 1979), the court observed that "[v]oluntary waiver of the right to remain silent is not mechanically to be determined but is to be determined from the totality of circumstances as a matter of fact." For example, in *United States v. Blocker,* 354 F. Supp. 1195 (D. D.C. 1973), a federal district court, citing decisions from the U.S. Court of Appeals for the Fifth Circuit, observed that a written waiver signed by the accused is not in itself conclusive evidence: "The court must still decide whether, in view of all the circumstances, defendant's subsequent decision to speak was a product of his free will." 354 F. Supp. at 1198 n. 11.

Although they must honor a suspect's refusal to cooperate, police are under no duty to inform a suspect who is considering whether to cooperate that arrangements have been made to provide counsel. In *Moran v. Burbine,* 475 U.S. 412, 106 S.Ct. 1135, 89 L.Ed.2d 410 (1986), police arrested a man on a burglary charge and subsequently linked him to an unsolved murder. The suspect's sister, not aware that a murder charge was about to be filed against her brother, arranged for a lawyer to represent her brother on the burglary charge. The attorney contacted the police to arrange a meeting with her client. The police did not mention the possible murder charge and told the attorney that her client was not going to be questioned until the next day. The police then began to interrogate Burbine, failing to tell him that a lawyer had been arranged for him and had attempted to contact him. Burbine waived his rights and eventually confessed to the murder. The Supreme Court upheld the use of the confession in evidence.

Coerced Confessions

Even where police officers provide the *Miranda* warnings and the suspect agrees to talk to police without having counsel present, a confession elicited from the suspect is inadmissible if it is obtained through coercion, whether physical intimidation or psychological pressure. *United States v. Tingle,* 658 F.2d 1332 (9th Cir. 1981). A classic example of psychological coercion is the so-called Mutt-and-Jeff strategy. Under this tactic, one police officer, the "bad guy," is harsh, rude, and aggressive, while another police officer, the "good guy," is friendly and sympathetic to the suspect. Obviously the objective of the strategy is to get the accused to confess to the "good guy," and there is reason to believe that it is an effective technique. There is controversy about whether the Mutt-and-Jeff tactic is a constitutional means of eliciting a confession from a suspect who has waived his or her *Miranda* rights and agreed to talk to police without the presence of counsel. In *Miranda*, the Supreme Court alluded to the Mutt-and-Jeff routine as a possible example of impermissible psychological coercion. 384 U.S. at 452, 86 S.Ct. at 1614, 16 L.Ed.2d at 711. Yet, absent other indications of coercion, courts have generally acquiesced in the practice.

Police Deception

The use of tricks or factual misstatements by police in an effort to induce a defendant to confess does not automatically invalidate a confession. A misstatement by police may affect the **voluntariness of a confession,** but the effect of any misstatements must be considered in light of the totality of surrounding circumstances. In *Frazier v. Cupp,* 394 U.S. 731, 89 S.Ct. 1420, 22 L.Ed.2d 684 (1969), the Supreme Court reversed a conviction where the police had falsely informed a suspect that his codefendant had confessed. Although the Supreme Court found the misstatement relevant to the issue of whether the confession had been given voluntarily, it did not find that the misstatement per se made the confession inadmissible. The Nebraska Supreme Court has held that even deceptive statements referring to nonexistent autopsies of victims will not automatically render a confession involuntary. *State v. Norfolk,* 381 N.W.2d 120 (Neb. 1986).

How far may police go in their use of deception? In 1989 a Florida appellate court affirmed a trial judge's order holding a confession involuntary where police had presented fabricated laboratory reports to the defendant to secure a confession. The "reports," which were on the stationery of a law enforcement agency and a DNA testing firm, indicated that traces of the defendant's semen had been found on the victim's underwear. Among the factors cited by the appellate court in support of the exclusion of the confession were the indefinite life span of manufactured documents, their self-authenticating character, and the ease of duplication. The court expressed concern that false documents could find their way into police files or the courtroom and be accepted as genuine. *State v. Cayward,* 552 So.2d 971 (Fla. App. 1989).

In *State v. Patton,* 826 A.2d 783 (N.J. Sup. 2003), a police officer, posing as an eyewitness, was "interviewed" on an audiotape and fabricated an account of the victim's murder. The tape was later played to the defendant. Despite his earlier denials of involvement, upon hearing the audiotape, the defendant confessed to the murder. The fabricated audiotape, identified as such, was later introduced into evidence at trial, and the defendant was found guilty. Relying heavily on the Florida court's opinion in *State v. Cayward,* supra, the New Jersey appellate court held this fabrication of evidence violated due process. The court found the defendant's resulting confession to be inadmissible and reversed the defendant's conviction.

Police deception must be distinguished from cases where the police use or threaten force or promise leniency to elicit a confession. In instances where force is used or leniency is promised, courts will suppress confessions obtained. See *Spano v. New York,* 360 U.S. 315, 79 S.Ct. 1202, 3 L.Ed.2d 1265 (1959). Moreover, when the police furnish a suspect an incorrect or incomplete advisory statement of the penalties provided by law for a particular crime, courts will generally suppress the suspect's confession. See, for example, *People v. Lytle,* 704 P.2d 331 (Colo. App. 1985).

Factors Considered by Judges in Evaluating Confessions

Judges consider several variables in determining whether a challenged confession was voluntary. These include the duration and methods of the interrogation, the length of the delay between arrest and appearance before a magistrate, the conditions of detention, the attitudes of the police toward the defendant, the defendant's physical and psychological state, and anything else that might bear on the defendant's resistance. *Commonwealth v. Kichline,* 361 A.2d 282, 290 (Pa. 1976). Courts are particularly cautious in receiving confessions by juveniles. See, for example, *Haley v. Ohio,* 332 U.S. 596, 68 S.Ct. 302, 92 L.Ed. 224 (1948).

Go to the Scheb/ Scheb Criminal Law and Procedure 6e website at academic .cengage.com/criminaljustice/ scheb for an edited version of *Arizona v. Fulminante.*

In a landmark ruling, *Arizona v. Fulminante,* 499 U.S. 279, 111 S.Ct. 1246, 113 L.Ed.2d 302 (1991), the Supreme Court said that the use of a confession that should have been suppressed does not automatically require reversal of a defendant's conviction. Rather, the appellate court must determine whether the defendant would have been convicted in the absence of the confession. If so, the admission of the confession is deemed to be a harmless error that does not require reversal. See, for example, *State v. Tart,* 672 So.2d 116 (La. 1996).

Identification Procedures

Police identification procedures include those in which victims and witnesses are asked to identify perpetrators, such as **lineups, showups,** and **photo packs.** They also encompass scientific techniques comparing **forensic evidence** taken from a suspect with that found at a crime scene. All of these procedures are extremely important in police work, but each poses unique legal problems.

Forensic Methods

Forensic methods involve the application of scientific principles to legal issues. In the context of police work, forensic methods commonly include fingerprint identification, comparison of blood samples, matching of clothing fibers, head and body hair comparisons, identification of semen, and, more recently, DNA tests. When these methods are conducted by qualified persons, the results are usually admissible in evidence. Indeed, the courts have ruled that obtaining such physical evidence from suspects does not violate the constitutional prohibition of compulsory self-incrimination. *Schmerber v. California,* 384 U.S. 757, 86 S.Ct. 1826, 16 L.Ed.2d 908 (1966).

In *Gilbert v. California,* 388 U.S. 263, 87 S.Ct. 1951, 18 L.Ed.2d 1178 (1967), the U.S. Supreme Court held that a suspect could be compelled to provide a **handwriting exemplar,** explaining that it is not testimony but an identifying physical characteristic. Similarly, in *United States v. Dionisio,* 410 U.S. 1, 93 S.Ct. 764, 35 L.Ed.2d 67 (1973), the Court held that a suspect could be compelled to provide a **voice exemplar** on the ground that the recording is being used only to measure the physical properties of the suspect's voice, as distinct from the content of what the suspect has said.

Of course, police may not use methods that "shock the conscience" in obtaining physical evidence from suspects. *Rochin v. California,* 342 U.S. 165, 72 S.Ct. 205, 96 L.Ed. 183 (1952). Courts will scrutinize closely procedures that subject the suspect to major bodily intrusions. For example, in *Winston v. Lee,* 470 U.S. 753, 105 S.Ct. 1611, 84 L.Ed.2d 662 (1985), the prosecution sought a court order requiring a suspect to have surgery to remove a bullet lodged in his chest. The prosecution believed that ballistics tests on the bullet would show that the suspect had been wounded during the course of a robbery. The Supreme Court, weighing the risks to the suspect against the government's need for evidence and noting that the prosecution had other evidence against the suspect, disallowed the procedure. The Court declined to formulate a broad rule to govern such cases. Rather, courts must consider such matters on a case-by-case basis, carefully weighing the interests on both sides.

As the 1995 O. J. Simpson murder trial demonstrated, defense lawyers can attack the methodology of forensic procedures as well as the qualifications of those administering them. If the evidence is inherently unreliable, it is inadmissible regardless of whether there were violations of the suspect's constitutional rights. In 1996 the FBI crime laboratory was criticized for allegedly sloppy procedures in the conduct of DNA and other forensic tests. This encouraged defense lawyers to challenge the reliability of the evidence in several cases where prosecutors were using evidence analyzed by the FBI crime lab.

With the rapid progress of science and technology, forensic procedures are constantly evolving and new procedures becoming available to the police. Evidence obtained through scientific and technological innovations can be both relevant and probative in a criminal case. Yet care must be taken to ensure that a new method is clearly supported by research.

Until recently, federal and state courts followed the test articulated in *Frye v. United States,* 293 F. 1013 (D.C. Cir. 1923), and admitted scientific evidence only if it was based on principles or theories generally accepted in the scientific community. In *Daubert v. Merrell Dow Pharmaceuticals, Inc.,* 509 U.S. 579, 113 S.Ct. 2786, 125 L.Ed.2d 469 (1993), the Supreme Court held that the Federal Rules of Evidence supersede *Frye* and govern the admissibility of scientific evidence in the federal courts. This approach causes admissibility of scientific evidence to hinge on such factors as whether the evidence can be tested and whether it has been subjected to peer review. State courts are now divided on whether to accept the newer *Daubert* standard or remain with the classic standard announced in 1923 in *Frye.* (This topic is discussed further in Chapter 18.)

Lineups

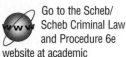
Go to the Scheb/ Scheb Criminal Law and Procedure 6e website at academic .cengage.com/criminaljustice/ scheb for an edited version of *Rochin v. California.*

Eyewitness identification may be more persuasive to juries than forensic evidence, but it can also present problems. One of the most common nonscientific methods of identification is the lineup. In a lineup, a group of individuals, one of whom is the suspect in custody, appears before a victim or witness, who is usually shielded from the suspect's view. Often, the individuals in the lineup are asked to walk, turn sideways, wear certain items of clothing, or speak to assist the victim or eyewitness in making a positive identification. The Supreme Court has held that there is no Fifth Amendment immunity against being placed in a lineup as an identification procedure. *United States v. Wade,* 388 U.S. 218, 87 S.Ct. 1926, 18 L.Ed.2d 1149 (1967). However, courts must guard against the possibility that identification procedures, especially lineups, are unfair when a victim or witness is prompted to identify a particular suspect as

Go to the Scheb/ Scheb Criminal Law and Procedure 6e website at academic .cengage.com/criminaljustice/ scheb for an edited version of *U.S. v. Wade.*

the perpetrator. See, for example, *Foster v. California,* 394 U.S. 440, 89 S.Ct. 1127, 22 L.Ed.2d 402 (1969). Obviously, if the perpetrator is known to be black, it is impermissibly suggestive for police to place one African American suspect in a lineup with five white individuals. In practice, however, the more subtle suggestiveness of lineups causes problems for the courts. To avoid such problems, police should place several persons with similar physical characteristics in a lineup.

To further protect the rights of the accused, the Supreme Court has said that after formal charges have been made against a defendant, the defendant has the right to have counsel present at a lineup. *Kirby v. Illinois,* 406 U.S. 682, 92 S.Ct. 1877, 32 L.Ed.2d 411 (1972). To ensure that police and prosecutors honor that right, the Supreme Court has said that a pretrial identification obtained in violation of the right to counsel is per se inadmissible at trial. *Gilbert v. California,* supra. A per se exclusionary rule was deemed necessary to ensure that the police and the prosecution would respect the defendant's right to have counsel present at a lineup. On the other hand, a pretrial identification obtained through impermissibly suggestive identification procedures is not per se inadmissible. Instead, such an identification may be introduced into evidence if the trial judge first finds that the witness's in-court identification is reliable and based on independent recall. In making this determination, the trial judge must consider (1) the opportunity of the witness to view the accused at the time of the crime, (2) the witness's degree of attention, (3) the accuracy of the witness's prior description of the accused, (4) the level of certainty demonstrated at the confrontation, and (5) the time that elapsed between the crime and the confrontation. *Neil v. Biggers,* 409 U.S. 188, 93 S.Ct. 375, 34 L.Ed.2d 401 (1972); see also *Wethington v. State,* 560 N.E.2d 496 (Ind. 1990).

Showups

The showup is a frequently used method of identification of a suspect. In a showup, the police usually take the victim to the suspect to determine whether the victim can make an identification, and at least one state supreme court has held the that police may transport a person stopped for an investigatory stop a short distance for purposes of a showup. *People v. Lippert,* 432 N.E.2d 605 (Ill. 1982).

In 1967 the U.S. Court of Appeals for the District of Columbia Circuit approved the use of showups, commenting, "[W]e do not consider a prompt identification of a suspect close to the time and place of an offense to diverge from the rudiments of fair play that govern the due balance of pertinent interests that suspects be treated fairly while the state pursues its responsibility of apprehending criminals." *Wise v. United States,* 383 F.2d 206, 210 (D.C. Cir. 1967).

In *Stovall v. Denno,* 308 U.S. 293, 87 S.Ct. 198, 18 L.Ed.2d 1199 (1967), the Supreme Court recognized a defendant's due process right to exclude identification testimony that results from unnecessarily suggestive procedures that may lead to an irreparably mistaken identification. This form of "on-the-scene" confrontation between an eyewitness and a suspect is inherently suggestive because it is apparent that when law enforcement takes a victim for a showup of a suspect, they usually believe they have caught the offender. Therefore, courts review identification testimony carefully to make sure a witness's identification testimony is not based on impermissibly suggestive identification procedures. In making such a determination, courts often look to the length of time between the crime and the confrontation and the level of certainty demonstrated by the witness at the confrontation.

Although critics complain of the use of showups, such a confrontation may be justified by the necessity to preserve a witness's memory of a suspect before the suspect has had an opportunity to alter his or her clothing and appearance. Appellate courts consistently admonish caution in the use of showups; however, they generally approve of their use when the identification occurs shortly after the crime has been committed and the showup is conducted near the scene of the crime under circumstances that are not unduly suggestive. In approving showups, some courts have pointed out that a victim's or eyewitness's on-the-scene identification is likely to be more reliable than a later identification because the memory is fresher. See, for example, *Jones v. State,* 600 P.2d 247, 250 (Nev. 1979). Courts base their judgments on the reliability of showups based on many factors and circumstances. For example, in *United States v. Bautista,* 23 F.3d 726 (2d Cir. 1994), in its review of a challenge to an on-the-scene identification immediately following a nighttime narcotics raid, the court observed, "The fact that the suspects were handcuffed, in the custody of law enforcement officers, and illuminated by flashlights … did not render the pre-trial identification procedure unnecessarily suggestive." *Id.* at 731. The court went on to explain that because the on-the-scene identification was necessary to allow the officers to release the innocent, the incidents of that identification were also necessary.

Photo Packs

A photo pack is simply a set of "mug shots" that are shown individually to the victim or eyewitness in the hope of being able to identify the perpetrator. To produce a reliable, hence admissible, identification, the presentation of the photo pack should not emphasize one photo over the others. For example, in *Commonwealth v. Thornley,* 546 N.E.2d 350 (1989), the Supreme Judicial Court of Massachusetts found that the photographic array was impermissibly suggestive because the witnesses admitted they made their selection of the defendant's photograph because the man in the photo was wearing glasses. The defendant was the only one of thirteen men in the photo array who was wearing glasses.

The words and actions of the officers making the presentation must manifest an attitude of disinterest. *State v. Thamer,* 777 P.2d 432 (Utah 1989). In analyzing a defendant's claim of being the victim of an impermissibly suggestive photo pack identification, courts generally apply a two-part test. First, did the photo array present the defendant in an impermissibly suggestive posture? Second, if so, under the totality of circumstances, did the procedure give rise to a substantial likelihood of misidentification? *State v. Bedwell,* 417 N.W.2d 66 (Iowa 1987).

■ CONCLUSION

Police are permitted broad discretion in their interactions with the public. There are no legal prerequisites to the many consensual encounters through which police routinely perform their investigative and preventive duties. Nonconsensual encounters are subject to legal requirements. To stop and frisk a person requires reasonable suspicion; to make an arrest, police must have probable cause to believe that a crime has been committed. When practicable, it is desirable that police obtain an arrest warrant, but this is not always essential to legitimize an arrest based on probable cause.

Even without probable cause, police are permitted to stop and frisk persons where there is reasonable suspicion that a crime is about to take place. This stop-and-frisk exception also applies to investigatory stops of motor vehicles. In determining whether police had reasonable suspicion to conduct an investigatory detention, courts consider the totality of circumstances known to the officer at the time. Courts are still struggling with the permissible length and scope of such field detentions.

Persons who are detained or arrested by police possess a constitutional right to remain silent. Under normal circumstances, police may not compel even a suspicious person to identify himself or herself. In many states, "cite and release" statutes provide for officers to "ticket" those who commit minor traffic offenses.

Police officers are allowed to use such force as is reasonably necessary to effect an arrest; however, they are not permitted to use deadly force against fleeing suspects when there is no threat to the officer or the public. When police make an arrest, they must inform the suspect of the constitutional rights to remain silent and consult with counsel. Failure to do so jeopardizes the admissibility of incriminating statements that the suspect might make even voluntarily. It also jeopardizes the use of physical evidence discovered as a result of statements that are later held to be inadmissible. Although the courts are willing to recognize certain exceptional situations, the prudent police officer will "Mirandize" the suspect immediately on arrest. Persons arrested must be brought promptly before a court of law.

There is no constitutional prohibition against police taking fingerprints, voice samples, handwriting exemplars, and the like from suspects. Nor is there any prohibition against forcing suspects to appear in lineups for identification by a witness or victim, as long as police avoid suggesting the person to be identified.

Despite the increased scrutiny of courts over the last several decades, law enforcement officers retain considerable discretion in making arrests, conducting investigations, and interviewing suspects. These investigatory procedures have been extended, subject to certain restrictions, to conducting roadblocks and sobriety checkpoints. As long as certain essential safeguards are observed, police are not seriously hampered in their efforts to ferret out crime.

■ KEY TERMS

arrest, 431
request for information or
    identification, 431
interrogation, 431
identification procedures, 431
arrest warrant, 432
capias, 432
warrantless arrest, 433
plain view, 433
citizen's arrest, 437
investigatory detention, 439
pat-down search, 439
Terry-stop, 441
pretextual stops, 443
racial profiling, 444
roadblocks, 445

coerced confession, 448
Miranda warnings, 449
derivative evidence, 449
independent source doctrine, 449
inevitable discovery doctrine, 449
public safety exception, 451
incriminating statements, 451
waiver of *Miranda* rights, 451
voluntariness of a confession, 452
police deception, 453
lineups, 453
showups, 453
photo packs, 453
forensic evidence, 453
handwriting exemplar, 453
voice exemplar, 453

■ WEB-BASED RESEARCH ACTIVITY

Use www.findlaw.com or some other Internet resource to locate the U.S. Supreme Court's most recent decisions in the areas of arrest and interrogation. Try to determine whether the Court has agreed to hear new cases in these areas and, if so, what issues these cases present.

Find the Web site for the U.S. Court of Appeals for the circuit in which your state is located. Search the recent decisions of that court in an effort to locate a recent decision on arrest or interrogation. Is this case likely to be reviewed by the U.S. Supreme Court?

■ QUESTIONS FOR THOUGHT AND DISCUSSION

1. Practically speaking, what is the difference between "probable cause" and "reasonable suspicion"? How long can police detain a suspect based on reasonable suspicion?

2. What are the practical arguments for and against allowing private citizens to make arrests when they observe criminal activity taking place? What is the law in your state governing "citizen's arrests"?

3. Does your state make any distinction between minor and serious traffic offenses in permitting arrests? Is the use of arrest procedures for relatively minor traffic offenses unnecessary? Is it better to give the individual police officer discretion in these matters or to adopt laws decriminalizing such infractions?

4. In the *Miranda* case, the Supreme Court released a convicted rapist to impose a requirement that police advise suspects of their constitutional rights before conducting interrogations. Was the Court's decision a wise one? What has been the impact of the *Miranda* decision on law enforcement?

5. What factors do courts consider in determining whether an individual is "in custody" when a police interrogation takes place?

6. What limitations do courts impose on police in the use of deception in interrogations of suspects?

7. How might police coerce a suspect into waiving the right to counsel and to remain silent during interrogation? How can courts ensure that cooperation with police was voluntary?

8. What factors do courts consider in evaluating whether a confession has been coerced?

9. Are the courts correct in limiting the scope of the Fifth Amendment Self-Incrimination Clause to verbal statements so that there is no constitutional protection against compulsory police identification procedures? What would be the implications for law enforcement if the courts included physical evidence like fingerprints or handwriting samples within the scope of the Fifth Amendment privilege?

10. Describe the methods of nonscientific identification used by law enforcement in their attempts to identify suspects. Which do you think is the most reliable?

11. Would it be permissible for police to construct a lineup including four visibly overweight persons along with a slim suspect where the victim told police that her assailant was "very thin"?

12. Discuss racial profiling, which results in a disproportionate number of minorities being stopped for disobeying traffic laws. Should this problem be addressed by (a) courts' dismissing charges or suppressing evidence seized as a result of racial profiling based on denial of due process and equal protection of the law, (b) civil litigation seeking financial redress, (c) disciplinary action against law enforcement officers responsible for racial profiling, or (d) some other proposed remedy?

■ PROBLEMS FOR DISCUSSION AND SOLUTION

1. Police obtained a warrant to search a single-family residence for "illegal amphetamines and equipment used in the manufacture of same." The warrant also authorized the search of the person of Harry Hampton, described in the warrant as

a white male, 32 years of age, 6 ft. 2 in., and 225 lbs. When police arrived at the scene, one officer began to search Hampton. When that search yielded contraband, another officer detained a second man sitting on the porch (he was later identified as Jimmy Jaffers). The officer subjected Jaffers to a pat-down search. No weapons were discovered on Jaffers's person, but the officer, having felt a "suspicious lump" in Jaffers's front pants pocket, retrieved a plastic bag of capsules that later proved to be illegal amphetamines. In a pretrial motion, Jaffers's counsel moves to suppress the contraband, arguing that his client was the victim of an unreasonable search. Is Jaffers likely to prevail in this contention? Why or why not?

2. A police officer on night patrol saw a car parked off a dirt road in an area known to be a "lovers' lane." As his cruiser approached the car, he observed a male and a female sitting inside. He noticed the male occupant make a movement that the officer interpreted as an attempt to hide something under the seat. The officer approached the vehicle and directed the occupants to get out. As they did, he observed a marijuana "roach" in the open ashtray. The officer then reached under the front seat and retrieved a small quantity of marijuana. The officer placed both individuals under arrest. In court, the officer admitted that he was not concerned for his safety but simply had a "hunch" that the couple could be "doing drugs." Did the officer make a legal arrest? Why or why not?

CHAPTER 17

The Pretrial Process

**CHAPTER
OUTLINE**

Introduction

The U.S. Constitution and the constitutions of all fifty states guarantee due process of law to all persons accused of criminal wrongdoing. Due process requires that persons accused of crimes be given fair notice of criminal charges and an adequate opportunity to contest them. As the Supreme Court has said,

> No principle of procedural due process is more clearly established than that of notice of the specific charge, and a chance to be heard in a trial of the issues raised by that charge, if desired, are among the constitutional rights of every accused in a criminal proceeding, in all courts, state or federal. *Cole v. Arkansas,* 333 U.S. 196, 201, 68 S.Ct. 514, 517, 92 L.Ed. 644, 647 (1948).

For **petty offenses** (minor misdemeanors), due process may require no more than the opportunity for the accused to contest the charge before a magistrate in a single, summary proceeding. For more serious offenses (treason, felonies, and major misdemeanors), the federal and state constitutions impose more elaborate procedural requirements.

As a practical matter, judicial decisions interpreting the generalities of the federal and state constitutions have greatly expanded the procedural rights that must be observed in criminal prosecutions. One result of this judicial activity is that the area of law known as criminal procedure has developed substantially over the past several decades.

Although many people equate the term **criminal procedure** with the criminal trial, the former term is actually much broader. Criminal procedure includes search and seizure, arrest, and interrogation (see Chapters 15 and 16), as well as a variety of other procedures that must occur before a trial can take place. The main components of the pretrial process are the **initial appearance** before a magistrate, the **preliminary hearing,** the **grand jury proceeding,** and the **arraignment** (see Figure 17.1). In addition, judges consider various motions made by the defense and prosecution at pretrial hearings. These pretrial procedures are designed to eliminate from the system

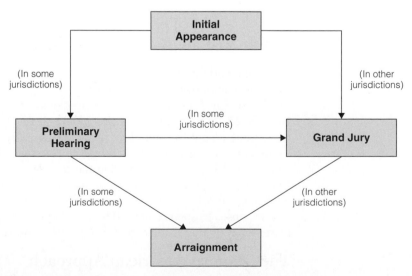

FIGURE 17.1 Major Components of the Pretrial Process in Felony Cases

those cases for which there is insufficient evidence of criminal wrongdoing and to set the stage for a fair and orderly resolution of cases for which the evidence is sufficiently strong to proceed to trial.

Although pretrial proceedings in most cases attract relatively little attention, the American public was made aware of the importance of the pretrial process during the latter months of 1994, when the media provided extensive coverage of pretrial procedures in the O. J. Simpson case. What happens during the pretrial process often determines the outcome of a criminal case. Indeed, the overwhelming majority of criminal cases never make it to trial. Some cases are dropped or dismissed for lack of sufficient evidence; many others result in convictions pursuant to guilty pleas. A substantial number of these guilty pleas result from negotiations between prosecutors and defense counsel. In such cases, trials are unnecessary. Where a defendant pleads guilty or no contest to an offense, there is a factual basis for the plea, and the court is satisfied that the plea has been entered voluntarily, guilt is pronounced and the process moves along to the sentencing stage. Given the relative infrequency of trials, pretrial procedures have great importance in the day-to-day operation of the criminal justice system.

The Right to Counsel

Before undertaking a detailed examination of pretrial procedures, we must consider the contours of the **right to counsel,** which is essential to preserving the fundamental fairness of all criminal procedures. The defense attorney not only represents the accused in pretrial court proceedings but also advises on strategy and often serves as the negotiator between the defendant and the prosecutor. Thus, the attorney for the defense plays an essential role in the criminal process. Indeed, in our adversarial legal system, the right to counsel may be the single most important right possessed by persons accused of serious crimes. As the Supreme Court has observed, "[T]he right of one charged with crime to counsel may not be deemed fundamental and essential in some countries, but it is in ours." *Gideon v. Wainwright*, 372 U.S. 335, 344, 83 S.Ct. 792, 796, 9 L.Ed.2d 799, 805 (1963).

Common-Law Background of the Right to Counsel

Under the early English common law, there was no right to counsel for persons accused of treason or felonies. Somewhat ironically, by modern standards, the common law did recognize a right to counsel in misdemeanor cases. See *Argersinger v. Hamlin*, 407 U.S. 25, 92 S.Ct. 2006, 32 L.Ed.2d 530 (1972). In 1698 Parliament enacted a law recognizing a right to counsel in cases of treason. By the late eighteenth century, the common law recognized a limited right to counsel in felony cases, and in 1836 Parliament passed legislation recognizing the right to counsel for all criminal defendants. Under the common law and the aforementioned acts of Parliament, the right to counsel meant the right to hire a barrister (a lawyer admitted to trial practice) at a person's own expense. It was not until 1903 that Parliament passed the Poor Prisoner's Defense Act, requiring that indigent defendants be provided counsel at public expense.

The Modern American Approach

In the United States, the right to counsel has likewise evolved through both judicial decisions and legislation. As the Sixth Amendment to the U.S. Constitution provides,

"In all criminal prosecutions, the accused shall enjoy the right ... to have the Assistance of Counsel for his defense."

The Sixth Amendment has been consistently interpreted to allow defendants to employ counsel in all federal prosecutions, including treason, felony, and misdemeanor cases. Similar provisions in the fifty state constitutions have been interpreted to allow defendants to retain counsel in state criminal prosecutions. Irrespective of state constitutional protection, the accused is protected by the federal constitution. In 1963 the Supreme Court held that the Sixth Amendment right to counsel applies to prosecutions in the state courts by way of the Due Process Clause of the Fourteenth Amendment. *Gideon v. Wainwright,* supra. Today, criminal defendants have the right to retain attorneys to represent them in all types of criminal prosecutions, whether in state court, in federal court, or before military tribunals.

Indigency and the Right to Counsel

Although criminal defendants have the right to employ attorneys to represent them, many defendants are too poor to afford private counsel. To what extent does the law mandate that they be provided counsel at public expense?

In 1790 Congress first addressed the issue of **indigency** in the context of federal criminal prosecutions for capital crimes. The Judiciary Act of 1790 required federal judges to assign counsel to indigent defendants in capital cases, at least where defendants requested representation. 1 Stat. 112, § 29 (1790). Some states emulated the act of Congress by providing for appointed counsel in capital cases, but most did not.

THE SCOTTSBORO CASE

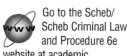

Go to the Scheb/ Scheb Criminal Law and Procedure 6e website at academic .cengage.com/criminaljustice/ scheb for an edited version of *Powell v. Alabama.*

In a highly publicized case in the early 1930s, the Supreme Court held that the Fourteenth Amendment required states to observe the requirement long since imposed on federal courts by Congress. *Powell v. Alabama,* 287 U.S. 45, 53 S.Ct. 55, 77 L.Ed. 158 (1932). In the "Scottsboro case," as it has become known, several black youths were charged with raping two white women. Within a week of being arrested, the defendants were tried, convicted, and sentenced to death, all without meaningful assistance of counsel. The Supreme Court reversed their convictions:

> In light of the ... ignorance and illiteracy of the defendants, their youth, the circumstances of public hostility, the imprisonment and the close surveillance of the defendants by the military forces, the fact that their friends and families were all in other states and communication with them necessarily difficult, and above all that they stood in deadly peril of their lives ... we think that ... the failure of the trial court to make an effective appointment of counsel was ... a denial of due process within the meaning of the Fourteenth Amendment. 287 U.S. at 71, 53 S.Ct. at 65, 77 L.Ed. at 171 (1932).

Relying heavily on its reasoning in *Powell v. Alabama,* the Supreme Court held four years later that the Sixth Amendment requires federal courts to appoint counsel for indigent defendants in all felony cases. *Johnson v. Zerbst,* 304 U.S. 458, 58 S.Ct. 1019, 82 L.Ed. 1461 (1938). Subsequently, Congress enacted the Criminal Justice Act of 1964, 18 U.S.C.A. § 3006A, which provided that all indigent defendants in federal criminal cases are entitled to appointed counsel.

In the wake of *Powell v. Alabama,* many states adopted laws creating a right to counsel at state expense, at least in capital cases. Some states went further by providing counsel for all indigent defendants in felony prosecutions. In states where appointed counsel was not a legal requirement, it was not uncommon for trial judges to appoint new members of the bar to represent indigent felony defendants *pro bono* (free of charge). In so doing, these judges may have anticipated a landmark court decision that was to have a tremendous impact on the criminal justice system.

THE *GIDEON* DECISION

In 1963 the Supreme Court decided that the Fourteenth Amendment requires states to provide counsel to indigent defendants in all felony cases, observing that "any person haled into court, who is too poor to hire a lawyer, cannot be assured a fair trial unless counsel is provided for him." *Gideon v. Wainwright,* supra. The impact of the *Gideon* decision was amplified because it was made retroactive. In Florida, where the *Gideon* case originated, the state was forced to release or retry hundreds of convicted criminals. Other states experienced similar problems. Today, the *Gideon* decision has come to be widely accepted by state officials who recognize that representation by counsel is essential to the fair and effective functioning of the adversary system of justice.

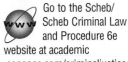

Go to the Scheb/ Scheb Criminal Law and Procedure 6e website at academic .cengage.com/criminaljustice/ scheb for an edited version of *Gideon v. Wainwright.*

INDIGENT MISDEMEANOR DEFENDANTS

In 1972 the Supreme Court extended the *Gideon* decision to encompass defendants who were sentenced to jail terms for misdemeanors. *Argersinger v. Hamlin,* supra. But the Court's decision left unresolved the question of whether counsel had to be provided to misdemeanor defendants who faced possible jail terms, as distinct from those who are actually sentenced to jail. In 1979 the Court opted for the **actual imprisonment standard.** *Scott v. Illinois,* 440 U.S. 367, 99 S.Ct. 1158, 59 L.Ed.2d 383 (1979). The actual imprisonment standard poses a problem for judges, for if an indigent defendant to a misdemeanor charge is denied counsel and is subsequently found guilty, the judge is barred from imposing a jail term. To do so would be a constitutional violation likely to result in a reversal of the defendant's conviction. This places the judge in the anomalous position of having to consider the sentence before determining the guilt or innocence of the accused. As a result, several states have gone beyond the federal constitutional requirement announced in *Scott v. Illinois* by providing counsel to indigent defendants in all misdemeanor cases where defendants face possible jail terms.

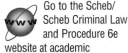

Go to the Scheb/ Scheb Criminal Law and Procedure 6e website at academic .cengage.com/criminaljustice/ scheb for an edited version of *Scott v. Illinois.*

REPRESENTATION OF INDIGENT PERSONS AT PRETRIAL PROCEEDINGS

Most people think of the right to counsel in terms of a defendant being represented at trial. Although this might be the most important stage of the criminal process for a defendant who pleads not guilty, most criminal cases do not go to trial. For the defendant who elects to plead guilty, the pretrial procedures are critically important. The right of indigent persons to be provided counsel extends to many pretrial procedures. The U.S. Supreme Court has specifically identified a number of critical stages where counsel must be provided to indigent persons. Such **critical pretrial stages** include preliminary hearings, *White v. Maryland,* 373 U.S. 59, 83 S.Ct. 1050, 10 L.Ed.2d 193 (1963); lineups after charges have been filed against the accused, *United States v. Wade,* 388 U.S. 218, 87 S.Ct. 1926, 18 L.Ed.2d 1149 (1967); post-indictment interrogations, *Massiah v. United States,* 377 U.S. 201, 84 S.Ct. 1199, 12 L.Ed.2d 246 (1964); and arraignments, *Hamilton v. Alabama,* 368 U.S. 52, 82 S.Ct. 157, 7 L.Ed.2d 114 (1961).

ALTERNATIVE MEANS OF PROVIDING COUNSEL TO INDIGENT PERSONS

The representation provided to indigent defendants may take the form of a public defender or an attorney appointed ad hoc by the court. Many states have established successful public defender systems. In most states that use this system, the public defender is an elected official provided with funds to hire a staff of lawyers, much like the public prosecutor. In other states, indigent defendants still depend largely on ad hoc appointment of counsel. Very often the attorneys appointed to represent indigent defendants in noncapital cases are new members of the bar with limited trial experience. Remuneration for appointed counsel tends to be modest.

There remains considerable controversy over which method of providing counsel is more cost effective and which method more effectively meets a state's constitutional responsibilities. Proponents of the public defender system note that public defenders are full-time specialists in criminal law, whereas appointed counsel may be relatively inexperienced in the field. Critics of the public defender system express concern about the constant contact between public defenders and prosecutors. They argue that this undermines the adversary system, resulting in a routinization of the criminal process in which the interests of the accused become subordinated to a bureaucratic effort to maximize efficiency in the processing of cases.

Sometimes the public defender's office has a conflict in which codefendants want to pursue inconsistent defenses. In such instances, an outside attorney should be appointed. If trial counsel representing multiple defendants brings a conflict of interest to the judge's attention, separate counsel must be appointed unless the judge determines that the risk of conflict is remote. *Holloway v. Arkansas,* 435 U.S. 475, 98 S.Ct. 1173, 55 L.Ed.2d 426 (1978). Most states have statutes providing for the appointment of private counsel in instances where public defenders have conflicts, but even in the absence of such statutes, courts generally take the position that they have the inherent authority to make such appointments.

DETERMINING WHO IS INDIGENT

Federal law leaves the determination of indigency to the discretion of the courts. This is also the case in most states. See, for example, Ala. Rule Crim. Proc. 6.3. Courts tend to be liberal in this regard, refusing to equate indigency with destitution, and are generally inclined to appoint counsel if the cost of hiring a lawyer would prevent the defendant from making **bail** (posting a bond to secure pretrial release).

After arrest, the accused is asked to complete a form to elicit information about employment, income, assets, and liabilities. Before the defendant's first appearance in court, judicial staff persons will attempt to verify the accuracy of the defendant's statement. This information is then passed along to assist the magistrate in determining whether the defendant is entitled to appointed counsel. In most jurisdictions, more than 75 percent of felony defendants are classified as indigent. Some state statutes provide for an assessment of an attorney's fee against a defendant who is represented by the public defender's office. See, for example, West's Ann. Cal. Penal Code § 987.8. An indigent defendant may be assessed the costs of appointed counsel, and these costs may be collected at some later time if the defendant becomes solvent. See *Fuller v. Oregon,* 417 U.S. 40, 94 S.Ct. 2116, 40 L.Ed.2d 642 (1974).

Self-Representation

The Supreme Court has held that there is a constitutional right to represent oneself in a criminal prosecution. *Faretta v. California,* 422 U.S. 806, 95 S.Ct. 2525, 45 L.Ed.2d 562 (1975). In *Faretta,* the Court said that the defendant's legal knowledge or skill has no bearing on the right to **self-representation.** However, the Court stressed that the defendant who waives the right to counsel and proceeds *pro se* (Latin meaning "for oneself") must do so "knowingly and intelligently." Critics of the *Faretta* decision believe that criminal law and procedure have become too complex and technical to permit the nonlawyer defendant to engage in effective self-representation. They argue that due process requires that defendants be represented by trained counsel, lest fundamental fairness be denied. As the Supreme Court recognized in *Powell v. Alabama,*

> Even the intelligent and educated layman has small and sometimes no skill in the science of the law. If charged with a crime, he is incapable, generally, of determining for himself whether the indictment is good or bad. He is unfamiliar with the rules of evidence. Left without the aid of counsel he may be put on trial without a proper charge, and convicted upon incompetent evidence, or evidence irrelevant to the issue or otherwise inadmissible. He lacks both the skill and knowledge adequately to prepare his defense, even though he may have a perfect one. He requires the guiding hand of counsel at every step in the proceedings against him. Without it, though he be not guilty, he faces a danger of conviction because he does not know how to establish his innocence. 287 U.S. 45, 69, 53 S.Ct. 55, 64, 77 L.Ed. 158, 170 (1932).

Despite the potential dangers of the *pro se* defense, the Supreme Court held in *Faretta* that the Constitution places the defendant's "free choice" above the need for effective representation in a criminal trial. The constitutional issue aside, many lawyers have said that "the defendant who chooses to represent himself has a fool for a client."

CASE-IN-POINT

The Right to Self-Representation: The Case of the Long Island Railroad Massacre

On the evening of December 7, 1993, Jamaican-born Colin Ferguson boarded a commuter train in Long Island, New York, and began shooting passengers at random. Six people were killed and nineteen more were injured in the rampage. When Ferguson paused to reload his handgun, he was subdued by several passengers. Initially, Ferguson was represented by two prominent civil rights lawyers, William Kuntsler and Ron Kuby, who undertook the case *pro bono.* But Ferguson disapproved of the defense they intended to put on, namely, that Ferguson was legally insane at the time of the shooting due to an uncontrollable "black rage." Ferguson dismissed Kuntsler and Kuby and insisted on representing himself at trial.

The evidence produced at trial as to Ferguson's mental state as well as his bizarre behavior in the courtroom suggested that an insanity defense might have been effective, but Ferguson's defense amounted to little more than a denial and an insistence that he was a victim of mistaken identity. After hearing from a number of eyewitnesses to the shooting, the jury had little difficulty in convicting Ferguson of six counts of second-degree murder, nineteen counts of attempted second-degree murder, reckless endangerment, and criminal possession of a firearm. Ferguson was sentenced to consecutive prison terms that exceeded two hundred years. Today, he remains confined in New York's Attica prison. Critics of the trial questioned how the trial judge could find Ferguson competent to stand trial, let alone to represent himself. However, in reviewing the case the Appellate Division of the New York Supreme Court determined that the trial court had properly determined that Ferguson was competent to stand trial, noting that "[t]he People sustained their burden of establishing the defendant's fitness through the expert testimony of two psychiatrists."

The court observed, "Contrary to the defendant's contentions, neither the fact that the defense-retained psychiatrist disagreed with the conclusion of the two court-appointed experts, nor the fact that the defendant opted to reject a 'black rage' insanity defense dictated a ruling that he was unfit for trial." The appellate court held further that the trial court "properly permitted the defendant to appear *pro se* [represent himself], since a defendant who is competent to stand trial is necessarily competent to waive his right to counsel and proceed *pro se.*"

People v. Ferguson, 248 A.D.2d 725, 670 N.Y.S.2d 327 (N.Y. App. 1998).

In 1984 the Supreme Court ruled that "a defendant does not have a constitutional right to receive personal instruction from the trial judge on courtroom procedure. Nor does the Constitution require judges to take over chores for a *pro se* defendant that would normally be attended to by trained counsel as a matter of course." *McKaskle v. Wiggins*, 465 U.S. 168, 183–184, 104 S.Ct. 944, 954, 79 L.Ed.2d 122, 136–137 (1984). Numerous appellate decisions from state courts have emphasized that before approving self-representation by a criminal defendant, the trial court must conduct a thorough *Faretta* hearing to determine whether the defendant has competently and intelligently exercised the right to choose self-representation. Basic to the conduct of such hearing is for the trial judge to make the defendant aware of the dangers and disadvantages of self-representation. The objective is to ensure that the defendant seeking to represent himself or herself makes such choice only after being fully informed of the disadvantages of self-representation. Failure to conduct a thorough *Faretta* hearing can result in reversal of a conviction. See, for example, *State v. Chavis*, 644 P.2d 1202 (Wash. App. 1982) (The trial judge's questions to the defendant must reveal the defendant's understanding and not merely consist of questions that call for a simple yes or no response.).

But once a defendant has made the choice "knowingly and intelligently," the trial court is not required to give the defendant instructions on the law. This is illustrated by a 1993 decision of the California Supreme Court, reversing lower state courts. In *People v. Barnum*, 64 P.3d 788 (Cal. 2003), the supreme court ruled that a trial court is not required to advise self-represented defendants of the privilege against compelled self-incrimination. Moreover, the constitutional right to self-representation does not imply a right to obstruct the workings of the criminal process. A trial judge may terminate self-representation by a defendant who engages in obstructionist conduct. *Illinois v. Allen*, 397 U.S. 337, 90 S.Ct. 1057, 25 L.Ed.2d 353 (1970).

Judges sometimes appoint standby counsel to assist defendants who choose self-representation. There are two principal advantages: (1) standby counsel can be available to answer questions by a *pro se* defendant, and (2) if it is necessary to terminate the *pro se* defense because of misconduct, standby counsel is available to complete the case.

Although a defendant has the right to self-representation, he or she may not be represented by another person who is not a member of the bar. Nor may a defendant force an unwilling attorney to represent him or her. *Wheat v. United States*, 486 U.S. 153, 108 S.Ct. 1692, 100 L.Ed.2d 140 (1988). By the same token, a trial judge does have the discretion to deny an attorney's motion to withdraw from representation—after, of course, examining counsel's reasons for wanting to withdraw.

Disposition of Petty Offenses

As we noted in Chapter 12, many states have decriminalized routine traffic violations. This means that an officer who stops a motorist for committing such an infraction has no authority to make an arrest (unless, of course, there is probable cause to believe the motorist has committed another offense for which he or she may be arrested). Rather, the officer simply issues the motorist a **citation.** In other jurisdictions in which minor traffic violations are still considered criminal offenses, legislatures have passed **cite and release statutes** that instruct officers to issue citations rather than arresting motorists who are stopped only for minor traffic offenses.

One who is cited for an infraction or minor misdemeanor may simply elect to waive the right to appear in court to contest the charge, in which case he or she is required to pay a predetermined fine. If the individual appears in court to contest the charges, the entire matter is typically resolved in one proceeding. Under most statutes decriminalizing minor traffic violations, the court must find there is a preponderance of evidence to support the citation. If the court so finds, the cited party is ordered to pay a fine (along with court costs), but there is no criminal record because the infraction is a civil one. In the case of the minor misdemeanor, the accused may plead guilty or no contest, in which case guilt is pronounced and the sentence is imposed immediately. If the plea is not guilty, the court conducts a **summary trial** and determines guilt or innocence according to the reasonable doubt standard.

Although defendants clearly have a right to hire attorneys to represent them in minor misdemeanor cases, few exercise this right. Most people would rather go it alone before the magistrate. If they lose, which is highly probable, they typically pay a fine, which tends to be substantially less expensive than hiring an attorney. As noted earlier, the Supreme Court has said that there is no constitutional right for indigent persons to have counsel appointed in such minor cases except where defendants are actually sentenced to jail terms. *Scott v. Illinois,* supra.

The Initial Court Appearance

In major misdemeanor and felony cases, the procedure is much more complex and protracted. Typically, individuals charged with felonies are placed under arrest before any appearance in court. However, all persons placed under arrest must promptly be taken before a court of law. The purpose of the initial appearance is to begin the formal charging process. Essentially, the magistrate must perform three important functions at the initial appearance: (1) the charges must be read so that the accused knows exactly what he or she is being charged with; (2) the accused must be informed of relevant constitutional rights, including the right to remain silent and the right to counsel; and (3) a determination must be made of whether the accused should be released pending trial or remanded to custody to await the disposition of the case. As we shall discuss, the court may order the defendant to post bond in order to ensure future court appearances. If so, the amount of bail is determined at this time.

All jurisdictions require the prompt appearance of an arrestee before a court of law, but what constitutes "prompt"? Many jurisdictions require a suspect to be brought before a magistrate for an initial appearance within twenty-four hours after arrest. See, for example, Fla. R. Crim. P. Rule 3.130(a). However, the U.S. Supreme Court has ruled that suspects may be detained for as long as forty-eight hours before being taken before a magistrate. *County of Riverside v. McLaughlin,* 500 U.S. 44, 111 S.Ct. 1661, 114 L.Ed.2d 49 (1991).

Rule 5(a) of the Federal Rules of Criminal Procedure provides that a person arrested for a federal offense shall be taken before a magistrate "without unnecessary delay" for a first appearance. Under the so-called *McNabb–Mallory* rule (see *McNabb v. United States,* 318 U.S. 332, 63 S.Ct. 608, 87 L.Ed. 819 [1943], and *Mallory v. United States,* 354 U.S. 449, 77 S.Ct. 1356, 1 L.Ed.2d 1479 [1957]), confessions made during periods of detention that violate the prompt presentment requirement of Rule 5(a) are inadmissible at trial. Under 18 U.S.C.A. § 3501(c), however, Congress provided that a confession made within six hours after arrest is not rendered inadmissible solely because of a delay in bringing the accused before the magistrate.

In *Alvarez-Sanchez v. United States*, 975 F.2d 1396 (9th Cir. 1992), the U.S. Court of Appeals for the Ninth Circuit reversed a federal counterfeiting conviction based on the delay in the pretrial process. The defendant was originally arrested on a Friday by state authorities on state charges. A search of his home turned up evidence of counterfeit U.S. currency. On Monday, federal agents took the defendant into custody and obtained a confession. Because of congestion in court, the defendant was not taken before a federal magistrate until Tuesday. The Ninth Circuit held that the confession could not be used as evidence because of the delay in the first appearance. In reversing the Court of Appeals, the Supreme Court held that the promptness requirement is inapplicable where an accused person is first arrested on state charges and then later turned over to federal authorities on related charges. As Justice Clarence Thomas explained, "Until a person is arrested or detained for a federal crime, there is no duty, obligation, or reason to bring him before a judicial officer 'empowered to commit persons charged with offenses against the laws of the United States,' and therefore, no 'delay' under § 3501(c) can occur." *United States v. Alvarez-Sanchez,* 511 U.S. 350, 358, 114 S.Ct. 1599, 1604, 128 L.Ed.2d 319, 328.

Pretrial Release and Pretrial Detention

The most important thing to a person who has been arrested and confined to jail is to secure release as soon as possible. Beyond the obvious desirability of freedom, an accused who remains at liberty can be of considerable assistance to defense counsel in locating witnesses and being able to confer with counsel outside the jail setting. In addition, a person who remains at liberty can usually pursue gainful employment and discharge family responsibilities pending the disposition of the criminal charges.

Granting an accused **pretrial release** is commonly referred to as granting bail. Judicial authority to grant a defendant bail originated in English common law. Statutes or court rules commonly grant judges this authority today. In determining whether a defendant is entitled to pretrial release, the court usually considers the accused's prior convictions (if any), character, employment history, and ties to family and the community, as well as the nature and scope of the current charges. In making these determinations, judges rely on reports prepared by court personnel. In the federal system, these reports are prepared by an agency called Pretrial Services. Increasingly, courts are requiring that arrested persons be drug tested. Although not used as evidence, the results of the drug test help the judge decide whether to grant pretrial release and whether to impose conditions upon that release. As with probation and parole, pretrial release may be contingent on a defendant's willingness to abide by certain conditions, such as avoiding certain places or activities or remaining at home after dark.

Modes of Pretrial Release

Pretrial release can take several forms. The four most common are **release on personal recognizance,** release to the custody of another, posting an individual bond, and posting a **surety bond:**

- *Personal recognizance.* A recognizance is a person's promise to appear in court as required. The defendant signs a guarantee to appear at all required proceedings and, in some cases, acknowledges certain restrictions on his or her activities.

- *Release to the custody of another.* The magistrate may release the defendant to the custody of some responsible person, often the defendant's attorney, who agrees to exercise custodial supervision and to assume responsibility for the defendant's required court appearances.

- *Posting an individual bond.* The defendant posts a bond agreeing to appear in court as required. The defendant may or may not be required to post an amount of cash or other security to guarantee the undertaking.

- *Posting a surety bond.* Also known as a **bail bond,** this is the common method of securing pretrial release by paying a premium to a third party that agrees to post the bond for the accused. The magistrate sets the amount of a bond for the particular offense. Often, this is based on a schedule of bonds set by the judge of the court having jurisdiction over the offense. The defendant signs the bond, agreeing to appear as required. The bond is guaranteed by the defendant's surety, which means that should the defendant default, the surety, or bonding company, is bound to pay the court the amount of the bond (called the "penal sum"). A defendant usually pays a premium of about 10 percent of the amount of the bond and in most instances provides the surety with collateral to induce the surety to sign the bond. Sureties bonding a defendant are responsible for ensuring the defendant's appearance; therefore, they are commonly given the statutory authority to arrest an absconding defendant. To this end, sureties often employ **skip tracers,** who are, in effect, modern bounty hunters who seek out and return an absconding defendant. When a surety promptly produces a defendant, it can usually recover any money forfeited to the court because of the defendant's failure to appear.

The Issue of Excessive Bail

Recognizing the common-law practice of allowing pretrial release on bail, the Eighth Amendment to the federal constitution states that "excessive bail shall not be required." The Supreme Court has made it clear that the purpose of bail is to ensure the appearance of the accused in court, not to inflict punishment: "Bail set at a figure higher than an amount reasonably calculated to fulfill this purpose is 'excessive' under the Eighth Amendment." *Stack v. Boyle,* 342 U.S. 1, 5, 72 S.Ct. 1, 3, 96 L.Ed. 3, 6 (1951). However, the Supreme Court has never held that the Excessive Bail Clause of the Eighth Amendment is enforceable against the states via the Fourteenth Amendment, leaving the matter of **excessive bail** in state criminal cases to the state constitutions, legislatures, and courts.

Go to the Scheb/ Scheb Criminal Law and Procedure 6e website at academic .cengage.com/criminaljustice/ scheb for an edited version of *Stack v. Boyle.*

The Illinois Code of Criminal Procedure provides that "the amount of bail shall be: (1) Sufficient to assure compliance with the conditions set forth in the bail bond; (2) Not oppressive; (3) Considerate of the financial ability of the accused." SHA 725 ILCS 5/110-5(b). Similarly, the Texas Code of Criminal Procedure states that "the power to require bail is not to be so used as to make it an instrument of oppression." Vernon's Ann. Tex. Code Crim. P. art. 17.15(2).

Pretrial Detention

The Eighth Amendment prohibition of "excessive bail" is vague regarding the existence of a constitutional right to pretrial release. However, the Supreme Court has ruled that there is no right to bail under the Eighth Amendment. *United States v. Salerno,* 481 U.S. 739, 107 S.Ct. 2095, 95 L.Ed.2d 697 (1987). The **Federal Bail Reform Act of 1984,** 18 U.S.C.A. § 3141 *et seq.,* allows federal courts to detain arrestees without bail on the ground of the arrestee's danger to the community, as well as the need to ensure future court appearances. First, the court must determine whether the government has established "by a preponderance of the evidence that the defendant either has been charged with one of the crimes enumerated in Section 3142(f)(1) or that the defendant presents a risk of flight or obstruction of justice." *United States v. Friedman*, 837 F.2d 48, 49 (2d Cir. 1988). If the government satisfies that burden, the court must determine whether there are "conditions or a combination of conditions which reasonably will assure the presence of the defendant at trial." *United States v. Shakur*, 817 F.2d 189, 195 (2d Cir. 1987). Congress has set forth various factors that a court must consider in weighing the appropriateness of **pretrial detention.** Among these are the nature of the offense, the weight of the evidence against the suspect, the history and character of the person charged, and the nature and seriousness of the risk to the community. 18 U.S.C.A. § 3142(g). The statute provides for an adversary hearing on the issue of detention. The government must show by clear and convincing evidence that pretrial release will not reasonably ensure the appearance of the accused or the safety of other persons and the community. *United States v. Orta*, 760 F.2d 877 (8th Cir. 1985).

The judge or magistrate who denies pretrial release must prepare a written statement justifying the decision to detain the accused and direct that the detainee be afforded a reasonable opportunity for private consultation with counsel. 18 U.S.C.A. § 3142(i). Finally, the law provides for a prompt appellate review of the detention decision. 18 U.S.C.A. § 3145(c). In upholding the Bail Reform Act of 1984 against an Eighth Amendment challenge, the Supreme Court in *United States v. Salerno* said that "when Congress has mandated detention on the basis of a compelling interest other than prevention of flight, as it has here, the Eighth Amendment does not require release on bail." 481 U.S. at 754–755, 107 S.Ct. at 2105, 95 L.Ed.2d at 713–714.

The *Salerno* decision, although technically limited to the constitutionality of federal pretrial detention, suggests the validity of state laws or court decisions that deny bail to persons accused of violent crimes, especially where arrestees have a record of violent crime.

In many states, a defendant is ineligible for pretrial release if charged with a crime that is punishable by death or life imprisonment and if the "proof is evident or the presumption [of guilt] is great." See, for example, *State v. Arthur*, 390 So.2d 717, 718 (Fla. 1980). In the majority of these states, before denying pretrial release, courts must determine whether the facts, viewed in the light most favorable to the state, are legally sufficient to sustain a verdict of guilty. See *Fountaine v. Mullen*, 366 A.2d 1138 (R.I. 1976).

Go to the Scheb/ Scheb Criminal Law and Procedure 6e website at academic .cengage.com/criminaljustice/ scheb for an edited version of *U.S. v. Salerno*.

The Formal Charging Process

Prosecutors occupy a uniquely important role in the criminal justice system. The prosecutor decides whether to proceed with a criminal case and whether to negotiate charges with the defense, and must, at various stages of the process, demonstrate the veracity of the government's case to the satisfaction of the court. The prosecutor causes the court to issue **subpoenas** to compel the attendance of witnesses to testify, to bring in documents, and to provide nontestimonial physical evidence such as handwriting specimens, *United States v. Mara*, 410 U.S. 19, 93 S.Ct. 774, 35 L.Ed.2d 99 (1973), and voice exemplars, *United States v. Dionisio*, 410 U.S. 1, 93 S.Ct. 764, 35 L.Ed.2d 67 (1973).

State and federal prosecutors have broad discretion in deciding whether to proceed with criminal charges initiated by a complainant or the police. The prosecutor may decide to drop a case for a variety of reasons, ranging from insufficient evidence to a judgment that the criminal sanction is inappropriate in a given situation. Alternatively, the prosecutor may decide to proceed on a lesser charge.

The American Bar Association's *Standards Relating to the Prosecution and Defense Function* offers prosecutors guidelines for the exercise of their discretion in making the decision to charge. The standards admonish prosecutors not to be influenced by personal or political motivations and not to bring more charges, in number or degree, than can reasonably be supported at trial.

Prosecutorial discretion facilitates the widespread yet controversial practice of plea bargaining, which we discuss later in the chapter. Although very broad, prosecutorial discretion is not unlimited. The Equal Protection Clause of the Fourteenth Amendment is offended by selective prosecution. Prosecutors may not single out defendants for prosecution on the basis of race, religion, or other impermissible classifications. *Oyler v. Boles,* 368 U.S. 448, 82 S.Ct. 501, 7 L.Ed.2d 446 (1962).

Courts have not only cloaked prosecutors with broad discretion in determining whether to prosecute, but they have also long held prosecutors immune from civil actions for malicious prosecution, as long as they are acting within the scope of their offices. *Griffith v. Slinkard,* 44 N.E. 1001 (Ind. 1896). More recently, the U.S. Supreme Court has ruled that the same considerations that underlie **prosecutorial immunity** in tort actions require that prosecutors be immune from damages for deprivation of defendants' constitutional rights under 42 U.S.C.A. § 1983. See *Imbler v. Pachtman,* 424 U.S. 409, 96 S.Ct. 984, 47 L.Ed.2d 128 (1976).

Determining the Sufficiency of the Government's Case

Assuming that the prosecutor decides to proceed with criminal charges, an examination of the sufficiency of the evidence generally follows. The purpose of this procedure is to ensure that there is probable cause for trial. This determination is made by a magistrate, a grand jury, or both. In some jurisdictions, the prosecutor files a document called an **information** in the appropriate court of law. An information is a formal accusatorial document detailing the specific charges against a defendant. After the filing of the information, a preliminary hearing may be requested to determine the sufficiency of the evidence in support of the information. In other jurisdictions, the prosecutor must obtain an indictment from a grand jury. Some jurisdictions employ a combination of both mechanisms. In Tennessee, for example, a person accused of a felony must be indicted by a grand jury; a preliminary examination before the grand jury proceeding is available at the option of the accused. Tenn. R. Crim. P., Rule 5.

CASE-IN-POINT

Limitations on Prosecutorial Conduct

E. J. Reagan was charged with torturing a child and assault with intent to do great bodily harm. The prosecutor agreed to drop the charges if Reagan could pass a lie detector test. The defendant agreed and passed the test. Pursuant to the agreement, the prosecutor filed a *nolle prosequi* (Latin for "not wish to prosecute") and the charges were dismissed. Subsequently, the prosecutor became convinced that the polygraph examination was flawed. He then filed a new complaint on the same charges. The defendant was tried and convicted. The Michigan Supreme Court reversed the conviction and discharged the defendant. The court said that "a pledge of public faith in this instance gave force to an unwise agreement."

People v. Reagan, 235 N.W.2d 581 (Mich. 1975).

Racially Motivated Prosecution

One of the long-standing controversies in the criminal justice field is whether police and prosecutors unfairly target people on the basis of race in the enforcement of certain types of criminal prohibitions. In 1996 the U.S. Supreme Court made it more difficult for criminal defendants to make prosecutors respond to claims that they are engaging in racially motivated selective prosecution. Five African Americans charged with selling crack cocaine persuaded lower courts to dismiss the charges against them because prosecutors refused to explain how they chose which crack cocaine cases to pursue. Dividing 8–1, with only Justice John Paul Stevens in dissent, the Court held that defendants who make selective-prosecution claims must show

that people of other races were not prosecuted for the same crimes. "To establish a discriminatory effect in a race case, the claimant must show that similarly situated individuals of a different race were not prosecuted," Chief Justice William H. Rehnquist wrote for the court. Because the defendants did not make such a showing, the prosecutors were not required to respond to their allegation of discrimination. In his solo dissent, Justice Stevens stressed "the need for judicial vigilance over certain types of drug prosecutions," referring to the fact that the overwhelming majority of individuals charged with offenses involving crack cocaine are black.

United States v. Armstrong, 517 U.S. 456, 116 S.Ct. 1480, 134 L.Ed.2d 687 (1996).

The Preliminary Hearing

In a preliminary hearing (not to be confused with the initial appearance), a judge or magistrate examines the state's case to determine whether there is probable cause to bind the accused over to the grand jury or (in the absence of a grand jury requirement) hold the accused for trial. The Supreme Court has said that when an arrest is made without a warrant, a preliminary hearing is constitutionally required in the absence of grand jury review to determine the sufficiency of an information. *Gerstein v. Pugh,* 420 U.S. 103, 95 S.Ct. 854, 43 L.Ed.2d 54 (1975). However, *Gerstein* does not require preliminary hearings to be full-blown adversarial proceedings. Nevertheless, most states do provide for open hearings with both parties represented. Typically, in a preliminary hearing the defense has the privilege of cross-examining witnesses for the prosecution and can learn the details and strengths of the state's case. The state can preserve testimony of witnesses who may balk at testifying at the trial. Thus, the preliminary hearing serves the interests of both the prosecution and the defense by providing an inquiry into probable cause for arrest and detention, a screening device for prosecutors, and an opportunity for the defense to discover the prosecutor's case.

The Grand Jury

In many jurisdictions, prosecutors must obtain an indictment or "true bill" from the grand jury in addition to, or instead of, the preliminary hearing. The Fifth Amendment to the U.S. Constitution states that "[n]o person shall be held to answer for a capital, or otherwise infamous crime, unless on a presentment or indictment of a grand jury."

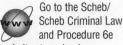

Go to the Scheb/ Scheb Criminal Law and Procedure 6e website at academic .cengage.com/criminaljustice/ scheb for an edited version of *Hurtado v. California.*

The Supreme Court has held that states are not bound by the Fourteenth Amendment to abide by the grand jury requirement imposed on the federal courts by the Fifth Amendment. *Hurtado v. California,* 110 U.S. 516, 4 S.Ct. 111, 28 L.Ed. 232 (1884). Nevertheless, about half the states have constitutional provisions or statutes requiring the use of grand juries in certain types of criminal cases. Other states use grand juries primarily in an investigatory or supervisory capacity.

The grand jury is an institution deeply rooted in the common law. For detailed discussion, see *Costello v. United States,* 350 U.S. 359, 362, 76 S.Ct. 406, 408, 100 L.Ed. 397, 401 (1956). At common law, the grand jury comprised twenty-three persons, at least twelve of whom had to agree to hand down an indictment. Today, federal grand juries comprise sixteen to twenty-three persons, Fed. R. Crim. P. 6(a), but the "12-votes for indictment" rule applies in every case, Fed. R. Crim. P. 6(f). States vary in the size of grand juries, but in every state at least a majority of grand jurors must agree that there is probable cause for trial in order to hand down an indictment against the accused. In Texas, for example, the grand jury consists of twelve jurors. Texas Const., Art. V, § 13. At least nine grand jurors must agree to hand down an indictment. Vernon's Ann. Tex. Code Crim. P. Art. 20.19.

Exclusion of Minorities from Grand Juries

As with trial jurors, the selection of grand jurors must not systematically exclude certain groups in the community. A defendant may be able to obtain a reversal of a conviction on this basis. For example, in *Castaneda v. Partida,* 430 U.S. 482, 97 S.Ct. 1272, 51 L.Ed.2d 498 (1977), the Supreme Court reversed a conviction after finding that Mexican Americans had been grossly underrepresented on a grand jury that indicted a Mexican American defendant. In his opinion for the Court, Justice Harry Blackmun outlined the necessary steps to make a case that such a violation has occurred:

> [I]n order to show that an equal protection violation has occurred in the context of grand jury selection, the defendant must show that the procedure employed resulted in substantial underrepresentation of his race or of the identifiable group to which he belongs. The first step is to establish that the group is one that is a recognizable, distinct class, singled out for different treatment under the laws, as written or as applied…. Next, the degree of underrepresentation must be proved, by comparing the proportion of the group in the total population to the proportion called to serve as grand jurors, over a significant period of time…. This method of proof, sometimes called the "rule of exclusion," has been held to be available as a method of proving discrimination in jury selection against a delineated class…. Finally, … a selection procedure that is susceptible of abuse or is not racially neutral supports the presumption of discrimination raised by the statistical showing…. Once the defendant has shown substantial underrepresentation of his group, he has made out a *prima facie* case of discriminatory purpose, and the burden then shifts to the State to rebut that case. 430 U.S. at 494, 97 S.Ct. at 1280, 51 L.Ed.2d at 510–511 (1977).

Functions and Powers of the Grand Jury

Historically, the grand jury acted as a shield to prevent unfounded charges and arbitrary and overzealous prosecution. Today, grand juries seldom refuse to hand down indictments sought by prosecutors, causing some critics to question the institution's use as a safeguard for the rights of the accused. Perhaps this perception has led several states to adopt the information/preliminary hearing mechanism in lieu of the grand jury. In most midwestern and western states, the grand jury is seldom used to charge persons with crimes.

The grand jury, like the magistrate presiding over the preliminary hearing, examines testimony and other evidence the prosecution has collected against the accused. Unlike the preliminary hearing, the grand jury proceeding is normally closed: the defendant is generally not represented by counsel or even present at the proceeding. Testimony before the grand jury is not always transcribed, and if it is, access to transcripts is either limited or nonexistent. Although controversial, grand jury secrecy encourages uninhibited testimony by witnesses and prevents the circulation of derogatory statements about persons who are ultimately not indicted. *Pittsburgh Plate Glass Co. v. United States,* 360 U.S. 395, 79 S.Ct. 1237, 3 L.Ed.2d 1323 (1959). Grand jury secrecy also protects grand jurors from intimidation and possible reprisals.

After the prosecutor has presented testimony and physical evidence, the members of the grand jury vote on whether to hand down an indictment. Rules that determine grand jury indictments vary among jurisdictions, but in no case can a grand jury return a true bill unless a majority of grand jurors vote to indict.

Grand juries possess the authority to compel the appearance of witnesses, to subpoena documents, to hold individuals in contempt, and to grant immunity from prosecution in exchange for testimony. Immunity is of two kinds. Transactional immunity bars any further prosecution of the witness for the specific transaction to which the witness testified. Use immunity is more limited, barring only the use of the witness's testimony against the witness in a subsequent prosecution. Federal grand juries are authorized to grant use immunity. 18 U.S.C.A. § 6002. The basic purpose of granting immunity is to permit compulsion of testimony that otherwise would be privileged by the Fifth Amendment. *United States v. Weiss,* 599 F.2d 730 (5th Cir. 1979). Many states follow the federal statute; some states go further and permit grand juries to grant transactional immunity. The federal statutory bar against the use of immunized testimony applies equally to federal and state proceedings. *In re Grand Jury Proceedings,* 860 F.2d 11 (2d Cir. 1988).

Rights of Witnesses and Suspects

The Supreme Court has held that grand jury witnesses retain their Fifth Amendment privileges against compulsory self-incrimination. *Lefkowitz v. Turley,* 414 U.S. 70, 94 S.Ct. 316, 38 L.Ed.2d 274 (1973). Nevertheless, through a limited grant of immunity, a grand jury can override a witness's refusal to answer questions on Fifth Amendment grounds. The Supreme Court has also held that a grand jury's grant of immunity must be coextensive with the privilege against self-incrimination. Use immunity satisfies this requirement; transactional immunity is not required by the Constitution. *Kastigar v. United States,* 406 U.S. 441, 92 S.Ct. 1653, 32 L.Ed.2d 212 (1972). Witnesses testifying before grand juries have no right to be represented by counsel, *In re Groban's Petition,* 352 U.S. 330, 77 S.Ct. 510, 1 L.Ed.2d 376 (1957), although some jurisdictions allow witnesses to consult with counsel outside the grand jury room. An attorney's appearance before a grand jury on behalf of a witness is generally thought to cause unnecessary delays and violate the secrecy of the proceeding.

In only a few states does the defendant have a right to appear before the grand jury to confront his or her accusers. Like witnesses, a suspect has no federal constitutional right to be represented by counsel inside the grand jury room. *United States v. Mandujano,* 425 U.S. 564, 96 S.Ct. 1768, 48 L.Ed.2d 212 (1976).

Evidence Before the Grand Jury

Many rules of evidence that apply to the criminal trial do not apply to the grand jury. *Costello v. United States,* 350 U.S. 359, 76 S.Ct. 406, 100 L.Ed. 397 (1956). For example, hearsay evidence is generally admissible, whereas at trial, it is not admitted over the defendant's objection. Moreover, evidence excluded from trial on Fourth or Fifth Amendment grounds is admissible before the grand jury. *United States v. Calandra*, 414 U.S. 338, 94 S.Ct. 613, 38 L.Ed.2d 561 (1974). The theory is, of course, that the grand jury is an investigative body and that any infringement of the rights of the accused can be corrected in subsequent adversary court proceedings. Notwithstanding that a grand jury may consider evidence that is inadmissible at trial, it may not violate a valid evidentiary privilege (see Chapter 18) whether established by the Constitution, statutes, or the common law. *Branzburg v. Hayes*, 408 U.S. 665, 92 S.Ct. 2646, 33 L.Ed.2d 626 (1972).

 Go to the Scheb/ Scheb Criminal Law and Procedure 6e website at academic .cengage.com/criminaljustice/ scheb for an edited version of *U.S. v. Calandra.*

Right to a Prompt Indictment

Under federal law an indictment must be filed within thirty days of arrest, 18 U.S.C.A. § 3161. Where delay in filing an indictment prejudices the presentation of a defense and is engaged in for an improper purpose, it violates the Due Process Clause. *United States v. Lovasco*, 431 U.S. 783, 795, 97 S.Ct. 2044, 52 L.Ed.2d 752 (1977). Prejudice in this context means the sort of deprivation that impairs a defendant's right to a fair trial. See *United States v. Elsbery*, 602 F.2d 1054 (2d Cir. 1979). In *United States v. Mmahat*, 106 F.3d 89 (5th Cir. 1997), the court said the defendant must show actual prejudice and deliberate design by the government to gain tactical advantage to establish a claim of preindictment delay. Usually a defendant attempts to meet this standard by demonstrating that the prosecution's delay resulted in the loss of documentary evidence or the unavailability of a key witness.

State courts generally take a similar the approach. Illustrative is *State v. Smith*, 699 P.2d 711 (Utah 1985), where the court observed:

> A hard and fast rule that a prosecutor must file charges as soon as he has probable cause could result in the charging of innocent persons. Such a rule could also result in the acquittal of guilty persons by hampering the investigation of crimes. Therefore, a prosecutor is not required to file charges as soon as probable cause exists but before the prosecutor is reasonably satisfied that he will be able to establish the suspect's guilt beyond a reasonable doubt. For preaccusation delay to constitute reversible error, the delay must cause actual prejudice to the defendant's case and result in a tactical advantage for the prosecutor. *Id.* at 713.

Extradition

Extradition is the surrender, on demand, of an individual accused or convicted of an offense committed within the territorial jurisdiction of the demanding government and outside the territory of the ceding government. See *Terlinden v. Ames,* 184 U.S. 270, 22 S.Ct. 484, 46 L.Ed. 534 (1902). The objective is to prevent the escape of persons who stand accused or convicted of crimes and to secure their return to the jurisdiction from which they fled.

In a mobile society such as ours, it is not uncommon for persons accused of crimes to flee across state lines to avoid prosecution. Anticipating this problem, Article IV, Section 2 of the Constitution provides that

> [a] Person charged in any State with Treason, Felony or any other crime, who shall flee from Justice, and be found in another state, shall on demand of the executive Authority of the State from which he fled, be delivered up, to be removed to the State having Jurisdiction of the crime.

To effectuate the constitutional provision, Congress has enacted statutes governing interstate extradition. 18 U.S.C.A. § 3182. Interstate extradition is a summary executive proceeding designed to enable each state to bring offenders to trial swiftly in the state where the alleged crime was committed. *Michigan v. Doran,* 439 U.S. 282, 99 S.Ct. 530, 58 L.Ed.2d 521 (1978). Every offense punishable by law of a jurisdiction where it was committed can be subject to extradition, but extradition is usually sought only in serious offenses. Frequently it is used to regain custody of parole violators, prison escapees, or those persons who have "jumped bail."

Most states have adopted the Uniform Criminal Extradition Law, which sets out procedural rules for handling interstate extradition. The governor of the "demanding" state issues a requisition warrant seeking return of the fugitive. This is presented to the governor of the "asylum" state (that is, the state in which the fugitive is located). After investigation, the governor of the asylum state issues a warrant for the fugitive's arrest. An opportunity exists for the person sought as a fugitive to contest the extradition in a court of law in the asylum state. Often this challenge takes the form of a petition for a writ of habeas corpus challenging whether the petitioner is in fact the person charged or attacking the regularity of the proceedings. See, for example, N.J. Stat. Ann. § 2A: 160–18. Such proceedings seek the release of the prisoner who is to be extradited but do not focus on the issue of the prisoner's guilt or innocence.

Jurisdiction and Venue

Before it may hear and adjudicate a case, a court must possess jurisdiction over the subject matter and the parties to the case. State courts have jurisdiction only over persons who commit crimes in their particular states. Of course, it is necessary for a court to acquire jurisdiction over a person before that individual can be tried for an offense. When a person is arrested, a court with jurisdiction over the offense acquires jurisdiction over that person. In other instances, the court acquires jurisdiction when an arrest warrant is issued following an indictment or after a capias is issued once a prosecutor files an information.

The term **venue** is sometimes confused with the concept of jurisdiction, but it is a distinct concept. Venue refers to the place of the trial, and its importance is underscored by the fact that it is twice mentioned in the U.S. Constitution. As Article III, Section 2 provides, in part,

> Trial shall be held in the State where the said crimes shall have been committed; but when not committed within the State, the Trial shall be at such Place or Places as the Congress may by law have directed.

As the Sixth Amendment provides, "In all criminal prosecutions, the accused shall enjoy the right to a … public trial, by an impartial jury of the State and district wherein the crime shall have been committed."

The Sixth Amendment applies to state criminal trials via the Fourteenth Amendment. *Duncan v. Louisiana,* 391 U.S. 145, 88 S.Ct. 1444, 20 L.Ed.2d 491 (1968). State constitutions, statutes, or court rules usually mirror the provisions of the Sixth Amendment.

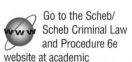 Go to the Scheb/ Scheb Criminal Law and Procedure 6e website at academic .cengage.com/criminaljustice/ scheb for an edited version of *Duncan v. Louisiana.*

Federal courts sit in all fifty states, as well as in federal territories. In some states, federal court jurisdiction is divided into two or more districts. A federal offense is normally tried in the particular federal district where the crime was committed. State courts are usually organized by districts of one or more counties. Likewise, a state criminal case is tried in the particular jurisdiction (district, county, circuit, and so forth) where the offense was committed.

Although venue lies in the district where the offense was committed, there are unique situations in which the nature of the crime makes it difficult to determine in which of two districts the crime occurred. For example, consider the situation where a person fires a rifle across a county or state line, killing a victim in the adjoining county or state. A more probable scenario is a kidnapping in which the perpetrator takes the victim across county or state lines. Courts must resolve these jurisdictional quandaries according to the relevant statutes and precedents.

Defendants commonly seek a **change of venue** if they believe it is impossible to obtain a fair trial in the venue in which the crime occurred. Rule 21(a) of the Federal Rules of Criminal Procedure stipulates:

> Upon the defendant's motion, the court must transfer the proceeding as to that defendant to another district … if the court is satisfied that there exists in the district where the prosecution is pending so great a prejudice against the defendant that the defendant cannot obtain a fair and impartial trial at any place fixed for holding court in that district.

State statutes and court rules generally contain similar provisions. Indeed, some states permit prosecutors, as well as defendants, to seek a change of venue. See, for example, Fla. R. Crim. P. 3.240. In determining whether to grant a change of venue, courts consider a variety of factors, including (1) the nature of the pretrial publicity and the degree to which it has circulated in the community, (2) the connection of government officials with the release of the publicity, (3) the length of time elapsing between the dissemination of the publicity and the trial, (4) the severity and notoriety of the offense, (5) the area from which the jury is to be drawn, (6) other events occurring in the community that either affect or reflect the attitude of the community or individual jurors toward the defendants, and (7) any factor likely to affect the candor and veracity of the prospective jurors. See, for example, *State v. Bell*, 315 So.2d 307 (La. 1975).

A defendant seeking a change of venue bears the burden of showing the necessity for the change. Changing venue can offend the community sense of justice in not having a trial take place within the community. In addition, it can create hardships and inefficiencies because of the need to transport witnesses and court personnel to sometimes distant locations. Because a decision to change venue depends on many factors that can best be determined by the local judge, trial courts are accorded considerable discretion in determining whether to grant a motion to change venue in a criminal case.

Joinder and Severance

Very often, a defendant stands accused of several distinct offenses arising from one set of related facts. Conceivably, each offense could be prosecuted separately, but it would be more efficient, in most instances, to prosecute such offenses jointly.

Most state rules of criminal procedure follow the federal rule on **joinder of offenses:**

> (a) Joinder of Offenses. The indictment or information may charge a defendant in separate counts with 2 or more offenses if the offenses charged—whether felonies or misdemeanors or both—are of the same or similar character, or are based on the same act or transaction, or are connected with or constitute parts of a common scheme or plan.
>
> Fed. R. Crim. Proc. 8(a).

In determining whether to proceed on multiple criminal charges jointly or separately, a prosecutor must consider the Double Jeopardy Clause of the Fifth Amendment. This clause bars successive prosecutions for the "same offense." A particular set of actions by the defendant may constitute distinct violations of criminal law and yet be considered part of the same offense under the Double Jeopardy Clause. For example, in *Harris v. Oklahoma,* 433 U.S. 682, 97 S.Ct. 2912, 53 L.Ed.2d 1054 (1977), the Supreme Court held that a defendant could not be prosecuted for armed robbery after being convicted of felony murder for a homicide committed during the armed robbery "because proof of the underlying felony, i.e., armed robbery, was required to prove the intent necessary for the felony-murder conviction."

The basic test laid down by the Supreme Court for determining whether there are two separate offenses is "whether each provision [of the criminal law] requires proof of an additional fact that the other does not." *Blockburger v. United States,* 284 U.S. 299, 304, 52 S.Ct. 180, 182, 76 L.Ed. 306, 309 (1932). Separate statutory crimes need not be identical—either in constituent elements or in actual proof—to be the "same offense" within the meaning of the Double Jeopardy Clause of the Fifth Amendment. Thus, a defendant cannot be convicted of an offense and a lesser included offense. *Brown v. Ohio,* 432 U.S. 161, 97 S.Ct. 2221, 53 L.Ed.2d 187 (1977). State courts have held that a person cannot be convicted of two separate homicide charges where there is only one victim. See, for example, *Wilcox v. Leapley,* 488 N.W.2d 654 (S.D. 1992).

Severance of Charges

Where two or more related offenses are charged in a single indictment or information, the trial judge ordinarily grants a **severance of the charges** on the motion of either the defense or prosecution if it is necessary to achieve a fair determination of the defendant's guilt or innocence on each offense. A defendant seeking severance bears the burden of showing that a joint trial would be so unfairly prejudicial that it would result in a miscarriage of justice. *United States v. Williams,* 10 F.3d 1070 (4th Cir. 1993).

Trial judges have considerable discretion in this area, but there are certain situations in which severance seems mandatory. For example, a defendant charged with two offenses might want to testify in one case but decline to testify in the other. Or a defendant might be charged in one case with possession of a firearm by a convicted felon and in another case with robbery. To sustain the charge in the firearm case, the prosecution would have to show the defendant's prior conviction of a felony. Such a showing would obviously be prejudicial to defense of the robbery charge being heard by the same jury.

Joinder and Severance of Parties

As with multiple offenses, prosecutors generally have broad discretion in deciding whether to prosecute multiple defendants separately or jointly. However, here too there are constitutional considerations. For example, it has been held that separate trials are required where the prosecution plans to use against one defendant evidence that has no relevance to the other defendants. *Kotteakos v. United States,* 328 U.S. 750, 66 S.Ct. 1239, 90 L.Ed. 1557 (1946).

Rule 8(b) of the Federal Rules of Criminal Procedure authorizes joinder of two or more defendants in the same indictment "if they are alleged to have participated in the same act or transaction or the same series of acts or transactions constituting an offense or offenses." However, rule 14(a) states that the court "may grant" a severance "if it appears that a defendant or the government is prejudiced by a joinder of offenses or of defendants." Thus, federal judges try to determine whether the failure to sever prevents the moving party from getting a fair trial. Denial of a motion for severance is generally held to be an abuse of discretion if the defendants present conflicting and irreconcilable defenses and if there is a danger that the jury will infer that such conflict demonstrates that both are guilty. *United States v. Tarantino,* 846 F.2d 1384 (D.C. Cir. 1988).

Rules governing **joinder and severance of parties** are usually spelled out in the rules of criminal procedure in each jurisdiction. The purpose of such rules is to ensure that when two or more persons are charged jointly, each will receive a fair determination of guilt or innocence. The Tennessee Rules of Criminal Procedure are fairly typical in this respect:

> The Court, on motion of the State or on motion of the defendant … shall grant a severance of defendants if:
>
> I. before trial, it is deemed necessary to protect a defendant's right to a speedy trial or it is deemed appropriate to promote a fair determination of the guilt or innocence of one or more defendants; or
>
> II. during trial, with the consent of the defendant to be severed, it is deemed necessary to promote a fair determination of the guilt or innocence of one or more defendants.
>
> Tenn. R. Crim. Proc., Rule 14(c)(2).

Severance of defendants is almost always granted when jointly charged defendants pursue inconsistent defenses, when their interests are otherwise antagonistic, or when one defendant chooses to testify and the other does not. Severance can be crucial when a codefendant's confession implicates another, nontestifying codefendant. The Supreme Court addressed the problem in *Bruton v. United States,* 391 U.S. 123, 88 S.Ct. 1620, 20 L.Ed.2d 476 (1968). Bruton and Evans were charged with the same robbery and were tried jointly before the same jury. Evans had confessed that he and Bruton had committed the robbery. Although Evans did not testify, his confession incriminating Bruton was read to the jury. The trial judge instructed the jury to consider the confession as evidence only against Evans. Both were convicted. The Supreme Court reversed Bruton's conviction, finding that the introduction of Evans's confession at the joint trial violated Bruton's rights under the Confrontation Clause of the Sixth Amendment.

The Florida courts developed the following procedural rule to cope with the *Bruton* problem. The rule gives the state three options when the trial court determines that a defendant's statement is not admissible against a codefendant.

> If a defendant moves for a severance of defendants on the ground that an oral or written statement of a co-defendant makes reference to him but is not admissible against him, the court shall determine whether the State will offer evidence of the statement at the trial. If the State intends to offer the statement in evidence, the court shall order the State to submit its evidence of such statement for consideration by the court and counsel for defendants and if the court determines that such statement is not admissible against the moving defendant, it shall require the State to elect one of the following courses: (i) a joint trial at which evidence of the statement will not be admitted; (ii) a joint trial at which evidence of the statement will be admitted after all references to the moving defendant have been deleted, provided the court determines that admission of such evidence with deletions will not prejudice the moving defendant; or (iii) severance of the moving defendant. Florida R. Crim. P. 3.152.

Go to the Scheb/ Scheb Criminal Law and Procedure 6e website at academic .cengage.com/criminaljustice/ scheb for an edited version of *Bruton v. U.S.*

Go to the Scheb/ Scheb Criminal Law and Procedure 6e website at academic .cengage.com/criminaljustice/ scheb to find *Cook v. State* (1977), where a Florida appellate court discusses Florida R. Crim. P. 3.152.

REDACTION OF INCRIMINATING STATEMENTS INTRODUCED IN A JOINT TRIAL

One of the options allowed by the rule is **redaction** (editing) of a confession or incriminating statement made by one defendant so that it may be used at a joint trial without implicating any other defendant. In *Gray v. Maryland,* 523 U.S. 185, 118 S.Ct. 1151,

140 L.Ed.2d. 294 (1998), the Supreme Court addressed the redaction problem in a case that resulted in Kevin Gray's conviction for involuntary manslaughter. Gray's codefendant, Bell, had given a confession to the police in which he said that Bell, Gray, and Vanlandingham had participated in a beating that resulted in the victim's death. Vanlandingham later died, and Bell and Gray were tried jointly for murder. The trial judge, after denying Gray's motion for a separate trial, permitted a police detective to read Bell's redacted confession into evidence. The detective said the word "deleted" or "deletion" whenever Gray's name or Vanlandingham's name appeared. The state then introduced into evidence a written copy of Bell's confession with Gray's and Vanlandingham's names omitted, leaving in their place blank white spaces separated by commas. The Maryland Court of Appeals upheld Gray's conviction. A sharply divided Supreme Court vacated the decision and stated that "redactions that replace a proper name with an obvious blank, the word 'delete,' a symbol, or similarly notify the jury that a name has been deleted are similar enough to *Bruton's* unredacted confession as to warrant the same legal results." 523 U.S. at 195, 118 S.Ct. at 1156, 140 L.Ed.2d. at 302. Writing for the Court's four dissenters, Justice Antonin Scalia contended that allowing the confession to be admitted with limiting instructions "represents a reasonable practical accommodation of the interests of the state and the defendant in the criminal justice process." 523 U.S. at 200, 118 S.Ct. at 1159, 140 L.Ed.2d. at 306.

SEVERANCE IN CASES WHERE DEFENDANTS PURSUE MUTUALLY CONTRADICTORY DEFENSES

Lower federal courts have generally taken the position that rule 14 entitles defendants to separate trials if their defenses are mutually contradictory. See, for example, *United States v. Tarantino*, supra. In 1993 the U.S. Supreme Court addressed the issue. Writing for the Court, Justice Sandra Day O'Connor made it clear that severance of defendants is not required, as a matter of law, when defendants present mutually antagonistic defenses. Rather, severance is required only if the trial court finds a serious risk that a joint trial would compromise a specific trial right of a properly joined defendant or prevent the jury from making a reliable judgment about guilt or innocence. Circumstances that may require a severance include a case in which joinder results in the admission of evidence that the jury could consider against one defendant but not another, or a case in which evidence exculpating one defendant would have to be excluded at a joint trial. But in federal courts, reliance simply on antagonistic defenses without articulating any specific prejudice is not sufficient to require that a trial court sever the trial of a codefendant. *Zafiro v. United States*, 506 U.S. 534, 113 S.Ct. 933, 122 L.Ed.2d 317 (1993).

Pretrial Motions

Pretrial motions are written requests to the court on behalf of the government or the defendant. They are the means by which defense counsel and prosecutors seek to attain certain objectives before trial. Typically, many motions are available to both the defense and the prosecution during the pretrial phase of a criminal case. One common set of motions deals with joinder and severance of offenses and defendants, as previously discussed. Other common pretrial motions include the following:

1. *Motion to dismiss.* Frequently the defense files a **motion to dismiss** the indictment or information, alleging (a) that the government's allegations, assuming the

truth thereof, do not allege a crime, or that the accusatorial document is not correct in form; or (b) that the undisputed facts do not establish a case of *prima facie* guilt against the defendant. Often the court's determination on a motion to dismiss is not final, as the government may be given an opportunity to amend its documentation. In addition, a defendant may file a motion to dismiss on grounds of double jeopardy or having been granted immunity.

2. *Motion to determine the competency of the accused to stand trial.* In cases where the defendant is mentally disturbed, the defendant may be declared incompetent to stand trial on the motion of the defense. In federal cases the trial judge must determine whether the defendant has (1) a rational and factual understanding of the pending proceedings and (2) the ability to consult with his or her lawyer with a reasonable degree of rational understanding. *Dusky v. United States,* 362 U.S. 402, 80 S.Ct. 788, 4 L.Ed.2d 824 (1960). State courts use varying standards to determine whether an accused person is competent to stand trial. The differences are largely semantic. Some state courts apply the federal standard, with the additional requirement that the accused must understand the range of penalties that would attend conviction and be able to perceive the adversarial nature of the trial process. A person restored to competency may then be tried for the criminal offense originally charged. States generally require a defendant to prove incompetency by a preponderance of the evidence. In *Cooper v. Oklahoma,* 517 U.S. 348, 116 S.Ct. 1373, 134 L.Ed.2d 498 (1996), the Supreme Court held that a law that required defendants to prove incompetence to stand trial by clear and convincing evidence violated the Due Process Clause.

3. *Motion to suppress evidence obtained through unlawful search or seizure.* Evidence obtained in violation of a defendant's Fourth Amendment rights cannot be used against the defendant in a criminal trial. *Weeks v. United States,* 232 U.S. 383, 34 S.Ct. 341, 58 L.Ed. 652 (1914); *Mapp v. Ohio,* 367 U.S. 643, 81 S.Ct. 1684, 6 L.Ed.2d 1081 (1961). When the defense moves to suppress evidence on Fourth Amendment grounds, the court generally holds an evidentiary hearing. If the defense is successful in causing the **suppression of evidence,** it may undermine the government's case, leading to a favorable ruling on a subsequent defense motion to dismiss. When the state's case depends solely on the evidence sought to be suppressed, the defense's attempt is often referred to as a **dispositive motion.**

Go to the Scheb/ Scheb Criminal Law and Procedure 6e website at academic .cengage.com/criminaljustice/ scheb for an edited version of *Weeks v. U.S.*

4. *Motion to suppress confessions, admissions, or other statements made to the police.* A defendant is constitutionally entitled to a determination by the court whether a confession is voluntary before the confession is made known to the jury. *Jackson v. Denno,* 378 U.S. 368, 84 S.Ct. 1774, 12 L.Ed.2d 908 (1964). The motion to suppress the confession is the means of bringing this issue before the court. The motion can initiate a number of related inquiries, such as whether the confession was obtained in violation of the *Miranda* rules. Generally, before ruling on a motion to suppress a confession, the court holds an evidentiary hearing. Again, the disposition of such a motion can have a significant impact on the prosecution of a criminal case. If the confession is crucial to the prosecution's case, a favorable ruling on the motion to suppress may lead to a dismissal of the charges.

5. *Motion to suppress a pretrial identification of the accused.* This motion by the defendant is designed to determine whether the pretrial identification procedures employed by the police in having an eyewitness identify the accused violated the due process standards outlined in *Neil v. Biggers,* 409 U.S. 188, 93 S.Ct. 375, 34 L.Ed.2d 401 (1972). The court's inquiry here focuses on whether the identification procedures were impermissibly suggestive to the witness (see Chapter 16).

6. *Motion to require the prosecution to disclose the identity of a confidential informant.* The prosecution is not ordinarily required to disclose the identity of a confidential informant who merely furnishes the probable cause on which an arrest or search is predicated. Nevertheless, if the informant was an "active participant" in the offense, the prosecution may be required to disclose the informant's identity. The test calls for balancing the public interest in protecting the free flow of information to the police against the individual's right to prepare a defense. See *Roviaro v. United States*, 353 U.S. 53, 77 S.Ct. 623, 1 L.Ed.2d 639 (1957). Trial judges have considerable discretion in ruling on this motion.

7. *Motion for change of venue.* The defendant, and in some instances the government, may move for a change of venue (that is, place of trial) on the ground that a fair and impartial trial cannot be had where the case is pending. In recent years, heightened media coverage of crime and criminal prosecutions has generated tremendous concern over the ability of defendants to receive a fair trial. The concern usually focuses on the difficulty of selecting an impartial jury when potential jurors have been exposed to intensive newspaper, radio, and television coverage of a crime. The Supreme Court, in *Sheppard v. Maxwell*, 384 U.S. 333, 86 S.Ct. 1507, 16 L.Ed.2d 600 (1966), established some guidelines for dealing with the effects of pretrial publicity (see Chapter 18). Since then, an increasing number of defendants have filed motions seeking a change of venue.

Go to the Scheb/ Scheb Criminal Law and Procedure 6e website at academic .cengage.com/criminaljustice/ scheb for an edited version of *Sheppard v. Maxwell.*

8. *Motion for a continuance.* Either the government or the defendant may seek a **continuance,** or postponement, of the trial. A variety of grounds may be asserted, including illness or emergency that makes it difficult or impossible for the defendant, prosecutor, defense counsel, or an important witness to be present as scheduled; the unavailability of a significant witness or piece of documentary evidence; or the lack of adequate time to prepare for trial. Appellate courts consistently hold that there is no abuse of discretion unless a party can show that specific prejudice has resulted to the defendant as a result of the denial of the requested continuance.

9. *Other pretrial motions.* Other common pretrial motions include motions to take a **deposition;** to preserve the testimony of an infirm witness or one who might not be available for trial; to appoint an interpreter; to inspect the minutes of the grand jury proceeding; to compel the prosecutor to disclose evidence that might be favorable to the accused; and to disqualify the trial judge on grounds of bias, close relationship to parties, or that the judge will be a material witness.

Arraignment

The arraignment is the accused's first appearance before a court of law with the authority to conduct a criminal trial. At this stage of the process, the accused must enter a plea to the charges contained in the indictment or information. There are several options. The accused may choose to enter a **plea of not guilty,** in which case the plea is noted and a trial date is set. The accused may enter a **plea of guilty,** in which case no trial is necessary. Instead, guilt is simply pronounced and sentencing follows, either immediately or at some future court appearance, after a presentence investigation has been completed (see Chapter 19). A plea of guilty containing a protestation of innocence, sometimes called an *Alford* **plea,** can be made when a defendant intelligently concludes that his or her interests require the entry of a guilty plea. *North Carolina v. Alford,*

400 U.S. 25, 91 S.Ct. 160, 27 L.Ed.2d 162 (1970). In some jurisdictions, the accused has the option of pleading *nolo contendere* (no contest). The **no contest plea,** although functionally equivalent to a guilty plea in a criminal trial, provides the accused the advantage that it generally cannot be construed as an admission of guilt in a related civil suit. Although a judgment is entered on a no-contest plea, the defendant neither admits nor denies anything.

Because a plea of guilty or *nolo contendere* represents a waiver of constitutional rights, it is essential that the plea be made knowingly and voluntarily. The Federal Rules of Criminal Procedure preclude trial judges from accepting such a plea unless the court determines the plea is "voluntary and not the result of force or threats or of promises apart from a plea agreement." Fed. R. Crim. P. 11(b)(2). In addition to determining voluntariness, a judge must decide whether a **factual basis** exists for a plea of guilty or *nolo contendere.* A factual basis is necessary to ensure that the accused does not admit to an offense when his or her conduct does not fall within the bounds of the government's accusations. See, for example, *United States v. Montoya-Camacho,* 644 F.2d 480 (5th Cir. 1981).

Most states have adopted similar rules of procedure to ensure that pleas are voluntary and comply with constitutional requirements. For example, rule 3.170(k) of the Florida Rules of Criminal Procedure specifies that "[n]o plea of guilty or *nolo contendere* shall be accepted by a court without first determining … that the circumstances surrounding the plea reflect … its voluntariness and that there is a factual basis for the plea."

Rules concerning voluntariness and factual basis generally do not specify any precise method to be followed by the court. Judges employ various methods to determine voluntariness. Often these methods include interrogation of the defendant by the judge and sometimes by the prosecutor and defense counsel. The extent of questioning often depends on the defendant's educational level and maturity. Frequently, judges ask indigent defendants about their satisfaction with court-appointed counsel. The objective is to establish that no improper inducements have been made to secure a plea, that the defendant understands the basic constitutional rights incident to a trial, that these rights are being waived, and that he or she comprehends the consequences of the plea. *Boykin v. Alabama,* 395 U.S. 238, 89 S.Ct. 1709, 23 L.Ed.2d 274 (1969).

Go to the Scheb/ Scheb Criminal Law and Procedure 6e website at academic .cengage.com/criminaljustice/ scheb for an edited version of *Boykin v. Alabama.*

In determining that a factual basis exists for the defendant's plea, judges often have the prosecutor briefly outline available proof to establish a *prima facie* case of the defendant's guilt. A more extensive inquiry is usually necessary for specific-intent crimes. The thoroughness of the court's determination of voluntariness and factual basis becomes important if a defendant later moves to withdraw a plea and enter a plea of not guilty.

Plea Bargaining

In most jurisdictions, more than 90 percent of felony suspects arraigned plead guilty or no contest. Very often the guilty plea is the result of a bargain struck between the defense and the prosecution. In a plea bargain, the accused agrees to plead guilty in exchange for a reduction in the number or severity of charges or a promise by the prosecutor not to seek the maximum penalty allowed by law. Often bargains are quite specific in terms of punishment to be imposed, conditions of probation, restitution to the victim, and so forth.

Plea negotiations are subject to the approval of the trial court. In most instances, the bargain is arranged by experienced and knowledgeable counsel on both sides and is readily approved by the court. If the court is unwilling to approve the plea bargain, the defendant must choose between withdrawing the guilty plea (and thus going to trial) and accepting the plea bargain with such modifications as the judge may approve. Once the court has accepted a guilty plea pursuant to a plea bargain, the court cannot unilaterally alter it without permitting the defendant the opportunity to withdraw the plea.

In some jurisdictions, judges participate directly in plea-bargaining discussions. The justification for this practice is that a judge can guide the parties to an equitable and expeditious resolution of the case. On the other hand, some courts disfavor the participation of a trial judge in plea-bargaining discussions on the basis that the power and position of the judge may improperly influence the defendant to enter a guilty plea. See, for example, *Perkins v. Court of Appeals,* 738 S.W.2d 276, 282 (Tex. Crim. App. 1987).

Plea bargaining has been sharply criticized by observers with different perspectives on the criminal process. Some critics fault plea bargaining for reducing the severity of criminal penalties. Others view plea bargaining as an unconstitutional effort to deprive defendants of their right to a fair trial. Plea bargaining has never been popular, but few who oppose the practice stop to consider the tremendous costs and delays that would result if the numerous cases currently resolved through plea bargaining were to go to trial.

Despite frequent criticism, the practice of plea bargaining is widespread among American jurisdictions today. In addition to permitting a substantial conservation of prosecutorial and judicial resources, plea bargaining provides a means by which, through mutual concession, the parties can obtain a prompt resolution of criminal proceedings with the benefits that flow from final disposition of a case. The plea bargain, or negotiated sentence, enables the parties to avoid the delay and uncertainties of trial and appeal, and it permits swift and certain punishment of law violators with a sentence tailored to the circumstances of the case at hand.

Despite constitutional attacks, the Supreme Court has upheld the practice of plea bargaining. In *Brady v. United States,* 397 U.S. 742, 753, 90 S.Ct. 1463, 1471, 25 L.Ed.2d 747, 759 (1970), the Court said that "we cannot hold that it is unconstitutional for the State to extend a benefit to a defendant who in turn extends a substantial benefit to the State." In a subsequent case, the Court was even more sanguine about plea bargaining:

CASE-IN-POINT

The Realities of Plea Bargaining

Paul LaVallee was charged in a New Hampshire court with the crime of aggravated assault. He elected to plead not guilty, was convicted at trial, and was sentenced to ten to thirty years in prison. LaVallee brought a habeas corpus action challenging his sentence, arguing that it was disproportionate to the sentences given defendants who agreed to plead guilty. He claimed that it was impermissible for the courts to give harsher sentences to defendants who insist on their constitutional right to a trial. The state supreme court rejected LaVallee's challenge. The court said that the defendant's argument ignored "the realities of the plea bargaining process." Further, it noted that "[i]n this state, we have rejected the notion that it is impermissible to compensate one who pleads guilty by extending him a proper degree of leniency."

LaVallee v. Perrin, 466 A.2d 932 (N.H. 1983).

The disposition of criminal charges by agreement between the prosecutor and the accused, sometimes loosely called "plea bargaining," is an essential component of the administration of justice. Properly administered, it is to be encouraged. If every criminal charge were subjected to a full-scale trial, the States and the Federal Government would need to multiply by many times the number of judges and court facilities. *Santobello v. New York,* 404 U.S. 257, 260, 92 S.Ct. 495, 498, 30 L.Ed.2d 427, 432 (1971).

The plea bargain necessarily entails a waiver of the constitutional right to trial, so it must be examined by the trial court to determine whether the accused has knowingly waived his or her rights and agreed to plead guilty without coercion by the state. *Boykin v. Alabama,* supra. Despite such procedural protections, cases still arise challenging the fundamental fairness of certain plea-bargaining tactics. See, for example, *Bordenkircher v. Hayes,* 434 U.S. 357, 98 S.Ct. 663, 54 L.Ed.2d 604 (1978), where the Court found no due process violation when the prosecutor threatened during plea negotiations to reindict the defendant on a more serious charge if the defendant refused to plead guilty to the lesser crime originally charged.

Go to the Scheb/ Scheb Criminal Law and Procedure 6e website at academic .cengage.com/criminaljustice/ scheb for an edited version of *Borden-kircher v. Hayes.*

Availability of Compulsory Process

The Sixth Amendment to the Constitution guarantees a defendant in a criminal case the right to "have the **compulsory process** of the law to obtain witnesses in his favor." The "compulsory process" clause was applied to the states in *Washington v. Texas,* 388 U.S. 14, 87 S.Ct. 1920, 18 L.Ed.2d 1019 (1967), although the right previously existed in state constitutions and laws. The method of securing this right is through use of a subpoena, a formal written demand available in all federal and state jurisdictions. Subpoenas are available to both the prosecution and defense.

Rule 17 of the Federal Rules of Criminal Procedure implements this right at the federal level by allowing a defendant to have the court issue a subpoena for witnesses, documents, and objects and providing for service of such subpoenas. Court clerks, and sometimes judges, issue subpoenas. They are usually served by a marshal in the federal system and a sheriff or process server in the state system. There are costs associated with subpoenas, but the federal rule provides for issuance without cost when a defendant is financially unable to pay the costs, as long as the witness is "necessary to an adequate defense." States generally have statutes or court rules closely paralleling the federal rule.

In the pretrial stages, challenges may be made to the right to subpoena a witness, document, or object. Challenges are usually based on the contention that such witnesses or items are not material to issues in the case. Judges have considerable discretion in ruling on these challenges.

Pretrial Discovery

The courts have long recognized a prosecutorial duty to disclose to the defense exculpatory information (that is, information that tends to vindicate the accused). This duty is based on the fundamental concept of our system of justice—that individuals accused of crimes must be treated fairly. The Supreme Court has stated that "the suppression by the prosecution of evidence favorable to the accused upon request violates due process where the evidence is material either to guilt or punishment, irrespective of the good faith or bad faith of the prosecution." *Brady v. Maryland,* 373 U.S. 83, 87, 83 S.Ct. 1194, 1996, 10 L.Ed.2d 215, 218 (1963).

The Supreme Court has held that, in addition to substantive exculpatory evidence, evidence tending to impeach (i.e., challenge the credibility of) prosecution witnesses falls within *Brady's* definition of evidence favorable to an accused. Therefore, under *Brady* a defendant is entitled to disclosure of information that might be used to impeach government witnesses. See *United States v. Bagley,* 473 U.S. 667, 105 S.Ct. 3375, 87 L.Ed.2d 481 (1985).

Generally, the defense must request the disclosure of the **exculpatory evidence.** If the defense is unaware of the existence of the evidence, however, such a request is impossible. The Supreme Court has held that failure to request disclosure is not necessarily fatal to a later challenge based on *Brady,* but it may significantly affect the standard for determining materiality. *United States v. Agurs,* 427 U.S. 97, 96 S.Ct. 2392, 49 L.Ed.2d 342 (1976).

In a similar vein, it has been held to be a denial of due process if a prosecutor knowingly allows perjured testimony to be used against the accused. *Mooney v. Holohan,* 294 U.S. 103, 55 S.Ct. 340, 79 L.Ed. 791 (1935); *Alcorta v. Texas,* 355 U.S. 28, 78 S.Ct. 103, 2 L.Ed.2d 9 (1957).

Evidence that impeaches the credibility of a prosecution witness is considered to be exculpatory. The Supreme Court of Virginia in 1993 held that before the prosecution is obliged to produce evidence, it must be established that the undisclosed evidence is exculpatory and material to the defendant's guilt or punishment. Accordingly, where the record did not establish that there was any exculpatory evidence in the defendant's accomplices' polygraph tests, the state supreme court said that the trial court did not err in denying the defendant's motion seeking to discover the results of the tests. *Ramdass v. Commonwealth,* 437 S.E.2d 566 (Va. 1993).

Most states have now adopted liberal rules pertaining to **pretrial discovery,** rules designed to avoid unfairness to the defense resulting from abdications of prosecutorial duty. Using appropriate pretrial motions, the defense and prosecution can gain access to the evidence possessed by the opposing party. Thus, pretrial discovery not only enhances the fairness of the criminal process but also militates against surprises at trial.

CASE-IN-POINT

Pretrial Discovery

Police obtained a warrant to search Barton's home based on an officer's affidavit that he had smelled marijuana during a prior consensual entry of the home. At a pretrial suppression hearing, Barton claimed that the officer could not have smelled the marijuana plants that were seized because they had no odor. But by the time of the suppression hearing, the plants had rotted because the police had not ventilated the bag in which they stashed the plants. The court recognized that the destruction by the government of evidence that tends to impeach allegations in an affidavit demonstrating probable cause for a search warrant may violate due process principles. Nevertheless, the defendant did not prevail. Rather, the *Barton* court relied upon the principle declared by the U.S. Supreme Court in *Arizona v. Youngblood,* 488 U.S. 51, 109 S.Ct. 333, 102 L.Ed.2d 281 (1988). There, the Court held that the failure of law enforcement officers through mere negligence and not in bad faith to preserve evidence that might have been helpful to the defendant does not violate a defendant's right to due process of law.

United States v. Barton, 995 F.2d 931 (9th Cir. 1993).

Discovery in the Federal Courts

Discovery in a criminal case is somewhat more limited in federal courts than in state courts. Under the provisions of 18 U.S.C.A. § 3500, a federal criminal defendant is not entitled to inspect a statement or report prepared by a government witness "until said witness has testified on direct examination in the trial of the case." After a witness testifies, the government, on proper request of the defense, must then produce that portion of any statement or report that relates to the subject matter on which the witness has testified. The federal statute is commonly referred to as the **Jencks Act** because its effect was first recognized in *Jencks v. United States,* 353 U.S. 657, 77 S.Ct. 1007, 1 L.Ed.2d 1103 (1957). In *Jencks,* a defendant was allowed to obtain

SUPREME COURT PERSPECTIVE

Strickler v. Greene, 527 U.S. 263, 119 S.Ct. 1936, 144 L.Ed.2d 286 (1999)

In this 1999 decision, the Supreme Court refused to overturn a murder conviction and concomitant death sentence that the petitioner challenged on the basis of the Sixth Amendment right to counsel. The petitioner argued that his trial lawyer was less than reasonably effective for failing to file a motion to require the prosecutor to turn over certain potentially exculpatory evidence. The prosecutor had denied withholding the evidence, stating that the office maintained an "open file policy." The Supreme Court held that the petitioner had failed to show a reasonable probability that disclosure of the evidence in question would have changed the outcome of the trial. In his opinion for the Court, Justice John Paul Stevens discussed the *Brady* decision, the obligation it imposes on prosecutors, and the benefits it confers on defendants.

JUSTICE STEVENS delivered the opinion of the Court, saying in part:

In Brady this Court held "that the suppression by the prosecution of evidence favorable to an accused upon request violates due process where the evidence is material either to guilt or to punishment, irrespective of the good faith or bad faith of the prosecution." ... We have since held that the duty to disclose such evidence is applicable even though there has been no request by the accused, ... and that the duty encompasses impeachment evidence as well as exculpatory evidence.... Such evidence is material "if there is a reasonable probability that, had the evidence been disclosed to the defense, the result of the proceeding would have been different." ...

Moreover, the rule encompasses evidence "known only to police investigators and not to the prosecutor." ... In order to comply with Brady, therefore, "the individual prosecutor has a duty to learn of any favorable evidence known to the others acting on the government's behalf in this case, including the police."

These cases, together with earlier cases condemning the knowing use of perjured testimony, illustrate the special role played by the American prosecutor in the search for truth in criminal trials. Within the federal system, for example, we have said that the United States Attorney is "the representative not of an ordinary party to a controversy, but of a sovereignty whose obligation to govern impartially is as compelling as its obligation to govern at all; and whose interest, therefore, in a criminal prosecution is not that it shall win a case, but that justice shall be done."

This special status explains both the basis for the prosecution's broad duty of disclosure and our conclusion that not every violation of that duty necessarily establishes that the outcome was unjust. Thus the term "Brady violation" is sometimes used to refer to any breach of the broad obligation to disclose exculpatory evidence—that is, to any suppression of so-called "Brady material"—although, strictly speaking, there is never a real "Brady violation" unless the nondisclosure was so serious that there is a reasonable probability that the suppressed evidence would have produced a different verdict. There are three components of a true Brady violation: The evidence at issue must be favorable to the accused, either because it is exculpatory, or because it is impeaching; that evidence must have been suppressed by the State, either willfully or inadvertently; and prejudice must have ensued.

Sidebar   Illinois Discovery Rules

The Illinois Supreme Court has promulgated rules governing discovery procedures in criminal cases. In part, those rules are as follows:

Supreme Court Rule 412.
Disclosure to Accused

(a) Except as is otherwise provided in these rules ... , the State shall, upon written motion of defense counsel, disclose ... the following information or material within its possession or control:

(i) the names and last known addresses of persons whom the State intends to call as witnesses, together with their relevant written or recorded statements ... ;

(ii) any written or recorded statements and the substance of any oral statements made by the accused or by a codefendant, and a list of witnesses to the making and acknowledgment of such statements;

(iii) a transcript of those portions of grand jury minutes containing testimony of the accused and relevant testimony of persons whom the prosecuting attorney intends to call as witnesses at the hearing or trial;

(iv) any reports or statements of experts, made in connection with the particular case, including results of physical or mental examinations and of scientific tests, experiments, or comparisons, and a statement of the qualifications of the expert;

(v) any books, papers, documents, photographs or tangible objects which the prosecuting attorney intends to use in the hearing or trial or which were obtained from or belong to the accused; and

(vi) any record of prior criminal convictions, which may be used for impeachment, of persons whom the State intends to call as witnesses at the hearing or trial....

Supreme Court Rule 413.
Disclosure to Prosecution

(a) The person of the accused. Notwithstanding the initiation of judicial proceedings, and subject to constitutional limitations, a judicial officer may require the accused, among other things, to:

(i) appear in a line-up;

(ii) speak for identification by witnesses to an offense;

(iii) be fingerprinted;

(iv) pose for photographs not involving reenactment of a scene;

(v) try on articles of clothing;

(vi) permit the taking of specimens material under his fingernails;

(vii) permit the taking of samples of his blood, hair and other materials of his body which involve no unreasonable intrusion thereof;

(viii) provide a sample of his handwriting; and

(ix) submit to a reasonable physical or medical inspection of his body.

(b) [provision for appearance of accused and counsel at foregoing]

(c) Medical and scientific reports....

(d) Defenses. Subject to constitutional limitations and within reasonable time after the filing of a written motion by the State, defense counsel shall inform the State of any defenses which he intends to make at a hearing or trial and shall furnish the state with the following material and information within his possession or control:

(i) the names and last known addresses of persons he intends to call as witnesses together with their relevant written or recorded statements....

(ii) any books, papers, documents, photographs, or tangible objects he intends to use as evidence or for impeachment at a hearing or trial;

(iii) and if the defendant intends to prove an alibi, specific information as to the place where he maintains he was at the time of the alleged offense.

(e) Additional disclosure. Upon a showing of materiality, and if the request is reasonable, the court in its discretion may require disclosure to the State of relevant material and information not covered by this rule.

for impeachment purposes previous statements made to government agents by prosecution witnesses. Courts have indicated that the principal purpose of the *Jencks* Act is to aid a defendant's right to cross-examination. In some instances the trial judge must make an ***in camera* inspection** of documents where the government asserts that the documents contain statements not relevant to the subject matter to which the witness has testified. The government is not required under the *Jencks* Act to turn over victims' statements to defendants during a pretrial suppression hearing. *United States v. Williams,* 10 F.3d 1070 (4th Cir. 1993).

The Right to a Speedy Trial

The Sixth Amendment to the Constitution guarantees the defendant the **right to a speedy trial.** In *Barker v. Wingo,* 407 U.S. 514, 92 S.Ct. 2182, 33 L.Ed.2d 101 (1972), the Supreme Court refused to mandate a specific time limit between the filing of charges and the commencement of trial but did adopt a balancing test to determine whether a defendant was denied the right to a speedy trial. Under this test, courts must consider (1) the length of the delay, (2) the reasons for the delay, (3) the defendant's assertion of the right, and (4) prejudice to the defendant.

In response to the Court's decision in *Barker v. Wingo,* Congress enacted the **Speedy Trial Act of 1974,** 18 U.S.C.A. § 3161. The act provides specific time limits for pretrial and trial procedures in the federal courts. For example, an indictment must be filed within thirty days of arrest, and trial must commence within seventy days after the indictment. If the defendant's trial does not begin within the time limitations and the defendant enters a motion—before the trial's start or entry of a guilty plea—to dismiss the charges, the district court must dismiss the charges. There are a number of exceptions to the time limits, especially where delays are caused by defendants' motions. Questions have arisen in the lower federal courts as to whether a defendant can simply waive the application of the Speedy Trial Act. In *Zedner v. United States,* ___ U.S. ___, 126 S.Ct. 1976, 164 L.Ed.2d 749 (2006), the Supreme Court ruled that a defendant's prospective waiver of the application of the Speedy Trial Act was ineffective.

The Speedy Trial Clause of the Sixth Amendment applies to the states through the Fourteenth Amendment. *Klopfer v. North Carolina,* 386 U.S. 213, 87 S.Ct. 988, 18 L.Ed.2d 1 (1967). Most states have adopted legislation or court rules similar to the federal speedy trial law. See, for example, Ill. S.H.A. § 725 ILCS 5/103–5. State laws frequently provide that the right to a speedy trial is activated either on the date of the filing of an indictment, information, or other formal accusatorial document or on the date that the accused is taken into custody. In *People v. Hillsman,* 769 N.E.2d 1100 (Ill. App. 2002), the court cites a number of Illinois appellate court decisions holding that an accused is entitled to discharge if his trial begins more than 120 days after he was placed in custody, and a defendant in such a position is entitled to discharge on the day of his scheduled trial.

■ CONCLUSION

The rights afforded by the Fourth, Fifth, Sixth, and Eighth amendments to the U.S. Constitution (and similar provisions in the state constitutions) vitally affect the procedures used in criminal cases. Many of these rights were redefined or enlarged by the courts during the 1960s and 1970s, and they become significant considerations long before a criminal prosecution reaches the trial stage. Of particular importance are the right to counsel guaranteed by the Sixth Amendment and the right of pretrial discovery.

Because most criminal cases never reach the trial stage, it is essential that the student of criminal justice have a good grasp of the various pretrial procedures, such as the role of motions seeking relief, that often influence—and frequently determine—the outcome of a criminal case. It is equally important to understand the substantial discretion vested in key actors in the pretrial process, especially in the prosecutor. The prosecutor's discretion is manifested not only in the charging process but also in the pervasive and highly controversial practice of plea bargaining. When the exercise of prosecutorial discretion and the efforts of defense counsel fail to achieve a negotiated guilty plea, then a trial must be held. In the next chapter, we discuss procedures pertaining to the criminal trial.

■ KEY TERMS

petty offenses, 461
criminal procedure, 461
initial appearance, 461
preliminary hearing, 461
grand jury proceeding, 461
arraignment, 461
right to counsel, 462
indigency, 463
actual imprisonment standard, 464
critical pretrial stages, 464
bail, 465
self-representation, 465
citation, 467
cite and release statutes, 467
summary trial, 468
pretrial release, 469
release on personal recognizance, 469
surety bond, 469
bail bond, 470
skip tracers, 470
excessive bail, 470
Federal Bail Reform Act of 1984, 470
pretrial detention, 471
subpoenas, 471
prosecutorial discretion, 472
prosecutorial immunity, 472

information, 472
extradition, 476
venue, 477
change of venue, 478
joinder of offenses, 478
severance of the charges, 479
joinder and severance of parties, 480
redaction, 480
pretrial motions, 481
motion to dismiss, 481
suppression of evidence, 482
dispositive motion, 482
continuance, 483
deposition, 483
plea of not guilty, 483
plea of guilty, 483
Alford plea, 483
no contest plea, 484
factual basis, 484
compulsory process, 486
exculpatory evidence, 487
pretrial discovery, 487
Jencks Act, 488
in camera inspection, 490
right to a speedy trial, 490
Speedy Trial Act of 1974, 490

■ WEB-BASED RESEARCH ACTIVITY

 Use Web-based resources to determine the role of grand juries in your state's criminal justice system. How are grand jurors selected? How long do they serve? What powers does the grand jury possess? Have there been calls for reforming the grand jury in your state?

■ **QUESTIONS FOR THOUGHT AND DISCUSSION**

1. Have the courts gone too far or not far enough in requiring that indigent defendants be represented by counsel at public expense?

2. What are the arguments for and against allowing defendants without any legal training to represent themselves in felony prosecutions? How far should a trial judge go in advising a defendant of the pitfalls of proceeding without legal counsel?

3. In your opinion, does the Eighth Amendment guarantee the right to pretrial release on bail in a felony case? What about a misdemeanor case? Did the Supreme Court decide the *Salerno* case correctly? Why or why not?

4. How does a magistrate determine how much bail is appropriate and how much is "excessive"? What alternatives, if any, do you see to the traditional bail-bond system to ensure the appearance of the defendant in court?

5. Can you imagine a situation in which a prosecutor would run afoul of the Constitution by engaging in selective prosecution? In your state, can a prosecutor be sued for malicious prosecution? How is this proved?

6. Why does the law insist on a determination of voluntariness and a factual basis when a defendant pleads guilty or *nolo contendere*?

7. Do the courts in your state permit the *nolo contendere* plea? If so, what tactical advantage does the defendant gain by pleading *nolo contendere* rather than guilty?

8. How might a prosecutor persuade a defendant to plead guilty to a criminal charge without running afoul of due process? What prosecutorial tactics are likely to be viewed as fundamentally unfair?

9. Compare the advantages and disadvantages to the defendant of insisting on the right to a speedy trial.

10. Why do you think the U.S. Supreme Court has never held that the Fifth Amendment requirement of indictment by a grand jury applies to the states as well as to the federal government?

11. Does the grand jury still play a viable role in the criminal justice system? Are the criticisms of the grand jury valid? Why or why not?

12. Should plea bargaining be abolished? If not, what modifications might be necessary to protect (a) the defendant and (b) the public?

■ **PROBLEMS FOR DISCUSSION AND SOLUTION**

1. Samuel Penurio was president of a community bank in a small town. He was well thought of in the community, but he was known to drink to excess occasionally. One June evening his bank hosted a cocktail party. About 10:00 P.M., after the party was over, Penurio offered to drive his secretary home. Each had drunk several cocktails. En route to her home, Penurio drove through an intersection controlled by a signal light. His car crashed into a car of four students who had just left their high school football game. One student, the popular head female cheerleader, died as a result of the injuries she received from the accident. Penurio's blood-alcohol level was 1.0. He was charged with vehicular homicide, which carries a maximum punishment of life imprisonment. Penurio and his secretary claim that he drove through the intersection just as the light was changing and that the car occupied by the students drove through the intersection at an

excessive rate of speed. The driver of the students' car had not been drinking, and the surviving students all say Penurio drove through the red light. The local newspaper ran a front-page story with pictures of the students holding a school-wide memorial service for the deceased cheerleader, describing the students' version of the accident, and pointing out that Penurio had been convicted of DWI just a year earlier. Over the next several days, the newspaper and the local radio station carried adverse comments from their readers and listeners about Penurio's conduct. Penurio's counsel has filed a motion for a change of venue. Do you think it likely the court will grant the motion? What, if any, additional information should be sought to support the motion?

2. Willy Doolittle, age thirty-eight, is an unemployed male construction worker. He is married with two children in middle school. He has been unable to support his family for the past few weeks because of lack of work. His wife takes care of their rented home, but, in addition to being a high school dropout, she receives Medicaid assistance for a series of physical problems. One night after having a few beers, Doolittle, using a key he had kept from when he had worked in a grocery warehouse, entered the warehouse without permission and stole approximately $1,000 worth of snack foods. The state charged Doolittle with burglary. His bail was set under a standard schedule that calls for $10,000 cash or bond. Doolittle has no means to post cash or a bond. The public defender (PD) was appointed to represent him. Doolittle has no prior criminal record and has lived in the community for three years. He wants to be released, and the PD thinks he may be able to represent him more effectively if Doolittle is released and obtains employment. A social worker reports that the family is in need of support and has offered to assist Doolittle in obtaining employment at a new construction site. The PD asks you to prepare a memorandum to support an application for pretrial release without posting cash or bond. What additional information should you seek? In seeking to obtain Doolittle's release without posting cash or bond, what conditions of release should the PD propose to the court?

CHAPTER **18**

The Criminal Trial

CHAPTER OUTLINE

Introduction

Constitutional Rights Pertaining to the Criminal Trial

Selection of the Jury

Free Press versus Fair Trial

"Order in the Court"

The Rules of Evidence

The Trial Process

Introduction

More than 90 percent of felony charges and an even higher percentage of misdemeanor offenses are disposed of before trial. Nevertheless, the criminal trial is the centerpiece of the criminal justice system for several reasons. First, trials are generally held before juries drawn from the community. Second, trials are the most visible aspect of the justice system and often attract widespread media coverage. Finally, cases disposed of by trial often have an important impact on the administration of justice.

Before the arrival of William the Conqueror in England in 1066, criminal trials took the forms of compurgation or ordeal. In a trial by compurgation, a defendant who had denied guilt under oath attempted to recruit a body of men to attest to his or her honor. If a group would swear to the defendant's innocence, the law considered the defendant to be innocent. In a trial by ordeal, the defendant was tortured by fire or water. If the defendant survived the ordeal, God had intervened to prove the defendant's innocence before the law.

Jury trials as we know them today originated with the Magna Charta, which the English nobles forced King John to sign at Runnymede in 1215. The Magna Charta granted freemen the right of trial by their peers. Early juries comprised persons who had knowledge of the facts of a case—it was centuries before trial juries functioned in the role they now perform. The jury became characteristic of the English common law, a feature that distinguished it from the law of the European continent, which was based on Roman law.

Constitutional Rights Pertaining to the Criminal Trial

Despite the protections of the common law, English subjects accused of crime were not always afforded fair trials. The notorious Star Chamber was established in the fifteenth century to punish offenses outside the common law. Its real purpose was to punish opponents of the monarch. It met in secret, dispensed with jury trials, and offered no legal protections to the accused. Before the Star Chamber, accusation was tantamount to conviction. Its punishments were unduly harsh, often involving torture and disfigurement. Although the Star Chamber was abolished by Parliament in 1641, the framers of the American Bill of Rights wanted to make sure that no such institution would ever be established in this country. Thus, as the Sixth Amendment provides,

> In all criminal prosecutions, the accused shall enjoy the right to a speedy and public trial, by an impartial jury of the State and district wherein the crime shall have been committed, which district shall have been previously ascertained by law, and to be informed of the nature and cause of the accusation; to be confronted with the witnesses against him; to have compulsory process for obtaining witnesses in his favor, and to have the Assistance of Counsel for his defence.

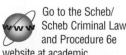
Go to the Scheb/ Scheb Criminal Law and Procedure 6e website at academic .cengage.com/criminaljustice/ scheb for edited versions of *Gideon v. Wainwright* and *Duncan v. Louisiana*.

Because they are deemed to be fundamentally important in securing liberty and ensuring fairness, the various rights protected by the Sixth Amendment are made applicable to state criminal trials by the Fourteenth Amendment. See, for example, *Gideon v. Wainwright*, 372 U.S. 335, 344, 83 S.Ct. 792, 796, 9 L.Ed.2d 799, 805 (1963); *Pointer v. Texas*, 380 U.S. 400, 85 S.Ct. 1065, 13 L.Ed.2d 923 (1965); *Duncan v. Louisiana*, 391 U.S. 145, 88 S.Ct. 1444, 20 L.Ed.2d 491 (1968).

The Right to Compulsory Process

The Sixth Amendment guarantees a defendant the right "to have compulsory process for obtaining witnesses in his favor." This affords the defendant the right to obtain court process (a subpoena) to compel witnesses to appear in court. There are some restrictions (for example, a defendant cannot cause numerous witnesses to be subpoenaed simply to give cumulative testimony), but courts allow defendants a fair degree of liberality in causing witnesses to be subpoenaed. Of course, the prosecution can also compel the attendance of witnesses.

The Right to an Open Public Trial

The Sixth Amendment guarantees "the right to a speedy and public trial." Although the right to an **open public trial** is central to our system of justice, that right is not absolute. After pointing out that a public trial is for the benefit of the accused and to ensure that the judge and prosecutor carry out their duties responsibly, the Supreme Court in *Waller v. Georgia*, 467 U.S. 39, 45, 104 S.Ct. 2210, 2215, 81 L.Ed.2d 31, 38 (1984), explained that

> the right to an open trial may give way in certain cases to other rights or interests, such as the defendant's right to a fair trial or the government's interest in inhibiting disclosure of sensitive information. Such circumstances will be rare, however, and the balance of interest must be struck with special care.

The Supreme Court has ruled that the requirement for openness extends to all phases of the trial. Consequently, in 1982 it declared invalid a state statute requiring mandatory closing of the courtroom during the testimony of victims of sexual offenses. The Court said the issue of closing should be left to the discretion of the trial judge to determine on a case-by-case basis when the state's legitimate interests for the victim's well-being necessitate closing the courtroom. *Globe Newspaper Company v. Superior Court*, 457 U.S. 596, 102 S.Ct. 2613, 73 L.Ed.2d 248 (1982). Two years later, the Court held that *voir dire* proceedings (discussed later in this chapter) in criminal trials can be closed only by overcoming the presumption of openness. Accordingly, before a trial court orders the closing of court proceedings, it must make specific findings that such closing is essential and explain why available alternatives are inadequate. *Press-Enterprise Company v. Superior Court of California*, 464 U.S. 501, 104 S.Ct. 819, 78 L.Ed.2d 629 (1984).

Among the reasons frequently cited by courts for limiting public access to criminal proceedings are the need to protect rape victims or children who have been molested and the need to protect witnesses and jurors from embarrassment, trauma, or intimidation.

The Sixth Amendment right to a public trial, even if waived by the defendant, does not allow a defendant to invoke the converse of that right—that is, there is no right to a private trial. *Singer v. United States*, 380 U.S. 24, 34–35, 85 S.Ct. 1783, 790, 13 L.Ed.2d 630, 638 (1965).

The Right to Trial by Jury

The Sixth Amendment also ensures the right to trial by jury. However, the amendment leaves unanswered questions concerning the qualifications of jurors, the method of their selection, and the requirements for a jury to convict a person accused of a crime.

An accused may waive the right to a **jury trial.** Indeed, many persons who plead not guilty to misdemeanor charges elect a **bench trial.** On the other hand, most defendants who plead not guilty to felony charges choose to be tried by jury. The U.S. Supreme Court has ruled that the constitutional right to a jury trial extends to the class of cases for which an accused was entitled to a jury trial when the Constitution was adopted. This did not include juvenile cases; hence, there is no right to a jury trial for juveniles under the federal constitution. *McKeiver v. Pennsylvania,* 403 U.S. 528, 91 S.Ct. 1976, 29 L.Ed.2d 647 (1971). Furthermore, the right to trial by jury is not applicable to military tribunals. *Ex parte Quirin,* 317 U.S. 1, 63 S.Ct. 1, 87 L.Ed. 3 (1942).

 Go to the Scheb/ Scheb Criminal Law and Procedure 6e website at academic .cengage.com/criminaljustice/ scheb for an edited version of *Ex parte Quirin.*

The constitutional requirement of a jury trial applies to the states, thereby guaranteeing a defendant a right to a jury trial in a state criminal prosecution if such a right would exist in a federal prosecution. *Duncan v. Louisiana,* supra. Interestingly, the Sixth Amendment right to a jury trial does not afford a defendant the corresponding right to be tried before a judge without a jury. *Singer v. United States,* 380 U.S. 24, 85 S.Ct. 783, 13 L.Ed.2d 630 (1965).

As now interpreted, the Sixth Amendment guarantees an accused the right to a jury trial in criminal cases where a penalty of more than six months' imprisonment can be imposed. *Codispoti v. Pennsylvania,* 418 U.S. 506, 94 S.Ct. 2687, 41 L.Ed.2d 912 (1974). Offenses that carry a possible penalty of no more than six months' imprisonment are generally termed "petty offenses," and a jury trial is not required under the Constitution. *Baldwin v. New York,* 399 U.S. 66, 90 S.Ct. 1886, 26 L.Ed.2d 437 (1970).

In *Blanton v. City of North Las Vegas,* 489 U.S. 538, 109 S.Ct. 1289, 103 L.Ed.2d 550 (1989), the Supreme Court observed that a defendant might be entitled to a jury trial even if the penalty was no more than six months' imprisonment. The Court said this could occur where additional statutory penalties, in conjunction with the maximum authorized period of incarceration, are so severe as to clearly reflect a legislative determination that the offense is a "serious" one. But the Court held that the prospect of a $1,000 fine, attendance at an alcohol abuse clinic, and the loss of a driver's license for ninety days were not sufficient to make the offense of driving while intoxicated so "serious" as to require a jury trial.

In 1996, in a 5–4 decision, the Supreme Court ruled that a defendant charged with multiple petty offenses is not entitled to a jury trial under the federal constitution even though the possible sentence may add up to more than six months in prison. *Lewis v. United States,* 518 U.S. 322, 116 S.Ct. 2163, 135 L.Ed.2d 590 (1996).

Notwithstanding the federal constitutional requirements, under some states' constitutions or statutory laws, an accused has the right to a jury trial for certain offenses even though they may be classified as "petty offenses" from a federal constitutional standpoint. In Florida, for example, a defendant is entitled to a jury trial under the state constitution for any offense that was a *malum in se* and indictable at common law even though the maximum punishment is less than six months' imprisonment. *Reed v. State,* 470 So.2d 1382 (Fla. 1985).

ANONYMOUS JURIES

Ordinarily, the identities of members of a jury are a matter of public information. But in some cases courts find it necessary to impanel an anonymous jury, where information about the jurors such as their names, residences, employment information, and so forth is not disclosed to the public. Anonymous juries were unknown at common law; the first one was impanelled in the United States in 1979. Courts now employ anonymous juries where necessary to protect potential jurors and their families from threats, harassment, or intimidation, which can occur from organized crime, gang activity, or other sources. In *United States v. Paccione,* 949 F.2d 1183 (2nd Cir. 1991), the court said a trial court "should not order the empanelling of an anonymous jury without (a) concluding that there is strong reason to believe the jury needs protection, and (b) taking reasonable precautions to minimize any prejudicial effects on the defendant and to ensure that his fundamental rights are protected." 949 F.2d at 1192.

In *United States v. Krout,* 66 F.3d 1420 (5th Cir. 1995), defendants were convicted in a federal district court of participating in a continuing criminal enterprise of murder, drug distribution, and firearms offenses. One ground asserted in their appeal was that they were denied a fair trial because the identities of the jurors who found them guilty were not publicly revealed. The U.S. Court of Appeals for the Fifth Circuit rejected their challenge and held that the trial court did not abuse its discretion in impaneling an anonymous jury. The appellate court mentioned that one of the objectives of the defendants' criminal organization was to interfere with potential witnesses. *United States v. Krout,* 66 F.3d 1420 (5th Cir. 1995).

In *State v. Ivy,* 188 S.W.3d 132 (Tenn. 2006), the Tennessee Supreme Court reviewed a defendant's murder conviction. Among other issues on appeal, the defendant argued that the trial court erred in impanelling an anonymous jury. The issue of impanelling anonymous juries was one of first impression with the court. The court upheld the trial court's finding that strong reasons existed to protect the jury, as one of the defendant's apparent motives in committing the charged offense included the defendant's desire to prevent the victim from going to the police. Following the rationale of federal appellate court decisions, the court approved the use of an anonymous jury where there is a strong reason to believe the jury needs protection and where reasonable precautions are taken to ensure that the defendant's fundamental rights are protected.

COMPOSITION OF THE TRIAL JURY

At common law, a jury consisted of twelve men. Rule 23(b), Federal Rules of Criminal Procedure, requires a twelve-member jury in criminal cases in federal courts unless the defendant stipulates fewer in writing. If the court finds it necessary to excuse a juror after the jury has retired to consider its verdict, at the discretion of the court, a valid verdict may be returned by the remaining eleven jurors. All states require twelve-member juries in capital cases. Most require the same number for all felony prosecutions. However, many now use fewer than twelve jurors in misdemeanor cases. Florida uses six-person juries for all but capital felonies. Fla. R. Crim. P. 3.270. In *Williams v. Florida,* 399 U.S. 78, 90 S.Ct. 1893, 26 L.Ed.2d 446 (1970), the Supreme Court upheld the use of six-person juries in the trial of felony offenses in Florida. Subsequently, in *Ballew v. Georgia,* 435 U.S. 223, 98 S.Ct. 1029, 55 L.Ed.2d 234 (1978), the Court held that a jury of only five persons was not acceptable under the Sixth Amendment.

In federal courts and in the great majority of state courts, a jury verdict in a criminal trial must be unanimous. However, a few states accept less than unanimous verdicts. The Supreme Court has approved nonunanimous verdicts rendered by twelve-person juries. *Johnson v. Louisiana,* 406 U.S. 356, 92 S.Ct. 1620, 32 L.Ed.2d 152 (1972); *Apodaca v. Oregon,* 406 U.S. 404, 92 S.Ct. 1628, 32 L.Ed.2d 184 (1972). But the Court held that a conviction by a nonunanimous six-person jury in a state trial for a nonpetty offense violates the right to trial by jury guaranteed by the Sixth and Fourteenth Amendments to the U.S. Constitution. *Burch v. Louisiana,* 441 U.S. 130, 99 S.Ct. 1623, 60 L.Ed.2d 96 (1979).

The Right to Counsel

The Sixth Amendment right to counsel at a criminal trial is well established. But a defendant also has a constitutional right of self-representation, and at times the defendant does not exercise that right until the trial. If the defendant does choose self-representation, the trial judge must determine whether the defendant has made a voluntary and intelligent decision. If a careful inquiry by the judge indicates that the defendant's

Go to the Scheb/
Scheb Criminal Law and Procedure 6e website at academic
.cengage.com/criminaljustice/
scheb for an edited version of *Williams v. Florida.*

election is voluntary and intelligent, then it is incumbent on the court to allow self-representation. Any such waiver of counsel must be carefully documented in the court records, and the court, at its option, may appoint **standby counsel** to assist the defendant. *Faretta v. California*, 422 U.S. 806, 95 S.Ct. 2525, 45 L.Ed.2d 562 (1975). In *State v. Bakalov*, 862 P.2d 1354 (Utah 1993), the Supreme Court of Utah cautioned trial judges to advise a defendant who elects to proceed *pro se* of the risks of presenting a *pro se* defense. A Pennsylvania appellate court has ruled that before the right to counsel may be waived, the trial court is required "to make searching and formal on-the-record inquiry to ascertain (1) whether the defendant is aware of his right to counsel and (2) whether the defendant is aware of the consequences of waiving that right or not." *Commonwealth v. Owens,* 750 A.2d 872, 875 (Pa. Super. 2000).

At trial, a defense counsel who represents multiple defendants might discover a possible conflict in his or her representation of the defendants. In such an instance, it is the trial court's duty "either to appoint separate counsel or to take adequate steps to ascertain whether the risk was too remote to warrant separate counsel." *Holloway v. Arkansas*, 435 U.S. 475, 484, 98 S.Ct. 1173, 1178, 55 L.Ed.2d 426, 434 (1978).

In 1976 the Supreme Court ruled that it is a violation of a defendant's Sixth Amendment right to counsel for a trial judge to bar the defendant from conferring with defense counsel during an overnight recess of a trial. *Geders v. United States*, 425 U.S. 80, 96 S.Ct. 1330, 47 L.Ed.2d 592 (1976). More than a decade later, the Court held it was not a denial of the right to counsel for a trial judge to bar a defendant from conferring with counsel during a brief trial recess that occurred after the defendant testified on direct examination but before cross-examination by the prosecutor. *Perry v. Leeke*, 488 U.S. 272, 109 S.Ct. 594, 102 L.Ed.2d 624 (1989). The Court's holdings in these cases acknowledge the importance of a close relationship between attorney and client during a trial but also recognize that the pursuit of truth is the purpose of the in-court examination of witnesses. Thus, there are valid reasons not to allow any witness to confer with counsel between the direct examination and the cross-examination.

Selection of the Jury

State and federal laws prescribe certain basic qualifications for jurors. Statutes commonly require that jurors be at least eighteen years of age and registered voters in the state or district from which they are to be selected. In contrast with past practices, laws prescribing qualifications cannot discriminate to prevent women as a class from serving as jurors. *Taylor v. Louisiana*, 419 U.S. 522, 95 S.Ct. 692, 42 L.Ed.2d 690 (1975). Convicted felons whose civil rights have not been restored are usually excluded from serving on juries. Beyond this, statutes frequently carve out exemptions for expectant mothers and mothers with young children, for persons over seventy years of age, and for physicians, dentists, attorneys, judges, teachers, elected officials, police, firefighters, and emergency personnel. The trend has been for states to restrict exemptions from jury duty so that the pool of prospective jurors reflects a representative cross-section of the community.

The Jury Selection and Service Act of 1968, 28 U.S.C.A. § 1861ff, was enacted to ensure that jury panels in federal courts are selected at random from a fair cross-section of the community. States also have statutes prescribing the process of selection. Local officials compile a list of persons qualified to serve as jurors, generally from the rolls of registered voters, driver's license lists, or some combination thereof. From this list, prospective jurors are randomly selected and summoned to court.

Compensation paid to trial jurors ranges from meager to modest amounts for their travel and per diem expenses. Most states prohibit an employer from discharging an employee who has been summoned for jury duty.

The body of persons summoned to be jurors is referred to as the **venire.** After outlining the case to be tried and reciting the names of those expected to participate, the judge may excuse those whose physical disabilities or obvious conflicts of interest based on family relationships or business connections disqualify them from serving. After excusing those who do not qualify, the judge swears in the remaining members of the venire to answer questions put to them by the court and counsel. Then six or twelve of these prospective jurors are called at random to take their seats in the jury box, where either the judge or counsel for each side may ask further questions. This process is called the *voir dire.*

The *Voir Dire*

Lawyers for the prosecution and the defense are permitted to challenge prospective jurors either for cause or peremptorily. A challenge is a request that a juror be excused from serving. Challenges are customarily asserted at the *voir dire* (from the French, meaning "to tell the truth"). The function of the *voir dire* is to enable the court and counsel to obtain the information necessary to ensure the selection of a fair and impartial jury. To assist in obtaining background information and thereby expedite the *voir dire* process, it is not uncommon for courts to submit a series of written questions to be answered by prospective jurors in advance of their appearance in court. In some courts, the *voir dire* examination is conducted by the trial judge, who may invite the lawyers to suggest questions to ask the prospective jurors. In others, lawyers for each side conduct the *voir dire.* In either event, the presiding judge exercises broad discretion to keep the questioning within proper bounds. A *voir dire* examination is generally conducted before the six or twelve prospective jurors initially selected; however, under certain circumstances some courts have allowed the examination of individual jurors apart from the collective group.

The objective of the *voir dire* examination is to select jurors who can render a verdict fairly and impartially. However, it would be naive to expect that the prosecutor and defense counsel are both striving to seat a wholly objective panel of jurors. Obviously, each trial lawyer wants jurors who will be sympathetic to the cause he or she advocates. To accomplish this, trial lawyers must be well versed in the facts of the case and the relevant law. They must also display ingenuity in questioning the prospective jurors to determine whether to exercise their right to challenge jurors' qualifications to serve. Lawyers must be conversant with local court practices because judges have broad discretion in conducting the *voir dire.* Trial lawyers have their own theories on how to conduct a *voir dire* examination, but most would agree that a practical knowledge of psychology is helpful. In recent years, some have even retained social scientists for advice and assistance in the jury selection process. The process of excusing prospective jurors is accomplished by counsel exercising challenges, either "for cause" or "peremptorily"—that is, without assigning a reason.

Challenges for Cause

Challenges for cause may be directed to the venire on the basis of the panel having been improperly selected. An example is when the defense counsel contends that the selection procedures exclude minority members. More commonly, challenges for cause are directed to a prospective juror individually concerning some fact that would disqualify that person from serving on the particular case. Among the more common reasons for disqualification are having a close relationship with counsel, being significantly involved in the case as a witness or in some other capacity, or having formed a definite opinion about the case. However, it is not expected that the jurors be totally ignorant of the facts and issues involved in the case. Forty years ago, Justice Tom C. Clark, writing for the Supreme Court, observed:

> In these days of swift, widespread and diverse methods of communication, an important case can be expected to arouse the interest of the public in the vicinity, and scarcely any of those best qualified to serve as jurors will not have formed some impression or opinion as to the merits of the case. *Irvin v. Dowd,* 366 U.S. 717, 722, 81 S.Ct. 1639, 1642, 6 L.Ed.2d 751, 756 (1961).

With our widespread access to television and the Internet, Justice Clark's observation is even more compelling today than in 1961. Nevertheless, prospective jurors who acknowledge that they have formed an opinion on the merits of the case and cannot disregard this opinion are generally excused for cause. Absent unusual circumstances concerning the parties involved in a case, a person would not be excused for cause because of religious or political affiliations.

The Problem of "Death-Qualified" Juries

In 1970 the Supreme Court expressed concern about some courts automatically excluding from juries trying capital cases persons who oppose or who have conscientious scruples against capital punishment. The Court held that opponents of capital punishment could not be excluded from juries impaneled to hear cases where the death penalty could be imposed unless the prospective jurors indicated that they could not make an impartial decision on the issue of guilt or could never vote to impose the death penalty. *Witherspoon v. Illinois,* 391 U.S. 510, 88 S.Ct. 1770, 20 L.Ed.2d 776 (1968).

In *Wainwright v. Witt,* 469 U.S. 412, 424, 105 S.Ct. 844, 852, 83 L.Ed.2d 841, 851–852 (1985), the Court articulated the proper standard for determining when a prospective juror may be excluded for cause because of views on capital punishment. The test, the Court said, is whether the juror's views would "prevent or substantially impair the performance of his duties as a juror in accordance with his instructions and oath." Justice William J. Brennan, with whom Justice Thurgood Marshall joined in dissent, observed that "basic justice demands that juries with the power to decide whether a capital defendant lives or dies not be poisoned against the defendant." 469 U.S. at 439, 105 S.Ct. at 860, 83 L.Ed.2d at 861. In capital cases, the jury first hears the evidence bearing on the defendant's guilt or innocence; then, only if a guilty verdict is rendered, the jury receives evidence on whether the death penalty should be imposed. This practice is referred to as a bifurcated trial (see Chapter 19). The Supreme Court has said that the **death qualification of a jury** (that is, the exclusion of prospective jurors who will not under any circumstances vote for imposition of the death penalty) is designed to obtain a jury that can properly and impartially apply the law to the facts at both the guilt and sentencing phases of a capital trial. On this rationale, the Court held that removal before the guilt phase in a capital trial of prospective jurors whose opposition to the death penalty would impair or prevent performance of their duties at the sentencing phase is not unconstitutional. *Lockhart v. McCree,* 476 U.S. 162, 106 S.Ct. 1758, 90 L.Ed.2d 137 (1986).

Peremptory Challenges of Jurors

It is not always possible to articulate a basis for dismissing a juror who appears to be biased. Therefore, each side in a criminal trial is also allowed a limited number of **peremptory challenges** that may be exercised on *voir dire* to excuse prospective jurors without stating any reason. The number of peremptory challenges is usually provided by statute or court rules.

In federal courts, each party in a criminal case is allowed twenty peremptory challenges where the offense is punishable by death. If the offense is punishable by more than one year in prison, the government is allowed six and the defendant is allowed ten. Each side is allowed three peremptory challenges where the offense carries a punishment of less than one year in prison. Fed. R. Crim. P. 24(b).

States vary in the number of peremptory challenges allowed in criminal trials. Rather typical is Article 35.15 of the Vernon's Annotated Texas Code of Criminal Procedure, which allows the state and the defendant fifteen peremptory challenges each in capital cases where the state seeks the death penalty. Where two or more defendants are tried together, the state is entitled to eight peremptory challenges for each defendant, and each defendant is entitled to eight as well. In noncapital felony cases and in capital cases where the state does not seek the death penalty, the state and defendant are each entitled to ten peremptory challenges. Where two or more defendants are tried together, each defendant is entitled to six peremptory challenges, and the state is likewise entitled to six for each defendant. In misdemeanor cases, each side is allowed either three or five peremptory challenges, depending on the level of court where the defendant is tried.

To determine whether to exercise a peremptory challenge, an attorney conducting a *voir dire* examination attempts to determine the attitudes, backgrounds, and personalities of prospective jurors. Trial courts limit the questions that may be asked of prospective jurors, depending on the nature of the case. Some areas of questioning are considered very delicate and usually will not be permitted. For example, in *Alderman v. State,* 327 S.E.2d 168 (Ga. 1985), the Supreme Court of Georgia upheld a trial judge's refusal to allow a defendant to ask prospective jurors questions concerning the kinds of books and magazines they read, whether they were members of any political organizations, and what kinds of bumper stickers they had on their vehicles.

RACIALLY BASED PEREMPTORY CHALLENGES

To reduce the potential for racial discrimination in the exercise of **racially based peremptory challenges,** courts have recently reassessed the historic freedom accorded counsel in exercising peremptory challenges. In 1965, in *Swain v. Alabama,*

CASE-IN-POINT

When Should a Juror Be Excused for Cause?

The defendant was tried by jury for rape, sodomy, and some weapons offenses. Prospective jurors were not asked during the *voir dire* if they had ever been raped or had a family member or friend who had been raped. After the jury had been selected, a female juror suggested to the court that she should be excused because her daughter had been raped five years earlier. After being closely questioned by the judge and defense lawyer, she expressed convincingly that she and her daughter had effectively recovered from the trauma of the rape and that she could be a fair and impartial juror. The court refused to excuse her from the jury panel. The defendant was convicted and appealed.

The Georgia Court of Appeals affirmed the defendant's conviction. In rejecting the defendant's argument that the trial court erred in not excusing the juror for cause, the court said that the trial court had an ample basis upon which to believe the juror would perform her duty justly.

Jamison v. State, 295 S.E.2d 203 (Ga. App. 1982).

Go to the Scheb/ Scheb Criminal Law and Procedure 6e website at academic .cengage.com/criminaljustice/ scheb for an edited version of *Batson v. Kentucky*.

380 U.S. 202, 85 S.Ct. 824, 13 L.Ed.2d 759, the Supreme Court said that it was a violation of the Equal Protection Clause of the Fifth Amendment to systematically exclude someone from serving on a jury because of the person's race. To make a *prima facie* case of purposeful discrimination, the defendant faced the formidable task of proving that the peremptory challenge system as a whole was being perverted. There was considerable criticism of the Court's ruling in *Swain v. Alabama,* and the Court again addressed the problem in *Batson v. Kentucky,* 476 U.S. 79, 106 S.Ct. 1712, 90 L.Ed.2d 69 (1986).

In *Batson,* the Supreme Court held that a prosecutor's peremptory challenges to exclude African Americans from a jury trying African American defendants was ground for a defendant to claim discrimination under the Equal Protection Clause of the Fourteenth Amendment to the Constitution. *Batson* became the basis for trial courts to deny the prosecution's use of a peremptory challenge for exclusion of an African American juror from a trial of a person of that race if the court was persuaded the challenge was racially motivated. In 1991 the Supreme Court broadened the rule so that the racial motivation of the prosecutor became subject to challenge irrespective of the defendant and prospective juror being of the same race. *Powers v. Ohio,* 499 U.S. 400, 111 S.Ct. 1364, 113 L.Ed.2d 411 (1991).

In 1992 the Court revisited this area of the law and extended the *Batson* rule by holding that a defendant's exercise of peremptory challenges was state action and that the Equal Protection Clause also prohibits defendants from engaging in purposeful discrimination on the ground of race. *Georgia v. McCollum,* 505 U.S. 42, 112 S.Ct. 2348, 120 L.Ed.2d 33 (1992). And in 2000, the Court suggested that the *Batson* rule applies to ethnicity as well as race. *United States v. Martinez-Salazar,* 528 U.S. 304, 120 S.Ct. 774, 145 L.Ed.2d 792 (2000). In *Rico v. Byrd,* 340 F.3d 178 (3rd Cir. 2003), the U.S. Court of Appeals for the Third Circuit relied on that dictum in holding that peremptory challenges to Italian American prospective jurors are within the scope of the *Batson* rule.

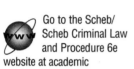

Go to the Scheb/ Scheb Criminal Law and Procedure 6e website at academic .cengage.com/criminaljustice/ scheb for an edited version of *Rico v. Byrd*.

GENDER-BASED PEREMPTORY CHALLENGES

In the late 1980s and early 1990s, courts moved to restrict **gender-based peremptory challenges.** By 1993, federal appellate courts had issued disparate rulings on the issue. Finally, in *J.E.B. v. Alabama ex rel. T.B.,* 511 U.S. 127, 114 S.Ct. 1419, 128 L.Ed.2d 89 (1994), the U.S. Supreme Court resolved that conflict and held that the Equal Protection Clause of the Fourteenth Amendment also prohibits gender-based peremptory challenges. Writing for the majority, Justice Harry Blackmun emphasized the relationship between racially based and gender-based peremptory challenges: "Failing to provide jurors the same protection against gender discrimination as race discrimination could frustrate the purpose of *Batson* itself." 511 U.S. at 148, 114 S.Ct. at 1430, 128 L.Ed.2d at 107. Now that peremptory challenges based on race, ethnicity, and gender have been invalidated as violations of equal protection, some observers wonder whether the peremptory challenge itself is on the way out.

Impaneling of the Jury

If the court anticipates that a trial might be protracted, it may have one or more alternate jurors selected to serve should any juror become ill or have to respond to an emergency. An alternate juror sits with the jury, but unless substituted for a regular juror, the alternate is excused just before the jury retires to deliberate. After selection of the jury is complete, it is sworn as a body by the judge or the clerk of the court to carry out its duties and is admonished not to discuss the case until instructed by the court to deliberate.

What Happens When a Juror Becomes Emotionally Disabled?

Fred Mills was convicted of aggravated robbery in Dallas County, Texas. On the morning of his trial, one of the jurors impaneled to hear the case requested permission to attend a memorial service for his grandfather, who had died the previous evening. The trial judge found the juror was "emotionally disabled" and would not be able to concentrate if not allowed to attend the memorial service. Attempts to postpone the trial disclosed conflicts for other jurors and schedules for other docketed cases, so over Mills's objection, the judge proceeded with the trial with the remaining eleven jurors. On federal habeas corpus review, the U.S. Court of Appeals for the Fifth Circuit noted that Article 36.29 of the Texas Code of Criminal Procedure specifies a norm of twelve jurors in felony cases, yet it provides that if one juror becomes "disabled," the remaining eleven can render a verdict. The court declined to review the Texas court's finding that the juror was emotionally disabled due to death of a relative. Citing *Williams v. Florida*, 399 U.S. 78, 90 S.Ct. 1893, 26 L.Ed.2d 446 (1970), the court denied Mills's petition. The court observed that "since Texas provided Mills with a jury possessing the fundamental attributes of the jury guaranteed by the Sixth and Fourteenth Amendments, Mills has no claim for relief."

Mills v. Collins, 924 F.2d 89 (5th Cir. 1991).

Proposals for Jury Reform

In the nationally televised O. J. Simpson case in 1995, the public witnessed considerable bickering between counsel and long delays in impaneling a jury. A protracted jury trial with many delays ensued. Thus, the Simpson trial became a catalyst for reform in the jury processes. Polls taken after that trial revealed a great decline in interest in serving on juries. Many who have been called to serve complain of "just sitting around the courthouse and wasting time" with no explanation for the delay. They are demanding that court officials show them more concern and respect. Although some progress has been made in allowing jurors to remain on call until needed, there remains room for improvement in many jurisdictions.

Many who have served on juries feel that the jury selection process has become too competitive, with little focus on the goal of obtaining a fair and impartial jury. Others emphasize the need not only to expedite the process of impaneling a jury but also for jurors to be given a greater role during the trial. Suggestions for reform have included limiting the number of peremptory challenges by counsel, allowing jurors to take written notes as a trial proceeds, and permitting questioning of witnesses by jurors. Over the last decade, courts have been increasingly willing to allow jurors to play a more active role in the trial. (For further discussion, see the section entitled "Conduct of the Jury during the Trial" on page 526.)

Free Press versus Fair Trial

First Amendment guarantees of freedom of the press often collide with a defendant's right to a fair trial before an impartial jury. This is particularly true when heightened public interest results in mass media coverage of a trial, with potential prejudicial effects on witnesses and jurors. When this occurs, the trial court must protect the defendant's right to a fair trial by taking steps to prevent these influences from affecting the rights of the defendant. Failure to do so can result in a verdict of guilty being overturned by an appellate tribunal.

In a high-profile homicide case, a jury found Dr. Sam Sheppard guilty of the 1954 murder of his wife, Marilyn. His conviction was affirmed on appeal. But in *Sheppard v. Maxwell,* 384 U.S. 333, 86 S.Ct. 1507, 16 L.Ed.2d 600 (1966), the Supreme Court reversed a federal appeals court's denial of Sheppard's petition for habeas corpus. Observing that jurors at Sheppard's trial were constantly exposed to intense media coverage until their deliberations and that the "newsmen took over practically the entire courtroom," 384 U.S. at 355, 86 S.Ct. at 1518, 16 L.Ed.2d at 616, the Court found that the highly prejudicial publicity contributed to the denial of due process of law to the defendant. Acknowledging that nothing proscribes the press from reporting events in the courtroom, the Court suggested that trial courts can combat the problem through such measures as (1) proscribing out-of-court statements by lawyers, parties, witnesses, or court officials concerning matters that could be prejudicial to the accused and (2) insulating the witnesses and sequestering the jury to prevent exposure to reports by the media. The prosecution was given a reasonable time to retry Sheppard. On retrial in 1966, he was acquitted. Sheppard died in 1970, but his son, Sam Reese Sheppard, brought a civil suit against the state of Ohio claiming that his father was wrongfully imprisoned for the crime for which he was later acquitted. In an attempt to clear Sheppard's reputation, counsel attempted to establish that the DNA of a third person—not Sheppard or his wife—was present at the crime scene. On April 10, 2000, a jury in Cuyahoga County, Ohio, unanimously rejected the claim.

Although the media cannot "take over" the courtroom, it is equally clear that because of First Amendment rights, the public and the press cannot ordinarily be excluded from criminal trials. In 1980 Chief Justice Warren Burger, writing for the Supreme Court, traced the history of criminal trials in Anglo-American jurisprudence and concluded that public access is an indispensable element of criminal trials. Therefore, the Court concluded that trials may not be closed without findings sufficient to overcome the presumption of openness. *Richmond Newspapers, Inc. v. Virginia,* 448 U.S. 555, 100 S.Ct. 2814, 65 L.Ed.2d 973 (1980).

Go to the Scheb/ Scheb Criminal Law and Procedure 6e website at academic .cengage.com/criminaljustice/ scheb for an edited version of *Sheppard v. Maxwell.*

Cameras in the Courtroom

In 1965, in a 5–4 decision, the Supreme Court held that the defendant, Billy Sol Estes, was denied due process of law because the proceedings of his criminal trial were televised over his objection. *Estes v. Texas,* 381 U.S. 532, 85 S.Ct. 1628, 14 L.Ed.2d 543 (1965). This was consistent with the longtime ban that courts had imposed on allowing cameras in the courtroom. During the 1970s, many state courts began to allow radio, television, and still-camera coverage of court proceedings subject to limitations necessary to preserve the essential dignity of a trial (for example, equipment must be noiseless, and strong lights are not permitted). Also, judges may limit coverage by requiring pooling of media equipment. Nevertheless, rule 53 of the Federal Rules of Criminal Procedure still prohibits the taking of photographs in the courtroom during the progress of judicial proceedings in federal courts.

Florida is among the states that began permitting televising of trials in the late 1970s. *In re Post-Newsweek Stations, Florida, Inc.,* 370 So.2d 764 (Fla. 1979). Thereafter, Noel Chandler and another defendant, who were charged with several offenses, requested the trial court to exclude live television coverage from their jury trial. The court denied their request, and they were found guilty. A state appellate court affirmed their convictions. *Chandler v. State,* 366 So.2d 64 (Fla. App. 1978). The U.S. Supreme

Court granted review. At the outset, the Court acknowledged that it had no supervisory jurisdiction over state courts. Therefore, it confined its review to evaluating the constitutionality of Florida's program permitting radio, television, and photographic coverage of criminal proceedings over an accused's objection. The Court declined to prohibit television cameras from state courts but said that defendants have a right to show that such use prejudiced them in obtaining a fair trial. Finding that Chandler and his codefendant had not shown they were prejudiced in any way by the televising of their trials, the Court denied them any relief. *Chandler v. Florida,* 449 U.S. 560, 101 S.Ct. 802, 66 L.Ed.2d 740 (1981).

By 1993, cameras were allowed in the courtrooms of almost all state courts. And although there has been some backlash following the O. J. Simpson case, most still feel that cameras in the courtroom have enhanced the public's awareness of the judicial process. However, it is probably a fair generalization to conclude that, depending on the particular case, judges should be more assertive in exercising control over the televising of criminal proceedings.

The federal ban on cameras in the courtroom came to the forefront in March and April 1993, when four police officers, previously acquitted of criminal charges in a state court trial, were tried in a federal district court in Los Angeles on charges of violating the Fourth Amendment rights of Rodney King. Because this trial attracted widespread interest, the media voiced displeasure at their inability to bring to the public live camera coverage. Nevertheless, in 1994 the Judicial Conference of the United States voted to maintain the ban on television cameras in federal courts. There is less resistance to allowing television and still photography coverage of appellate proceedings. In March 1996, the U.S. Judicial Conference voted 14–12 to allow federal appeals courts to permit television, radio, and still photography in civil, but not criminal, appeals.

Almost all state courts now permit television and photographic coverage of court proceedings. In most states, the consent of the presiding judge is required, and judges generally have considerable discretion to control the coverage. Coverage of jurors is either prohibited or restricted, and most states prohibit coverage of cases involving juveniles and victims of sex crimes. Some states have such restrictive policies that television coverage of trials almost never takes place. In many states, television cameras that are permanent fixtures of the courtroom record court proceedings. Television stations and networks can simply pick up the signals, which they can edit or present live to their viewers.

The O. J. Simpson case, tried in California in 1995, shows how a sensational criminal trial can draw the mass media's attention. In that case, CNN and Court TV featured live coverage of many of the courtroom activities; other television networks carried daily "O. J. Updates" in their evening news programs.

"Order in the Court"

Occasionally a trial judge is confronted with a defendant or others in attendance at a trial whose disruptive behavior impedes the court from conducting a trial in a proper judicial atmosphere. As Justice Hugo Black observed, "The flagrant disregard in the courtroom of elementary standards of proper conduct should not and cannot be tolerated." *Illinois v. Allen,* 397 U.S. 337, 343, 90 S.Ct. 1057, 1061, 25 L.Ed.2d 353, 359 (1970).

This problem is more likely encountered in a so-called political trial, where there may be support for the cause the defendant claims to represent. One such highly publicized instance of courtroom disruption occurred in the 1969–1970 "Chicago Seven" conspiracy trial in federal court in Chicago. The seven defendants, including antiwar activist David T. Dellinger, were prosecuted under the Federal Anti-Riot Statute (18 U.S.C.A. §§ 2101–2102) for their actions at the August 1968 Democratic National Convention in Chicago. An eighth defendant, Black Panther party leader Bobby G. Seale, was tried separately on similar charges. Considerable antagonism developed between the trial judge, the defendants, and their counsel. As a result of their actions during their trials, all defendants and two of their attorneys were found guilty of contempt of court. Despite the number of unruly and disrespectful actions that took place, the contempt convictions were reversed because of procedural irregularities. *United States v. Seale,* 461 F.2d 345 (7th Cir. 1972); *In re Dellinger,* 461 F.2d 389 (7th Cir. 1972). Subsequently, the defendants' convictions were also reversed by the same federal court of appeals on the basis of judicial error. In this latter opinion the appellate court criticized the trial judge for his own antagonistic behavior during the trial. *United States v. Dellinger,* 472 F.2d 340 (7th Cir. 1972).

Unruly Defendants

It is not too difficult for judges to exercise control over members of the public who attend court trials. The problem that confronts judges is a defendant who becomes unruly. In most instances, judges control disruption and defiance by defendants and others through exercise of the **power of contempt.** Yet in recent years, some courts have had to go further. In *Illinois v. Allen,* supra, the Supreme Court recognized that there is no one formula for maintaining the appropriate courtroom atmosphere, but indicated that

> there are at least three constitutionally permissible ways for a trial judge to handle an obstreperous defendant … : (1) bind and gag him, thereby keeping him present; (2) cite him for contempt; (3) take him out of the courtroom until he promises to conduct himself properly. 397 U.S. at 343–344, 90 S.Ct. at 1061, 25 L.Ed.2d at 359.

The Sixth Amendment protects the defendant's right to be present at every critical stage of criminal proceedings. *Snyder v. Massachusetts,* 291 U.S. 97, 54 S.Ct. 330, 78 L.Ed. 674 (1934). The right to be present at trial is fundamental; however, it may be forfeited if the defendant is disruptive or fails to comply with reasonable standards of the court. For example, in New York a defendant repeatedly insisted on appearing in court while wearing only his underwear covered by a sheet. After warning him of the consequences of not wearing proper attire to court, the trial court allowed the trial to proceed in the defendant's absence. On appeal, the trial court's action was affirmed. *People v. Hinton,* 550 N.Y.S.2d 438 (N.Y. App. Div. 1990).

The Supreme Court in *Illinois v. Allen,* 397 U.S. 337, 90 S.Ct. 1057, 25 L.Ed.2d 353 (1970), explained that a trial judge is justified in employing necessary security measures to control a disruptive defendant. Accordingly, all courts insist that a defendant not disrupt courtroom proceedings. Thus, if there is a real threat of serious disruption by a defendant, or where threats of escape or danger to those in and around the courtroom exist, a defendant may be shackled. Federal and state courts are reluctant to shackle a defendant unless it becomes imperative because, in addition to concerns over the appearance of the defendant, shackling may have a prejudicial effect on a defendant's decision to testify at trial. See *People v. Duran,* 545 P.2d 1322 (Cal. 1976). Moreover, in some cases such restraints "may … impair [the defendant's] ability to confer with counsel, and significantly affect the trial strategy he chooses to follow." *Zygadlo v. Wainwright,* 720 F.2d 1221, 1223 (11th Cir. 1983).

Most state courts probably take the view of the Missouri Supreme Court. In 1996 that court observed that the use of restraints for courtroom security purposes is a matter within the discretion of the trial court. *State v. Kinder,* 942 S.W.2d 313 (Mo. 1996). In 1999 the Illinois Supreme Court, citing one of its earlier decisions, enumerated the following factors a trial judge should consider in determining whether to shackle a defendant:

> the seriousness of the present charge against the defendant; defendant's temperament and character; his age and physical attributes; his past record; past escapes or attempted escapes, and evidence of a present plan to escape; threats to harm others or cause a disturbance; self-destructive tendencies; the risk of mob violence or of attempted revenge by others; the possibility of rescue by other offenders still at large; the size and mood of the audience; the nature and physical security of the courtroom; and the adequacy and availability of alternative remedies. *People v. Buss,* 718 N.E.2d 1, 40 (Ill. 1999).

Behavior of Counsel

Dramatic, fictional presentations of courtroom proceedings now occupy a considerable part of television entertainment. A viewer is quite likely to gain an erroneous impression of courtroom proceedings, particularly in respect to the standards of conduct enforced against lawyers in criminal trials. Lawyers are seen asking inflammatory questions of a witness and expressing personal opinions concerning facts in issue. Others persist in interrogating a witness after the court has sustained an objection to such a line of questioning. It is not uncommon to see a lawyer continuing to press a point of law after the trial judge has made a ruling. Some actually appear to practice deceptive tactics on behalf of a client, justifying the means by the ultimate goal of helping a client. A prospective criminal justice professional could misapprehend the true role of a prosecutor or defense lawyer. Moreover, a prospective client who sees lawyers on television dramatically pursue such flagrant tactics may gain a false expectation of what a lawyer's role is in the courtroom and as a result may someday expect his or her own lawyer to pursue such tactics.

In reality, in federal and state courts lawyers are subject to rather strict legal and ethical rules in presenting evidence, following trial procedures, and courtroom decorum. When making an opening statement, a lawyer must not express personal knowledge or opinion concerning facts in issue. Lawyers must avoid misstating a fact or point of law; must address their arguments to the court, not to opposing counsel; and must avoid disparaging remarks toward opposing counsel. They are expected to refer to adult witnesses by their surnames and refrain from any gestures of approval or disapproval during a witness's testimony. A lawyer is not permitted to express a personal opinion as to the guilt or innocence of a defendant, but may argue whether the evidence shows guilt or innocence. Finally, a lawyer should abstain from flattery or other comments designed to curry favor with a juror. And it goes without saying that a trial judge must maintain a position of dignity and neutrality during the course of a trial.

It is understandable that emotions can run high during a trial, but trial judges generally insist on proper decorum in the courtroom. The court may discipline a lawyer who fails to abide by these rules. An offending lawyer may be found in contempt of court and fined or even jailed in instances of egregious misconduct. However, because of the possible adverse effect on a case, trial judges are hesitant to reprimand a lawyer, particularly defense counsel, in the presence of a jury. Other forms of disciplinary action may be initiated by a bar association and can range from public reprimands to suspension or even disbarment where a lawyer intentionally deceives the court, knowingly makes a false statement or submits a false document, or improperly withholds material information that causes serious injury to a party or a significant adverse effect on a legal proceeding.

The Rules of Evidence

In our adversary system, the purpose of a trial is to search for the truth. Guilt or innocence is determined based on the evidence produced at a trial. Evidence consists of verbal statements, writings, documents, photographs, and tangible items that tend to prove or disprove some fact in issue. Certain rules govern the introduction of evidence in a court of law. Sometimes a judge will tend to relax these rules in a nonjury trial because the judge is trained to "sort out" the probative evidence from the nonprobative. However, in a jury trial in a criminal case, the rules of evidence are strictly enforced.

The subject of evidence is complex. The rules of evidence prescribed by Congress for use in federal courts are known as the Federal Rules of Evidence and are found in Title 28 of the U.S. Code Annotated. Some states have legislatively or judicially adopted codes of evidence; in other states, the rules of evidence must be gleaned from a study of the decisional law of the state. Volumes have been written on the subject, and thousands of court decisions address its various aspects and refinements of general rules. From a basic text on criminal law and procedure, the reader can expect to gain only a very basic grasp of the principles involved.

Judicial Notice

Facts commonly known are accepted by courts without formal proof, a process known as the court taking **judicial notice** of certain established facts. Usually there is a request by counsel, but in some instances courts take judicial notice without request. The rationale for the doctrine of judicial notice is that courts should not exclude consideration of matters of general knowledge that are well known to informed members of the public. To illustrate, courts take judicial notice of who is president of the United States, that a particular date in a given month was on a certain day of the week, or that whiskey is an intoxicating liquor. In some instances it may be necessary to bring such commonly accepted facts to the court's attention by presentation of a calendar or an almanac. Courts in a particular area may be asked to take judicial notice of certain facts within the geographic area of the court's jurisdiction. However, judicial notice of a fact must never be used as a substitute for proof of an essential element of a crime. *State v. Welch*, 363 A.2d 1356 (R.I. 1976). Taking judicial notice is not conclusive because a party can always offer proof to the contrary.

Courts also take judicial notice of the law. All courts take judicial notice of the U.S. Constitution and general acts of Congress, and federal courts take judicial notice of the federal laws and the laws of each state, whether depending upon statutes or judicial opinions. *Lamar v. Micou*, 114 U.S. 218, 5 S.Ct. 857, 29 L.Ed. 94 (1885). State courts take judicial notice of their own state constitutions and state laws. Municipal ordinances and the laws of other states generally must be established by formal proof, but attorneys frequently stipulate as to the text of these laws. Of course, courts can require counsel to submit memoranda relative to the status of laws and judicial opinion to be judicially noticed.

Proof beyond a Reasonable Doubt

Go to the Scheb/ Scheb Criminal Law and Procedure 6e website at academic .cengage.com/criminaljustice/ scheb to find *Jackson v. State (1987),* where a Florida appellate court finds that the circumstantial evidence of the defendant's guilt is insufficient to uphold the defendant's conviction for first-degree murder and armed burglary.

Historically, the requirement for **proof beyond a reasonable doubt** in a criminal trial has required proof whereby the fact finder would have "an abiding conviction, to a moral certainty, of the truth of the charge." *Commonwealth v. Webster,* 59 Mass. (5 Cush.) 295, 320 (1850). The historical requirement was elevated to a constitutional mandate in *In re Winship,* 397 U.S. 358, 90 S.Ct. 1068, 25 L.Ed.2d 368 (1970). There, the Supreme Court held that the Due Process Clause of the Fourteenth Amendment requires the prosecution to establish the elements of a charged crime beyond a reasonable doubt. Judges have defined "beyond a reasonable doubt" in a variety of ways. In *Victor v. Nebraska,* 511 U.S. 1, 114 S.Ct. 1239, 127 L.Ed.2d 583 (1994), the Supreme Court held that the Constitution does not require that any one particular form of words be employed. Rather, judges have wide discretion in instructing juries on the meaning of the reasonable doubt standard. In evaluating jury instructions on this issue, the question is whether the court's instruction, taken as a whole, conveys a correct sense of the concept of reasonable doubt. In *Victor,* the Court avoided defining reasonable doubt directly but said that trial courts must avoid definitions of reasonable doubt that permit juries to convict a person on a standard that is less than what is required by due process of law.

Evidentiary Presumptions

This standard of requiring proof beyond a reasonable doubt is central to judicial consideration of the validity of **evidentiary presumptions.** At common law, a child younger than seven years old was conclusively presumed to be incapable of committing a crime. A legal presumption of this type is called an irrebuttable presumption. In other words, no evidence can be introduced in court to overcome it. In criminal law, an irrebuttable presumption that provides, based on proof of one fact, that the fact finder (judge or jury) must conclusively find the existence of another fact is troublesome because it encroaches on a defendant's due process right to have the prosecution prove the defendant guilty beyond a reasonable doubt.

Today, most presumptions in criminal law are permissive. These are evidentiary devices designed to aid a party who has the burden of proof. For example, under this type of presumption, once evidence establishes a fact, the jury may infer that something else is true, provided there is a rational connection between the basic fact and the presumed fact.

In *County Court of Ulster County, New York v. Allen,* 442 U.S. 140, 99 S.Ct. 2213, 60 L.Ed.2d 777 (1979), the Supreme Court upheld the application of a New York statutory presumption that occupants of a car in which firearms were present were in illegal possession of them, as applied to a case in which three adults and a juvenile were tried for illegal possession of handguns. When the police stopped the vehicle in which the suspects were riding, they saw the handguns located crosswise in an open handbag. The juvenile admitted ownership of the bag. At the conclusion of the trial, the judge instructed the jury, in part, that "you may infer and draw a conclusion that such prohibited weapon was possessed by each of the defendants who occupied the automobile at the time when such instruments were found. The presumption, or presumptions, is effective only so long as there is no substantial evidence contradicting the conclusion flowing from the presumption, and the presumption is said to disappear when such contradictory evidence is adduced." The Supreme Court pointed out that "the presumption was merely a part of the prosecution's case, that it gave rise to a permissive inference available only in certain circumstances, rather than a mandatory conclusion of possession, and that it could be ignored by the jury even if there was no affirmative proof offered by defendants in rebuttal." 442 U.S. at 160–161, 99 S.Ct. at 2213, 60 L.Ed.2d at 794.

Shortly thereafter, in *Sandstrom v. Montana,* 442 U.S. 510, 99 S.Ct. 2450, 61 L.Ed.2d 39 (1979), the Court reviewed a case in which the State of Montana charged the defendant, David Sandstrom, with a homicidal crime where intent was a necessary element of the offense. The trial court instructed the jury that "the law presumes that a person intends the ordinary consequences of his voluntary act." Historically, many trial courts commonly instructed juries substantially as quoted. But in *Sandstrom,* the Supreme Court noted that because the jury was not told that the presumption could be rebutted, it may have interpreted the presumption as being conclusive or as shifting to the defendant the burden of persuasion on the element of intent. Thus, the Court viewed the issue to be whether such an instruction relieved the state of its burden to prove the defendant guilty beyond any reasonable doubt. The Court found that the instruction mandated a conclusive presumption that removed the need to prove the essential element of intent and ruled that such a presumption violated the defendant's due process rights under the Fourteenth Amendment.

A decade later, the Court reiterated the principle announced in *Sandstrom.* A defendant had been prosecuted for violating a statute that provided as follows:

> Whenever any person who has … rented a vehicle willfully and intentionally fails to return the vehicle to its owner within 5 days after the … rental agreement has expired, … shall be presumed to have embezzled the vehicle.

The Court held that the jury instruction that included the mandatory presumption of the statute violated the defendant's due process rights. *Carella v. California,* 491 U.S. 263, 109 S.Ct. 2419, 105 L.Ed.2d 218 (1989).

Requirements of Admissibility

As we pointed out in Chapter 16, a defendant has certain constitutional protections concerning the prosecution's use of forced admissions and confessions and of other evidence that has been illegally obtained. In addition, before evidence may be admitted in court, whether real or testimonial and whether direct or circumstantial, it must meet certain legal requirements. First, all evidence must be relevant (that is, it must tend to prove or disprove a material fact in issue). For example, assume that a defendant is charged with armed robbery. It would be relevant to show where the defendant and victim were located when the offense occurred, the money or other articles stolen, the force applied by the defendant, details of any weapon used, the victim's resistance, and the defendant's fingerprints. Flight by the defendant when the police sought to make an arrest and, of course, any admissions or confessions of the defendant material to the crime would also be relevant. But offenses committed by the defendant completely unrelated to the crime of robbery would be irrelevant, as would be the defendant's individual likes, dislikes, and lifestyle.

Similar Fact Evidence

So-called **similar fact evidence** consists of facts similar to the facts in the crime charged. Such evidence might reveal the commission of a collateral crime. The test of admissibility is whether such evidence is relevant and has a probative value in establishing a material issue. Thus, under some limited circumstances, evidence of other crimes or conduct similar to that charged against the defendant may be admitted in evidence in a criminal prosecution. Although such evidence cannot be admitted to prove the defendant's bad character or propensity to commit a crime, in some instances it may be admitted to show motive, identity, or absence of mistake or accident. See, for example, *Williams v. State,* 110 So.2d 654 (Fla. 1959). This is a very technical area of the law of evidence and is subject to varying interpretations by federal and state courts.

The trend is to admit similar fact evidence in cases involving prosecutions for sexual abuse of children. In these cases, it often becomes important to establish opportunity, motive, intent, identity, or the absence of a mistake or accident or even to establish a child's credibility as a witness if such credibility is attacked by the defendant. This last point is illustrated by *Gezzi v. State,* 780 P.2d 972 (Wyo. 1989). There, the Wyoming Supreme Court reviewed a defendant's conviction on two counts of committing indecent acts with the younger of his two daughters. During the defendant's trial, the older sister testified to a course of sexual misconduct occurring between her and the defendant similar to the molestation occurring between the defendant and the younger sister. Admission of this testimony was upheld because the younger sister's credibility was attacked and the evidence admitted at trial was inconclusive as to the cause of the younger sister's physical symptoms. In affirming the defendant's conviction, the court included an exhaustive footnote showing that about half of state courts now liberally recognize the admissibility of prior bad acts (similar acts) as evidence in sexual offenses for various purposes.

Classifications of Evidence

There are several classifications of evidence. First, evidence may be real or testimonial. **Real evidence** consists of maps, blood samples, X-rays, photographs, stolen goods, fingerprints, knives, guns, and other tangible items. **Testimonial evidence** consists of sworn statements of witnesses. Watching a television drama might give the impression that a criminal trial consists largely of real evidence, but the great majority of evidence presented in criminal trials comes from the mouths of the witnesses, both lay and expert.

Next, evidence may be direct or indirect. **Direct evidence** includes **eyewitness testimony,** whereas **indirect evidence** usually consists of circumstantial evidence— that is, attendant facts from which inferences can be drawn to establish other facts in issue at the trial. To illustrate, a person who testifies to having seen the defendant enter the victim's house is giving direct evidence. Testimony that reveals that the defendant's fingerprints were found on a windowpane of that house shortly after it was broken into is **circumstantial evidence** from which, depending on the circumstances, it may be inferred that the defendant entered the house through that window. The admissibility of circumstantial evidence in criminal trials is well established in American law. *Tot v. United States,* 319 U.S. 463, 63 S.Ct. 1241, 87 L.Ed. 1519 (1943).

The same evidence can be direct regarding one fact and circumstantial regarding another. The witness who testifies that the defendant had possession of a pistol is giving direct evidence of that fact. Depending on other circumstances, it might be inferable from proof of that fact that the defendant attacked the victim.

Actually, there is no real difference in the weight given circumstantial as opposed to real evidence. Circumstantial evidence may once have been suspect, yet lawyers and judges can point to many instances where circumstantial evidence has proven to be more reliable than testimonial evidence. As the Supreme Court has observed,

[C]ircumstantial evidence may in some cases point to a wholly incorrect result. Yet this is equally true of testimonial evidence. In both instances, a jury is asked to weigh

CASE-IN-POINT

Conviction Based Solely on Circumstantial Evidence Must Exclude Every Reasonable Hypothesis of a Defendant's Innocence

A Florida jury found John William Jackson guilty of first-degree murder and armed burglary based entirely on circumstantial evidence. On appeal, Jackson argued that the trial court erred in denying his motion for a judgment of acquittal.

The state's evidence revealed that on December 19, 1983, around 4:30 A.M., the victim was raped and stabbed in her house trailer. She sought help from a neighbor and described her assailant as "an orange picker, Michigan tag." Shortly thereafter she died from multiple stab wounds to her neck. The police arrived at the scene later that day and collected blood, semen, and saliva stains; fingerprints; and hair samples. Jackson later gave the police his fingerprints, impressions of his teeth, and samples of his pubic and head hair and his blood. An autopsy revealed that a bruise on the victim's right wrist was a bite mark. Jackson, a 31-year-old Caucasian male, had lived in the vicinity of the victim's trailer from approximately July 1983 until a few days before the crime, when he moved a few miles away.

Dr. Richard Souviron, a forensic odontologist, testified that the bite mark on the victim's wrist was consistent with Jackson's teeth impressions. On January 31, 1984, Jackson had a conversation with Charles and Patricia Fuller, on whose property he had lived during the latter part of 1983. Jackson mentioned to them that when the police interrogated him, he learned that the victim had been raped, stabbed, and bitten. This occurred before the police had released the information that the victim had been bitten. Mrs. Fuller acknowledged that Jackson had told her that he had been picking oranges. Mr. Fuller testified that during the time he knew him, the defendant had worked as a heavy equipment operator. FBI Agent Michael Malone, an expert in hair and fiber analysis, identified two head hairs found on the victim's pajama top as being indistinguishable from Jackson's hair sample. Agent Malone also said that Negroid hairs were found in a window screen and a Negroid pubic hair found in the combed pubic hair of the victim.

The appellate court found that the prosecution presented three items of crucial evidence: first, the consistent bite mark; second, Jackson's statement to

the Fullers that the victim had been bitten; and third, the strands of hair found on the victim matching Jackson's hair. The court noted that although Dr. Souviron concluded that the bite marks on the victim's wrist were consistent with Jackson's teeth impression, he added "this was not a positive bite.... I certainly hope [the detective] didn't arrest John Jackson on this bite." The court found that the fact that Jackson knew the victim had been bitten was not probative of his guilt. The court pointed out that prior to Jackson's conversation with the Fullers, the police had taken impressions of his teeth, an event that would be a strong indication to anyone that a bite mark was involved. The only other significant evidence against Jackson, the court noted, was Agent Malone's testimony that two strands of hair found on the victim's pajamas matched the defendant's hair samples. But Agent Malone also agreed that hair comparisons do not constitute a basis for positive personal identification and added, "It's not a fingerprint, no. I cannot say that that hair came from John Jackson and nobody else."

"Jackson's conviction," the court concluded, "hinges on two hairs found on the victim's clothing which match his hair sample. Hair comparison testimony, while admissible, does not result in identifications of absolute certainty. There was no evidence placing the defendant at the scene of the crime, no indication of a relationship of any kind between the defendant and the victim, or that they even knew each other. The victim's dying words pointed to an 'orange picker, Michigan tag.' Jackson's car, however, had a Florida tag. None of the fingerprints found at the scene of the crime matched Jackson's. This, plus the presence of Negroid pubic hair in the victim's pubic hair combings, adds support to a reasonable hypothesis that someone else committed the crime." Finally, the court explained, "[w]here the only proof of guilt is circumstantial, no matter how strongly the evidence may suggest guilt a conviction cannot be sustained unless the evidence is inconsistent with any reasonable hypothesis of innocence." Because the state failed to present evidence sufficient to enable the jury to exclude every reasonable hypothesis of the defendant's innocence, the court vacated the defendant's convictions.

Jackson v. State, 511 So.2d 1047 (Fla. App. 1987).

the chances that the evidence correctly points to guilt against the possibility of inaccuracy or ambiguous inference. In both the jury must use its experience with people and events in weighing the probabilities. *Holland v. United States,* 348 U.S. 121, 140, 75 S.Ct. 127, 137–138, 99 L.Ed. 150, 166–167 (1954).

The Requirement of Competency

To be admissible in court, evidence must also be competent. In determining whether a witness is **competent to testify,** the trial judge must consider the ability of the witness to receive and recollect impressions, to understand questions, and to appreciate the moral duty to tell the truth. A very young child may or may not be competent to testify. This depends on the court's finding regarding the child's ability to understand the meaning of telling the truth. No precise rule can be set forth about when a young child may be competent to testify. Rather, it is a matter for determination in the sound discretion of the trial judge, and considerations include the child's age, intelligence, and capacity to appreciate the requirement to tell the truth. See *Wheeler v. United States,* 159 U.S. 523, 16 S.Ct. 93, 40 L.Ed. 244 (1895). A determination that a child is competent to testify will generally not be overturned by an appellate court unless the trial court's judgment is clearly erroneous. *Trujillo v. State,* 880 P.2d 575 (Wyo. 1994). Persons of unsound mind may not be competent to testify, but again, a judge must determine this. The presiding judge and members of the jury would not be competent to testify at a trial where they serve.

Expert Witnesses

Today, **forensic experts** in nearly every field make a specialty of testifying in court. To qualify as an expert, a witness must present proper credentials and be received by the trial court as an expert. A court may call experts on its own motion, but usually the prosecution or defense produces experts. After one side offers a witness as an expert, opposing counsel may cross-examine the prospective witness about his or her qualifications. For example, a physician who is to give evidence as to the cause of death of someone is first asked to relate his or her educational background and experience in the specialized area of medical practice in question. In many cases, attorneys for the prosecution and defense will stipulate that a particular witness is an expert in the field. The trial judge has considerable discretion in determining whether a witness is to be received as an expert.

Unlike lay witnesses, an expert witness may respond to **hypothetical questions** and may express opinions within the realm of his or her expertise. Fingerprint identification, ballistics tests, handwriting exemplars, and medical tests have been prominent among areas where expert evidence is commonly received in criminal cases. More recently, evidence of speed-detection devices, Intoximeters, and other devices to test blood-alcohol content has become commonplace. Judges and jurors are not necessarily scientists. Indeed, it is unlikely that many of them have more than a basic knowledge of scientific principles. Yet courts must make rational judgments about new scientific advances to determine their admissibility in court. To accomplish this, courts must depend on experts in the field.

An expert who has knowledge from personal observation may testify on that basis. For example, a psychiatrist who has examined the accused may offer an opinion as to the accused's sanity. If the expert is not acquainted with the person or subject from personal observation, the expert's opinion can be based on hypothetical questions that assume the existence of facts the evidence tends to establish. Medical experts and handwriting experts frequently are asked hypothetical questions in court, and experts on the subject of accident reconstruction frequently offer testimony about speed, braking, and other factors relevant to determining fault in cases involving auto accidents.

Scientific Evidence in the Courtroom

Evidence obtained through scientific and technological innovations can be both relevant and probative in a criminal case. Yet care must be taken to ensure that a new principle or technique is well supported by research and is generally accepted by the scientific community. The basic issue the courts face is whether the expert **scientific evidence** is reliable. In *Frye v. United States,* 293 F. 1013 (D.C. Cir. 1923), the court said that "in admitting expert testimony deduced from a well-recognized scientific principle or discovery, the thing from which the deduction is made must be sufficiently established to have gained general acceptance in the particular field in which it belongs." 293 F. at 1014.

For seventy years the *Frye* test, or **general acceptance test,** was commonly applied in federal and most state courts faced with the issue of whether new scientific tests should be admitted into evidence in criminal trials. In 1993, however, in *Daubert v. Merrell Dow Pharmaceuticals, Inc.,* 509 U.S. 579, 113 S.Ct. 2786, 125 L.Ed.2d 469, the U.S. Supreme Court rejected the general acceptance test. Rather, the Court ruled that the federal rules of evidence supersede *Frye.* The Court held that admissibility of scientific evidence must be based on several factors, including whether the evidence can be tested and whether it can be subjected to peer review. Under *Daubert,* the trial judge must make a preliminary assessment of whether the reasoning or methodology underlying the expert's testimony is scientifically valid and whether that reasoning or methodology can be applied to the facts in issue. Once the court determines admissibility, the jury then determines the weight to give to such evidence. Because the Court's ruling in *Daubert* is not one of constitutional dimension, state courts are not required to follow it. As we pointed out in Chapter 16, state courts are now divided on whether to accept the newer *Daubert* standard or remain with the classic standard announced in 1923 in *Frye v. United States.*

Hypnotically Enhanced Testimony

One controversial area of expert testimony concerns whether **hypnotically enhanced testimony** is admissible in a criminal trial. After examining extensive scientific literature, research, and testimony on the reliability of hypnotically refreshed memory and determining that the scientific community was divided on the subject, the California Supreme Court determined that hypnotically refreshed memory should not be admitted in judicial proceedings. *People v. Shirley,* (Cal. 1982). In earlier years, some courts tended to admit such evidence—see, for example, *Harding v. State,* 246 A.2d 302 (Md. App. 1968)—however, the trend seems to have moved in the direction of not allowing such evidence. The majority of courts in the last decade have held that hypnotically enhanced testimony is not sufficiently reliable to be admissible. In *State v. Tuttle,* 780 P.2d 1203 (Utah 1989), the Utah Supreme Court published an exhaustive opinion analyzing the status of the law in this area and held that hypnotically enhanced testimony, as well as testimony regarding anything first recalled from the time of a hypnotic session forward, is inadmissible as evidence.

In *Rock v. Arkansas,* 483 U.S. 44, 107 S.Ct. 2704, 97 L.Ed.2d 37 (1987), the U.S. Supreme Court held that excluding hypnotically enhanced testimony, when applied to prevent an accused from testifying to his or her own posthypnotic recall, violated her constitutional right to testify on her own behalf. Accordingly, the position of the majority of courts to exclude all hypnotically induced testimony should not prevent an accused from testifying to his or her own posthypnotic recall. Recently some state and federal courts have allowed hypnotically enhanced testimony, but only after first conducting a determination of reliability.

Polygraph Evidence

Known in the vernacular as a lie detector, a polygraph records a subject's respiration, blood pressure, and heartbeat as the subject is questioned by an examiner. The examiner poses certain questions and records the subject's responses. The premise of the polygraph is that deception is accompanied by stress that is manifested in increased respiration, pulse, and blood pressure. The use of a polygraph is controversial. Polygraph operators argue that a properly administered polygraph test is effective in detecting deception, and they cite impressive figures attesting to the accuracy of results. However, some critics argue that an individual can so control physiological responses as to distort the findings.

Historically, federal and state courts have declined to admit **polygraph evidence.** As late as 1989, the Minnesota Supreme Court held that the results of polygraph tests, as well as any direct or indirect references to the taking of or refusal to take such tests, are inadmissible. *State v. Fenney,* 448 N.W.2d 54 (Minn. 1989). Most state courts

SUPREME COURT PERSPECTIVE

United States v. Scheffer, 523 U.S. 303, 118 S.Ct. 1261, 140 L.Ed.2d 413 (1998)

In this case the Supreme Court upheld a ban on the use of polygraph evidence in military courts.

JUSTICE CLARENCE THOMAS delivered the opinion of the Court, saying in part:
State and federal governments unquestionably have a legitimate interest in ensuring that reliable evidence is presented to the trier of fact in a criminal trial. Indeed, the exclusion of unreliable evidence is a principal objective of many evidentiary rules....

[T]here is simply no consensus that polygraph evidence is reliable. To this day, the scientific community remains extremely polarized about the reliability of polygraph techniques.... Some studies have concluded that polygraph tests overall are accurate and reliable.... Others have found that polygraph tests assess truthfulness significantly less accurately—that scientific field studies suggest the accuracy rate of the 'control question technique' polygraph is 'little better than could be obtained by the toss of a coin,' that is, 50 percent.... This lack of scientific consensus is reflected in the disagree-

ment among state and federal courts concerning both the admissibility and the reliability of polygraph evidence.

Although some Federal Courts of Appeal have abandoned the per se rule excluding polygraph evidence, ... at least one Federal Circuit has recently reaffirmed its per se ban, ... and another recently noted that it has 'not decided whether polygraphy has reached a sufficient state of reliability to be admissible.' ... Most States maintain per se rules excluding polygraph evidence....

Whatever their approach, state and federal courts continue to express doubt about whether such evidence is reliable....

[E]xcluding polygraph evidence in all military trials is a rational and proportional means of advancing the legitimate interest in barring unreliable evidence. Although the degree of reliability of polygraph evidence may depend upon a variety of identifiable factors, there is simply no way to know in a particular case whether a polygraph examiner's conclusion is accurate, because certain doubts and uncertainties plague even the best polygraph exams. Individual jurisdictions therefore may reasonably reach differing conclusions as to whether polygraph evidence should be admitted.

agree and hold that the reliability of polygraph testing has not been scientifically demonstrated to such a degree of certainty as to permit its use in evidence. However, some courts allow the results of polygraph testing to be admitted in court on stipulation of the prosecution and the defense. See, for example, *State v. Souel,* 372 N.E.2d 1318 (Ohio 1978); *State v. Valdez,* 371 P.2d 894 (Ariz. 1962). Other state supreme courts have held that polygraph evidence is not admissible in a criminal trial even when the parties stipulate to its admissibility. See, for example, *People v. Baynes,* 430 N.E.2d 1070 (Ill. 1981).

The prognosis for the use of polygraph evidence remains uncertain. Advocates of polygraph evidence were heartened in 1989 when the Eleventh Circuit Court of Appeals observed that polygraph testing has gained increasingly widespread acceptance as a useful and reliable scientific tool: "We agree with those courts which have found that a per se rule disallowing polygraph evidence is no longer warranted." *United States v. Piccinonna,* 885 F.2d 1529, 1535 (11th Cir. 1989). But on March 31, 1998, the U.S. Supreme Court upheld a ban on the use of polygraph evidence in military courts. *United States v. Scheffer,* 523 U.S. 303, 118 S.Ct. 1261, 140 L.Ed.2d 413 (1998). A military appeals court had ruled that an airman should not have been barred from introducing lie-detector evidence during his court-martial on charges of using drugs and writing bad checks. In reversing that decision, the Court, in an opinion by Justice Clarence Thomas, observed that there was no consensus that such evidence is reliable and ruled that the military ban on the use of such evidence did not unconstitutionally abridge the airman's right to present a defense. However, four of the justices in the court's eight-member majority recognized that in some future case, the polygraph test might be so crucial that its results should be allowed (see the Supreme Court Perspective on page 516).

Battered Woman Syndrome

Expert testimony concerning the battered woman syndrome has gained substantial scientific acceptance, and in the past several years such testimony has been received in many courts in cases where women claim to have acted in self-defense. In 1989 the Ohio Supreme Court receded from its 1981 decision declaring such evidence inadmissible. The court took a fresh look at the literature published in this area since 1981 and said that "expert testimony on the battered woman syndrome would help dispel the ordinary lay person's perception that a woman in a battering relationship is free to leave at any time. Popular misconceptions about battered women should be put to rest, including beliefs that the women are masochistic." *State v. Koss,* 551 N.E.2d 970, 971 (Ohio 1990). To some extent, a woman's reliance on evidence of the battered woman syndrome depends on whether state law imposes a duty to retreat before defending oneself with deadly force. We discuss this subject in Chapter 14 concerning defenses.

DNA Evidence

Since its introduction in the late 1980s, **DNA testing** has had a profound impact on law enforcement and criminal procedure. DNA is an abbreviation of deoxyribonucleic acid, the chemical that carries an individual's genetic information. DNA is extracted from a biological specimen (for example, white blood cells, semen, body hair, and tissue). Through sophisticated testing results, DNA printing tests compare DNA molecules extracted from a suspect's specimen with DNA molecules extracted from specimens found at a crime scene to determine whether the samples match.

Scientists and law enforcement officers attempt to develop what a layperson might call "genetic fingerprints."

In one of the first uses of DNA evidence in a criminal trial in the United States, Tommy Lee Andrews was convicted of rape by a Florida court in 1987 after his DNA was matched to that of semen traces obtained from the victim's body. *Andrews v. State*, 533 So.2d 841, 842-43 (Fla. App. 1989). Since then the use of DNA printing has proliferated, especially in rape and homicide cases.

When it was introduced, DNA profiling was widely heralded by prosecutors. Defense counsel usually accepted the validity of the evidence without presenting their own experts to challenge it. Courts, too, were extremely impressed with this new form of evidence. One federal court referred to the reliability and accuracy of DNA profiling as justifying "an aura of amazement." See *United States v. Jakobetz*, 747 F. Supp. 250, 258 (D. Vt. 1990). During the 1990s, defense counsel began to challenge DNA evidence principally on the basis of the test results. Courts became increasingly concerned over the issue of reliability of test results due to documented instances of false positive and false negative entries by DNA laboratories. See, for example, *State v. Cauthron*, 846 P.2d 502 (Wash. 1993); *People v. Barney*, 10 Cal. Rptr.2d 731 (Cal. App. 1992).

Introduction of DNA evidence must satisfy the tests for scientific evidence. As previously noted, federal and several state courts follow the *Daubert* ruling (*Daubert v. Merrell Dow Pharmaceuticals, Inc.*, supra), where the trial judge assesses whether the reasoning or methodology underlying an expert's testimony is scientifically valid and can be applied to the facts in issue. Many state courts continue to follow the *Frye* "general acceptance test" (*Frye v. United States*, supra). Irrespective of the test courts follow for admission of DNA evidence, the trend has been to take a more rigorous approach.

In *Turner v. State*, 746 So.2d 355 (Ala. 1998), the Alabama Supreme Court stated that although the *Frye* test remains the standard of admissibility for scientific evidence generally, trial courts must follow additional specific requirements in determining the admissibility of DNA evidence. The court noted that evidence concerning the use of genetic markers contained in or derived from DNA for identification purposes is admissible provided "the trial court shall be satisfied that the expert testimony or evidence meets the criteria for admissibility as set forth by the U.S. Supreme Court in *Daubert v. Merrell Dow Pharmaceuticals, Inc.*" *Id.* at 360. The court cautioned, "Trial courts should use the flexible *Daubert* analysis in making the 'reliability' (scientific validity) assessment. In making that assessment, the courts should employ the following factors: (1) testing; (2) peer review; (3) rate of error; and (4) general acceptance admissibility standard established in *Daubert*." *Id.* at 361.

The Florida Supreme Court continues to follow the *Frye* standard for admissibility of scientific evidence but now requires proof of a two-step DNA testing process. "The first step relies on principles of molecular biology and chemistry to determine that two DNA samples match, while a second statistical step is needed to give significance to the match. The second step relies on principles of statistics and population genetics, and the calculation techniques used in determining and reporting DNA population frequencies must also satisfy the *Frye* test." *Brim v. State*, 695 So.2d 268, 269 (Fla. 1997).

Although their requirements for the introduction of DNA evidence vary, no court has rejected DNA evidence on the ground that it is invalid from a scientific basis. But the admissibility of DNA evidence must satisfy the requirements for courts to receive scientific evidence. One current legal issue concerns the extent to which defense attorneys are entitled to discover the underlying data necessary to challenge the reliability of methods used in gathering, testing, and processing DNA evidence.

"Your Honor, I Object"

Anyone who has observed a criminal trial, or even a television drama depicting one, is familiar with the advocates frequently addressing the court: "Your honor, I object." To this, the objecting lawyer might add "on the ground that the testimony is irrelevant." This is called a **general objection.** Or the lawyer might make a **specific objection** and add "because the testimony sought would be hearsay," "because the answer calls for an opinion of the witness which the witness is not qualified to give," or another specific reason. There are numerous other grounds for specific objections. We consider some of the more common objections in the following sections.

ON THE GROUND OF HEARSAY

Hearsay evidence refers to an oral or written statement by a person other than the one testifying in court. The general rule is often stated as follows: a witness may not testify as to a statement made by another if that statement is offered as proof of the matter asserted. Thus, a witness who testifies "I know the defendant was home on the night of the offense because my sister told me so" would be giving hearsay testimony. The real test of hearsay is whether a lawyer can cross-examine the person responsible for the contents of a statement.

The hearsay rule has many exceptions. Sometimes a hearsay statement is admissible to prove something other than the truth of the statement itself. Spontaneous or excited utterances, a person's dying declaration, evidence of a person's reputation, matters contained in old family records, and certain business and public records are among the most common exceptions recognized by courts. Likewise, a defendant's out-of-court statement generally may be used if it is an admission, confession, or some other statement against the defendant's interest. But the use of hearsay evidence in criminal trials presents some unique constitutional issues. When a hearsay declarant is not present for cross-examination, the declarant's statement can be admitted in evidence if it bears what courts refer to as "adequate indicia of reliability." Courts have usually taken the view that the Confrontation Clause of the Sixth Amendment to the U.S. Constitution is met as long as the court found the hearsay statements reliable even though the defendant had no opportunity to cross-examine the declarant. This view was espoused by the U.S. Supreme Court in *Ohio v. Roberts,* 448 U.S 56, 100 S.Ct. 2531, 65 L.Ed.2d 597 (1980).

This principle changed dramatically after the Supreme Court's 2004 decision in *Crawford v. Washington,* 541 U.S. 36, 124 S.Ct. 1354, 158 L.Ed.2d 177. In 1999, Michael D. Crawford was charged with assault and attempted murder for the alleged stabbing of Kenneth Lee. Sylvia Crawford, the defendant's wife, witnessed the incident. In a tape-recorded statement to a police officer, she indicated that Crawford's actions were not in self-defense. Under the state's marital privilege, Ms. Crawford was not permitted to testify against her husband. When the State sought to introduce Ms. Crawford's recorded statement to the police as an exception to the hearsay rule, the defendant objected on the ground that admitting her statement would violate his constitutional right to confront witnesses against him. Eventually this issue reached the Supreme Court.

In an opinion by Justice Antonin Scalia, the Supreme Court held that admission of Ms. Crawford's out-of-court recorded statement to police officers regarding the incident violated the Confrontation Clause, which provides that "[i]n all criminal prosecutions, the accused shall enjoy the right … to be confronted with the witnesses against him." The decision overrules the Court's decision in *Ohio v. Roberts* and effectively bars out-of-court testimonial statements by a witness unless the witness is unavailable and the defendant has had a prior opportunity to cross-examine the witness.

The Court's 2004 decision in *Crawford* left unanswered the precise meaning of *testimonial* statements, thereby creating considerable uncertainty. On June 19, 2006, in another opinion by Justice Scalia, the Supreme Court attempted to clarify its holding in *Crawford.* The Court in *Davis v. Washington,* ___ U.S. ___, 126 S.Ct. 2266, 165 L.Ed.2d 224, held that statements in response to a 9-1-1 operator are nontestimonial unless the circumstances objectively indicate that there is no such emergency. The Court went on to explain that if interrogation is intended primarily to "establish or prove past events," the resulting statements are testimonial and subject to the requirements of the Confrontation Clause. Confrontation issues frequently arise in out-of-court statements in cases involving charges of sexual abuse of children, and the dichotomy between testimonial and nontestimonial will be the subject of further litigation in the lower courts.

ON THE GROUND OF THE BEST EVIDENCE RULE

Ordinarily, the **best evidence** of a transaction must be offered in court. This rule applies to writings and means that an original document must be offered unless the party who offers a copy can present a plausible explanation of why the original is not available. For example, historically the original check allegedly forged by the defendant had to be produced rather than a photocopy of it. But the Federal Check Clearing for the 21st Century Act, PL 108-100 (Check 21 Law) became effective on October 28, 2004. Among its many provisions, the act provides that a substitute check is the legal equivalent of the original check.

ON THE GROUND THAT THE QUESTION CALLS FOR AN OPINION FROM THE WITNESS

A lay witness is supposed to testify regarding facts of which he or she has personal knowledge. In addition, lay witnesses are generally permitted to testify about such matters perceived through their physical senses and matters that are within the common knowledge of most people, such as the speed of a vehicle, sizes, distances, or the appearance of a person. They cannot give opinions on matters beyond the common experience and understanding of laypersons. To illustrate, a driver can give an estimate of the speed of a vehicle he or she observed traveling on the street, but a witness must be qualified as an expert to be permitted to testify as to the speed of a car based on observation of the car's skid marks on the pavement. Such an opinion must generally be based on facts perceived by the witness and not on hearsay statements. Rule 701 of the Federal Rules of Evidence limits lay witnesses to testifying to those opinions rationally based on the perception of the witness and helpful to an understanding of the testimony or determination of a fact in issue. States have similar rules of evidence.

A trial judge has considerable discretion to determine whether to admit **opinion evidence** from a lay witness. Although it is difficult to formulate precise rules, two illustrations shed light on the views of appellate courts. In *State v. Anderson,* 390 So.2d 878 (La. 1980), the Louisiana Supreme Court held that it was an error for the trial court to have allowed a police detective to give his opinion regarding the reasons he received an anonymous call in a homicide case; however, the court found the error harmless under the circumstances of the case. In *State v. Lagasse,* 410 A.2d 537 (Me. 1980), the court held that a lay witness's opinion testimony that a girl "looked like she had been slapped" was admissible.

Privileged Communications

The rules of evidence also recognize certain **privileges** that limit testifying. Privileges raise difficult issues by requiring the law, in the search for truth, to choose between protecting a person's confidentiality and allowing testimony that can result in full disclosure of all relevant evidence.

At common law, individuals who were in certain close relationships were privileged not to testify about certain matters. Today, statutes, court rules of evidence, and judicial decisions protect parties in certain relationships from being required to testify. These protections are known as privileges, and a person who asserts a privilege must establish the existence of the required relationship. We discuss the most common evidentiary privileges, which protect communications between attorney and client, husband and wife, and clergy and penitent.

ATTORNEY–CLIENT PRIVILEGE

The **attorney–client privilege** can be claimed either by the client or by the attorney on behalf of the client regarding communications between them in the course of the attorney's legal representation. The privilege belongs to the client, and if the client waives that privilege, the attorney can be required to disclose the communication. *Hunt v. Blackburn,* 128 U.S. 464, 9 S.Ct. 125, 32 L.Ed. 488 (1888). Several state supreme courts have ruled that the privilege survives the client's death. There was doubt as to whether this prevailed at the federal level; however, in a 1998 case involving activities of the Independent Counsel, the U.S. Supreme Court in a 7–2 decision ruled that the attorney–client privilege does survive the client's death. *Swidler & Berlin v. United States*, 524 U.S. 399, 118 S.Ct. 2081, 1421 L.Ed.2ds 379 (1998).

Go to the Scheb/
Scheb Criminal Law
and Procedure 6e
website at academic
.cengage.com/criminaljustice/
scheb for an edited version of
In re Death of Eric Miller.

In 2003 the North Carolina Supreme Court recognized an exception to the principle that attorney–client privilege survives the client's death. The court held that in the context of a pretrial criminal investigation, if a trial court "determines that some or all of the communications between a client and an attorney do not relate to a matter that affected the client at the time the statements were made, about which the attorney was professionally consulted ... , such communications are not privileged and may be disclosed." *In re Death of Eric Miller,* 565 S.E.2d 663 (N.C. 2003).

MARITAL PRIVILEGE

A husband and wife enjoy a privilege as to confidential communications between them during their marriage. This **marital privilege** emanates from the common law but has been codified by statutes and court rules in most jurisdictions. The privilege is based on the policy of promoting and preserving domestic harmony and the repugnance against convicting one person through the testimony of another who shares intimate secrets of domestic life. Either spouse may assert the privilege to prevent disclosing privileged matters; either may assert it to prevent the other spouse from testifying about privileged matters. Federal and state courts recognize the privilege, although the ramifications of it vary somewhat in different jurisdictions. The privilege does not preclude a spouse from testifying as to observations of the other's criminal activities and generally does not apply where one spouse is charged with a crime against the other or against a child of either.

A number of appellate court decisions recognize that the marital privilege survives the termination of a marriage by death or divorce. Some states have enacted statutes to so provide. See, for example, section 57-3-4 of the West Virginia Code, which states,

> Neither husband nor wife shall, without the consent of the other, be examined in any
> case as to any confidential communication made by one to the other while married,
> nor shall either be permitted, without such consent, to reveal in testimony after the
> marriage relation ceases any such communication made while the marriage existed.

The spousal privilege can apply to confidential communications between parties to a valid common-law marriage where such marriage is recognized by law, but numerous appellate courts have held the privilege does not extend to unmarried cohabitants. See, for example, *People v. Delph,* 156 Cal. Rptr. (Cal. App. 1979). But under Vermont's civil union law that became effective July 1, 2000, same-sex couples registered under the law have the benefit of "laws relating to immunity from compelled testimony and the marital communication privilege." 15 Vt. Stat. Ann. § 1204(e)(15).

CLERGY–PENITENT PRIVILEGE

Generally priests, ministers, and rabbis are prohibited from testifying about matters related to them by the penitent in confidence. This is known as the **clergy–penitent privilege,** and the clergyperson can assert the privilege on behalf of the penitent. This privilege is rooted in the English common law but is recognized by federal statute and by statutes in all fifty states. It is not based on the Religion Clauses of the First Amendment. In *Commonwealth v. Kane,* 445 N.E.2d 598 (Mass. 1983), the Massachusetts Supreme Judicial Court held that the privilege could be asserted only by the defendant and that a cleric may not refuse to answer questions where the defendant has waived the privilege. In that case, a defendant maintained that he had confessed nothing that was incriminating and wanted his priest to corroborate that position. The priest refused and was held in contempt by the trial court.

OTHER PRIVILEGES

Some jurisdictions also recognize testimonial privileges between a physician and a patient, between a psychotherapist and a patient, and between an accountant and a client. These expand the common-law concept of testimonial privilege, so the statutes and judicial decisions of a particular jurisdiction must be consulted.

The common law did not provide any testimonial privilege for confidential communications between a parent and a child, and most courts have rejected such a privilege. In a few states the legislature has provided that a parent or the parent's minor child may not be examined as to any communication made in confidence by the minor to the minor's parent. See, for example, Minn. Stat. Ann. § 595.02.

The Trial Process

The trial is the centerpiece of the criminal justice system, and in American courts the trial judge is the person most responsible for ensuring that the system operates in a fair, efficient, and impartial manner. Trial judges come into office through election or appointment. Ideally, they are selected because of their scholarship, integrity, and the patience and compassion the public associates with the fair and impartial administration of justice. To those appearing before the court and to the jurors and court personnel, the black-robed judge stands as a symbol of justice. In previous chapters, we have pointed out that judges perform numerous functions in the pretrial phases of the criminal justice system, but the most visible aspects of the judge's work are presiding at trials and, when convictions result, setting punishments.

During a trial, the judge serves as an umpire in many respects. The judge rules on the questions that may be asked of potential jurors, determines whether witnesses are competent to testify, controls the scope of interrogation of lay and expert witnesses, and instructs the jury on the law applicable to the particular case. The judge also determines all important judicial and administrative matters concerning the trial. Trial judges are held accountable by appellate courts sitting to review judgments and sentences and to correct harmful errors. Yet in numerous administrative and procedural areas (for example, whether to grant a postponement of a trial or to limit the number of expert witnesses), a judge's actions are discretionary, and appellate review in such areas is limited to determining whether the trial judge abused that discretion. "In discharging his responsibilities, the trial judge may properly caution, correct, advise, admonish, and, to a certain extent, criticize counsel during the case, provided it is done in such manner as not to subject counsel to contempt or ridicule, or to prejudice accused in the minds of the jurors." *M.T. v. State,* 677 So.2d 1223, 1229 (Ala. Cr. App. 1995). Nevertheless, trial judges must be very cautious of being critical of attorneys, especially in a jury trial, because jurors place great importance on the judge's attitude. A trial judge who is critical of a defendant's attorney might hold that attorney up to ridicule in the eyes of the jury and thereby impede the fairness of the trial. In *Earl v. State,* 904 P.2d 1029 (1995), the trial judge made many derogatory remarks concerning the defense counsel's capacity as a lawyer before the jury. The appellate court reversed the defendant's conviction and remanded the case for a new trial, noting that the trial judge's comments toward the defense attorney cumulatively prejudiced the defendant's case. In *State v. Jenkins,* 445 S.E.2d 622 (N.C. App. 1994), the court reversed a defendant's convictions because the judge turned his back to the defendant and the jury during the defendant's testimony. The appellate court was concerned that the jury may have interpreted the judge's action to mean that he did not believe the defendant's testimony to be credible.

Usually, either or both sides in a criminal trial request the court to invoke the traditional rule that requires all witnesses except the defendant to remain outside the courtroom except when testifying. The purpose of **putting witnesses under the rule,** as lawyers commonly refer to it, is to prevent witnesses from matching narratives. Whether witnesses should be excluded from the courtroom is a matter within the sound discretion of the trial court, *Witt v. United States,* 196 F.2d 285 (9th Cir. 1952); however, the request is generally granted.

Witnesses are interrogated by counsel in the adversary system of American justice; however, it is the right, and sometimes becomes the duty, of a judge to interrogate a witness. This is another delicate area, and appellate courts have emphasized that questioning from the bench should not show bias or feeling and should not be protracted. *Commonwealth v. Hammer,* 494 A.2d 1054, 1060 (Pa. 1985).

The Opening Statements

Once the jury is in place, the trial is ready to begin. The prosecution and the defense are each allowed to make an **opening statement** outlining their respective theories of the case and the evidence to be presented. These opening statements must not be argumentative, nor may counsel make disparaging remarks against one another. Often a defense lawyer defers making an opening statement until the prosecution rests its case. Opening statements are designed to orient the jury; therefore, if the defendant elects a bench trial, they are frequently waived. If not waived, opening statements of counsel are usually very brief in bench trials. After the opening statements have been presented, the prosecution calls its first witness to take the stand.

The Case for the Prosecution

Prosecutors are ever mindful that when a defendant pleads not guilty, the government must establish the defendant's guilt beyond any reasonable doubt. In presenting the government's case, the prosecuting attorney usually calls as witnesses police officers, the victim, and any other available witnesses whose testimony can support the charge against the defendant. The government's witnesses may also include experts. For example, in a homicide prosecution the prosecutor usually calls a physician; in a drug trafficking case, a chemist; in a forgery prosecution, a handwriting expert. In a DUI case the prosecution often calls the technician who performed a breath test on the defendant. A scientist who has conducted laboratory tests on DNA samples is often called to testify in homicide and sexual battery cases.

The Right to Confrontation and Cross-Examination

The Sixth Amendment to the Constitution guarantees the defendant the right to be confronted with the witnesses who offer evidence against the defendant. This means that the defendant has the right to be present at trial, *Illinois v. Allen,* supra, and to cross-examine each witness. As explained in *California v. Green,* this right of confrontation

1. insures that the witness will give his statements under oath....

2. forces the witness to submit to cross examination, the "greatest legal engine ever invented for the discovery of truth" [and]

3. permits the jury ... to observe the demeanor of the witness ... thus aiding the jury in assessing his credibility. 399 U.S. 149, 158, 90 S.Ct. 1930, 1935, 26 L.Ed.2d 489, 497 (1970).

The **right of cross-examination** of an adversary's witness is absolute. *Alford v. United States,* 282 U.S. 687, 51 S.Ct. 218, 75 L.Ed. 624 (1931). However, the permissible scope of cross-examination varies somewhat in different jurisdictions and is a matter largely within the discretion of the trial court. *Smith v. Illinois,* 390 U.S. 129, 88 S.Ct. 748, 19 L.Ed.2d 956 (1968). Courts generally agree that the right of cross-examination is limited to (1) questioning the witness about matters he or she testified to on direct examination and (2) asking any questions that might tend to impeach the witness's credibility or demonstrate any bias, interest, or hostility of the witness.

The right of cross-examination is available to both the prosecutor and the defense counsel and is extremely valuable in criminal trials. Although in most instances it is objectionable for a lawyer who is examining a witness to ask **leading questions** on direct examination, the rules of evidence permit a cross-examiner to ask leading questions. When skillfully employed, cross-examination often develops facts favorable to the cross-examiner's side of the case. Frequently, a cross-examiner is successful in bringing out inconsistencies, contradictions, and any bias or hostility of the witness. A witness may also be subject to **impeachment**—that is, having his or her credibility attacked on cross-examination. A witness's credibility may be attacked in the following ways:

- Showing the witness's inability to have viewed or heard the matters the witness has testified to, or inability to recall the event testified to

- Demonstrating that the witness has made prior conflicting statements on an important point

- Showing the witness has been convicted of a crime

- Establishing that the witness bears a bad reputation for truthfulness in the community

- Showing bias, prejudice, or motive to misrepresent the facts, or that the witness has a definite interest in the result of the trial

The defendant's **right of confrontation** guaranteeing a face-to-face meeting with witnesses appearing before the judge or jury is not absolute. It must occasionally give way to considerations of public policy and the necessities of the case. *Thomas v. People*, 803 P.2d 144 (Colo. 1990).

The constitutional right of confrontation came into sharp focus in 1988, when the Supreme Court held that a defendant's Sixth Amendment right to confront witnesses was violated in a sexual abuse case in which the trial judge, pursuant to an Iowa law, allowed a screen to be erected between the defendant and the two thirteen-year-old girls that he was accused of assaulting. The two children were situated so they could not see the defendant during their testimony. *Coy v. Iowa*, 487 U.S. 1012, 108 S.Ct. 2798, 101 L.Ed.2d 857 (1988). The Court left open the question of whether a procedure that shields a child sex abuse victim may be constitutionally acceptable if there is an individualized finding that the witness is in need of such protection. Two years later, in *Maryland v. Craig*, 497 U.S. 836, 110 S.Ct. 3157, 111 L.Ed.2d 666 (1990), the Court held that the Confrontation Clause of the Sixth Amendment does not absolutely prohibit states from using one-way closed circuit television to receive a child's testimony in a case involving child abuse.

Since the Supreme Court's decision in *Coy*, several states have refined their **child shield statutes** affecting children who are victims of sexual abuse. These revised statutes have met with varying reactions from state appellate courts. However, one thing seems clear: to avoid the constitutional requirements of the Confrontation Clause, the prosecution must show and the trial judge must make particularized findings that a child victim of sexual abuse would suffer unreasonable and unnecessary mental or emotional harm if the child were to testify in the presence of the defendant. In view of the Supreme Court's March 8, 2004, decision in *Crawford v. Washington*, supra, requiring testimonial evidence to comport with the Sixth Amendment right of confrontation, the validity of child protective statutes may be subject to further review. Of course, *Crawford* focuses on out-of-court statements and arguably might not affect the in-court procedures addressed by child shield statutes.

It must be remembered that all evidence, whether from the prosecution or defense, must comport with the rules of evidence as previously outlined. When the prosecution rests its case, the next move is up to the defense.

The Defense Strategy in Moving for a Judgment of Acquittal

At the close of the prosecution's evidence, the defense counsel will frequently move the court to grant a **directed verdict** or, as it is called in federal courts and some state courts, a **judgment of acquittal.** The purpose of such a motion is to have the trial judge determine whether the evidence presented by the prosecution is legally sufficient to support a verdict of guilty. For the purpose of ruling on the motion, the trial judge must view the prosecution's evidence in the light most favorable to the government. The trial judge's authority to direct a verdict has long been recognized. *France v. United States*, 164 U.S. 676, 17 S.Ct. 219, 41 L.Ed. 595 (1897).

Should the motion be granted, the defendant is discharged. If, as in most cases, the motion is denied, defense counsel proceeds with the case on behalf of the defendant, and if additional evidence is offered, defense counsel may renew the motion at the close of the evidence. Federal appellate courts will not review the sufficiency of the evidence to support a verdict unless a motion for a judgment of acquittal was made at the close of all the evidence in the trial court. See, for example, *Corbin v. United States*, 253 F.2d 646 (10th Cir. 1958). This principle also prevails in many state appellate courts.

The Defense Case: Will the Defendant Take the Stand?

Under the Fifth Amendment, the defendant does not have to testify in a criminal case, and often defendants choose to rely simply on cross-examination of the government's witnesses in an effort to obtain an acquittal. Or the defendant may present witnesses in support of an alibi, to contradict the prosecution's witnesses, or to establish an affirmative defense (see Chapter 14).

Perhaps the major tactical decision a defendant and defense counsel must make at trial is whether the defendant will take the stand and testify on his or her behalf. The Fifth Amendment privilege against self-incrimination that applies to the states through the Fourteenth Amendment, *Malloy v. Hogan,* 378 U.S. 1, 84 S.Ct. 1489, 12 L.Ed.2d 653 (1964), protects the defendant from being required to testify, absent a grant of immunity. Moreover, it also forbids any direct or indirect comment by the prosecution on the accused's failure to testify. *Griffin v. California,* 380 U.S. 609, 85 S.Ct. 1229, 14 L.Ed.2d 106 (1965).

When an accused chooses to testify on his or her behalf, the prosecution may cross-examine the accused about his or her testimony with the same latitude as with any other witness. *Fitzpatrick v. United States,* 178 U.S. 304, 20 S.Ct. 944, 44 L.Ed. 1078 (1900). Moreover, even though illegally obtained evidence cannot be used to prove the government's case, in recent years it has been held that there is no federal constitutional prohibition that prevents the prosecution from using such evidence to impeach statements made by the defendant on cross-examination. *United States v. Havens,* 446 U.S. 620, 100 S.Ct. 1912, 64 L.Ed.2d 559 (1980); *Harris v. New York,* 401 U.S. 222, 91 S.Ct. 643, 28 L.Ed.2d 1 (1971). These realities must weigh heavily in a defendant's decision whether to testify because the threat of contradiction and impeachment always exists in cross-examination. Regardless of whether the defendant testifies, any witnesses presented by the defendant are subject to cross-examination by the prosecution.

The Rebuttals

At the conclusion of the defendant's case, the prosecution is entitled to present **rebuttal witnesses** to dispute the testimony of the defendant's witnesses. After examination by the prosecution and cross-examination by the defense counsel, the defense may then present its rebuttal witnesses. They, in turn, are subject to examination by the defense counsel and to cross-examination by the prosecutor. This usually concludes the evidentiary phase of the trial.

Conduct of the Jury during the Trial

The traditional role of the juror has been to attentively listen to the evidence as presented by the prosecution and defense, to avoid any outside influences, and to withhold judgment until all the evidence has been presented and the jury retires to deliberate. Most trial judges today allow jurors to take notes. In recent years trial courts have increasingly allowed jurors to submit questions to witnesses.

Historically judges have been reluctant to allow jurors to question witnesses in criminal trials. One principal concern has been that the questions may be improper, yet counsel may hesitate to object to a juror's question. In *United States v. Witt,* 215 F.2d 580 (2d Cir. 1954), the court said it was within the discretion of the trial judge to permit jurors to put questions to witnesses and receive answers. Other federal courts have allowed jurors to ask questions, but the practice has never been encouraged. In *United States v. Land,* 877 F.2d 17, 19 (8th Cir. 1989), the court noted that the practice of allowing jurors to submit questions to witnesses is "fraught with dangers which can undermine the orderly progress of the trial to verdict." Nevertheless, every federal circuit court and virtually every state appellate court that has considered this practice has permitted it. In *United States v. Richardson*, 233 F.3d 1285 (11th Cir. 2000), the U.S. Court of Appeals for the Eleventh Circuit rejected an appellant's claim that the trial judge's decision to allow jurors to submit questions to witnesses violated her right to a fair trial. The court, however, cautioned that "jurors should not be permitted to directly question a witness but rather should be required to submit their questions in writing to the trial judge, who should pose the questions to the witness in a neutral manner." 233 F.3d at 1290.

 Go to the Scheb/ Scheb Criminal Law and Procedure 6e website at academic .cengage.com/criminaljustice/ scheb to find *U.S. v. Richardson.*

Based on the premise that allowing juror questions in criminal cases would impact juror impartiality and relieve the prosecution of its burden of proof, the Minnesota Supreme Court recently held that no court shall permit jurors to question witnesses in a criminal trial. *State v. Costello*, 646 N.W.2d 204 (Minn. 2002). In *Coates v. State*, 855 So.2d 223 (Fla. App. 2003), the appellant contended that the trial court abused its discretion in allowing any jury questioning. He argued that allowing jurors to ask questions compels them to become advocates rather than neutral finders of fact. The appellate court, however, pointed out that the trial judge instructed the jurors to write out their questions and hand them to the bailiff. Jurors were then asked to leave the courtroom while the judge ruled on any objections by attorneys. Thereafter, the jury was returned to the courtroom and the judge asked the questions of the witness, with each attorney afforded an opportunity to ask follow-up questions. The court found the trial court had not abused its discretion in handling the questioning in such a controlled manner.

The Jury Instructions Conference

After all evidence has been presented in a jury trial, the trial judge customarily confers with counsel outside the presence of the jury concerning the instructions on the law that the judge will give to the jury. The prosecutor and defense counsel may be asked to present proposed instructions for the court to consider. More commonly, the trial judge announces that the court will give certain standard instructions and offers to supplement them with specific instructions to be chosen from those submitted by counsel. A defendant is entitled to have the jury instructed on the law applicable to any legitimate theory of defense that is supported by the evidence presented. See *United States v. Creamer*, 555 F.2d 612 (7th Cir. 1977). **Jury instructions** are settled in advance of closing arguments by counsel so that the prosecutor and defense counsel can present their arguments knowing how the judge will instruct the jury.

The Closing Arguments of Counsel

The Sixth Amendment guarantee of the right to assistance of counsel has been interpreted to include the right to present **closing arguments** in a criminal case, whether the case is tried before a jury or before a judge. *Herring v. New York*, 422 U.S. 853, 95 S.Ct. 2550, 45 L.Ed.2d 593 (1975). A defendant represented by counsel has no right to share the closing argument with his or her counsel, but if the defendant is *pro se*—that is, representing self—the court must allow the defendant to make a closing argument. *State v. Plaskonka*, 577 A.2d 729 (Conn. App. 1990). Although the constitutional guarantee accords the right of closing arguments to the defendant, by statute or rules of court the government and the defendant are each accorded the right for counsel to make closing arguments. The order of the arguments may be set by statute or court rule, but the trial judge retains control of the extent of the argument. The prosecutor usually argues first, followed by the defense counsel, with the prosecutor having an opportunity for a brief rebuttal.

Closing arguments are designed to assist the jury in recalling and evaluating the evidence and in drawing inferences therefrom. Many lawyers begin by recapitulating the evidence in the light most favorable to their client. After that, the arguments frequently become emotional, with each side entreating the jury to "do its duty" by either convicting or acquitting the defendant, arguing why the jury should by its interpretation of the evidence thereby either convict or acquit.

In closing arguments, counsel may comment on the weight of the evidence and the credibility of the witnesses, but it is improper for either the prosecutor or defense counsel to state a personal belief about the guilt or innocence of the accused. Likewise, it is improper for counsel to refer to any matters—other than those of common, everyday knowledge—that have not been introduced in evidence. Because a judge is trained in evaluating evidence, counsel in nonjury cases frequently waive their right to make closing arguments; otherwise, the arguments are generally quite brief.

Although prosecutors may use every legitimate method to obtain a conviction, a legion of appellate court opinions admonishes them to be fair and objective in their presentations to a jury. Characteristically, the Wisconsin Supreme Court observed that the prosecutor's role should be "to analyze the evidence and present facts with a reasonable interpretation to aid the jury in calmly and reasonably drawing just inferences and arriving at a just conclusion.... " *State v. Genova*, 8 N.W.2d 260, 263 (Wis. 1943).

Prosecutors are prohibited from making inflammatory remarks to the jury. If a prosecutor does make inflammatory remarks or statements that have no basis in the evidence or that can be interpreted as a comment on the defendant's failure to testify, the judge may admonish the prosecutor. Usually this is followed by a cautionary instruction directing the jury to disregard such remarks. If the defendant objects and the trial judge fails to take appropriate action, or if the prosecutor's remarks are so prejudicial that they cannot be erased from the minds of the jurors, the defendant may be able to obtain a mistrial or, if convicted, win a new trial from an appellate court.

Perhaps because the government cannot ordinarily appeal on the basis of improper comments by a defense counsel, the law seems to indulge a defendant in a somewhat wider latitude in jury arguments. Nevertheless, there are restraints, and sanctions for violations may take the form of an admonition by the trial judge or even disciplinary action where a defense lawyer's performance is egregious. Despite the fact that counsel must strive for acquittal of a client in our adversary system of justice, courts frequently remind defense lawyers that they, too, are officers of the court. Accordingly, they must aid in the administration of justice to the end that the lawful rights and privileges of the defendant are not violated. See, for example, *State v. Leaks*, 10 A.2d 281 (N.J. 1940).

The Judge Instructs the Jury

Typically, at the conclusion of the closing arguments the judge either reads the indictment or information or explains the charges against the defendant to the jury. This is followed by an admonition that the defendant is presumed innocent unless and until the government proves the defendant guilty of each element of the crime beyond a reasonable doubt. The judge defines the elements of any crime charged and explains any technical legal terms. Where applicable, the court generally instructs on an attempt to commit the crime charged as well. Where the jury may convict the defendant of a lesser offense, the judge must go further than merely defining the crime charged. For example, if the defendant is charged with first-degree murder, the judge must describe the lesser degrees of murder as well as manslaughter and excusable and justifiable homicide.

These instructions on the crimes may be followed by an explanation of any defenses pled by the defendant and the burden of proof, if any, on the defendant to sustain such defenses. A defendant is entitled to an instruction about any defense sustained by the evidence. On the request of the defendant, the judge usually informs the jury that it should not consider any inference of guilt because the defendant exercised the right not to testify. However, many defense lawyers prefer not to have the judge give this instruction.

The trial judge always explains to the jury that its role is to be the sole judge of the facts and advises the jury about some of the things it should consider in evaluating the credibility of the evidence presented. If expert witnesses have testified, the judge explains their role and informs the jury that it is free to accept or reject their opinions. In America, in contrast with the English practice, the trial judge generally is not permitted to summarize the evidence or express an opinion on the weight of that evidence or the credibility of the witnesses.

Rule 31(c) of the Federal Rules of Criminal Procedure provides,

> The defendant may be found guilty of an offense necessarily included in the offense charged or of an attempt to commit either the offense charged or of an offense necessarily included therein if the attempt is an offense in its own right.

A defendant is entitled to have the jury instructed on any lesser included offense whenever (1) the elements of the lesser offense are a subset of elements of the charged offense and (2) the evidence at trial is such that a jury could rationally find the defendant guilty of the lesser offense yet acquit the defendant of the greater offense. *Schmuck v. United States*, 489 U.S. 705, 109 S.Ct. 1443, 103 L.Ed.2d 734 (1989).

Practices in state courts vary in the extent to which the trial judge must instruct a jury on offenses that are lesser than the offense charged against a defendant. Some courts distinguish between those offenses that are necessarily included in the offense charged and those that may be included based on the allegations of the offense charged and the evidence presented at trial. In state courts, a defendant is generally entitled to an instruction of an offense of a less serious nature than the one charged if the elements of the charged offense can constitute the lesser crime. If the evidence is such that no rational jury could conclude the lesser offense was proper, however, then the trial court's refusal to give the lesser offense instruction is not necessarily considered a reversible error by most appellate courts. See, for example, *People v. Tucker*, 542 N.E.2d 804 (Ill. App. 1989).

In a few states, juries determine sentences. In these jurisdictions, the judge must also instruct the jury on the range of sentences permitted. In most states that have the death penalty, a jury trial in a capital case is bifurcated, with the jury first determining guilt or innocence. If the jury finds the defendant guilty, a second phase ensues, during which the jury hears evidence of aggravating and mitigating circumstances and determines whether the death penalty should be imposed (see Chapter 19).

The judge's instructions are given orally, and in some instances the jury is given a copy of the instructions. The clerk furnishes the jury forms of verdicts so they may find the defendant not guilty, guilty as charged, or guilty of some degree of the offense charged or of a lesser included offense. In federal criminal trials and in most state courts, the judge explains the requirement for a unanimous verdict. In some states, the judge is required to inform the jury of the penalties that can be imposed for the offense charged. Finally, the jury is directed to retire, select one of its members as **foreperson,** and deliberate on its verdict. Usually a jury is allowed to take with it to the jury room all exhibits received in evidence.

Improper Argument by a Prosecutor

Defendant Larry Witted was charged with attempted murder and armed robbery. At his jury trial, the chief issue was whether the victim had correctly identified the defendant as the person who robbed him. While the victim's testimony was positive, it was uncorroborated by any other evidence. During closing arguments, the defense counsel argued that the process used to identify the defendant as the perpetrator was unduly suggestive. In rebuttal, the prosecutor implied that witnesses for the defense had perjured themselves at the request of defense counsel and that the defendant had a criminal background that the defense was hiding from the jury. Because the prosecutor's remarks were made during his rebuttal closing argument, the defense had no opportunity to challenge the inferences that were made. Witted was convicted, but the court awarded him a new trial, citing the prosecutor's misconduct during closing arguments.

People v. Witted, 398 N.E.2d 68 (Ill. App. 1979).

The Jury Deliberates and Returns Its Verdict

When directed to deliberate, the jurors are escorted to their quarters by a court bailiff. In some cases, the judge orders the jury sequestered, which means the jury must remain together until it reaches its verdict. **Sequestration** often requires the bailiff to escort the jurors to a hotel and to be present with them during meals to ensure that no outside influences are brought to bear on their judgment. Once in the jury room, the jurors' first order of business is to elect a foreperson. Then they are ready to commence their deliberations.

Because jury deliberations are secret, we can only speculate about the reasoning processes of jurors. However, we do know that juries usually take a preliminary vote shortly after electing a foreperson. In most cases, the jury probably arrives at its verdict without much discussion. In the famous "Monkey Trial" of John Scopes in Dayton, Tennessee, in 1925, the jury deliberated only eight minutes before convicting Scopes of unlawfully teaching the theory of evolution in his high school biology class. More recently, in the O. J. Simpson case the jury returned its verdict of not guilty after only four hours. In other instances, jurors may deliberate for hours or days, and many votes may be taken. In the murder trial of Charles Manson in 1971, the jury deliberated about forty-two hours.

The Deadlocked Jury

Sometimes juries become "hung"—that is, they cannot agree on a verdict. This was illustrated in 1988, when a young man was tried in New York City for allegedly strangling a young woman in Central Park. The so-called "yuppie murder case" drew national attention, partly because the testimony revealed that the victim's death resulted from "a rough sexual encounter" between the defendant and the victim. After a twelve-week trial, a panel of eight men and four women deliberated for nine days. They then sent a note to the judge saying they had reached an impasse. At that point, in a desire to conclude the proceedings—and perhaps rather than risk another trial—the defendant entered a negotiated plea of guilty to manslaughter, a lesser offense than that charged.

If a jury reports that it is a **deadlocked jury,** the trial judge can either declare a mistrial or urge the jury to make further attempts to arrive at a verdict. One tool that both federal and state trial judges sometimes employ is to give the jury a supplemental instruction called an ***Allen* charge.** The instruction takes its name from an opinion issued by the Supreme Court at the turn of the century, *Allen v. United States,* 164 U.S. 492, 17 S.Ct. 154, 41 L.Ed. 528 (1896). A number of modifications have been made to the original *Allen* charge, but the basic thrust remains to urge

> that if much the larger number were for conviction, a dissenting juror should consider whether his doubt was a reasonable one.... If, upon the other hand, the majority were for acquittal, the minority ought to ask themselves whether they might not reasonably doubt the correctness of a judgment that was not concurred in by the majority. 164 U.S. at 501, 17 S.Ct. at 157, 41 L.Ed. at 531.

In Colorado the *Allen* charge is called "the third-degree instruction," and New Mexico courts have referred to it as the "shotgun instruction." *Leech v. People,* 146 P.2d 346, 347 (Colo. 1944); *State v. Nelson,* 321 P.2d 202, 204 (N.M. 1958).

The use of the *Allen* charge in its original or in its many modified forms has been criticized as having a coercive effect for implying that the majority view is the correct one and for importuning the minority to change their views. In a few states, the state supreme court has banned its use. See, for example, *State v. Randall,* 353 P.2d 1054 (Mont. 1960). Nevertheless, federal and most state courts have generally approved the use of some version of the instruction when it has been cautiously given. See, for example, *Benscoter v. United States,* 376 F.2d 49 (10th Cir. 1967).

Jury Pardons

At times, juries disregard the evidence and the judge's instructions on the law and acquit a defendant or convict the defendant for a lesser offense than charged. This is referred to as **jury nullification** or as granting the defendant a **jury pardon.** Jurors, of course, take an oath to follow the law as charged by the judge and are expected to do so. *United States v. Powell,* 469 U.S. 57, 105 S.Ct. 471, 83 L.Ed.2d 461 (1984). But it is also recognized that a jury has the prerogative to exercise its judgment and bring in a verdict of not guilty or guilty of a lesser offense.

CASE-IN-POINT

Factors Considered in Approving a Trial Court's Use of the *Allen* Charge Where the Jury Is Deadlocked

Defendant Lindel and others were charged in U.S. District Court with thirty-five counts of various crimes stemming from a marijuana importation scheme. They were convicted on several counts and then appealed. Among their points on appeal, the defendants contended that when the jury sent notes that it was hopelessly deadlocked, the trial court should have declared a mistrial instead of giving an *Allen* charge to the jury. In rejecting the defendants' challenge, the U.S. Court of Appeals for the Fifth Circuit first noted that the language in the judge's charge to the jury comported with the modified *Allen*

charge language repeatedly approved. Then the court pointed out that the trial lasted for three weeks, that the verdict was a discriminating one returning both guilty and not guilty verdicts on the various counts, that in giving the *Allen* charge the judge did not set a deadline on deliberations, and that the verdict was not returned until two days after the *Allen* charge was given. Considering these factors, the court found no abuse of discretion in the trial judge's having given the charge, and after rejecting other points raised by the defendants, the court of appeals affirmed the defendants' convictions.

United States v. Lindel, 881 F.2d 1313 (5th Cir. 1989).

In death penalty cases, there has been explicit recognition of the principle. For instance, in *Beck v. Alabama,* 447 U.S. 625, 100 S.Ct. 2382, 65 L.Ed.2d 392 (1980), the Supreme Court held that the death penalty may not be imposed if the jury is not permitted to consider a verdict of guilt of a lesser included noncapital offense when the evidence would have supported such a verdict. The Court explained that "the nearly universal acceptance of the rule in state and federal courts establishes the value to the defendant of this procedural safeguard." 447 U.S. at 637, 100 S.Ct. at 2389, 65 L.Ed.2d at 402.

In trials for noncapital offenses, the reality of jury nullification exists, but there is no requirement for a judge to inform the jury of that power. See, for example, *United States v. Dougherty,* 473 F.2d 1113 (D.C. Cir. 1972). Acquittals by juries are not subject to appeal, so it is difficult to know when jury nullification occurs, but undoubtedly some defendants are acquitted or convicted of lesser offenses as a result of a jury pardon. In *United States v. Dougherty,* the court in footnote 33 cites a number of examples taken from a study undertaken at the University of Chicago Law School of the types of cases in which a jury voted to acquit because of its empathy with the defendant. The examples mentioned include statutory rape of a promiscuous female, sale of liquor to a minor who is a member of the armed forces, and violence erupting after domestic strife.

The Verdict

As we pointed out earlier in this chapter, the Sixth Amendment to the U.S. Constitution requires a unanimous **verdict** in federal cases. *Andres v. United States,* 333 U.S. 740, 68 S.Ct. 880, 92 L.Ed. 1055 (1948); see also Fed. R. Crim. P. 31(a). A few states permit a less than unanimous verdict in criminal cases. State constitutional and statutory provisions that authorize a less than unanimous verdict by a twelve-person jury have been held not to violate the federal constitution, *Johnson v. Louisiana,* supra, although verdicts by six-person juries must be unanimous, *Burch v. Louisiana,* supra.

When a jury has concluded its deliberations, it returns to the courtroom and delivers its written verdict. The verdict is usually first handed to the judge, who reviews it to determine whether it is in proper form. If it is, the judge hands the verdict to the clerk or jury foreperson to be read aloud in open court. A defendant who is acquitted by a jury is immediately discharged. If a jury finds the defendant guilty, the defendant is generally taken into custody to await sentencing. In some instances, the defendant may be continued on bail, pending application for a new trial or an appeal. We discuss sentencing and appellate procedures in Chapters 19 and 20, respectively.

Polling the Jury

After a verdict has been read, the court or any party may have the jury polled individually. The clerk or judge handles **polling the jury** by asking each juror, "Is this your verdict?" or words to that effect. In most cases, each juror responds affirmatively and the jury is discharged. If, on the other hand, a juror expresses dissent from the verdict, the trial judge may either direct the jury to retire for further deliberation or discharge the jury. See *People v. Kellogg,* 397 N.E.2d 835 (Ill. 1979).

Posttrial Motions

A convicted defendant may, and frequently does, file a **motion for a new trial,** alleging that errors were committed at trial. This type of motion affords the trial judge an opportunity to rectify errors by awarding the defendant a new trial. In most instances, however, it is a *pro forma* prelude to an appeal and is denied by the trial court. A defendant may also seek bail pending appeal (see Chapter 20). When the court disposes of these motions, the process moves into sentencing (see Chapter 19).

■ CONCLUSION

Despite the relatively small percentage of criminal cases that go to trial, the criminal trial remains a vital part of the criminal justice system. Adjudications at trial set the overall tone for the administration of the criminal law in the community. Jury verdicts become "weather vanes" of the public's attitude on the enforcement of the law.

Criminal trials also have an important bearing on the reshaping of both the statutory and decisional law in light of contemporary community values. With counsel now readily available to indigent defendants for handling their appeals as well as for representation at trial, appellate courts have the opportunity to update precedents and refine trial court procedures based on present constitutional standards.

Court procedures are slow to change, but changes are occurring and will continue into the future. Scientific evidence now plays a more important role in criminal trials, especially in sexual assaults, homicide offenses, and offenses involving intoxication. With the emphasis on DNA testing, that role will become very significant. Increasingly, videotapes and other photographic means are being used to present evidence at trials. With the increased emphasis on efficiency, state legislative bodies and courts may soon find it advisable to reexamine the need for a jury of twelve persons as well as the traditional requirement for a unanimous verdict.

The increased criminal caseload in the federal and state courts can be alleviated to a considerable extent by the decriminalization of most traffic offenses, further institution of drug courts, and resort to pretrial diversionary programs for first offenders charged with misdemeanor or, in some instances, nonviolent felony offenses.

In contrast with our earlier history, most jurors today are well educated. They respond favorably when the trial judge, at the inception of a trial, gives a basic orientation on the standard of proof and definition of crimes and an explanation of the trial procedures that are about to take place. This initial orientation is especially useful because the trial judge's jury instructions given just before the jury retires to deliberate on the verdict are often lengthy and complex. Modern technology makes it feasible for the trial judge's instructions on the law to be recorded and copies handed to the jury before it commences deliberations.

Despite changes, the basic function of the criminal trial by a jury of one's peers will remain. It must because it is not only each citizen's protection against overzealous law enforcement and prosecutions; it also ensures the public that no defendant will gain preferred status by virtue of prominence or be dealt with unfairly because of lowly status.

■ KEY TERMS

open public trial, 496
jury trial, 497
bench trial, 497
standby counsel, 499
venire, 500
voir dire, 500
challenges for cause, 500
death qualification of a jury, 501
peremptory challenges, 501

racially based peremptory
   challenges, 502
gender-based peremptory
   challenges, 503
power of contempt, 507
judicial notice, 509
proof beyond a reasonable doubt, 510
evidentiary presumptions, 510
similar fact evidence, 511

◼ WEB-BASED RESEARCH ACTIVITY

Go to the Court TV website at http://www.courtv.com. Follow Court TV's coverage of a current trial. Write a memorandum to your instructor summarizing the major factual and legal issues before the court.

◼ QUESTIONS FOR THOUGHT AND DISCUSSION

1. Jurors are generally selected from among those citizens who have registered to vote or who have registered motor vehicles. Do these methods produce juries drawn from a "representative cross-section of the community"? Can you suggest a better way of selecting jurors?

2. In England, the *voir dire* process is conducted by the trial judge and is extremely limited. Do you think the American system of criminal justice would have more credibility if the *voir dire* were conducted exclusively by the judge, with only challenges for cause permitted? Explain your view.

3. What factors do you think a defense attorney considers in deciding whether to advise a client to testify in his or her own behalf at trial?

4. In 1965 Justice Tom Clark, writing for the Supreme Court in *Estes v. Texas,* observed that "[t]rial by television is … foreign to our system." Evaluate Justice Clark's statement in view of contemporary attitudes toward communications technology.

5. Many rules of evidence applied in jury trials are derived from the early common law, when jurors were largely uneducated. These rules were designed to prevent jurors from hearing evidence that might prejudice their judgment in the case. Given the educational standards in the United States, should these rules be made less restrictive regarding evidence that can be presented in courts? What

constitutional problems would arise by allowing hearsay evidence to be presented against a defendant?

6. What testimonial privileges are available to witnesses in your state? What is the rationale for each?

7. Do you think a trial judge should be allowed to summarize the evidence for the jury's benefit before the jurors retire to deliberate? What advantages and disadvantages can you see in such a practice? Would it be constitutional?

8. In some jurisdictions, a judge instructs the jury regarding its general duties and responsibilities at the beginning of the trial rather than waiting until the evidence has been presented. Do you favor this approach? Why or why not?

9. Do you think that the trial judge should inform a jury that it has the power to issue a jury pardon despite the evidence of the defendant's guilt when the jury feels that in "good conscience" the defendant should not be convicted of the crime charged or any lesser crime supported by the evidence at trial? Give reasons for your view.

10. The Supreme Court has said that state criminal trial juries need not observe the unanimity principle that prevails in the federal courts. Could it not be argued that the reasonable doubt standard necessarily entails the unanimity principle, as the doubt of one juror is sufficient to suggest a reasonable doubt about the guilt of the accused?

▪ PROBLEMS FOR DISCUSSION AND SOLUTION

1. A defendant is tried before a jury on a DWI charge. At the conclusion of the trial the judge instructs the jury: "If you find from the evidence that the defendant had a blood-alcohol content of .10, you may presume she was intoxicated." Should the defendant's attorney object to this instruction? On what basis?

2. A defendant is being tried for first-degree murder. The prosecutor presents an eyewitness to the victim's being shot. After asking the witness some preliminary questions, the prosecutor begins a question with, "When the defendant shot and killed the victim …" Should the defense attorney pose an objection to this question? On what ground?

3. In response to the prosecutor's questions, a lay witness who is a high school graduate testifies as follows: "I measured the defendant's skid marks, and I believe he was driving at a speed of at least 65 miles per hour." "In my opinion, anyone who drinks two beers becomes intoxicated." "When I saw the defendant right after the accident, his face appeared flushed and he staggered as he walked." "My sister told me that the defendant did a lot of drinking at the nearby bar." What objections should the defense make to each one of the witness's statements?

4. Luke Lumberjack is being tried for raping a woman he has known for a year. The state's evidence disclosed that Lumberjack, age twenty-three, had spent an evening with the female complainant, age twenty-one. Afterward, at his invitation, they went to his apartment and had a few beers. The complainant testified that Lumberjack, a large, husky male, forced her to have sex with him, despite her stated unwillingness. During cross-examination, the complainant admitted having once before had a consensual sexual relationship with the defendant. During the state's closing argument, in referring to the defendant, the prosecutor told the jury, "This big hunk of cruelty is an animal, one who must be put away to protect the young women of this community. It's important to do your

duty by convicting him to send a message to the community." Defense counsel objected on the ground that the prosecutor's comments were inflammatory, prejudicial, and unfair. He requested that the trial judge strike the prosecutor's comments, inform the jury that they should be disregarded, and admonish the prosecutor for having made such statements. What do you think the trial judge's ruling should be?

CHAPTER **19**

Sentencing and Punishment

CHAPTER OUTLINE

Introduction

The concept of criminal punishment is an ancient one. The Code of Hammurabi, promulgated in Babylonia nearly two thousand years before the birth of Christ, contained a detailed schedule of crimes and punishments and first codified the notion of "an eye for an eye." In a similar vein, the Old Testament mandated severe but proportionate punishment based on this principle of **retribution.**

While it is sometimes equated with legalized vengeance, the concept of retribution was a great leap forward in the evolution of criminal punishment. It replaced the personal or familial (and often excessive) acts of vengeance that frequently followed injuries to persons or property. Moreover, retribution carried with it a sense of **proportionality,** which continues to have relevance in criminal sentencing today.

Most ancient legal systems prescribed severe punishments for those who committed the kinds of acts we now consider *mala in se*. Execution, torture, mutilation, and banishment from the community were not uncommon. But ancient legal systems also employed economic sanctions such as forfeiture of property, especially when members of the upper classes committed transgressions against members of the lower classes.

The Common-Law Background

By contemporary standards, the English common law was quite severe—the death penalty was prescribed for most felonies. In the early days of the common law, nobles who committed **capital crimes** were shown mercy by simply being beheaded. Commoners who were sentenced to death were often subjected to more grisly forms of punishment—they were broken on the wheel, burned at the stake, or drawn and quartered. Eventually, the comparatively humane method of hanging was adopted as the principal means of execution in England.

Persons convicted of misdemeanors were generally subjected to nonlethal **corporal punishment** such as flogging. The misdemeanant was taken into the public square, bound to the whipping post, and administered as many lashes as were prescribed by law for the offense.

In England—indeed, throughout Europe—the administration of punishment was intentionally a matter of public spectacle. The idea was that public display of painful and humiliating punishment would deter others from engaging in criminal acts. This theory, known as **general deterrence,** is still prevalent today.

During the colonization of the New World, English subjects convicted of misdemeanors were often sent to penal colonies in America to do hard labor. After the American Revolution, they were sent to Australia.

The American Experience

In colonial America, criminal punishment followed common-law practice, although the Massachusetts Code of 1648 mandated capital punishment in cases of idolatry, witchcraft, blasphemy, sodomy, adultery, and "man stealing," as well as for the common-law capital crimes. At the time of the American Revolution, the death penalty was in wide use for a variety of felonies. And corporal punishment, primarily flogging, was widely used for a variety of crimes, including many misdemeanors.

The American Bill of Rights, ratified in 1791, prohibited the imposition of "cruel and unusual punishments." The framers of the Bill of Rights sought to prevent the use of torture, which had been common in Europe as late as the eighteenth century. However, they did not intend to outlaw the death penalty, nor did they intend to abolish all forms of corporal punishment.

During the nineteenth century, reformers introduced the concept of the penitentiary—literally, "a place to do penance." The idea was that criminals could be reformed through isolation, Bible study, and hard labor. This gave rise to the notion of **rehabilitation,** the idea that the criminal justice system could reform criminals and reintegrate them into society. Many of the educational, occupational training, and psychological programs found in modern prisons are based on this theory.

By the twentieth century, **incarceration** replaced corporal punishment as the mainstay of criminal sentencing. All states, as well as the federal government, constructed prisons to house persons convicted of felonies. Even cities and counties constructed jails to confine persons convicted of misdemeanors. However, the **death penalty** remained in wide use for the most serious violent felonies. But it was rendered more "humane" as the gallows were replaced by the firing squad, the gas chamber, the electric chair, and, eventually, lethal injection. The death penalty remains in effect today in more than half the states, although its use is now limited to the most aggravated cases of murder. Yet it remains one of the most intensely controversial aspects of the American system of criminal justice.

Today the focus of criminal punishment is on the goal of **incapacitation.** Incapacitation means that offenders are prevented from committing further criminal acts. In ancient societies, banishment was sometimes used to protect the community from those whose presence was regarded as unduly threatening. Contemporary American society resorts to imprisonment or, in extreme cases, execution to rid itself of seriously threatening behavior. Although nearly everyone favors incapacitation of violent offenders, in practice incapacitation extends beyond execution or incarceration. When a state revokes a person's driver's license for driving while intoxicated, the purpose is primarily incapacitation. Similarly, some states have laws offering convicted rapists the option of taking a drug to render them incapable of committing rape. Other forms of incapacitation can be extremely controversial. For example, may a judge order a convicted child abuser to refrain from having any more children to prevent future child abuse?

Those who favor incapacitation to the exclusion of the other purposes of punishment are likely to favor harsh sentences, even for relatively minor crimes. They prefer to "lock 'em up and throw away the key." Again, we must consider the issue of proportionality: Crime control is not the only goal of the criminal justice system—dispensing justice is equally important.

Legal Constraints on Sentencing and Punishment

There are procedural as well as substantive issues in the area of sentencing and punishment. Sharp disagreements exist regarding the roles that legislatures, judges, and corrections officials should play in determining punishments. Generally, judges are required to impose sentences that fall within the parameters of appropriate punishment specified by statute, yet within these parameters, courts exercise substantial discretion. Recent concern about sentencing disparities has resulted in a variety of measures aimed at reducing the range of judicial discretion in sentencing.

Just as judges' sentencing decisions are constrained by statutes, statutory penalties must comport with substantive and procedural requirements imposed by the federal and state constitutions. Specifically, criminal punishment is limited by the Eighth Amendment prohibition of cruel and unusual punishments, the Due Process Clauses of the Fifth and Fourteenth Amendments, and similar provisions in all fifty state constitutions. Recent judicial activity in the areas of sentencing and punishment has focused on the need for procedural regularity in sentencing and proportionality in punishment.

Contemporary Forms of Criminal Punishment

Today the criminal law provides for a variety of criminal punishments, including monetary fines, incarceration, probation, community service, and, of course, the death penalty. Although most people agree about the propriety of punishing criminal behavior, they disagree about the legality, morality, and efficacy of specific modes of criminal punishment. The death penalty in particular remains a hotly debated issue.

Fines

By far the most common form of criminal punishment today is the **monetary fine.** Most misdemeanors carry monetary fines, especially for first offenses. Some felonies, especially serious economic crimes defined by federal law, carry heavy monetary fines as penalties. For example, offenses against federal banking laws and securities and exchange laws are punishable by fines reaching into the millions of dollars. Increasingly, drug trafficking offenders are being punished by large fines.

In many states, a court can sentence a defendant to pay a fine in addition to a sentence of imprisonment or probation. In New Jersey, for example, such fines may range from $500 to $200,000, depending on the nature and degree of the offense. N.J. Stat. Ann. 2C: 43–3. Fines might be appropriate devices of retribution and deterrence for economic crimes, but they hardly seem suitable as punishments for criminal acts of violence. And many have questioned the fairness and effectiveness of established minimum and maximum fines that do not consider the economic circumstances of individual defendants.

Forfeiture of Property

Federal law provides for **forfeiture** of the proceeds of a variety of criminal activities. See, generally, 18 U.S.C.A. §§ 981–982. More controversial are the federal law provisions allowing forfeiture of property used in illicit drug activity. Under federal law, a "conveyance," which includes aircraft, motor vehicles, and vessels, is subject to forfeiture if it is used to transport controlled substances. 21 U.S.C.A. § 881(a)(4). Real estate may be forfeited if it is used to commit or facilitate commission of a drug-related felony. 21 U.S.C.A. § 881(a)(7). Many states have similar statutes. See, for example, Oklahoma's Uniform Controlled Dangerous Substances Act, 63 Okl. St. Ann. § 2–503. State courts dealing with forfeiture under state law generally review forfeitures under the "excessive fines" provisions of their state constitutions. See, for example, *In re King Properties*, 635 A.2d 128 (Pa. 1993), where the court found that forfeiture of a house used as a base of operations in an ongoing drug business was not excessive. Where a state constitutional provision exempts a homestead from forced sale, courts generally hold that it also prohibits civil or criminal forfeiture of homestead property. See, for example, *Butterworth v. Caggiano*, 605 So.2d 56 (Fla. 1992). However, a federal appeals court has ruled that federal law preempts—that is, overrides—state homestead exemptions when federal crimes have been committed. *United States v. Lot 5, Fox Grove, Alachua County, Fla.*, 23 F.3d 359 (11th Cir. 1994).

As we pointed out in Chapter 9, asset forfeiture may be accomplished through civil or criminal proceedings. In *Austin v. United States*, 509 U.S. 602, 113 S.Ct. 2801,

125 L.Ed.2d 488 (1993), the Supreme Court said that civil forfeiture "constitutes 'payment to a sovereign as punishment for some offense' … and, as such, is subject to the limitations of the Eighth Amendment's Excessive Fines Clause." 509 U.S. at 622, 113 S.Ct. at 2812, 125 L.Ed.2d at 505. However, the Court left it to state and lower federal courts to determine the tests of "excessiveness" in the context of forfeiture. In 1994 the Illinois Supreme Court said that three factors should be considered in this regard: (1) the gravity of the offense relative to the value of the forfeiture, (2) whether the property was an integral part of the illicit activity, and (3) whether illicit activity involving the property was extensive. *Waller v. 1989 Ford F350 Truck (Kusumoto),* 642 N.E.2d 460 (Ill. 1994).

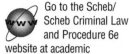

Go to the Scheb/ Scheb Criminal Law and Procedure 6e website at academic .cengage.com/criminaljustice/ scheb for an edited version of *Austin v. U.S.*

Incarceration

Confinement is generally regarded as the only effective way to deal with violent offenders. Although some question the efficacy of the prison, regarding it as little more than a factory for producing future criminals, incarceration does protect society from dangerous offenders. Prison is an effective incapacitator; it is rarely an effective rehabilitator. In fact, serving time in prison often reinforces criminal tendencies.

Today nearly 2.7 million inmates are housed in federal and state prisons or local jails. According to a press release issued by the U.S. Bureau of Justice Statistics (BJS) on October 23, 2005,

> As of December 31, 2004, there were 2,267,787 people behind bars in the United States, of which 1,421,911 were held in federal and state prisons (not including the 74,378 state and federal inmates incarcerated in local jails), 713,990 in local jails, 102,338 in juvenile facilities, 15,757 in U.S. Territory prisons, 9,788 in Bureau of Immigration and Customs Enforcement facilities, 2,177 in military prisons and 1,826 in Indian country jails (as of June 30, 2003).

The BJS press release also reported that the national "incarceration rate rose from 411 sentenced inmates per 100,000 U.S. residents in 1995 to 486 inmates per 100,000 at the end of [2004]—an 18 percent increase." For additional information, see Bureau of Justice Statistics, "Prisoners in 2004" (NCJ-210677), online at www .ojp.usdoj.gov/bjs/abstract/p04.htm.

Although the increase in the national incarceration rate has slowed somewhat since 2004, most state prisons are operating at or just below capacity. The federal system continues to operate well above its designed capacity. This problem has led to judicial intervention in many instances, yet society appears reluctant to provide additional resources to expand prison capacity. Imprisonment is expensive, costing taxpayers nearly $20 billion per year.

As criminologists have become increasingly dissatisfied with the effects of the prison system, judges have responded by imposing limits on prison populations and scrutinizing the conditions of confinement. Meanwhile, fiscal pressures prevent legislatures from appropriating the funds necessary to construct more prisons. Accordingly, attention has shifted to alternatives to incarceration, especially for less dangerous offenders. One of the most serious criticisms of all such alternatives emphasizes the difficulty of determining who should be eligible for an alternative form of punishment. In an age of overcrowded prisons, alternative punishments carry the real possibility that truly dangerous offenders will not be sufficiently controlled.

The Boot Camp: An Alternative to Prison?

One alternative to the traditional prison setting is the **boot camp,** a program designed to employ a system of discipline much like the one the military uses to instill discipline in its recruits. In early 1993, the American Correctional Association counted sixty-five adult boot camps in twenty-seven states and nineteen juvenile camps in eight states. The inmates are generally young, nonviolent offenders who have committed theft, burglary, forgery, and other nonviolent offenses, often brought about by their drug abuse. In lieu of a prison sentence, they elect to undergo three to six months of training that often includes drug rehabilitation and repairing roads and other public facilities. Ideally, their stint in boot camp is followed by a period of supervised probation. In addition to boot camps being less costly than traditional methods of incarceration, communities gain from the labor performed by the inmates, and their early release conserves financial resources essential to operating regular prisons.

The results of the boot camp experience have been somewhat disappointing. According to *Correctional Boot Camps: Lessons from a Decade of Research,* a report released in June 2003 by the Department of Justice, boot camps proliferated in the 1980s and early1990s, but by the mid-1990s their number declined and by 2000 only 51 camps remained. The report concluded that boot camps produced mixed results. Some short-term changes in behavior were realized but, with few exceptions, boot camps did little to reduce recidivism, in part because of insufficient focus on the offender's reentry into the community.

In January 2006, a fourteen-year-old boy died after being roughed up by guards at a sheriff's boot camp in Panama City, Florida. The boy's death led to the dismantling of the Florida boot camp program. After a lengthy investigation, in November 2006 the State charged seven former guards and a nurse at the facility with manslaughter arising out of the incident. The incident gave more impetus to criticism of boot camps nationwide, and it now appears that the national boot camp experiment is coming to an end.

Probation

Of the various alternatives to incarceration, **probation** is by far the most common. According to a November 2, 2005, press release from the federal Bureau of Justice Statistics, more than 4.1 million adult men and women were under federal, state, or local probation at the end of 2004.

An outgrowth of nineteenth and twentieth century developments in criminal justice, probation is the conditional release of a convicted offender by a trial court. If prisons have become little more than factories for producing future criminals, then probation seems to be a viable alternative to prison terms, especially for non-violent, first-time offenders. The primary purpose of probation is to rehabilitate the defendant. Thus, the defendant is released under the supervision of a probation officer, who is responsible to the court for making sure that the offender abides by the **conditions of probation.**

The mandatory and discretionary conditions for probation for federal offenses are set out in 18 U.S.C.A. § 3563. By 1967 all states provided for probation, often varying in the offenses and defendants eligible. State laws generally provide for certain mandatory conditions. A sentencing judge is afforded broad discretion in formulating additional conditions of a defendant's probation. Certain conditions are relatively standard, for example, that the probationer will not commit further crimes, will avoid certain persons or places, will maintain gainful employment and support any dependents, and will not travel outside the court's jurisdiction without permission of the court or probation officer. The sentencing judge, however, can tailor additional conditions to the defendant's rehabilitation, even to the extent of imposing conditions that infringe a probationer's constitutional rights, including First Amendment rights of free speech and association, as long as those conditions are related to the goal of rehabilitation. *Malone v. United States,* 502 F.2d 554 (9th Cir. 1974); *Porth v. Templar,* 453 F.2d 330 (10th Cir. 1971).

Conditions of Probation

In 1990 the Supreme Court of Ohio reviewed the conviction of a defendant on a charge of contributing to the delinquency of a child by furnishing alcohol to three young boys. The court focused on a single point: whether the trial court abused its discretion in imposing a condition of probation stipulating that the defendant "have no association or communication, direct or indirect, with anyone under the age of 18 years not a member of his immediate family." The court noted that while a trial judge is granted broad discretion in setting conditions of probation, that discretion is not limitless, and courts must guard against overly broad conditions that impinge upon the probationer's liberty. Nevertheless, the court found the restriction imposed against the defendant "reasonably related to rehabilitating [the defendant] without being unduly restrictive." Citing various state and federal authorities, the court said that in setting conditions of probation, trial judges should consider whether a condition to be imposed (1) is reasonably related to rehabilitating the offender, (2) has some relationship to the crime for which the offender was convicted, and (3) relates to conduct that is criminal or reasonably related to future criminality.

State v. Jones, 550 N.E.2d 469 (Ohio 1990).

The U.S. Supreme Court has had little to say on the subject of probation since mentioning that probation conditions must serve "the ends of justice and the best interest of both the public and the defendant." *Burns v. United States,* 287 U.S. 216, 220, 53 S.Ct. 154, 156, 77 L.Ed.266, 268 (1932). In *Higdon v. United States,* 627 F.2d 893 (9th Cir. 1980), a leading federal decision, the court noted, "The only factors which the trial judge should consider when deciding whether to grant probation are the appropriateness and attainability of rehabilitation and the need to protect the public by imposing conditions which control the probationer's activities." *Id.* at 897. The court fashioned a two-step process for reviewing conditions of probation. The court first determines whether the conditions are permissible, and if so, it then looks to whether there is a reasonable relationship between the conditions imposed and the purpose of the probation.

Most probationary sentences are imposed by state courts, which frequently cite *People v. Dominguez,* 64 Cal. Rptr. 290 (Cal. App. 1967), as the standard for judging the reasonableness of conditions of probation. There the court established that a condition of probation that (1) has no relationship to the crime of which the offender was convicted, (2) relates to conduct which is not in itself criminal, and (3) requires or forbids conduct which is not reasonably related to future criminality does not serve the ends of probation and is invalid. *Id.* at 293. In *Dominguez,* the court reasoned that a condition that the probationer not become pregnant without being married was unrelated to her offense or to future criminality and thus was invalid.

Because most probationers are grateful to receive a probationary sentence and avoid incarceration, constitutional challenges to conditions are not too common. Nevertheless, some courts that have reviewed such conditions have ruled there are limits to probation conditions. In *Biller v. State,* 618 So.2d 734 (Fla. 1993), the Florida Supreme Court invalidated a probation order that required the probationer to refrain from using or possessing alcoholic beverages. The court pointed out that nothing in the record showed any connection between alcohol consumption and the weapons violation of which the probationer had been convicted.

In *Commonwealth v. LaFrance,* 525 N.E.2d 379 (Mass. 1988), the Supreme Judicial Court of Massachusetts invalidated a condition of probation that required the defendant to submit to a search of herself, her possessions, and any place where she may be, with or without a search warrant, on request of a probation officer. Although the court determined that condition violated the defendant's rights, the court suggested that the following condition could be substituted: "On the basis of a reasonable suspicion that a condition of the probationer's probation has been violated, a probation officer, or any law enforcement officer acting on the request of the probation office, may search the probationer, her property, her residence, and any place where she may be living, and may do so with or without a search warrant depending on the requirements of law." *Id.* at 383.

Courts tend to scrutinize conditions that restrict such fundamental rights as procreation. A Florida appellate court held that although a condition of probation prohibiting custody of children had a clear relationship to the crime of child abuse and was valid, conditions prohibiting marriage and pregnancy nevertheless added nothing to decrease the possibility of further child abuse and were found to be invalid. *Rodriguez v. State,* 378 So.2d 7 (Fla. App. 1979). Three years later, the same court struck down a condition of probation that required that the defendant "must not father any children during [the] probation period." *Burchell v. State,* 419 So.2d 358 (Fla. App. 1982). In *State v. Mosburg,* 768 P.2d 313 (Kan. App. 1989), the court held that a probation condition requiring a defendant who was convicted of endangering a child to refrain from becoming pregnant during the term of probation unduly intruded on the defendant's right to privacy. At a time when some in society equated long hair with unacceptable behavior, in *Inman v. State,* 183 S.E.2d 413 (Ga. App. 1971), a Georgia appellate court held invalid a condition of probation that required a male defendant to maintain a short haircut as not related to his rehabilitation and therefore unconstitutionally invasive of his right of self-expression. (Interestingly, the court observed that its State Judicial Building contains busts of three eminent justices with magnificent, shoulder-length locks).

Different factual scenarios can result in different judicial approaches and reach different conclusions. Consider the recent approach of the Wisconsin Supreme Court. In *State v. Oakley,* 629 N.W.2d 2001 (Wis. 2001), David Oakley, the father of nine children, pled no contest to intentionally refusing to provide child support. The trial judge placed him on probation to enable him to make meaningful payments of support that would not be possible if he was incarcerated. As a condition of Oakley's probation, the judge stipulated, "Oakley cannot father any additional children unless he can demonstrate that he has the financial ability to support them, and that he is supporting the children he has." *Id.* at 203. In rejecting his challenge based on his constitutional right to procreate, the court pointed out that Wisconsin law grants judges broad discretion in fashioning probation conditions and concluded, "[B]ecause Oakley can satisfy this condition by not intentionally refusing to support his current nine children and any future children required by the law, we find that the condition is narrowly tailored to serve the State's compelling interest of having parents support their children." *Id.* at 212.

Conditions of probation recently imposed on offenders convicted of child pornography offenses have included some innovative approaches. In *United States v. Zinn,* 321 F.3d 1084 (11th Cir. 2003), the court ruled that it was not an abuse of discretion for the district court to require the defendant to submit to polygraph testing reasonably related to his child pornography offense and his personal history.

In imposing conditions of probation, other courts have noted the strong link between child pornographers and their use of the Internet, and the need to protect children from sex offenders. For example, in *United States v. Rearden,* 349 F.3d 608, 620 (9th Cir. 2003), the defendant was convicted of shipping child pornography (over the Internet) in violation of 18 U.S.C.A. § 2252A(a)(1). The appellate court said the district court did not err in imposing conditions of supervised release that prohibited him from possessing or using a computer with Internet access without prior approval of his probation officer.

In *State v. Ehli*, 681 N.W.2d 808 (N.D. 2004), the defendant pleaded guilty to sexual abuse of a young child. He had used pornography from the Internet to "instruct" the child on certain adult sexual acts. The state supreme court rejected the defendant's challenge to the suspended part of his sentence that included conditions of probation that prohibited him from having access to the Internet.

In *People v. Harrisson,* 134 Cal. App. 637 (2005), the defendant pleaded no contest to possession of child pornography after having used his computer to send pornographic images to an undercover police officer. The court rejected his contention that the probationary part of his sentence that prohibited him access to the Internet violated his constitutional rights.

Community Service

Another alternative to incarceration, **community service** is growing in popularity. Community service refers to sentences whereby offenders are required to perform a specified number of hours of service to the community doing specified tasks. Often, community service is required as one of several conditions of probation.

Community service has the virtues of keeping the offender out of the undesirable prison environment and exacting a penalty that is useful to the community. Ideally, it seems like an excellent way to instill in the offender a sense of responsibility to the community for having committed criminal actions, but community service also has its drawbacks. It is difficult for the community to reap any real benefit without providing a degree of training for and supervision of the offender. Training and supervision can be costly and can, in many instances, exceed the value of the community service to be performed.

Community Control

Another alternative to incarceration is **community control,** a neologism for an ancient practice known as **house arrest.** Under this alternative, an offender is allowed to leave home only for employment and approved community service activities. Increasingly, house arrest is monitored electronically by requiring persons to wear bracelets that permit officials to track their whereabouts. Community control is generally employed when incarceration is not warranted but probation is not considered sufficiently restrictive. Community control requires intensive surveillance and supervision and might not be practical in many cases. For example, consider a convicted rapist whose occupation is plumbing. To allow this offender to carry on his trade may pose a significant risk to householders. Comparable risks often militate against placing offenders under community control.

Creative Alternatives to Confinement

Judges seeking alternatives to jail or prison have been increasingly creative recently. One judge in Houston, Texas, has been known to require offenders to clean out the police department stables as part of their "community service." Some juvenile courts require offenders to make public apologies to their victims. In a few cities, billboards have been erected bearing the names of persons convicted for driving while under the influence of intoxicating substances. Some jurisdictions even publish the names of persons who patronize prostitutes. These actions are intended to shame offenders by drawing public attention to their misconduct. In seventeenth-century Massachusetts,

Involuntary Confinement Not a Criminal Proceeding

In 1994 Kansas enacted the Sexually Violent Predator Act. The act establishes procedures for the civil commitment of persons who, because of mental abnormality or personality disorder, are likely to engage in "predatory acts of sexual violence." Leroy Hendricks, an inmate with a history of sexually molesting children, was scheduled for release from prison soon after the act became effective. The State invoked the act to commit him to custody. After hearing testimony, which included Hendricks's own testimony that when he gets "stressed" he continues to be unable to control his sexual desires for children, a jury determined he was a sexually violent predator. The court ordered him confined. On appeal, the Kansas Supreme Court invalidated the act, and the State of Kansas sought review in the U.S. Supreme Court.

In a 5–4 decision, the U.S. Supreme Court rejected Hendricks's arguments. The Court held that the act does not offend the constitutional prohibitions against *ex post facto* laws and double jeopardy because it does not criminalize conduct that was legal before its enactment and because it does not constitute punishment. Writing for the majority, Justice Clarence Thomas stated that "[t]he State may take measures to restrict the freedom of the dangerously mentally ill. This is a legitimate nonpunitive governmental objective." Dissenting justices argued that the act was not simply an effort to commit Hendricks civilly but rather an effort to inflict further punishment upon him for crimes committed prior to enactment of the act.

Kansas v. Hendricks, 521 U.S. 346, 117 S.Ct. 2072, 138 L.Ed.2d 501 (1997).

women found guilty of adultery were required to wear a scarlet "A." This idea that offenders need to experience shame appears to be making a comeback.

In 1987 a convicted child molester was sentenced by an Oregon court to five years' probation on the condition that he display on his front door and automobile a warning sign: "Dangerous Sex Offender: No Children Allowed." Although the unusual sentence drew praise from prosecutors and many citizens' groups, civil libertarians objected.

One county judge in Sarasota, Florida, made national news in 1986 by requiring that DWI offenders—as a condition of probation—place bumper stickers on their cars to alert the driving public to their convictions. On appeal, the practice was upheld against an Eighth Amendment attack. As the appellate court said, "The mere requirement that a defendant display a 'scarlet letter' as part of his punishment is not necessarily offensive to the Constitution." *Goldschmitt v. State,* 490 So.2d 123, 125 (Fla. App. 1986). On the other hand, the New York Court of Appeals invalidated a condition of probation that ordered the defendant to attach a "Convicted DWI" sign to the license plate of any car driven by the defendant on the ground that it bore no relationship to the goal of rehabilitation. *People v. Letterlough,* 655 N.E.2d 146 (N.Y. 1995). Obviously, there is room for judicial disagreement on such matters.

The Death Penalty

The death penalty remains the single most controversial issue in the realm of criminal punishment. Although the death penalty has deep roots in religious and legal traditions, the twentieth century witnessed widespread abolition of **capital punishment.** At present, the United States is the only Western democracy that retains the death penalty. Thirty-eight states currently authorize capital punishment for first-degree murder or other types of aggravated homicide.

Historical Background

The framers of the Bill of Rights did not intend for the Cruel and Unusual Punishments Clause of the Eighth Amendment to abolish the death penalty. The Bill of Rights assumes the existence of capital punishment. Indeed, the Fifth Amendment refers specifically to "capital" crimes and the deprivation of life. A reform movement in the nineteenth century succeeded in limiting public executions and reducing the range of capital offenses. The movement to eliminate the death penalty achieved its first victory in 1847, when Michigan abolished capital punishment. This movement grew steadily throughout the twentieth century. By the 1960s, it appeared that the death penalty was on the way out. Public opinion no longer favored it; many states abolished it. In those that did not, the courts began to impose restrictions on its use. In 1967 two persons were executed in the United States. Ten years passed before another person was put to death. When the Supreme Court declared Georgia's death penalty law unconstitutional in *Furman v. Georgia,* 408 U.S. 238, 92 S.Ct. 2726, 33 L.Ed.2d 346 (1972), some observers thought it signaled the abolition of the death penalty in America.

Revival of the Death Penalty

Go to the Scheb/ Scheb Criminal Law and Procedure 6e website at academic .cengage.com/criminaljustice/ scheb for an edited version of *Furman v. Georgia.*

The Supreme Court's 1972 decision striking the Georgia death penalty concentrated on the virtually unlimited discretion the state placed in trial juries empowered to impose death sentences. According to Justice Potter Stewart's concurring opinion in *Furman,* Georgia's administration of the death penalty was unpredictable to the point of being "freakishly imposed." 408 U.S. 238, 310, 92 S.Ct. 2726, 2763, 33 L.Ed.2d 346, 390 (1972). In the wake of the *Furman* decision, Georgia and most other states revised their death penalty laws to address the concerns raised by the Court.

Under the revised Georgia statute, a **bifurcated trial** is held in cases where the state seeks the death penalty. In the first stage, guilt is determined according to the usual procedures, rules of evidence, and standard of proof. If the jury finds the defendant guilty, the same jury considers the appropriateness of the death sentence in a separate proceeding where additional evidence is received to determine aggravation or mitigation of the punishment. To impose the death penalty, the jury must find at least one of several **aggravating factors** specified in the statute. The purpose of requiring aggravating factors before imposing the death penalty is to narrow the cases and persons eligible for capital punishment and make the imposition of the death penalty more predictable.

Under Georgia law, the specific aggravating factors to be considered by the jury are whether

1. The offense … was committed by a person with a prior record of conviction for a capital felony;

2. The offense … was committed while the offender was engaged in … another capital felony or aggravated battery, or the offense of murder was committed while the offender was engaged in the commission of another capital felony or aggravated battery or … burglary or arson in the first degree;

3. The offender … knowingly created a great risk of death to more than one person in a public place by means of a weapon or device which would normally be hazardous to the lives of more than one person;

4. The offender committed the offense of murder for himself or another for the purpose of receiving money or any other thing of monetary value;

5. The murder of a judicial officer, former judicial officer, a district attorney or solicitor-general, or former district attorney, solicitor or solicitor-general was committed during or because of the exercise of his or her official duties;

6. The offender caused or directed another to commit murder or committed murder as an agent or employee of another person;

7. The offense … was outrageously or wantonly vile, horrible or inhuman in that it involved torture, depravity of mind or an aggravated battery to the victim;

8. The offense of murder was committed against any peace officer, corrections employee, or fireman while engaged in the performance of his official duties;

9. The offense of murder was committed by a person in, or who has escaped from, the lawful custody of a peace officer or place of lawful confinement; or

10. The murder was committed for the purpose of avoiding, interfering with, or preventing a lawful arrest or custody in a place of lawful confinement, of himself or another; or

11. The offense of murder, rape, or kidnapping was committed by a person previously convicted of rape, aggravated sodomy, aggravated child molestation, or aggravated sexual battery.

Official Ga. Code Ann. § 17–10–30(b).

To hand down a death sentence, a Georgia jury must find that at least one of these aggravating circumstances was present in the crime. The jury must then weigh the aggravating factors against any **mitigating factors** presented by the defense. See Official Ga. Code Ann. § 17–10–31. Should the jury make this finding and opt for the death penalty, the statute provides for automatic appeal to the state supreme court. That court is required to consider

1. Whether the sentence of death was imposed under the influence of passion, prejudice or any other arbitrary factor; and

2. Whether … the evidence supports the jury's or judge's finding of a statutory aggravating circumstance … , and

3. Whether the sentence of death is excessive or disproportionate to the penalty imposed in similar cases, considering both the crime and the defendant.

Official Code Ga. Ann. § 17–10–35(c).

Go to the Scheb/ Scheb Criminal Law and Procedure 6e website at academic .cengage.com/criminaljustice/ scheb for an edited version of *Gregg v. Georgia.*

In *Gregg v. Georgia*, 428 U.S. 153, 96 S.Ct. 2909, 49 L.Ed.2d 859 (1976), the Supreme Court upheld Georgia's revised death penalty statute by a vote of 7–2. Apparently, the Court was satisfied that this scheme had sufficiently addressed the evils identified in *Furman*. Thirty-eight states now have death penalty statutes modeled along the lines of the law upheld in *Gregg*.

Shortly after the death penalty was effectively reinstated by the Supreme Court's *Gregg* decision, executions in the United States began anew. On January 17, 1977, the state of Utah executed convicted murderer Gary Gilmore by firing squad. Between the date of the Gilmore execution and the end of 2005, a total of 1,004 prisoners were executed in the United States. At the end of 2005, there were 3,254 persons under sentence of death in thirty-eight jurisdictions (thirty-six states, the U.S. military, and the federal government). U.S. Department of Justice, Bureau of Justice Statistics, *Capital Punishment 2005*, December 2006, NCJ 215083.

The Federal Death Penalty

In August 1997, Timothy McVeigh was sentenced to death by lethal injection for his role in the bombing of the federal office building in Oklahoma City in 1995. In his federal trial, McVeigh was convicted of twenty-eight counts of murder of a federal law enforcement agent on active duty. See 18 U.S.C.A. § 1114. Under federal law, executions are carried out in the state where the defendant was sentenced unless that state has no death penalty, in which case the prisoner is transferred to another state for execution. 18 U.S.C.A. § 3596. McVeigh was executed at the federal prison in Terre Haute, Indiana, in June 2001. Prior to the McVeigh execution, the federal government had not put anyone to death since 1963.

The Anti-Drug Abuse Act of 1988, 21 U.S.C.A. § 848(e), allows the death penalty for so-called "drug kingpins" who control "continuing criminal enterprises" whose members intentionally kill or procure others to kill in furtherance of the enterprise. In 1993 Juan Raul Garza was sentenced to death under this statute for three murders committed as head of a Texas-based drug trafficking organization. The conviction and sentence were affirmed by the U.S. Court of Appeals for the Fifth Circuit. *United States v. Flores & Garza,* 63 F.3d 1342 (5th Cir. 1995). A federal district judge set Garza's execution for August 5, 2000, but in July of that year President Bill Clinton ordered the execution delayed to allow Garza to request executive clemency under new rules promulgated by the Justice Department. After President George W. Bush denied his plea for clemency, Garza was finally put to death in June 2001.

Go to the Scheb/ Scheb Criminal Law and Procedure 6e website at academic .cengage.com/criminaljustice/ scheb for an edited version of *Coker v. Georgia.*

In 1994, Congress enacted the **Federal Death Penalty Act (FDPA),** 18 U.S.C.A. §§ 3591 *et seq.* Section 3592 lists the mitigating and aggravating factors affecting a decision of whether to impose the death penalty. Section 3593 provides for a special hearing to determine whether a sentence of death is justified in a particular case (see Supreme Court Perspective below). The FDPA dramatically increased the number of federal crimes eligible for the death penalty. Capital punishment is now authorized for dozens of federal crimes, including nonhomicidal offenses such as treason and large-scale drug trafficking. It remains to be seen whether the federal courts will permit the death penalty for nonhomicidal crimes. In *Coker v. Georgia,* 433 U.S. 584, 97 S.Ct. 2861, 53 L.Ed.2d 982 (1977), the Supreme Court prohibited capital punishment for the crime of rape. *Coker* suggests that the death penalty is an inappropriate punishment for any crime that does not involve the taking of a human life.

Go to the Scheb/ Scheb Criminal Law and Procedure 6e website at academic .cengage.com/criminaljustice/ scheb for an edited version of *Jones v. U.S.*

SUPREME COURT PERSPECTIVE

Jones v. United States, 527 U.S. 373, 119 S.Ct. 2090, 144 L.Ed.2d 370 (1999)

In this case the Supreme Court considered a number of issues relative to the Federal Death Penalty Act. In his opinion for the Court, Justice Thomas made the following observations about the process of capital sentencing:

To be sure, we have said that the Eighth Amendment requires that a sentence of death not be imposed arbitrarily.... In order for a capital sentencing scheme to pass constitutional muster, it must perform a narrowing function with respect to the class of persons eligible for the death penalty and must also ensure that capital sentencing decisions rest upon an individualized

inquiry. Our cases have held that in order to satisfy the requirement that capital sentencing decisions rest upon an individualized inquiry, a scheme must allow a "broad inquiry" into all "constitutionally relevant mitigating evidence."

Ensuring that a sentence of death is not so infected with bias or caprice is our "controlling objective when we examine eligibility and selection factors for vagueness." ... *Our vagueness review, however, is "quite deferential." As long as an aggravating factor has a core meaning that criminal juries should be capable of understanding, it will pass constitutional muster.*

Death, Deterrence, Retribution, and Incapacitation

One of the most intense battles among academicians in the field of criminal justice has been waged over the alleged deterrent value of the death penalty. At this point, the evidence appears to be mixed, making firm conclusions impossible. Whatever the possible deterrent value of the death penalty, its actual deterrent effect is reduced by the years of delay between sentencing and execution. Obviously, the death penalty has no value as a means of rehabilitation. Therefore, if the death penalty is to be justified, it must be primarily on grounds of retribution and incapacitation. Supporters of the death penalty argue, perhaps ironically, that the value of human life is underscored by imposing the severest of sanctions on those who commit murder. Certainly the death penalty is proportionate to the crime of murder. Indeed, the Supreme Court has made it clear that murder is the only crime for which the death penalty is permissible. *Coker v. Georgia,* supra.

Advocates of capital punishment also stress the incapacitation of the offender, and it is difficult to argue that death is not a complete incapacitator. But are retribution and incapacitation sufficient justifications for the death penalty?

Is the Death Penalty Racially Discriminatory?

Whether the Court achieved the evenhandedness in the administration of capital punishment it sought through its decisions in *Furman* and *Gregg* is questionable. Critics have long charged that the death penalty is racially discriminatory. During the 1970s, criminologist David Baldus collected data on more than one thousand murder cases in Georgia and found significant disparities in the imposition of the death penalty based primarily on the race of the murder victims and, to a lesser extent, on the race of the defendants. The data reveal that blacks who killed whites were more than seven times more likely to receive the death sentence than were whites who killed blacks.

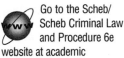
Go to the Scheb/ Scheb Criminal Law and Procedure 6e website at academic .cengage.com/criminaljustice/ scheb for an edited version of *McCleskey v. Kemp.*

In April 1987, the Supreme Court reviewed the death sentence of a black man convicted of killing a white police officer in Georgia. The Court refused to accept statistical evidence derived from the Baldus study as a basis for reversing the death sentence. In the Court's view, even if there is statistical evidence of race discrimination, a defendant sentenced to death cannot prevail on appeal unless the defendant can show that the death sentence was imposed because of race discrimination in this case. *McCleskey v. Kemp,* 481 U.S. 279, 107 S.Ct. 1756, 95 L.Ed.2d 262 (1987). Obviously, this would be difficult, although certainly not impossible, for a defendant to demonstrate.

In a 1990 report, the U.S. General Accounting Office concluded that available research demonstrated "a pattern of evidence indicating racial disparities in the charging, sentencing, and imposition of the death penalty." Similarly, in 1994 the U.S. House of Representatives Subcommittee on Civil and Constitutional Rights concluded that members of racial minorities were being disproportionately prosecuted under the federal death penalty law. According to the Death Penalty Information Center, of the 133 defendants authorized for death penalty prosecution from 1988 to 1998, 76 percent were members of racial minorities. Of the 3,254 death row inmates in the United States at the end of 2005, 42 percent were African American. U.S. Department of Justice, Bureau of Justice Statistics, *Capital Punishment 2005,* December 2006, NCJ 215083. Certainly these statistics provide a basis for concern about the fairness with which the death penalty has been administered in this country.

Capital Punishment of Juvenile Offenders

One very difficult issue that the Supreme Court faced during the 1980s was whether, and under what circumstances, a juvenile may be executed when convicted of a capital crime. The Court responded in three decisions. In *Thompson v. Oklahoma,* 487 U.S. 815, 108 S.Ct. 2687, 101 L.Ed.2d 702 (1988), the Court ruled in a 6–3 decision that the Constitution forbids executing a juvenile who was fifteen years of age or younger at the time of commission of a capital crime. The following year, in *Stanford v. Kentucky,* 492 U.S. 361, 109 S.Ct. 2969, 106 L.Ed.2d 306 (1989), the Supreme Court split 5–4 in holding that a juvenile sixteen or older at the time of the crime may be sentenced to death. Concurring in *Stanford,* Justice Sandra Day O'Connor commented that "it is sufficiently clear that no national consensus forbids the imposition of capital punishment on 16- or 17-year-old capital murderers." 492 U.S. at 381, 109 S.Ct. at 2981, 106 L.Ed.2d at 325. In both *Thompson* and *Stanford,* the Court referred to "evolving standards of decency" as the proper test for judging the constitutionality of whether a juvenile may be executed. Applying that test, the Court in *Roper v. Simmons,* 543 U.S. 551, 125 S.Ct. 1183, 161 L.Ed.2d 1 (2005), forbade the execution of anyone who was under eighteen at the time of their offense.

Writing for the Court in *Roper,* Justice Anthony Kennedy noted the decreasing frequency with which juvenile offenders were being sentenced to death as evidence of an emerging national consensus against capital punishment for juveniles. At the time of the *Roper* decision, only twenty states still allowed juveniles to be executed, and since 1995 only three states (Oklahoma, Texas, and Virginia) had actually executed inmates for crimes committed as juveniles. Moreover, five of the states that allowed the juvenile death penalty when *Stanford v. Kentucky* was decided in 1989 have since done away with it.

Execution of Prisoners Who Have Become Insane

In 1974 Alvin Ford was convicted of murder and sentenced to death by a Florida court. There was no indication that he was mentally incompetent at the time of the trial. However, while in prison awaiting execution, Ford began to exhibit profound changes in behavior and to experience bizarre delusions. In 1983 a prison psychiatrist diagnosed Ford as suffering from a severe and uncontrollable mental disease closely resembling paranoid schizophrenia. Ford's attorney then invoked procedures under Florida law governing the determination of competency of a condemned prisoner. A panel of psychiatrists examined Ford, and although they differed in their specific diagnoses, all agreed that Ford was not insane under Florida law.

On April 30, 1984, Governor Bob Graham signed Ford's death warrant. Ford's attorney then filed a petition for habeas corpus in the U.S. District Court, seeking an evidentiary hearing on his client's sanity. The district court denied relief, and the court of appeals affirmed. The U.S. Supreme Court agreed to review the case to resolve the issue of whether the Eighth Amendment prohibits the execution of a person who is insane. On June 26, 1986, the Supreme Court announced its decision in *Ford v. Wainwright,* 477 U.S. 399, 106 S.Ct. 2595, 91 L.Ed.2d 335 (1986). The Court held that the Eighth Amendment bars the execution of a person who is insane. Writing for a plurality of justices, Justice Thurgood Marshall declared that "[i]t is no less abhorrent today than it has been for centuries to exact in penance the life of one whose mental illness prevents him from comprehending the reasons for the penalty or its implications." 477 U.S. at 417, 106 S.Ct. at 2606, 91 L.Ed.2d at 351. The Court also held that Florida's procedures for determining the sanity of a death row prisoner violated due process. The Court ruled that Ford was entitled to a *de novo* evidentiary hearing in the district court on the question of his competence to be executed.

Go to the Scheb/ Scheb Criminal Law and Procedure 6e website at academic .cengage.com/criminaljustice/ scheb for an edited version of *Ford v. Wainwright.*

Execution of Mentally Retarded Persons

Even many supporters of the death penalty are troubled by the prospect of executing a mentally retarded offender. In *Penry v. Lynaugh*, 492 U.S. 302, 109 S.Ct. 2934, 106 L.Ed.2d 256 (1989), the U.S. Supreme Court held that execution of a mentally retarded prisoner does not necessarily violate the Cruel and Unusual Punishments Clause. However, the Court held that juries must be allowed to consider evidence of mental retardation as a mitigating factor in the sentencing phase of a capital trial. Justice O'Connor wrote the opinion of the Court, observing that

> mental retardation is a factor that may well lessen a defendant's culpability for a capital offense. But we cannot conclude today that the Eighth Amendment precludes the execution of any mentally retarded person of Penry's ability convicted of a capital offense simply by virtue of his or her mental retardation alone. So long as sentencers can consider and give effect to mitigating evidence of mental retardation in imposing sentence, an individualized determination whether "death is the appropriate punishment" can be made in each particular case. While a national consensus against execution of the mentally retarded may someday emerge reflecting the "evolving standards of decency that mark the progress of a maturing society," there is insufficient evidence of such a consensus today. 92 U.S. at 340, 109 S.Ct. at 2958, 106 L.Ed.2d at 292.

By 2001 eighteen of the thirty-eight states that allowed the death penalty had, either by statute or judicial decision, outlawed the execution of retarded prisoners. In *Atkins v. Virginia*, 536 U.S. 304, 122 S.Ct. 2242, 153 L.Ed.2d 335 (2002), the U.S. Supreme Court reconsidered the issue and held that there was a sufficient national consensus for the Court to prohibit the execution of mentally retarded persons via the Eighth Amendment. Writing for a majority of six justices, Justice John Paul Stevens concluded that

> mentally retarded persons who meet the law's requirements for criminal responsibility should be tried and punished when they commit crimes. Because of their disabilities in areas of reasoning, judgment and control of their impulses, however, they do not act with the level of moral culpability that characterizes the most serious adult criminal conduct. 536 U.S. at 306, 122 S.Ct. at 2244, 153 L.Ed.2d at 341.

 Go to the Scheb/ Scheb Criminal Law and Procedure 6e website at academic .cengage.com/criminaljustice/ scheb for an edited version of *Atkins v. Virginia.*

Writing for the three dissenters, Justice Antonin Scalia argued that the decision had "no support in the text or history of the Eighth Amendment." Justice Scalia accused the majority of making policy rather than law, saying, "Seldom has an opinion of this Court rested so obviously upon nothing but the personal views of its members." 536 U.S. at 338, 122 S.Ct. at 2259, 153 L.Ed.2d at 363.

Methods of Execution

Currently, five methods of execution exist in the United States: electric chair, lethal injection, gas chamber, firing squad, and hanging. Hanging is by far the least common and, with the possible exception of the gas chamber, is also the least humane mode of capital punishment. Nevertheless, a federal appeals court ruled in 1994 that hanging, as it is administered by the State of Washington, is not cruel and unusual punishment. *Campbell v. Wood*, 18 F.3d 662 (9th Cir. 1994). The court discussed at some length the grisly mechanics of hanging and concluded that hanging, as practiced in Washington, is likely to produce a quick and painless death. In a subsequent decision, however, a federal district court in Washington forbade the hanging of a 409-pound man, saying that there was a significant risk that hanging a person of that weight would result in decapitation. The court said that such an execution would be akin to beheading by ax or guillotine and would be inconsistent with the concept of human dignity underlying the Eighth Amendment. *Rupe v. Wood*, 863 F. Supp. 1315 (D.C. W.Wash. 1994).

THE GAS CHAMBER CONTROVERSY

In a related case, a federal district court in California ruled that execution by means of the gas chamber is unconstitutional. The court found that the gas chamber produces a lingering death accompanied by intense pain, anxiety, and muscle spasms. *Fierro v. Gomez,* 865 F. Supp. 1387, 1389 (N.D. Cal. 1994). Interestingly, the district court relied on the Ninth Circuit's decision in *Campbell v. Wood,* supra, which the district court interpreted to forbid unnecessarily cruel means of execution. In 1996 the Ninth Circuit Court of Appeals upheld the prohibition on the gas chamber. *Fierro v. Gomez,* 77 F.3d 301 (9th Cir. 1996). Later that year, however, the Supreme Court granted certiorari and remanded the case to the Ninth Circuit for reconsideration in light of an amended California statute. *Gomez v. Fierro,* 519 U.S. 918, 117 S.Ct. 285, 136 L.Ed.2d 204 (1996). On remand, the Ninth Circuit held that Gomez lacked standing to challenge the constitutionality of execution by lethal gas because the amended California death penalty statute affords the choice of either lethal gas or lethal injection, with lethal injection being the default method in absence of an election. Because Gomez did not elect the lethal gas option, he had no standing to challenge that method of execution. *Fierro v. Tehune,* 147 F.3d 1158 (9th Cir. 1998).

THE ELECTRIC CHAIR DEBATE

The electric chair was introduced in the 1890s as a "humanitarian" alternative to the gallows. "The chair" is now employed in only six states: Alabama, Florida, Georgia, Kentucky, Nebraska, and Tennessee. This method of execution subjects the inmate to approximately 2,000 volts of electricity conducted through copper electrodes attached to the head. Usually, the first jolt of electricity causes death by cardiac arrest and respiratory paralysis, although there have been several instances where multiple jolts have had to be applied. In some cases, the administration of electricity produces smoke and even fire. In March 1997, some observers were shocked when white smoke and flames nearly a foot high issued from the head of Pedro Medina when he was executed in "Old Sparky," Florida's seventy-four-year-old electric chair. Later that year a Florida trial judge rejected a death row inmate's constitutional challenge to the use of the electric chair. And in *Jones v. State,* 701 So.2d 76 (Fla. 1997), the Florida Supreme Court in a 4–3 decision upheld the constitutionality of using the electric chair. Three dissenting justices described its use as archaic and barbaric.

The *Jones* decision prompted the Florida legislature to revise the law to provide persons under sentence of death with the option of being executed by lethal injection. As amended in 2000, Section 922.105, Florida Statutes now provides the following:

(1) A death sentence shall be executed by lethal injection, unless the person sentenced to death affirmatively elects to be executed by electrocution....

(2) A person convicted and sentenced to death for a capital crime at any time shall have one opportunity to elect that his or her death sentence be executed by electrocution. The election for death by electrocution is waived unless it is personally made by the person in writing and delivered to the warden of the correctional facility within 30 days after the issuance of mandate pursuant to a decision by the Florida Supreme Court affirming the sentence of death.

(3) If electrocution or lethal injection is held to be unconstitutional by the Florida Supreme Court under the State Constitution, or held to be unconstitutional by the United States Supreme Court under the United States Constitution, or if the United States Supreme Court declines to review any judgment holding a method of execution to be unconstitutional under the United Sates Constitution made by the Florida Supreme Court or the United States Court of Appeals that has jurisdiction over

Florida, all persons sentenced to death for a capital crime shall be executed by any constitutional method of execution.

CONTROVERSY OVER LETHAL INJECTION

Although lethal injection was hailed as a more humane alternative to the electric chair and the gas chamber, critics of the death penalty are now attacking lethal injection as cruel and unusual punishment. In particular, they claim that the paralyzing agent used as part of the lethal combination of drugs masks the suffering of the person being executed. There are numerous lawsuits challenging lethal injection pending in the courts. On December 15, 2006, a federal judge in California enjoined the use of lethal injection in that state, ruling that "implementation of lethal injection is broken, but it can be fixed." On the same day, Florida governor Jeb Bush imposed a moratorium on executions by lethal injection. The governor's pronouncement came days after the execution of Angel Nieves Diaz. Diaz's execution took thirty-four minutes, twice as long as it normally takes to produce death, because the needle that administered the lethal cocktail was not properly inserted into the vein. Governor Bush appointed a panel to study the matter but indicated that he would not sign any more execution orders until the panel's report was concluded. Around the country, opponents of the death penalty were buoyed by the developments in Florida and California. If lethal injection is ultimately banned as inhumane punishment, it could possibly signal the demise of the death penalty.

The Sentencing Stage of the Criminal Process

Every jurisdiction requires that criminal sentences for adults be imposed in open court, although in many instances juvenile offenders may be sentenced *in camera*. In misdemeanor cases, sentencing usually occurs immediately on conviction. In felony cases, where penalties are greater, sentencing may be postponed to allow the court to conduct a **presentence investigation.**

The Presentence Report

In many states as well as in the federal system, the court is required to order a **presentence report** when the offender to be sentenced is a first offender or is under a certain age. In other state jurisdictions, the sentencing judge is accorded discretion in this area. For example, rule 702 of the Pennsylvania Rules of Criminal Procedure provides as follows:

A. Presentence Investigation Report.

1. The sentencing judge may, in the judge's discretion, order a presentence investigation report in any case.

2. The sentencing judge shall place on the record the reasons for dispensing with the presentence investigation report if the judge fails to order a presentence report in any of the following instances:

(a) when incarceration for one year or more is a possible disposition under the applicable sentencing statutes; or

(b) when the defendant is less than twenty-one years old at the time of conviction or entry of a plea of guilty; or

(c) when a defendant is a first offender in that he or she has not heretofore been sentenced as an adult.

3. The presentence investigation report shall include information regarding the circumstances of the offense and the character of the defendant sufficient to assist the judge in determining sentence.

4. The presentence investigation report shall also include a victim impact statement as provided by law.

Rule 703 makes the reports confidential and available only to the sentencing judge, counsel for the state and the defense, and experts appointed by the court to assist the court in sentencing.

In some states, statutes, court rules, or judicial interpretations mandate that courts release a presentence report to the defendant or defendant's counsel, usually allowing some exemptions for sensitive material. In other states, courts have ruled that this is a matter within the discretion of the sentencing judge. In some instances, courts will reveal factual material such as police reports but decline to disclose statements made in confidence to investigators. Often the judicial interpretation depends on the language of the statute or court rule. The Supreme Court requires the release of presentence reports to defendants who may be sentenced to death.

The presentence report sets forth the defendant's history of delinquency or criminality, medical history, family background, economic status, education, employment history, and so forth. Much of this information is obtained by probation officers, who interview defendants' families, friends, employers, and so on. In addition, most jurisdictions allow courts to order physical or mental examinations of defendants. This information can be very useful to a judge who must determine a sentence that is at once fair, humane, and meaningful.

The Sentencing Hearing

Go to the Scheb/ Scheb Criminal Law and Procedure 6e website at academic .cengage.com/criminaljustice/ scheb for an edited version of *Mempa v. Rhay.*

After the presentence report is completed, a **sentencing hearing** is held. At this hearing, the court considers the evidence received at trial, the presentence report, any evidence offered by either party in aggravation or mitigation of sentence, and any statement the defendant wishes to make. In addition, most jurisdictions require judges to hear arguments concerning various sentencing alternatives. Sentencing is a critical stage of the criminal process, and counsel must be supplied to indigent defendants. *Mempa v. Rhay,* 389 U.S. 128, 88 S.Ct. 254, 19 L.Ed.2d 336 (1967).

CASE-IN-POINT

Presentence Reports

Daniel Gardner was found guilty of first-degree murder, and the jury recommended a sentence of life imprisonment. The jury's recommendation was based on its finding that mitigating factors outweighed the aggravating circumstances of the crime. However, the trial judge sentenced Gardner to death, relying on a confidential portion of a presentence report that had not been made available to the defense. The U.S. Supreme Court vacated the sentence and directed the trial court to conduct another sentencing proceeding in which the defendant would have an opportunity to deny or explain the contents of the presentence report.

Gardner v. Florida, 430 U.S. 349, 97 S.Ct. 1197, 51 L.Ed.2d 393 (1977).

Pronouncement of Sentence

After the judge has digested the sentencing report, heard arguments from counsel and the defendant's statement, and considered the relevant provisions of law, the sentence is pronounced in open court. The **pronouncement of sentence** is the stage when the trial court imposes a penalty on a defendant for the offense of which the defendant has been adjudged guilty. Sentences are usually pronounced by the judge who presided at the defendant's trial or the entry of plea. In misdemeanor cases, sentencing often occurs immediately after the entry of a plea or a finding of guilty by the judge or jury. In felony cases, the pronouncement is often delayed until the court has received a presentence investigation report or until the prosecutor and defense counsel have had an opportunity to prepare a presentation.

The rules of evidence are relaxed during a sentencing proceeding. Traditionally, a defendant has been afforded an opportunity to make a statement on his or her own behalf, a procedure often referred to as the **right of allocution.** Generally, special rules govern the sentencing of a defendant who is insane, and often sentencing must be deferred for a female defendant who is pregnant.

The procedure at the pronouncement stage is generally outlined in the criminal procedure rules of each jurisdiction. Typically, rule 704 of the Pennsylvania Rules of Criminal Procedure, provides the following:

C. Sentencing Proceeding

(1) At the time of sentencing, the judge shall afford the defendant the opportunity to make a statement in his or her behalf and shall afford counsel for both parties the opportunity to present information and argument relative to sentencing.

(2) The judge shall state on the record the reasons for the sentence imposed.

(3) The judge shall determine on the record that the defendant has been advised of the following:

(a) of the right to file a post-sentence motion and to appeal, of the time within which the defendant must exercise those rights, and of the right to assistance of counsel in the preparation of the motion and appeal;

(b) of the rights,

(i) if the defendant is indigent, to proceed *in forma pauperis* and to proceed with appointed counsel as provided in Rule 122; or

(ii) if represented by retained counsel, to proceed with retained counsel unless the court has granted leave for counsel to withdraw pursuant to Rule 120(B);

(c) of the time limits within which post-sentence motions must be decided;

(d) that issues raised before or during trial shall be deemed preserved for appeal whether or not the defendant elects to file a post-sentence motion; and

(e) of the defendant's qualified right to bail under Rule 521(B).

(4) The judge shall require that a record of the sentencing proceeding be made and preserved so that it can be transcribed as needed. The record shall include:

(a) the record of any stipulation made at a pre-sentence conference; and

(b) a verbatim account of the entire sentencing proceeding.

CREDIT FOR TIME SERVED

When the trial court sentences a defendant to incarceration, it generally allows the defendant credit against any term of incarceration for all time spent in custody as a result of the charge for which the sentence is imposed. The following Pennsylvania law specifically recognizes this option:

> **§ 9760. Credit for time served**
>
> After reviewing the information submitted under section 9737 (relating to report of outstanding charges and sentences) the court shall give credit as follows:
>
> (1) Credit against the maximum term and any minimum term shall be given to the defendant for all time spent in custody as a result of the criminal charge for which a prison sentence is imposed or as a result of the conduct on which such a charge is based. Credit shall include credit for time spent in custody prior to trial, during trial, pending sentence, and pending the resolution of an appeal.
>
> (2) Credit against the maximum term and any minimum term shall be given to the defendant for all time spent in custody under a prior sentence if he is later reprosecuted and resentenced for the same offense or for another offense based on the same act or acts. This shall include credit in accordance with paragraph (1) of this section for all time spent in custody as a result of both the original charge and any subsequent charge for the same offense or for another offense based on the same act or acts.
>
> (3) If the defendant is serving multiple sentences, and if one of the sentences is set aside as the result of direct or collateral attack, credit against the maximum and any minimum term of the remaining sentences shall be given for all time served in relation to the sentence set aside since the commission of the offenses on which the sentences were based.
>
> (4) If the defendant is arrested on one charge and later prosecuted on another charge growing out of an act or acts that occurred prior to his arrest, credit against the maximum term and any minimum term of any sentence resulting from such prosecution shall be given for all time spent in custody under the former charge that has not been credited against another sentence. 42 Pa. Stat. Ann. § 9760.

SUSPENDED SENTENCES

In most instances where defendants are convicted of **noncapital crimes,** courts are authorized to suspend the imposition of the sentence and place defendants on probation or under community control for some determinate period. Statutes often require courts to impose certain conditions (similar to probation conditions) on a defendant whose sentence is suspended. See, for example, N.J. Stat. Ann. 2C: 45–1. Of course, if the defendant violates conditions set by the court, the original sentence may be imposed. A **suspended sentence** is most often used for first offenses or nonviolent offenses. Authority to suspend a felony conviction is generally limited to only a first conviction. See, for example, La. C. Cr. P. Art. 83.

Concurrent and Consecutive Sentences

A defendant who is convicted of multiple crimes must be given separate sentences for each offense. These sentences may run consecutively or concurrently, usually at the discretion of the sentencing judge. See, for example, Pa. R. Crim. P. 705. **Concurrent sentencing** in a given case may simply reflect the court's view that **consecutive sentencing** would result in a punishment that is too harsh for the crime.

Sentencing in Capital Cases

In those cases where the prosecution is permitted by law to seek the death penalty, the sentencing procedure is considerably more complex. As we noted in the discussion of the death penalty, a bifurcated trial is employed. Following the conviction of a defendant for a capital crime, the jury hears testimony in aggravation or mitigation of the sentence. For the jury to hand down the death penalty, it must find beyond a reasonable doubt that the aggravating factors outweigh the mitigating ones. The aggravating factors are specified by law; the mitigating factors are those characteristics of the defendant or the crime that suggest that leniency might be appropriate. Quite often the defense attorney will put the defendant's relatives on the stand to testify about the defendant's redeeming qualities or to generally plead for mercy.

VICTIM IMPACT EVIDENCE

Prosecutors counter emotional pleas on the defendant's behalf by presenting **victim impact evidence.** This evidence takes the form of testimony addressing the impact of the murder on the victim and the victim's family, including the physical, economic, and psychological effects of the crime. For example, the victim's surviving spouse might be called to testify to the toll the homicide has taken on the family. Needless to say, such testimony is often fraught with emotion and can have a powerful impact on the jury.

In 1987 the U.S. Supreme Court struck down a Maryland statute requiring that a **victim impact statement** be considered during the penalty phase of capital cases. *Booth v. Maryland,* 482 U.S. 496, 107 S.Ct. 2529, 96 L.Ed.2d 440 (1987). The Court said that such statements raised the real possibility that death sentences would be based on irrelevant considerations. Four years later, however, in *Payne v. Tennessee,* 501 U.S. 808, 111 S.Ct. 2597, 115 L.Ed.2d 720 (1991), the Court overruled its decision in *Booth.* According to Chief Justice William Rehnquist, who wrote the majority opinion in *Payne,* the *Booth* decision "deprives the State of the full moral force of its evidence and may prevent the jury from having before it all the information necessary to determine the proper punishment for a first-degree murder." 501 U.S. at 825, 111 S.Ct. at 2608, 115 L.Ed.2d at 735. Notwithstanding the Supreme Court's decision in *Payne v. Tennessee,* appellate courts may still find that a particular victim impact statement has impermissibly injected too much emotionalism into the jury's sentencing deliberations.

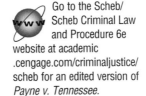

Go to the Scheb/ Scheb Criminal Law and Procedure 6e website at academic .cengage.com/criminaljustice/ scheb for an edited version of *Payne v. Tennessee.*

WHAT ARE JURIES ENTITLED TO KNOW ABOUT THE DEFENDANT?

In 1994 the Supreme Court also decided two important cases dealing with the information that juries may consider in deciding whether to impose the death penalty. In *Romano v. Oklahoma,* 512 U.S. 1, 114 S.Ct. 2004, 129 L.Ed.2d 1 (1994), the Court held that neither the Eighth Amendment nor the Due Process Clause of the Fourteenth Amendment prohibits capital-sentencing juries from being informed that the defendant is already under sentence of death for another crime. Petitioner John Romano had already been sentenced to death for robbing and murdering one man when he was tried for another robbery-murder. During the sentencing phase, the prosecution sought to introduce evidence of the former crime and sentence. Romano's attorney objected, claiming that for the jury to know of the previous death sentence would diminish its sense of responsibility in imposing another death sentence. The trial judge overruled the objection, and Romano was sentenced to death. Writing for the Supreme Court, Chief Justice Rehnquist observed that although the prior death sentence was irrelevant, the Constitution "does not establish a federal code of evidence to supersede state evidentiary rules in capital sentencing proceedings." 512 U.S. at 12, 114 S.Ct. at 2011, 129 L.Ed.2d at 13.

Chief Justice Rehnquist's observation in *Romano* notwithstanding, the Court in *Simmons v. South Carolina,* 512 U.S. 154, 114 S.Ct. 2187, 129 L.Ed.2d 133 (1994), held that defendants facing the death penalty have a right to tell juries if the only alternative to a death sentence is life imprisonment without the possibility of parole. Jonathan Simmons was convicted of murdering a seventy-nine-year-old woman in her home. Because Simmons had been convicted twice before of sexually assaulting elderly women, South Carolina law provided that he would be ineligible for parole if sentenced to prison. Over defense counsel's objection, the trial judge granted the prosecution's motion to exclude any mention of parole during the trial. During the sentencing phase, the court denied the defense counsel's request to explain to the jury that a life sentence carried no possibility of parole. Finally, during deliberations the judge told the jury not to consider whether Simmons could be paroled if he was sentenced to life imprisonment. Simmons was sentenced to death. The Supreme Court remanded the case for re-sentencing, saying that the trial judge's refusal to provide the requested instruction constituted a denial of due process. In dissent, Justice Scalia accused the Court of trying to impose on the states a "Federal Rules of Death Penalty Evidence." 512 U.S. at 185, 114 S.Ct. at 2205, 129 L.Ed.2d at 156.

THE ROLE OF THE JUDGE IN CAPITAL SENTENCING

States vary as to the role of the trial judge in determining death sentences. Under the capital sentencing procedures in Georgia, where the jury finds at least one statutory aggravating circumstance and recommends the death penalty, the trial judge must sentence the defendant to death. Official Ga. Code Ann. § 17-10-31. In other states, a different method is employed. For example, in Florida the trial court decides whether to accept a jury's recommendation of death or life imprisonment. See *Spaziano v. Florida,* 468 U.S. 447, 104 S.Ct. 3154, 82 L.Ed.2d 340 (1984). Where a jury recommends life imprisonment and the trial court overrides that recommendation and imposes the death penalty, the decision is carefully scrutinized by the Florida Supreme Court. For the trial court's override to be sustained, the life imprisonment recommendation by the jury must have been unreasonable. If the supreme court's review finds there was a reasonable basis for the jury's recommendation, it reverses the court's imposition of the death penalty and remands the case for a sentence as recommended by the jury. *Buford v. State,* 570 So.2d 923 (Fla. 1990).

WHAT HAPPENS WHEN THE CAPITAL JURY IS DEADLOCKED ON THE SENTENCE?

When the jury in a capital case cannot agree on the appropriate sentence, sentencing normally reverts to the judge. As we have seen, in some jurisdictions, the judge is barred from imposing the death penalty without a jury recommendation. In such instances, the judge must sentence the defendant to any lesser sentence authorized by law. The judge is not required to instruct the jury with regard to the consequences of deadlock, however. *Jones v. United States,* 527 U.S. 373, 119 S.Ct. 2090, 144 L.Ed.2d 370 (1999).

 Go to the Scheb/ Scheb Criminal Law and Procedure 6e website at academic .cengage.com/criminaljustice/ scheb for an edited version of *Jones v. U.S.*

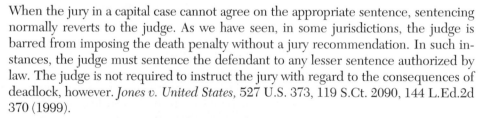

Granting and Revoking Probation

Probation is a sentencing option in the federal courts and in most state courts. Under federal law, a defendant who has been found guilty of an offense may be sentenced to a term of probation unless (1) the offense is a felony where the maximum term of imprisonment authorized is twenty-five years or more, life imprisonment, or death; (2) the offense is one for which probation has been expressly precluded; or (3) the defendant is sentenced at the same time to a term of imprisonment for the same or a different offense. A defendant who has been convicted for the first time of a domestic violence crime must be sentenced to a term of probation if not sentenced to a term of imprisonment. 18 U.S.C.A. § 3561. Probation terms for a felony must not be less than one nor more than five years and for a misdemeanor not more than five years. 18 U.S.C.A. § 3561. Certain conditions of probation are mandatory, and others are discretionary with the federal judge who imposes probation. 18 U.S.C.A. § 3563.

In most states, the term of probation is limited to the maximum statutory term of confinement for the particular offense. Probation is granted on the condition that the defendant abides by various stipulations. In some instances, mandatory conditions are imposed by statute, but the trial court may impose additional conditions. Probation is often combined with a fine, restitution to the victim, or a short term of incarceration to give the probationer "a taste of jail." Because the procedures in state courts vary widely, it is difficult to generalize; however, it is important for the probationer to receive a written order incorporating the terms of probation and outlining his or her responsibilities to the probation officer and the court. Courts must guard against imposing vague conditions of probation or delegating overly broad authorities to probation officers.

Revocation of Probation

In every jurisdiction, the commission of a felony while on probation is grounds for revocation. In many jurisdictions, certain misdemeanors qualify as grounds for revocation. In addition, the violation of any substantive condition of probation is grounds for revocation. Typically, a probation officer is vested with broad discretion in determining when to seek revocation of probation. A probationer facing the loss of freedom is entitled to a fair hearing. At this hearing the probationer has the right to call favorable witnesses, to confront hostile witnesses, and to be represented by counsel. *Gagnon v. Scarpelli,* 411 U.S. 778, 93 S.Ct. 1756, 36 L.Ed.2d 656 (1973). In *Gagnon,* the Supreme Court said that indigent probationers may have a constitutional right to have counsel appointed at revocation hearings, depending on the complexity of the issues involved, and that if counsel is not provided, the judge must state the reason. In practice, counsel is usually provided. There is a statutory right to appointment of counsel for those financially unable to obtain counsel in federal probation revocation proceedings. 18 U.S.C.A. § 3006A.

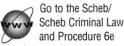

Go to the Scheb/ Scheb Criminal Law and Procedure 6e website at academic .cengage.com/criminaljustice/ scheb for an edited version of *Gagnon v. Scarpelli.*

The Federal Rules of Criminal Procedure require a two-step process before probation can be revoked:

(1) Preliminary Hearing.

(A) In General. If a person is in custody for violating a condition of probation or supervised release, a magistrate judge must promptly conduct a hearing to determine whether there is probable cause to believe that a violation occurred. The person may waive the hearing.

(B) Requirements. The hearing must be recorded by a court reporter or by a suitable recording device. The judge must give the person:

(i) notice of the hearing and its purpose, the alleged violation, and the person's right to retain counsel or to request that counsel be appointed if the person cannot obtain counsel;

(ii) an opportunity to appear at the hearing and present evidence; and

(iii) upon request, an opportunity to question any adverse witness, unless the judge determines that the interest of justice does not require the witness to appear.

(C) Referral. If the judge finds probable cause, the judge must conduct a revocation hearing. If the judge does not find probable cause, the judge must dismiss the proceeding.

(2) Revocation Hearing. Unless waived by the person, the court must hold the revocation hearing within a reasonable time in the district having jurisdiction. The person is entitled to:

(A) written notice of the alleged violation;

(B) disclosure of the evidence against the person;

(C) an opportunity to appear, present evidence, and question any adverse witness unless the court determines that the interest of justice does not require the witness to appear;

(D) notice of the person's right to retain counsel or to request that counsel be appointed if the person cannot obtain counsel; and

(E) an opportunity to make a statement and present any information in mitigation. Fed. R. Crim. P. 32.1(b).

The rules of evidence applicable at criminal trials are relaxed at probation revocation hearings. For example, in federal courts hearsay evidence may be received over a probationer's objection because a probation revocation hearing is not a criminal trial. *United States v. Miller,* 514 F.2d 41 (9th Cir. 1975). In most state courts, "reliable" hearsay evidence is admissible in probation revocation proceedings. This most commonly applies to laboratory reports and other documentation. Nevertheless, a legion of state appellate court decisions hold that probation cannot be revoked solely on the basis of hearsay evidence. See *Turner v. State,* 293 So.2d 771 (Fla. App. 1974). Thus, an appellate court found insufficient evidence that a defendant violated a condition of his probation prohibiting changing residence without permission where the only evidence of violation was hearsay testimony from the defendant's probation officer that the probationer's mother stated that she did not know where he was. *Cito v. State,* 721 So.2d 1192 (Fla. App. 1998). Some state courts hold hearsay evidence to be inadmissible in probation revocation proceedings. See, for example, *Wolcott v. State,* 604 S.E.2d 478 (Ga. 2004), where the Georgia Supreme Court held that hearsay evidence is inadmissible but found it harmless in the particular case because it was cumulative to other admissible evidence that established the defendant had committed an offense that constituted probation violation.

As noted, a large number of state appellate court decisions make it clear that hearsay evidence alone is not sufficient to revoke probation. See *Nadeau v. State,* 920 So.2d 206 (Fla. App. 2006). Most revocation cases do not reach the highest state courts, but in 1993 the Tennessee Supreme Court held that probation could not be revoked based solely on a lab test indicating that the probationer had used illicit drugs where the technician who performed the drug test was not available to be cross-examined at the revocation hearing. *State v. Wade,* 863 S.W.2d 406 (Tenn. 1993).

Courts have frequently articulated that the standard to be applied at revocation hearings is not "reasonable doubt" or "preponderance of evidence" but whether from the evidence presented the court is reasonably satisfied of the probationer's violation. Nor is there any requirement that a probationer be granted a jury trial in revocation proceedings, even when those proceedings are predicated on a violation of a criminal law. *United States v. Czajak,* 909 F.2d 20 (1st Cir. 1990). Often a court will modify rather than revoke a defendant's probation, but if the court does revoke probation, statutory and decisional law generally permit it to sentence the defendant to any term that would have been appropriate for the underlying offense. And although a probationer may not be sentenced on revocation for the conduct that constituted the probation violation, it is proper for the trial court to consider the probationer's conduct while on probation to assess a potential for rehabilitation. See, for example, *People v. Vilces,* 542 N.E.2d 1269 (Ill. App. 1989).

Revocation of Probation Requires a Willful Violation

Danny Bearden pled guilty to charges of burglary and theft. Pursuant to Georgia's First Offenders Act, Official Code Ga. Ann. § 27–2727 *et seq.*, current version at § 42–8–60, he was placed on three years' probation. As a condition of his probation, Bearden was required to pay a $500 fine and make restitution of $250, according to a court-imposed payment schedule. After making some payments, Bearden was laid off from work and became unable to continue making payments. As a result, the trial court revoked his probation and sentenced him to serve the remaining portion of his term of probation in prison. The U.S. Supreme Court reversed the revocation of probation because the trial court had made no finding that Bearden was responsible for his failure to make the required payments. Nevertheless, the Court said, "If the probationer willfully refused to pay or failed to make sufficient bona fide efforts legally to acquire the resources to pay, the court may revoke probation."

Bearden v. Georgia, 461 U.S. 660, 672, 103 S.Ct. 2064, 2073, 76 L.Ed.2d 221, 233 (1983).

The violation of any valid substantive condition is grounds for revocation of probation, but in practice courts may hold that a minor or technical violation such as a probationer's being a day late in filing a monthly report is not sufficient for a court to revoke probation.

Statutory Approaches to Incarceration

Once it has been determined that a defendant is to be incarcerated, several variations of the type and extent of the defendant's sentence may be available. The legislative trend has been to limit judicial discretion in imposing incarceration by statutorily providing whether the defendant is subject to an indeterminate or determinate sentence and whether a minimum mandatory term is to be imposed. In recent years, in an attempt to cope with the problem of recidivism, legislatures have enacted laws providing for enhanced terms of incarceration.

Indeterminate Sentencing

For much of the twentieth century, legislatures commonly allowed judges to sentence criminals to imprisonment for indeterminate periods. This was designed to assist corrections officials in rehabilitating offenders. Officials were permitted to hold the criminal in custody until they determined that he or she was rehabilitated. Under this system, release from prison took the form of parole. Abuses of the system, combined with the decline of popular support for rehabilitation, have led most jurisdictions to abandon the concept of **indeterminate sentencing.**

Notwithstanding the trend away from indeterminate sentencing, a number of state laws retain indeterminate sentencing for youthful offenders. For example, New Jersey law specifies the following:

Any person who, at time of sentencing, is less than 26 years of age and who has been convicted of a crime may be sentenced to an indeterminate term at the Youth Correctional Institution Complex, … in the case of men, and to the Correctional Institute for

Women, … in the case of women, instead of the sentences otherwise authorized by the code. N.J. Stat. Ann. 2C: 43–5.

In *State v. Styker,* 619 A.2d 1016 (N.J. Super. 1993), the court pointed out that while the youthful offender law offers the benefits of rehabilitation in certain instances, "its application is now merely an option, the exercise of which is reserved solely for those limited cases where the sentencing court, in its sound discretion, deems it to be appropriate." *Id.* at 1024.

Definite and Determinate Sentencing

At the opposite extreme from indeterminate sentencing is **definite sentencing.** The concept here is to eliminate discretion and ensure that offenders who commit the same crimes are punished equally. The definite sentence is set by the legislature, with no leeway for judges or corrections officials to individualize punishment. Under **determinate sentencing,** a variation of the definite sentence, the judge sets a fixed term of years within statutory parameters, and the offender is required to serve that term without the possibility of early release. Although the sentence is for a fixed term, these laws often allow the trial court to increase the term if it finds one or more aggravating circumstances.

Indefinite Sentencing

The most common statutory approach to sentencing is referred to as **indefinite sentencing.** Here, there is judicial discretion to impose sentences within a range of prescribed minimum and maximum penalties for specific offenses. What distinguishes indefinite from determinate sentencing is that indefinite sentencing allows early release from prison on parole. An example of a statute that permits indefinite sentencing can be drawn from the New Jersey Code:

> Except as otherwise provided, a person who has been convicted of a crime may be sentenced to imprisonment, as follows: (1) In the case of a crime of the first degree,

CASE-IN-POINT

Penalty Enhancement Based on Aggravating Circumstances

John Cunningham was tried by jury and convicted in a California court of continuous sexual abuse of a child under the age of fourteen. The jury found him guilty but made no factual findings. The California determinate sentencing law required the trial court to sentence Cunningham to twelve years unless it found one or more additional facts in aggravation. The trial court found several aggravating factors and sentenced Cunningham to an additional four years' imprisonment. The sentence was affirmed by the state courts. The U.S. Supreme Court granted review and on January 22, 2007, held that California's determinate sentencing law, which authorized a judge, not a jury, to find facts exposing a convicted defendant to an elevated sentence, violated a defendant's right to trial by jury. Writing for a 6–3 majority, Justice Ruth Bader Ginsburg observed that the jury's verdict alone limited the permissible sentence to twelve years and that by sentencing Cunningham to an additional four years based on the trial court's fact finding, the trial court deprived him of his right to a jury trial under the Sixth Amendment.

Cunningham v. California, ___ U.S. ___, 127 S.Ct. 856, ___ L.Ed.2d ___ (2007).

for a specific term of years which shall be fixed by the court and shall be between 10 years and 20 years; (2) In the case of a crime of the second degree, for a specific term of years which shall be fixed by the court and shall be between 5 years and 10 years; (3) In the case of a crime of the third degree, for a specific term of years which shall be fixed by the court and shall be between 3 years and 5 years; (4) In the case of a crime of the fourth degree, for a specific term which shall be fixed by the court and shall not exceed 18 months. N.J. Stat. Ann. 2C: 43–6(a).

Except for certain offenses where a mandatory minimum sentence applies, New Jersey judges retain discretion to impose probation, fines, or other alternatives to incarceration. N.J. Stat. Ann. 2C: 43–2. If the judge opts for imprisonment, the judge's discretion is channeled as indicated earlier. The New Jersey scheme qualifies as indefinite sentencing because in most cases the law allows offenders to be released on parole before the completion of their prison terms.

Mandatory Minimum Sentencing

Mandatory sentences result from legislative mandates that offenders who commit certain crimes must be sentenced to prison terms for minimum periods. Under mandatory minimum sentencing, judges have no option to place offenders on probation. Most often, mandatory sentences are required for violent crimes, especially those involving the use of firearms. For example, Iowa law mandates that persons who use firearms in the commission of "forcible felonies" must be sentenced to a five-year minimum prison term with no eligibility for parole until the person has served the minimum sentence of confinement. Iowa Code Ann. § 902.7.

As a result of the "war on drugs" launched in the 1980s, federal law now mandates minimum prison terms for serious drug crimes prosecuted in federal courts. For example, a person charged with possession with the intent to distribute more than five kilograms of cocaine is subject to a mandatory minimum sentence of ten years in prison. See 21 U.S.C.A. § 841(b)(1)(A). In *Melendez v. United States,* 518 U.S. 120, 116 S.Ct. 2057, 135 L.Ed.2d 427 (1996), the U.S. Supreme Court made it clear in a unanimous decision that federal courts have no authority to impose lesser sentences than those mandated by Congress unless prosecutors specifically request such departures. This, of course, provides federal prosecutors substantial leverage in persuading defendants to provide evidence against other suspects, which is particularly useful in prosecuting drug distribution conspiracies.

Habitual Offender Statutes

In an effort to incapacitate habitual offenders, the laws of many states require automatic increased penalties for persons convicted of repeated felonies. For example, as Iowa law states:

> An habitual offender is any person convicted of a class "C" or a class "D" felony, who has twice before been convicted of any felony in a court of this or any other state, or of the United States. An offense is a felony if, by the law under which the person was convicted, it is so classified at the time of the person's conviction. A person sentenced as an habitual offender shall not be eligible for parole until he or she has served the minimum sentence of confinement of three years. Iowa Code Ann. § 902.8.

Most courts hold that habitual offender status is not established if a defendant committed the present offense before having been convicted of a prior offense. Courts have struggled with the issue of whether multiple convictions entered on one day are to be treated as separate or as one conviction, but they usually treat these multiple convictions as one irrespective of whether they arise from one or multiple criminal transactions.

In *Rummel v. Estelle*, 445 U.S. 263, 100 S.Ct. 1133, 63 L.Ed.2d 382 (1980), the U.S. Supreme Court upheld a life sentence imposed under the Texas habitual offender statute mandating life terms for persons convicted of three felonies. Rummel was convicted of obtaining $120.75 under false pretenses after previously being convicted of the fraudulent use of a credit card to obtain $80 worth of goods and passing a forged check for $28.36. After his third felony conviction, Rummel was sentenced to life imprisonment.

In *Solem v. Helm*, 463 U.S. 277, 103 S.Ct. 3001, 77 L.Ed.2d 637 (1983), the Court vacated a life sentence without parole under a South Dakota **habitual offender statute.** Because the defendant's convictions involved nonviolent felonies, the Court found the life sentence to be "significantly disproportionate" and thus invalid under the Eighth Amendment.

Go to the Scheb/ Scheb Criminal Law and Procedure 6e website at academic .cengage.com/criminaljustice/ scheb for an edited version of *Solem v. Helm*.

"Three Strikes and You're Out"

A variation on the habitual offender law is known colloquially as **three strikes and you're out.** In 1994 California voters overwhelmingly approved a ballot initiative under which persons convicted of a third violent or "serious" felony would be incarcerated for twenty-five years to life. Prosecutors immediately availed themselves of this new weapon, but in many instances the new law led to controversial results. In one well-known case, a man received twenty-five years to life after being convicted of robbery stemming from an incident where he stole a slice of pizza. *People v. Romero*, 917 P.2d 628 (Cal. 1996). In reversing the sentence, the California Supreme Court said that judges must retain the power to set sentences in furtherance of justice.

The 1994 Federal Crime Bill provided for mandatory life sentences for persons convicted in federal court of a "serious violent felony" after having been previously convicted, in federal or state court, of two "serious violent felonies" or "one or more serious violent felonies and one or more serious drug offenses; and each serious violent felony or serious drug offense used as a basis for sentencing under this subsection, other than the first, was committed after the defendant's conviction of the preceding serious violent felony or serious drug offense." 18 U.S.C.A. § 3559. Currently, the federal government and most states have some form of habitual offender or "three strikes" statute. In most states, prosecutions under these statutes are relatively infrequent.

In 2003 the U.S. Supreme Court upheld California's three strikes law against a constitutional challenge based on the Eighth Amendment's Cruel and Unusual Punishments Clause. The defendant in the case, Gary Ewing, was convicted of grand theft for stealing several golf clubs worth nearly $1,000. In 2000, when Ewing committed this crime, he was on parole after having served six years in prison for robbery and burglary committed in the fall of 1993. Aptly described by the Supreme Court as "no stranger to the criminal justice system," Ewing had previously been convicted of grand theft auto (1988), petit theft (1990), battery (1992), burglary (January 1993), possession of drug paraphernalia (February 1993), appropriating lost property (July 1993), and unlawful possession of a firearm and trespassing (September 1993). After being convicted of grand theft for stealing the golf clubs, Ewing was sentenced under the three strikes law to twenty-five years to life. In a 5–4 decision, the Supreme Court upheld Ewing's sentence and the three strikes statute on which it was based. *Ewing v. California*, 538 U.S. 11, 123 S.Ct. 1179, 155 L.Ed.2d 108 (2003). However, the Court failed to produce a majority opinion. Writing for a plurality of three justices, Justice O'Connor concluded that Ewing's sentence was constitutionally permissible as it was not "grossly disproportionate" to his offenses. The remaining members of the majority, Justices Thomas and Scalia, rejected the approach taken by Justice O'Connor. In their view, the Eighth Amendment "was aimed at excluding only certain *modes* of punishment, and was not a 'guarantee against disproportionate sentences.'" 538 U.S. at 31, 123 S.Ct. at 1190, 155 L.Ed.2d at 123. Writing for the four dissenters, Justice Stephen Breyer concluded that Ewing's sentence was "grossly disproportionate" inasmuch as it was "2 to 3 times the length of sentences that other jurisdictions would impose in similar circumstances." 538 U.S. at 52, 123 S.Ct. at 1202, 155 L.Ed.2d at 137.

Truth in Sentencing

Truth in sentencing refers to a movement that began in the 1980s to close the gap between the sentences imposed by courts and the time actually served in prison. Prior to the enactment of truth in sentencing laws, the average prisoner served less than half the sentence in prison before being paroled. The **Federal Sentencing Reform Act of 1984** dramatically toughened federal sentencing policies by abolishing parole, ending **good time credit** (time off for good behavior in prison), and prohibiting judges from imposing suspended sentences. Of course, these reforms applied only to the federal justice system. In 1994 Congress provided a strong financial incentive to the states to change their sentencing laws. The Violent Crime Control and Law Enforcement Act of 1994 provided federal grants to states that conform to the federal truth in sentencing guideline, which mandates actual confinement for at least 85 percent of the court-imposed prison sentence. By 2001, more than two-thirds of the states had adopted truth in sentencing laws to comply with the federal guideline. Since then, budgetary pressures have led some states to repeal or liberalize these laws.

Penalty Enhancement

Another approach to sentencing that has gained popularity in recent years is enhancing or extending penalties based on characteristics of the crime or the victim. For example, in an effort to strengthen law enforcement in the war on drugs, the Violent Crime Control and Law Enforcement Act of 1994 included several provisions for enhanced penalties. Drug trafficking in prisons and "drug-free" zones and illegal drug use in or smuggling drugs into federal prisons are now subject to enhanced penalties. See 42 U.S.C.A. §§ 14051, 14052.

ENHANCED PENALTIES FOR HATE CRIMES

As we noted in Chapter 6, recent years have seen growing concern over "hate crimes," crimes where victims are targeted on the basis of race, gender, or other characteristics. The federal government and many states currently have laws increasing the severity of punishment in hate crime cases. In 1993 the U.S. Supreme Court upheld a Wisconsin statute of this type. *Wisconsin v. Mitchell*, 508 U.S. 476, 113 S.Ct. 2194, 124 L.Ed.2d 436 (1993). Stressing that the statute was aimed at conduct rather than belief, the Court held that increasing punishment because the defendant targeted the victim on the basis of his race does not infringe the defendant's freedom of conscience as protected by the First Amendment.

Typically, **penalty enhancement statutes** require that a judge find by a preponderance of the evidence that a crime was racially motivated before applying penalty enhancement during sentencing. In a decision with far-reaching implications, the U.S. Supreme Court in June 2000 ruled that any fact that increases criminal punishment beyond the statutory maximum (other than a prior conviction) must be submitted to a jury and proved beyond a reasonable doubt. *Apprendi v. New Jersey*, 530 U.S. 466, 120 S.Ct. 2348, 147 L.Ed.2d 435 (2000). This 5–4 decision raises questions about numerous statutory sentencing schemes under which particular sentencing determinations are based on facts found by judges during sentencing rather than by juries as part of the trial.

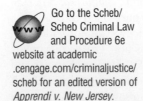

Go to the Scheb/ Scheb Criminal Law and Procedure 6e website at academic .cengage.com/criminaljustice/ scheb for an edited version of *Apprendi v. New Jersey.*

Sidebar — Justice Anthony Kennedy Speaks Out on Mandatory Sentencing

In a speech to a convention of the American Bar Association in San Francisco on August 9, 2003, Associate Justice Kennedy made the following observations about mandatory sentencing:

I accept neither the wisdom, the justice nor the necessity of mandatory minimums. In all too many cases they are unjust. I'll give you an example of how this works. A young man is on the George Washington Parkway which is a federal highway under the jurisdiction of federal park police, so federal law applies. He's stopped because he's not wearing a seat belt. He's eighteen years old. A search of the car reveals that he has a plastic bag with just over five grams of crack cocaine. His mandatory minimum sentence is five years.

Ladies and gentlemen I submit to you an eighteen year old doesn't know how long five years is. Our United States Marshals, a wonderful law enforcement agency, tell me time after time of going to the home to pick up a young man to serve and his mother says, "How long is my boy going to be gone?" and they will say five years or ten years or fifteen years. I could have given you some simple examples where there's ten and fifteen year minimums.

Every day in prison is much longer than most any day you have ever spent. One of the great classics of our time written by Alexander Solzhenitsyn talks about just one day in prison. Called *One Day in the Life of Ivan Denisovich,* … the book is one in which Denisovich realizes that he's survived another day of peril and agony. And he multiplies his ten year sen-

tence, he has a ten year sentence, by the number of days in the year. And the final passage of the book is something like this, "It was an almost sunny day. It was an almost happy day. One day in a sentence of three thousand six hundred and fifty three days from bell to bell." The three extra days were for leap years.

Now, part of the federal mandatory minimums have resulted because there's a shift in discretion from the courts to the prosecutors—sometimes to an assistant U.S. attorney not much older than the defendant. There is a shift from the one actor in the system that is trained in the use of the discretion. That gives reasons for it. That exercises it openly. And that's the judge. But the transfer is to the hidden parts of the prosecutor's office. And these are young prosecutors who often, probably in most cases, are conscientious about their duties. But it is simply unwise to take away our discretion from our United States judges….

The court on which I sit, on which I serve, and many other courts, have upheld very rigorous and severe sentencing schemes. But please remember that because a court has said something is permissible, it is not necessarily wise. And this is a mistake that we see all too often in our public and civic discourse. And in the accounts of what our court has done, in the press. It is simply not proper, as a matter of self governance, as a matter of exercising your political will, as a matter of discharging your political responsibility, to just pass off policy issues to the courts.

Sentencing Guidelines

Facing considerable criticism of judicial discretion, which often resulted in great disparities in sentences, Congress and a number of state legislatures adopted **sentencing guidelines.** Some states have adopted voluntary guidelines; others have mandated that sentencing conform to guidelines absent a compelling reason for departing from them.

THE SENTENCING REFORM ACT OF 1984

The federal guidelines came into being with the enactment of the Sentencing Reform Act of 1984, now codified at 18 U.S.C.A. §§ 3551 *et seq.* 28 U.S.C.A. §§ 991–998. The new act applies to all crimes committed after November 1, 1987. Its stated purpose was "to establish sentencing policies and practices for the federal criminal justice system that will assure the ends of justice by promulgating detailed guidelines prescribing the appropriate sentences for offenders convicted of federal crimes." To accomplish this, the act created the **United States Sentencing Commission** to establish sentencing guidelines. The commission promulgated guidelines that drastically reduced the discretion of federal judges by establishing a narrow sentencing range, with the requirement that judges who depart from these ranges state in writing their reasons for doing so. In addition, the new act provides for appellate review for sentences and abolishes the U.S. Parole Commission.

In *United States v. Scroggins,* 880 F.2d 1204 (11th Cir. 1989), the Eleventh Circuit Court of Appeals discussed the mechanics of sentencing under the new federal guidelines:

> [T]he district court begins the guidelines sentencing process by determining the circumstances of the defendant's offense conduct, the defendant's criminal history, and any other facts deemed relevant by the guidelines. The court then proceeds to assess the severity of the defendant's offense by applying the guidelines to the facts and circumstances of the defendant's offense conduct…. This process yields a numeric "total offense level" that consists of three elements: a "base offense level," which reflects the seriousness of the average offense sentenced under that particular guideline; "specific offense characteristics," which increase or decrease the base offense level in light of various factors considered relevant to the defendant's offense conduct; and "adjustments," which increase or decrease the offense level in light of certain factors considered generally relevant for sentencing purposes. The resulting total offense level can range from 1 (least serious) to 43 (most serious).
>
> Having determined the total offense level, the court next surveys the criminal history of the offender…. This inquiry places the defendant within a "criminal history category" that evaluates the need to increase his sentence incrementally to deter him from further criminal activity. By correlating the offense level with the offender's criminal history category on the sentencing table developed by the Sentencing Commission, the court then identifies the "guideline range" for the offender's sentence…. In general, the district court must sentence the offender within this range.

DEPARTURE FROM THE GUIDELINES

The sentence prescribed by the guidelines was not intended to be absolute. The sentencing court is permitted to depart from the guidelines if it "finds that there exists an aggravating or mitigating circumstance of a kind, or to a degree, not adequately taken into consideration … in formulating the guidelines that should result in a sentence different from that described." *United States v. Aguilar-Pena,* 887 F.2d 347, 349 (1st Cir. 1989). Of course, it is impermissible to depart from the guidelines on the basis of the defendant's race, sex, national origin, religion, or socioeconomic status. *United States v. Burch,* 873 F.2d 765 (5th Cir. 1989). Other factors not ordinarily deemed relevant in determining whether to depart include the defendant's age, education, mental and physical condition, employment history, and family and community ties. *United States v. Lira-Barraza,* 897 F.2d 981 (9th Cir. 1990), n. 5.

In *Nichols v. United States,* 511 U.S. 738, 114 S.Ct. 1921, 128 L.Ed.2d 745 (1994), the Supreme Court overruled precedent and held that a prior misdemeanor conviction in which the defendant was not represented by counsel could form the basis for a two-year sentence enhancement under the federal sentencing guidelines. Acting without counsel, Kenneth Nichols had pleaded no contest to a DUI charge in 1983. In 1990, then represented by counsel, Nichols was convicted of a federal drug conspiracy offense. The judge gave Nichols an enhanced sentence based on the prior DUI conviction. The Supreme Court upheld the enhanced sentence, saying that the sentencing process is a broad inquiry that may bring in information regarding the defendant's past misconduct even if it had not resulted in a criminal conviction. The Court thus went well beyond the facts of the case to permit federal judges broad discretion in handing

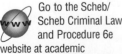

Go to the Scheb/ Scheb Criminal Law and Procedure 6e website at academic .cengage.com/criminaljustice/ scheb to find *Koon v. U.S.* (1996), where the U.S. Supreme Court discusses standards for downward departures from the federal sentencing guidelines.

down enhanced sentences under the sentencing guidelines. Critics of the Court's decision in *Nichols* pointed out that the reason the guidelines were adopted was to reduce judicial discretion in sentencing.

Blakely v. Washington, 542 U.S. 296, 124 S.Ct. 2531, 159 L.Ed.2d 403 (2004), involved a challenge to the Washington sentencing guidelines, which like the federal guidelines, permitted the trial court to enhance a defendant's sentence based on facts that were not found by a jury. The Supreme Court held that the state trial court's sentencing of a defendant to a prison term above the statutory maximum of the standard range for his offense, on the basis of the sentencing judge's finding that the defendant acted with deliberate cruelty, violated the defendant's Sixth Amendment right to a trial by jury.

Although Congress intended the federal sentencing guidelines to be mandatory, the U.S. Supreme Court's decision in *United States v. Booker,* 543 U.S. 220, 125 S.Ct. 738, 160 L.Ed.2d 621 (2005), effectively relegated the guidelines to an advisory position. Relying on its 2000 decisions in *Apprendi v. New Jersey,* supra, and its 2004 decision in *Blakely v. Washington,* supra, the Court in *Booker* held that, as originally constituted, the guidelines violated the Sixth Amendment right to trial by jury inasmuch as they authorized judges to increase sentences based on factual determinations not made by juries. Rather than invalidate the guidelines altogether, the *Booker* Court chose to strike down the provisions making them mandatory. In the wake of *Booker,* federal judges are not required to use the sentencing guidelines, but many still do use them on an "advisory" basis. To help eliminate some of the confusion that has followed the *Booker* decision, the Supreme Court in November 2006 granted review in *Claiborne v. United States,* 06-5618, and *Rita v. United States,* 06-5754, two of many cases reflecting the uncertainty of the lower federal courts with respect to the sentencing guidelines. Unfortunately, at the time that this book was being revised, those decisions were months away.

THE STATE EXPERIENCE

States have experimented with sentencing guidelines with varying results. Minnesota, the first state to adopt presumptive sentencing guidelines, in 1970, has a relatively simple system that has proven to be workable, although it has resulted in a higher incarceration rate. Washington's sentencing guidelines worked reasonably well until the state legislature began to mandate increased penalties overall as well as harsher minimum sentences for particular crimes. This has necessitated that the guidelines be revised. In Tennessee, the commission that established sentencing guidelines was terminated, although the guidelines themselves remain in effect. In Wisconsin, one of the early states to adopt sentencing guidelines, the sentencing commission as well as the guidelines it promulgated have been abolished by the state legislature because of political forces and fiscal pressures.

In 1990 the North Carolina legislature created the Sentencing and Policy Advisory Commission to study and repair a system of sentencing that had become dysfunctional. Due to prison overcrowding, felons were being paroled to the point that the system had become a revolving door. Thus, sentencing guidelines in North Carolina originated not so much from concern for sentencing disparity but from a desire to rationalize a system that had become chaotic. The commission followed the example of states such as Washington and Minnesota in adopting a simplified model of sentencing guidelines. Whereas the federal sentencing guidelines contain forty-three levels of felony offenses, the North Carolina guidelines contain ten levels. Thus far, the system seems to have worked reasonably well. However, it should be noted that North Carolina has eased pressure on the prison system by adopting intermediate measures such as house arrest and electronic monitoring for less serious offenders.

There is still considerable uncertainty about the efficacy of sentencing guidelines. There is evidence that they have reduced sentencing disparities, but they clearly have not eliminated this problem altogether. There is also concern that sentencing guidelines have generally promoted higher incarceration rates and have thus contributed to the problem of prison overcrowding. It is fair to say that to be successful, sentencing guidelines must be accompanied by policies designed to effectively manage prison populations.

Finally, state sentencing guidelines must now be viewed in the wake of the U.S. Supreme Court's decision in *Blakely v. Washington,* supra, where the Court held the State of Washington's sentencing guidelines unconstitutional to the extent they allowed a judge to enhance a defendant's criminal sentences based on facts other than those decided by a jury or confessed to by a defendant.

The Rights of Prisoners

Contrary to popular mythology, America's prisons are not country clubs. Although some **minimum security facilities** (like the military base where the Watergate conspirators were confined) are reasonably comfortable, **maximum security prisons** are another story. They are sometimes unsanitary; they are almost all overcrowded. All are violent, dangerous places to live.

The federal courts have made it clear that the Eighth Amendment's prohibition of cruel and unusual punishments imposes obligations on prison administrators to maintain certain standards of confinement. A sizable number of state prison systems have been or are currently under court orders to improve conditions of confinement or reduce overcrowding. Recently, some state courts have begun to focus their attention on the deplorable conditions existing in many city and county jails.

Historically, courts were quite unreceptive to claims brought by prisoners. They essentially adopted a "hands-off" policy, allowing prison officials free rein. In the late 1960s, that began to change as federal and state tribunals examined prison conditions and policies. As the courts signaled their willingness to scrutinize the prisons, litigation in this area mushroomed.

In one dramatic case involving prison conditions, Federal District Judge Frank M. Johnson Jr. found that the **conditions of confinement** in the Alabama system were barbarous and inhumane, thus violating the Eighth Amendment. Judge Johnson issued a detailed set of requirements to remedy the situation and appointed a special committee to oversee implementation of the order. Moreover, he threatened to close down the prison system unless his requirements were met. *Pugh v. Locke,* 406 F. Supp. 318 (M.D. Ala. 1976), aff'd sub. nom. *Newman v. Alabama,* 559 F.2d 283 (5th Cir. 1977).

Perhaps the most notorious story of prison conditions is that of the Arkansas prison system, which was scrutinized in a series of federal lawsuits beginning in 1969. *Holt v. Sarver,* 309 F. Supp. 362 (E.D. Ark. 1970), aff'd., 442 F.2d 304 (8th Cir. 1971). The most egregious conditions occurred at prison farms run largely by "trusties," senior prisoners entrusted with the job of controlling their fellow inmates. It should be noted that the trusty system is widely condemned by penologists. Under the Arkansas system, trusties smuggled in weapons, liquor, and drugs and sold them to the other inmates. Trusties hoarded food purchased with taxpayers' money and forced the other inmates to pay for their meals. Violence and even torture were commonly used by the trusties in maintaining their grip over the other prisoners. Medical care was almost totally lacking, and conditions of sanitation were miserable. Some prisoners were held in punitive isolation cells for months at a time. Overall, the penal farms were characterized by pervasive filth, disease, and violence.

In a series of decisions handed down during the 1970s, the federal district court issued detailed orders aimed at remedying the conditions in the Arkansas prison system. Especially controversial was an order placing a maximum limit of thirty days on the use of punitive isolation. The Supreme Court had little difficulty upholding this measure on appeal. *Hutto v. Finney,* 437 U.S. 678, 98 S.Ct. 2565, 57 L.Ed.2d 522 (1978).

Go to the Scheb/ Scheb Criminal Law and Procedure 6e website at academic .cengage.com/criminaljustice/ scheb for an edited version of *Hutto v. Finney.*

As currently interpreted, the Eighth Amendment requires that prisoners must be provided with reasonably adequate food, clothing, shelter, medical care, and sanitation. There must also be a reasonable assurance of their personal safety. Nevertheless, the Eighth Amendment does not require that prisoners be furnished everything they deem essential to their physical or psychological well-being. *Newman v. Alabama,* supra. Air conditioning, television, weightlifting equipment, and other nonessential items can be provided or removed at the discretion of prison authorities.

In 1992 the Supreme Court held that a prisoner who is beaten maliciously by guards may bring a civil action for damages based on a claim of cruel and unusual punishment, even if the prisoner does not suffer "significant injuries." *Hudson v. McMillian,* 503 U.S. 1, 112 S.Ct. 995, 117 L.Ed.2d 156 (1992). During the 1990s, prisoners began litigating the question of whether being subjected to environmental tobacco smoke (ETS) amounts to a violation of a prisoner's right to be free from cruel and unusual punishment under the Eighth Amendment. Lower federal courts recognized that the government has a duty to provide a safe environment for those incarcerated in its institutions but had disagreed as to whether exposure to ETS in a penitentiary setting constituted cruel and unusual punishment.

In 1993, the Supreme Court in *Helling v. McKinney,* 509 U.S. 25, 113 S.Ct. 2475, 125 L.Ed.2d 22, squarely faced the issue of whether the health risk posed by involuntary exposure of a prison inmate to ETS can be the basis of a claim for relief under the Eighth Amendment. In its landmark decision, the Court held that a prisoner who alleged that the prison system had, with "deliberate indifference," exposed him to levels of environmental tobacco that posed an unreasonable risk of serious damage to his future health stated an actionable claim under the Eighth Amendment against his custodians.

The Overcrowding Issue

Much of the current litigation challenging conditions of criminal confinement focuses on the problem of prison overcrowding. During the 1980s, the prison population in the United States nearly doubled. Rising crime rates and an increasingly punitive posture adopted by legislatures and courts, combined with fiscal stress, led to an overcrowding crisis in many prison systems. As mandatory sentence laws and sentencing guidelines have required judges to imprison larger numbers of convicted criminals, the number of prisoners has far outstripped the capacity of prisons in the United States. Today most state prisons are filled well beyond design capacity.

Throughout the 1980s, litigation in the federal courts by prisoners increased dramatically. Although the Supreme Court has said that "the Constitution does not mandate comfortable prisons," *Rhodes v. Chapman,* 452 U.S. 337, 101 S.Ct. 2392, 69 L.Ed.2d 59 (1981), lower federal courts have intervened to limit the number of inmates who can be housed in some prisons. The public is relatively unconcerned about prison overcrowding, but prison officials often welcome judicial intervention. Prison overcrowding makes it considerably more difficult to control inmate populations.

The Problem of Prison Rape

One of the most serious problems that a prison inmate can encounter is rape by a fellow inmate. Prison officials have not succeeded in eliminating this brutal aspect of prison life. Smaller, weaker inmates, especially those not aligned with a particular gang, are the most vulnerable to such attack. In recent years the problem has gained national attention, and in July 2003 Congress enacted the Prison Rape Reduction Act. The new act created a commission to examine all issues relating to the problem and requires the Department of Justice to provide assistance to federal, state, and local officials. It envisions the development of national standards applicable to the federal prisons with provisions for grants to encourage the states and local authorities to adopt such standards.

Other Rights of Prisoners

In addition to Eighth Amendment challenges to prison conditions, numerous lawsuits have sought to persuade the courts to recognize other **constitutional rights of prison inmates.** Traditionally, convicted felons were viewed as having forfeited most, if not all, of their constitutional rights. Thus, even reform-minded judges have been cautious in this area. For the most part they have deferred to prison officials, stressing the traditional view that "lawful incarceration brings about the necessary withdrawal or limitation of many privileges and rights, a retraction justified by the considerations underlying our penal system." *Price v. Johnston,* 334 U.S. 266, 285, 68 S.Ct. 1049, 92 L.Ed. 1356, 1369 (1948). Nevertheless, certain constitutional rights have been recognized. The Supreme Court has held that a prison inmate retains those First Amendment rights "that are not inconsistent with his status as a prisoner or with the legitimate penological objectives of the corrections system." *Pell v. Procunier,* 417 U.S. 817, 822, 94 S.Ct. 2800, 2804, 41 L.Ed.2d 495, 501 (1974).

For example, consider rights arising under the free exercise of religion clause of the First Amendment. Courts are generally receptive to prisoners' rights to possess Bibles, prayer books, and other religious materials, as well as inmates' rights to be visited by the clergy. On the other hand, courts have generally upheld restrictions on religious exercises if they disrupt prison order or routine. See, for example, *O'Lone v. Estate of Shabazz,* 482 U.S. 342, 107 S.Ct. 2400, 96 L.Ed.2d 282 (1987). If prison officials allow inmates who belong to mainstream religious denominations to attend worship services, however, then members of other religious sects must be given a reasonable opportunity to exercise their religious beliefs as well. *Cruz v. Beto,* 405 U.S. 319, 92 S.Ct. 1079, 31 L.Ed.2d 263 (1972).

One of the most firmly established rights of prisoners is the right of access to the courts. The Supreme Court made it clear decades ago that prison officials may not deny inmates access to the courts or penalize them for using that access. *Ex parte Hull,* 312 U.S. 546, 61 S.Ct. 640, 85 L.Ed. 1034 (1941). Similarly, courts have held that indigent inmates must be furnished writing materials and notary services to assist them in filing petitions and seeking writs from courts. Courts have generally upheld the right of prisoners to meet with counsel in privacy and, in the absence of other forms of legal assistance, to have access to law libraries. See *Bounds v. Smith,* 430 U.S. 817, 97 S.Ct. 1491, 52 L.Ed.2d 72 (1977).

The courts have also recognized that prisoners are entitled to limited rights of expression. For example, prisoners retain a limited right to communicate with the outside world via the mails, although prison officials may limit and censor the mail prisoners send and receive, provided there is no interference with attorney–client relationships. *Lee v. Tahash,* 352 F.2d 970 (8th Cir. 1965).

Prison officials also have broad latitude to restrict visitation privileges if there is reason to believe that an inmate is receiving contraband being smuggled into the prison by visitors. *Kentucky Department of Corrections v. Thompson,* 490 U.S. 454, 109 S.Ct. 1904, 104 L.Ed.2d 506 (1989). Likewise, prison regulations impinging on inmates' interests in free assembly and association have been consistently upheld. See, for example, *Jones v. North Carolina Prisoners' Labor Union, Inc.,* 433 U.S. 119, 97 S.Ct. 2532, 53 L.Ed.2d 629 (1977), where the Supreme Court refused to extend First Amendment protection to an effort to organize a labor union among prisoners. Obviously, prison is by definition antithetical to the ideas of freedom of assembly and freedom of association. Congress enacted the Ensign Amendment as part of the Omnibus Consolidated Appropriations Act of 1997. Pub. L. No. 104-208, § 614, 110 Stat. 3009-66 (1996). The Ensign Amendment prohibits prisons from using federal funds to distribute any information or material that is sexually explicit or features nudity. The law exempts any nudity featured for purposes of medical, educational, or anthropological content.

Prison Disciplinary Measures

The federal courts have imposed limits on **prison disciplinary measures** such as corporal punishment and the extended use of **punitive isolation.** Today, at least in most state prisons, discipline is largely accomplished by granting and removing good-time credit—that is, early release for good behavior. If officials pursue this policy, then due process demands that certain procedural requirements be observed before good time credit is removed for disciplinary purposes. Specifically, there must be written notice of the disciplinary action, and the inmate has the right to an administrative hearing with a written record. The inmate must be accorded the right to produce evidence refuting the charges of misconduct and may even call witnesses on his or her behalf. *Wolff v. McDonnell,* 418 U.S. 539, 94 S.Ct. 2963, 41 L.Ed.2d 935 (1974). These rights have not been extended to allow an inmate to have counsel present at such a hearing. *Baxter v. Palmigiano,* 425 U.S. 308, 96 S.Ct. 1551, 47 L.Ed.2d 810 (1976).

Parole and Its Revocation

Historically, the federal government and most states provided for early release from prison on **parole** for those inmates who could demonstrate to the parole board's satisfaction their willingness to conform their conduct to the requirements of the law. In recent years, parole has been abolished or restricted greatly in many jurisdictions. This generally corresponds to the "truth in sentencing" movement described above.

Naturally, there are also provisions by which parole can be revoked if the offender violates the conditions of release. As with internal prison disciplinary actions, the revocation of parole is affected by due process considerations. Essentially, before parole can be revoked, the parolee has the right to a hearing within a reasonable time after being retaken into custody. *Morrissey v. Brewer,* 408 U.S. 471, 92 S.Ct. 2593, 33 L.Ed.2d 484 (1972). However, the Supreme Court has stressed the informality of this hearing, saying that "the process should be flexible enough to consider evidence including letters, affidavits, and other material that would not be admissible in an adversary criminal trial." 408 U.S. at 489, 92 S.Ct. at 2604, 33 L.Ed.2d at 499. In practice, courts generally admit any relevant evidence that is not privileged, but as previously pointed out in respect to revocation of probation, courts generally do not allow revocation of parole based solely on hearsay evidence. See, for example, *Grello v. Commonwealth,* 477 A.2d 45 (Pa. Cmwlth. 1984). A year after its decision in *Morrissey v. Brewer,* the Supreme Court held that the right to counsel may apply to **parole revocation hearings,** depending on the complexity of the issues involved. *Gagnon v. Scarpelli,* supra.

The Rights of Crime Victims

Although crime is by definition an injury against society as a whole, we must not forget that most serious crimes injure individual victims, often quite severely. The injury may transcend physical or economic injury to include emotional hardship. During the 1960s the dominant concern of the criminal law was for the rights of the accused. In the 1990s the trend was to recognize the rights of crime victims. Most states have adopted constitutional amendments specifically recognizing **victims' rights,** while others have adopted statutes along these lines. See, for example, West's Ann. Cal. Penal Code § 679 *et seq.* Recently, a proposal to add a victims' rights amendment to the U.S. Constitution surfaced in Congress. Clearly, substantial public support exists for efforts to recognize and enhance victims' rights.

The Uniform Victims of Crime Act

The **Uniform Victims of Crime Act** (UVCA) is an attempt to lend uniformity to the patchwork of victims' rights laws that now exists at the state level. The UVCA was developed by the Uniform Law Commission, a voluntary association representing the legal profession. Like the Model Penal Code developed by the American Law Institute, the UVCA has no status as law unless and until it is adopted by a state legislature.

Under the UVCA, prosecutors or court personnel must notify victims of their rights under the act, as well as the times of any court proceedings involving the person or persons who allegedly victimized them. A crime victim has the right to be present at any court proceeding that the defendant has the right to attend. If the defendant is convicted, the victim has the right to make an impact statement during the sentencing hearing and assert an opinion as to the proper sentence. Finally, the UVCA provides for victims to be compensated by the state, up to $25,000, for any physical or emotional injuries suffered as the result of the victimization. However, this amount may be denied or reduced if the victim receives compensation through insurance or restitution from the defendant.

Restitution

Restitution is a time-honored means of protecting the interests of crime victims. Restitution refers to "the return of a sum of money, an object, or the value of an object that the defendant wrongfully obtained in the course of committing the crime." *State v. Stalheim,* 552 P.2d 829, 832 (Or. 1976). Although restitution was practiced under the early common law, it was eventually abandoned as a remedy in criminal cases in favor of fines payable to the Crown. In modern America, however, restitution is making a comeback in the criminal law. Several states have enacted laws allowing trial courts to require restitution as a condition of probation in lieu of sentencing offenders to prison. In states that have adopted restitution laws, courts have held that

(1) restitution is not necessarily incompatible with incarceration, *State v. Murray,* 621 P.2d 334 (Hawaii 1980); (2) restitution may be ordered for damages caused by the defendant during a criminal episode, irrespective of whether the loss is directly related to a specific conviction, *People v. Gallagher,* 223 N.W.2d 92 (Mich. App. 1974); and (3) a defendant may be ordered to pay restitution to a party other than the victim, *Shenah v. Henderson,* 476 P.2d 854 (Ariz. 1970).

Restitution is not practical in many criminal cases. Many offenders are not suited to probation, and even among those who are, there is no guarantee that they will be able to make payments to the victim. Recognizing this problem, several states have established victims' compensation commissions. For example, the Florida Crimes Compensation Act of 1977 makes victims and certain relatives eligible for compensation from a state commission where a crime results in injuries and is reported within seventy-two hours. Awards are limited to meeting the victims' actual needs. West's Fla. Stat. Ann. §§ 960.001–960.298.

■ CONCLUSION

The various forms of punishment meted out to convicted criminals rest on differing assumptions about crime and human nature. These assumptions lead to differing philosophies of punishment that stress retribution, deterrence, incapacitation, or rehabilitation. A great debate continues regarding both the propriety of these goals and the efficacy of the measures designed to achieve them. In particular, the deterrent value of the death penalty and the rehabilitative value of incarceration have been seriously questioned.

Courts of law tend to avoid the philosophical, theoretical, and empirical questions that surround the various forms of criminal punishment. Rather, they focus on the substantive and procedural limitations that the federal and state constitutions impose on the criminal justice system. In so doing, they tend to reflect the dominant values of the society. Thus, courts have not hesitated to invalidate torture and flogging as cruel and unusual punishments forbidden by the Eighth Amendment, yet they have been extremely reluctant to reach similar conclusions regarding the death penalty.

One current issue in criminal justice is the problem of sentencing disparity. The death penalty has been challenged, albeit unsuccessfully, as being racially discriminatory. But the allegations of disparity extend well beyond the death penalty to encompass the entire regime of criminal punishment. One approach to reducing sentencing disparity is to limit judicial discretion through more determinate sentencing. The Supreme Court has limited a trial judge from varying such sentences based on facts not found by a jury. Another approach to reducing sentencing disparity is the development of sentencing guidelines; however, recent Supreme Court rulings also limit enhancement of sentences to factors confessed by a defendant or found by a jury.

With rising crime rates in the 1970s and 1980s, the public demanded harsher sentences, especially for violent and repeat offenders. Legislative bodies responded by imposing mandatory minimum sentences for certain offenses. Advocates of mandatory sentencing point to the deterrent effects of requiring equal treatment of offenders, especially those who commit certain violent crimes and major drug offenses. Yet the concept of mandatory sentences evokes considerable controversy among many academicians, judges, and criminal justice professionals. The threat of a mandatory sentence may be a deterrent to crime, yet when a legislative body makes a predetermination of a sentence it removes the ability of a judge to consider the circumstances of an offense, the background and character of the defendant, and available sentencing options. It is contrary to the practice of individualized sentencing that many associate with the dispensing of justice.

Over the last several decades, courts have become more active in the area of prisoners' rights. Decisions have protected inmates' access to counsel and the courts, invalidated extreme conditions of confinement, and recognized limited First Amendment freedoms. Courts have imposed minimal due process requirements on prison disciplinary proceedings and on parole and probation revocation decisions as well. On the other hand, courts have tended to defer to corrections officials regarding most substantive restrictions on inmate behavior. In most instances, the public has shown little concern for conditions of confinement and rights of prisoners.

There is profound dissatisfaction with the nation's prison system. Little evidence exists that prisons provide any sort of meaningful rehabilitation. Yet few observers have proposed viable alternatives for dealing with violent criminals. As crime rates soared over the last three decades, the public began to demand stiffer sentences, especially for repeat offenders. The result is a prison system that is grossly overcrowded. In truth, our nation's correctional system is in a state of crisis. As the crisis worsens, policy makers face three choices: (1) change the criminal laws to make sentencing more lenient, (2) appropriate more revenues to construct new prison facilities, or (3) develop effective alternatives to confinement. Society appears reluctant to follow either of the first two courses, so exploring meaningful alternatives to incarceration is essential.

■ KEY TERMS

■ WEB-BASED RESEARCH ACTIVITY

 Go to the Web. Locate your state's statutes pertaining to criminal procedure. Does your state impose a mandatory minimum sentence for a defendant who is convicted of carrying a firearm during the commission of any offense? What sentence must be imposed?

■ QUESTIONS FOR THOUGHT AND DISCUSSION

1. Why have the courts generally viewed corporal punishment as "cruel and unusual" yet been unwilling to take the same view of capital punishment?

2. How could a prisoner on death row establish that his or her death sentence was the result of racial discrimination?

3. Does your state impose the death penalty? If so, what does the state law provide with respect to juries considering aggravating and mitigating factors? Do you think your state's law governing the death penalty should be amended? If so, explain why and how.

4. What alternatives to imprisonment exist to deal with violent criminals who are repeat offenders? What alternatives, if any, would you propose? What legal problems are implicit in these alternatives to incarceration?

5. Discuss the pros and cons of mandatory sentences. Do mandatory sentences remove discretion from the sentencing judge and vest discretion in the prosecutor who may elect to charge a defendant with a lesser offense to avoid imposition of a mandatory sentence?

6. Suppose you were a probation officer and a judge asked you to recommend probation conditions for a first-time offender convicted of the sale and possession of cocaine. What specific conditions would you propose?

7. Should a defendant always be permitted to view the contents of a presentence report? What are the arguments for and against this?

8. In August of 2003, Justice Kennedy made a speech in which he strongly criticized mandatory sentencing laws. (Excerpts from the speech are contained in a sidebar on page 567.) Do you agree or disagree with Justice Kennedy? Why?

9. What implications do the U.S. Supreme Court's recent decisions in *Apprendi v. New Jersey* (2000), *Blakely v. Washington* (2004), and *United States v. Booker* (2005) have for future use of sentencing guidelines?

10. What is the rationale for granting only minimal due process rights to parolees and probationers and to prisoners in disciplinary proceedings?

11. To what extent have the legal rights of prisoners been expanded since the 1960s? Have the courts been unduly solicitous in entertaining lawsuits brought by prison inmates?

12. Do you think that the introduction of a victim impact statement during the sentencing phase of a capital trial is appropriate, or do you think it might inject too much emotionalism into the process?

■ PROBLEMS FOR DISCUSSION AND SOLUTION

1. Inmate Jay Leburd has brought suit in federal court challenging the conditions of his confinement in the Intensive Management Unit (IMU) of a maximum

security state prison. Specifically, Leburd argues that the lack of any opportunity for outdoor exercise, total lack of reading materials, and absence of radio and television amount to "cruel and unusual punishment" in violation of the Eighth Amendment. Responding to the suit, the state prison system has conceded that the conditions in the IMU are "substantially as described by plaintiff." Nevertheless, the state has asked the court to dismiss the suit on the ground that "the Eighth Amendment does not guarantee fresh air and sunshine to inmates in solitary confinement, nor does it require that they be entertained." What is the federal judge likely to do? What do you think the judge should do?

2. In 1987 Douglas Deville was convicted in a state court for felonious possession of cocaine. He received probation for that offense. Three years later, Deville was found guilty of another drug-related felony in the same state. For that offense, he served five years in state prison. Three months after being released from prison, Deville was arrested for possession of 100 grams of cocaine base and 400 grams of marijuana. This time the case was prosecuted in federal court, where Deville was convicted of felony possession with intent to distribute. Because this was his third drug-related felony, Deville was sentenced to life imprisonment without parole under 21 U.S.C.A. § 841(b)(1)(A) (1994). On appeal, Deville claims that this sentence is "utterly disproportionate to his offense" and that, accordingly, it constitutes a violation of the Eighth Amendment's Cruel and Unusual Punishment Clause. Deville is relying on the U.S. Supreme Court's opinion in *Solem v. Helm,* 463 U.S. 277 (1983). Does Deville have a case? Is he likely to prevail? In your opinion, is Deville's sentence fair and just? Is it constitutional?

CHAPTER 20

Appeal and Postconviction Relief

CHAPTER OUTLINE

Introduction

Society's commitment to standards of fairness and procedural regularity is reflected in the opportunities that exist for defendants in criminal cases to seek judicial review of adverse court decisions. These opportunities have increased in recent decades, largely through judicial interpretation of various constitutional and statutory provisions.

Forms of review in criminal cases include **trial *de novo*, appeal of right, discretionary review,** and **postconviction relief.** Trial *de novo* occurs when a trial court of general jurisdiction reviews a conviction rendered by a court of limited jurisdiction. Appeal of right, the most common form of appeal, refers to an appellate court's review of a criminal conviction rendered by a trial court of general jurisdiction. A defendant whose conviction is affirmed on appeal may seek further review by a higher court by petitioning for discretionary review. Finally, a defendant confined to prison may seek additional review of his or her conviction or sentence by applying for a **writ of habeas corpus** or seeking another form of postconviction relief. The writ of habeas corpus allows a court of competent jurisdiction to review the legality of a prisoner's confinement. This device permits prisoners to raise a variety of legal issues in attacking their convictions and sentences. Each mechanism plays an important part in determining cases that move beyond the trial stage of the criminal process. In addition to correcting errors made by lower courts, appeals allow higher courts to refine and standardize both the substantive and procedural law.

Error Correction and Lawmaking Functions of Appellate Courts

Appellate courts perform dual functions in the criminal process: **error correction** and **lawmaking.** Most criminal appeals are reviewed by intermediate federal or state appellate courts, although in the less populous states, routine appeals are handled by the highest court of the state (see Figure 20.1). In these routine appeals, the primary function of appellate courts is correcting errors made by trial courts. Appellate review is designed to ensure that substantive justice has been accomplished under constitutional standards of due process of law. Because of gaps in the statutory law and the inevitable need to interpret both statutory and constitutional provisions, appellate courts in effect must "make law." This lawmaking function is more characteristic of the highest levels of courts than of intermediate appellate tribunals.

The Common-Law Background

Before the eighteenth century, there was no common-law right to appeal from a criminal conviction. On rare occasions, the Crown issued a writ of error to require a new trial, but there was no appeal in the modern sense. Indeed, the term "appeal" at common law had a very different usage from ours. At common law, appeal referred to an effort by a person convicted of treason to obtain a pardon from the Crown by accusing others of being accomplices to the treasonable act.

In a landmark decision, the Court of King's Bench ruled in 1705 that a **writ of error** had to be issued where a person convicted of a misdemeanor made proper application for the writ. *Paty's Case,* 91 Eng. Rep. 431 (K.B. 1705). In cases of felony and treason, the writ of error continued to be discretionary, although after 1700 the courts became more liberal in their issuance of the writ. The writ of error was finally

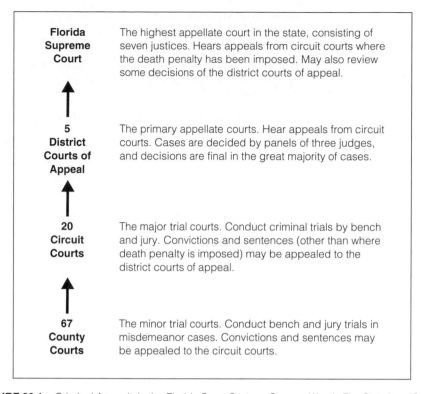

Florida Supreme Court — The highest appellate court in the state, consisting of seven justices. Hears appeals from circuit courts where the death penalty has been imposed. May also review some decisions of the district courts of appeal.

5 District Courts of Appeal — The primary appellate courts. Hear appeals from circuit courts. Cases are decided by panels of three judges, and decisions are final in the great majority of cases.

20 Circuit Courts — The major trial courts. Conduct criminal trials by bench and jury. Convictions and sentences (other than where death penalty is imposed) may be appealed to the district courts of appeal.

67 County Courts — The minor trial courts. Conduct bench and jury trials in misdemeanor cases. Convictions and sentences may be appealed to the circuit courts.

FIGURE 20.1   Criminal Appeals in the Florida Court System. Source: West's Fla. Stat. Ann. Const. Art. V. §§ 1–6; West's Fla. Stat. Ann. chs. 26, 34, 35.

abolished when Parliament enacted the Criminal Appeal Act of 1907, giving defendants the right to appeal their convictions.

Appeal of Right

The federal constitution makes no mention of the right to appeal from a criminal conviction, although some might argue that the right to appeal is implicit in the Due Process Clauses of the Fifth and Fourteenth Amendments. In 1894 the U.S. Supreme Court held that the federal constitution provides no right to appeal from a criminal conviction. *McKane v. Durston,* 153 U.S. 684, 14 S.Ct. 913, 38 L.Ed. 867 (1894). Given the recent expansion of the concept of due process, it is likely that the Court would reconsider this holding but for the fact that federal and state statutes allow criminal defendants to appeal their convictions and seek other forms of postconviction relief. Defendants convicted after entering a plea of not guilty are entitled under federal and state law to one appeal as a matter of right.

Appeals of right in federal criminal cases are heard by U.S. courts of appeals (circuit courts). State criminal appeals are heard by state supreme courts, by intermediate appellate courts, and—in Alabama, Oklahoma, Tennessee, and Texas—by specialized appellate courts that hear only criminal appeals. Beyond these appeals of right, opportunities exist for defendants to have their cases reviewed by the highest state courts and the U.S. Supreme Court, which may review convictions by issuing

writs of certiorari. Many states provide automatic appeals of death sentences to their highest court (see Chapter 19).

A party who takes an appeal of right is called the **appellant;** the party against whom the appeal is taken is the **appellee.** A party who seeks further review is referred to as the **petitioner;** the other party is designated the **respondent.**

What Defendants May Challenge on Appeal

In a direct appeal from a criminal conviction, a defendant may challenge any act of the trial court objected to by the defendant during the pretrial, trial, or posttrial phases of the defendant's case. Irrespective of whether an objection was made in the trial court, a defendant may challenge the trial court's jurisdiction and those trial court actions or rulings considered to be **fundamental errors.** Appellate courts take different approaches to how serious an error must be to be classified as fundamental. Essentially, the courts will deem an error to be fundamental if it undermines confidence in the integrity of the criminal proceeding. When the defendant has been convicted of a capital crime, courts are more liberal in reviewing errors first challenged at the appellate stage. Indeed, the U.S. Supreme Court has said that those fundamental errors not specifically challenged by the appellant should be corrected when a person's life is at stake. *Fisher v. United States,* 328 U.S. 463, 66 S.Ct. 1318, 90 L.Ed. 1382 (1946).

In practice, a defendant usually raises from one to six major points on appeal as a basis for reversal of the trial court's judgment or sentence. Often these points are referred to as **assignments of error.** The most common assignments of error on direct appeal are claims that the trial court erred in rulings in one or more of the following areas:

1. Pretrial violations of the defendant's rights, particularly those rights guaranteed by the Fourth, Fifth, and Sixth Amendments to the federal constitution
2. Procedural matters, especially trial court rulings admitting or excluding evidence
3. Irregularities in the impaneling or conduct of the jury
4. Failure to give jury instructions requested by the defendant or giving instructions objected to by the defendant
5. Prosecutorial misconduct such as improper remarks or arguments

Sidebar   **Success Rates of Types of Claims on Appeal in State Courts**

A 1989 study conducted for the National Center for State Courts looked at the distribution of outcomes in five representative appellate courts across the country. Nearly 80 percent of all judgments were affirmed in these courts during the period under study. Of the reversals, the most frequent outcome was a remand for resentencing. In less than 10 percent of these reversals did defendants win outright acquittal. The most frequent claims of error in criminal appeals in these five appellate courts involved the admissibil-ity of challenged evidence. Yet less than 8 percent of these claims resulted in reversals. The second-most commonly raised issue involved the trial judge's instructions to the jury. Roughly 10 percent of these claims resulted in reversals.

See Joy A. Chapper and Roger A. Hanson, "Understanding Reversible Error in Criminal Appeals," *Final Report Submitted to the State Justice Institute,* National Center for State Courts, October 1989, p. 5.

6. Sufficiency of the evidence to support a finding of the defendant's guilt beyond a reasonable doubt

7. Interpretations of statutes or ordinances

8. The legality and, in some jurisdictions, the reasonableness of the sentence imposed

9. Jury selection, deliberation, and misconduct

10. The voluntariness of a guilty plea

The Doctrine of Harmless Error

Although appellate review is designed to correct errors that occur before, during, or after trial, not all errors necessitate reversal. To obtain reversal of a judgment, the appellant must generally show that some prejudice resulted from the error and that the outcome of the trial or the sentence imposed would probably have been different in the absence of the error. Although specific standards vary among jurisdictions, all appellate courts operate on the principle that reversal is required only when substantial, as distinct from merely technical, errors are found in the record. This approach is illustrated by a provision of the California constitution that permits reversal on appeal only to prevent a **miscarriage of justice.** The California Supreme Court has interpreted this standard as follows:

> [A] "miscarriage of justice" should be declared only when the court, after an examination of the entire cause, including the evidence, is of the opinion that it is reasonably probable that a result more favorable to the appealing party would have been reached in the absence of the error. *People v. Watson,* 299 P.2d 243, 254 (Cal. 1956).

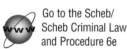 Go to the Scheb/ Scheb Criminal Law and Procedure 6e website at academic .cengage.com/criminaljustice/ scheb for an edited version of *Chapman v. California.*

Appellate courts frequently find that technical errors cited by appellants are harmless and do not merit a reversal; however, the U.S. Supreme Court has imposed a strict standard on the finding of harmless error. Where an error at trial involves provisions of the federal constitution, the Supreme Court has said that appellate courts must find beyond a reasonable doubt that the error was harmless if they are to affirm the trial court. *Chapman v. California,* 386 U.S. 18, 87 S.Ct. 824, 17 L.Ed.2d 705 (1967).

The **doctrine of harmless error** is subject to certain qualifications. For example, appellate courts generally do not consider each error at trial in isolation. Rather, they often consider the cumulative effect of a series of errors. Thus, an appellant might secure reversal of a conviction where the trial was replete with error, even though each particular error might be considered harmless by itself.

When an Appeal May Be Taken by a Defendant

Generally, only a defendant who has pled not guilty has the right to appeal, and that appeal must wait until the defendant has been convicted and sentenced. However, there are some instances in which courts permit other appeals by defendants. For example, an order modifying or revoking probation is usually appealable.

Typically, a defendant who pleads guilty may raise on appeal only those issues relating to the trial court jurisdiction, the voluntariness of the guilty plea, and the legality of the sentence imposed. Even then, an appellate court may refuse to review these aspects of a case, other than the issue of jurisdiction, unless the trial court has refused the defendant's request to withdraw the plea of guilty.

Federal Rule of Criminal Procedure 11(a)(2) provides, "With the consent of the court and the government, a defendant may enter a conditional plea of guilty or *nolo contendere,* reserving in writing the right to have an appellate court review an adverse determination of a specified pretrial motion. A defendant who prevails on appeal may then withdraw the plea."

Some state jurisdictions also permit a defendant to plead *nolo contendere* or guilty and reserve the right to appeal a specific ruling of the trial court. See, for example, Fla. Stat. § 924.051. Defendants who unsuccessfully employ a constitutional defense frequently rely on this procedure. For instance, a defendant may file a pretrial motion to suppress certain evidence on the ground that it was obtained in violation of the Fourth Amendment, or a motion challenging the legal sufficiency of the charging document or constitutionality of a controlling statute. If the trial judge denies the motion, the defendant can plead *nolo contendere,* reserving the right to appeal that specific point of law. Generally the point reserved must be one that would be dispositive of the appeal.

Appeals by the Prosecution

Early rulings by American state courts uniformly denied state governments the right to appeal acquittals of criminal defendants. The U.S. Supreme Court adopted this position in 1892, when it ruled that the federal government had no right to appeal an acquittal. *United States v. Sanges,* 144 U.S. 310, 12 S.Ct. 609, 36 L.Ed. 445 (1892). This prohibition is sensible inasmuch as the Double Jeopardy Clause of the Fifth Amendment (applicable to the states through the Fourteenth Amendment) prohibits a defendant who has been acquitted from being tried again for the same offense.

Texas law makes the following provisions regarding the prosecution's right to appeal:

(a) The state is entitled to appeal an order of a court in a criminal case if the order:

(1) dismisses an indictment, information, or complaint or any portion of an indictment, information, or complaint;

(2) arrests or modifies a judgment;

(3) grants a new trial;

(4) sustains a claim of former jeopardy;

(5) grants a motion to suppress evidence, a confession, or an admission, if jeopardy has not attached in the case and if the prosecuting attorney certifies to the trial court that the appeal is not taken for the purpose of delay and that the evidence, confession, or admission is of substantial importance in the case;

(6) is issued under Chapter 64 [refers to orders concerning DNA testing].

(b) The state is entitled to appeal a sentence in a case on the ground that the sentence is illegal.

(c) The state is entitled to appeal a ruling on a question of law if the defendant is convicted in the case and appeals the judgment....

(d) The state is entitled to appeal an order granting relief to an applicant for a writ of habeas corpus....

Vernon's Tex. Code Crim. Proc. Art. 44.01.

Either by statute or rule of court, most states afford similar opportunities for appeals by the prosecution. Similarly, 18 U.S.C.A. § 3731 permits the federal government to appeal an order of a federal district court (a) dismissing an indictment, (b) granting a new trial after judgment or verdict, (c) releasing a defendant before trial or after conviction, or (d) suppressing evidence before the time that the defendant is put in jeopardy. Both the government and the defendant have the right to appeal from a sentence imposed in violation of law, one that results from an erroneous application of a sentencing guideline, or one that is imposed by the court in violation of the terms of a plea agreement. Appeals by the prosecution from sentencing require prior approval by the office of the Attorney General or Solicitor General. 18 U.S.C.A. § 3742(a)&(b).

The constitutional proscription of double jeopardy does not prevent appeals by the prosecutor of pretrial orders because jeopardy does not apply before the impaneling of a jury or the taking of evidence in a nonjury trial. *Crist v. Bretz,* 437 U.S. 28, 98 S.Ct. 2156, 57 L.Ed.2d 24 (1978); *Serfass v. United States,* 420 U.S. 377, 95 S.Ct. 1055; 43 L.Ed.2d 265 (1975).

Trial *de Novo* in Minor Misdemeanor Cases

Most criminal appeals are heard "on the record." This means that the appellate court is asked to scrutinize the official record of the pretrial, trial, and posttrial proceedings for procedural errors that would require reversal of the judgment. Many misdemeanor cases are tried in local courts that are not courts of record; therefore, no record of the proceedings is available for review. Most of these involve summary justice. Trial is before a judge or magistrate without a jury in what is commonly called a bench trial. Counsel is rarely present, and frequently the only witnesses for the prosecution are police officers. The defendant may or may not choose to testify. Yet persons convicted of misdemeanors are generally entitled to an appeal by law. Where no record has been made of the proceedings, a trial *de novo* (literally, a "new trial") is held in a trial court of superior jurisdiction. In many instances, persons convicted at trial *de novo* may take an appeal to a higher court, but further review of such cases is generally discretionary.

Discretionary Review

A defendant whose conviction has been sustained by an intermediate appellate court may petition a court of last resort for discretionary review. In the U.S. Supreme Court and most state supreme courts, discretionary review occurs through the grant of a writ of certiorari. Rule 13 of the Rules of the U.S. Supreme Court states that a "petition for a writ of certiorari ... shall be in time when it is filed ... within 90 days after the entry of the judgment" of the lower court. The highest court in each state (usually the state supreme court) may entertain petitions if they are filed within the time prescribed by the court's rules, usually thirty days after the intermediate appellate court enters its decision.

"**Cert petitions,**" as they are commonly called, are granted at the discretion of the reviewing court. In deciding whether to exercise its discretion, the U.S. Supreme Court evaluates whether a **substantial federal question** is involved. If so, the Court is then interested in whether the petitioner has exhausted all other remedies available. In deciding whether to grant certiorari, the Court follows the **rule of four,** meaning that at least four of the nine justices must vote to place a case on the docket.

In determining whether to grant review, the high state appellate tribunals usually have unlimited discretion. The U.S. Supreme Court's rule of four serves as a model for some state supreme courts; however, others are guided by formal or informal rules in determining whether to "grant cert." Among the criteria frequently employed are whether the intermediate appellate court's decision conflicts with a decision of another intermediate court or the supreme court, is without authoritative precedent, or departs from the essential requirements of the law.

Steps in the Appellate Process

Usually the appellate process in a criminal appeal will take between nine and twelve months, depending on whether counsel must seek extensions of permitted times for record preparation and briefing, whether the case is orally argued, and the court's caseload. The following describes the usual steps in a direct appeal of right to a state or federal appellate court.

1. **Filing a notice of appeal by appellant** (usually filed with the clerk of a lower court with a copy served on the opposing party).

2. **Filing a record of lower court proceedings,** and, where there has been a trial, evidentiary exhibits, transcript of trial testimony, and the judge's instructions to the jury. Although this is a function of the court reporter and clerk of the lower court, the appellant is responsible for ensuring that the record is properly completed and filed in the appellate court.

3. **Filing by the appellant of an initial brief** raising the issues to be argued, supported by citations to the record on appeal and relevant constitutional provisions, statutes, and judicial decisions.

4. **Filing of motions** by the appellant (and sometimes the appellee) seeking interim forms of relief such as bail reductions, stay orders, extensions of time requirements for filing briefs, continuances of oral arguments, supplementing the record on appeal, striking sections of briefs, etc.

5. **Rulings** by the appellate court on motions.

6. **Filing of an application for oral argument,** if desired by the appellant.

7. **Filing by the appellee of an answer brief** refuting the appellant's arguments, likewise supported by citations to the record on appeal and relevant constitutional provisions, statutes, and judicial decisions.

8. **Filing an application for oral argument,** if desired, by the appellee (if not already requested by the appellant).

9. **Filing by the appellant of a brief in reply** to the appellee's answer brief.

10. **Review of the record on appeal and briefs by the judges** who are assigned to hear and decide the appeal.

11. **Oral argument by counsel,** where requested by counsel and granted by the court.

12. **Conference of judges** assigned to decide the case, often resulting in a tentative decision and assignment of a judge to prepare the court's decision.

13. **Additional research** by the appellate court's staff attorneys, where necessary.

14. **Drafting of proposed decision** by assigned judge and circulation of it to remaining judges who have participated in the case, followed by their agreement with the proposed decision or by offering a dissenting opinion.

15. **Issuance of the court's decision** by the clerk of the appellate court and circulation of that decision to counsel for the parties.

16. **Motion by the losing party for a rehearing** or issuance of a clarifying decision usually based on an allegation of the court's having overlooked some significant fact or point of law, followed by the court's ruling on the motion.

17. **Motion for *en banc* rehearing** (assuming the case was heard by fewer than all judges on the court).

18. **Ruling on motion for *en banc* review.** If granted, the court proceeds to rehear the case *en banc* and issues a decision by all judges who participate.

19. **Issuance of mandate.** After time for motions for rehearing to be filed, and, if granted, disposed of, the appellate court issues a mandate commanding the court's decision be followed. This is served on counsel and filed in the lower court.

The Appellate Process

To the layperson, the jurisdictional requirements and procedures of appellate courts appear complex. Although these procedures vary in detail, they essentially follow the same basic path. In some instances the defendant must first file a motion for a new trial before making an appeal. This is often a *pro forma* measure, but it affords the trial judge an opportunity to review the defendant's claim of error and award a new trial if necessary.

Release of Defendant on Bail Pending Appeal

Federal and state statutes and rules of court usually specify criteria for the release of a convicted defendant pending appeal. Admission to bail after conviction is not a matter of right but is at the discretion of the trial court. A defendant wanting to appeal is not aided by a presumption in favor of release on bail. Principally, the trial judge attempts to determine whether an appeal is taken in good faith and whether it presents a debatable point of law for appellate review. An appeal must not be frivolous or taken for the purpose of delay. *Birge v. State,* 230 S.E.2d 895 (Ga. 1976).

Trial judges typically consider several factors in exercising their discretion to grant or deny bail pending appeal. Among those factors are the defendant's habits and respect for the law, family and community ties, and the severity of punishment imposed. If the term of imprisonment imposed is relatively short, the court may also consider whether the denial of bail would render the defendant's right to appeal meaningless. Rules of criminal procedure generally provide for prompt appellate review of a decision denying bail to a convicted defendant or setting that bail unreasonably high. Absent such procedures, a defendant may seek a writ of habeas corpus.

If the State takes an appeal, the defendant is often released on personal recognizance during the **pendency of the appeal**—that is, while the appeal is being decided. Most states provide for the release of defendants pending an appeal by the prosecution. In Illinois, for example, "a defendant shall not be held in jail or to bail during the pendency of an appeal by the State … unless there are compelling reasons for his continued detention or being held to bail." Ill. Sup. Ct. Rule 604(a)(3).

RELEASE OF THE DEFENDANT IN FEDERAL APPEALS

Under the Federal Bail Reform Act of 1966 (repealed in 1984), the defendant in a federal court was entitled to bail unless there was "reason to believe that no one or more conditions of release will reasonably assure that the person will not flee, or pose a danger to any other person or any other community." The **Bail Reform Act of 1984,** 18 U.S.C.A. §§ 3141–3150, reversed that presumption of entitlement. Under the 1984 act, the defendant now has the burden of proving an entitlement to bail based on criteria specified in the law. Before granting bail pending appeal, the court must find

1. that the defendant is not likely to flee or pose a danger to the safety of any other person or the community if released;

2. that the appeal is not for the purpose of delay;

3. that the appeal raises a substantial question of law or fact; and

4. that if that substantial question is determined favorably to defendant on appeal, that decision is likely to result in reversal or an order for a new trial of all counts on which imprisonment has been imposed. *United States v. Miller,* 753 F.2d 19, 24 (3d Cir. 1985).

In an earlier topic, we pointed out that the federal government can take an appeal from certain pretrial orders under 18 U.S.C.A. § 3731 or from sentencing or plea agreement violations under 18 U.S.C.A. § 3742(b). Where an appeal is taken under section 3731, the Bail Reform Act ordinarily governs release of the defendant pending the appeal. If the government's appeal is taken under section 3742 and the defendant has been sentenced to imprisonment, the defendant is ordinarily not released pending the appeal.

Right to Counsel on Appeal

As we pointed out in Chapter 17, the U.S. Supreme Court has interpreted the Constitution to require that indigent defendants be furnished assistance of counsel in criminal prosecutions. To what extent does the Constitution require the appointment of counsel for indigent defendants who appeal their convictions to higher courts? In *Douglas v. California,* 372 U.S. 353, 83 S.Ct. 814, 9 L.Ed.2d 811 (1963), the Supreme Court said that states must provide counsel to indigent persons convicted of felonies who exercise their statutory right to appeal. In *Ross v. Moffitt,* 417 U.S. 600, 94 S.Ct. 2437, 41 L.Ed.2d 341 (1974), however, the Supreme Court held that a state's failure to provide counsel to an indigent defendant seeking discretionary review in the state and federal supreme courts did not violate due process or equal protection. Thus, the government must provide counsel as a matter of course when defendants have a statutory right to be heard in an appellate court. At later stages of the appeals process, there is no such requirement.

Go to the Scheb/ Scheb Criminal Law and Procedure 6e website at academic .cengage.com/criminaljustice/ scheb for an edited version of *Douglas v. California.*

The Supreme Court's decision in *Douglas v. California* produced a tremendous increase in appellate caseloads. Providing counsel at public expense aggravated the problem of **frivolous appeals** (that is, appeals lacking any arguable basis for reversal). In such cases, appointed counsel will often attempt to withdraw.

In *Anders v. California,* 386 U.S. 738, 87 S.Ct. 1396, 18 L.Ed.2d 493 (1967), the Supreme Court invalidated a state rule that allowed appointed counsel to withdraw by merely stating that an appeal had no merit. Reasoning that the right to counsel meant the right to have an effective advocate on appeal, the Court held that appointed counsel could withdraw only after submitting a brief claiming that the appeal was wholly frivolous and referring to any arguable issues. Recently, California developed a new procedure for handling criminal appeals by indigents. An appointed attorney may now write a "no merit brief" summarizing the procedural and factual history of the case. The court orders a briefing by counsel only if it finds arguable issues. Therefore, before rejecting the appeal, both counsel and the court have to find the appeal lacking in arguable issues. In January 2000, in *Smith v. Robbins,* 528 U.S. 259, 120 S.Ct. 746, 145 L.Ed.2d 756, the U.S. Supreme Court ruled that such "no merit brief" procedure satisfies the requirements of *Anders v. California.* The basic *Anders* approach is followed in most jurisdictions, and when an appellate court accepts an ***Anders* brief,** it usually notifies the defendant of the appointed counsel's withdrawal and permits the defendant to file a memorandum pointing to any claim of error. With the proliferation of criminal appeals by indigent defendants, the *Anders* brief has become a commonplace element of appellate procedure.

SELF-REPRESENTATION ON APPEAL

In Chapter 18, we pointed out that it is incumbent on a trial judge to allow self-representation by a defendant who voluntarily and intelligently elects to proceed in the trial court without counsel. *Faretta v. California,* 422 U.S. 806, 95 S.Ct. 2525, 45 L.Ed.2d 562 (1975). Many appellate courts allow convicted defendants to file *pro se* petitions for habeas corpus but generally do not allow defendants to handle direct appeals on a *pro se* basis. After Salvador Martinez represented himself before a trial court, the California courts denied him the right to represent himself in the California Court of Appeal. He obtained review in the U.S. Supreme Court, and on January 12, 2000, the Court upheld California's denial of his right to handle his appeal without counsel. The Court observed that although the Sixth Amendment to the

Constitution provides a basis for self-representation at the trial level, it does not include any right to appeal. The Court pointed to significant differences between the trial and appellate stages of a criminal proceeding and emphasized the need for a defendant to have counsel when attempting to overturn a criminal conviction. The Court recognized that states are free to determine whether to allow a defendant to proceed in an appellate court without counsel; nevertheless, it held that a criminal defendant does not have the right under the U.S. Constitution to elect self-representation on a direct appeal from a judgment of conviction. *Martinez v. California Court of Appeal,* 528 U.S. 152, 120 S.Ct. 684, 145 L.Ed.2d 597 (2000).

Filing the Appeal

Once the appellant has determined the correct forum for an appeal or a petition for discretionary review, the process is governed by federal or state rules of appellate procedure. The notice of appeal or petition for review must be filed in the appropriate court within a specified period of time. The time requirement tends to be strictly enforced because this notice or petition confers jurisdiction for the appellate court to act on the case.

Rule 4(b) of the **Federal Rules of Appellate Procedure** provides that an appeal by a defendant from a judgment and sentence in a federal district court must be filed within ten days after the entry of the judgment or the filing of the government's notice of appeal. Under certain circumstances, the time period may be extended but cannot exceed an additional thirty days. If a defendant makes a timely motion for judgment of acquittal, for a new trial, or for arrest of a judgment, then the **notice of appeal** must be filed within ten days after the trial court enters an order disposing of such motion(s). When an appeal by the government is authorized by statute, the notice of appeal must be filed within thirty days after the entry of judgment.

In state courts, an aggrieved party usually has thirty days after entry of judgment and sentence to file an appeal. For example, Maryland requires that the notice of appeal must be filed within thirty days after the trial court has entered its judgment or denied a motion for a new trial. Md. R. 8–202. The filing of a notice of appeal must be accompanied by the payment of a required filing fee unless the appellant is represented by the public defender's office or other counsel assigned by any other legal services organization that accepts as clients only those persons meeting the financial eligibility criteria established by the Federal Legal Services Corporation or other appropriate governmental agency. Md. Rule 8.201.

Motions

During the early stages of the appellate process, counsel for both parties frequently file motions in the appellate court. Some motions address substantive issues—for example, a motion asserting legal grounds to dismiss the appeal. More commonly, counsel use motions to draw the court's immediate attention to procedural matters outside the routine of the appellate process. For example, counsel may request additional time to meet deadlines for filing petitions and briefs. Occasionally, counsel will move for expedited consideration of an appeal. By appropriate motions, separate appeals may be consolidated; multiple appeals may be severed. Ordinarily, filing an appeal does not stay the judgment or sentence. However, on a showing of good cause, an appellate court may stay a judgment or sentence pending resolution of the appeal.

After a notice of appeal or a petition for discretionary review has been filed, a series of procedural steps are set in motion. It is incumbent on the appellant or petitioner to have the clerk of the trial court forward to the appellate tribunal certified copies of pertinent records and transcripts of testimony relevant to the issues to be raised on appeal. Beyond this, procedures vary somewhat, depending largely on whether the appeal is one of right or whether the defendant is seeking discretionary relief.

Submission of Briefs

In an appeal of right, the appellant files a **brief** summarizing the legal posture and the factual background of the case in the lower tribunal, the issues on appeal, and the legal authorities that support a reversal of the trial court's rulings. Briefs are the principal instruments used to persuade the appellate court to reverse, affirm, or modify the decision being appealed. They are usually heavily laden with citations to constitutional provisions, statutes, and court decisions regarded as persuasive by the advocates. The extent of background information contained in the briefs depends on the points to be presented to the appellate court. The appellee is permitted to respond to the appellant's contentions by filing an **answer brief,** and the appellant is usually permitted a **reply brief.** The whole process resembles the order of a classroom debate, where the affirmative presents its case, followed by the negative and a rebuttal by the affirmative.

Where a petitioner seeks discretionary review, the appellate court must first decide whether to accept or deny the request to take jurisdiction. If the court determines to proceed on the petition, it will order all affected parties to furnish the court a written response. As in an appeal of right, often the petitioner is permitted to file a reply to that response. The petition and response may be supplemented by such briefs as the court requires.

The format and submission of briefs must adhere closely to the requirements of the particular jurisdiction. Counsel must always furnish copies of briefs and other materials to their adversaries.

Oral Argument

After briefs have been submitted and reviewed by the appellate court, an **oral argument** may be held where counsel for both parties appear. Typically, appellate courts conduct oral arguments in about half the cases they decide. During oral arguments, counsel for both parties summarize their positions orally and then respond to questions from the bench.

The appellate rules of courts in many jurisdictions set out the time allowed for oral argument. For example, as rule 24 of the Rhode Island Rules of Appellate Procedure stipulates, "Counsel on each side will be allowed a period not in excess of thirty minutes for presentation of argument, and a period not in excess of ten minutes will be allowed the moving party for reply." Rule 28 of the U.S. Supreme Court provides, "Oral argument should emphasize and clarify the written arguments in the briefs on the merits. Counsel should assume that all Justices have read the briefs before oral argument." It further states, "Unless the Court directs otherwise, each side is allowed one-half hour for argument." Rule 34(d) of the U.S. Court of Appeals for the Fourth Circuit allows either fifteen or twenty minutes, depending on the type of appeal. Rather than stipulating a specific time, rules in some federal and state jurisdictions provide that the appellate court will specify the times for oral argument on the court calendar. Most state appellate courts allow twenty or thirty minutes for oral argument, but of course the court always reserves the right to shorten or lengthen the time allocated.

The Judicial Conference

Appellate judges customarily confer about the disposition of appeals. The **judicial conference** is regarded as an essential part of the collegial process that distinguishes the appellate role from that of the trial court. If there has been oral argument, it is common for the panel of judges that heard the case to confer shortly thereafter. At that time the panel frequently attempts to determine the disposition of the appeal but, in some instances, finds it necessary to further canvass the record or call on counsel or the court's own staff lawyers for additional legal research. Where there has been no oral argument, the panel of judges assigned to the case usually confers after each judge has reviewed the briefs, pertinent records, and results of any research assignments given to the court's legal staff.

Judgment of the Court

Essentially, an appellate court has three options in addressing a case before it. First, it may dismiss the appeal. This is uncommon in appeals of right unless the appeal is untimely. Dismissal is more common in cases of discretionary review. For example, the U.S. Supreme Court will sometimes dismiss a petition for certiorari as having been improvidently granted even after the case has been fully argued. When an appeal or cert petition is dismissed, the judgment of the lower court remains undisturbed. The second option of the appellate court is to **affirm** the decision being reviewed, which preserves the judgment of the lower court. The third option is to **reverse** the judgment of the lower court. A reversal is usually accompanied by an order to **remand** the case to the lower court for further proceedings consistent with the higher court's opinion. In the criminal context, this may mean the defendant receives a new trial or new sentencing hearing. When a court of last resort remands a case to an intermediate appellate court, the latter must reconsider the case based on the higher court's decision.

Appellate Court Opinions

After an appellate court has arrived at a decision, the court will issue an opinion announcing its decision. Some opinions simply announce the court's decision; others are quite lengthy in considering the arguments of counsel and articulating the reasons for the court's decision. Opinions are generally prepared by an individual judge or justice. If responsibility for the preparation of an opinion has not been previously given to one judge, that responsibility is usually assigned at conference by the senior judge or the senior judge voting with the majority of the panel.

There are two basic types of appellate court opinions: *per curiam* and signed. A ***per curiam* opinion** represents the appellate court as a whole; it is not attributed to any individual judge or group of judges on the court. More commonly the decision of the appellate court is announced in an **opinion of the court** authored by one judge and joined by other judges constituting a majority. A judge who disagrees with the decision of the court may write a **dissenting opinion.** A judge who agrees with the court's decision but wants to address or emphasize certain arguments not addressed or emphasized in the opinion of the court may write a separate **concurring opinion.** Sometimes, a separate opinion is listed as **concurring in the judgment** only, meaning that it supports the decision of the court but for reasons other than those articulated in the court's opinion.

Publication of Appellate Decisions

Most decisions of appellate courts in America are published in books known as **reporters.** The publication of appellate decisions plays an important role in developing the law because judges and lawyers regularly consult the case reporters for guidance in pending cases. Today, it is common for appellate opinions to become immediately available via the Internet. The U.S. Supreme Court, each of the federal circuits, and most state appellate courts maintain websites from which opinions are downloadable at no cost. (Access to published opinions, both through electronic and traditional means, is discussed in some detail in Appendix A.)

Motions for Rehearing

Rules of appellate procedure uniformly permit the filing of a motion asking the appellate court to reconsider its decision in a given case. A **motion for rehearing** is designed to address some misstatement of material fact or to direct the court's attention to an overlooked or misapprehended proposition of law. In the U.S. courts of appeals and in many state appellate courts, where cases are decided by panels of judges, a party may request that all judges (or a majority of the judges in appellate courts consisting of a large number of judges) of the court participate in an ***en banc rehearing.*** The likelihood of an appellate court's granting a motion for *en banc* rehearing is greater when there are conflicting opinions between or among panels of judges within the court. Appellate courts view many motions for rehearing as little more than attempts by dissatisfied parties to have another chance to persuade the court of their position. Accordingly, motions for rehearing are seldom granted.

Postconviction Relief

Normally, an appeal of a lower court decision must be made in a timely manner, usually within thirty days after that court's judgment or sentence. Petitions for certiorari (or other forms of discretionary review) are also subject to time limits. Yet incarcerated criminals may seek review of their convictions long after their rights to appeal have been exhausted or expired by means of a mechanism known as the writ of habeas corpus. It is available in the federal courts and in all fifty state judicial systems.

"Habeas corpus" is a Latin term meaning "you have the body." In law, it refers to a writ issued by a court to a person who is holding another in custody, requiring that the former show cause for holding the latter. Habeas corpus has roots deep in the common law. Blackstone called it "the most celebrated writ in the English law." 3 W. Blackstone, *Commentaries* 129. The framers of the American Constitution explicitly recognized habeas corpus as a fundamental right of citizens by declaring that "[t]he Privilege of the Writ of Habeas Corpus shall not be suspended unless when in Cases of Rebellion or Invasion the public Safety may require it." U.S. Const., Art. 1, Sec. 9. Only once in our history, during the Civil War, was the writ of habeas corpus suspended throughout the federal courts. This thoroughgoing suspension was subsequently declared unconstitutional. *Ex parte Milligan,* 71 U.S. (4 Wall.) 2, 18 L.Ed. 281 (1866).

Challenging State Court Convictions in Federal Court

The U.S. Supreme Court can review only a minute proportion of the thousands of petitions for certiorari through which persons convicted in state courts challenge their convictions on federal constitutional grounds. In recent decades, **federal habeas corpus review** of state criminal convictions has become a common form of appellate procedure. It has also greatly multiplied the opportunities for persons convicted of state offenses to obtain relief. Consequently, it has become the focus of considerable controversy.

The Judiciary Act of 1789, 1 Stat. 82 (1789), recognized the power of federal courts to issue writs of habeas corpus only for federal prisoners. In 1867 federal law was amended, 14 Stat. 385, 386, to allow federal courts to entertain habeas corpus petitions from state prisoners who allege that their incarceration violates provisions of the U.S. Constitution or federal statutes or treaties. The federal law on habeas corpus currently provides the following:

> The Supreme Court, a Justice thereof, a circuit judge, or a district court shall entertain an application for a writ of habeas corpus in behalf of a person in custody pursuant to the judgment of a State court only on the ground that he is in custody in violation of the Constitution or laws or treaties of the United States. 28 U.S.C.A. § 2254(a).

Before the twentieth century, the federal habeas corpus jurisdiction was seldom used to review state criminal convictions. When habeas corpus was granted, it was merely to ascertain that the state trial court had jurisdiction over the person being tried. In *Frank v. Mangum*, 237 U.S. 309, 35 S.Ct. 582, 59 L.Ed. 969 (1915), the Supreme Court broadened federal habeas corpus review to ensure that states supplied some "corrective process" whereby criminal defendants could seek to vindicate their federal constitutional rights. In 1953 the Court held that federal courts could use habeas corpus review to readjudicate federal constitutional issues that had been addressed in state court proceedings. *Brown v. Allen*, 344 U.S. 443, 73 S.Ct. 397, 97 L.Ed. 469 (1953).

Federal law had long provided that federal habeas corpus relief was available only to state prisoners who had exhausted all available remedies in the state courts. In 1963 the Supreme Court held that a state prisoner did not have to take a direct appeal to the state supreme court to seek federal habeas corpus review. Nor was the prisoner barred from raising constitutional issues in federal court merely because the issues had not been raised on direct appeal in state courts. *Fay v. Noia*, 372 U.S. 391, 83 S.Ct. 822, 9 L.Ed.2d 837 (1963).

The Supreme Court's efforts to broaden the availability of federal habeas corpus review coincided with its expansion of the constitutional rights of the accused. No doubt, the Court was initially reluctant to depend on state courts to implement these expanded rights, so it broadened the power of the federal district courts to review state criminal convictions. This resulted in numerous state convictions being overturned by the federal courts, often on Fourth or Fifth Amendment grounds. Indeed, many observers came to see state criminal trials merely as precursors to inevitable federal intervention.

Assistance of Counsel in Federal Habeas Corpus Cases

As we have seen, there is no federal constitutional right to counsel beyond the appeal of right. Congress has provided for representation of federal prisoners seeking habeas corpus relief in federal court, see 18 U.S.C.A. § 3006A, but has not provided for counsel for state prisoners seeking federal habeas corpus review. Representation in such cases is sometimes provided *pro bono* by groups such as the American Civil Liberties Union or the Legal Aid Society. In some instances, prisoners write their own petitions for federal habeas corpus review or get fellow inmates to do this for them.

Ineffective Counsel as a Basis for Postconviction Relief

The Supreme Court has recognized that the right to counsel means little unless counsel provides a defendant effective representation. *McMann v. Richardson,* 397 U.S. 759, 90 S.Ct. 1441, 25 L.Ed.2d 763 (1970). Failure of counsel, whether appointed or retained, to be an effective advocate for the defendant constitutes a basis to award a defendant a new trial. *Cuyler v. Sullivan,* 446 U.S. 335, 100 S.Ct. 1708, 64 L.Ed.2d 333 (1980). Some examples of ineffective representation where relief might well be afforded include failure of counsel to present evidence favorable to the accused, failure to challenge the admissibility of evidence presented by the prosecution, and failure to challenge prosecutorial misconduct.

The requirement to furnish counsel to indigent defendants has probably contributed to a rise in claims of **ineffective assistance of counsel.** Indigent defendants are sometimes distrustful of public defenders and other appointed counsel. If convicted, these defendants may be more likely to feel that their representation was ineffective compared with that provided by privately retained attorneys.

A defendant's claim of error or deficiency in counsel's performance is rarely challenged in the trial court, so it is not generally subject to being raised on direct appeal. But in some instances where the record of the trial shows on its face that counsel was ineffective, an appellate court will consider the issue on direct appeal. For example, in *Eure v. State,* 764 So.2d 798 (Fla. App. 2000), on a direct appeal from the defendant's conviction for possession and sale of cocaine, a Florida appellate court reversed the defendant's conviction because it found the defendant's counsel was ineffective for failing to object to a series of improper arguments by the prosecutor.

In *Strickland v. Washington,* 466 U.S. 668, 104 S.Ct. 2052, 80 L.Ed.2d 674 (1984), the Supreme Court articulated a uniform constitutional standard for determining the issue of ineffective counsel:

> First, the defendant must show that counsel's performance was deficient. This requires showing that counsel made errors so serious that counsel was not functioning as the "counsel" guaranteed the defendant by the Sixth Amendment. Second, the defendant must show that the deficient performance prejudiced the defense. This requires showing that counsel's errors were so serious as to deprive the defendant of a fair trial, a trial whose result is reliable. Unless a defendant makes both showings, it cannot be said that the conviction … resulted from a breakdown in the adversary process that renders the result unreliable. 466 U.S. at 687, 104 S.Ct. at 2063, 80 L.Ed.2d at 693.

The standard announced in *Strickland v. Washington* has been criticized by numerous commentators as being too lax. Only twice since 1984 has the Supreme Court upheld a claim of ineffective assistance on the basis of the *Strickland* test. In the first of these decisions, *Williams v. Taylor,* 529 U.S. 362, 120 S.Ct. 1495, 146 L.Ed.2d 389 (2000), the Court upheld a lower court determination that the attorneys representing Terry Williams in a capital murder case failed to provide effective assistance during the sentencing phase and that it was reasonably probable that Williams would not have received the death penalty if his attorneys had presented and fully explained to the jury all of the available evidence pertaining to mitigating factors. More recently, in *Wiggins v. Smith,* 539 U.S. 510, 123 S.Ct. 2527,156 L.Ed.2d 471 (2003), the Court found that the performance of the assistant public defenders representing Kevin Wiggins in the sentencing phase of his capital murder trial was constitutionally deficient. Writing for a majority of five justices, Justice Sandra Day O'Connor noted, "Wiggins' sentencing jury heard only one significant mitigating factor—that Wiggins had no prior convictions." 539 U.S. at 537, 123 S.Ct. at 2543, 156 L.Ed.2d at 495. In O'Connor's view, "Had the jury been able to place petitioner's

Go to the Scheb/ Scheb Criminal Law and Procedure 6e website at academic .cengage.com/criminaljustice/ scheb for an edited version of *Wiggins v. Smith.*

CASE-IN-POINT

Does a Lawyer's Failure to File a Notice of Appeal Constitute Ineffective Assistance of Counsel?

The question sometimes arises whether the failure of a defendant's lawyer to file a notice of appeal constitutes ineffective counsel. In 2000, the U.S. Supreme Court rejected any bright line rule that counsel must always consult with a defendant regarding an appeal. Rather, the Court held that counsel has a constitutionally imposed duty to consult with the defendant about taking an appeal where there is either a rational basis for an appeal or the defendant has demonstrated to counsel an interest in appealing.

Roe v. Flores-Ortega, 528 U.S. 470, 120 S.Ct. 1029, 145 L.Ed.2d 985 (2000).

excruciating life history on the mitigating side of the scale, there is a reasonable probability that at least one juror would have struck a different balance." 539 U.S. at 536, 123 S.Ct. at 2543, 156 L.Ed.2d at 495. The Court's decisions in the *Williams* and *Wiggins* cases suggest that the Court may be willing to scrutinize more closely the performance of counsel in cases where defendants' lives are at stake.

The Supreme Court Restricts Access to Federal Habeas Corpus

A growing criticism of federal court intervention, coupled with the increasing professionalism of the state judiciaries, persuaded the Supreme Court to restrict access to federal habeas corpus relief. During the 1970s, a more conservative Supreme Court began to narrow access to federal habeas corpus relief. In a seminal case, *Stone v. Powell*, 428 U.S. 465, 96 S.Ct. 3037, 49 L.Ed.2d 1067 (1976), the Court held that state prisoners could not use federal habeas corpus hearings to challenge searches and seizures where they had been provided an opportunity for full and fair litigation of a Fourth Amendment claim in the state courts.

Despite *Stone v. Powell*, federal habeas corpus review remains available to state prisoners seeking to challenge their convictions on a variety of constitutional grounds. For instance, the Supreme Court has said that federal habeas corpus review must remain available to state prisoners alleging racial discrimination in their indictments or convictions, regardless of their opportunity to raise such objections in the state courts. *Rose v. Mitchell*, 443 U.S. 545, 99 S.Ct. 2993, 61 L.Ed.2d 739 (1979). In another significant decision in 1979, *Jackson v. Virginia*, 443 U.S. 307, 99 S.Ct. 2781, 61 L.Ed.2d 560, the Court held that a federal court reviewing a state conviction on habeas corpus must consider whether any reasonable trier of fact could have found a defendant guilty beyond a reasonable doubt. Before *Jackson*, federal courts would not reverse state convictions for insufficient evidence if there was "any evidence" of the defendant's guilt.

In *Engle v. Isaac*, 456 U.S. 107, 102 S.Ct. 1558, 71 L.Ed.2d 783 (1982), the Supreme Court refused to allow a state prisoner to use federal habeas corpus to challenge a questionable jury instruction to which he failed to object during trial. Other decisions of the Court during the 1980s chipped away at the Court's earlier expansive interpretations of federal habeas corpus relief. See, for example, *Kuhlmann v. Wilson*, 477 U.S. 436, 106 S.Ct. 2616, 91 L.Ed.2d 364 (1986); *Straight v. Wainwright*, 476 U.S. 1132, 106 S.Ct. 2004, 90 L.Ed.2d 683 (1986).

RESTRICTING SUCCESSIVE HABEAS PETITIONS

During the early 1990s, the Supreme Court continued the trend toward limiting access to federal habeas corpus. In 1991 the Court said that Warren McCleskey, a prisoner on death row in Georgia, had abused the writ of habeas corpus when he filed a second federal habeas corpus petition. *McCleskey v. Zant,* 499 U.S. 467, 111 S.Ct. 1454, 113 L.Ed.2d 517 (1991). In the *McCleskey* case, the Court held that a state need not prove that a petitioner deliberately abandoned a constitutional claim in his or her first habeas corpus petition for the petitioner to be barred from raising the claim in a subsequent petition. The Court thus moved away from the "deliberate abandonment" standard it had previously articulated in *Sanders v. United States,* 373 U.S. 1, 83 S.Ct. 1068, 10 L.Ed.2d 148 (1963).

Similarly, in *Keeney v. Tamayo-Reyes,* 504 U.S. 1, 112 S.Ct. 1715, 118 L.Ed.2d 318 (1992), the Court overruled another earlier habeas corpus decision, *Townsend v. Sain,* 372 U.S. 293, 83 S.Ct. 745, 9 L.Ed.2d 770 (1963). In *Townsend,* the Court had held that a petitioner could challenge a state conviction despite a failure to develop a material fact in state proceedings unless it was determined that the petitioner deliberately bypassed the opportunity to develop the fact in the state courts. In *Keeney v. Tamayo-Reyes,* supra, the Court held that a petitioner's failure to develop a claim in state court proceedings should be excused only if he or she can show that a fundamental miscarriage of justice would result from failure to hold a federal evidentiary hearing.

The Supreme Court's decisions in *McCleskey v. Zant* and *Keeney v. Tamayo-Reyes* came when many in Congress were calling for legislative restrictions on federal habeas corpus. Both the Supreme Court and Congress were responding to a widespread perception that state prisoners were being afforded excessive opportunities to challenge their convictions in federal courts. Indeed, some conservative commentators questioned the need for federal postconviction review of state criminal cases altogether. Although federal habeas corpus has been subject to abuse by state prisoners, eliminating this aspect of federal jurisdiction altogether would remove some of the pressure that has led to an increased awareness of and appreciation for defendants' rights in the state courts. Indeed, in the *McCleskey* case, the Supreme Court expressed a commitment to the continued efficacy of habeas corpus to prevent miscarriages of justice in the state courts.

DEFLECTING CLAIMS OF ACTUAL INNOCENCE

In *Herrera v. Collins,* 506 U.S. 390, 113 S.Ct. 853, 122 L.Ed.2d 203 (1993), the Court held that a belated claim of innocence does not entitle a state prisoner on death row to a federal district court hearing before being executed. Writing for the Court, Chief Justice William Rehnquist noted, "Claims of actual innocence based on newly discovered evidence have never been held to state a ground for federal habeas relief absent an independent constitutional violation occurring in the underlying state criminal proceeding." 506 U.S. at 400, 113 S.Ct. at 860, 122 L.Ed.2d at 216. Noting that the State of Texas provided no mechanism for the litigation of a belated claim of innocence, the three dissenting justices (Blackmun, Stevens, and Souter) chastised the majority for its insensitivity to the plight of one who is actually innocent but not afforded an opportunity to demonstrate his innocence in court: "Nothing could be more contrary to contemporary standards of decency … or more shocking to the conscience … than to execute a person who is actually innocent." 506 U.S. at 430, 113 S.Ct. at 876, 122 L.Ed.2d at 236. Justice Harry Blackmun went so far as to write, "The execution of a person who can show that he is innocent comes perilously close to simple murder." 506 U.S. at 446, 113 S.Ct. at 864, 122 L.Ed.2d at 246.

 Go to the Scheb/ Scheb Criminal Law and Procedure 6e website at academic .cengage.com/criminaljustice/ scheb for an edited version of *Herrera v. Collins.*

Two years later the Supreme Court again addressed a claim of actual innocence of a prisoner under sentence of death. In *Schlup v. Delo,* 513 U.S. 298, 115 S.Ct. 851, 130 L.Ed.2d 808 (1995), the Court mitigated somewhat the harshness of *Herrera v. Collins.* Schlup, an inmate in a Missouri state prison, was sentenced to death after being convicted of the murder of a fellow inmate. After exhausting his remedies in the state courts, Schlup filed a petition for federal habeas corpus relief, claiming that his trial counsel had been ineffective. After failing in this effort, he filed a second federal habeas corpus petition claiming that he was actually innocent, offering proof of this claim, asserting that prosecutors had failed to disclose exculpatory evidence, and reasserting the claim of ineffective assistance of counsel. The lower federal courts denied relief, holding that Schlup was procedurally barred from raising these issues in a second federal habeas corpus petition. The Supreme Court reversed, however, holding that where claims of actual innocence are coupled with assertions of constitutional violations, in order to prevent a miscarriage of justice, a federal court may grant habeas corpus relief that would normally be procedurally barred. Writing for the Court, Justice John Paul Stevens observed that Schlup

> accompanies his claim of innocence with an assertion of constitutional error at trial. For that reason, Schlup's conviction may not be entitled to the same degree of respect as one, such as Herrera's, that is the product of an error-free trial. Without any new evidence of innocence, even the existence of a concededly meritorious constitutional violation is not in itself sufficient to establish a miscarriage of justice that would allow a habeas court to reach the merits of a barred claim. However, if a petitioner such as Schlup presents evidence of innocence so strong that a court cannot have confidence in the outcome of the trial unless the court is also satisfied that the trial was free of non-harmless constitutional error, the petitioner should be allowed to pass through the gateway and argue the merits of his underlying claims.
> 513 U.S. at 316, 115 S.Ct. at 861, 130 L.Ed.2d at 829.

REVERSING THE BURDEN OF PROOF

In *Brecht v. Abrahamson,* 507 U.S. 619, 113 S.Ct. 1710, 123 L.Ed.2d 353 (1993), the Supreme Court ruled that federal district courts may not overturn state criminal convictions unless the petitioner can show that he or she suffered "actual prejudice" from the errors cited in the habeas corpus petition. Previously, the state carried the burden of proving beyond a reasonable doubt that any constitutional error committed during or before trial was "harmless"—that is, not prejudicial to the defendant. *Brecht v. Abrahamson* had the effect of shifting the burden of proof from the state to the petitioner in a federal habeas corpus hearing.

REQUIRING PRISONERS TO EXHAUST STATE REMEDIES PRIOR TO SEEKING FEDERAL HABEAS CORPUS RELIEF

Under 28 U.S.C.A. § 2254(c), federal habeas corpus relief is available to state prisoners only after they have exhausted their remedies in state court. Prior to 1999, this was interpreted to apply only to appeals of right, not to discretionary review before state courts of last resort. In 1977 Darren Boerckel was convicted in an Illinois court of rape, burglary, and aggravated battery. The Illinois Appellate Court affirmed the conviction, and the Illinois Supreme Court denied Boerckel's petition for discretionary review. Boerckel then initiated a federal habeas corpus action in which he raised six federal constitutional claims. The federal district court denied the petition, finding that Boerckel had "procedurally defaulted" his first three claims by failing to include them in his petition for discretionary review to the Illinois Supreme Court. On appeal, the Seventh Circuit reversed, holding that filing for discretionary review by the state's highest court is not necessary to exhaust one's state court remedies for purposes of the federal habeas corpus statute. Reviewing the case on certiorari, the Supreme Court reversed again, holding that a state prisoner must present his claims to a state supreme court in a petition for discretionary review when such review is part of the State's "ordinary appellate review procedure." Failure to do so constitutes procedural default and precludes these issues being raised on federal habeas corpus review. *O'Sullivan v. Boerckel,* 526 U.S. 838, 119 S.Ct. 1728, 144 L.Ed.2d 1 (1999).

Congress Modifies the Federal Habeas Corpus Procedure

On April 24, 1996, President Clinton signed into law the Antiterrorism and Effective Death Penalty Act of 1996. One provision of this statute curtails second habeas corpus petitions by state prisoners who have already filed such petitions in federal court. Under the new statute, any second or subsequent habeas petition must meet a particularly high standard and must pass through a gatekeeping function exercised by the U.S. courts of appeals. The grant or denial of an authorization by a court of appeals for an inmate to file a second or successive petition for habeas corpus in the district

SUPREME COURT PERSPECTIVE

Calderon v. Thompson, 523 U.S. 538, 118 S.Ct. 1489, 140 L.Ed.2d 728 (1998)

In this habeas corpus case the Supreme Court denied relief to a convicted murderer awaiting execution in California. In his opinion for the Court, Justice Anthony Kennedy reflects on the need for finality in the criminal justice system.

JUSTICE KENNEDY delivered the opinion of the Court, saying in part:

In light of "the profound societal costs that attend the exercise of habeas jurisdiction," we have found it necessary to impose significant limits on the discretion of federal courts to grant habeas relief....

These limits reflect our enduring respect for "the State's interest in the finality of convictions that have survived direct review within the state court system." ... Finality is essential to both the retributive and the deterrent functions of criminal law. "Neither innocence nor just punishment can be vindicated until the final judgment is known." ... "Without finality, the criminal law is deprived of much of its deterrent effect." ...

Finality also enhances the quality of judging. There is perhaps "nothing more subversive of a judge's sense of responsibility, of the inner subjective conscientiousness which is so essential a part of the difficult and subtle art

of judging well, than an indiscriminate acceptance of the notion that all the shots will always be called by someone else." ...

Finality serves as well to preserve the federal balance. Federal habeas review of state convictions frustrates "both the States' sovereign power to punish offenders and their good-faith attempts to honor constitutional rights." ... "Our federal system recognizes the independent power of a State to articulate societal norms through criminal law; but the power of a State to pass laws means little if the State cannot enforce them." ... A State's interests in finality are compelling when a federal court of appeals issues a mandate denying federal habeas relief. At that point, having in all likelihood borne for years "the significant costs of federal habeas review," ... the State is entitled to the assurance of finality. When lengthy federal proceedings have run their course and a mandate denying relief has issued, finality acquires an added moral dimension. Only with an assurance of real finality can the State execute its moral judgment in a case. Only with real finality can the victims of crime move forward knowing the moral judgment will be carried out.... To unsettle these expectations is to inflict a profound injury to the "powerful and legitimate interest in punishing the guilty," ... an interest shared by the State and the victims of crime alike.

court is not appealable and is not subject to a petition for rehearing or for a writ of certiorari. 28 U.S.C.A. § 2244(b)(3).

In *Felker v. Turpin,* 518 U.S. 651, 116 S.Ct. 2333, 135 L.Ed.2d 827 (1996), an inmate awaiting execution in Georgia challenged the constitutionality of this provision, posing two constitutional objections: (1) that the new law amounted to an unconstitutional "suspension" of the writ of habeas corpus and (2) that the prohibition against Supreme Court review of a circuit court's denial of permission to file a subsequent habeas petition is an unconstitutional interference with the Supreme Court's jurisdiction as defined in Article III of the Constitution. In a unanimous decision rendered less than one month after the case was argued, the Supreme Court rejected these challenges and upheld the statute. In a "saving construction" of the statute, the Court interpreted the law in such a way as to preserve the right of state prisoners to file habeas corpus petitions directly in the Supreme Court. However, the Court stated that it would exercise this jurisdiction only in "exceptional circumstances."

Go to the Scheb/ Scheb Criminal Law and Procedure 6e website at academic .cengage.com/criminaljustice/ scheb for an edited version of *Felker v. Turpin.*

Collateral Attack in State Court

At one time federal habeas corpus review was the only real means of postconviction relief available to state prisoners who had exhausted their appeals of right in the state courts. Today, most states have statutes or court rules that permit state prisoners, under appropriate circumstances, to challenge illegal convictions or sentences even after their ordinary appeals have been exhausted. These procedures, known as **collateral attack** or postconviction relief, provide for state-level judicial review of judgments and sentences imposed in violation of the federal or state constitutions. As access to federal habeas corpus relief has been constricted by Congress and the Supreme Court, these state-level mechanisms take on even greater importance.

North Carolina statutes that provide opportunities for collateral relief to convicted defendants appear typical of the grounds for postconviction relief available to defendants convicted in state courts. The grounds that a defendant may assert by a motion for collateral relief include the following:

- the trial court lacked jurisdiction over the defendant;
- the defendant's conviction was obtained in violation of the U.S. or North Carolina Constitutions;
- a significant change has occurred in the law applied in the proceedings leading to the defendant's conviction or sentence and such changed law must be applied retroactively;
- the defendant's sentence is illegal; or the defendant is entitled to release for having fully served the sentence imposed.

In addition, within a reasonable time after discovery, a defendant may assert that evidence is available that was unknown or unavailable to the defendant at trial and that has a direct and material bearing on the defendant's eligibility for the death penalty or the defendant's guilt or innocence. West's N.C.G.S.A. § 15A–1415. This is particularly significant in light of the Supreme Court's decision in *Herrera v. Collins,* supra, that federal habeas corpus review is not the proper mechanism for litigation of belated claims of actual innocence brought by persons convicted in state courts.

DNA Evidence as a Basis for Postconviction Relief

As we pointed out in Chapter 18, the introduction of DNA testing has had an enormous impact on criminal trials, especially in rape and homicide prosecutions. But

DNA evidence is not only useful to prosecutors seeking convictions, it is also extremely valuable as a mean of proving the actual innocence of persons who were convicted of rape or homicide on the basis of eyewitness testimony or circumstantial evidence. According to research conducted by the Innocence Project, there have been more than 180 DNA exonerations in the United States since the first one in 1989. Fourteen of these exonerees were death-row inmates wrongly convicted of murder. See www.innocenceproject.org/docs/DNAExonerationFacts_WEB.pdf.

Most states now recognize newly discovered evidence as a basis for postconviction relief. In the case of DNA evidence, though, testing of genetic material is required before such evidence can be obtained. In most cases, a convicted person needs to get access to evidence through a sort of postconviction discovery process. Yet many jurisdictions have not established standards or procedures to govern such discovery. In some states, courts have formulated standards and procedures based on norms of due process and expressed through judicial opinions. In other states, prisoners seeking to demonstrate their innocence on the basis of DNA evidence must apply for executive clemency. A few states now have statutes addressing this problem. For example, New York law provides that

> in cases of convictions … where the defendant's motion requests the performance of a forensic DNA test on specified evidence, and upon the court's determination that any evidence containing deoxyribonucleic acid (DNA) was secured in connection with the trial resulting in the judgment, the court shall grant the application for forensic DNA testing of such evidence upon its determination that if a DNA test had been conducted on such evidence, and if the results had been admitted in the trial resulting in the judgment, there exists a reasonable probability that the verdict would have been more favorable to the defendant. McKinney's N.Y. Crim. Proc. Law § 440.30 (1-a)(a).

Unlike New York, some states, through legislation or rules of court, impose time limits on applications for postconviction DNA testing. Florida Rule of Criminal Procedure 3.853 originally imposed a deadline, but the Supreme Court of Florida has extended the deadline several times. The most recent version of the rule removes the deadline for filing an application. See *In re Amendments to Florida Rule of Criminal Procedure 3.853(d)*, 938 So.2d 977 (Fla. 2006).

Likewise the requirements for seeking DNA testing vary under various state statutes and rules of court. Florida Rule of Criminal Procedure 3.853(b) requires that a motion for postconviction DNA testing must be under oath and must include:

> (1) a statement of the facts relied on in support of the motion, including a description of the physical evidence containing DNA to be tested and, if known, the present location or last known location of the evidence and how it originally was obtained;

> (2) a statement that the evidence was not tested previously for DNA, or a statement that the results of previous DNA testing were inconclusive and that subsequent scientific developments in DNA testing techniques likely would produce a definitive result;

> (3) a statement that the movant is innocent and how the DNA testing requested by the motion will exonerate the movant of the crime for which the movant was sentenced, or a statement how the DNA testing will mitigate the sentence received by the movant for that crime;

> (4) a statement that identification of the movant is a genuinely disputed issue in the case and why it is an issue or an explanation of how the DNA evidence would either exonerate the defendant or mitigate the sentence that the movant received;

> (5) a statement of any other facts relevant to the motion; and

> (6) a certificate that a copy of the motion has been served on the prosecuting authority.

DNA Evidence Used to Exonerate a Man Falsely Convicted of Rape

In 1983, Bernard Webster was convicted of rape and sentenced to thirty years in prison by a Maryland court after a schoolteacher identified him as the man who sexually assaulted her in her apartment. Twenty years later, Webster was exonerated after DNA testing was performed on semen residues that had been obtained from the victim shortly after the rape occurred in 1982. In proving his innocence, Webster took advantage of a Maryland statute enacted in 2001 that requires judges to order DNA testing pursuant to motions for postconviction relief in murder and rape cases where there is "reasonable probability" that testing will produce evidence of actual innocence. In securing postconviction relief, Webster was aided by the Innocence Project, a *pro bono* group dedicated to assisting persons who were wrongfully convicted of crimes. According to a study conducted by the Center for Wrongful Convictions at Northwestern University, false identification by eyewitnesses is a leading cause of wrongful convictions.

Advocates of expanding prisoners' access to postconviction relief based on DNA evidence believe that prosecutors should be required to maintain biological evidence used to secure a conviction as long as that person is incarcerated. They also argue that statutes of limitations on postconviction relief should be abolished and that funding should be provided so that prisoners seeking postconviction relief can have adequate legal representation throughout the process.

Exonerations of convicted persons, especially those on death row, based on DNA testing have received enormous media coverage and have shocked the conscience of the public. While prosecutors often resist efforts to undo convictions through DNA testing, there is growing public sentiment that the need for finality in the judicial process must give way to the search for truth when such powerful scientific means of seeking the truth are now available.

THE U.S. SUPREME COURT GRANTS RELIEF BASED ON NEWLY DISCOVERED DNA EVIDENCE

In *House v. Bell,* ___ U.S. ___, 126 S.Ct. 2064, 165 L.Ed.2d 1 (2006), a case reminiscent of *Schlup v. Delo,* supra, the Supreme Court, in a 5–3 decision, granted Paul Gregory House, a Tennessee death row inmate, a hearing in federal district court to litigate a procedurally defaulted claim of ineffective assistance of counsel on the basis on newly discovered DNA evidence.

Writing for the majority, Justice Kennedy summed up the case as follows:

This is not a case of conclusive exoneration. Some aspects of the State's evidence ... still support an inference of guilt. Yet the central forensic proof connecting House to the crime ... has been called into question, and House has put forward substantial evidence pointing to a different suspect. Accordingly, and although the issue is close, we conclude that this is the rare case where—had the jury heard all the conflicting testimony—it is more likely than not that no reasonable juror viewing the record as a whole would lack reasonable doubt. ___ U.S. at ___, 126 S.Ct. at 2086, 165 L.Ed.2d at 31.

Nonjudicial Remedies Available to Persons Convicted of Crimes

Under the English common law, appeal to the Crown predated appeal to higher courts as the remedy for an unjust conviction or unreasonable sentence. In addition, because a crime was viewed as an offense against the Crown, the monarch possessed the authority to forgive the wrongdoer or grant **clemency.** In contemporary America, the appeal to executive authority remains as a carryover from the common law and as a supplement to judicial review.

Presidential Pardons

Article II, Section 2, Clause 1 of the U.S. Constitution states that the president "shall have Power to grant Reprieves and Pardons for Offences against the United States, except in Cases of Impeachment." This broad power includes the right to commute sentences, remit fines and penalties, and even grant conditional pardons. Indeed, the presidential **pardon** may be issued before conviction, as was amply demonstrated in 1974, when President Gerald Ford pardoned former president Richard Nixon for his role in the Watergate scandal. It was demonstrated again in December 1992, when President George Bush granted a pardon to Caspar Weinberger, the former Secretary of Defense, and five others who allegedly were involved in the much-publicized controversy concerning the trading of arms for hostages. However, the controversies that followed President Ford's pardon of Richard Nixon and President Bush's pardon of Caspar Weinberger paled in comparison to President Clinton's last-minute pardon of Marc Rich, a fugitive from a 1983 indictment for federal income tax evasion. The Rich pardon, which was given without the normal consultation with the Department of Justice, prompted congressional hearings and an investigation by federal prosecutors. Investigators looked into the possibility that Rich purchased a presidential pardon by passing money through his former wife, who made large contributions both to the Clinton presidential library foundation and to Hillary Clinton's 2000 Senate campaign.

The Supreme Court has said that "[t]he plain purpose of the broad power conferred … was to allow … the President to 'forgive' the convicted person in part or entirely, to reduce a penalty in terms of a specified number of years, or to alter it with conditions which are in themselves constitutionally unobjectionable." *Schick v. Reed,* 419 U.S. 256, 266, 95 S.Ct. 379, 385, 42 L.Ed.2d 430, 438–439 (1974). Therefore, a full presidential pardon totally restores any civil rights the recipient may have lost as a result of conviction. In effect, the full pardon makes an individual as innocent as if the crime had never been committed. *Ex parte Garland,* 71 U.S. (4 Wall.) 333, 18 L.Ed. 366 (1866).

Clemency at the State Level

Either by constitutional or statutory provisions, executive authorities in all fifty states are likewise granted broad powers to pardon and commute sentences of persons convicted of violations of state criminal law. In many states, the pardoning power is vested exclusively in the governor. In a few states, the governor is limited to granting pardons approved by a state commission. In some states, the pardoning power is vested entirely in a state commission.

In recent years, a number of state prisoners convicted of rape and murder have sought executive clemency based on DNA testing that shows their innocence. Increasingly, such claims are handled judicially through motions for postconviction relief as courts and legislatures recognize the need to allow persons who claim to have been wrongfully convicted of crimes to prove their innocence through DNA testing.

One of the most dramatic uses of executive clemency in American history took place in January 2003 when Governor George Ryan commuted the death sentences of 156 inmates awaiting execution in Illinois. All but three of the inmates had their sentences commuted to life in prison without possibility of parole; the other three were given life sentences with the possibility of seeking parole. Governor Ryan's dramatic and controversial order came three years after he announced a moratorium on the death penalty in Illinois and appointed a commission to study the issue. After receiving the commission's report, which identified various problems with trials, sentencing, and the appeals process, Governor Ryan concluded that the system was "haunted by the demon of error, error in determining guilt, and error in determining who among the guilty deserves to die."

■ CONCLUSION

Under the early English common law, the right to appeal was nonexistent. Eventually, through court decisions and statutes, defendants gained the right to appeal criminal convictions. In America, statutes and judicial decisions have created numerous opportunities for appeal in criminal cases. Federal and state statutes guarantee at least one appeal of right to defendants who are convicted after entering a plea of not guilty. Beyond these appeals of right, defendants may seek review from higher courts by filing petitions for certiorari or discretionary review. Today the mechanics of the appellate process are remarkably similar in federal and state courts of appeal. Finally, the historic writ of habeas corpus provides an avenue of postconviction relief in state and federal tribunals. In many states, postconviction relief has become structured under criteria specified by statute or rules of court.

Recently, there has been much criticism of the seemingly inexhaustible routes of appellate review. Some would argue that the numerous opportunities for defendants to obtain review of their convictions by higher courts result in unnecessary delays in dispensing justice. On the premise that "justice is due the accuser as well as the accused," critics would cite the old aphorism that "justice delayed is justice denied."

Certainly, an abundance of cases supports the criticism. Many involve the controversial issue of capital punishment. Such cases attract the media's attention and arouse the public. There is an unfortunate tendency to assume that such cases are typical and that the appellate process is incapable of moving expeditiously. The public is generally unaware of the thousands of appeals that are resolved in a timely manner for each one that becomes a case study in delay.

Perhaps as a response to such criticism, the U.S. Supreme Court has narrowed the access of state prisoners to federal postconviction relief. Today, federal habeas corpus review tends to focus largely on capital cases. Yet substantial opportunities remain for prisoners to seek postconviction review by state and federal tribunals. One of the most common issues raised on postconviction review is whether defendants received effective assistance of counsel at trial.

More dramatic has been the recent trend for courts to accept DNA evidence as proof of innocence of persons convicted of rape and homicide crimes on the basis of eyewitness testimony or circumstantial evidence.

Although it must be conceded that the appellate process does often delay the imposition of criminal punishments, such delay must be weighed against our society's deep and historic commitment to fundamental fairness. In America, criminal law and criminal procedure are guided by due process values as well as by society's need for crime control.

■ KEY TERMS

trial *de novo*, 580	Federal Rules of Appellate
appeal of right, 580	Procedure, 589
discretionary review, 580	notice of appeal, 589
postconviction relief, 580	brief, 590
writ of habeas corpus, 580	answer brief, 590
error correction, 580	reply brief, 590
lawmaking, 580	oral argument, 590
writ of error, 580	judicial conference, 591
writs of certiorari, 582	affirm, 591
appellant, 582	reverse, 591
appellee, 582	remand, 591
petitioner, 582	*per curiam* opinion, 591
respondent, 582	opinion of the court, 591
fundamental errors, 582	dissenting opinion, 591
assignments of error, 582	concurring opinion, 591
miscarriage of justice, 583	concurring in the judgment, 591
doctrine of harmless error, 583	reporters, 592
cert petitions, 585	motion for rehearing, 592
substantial federal question, 585	*en banc* rehearing, 592
rule of four, 585	federal habeas corpus review, 593
pendency of the appeal, 587	ineffective assistance of counsel, 594
Bail Reform Act of 1984, 587	collateral attack, 599
frivolous appeals, 588	clemency, 602
Anders brief, 588	pardon, 602

■ WEB-BASED RESEARCH ACTIVITY

 Locate your state's online resources on the Web. Find the opinions of the appellate court or courts that review routine criminal appeals. Determine whether that court's opinions are posted online. If so, examine the ten or twenty most recently posted decisions. Categorize these decisions by the issue(s) presented on appeal. From this sample, what kinds of issues are being raised in criminal appeals in your state? How do they compare with the kinds of issues discussed in this chapter?

■ QUESTIONS FOR THOUGHT AND DISCUSSION

1. What court or courts in your state have jurisdiction to hear appeals from felony convictions? What changes, if any, would you propose for your state's system of appellate courts?

2. Is the right to appeal a necessary concomitant of due process of law? In the absence of statutory rights to appeal, would the current Supreme Court find a constitutional right to appeal implicit in the due process requirements of the Constitution?

3. What new or revised procedures would expedite the resolution of criminal appeals? Would such procedures detract from the fair and deliberative review essential to determine whether the decision of the trial court in a criminal case was arrived at fairly and accurately?

4. In addition to determining whether a sentence imposed on a convicted defendant is within the statutory bounds, do you think an appellate court is an appropriate forum to reconsider the reasonableness of the sentence imposed by the trial court?

5. How has the "nationalization" of the criminal law that occurred through decisions of the U.S. Supreme Court during the 1960s and 1970s affected the appellate process?

6. The U.S. Supreme Court has recognized a constitutional right to represent oneself in a criminal trial. Could a person who insisted on self-representation at trial later challenge his or her conviction by claiming ineffective assistance of counsel?

7. Where a defendant has had an opportunity for a full and fair review of his or her trial through an appeal, what justifies the availability of additional avenues of review through collateral attack?

8. After studying briefs submitted by counsel and hearing oral arguments in a proceeding open to the public, appellate judges retire to privately discuss and decide the merits of criminal appeals. Should these deliberations be open to the public? Why or why not?

9. In a substantial number of criminal appeals, some state appellate courts routinely issue decisions merely stating "Judgment Affirmed." When an appellate court rejects a defendant's issues on appeal, should it be required to issue an opinion justifying its decision? In discussing this issue, consider whether such a requirement would (a) require greatly increasing the number of judges and support staff and the additional costs thereof and (b) detract from the court's ability to direct its efforts to writing opinions on novel questions of law.

10. Do you think the ability of a convicted defendant to secure DNA testing rises to an issue of due process of law? Does Congress have a role to play in providing a standardized process throughout the country? Should the process be governed by federal statute, or should state legislatures and courts be left free to develop their own procedures?

■ PROBLEMS FOR DISCUSSION AND SOLUTION

1. John Dunnit was convicted of aggravated sexual battery and was sentenced to state prison. After exhausting his appellate remedies in the state courts, Dunnit filed a federal habeas corpus application, which was denied. Dunnit appealed the denial of relief to the federal circuit court and was denied relief. Dunnit filed a second federal habeas corpus petition after President Clinton signed the Antiterrorism and Effective Death Penalty Act of 1996 amending the federal habeas corpus statute. How does this new law affect Dunnit's case? Is Dunnit's second application for a writ of habeas corpus affected by recent Supreme Court decisions mentioned in this chapter?

2. Culp Able was convicted of murder in state court. Central to the state's case was a confession that Able uttered before being given his *Miranda* warnings. The trial judge received the confession in evidence over the defendant's objection,

and Able was convicted. On appeal, the state intermediate appellate court and state supreme court considered and rejected Able's challenge to the admissibility of the confession. Then Able filed an application for federal habeas corpus relief, citing only the alleged *Miranda* violation as a basis for the reversal of his conviction. Relying on *Stone v. Powell* (1976), the state argues that the petition should be dismissed because Able was afforded "a full and fair opportunity to litigate his Fifth Amendment claim in the state courts." If you were the federal district judge, how would you rule? Should Able get his day in federal court?

Access to the Law through Legal Research

The Nature of Legal Research

Successful legal research requires a systematic method of finding the law applicable to a particular problem or set of facts. Before beginning research, it is helpful, if not essential, for the criminal justice professional or student to have a basic understanding of the law and the legal system.

After assembling the relevant facts and completing a preliminary analysis of the problem, the researcher must find the applicable constitutional and statutory materials and then search for authoritative interpretations of the law. Interpretations are usually found in appellate court decisions construing the particular constitutional provision or statute in analogous situations. These judicial decisions are referred to as cases in point. Legislative and judicial sources of the law are referred to as primary sources because they are authoritative.

A variety of other legal materials, called secondary sources, are available to the researcher. These consist of legal encyclopedias, textbooks by scholars and practitioners, law reviews published by law schools, and journals and periodicals published by various legal organizations. These secondary sources are extremely helpful to the researcher, especially to one unfamiliar with the law in a given area.

Getting Started in Legal Research

Once you become knowledgeable about the sources of the law and the process of its development by courts and you develop the skill of analyzing a problem, you can get started in legal research. Here is a suggestion that can help. If you attend a college at or near a law school, a law librarian might help you in the use of law books or electronic sources. Or you might get assistance from law students, as they usually take a course in legal research in their first year. If you are working from home, do not overlook the fact that in many communities, local governments, courthouses, and bar associations have established law libraries that are usually available to the public; some of these may even offer the free use of legal research databases and other electronic sources.

Legal research has changed rapidly due to the Internet, and more information is becoming available online every day. But before undertaking online research, it is essential that the legal researcher become knowledgeable about the books that are the traditional professional tools for legal research, when those books are the best sources to use, and when to go online instead.

Primary Legal Sources

Federal and state constitutions are often the beginning points in legal research in the criminal justice area because they provide the framework for our government and guarantee certain basic rights to the accused. As explained in this text, the rights of an accused are protected by several provisions of the federal constitution and the Bill of Rights. Most state constitutions afford criminal defendants similar protections. Thus, a person concerned about the legality of an arrest, search, or seizure would examine the relevant federal and state constitutional provisions and then seek to determine how the courts have construed the law in analogous situations.

Federal offenses are defined in statutes enacted by the U.S. Congress, and state offenses are defined in statutes enacted by state legislatures. Federal statutes (in sequence of their adoption) are published annually in the *United States Statutes at Large*. Most states have similar volumes, called session laws, that incorporate the laws enacted during a given session of the legislature. These federal and state laws are initially compiled in sequence of their adoption. Later they are merged into legal codes that systematically arrange the statutes by subject and provide an index. Of far greater assistance to the criminal justice researcher are commercially prepared versions of these codes that classify all federal and state laws of a general and permanent nature by subject and include reference materials and exhaustive indexes. These volumes are kept current by periodic supplements and revised volumes.

The *United States Code Annotated*

One popular compilation of the federal law widely used by lawyers, judges, and criminal justice professionals is the *United States Code Annotated*. The "U.S.C.A.," as it is known, is published by the West Group of St. Paul, Minnesota. The U.S.C.A. consists of fifty separate titles that conform to the text of the Official Code of the Laws of the United States. For instance, Title 18 is titled "Crimes and Criminal Procedure" and is of particular interest to the criminal justice researcher. Each section of statutory law in the U.S.C.A. is followed by a series of annotations consisting of court decisions interpreting the particular statute, along with historical notes, cross-references, and other editorial features. The U.S.C.A. also has a General Index, printed annually, that will guide the researcher to a particular title and section number by subject. If the researcher knows only the popular name of a federal statute, the corresponding U.S. Code title and section number can be found in the Popular Name Table. A sample page from the U.S.C.A. is included as Exhibit 1. A sample page from the Popular Name Table is included as Exhibit 2. The U.S.C.A. is kept up to date by the use of "pocket parts," annual updates with the latest laws and amendments, which are slipped into the back pockets of the individual volumes so that the researcher can easily find the latest versions of the laws.

Annotated State Codes

Most states have annotated statutes published by either the state or a private publisher. For example, *West's Annotated California Codes* follows the same general format as the U.S.C.A. A sample page is included as Exhibit 3 on page 611. Annotated statutes are popular aids to legal research and can save the researcher valuable time in locating cases in point. They are especially effective tools for locating interpretations of criminal statutes.

CHAPTER 87—PRISONS

Sec.
1791.   Traffic in contraband articles.
1792.   Mutiny, riot, dangerous instrumentalities prohibited.

Cross References

Escape and rescue, see section 751 et seq. of this title.

§ 1791.   Traffic in contraband articles

Whoever, contrary to any rule or regulation promulgated by the Attorney General, introduces or attempts to introduce into or upon the grounds of any Federal penal or correctional institution or takes or attempts to take or send therefrom anything whatsoever, shall be imprisoned not more than ten years.

(June 25, 1948, c. 645, 62 Stat. 786.)

Historical and Revision Notes

Reviser's Note. Based on Title 18, U.S.C., 1940 ed., §§ 753j, 908 (May 14, 1930, c. 274, § 11, 46 Stat. 327; May 27, 1930, c. 339, § 8, 46 Stat. 390).

Section consolidates sections 753j and 908 of Title 18, U.S.C., 1940 ed. The section was broadened to include the taking or sending out of contraband from the institution. This was suggested by representatives of the Federal Bureau of Prisons and the Criminal Division of the Department of Justice. In other respects the section was rewritten without change of substance.

The words "narcotic", "drug", "weapon" and "contraband" were omitted, since the insertion of the words "contrary to any rule or regulation promulgated by the attorney general" preserves the intent of the original statutes.

Words "guilty of a felony" were deleted as unnecessary in view of definitive section 1 of this title. (See also reviser's note under section 550 of this title.)

Minor verbal changes also were made.

Cross References

Bureau of Prisons employees, power to arrest without warrant for violations of this section, see section 3050 of this title.

West's Federal Forms

Sentence and fine, see § 7531 et seq.

Code of Federal Regulations

Federal penal and correctional institutions, traffic in contraband articles, see 28 CFR 6.1.

Library References

Prisons ☞17½.
C.J.S. Prisons § 22.

Notes of Decisions

Aiding and abetting 7
Admissibility of evidence 13

Articles prohibited 3
Assistance of counsel 11

585

EXHIBIT 1   *United States Code Annotated.* Source: Reprinted with permission from 18 U.S.C.A. § 1791. Copyright 1984 by West Publishing Co., 1-800-328-9352.

Crimes and Criminal Procedure—Continued

Oct. 28, 1992, Pub.L. 102–550, Title XIII, Subtitle A, § 1353, Title XV, Subtitle A, §§ 1504(c), 1512(a), (c), 1522(a), 1523(a), 1524, 1525(c)(1), 1526, 1527, 1528, 1530, 1531, 1533, 1534, 1536, Subtitle D, § 1543, Subtitle E, §§ 1552, 1553, 1554, 106 Stat. 3970, 4055, 4057, 4063, 4064, 4065, 4066, 4067, 4069, 4070, 4071 (Title 18, §§ 474, 474A, 504, 981, 982, 984, 986, 1510, 1905, 1956, 1957, 1960, 6001)

Oct. 28, 1992, Pub.L. 102–561, 106 Stat. 4233 (Title 18, § 2319)

Oct. 29, 1992, Pub.L. 102–572, Title I, § 103, Title VII, §§ 701, 703, 106 Stat. 4507, 4514, 4515 (Title 18, §§ 3143, 3154, 3401, 3603)

Criminal Appeals Act

Mar. 2, 1907, ch. 2564, 34 Stat. 1246 (See Title 18, § 3731)

Criminal Code

Mar. 4, 1909, ch. 321, 35 Stat. 1088 (See Title 18, chapters 1–15)
June 25, 1910, ch. 431, § 6, 36 Stat. 857 (See Title 18, §§ 1853, 1856)
Mar. 4, 1921, ch. 172, 41 Stat. 1444 (See Title 18, §§ 831–835)
Mar. 28, 1940, ch. 73, 54 Stat. 80 (See Title 18, § 1382)
Apr. 30, 1940, ch. 164, 54 Stat. 171 (See Title 18, § 1024)
June 6, 1940, ch. 241, 54 Stat. 234 (See Title 18, § 13)
June 11, 1940, ch. 323, 54 Stat. 304 (See Title 18, § 7)
Apr. 1, 1944, ch. 151, 58 Stat. 149 (See Title 18, § 491)
Sept. 27, 1944, ch. 425, 58 Stat. 752 (See Title 18, § 371)
June 8, 1945, ch. 178, 59 Stat. 234 (See Title 18, §§ 371, 1503, 1505)

Criminal Fine Enforcement Act of 1984

Pub.L. 98–596, Oct. 30, 1984, 98 Stat. 3134 (Title 18, §§ 1, 1 note, 3565, 3565 note, 3569, 3579, 3591 to 3599, 3611 note, 3621 to 3624, 3651, 3655, 4209, 4214; Title 18, F.R.Crim.Proc. Rules 12.2, 12.2 note)

Criminal Fine Improvements Act of 1987

Pub.L. 100–185, Dec. 11, 1987, 101 Stat. 1279 (Title 18, §§ 1 note, 18, 19, 3013, 3559, 3571, 3572, 3573, 3611, 3611 note, 3612, 3663; Title 28, § 604)

Criminal Justice Act Revision of 1984

Pub.L. 98–473, Title II, § 1901, Oct. 12, 1984, 98 Stat. 2185 (Title 18, § 3006A)

Criminal Justice Act Revision of 1986

Pub.L. 99–651, Title I, Nov. 14, 1986, 100 Stat. 3642 (Title 18, § 3006A)

Criminal Justice Act of 1964

Pub. L. 88–455, Aug. 20, 1964, 78 Stat. 552 (Title 18, § 3006A)

Criminal Law and Procedure Technical Amendments Act of 1986

Pub.L. 99–646, Nov. 10, 1986, 100 Stat. 3592 (Title 18, §§ 1 note, 3, 17, 18, 113, 115, 201, 201 note, 203, 203 note, 209, 219, 351, 373, 513, 524, 666, 1028, 1029, 1111, 1153, 1201, 1366, 1512, 1515, 1791, 1791 note, 1793, 1961, 1963, 2031, 2032, 2113, 2232, 2241, 2241 notes, 2242, 2243, 2244, 2245, 2315, 2320, 3050, 3076, 3141, 3142, 3143, 3143 note, 3144, 3146, 3147, 3148, 3150a, 3156, 3156 note, 3185, 3522, 3551 note, 3552, 3552 note, 3553, 3553 notes, 3556, 3561, 3561 note, 3563, 3563 notes, 3579, 3579 notes, 3583, 3583 note, 3603, 3603 note, 3624, 3624 note, 3671, 3671 note, 3672, 3672 note, 3673, 3673 note, 3681, 3682, 3731, 3742, 4044, 4045, 4082, 4203, 4204, 4208, 4209, 4210, 4214, 4217, 5003, 5037, 5037 note; Title 18, F.R.Crim.Proc. Rules 12.2, 29, 29 note, 32, 32 note, 32.1, 32.1 note; Title 21, §§ 802, 812, 845a, 875, 878, 881; Title 28, §§ 546, 992, 993, 994, 1921, 1921 note; Title 42, §§ 257, 300w–3, 300w–4, 9511, 10601, 10603, 10604)

Pub.L. 100–185, § 4(c), Dec. 11, 1987, 101 Stat. 1279 (Title 18, § 18)

Pub.L. 100–690, Title VII, §§ 7012 to 7014, Nov. 18, 1988, 102 Stat. 4395 (Title 18, §§ 18, 1961, 4217)

Criminal Victims Protection Act of 1990

Pub.L. 101–581, Nov. 15, 1990, 104 Stat. 2865 (Title 11, §§ 101 note, 523, 523 note, 1328)

Pub.L. 101–647, Title XXXI, Nov. 29, 1990, 104 Stat. 4916 (Title 11, §§ 101 note, 523, 523 note, 1328)

Critical Agricultural Materials Act

Pub.L. 95–592, Nov. 4, 1978, 92 Stat. 2529 (Title 7, §§ 178, 178a to 178n, 1314f); Pub.L. 98–284, May 16, 1984, 98 Stat. 184 (Title 7, §§ 178, 178 note, 178a to 178i, 178k to 178n)

Pub.L. 99–198, Title XIV, § 1439, Dec. 23, 1985, 99 Stat. 1559 (Title 7, § 178c)

Pub.L. 101–624, Title XVI, § 1601(e), Nov. 28, 1990, 104 Stat. 3704 (Title 7, § 178n)

EXHIBIT 2 Popular Name Table (from U.S.C.A.). Source: Reprinted with permission from U.S.C.A. Copyright 1992 by West Publishing Co., 1-800-328-9352.

Title 12   **SEARCH WARRANTS**   **§ 1524**

warrant. People v. Golden (1971) 97 Cal.Rptr. 476, 20 C.A.3d 211.

4. Affidavits

"Oral" procedure is permitted only as to affidavit in support of search and warrant itself must be in writing. Bowyer v. Superior Court of Santa Cruz County (1974) 111 Cal.Rptr. 628, 37 C.A.3d 151, rehearing denied 112 Cal.Rptr. 266, 37 C.A.3d 151.

For an affidavit based on informant's hearsay statement to be legally sufficient to support issuance of a search warrant, two requirements must be met: (1) affidavit must allege the informant's statement in language that is factual rather than conclusionary and must establish that informant spoke with personal knowledge of the matters contained in such statement, and (2) the affidavit must contain some underlying factual information from which magistrate issuing the warrant can reasonably conclude that informant was credible or his information reliable. People v. Hamilton (1969) 77 Cal.Rptr. 785, 454 P.2d 681, 71 C.2d 176.

5. Arrest

An arrest without a warrant may not be made on a belief, founded on information received from a third person, that a misdemeanor is being committed. Ware v. Dunn (1947) 183 P.2d 128, 80 C.A.2d 936.

Arrest under warrant issued by justice of peace directed to any sheriff "in the state," where proper sheriff did receive warrant and executed it, and person arrested was not prejudiced, and was not ground for complaint by person arrested, notwithstanding under statutes warrant should have been directed to any sheriff "in the county". Elliott v. Haskins (1937) 67 P.2d 698, 20 C.A.2d 591.

6. Unreasonable searches

Alleged action of city police on specified occasions in blocking off designated portions of city and stopping all persons and automobiles entering or leaving the blocked off area and searching them with-

out first obtaining a search warrant and without having probable cause for believing the searched individuals to have violated some law or that automobiles were carrying contraband, would be unconstitutional as being "unreasonable searches and seizures". Wirin v. Horrall (1948) 193 P.2d 470, 85 C.A.2d 497.

7. Admissibility of evidence

Rule excluding in criminal prosecutions evidence obtained through unlawful searches and seizures by police and governmental officers does not apply to evidence obtained by a private person, not employed by nor associated with a governmental unit. People v. Johnson (1957) 315 P.2d 468, 153 C.A.2d 870.

Evidence obtained in violation of constitutional guarantees against unreasonable searches and seizures is inadmissible. People v. Cahan (1955) 282 P.2d 905, 44 C.2d 434, 50 A.L.R.2d 513.

In a prosecution for burglary in the second degree, the fact that articles claimed to have been taken were seized from the person of accused without warrant in violation of Const.Art. 1, § 19 (repealed; see, now, Const.Art. 1, § 13) did not render their introduction in evidence error, although the court overruled the motion of accused to have the articles returned to him. People v. Watson (1922) 206 P. 648, 57 C.A. 85.

8. Federal and state warrants distinguished

Although a California municipal court judge is a "judge of a court of record" and thus authorized to issue federal warrants, the search warrant in question was clearly issued under state, not federal, authority, where it was issued by a California municipal judge on a California form, on the application of a California narcotics agent, and where there was no attempt to comply with the requirements of Fed. Rules of Cr.Proc. rule 41, 18 U.S.C. A. U. S. v. Radlick (C.A.1978) 581 F.2d 225.

§ 1524. Issuance; grounds; special master

(a) A search warrant may be issued upon any of the following grounds:

(1) When the property was stolen or embezzled.

(2) When the property or things were used as the means of committing a felony.

(3) When the property or things are in the possession of any person with the intent to use it as a means of committing a public of-

---

EXHIBIT 3 *West's Annotated California Code.* Source: Reprinted with permission from *West's Annotated California Codes*, Vol. 51A, § 1524. Copyright 1982 by West Publishing Co., 1-800-328-9352.

The National Reporter System

Volumes containing appellate court decisions are referred to as reporters. The National Reporter System, by West Publishing, includes decisions from the U.S. Supreme Court, the lower federal courts, and the state appellate courts. Reporters are available in bound volumes, on CD-ROM, and online through Westlaw.

Decisions of the U.S. Supreme Court are officially published in the *United States Reports* (abbreviated U.S.). Two private organizations also report these decisions in hardcover volumes. The *Supreme Court Reporter* (abbreviated S.Ct.) is published by West Group, and *Lawyers Edition,* now in its second series (abbreviated L.Ed.2d), is published by West Group/Lawyers Cooperative. Although the three reporters have somewhat different editorial features, the opinions of the Supreme Court are reproduced identically in all three reporters.

References to judicial decisions found in the reporters are called citations. U.S. Supreme Court decisions are often cited to all three publications—for example, *Miranda v. Arizona,* 384 U.S. 436, 86 S.Ct. 1602, 16 L.Ed.2d 694 (1966). With each of these publications, the citation tells you exactly where the case is published: for example, "384 U.S. 436" means that the *Miranda* case is in volume 384 of the United States Reports on page 436. A sample page from West's *Supreme Court Reporter* is included as Exhibit 4.

Since 1889, the decisions of the U.S. courts of appeals have been published in *West's Federal Reporter,* now in its third series (abbreviated F.3d). Decisions of federal district (trial) courts are published in *West's Federal Supplement,* which is now in its second series (abbreviated F. Supp. 2d). A citation to a case in *Federal Reporter* will read, for example, *Newman v. United States,* 817 F.2d 635 (10th Cir. 1987). This refers to a 1987 case reported in volume 817, page 635 of the *Federal Reporter,* second series, decided by the United States Court of Appeals for the Tenth Circuit. A citation to *United States v. Klopfenstine,* 673 F. Supp. 356 (W.D. Mo. 1987), refers to a 1987 federal district court decision from the western district of Missouri, reported in volume 673, page 356 of the *Federal Supplement.*

Additional federal reporters publish the decisions from other federal courts (for example, bankruptcy and military appeals), but the federal reporters referred to earlier are those most frequently used by criminal justice professionals.

The Regional Reporters

The decisions of the highest state courts (usually but not always called supreme courts) and the decisions of other state appellate courts (usually referred to as intermediate appellate courts) are found in seven regional reporters, West's *California Reporter,* and the *New York Supplement.* Regional reporters, with their abbreviations in parentheses, include decisions from the following states:

- *Atlantic Reporter* (A. and A.2d): Maine, Vermont, New Hampshire, Connecticut, Rhode Island, Pennsylvania, New Jersey, Maryland, Delaware, and the District of Columbia
- *North Eastern Reporter* (N.E. and N.E.2d): Illinois, Indiana, Massachusetts, New York (court of last resort only—other New York appellate courts have their opinions in the New York Supplement), and Ohio
- *North Western Reporter* (N.W. and N.W.2d): North Dakota, South Dakota, Nebraska, Minnesota, Iowa, Michigan, and Wisconsin

1602   **86 SUPREME COURT REPORTER**   **384 U.S. 436**

384 U.S. 436

Ernesto A. MIRANDA, Petitioner,

v.

STATE OF ARIZONA.

Michael VIGNERA, Petitioner,

v.

STATE OF NEW YORK.

Carl Calvin WESTOVER, Petitioner,

v.

UNITED STATES.

STATE OF CALIFORNIA, Petitioner,

v.

Roy Allen STEWART.

Nos. 759–761, 584.

Argued Feb. 28, March 1 and 2, 1966.

Decided June 13, 1966.

Rehearing Denied No. 584
Oct. 10, 1966.

See 87 S.Ct. 11.

Criminal prosecutions. The Superior Court, Maricopa County, Arizona, rendered judgment, and the Supreme Court of Arizona, 98 Ariz. 18, 401 P.2d 721, affirmed. The Supreme Court, Kings County, New York, rendered judgment, and the Supreme Court, Appellate Division, Second Department, 21 A.D.2d 752, 252 N.Y.S.2d 19, affirmed, as did the Court of Appeals of the State of New York at 15 N.Y.2d 970, 259 N.Y.S.2d 857, 207 N.E.2d 527. The United States District Court for the Northern District of California, Northern Division, rendered judgment, and the United States Court of Appeals for the Ninth Circuit, 342 F.2d 684, affirmed. The Superior Court, Los Angeles County, California, rendered judgment and the Supreme Court of California, 62 Cal.2d 571, 43 Cal. Rptr. 201, 400 P.2d 97, reversed. In the first three cases, defendants obtained certiorari, and the State of California obtained certiorari in the fourth case. The Supreme Court, Mr. Chief Justice Warren, held that statements obtained from defendants during incommunicado interrogation in police-dominated atmosphere, without full warning of constitu-

tional rights, were inadmissible as having been obtained in violation of Fifth Amendment privilege against self-incrimination.

Judgments in first three cases reversed and judgment in fourth case affirmed.

Mr. Justice Harlan, Mr. Justice Stewart, and Mr. Justice White dissented; Mr. Justice Clark dissented in part.

1. Courts ⚖═397½

Certiorari was granted in cases involving admissibility of defendants' statements to police to explore some facets of problems of applying privilege against self-incrimination to in-custody interrogation and to give concrete constitutional guidelines for law enforcement agencies and courts to follow.

2. Criminal Law ⚖═393(1), 641.1

Constitutional rights to assistance of counsel and protection against self-incrimination were secured for ages to come and designed to approach immortality as nearly as human institutions can approach it. U.S.C.A.Const. Amends. 5, 6.

3. Criminal Law ⚖═412.1(4)

Prosecution may not use statements, whether exculpatory or inculpatory, stemming from custodial interrogation of defendant unless it demonstrates use of procedural safeguards effective to secure privilege against self-incrimination. U. S.C.A.Const. Amend. 5.

4. Criminal Law ⚖═412.1(4)

"Custodial interrogation", within rule limiting admissibility of statements stemming from such interrogation, means questioning initiated by law enforcement officers after person has been taken into custody or otherwise deprived of his freedom of action in any significant way. U.S.C.A.Const. Amend. 5.

See publication Words and Phrases
for other judicial constructions and
definitions.

EXHIBIT 4 *Supreme Court Reporter.* Source: Reprinted with permission from 86 S.Ct. 1602. Copyright 1967 by West Publishing Co., 1-800-328-9352.

- *Pacific Reporter* (P. and P.2d): Washington, Oregon, California, Montana, Idaho, Nevada, Utah, Arizona, Wyoming, Colorado, New Mexico, Kansas, Oklahoma, Alaska, and Hawaii
- *Southern Reporter* (So. and So.2d): Florida, Alabama, Mississippi, and Louisiana
- *South Eastern Reporter* (S.E. and S.E.2d): Virginia, West Virginia, North Carolina, South Carolina, and Georgia
- *South Western Reporter* (S.W. and S.W.2d): Texas, Missouri, Arkansas, Kentucky, and Tennessee

For many states (in addition to New York and California), West publishes separate volumes reporting the decisions as they appear in the regional reporters. *Pennsylvania Reporter* and *Texas Cases* are examples of this.

The following examples of citation forms appear in some of the regional reporters:

- *State v. Hogan,* 480 So.2d 288 (La. 1985). This refers to a 1985 decision of the Louisiana Supreme Court found in volume 480, page 288 of the *Southern Reporter,* second series.
- *State v. Nungesser,* 269 N.W.2d 449 (Iowa 1978). This refers to a 1978 decision of the Iowa Supreme Court found in volume 269, page 449 of the *North Western Reporter,* second series.
- *Henry v. State,* 567 S.W.2d 7 (Tex. Cr. App. 1978). This refers to a 1978 decision of the Texas Court of Criminal Appeals found in volume 567, page 7 of the *South Western Reporter,* second series.

A sample page from *Southern Reporter,* second series, is included as Exhibit 5.

Syllabi, Headnotes, and Key Numbers

The National Reporter System and the regional reporters contain not only the official text of each reported decision but also a brief summary of the decision, called the syllabus, and one or more topically indexed "headnotes." These headnotes briefly describe the principles of law expounded by the court and are indexed by a series of topic "key numbers." West assigns these key numbers to specific points of decisional law. For instance, decisions dealing with first-degree murder are classified under the topic "homicide" and assigned a key number for each particular aspect of that crime. Thus, a homicide case dealing with the intent requirement in first-degree murder may be classified as "Homicide 9—Intent and design to effect death." Using this key number system, a researcher can locate headnotes of various appellate decisions on this aspect of homicide and is, in turn, led to relevant decisional law.

In addition, each of these volumes contains a table of statutes construed in the cases reported in that volume, with reference to the American Bar Association's *Standards for Criminal Justice.*

United States Law Week

United States Law Week, published by the Bureau of National Affairs, Inc., Washington, D.C., presents a weekly survey of American law. *Law Week* includes all the latest decisions from the U.S. Supreme Court as well as significant current decisions from other federal and state courts.

288 La.   **480 SOUTHERN REPORTER, 2d SERIES**

imprisonment. It is indeed unlikely that the enactment of art. 893.1 was designed to punish more severely those who commit negligent homicide than perpetrators of second degree murder, manslaughter, aggravated battery, etc.

In summary, therefore, we find as regards defendant's second assignment of error that the art. 893.1 enhancement is not constitutionally infirm as cruel, unusual and excessive punishment; that the absence of art. 894.1 sentence articulation in this case was harmless, there existing in this record sufficient factors to support this penalty which is well within the statutory range; that the two year penalty imposed in this case under § 14:95.2 is illegal; that art. 893.1 is applicable to all felonies, including those specially enumerated in § 14:95.2 and that therefore the art. 893.1 enhancement in this case is valid.

Decree

Accordingly, defendant's conviction is affirmed; his sentence is reversed and the case remanded for resentencing in accordance with the views expressed herein and according to law.

CONVICTION AFFIRMED; SENTENCE REVERSED; CASE REMANDED.

DIXON, C.J., and DENNIS, J., concur.

WATSON, J., dissents as to requiring notice.

STATE of Louisiana

v.

Patrick HOGAN.

No. 84–K–1847.

Supreme Court of Louisiana.

Dec. 2, 1985.

Defendant was convicted in the First Judicial District Court, Parish of Caddo, Charles R. Lindsay, J., of aggravated battery, and he appealed. The Court of Appeal, 454 So.2d 1235, affirmed, and defendant's petition for writ of review was granted. The Supreme Court, Calogero, J., held that: (1) sentence enhancement by reason of use of a firearm in commission of a felony was not constitutionally infirm as cruel, unusual and excessive; (2) existence of some mitigating factors did not preclude enhancement; (3) imposition of an additional two-year penalty for use of a gun while attempting commission of a specified felony was impermissible when not preceded by an appropriate notice; and (4) enhancement was not invalid, however, since minimum sentence mandated by use of firearm was applicable to all felonies.

Conviction affirmed, sentence reversed, and case remanded.

Dennis, J., concurred.

Watson, J., dissented as to requiring notice.

1. Criminal Law ⚷1206.1(1), 1213.2(1)

General sentencing enhancement statute [LSA-R.S. 14:34, 14:95; LSA-C.Cr.P. art. 893.1] applicable when a firearm is used in commission of a felony, does not impose cruel, unusual, and excessive punishment and is not constitutionally infirm on its face or as applied. U.S.C.A. Const. Amend. 8.

2. Criminal Law ⚷1213.8(7)

Imposition of mandatory minimum sentence under enhancement statute [LSA-R.S. 14:34, 14:95; LSA-C.Cr.P. art. 893.1]

EXHIBIT 5   *Southern Reporter.* Source: Reprinted with permission from 480 So.2d 288. Copyright 1986 by West Publishing Co., 1-800-328-9352.

Criminal Law Reporter

Published by the Bureau of National Affairs, Inc., Washington, D.C., the weekly *Criminal Law Reporter* reviews contemporary developments in the criminal law. It is an excellent source of commentaries on current state and federal court decisions in the criminal law area.

The Digests

West also publishes *Decennial Digests,* which topically index all the appellate court decisions from the state and federal courts. Digests are tools that enable the researcher to locate cases in point through topics and key numbers. By finding a particular topic and key number and looking it up in the pertinent digest, the researcher can locate other cases on the narrow point of law covered by that key number. The *Decennial Digests* are kept current by a set called the General Digests so that the researcher can always find the latest cases. The latest *Decennial Digest* covers cases from 1996 to 2001.

A series of federal digests contains key number headnotes for decisions of the federal courts. The current series published by West is *Federal Practice Digest 4th.* In addition, separate digests are published for some states as well as for the Atlantic, North Western, Pacific, and South Eastern reporters.

The index at the beginning of each topic identifies the various points of law by numerically arranged key numbers. In addition to the basic topic of criminal law, many topics in the field of criminal law are listed by specific crimes (such as homicide, forgery, and bribery). Procedural topics such as arrest and search and seizure are also included. The digests contain a descriptive word index and a table of cases sorted by name, listing the key numbers corresponding to the decisions. Thus, the researcher can find, by key number, reference topics that relate to the principles set out in the headnotes prepared for each judicial decision. A researcher who locates a topic and key number has access to all reported decisions on this point of law. A sample page from the *Texas Digest,* second series, is reprinted as Exhibit 6.

Shepard's Citations

Shepard's Citations is a series that provides the judicial history of cases by reference to the volume and page number of the cases in the particular reporters. Because the law is constantly changing and new laws and decisions come out all the time, it is essential that a researcher keep up to date and know if there are new cases or what might have happened to a case the researcher has found. By using the symbols explained in this work, the researcher can determine whether a particular decision has been affirmed, followed, distinguished, modified, or reversed by subsequent court decisions. Most attorneys "Shepardize" the cases they cite in their law briefs to support various principles of law. There is a separate set of *Shepard's Citations* for the U.S. Supreme Court reports, for the federal appellate and district courts, for each regional reporter, and for each state that has an official reporter. *Shepard's* can also be found on Lexis.

KeyCite

Another source that is used for updating a case history, and locating cases that refer to it, is KeyCite, available online as part of Westlaw. Like *Shepard's* (both print and computer versions), KeyCite gives the history of a case and subsequent cases that have cited it. Among other useful features that KeyCite has is a ranking system for

6 Tex D 2d—155   **ARREST**   ⟜63.3

For references to other topics, see Descriptive-Word Index

was observed in act of smoking a marihuana cigarette, for violation of narcotics laws, was legal. Code Cr.Proc.Tex.1925, arts. 212, 215; 26 U.S.C.A. §§ 2557(b) (1), 2593(a).

Rent v. U. S., 209 F.2d 893.

D.C.Tex. 1975. Arrest and subsequent detention of husband plaintiff by deputies without warrant was not unlawful where husband plaintiff appeared to be intoxicated in public place. 28 U.S.C.A. § 1343; 42 U.S.C.A. §§ 1983, 1985; U.S.C.A.Const. Amend. 4; Vernon's Ann.Tex.C.C.P. art. 14.01.

Lamb v. Cartwright, 393 F.Supp. 1081, affirmed 524 F.2d 238.

D.C.Tex. 1972. The "presence" of the officer, under Texas statute providing that a police officer may arrest an offender without a warrant for any offense committed in his "presence" or within his view, is satisfied if the violation occurs within reach of the officer's senses. Vernon's Ann.Tex.C.C.P. art. 14.01(b).

Taylor v. McDonald, 346 F.Supp. 390.

D.C.Tex. 1967. It is not the case that officer may arrest person committing felony in his presence irrespective of whose privacy officer must violate in order to place commission of felony in his presence.

Gonzales v. Beto, 266 F.Supp. 751, affirmed State of Tex. v. Gonzales, 388 F.2d 145.

Tex.Cr.App. 1981. Observation by police officer of the exchange of money between defendant and another person for tinfoil bindles coupled with officer's knowledge that heroin is normally packaged in tinfoil bindles was sufficient to provide probable cause to believe that an offense had been committed and, thus, defendant's warrantless arrest was valid under statute which allows peace officer to arrest an offender without a warrant "for any offense committed in his presence or within his view." Vernon's Ann.C.C.P. art. 14.01(b).

Boyd v. State, 621 S.W.2d 616.

Tex.Cr.App. 1981. Where defendant was observed in supermarket placing a steak and bottle of bath oil in her purse and observed leaving the store without paying for such items and was apprehended and placed in custody of city police officer who had been summoned by the manager, defendant's arrest was lawful. Vernon's Ann.C.C.P. art. 18.16.

Stewart v. State, 611 S.W.2d 434.

Tex.Cr.App. 1980. Peace officer need not determine whether material in question is in fact obscene in order to make a valid arrest for offense of commercially distributing obscene material; warrantless arrest is proper if there is probable cause to believe the publication commercially distributed in officer's pres-

see Vernon's Annotated Texas Statutes

ence or within his view was obscene. Vernon's Ann.C.C.P. art. 14.01(b); V.T.C.A., Penal Code § 43.21(1).

Carlock v. State, 609 S.W.2d 787.

Tex.Cr.App. 1980. Fact that defendants were in possession of a stolen gun several hours prior to their arrest was not a sufficient basis for the officers' conclusion that defendants were committing an offense within their presence so as to justify a warrantless arrest.

Green v. State, 594 S.W.2d 72.

Tex.Cr.App. 1979. Defendant had no reasonable expectation of privacy while sitting in a restaurant, so that, upon observing drug transaction in plain view from public vantage point outside the restaurant and recognizing it as offense, officers were authorized to make warrantless arrest. Vernon's Ann.C.C.P. art. 14.01.

Hamilton v. State, 590 S.W.2d 503.

Tex.Cr.App. 1979. Where defendants' vehicle was not stopped by any overt action on the part of off-duty police officers, who simply turned around and began to follow defendants' vehicle after spotting it traveling in the opposite direction and noting that defendants appeared to be smoking a marihuana cigarette, where it was only after defendants stopped at a traffic light that one officer was able to approach the vehicle and then noticed the odor of marihuana, and where it was at that point that the officer directed defendants to pull over to the side of the street and get out of their car, the arrest and subsequent search were reasonable under the circumstances. Vernon's Ann.C.C.P. art. 14.01(b).

Isam v. State, 582 S.W.2d 441.

Tex.Cr.App. 1979. Although detective did not view any of the reading matter of the magazine before making warrantless arrest of seller, the magazine's front and back covers, depicting an act of fellatio on a nude male and an act of cunnilingus on a nude female, gave the officer sufficient probable cause to reasonably believe that a violation of the obscenity statute had occurred in his presence and within his view justifying a warrantless arrest. V.T.C.A., Penal Code § 43.21(1); Vernon's Ann.C.C.P. art. 14.01(b).

Price v. State, 579 S.W.2d 492.

Tex.Cr.App. 1979. Though the scope of an investigation cannot exceed the purposes which justify initiating the investigation, if, while questioning a motorist regarding the operation of his vehicle, an officer sees evidence of a criminal violation in open view or in some other manner acquires probable cause with respect to a more serious charge, the officer may arrest for that offense and, incident thereto, conduct an additional search for physical evidence. Vernon's Ann.Civ.St. art.

EXHIBIT 6 *Texas Digest 2d.* Source: Reprinted with permission from West's *Texas Digest 2d,* Vol. 6, Page 155. Copyright 1982 by West Publishing Co., 1-800-328-9352.

the later cases, which shows which cases have discussed or explained the original one in detail and which give a mere mention of the case. This is of great help to the researcher who might otherwise be faced with a long list of cases to read and no way to differentiate their value.

Secondary Sources

Legal authorities other than constitutions, statutes, ordinances, regulations, and court decisions are called secondary sources, yet they are essential tools in legal research. A basic necessity for any legal researcher's work is a good law dictionary. Several are published, and *Black's Law Dictionary* (8th ed.), published by West Group is one of the best known. *Black's* is available both in print and computer disk media.

Legal Encyclopedias

Beyond dictionaries, the most common secondary legal authorities are legal encyclopedias. These are arranged alphabetically by subject and are used much like any standard encyclopedia. There are two principal national encyclopedias of the law: *Corpus Juris Secundum* (C.J.S.), published by West Group, and *American Jurisprudence*, second edition (Am.Jur.2d), published by West Group/Lawyers Cooperative. A sample page from C.J.S. appears as Exhibit 7. Appellate courts frequently include citations to these encyclopedias, as well as to cases in the reporters, to document the rules and interpretations contained in their opinions. Each of these encyclopedias is an excellent set of reference books; one significant difference is that *Corpus Juris Secundum* cites more court decisions, whereas *American Jurisprudence 2d* limits footnote references to the leading cases pertinent to the principles of law in the text. *Corpus Juris Secundum* includes valuable cross-references to West topic key numbers and other secondary sources, including forms. *American Jurisprudence 2d* includes valuable footnote references to another of the company's publications, *American Law Reports*, now in its fifth series. These volumes (cited as A.L.R.) include annotations to the decisional law on selected topics. For example, a 1987 annotation from A.L.R. entitled "Snowmobile Operation as D.W.I. or D.U.I." appears in 56 A.L.R. 4th 1092. Both *Corpus Juris Secundum* and *American Jurisprudence 2d* are supplemented annually by cumulative pocket parts and are exceptionally well indexed. They serve as an excellent starting point for a researcher because they provide a general overview of topics. A general index for each is published annually, and researchers should use this first to find their specific subjects and section numbers.

For example, a person researching the defenses available to a defendant charged with forgery would find a good discussion of the law in this area in either of these encyclopedias. A citation to the text on defenses to forgery found in *Corpus Juris Secundum* would read as follows: 37 C.J.S. Forgery § 41; in *American Jurisprudence 2d* it would read like this: 36 Am.Jur.2d Forgery § 42. In addition to these major national encyclopedias, some states have encyclopedias for the jurisprudence of their state—for example, *Pennsylvania Law Encyclopedia* and *Texas Jurisprudence*. Like the volumes of *Corpus Juris Secundum* and *American Jurisprudence 2d,* most encyclopedias of state law are annually supplemented with cumulative pocket parts.

religious beliefs.[38] The burden falls on prison officials to prove that the food available to a religious inmate is consistent with his dietary laws and provides adequate nourishment.[39] Thus, a prisoner who strictly adheres to Jewish dietary laws may be entitled to prepare his own meals during the Passover holiday,[40] and Muslim inmates may be entitled to a diet that provides them with adequate nourishment without requiring them to eat pork.[41]

However, where Muslim inmates are able to practice their religion conscientiously and still receive a sufficiently nutritious diet, the prison is not obligated to provide them with a special diet.[42]

Prison authorities are not required to supply a prisoner with a special religious diet where the prisoner's beliefs are not religious in nature.[43]

§ 95. Religious Names

Although under some authorities prisoners lose the right to change their names for religious purposes, other authorities generally preclude a categorical refusal to accord legal recognition to religious names adopted by incarcerated persons.

Library References
Prisons ⬤⇒4(14).

Although it has been held that a common-law name change, even for religious purposes, is among the rights that inmates lose as inconsistent with their status as prisoners,[44] it has also been held that a state's categorical refusal to accord legal recognition to religious names adopted by incarcerated persons is not reasonably and substantially justified by considerations of prison discipline and order.[45]

Thus, the inmates' free exercise of religion may be burdened by prison officials who continue for all purposes to use the names under which the inmates were committed,[46] and it may be unlawful for the state to refuse to deliver mail addressed to the prisoner under his legal religious name.[47]

On the other hand, inmates are not entitled to have prison officials use their new names for all purposes.[48] For example, correctional authorities generally do not have to reorganize institutional records to reflect prisoners' legally adopted religious names.[49]

E. COMMUNICATIONS AND VISITING RIGHTS AND RESTRICTIONS

§ 96. Communications in General

Prison inmates have a right to communicate with people living in free society, but this right is not unfettered and may be limited by prison officials in order to promote legitimate institutional interests.

Library References
Prisons ⬤⇒4(5, 6).

Prison inmates have a constitutional right to communicate with people living in free society.[50] However, this right is not absolute, and is subject

---

38. U.S.—Prushinowski v. Hambrick, D.C.N.C., 570 F.Supp. 863.

39. U.S.—Prushinowski v. Hambrick, D.C.N.C., 570 F.Supp. 863.

40. U.S.—Schlesinger v. Carlson, D.C.Pa., 489 F.Supp. 612.

41. U.S.—Masjid Muhammad-D.C.C. v. Keve, D.C.Del., 479 F.Supp. 1311.

42. U.S.—Masjid Muhammad-D.C.C. v. Keve, D.C.Del., 479 F.Supp. 1311.

43. U.S.—Africa v. Commonwealth of Pennsylvania, C.A.Pa., 662 F.2d 1025, certiorari denied 102 S.Ct. 1756, 456 U.S. 908, 72 L.Ed.2d 165.

44. U.S.—Salahuddin v. Coughlin, D.C.N.Y., 591 F.Supp. 353.

45. U.S.—Barrett v. Commonwealth of Virginia, C.A.Va., 689 F.2d 498.

46. U.S.——Masjid Muhammad-D.C.C. v. Keve, D.C.Del., 479 F.Supp. 1311.

47. U.S.——Barrett v. Commonwealth of Virginia, C.A.Va., 689 F.2d 498.

Masjid Muhammad-D.C.C. v. Keve, D.C.Del., 479 F.Supp. 1311.

48. U.S.—Azeez v. Fairman, D.C.Ill., 604 F.Supp. 357—Masjid Muhammad-D.C.C. v. Keve, D.C.Del., 479 F.Supp. 1311.

49. U.S.—Barrett v. Commonwealth of Virginia, C.A.Va., 689 F.2d 498.

Azeez v. Fairman, D.C.Ill., 604 F.Supp. 357.

Failure to follow statutory mechanism

Inmates' constitutional rights were not violated by failure of prison officials to recognize their use of Muslim names in records of department of correctional services, where inmates had not followed statutory mechanism for name change.

U.S.—Salahuddin v. Coughlin, D.C.N.Y., 591 F.Supp. 353.

50. U.S.—Pell v. Procunier, Cal., 94 S.Ct. 2800, 417 U.S. 817, 41 L.Ed.2d 495.

Inmates of Allegheny County Jail v. Wecht, D.C.Pa., 565 F.Supp. 1278.

Friends and relatives

U.S.—Hutchings v. Corum, D.C.Mo., 501 F.Supp. 1276.

EXHIBIT 7 *Corpus Juris Secundum.* Source: Reprinted with permission from *Corpus Juris Secundum,* Vol. 72, Prisons § 96, p. 501. Copyright 1987 by West Publishing Co., 1-800-328-9352.

Textbooks

Textbooks and other treatises on legal subjects often read much like encyclopedias; however, most address specific subjects in great depth. One of the better-known textbooks is LaFave and Scott, *Criminal Law*, published by the West Group.

Law Reviews

In addition, most leading law schools publish law reviews that contain articles, commentaries, and notes by academics, judges, lawyers, and law students who exhaustively research topics. Law review articles can be excellent sources of in-depth analyses and background information on specific legal topics. A citation for a recent law review article in the criminal justice field, "Consequences of Refusing Consent to a Search and Seizure," 75 S. Cal. L. Rev. 901 (2002), refers to a scholarly article published in volume 75 at page 901 of the *Southern California Law Review*.

Professional Publications and Other Useful Secondary Sources

An example of a professional publication is the *Criminal Law Bulletin*, published bimonthly by Warren, Gorham and Lamont of Boston. It contains many valuable articles of contemporary interest. For instance, "Probable Cause and the Fourth Amendment" was published in the September 2003 issue. The American Bar Association and most state bar associations publish numerous professional articles in their journals and reports. Some of these present contemporary views on the administration of justice; often they provide more about how the law is actually applied, not just the theory behind it that law review articles sometimes focus on.

The *Index to Legal Periodicals*, published by H. W. Wilson Company of the Bronx, New York, indexes articles from leading legal publications by subject and author. Another index for legal articles is the *Current Law Index*, published by Information Access. These valuable research tools are found in many law libraries and are kept current by periodic supplements; many college and law school libraries also have these available online. Periodicals published by law schools, bar associations, and other professional organizations can be valuable both in doing research and in gaining a perspective on many contemporary problems in the criminal justice field. The federal government also publishes numerous studies of value to the criminal justice professional and student.

Words and Phrases, another West publication, consists of numerous volumes alphabetically arranged in dictionary form. Hundreds of thousands of legal terms are defined with citations to appellate court decisions. The volumes are kept current by annual pocket part supplements. A sample page from *Words and Phrases* is reprinted as Exhibit 8.

Computerized Legal Research

Increasingly, legal research is being done electronically using computerized legal databases such as Westlaw. Westlaw operates from a central computer system at the West headquarters in St. Paul, Minnesota, and has databases for state and federal

RESISTANCE

RESISTANCE—Cont'd

Where a contract for the purchase of defendant's stock in plaintiff corporation provided that defendant should not concern himself in the manufacture or sale of resistance or steel armature binding wire, sheet, or strip, such manufactures must be understood as some alloy of copper used in the manufacture of electric apparatus which does not conduct electricity as freely as pure copper, which is the best conductor, and hence is called "resistance, wire, sheet, or strip." Driver-Harris Wire Co. v. Driver, 62 A. 461, 463, 70 N.J.Eq. 34.

Breaking of glass bottles on roadway over which pneumatic-tired trucks, which were loaded with goods being removed from building by United States Marshal under writ of replevin, were required to pass, held criminal contempt of court, since "resistance" as used in contempt statute includes willful purpose and intent to prevent execution of process of court. Russell v. United States, C.C.A.Minn., 86 F.2d 389, 394, 109 A.L.R. 297.

RESIST HORSES, CATTLE AND LIVE STOCK

Under the statute which requires railroad companies to maintain fences sufficient to "resist horses, cattle and live stock," an instruction that a company was required to maintain one sufficient to "turn stock" was not improper; the quoted terms being synonymous. Deal v. St. Louis, I. M. & S. Ry. Co., 129 S.W. 50, 52, 144 Mo.App. 684.

Under Rev.St.1899, § 1105, Mo.St.Ann. § 4761, p. 2144, requiring a railroad company to construct and maintain fences sufficient to prevent stock getting on the track, an instruction in an action under such section for injuries to stock, which defined a lawful fence as one sufficient "to resist horses, cattle, swine, and like stock," was not erroneous for using the phrase "to resist"; such phrase not being as strong as the phrase "to prevent" in the statute. Hax v. Quincy, O. & K. C. R. Co., 100 S.W. 693, 695, 123 Mo.App. 172.

RESISTING AN OFFICER

To constitute the offense of "resisting an officer," under Act March 8, 1831, § 9, it is not necessary that the officer should be assaulted, beaten, or bruised. Woodworth v. State, 26 Ohio St. 196, 200.

RESISTING AN OFFICER—Cont'd

A justice of the peace being a conservator of the peace, under Const. art. 7, § 40, and being, under Crawford & Moses' Dig. § 2906, without authority to make an arrest himself, act of one in resisting an arrest by a justice does not constitute offense of "resisting an officer," in violation of section 2585 et seq. Herdison v. State, 265 S.W. 84, 86, 166 Ark. 33.

"Resist," as used in Code, § 4476, providing for the punishment of any person who shall knowingly and willfully obstruct, resist, or oppose any officer or other person duly authorized in serving or executing any lawful process, imports force. The words "obstruct," "resist," or "oppose" mean the same thing, and the word "oppose" would cover the meaning of the word "resist" or "obstruct." It does not mean to oppose or impede the process with which the officer is armed, or to defeat its execution, but that the officer himself shall be obstructed. Davis v. State, 76 Ga. 721, 722.

RESISTING AN OFFICER IN DISCHARGE OF HIS DUTY

Where police officers investigated defendant's premises to determine whether he was killing sheep or cattle in alleged violation of an ordinance and after failing to discover indications of such killing one of officers informed defendant that he was under arrest and attempted to put upon his hand a wrist chain and defendant resisted such action for three or four minutes and then submitted quietly, defendant's actions did not constitute "resisting an officer in discharge of his duty" since officers had no right to arrest defendant. City of Chicago v. Delich, 1st Dist. No. 20,686, 193 Ill.App. 72.

Where police officers investigated defendant's premises to determine whether he was killing sheep or cattle in alleged violation of an ordinance and after failing to discover indications of such killing one of officers informed defendant that he was under arrest and attempted to put upon his hand a wrist chain and defendant resisted such action for three or four minutes and then submitted quietly, action of wife who took some part in the altercation with the officers did not constitute "resisting an officer in discharge of his duty," since officers had no right to arrest defendant. City of Chicago v. Delich, 1st Dist., No. 20,687, 193 Ill. App. 74.

612

EXHIBIT 8 *Words and Phrases.* Source: Reprinted with permission from *Words and Phrases,* Vol. 37, p. 612. Copyright 1992 by West Publishing Co., 1-800-328-9352.

statutes, appellate decisions, attorney general opinions, and certain legal periodicals. For example, the law review article referred to earlier, "Consequences of Refusing Consent to a Search and Seizure," 75 S. Cal. L. Rev. 901 (2002), is available on West-law in the ScALR database and can be quickly retrieved by typing the citation—75 S. Cal. L. Rev. 901—into the "find this document" box on the welcome page. Subscribers can access Westlaw through the Internet. Westlaw users enter queries into the system to begin research, using connectors recognized by the system. A properly formulated query pinpoints the legal issue to be researched and instructs Westlaw to retrieve all data relevant to the query.

Westlaw also has a searching method that uses natural language, which allows queries to be entered in plain English without special terms or connectors. The statutes, cases, and other research results found on Westlaw can be printed, downloaded, or e-mailed. One of the most useful features of Westlaw is the ability to check the history of cases using KeyCite. When the researcher needs to update a large number of cases, Westlaw can save a tremendous amount of time and substantially reduce the possibility of error.

Lexis/Nexis is an excellent competing system. As with Westlaw, researchers can use Lexis/Nexis to find cases and statutes, search for items either by forming queries or using natural language, and find cases by typing in the citations. Unlike Westlaw, which has KeyCite to check citation history, Lexis/Nexis has an electronic version of *Shepard's* to check cites. It is a bit easier to use and more up to date than the printed *Shepard's* volumes.

Legal Research Using the Internet

The phenomenal growth of the Internet makes it impossible to firmly state what legal sources or sites might be available because new things are being added constantly. The federal and state governments are among those rapidly adding data to the Internet, and for that reason a person looking for government information, or statutes and codes, is likely to find it on the Internet. Among the best ways to search for legal information is to use a comprehensive legal site such as ALSO—American Law Sources Online (www.lawsource.com)—which has a detailed page of law sites for each state and for federal sources. ALSO provides links to official sites such as those of government agencies, courts, and codes available online, as well as other helpful sites such as state bar associations and legal aid groups. Another major site is Findlaw (www.findlaw.com), which uses categories to neatly divide legal information so that a user can search for the appropriate category and then find the information available on that topic or issue. Among Findlaw's categories are state law (further divided into categories for each individual state) and international law (indeed, the Internet is currently the best source for locating law from other countries). Another excellent source for federal information is Thomas (thomas.loc.gov), the Library of Congress website, which contains pending bills, federal laws, and links to other federal sites.

Findlaw's Supreme Court category offers U.S. Supreme Court opinions dating back to 1893 in a searchable format. In addition, the Legal Information Institute (LII) at Cornell University (supct.law.cornell.edu/supct/) offers downloadable Supreme Court opinions. The LII archive now contains all opinions of the Court issued since May 1990 as well as hundreds of the most important historical decisions of the Court. The Supreme Court itself now has its own website, useful for finding information about pending or recently decided cases, at www.supremecourtus.gov.

More and more lower courts, both at the federal and state levels, are putting up their own websites, and often very recently decided cases can be found on them.

ALSO is a good place to begin in trying to locate these sites, as its listing for each state includes links to courts of that state. (The researcher may notice that many states have websites that cover all of their courts; for example, www.flcourts.org, the Florida courts website, has links to extensive information from all Florida appellate courts and many of the trial level courts too.) Findlaw also can help the researcher find the statutes, court decisions, and court rules of most states, almost all of which are now on the Internet. Also, regular search engines such as Google and Yahoo can be very helpful in locating court sites and other legal information. When using one of these search engines to locate a particular court decision, it is important to be very specific. One might try a docket number or an obscure or unique term that is found in the case.

Although the Internet is convenient and low in cost, there are limitations to consider in doing research there. The Internet is a solid source for finding up-to-date information, such as current state statutes and some recent court decisions; it is also a good source for finding factual material, such as statistics and background information. Because most legal research involves finding more than just the latest cases and laws, however, a researcher will usually need to use other written or computer resources in addition to the Internet. When that is the case, the researcher will need to fall back on traditional methods of research.

How to Research a Specific Point of Law

The following example demonstrates how a legal researcher might employ the research tools discussed earlier to find the law applicable to a given set of facts. Consider this hypothetical scenario:

> Mary Jones, a student at a Florida college, filed a complaint accusing Jay Grabbo for taking her purse while she was walking across campus on November 20, 2005. In her statement to the police, Jones was vague on whether Grabbo had used any force in taking the purse and whether she had offered any resistance. She stated that she had recently purchased the purse for $49 and that it contained $22 in cash plus a few loose coins and personal articles of little value. Further inquiry by the police revealed that Grabbo was unarmed.

A researcher who needs to gain a general background on the offense of robbery and how it differs from theft can profitably consult one of the legal encyclopedias mentioned earlier. Someone with a general knowledge of criminal offenses might still need to review the offense of robbery from the standpoint of state law. If so, *Florida Jurisprudence 2d* or some similar text should be consulted.

Given a general knowledge of the crimes of theft and robbery, a likely starting point would be the state statutes. In this instance, reference could be made to the official Florida Statutes. But from a research standpoint, it might be more productive to locate the statutes proscribing theft and robbery in the index to *West's Florida Statutes Annotated* and review the statutes and pertinent annotations in both the principal volume and the pocket part. The researcher would quickly find the offense of theft defined in section 812.014 and the offense of robbery defined in section 812.13.

Research of the statutory law would disclose that under Florida law, the theft of Jones's purse would be petit theft in the second degree if the total value was less than $100. West's Fla. Stat. Ann. § 812.014. This offense is a misdemeanor for which the maximum penalty is sixty days in jail and a $500 fine. West's Fla. Stat. Ann. § 775.082 and § 775.083. Unarmed robbery, on the other hand, is defined as

> the taking of money or other property which may be the subject of larceny from the person or custody of another, with intent to either permanently or temporarily deprive the person or the owner of the money or other property, when in the course of the taking there is the use of force, violence, assault, or putting in fear and where the perpetrator is unarmed.

It is a second-degree felony that subjects the offender to a maximum fifteen years' imprisonment and a maximum fine of $10,000. West's Fla. Stat. Ann. § 812.13, § 775.082, and § 775.083. Therefore, it is very important to determine whether Grabbo should be charged with petit theft or robbery.

The researcher would then proceed to references noted under the topics of "force" and "resistance" following the text of the robbery statute. The annotated statutes would identify pertinent Florida appellate decisions on these points. For example, the researcher would find a note to *Mims v. State,* 342 So.2d 116 (Fla. App. 1977), indicating that purse snatching is not robbery if no more force is used than is necessary to physically remove the property from a person who does not resist. If the victim does resist and that resistance is overcome by the force of the perpetrator, however, the crime of robbery is complete. Another reference points the researcher to *Goldsmith v. State,* 573 So.2d 445 (Fla. App. 1991), which held that the slight force used in snatching a $10 bill from a person's hand without touching the person was insufficient to constitute robbery and instead constituted petit theft. Additional decisions refer to these and related points of law. For example, *Robinson v. State,* 680 So.2d 481 (Fla. App. 1999), indicates that while a stealthful taking may be petit theft, the force required to take someone's purse can make the offense robbery.

A further check into *West's Florida Statutes Annotated* reveals that the legislature enacted a new statute called "Robbery by Sudden Snatching" effective October 1, 1999. The new statute has been indexed as section 812.131 and provides,

> (1) "Robbery by sudden snatching" means the taking of money or other property from the victim's person, with intent to permanently or temporarily deprive the victim or the owner of the money or other property, when, in the course of the taking, the victim was or became aware of the taking. In order to satisfy this definition, it is not necessary to show that:
>
> > (a) The offender used any amount of force beyond that effort necessary to obtain possession of the money or other property; or
> >
> > (b) There was any resistance offered by the victim to the offender or that there was injury to the victim's person.

The new offense is a third-degree felony, which is punishable by a maximum of five years' imprisonment and a fine of $5,000. West's Fla. Stat. Ann. § 775.082 and § 775.083.

Annotations to Fla. Stat. § 812.131 show that in *Brown v. State,* 848 So.2d 361 (Fla. App. 2003), the court reversed a defendant's conviction for robbery by sudden snatching. The court noted that the offense requires that property be taken from the victim's actual, physical possession and that because the evidence at the defendant's trial revealed that the victim was unaware of the snatching until after it had been accomplished, the defendant should be acquitted of the charge of robbery by sudden snatching.

After locating these and other pertinent references, the researcher should go to the *Southern Reporter 2d* and read the located cases. After concluding the search, the researcher should "Shepardize" or "KeyCite" the decisions to determine whether they have been subsequently commented on, distinguished, or even reversed.

In view of the newer statute and the recent appellate court interpretation, before arriving at a conclusion, the researcher will likely need additional information as to whether the victim was actually aware of Grabbo's taking her purse. If the research is undertaken for the prosecutor or the police, they can determine once it is completed whether any further factual investigation is necessary. They can decide the charge to place against Grabbo and the proof required to sustain that charge. On the other hand, if the research is undertaken for a defense attorney, it may be that the attorney can obtain more precise information from the victim's testimony through discovery. That, along with the results of the legal research, would assist counsel in advising Grabbo, assuming he is charged with a crime, on how to plead and what defenses may be available.

The steps outlined here are basic and are designed to illustrate rudimentary principles of gaining access to the criminal law on a particular subject. As previously indicated, another method might involve using digests with the key number system of research. Moreover, there will often be issues of interest still undecided by courts in a particular state. If so, then research into the statutes and court decisions of other states may be undertaken. The methodology and level of research pursued will often depend on the researcher's objective, knowledge of the subject, and experience in conducting legal research.

Conclusion

Understanding how to gain access to the primary and secondary sources of the criminal law is tremendously important. The ability to assemble relevant facts, analyze a problem, and conduct a systematic search for applicable authoritative statements of constitutional, statutory, and decisional law is a skill to be acquired by both the criminal justice student and the working professional. Professionally trained lawyers, who must make the critical judgments concerning the prosecution and defense of criminal actions, increasingly assign basic legal research to paralegal and criminal justice staff personnel. The ability to access the law through traditional as well as computerized methods will assist the student and professional in becoming better acquainted with the dynamics of the criminal law. Moreover, the honing of such skill will enhance a person's ability to carry out specific research assignments and to support his or her recommendations with relevant legal authorities.

The Constitution of the United States of America

We the People of the United States, in Order to form a more perfect Union, establish Justice, insure domestic Tranquility, provide for the common defence, promote the general Welfare, and secure the Blessings of Liberty to ourselves and our Posterity, do ordain and establish this Constitution for the United States of America.

Article I

Section 1. All legislative Powers herein granted shall be vested in a Congress of the United States, which shall consist of a Senate and House of Representatives.

Section 2. (1) The House of Representatives shall be composed of Members chosen every second Year by the People of the several States, and the Electors in each State shall have the Qualifications requisite for Electors of the most numerous Branch of the State Legislature.

(2) No Person shall be a Representative who shall not have attained to the age of twenty-five Years, and been seven Years a Citizen of the United States, and who shall not, when elected, be an Inhabitant of that State in which he shall be chosen.

(3) Representatives and direct Taxes shall be apportioned among the several States which may be included within this Union, according to their respective Numbers, which shall be determined by adding to the whole Number of free Persons, including those bound to Service for a Term of Years, and excluding Indians not taxed, three fifths of all other Persons. The actual Enumeration shall be made within three Years after the first Meeting of the Congress of the United States, and within every subsequent Term of ten Years, in such Manner as they shall by Law direct. The Number of Representatives shall not exceed one for every thirty Thousand, but each State shall have at Least one Representative; and until such enumeration shall be made, the State of New Hampshire shall be entitled to chuse three, Massachusetts eight, Rhode Island and Providence Plantations one, Connecticut five, New York six, New Jersey four, Pennsylvania eight, Delaware one, Maryland six, Virginia ten, North Carolina five, South Carolina five, and Georgia three.

(4) When vacancies happen in the Representation from any State, the Executive Authority thereof shall issue Writs of Election to fill such Vacancies.

(5) The House of Representatives shall chuse their Speaker and other Officers; and shall have the sole Power of Impeachment.

Section 3. (1) The Senate of the United States shall be composed of two Senators from each State, chosen by the Legislature thereof, for six Years; and each Senator shall have one Vote.

(2) Immediately after they shall be assembled in Consequence of the first Election, they shall be divided as equally as may be into three Classes. The Seats of the Senators of the first Class shall be vacated at the Expiration of the second Year, of the second Class at the Expiration of the fourth Year, and of the third Class at the Expiration of the sixth Year, so that one third may be chosen every second Year; and if Vacancies happen by Resignation, or otherwise, during the Recess of the Legislature of any State, the Executive thereof may make temporary Appointments until the next Meeting of the Legislature, which shall then fill such Vacancies.

(3) No Person shall be a Senator who shall not have attained, to the Age of thirty Years, and been nine Years a Citizen of the United States, and who shall not, when elected, be an Inhabitant of that State for which he shall be chosen.

(4) The Vice President of the United States shall be President of the Senate, but shall have no Vote, unless they be equally divided.

(5) The Senate shall chuse their other Officers, and also a President pro tempore, in the Absence of the Vice President, or when he shall exercise the Office of the President of the United States.

(6) The Senate shall have the sole Power to try all Impeachments. When sitting for that Purpose, they shall be on Oath or Affirmation. When the President of the United States is tried, the Chief Justice shall preside: And no Person shall be convicted without the Concurrence of two thirds of the Members present.

(7) Judgment in Cases of Impeachment shall not extend further than to removal from Office, and disqualification to hold and enjoy any Office of honor, Trust or Profit under the United States: but the Party convicted shall nevertheless be liable and subject to Indictment, Trial, Judgment and Punishment, according to Law.

Section 4. (1) The Times, Places and Manner of holding Elections for Senators and Representatives, shall be prescribed in each State by the Legislature thereof; but the Congress may at any time by Law make or alter such Regulations, except as to the Places of chusing Senators.

(2) The Congress shall assemble at least once in every Year, and such Meeting shall be on the first Monday in December, unless they shall by Law appoint a different Day.

Section 5. (1) Each House shall be the Judge of the Elections, Returns and Qualifications of its own Members, and a Majority of each shall constitute a Quorum to do Business; but a smaller Number may adjourn from day to day, and may be authorized to compel the Attendance of absent Members, in such Manner, and under such Penalties as each House may provide.

(2) Each House may determine the Rules of its Proceedings, punish its Members for disorderly Behaviour, and, with the Concurrence of two thirds, expel a Member.

(3) Each House shall keep a Journal of its Proceedings, and from time to time publish the same, excepting such Parts as may in their Judgment require Secrecy; and the Yeas and Nays of the Members of either House on any question shall, at the Desire of one fifth of those Present, be entered on the Journal.

(4) Neither House, during the Session of Congress, shall, without the Consent of the other, adjourn for more than three days, nor to any other Place than that in which the two Houses shall be sitting.

Section 6. (1) The Senators and Representatives shall receive a Compensation for their Services, to be ascertained by Law, and paid out of the Treasury of the United States. They shall in all Cases, except Treason, Felony and Breach of the Peace, be privileged from Arrest during their Attendance at the Session of their respective Houses, and in going to and returning from the same; and for any Speech or Debate in either House, they shall not be questioned in any other Place.

(2) No Senator or Representative shall, during the Time for which he was elected, be appointed to any civil Office under the Authority of the United States, which shall have been created, or the Emoluments whereof shall have been increased during such time; and no Person holding any Office under the United States, shall be a Member of either House during his Continuance in Office.

Section 7. (1) All Bills for raising Revenue shall originate in the House of Representatives; but the Senate may propose or concur with Amendments as on other Bills.

(2) Every Bill which shall have passed the House of Representatives and the Senate, shall, before it become a Law, be presented to the President of the United States; If he approve he shall sign it, but if not he shall return it, with his Objections to that House in which it shall have originated, who shall enter the Objections at large on their Journal, and proceed to reconsider it. If after such Reconsideration two thirds of that House shall agree to pass the Bill, it shall be sent, together with the Objections, to the other House, by which it shall likewise be reconsidered, and if approved by two thirds of that House, it shall become a Law. But in all such Cases the Votes of both Houses shall be determined by Yeas and Nays, and the Names of the Persons voting for and against the Bill shall be entered on the Journal of each House respectively. If any Bill shall not be returned by the President within ten Days (Sunday excepted) after it shall have been presented to him, the Same shall be a Law, in like Manner as if he had signed it, unless the Congress by their Adjournment prevent its Return, in which Case it shall not be a Law.

(3) Every Order, Resolution, or Vote to which the Concurrence of the Senate and House of Representatives may be necessary (except on a question of Adjournment) shall be presented to the President of the United States; and before the Same shall take Effect, shall be approved by him, or being disapproved by him, shall be repassed by two thirds of the Senate and House of Representatives, according to the Rules and Limitations prescribed in the Case of a Bill.

Section 8. (1) The Congress shall have Power To lay and collect Taxes, Duties, Imposts and Excises, to pay the Debts and provide for the common Defence and general Welfare of the United States; but all Duties, Imposts and Excises shall be uniform throughout the United States;

(2) To borrow Money on the credit of the United States;

(3) To regulate Commerce with foreign Nations, and among the several States, and with the Indian Tribes;

(4) To establish an uniform Rule of Naturalization, and uniform Laws on the subject of Bankruptcies throughout the United States;

(5) To coin Money, regulate the Value thereof, and of foreign Coin, and to fix the Standard of Weights and Measures;

(6) To provide for the Punishment of counterfeiting the Securities and current Coin of the United States;

(7) To establish Post Offices and post Roads;

(8) To promote the Progress of Science and useful Arts, by securing for limited Times to Authors and Inventors the exclusive Right to their respective Writings and Discoveries;

(9) To constitute Tribunals inferior to the supreme Court;

(10) To define and punish Piracies and Felonies committed on the high Seas, and Offenses against the Law of Nations;

(11) To declare War, grant Letters of Marque and Reprisal, and make Rules concerning Captures on Land and Water;

(12) To raise and support Armies, but no Appropriation of Money to that Use shall be for a longer Term than two Years;

(13) To provide and maintain a Navy;

(14) To make Rules for the Government and Regulation of the land and naval Forces;

(15) To provide for calling forth the Militia to execute the Laws of the Union, suppress Insurrections and repel Invasions;

(16) To provide for organizing, arming, and disciplining, the Militia, and for governing such Part of them as may be employed in the Service of the United States, reserving to the States respectively, the Appointment of the Officers, and the Authority of training the Militia according to the discipline prescribed by Congress;

(17) To exercise exclusive Legislation in all Cases whatsoever, over such District (not exceeding ten Miles square) as may, by Cession of particular States, and the Acceptance of Congress, become the Seat of the Government of the United States, and to exercise like Authority over all Places purchased by the Consent of the Legislature of the State in which the Same shall be, for the Erection of Forts, Magazines, Arsenals, dock-Yards, and other needful Buildings;—And

(18) To make all Laws which shall be necessary and proper for carrying into Execution the foregoing Powers, and all other Powers vested by this Constitution in the Government of the United States, or in any Department or Officer thereof.

Section 9. (1) The Migration or Importation of such Persons as any of the States now existing shall think proper to admit, shall not be prohibited by the Congress prior to the Year one thousand eight hundred and eight, but a Tax or Duty may be imposed on such Importation, not exceeding ten dollars for each Person.

(2) The Privilege of the Writ of Habeas Corpus shall not be suspended unless when in Cases of Rebellion or Invasion the public Safety may require it.

(3) No Bill of Attainder or expost facto Law shall be passed.

(4) No Capitation, or other direct, Tax shall be laid, unless in Proportion to the Census or Enumeration herein before directed to be taken.

(5) No Tax or Duty shall be laid on Articles exported from any State.

(6) No Preference shall be given by any Regulation of Commerce or Revenue to the Ports of one State over those of another; nor shall Vessels bound to, or from, one State, be obliged to enter, clear or pay Duties in another.

(7) No Money shall be drawn from the Treasury, but in Consequence of Appropriations made by Law; and a regular Statement and Account of the Receipts and Expenditures of all public Money shall be published from time to time.

(8) No Title of Nobility shall be granted by the United States: And no Person holding any Office of Profit or Trust under them, shall, without the Consent of the Congress, accept of any present, Emolument, Office, or Title, of any kind whatever, from any King, Prince or foreign State.

Section 10. (1) No State shall enter into any Treaty, Alliance, or Confederation; grant Letters of Marque and Reprisal; coin Money; emit Bills of Credit; make any Thing but gold and silver Coin a Tender in Payment of Debts; pass any Bill of Attainder, expost facto Law, or Law impairing the Obligation of Contracts, or grant any Title of Nobility.

(2) No State shall, without the Consent of Congress, lay any Imposts or Duties on Imports or Exports, except what may be absolutely necessary for executing its inspection Laws: and the net Produce of all Duties and Imposts, laid by any State on Imports or Exports, shall be for the Use of the Treasury of the United States; and all such Laws shall be subject to the Revision and Control of the Congress.

(3) No State shall, without the Consent of Congress, lay any Duty of Tonnage, keep Troops, or Ships of War in time of Peace, enter into any Agreement or Compact with another State, or with a foreign Power, or engage in War, unless actually invaded, or in such imminent Danger as will not admit of Delay.

Article II

Section 1. (1) The executive Power shall be vested in a President of the United States of America. He shall hold his Office during the Term of four Years, and, together with the Vice President, chosen for the same Term, be elected, as follows:

(2) Each State shall appoint, in such Manner as the Legislature thereof may direct, a Number of Electors, equal to the whole Number of Senators and Representatives to which the State may be entitled in the Congress: but no Senator or Representative, or Person holding an Office of Trust or Profit under the United States, shall be appointed an Elector.

The Electors shall meet in their respective States, and vote by Ballot for two Persons, of whom one at least shall not be an Inhabitant of the same State with themselves. And they shall make a List of all the Persons voted for, and of the Number of Votes for each; which List they shall sign and certify, and transmit sealed to the Seat of the Government of the United States, directed to the President of the Senate. The President of the Senate shall, in the presence of the Senate and House of Representatives, open all the Certificates, and the Votes shall then be counted. The Person having the greatest Number of Votes shall be the President, if such Number be a Majority of the whole Number of Electors appointed; and if there be more than one who have such Majority, and have an equal Number of Votes, then the House of Representatives shall immediately chuse by Ballot one of them for President; and if no Person have a Majority, then from the five highest on the List the said House shall in like Manner chuse the President. But in chusing the President, the Votes shall be taken by States, the Representation from each State having one Vote; a quorum for this Purpose shall consist of a Member or Members from two thirds of the States, and a Majority of all the States shall be necessary to a Choice. In every Case, after the Choice of the President, the Person having the greatest Number of Votes of the Electors shall be the Vice President. But if there should remain two or more who have equal Votes, the Senate shall chuse from them by Ballot the Vice President.

(3) The Congress may determine the Time of chusing the Electors, and the Day on which they shall give their Votes; which Day shall be the same throughout the United States.

(4) No Person except a natural born Citizen, or a Citizen of the United States, at the time of the Adoption of this Constitution, shall be eligible to the Office of President; neither shall any Person be eligible to that Office who shall not have attained to the Age of thirty five Years, and been fourteen Years a Resident within the United States.

(5) In Case of the Removal of the President from Office, or of his Death, Resignation, or Inability to discharge the Powers and Duties of the said Office, the Same shall devolve on the Vice President, and the Congress may by Law provide for the Case of Removal, Death, Resignation or Inability, both of the President and Vice President, declaring what Officer shall then act as President, and such Officer shall act accordingly, until the Disability be removed, or a President shall be elected.

(6) The President shall, at stated Times, receive for his Services, a Compensation, which shall neither be increased nor diminished during the Period for which he shall have been elected, and he shall not receive within that Period any other Emolument from the United States, or any of them.

(7) Before he enter on the Execution of his Office, he shall take the following Oath or Affirmation:—"I do solemnly swear (or affirm) that I will faithfully execute the Office of President of the United States, and will to the best of my Ability, preserve, protect and defend the Constitution of the United States."

Section 2. (1) The President shall be Commander in Chief of the Army and Navy of the United States, and of the Militia of the several States, when called into the actual Service of the United States; he may require the Opinion, in writing, of the principal Officer in each of the executive Departments, upon any Subject relating to the Duties of their respective Offices, and he shall have Power to grant Reprieves and Pardons for Offenses against the United States, except in Cases of Impeachment.

(2) He shall have Power, by and with the Advice and Consent of the Senate, to make Treaties, provided two thirds of the Senators present concur; and he shall nominate, and by and with the Advice and Consent of the Senate, shall appoint Ambassadors, other public Ministers and Consuls, Judges of the supreme Court, and all other Officers of the United States, whose Appointments are not herein otherwise provided for, and which shall be established by Law: but the Congress may by Law vest the Appointment of such inferior Officers, as they think proper, in the President alone, in the Courts of Law, or in the Heads of Departments.

(3) The President shall have Power to fill up all Vacancies that may happen during the Recess of the Senate, by granting Commissions which shall expire at the End of their next Session.

Section 3. He shall from time to time give to the Congress Information of the State of the Union, and recommend to their Consideration such Measures as he shall judge necessary and expedient; he may, on extraordinary Occasions, convene both Houses, or either of them, and in Case of Disagreement between them, with Respect to the Time of Adjournment, he may adjourn them to such Time as he shall think proper; he shall receive Ambassadors and other public Ministers; he shall take Care that the Laws be faithfully executed, and shall Commission all the Officers of the United States.

Section 4. The President, Vice President and all Civil Officers of the United States, shall be removed from Office on Impeachment for, and Conviction of, Treason, Bribery, or other high Crimes and Misdemeanors.

Article III

Section 1. The judicial Power of the United States, shall be vested in one supreme Court, and in such inferior Courts as the Congress may from time to time ordain and establish. The Judges, both of the supreme and inferior Courts, shall hold their Offices during good Behaviour, and shall, at stated Times, receive for their Services, a Compensation, which shall not be diminished during their Continuance in Office.

Section 2. (1) The judicial Power shall extend to all Cases, in Law and Equity, arising under this Constitution, the Laws of the United States, and Treaties made, or which shall be made, under their Authority;—to all Cases affecting Ambassadors, other public Ministers and Consuls;—to all Cases of admiralty and maritime Jurisdiction;—to Controversies to which the United States shall be a party;—to Controversies between two or more States;—between a State and Citizens of another State;—between Citizens of different States;—between Citizens of the same State claiming Lands under Grants of different States, and between a State, or the Citizens thereof, and foreign States, Citizens or Subjects.

(2) In all Cases affecting Ambassadors, other public Ministers and Consuls, and those in which a State shall be Party, the supreme Court shall have original Jurisdiction. In all the other Cases before mentioned, the supreme Court shall have appellate Jurisdiction, both as to Law and Fact, with such Exceptions, and under such Regulations as the Congress shall make.

(3) The Trial of all Crimes, except in Cases of Impeachment, shall be by Jury; and such Trial shall be held in the State where the said Crimes shall have been

committed; but when not committed within any State, the Trial shall be at such Place or Places as the Congress may by Law have directed.

Section 3. (1) Treason against the United States, shall consist only in levying War against them, or in adhering to their Enemies, giving them Aid and Comfort. No Person shall be convicted of Treason unless on the Testimony of two Witnesses to the same overt Act, or on Confession in open Court.

(2) The Congress shall have Power to declare the Punishment of Treason, but no Attainder of Treason shall work Corruption of Blood, or Forfeiture except during the Life of the Person attainted.

Article IV

Section 1. Full Faith and Credit shall be given in each State to the public Acts, Records, and judicial Proceedings of every other State. And the Congress may by general Laws prescribe the Manner in which such Acts, Records and Proceedings shall be proved, and the Effect thereof.

Section 2. (1) The Citizens of each State shall be entitled to all privileges and Immunities of Citizens in the several States.

(2) A Person charged in any State with Treason, Felony, or other Crime, who shall flee from Justice, and be found in another State, shall on Demand of the executive Authority of the State from which he fled, be delivered up, to be removed to the State having Jurisdiction of the Crime.

(3) No Person held to Service of Labour in one State, under the Laws thereof, escaping into another, shall, in Consequence of any Law or Regulation therein, be discharged from such Service or Labour, but shall be delivered up on Claim of the Party to whom such Service or Labour may be due.

Section 3. (1) New States may be admitted by the Congress into this Union; but no new State shall be formed or erected within the Jurisdiction of any other State; nor any State be formed by the Junction of two or more States, or Parts of States, without the Consent of the Legislatures of the States concerned as well as of the Congress.

(2) The Congress shall have power to dispose of and make all needful Rules and Regulations respecting the Territory or other Property belonging to the United States; and nothing in this Constitution shall be so construed as to Prejudice any Claims of the United States, or of any particular State.

Section 4. The United States shall guarantee to every State in this Union a Republican Form of Government, and shall protect each of them against Invasion; and on Application of the Legislature, or of the Executive (when the Legislature cannot be convened) against domestic Violence.

Article V

The Congress, whenever two thirds of both Houses shall deem it necessary, shall propose Amendments to this Constitution, or, on the Application of the Legislatures of two thirds of the several States, shall call a Convention for proposing Amendments, which, in either Case, shall be valid to all Intents and Purposes, as Part of this Constitution, when ratified by the Legislatures of three fourths of the several States, or by Conventions in three fourths thereof, as the one or the other Mode of Ratification may be proposed by the Congress; Provided that no Amendment which may be made prior to the Year One thousand eight hundred and eight shall in any Manner affect the first and fourth Clauses in the Ninth Section of the first Article; and that no State, without its Consent, shall be deprived of its equal Suffrage in the Senate.

Article VI

(1) All Debts contracted and Engagements entered into, before the Adoption of this Constitution, shall be as valid against the United States under this Constitution, as under the Confederation.

(2) This Constitution, and the Laws of the United States which shall be made in Pursuance thereof; and all Treaties made, or which shall be made, under the Authority of the United States, shall be the supreme Law of the Land; and the Judges in every State shall be bound thereby, any Thing in the Constitution or Laws of any State to the Contrary notwithstanding.

(3) The Senators and Representatives before mentioned, and the Members of the several State Legislatures, and all executive and judicial Officers, both of the United States and of the several States, shall be bound by Oath or Affirmation, to support this Constitution; but no religious Test shall ever be required as a Qualification to any Office or public Trust under the United States.

Article VII

The Ratification of the Conventions of nine States, shall be sufficient for the Establishment of this Constitution between the States so ratifying the Same.

Articles in Addition to, and Amendment of, the Constitution of the United States of America, Proposed by Congress, and Ratified by the Several States, Pursuant to the Fifth Article of the Original Constitution

Amendment I (1791)

Congress shall make no law respecting an establishment of religion, or prohibiting the free exercise thereof; or abridging the freedom of speech, or of the press; or the right of the people peaceably to assemble, and to petition the Government for a redress of grievances.

Amendment II (1791)

A well regulated Militia, being necessary to the security of a free state, the right of the people to keep and bear Arms, shall not be infringed.

Amendment III (1791)

No Soldier shall, in time of peace be quartered in any house, without the consent of the Owner, nor in time of war, but in a manner to be prescribed by law.

Amendment IV (1791)

The right of the people to be secure in their persons, houses, papers, and effects, against unreasonable searches and seizures, shall not be violated, and no Warrants shall issue, but upon probable cause, supported by Oath or affirmation, and particularly describing the place to be searched, and the persons or things to be seized.

Amendment V (1791)

No person shall be held to answer for a capital, or otherwise infamous crime, unless on a presentment or indictment of a Grand Jury, except in cases arising in the land or naval forces, or in the Militia, when in actual service in time of War or public danger; nor shall any person be subject for the same offence to be twice put in jeopardy of life or limb; nor shall be compelled in any criminal case to be a witness against himself, nor be deprived of life, liberty, or property, without due process of law; nor shall private property be taken for public use, without just compensation.

Amendment VI (1791)

In all criminal prosecutions, the accused shall enjoy the right to a speedy and public trial, by an impartial jury of the State and district wherein the crime shall have been committed, which district shall have been previously ascertained by law, and to be informed of the nature and cause of the accusation; to be confronted with the witnesses against him; to have compulsory process for obtaining witnesses in his favor, and to have the Assistance of Counsel for his defence.

Amendment VII (1791)

In Suits at common law, where the value in controversy shall exceed twenty dollars, the right of trial by jury shall be preserved, and no fact tried by a jury, shall be otherwise re-examined in any Court of the United States, than according to the rules of the common law.

Amendment VIII (1791)

Excessive bail shall not be required, nor excessive fines imposed, nor cruel and unusual punishments inflicted.

Amendment IX (1791)

The enumeration in the Constitution, of certain rights, shall not be construed to deny or disparage others retained by the people.

Amendment X (1791)

The powers not delegated to the United States by the Constitution, nor prohibited by it to the States, are reserved to the States respectively, or to the people.

Amendment XI (1798)

The Judicial power of the United States shall not be construed to extend to any suit in law or equity, commenced or prosecuted against one of the United States by Citizens of another State, or by Citizens or Subjects of any Foreign State.

Amendment XII (1804)

The Electors shall meet in their respective states and vote by ballot for President and Vice-President, one of whom, at least, shall not be an inhabitant of the same state with themselves; they shall name in their ballots the person voted for as President, and in distinct ballots the person voted for as Vice-President, and they shall make distinct lists of all persons voted for as President, and of all persons voted for as Vice-President, and of the number of votes for each, which lists they shall sign and certify, and transmit sealed to the seat of the government of the United States, directed to the President of the Senate;—The President of the Senate shall, in the presence of the Senate and House of Representatives, open all the certificates and the votes shall then be counted;—The person having the greatest number of votes for President, shall be the President, if such number be a majority of the whole number of Electors appointed; and if no person have such majority, then from the persons having the highest numbers not exceeding three on the list of those voted for as President, the House of Representatives shall choose immediately, by ballot, the President. But in choosing the President, the votes shall be taken by states, the representation from each state having one vote; a quorum for this purpose shall consist of a member or members from two-thirds of the states, and a majority of all the states shall be necessary to a choice. And if the House of Representatives shall not choose a President whenever the right of choice shall devolve upon them, before the fourth day of March next following, then the Vice-President shall act as President, as in the case of the death or other constitutional disability of the President—The person having the greatest number of votes as Vice-President, shall be the Vice-President, if such number be a majority of the whole number of Electors appointed, and if no person have a majority, then from the two highest numbers on the list, the Senate shall choose the Vice-President; A quorum for the purpose shall consist of two-thirds of the whole number of Senators, and a majority of the whole number shall be necessary to a choice. But no person constitutionally ineligible to the office of President shall be eligible to that of Vice-President of the United States.

Amendment XIII (1865)

Section 1. Neither slavery nor involuntary servitude, except as a punishment for crime whereof the party shall have been duly convicted, shall exist within the United States, or any place subject to their jurisdiction.
Section 2. Congress shall have power to enforce this article by appropriate legislation.

Amendment XIV (1868)

Section 1. All persons born or naturalized in the United States and subject to the jurisdiction thereof, are citizens of the United States and of the State wherein they reside. No State shall make or enforce any law which shall abridge the privileges or immunities of citizens of the United States; nor shall any State deprive any person of life, liberty, or property, without due process of law; nor deny to any person within its jurisdiction the equal protection of the laws.
Section 2. Representatives shall be apportioned among the several States according to their respective numbers, counting the whole number of persons in each State, excluding Indians not taxed. But when the right to vote at any election for the choice of electors for President and Vice-President of the United States, Representatives in Congress, the Executive and Judicial officers of a State, or the members of the Legislature thereof, is denied to any of the male inhabitants of such State, being twenty-one years of age, and citizens of the United States, or in any way abridged, except for participation in rebellion, or other crime, the basis of representation therein shall be reduced in the proportion which the number of such male citizens shall bear to the whole number of male citizens twenty-one years of age in such State.
Section 3. No person shall be a Senator or Representative in Congress, or elector of President and Vice-President, or hold any office, civil or military, under the United States, or under any State, who, having previously taken an oath, as a member of Congress, or as an officer of the United States, or as a member of any State legislature, or as an executive or judicial officer of any State, to support the Constitution of

the United States, shall have engaged in insurrection or rebellion against the same, or given aid or comfort to the enemies thereof. But Congress may by a vote of two-thirds of each House, remove such disability.

Section 4. The validity of the public debt of the United States, authorized by law, including debts incurred for payment of pensions and bounties for services in suppressing insurrection or rebellion, shall not be questioned. But neither the United States nor any State shall assume or pay any debt or obligation incurred in aid of insurrection or rebellion against the United States, or any claim for the loss or emancipation of any slave; but all such debts, obligations and claims shall be held illegal and void.

Section 5. The Congress shall have power to enforce, by appropriate legislation, the provisions of this article.

Amendment XV (1870)

Section 1. The right of citizens of the United States to vote shall not be denied or abridged by the United States or by any State on account of race, color, or previous condition of servitude.

Section 2. The Congress shall have power to enforce this article by appropriate legislation.

Amendment XVI (1913)

The Congress shall have power to lay and collect taxes on incomes, from whatever source derived, without apportionment among the several States, and without regard to any census or enumeration.

Amendment XVII (1913)

The Senate of the United States shall be composed of two Senators from each State, elected by the people thereof, for six years; and each Senator shall have one vote. The electors in each State shall have the qualifications requisite for electors of the most numerous branch of the State legislatures.

When vacancies happen in the representation of any State in the Senate, the executive authority of such State shall issue writs of election to fill such vacancies: Provided, That the legislature of any State may empower the executive thereof to make temporary appointments until the people fill the vacancies by election as the legislature may direct.

This amendment shall not be so construed as to affect the election or term of any Senator chosen before it becomes valid as part of the Constitution.

Amendment XVIII (1919)

Section 1. After one year from the ratification of this article the manufacture, sale, or transportation of intoxicating liquors within, the importation thereof into, or the exportation thereof from the United States and all territory subject to the jurisdiction thereof for beverage purposes is hereby prohibited.

Section 2. The Congress and the several States shall have concurrent power to enforce this article by appropriate legislation.

Section 3. This article shall be inoperative unless it shall have been ratified as an amendment to the Constitution by the legislatures of the several States, as provided in the Constitution, within seven years from the date of the submission hereof to the States by the Congress.

Amendment XIX (1920)

The right of citizens of the United States to vote shall not be denied or abridged by the United States or by any State on account of sex.

Congress shall have power to enforce this article by appropriate legislation.

Amendment XX (1933)

Section 1. The terms of the President and Vice President shall end at noon on the 20th day of January, and the terms of Senators and Representatives at noon on the 3rd day of January, of the years in which such terms would have ended if this article had not been ratified; and the terms of their successors shall then begin.

Section 2. The Congress shall assemble at least once in every year, and such meeting shall begin at noon on the 3rd day of January, unless they shall by law appoint a different day.

Section 3. If, at the time fixed for the beginning of the term of the President, the President elect shall have died, the Vice President elect shall become President. If a President shall not have been chosen before the time fixed for the beginning of his term, or if the President elect shall have failed to qualify, then the Vice President elect shall act as President until a President shall have qualified; and the Congress may by law provide for the case wherein neither a President elect nor a Vice President elect shall have qualified, declaring who shall then act as President, or the manner in which one who is to act shall be selected, and such person shall act accordingly until a President or Vice President shall have qualified.

Section 4. The Congress may by law provide for the case of the death of any of the persons from whom the House of Representatives may choose a President whenever the right of choice shall have devolved upon them, and for the case of the death of any of the persons from whom the Senate may choose a Vice President whenever the right of choice shall have devolved upon them.

Section 5. Sections 1 and 2 shall take effect on the 15th day of October following the ratification of this article.

Section 6. This article shall be inoperative unless it shall have been ratified as an amendment to the Constitution by the legislatures of three-fourths of the several States within seven years from the date of its submission.

Amendment XXI (1933)

Section 1. The eighteenth article of amendment to the Constitution of the United States is hereby repealed.

Section 2. The transportation or importation into any State, Territory or possession of the United States for delivery or use therein of intoxicating liquors, in violation of the laws thereof, is hereby prohibited.

Section 3. This article shall be inoperative unless it shall have been ratified as an amendment to the Constitution by conventions in the several States, as provided in the Constitution, within seven years from the date of the submission hereof to the States by the Congress.

Amendment XXII (1951)

Section 1. No person shall be elected to the office of the President more than twice, and no person who has held the office of President, or acted as President, for more than two years of a term to which some other person was elected President shall be elected to the office of the President more than once. But this Article shall not apply to any person holding the office of President when this Article was proposed by the Congress, and shall not prevent any person who may be holding the office of President, or acting as President, during the term within which this Article becomes operative from holding the office of President or acting as President during the remainder of such term.

Section 2. This Article shall be inoperative unless it shall have been ratified as an amendment to the Constitution by the legislatures of three-fourths of the several States within seven years from the date of its submission to the States by the Congress.

Amendment XXIII (1961)

Section 1. The District constituting the seat of Government of the United States shall appoint in such manner as the Congress may direct:

A number of electors of President and Vice President equal to the whole number of Senators and Representatives in Congress to which the District would be entitled if it were a State, but in no event more than the least populous State; they shall be in addition to those appointed by the States, but they shall be considered, for the purposes of the election of President and Vice President, to be electors appointed by a State; and they shall meet in the District and perform such duties as provided by the twelfth article of amendment.

Section 2. The Congress shall have power to enforce this article by appropriate legislation.

Amendment XXIV (1964)

Section 1. The right of citizens of the United States to vote in any primary or other election for President or Vice President, for electors for President or Vice President, or for Senator or Representative in Congress, shall not be denied or abridged by the United States or any State by reason of failure to pay any poll tax or other tax.

Section 2. The Congress shall have power to enforce this article by appropriate legislation.

Amendment XXV (1967)

Section 1. In case of the removal of the President from office or of his death or resignation, the Vice President shall become President.

Section 2. Whenever there is a vacancy in the office of the Vice President, the President shall nominate a Vice President who shall take office upon confirmation by a majority vote of both Houses of Congress.

Section 3. Whenever the President transmits to the President pro tempore of the Senate and the Speaker of the House of Representatives his written declaration that he is unable to discharge the powers and duties of his office, and until he transmits to them a written declaration to the contrary, such powers and duties shall be discharged by the Vice President as Acting President.

Section 4. Whenever the Vice President and a majority of either the principal officers of the executive departments or of such other body as Congress may by law provide, transmit to the President pro tempore of the Senate and the Speaker of the House of Representatives their written declaration that the President is unable to discharge the powers and duties of his office, the Vice President shall immediately assume the powers and duties of the office as Acting President.

Thereafter, when the President transmits to the President pro tempore of the Senate and the Speaker of the House of Representatives his written declaration that no inability exists, he shall resume the powers and duties of his office unless the Vice President and a majority of either the principal officers of the executive department or of such other body as Congress may by law provide, transmit within four days to the President pro tempore of the Senate and the Speaker of the House of Representatives their written declaration that the President is unable to discharge the powers and duties of his office. Thereupon Congress shall decide the issue, assembling within forty-eight hours for that purpose if not in session. If the Congress, within twenty-one days after receipt of the latter written declaration, or, if Congress is not in session, within twenty-one days after Congress is required to assemble, determines by two-thirds vote of both Houses that the President is unable to discharge the powers and duties of his office, the Vice President shall continue to discharge the same as Acting President; otherwise, the President shall resume the powers and duties of his office.

Amendment XXVI (1971)

Section 1. The right of citizens of the United States, who are eighteen years of age or older, to vote shall not be denied or abridged by the United States or by any State on account of age.

Section 2. The Congress shall have power to enforce this article by appropriate legislation.

Amendment XXVII (1992)

No law, varying the compensation for the services of the Senators and Representatives, shall take effect, until an election of Representatives shall have intervened.

Glossary

abandoned property   Property over which the former owner has relinquished any claim of ownership.

abortion   The intentional termination of a pregnancy.

abuse of the elderly   Infliction of physical or mental harm on elderly persons.

access device fraud   The crime of using a stolen, canceled, counterfeit, or altered card, personal identification number, or password to wrongfully obtain access electronically to money or anything of value.

access devices   Cards, plates, codes, electronic serial numbers, mobile identification numbers, personal identification numbers, and telecommunications services, equipment, or instrument identifiers or other means that can be used to obtain goods or services.

accessory after the fact   A person who, with knowledge that a crime has been committed, conceals or protects the offender.

accessory before the fact   A person who aids or assists another in commission of an offense.

accomplice   A person who voluntarily unites with another in commission of an offense.

act of omission   The failure to perform an act required by law.

actual imprisonment standard   The standard governing the applicability of the federal constitutional right of an indigent person to have counsel appointed in a misdemeanor case. For the right to be violated, the indigent defendant must actually be sentenced to jail or prison after having been tried without appointed counsel.

actual possession   Possession of something with the possessor having immediate control.

actus reus   A "wrongful act" that, combined with other necessary elements of crime, constitutes criminal liability.

administrative searches   Searches of premises by a government official to determine compliance with health and safety regulations.

administrative-type acts   Ministerial acts performed by executive officers in carrying out duties assigned by law.

adultery   Voluntary sexual intercourse where at least one of the parties is married to someone other than the sexual partner.

affiant   A person who makes an affidavit.

affidavit   A written document attesting to specific facts of which the affiant has knowledge, and sworn to or affirmed by the affiant.

affirm   To uphold, ratify, or approve.

affirmative defense   Defense to a criminal charge where the defendant bears the burden of proof. Examples include automatism, intoxication, coercion, and duress.

aggravated assault   An assault committed with a dangerous weapon or with intent to commit a felony.

aggravated battery   A battery committed by use of an instrument designed to inflict great bodily harm on the victim.

aggravated robbery   A robbery committed by a person armed with a dangerous weapon.

aggravating factors   Factors attending the commission of a crime that make the crime or its consequences worse.

aiding and abetting   Assisting in or otherwise facilitating the commission of a crime.

***Alford* plea**   A plea of guilty with a protestation of innocence.

ALI standard   A test proposed by American Law Institute to determine if a defendant is legally insane. See substantial capacity test.

alibi   Defense to a criminal charge that places the defendant at some place other than the scene of the crime at the time the crime occurred.

***Allen* charge**   A judge's instruction to jurors who are deadlocked, encouraging them to listen to one another's arguments and reappraise their own positions in an effort to arrive at a verdict.

Anders **brief**   A law brief submitted to an appellate court by publicly appointed defense counsel in which counsel explains that the defendant's appeal is nonmeritorious and requests release from further representation of the defendant.

answer brief   The appellee's written response to the appellant's law brief filed in an appellate court.

anticipatory search warrant   A search warrant issued based on an affidavit that at a future time evidence of a crime will be at a specific place.

antismoking laws   Statutes or ordinances prohibiting or restricting smoking in all or specified public places.

Antiterrorism and Effective Death Penalty Act of 1996   A federal statute designed to effectuate reforms in administration of the death penalty by curtailing successive petitions for habeas corpus by prisoners sentenced to death.

antitrust violations   Violations of laws designed to protect the public from price fixing, price discrimination, and monopolistic practices in trade and commerce.

appeal of right   An appeal that a defendant is entitled to make as a matter of law.

appellant   A person who takes an appeal to a higher court.

appellate courts   Judicial tribunals that review decisions from lower tribunals.

appellee   A person against whom an appeal is taken.

arraignment   An appearance before a court of law for the purpose of pleading to a criminal charge.

arrest   To take someone into custody or otherwise deprive that person of freedom of movement.

arrest warrant   A document issued by a magistrate or judge directing that a named person be taken into custody for allegedly having committed an offense.

arson   The crime of intentionally burning someone else's house or building—now commonly extended to other property as well.

asportation   The carrying away of something: in kidnapping, the carrying away of the victim; in larceny, the carrying away of the victim's property.

assault   The attempt or threat to inflict bodily injury upon another person.

assignments of error   A written presentation to an appellate court identifying the points that the appellant claims constitute errors made by the lower tribunal.

assisted suicide   An offense (in some jurisdictions) of aiding or assisting a person to take his or her life.

attempt   An intent to commit a crime coupled with an act taken toward committing the offense.

Attorney General   The highest legal officer of a state or of the United States.

attorney–client privilege   The right of a person (client) not to testify about matters discussed in confidence with an attorney in the course of the attorney's representation.

automatism   The condition under which a person performs a set of actions during a state of unconsciousness.

automobile exception   Exception to the Fourth Amendment warrant requirement. The exception allows the warrantless search of a vehicle by police who have probable cause to search but because of exigent circumstances are unable to secure a warrant.

bail   The conditional release of a person charged with a crime.

bail bond   Sum of money posted to ensure a defendant's subsequent appearance in court.

Bail Reform Act of 1984   See Federal Bail Reform Act of 1984.

bankruptcy fraud   Dishonest or deceitful acts committed by one who seeks relief under laws designed to protect honest debtors from their creditors.

battered child syndrome   A group of symptoms typically manifested by a child who has suffered continued physical or mental abuse, often from a parent or person having custody of the child.

battered woman syndrome   A group of symptoms typically manifested by a woman who has suffered continued physical or mental abuse, usually from a male with whom she lives.

battery   The unlawful use of force against another person that entails some injury or offensive touching.

bench trial   A trial held before a judge without a jury present.

best evidence   Primary evidence used to prove a fact—usually an original written document that evidences a communication or transaction.

beyond a reasonable doubt   The standard of proof that is constitutionally required to be introduced before a defendant can be found guilty of a crime or before a juvenile can be adjudicated as a delinquent.

bid rigging   An illegal manipulation in submitting bids to obtain a contract, usually from a public body.

bifurcated trial   A capital trial with separate phases for determining guilt and punishment.

bigamy   The crime of being married to more than one person at the same time.

bill of attainder   A legislative act imposing punishment without trial upon persons deemed guilty of treason or felonies (prohibited by the U.S. Constitution).

Bill of Rights   A written enumeration of basic rights, usually annexed to a written constitution—for example, the first ten amendments to the U.S. Constitution.

blackmail   Extortion of money, property, or services from a person by threatening to expose embarrassing or harmful information about that person.

Blackstone's *Commentaries*   A massive treatise on the English common law published in 1769 by Sir William Blackstone, a professor at Oxford University. In America, Blackstone's *Commentaries* became something of a legal bible.

***Blockburger* test**   A test applied by courts to determine if the charges against a defendant would constitute a violation of the constitutional prohibition against double jeopardy—that is, being tried twice for the same offense. The *Blockburger* test holds that it is not double jeopardy for a defendant to be tried for two offenses if each offense includes an element that the other offense does not.

boot camp   An institution that provides systematic discipline in a military-like environment designed to rehabilitate an offender; employed as a sentencing alternative.

bootlegging   The crime of knowingly trafficking in counterfeit labels affixed or designed to be affixed to copies of musical recordings, computer programs, motion pictures, etc.

border search   A search of persons entering the borders of the United States.

Brady Bill   Legislation passed by Congress in 1993 requiring a five-day waiting period before the purchase of a handgun, during which time a background check is conducted of the buyer.

brain death   The cessation of activity of the central nervous system.

breach of contract   The violation of a provision in a legally enforceable agreement that gives the damaged party the right to recourse in a court of law.

breach of the peace   The crime of disturbing the public tranquility and order; a generic term encompassing disorderly conduct, riot, etc.

breaking and entering   Forceful, unlawful entry into a building or conveyance.

breathalyzer   A device that detects the amount of alcohol in a sample of a person's breath.

bribery   The crime of offering, giving, requesting, soliciting, or receiving something of value to influence a decision of a public official.

brief   A document filed by a party to a lawsuit to convince the court of the merits of that party's case.

burden of production of evidence   The obligation of a party to produce some evidence in support of a proposition asserted.

canons of construction   Rules governing the judicial interpretation of constitutions, statutes, and other written instruments.

capias   "That you take." A general term for various court orders requiring that some named person be taken into custody.

capital crime   A crime for which death is a permissible punishment.

capital punishment   The death penalty.

carjacking   Taking a motor vehicle from someone by force and violence or by intimidation.

carnal knowledge   Sexual intercourse.

castle doctrine   "A man's home is his castle." At common law, the right to use whatever force is necessary to protect one's dwelling and its inhabitants from an unlawful entry or attack.

causation   An act that produces an event or an effect.

cert petition   A petition to a higher court asking the court to review a lower court decision.

challenge for cause   Objection to a prospective juror on some specified ground (for example, a close relationship to a party in the case).

change of venue   The removal of a legal proceeding, usually a trial, to a new location.

child abuse   Actions that physically, mentally, or morally endanger the welfare of a child.

child pornography   Material depicting persons under the age of legal majority in sexual poses or acts.

child shield statutes   Laws that allow a screen to be placed between a child victim of sexual abuse and a defendant while the child testifies in court.

child snatching   Action by one parent in deliberately retaining or concealing a child from the other parent.

churning   Making purchases and sales of securities in a client's account simply to generate commissions for the broker.

circumstantial evidence   Indirect evidence from which the existence of certain facts may be inferred.

citation   (1) A summons to appear in court, often used in traffic violations. (2) A reference to a statute or court decision, often designating a publication where the law or decision appears.

cite and release statutes   Laws permitting or requiring police officers to issue citations instead of making arrests for traffic violations or other minor misdemeanors or infractions.

citizen's arrest   An arrest made by a person who is not a law enforcement officer.

civil action   A lawsuit brought to enforce private rights and to remedy violations thereof.

civil contempt   Being held in contempt of court pending the performance of some court-ordered act.

civil forfeiture   Taking of property used in or obtained through unlawful activity pursuant to a civil proceeding in which the property itself is named as the defendant.

civil infractions   Noncriminal violation of a law, often referring to minor traffic violations.

civil rights   Rights protected by the federal and state constitutions and statutes. The term is often used to denote the right to be free from unlawful discrimination.

Clean Air Act   A federal statute designed to deter polluters and thereby enhance the quality of the air.

Clean Water Act   A federal statute designed to deter polluters and thereby enhance the quality of bodies of public water.

clear and convincing evidence standard   An evidentiary standard that is higher than the standard of "preponderance of the evidence" applied in civil cases but lower than the standard of "beyond a reasonable doubt" applied in criminal cases. For example, under the new federal standard for the affirmative defense of insanity, the defendant must establish the defense of insanity by "clear and convincing evidence."

clear and present danger doctrine   In constitutional law, the doctrine that the First Amendment does not protect those forms of expression that pose a "clear and present danger" of bringing about some substantive evil that government has a right to prevent.

clemency   A grant of mercy by an executive official commuting a sentence or pardoning a criminal.

clergy–penitent privilege   The exemption of a clergyperson and a penitent from disclosing communications made in confidence by the penitent.

closing arguments   Arguments presented at trial by counsel at the conclusion of the presentation of evidence.

coerced confession   A confession or other incriminating statements obtained from a suspect by police through force, violence, threats, intimidation, or undue psychological pressure.

collateral attack   The attempt to defeat the outcome of a judicial proceeding by challenging it in a different proceeding or court.

commercial bribery   Offering, soliciting, or accepting a benefit or consideration in respect to a business or professional matter in violation of a person's duty of fidelity.

common-law rape   Sexual intercourse by a male with a female, other than his wife, by force and against the will of the female.

community control   A sentence imposed on a person found guilty of a crime that requires that the offender be placed in an individualized program of noninstitutional confinement.

community policing   Style of police work that stresses development of close ties between police officers and the communities they serve.

community service   A sentence requiring that the criminal perform some specific service to the community for some specified period of time.

compelling government interest   A government interest sufficiently strong that it overrides the fundamental rights of persons adversely affected by government action or policy.

competent to testify   A person who has the legal capacity to offer evidence under oath in court.

compounding a crime   The acceptance of money or something else of value in exchange for an agreement not to prosecute a person for committing a crime.

Comprehensive Environmental Response, Compensation, and Liability Act   A Congressional enactment commonly known as the Superfund Law. Its purpose is to finance cleanup and provide for civil suits by citizens. The act also imposes reporting requirements for the collection and disposal of solid wastes.

compulsory process   See subpoena.

computer fraud   An offense consisting of obtaining property or services by false pretenses through use of a computer or computer network.

Computer Fraud and Abuse Act   Federal law criminalizing fraud and related activity in connection with computers.

computer trespass   An offense consisting of the unauthorized copying, alteration, or removal of computer data, programs, or software.

concealed weapon   A weapon carried on or about a person in such a manner as to hide it from the ordinary sight of another person.

concurrent sentencing   The practice in which a trial court imposes separate sentences to be served at the same time.

concurring in the judgment   An opinion by a judge or justice agreeing with the judgment of an appellate court without agreeing with the court's reasoning process.

concurring opinion   Opinion handed down by a judge that supports the judgment of the court but often through different reasoning.

conditions of confinement   The conditions under which inmates are held in jails and prisons. These conditions are subject to challenge under the Eighth Amendment's Cruel and Unusual Punishments Clause.

conditions of probation   A set of rules that must be observed by a person placed on probation.

confidential informant (CI)   An informant known to the police but whose identity is held in confidence.

consanguinity   Kinship; the state of being related by blood.

consecutive sentencing   The practice in which a trial court imposes a sentence or sentences to be served following completion of a prior sentence or sentences.

consent   Voluntarily yielding to the will or desire of another person.

consent to a search   The act of a person voluntarily permitting police to conduct a search of person or property.

consideration, prize, and chance   The legal elements that constitute gambling under most statutes that make it an offense to gamble.

conspiracy   The crime of two or more persons' agreeing or planning to commit a crime. The crime of conspiracy is distinct from the crime contemplated by the conspirators (the target crime).

constitutional right of privacy   See privacy, constitutional right of.

constitutional rights of prison inmates   Under modern interpretation of the federal and state constitutions, prisoners retain those constitutional rights that are not inconsistent with the fact that they are confined in a secure environment.

constitutional supremacy   The doctrine that the Constitution is the supreme law of the land and that all actions and policies of government must be consistent with it.

constructive intent   Intent inferred by law as a result of circumstances surrounding a party's actions.

constructive possession   Being in the position to effectively control something, even if it is not actually in one's possession.

contemnor   A person found to be in contempt of court.

continuance   Delay of a judicial proceeding on the motion of one of the parties.

contraband   Any property that is inherently illegal to produce or possess.

contractual immunity   A grant by a prosecutor with approval of a court that makes a witness immune from prosecution in exchange for the witness's testimony.

controlled substance   A drug designated by law as contraband.

Controlled Substances Act   A federal law listing controlled substances according to their potential for abuse. States have similar statutes.

copyright   A form of legal protection provided to the authors of original musical, artistic, and architectural works as well as videos and computer software and databases.

corporal punishment   Punishment that inflicts pain or injury to a person's body.

corporate defendants   Corporations charged with criminal offenses.

corpus delicti   "The body of the crime." The material thing upon which a crime has been committed (for example, a burned-out building in a case of arson).

corrections system   The system of prisons, jails, and other penal and correctional institutions.

counterfeiting   Making an imitation of something with the intent to deceive—for example, the offense of making imitations of U.S. coins and currency.

Court of Appeals for the Armed Forces   The court (formerly known as the Court of Military Appeals) consisting of five civilian judges that reviews sentences affecting a general or flag officer or imposing the death penalty and that reviews cases certified for review by the judge advocate general of a branch of service. May grant review of convictions and sentences on petitions by service members.

court-martial   A military tribunal convened by a commander of a military unit to try a person subject to the Uniform Code of Military Justice who is accused of violating a provision of that code.

courts of general jurisdiction   Courts that conduct trials in felony and major misdemeanor cases. Also refers to courts that have jurisdiction to hear civil as well as criminal cases.

courts of limited jurisdiction   Courts that handle pretrial matters and conduct trials in minor misdemeanor cases.

crime syndicates   An association or group of people that carries out organized crime activities.

criminal contempt   Punishment imposed by a judge against a person who violates a court order or otherwise intentionally interferes with the administration of the court.

criminal forfeiture   Government confiscation of private property obtained through or otherwise involved in criminal activity pursuant to a criminal conviction of the owner of said property.

criminal negligence   Conduct involving the reckless and flagrant disregard of the life or safety of another.

criminal procedure   The rules of law governing the procedures by which crimes are investigated, prosecuted, adjudicated, and punished.

criminal responsibility   Refers to the set of doctrines under which individuals are held accountable for criminal conduct.

criminal trial   A trial in a court of law to determine the guilt or innocence of a person charged with a crime.

critical pretrial stages   Significant procedural steps that occur before a criminal trial. A defendant has the right to counsel at these critical stages.

cruel and unusual punishment   Punishment that shocks the moral conscience of the community—for example, torturing or physically beating a prisoner.

curfew ordinances   Ordinances typically requiring minors to be off the streets by a certain time of night.

curtilage   At common law, the enclosed space surrounding a dwelling house; in modern codes, this space has been extended to encompass other buildings.

deadlocked jury   A jury made up of jurors who cannot agree on a verdict.

deadly force   The degree of force that may result in the death of the person against whom the force is applied.

death penalty   Capital punishment; a sentence to death for the commission of a crime.

death qualification of a jury   Obtaining a trial jury composed of people who do not entertain scruples against imposing a death sentence.

decisional law   Law declared by appellate courts in their written decisions and opinions.

decriminalization of routine traffic offenses
The recent trend toward treating minor motor vehicle offenses—for example, speeding—as civil infractions rather than crimes.

defense attorney   A lawyer who represents defendants in criminal cases.

defense of habitation and other property   The right of a defendant charged with an offense to assert that he or she used reasonable force to protect his or her home or property.

defense of others   The defense asserted by one who claims the right to use reasonable force to prevent the commission of a felony against another person.

definite sentencing   Legislatively determined sentencing with no discretion given to judges or corrections officials to individualize punishment.

Department of Justice   The department within the executive branch of the federal government that is headed by the Attorney General and staffed by U.S. Attorneys.

deposition   The recorded sworn testimony of a witness; not given in open court.

depraved mind or heart   A serious moral deficiency; a high level of malice often linked to second-degree murder.

derivative evidence   Evidence that is derived from or obtained only as a result of other evidence.

determinate sentencing   The process of sentencing whereby the judge sets a fixed term of years within statutory parameters and the offender must serve that term without possibility of early release.

diplomatic immunity   A privilege to be free from arrest and prosecution granted under international law to diplomats, their staffs, and their household members.

direct contempt   An obstructive or insulting act committed by a person in the immediate presence of the court.

direct evidence   Evidence that applies directly to proof of a fact or proposition. For example, a witness who testifies to having seen an act done or heard a statement made is giving direct evidence.

directed verdict   A verdict rendered by a jury by direction of the presiding judge.

discretionary review   Form of appellate court review of lower court decisions that is not mandatory but occurs at the discretion of the appellate court. See also writ of certiorari.

disorderly conduct   Illegal behavior that disturbs the public peace or order.

disorderly intoxication   An offense consisting of misbehavior by a person who is drunk that results in disturbing the public peace or safety.

dispositive motion   A motion made to a court where the ruling on the motion will determine the outcome of the case.

dissenting opinion   An opinion rendered by a judge disavowing or disagreeing with the decision of a collegial court.

DNA testing   Laboratory tests that compare DNA molecules extracted from a suspect's specimen with DNA molecules extracted from specimens found at a crime scene to determine whether the samples match.

doctrine of harmless error   The doctrine that minor or harmless errors during a trial do not require reversal of the lower court's judgment by an appellate court.

doctrine of incorporation   See incorporation, doctrine of.

doctrine of overbreadth   See overbreadth doctrine.

double jeopardy   The condition of being tried twice for the same criminal offense.

driving under the influence (DUI)   The crime of driving under the influence of alcohol or drugs.

driving while intoxicated (DWI)   The crime of driving while intoxicated by alcohol or drugs.

driving with an unlawful blood-alcohol level (DUBAL)
The offense of operating a motor vehicle while one's blood-alcohol level is higher than allowed by law.

drug courier profiling   Employing a set of characteristics thought to typify people engaged in drug smuggling to identify suspects.

drug court   A specialized court or division of a court designed to deal specifically with defendants charged with violating laws proscribing the possession and use of controlled substances. Drug courts emphasize rehabilitation of offenders.

drug paraphernalia   Items closely associated with the use of illegal drugs.

drug-testing requirements   Laws, regulations, or policies that require students or employees to undergo chemical testing of their urine to determine whether they are free of illicit drugs.

Due Process Clause   The clause of the Fifth Amendment to the U.S. Constitution that prohibits the federal government from depriving persons within its jurisdiction of life, liberty, or property without due process of law. A similar provision in the Fourteenth Amendment imposes the same prohibition on state governments.

due process of law   Procedural and substantive rights of citizens against government actions that threaten the denial of life, liberty, or property.

duress The use of illegal confinement or threats of harm to coerce someone to do something he or she would not do otherwise.

***Durham* test** A test for determining insanity developed by the U.S. Court of Appeals for the District of Columbia Circuit in the case of *Durham v. United States* (1954). Under this test, a person is not criminally responsible for an unlawful act if it was the product of a mental disease or defect.

electronic eavesdropping Covert listening to or recording of a person's conversations by electronic means.

embezzlement The crime of using a position of trust or authority to transfer or convert the money or property of another to oneself.

emergency searches A search by law enforcement officers in response to an emergency. In such an instance, police can seize evidence in plain view despite not having a search warrant.

***en banc* hearing** A hearing in an appellate court in which all or a majority of the judges participate.

***en banc* rehearing** A rehearing in an appellate court in which all or a majority of the judges participate.

Endangered Species Act A 1973 act of Congress designed to conserve ecosystems by preserving wildlife, fish, and plants. The act imposes criminal penalties against any person who knowingly violates regulations issued under the act.

endangering the welfare of a child Knowingly acting in a manner likely to be injurious to the physical, mental, or moral welfare of a child.

English common law The body of decisional law based largely on custom as declared by English judges after the Norman Conquest of 1066. See also *stare decisis.*

enterprise An individual, partnership, corporation, association, or other legal entity; a union or group of individuals although not a legal entity.

entrapment The act of government agents in inducing someone to commit a crime that the person would not otherwise be disposed to commit.

enumerated powers Powers explicitly granted governments by their constitutions.

environmental crime A violation of a criminal provision of an environmental statute such as the Clean Water Act.

Environmental Protection Agency Agency within the executive branch of the national government with principal responsibility for the enforcement of environmental laws, promulgation of environmental regulations, and administration of environmental programs.

equal protection of the laws Constitutional requirement that the government afford the same legal protection to all persons.

error correction function One of the principal functions of an appellate court—that is, to correct errors of trial courts.

escape Unlawfully fleeing to avoid arrest or confinement.

espionage The crime of turning over state secrets to a foreign government.

evanescent evidence Evidence that tends to disappear or be destroyed. Often, police seek to justify a warrantless search on the ground that destruction of the evidence is imminent.

evidentiary presumption Establishment of one fact allows inference of another fact or circumstance.

***ex post facto* law** A retroactive law that criminalizes actions that were legal at the time they were taken or increases punishment for a criminal act after it was committed.

excessive bail Where a court requires a defendant to post an unreasonably large amount or imposes unreasonable conditions as a prerequisite for a defendant to be released before trial. The Eighth Amendment to the U.S. Constitution prohibits courts from requiring "excessive bail."

excessive noise Unnecessarily loud sounds that interfere with the public peace and endanger the public peace, health, and welfare; sounds emitted that exceed the levels permitted by law or ordinance.

exclusionary rule Judicial doctrine forbidding the use of evidence in a criminal trial where the evidence was obtained in violation of the defendant's constitutional rights.

exculpatory evidence That which exonerates or tends to exonerate a person from fault or guilt.

excusable homicide A death caused by accident or misfortune.

exigent circumstances Unforeseen situations that demand unusual or immediate action.

extortion The crime of obtaining money or property by threats of force or the inducement of fear.

extradition The surrender of a person by one jurisdiction to another for the purpose of criminal prosecution.

eyewitness testimony Testimony given by a person based on personal observation of an event.

factual basis Judicial determination that there are factual grounds to support a defendant's entry of a plea of guilty or no contest.

factual impossibility That which is in fact impossible to achieve.

fair hearing A hearing in which both parties have a reasonable opportunity to be heard—to present evidence and make arguments. A fundamental element of due process of law.

fair notice The requirement, stemming from due process, that government provide adequate notice to a person before it deprives that person of life, liberty, or property.

False Claims Act   A federal statute that makes it unlawful for a person to knowingly present a false or fraudulent claim to the U.S. government.

false imprisonment   The tort or crime of unlawfully restraining a person.

false pretenses   The crime of obtaining money or property through misrepresentation.

False Statements Act   A federal statute making it a crime for a person to knowingly make a false and material statement to a U.S. government agency to obtain a government benefit or in connection with performing work for the government.

Federal Anti-Riot Act   A federal law enacted in 1968 making it a crime to travel or use interstate or foreign commerce facilities in connection with inciting, participating in, or aiding acts of violence.

Federal Bail Reform Act of 1984   An act that provides that a defendant charged with a federal crime may be denied bail if the prosecution can show that the defendant poses a threat to public safety.

Federal Bureau of Investigation (FBI)   The primary federal agency charged with investigating violations of federal criminal laws.

Federal Gun Control Act   This 1968 statute prohibits firearms dealers from transferring handguns to people who are younger than twenty-one, nonresidents of the dealer's state, and those who are otherwise prohibited by state or local laws from purchasing or possessing firearms. It also forbids possession of a firearm by, and transfer of a firearm to, people in a number of categories, including convicted felons, users of controlled substances, those adjudicated as incompetent or committed to mental institutions, illegal aliens, those dishonorably discharged from the military, those who have renounced their citizenship, and fugitives from justice.

federal habeas corpus review   Review of a state criminal trial by a federal district court on a writ of habeas corpus after the defendant has been convicted, has been incarcerated, and has exhausted appellate remedies in the state courts.

Federal Rules of Appellate Procedure   Rules governing the practice of law in the U.S. courts of appeals.

Federal Sentencing Reform Act of 1984   A federal act directing the promulgation of sentencing guidelines.

federalism   The constitutional distribution of government power and responsibility between the national government and the states.

felony   A serious crime for which a person may be imprisoned for more than one year.

felony murder   A homicide committed during the course of committing another felony other than murder (for example, armed robbery). The felonious act substitutes for the malice aforethought ordinarily required in murder.

field sobriety test   A test administered by police to people suspected of driving while intoxicated. Usually consists of requiring the suspect to demonstrate the ability to perform such physical acts as touching one's finger to one's nose or walking backward.

fighting words   Utterances that are inherently likely to provoke a violent response from the audience.

fines   See monetary fines.

First Amendment   Amendment to the U.S. Constitution. Establishes freedoms of expression, religion, and assembly.

first-degree murder   The highest degree of unlawful homicide, usually defined as "an unlawful act committed with the premeditated intent to take the life of a human being."

force   The element of compulsion in such crimes against persons as rape and robbery.

forcible rape   Sexual intercourse by force and against the will of the victim.

forensic evidence   Evidence obtained through scientific techniques of analyzing physical evidence.

forensic experts   Persons qualified in the application of scientific knowledge to legal principles, usually applied to those who participate in discourse or who testify in court.

foreperson   The person selected by fellow jurors to chair deliberations and report the jury's verdict.

forfeiture   Sacrifice of ownership or some right (usually property) as a penalty.

forgery   The crime of making a false written instrument or materially altering a written instrument (such as a check, promissory note, or college transcript) with the intent to defraud.

fornication   Sexual intercourse between unmarried persons; an offense in some jurisdictions.

Fourteenth Amendment   Amendment to the U.S. Constitution ratified after the Civil War in 1868. Prohibits states from denying due process and equal protection of law to persons within their jurisdictions and provides Congress legislative power to enforce these prohibitions.

***Franks* hearing**   A pretrial proceeding that allows a defendant to challenge the veracity of an affiant's statements in the affidavit that supports the issuance of a search warrant.

freedom of expression   The right of the individual to express thoughts and feelings through speech, writing, and other media of expression; protected by the First Amendment to the U.S. Constitution.

freedom of religion   The First Amendment right to the free exercise of one's religion.

frivolous appeals   Appeals wholly lacking in legal merit.

fruit of the poisonous tree doctrine   A doctrine based on the judicial interpretation of the Fourth Amendment that holds that evidence derived from other, illegally seized evidence cannot be used by the prosecution.

***Frye* test**   See general acceptance test.

fundamental error   An error in a judicial proceeding that adversely affects the substantial rights of the accused.

fundamental rights   Those constitutional rights that have been declared to be fundamental by the courts. Includes First Amendment freedoms, the right to vote, and the right to privacy.

gambling   Operating or playing a game for money in the expectation of gaining more than the amount played.

gender-based peremptory challenges   A challenge to a prospective juror's competency to serve based solely on the prospective juror's gender.

gender-neutral offense   A crime that may be committed by members of either sex against members of either sex.

general acceptance test   Also known as the *Frye* test, this test is used by many state courts to determine whether to admit expert testimony in scientific matters. It must be established that the scientific principle from which the expert's deduction is made has gained general acceptance in its field.

general deterrence   The theory that punishment serves to deter others from committing crimes.

general intent   The state of mind to do something prohibited by law without necessarily intending to accomplish the harm that results from the illegal act.

general objection   An objection raised against a witness's testimony or introduction of evidence when the objecting party does not recite a specific ground for the objection.

general warrant   A search or arrest warrant that is not particular as to the person to be arrested, place to be searched, or property to be seized.

general-intent statutes   Statutes defining crimes that require only general intent, as distinct from specific intent, on the part of the violator.

good time credit   Credit toward early release from prison based on good behavior during confinement (often referred to as gain time).

good-faith exception   An exception to the exclusionary rule (which bars the use of evidence obtained by a search warrant found to be invalid). The exception allows use of the evidence if the police relied in good faith on the search warrant, even though the warrant is subsequently held to be invalid.

grand jury   See grand jury proceeding.

grand jury proceeding   A group of citizens designated by law to make an investigation or to determine whether there is sufficient evidence to prosecute someone for a crime.

grand theft   Theft of a sufficient value of property to make the crime a felony.

guilty but mentally ill   A form of verdict that may be rendered in some states where the jury finds that the defendant's mental illness does not deprive the defendant of substantial capacity sufficient to satisfy the insanity test but warrants the defendant's treatment in addition to incarceration.

gun control laws   Laws regulating the manufacture, importation, sale, distribution, possession, or use of firearms.

Gun-Free School Zones Act   Federal statute making it a crime "for any individual knowingly to possess a firearm at a place that the individual knows, or has reasonable cause to believe, is a school zone." This law was declared unconstitutional by the U.S. Supreme Court in *United States v. Lopez* (1995).

habitual offender statute   A law that imposes an additional punishment on a criminal who has previously been convicted of crimes.

Hale's Rule   English common law credited to Sir Matthew Hale, Lord Chief Justice in the seventeenth century, holding that a husband could not be charged with the rape of his wife.

handwriting exemplar   A sample of a suspect's handwriting.

hard-core pornography   Pornography that is extremely graphic in its depiction of sexual conduct.

hate crimes   Crimes in which the victim is selected on the basis of race, religion, sexual orientation, or ethnicity.

hate speech   Offensive speech directed at members of racial, religious, sexual, or ethnic minorities.

hearsay evidence   Statements made by someone other than a witness offered in evidence at a trial or hearing to prove the truth of the matter asserted.

heat of passion   A violent and uncontrollable rage resulting from a provocation that would cause such a response by a reasonable person—for example, a person who views his or her spouse in the act of committing adultery.

Hobbs Act   A 1946 act of Congress authorizing criminal penalties for whoever in any way or degree obstructs, delays, or affects commerce or the movement of any article or commodity in commerce, by robbery or extortion or attempts or conspires so to do, or commits or threatens physical violence to any person or property in furtherance of a plan or purpose to do anything in violation of this section.

homicide   The killing of a human being.

hostage taking   The act in which the perpetrator of a robbery or some other crime forcibly detains innocent bystanders.

hot pursuit   (1) The right of police to cross jurisdictional lines to apprehend a suspect or criminal; (2) the Fourth Amendment doctrine allowing warrantless searches and arrests where police pursue a fleeing suspect into a protected area.

house arrest   A sentencing alternative to incarceration where the offender is allowed to leave home only for employment and approved community service activities.

hypnotically enhanced testimony   Testimony offered by a witness whose memory has been refreshed through hypnosis.

hypothetical question   A question based on an assumed set of facts. Hypothetical questions may be asked of expert witnesses in criminal trials.

identification procedures   Scientific and nonscientific procedures employed by police to assist in the identification of suspects.

identity theft   The crime of using someone else's personal information—such as their name, Social Security number, or credit card number—without their permission to commit fraud or other crimes.

immigration offenses   Criminal violations of federal laws regarding entry to the United States by foreign nationals.

imminent lawless action   Unlawful conduct that is about to take place and that is inevitable unless there is intervention by the authorities.

immunity   Exemption from civil suit or prosecution.

impeachment   (1) A legislative act bringing a charge against a public official that, if proven in a legislative trial, will cause his or her removal from public office; (2) impugning the credibility of a witness by introducing contradictory evidence or proving his or her bad character.

implied consent   An agreement or acquiescence manifested by a person's actions or inaction.

implied consent statutes   Laws providing that by accepting a license, a driver arrested for a traffic offense consents to urine, blood, and breath tests to determine blood-alcohol content.

implied exception   An exclusion that can reasonably be inferred or assumed based on the purpose and intent of an ordinance, statute, or contract.

implied powers   Powers not expressly granted to government by a constitution but fairly implied by the document.

impotency   Lacking in power; in reference to a male, the inability to copulate.

in camera inspection   Inspection of documents in the judge's chambers as opposed to in open court.

incapacitation   Punishment making it impossible for an offender to reoffend.

incarceration   Imprisonment.

incest   Sexual intercourse with a close blood relative or, in some cases, a person related by affinity.

inchoate offenses   Offenses preparatory to committing other crimes. Inchoate offenses include attempt, conspiracy, and solicitation.

inciting a riot   The crime of instigating or provoking a riot.

incorporation, doctrine of   The doctrine under which provisions of the Bill of Rights are held to be incorporated within the Due Process Clause of the Fourteenth Amendment and are thereby made applicable to actions of the state and local governments.

incriminating statements   Statements typically made to police that increase the likelihood that one will be found guilty of a crime.

indecent exposure   The intentional exposure in public of private areas of a person's body.

indefinite sentencing   Form of criminal sentencing whereby a judge imposes a term of incarceration within statutory parameters and corrections officials determine actual time served through parole or other means.

independent counsel   A special prosecutor appointed to investigate and, if warranted, prosecute official misconduct.

independent source doctrine   The doctrine that permits evidence to be admitted at trial as long as it was obtained independently from illegally obtained evidence.

indeterminate sentencing   Form of criminal sentencing where criminals are sentenced to prison for unspecified periods until corrections officials determine that rehabilitation has been accomplished.

indictment   A formal document handed down by a grand jury accusing one or more persons of the commission of a crime or crimes.

indigency   Poverty.

indigent defendants   Defendants who cannot afford to retain private legal counsel and are therefore entitled to be represented by a public defender or a court-appointed lawyer.

indirect contempt   An act committed outside the presence of the court that insults the court or obstructs a judicial proceeding.

indirect evidence   Inferences and presumptions that are probative of various facts in issue.

ineffective assistance of counsel   Deficient performance by a lawyer representing a defendant that results in serious errors that prejudice the right of a defendant to a fair trial.

inevitable discovery doctrine   The doctrine that holds that evidence derived from inadmissible evidence is admissible if it inevitably would have been discovered independently by lawful means.

infancy   The condition of being below the age of legal majority.

information   A document filed by a prosecutor under oath charging one or more persons with commission of a crime.

initial appearance   After arrest, the first appearance of the accused before a judge or magistrate.

insanity A degree of mental illness that negates the legal capacity or responsibility of the affected person.

Insanity Defense Reform Act of 1984 An act of Congress that specifies that insanity is an affirmative defense to a prosecution under a federal statute and details the requirements for establishing such a defense.

insider trading Transactions in securities by a person who operates inside a corporation and, by using material nonpublic information, trades to his or her advantage without first disclosing that information to the public.

insufficient evidence Evidence that falls short of establishing what is required by law, usually referring to evidence that does not legally establish an offense or a defense.

intellectual property Rights to the products of the human intellect, such as patents, copyrights, trademarks, and trade secrets.

intent to deprive The willful design to take goods or services from another without permission or authority of law.

intentionally Willfully; with a mental purpose to act.

intermediate appellate courts Judicial tribunals consisting of three or more judges that review decisions of trial courts but that are subordinate to the final appellate tribunals.

interrogation Questioning of a suspect by police or questioning of a witness by counsel.

interstate commerce Economic activity between or among states or affecting more than one state.

intoxication Condition in which a person has impaired physical or mental capacities due to the ingestion of drugs or alcohol.

inventory search An exception to the warrant requirement that allows police who legally impound a vehicle to conduct a routine inventory of the contents of the vehicle.

investigatory detention Brief detention of suspects by a police officer who has reasonable suspicion that criminal activity is afoot. See also stop-and-frisk.

involuntary intoxication Intoxication that is not the result of a person's intentional ingestion of an intoxicating substance. A person may become involuntarily intoxicated through the trickery or fraud of another person or through the inadvertent ingestion of medicine.

involuntary manslaughter The unintentional killing of another person as the result of gross or wanton negligence.

irresistible impulse A desire that cannot be resisted due to impairment of the will by mental disease.

Jencks **Act** The common name for a federal statute that permits a defendant to review a witness's prior written or recorded statement, but only after the witness has testified on direct examination for the government.

joinder and severance of parties The uniting or severing of two or more parties charged with a crime or crimes.

joinder of offenses The uniting of different charges or counts alleged in an information or indictment into one case for trial.

judgment of acquittal In a nonjury trial, a judge's order exonerating a defendant based on a finding that the defendant is not guilty. In a case heard by a jury finding a defendant guilty, a judge's order exonerating a defendant on the ground that the evidence was not legally sufficient to support the jury's finding of guilt.

judicial conference A meeting of judges to deliberate on the disposition of a case.

judicial notice The act of a court recognizing, without proof, the existence of certain facts that are commonly known. Such facts are often brought to the court's attention through the use of a calendar or almanac.

judicial review The power of courts of law to review governmental acts and declare them null and void if they are found to be unconstitutional.

jurisdiction The authority of a court to hear and decide certain categories of legal disputes. Jurisdiction relates to the authority of a court over the person, subject matter, and geographical area.

jury A group of citizens convened for the purpose of deciding factual questions relevant to a civil or criminal case.

jury instructions A judge's explanation of the law applicable to a case being heard by a jury.

jury nullification The fact of a jury disregarding the court's instructions and rendering a verdict on the basis of the consciences of the jurors.

jury pardon An action taken by a jury, despite the quality of the evidence, acquitting a defendant or convicting the defendant of a lesser crime than charged.

jury trial A judicial proceeding to determine a defendant's guilt or innocence conducted before a body of people sworn to render a verdict based on the law and the evidence presented.

justifiable homicide Killing another in self-defense or defense of others when there is serious danger of death or great bodily harm to self or others or when authorized by law.

justifiable use of force The necessary and reasonable use of force by a person in self-defense, defense of another, or defense of property.

juvenile court A judicial tribunal having jurisdiction over minors defined as juveniles who are alleged to be status offenders or to have committed acts of delinquency.

juvenile delinquency Actions of a juvenile in violation of the criminal law.

kidnapping The forcible abduction and carrying away of a person against that person's will.

kidnapping for ransom   The offense of unlawfully taking and confining a person until a specified payment is made to the offender.

knock-and-announce rule   The provision under federal and most state laws that requires a law enforcement officer to first knock and announce his or her presence and purpose before entering a person's home to serve a search or arrest warrant.

knowingly   Consciously, i.e., with knowledge.

larceny   At common law, the unlawful taking of property with the intent of permanently depriving the owner of same.

lawmaking function   One of the principal functions of an appellate court, often referred to as the law development function.

leading questions   A question that suggests an answer. Leading questions are permitted at a criminal trial on cross-examination of witnesses and in other limited instances.

legal impossibility   A defense allowed in some jurisdictions when, although the defendant intended to commit a crime, it was impossible to do so because the completed act is not a crime.

legislative intent   The purpose the legislature sought to achieve in enacting a particular provision of law.

legislature   An elected lawmaking body such as the Congress of the United States or a state assembly.

lewd and lascivious conduct   Indecent exposure of a person's private parts in public; indecent touching or fondling of a child.

lineup   A police identification procedure where a suspect is included in a group with other persons and the group is exhibited to a victim.

littering   The crime of disposing of garbage along a public street or road.

loan sharking   The practice of lending money at illegal rates of interest.

loitering   The offense of standing around idly in a public place.

lottery   A drawing in which prizes are distributed to winners selected by lot from among those who have participated by paying a consideration.

M'Naghten Rule   Under this rule, for a defendant to be found not guilty by reason of insanity, it must be clearly proved that, at the time of committing the act, the defendant was suffering such a defect of reason, from disease of the mind, as not to know the nature and quality of the act he was doing; or, if he did know it, that he did not know what he was doing was wrong.

mail fraud   A scheme devised or intended to defraud or to obtain money or property by fraudulent means, or the use or causing to use the mails in furtherance of the fraudulent scheme.

mala in se   "Evil in itself."

mala in se **offenses**   Crimes such as murder that are universally condemned.

mala prohibita   "Prohibited evil."

mala prohibita **offenses**   Crimes that are wrong primarily because the law declares them to be wrong.

malice aforethought   The mental predetermination to commit an illegal act.

malicious mischief   The crime of willful destruction of the personal property of another.

mandatory child restraint laws   Laws requiring that children below a specified age be restrained by approved safety devices when riding in automobiles.

mandatory minimum sentence   A sentence in which the minimum duration of incarceration is specified by law.

mandatory seat belt laws   Laws requiring automobile drivers and passengers to wear seat belts.

manifest necessity   That which is clearly or obviously necessary or essential.

manslaughter   The crime of unlawfully killing another person without malice.

marital exception   The traditional common-law principle that a husband could not be guilty of raping his wife.

marital privilege   The privilege of married persons not to be compelled to testify against each other.

maximum security prisons   Prisons designed to minimize the movement and maximize the surveillance and control of inmates.

mayhem   At common law, the crime of injuring someone so as to render that person less able to fight.

Megan's law   Name applied to statutes that require convicted sex offenders, upon release from prison, to register with local law enforcement agencies (named in memory of Megan Kanka, who died in 1994 at the hands of a released offender).

mens rea   "Guilty mind"; criminal intent.

Migratory Bird Conservation Act   Act of Congress protecting certain species of migratory birds from hunting within the United States and its territories.

minimum security facilities   Prisons and jails that offer inmates the most freedom of movement within the least secure environment.

Miranda **warning**   Based on the Supreme Court's decision in *Miranda v. Arizona* (1966), this warning is given by police to individuals who are taken into custody before they are interrogated. The warning informs persons in custody that they have the right to remain silent and to have a lawyer present during questioning, and that anything they say can and will be used against them in a court of law.

miscarriage of justice   Decision of a court that is inconsistent with the substantial rights of a party to a case.

misdemeanor   A minor offense usually punishable by fine or imprisonment for less than one year.

misprision of felony   The crime of concealing a felony committed by another.

misrepresentation   An untrue statement of fact made to induce action.

mistake of law   An erroneous opinion of legal principles applied to a set of facts.

mitigating factors   Circumstances or factors that tend to lessen culpability.

Model Penal Code (MPC)   Published by the American Law Institute (ALI), the MPC consists of general provisions concerning criminal liability, sentences, defenses, and definitions of specific crimes. The MPC is not law; rather, it is designed to serve as a model code of criminal law for all states.

monetary fines   Sums of money that offenders are required to pay as punishment for the commission of crimes.

money laundering   The offense of disguising illegal income to make it appear legitimate.

motion for a new trial   A formal request made to a trial court to hold a new trial in a particular case that has already been adjudicated.

motion for rehearing   A formal request made to a court of law to convene another hearing in a case in which the court has already ruled.

motion to dismiss   A formal request to a trial court to dismiss the criminal charges against the defendant.

motive   A person's conscious reason for acting.

motor vehicle violation   Minor crime involving the operation of motor vehicles.

necessity   A condition that compels or requires a certain course of action.

negative defense   Any criminal defense not required to be specifically pled.

no bill   "Not found"; conclusion of a grand jury that declines to return an indictment.

no contest plea   A plea to a criminal charge that, although it is not an admission of guilt, generally has the same effect as a plea of guilty.

noise control ordinances   Local laws prohibiting loud noises during certain hours of the night, typically midnight to 6 A.M.

noise ordinances   Local laws restricting the making of noise.

nolle prosequi   A formal entry by a prosecutor who declines to proceed further in the prosecution of an offense; commonly called a *nol pros*.

noncapital crimes   Crimes that do not carry the ultimate penalty, whether death or life in prison with no possibility of parole.

nondeadly force   Force that does not result in death.

not guilty by reason of insanity   A plea that admits criminal conduct but raises the insanity defense.

notice of appeal   Document filed notifying an appellate court of an appeal from a judgment of a lower court.

novel and innovative defenses   New defenses based on heretofore unaccepted principles of criminal responsibility.

nuisance   An unlawful or unreasonable use of a person's property that results in an injury to another or to the public.

nullen crimen, nulla poena, sine lege   "There is no crime, there is no punishment, without law." Refers to the doctrine that one cannot be found guilty of a crime unless there is a violation of an existing provision of law defining the applicable criminal conduct.

numbers racket   A common form of illegal gambling in which one places a bet on a number with the hope that it will correspond to a preselected number.

objective test   A legal test based on external circumstances rather than the perceptions or intentions of an individual actor.

objective test for the use of deadly force   Under this test, the judge or jury places themselves in the shoes of a hypothetical reasonable and prudent person to determine whether a defendant's use of deadly force was permissible.

objective test of entrapment   Under this approach to determining whether police engaged in entrapment, a court inquires whether the police methods were so improper that they were likely to induce or ensnare a reasonable person into committing a crime.

obscenity   Explicit sexual material that is patently offensive, appeals to a prurient or unnatural interest in sex, and lacks serious scientific, artistic, or literary content.

obstruction of justice   The crime of impeding or preventing law enforcement or the administration of justice.

one year and a day rule   A common-law rule that to convict a defendant of homicide, not more than a year and a day can intervene from the defendant's criminal act to the death of the victim.

open fields doctrine   The doctrine that the Fourth Amendment does not apply to the open fields around a home, even if these open fields are private property.

open public trial   A trial that is held in public and is open to spectators.

opening statement   A prosecutor's or defense lawyer's initial statement to the judge or jury in a trial.

opinion evidence   Testimony in which the witness expresses an opinion, as distinct from expressing knowledge of specific facts.

opinion of the court   The opinion expressing the views of the majority of judges participating in a judicial decision.

oral argument   Verbal presentation made to an appellate court in an attempt to persuade the court to affirm, reverse, or modify a lower court decision.

order maintenance   The police officer's function of keeping the peace, as distinct from enforcement of the law.

ordinance   An enactment of a local governing body such as a city council or commission.

organized crime   Syndicates involved in racketeering and other criminal activities.

Organized Crime Control Act of 1970   Federal law dealing with organized crime. Title IX of the act is entitled "Racketeer Influenced and Corrupt Organizations" and is commonly referred to by the acronym RICO.

overbreadth doctrine   First Amendment doctrine that holds that a law is invalid if it can potentially be applied to punish people for engaging in constitutionally protected expression.

overt act   A visible act by an individual.

panhandling   Begging for money in public.

pardon   An executive action that mitigates or sets aside punishment for a crime.

parens patriae   "The parent of the country." Refers to the role of the state as the guardian of minors or other legally disabled persons.

Parental Kidnapping Prevention Act (PKPA)   A federal act adopted in 1980 designed to prevent jurisdictional conflicts over child custody matters. The primary goal of the statute is to reduce any incentive for parental child snatching.

parole   Conditional release from jail or prison of a person who has served part of his or her sentence.

parole revocation hearing   An administrative hearing held for the purpose of determining whether an offender's parole should be revoked.

partial birth abortion   A method of abortion in which the fetus is partially delivered before its life is terminated and it is removed from the mother's body.

pat-down search   A manual search by a police officer of the exterior of a suspect's outer garments.

patent   A government grant of the right to exclude others from producing or using a discovery or invention for a certain period of time.

patently offensive   That which is obviously offensive or disgusting.

pattern of racketeering   To obtain a conviction under the federal RICO statute, the government must establish the defendant's involvement in a "pattern of racketeering" that requires proof of at least two predicate acts of racke-

teering having occurred within a period of ten years, excluding any period of imprisonment.

pen register   Device that enables law enforcement to obtain the numbers that have been dialed by use of a specific telephone instrument.

penalty enhancement statutes   Sentencing laws that provide for increased penalties when certain conditions were present in crimes—for example, the racial motivations of the perpetrator.

pendency of the appeal   The period after an appeal is filed but before the appeal is adjudicated.

penitentiary   Prison.

per curiam **opinion**   An opinion rendered "by the court" as distinct from one attributed to one or more judges.

peremptory challenge   An objection to the selection of a prospective juror in which the attorney making the challenge is not required to state the reason for the objection.

perjury   The crime of making a material false statement under oath.

perjury by contradictory statements   Commission of the offense of perjury by a witness who makes conflicting statements under oath.

petit (trial) jury   A trial jury, usually composed of either six or twelve persons.

petit theft   Minor form of larceny; theft of property of sufficiently small value that the offense is classified as a misdemeanor.

petitioner   A person who brings a petition before a court of law.

petty (petit) offenses   Minor crimes for which fines or short jail terms are the only prescribed modes of punishment.

photo pack   A collection of "mug shots" to be exhibited to a victim or witness in an attempt to identify the perpetrator of a crime.

Pinkerton **Rule**   Rule enunciated by the Supreme Court in *Pinkerton v. United States* (1946) holding that a member of a conspiracy is liable for all offenses committed in furtherance of the conspiracy.

plain meaning rule   The judicial doctrine holding that if the meaning of a text is plain, a court may not interpret it but must simply apply it as written.

plain view   Readily visible to the naked eye.

plain view doctrine   The Fourth Amendment doctrine under which a police officer may seize evidence of a crime that is readily visible to the officer's naked eye as long as the officer is legally in the place where the evidence becomes visible.

plea bargaining   Agreement between a defendant and a prosecutor whereby the defendant agrees to plead guilty in exchange for some concession (such as a reduction in the number of charges brought).

plea of guilty   A formal answer to a criminal charge in which the accused acknowledges guilt and waives the right to trial.

plea of not guilty   A formal answer to a criminal charge in which the accused denies guilt and thus exercises the right to a trial.

poaching   Taking of game illegally, either by hunting protected species, hunting out of season, hunting in areas in which hunting is prohibited, or violating restrictions as to the number or size of animals that may be taken.

point source   A fixed point in space from which pollutants are emitted, such as a smokestack.

police deception   Intentional deception by police in order to elicit incriminating statements from a suspect.

police departments   Organizations established by municipalities and sometimes states whose function is to enforce the criminal laws within their respective jurisdictions.

police power   The power of government to legislate to protect public health, safety, welfare, and morality.

polling the jury   Practice in which a trial judge asks each member of the jury whether he or she supports the jury's verdict.

polygraph evidence   Results of lie detector tests (generally inadmissible into evidence).

pornography   Material that appeals to the sexual impulse or appetite.

possession   The actual or constructive control or occupancy of real or personal property. See also actual possession; constructive possession.

possession of burglar's tools   The knowing control of instruments, machines, or substances designed to enable one to forcefully break into buildings or vaults in order to carry out the intent to steal or destroy property.

postconviction relief   Term applied to various mechanisms a defendant may use to challenge a conviction after other routes of appeal have been exhausted.

power of contempt   The authority of a court of law to punish someone who insults the court or flouts its authority.

predicate acts   Prior acts of racketeering used to demonstrate a pattern of racketeering in a RICO prosecution.

preliminary hearing   A hearing held to determine whether there is sufficient evidence to hold an accused for trial.

premeditation   Deliberate decision or plan to commit a crime.

preparatory conduct   Actions taken to prepare to commit a crime.

preponderance of the evidence   Evidence that has greater weight than countervailing evidence.

presentence investigation   An investigation held to aid the court in determining the appropriate punishment before sentencing a convicted criminal.

presentence report   A report containing the results of a presentence investigation.

presumption of innocence   In a criminal trial, the accused is presumed innocent until proven guilty.

pretextual stop   An incident in which police stop a suspicious vehicle on the pretext of a motor vehicle infraction.

pretrial detention   Holding a defendant in jail pending trial.

pretrial discovery   The process by which the defense and prosecution interrogate witnesses for the opposing party and gain access to the evidence possessed by the opposing party prior to trial.

pretrial diversion program   A program in which a first-time offender is afforded the opportunity to avoid criminal prosecution by participating in some specified treatment, counseling, or community service.

pretrial motion   A request for a ruling or an order before the commencement of a trial.

pretrial release   Release of a defendant on bail or personal recognizance pending adjudication of criminal charges.

price fixing   Sellers unlawfully entering into agreements as to the price of products or services.

principal   A perpetrator of or an aider and abettor in the commission of a crime (as distinguished from an accessory).

principals   People whose conduct involves direct participation in a crime.

principle of legality   The principle that there can be no crime or punishment in the absence of law.

prison disciplinary measures   Steps taken by prison officials to punish prisoners for misconduct, largely accomplished by removing good-time credits that prisoners earn for exemplary behavior in prison.

privacy, constitutional right of   Implied constitutional right allowing individuals to be free of government interference in intimate activities, especially those involving sex and reproduction.

privacy, reasonable expectations of   Doctrine holding that the Fourth Amendment protects persons from official intrusions as long as they have a subjective expectation of privacy that society is prepared to accept.

privileges   Rights extended to persons by virtue of law—for example, the right accorded a spouse in not being required to testify against the other spouse.

probable cause   A reasonable ground for belief in certain alleged facts.

probation   Conditional release of a convicted criminal in lieu of incarceration.

procedural criminal law   The branch of the criminal law that deals with the processes by which crimes are investigated, prosecuted, and punished.

profanity   Irreverence toward sacred things; foul language.

pronouncement of sentence   Formal announcement of a criminal punishment by a trial judge.

proof beyond a reasonable doubt   The standard of proof in a criminal trial or a juvenile delinquency hearing.

proportionality   The degree to which a particular punishment matches the seriousness of a crime or matches the penalty other offenders have received for the same crime.

prosecutor   A public official empowered to initiate criminal charges and conduct prosecutions.

prosecutor's information   An accusatorial document filed under oath by a prosecutor charging a person with one or more violations of the criminal law; similar to an indictment issued by a grand jury.

prosecutorial discretion   The leeway afforded prosecutors in deciding whether or not to bring charges and to engage in plea bargaining.

prosecutorial immunity   A prosecutor's legal shield against civil suits stemming from his or her official actions.

prostitution   The practice of selling sexual favors.

provocation   Refers to conduct that prompts another person to react through criminal conduct.

proximate cause   The cause that is nearest a given effect in a causal relationship.

prurient interest   An excessive or unnatural interest in sex.

public defender   An attorney responsible for defending indigent persons charged with crimes.

public drunkenness   The offense of appearing in public while intoxicated.

public forum   A public space generally acknowledged as appropriate for public assemblies or expressions of views.

public health   The effort to protect society from the spread of diseases and toxins.

public indecency   Vulgar, lewd, immoral, or obscene acts committed in public that are defined as offensive by law in accordance with constitutional standards.

public safety exception   Exception to the requirement that police officers promptly inform suspects taken into custody of their rights to remain silent and have an attorney present during questioning. Under the public safety exception, police may ask suspects questions motivated by a desire to protect public safety without jeopardizing the admissibility of suspects' answers to those questions or subsequent statements.

punitive isolation   Solitary confinement of a person who is incarcerated.

Pure Food, Drug, and Cosmetic Act   Federal law that prohibits traffic in food, drugs, and cosmetics prepared or handled under unsanitary circumstances or under conditions that render them injurious to health.

putting witnesses under the rule   Placing witnesses under the traditional rule that requires them to remain outside the courtroom except when testifying.

Quiet Communities Act   Federal law enacted in 1978 to protect the environment against noise pollution.

racial profiling   Practice of singling out members of minority groups by law enforcement officers.

racially based peremptory challenges   Peremptory challenges to prospective jurors that are based solely on racial animus or racial stereotypes.

Racketeer Influenced and Corrupt Organizations (RICO)   This section of the Organized Crime Control Act of 1970 prohibits the infiltration of legitimate organizations by racketeers where foreign or interstate commerce is affected.

racketeering   Illegal enterprises that engage in extortion.

rape shield law   A law that protects the identity of a rape victim or prevents disclosure of a victim's sexual history.

rape trauma syndrome   A recurring pattern of physical and emotional symptoms experienced by rape victims.

rational basis test   The judicial requirement that legislation must be rationally related to a legitimate government objective in order to survive constitutional challenge.

real evidence   Refers to maps, blood samples, X-rays, photographs, stolen goods, fingerprints, knives, guns, and other tangible items introduced into evidence.

reasonable doubt standard   The required standard of proof in a criminal case. Guilt must be proved beyond a reasonable doubt. Held by the Supreme Court to be an implicit requirement of constitutional due process.

reasonable expectation of privacy   A person's expectations of privacy that society is prepared to recognize as reasonable and legitimate.

reasonable force   The maximum degree of force that is necessary to accomplish a lawful purpose.

reasonable suspicion   A police officer's belief based on all relevant circumstances that criminal activity is afoot.

rebuttal witnesses   Witnesses called to dispute the testimony of the opposing party's witnesses.

recantation   The withdrawal or repudiation of previous statements. In some instances, a person who has lied under oath is permitted to recant to avoid being charged with perjury.

receiving stolen property   Knowingly receiving possession and control of personal property belonging to another with the intent to permanently deprive the owner of possession of such property.

recklessly   Without regard to consequences.

redaction   Editing out portions of a transcript in order to maintain secrecy of someone's identity or other information.

regulatory offenses   Strict-liability criminal offenses dealing with public health and the environment.

rehabilitation   Restoring someone or something to its former status; a justification for punishment emphasizing reform rather than retribution.

release on personal recognizance   Pretrial release of a defendant based solely on the defendant's promise to appear for future court dates.

remand   To send back, usually with instructions.

reply brief   A brief submitted by an appellant in response to an appellee's answer brief.

reporters   Books containing judicial decisions and accompanying opinions.

request for information or identification   A police–citizen encounter in which the police officer requests the citizen to provide identification or provide certain information.

resisting arrest   The crime of obstructing or opposing a police officer making an arrest.

Resource Conservation and Recovery Act (RCRA)   Enacted in 1976, RCRA is the major federal law dealing with the transportation, storage, and disposal of hazardous waste.

respondent   A person asked to respond to a lawsuit or writ.

responsible corporate officer   A person holding a supervisory position in an organization who may be subject to criminal liability for regulatory offenses committed by subordinates.

restitution   The act of compensating someone for losses suffered.

retreat rule   The common-law requirement that a person being attacked "retreat to the wall" before using deadly force in self-defense.

retribution   Something demanded as payment; the theory of punishment that stresses just desserts.

retroactive   Having an effect on things or actions in the past.

reverse   To set aside a decision on appeal.

right from wrong test   See *M'Naghten* Rule.

right of allocution   The right of a criminal defendant to make a statement on his or her own behalf before the sentence is pronounced.

right of confrontation   The right to face one's accusers in a criminal case.

right of cross-examination   The right to question witnesses for the opposing side in a criminal trial.

right of privacy   Constitutional right to engage in intimate personal conduct or make fundamental life decisions without interference by the government.

right to a speedy trial   Constitutional right to have an open public trial conducted without unreasonable delay.

right to counsel   (1) The right to retain an attorney to represent oneself in court; (2) the right of an indigent person to have an attorney provided at public expense.

right to die   Controversial "right" to terminate one's own life under certain circumstances.

right to keep and bear arms   Right to possess certain weapons, protected against federal infringement by the Second Amendment to the U.S. Constitution.

right to refuse medical treatment   The right of a patient—or patient's surrogate in some instances—to refuse to allow doctors to administer medical treatment.

riot   A public disturbance involving acts of violence, usually by three or more persons.

Rivers and Harbors Act   An 1899 act of Congress making it a misdemeanor to discharge refuse into the navigable waters of the United States.

roadblocks   Barriers set up by police to stop motorists.

robbery   The crime of taking money or property from a person against that person's will by means of force.

rout   At common law, a disturbance of the peace similar to a riot but without carrying out the intended purpose.

rule of four   U.S. Supreme Court rule whereby the Court grants certiorari only on the agreement of at least four justices.

rule of law   The idea that law, not the discretion of officials, should govern public affairs.

rules of evidence   Legal rules governing the admissibility of evidence at trial.

rules of procedure   Rules promulgated by courts of law under constitutional or statutory authority governing procedures for trials and other judicial proceedings.

rules of statutory interpretation   Rules developed by courts to determine the meaning of legislative acts.

rules of the road   Rules for the operation of motor vehicles on the public streets.

sabotage   The crime of infiltrating and destroying a nation's war-making capabilities.

same elements test   Test based on the Double Jeopardy Clause of the Fifth Amendment that bars separate punishment for offenses that have the same elements, or for one offense that includes or is included in another offense.

same evidence test   A test applicable to the Double Jeopardy Clause of the Fifth Amendment. If to establish an essential element of an offense charged the government will prove conduct that constitutes an offense for which the defendant has already been prosecuted, a second prosecution is barred.

scientific evidence   Evidence obtained through scientific and technological innovations.

scope of an agent's authority   In white-collar crime cases, the scope of an agent's authority depends on whether the commission of the offense was authorized, requested, commanded, performed, or recklessly tolerated by the board of directors or by a high managerial agent acting in behalf of the corporation within the scope of his or her office or employment.

search   Inspection; attempt to locate a particular person or object.

search incident to a lawful arrest   Search of a person placed under arrest and the area within the arrestee's grasp and control.

second-degree murder   Typically refers to a killing perpetrated by any act imminently dangerous to another and evincing a depraved mind regardless of human life, although without any premeditated design to effect the death of any particular individual.

Securities and Exchange Act   The 1934 act of Congress regulating the sale of securities in interstate commerce.

sedition   The crime of advocating or working toward the violent overthrow of one's own government.

seduction   The common-law crime of inducing a woman to have sexual intercourse outside of wedlock on the promise of marriage.

seizure   Action of police in taking possession or control of property or persons.

selective prosecution   Singling out defendants for prosecution on the basis of race, religion, or other impermissible classifications.

self-defense   The protection of one's person against an attack.

self-representation   Representing oneself in a criminal case.

sentencing guidelines   Legislative guidelines mandating that sentencing conform to guidelines absent a compelling reason for departing from them.

sentencing hearing   A hearing held by a trial court before the sentence is pronounced.

separation of powers   Constitutional assignment of legislative, executive, and judicial powers to different branches of government.

sequestration   Holding jurors incommunicado during trial and deliberations.

session laws   Collection of laws enacted during a particular legislative session.

severance of charges   Conducting multiple trials for multiple charges, as distinct from joinder, which refers to trying all charged offenses at once. Where two or more related offenses are charged in a single indictment or information, the trial judge often grants a severance of the charges on the motion of either the defense or the prosecution.

sexual contact   The intentional touching of the victim's intimate parts or the intentional touching of the clothing covering the immediate area of the victim's intimate parts, if that intentional touching can reasonably be construed as being for the purpose of sexual arousal or gratification.

sexual penetration   Sexual intercourse, cunnilingus, fellatio, anal intercourse, or any other intrusion, however slight, of any part of a person's body or by any object into the genital or anal openings of another person's body.

sheriff   The chief law enforcement officer of the county.

Sherman Antitrust Act   A federal statute prohibiting any contract, combination, or conspiracy in restraint of trade. The act is designed to protect and preserve a system of free and open competition. Its scope is broad and reaches individuals and entities in profit and nonprofit activities as well as local governments and educational institutions.

showup   An event in which a crime victim is taken to see a suspect to make an identification.

similar fact evidence   Refers to evidence of facts similar to the facts in the crime charged. The test of admissibility is whether such evidence is relevant and has a probative value in establishing a material issue. Under some limited circumstances, evidence of other crimes or conduct similar to that charged against the defendant may be admitted in evidence in a criminal prosecution.

simple kidnapping   The abduction of another person without a demand for ransom.

skip tracer   A person who tracks down alleged offenders who have fled to avoid prosecution.

sobriety checkpoints   Roadblocks set up for the purpose of administering field sobriety tests to motorists who appear to be intoxicated.

sodomy   Oral or anal sex between persons or sex between a person and an animal, the latter commonly referred to as bestiality.

solicitation   The inchoate offense of requesting or encouraging someone to engage in illegal conduct.

special agents   Officers of the Federal Bureau of Investigation with the power to make arrests and use force in the enforcement of federal law.

specific intent   The mental purpose to accomplish a specific act prohibited by law.

specific objection   Counsel's objection to a question posed to a witness by opposing trial counsel where a specific reason is given for the objection—for example, that the question calls for hearsay evidence.

specific-intent statute   A statute defining criminal conduct in which the offender must harbor a specific intent to accomplish a prohibited result.

speedy and public trial   An open and public criminal trial held without unreasonable delay.

Speedy Trial Act of 1974   This federal statute provides specific time limits for pretrial and trial procedures in the federal courts. For example, an indictment must be filed within thirty days of arrest, and trial must commence within seventy days after the indictment.

sports bribery   Offering anything of value to a participant or official in an amateur or professional athletic contest to vary his or her performance.

spousal abuse   Physical, emotional, or sexual abuse of one's husband or wife.

stalking   Following or placing a person under surveillance and threatening that person with bodily harm, sexual assault, confinement, or restraint, or placing that person in reasonable fear of bodily harm, sexual assault, confinement, or restraint.

standby counsel   An attorney appointed to assist an indigent defendant who elects to represent himself or herself at trial.

standing   The right to initiate a legal action or challenge based on the fact that one has suffered or is likely to suffer a real and substantial injury.

stare decisis   The doctrine of deciding cases based on precedent.

state supreme court   The highest appellate court of a state.

state's attorney   A state prosecutor.

status   One's condition or situation.

status offenses   Noncriminal conduct on the part of juveniles that may subject juveniles to the authority of a juvenile court.

statute   A generally applicable law enacted by a legislature.

statute of limitations   A law proscribing prosecutions for specific crimes after specified periods of time.

statutory rape   The strict liability offense of having sexual intercourse with a minor, irrespective of the minor's consent.

stop-and-frisk   An encounter between a police officer and a suspect during which the latter is temporarily detained and subjected to a pat-down search for weapons.

strict judicial scrutiny   Judicial review of government action or policy in which the ordinary presumption of constitutionality is reversed.

strict liability   Criminal responsibility based solely on the commission of a prohibited act.

strict liability offenses   Offenses that do not require proof of the defendant's intent.

strip searches   Searches of suspects' or prisoners' private parts.

structuring   Engaging in multiple smaller transactions to avoid currency reporting requirements.

subjective standard of reasonableness   A test used by courts to determine whether it was appropriate for a defendant to use deadly force in self-defense. Under this approach, the jury is asked to place itself in the shoes of the defendant.

subjective test of entrapment   Whether the defendant's criminal intent originated in the mind of the police officer or the defendant was predisposed to commit the offense.

subornation of perjury   The crime of procuring someone to lie under oath.

subpoena   A judicial order to appear at a certain place and time to give testimony.

subpoena duces tecum   A judicial order requiring a particular party to produce certain records, papers, books, or documents in court.

substantial capacity test   The doctrine that a person is not responsible for criminal conduct if at the time of such conduct, as a result of mental disease or defect, the person lacks substantial capacity either to appreciate the wrongfulness of his or her conduct or to conform his or her conduct to the requirements of the law.

substantial federal question   A significant legal question pertaining to the U.S. Constitution, a federal statute, treaty, regulation, or judicial interpretation of any of the foregoing.

substantial step   A significant step toward completion of an intended result.

substantive criminal law   That branch of the criminal law that defines criminal offenses and defenses and specifies criminal punishments.

suicide   The intentional taking of a person's own life.

suppression of evidence   See exclusionary rule.

surety bond   A sum of money or property that is posted or guaranteed by a party, usually an insurer, to ensure the future court appearance of another person.

suspended sentence   Trial court's decision to place a defendant on probation or under community control instead of imposing an announced sentence on the condition that the original sentence may be imposed if the defendant violates the conditions of the suspended sentence.

sworn officers   Law enforcement officers sworn to uphold the Constitution and laws of the United States and of their own states.

symbolic speech   Expression by symbols, gestures, and so forth.

tangible property   Property that has physical form, substance, and value in itself.

target crime   A crime that is the object of a conspiracy. For example, in conspiracy to traffic in illegal drugs, the offense of trafficking in illegal drugs is the target crime.

tax fraud   False or deceptive conduct performed with the intent of violating revenue laws, especially the Internal Revenue Code.

terrorism   Crime of inflicting terror on a population through the indiscriminate killing of people and destruction of property, often done with explosive devices.

Terry-**stop**   See stop-and-frisk.

testimonial evidence   Evidence received by a court from witnesses who have testified under oath.

theft of computer services   Stealing software, data, computer access codes, computer time, and so on.

third-party consent   Consent, usually to a search, given by a person on behalf of another—for example, a college roommate who allows the police to search his or her roommate's effects.

three strikes and you're out   Popular term for a statute that provides for mandatory life imprisonment for a convicted felon who has been previously convicted of two or more serious felonies.

three strikes laws   Statutes that provide for mandatory life imprisonment for a convicted felon who has been previously convicted of two or more serious felonies.

time, place, and manner regulations   Government limitations on the time, place, and manner of expressive activities.

tolling   Ceasing. For example, one who conceals himself or herself from the authorities generally causes a tolling of the statutes of limitation on the prosecution of a crime.

tort   A wrong or injury other than a breach of contract for which the remedy is a civil suit for damages.

totality of circumstances   Circumstances considered in the aggregate as opposed to individually.

Toxic Substances Control Act   A federal statute authorizing the Environmental Protection Agency to prohibit the manufacture, distribution, or use of chemicals that present unreasonable risks to the environment and to regulate the disposal of such chemicals.

trade secret   A formula, pattern, physical device, idea, process, compilation of information, or other information that provides a business with a competitive advantage.

trademark   A distinctive word, phrase, or graphic symbol used to distinguish a commercial product.

trademark counterfeiting   The offense of using a registered trademark to falsely market a product or service.

traffic court   Court of limited jurisdiction whose main function is the adjudication of traffic offenses and other minor misdemeanors.

transactional immunity   A grant of immunity applying to offenses that a witness's testimony relates to.

trap and trace device   Device that captures incoming electronic impulses that identify the originating number of a device from which an electronic communication was transmitted.

treason   The crime of making war against one's own government or giving aid and comfort to its enemies.

trial courts   Judicial tribunals usually presided over by one judge who conducts proceedings and trials in civil and criminal cases with or without a jury.

trial *de novo*   "A new trial." Refers to trial court review of convictions for minor offenses by courts of limited jurisdiction by conducting a new trial instead of merely reviewing the record of the initial trial.

true bill   An indictment handed down by a grand jury.

truth in sentencing   Term applied to laws abolishing parole and/or requiring offenders to serve a set proportion of their prison terms before being released.

truth in sentencing laws   Laws requiring that people sentenced to prison serve a specified proportion of their sentences.

two-witness rule   A requirement that to prove a defendant guilty of perjury, the prosecution must prove the falsity of the defendant's statements either by two witnesses or by one witness and corroborating documents or circumstances.

ultra vires   Beyond the scope of a prescribed authority.

unconstitutional as applied   Declaration by a court of law that a statute is invalid insofar as it is enforced in some particular context.

unconstitutional per se   A statute that is unconstitutional under any given circumstances.

Uniform Child Custody Jurisdiction Act (UCCJA)   A law in force in all fifty states that generally continues jurisdiction for custody of children in the home or resident state of the child.

Uniform Code of Military Justice (UCMJ)   A code of laws enacted by Congress that governs military service personnel and defines the procedural and evidentiary requirements in military law and the substantive criminal offenses and punishments.

Uniform Victims of Crime Act   A law proposed by the Uniform Law Commission designed to provide uniform rights and procedures concerning crime victims.

United States Code Annotated (U.S.C.A.)   An annotated version of the United States Code.

United States Congress   The national legislature of the United States, consisting of the Senate and the House of Representatives.

United States Sentencing Commission   A federal body that proposes guideline sentences for defendants convicted of federal crimes.

unlawful assembly   A group of individuals, usually five or more, assembled to commit an unlawful act or to commit a lawful act in an unlawful manner.

U.S. Attorneys Attorneys appointed by the president with consent of the U.S. Senate to prosecute federal crimes in specific federal judicial districts.

U.S. Code The comprehensive and systematic collection of federal laws currently in effect.

U.S. Courts of Appeals The twelve intermediate appellate courts of appeals in the federal system that sit in specified geographical areas of the United States and in which panels of appellate judges hear appeals in civil and criminal cases, primarily from the U.S. District Courts.

U.S. District Courts The principal trial courts in the federal system that sit in ninety-four districts. Usually, one judge hears proceedings and trials in civil and criminal cases.

U.S. Marshals Service Law enforcement officers of the U.S. Department of Justice who are responsible for enforcing federal laws, enforcing federal court decisions, and effecting the transfer of federal prisoners.

U.S. Supreme Court The highest court in the United States, consisting of nine justices, that has jurisdiction to review, by appeal or writ of certiorari, the decisions of lower federal courts and many decisions of the highest courts of each state.

USA PATRIOT Act Controversial act of Congress enacted in 2001 to strengthen the federal government's efforts to combat terrorism.

use immunity A grant of immunity that forbids prosecutors from using immunized testimony as evidence in criminal prosecutions.

uttering a forged instrument The crime of passing a false or worthless instrument, such as a check, with the intent to defraud or injure the recipient.

vagrancy The common-law offense of going about in public without any visible means of support (now defunct).

vagueness doctrine Doctrine of constitutional law holding unconstitutional (as a violation of due process) legislation that fails to clearly inform the person what is required or proscribed.

vandalism The willful destruction of the property of another person.

vehicular homicide Homicide resulting from the unlawful and negligent operation of a motor vehicle.

venire The group of citizens from whom a jury is chosen in a given case.

venue The location of a trial or hearing.

verdict The formal decision rendered by a jury in a civil or criminal trial.

vice crimes Crimes of immoral conduct, such as prostitution, gambling, and the use of narcotics.

victim A person who is the object of a crime or tort.

victim impact evidence Evidence relating to the physical, economic, and psychological impact that a crime has on the victim or victim's family.

victim impact statement Statement read into the record during the sentencing phase of a criminal trial to inform the court about the impact of the crime on the victim or victim's family.

victims' rights Refers to the various rights possessed by victims of crimes. See Uniform Victims of Crime Act.

Violent Crime Act See Violent Crime Control and Law Enforcement Act of 1994.

Violent Crime Control and Law Enforcement Act of 1994 Known generally as the Crime Bill, this federal statute dramatically increased the number of federal crimes eligible for the death penalty, authorized federal grants for drug court programs that include court-supervised drug treatment, and created the offense of interstate domestic violence.

voice exemplar A sample of a person's voice, usually taken by police for the purpose of identifying a suspect.

void for vagueness See vagueness doctrine.

voir dire "To speak the truth." The process by which prospective jurors are questioned by counsel and/or the court before being selected to serve on a jury.

voluntariness of a confession The quality of a confession having been freely given.

voluntary intoxication The state of becoming drunk or intoxicated of one's own free will.

voluntary manslaughter The intentional killing of a human without malice or premeditation and usually occurring during a sudden quarrel or in the heat of passion.

voyeurism The practice of seeking sexual gratification by observing the naked bodies or sexual acts of others, usually from a hidden vantage point.

waiver of *Miranda* rights A known relinquishment of the right against self-incrimination provided by the Fifth Amendment to the U.S. Constitution.

warrant A judicial writ or order directed to a law enforcement officer authorizing the doing of a specified act, such as an arrest or a search.

warrantless arrest An arrest made by police who do not possess an arrest warrant.

warrantless searches Searches made by police who do not possess search warrants.

weapons of mass destruction Weapons designed to kill large numbers of people and/or damage extensive areas. Includes nuclear, radiological, biological, and chemical weapons.

weapons offenses Violations of laws restricting or prohibiting the manufacture, sale, transfer, possession, or use of certain firearms.

weight of the evidence   The balance or preponderance of the evidence. Weight of the evidence is to be distinguished from "legal sufficiency of the evidence," which is the concern of an appellate court.

well-regulated Militia   This phrase, from the Second Amendment to the U.S. Constitution, refers to a citizen army subject to government regulations. In the early history of the United States, the militia was the set of able-bodied men who could be pressed into military service by the governor of the state. The National Guard is the modern counterpart.

Wharton's Rule   Named after Francis Wharton, a well-known commentator on criminal law, this rule holds that two people cannot conspire to commit a crime such as adultery, incest, or bigamy inasmuch as these offenses involve only two participants.

white-collar crimes   Various criminal offenses committed by people in the upper socioeconomic strata of society, often in the course of their occupation or profession.

wire fraud   A fraudulent scheme that uses interstate television, radio, or wire communications.

wiretap order   A court order permitting electronic surveillance for a limited period.

wiretapping   The use of highly sensitive electronic devices designed to intercept electronic communications.

worthless check statutes   Laws making it an offense to knowingly pass a worthless check.

writ   An order issued by a court of law requiring the performance of some specific act.

writ of certiorari   Writ issued by an appellate court to grant discretionary review of a case decided by a lower court.

writ of error   A writ issued by an appellate court for the purpose of correcting an error revealed in the record of a lower court proceeding.

writ of habeas corpus   A judicial writ requiring that a party be brought before a court. The primary function of habeas corpus is to release a person from unlawful confinement.

zoning ordinance   A local law regulating the use of land.

Case Index

Subject Index

A

Abandoned property, 392
Abortion, 66, 117, 144–145
Abortion clinics, 66
Abscam operation, 375
Abusive offenses
    abuse of the elderly, 148–149
    child abuse, 145–147
    sexual abuse, 512
    spousal abuse, 147–148
Access device fraud, 181–183
Access devices, 248
Accessories, 74, 86, 87–88
Accomplices, 86
    See also Accessories
Acid reflux defense, 225
Acquired immune deficiency syndrome
    (AIDS), 229
    See also AIDS testing
Acquittal, 525
Act
    administrative-type, 76
    attempt and, 93
    definition of, 75
    of omission, 75–76
    status as, 77
    See also Criminal act
Actual breaking, 184
Actual imprisonment standard, 464
Actual possession, 77, 231–232
Actus reus, 4
    See also Criminal act
"Adequate indica of reliability," 519
Administrative searches, 391–392
Administrative-type act, 76
Adulterated food, 268–269
Adultery, 122, 197, 201, 202
Advocacy, free speech and, 54
Affiant, 399
Affidavits, 399–401
Affirm, 591
Affirmative defense, 344–345
Aggravated assault, 109, 110–111
Aggravated battery, 109, 110–111

Aggravated robbery, 176
Aggravated stalking, 114
Aggravating factors, affecting capital
    punishment, 547–548
Aggressive panhandling, 307
Aguilar–Spinelli test, 401, 402
Aiding and abetting, 87, 101
AIDS testing, 267–268
Air passengers, 444
Air pollution statutes, 274, *282, 283*
Airports, 396
Alabama Criminal Code, 80, 82
Alcohol offenses
    consumption of alcohol by minors, 221
    driving under the influence, 222–225
    historical background, 220–221
    public intoxication, 222
Alcoholic beverages, 220–221
Alcoholism, 77, 222
Alford plea, 483–484
ALI standard, 349
Alibi, 353, 358–359
Alito, Samuel, 32
Allen charge, 531
ALSO, 622, 623
Amadou Diallo case, 435–436
American Bar Association, 472
American Civil Liberties Union (ACLU),
    305, 593
American Jurisprudence (Am.Jur.2d), 618
American Law Institute (ALI), 10, 80,
    349
American Law Reports (A.L.R.), 618
American Law Sources Online (ALSO),
    622, 623
Americans with Disabilities Act, 437
Ames, Aldrich, 313
Amish people, 59
Amobarbital, 227
Amphetamines, 227
Anabolic steroids, 227
Anders brief, 588
Andrews, Tommy Lee, 518
Animal cruelty, 216–217

Animal sacrifice, 60
Animus furundi, 162, 174
Annotated California Codes, 608, 611
Annotated codes
    federal, 608, 609, 610
    state, 608, 611
Anonymous informants, 401
Anonymous juries, 497–498
Anonymous tips
    automobile stops based on, 442–443
    as the basis of reasonable suspicion,
        442
    stop-and-frisk searches based on,
        413–414
Anslinger, Harry, 226
Answer briefs, 590
Anti-Car Theft Act of 1992, 177
Anticipatory search warrants, 404–405
Anti-Drug Abuse Act of 1988, 238, 549
Anti-Racketeering Act of 1934, 255
Antismoking statutes, 266, 285–286, 291
Antiterrorism and Effective Death Penalty
    Act of 1996, 315–316, 598
Antiterrorism legislation, 315–317
Antitrust violations, 247
Appeal
    common law background, 580–581
    court opinions, 591
    the court system and, 581–582
    current trends and issues in, 603–604
    discretionary review, 585
    doctrine of harmless error, 583
    filing, 589
    Florida court system, *581*
    historical background, 581
    judgment of the court, 591
    judicial conference, 591
    motions for rehearing, 592
    motions in, 589–590
    oral argument, 590
    by the prosecution, 584–585
    publication of appellate decisions, 592
    release on bail pending appeal, 587–588
    right to counsel, 588–589

Gardner, Daniel, 555
Gardner, Roger, 96
Gary, Lloyd, 109
Garza, Juan Raul, 549
Gas chamber, 553
Gaudin, Michael E., 330
Gay rights movement, 67
Gender-based peremptory challenges, 503
General acceptance test, 515, 518
General court-martial, 33
General deterrence theory, 538
General Digests, 616
General intent, 78–80
General-intent statutes, 79
General objections, 519
General warrants, 387
"Genetic fingerprints," 518
Geneva Conventions, 34
German Shepherds, 436
Gerulis, Andrea M., 168
Gideon, Clarence Earl, 27
Gideon decision, 464
Gilbert, Roswell, 68
Gilmore, Gary, 548
Ginsburg, Ruth Bader, 32, 143, 352, 563
Goldberg, Arthur, 448
Goldman, Ron, 7
Good time credit, 566
Good-faith exception to the exclusionary
    rule, 423–424
Google, 623
Grace, Mary, 298
Graham, Bob, 551
Grand juries
    evidence before, 475–476
    exclusion of minorities and, 474
    functions and powers of, *20,* 474–475
    indictments and, 473, 476
    overview of, 29, 474
    rights of witnesses and suspects, 475
Grand theft, 166, 168
Grant, Robert, 166
Granting bail, 469
Gray, Kevin, 481
"Great bodily harm," 111
Green, Thomas Arthur, 198
Green sea turtles, 289
Griswold, Estelle, 196
Guantanamo Bay detention center, 33,
    317–318
Guilty but mentally ill, 350–351
Gun control laws, 294
Gun-Free School Zone Act of 1990, 47, 311

H

H. W. Wilson Company, 620
Habeas corpus. *See* Federal habeas corpus
    review; Writ of habeas corpus
Habitation offenses, 183–187
Habitations
    defense of, 363–364
    See also Homes

Habitual offender statutes, 564–565
Hacking, 244
Hair (play), 209
Hale, Sir Matthew, 133, 138
Hale's Rule, 133, 138
Hall, Charles E., 132
Hallucinogens, *227*
Handwriting exemplar, 453
Hanging, 538, 552
Hanousek, Edward, Jr., 275–276
Hanssen, Robert, 313
Hard-core pornography, 206
Harlan, John M., 58, 212–213, 226, 395
Harmless error, doctrine of, 583
Harrison Act of 1914, 225–226
Hashish, *227*
Hate crimes, 155–156, 566
Hate Crimes Prevention Act, 155–156
Hate Crimes Statistics Act of 1990, 155
Hate speech, 55–56
Hauptmann, Bruno Richard, 151
Hazardous waste statutes, 278–280,
    282, 283
Hazing, 112–113
Headnotes, 614
Health care, False Claims Act and,
    249–250
Health Insurance Portability and Account-
    ability Act of 1996, 249–250
Hearings, preliminary, 473
Hearsay evidence, 102, 519–520, 561
Heat of passion, 116
Heightened security test, 305
Hemp. *See* Marijuana
Hendricks, Leroy, 546
Heroin, *227*
Hicks, Donald D., 180
Hill, Ronnie, 446
Hinckley, John, 348, 349
Hiss, Alger, 329
HIV testing, 267–268
Hobbs Act of 1951, 175, 255, 261–262
Holmes, Oliver Wendell, Jr., 53, 314, 391
Home(s)
    consent to search and, 394–395
    defense of, 363–364
    forcible entry for warrantless arrests,
        433–434
    searches and, 390
Homeless persons, 303–304
Homestead property, 540
Homicides
    causation requirement, 86
    at common law, 116
    corpus delicti, 126–128
    defenses to, 129
    excusable, 124
    felony murder, 118–119
    fetal, 126
    first-degree murder, 117–118
    justifiable, 125
    manslaughter, 121–123

modern statutory classifications, 116
    prosecutorial burdens, 126–129
    removal of life support systems,
        125–126
    second-degree murder, 119–121
    transferred intent, 84
    vehicular, 121, 123–124
Homosexual conduct, 67
Hong, James, 279
Hostage taking, 152
Hot pursuit, 410
House arrest, 545
Human immunodeficiency virus (HIV),
    127–128
Hung juries, 530–531
Hypnotically enhanced testimony,
    515–516
Hypothetical questions, 514–515

I

Identification
    police request for, 447, 448
    pretrial motion to dismiss, 482
Identification procedures, 431, 453–456
Identity theft, 169–170
Identity Theft and Assumption
    Deterrence Act of 1998 (ITADA),
    169–170
Idleness, 300
Illegal immigration, 318–319
Illinois, discovery rules, 489
ImClone, 254
Immigration offenses, 294–295, 318–319
Imminent lawless action, 54
Immunity, 367–378, 475
Impeachment, 524
Implied consent, 393
Implied consent statutes, 225
Implied exception, 22
Implied powers, 19, 20
Impotency, 143
In camera inspection, 135, 490
In rem forfeiture, 236, 237
Inadvertent discovery requirement, 408
Incapacitation, 539, 550
Incarceration
    current status of, 541
    for felonies, 15
    historical background, 39, 539
    statutory approaches to, 562–570
    See also Confinement; Corrections
        system; Penitentiaries; Prisons
Incest, 197–198, 202
Inchoate offenses
    attempt, 92–95
    conspiracy, 98–104
    overview of, 92, 104–105
    solicitation, 95–98
Inciting a riot, 294, 296, 300
Incorrigibility, 37
Incriminating statements, 451
    redaction in joint trials, 480–481

marijuana prohibition, 48
on *in rem* forfeiture, 237
on *Scheidler v. National Organization for Women,* 261
on sex offender registration laws, 143
on the trying of Guantanamo Bay detainees, 318
on unloaded guns as "dangerous weapons," 175
Stewart, Martha, 254
Stewart, Potter
on the death penalty, 547
on obscenity, 206
on privacy and electronic surveillance, 417
on rights of arrestees, 434
on Section 301(k) of the FDCA, 270
Stinson, Ricky, 363
Stogner, Marion, 52
Stolen property, receiving, 161, 163, 164
Stop-and-frisk, 439
on anonymous tips, 413–414
length of detention, 441
overview of, 413–414
reasonable suspicion, 440, 456
when police may conduct, 441
See also Investigatory detention
Story, Joseph, 51
Strickland test, 594
Strict judicial scrutiny, 69–70
Strict liability, 267, 291
Strict liability offenses, 4–5, 84–86, 269, 291
Strict scrutiny test, 305
Strip searches, 397
"Structuring" cash transactions, 253
Subjective standard of reasonableness, 360
Subjective test of entrapment, 373, 374
Subornation of perjury, 328, 330
Subpoenas, 471, 486
Subsistence defense, 290
Substantial capacity test, 349
Substantial federal question, 585
Substantial step, 92, 93, 100
Substantive criminal law, 3
Suicide, 129–132
Summary court-martial, 33
Summary trial, 468
Superfund Law, 281
Supervisory responsibility, 275–276
Suppression of evidence, 482
Supreme Court Reporter (S.Ct.), 32, 612, 613
Surety bonds, 470
Surveillance, 416
See also Electronic surveillance
Suspects, rights before grand juries, 475
Suspended sentences, 557
SWAT teams, 24
Sworn officers, 23
Syllabus (pl. syllabi), 614

Symbolic speech, 54–55

T

Tandy, Karen P., 230
Tangible property, 161
Target crime, 94
Tasers, 436–437
Tax fraud, 255–256
Tax perjury, 256
Tax violations, 256–257
Teachers, drug testing, 235
Television cameras, 505–506
Television intoxication, 379
Tellico Dam and Reservoir, 288
Temperance Movement, 220
Terri Schiavo case, 125
Terrorism
antiterrorism legislation, 315–317
contemporary acts of, 315
Terrorists, military tribunals and, 33–34
Terrorists captured abroad, detention and trial of, 317–318
Terry-stop, 413, 441
Testimony
hypnotically enhanced, 515–516
testimonial evidence, 512
testimonial statements, 519–520
Tetrahydrocannabinols, *227*
Texas Digest 2d, 617
Textbooks, law, 620
Theft of computer services, 167
Theft offenses
at common law, 161–164
computer crime, 167–168
evolution of, *164*
federal approaches, 164–165
prosecutorial burden, 168–169
state approaches, 165–167
"Third-degree instruction," 531
Third-party consent, 393–394
Thomas, Clarence, 32
on the capital sentencing, 549
on criminal intent, 82
on delay in the pretrial process, 469
on drug testing, 235
on *Ewing v. California,* 565–565
on the Kansas Sexually Violent Predator Act, 546
on marijuana use and necessity, 355
on polygraph evidence in military courts, 516, 517
on sodomy laws, 200
on *United States v. Dickerson,* 450
Thomas (Library of Congress Web site), 622
"Three strikes and you're out" laws, 40, 65, 565–566
"Ticketing," 438
Tickets, 308
Time, place, and manner regulations, 59
Timmendequas, Jesse, 142
Tips, 401–402

See also Anonymous tips
Tolling, 371
Topless sunbathing, 204
Torts, 7
Torture, 38
Totality of circumstances, 398, 402
Toxic Substances Control Act (TSCA), 274, 280–281
Trade secrets, theft of, 173–174
Trademark counterfeiting, 172–173
Trademark Counterfeiting Act of 1984, 173
Trademarks, 172
Traffic court, 308
Traffic offenses
decriminalization of, 308
pretextual stops and, 443
See also Motor vehicle violations
Transactional immunity, 367, 475
Transferred intent, 83–84
Trap and trace devices, 419, 420, 421
Treason, 49–50, 313
Trespass, 162
Trial by compurgation, 495
Trial by ordeal, 495
Trial courts, 11, 30, 35, 36
See also Criminal trials
Trial de novo, 580, 585
Trial judges
in capital sentencing, 559
criticism of attorneys and, 523
instruction to the jury, 528–529
roles of, 522–523
Trial jury
composition, 498
conduct during the trial, 526–527
deadlocked, 530–531, 559
deliberation, 530
features of, 29–30
foreperson, 529
impaneling, 503
instructions to, 528–529
jury instruction conference, 527
knowledge about the defendant, 558–559
polling, 532
right to, 29
selection of jurors, 499–504
sentencing, 529
the verdict, 532
See also Criminal trials; Juries
Tribal courts, 31
Trosclair, Angelo, 326
Truancy, 37
"True bill," 29, 473
See also Indictments
"Truth in sentencing" laws, 40, 566
Twelve Tables, 8
Twenty-first Amendment, 221
Twilight Zone, The (film), 121
2 Live Crew, 208
Two-witness rule, 328